Friedrich Nietzsche
A Philosophical Biography

In this beautifully written account, Julian Young provides the most comprehensive biography available today of the life and philosophy of the nineteenth-century German philosopher Friedrich Nietzsche. Young deals with the many puzzles created by the conjunction of Nietzsche's personal history and his work: why the son of a Lutheran pastor developed into the self-styled "Antichrist"; why this archetypical Prussian came to loathe Bismarck's Prussia; and why this enemy of feminism preferred the company of feminist women. Setting Nietzsche's thought in the context of his times – the rise of Prussian militarism, anti-Semitism, Darwinian science, the "Youth" and emancipationist movements and the "death of God" – Young emphasizes the decisive influence of Plato and of Richard Wagner on Nietzsche's attempt to reform Western culture. He also describes the devastating effect on Nietzsche's personality of his unhappy love for Lou Salomé and attempts to understand why, at the age of forty-four, he went mad.

This book includes a selection of more than thirty photographs of Nietzsche, his friends, and his work sites. Seventeen of the philosopher's musical compositions, which are key to a deeper understanding of his intellectual project, are available online.

Educated at Cambridge University and the University of Pittsburgh, Julian Young is Kenan Professor of Humanities at Wake Forest University, Professor of Philosophy at the University of Auckland, and Honorary Research Professor at the University of Tasmania. A scholar of nineteenth- and twentieth-century German philosophy, he is the author of nine books, most recently *Nietzsche's Philosophy of Religion*, and has been invited to speak at universities and conferences throughout the world.

Note

Chapters and sections with headings in italics discuss Nietzsche's works. The remainder discuss his life. There are thus three ways of reading this book. One can read about Nietzsche's life, about his works, or, best of all, about both his life and his works.

Seventeen of Nietzsche's musical compositions, together with a commentary, are available on the book's Web site, http://www.cambridge.org/9780521871174.

FRIEDRICH NIETZSCHE

A
Philosophical
Biography

JULIAN YOUNG

CAMBRIDGE
UNIVERSITY PRESS

CAMBRIDGE UNIVERSITY PRESS
Cambridge, New York, Melbourne, Madrid, Cape Town,
Singapore, São Paulo, Delhi, Tokyo, Mexico City

Cambridge University Press
32 Avenue of the Americas, New York, NY 10013-2473, USA

www.cambridge.org
Information on this title: www.cambridge.org/9780521871174

First published 2010
Reprinted 2010 (twice), 2011

Printed in the United States of America

A catalog record for this publication is available from the British Library.

Library of Congress Cataloging in Publication Data
Young, Julian.
Friedrich Nietzsche : a philosophical biography / Julian Young.
p. cm.
Includes bibliographical references and index.
ISBN 978-0-521-87117-4 (hardback)
1. Nietzsche, FriedrichWilhelm, 1844–1900. I. Title.
B3316.Y68 2010
193 – dc22 2009023342

ISBN 978-0-521-87117-4 Hardback

Contents

PART THREE · THE NOMAD

List of Illustrations

Acknowledgments

I AM DEEPLY grateful to the following: Curt Paul Janz for an illuminating correspondence concerning the infamous 'whip' photograph; Professor Gerhard Schaumann, who spent an entire day showing me round Tautenburg, the place of Nietzsche's tête-à-tête with Lou Salomé, and his wife, Karin, who introduced me to the Saale-Unstrut wines with which Nietzsche grew up; Frau Petra Dorfmüller, the archivist of Schulpforte, who gave me great insight into the school as it was in Nietzsche's time; Dr. Gudrun Föttinger, acting director of the Wagner Museum in Bayreuth, who, in the midst of the 2007 Festival, talked to me at length about early Wagner productions; Professor Mario Russo, who enabled me finally to track down what remains of the Villa Rubinacci in Sorrento; Wolfgang Bottenberg, who, as well as producing the recordings of Nietzsche's music available on the Web site for this book, illuminated many aspects of his life and thought; Joanna Bottenberg for being similarly illuminating and for wonderful hospitality in Montreal; Peter Loptson, who, as usual, kept me up to the mark philosophically, as well as correcting me on several points of nineteenth-century history; Friedrich Voit, as always my backstop on difficult issues of translation; Christine Swanton, who on countless occasions directed me away from the false and towards the true; my proof-reader, Mary Montgomery, who saved me from numerous grammatical solecisms; and my editor, Beatrice Rehl, who has been consistently enthusiastic and wise. Above all, I am grateful to Anja van Polanen Petel: only a superwoman could have borne, year after year, a husband vanished without trace into the depths of the nineteenth century.

The completion of this book has been made possible by sabbatical leave from the University of Auckland in 2006 and a Writing Fellowship in 2007, as well as a Discovery Project Grant from the Australian Research Council for 2008–9. Parts of Chapter 5 appeared in my essay 'Schopenhauer, Nietzsche, Death and Salvation' in the *European Journal of Philosophy* Vol. 16, No. 2, 2008, pp. 311–24, and parts of Chapter 7 in my 'Richard Wagner and the Birth of *The Birth of Tragedy*' in the *International Journal of Philosophical Studies* Vol. 16, No. 2, 2008, pp. 217–45. I am grateful to the editors of those journals for permission to reuse this material.

List of Abbreviations

WORKS BY NIETZSCHE

The works Nietzsche himself published are cited using the following abbreviations: Roman numerals refer to major parts of the works, Arabic numerals refer to sections, not pages. References to KGW and KSA cite a volume number followed by the notebook number and, in brackets, the note number (e.g., KSA 13 14 [204]). References to KGB cite a volume number followed by a letter number (e.g., KGB 11.3 393). The translations of KGB, KGW, and KSA are entirely my own. I have sometimes modified the translations of Nietzsche's published works that I cite.

A   *The Antichrist* in *The Anti-Christ, Ecce Homo, Twilight of the Idols and Other Writings*, ed. A. Ridley, trans. J. Norman (Cambridge: Cambridge University Press, 2005). Hereafter 'Ridley and Norman'.

AOM   *Assorted Opinions and Maxims* in *Human, All-Too-Human*, ed. E. Heller, trans. R. Hollingdale (Cambridge: Cambridge University Press, 1986). Hereafter 'Heller and Hollingdale'.

BGE   *Beyond Good and Evil*, ed. R.-P. Horstmann and J. Norman, trans. J. Norman (Cambridge: Cambridge University Press, 2002).

BT   *The Birth of Tragedy* in *The Birth of Tragedy and Other Writings*, ed. R. Geuss and R. Speirs, trans. R. Speirs (Cambridge: Cambridge University Press, 1999).

D   *Daybreak* ed. M. Clark and B. Leiter, trans. R. Hollingdale (Cambridge: Cambridge University Press, 1997). Referred to by me as *Dawn*.

EH   *Ecce Homo* in Ridley and Norman.

EI   *On the Future of Our Educational Institutions*, trans. M. W. Grenke (South Bend, IN: St. Augustine's Press, 2004).

GM   *On the Genealogy of Morals*, ed. K. Ansell-Pearson, trans. C. Diethe (Cambridge: Cambridge University Press, 1994).

GS   *The Gay Science*, ed. B. Williams, trans. J. Naukhoff (Cambridge: Cambridge University Press, 2001).

HH   *Human, All-Too-Human* in Heller and Hollingdale.

HKG   *Friedrich Nietzsche: Werke und Briefe: Historisch-kritische Gesamtausgabe*, Vol. II, ed. Hans Joachim Mette (Munich: Beck, 1933).

KGB   *Nietzsche Briefwechsel: Kritische Gesamtausgabe* (25 vols.), ed. G. Colli and M. Montinari (Berlin: de Gruyter, 1975–2004).

KGW   *Nietzsche Werke: Kritische Gesamtausgabe* (24 vols. + 4 CDs), ed. G. Colli and M. Montinari (Berlin: de Gruyter, 1967–2006).

KSA   *Kritische Studienausgabe* (15 vols.), ed. G. Colli and M. Montinari (Berlin: de Gruyter, 1999).

NCW *Nietzsche Contra Wagner* in *The Portable Nietzsche*, ed. W. Kaufmann (New York: Penguin, 1982).

PTA *The Complete Works of Friedrich Nietzsche*, Vol. 2, *Early Greek Philosophy*, ed. O. Levy, trans. M. A. Mügge (New York: Russell & Russell, 1964).

S *Nietzsche: Werke in Drei Bänden* (3 vols.), ed. K. Schlechta (Munich: Hanser, 1965).

TI *Twilight of the Idols* in Ridley and Norman.

UM *Untimely Meditations*, ed. D. Breazeale, trans. R. Hollingdale (Cambridge: Cambridge University Press, 1997). Hereafter 'Breazeale and Hollingdale'.

WB *Wagner in Bayreuth* in Breazeale and Hollingdale.

WC *The Case of Wagner: A Musician's Problem* in Ridley and Norman.

WP *The Will to Power*, ed. W. Kaufmann, trans. W. Kaufmann and R. Hollingdale (New York: Vintage, 1968).

WS *The Wanderer and His Shadow* in Heller and Hollingdale.

Z *Thus Spoke Zarathustra*, trans. and ed. G. Parkes (New York: Oxford University Press, 2005).

OTHER WORKS

BM *On the Basis of Morality*, Arthur Schopenhauer, trans. E. F. J. Payne (New York: Bobbs-Merrill, 1965).

C *Friedrich Nietzsche: Chronik in Bildern und Texten*, ed. R. Benders and S. Oettermann for the Stiftung Weimarer Klassik (Munich–Vienna: Hanser, 2000).

J *Friedrich Nietzsche: Biographie* (3 vols.), C. P. Janz (Munich–Vienna: Hanser, 1978).

FR *The Fourfold Root of the Principle of Sufficient Reason*, Arthur Schopenhauer, trans. E. F. J. Payne (La Salle, IL: Open Court, 1974).

LN *The Lonely Nietzsche*, Elizabeth Förster-Nietzsche, trans. P. Cohn (London: Heinemann, 1915).

PP *Parerga and Paralipomena* (2 vols.), Arthur Schopenhauer, trans. E. Payne (Oxford: Clarendon Press, 1974).

WMD *Wagner on Music and Drama*, Richard Wagner, ed. A. Goldman and E. Sprinchorn, trans. W. Aston Ellis (London: Gollancz, 1964).

WN *On the Will in Nature*, Arthur Schopenhauer, trans. E. Payne (New York: Berg, 1992).

WPW *Richard Wagner's Prose Works*, Vol. 5, Richard Wagner, trans. W. Ashton Ellis (London: Kegan Paul, Trench, Trübner and Co., 1896).

WR *The World as Will and Representation* (2 vols.), Arthur Schopenhauer, trans. E. Payne (New York: Dover, 1969).

YN *The Young Nietzsche*, Elizabeth Förster-Nietzsche, trans. A. Ludovici (London: Heinemann, 1912).

1. Karl Ludwig Nietzsche (Nietzsche's father).

2. Franziska Nietzsche (Nietzsche's mother) aged about 25.

3. The vicarage in Röcken, where Nietzsche was born, with his father's church behind.

4. 18 Weingarten, Franziska Nietzsche's house in Naumburg.

5. Nietzsche, aged 17.

6. Friedrich Ritschl, Nietzsche's beloved professor in Leipzig.

7. Paul Deussen, aged about 19.

8. Nietzsche, aged 24, at the time of his military service.

9. Arthur Schopenhauer, the 'heavenly picture of our master' by Jules Luntenschütz.

10. Franz Overbeck.

11. The Wagners' house at Tribschen, Lucerne.

12. Richard and Cosima Wagner in May 1872, the time of their transfer to Bayreuth.

13. Nietzsche with his friends Erwin Rohde (on left) and Carl von Gersdorff, October 1871.

14. Wahnfried, the Wagners' house in Bayreuth.

Here where my
delusions found
peace

WAHNFRIED

I name this
house.

15. The Festival Theatre in Bayreuth.

16. Malwida von Meysenbug.

17. Elizabeth Förster-Nietzsche (Nietzsche's sister), aged about 30.

18. Paul Rée.

19. Heinrich Köselitz ('Peter Gast').

20. Mathilde Trampedach.

21. The Durisch house in Sils Maria. Nietzsche's room top right, at the back.

22. Nietzsche's room in the Durisch house.

23. The 'mighty pyramidal block of stone' by Lake Silvaplana where the thought of 'eternal return' first came to Nietzsche.

24. Lou Salomé in 1882, the year of the 'Salomé affair'.

25. 'You are going to women?
Then don't forget the whip'. Lou Salomé, Paul Rée, and Nietzsche, Lucerne, May 1882.

OH MENSCH! GIEB ACHT!
WAS SPRICHT DIE TIEFE MITTERNACHT?
»ICH SCHLIEF, ICH SCHLIEF–,
»AUS TIEFEM TRAUM BIN ICH ERWACHT:–
»DIE WELT IST TIEF,
»UND TIEFER ALS DER TAG GEDACHT.
»TIEF IST IHR WEH–,
»LUST – TIEFER NOCH ALS HERZELEID:
»WEH SPRICHT: VERGEH!
»DOCH ALLE LUST WILL EWIGKEIT–,
»– WILL TIEFE, TIEFE EWIGKEIT!«

MDCCC   FRIEDRICH NIETZSCHE.

26. Memorial to Nietzsche on Chasté peninsula, with quotation from *Zarathustra*'s 'Intoxicated Song'. Erected in 1900 by Carl Fuchs and Walther Lampe.

27. Resa von Schirnhofer.

28. Meta von Salis-Marschlins.

29. Lake Silvaplana, looking towards Sils Maria.

30. The Nietzsche Archive, formerly Villa Silberblick, Weimar.

31. Nietzsche in May 1899, shortly before his death.

32. Elizabeth Förster-Nietzsche and Chancellor Adolf Hitler.

PART ONE

Youth

1

Da Capo

Röcken

NIETZSCHE'S GREATEST inspiration, he believed, was the idea that if one is in a state of perfect mental health one should be able to survey one's entire life and then, rising ecstatically to one's feet, shout '*Da capo!* – Once more! Once more! Back to the beginning!' – to 'the whole play and performance'. In perfect health one would 'crave nothing more fervently' than the 'eternal return' of one's life throughout infinite time – not an expurgated version with the bad bits left out, but *exactly* the same life, down to the very last detail, however painful or shameful. His own particular task was to become able to do this, to reach a point where he could shout '*Da capo!*' to his own life. Let us see what he had to contend with before reaching that point.

Friedrich Nietzsche, 'Fritz', was born (exactly a week before one of his divinities, Sarah Bernhardt) on October 15, 1844, in the Saxon village of Röcken. Two facts about this birthplace are important.

The first is that Röcken lay in that part of Saxony which had been annexed in 1815 by the rising power of Prussia. This was a punishment for the Saxon king's alliance with Napoleon, whom the Prussians, together with their allies, the Russians, Austrians, and Swedes, had defeated in the battle of Leipzig in 1813. (Nietzsche recalls that, unlike the rest of the family, his paternal grandmother had been a great admirer of Napoleon,[1] an attribute which, later on, would become an important part of his own political outlook.)

As we shall see, Prussia looms large in Nietzsche's intellectual landscape. In his youth he was intensely proud of his Prussian nationality – 'I am a Prussian', he declared in a moment of summary self-definition – and was a strong admirer of Otto von Bismarck, Prime Minister of Prussia and later Chancellor of the united German *Reich*. After the horrors of the Franco-Prussian war (1870–71), Bismarck's 'war of choice' initiated in order to compel the German states to unite against a common enemy, Nietzsche became more and more appalled at the use made of Prussian power by the 'blood and iron' Chancellor, and by the complacent, jingoistic philistinism growing up behind its shield. Yet, as a result of being brought up in a passionately Prussian household and in the Prussian education system, he acquired, I shall suggest, an archetypically Prussian personality. That the philosopher who demanded that one organise one's life as a ramrod 'straight line' towards a single 'goal',[2] and that one achieve a 'rank-ordering' in both the soul and the state, should have been claimed as the godfather of contemporary 'postmodernism' is a tribute to the almost unlimited capacity of philosophers wilfully to misunderstand each other.

The second important fact about the location of Nietzsche's birthplace is its position in the heartland of the Protestant Reformation: Röcken is about seventy kilometres from Eisleben, the birthplace of Martin Luther, about twenty-five kilometres southwest of Leipzig, where Johann Sebastian Bach worked and died, and about fifty kilometres from Halle, where Georg Friedrich Händel (or Handel) was born and worked. Both Bach and Handel – the two great musical voices of German Lutheranism and of Nietzsche's homeland – were of great importance to the profoundly musical Fritz. He records that on hearing the Hallelujah Chorus from Handel's *Messiah* during his ninth year, he felt 'as if I had to join in ... the joyful singing of angels, on whose billows of sound Jesus ascended to heaven' and decided to try to write something similar (track 1 on the Web site for this book).[3]

That the future self-styled 'Antichrist' should be born into the cradle of Protestantism creates a paradox we shall have to try to resolve. How was it, we will need to ask, that German Protestantism nursed such a viper in its bosom?

* * *

Fritz was christened 'Friedrich Wilhelm' because he was born on the birthday of the King of Prussia, Friedrich Wilhelm IV, and because his father, Karl Ludwig (see Plate 1), was passionately *Königstreu*, a passionate royalist.

Ludwig, as Nietzsche's father was known, had been born in 1813, the son of Friedrich August (1756–1826), a 'superintendent' (roughly, archdeacon) in the Lutheran church and a writer of treatises on moral and theological subjects. Ludwig's mother, Erdmuthe, was descended from five generations of Lutheran pastors. That Ludwig was a Prussian royalist was at least partly a matter of gratitude. Having completed his theological studies at Halle University, he became tutor to the three daughters of the Duke of Sax-Altenburg, a small principality which, like Röcken, lay in Prussian Saxony. It was here that he acquired a somewhat dandyish taste in dress – far removed from the usual clerical drabness – a taste his son would inherit. And it was here that he met the King of Prussia, on whom he must have made a good impression, since it was by royal decree that, in 1842, he received the living of Röcken together with the neighbouring villages of Michlitz and Bothfeld.

In the same year the twenty-nine-year-old Ludwig met the seventeen-year-old Franziska Oehler (see Plate 2), daughter of David Ernst Oehler, pastor in the nearby village of Pobles. His fine clothes, courtly manners, and talented piano playing – a gift again inherited by his son – must have made a favourable impression, since they were married the following year.

Nietzsche was thus surrounded by Lutheran pastors, wall to wall, as it were. But it would be a mistake to see his later attempted assassination of Christianity as a reaction against a fundamentalist or puritanical background. His family was neither of these, as he himself affirms in *Ecce Homo*, the quasi-autobiography he wrote at the end of his career: 'If I wage war against Christianity, I am the right person to do so, since it never caused me personally any great misfortune or constricted my life – committed Christians have always been well-disposed towards me'.[4]

Nietzsche's father, that is to say, was a man of wide – especially musical – culture who was uninterested in dogma and held the niceties of theological belief to belong within the privacy of individual conscience. And Erdmuthe Nietzsche, as Fritz's sister, Elizabeth, recollects, 'had grown up at a period of dry rationalism . . . and consequently felt ill at ease during the orthodox revival of the 1850s, when people were beginning to be "born again" and denounce themselves in public as desperate sinners'.⁵ The same anti-fanaticism was true of Fritz's maternal grandfather, to whose 'cosy [*gemütlich*]' and indulgent household the young Fritz became extremely attached. David Oehler was the son of a weaver who, through intelligence, education, and marriage, had elevated himself into the landed gentry and was thus able to live the life of a country squire. He fathered eleven children, enjoyed playing cards, and was a farmer and a keen huntsman. He was a gifted musician who organised regular musical gatherings to liven up the winter evenings and possessed a large library that became one of Fritz's favourite haunts.

The Lutheran Church was, in fact, much like the Anglican. It was a path to social advancement and a life of relative gentility. Yet it would be a mistake to reach for the adjective 'Trollopian': to suppose that Christian faith meant nothing to the Nietzsche/Oehlers, that they observed merely its outward, social form. Their faith was genuine and unquestioned, untroubled for the most part by doubt.* It was the foundation of their lives. Elizabeth makes this clear:

> Throughout our childhood Christianity and religion never seemed to contain any element of restraint, but we actually had examples of both constantly before us in the most sublime manifestations of natural submission.⁶

The Nietzsche/Oehlers surrounded the children with authentic Christian lives, with the unforced manifestation of Christian virtue.

This is what makes the ferocity of the mature Nietzsche's attack on Christianity a biographical puzzle. Christianity was the material and emotional foundation of an extended family that filled his childhood with love and security, a warmth he never ceased to value. To his father, in particular, Fritz was intensely attached. In the autobiographical reflections written when he was thirteen, he recalls him as

> the very model of a country parson! Gifted with spirit and a warm heart, adorned with all the virtues of a Christian, he lived a quiet, simple, yet happy life, and was loved and respected by all who knew him. His good manners and cheerful demeanour graced many a

---

* There is one recorded exception to this, which appears in a letter Nietzsche's uncle, Edmund Oehler, wrote him in 1862: 'You will want to know how I am. I'm very well now, thank God. The melancholy, damp fogs are past and there is again pure, fresh air . . . After a time of dark night and great inner suffering a new day and a new life begins to break. Jesus Christ, crucified and resurrected and ascended into heaven, still lives and rules today; he is now my only Lord and the king of my heart, him alone will I follow, for him will I live and die and work. For a considerable time I lived in doubt due to following men, my own reason, and worldly wisdom. As you indeed know, the opinions of men constantly cancel each other out, which means that a searching soul can find no firm foundation. Now, however, that Jesus has become lord of my heart the time of doubt is past. Now I have a firm foundation, for Jesus remains always one and the same . . . My dear Fritz, I know from our conversations that you too are a searching, struggling, conflicted soul. Follow my advice and make Jesus your Lord, whom alone you follow . . . not any human system. Jesus alone, Jesus alone, and again Jesus alone . . . Jesus alone' (KGB 1.1 To Nietzsche 58). This seems to suggest that Nietzsche's uncle Edmund, after a religious crisis, emerged into a 'born again' Christianity which, in the main, the Nietzsche/Oehlers found quite alien.

social occasion to which he had been invited, and made him straight away loved by all. His leisure hours he occupied with the delights of science and with music. In his piano playing he had achieved a notable skill, especially in improvising variations on a theme...[7]

— a skill in which Fritz, too, would soon excel. Elizabeth qualifies this picture of their father with a slightly repressive nuance, recalling that no discord was allowed to come to his attention since

he was an extraordinarily sensitive man, or, as was said of him at the time, he took everything so much to heart. Any sign of discord either in the parish or in his own family was so painful to him that he would withdraw to his study and refuse to eat or drink, or speak with anyone.[8]

Yet not for a moment does she doubt Fritz's intense devotion to him:

Our father used to spend much of his time with us, but more especially with his eldest son, Fritz, whom he called his 'little friend', and whom he allowed to be with him even when he was busy, as he [Fritz] knew how to sit still and would thoughtfully watch his father at work. Even when Fritz was only a year old he was so delighted by his father's music that whenever he cried for no apparent reason our father was begged to play the piano to him. Then the child would sit upright in his little pram, as still as a mouse, and would not take his eyes off the musician.[9]

In *Ecce Homo*, Nietzsche states that he

regard[s] it as a great privilege to have had such a father; it even seems to me that whatever else of privileges I possess is thereby explained...Above all, that it requires no intention on my part, but only a mere waiting, for me to enter involuntarily into a world of exalted and delicate things [the world of books]: there I am at home, only there does my innermost passion become free.[10]

Whatever, therefore, the grounds for Nietzsche's turn against Christianity, they are not to be found in any Oedipal desire to 'kill the father'.

* * *

The Röcken vicarage (see Plate 3) was presided over by women — by Ludwig's widowed mother, Erdmuthe, a kind but sickly woman sensitive to noise, and by his spinster stepsisters: Auguste, who ran the household and was a victim of gastric troubles, and Rosalie, who was mildly domineering, suffered from 'nerves', was interested in politics, and — unusual for a woman of her times — read the newspapers. Fritz was fond of them all.

Franziska, eighteen when she gave birth to Fritz, was a woman of some spirit, a warm heart, a modest education, simple faith, and the narrow, conservative outlook typical for a girl of rural upbringing. To her teenage son she would complain of his 'desire to be different'. He in turn would complain of her, and Elizabeth's, 'Naumburg virtue', a term denoting narrow, legalistic, oppressive small-town morality taken from the name of the town to which they would soon move.

Fritz's sister, Elizabeth, born on July 10, 1846, was christened Elizabeth Therese Alexandra after the three princesses her father had tutored at the court of Sax-Altenburg. Elizabeth, or 'Llama', as Fritz nicknamed her, worshipped her elder brother, who in turn patronised her in a lordly, though kindly, manner. Elizabeth recalls that after entering grammar school he started calling her 'little girl', even though they were less than two years apart, and, in the street, insisted on walking five paces ahead of her and any female companion she might have.* From an early age, she developed the habit of squirreling away anything Fritz had written, the origin of the remarkably extensive collection of unpublished material (the *Nachlass*) that survived Nietzsche's death. Devoid of any capacity for abstract thought and given to sentimentality (her writing would be so much better if she could get over all the 'ohs' and 'ahs', Nietzsche complained to their mother),[11] Elizabeth nonetheless developed a capacity for shrewd (eventually criminal) entrepreneurship which, as we shall see, enabled her to make a good living from her brother's name after his descent into madness.

Since Franziska was not responsible for running the household and since she was almost as close in age to her children as to the adults of the household, she became as much an older sister as a mother to Fritz and Elizabeth.

* * *

Here is how the seventeen-year-old Nietzsche recalls the village of his birth in one of the nine autobiographical fragments he wrote during his teenage years:

> I was born in Röcken, a village which lies along the high road and is near to Lützen. Enclosing it are woods of willows as well as a few poplars and elms, so that from a distance only the chimneys and the tower of the ancient church are visible above the tree tops. Inside the village are large ponds, separated from each other only by narrow strips of land. Around them are bright green, knotty willows. Somewhat higher lies the vicarage and the church, the former surrounded by a garden and orchard. Adjacent is the cemetery full of gravestones partially collapsed into the earth. The vicarage itself is shaded by three fine, broad-branched elms whose stately height and shape makes a pleasing impression on the visitor...Here I lived in the happy circle of my family untouched by the wide world beyond. The village and its immediate environs were my world, the everything beyond it an unknown, magical region.[12]

Three years earlier his recollections, though in the main as sunny as this, are touched by some gothic shadows:

> The village of Röcken...looks quite charming with its surrounding woods and its ponds. Above all, one notices the mossy tower of the church. I can well remember how one day

---

* In 1862, at the age of sixteen, Elizabeth was sent to Dresden, the cultural capital of Southeast Germany, to complete her education. The following letter reveals both Fritz's affection for and his schoolmasterly patronising of his sister: 'Dear, dear Lisbeth...I think of you almost always...even when I'm asleep I often dream of you and our time together...You will survive another couple of months in Dresden. Above all try to get to know well all the art treasures of Dresden, so that you can gain some real profit. You must visit the art galleries at least once or twice a week and it would be good if you look at only two or three pictures so that you can give me a detailed description – in writing, naturally' (KGB 1.1 302).

I walked with my dear father from Lützen back to Röcken and how half way we heard the uplifting ringing of the bells sounding the Easter festival. This ringing often echoes in me still and nostalgia carries me back to the distant house of my father. How often I interested myself in funeral biers and black crêpe and old gravestone inscriptions and memorials when I saw the old, old mortuary…Our house was built in 1820 and so was in excellent condition. Several steps led up to the ground floor. I can still remember the study on the top floor. The rows of books, among them many picture-books and scrolls, made it my favourite place. Behind the house lay the garden and orchard. Part of this tended to flood in spring as did the cellar. At the front of the house lay the courtyard with barn and stalls which led to the flower garden. I was usually to be found sitting in its shady spots. Behind the green wall lay the four ponds surrounded by willows. To walk among them, to see the rays of the sun reflecting off their surfaces and the cheerful little fishes playing was my greatest joy. I have yet to mention something that always filled me with secret horror: in the gloom of the church stood on one side an over-life-size image of St. George, carved in stone by a skilful hand. The impressive figure, the terrible weapon and the mysterious twilight always caused me to shrink back when I looked at it.* It is said that, once, his eyes flashed so terrifyingly that all who saw him were filled with horror. – Around the cemetery lay the farmhouses and gardens constructed in rustic style. Harmony and peace reigned over every roof, wild events entirely absent. The inhabitants seldom left the village, at most for the annual fair, when cheerful throngs of lads and lassies took off for busy Lützen to admire the crowds and the shiny wares for sale.[13]

Tranquil though Röcken was, the outside world was in a quite different condition:

While we in Röcken lived quietly and peaceably earth-shattering events shook almost all European nations. Years earlier the explosive material [the French Revolution of 1789] had been spread everywhere so it needed only a spark to set it on fire. – Then one heard from distant France the first clash of weapons and battle songs. The terrible February Revolution [of 1848] happened in Paris and spread with ever-increasing speed. 'Liberty, Equality, Fraternity' was the cry in every country, people, humble and elevated, took up the sword, sometimes in defence of the king and sometimes against him. The revolutionary war in Paris was imitated in most of the states of Prussia. And even though quickly suppressed, there remained for a long time a desire among the people for 'a German Republic'. These ructions never penetrated to Röcken, although I can still remember wagons filled with cheering crowds and fluttering flags passing by on the main road.[14]

In the royalist household at Röcken, there was of course no sympathy at all for this repetition of the French Revolution (a repetition that involved Richard Wagner in Dresden and Karl Marx in the Rhineland). On hearing that, in an effort to appease the crowd, the Prussian king had donned the red cockade of the socialist revolutionaries, Ludwig broke down and cried.[15] All his life, as we shall see, Nietzsche retained a hatred of Rousseau (who gave the French Revolution its battle-cry of 'Liberty, Equality, Fraternity'), of socialism, and

---

* This is a mistake. There has never been a statue of St. George in the Röcken church. Instead there are two wall-reliefs depicting medieval knights, each armed with a large sword.

indeed of revolution of any kind. And true to his father's royalism, he always thought of monarchy as the ideal form of government.[16]

* * *

During this, throughout Europe, tumultuous spring, Franziska gave birth to her third child, who was christened Joseph, in honour of Duke Joseph of Sax-Altenburg whom Karl Ludwig had once served. Flexing his precocious literary talent, the thirteen-year-old Nietzsche takes up the story:

> Up to now happiness and joy had shone upon us always: our life flowed on unperturbed, like a bright summer's day. But now black clouds piled up above us, lightning flashed, and hammer blows were sent from heaven to strike us. In September 1848 my beloved father suddenly became mentally ill. We consoled ourselves and him, however, with the hope he would soon recover. Whenever a better day did come he would preach and hold his confirmation lessons, for his active spirit was incapable of slothfulness. Several physicians endeavoured to discover the nature of his illness but in vain. Then we sent for the famous Dr. Opolcer, who was in Leipzig at the time, and he came to Röcken. This excellent man immediately recognised where the seat of the illness was to be found. To the horror of us all he diagnosed it as a softening of the brain, not yet hopelessly advanced, but already extremely dangerous. My father had to suffer terribly, but the illness would not diminish, on the contrary it grew worse from day to day. Finally the power of vision was extinguished, and he had to endure his sufferings in eternal darkness. He was bedridden until July 1849; then the day of his redemption drew nigh. On July 26th he sank into a deep slumber from which he awoke only fitfully. His last words were: 'Fränzchen – Fränzchen – come – mother – listen – O God!' Then he died, quietly and blessedly † † † † on July 27th 1849 [at the age of 35]. When I woke the next morning all around me I heard loud weeping and sobbing. My dear mother came to me with tears in her eyes and cried out 'O God! My good Ludwig is dead!'. Although I was very young and inexperienced, I still had some idea of death: the thought that I would be separated for ever from my dear father seized me and I wept bitterly. The next few days passed amid tears and preparations for the funeral. O God! I had become a fatherless orphan, my dear mother a widow! – On August 2nd the earthly remains of my beloved father were committed to the womb of the earth. The parish had prepared for him a stone-lined grave. At one o'clock in the afternoon the service began, with the bells pealing their loud knell. Oh, never will the deep-throated sound of those bells quit my ear; never will I forget the gloomy surging melody of the hymn 'Jesu, my trust'! The sound of the organ resounded through the empty spaces of the church.[17]

Since an autopsy revealed a quarter of the brain to be missing, it seems certain that Nietzsche lost his beloved father to some kind of brain disease. Though he was only five years old, the loss marked him for life. In 1885, having been awarded seven thousand Swiss francs in a court settlement against his publisher, the first thing he purchased after paying off bookstore debts was an engraved tombstone for his father's grave – thirty-six years after Ludwig's death.[18] It appears that it was Nietzsche himself (by now in full swing as the scourge of Christianity) who designed the stone on which is inscribed a quotation from St. Paul: 'Love never faileth (I Cor, 13, 8)'.

The death of his father, soon to be followed by the loss of the *Vaterhaus* [father-house], as Nietzsche always refers to the Röcken vicarage, was Nietzsche's first loss of security. A sense of homelessness became, and would remain, an obsessive theme in his poetry. In his fourteenth year, for instance, allowing feelings to surface that he could not easily express outside poetry, he composed the following:

> *Where to?*
> *Little bird in the air,*
> *Fly away with your song,*
> *And greet for me my dear,*
> *My beloved Home.*
>
> *O lark, take this blossom*
> *Tender with you.*
> *I plucked it as decoration*
> *For my far-away father's house.*
>
> *O nightingale fly down to me*
> *and take this rosebud*
> *to my father's grave.*[19]

* * *

Almost immediately, however, Fritz's desolation over the loss of his father was intensified by two further 'hammer blows from heaven'. The thirteen-year-old continues:

When a tree is deprived of its crown it withers and wilts, and the tiny birds abandon its branches. Our family had been deprived of its head. All joy vanished from our hearts and profound sadness overtook us. Yet when our wounds had only just begun to heal a new event painfully tore them open. – At that time I had a dream that I heard organ music in the church, the music I had heard during my father's funeral. When I perceived what lay behind these sounds, a grave-mound suddenly opened up and my father, wrapped in a linen shroud, emerged from it. He hurried into the church and returned a moment later with a child in his arms. The tomb yawned again, he entered it, and the cover closed over the opening. The stentorian sounds of the organ ceased instantly and I awoke. On the day that followed this night, little Joseph suddenly fell ill, seized by severe cramps, and after a few hours he died. Our grief knew no bounds. My dream had been fulfilled completely. The tiny corpse was laid to rest in his father's arms. – In this double misfortune, God in heaven was our sole consolation and protection. This happened [in]...the year 1850.[20]

Since the vicarage was needed for the new pastor, Fritz now lost not only father and brother, but also the *Vaterhaus*:

The time approached when we were to be separated from our beloved Röcken. I can still remember the last day and night we spent there. That evening I played with several local children, conscious of the fact that it would be for the last time. The vesper bell tolled its melancholy peal across the waters, dull darkness settled over the earth, and the moon and shimmering stars shone in the night sky. I could not sleep for very long. At one-thirty in the morning I went down again to the courtyard. Several wagons stood there, being loaded. The dull glimmer of their lanterns cast a gloomy light across the courtyard. I considered it absolutely impossible that I would ever feel at home in another place. How painful it was to abandon a village where one had experienced joy and sorrow, where the graves of my father and younger brother lay, where the village folk always surrounded me with love and friendliness. Scarcely had the dawning day shed its light on the meadows, when our wagon rolled out onto the high road that took us to Naumburg, where a new home awaited. – Adieu, adieu, dear *Vaterhaus*. [21]

* * *

Earlier, I raised the question of how it was that Christianity's great enemy could have grown up in the heartland of German Protestantism, in a family that provided him, to an exemplary degree, with warmth and love. How was it that, in his maturity, he came to attack the foundation on which his childhood security had been built? It might be, of course, that Nietzsche's philosophical commitment to telling the truth without fear or favour simply overrode all personal considerations. But it might also be that, already in earliest childhood, he was aware of shadowy corners within the sunlit world of his Lutheran homeland, that the worm of doubt was already present in his earliest experiences. Read carefully, I believe, the autobiographical fragments – written, it should be emphasised, by a still-committed Christian – suggest this to be the case.

The adult philosopher has an armoury of polemical descriptions of Christianity: 'madhouse', 'torture chamber', 'hangman God',[22] among others. One phrase, however, is of particular interest: 'Christian sick house and dungeon atmosphere'.[23] 'Sick house' is of interest since, from the end of Fritz's third year, the Nietzsche household was, literally, a 'sick house'. Though the recollections of his father in *Ecce Homo* are a eulogy, they contain, nonetheless, an emphasis on sickness: 'My father died at the age of thirty-six: he was delicate, loveable and morbid, like a being destined only temporarily for this world – a gracious reminder of life rather than life itself'.[24] And, in the remark quoted on p. 6 above what Nietzsche actually says (a major qualification I there omitted) is that he owes his father every 'privilege' of his nature *save for* 'life, the great Yes to life [which is] *not* included' in his debt. Putting these remarks together, we can see that Nietzsche remembers his father as 'morbid' not just physically but also spiritually, remembers him as, in his later terminology, a 'life-denier' rather than a 'life-affirmer': someone low in energy, withdrawn from life in the hope of finding his true home in another, better world. Recall, too, Elizabeth's remark that, even before the onset of his sickness, Ludwig was so sensitive that at the least sign of discord he would 'withdraw to his study and refuse to eat or drink, or speak with anyone' (p. 6 above). It seems to me possible that one of the things the mature Nietzsche held, at least unconsciously, against the Christian worldview was that, with its reduction of this world to a cold and draughty waiting-room we sinners are forced to inhabit prior to our departure for the 'true' world above, it deprived his father of the fullness of life he might have enjoyed had he not been in its grips – deprived him even, perhaps, of life itself.

As for the phrase 'dungeon atmosphere', this puts one in mind of Fritz's 'horror' (about which he could tell no one) before the threatening figure of 'St. George' with his 'terrible weapon' and 'flashing eyes' in the 'gloomy church' (p. 8 above). Could this, one wonders, be an early encounter with 'the hangman God'? And then the mortuary, the tombstones, the black crêpe and the funeral biers: the immediate environment of Nietzsche's childhood provided daily encounters with death and with the terror of its Christian meaning. Though Fritz's autobiographical reflections are, for the most part, conventionally sunny, they include enough of what I called a 'gothic' undertone – later, he will speak of Christianity as a sunless world of 'grey, frosty, unending mist and shadow'[25] – to suggest that some of the seeds of the later critique of Christianity lie in the earliest terrors of an imaginative child.

Naumburg

Compelled to vacate the Röcken vicarage, the Nietzsches moved in April 1850 to nearby Naumburg. Initially they took lodgings in the Neugasse, in the house of a rail-haulage agent, Herr Otto. (The railway connecting Naumburg to Leipzig in one direction and Weissenfels in the other had only just been completed.) Following the deaths of Aunt Augusta in 1855 and Grandmother Erdmuthe in the following year, however, Franziska moved to the house of a friend and then, relieved to escape the dominion of older women, to her own establishment. In the autumn of 1858 she moved once again, to 335 (today 18) Weingarten, where she remained the rest of her life (see Plate 4). It was from this house that Nietzsche left for boarding school in 1858, and to it that he returned, insane, thirty-two years later, to be cared for by his mother until her death in 1897.

* * *

Situated near the confluence of two slow-moving rivers, the Unstrut and the larger Saale, Naumburg is a small cathedral town. But, coming from a tiny hamlet, the five-year-old Fritz experienced it as a vast and frightening metropolis. Here is his recollection of his first encounter:

> Our grandmother together with Aunt Rosalie and the servant girl went on ahead [from Röcken] and we followed later, feeling very sad…For us [Fritz and Elizabeth] it was a terrible experience after living for so long in the countryside. So we avoided the gloomy streets and sought the open countryside, like a bird that flees its cage…I was amazed by the unaccustomed crowds of people. And then I was astonished when I observed that none of them were known to each other, for in the village everyone knew everyone else. What I found most unpleasant were the long, paved streets.[26]

Fritz, we saw, experienced the loss of his father as a 'wound'. The loss of Röcken and the transplantation to a strange and frightening environment was another. Soon, of course, it began to heal as, with a healthy boy's adaptability, he began to settle into life in Naumburg. But though the wound healed, it left a scar. As already remarked, the yearning for the security of a recovered homeland remained an undertone throughout Nietzsche's life.

* * *

Once Fritz had adjusted to the change of scale, one thing that may have helped him acquire at least relative security in Naumburg is the fact that the town was then enclosed by a medieval wall. Here is Elizabeth's description:

> It was surrounded by walls, and from ten o'clock at night to five o'clock in the morning five heavy gates closed it in on all sides from the outer world. It was only by dint of loud ringing, and the gift of a small donation, that the gatekeeper could be induced, often after a prolonged wait, to allow those standing outside to enter, so that anyone who spent the evenings outside the city in the vineyards on the hills would hasten his footsteps when he heard the little bell ring from the tower of the town-hall, giving warning, a few minutes beforehand, of the closing of the gates. All round the town there was a deep moat, bounded on the other side by a fine avenue of elms, which in its turn was surrounded by gardens, fields and vine-clad hills.[27]

At least until the beginning of his nomadic mode of life at the end of the 1870s, Nietzsche hated large cities. But small towns where one was protected from the dangers of the wide world by a wall, where one came to know one's neighbours and remained in contact with the countryside, he came to love, particularly Germany's old medieval towns. In 1874, for instance, he wrote to his friend Edwin Rohde [28] that he planned to leave the city of Basel and move to the walled (to this very day) medieval town of Rotenburg-ob-der-Tauber in Franconia since, unlike the cities of modernity, it was still '*altdeutsch*' [German in the old-fashioned way] and 'whole'.

Naumburg, too, spiritually as well as architecturally, was '*altdeutsch*'. It was, as Elizabeth writes, 'a thoroughly Christian, conservative town, loyal to the King and a pillar of Throne and Church'.[29] Here is Fritz, the thirteen-year-old royalist, recollecting the visit of his namesake, the King of Prussia:

> Our dear King honoured Naumburg with a visit [in 1854]. Great preparations were made for the occasion. All the schoolchildren were decked out with black-and-white favours [ribbons or badges signifying allegiance to the crown] and stood in the market place from eleven o'clock in the morning awaiting the arrival of the father of the country. Gradually the sky became overcast, rain poured down on us all – the king would not come! Twelve o'clock struck – the King did not come. Many of the children began to feel hungry. A fresh downpour occurred, all the streets were covered in mud. One o'clock struck – the impatience grew intense. Suddenly about two o'clock the bells began to ring and the sky smiled through its tears upon the joyously swaying crowd. Then we heard the rattle of the carriage; a boisterous cheer roared through the city; we waved our caps in exultation and cheered at the top of our voices. A fresh breeze set flying the myriad flags which hung from the roofs, all the bells of the town rang out, and the vast crowd shouted, hurrahed, and literally pushed the carriage in the direction of the cathedral. In its alcoves had been placed a large number of young girls with white dresses and garlands of flowers in their hair. The King alighted, praised the preparations and entered the residence prepared for him. That evening the whole town was lit up. Countless numbers of people thronged the streets. The pyramids of garlands on the town hall and cathedral were lit from top to bottom with tiny lamps. Thousands of banners decorated the houses. Fireworks were set off in the cathedral square so that from time to time the dark shape of the cathedral was lit up by an unearthly light.[30]

* * *

Shortly after arriving in Naumburg, Fritz was sent to the *Knaben-Bürgerschule*, the town's primary school for boys, rather than to a private school. The reason, as Elizabeth records, was that Grandmother Erdmuthe held the startlingly modern idea that, up to the age of ten, children of all social strata should be taught together since 'the children of the higher classes would thus acquire a better understanding of the attitude of mind peculiar to the lower orders'.[31] (This same thought, one supposes, motivates the British royal family's practice of having their sons do military service.) But though he did acquire his first real friends, the cousins Wilhelm Pinder and Gustav Krug, mixing the short-sighted, bookish Fritz with the rough boys from the 'lower orders' did not work particularly well. After a year, therefore, the three boys were transferred to the private school of a Herr Weber, devoted to preparing pupils for entry into grammar school. They stayed here until 1854, when they duly gained admission to the *Domgymnasium*, the Cathedral Grammar School, a building attached to the cathedral itself. Here, for the first time, Nietzsche began to suffer from the blinding headaches that would plague him for the rest of his life, and was often absent from school. Nonetheless he worked extremely hard, often until eleven or twelve at night, even though he had to get up at five o'clock the next morning.[32] As a result he won a scholarship to the prestigious boarding school Pforta, to which he transferred in the autumn of 1858.

* * *

Though bookish, the Fritz of the Naumburg years was also rather charmingly boyish. He recollects the life he and his two friends led at Weber's prep school:

> Herr Candidate [for ordination] Weber, a diligent, Christian teacher, knew of our friendship and did not seek to separate us. Here was laid the foundation of our future education. For along with excellent religious instruction, we received our first lessons in Greek and Latin. We were not overloaded with work, and had time therefore for physical activity. In summer we often made small excursions into the surrounding countryside. We visited the lovely Schönburg, castle Goseck Frieburg, as well as Rudelsburg and Saaleck, usually together with the whole Institute. Walking together in a group always makes one feel cheerful; patriotic songs sounded out, enjoyable games were played, and when the route went through a forest we decorated ourselves with leaves and twigs. The castles resounded with the wild cries of the revellers – it put me in mind of the carousing of the knights of old. In the courtyards and in the forest, too, we had horseback battles, imitating in miniature the most glorious time of the middle ages. Then we climbed the high towers and guard posts and surveyed the golden valley shimmering in the evening light, and when the mist descended on the meadows we returned homewards with our merry cries. Every spring we had a feast that was our version of the cherry festival. That is, we went off to Rossbach, a small village near Naumburg, where two birds awaited our crossbows. We shot enthusiastically, Herr Weber divided up the spoils and a great time was had by all. In the nearby woods we played cops and robbers.[33]

Apart from the idea of arming small boys with crossbows, these may strike one as pretty normal boys' games. In fact, however, the way Fritz played his war games evinces a precocious, creative intelligence.

In 1854, following Russian successes against the Turks in the Black Sea region, the British and French declared war on Russia, aiming to prevent its further westward expansion, which threatened the Mediterranean and their main overland routes to India. Major battles were fought at the River Alma, Balaclava, and Inkerman. In spite of major British incompetence – famously, the suicidal charge of the Light Brigade – the fall of the coastal Russian fortress of Sebastopol in September 1855 led finally to peace negotiations. The thirteen-year-old Fritz recalls how the Crimean War was viewed from Naumburg:

> The French and English equipped an army and fleet and sent them to help [the Turks]. The theatre of war was in the Crimea, and the huge army besieged Sebastopol where the great Russian army under Menschikoff made a stand. – We approved of that, so we immediately took up the Russian cause and angrily challenged anyone who sided with the Turks to battle. Since we possessed tin soldiers and a construction set we spared no effort in recreating the siege and the battle. We built walls of earth, everyone found new methods of making them properly stable. We all kept a small book which we called 'war lists', had lead balls poured

and increased the size of our armies with new purchases. Sometimes we dug a little pool following the plan of the harbour of Sebastopol, constructed the precise fortifications, and filled our harbour with water. We formed a lot of balls from pitch, sulphur and saltpetre and when they were alight hurled them at the paper ships. Soon bright flames blazed away; our excitement grew and it was really beautiful – since we often played late into the evening – to see the fiery balls whistling through the darkness. In the end the whole fleet as well as all the bombs were burned up; during the conflagration flames often rose two feet into the air. In such a manner I had happy times, not just with my friends [Pinder and Krug] but also with my sister. We, too, constructed fortifications with our construction kit and through much practice learned all the finer points of building ... We discussed at length everything we could discover about the science of war, so that I became pretty expert. War lexicons as well as recently published military books enriched our collections and already we wanted to write a great military dictionary.[34]

Another game exhibiting Fritz's freakish, multifaceted intelligence, as well as his royalist sentiments, is recalled by Elizabeth:

My brother and I ... created an imaginary world of our own in which tiny china figures of men and animals, lead soldiers, etc., all revolved round one central personality in the shape of a little porcelain squirrel about an inch and a half high whom we called King Squirrel I ... It never for a moment entered our heads that there is nothing regal about a squirrel; on the contrary, we considered that it had a most majestic presence ... this small king gave rise to all sorts of joyous little ceremonies. – Everything that my brother made was in honour of King Squirrel; all his musical productions were to glorify His Majesty; on his birthday ... poems were recited and plays acted, all of which were written by my brother. King Squirrel was a patron of art; he must have a picture gallery. Fritz painted one hung round with Madonnas, landscapes, etc., etc. A particularly beautiful picture represented a room in an old monastery in which an old-fashioned lamp burnt in a niche and filled the whole apartment with a quaint glow.[35]

* * *

Fritz had close and affectionate relations with both his sister and mother. But he also became very close to Wilhelm Pinder and Gustav Krug, who were, as observed, his first real friends. They remained friends throughout their schooldays, though they began drifting apart when Wilhelm and Gustav left to attend university in Heidelberg while Fritz went to Bonn.

Both friends came from families of higher social standing than the Nietzsches. Wilhelm, a gentle, somewhat fragile boy, lived with his father, a judge, and his grandmother in half of one of the best houses in town (the other half was occupied by the Krugs), a five-storied villa facing the marketplace, where both Frederick the Great and Napoleon were said to have stayed. A good friend of Fritz's grandmother, Grandmother Pinder was one of Naumburg's leading ladies, her house a gathering-place for all who were interested in literature and the arts. She and Erdmuthe encouraged the boys to become friends. Judge Pinder was of a literary disposition, and it was he who introduced Fritz to the works of Goethe, whom Nietzsche would come to admire more than any other human being. Poetry was the principal bond between Fritz and Wilhelm.

Gustav was of a more rugged disposition than Wilhelm. His father, as Fritz recalls,

> was a great music enthusiast and virtuoso. He had even written several significant composi-
> tions ... He possessed a wonderful grand piano so that I often stood spellbound in front of
> his house listening to Beethoven's sublime music. Mendelssohn was a close friend as well
> as the Müller brothers, those famous violin virtuosi whom I was once lucky enough to hear.
> In his house there often assembled a select group of friends of music, and virtually every
> virtuoso who wanted to perform in Naumburg sought Herr Krug's recommendation.[36]

Brought up in such a household, Gustav developed a passion for music as strong as Fritz's, and soon became a violinist of what must have been considerable ability, since in December 1863 he writes Fritz that he is playing the – extremely difficult – Mendelssohn violin concerto. Music was the principal bond between him and Fritz, a bond that was nourished by the wonderfully rich musical environment provided not just by the Krug household, but by Naumburg in general. Fritz recalls that as a boy

> I heard many oratorios. The breath-catching Requiem was what I heard first – how the
> words 'Dies irae, dies illa' touched me at the core. But oh the truly heavenly Benedictus! –
> I often attended rehearsals. Since the requiem mass was usually performed at funerals many
> of these occurred during the foggy, autumn evenings. In the sacred, semi-darkness of the
> cathedral I sat and listened to the noble melodies. At this point I must mention the cathe-
> dral's music director, Herr Wetig, an utterly committed musician who both conducted and
> composed. His small choir was always in first-rate order, and he rehearsed the choir of the
> choral society in an exemplary manner. On top of this he was accounted the best music
> teacher in Naumburg. His wife, a former opera singer, also did much to improve perfor-
> mances. Besides these we have two further music directors in Naumburg: Otto Claudius,
> conductor of the former *Liedertafel*, a diligent composer though somewhat vain and con-
> ceited; and Fuckel, who directed the town choir. – Also I heard Handel's *Judas Maccabaeus*
> and, above all, Haydn's *Creation*. And then I was at the performance of the tender and apt
> *Midsummer Night's Dream* by Mendelssohn.[37] This wonderful overture! It seemed to me as
> though elves in a moon-sparkling silver night were dancing in airy rings.[38]

* * *

Because he was shy and because he had high expectations, Nietzsche found it difficult to make friends. But once made he valued them deeply. Unsurprisingly, therefore, friendship is much discussed in his mature writings. In different places he proposes two elements of friendship, both of which should exist, to one degree or another, in a true friendship. The first of these, which may be called the 'agonistic' element, is based on his study of the Greek ideal of *agon* – aggressive competition contained within ultimately cooperative bounds. 'In your friend', says *Thus spoke Zarathustra*, 'you shall find your best enemy'.[39] The friendship with Krug seems to have been marked by a strongly agonistic element: Fritz records that 'we often looked at a musical score together, offered contrary opinions, tried this and that, playing alternately' on the piano.[40] As we shall see, it was Gustav's persistence which finally overcame Fritz's innate musical conservatism and persuaded him to become, for a fateful decade, an enthusiast for the *Zukunftsmusik* [music of the future] of Richard Wagner.

Nietzsche did not believe in exposing one's soul to the other: one should wear one's *best* clothes and not wish to appear before the friend with 'no clothes', says *Zarathustra*.[41] In place of soul-to-soul intimacy, he proposes, as the second element in true friendship, shared commitment to a common goal. It is this that constitutes the shared bounds to the agonistic struggle. Comradeship seems to have been strongly to the fore in the friendship with Pinder. He was, Nietzsche recalls, 'milder than Gustav, even the opposite', with the result that 'we worked almost always in harmony so that our opinions and ideas almost always agreed'.[42]

In the latter part of his creative life Nietzsche suffered acutely from loneliness. Like his alter ego, Zarathustra, he found himself alone on a (Swiss) mountain-top. But, intellectually at least, he accepted this condition. Since, he reasoned, a radical social critic, a 'free spirit' such as himself, sets himself ever more in opposition to the foundational agreements on which social life depends, he reduces the pool of possible comrades, and so of possible friends, to the vanishing point. But in his youth he was far from being a social critic. He was, rather, as we will shortly see, a social conformist, indeed a *passionate* social conformist. And so he by no means lacked friends. The accusation often made that he was constitutionally incapable of friendship is manifestly mistaken.

* * *

What was Fritz really like in those early, prepubescent years in Naumburg? First, of course, he was, though not a prodigy in the Mozartian mould, nonetheless prodigious. We have already noticed the unusual creative intelligence behind his boyhood games. In Naumburg he started piano lessons and was already playing the easier Beethoven piano sonatas after two years of study. (In British terms, that is, he reached Grade 8 within two years.) In his autobiographical reflections he lists forty-six poems written between the ages of eleven and thirteen (he had a passion for lists). And already in prepubescent days he liked nothing better than fossicking around in Grandfather Oehler's library and visiting the Leipzig bookshops with him.[43] As Elizabeth reports, it was in fact Grandfather Oehler who first spotted Fritz's unusual gifts, telling Franziska that he was the most talented boy he had ever seen, more talented than his own six sons put together.[44]

Less often noticed, but equally marked, is the fact that he was an extremely affectionate boy, affectionate towards his entire extended family, especially Grandfather Oehler, and towards his friends. Without his two 'noble, true, friends', he records,

> I would perhaps never have felt at home in Naumburg. But since I have won such lively friends, being here is dear to me, and it would be extremely painful to have to leave. For we three are never apart except when I make a holiday trip somewhere else with Mamma and my sister.[45]

Wilhelm supports this, calling Fritz, in his own recollections (also recorded in his teenage years), 'a very dear and loving friend to me'.[46]

It is true that Fritz also needed solitude. Here is his own, retrospective, character-assessment:

> I had, in my young life, already seen a great deal of tragedy and sadness and was therefore not as wild and jolly as children usually are. My schoolfellows used to tease me on account of my seriousness. This didn't just happen in the primary school but also in the Institute

[of Herr Weber] and even in grammar school. From childhood onwards I sought to be alone and felt best when I could be undisturbed by myself. And this was usually in the free temple of nature, where I found the truest joy. So a thunderstorm always made the deepest impression on me; the rumble of distant thunder and the brightly flickering lightning only increased my awe in the face of God.[47]

The twin human needs, for solitude and for society, are, presumably, universal. But there is no doubt that Nietzsche possessed the former to an abnormally high degree – in his maturity, largely because he had a great many things to say and an increasing sense that the time he had to say them in was short. Solitude, one might suggest, is the fate of the writer. Yet in the above self-assessment there is surely a degree of adolescent self-dramatisation. For, as we have seen, there was a great deal of normal boyish sociability, even boisterousness, in Fritz's early life. One should not, moreover, be tempted to discover any hint of misan-thropy in his delight in entering the 'free temple of nature'. The reason he finds there his 'truest joy' is not that there is no joy to be found among humans but rather that it is in the sublimity of nature that he discovers God.

God

For most of his youth, Nietzsche intended to enter the priesthood. Through, no doubt, identification with his dead father, he was given to priestly moments at an early age. Elizabeth records that he was nicknamed 'the little pastor' since, already in primary school, 'he could recite biblical texts and hymns with such feeling that he almost made one cry'.[48]

Yet there was more to Nietzsche's piety than theatre. The following private note from his thirteenth year contains a startling intensity of genuine religious feeling, feeling bound up with the need to believe that one day he would be reunited with his father:

I had already experienced so much – joy and sorrow, cheerful things and sad things – but in everything God has safely led me as a father leads his weak little child…I have firmly resolved within me to dedicate myself forever to His service. May the dear Lord give me strength and power to carry out my intentions and protect me on my life's way. Like a child I trust in his grace: He will preserve us all, that no misfortune may befall us. But His holy will be done! All He gives I will joyfully accept: happiness and unhappiness, poverty and wealth, and boldly look even death in the face, which shall one day unite us all in eternal joy and bliss. Yes, dear Lord, let Thy face shine upon us forever! Amen![49]

An important affirmation here is: 'All He gives I will joyfully accept'. This is an almost exact formulation of the doctrine of Nietzsche's maturity which he sometimes calls *amor fati* [love of fate] and sometimes 'willing the eternal return of the same': the doctrine that an ideal of human well-being is being able to say a joyful 'Yes' to *everything* that has happened and thus will its eternal return. This doctrine was formulated long after he had ceased to believe in the Christian God. But what the close similarity between it and Nietzsche's youthful Christian piety suggests is that at the heart of his mature thought is the effort to rediscover, even in God's absence, central elements of the passionate Christian's stance to existence.

Another aspect of Fritz's Christian piety which is reflected in the philosophy of his adult-hood is his love of Christmas. Partly, of course, he loves Christmas from a normal, boyish delight in high days, holidays and presents, but partly, too, out of something more. As a thirteen-year-old he asks himself why it is he loves Christmas even more than birthdays, and answers that Christmas is 'the most blessed festival of the year because it doesn't con-cern us alone, but rather the whole of mankind, rich and poor, humble and great, low and high. And it is precisely this universal joy which intensifies our own mood'.[50] This same deeply rooted yearning for union and harmony between all men appears in Fritz's record of a visit, in August 1860, to Gorenzen, a forest-encircled town not far from Luther's birth-place at Eisleben, on the southeast fringe of the Harz mountains, where his uncle Edmund Oehler was the pastor:

> And then it was Sunday. My uncle was very busy the whole morning. I saw him first outside the entrance to the church. The attendance was large and regular. And what a wonderful sermon he gave. He spoke about reconciliation, taking as his text "If you bring your gift to the altar, first make peace with your brother". It was the day for Communion. Immediately after the sermon two of the village officials, educated men but enemies of long standing, came forward and made peace, each reaching out his hand to the other.[51]

Despite his hostility to Christianity, the mature Nietzsche always retained his delight in the authentic spirit of Christmas. It reappears in his philosophy as the yearning for a time when 'all men...share the experience of those shepherds who saw the heavens brighten above them and heard the words "On earth peace, good will towards all men"'.[52] How Nietzsche could possibly combine this yearning for world peace with his celebration of the Greek *agon*, not to mention the 'will to power', is a matter we shall have to think about.

* * *

As well as *pious*, the young Nietzsche was also *good*, sometimes exaggeratedly so. In her memoirs, Elizabeth wishes she could recount at least one incident of genuine naughtiness on his part but regrets that she remembers not one. The nearest is her retrieval of an incident in which the two of them were praised for donating their very best toys for the missionaries to give to the 'black little heathens' in Africa, when, in fact, they had donated only rather inferior ones. Full of shame, Fritz says to her:

> "Lizzie, I wish I had given my box of cavalry". These were his finest and favourite soldiers. But I had still enough of the serpent and of Eve in me to answer with some hesitation: "Ought God really to demand the very best toys from us, Fritz?" (The idea of sending my best-loved dolls to black and probably exceedingly savage cannibals seemed utterly impossible to me.) But Fritz whispered in reply: "Yes indeed, Lizzie".[53]

Fritz was also deeply *obedient*, again in a sometimes exaggeratedly inflexible – 'Prussian' – manner. Elizabeth recollects a heavy downpour of rain causing all the boys to run like mad on their way home from primary school. All except Fritz, 'who was walking slowly with his cap covering his slate and his little handkerchief spread over the whole', oblivious to his mother's instructions to 'Run, child, run!'. When she remonstrated with him for coming home soaked he replied 'But Mamma, the school rules say that on leaving school, boys are forbidden to jump and run about in the street, but must walk home quietly and deco-rously'.[54]

In sum, on the eve of his departure for boarding school, Fritz was a precocious, shy, affectionate, pious, virtuous and obedient boy, unconventional only in the intensity of his devotion to the conventions of his Prussian-Lutheran upbringing. It is hard to discover even the remotest hint of the Samson who would one day pull down the pillars of the Christian temple.

2

Pforta

IN SEPTEMBER 1858 Franziska Nietzsche received a letter from the rector of Pforta boarding school offering Fritz a scholarship at the best and most famous secondary school in Germany. According to Elizabeth, news of the outstanding academic promise he had shown at the Cathedral Grammar School had reached the rector's ears via Naumburg relatives. Fritz had wanted to go to Pforta since the age of ten, expressing his desire in something less than magnificent verse:

> *There, where through her narrow door*
> *Pforta's pupils evermore*
> *Pass out into life so free*
> *There in Pforta would I be!*

And since the scholarship would secure his financial future for the next six years it was an offer Franziska – though bitterly regretting severance from the child of her heart – could not refuse. The following month Fritz became a Pforta pupil, and he would remain one until September 1864.

Originally a Cistercian abbey called Porta Coeli (Gate of Heaven), Pforta ('Gate' – now to education rather than heaven) had been transformed into a school in 1543 by the Prince-Elector Moritz of Saxony, a 'dissolution' and recycling of the monasteries that was a major plank of the Protestant Reformation. (Ten years later Edward VI, in a similar spirit, founded Christ's Hospital on the site of the former Greyfriars friary in the City of London.) Pforta, or Schulpforte (Pforta School), as it is known today, is about an hour's walk from Naumburg – Fritz sometimes walked home for the holidays. It lies just south of the ambling Saale River in a wooded valley that extends from the western edge of Naumburg to the narrow gorge of Kösen. The school estate comprises some seventy-three acres of gardens, orchards, groves of trees, buildings, and cloisters, protected from the outer world by a thick twelve-foot-high wall, which forms an almost perfect rectangle. A branch canal of the Saale flows through the middle of the enclosure, separating the work buildings and gardens and most of the teachers' houses from the school itself. Small and highly select, the school, in Nietzsche's day, accommodated some two hundred pupils.

A Divided Heritage

What sort of a place was Pforta? First, as the rector put it in 1843, in a speech celebrating the 300th anniversary of the school's foundation, it was a 'self-contained scholastic state', a 'state' within a state in which 'all parental rights are handed over to the alma mater' for the 'six most decisive years, from adolescence until entry into university', in order that the boys become 'divorced from all distractions associated with town life'.[1]

As well as in total isolation, Pforta pupils also existed under a condition of near-total control. One needed permission for virtually everything. The Nietzsche *Nachlass* contains innumerable chits written to his tutor requesting permission to go for a walk, have some pocket money, rent a piano, buy some cake, meet his family, etc., etc. Given such control, it was no idle boast of the rector's to claim that the school formed the 'totality' of a pupil's being, 'not just the development of their minds but also the formation of their morals and character', with the result that 'every Pforta boy, as a rule, leaves the institution with the definite stamp of a certain sound diligence which lasts him throughout his life'.[2]

'Sound diligence' is typical Pforta modesty. (Elizabeth comments that though the masters knew that Fritz was their most talented pupil in living memory, he was 'never allowed to suspect a word of this', for Pforta 'under no circumstances flattered its gifted scholars'.)[3] What the rector fails to mention is the school's tremendous esprit de corps. Intensely proud of its famous alumni – Klopstock, Novalis, Fichte, the Schlegel brothers, almost a roll call of the great names of German romanticism, as well as the great historian Leopold von Ranke – it saw its role as that of training young men for the *geistige Führung des Volkes*, the 'spiritual leadership of the people';[4] for the intellectual, cultural, spiritual, and, ultimately, more or less direct political leadership of the nation. How was this Pforta 'stamp' on the cultural aristocracy of the future to be achieved? Through, as the rector put it, a 'virile, severe, and powerful spirit of discipline' which taught the pupils 'obedience to the command and will of their superiors', 'the severe and punctual fulfilment of duty', 'self-control', and 'earnest work', while at the same time encouraging the development of 'original personal initiative'.[5] What this means will be familiar to anyone who has attended, even in recent times, a British boarding school: the classical techniques of Sparta – cold baths, a hierarchy of prefects and sub-prefects with the power of life and death over their subordinates, a regimented daily routine, lack of privacy save in the lavatories and sometimes not even there ('total observation' as Michel Foucault calls it), corporal punishment, and so on. All in all, Pforta closely resembled a Prussian military academy save for the fact that it produced 'officers' for, in the first instance, cultural rather than military leadership[6] – though, as we shall see, it produced the latter, too.

Fritz begins his description of the daily routine:

> I will now attempt to give a picture of everyday life in Pforta. As early as four in the morning the dormitory doors are thrown open, and from that time onwards anyone is free to rise who wishes to do so. But at five o'clock (in winter at six) everybody must be out of the room: as usual the school bell rings, the dormitory prefects peremptorily shout, 'Get up, get up;

make haste' and punish anyone who doesn't find it so easy to get out of bed. Then all the boys scramble into a few light garments as quickly as possible, and hurry to the washrooms to secure a place before they get too crowded. Rising and washing lasts ten minutes, after which everyone returns to their rooms where they dress properly. At twenty-five past the first prayer-bell sounds, and at the second everyone has to be in hall for prayers. Here the prefects keep order until the master comes . . . punctually at six (in the winter seven) the bell rings for the boys to go to their classrooms.[7]

Ronald Hayman's biography of Nietzsche has little time for Pforta. Referring to an episode in which Fritz held a lighted match to his hand to prove that his self-discipline was up to Roman standards, he observes that 'the sadism in authoritarian oppression always tends to generate masochism in the desire to excel through obedience' and suggests that Pforta transformed Nietzsche into a 'sado-masoch[ist]'.[8] Though clever, this seems to me to ignore, first, the fact that some people *enjoy* a life of obedience, and, second, the warmer side of Pforta.

To begin at the most basic level, the meals at Pforta (compared, at least, to my own boarding-school experience) were substantial, and, from a nutritional point of view, surprisingly sound. Since, moreover, the fruit and vegetables were all freshly gathered from the school's own orchards and gardens, they were probably enjoyable. Fritz's description of daily life continues:

The menu for the [mid-day meal] for the week is as follows:
Monday: soup, meat, vegetables, fruit.
Tuesday: soup, meat, vegetables, bread and butter.
Wednesday: soup, meat, vegetables, fruit.
Thursday: soup, boiled beef, vegetables, grilled kidneys and salad.
Friday: soup, roast pork, vegetables, and bread and butter; or soup, lentils, sausage, and bread and butter.
Saturday: soup, meat, vegetables, fruit.

And for the evening meal at 7.00 p.m.:

Monday and Friday: soup, bread and butter and cheese.
Tuesday and Saturday: soup, potatoes, herring, and bread and butter.
Wednesday: soup, sausage, mashed potatoes or pickled cucumber.
Thursday: soup, pancakes, plum sauce, bread and butter.
Sunday: soup, rice boiled in milk, bread and butter; or eggs, salad and bread and butter.[9]

Second, the discipline and regimentation were not, in fact, as total or as inflexible as the rector makes out. Plenty of time was allowed for walks, playing bowls, and swimming in, or, in winter, skating on, the Saale, both of which Fritz loved and became good at. In spite of the early rising at 4.00 a.m., bedtime was at 8.30 or 9.00 p.m., so the boys were actually allowed about eight hours sleep. And, as Fritz records, in summer, if the temperature reached 24°C, classes were cancelled for the rest of the day and the whole school went swimming. On Sundays, the boys were given wine (Saale-Unstrut is Germany's northernmost *appellation*) from the school's own vineyards.

Third, Fritz's school experience, so far as one can tell, seems to have been relatively free of the usual perils of boarding school, bullying and sexual abuse. It is possible that elements of school life were repressed in the letters he wrote home several times a week, but the general picture, apart from bouts of ill health, is of a happy schoolboy: about the only time he complains is when bad weather makes skating impossible or when his orders from home are not promptly filled. (He tends – a habit that persisted into adulthood – to treat his mother as a mail-order firm, demanding instant delivery of, among other items, strong glasses, ink bottles, steel pens, soap, cocoa, wafer biscuits, notebooks, writing pads, scissors, morning shoes, boot jacks, and a draughts set.)[10] Contra Hayman's suggestion of sadism, Elizabeth mentions how kind the prefects were to her brother. And it is certainly true that he liked and admired Oscar Krämer, the prefect to whom he was immediately answerable (and who, therefore, more than anyone, could make his life either hell or heaven), and whom he invited home to tea with his mother.[11] It was Krämer who knocked from his hand the lighted candle with which he was burning himself and told him not to be so stupid. (Barely out of his teens, Krämer died as a lieutenant in the battle of Sadowa in 1866, an event which certainly influenced the mature Nietzsche's loathing of warfare.)

Fourth, in spite of the rector's claim of total sequestration from town and home, there was in fact frequent contact with home. Not only were there the regular letters and supplies from home, but most Sundays Fritz would make the half-hour walk to Almrich – the midway point between Pforta and Naumburg – to spend the afternoon with his mother and sister.

Of course, uprooted from his second home and his two best friends, Fritz at first suffered terribly from homesickness. As he approached Pforta for the first time in the grey light of dawn, shivering with fear before an 'ominous future veiled in grey', the walls of Pforta looked, he wrote Wilhelm, 'more like a prison than an alma mater'.[12] Fortunately he found in his tutor (equivalent to a housemaster in the British system) a man of simple faith and great kindheartedness who offered him what Fritz calls 'the cure for homesickness (according to Professor Buddensieg)':

(1) If we want to learn anything of value we cannot always stay at home.
(2) Our dear parents do not wish us to remain at home; we should therefore fulfil their wishes.
(3) Our loved ones are in God's hands. We are continually accompanied by their thoughts.
(4) If we work diligently our sad thoughts will vanish.
(5) If none of the above helps, pray to God almighty.[13]

Though none of this may seem very effective, Fritz loved Robert Buddensieg dearly (fairly clearly, he was the first of Nietzsche's several substitute fathers) and wept bitter tears over his untimely death from typhus in August 1861.[14] Though he retained friendly relations with his new tutor, Max Heinze,* for the rest of his life, Heinze was no substitute for Buddensieg.

---

* Heinze became well known as an historian of philosophy. For a short time he became Nietzsche's colleague at the University of Basel before moving on to Leipzig. Among other things, he produced an edition of Lenin's writings, which suggests a man of considerable breadth of vision.

Fritz looked forward to school holidays with something approaching ecstasy. And going back to school was always an occasion for sounding like one of Schubert's lieder poets: 'The golden days of the holidays are over, vanished like a dream', 'my heart was darkened by clouds of sadness',[15] and so on. But none of this should be taken as showing that school was a place of sadistic torment. Fritz of course missed home and family. But what he really missed was *freedom*, the freedom to eat, drink, sleep, walk, read, write, play the piano when, where, and with whom he liked. 'Schooldays', as he himself observed, 'are difficult years...because the fresh spirit must confine itself in narrow limits'.[16]

* * *

The picture of Pforta as a sadistic machine designed to produce Prussian robots needs a further qualification: one needs to attend to the spirit of renaissance humanism pervading its worldview, which arose from the centrality of classics to the curriculum. Pforta humanism embraced a reverence for Rome, but above all for Greece, as the highest point of Western civilization. From this it derived a quiet, yet real, commitment to an ideal of freedom and republicanism based on the model of the Athenian city-state and the Roman Republic. Politically, the dominant culture at Pforta was 'liberal' in the nineteenth-century sense, which embraced liberation from authoritarian rule, extension of civil rights and the franchise (sometimes even to women), and moves towards democratic government. And, in the specifically German context, it embraced the cause of German unification. Though in the event, thanks to the authoritarian Bismarck and a benighted Emperor, the German Reich (which came into being in 1871) proved a great disappointment to them; liberals had supported its creation, hoping that it would bring an end to the multitude of petty states run, on feudal lines, by dukes and princes. Moreover, the 'deconstructive' spirit of classical philology, as soon as it extended itself beyond ancient texts, had an intrinsic tendency to undermine established convictions and authorities. (Later, Nietzsche refers to 'Voltairean deconstruction' as a salient effect of historical studies.)[17] At least as important as Darwinism in the undermining of Christian faith in the nineteenth century was the philological deconstruction of the Bible by scholars such as David Strauss (see pp. 168–70 below). (When Jacques Derrida told the radical students of 1968 that it was more important to deconstruct texts than to barricade the streets of Paris, he was simply recalling what philology had been doing for the past hundred years.)

Thus Pforta, like the best English boarding schools both then and now, was riddled with 'creative' contradictions. On the one hand, it venerated Prussian authority, but on the other, it quietly subverted all authority. On the one hand, it was oppressively Protestant – frequent doses of prayers and chapel were compulsory – but on the other, it venerated everything about antiquity, including the Greek (that is, *pagan*) gods. And though on the one hand oppressively loyal to the Prussian throne, on the other it was quietly republican.

Nietzsche never doubted that Pforta made him. And he was always loyal to the school and grateful, not only for the magnificent education in the humanities but also for the character 'formation' it had given him. Twenty-four years after leaving, he wrote,

> The most desirable thing of all...is under all circumstances to have severe discipline *at the right time*. i.e., at the age when it makes us proud that people should expect great things from us. For this is what distinguishes hard schooling from every other schooling, namely that a good deal is demanded; that goodness, nay even excellence itself, is required as if it were normal; that praise is scanty; that leniency is non-existent; that blame is sharp,

practical, and has no regard to talents or antecedents. We are all in every way in need of such a school; and this holds good of physical as well as spiritual things – it would be fatal to draw distinctions here! The same discipline makes the soldier and the scholar efficient; and, looked at more closely, there is no true scholar who has not the instincts of a true soldier in his veins.[18]

As I emphasised earlier, Nietzsche was, and would remain all his life, at heart a Prussian. His home predisposed him thus, but his unwavering commitment to Prussian discipline – to 'self-overcoming', in his own later terminology – was very largely Pforta's creation. But being itself a contradiction, Pforta produced, in Nietzsche, a contradiction. As the British public schools have produced the leaders of mainstream society but, at the same time, its disloyal opposition – communist spies such as Burgess, Maclean, Philby and Blunt – so Pforta produced, in Nietzsche, a Prussian anti-Prussian, Prussia's very own 'mole', someone who, in his maturity, would set out to undermine everything for which it stood.

The Curriculum

The heart of the Pforta curriculum was Greek and Latin and, to a lesser degree, the German classics. What the students breathed was not the air of modern Europe but that of Greece and Rome, Goethe and Schiller. Natural science and mathematics always came a poor third, disciplines to be specialised by the less able boys. Predictably, mathematics was badly taught, so that Fritz, after initially doing well, came to find it extremely boring. He became so bad at it that, when it came to his *Abitur*, the school-leaving exam, the maths teacher wished to fail him, prompting another examiner to ask quietly, 'But gentlemen, are we really going to fail the best pupil in living memory?' In the 1870s, developing a keen interest in natural science, Nietzsche became acutely aware of his lack of grounding following the perfunctory way the sciences were taught at Pforta. We had, he writes in 1881,

> mathematics and physics forced upon us *instead* of our being led into despair at our ignorance, and having our little daily life, our activities, and all that went on at home, in the work place, in the sky, in the countryside from morn to night, reduced to thousands of problems, to annoying, mortifying, irritating problems – so as to show that we *needed* a knowledge of mathematics and mechanics, and then to teach us our first *delight* in science ... If only we had been taught to *revere* the sciences.[19]

In addition to Latin and Greek, Fritz also studied French and Hebrew, the latter on account of his dutiful intention to follow his mother's desire that he study theology at university. In fact, however, he never completely mastered any foreign language, ancient or modern. Though one was supposed to be able to think in Latin, Fritz never quite managed it, his Latin compositions always looking like translations from German. In later life, though he spent much time in Italy, he understood comparatively little of the language. To read French he always needed a dictionary, while his English was nonexistent: Byron and Shakespeare, whom he loved, he read in German translation. These facts are of some importance since, though he came to style himself a 'good European' and to deplore

German chauvinism, he always thought in German and therefore, in a strong sense, *as* a German.

The *Germania* Society

Until his final year Fritz had no really close friends at school. Usually at or near the top of his class, he seemed to his fellows something of a *Streber* [striver] – a goody-goody who strives too obviously to be top. Reserved, earnest beyond his years, and not given to the physical rough-and-tumble of boarding-school life, he seemed to his fellows somewhat weird – as, given the hand-burning episode, he indeed was. For this reason, his normal boarding-school yearning for the holidays was a yearning not only for the comforts of home but also for the company of his only two friends, Wilhelm and Gustav.

In the summer holidays of 1860 the three friends decided to found a society for literature and the arts, to be called *Germania*.[20] This was the first glimmer of a very German phenomenon, the desire to found a 'circle', such as the Wagner Circle or, later, the Stefan George Circle, devoted to cultural regeneration, a desire which would persist throughout Nietzsche's life. Elizabeth recounts the founding of the *Germania* Society:

> [On July 5th] the friends bought a nine-Groschen bottle of red Naumburg wine and set forth in an earnest and dignified procession to the ruin of Schönburg, an hour's distance from the town. By means of an extremely rickety ladder they climbed to the highest ledge of the watch tower, from which there was a magnificent view over the picturesque Saale valley, and from this position, high above the misty regions of the plain, they discussed their plan for fulfilling their highest aspirations for culture.

The constitution of the society required that each member contribute a monthly subscription – which was used to purchase, *inter alia*, the works of the then highly avant garde poet Friedrich Hölderlin – as well as, each month, an original work of literature, art, or music (Nietzsche's compositions recorded as tracks 3–7 on the Web site for this book were all *Germania* contributions). The work would then be criticised in a rigorous but constructive manner by the other members. At the end of the founding ceremony, Elizabeth continues, 'the friends pledged themselves to the bond of friendship and community of ideas, baptized the society *Germania*, and hurled the empty bottle into the abyss'.[21]

Like most societies, *Germania* began with a burst of enthusiasm but, then, under the pressure of, in Fritz's words, 'school-work, dancing lessons, love affairs, political excitements',[22] gradually became moribund, and then bankrupt, and was finally wound up in July 1863. Fritz proved its most diligent member, at least partly because, having changed schools, he approached *Abitur* six months later than Wilhelm and Gustav.

During *Germania*'s lifetime the members contributed and discussed (in person during the holidays, by correspondence during term-time) numerous works by themselves and others. Their most significant purchases were, in 1861,[23] a piano reduction of the score of Wagner's *Tristan und Isolde* (four years before its first performance) and a subscription to the *Neue Zeitschrift für Musik*, a magazine founded by Schumann in 1834, now dedicated to explaining and defending *Zukunftsmusik* in general, and Wagner's music in particular.

The score of *Tristan* was the means by which Gustav finally converted Fritz to the cause. The conversion experience, which happened either in 1861 or 1862, consisted in the two of them playing through the piano reduction with four hands as well as singing all the parts. Elizabeth reports that the rendition of this 'music of the future' by their powerful voices reminded her of the howling of wolves and that 'a certain deaf woman who lived opposite us anxiously rushed to her window when she heard the fearful noise that seemed to have penetrated even her ears because she thought there must be a fire somewhere'.[24]

The original contributions[25] to the society consisted of poems and musical compositions as well as lectures of a literary, historical, musicological, and philosophical character. Fritz contributed, *inter alia*, four parts of a *Christmas Oratorio* (tracks 4,5 and 6 on the Web site for this book) inspired by Bach's eponymous work and numerous poems, including 'Six Serbian Folk Songs, translated by F. Nietzsche' (Wilhelm wondered how he could have done this given he knew no Serbo-Croatian),[26] as well as lectures on Byron and Napoleon III, and his first work of philosophy, 'Fate and Freedom', written in March 1862.

Meanwhile, at school, too, Fritz was beginning to produce works of significance. In addition to his classical studies, he wrote extended essays on, *inter alios*, Hölderlin and Byron, on the Ermanarich Saga and other Norse sagas, on the origin and nature of civilization and on the nature of homeland. As he gained insight into the principles of philological criticism, he was, moreover, beginning to take a more critical stance towards the Bible.

Religious Doubt

As we have seen, Fritz's childhood was marked by passionate, rather than merely conventional, piety, a piety that speaks unmistakably from his early musical compositions (listen to tracks 1, 2 and 3 on the Web site for this book). His attitude to the Bible was one of unqualified belief. Piety as well as poetry is what he had in common with his first genuine school friend, Paul Deussen, also the son of a pastor and also intending to enter the ministry. This pious phase culminated in the two being confirmed together in March 1861. Deussen recollects:

> I remember very well the holy, world-enchanting atmosphere which took possession of us during the weeks before and after our confirmation. We were quite prepared to depart this life, to be with Christ, and all our thinking, feeling, and striving was irradiated by an other-worldly cheerfulness.[27]

Almost immediately, however, fractures began to appear in the fabric of Fritz's piety. During the Easter holidays he had a serious quarrel with Franziska which resulted in a letter of apology in marked contrast to the sunny affection of their correspondence to date:

> And now, dear Mamma, a word for your ears alone. To me too it seems that the otherwise so wonderful Easter holiday was overshadowed and darkened by those ugly events, and it causes me great pain each time I think of it that I upset you so much. I beg you to forgive me, dear Mamma: it would be terrible if this incident were to damage our lovely relationship with each other. Forgive me, dear Mamma... From now on I will try as hard as I can, through my behaviour and love for you, to heal the breach.[28]

Almost certainly the quarrel concerned religion, Fritz having begun to read works whose 'scientific' approach to religion (in the broad German sense according to which any rational and disciplined enquiry counts as 'scientific') would have offended Franziska's simple traditionalism. She was certainly shocked when, in November, he recommended Karl von Hase's rationalistic *Life of Jesus* to his sister.[29] Deussen confirms that 'science' was beginning to undermine Fritz's Christian faith. The religious intoxication at the time of their confirmation, he writes,

> since it was an artificially cultivated plant, could not last, and under the influence of our daily education and life, dissipated as quickly as it arrived. Meanwhile we preserved a certain degree of belief until the *Abitur* exams were over. What undermined it, without our noticing, was the superb historical-critical method which we employed, in Pforta, to torment the ancients and which then, quite by itself, applied itself to biblical matters.[30]

The 'historical-critical method' is essentially what Nietzsche employs in his mature philosophy to undermine Christianity and Christian morality. In general terms, it is the 'hermeneutics of suspicion', close questioning of a text guided by the presumption that there is more (or perhaps less) to it than meets the eye and that what fails to meet the eye is probably, in one way or another, disreputable. But, as Deussen notes, the 'method' is essentially the (as noted, incipiently subversive) discipline of philology transferred from classical texts to the Bible. What was beginning to happen, therefore, was the resolution of one of the contradictions inherent in the Pforta worldview. 'Science' was beginning to undermine faith.

By the spring of 1862, in the 'Fate and History' lecture delivered to the audience of two that, together with the lecturer, constituted the 'synod' of the *Germania* society, Fritz insists on the need and right to take a 'free and unpartisan' view of Christianity even though one's upbringing made it seem almost a 'crime'. Yet, as we will see in discussing this essay, Fritz's aim is not *rejection* of Christianity but rather its *modernisation*. The Christian life-form, essential to the fabric of society, is too valuable to be discarded. But its theological beliefs must be recast so as to accord, rather than conflict, with modern science. This quest for a modernised Christianity, we shall see, was cemented by David Strauss's *Life of Jesus*, which Fritz read during his first year at university.

Teenage Rebellion

Fritz's emergence from naïve religiosity was accompanied by a foray into the general spirit of teenage rebellion. This lasted about a year, starting in the spring of 1862, after which he returned to his accustomed role and left Pforta in a blaze of glory. He began keeping company with the school's rebels, dubious characters such as Guido Meyer and Raimund Granier, denizens of Pforta's underground counterculture. Together they would make fun of the school's eager beavers as well as indulging in crimes such as secret drinking, smoking, and snuff-taking. Meyer was in fact expelled in March 1863 for illegal drinking, which Fritz described to his mother as a heavy-handed miscarriage of justice and his saddest day at Pforta.[31]

On the literary level, Fritz became enamoured of Byron as an icon of rebellion and set out on a path of blasphemous transgression. He wrote a novel-fragment, *Euphorion* – in which the eponymous hero impregnates a nun who then marries her brother – and then sent it to Granier, his partner in nihilism, proudly describing it as 'disgusting', worth using only as lavatory paper.[32] A death wish emerges in his poetry – 'O that I could, world-weary/Fly away/And like the swallow go south/Towards my grave'. In another poem a drunk hurls a bottle of schnapps at the crucified Christ.

Letters home now began with the pseudo-sophisticated 'dear People', as opposed to 'Dear Mamma', which earned him a reprimand. At school, too, there was trouble. Being a prefect, Fritz was required to conduct surveys and report anything needing repair in the classrooms or dormitories. As a gesture of mild rebellion, he succumbed to the temptation to insert into his reports little jokes such as 'the benches in the upper second, which were painted recently, became excessively attached to those who sat on them'. For this he was gated, missing a prearranged meeting with Franziska at Almrich. Once again – 'Dear Fritz' has been replaced by 'My dear son' – he receives a heavy-handed reprimand from home:

> Thank God that it is not a worse punishment, but frankly...I would have expected more tact from you. You will be again charged with the mistake of vanity, always wanting to do something different from the others, and I find the punishment quite justified, for it seems a terrible presumptuousness against the teachers to allow oneself to do something like this. So please in future be more careful in your mode of thought and action, follow always your better self and you will be preserved from all the strife and unquiet I have observed in you more and more.[33]

Teenage rebellion came to a head in April 1863 when Fritz was discovered by a master, completely drunk. This resulted in his being stripped of his status as a prefect and once more gated, so that again the Sunday meeting with mother and sister had to be cancelled. Again he had to write to his mother in a state of extreme embarrassment:

> Dear Mother – if I write today it's about one of the most unpleasant and painful incidents I've ever been responsible for. In fact I have misbehaved very badly and I do not know whether you can or will forgive me. I pick up my pen most reluctantly and with a heavy heart especially when I call to mind our lovely time together during the Easter holidays, which were never spoiled by discord. Last Sunday I got drunk and I have no excuse, except that I did not know how much I could take, and I was rather excited in the afternoon...[he was celebrating coming top in end-of-year exams]. You can imagine how ashamed and depressed I am to have caused you such sorrow with such an unworthy tale as I have never caused you in my life before. It also makes me feel very sorry on Pastor Kletschke's account [the school chaplain whom Fritz had chosen to succeed Heinze as his tutor, and who had made him a senior prefect]...Write me very soon and very strictly for I've deserved it as no one knows more than I...Write me very soon and don't be too cross, dear mother. Very depressed, Fritz.[34]

The magnitude of this incident seems to have lanced the boil of rebellion, since from now on his name makes no further appearance in the Pforta punishment book. But it left him with a lifelong distrust of alcohol. In *Ecce Homo* he attributes his preference for water over 'spirituous' drinks to 'having almost turned into a sailor' while at Pforta.[35]

* * *

Fritz's final year at Pforta was dominated by the question of what should become his *Brot-studium*, breadwinning course of study. As a scholarship boy from a poor background he had no option but to think seriously about breadwinning. Multitalented as he was, he complained that a choice of profession was 'a lotto-game'.[36] For a time he thought of music; 'everything seems to me dead when I can't hear music', he wrote his mother.[37] In the end, of course, he decided for that to which Pforta, both by training and ideology, had predestined him – classics, 'classical philology'. As he wrote in 1869,

> Only at the end of my Pforta life, having achieved proper self-knowledge, did I give up all artistic life-plans: into the resulting gap stepped philology. I needed, that is, to achieve equanimity in the face of the flux of disquieting inclinations, a discipline (*Wissenschaft*) that could be pursued with equanimity in the face of the changeable and disquieting flux of inclinations, a discipline which could be conducted with cool level-headedness and logical coldness – routine work – without its results stirring the heart.[38]

What this reveals, apart from Nietzsche's passion for Prussian *order*, is that, though he loved the Greeks, he did not love philology – a fact that would be scented out by Ulrich Wilamowitz in a review of his first book that, we shall see, was intended to drive him out of the profession. In choosing a career path for which he had no passion Nietzsche was storing up an agonising dilemma that, one day, he would have to resolve.

New Friends

During his final months at school, Fritz recognised with sadness that with Wilhelm and Gustav bound for university in Heidelberg, which did not recommend itself to a philologist, his friendship with them was weakening. Two new friendships, however, were beginning to blossom in their place: first, as noted, with Paul Deussen,* and soon after with Baron Carl von Gersdorff (see Plate 13), the atypical product of a Prussian Junker household.† At first Carl and Fritz were drawn together by a common interest in music, meeting each other for the first time in the Pforta music room. Carl was bowled over by Fritz's piano improvisation, remarking that he 'would have no difficulty in believing that even Beethoven did not improvise in more moving manner than Nietzsche, particularly when a thunder storm was threatening'.[39] By the time they left school they had moved

---

* Like Nietzsche, Deussen began academic life as a Greek philologist. But then, via Schopenhauer, he branched out into Eastern thought, becoming a full professor in Berlin and one of the great orientalists of his day.

† Following the Junker tradition, von Gersdorff fought in both the Austro-Prussian war of 1866 and the Franco-Prussian war of 1870–71. One of his elder brothers died in the former, another in the latter, the second being awarded the Iron Cross. Although he was forced to take over the administration of the family estate, von Gersdorff's real desire was to be an artist. He spoke at Nietzsche's funeral in 1900. In 1904, showing increasing symptoms of mental illness, he committed suicide by throwing himself out of a window.

from the formal to the familiar 'you' (from *Sie* to *du*), then, even more than now, a major step in personal relations between Germans.

In 2002 a book appeared entitled *Zarathustra's Secret*[40] in which – undeterred by the complete absence of evidence – the author made the sensational claim that 'Zarathustra's' (i.e., Nietzsche's) guilty 'secret' was that he was 'gay'. It is worth recording, therefore, that both Deussen and von Gersdorff were thoroughly heterosexual. And that Fritz himself, in his penultimate school year, was attracted to Anna Redtel, the sister of a school acquaintance, with whom, when she visited her grandparents in Kösen (between Pforta and Naumburg), he played piano duets. To her he dedicated a collection of his early compositions, lieder and piano pieces.[41]

Fritz and his male friends wrote to each other in the most fulsome terms. They 'miss' each other 'terribly' and 'long' for the holidays when they will be together once more. And as was the fashion throughout late Victorian Europe, they constantly exchanged photographs of each other. Whereas a healthy modern schoolboy would likely have photographs of large-breasted film stars on his walls, Fritz decorated the walls of his room with photographs of his friends.[42]

Were these 'gay' relationships? They were not. Flowing expressions of undying love for one's friend, though perhaps startling to someone brought up in the emotional constipation of today's male-to-male communication, were a Victorian commonplace. Were homoerotic feelings involved? Quite possibly. For Victorian men who had spent their formative years in single-sex boarding schools which encouraged them to idealise the lives of Greek aristocrats, it was natural to reserve their most intimate and tender feelings for those of their own sex. And in this regard, Fritz was no exception. But if Nietzsche was 'gay' then so were the great majority of middle-class Victorian men.

Leaving School

Fritz left Pforta, just short of his twentieth birthday, adjudged the finest pupil for many years. Superbly trained by teachers who would go back and forth between positions at Pforta and chairs at the best universities, he was already fully equipped to become a professional classical philologist. A brilliant future lay before him. Two clouds, however, hung over his head.

The first was his health. Given the Spartan regime of the school, one did not show up in the medical records unless one was unmistakably sick. Yet in his six years at Pforta Fritz was confined to the infirmary no less than eighteen times – an average of three times a year. On two occasions the illness was so severe that he was sent home to convalesce. Mainly he suffered from various kinds of flu, but these attacks were always accompanied by headaches, which also afflicted him on many other occasions. As we shall see, blinding and incapacitating headache-attacks accompanied by nausea and vomiting would plague his entire adult life.

Nietzsche's headaches may have had a physical cause. But they were likely exacerbated by his extreme short-sightedness and by the strain imposed by prodigious amounts of reading. (Often he read through an entire night, his foot in a bucket of freezing water to prevent him falling asleep.[43]) Moreover, there also seems to have been a psychosomatic element in at least the timing of the attacks: stress seems to have made him more vulnerable. The year 1862, for instance, was particularly bad – he appeared in the infirmary's medical record four times and was eventually sent home to convalesce – a period of ill-health that coincided with his flirtation with the confused nihilism of the Pforta counterculture. And in the following year, the extreme depression expressed in the April 16 letter home confessing the drunkenness episode (p. 30 above) was followed by confinement to the infirmary from April 24 until May 5 and then again from May 7 to May 20.

That a second cloud hung over Fritz's departure from Pforta is suggested by a poem written during his final days at school. It reads, in part,

> *Once more before I travel on*
> *And cast my glance forward*
> *In my solitude I raise my hands*
> *Up to you, my refuge,*
> *To whom in the deepest depths of my heart*
> *I have solemnly dedicated altars*
> *So that for all time*
> *Your voice always calls me back.*
> *On them, deeply engraved, shines*
> *The word: to the unknown god....*
> *I must know you, unknown one*
> *You who reach deep into my soul...* [44]

Philological sophistication, we have seen, deprived Nietzsche of the simple Naumburg faith of his childhood. Though this in no way led him to atheism – the *yearning* for God was undiminished – he no longer knew who God was. God had become 'the unknown god' (the Greek designation may have come to him via Hölderlin's 'In Lovely Blueness'). God had become a quest, and would remain so for the remainder of his life.

Literary Works 1858–1864

It would be easy to dismiss the literary works of the Pforta years as juvenilia. But that would be a mistake, since many of the major themes of his mature philosophy (the two exceptions are the 'will to power' and the 'eternal return of the same') receive their first airing in these teenage works. Nietzsche did not, of course, retain his teenage views unmodified throughout his life. Nonetheless, understanding these views is crucial to an understanding of what really concerned him. I shall order the discussion by topics rather than texts, discussing his views on religion, music, Greek tragedy, poetry, politics and morality, homeland versus cosmopolitanism, and freedom of the will in that order.

Religion

'On the Childhood of Peoples',[45] a lecture delivered to the *Germania*'s audience of two on March 24, 1861, contains the beginnings of Nietzsche's lifelong meditation on the origin of religion. From a sixteen-year-old, it is an impressive work.

The most fundamental possession of a *Volk* [people], Fritz argues, is a common language. This is true by definition, since a shared language is what constitutes a group of individuals as a people. But the next most fundamental feature is a shared religion. At the most primitive stage of civilization, Fritz hypothesises, peoples considered themselves God's children. Terrified by his power, which speaks to them in thunder and lightning, they seek his help and forgiveness for their sins through prayer and sacrifice. This first and most natural religion worships a God who is immanent in natural phenomena – the 'truth' that God is a supranatural rather than natural being remained unknown to them. In time, however, primordial monotheism acquired the 'heathen accretion' of polytheism. Even the Jews were polytheists, regarding Jehovah, the God of Israel, merely as the highest of the gods, occupying a kingly role with respect to the others. The various natural forces and the different seasons, seeming to represent different godly powers, generated the dim representation of a multiplicity of supernatural agencies governing the destiny of each individual. The notion that some of these spirits were benevolent and others malevolent arose in a natural way, and everyone became eager to enjoy the favour of the benevolent ones. Then profound men, presenting themselves as messengers of the gods, founded a new form of religion by attaching the foundations of morality to theological belief and propagating the resulting synthesis of gods and morals among their people. This is how the religions of the most spiritually rich nations of antiquity arose. But, Fritz concludes, history shows that

> ever-maturing religious thought leads towards a standpoint from which the demand for a pure, natural doctrine is satisfied, where enlightened philosophers return us to a single God as the primordial source of all being. It is the mission of the Christian religion to expedite this process, not through stepping in and destroying heathen religion by force, but by awakening the natural need for a kindlier teaching. [Fritz is surely thinking, here, of the German missionaries in Africa to whom he and Elizabeth, in their childhood, had donated their second-best toys.] Just as necessary, however, and required by the foundational idea of Christianity, is the love which leads them out of their unblessed condition and into the arms of the Church through which alone salvation can be attained.

This is clearly written within the parameters of Christian theology, which constrain him to postulate monotheism as the first and most natural idea of the divine – an implausible hypothesis he later rejects. Nonetheless, the fact that he thinks religion *has* an origin reveals already a certain detachment from Christian faith: as he says in the *Genealogy of Morals*, the mere recognition that religious belief *has* a history undermines the assumption that it is the product of divine revelation.

By the following year, however, Fritz's process of detaching himself from naive Christianity has become much more advanced. In the Easter holidays, in 'Fate and History',[46] another *Germania* lecture, he writes that

> If we could examine Christian doctrine and Church history with a free, unconstrained eye, we would be compelled to arrive at many conclusions which contradict generally accepted ideas. But restricted as we are from our first days by the yoke of habit and prejudice, restricted in the development of our intellects and predetermined in the development of our character by the stamp of childhood, we are forced to regard it as almost a sin [by, of course, Franziska] if we choose to adopt a free standpoint, and hit upon an unpartisan judgment about religion appropriate to the age in which we live.

So Fritz declares his right of detachment – later he will call this 'becoming a free spirit' – a desire to view religion from the perspective of the educated knowledge of his age. But with, for his years, a remarkably mature sense of intellectual responsibility to his community and its great tradition, he continues,

> such an attempt is not the work of a few weeks but of an entire lifetime. For how could we, armed with the results of mere adolescent broodings, annihilate the authority of two thousand years and the testimony of the greatest minds? How could one, with fantasies and immature ideas, discount all the deep joys, blessings and sorrows belonging to the development of religion in the history of the world? It is sheer arrogance to try to solve philosophical problems about which there have been conflicting opinions for two thousand years, or to overthrow beliefs which, according to the convictions of the highest intellects, are alone capable of elevating the animal man into a true man, or to unite natural science and philosophy without knowing the principal results of either. Or, finally, to construct a system of reality out of natural science and history, while the unity of world history and the fundamental principles thereof have not yet been revealed to the human mind.

And now we come to the first appearance of what may be called the 'Columbus image', the image of philosopher as seafarer, that recurs throughout his mature philosophy:

> To dare to launch out on the sea of doubt without compass or guide is death and destruction for undeveloped heads; most are struck down by storms, few discover new lands. From the midst of this immeasurable ocean of ideas one will often long to be back on firm land.

Nonetheless Fritz remains resolute in his commitment to the scientific outlook of his age: 'history and science, the wonderful legacy of our whole past and the herald of our future, are the sole foundation on which we can build the tower of our speculations'. And, anticipating *The Gay Science*'s forebodings concerning the consequences of the 'death of God', he does not disguise the fact that the consequences of the contemporary outlook are going to be traumatic:

> We stand at the threshold of a great revolution when the mass of mankind first grasps that the whole fabric of Christianity rests on [mere] assumptions: the existence of God, immortality, the authority of the Bible will always remain problematic.

And then (anticipating *The Gay Science*'s important line 'Only as creators can we destroy'[47] – an aphorism pointing to the fact that Nietzsche is not *just* a 'deconstructionist') he writes,

> I have made the attempt [*Versuch*] to deny everything. Oh, destruction is easy – but to construct! And even destruction seems easier than it really is since we are so influenced in our innermost being by the stamp of our childhood, the influence of our parents and education, so that these deeply embedded prejudices are by no means easily uprooted by rational arguments.

The result can often be the backsliding, the loss of intellectual integrity, which, in *Human, All-Too-Human*, will be pictured as the 'free spirit's' return to a 'lost love, whether she be called religion or metaphysics':[48]

> Force of habit, the need for something higher, [fear of] the dissolution of all social forms fight a determined battle with the suspicion of having been misled for two thousand years by a mirage ... until in the end sad and bitter experiences lead us back to the old childish beliefs.

None of the above, however, amounts as yet to a rejection of Christianity. What Fritz seeks, rather, is its modernisation, a reconciliation between religion and the naturalistic outlook of his age. Here is what he writes to Wilhelm and Gustav in April 1862:

> Christianity is not fatalistic ... only when we recognise that we are responsible for ourselves, and that a failure to live a meaningful life can be ascribed only to ourselves, not to any kind of a higher force, will the foundational idea of Christianity enter the kernel of our being. Christianity is essentially a matter of the heart: only when we embody it, when it has become our innermost nature, have we become true Christians. At bottom, the teaching of Christianity expresses only the fundamental ideas of the human heart. They are symbols ...[49]

In *The Antichrist*, virtually the last thing he ever wrote, Nietzsche claims that for the historical Jesus, 'the kingdom of heaven is in the heart'. The real Jesus, that is, was an ethical teacher, rather like the Buddha, who taught the achievement of a state of inner peace through the practice of universal and unconditional love. He had no metaphysical beliefs at all – the transformation of 'heaven' into a supernatural post-mortem destination was a perversion of his teachings by St. Paul. This is the point he makes here: being a Christian is a matter of living the ethics of love, not of believing in a life-governing, supernatural force. In an essay written at about the same time as 'Fate and History', Fritz attacks 'the delusion of a supernatural world' as something that 'leads mankind into a false stance towards the natural world': by making the supernatural the locus of all that is holy, metaphysical Christianity devalues, 'de-divinises' the natural, actual world. This quite 'wrong understanding' of Christianity is a naive product of the 'childhood of peoples' since 'that God became man shows only that man is not to seek his bliss in the infinite, but to seek it on earth'. And then Fritz remarks that 'only through bearing the burden of doubt and struggle does humankind arrive at its humanity: it recognises in itself the beginning, middle and end of religion'.[50]

The final remark here is in fact a quotation from Ludwig Feuerbach's *The Essence of Christianity* (translated into English by George Eliot).[51] Feuerbach's, at the time, revolutionary pronouncement was that all gods are human creations, projections of human conceptions of perfection – crudely put, 'role models'. This explains Fritz's claim that what Christianity deals in are essentially 'symbols'. Rightly understood, Jesus is not a gateway to another life but a role model for this one.

In sum, then, by 1862 Nietzsche had clearly rejected metaphysical Christianity, but equally clearly remained fully committed to ethical Christianity – precisely the position being adopted, at about the same time, by George Eliot. When, therefore, in *Twilight of the Idols*, he criticises her as a 'little moralistic female' lacking the brains to realise that

Christianity is a package deal, that its ethics makes no sense without its metaphysics,[52] he is also criticising his former self.

By 1862, then, Nietzsche, while remaining committed to its ethics, had abandoned the metaphysics of Christianity. The question remains, however, as to whether he had *completely* succumbed to the positivist spirit of his age: whether he had completely rejected the supranatural, or whether something beyond the physical, something 'meta-physical', remained in his outlook. To answer this question, we need to turn to his writings on art, above all on music.

Music

We saw in the first chapter the inseparable connexion in Nietzsche's childhood between music and religion. Nearly all his intense musical experiences were of sacred music; nearly all the choral compositions of his early years were sacred pieces. This connexion is enshrined in his earliest contribution to the philosophy of music in an autobiographical fragment of 1858:

> God has given us music so that *above all* it might lead us upwards. Music unites all qualities: it can exalt us, divert us, cheer us up, or break the hardest of hearts with the softness of its melancholy tones. But its principal task is to lead our thoughts to higher things, to elevate, even to make us tremble. Above all, this is the purpose of Church music ... The musical art often speaks in sounds more penetrating than the words of poetry, and takes hold of the most hidden crevices of the heart. But everything God sends to us can bring us to blessedness only when it is used in a wise and proper way. Thus song elevates our being and leads it to the good and the true. If, however, music serves only as a diversion or as a kind of vain ostentation it is sinful and harmful. Yet this fault is very frequent; almost all of modern music is guilty of it. Another regrettable phenomenon is that many modern composers try to write as obscurely as possible. But precisely these artificial efforts, which possibly charm the connoisseur, leave the healthy human ear cold ... above all so-called *Zukunftsmusik* of a Liszt, or a Berlioz [or a Wagner] that strives to be, at all costs, different.[53]

Three themes manifest themselves here. First, the puritanical conception that either music guides our thoughts to 'higher' things or else it is sinful. Second, the idea that sinful music comes in two forms, low entertainment and high obscurantism. And third, Fritz's innate musical conservatism: the autobiographical fragment goes on to speak of his 'hatred of all modern music', by which he means *Zukunftsmusik*. 'Mozart, Haidn (sic), Schubert, and Mendelssohn, Beethoven and Handel, these are the pillars on which alone German music and I myself are founded',[54] he states defiantly.

These same themes appear three years later in the following letter to Wilhelm and Gustav of January 1861, the year in which he wrote four parts of a *Christmas Oratorio* (p. 28 above):

> Although until now the oratorio has always been believed to hold the same place in spiritual music as does opera in worldly music, this opinion seems wrong to me, and even a disparagement of oratorio. In and of itself, the oratorio is already of a wonderful simplicity, and indeed, as uplifting and indeed strictly religiously uplifting music, it must be so. Hence the

oratorio spurns all those other means that opera uses for effects; no one can take it for just something incidental, as operatic music still is for the masses. It excites no other sense than our hearing. Its content, too, is infinitely simpler and more sublime and, for the most part, is familiar and easily comprehensible to even an uneducated audience. This is why I believe that, in its musical genus, oratorio stands at a higher level than opera in that its means are simpler, its effect more immediate, and its reception at least ought to be wider. If this is not the case the cause must be sought not in the type of music itself, but partly in the treatment and partly in the lack of seriousness of our times. How can a composition that is divided into many disconnected parts make a unified and, above all, holy impression? . . . Secondly, a disadvantage is in the much too artificial, 'authentic (*altväterisch*)' method of performance which belongs more in the study than in our churches and auditoriums, and ensures that music will be hard, indeed impossible, for the musically uneducated to understand . . . The principal reason, however, that the oratorio is not very popular is to be sought in the fact that its music often contains an unholy mixture of profane elements. And this is the principal requirement; that it carry in all its parts, the evident mark of the sacred, the divine.[55]

Again we find the demand that music lead our thoughts to the divine, and that it be accessible to ordinary people. This time, however, not wilful obscurity by composers but pettifogging insistence on 'authenticity' by performers – a pedantic insistence on an original style of performance rather than one suited to the contemporary ear – is identified as that which blocks accessibility. (Just as Christianity must modernise to remain a living phenomenon, so must musical performance.) And what we now find identified as the 'sinful' antithesis of the proper use of music is explicitly identified as 'opera'. This is interesting because after he became a Wagnerian the same puritanical rejection of 'opera' occurs. The only difference, as we shall see, is that, now, in place of oratorio, the Wagnerian music-drama has become the paradigm of good music. This is because, like Wagner himself, Nietzsche understands the music-drama as performing a religious function. And when he turns against Wagner it is because he has changed his mind about Wagner's music and decided that it is, after all, merely 'opera': cheap – sinful – entertainment. Continuous through all these changes is Nietzsche's musical piety. Even after the loss of his Christian faith, good music, I shall suggest, at least until the time he begins to lose his sanity, is, in one way or another, sacred music.

By 1862 Fritz has abandoned the naïve, metaphysical Christianity of his mother. Positivism, however, does not claim him. Thus, discussing 'the essence of music' in early 1863, he writes that the great composer must be inspired by 'an indefinable Something, the daemonic':

> the communication of this daemonic Something is the highest demand the artistic understanding must satisfy. This, however, is neither a sensation nor knowledge, but rather a dim intimation of the divine. Through movement there comes into being a feeling, from out of which heaven suddenly shines forth.[56]

Similar sentiments are expressed in July 1864, right at the end of his Pforta days, in a letter to a fellow pupil, Rudolf Buddensieg.[57] Buddensieg had sought to suggest that music produces its effects by stimulating the same parts of the nervous system as all the other higher arts. Fritz replies that this describes merely the 'physical effect' of music. Much more important is the fact that it produces

A spiritual intuition, which, by means of its uniqueness, greatness and suggestive power, works like a sudden miracle. Do not think that the ground of this emotional intuition lies in sensation: rather it lies in the highest and finest part of the knowing spirit. Isn't it the same for you, too – as though something beyond, unsuspected, is disclosed? Don't you sense, that you have been transported into another realm, which is normally hidden from men?...Nothing in art surpasses this effect...[Writing] to a friend more than two years ago I named the effect 'something daemonic'. If there can be intimations of higher worlds here is where they are concealed.[58]

Eight years later, the 'daemonic' appears in Nietzsche's first book, *The Birth of Tragedy*, as 'the Dionysian'. It constitutes 'the spirit of music' out of which Greek tragedy, the highest art ever produced, is born.

In his mature philosophy Nietzsche attacks what he calls 'art-deification':

Art raises its head when the religions relax their hold. It takes over a host of moods and feelings engendered by religion, lays them to its heart and itself grows more profound and soulful...The Enlightenment undermined the dogmas of religion and inspired a fundamental distrust of them; so that the feelings expelled from the sphere of religion by the Enlightenment throw themselves into art,[59]

above all into music. The important point here is that, first and foremost, this is autobiography. Fritz's own 'enlightenment' during the Pforta years required him to abandon the naïve theological dogma of his upbringing. The effect, however, was not – not yet – to turn him into a positivist, but to cause him to relocate the 'beyond' in a dogma-free domain accessible through art. Fritz's piety became a piety towards art.

* * *

As the continuation of religion by other means, music becomes, for Fritz, the primary form of art and therefore the primary activity of life. But it is also primary in two other connexions.

First, it is prior to language:

the older a language the richer in sounds it is, so that often it cannot be distinguished from song. The oldest languages, that is, had few words and no universal concepts. One can almost assert that they were languages of feeling rather than languages of words.[60]

This idea that the first form of human communication was more like wordless song than what we would recognise as language* leads, in Nietzsche's mature philosophy, to a suspicion of words, paradoxical in one of the supreme wordsmiths of the German language. The more 'wordy' we become, he suggests in *Wagner at Bayreuth*, the more distant we become from true feeling and insight.

The other context in which the primacy of music appears is in Fritz's analysis of the origin and nature of Greek tragedy.

---

* The idea originates with Rousseau, Condillac and Herder and plays an important role in Wagner's *Opera and Drama* (1852), which is possibly the more or less direct route by which it came to Nietzsche. It has recently been revived in the archaeologist Stephen Mithen's *The Singing Neanderthals* (Mithen 2005).

Tragedy

The full title of Nietzsche's first book, which appeared in 1872, is *The Birth of Tragedy out of the Spirit of Music*. Remarkably, however, the fragments remaining from the Pforta period make it clear that the most fundamental, revolutionary idea of this book had already been worked out before he left school.

In 'Thoughts Concerning Choral Music in Tragedy', written in the spring of 1864, Fritz writes that 'while the German dramas developed from the epic',

> the origin of Greek drama lay in the lyric, unified with musical elements...Still, in the oldest preserved tragedies of Aeschylus, the chorus has by far the most dominant role; the speeches in between often serve only to introduce a new motif which alters the mood of the chorus and necessitates a development of feeling. Admittedly the chorus gradually retreated as the action was moved out of it and into the parts between [the choral passages]. It retained significance only because it contained the musical element essential to tragedy if it were to have a genuinely tragic effect. Concerning this tragic effect the Greeks thought differently from us: it was introduced in the scenes of great pathos, great outpourings of emotion, mainly musical, in which action played only a small part. Lyrical feeling, by contrast [with us], was everything. The chorus in these scenes contained one of the most important, and, for the success of the tragedy, decisive moments, the music in the tragedy. It is certainly a well-grounded hypothesis to assert that at its highest point...the entire tragedy, and not just the choral parts, is governed by the order and proportions of a musical plan. What is strophe and anti-strophe other than a musical symmetry?

Not only is *The Birth*'s thesis of the primacy of the chorus presented in this essay, but so too (now he has been converted by Gustav) is its thesis of the rebirth of tragedy in Wagner's music-dramas: the 'meaninglessness' of today's opera, something which in their prime the 'fine-feeling Greeks' would never have tolerated, is something we need rescuing from by 'Richard Wagner's brilliant deeds and plans of reform'. In the great tragedies of the Greeks, Fritz concludes, the Wagnerian *Gesamtkunstwerk* (the 'collective artwork' in which all the individual arts are collected together) is prefigured: in the Greek tragedies we find 'that which the newest musical school sets forth as the "artwork of the future" [Wagner's term for the collective artwork], works in which the noblest of the arts found their way into a harmonic unity'.[61] That the Wagner-as-the-saviour-of-art-and-culture theme appears already in 1864 is important, for it shows that far from Wagner's hijacking Nietzsche's first book through force of personality, as is usually claimed, the theme was already in Fritz's mind well before he ever met Wagner.

By no means, however, is all of *The Birth* anticipated by the sixth-former. And in one conspicuous respect – the nature of the tragic effect – the 1864 reflections are quite different from those of 1872. Throughout his life Nietzsche returned again and again to the question of the nature of this paradoxical effect: the question of why tragedy does not play to empty houses, of what kind of satisfaction we could possibly derive from witnessing the destruction of the tragic hero, a figure who, in many respects, represents what is finest and wisest within us. In total, Nietzsche produces at least four different answers to this question, all of which seem to hit upon a genuine aspect of what draws us to tragic drama. In *The Birth*, we shall see, he will appeal to the idea of transcendence of individuality. But here he holds that the effect and aim of tragedy, revealed in, for example, the fate of Oedipus, is to guard against hubris, to remind us of the gap between men and gods (one the Greeks were liable to cross, finding it hard to tell the difference between a god and an Olympic champion). Tragedy reveals that 'the divinity often sends men unjustified suffering, not arbitrarily, but to preserve a customary world-order'.[62]

What this reveals is the seriousness with which the Greeks took the tragic festival, the fact that

> the highest aesthetic pleasure did not blind the judgment of the Athenians to the ethical and religious aspects [of tragedy], that they always held the religious origin before their eyes. The effect of their theatrical productions was therefore like neither that of our theatres nor of our churches, but they were rather mixed together and intertwined.[63]

Though *The Birth* abandons the foregoing account of the tragic effect – or at least chooses to emphasise another aspect – this idea of the essentially religious nature of the occasion is central to *The Birth* and to virtually all Nietzsche's later thinking about tragedy.

Poetry

Throughout the Pforta period Fritz continued to produce enormous numbers of poems. But he also wrote *about* poetry, in particular about the poetry of Friedrich Hölderlin (1770–1843).

Hölderlin had been a younger friend of Schiller and an intimate friend of his fellow university students at Tübingen, Schelling and Hegel. As much philosopher as poet, Hölderlin was the source of many of Hegel's main ideas. In 1806, at the age of thirty-six, he lapsed into a form of insanity which a modern diagnosis would probably classify as schizophrenia.

Hölderlin's poems, which he often called 'hymns', and his always lyrical prose works express a religious veneration for nature. Throughout his thinking runs an antithesis between 'clarity of presentation' and 'the fire from heaven'; between, that is, finite human reason and the infinitude of 'the holy'. He holds that Western modernity has been overtaken by 'clear' but shallow reason so that it has lost its sense of the divine, has fallen away from the West's 'great beginning' in ancient Greece. (A century later Max Weber would speak of Western modernity's 'dis-enchantment'.) The poet, standing nearer to the gods than other mortals, has the priestly task of restoring 'holy pathos'. 'What are poets for in destitute times?' Hölderlin asks in 'Bread and Wine'. They are, he answers, 'like the wine-god's holy priests/Who roamed from land to land in holy night'.

As 'roaming' suggests, Hölderlin felt that the price he – 'the poet' – paid for his closeness to the gods was estrangement from mortals. Sensing the approach of his madness, he began to experience himself as a 'false priest' about to be punished for his hubris, for overstepping the boundary between mortals and the gods.

Hölderlin first became a major figure during the First World War, when many of his greatest poems received their first publication. Relatively little known in Nietzsche's day, and if known dismissed on account of his unhappy end, he is now regarded as one of the two or three greatest German poets. He is a major presence in Nietzsche's works as he is in Heidegger's (a fact which establishes a profound, if subterranean, bond between them).

Heidegger observes that *The Birth of Tragedy*'s fundamental distinction between the realms of Apollo and of Dionysus, between the 'Apollonian' and the 'Dionysian', is actually a re-presentation of Hölderlin's 'clarity of presentation'/'fire from the heavens' distinction.[64] Given that Hölderlin's supra-rational realm of 'the holy' is, as the quotation from 'Bread and Wine' indicates, the realm of 'the wine god', of, in other words, Dionysus (or Bacchus), this is surely correct. Nietzsche's own poetry echoes with Hölderlin's sonorous musicality, and sometimes with direct quotation. Allusions to and semi-quotations from Hölderlin permeate the more poetic of Nietzsche's mature philosophical works, in particular *Thus Spoke Zarathustra*: Graham Parkes's excellent annotated translation spots no less than fifteen allusions, mostly to the poetic novel *Hyperion*, and there are, in fact, more.[65] Cosima Wagner noted in her diary in December 1873 the (as she sees it) somewhat dubious influence of Hölderlin on Nietzsche: 'Malwida [von Meysenbug] gave R[ichard Wagner] Hölderlin's works [for Christmas]. R and I realise, with some concern, the great influence this writer has exercised on P[rofessor] Nietzsche; rhetorical bombast, weirdly accumulated images (the north wind sings the blossoms etc.); but at the same time a beautiful, noble meaning'.[66]

* * *

As Gustav Krug introduced Fritz to Wagner, so it is likely that Wilhelm Pinder introduced him to Hölderlin.[67] Fritz's ever increasing passion for the poet was inspired not just by his works but also by his life, about which he was well informed[68] and with which he almost certainly felt a strong personal identification on account of the similarities between Hölderlin's life and his own. Like Nietzsche, Hölderlin lost his father at an early age, was much influenced by his mother, loved nature and wrote a great deal of nature poetry, attended a boarding school very like Pforta, had an aversion to all forms of vulgarity and a tendency to melancholy, made few friends at school but had a close friend at home, was distressed by the current state of German culture, and had a passion for Greece but had intended to study theology at university.

In adulthood, the similarities between the two lives continue. Hölderlin experienced an impossible love for Susette Gontard, the mother of the boy to whom he was tutor and whom he celebrated in verse as 'Diotima', while Nietzsche harboured an equally impossible love for Cosima Wagner, whom he celebrated as 'Ariadne'.[69] And, of course, the most striking similarity of all is that both Hölderlin and Nietzsche entered long nights of madness, the former's lasting from 1806 until his death in 1843, the latter's from 1889 until his death in 1900. Hölderlin, it seems likely, had a strong personal identification with Empedocles, the ancient Greek poet who, feeling himself more god than man, hurled himself into the Crater of Etna. As Fritz hypothesises in the essay I am about to discuss, Hölderlin may have understood his own approaching madness as a kind of falling into Etna: the 'melancholy tones' of his 'so significant, dramatic fragment' *The Death of Empedocles*, Fritz suggests, is permeated with a pre-echo of 'the future of the unhappy poet, the grave of a years-long madness'. But Nietzsche, too, via Hölderlin, may have come to identify with Empedocles' mode of dying. This thought raises the possibility, to which I shall return, that the manner of Nietzsche's entry into madness was, to a degree, 'scripted'.

* * *

In October 1861, Fritz was set by his German literature teacher the task of writing an essay under the title 'A Letter to a Distant [i.e., imaginary] Friend Recommending Him to

Read My Favourite Poet'. Indulging his passion, Fritz chooses to write on Hölderlin.[70] The essay[71] begins as follows:

> Some remarks in your last letter about Hölderlin have surprised me very much, and I feel compelled to enter the lists against you on behalf of my favourite poet…You say, "How Hölderlin can be your favourite poet I can't comprehend. On me, at least, these hazy, half-crazy outpourings from a fractured, ruptured mind can only make a sad, and also repellent, impression. Unclear language, ideas that belong in a madhouse, wild outbursts against the Germans, deification of the heathen world, sometimes naturalism, sometimes pantheism, sometimes polytheism all together in a chaotic mixture – his poetry is disfigured by all this, albeit composed in well-crafted Greek metres".

Fritz's general line of defence against the imagined attack, a mode of persuasion that will pervade his mature philosophy, is not to challenge the 'friend's' account of the facts but rather to offer a different perspective on them. He points out, first of all, that Hölderlin's lines are not just 'well-crafted' but represent virtuosity of the highest order. *Hyperion*, in particular, he suggests, sounds at times like 'the breaking of waves in the stormy sea' and is, in fact, with its alternation of 'soft, melting sounds' with 'painful dissonances', 'music' – for Fritz, as we know, the highest condition of art.

Concerning the criticism of the Germans, Fritz continues, Hölderlin does indeed tell them some hard truths about the desolation engulfing their culture, though what he hates is not the Germans, but rather the 'barbarism', the philistinism and reduction of human beings to mere 'cogs in the machine [*Fachmenschen*]', that is destroying their community. It is in other words a case of tough love, criticism springing from a 'love of the Father-land which Hölderlin possessed to the highest degree'. (Though he does not, Fritz could have strengthened his case by citing Hölderlin's 'Homecoming/To the Relatives', in which the poet, returning to his Swabian homeland from the Swiss Alps where he has joyfully encountered 'the Highest', is yet in a state of 'holy mourning' because the 'relatives', still being God-less, are not yet properly related to him. This is what establishes his poetic ministry of love: his mission of actualising their relatedness through, as he puts it elsewhere, his '[re]founding the holy'.)

Concerning the accusation of unclarity, Fritz responds that the seeming opacity of the works is in fact 'Sophoclean' depth created by their 'inexhaustible plenitude of profound thoughts'. To back up the claim of profundity he notes that Hölderlin is no mere poet but also the writer of works of philosophical prose which display his 'spiritual brotherhood' with Schiller and with his intimate friend, the deep-thinking Hegel.

What, according to Fritz, are the profound ideas to be found in Hölderlin? He quotes from a poem, 'Evening Fantasy':

> *In the evening sky a springtime flowers*
> *Innumerable the roses blossom and peaceful seems*
> *The golden world; Oh, take me there*
> *Crimson clouds! And there on high may*
> *In light and air, love and sorrow melt away! –*
> *But, as if scared by stupid request, the magic*

Takes flight. It becomes dark, and lonely
Beneath the heavens, I am as always.
Come now, soft slumber! Too much the heart
Desires, but at the last, youthfulness, you too will fade!
You restless dreamer!
Peaceful and serene is my old age then.

It is not difficult to understand why this beautiful poem (one can easily imagine it as one of Richard Strauss's 'Four Last Songs') seems to Nietzsche profound rather than mad: it expresses his own *Weltschmerz*, the spiritual homesickness he pours into innumerable poems with titles such as 'Alone', 'Homesickness' and 'Homecoming'. But here, clearly, homecoming is conceived in, to the young Nietzsche, a novel, post-Christian manner. It consists not in reunion with departed souls in a Christian heaven but in what Freud called the 'oceanic' feeling: the transcendence of individuality in an experience of unification with nature, with the totality of being, 'the All'.

This will become a major theme in Nietzsche's mature philosophy. In his first book, *The Birth of Tragedy*, he asserts that 'individuality [is]...the source of all suffering'[72] and offers its transcendence as the paradoxical joy that is the essence of the 'tragic effect'. And in his later thought, as we shall see, transcendence is his account of the 'Dionysian' perspective on the world, the key to the task of willing life's 'eternal return'.

* * *

Hölderlin's lyrical novel, *Hyperion*, which Fritz's essay singles out for special praise, expresses sentiments similar to those of 'Evening Fantasy'. It takes the form of a series of letters written by Hyperion, a Greek, to Bellarmin, a German friend. Hyperion, having spent some time travelling in Western Europe, and having absorbed certain modes of living characteristic of the West, discovers on his return to Greece that he has become cut off from the experience of wholeness he had once known in his ancient homeland.

Schiller distinguished between the 'sentimental' and the 'naïve' (neither term is pejorative). Poetry which expresses a simple, unreflective unity with nature of the kind enjoyed by a flower is 'naïve', poetry which yearns to recover such 'naïve' unity is 'sentimental'. The 'sentimental' yearning for 'naivety', Schiller suggests, resembles the sick person's yearning for health. The poetry of ancient Greece, in particular of Homer, he classified as 'naïve', that of nineteenth-century romantics, such as himself, as 'sentimental'. Hyperion's letters (and Nietzsche's poems) are 'sentimental'. They contrast an idealized picture of primal Greek experience with the dis-enchantment, the rationalization and mechanization, of Western modernity. The first letter evokes the primordial state of connectedness to all things, an experience Hyperion briefly recovers on his return home:

To be one with all – this is the life divine, this is man's heaven. To be one with all that lives, to return in blessed self-forgetfulness into the All of nature – this is the pinnacle of thoughts and joys, this the eternal mountain peak, the place of eternal rest.

In the primal wholeness of all that lives, death is overcome, since there exists only the youthfulness of ever-new being:

To be one with all that lives! At those words Virtue puts off her wrathful armour ... and Death vanishes from the confederacy of beings, and eternal indivisibility and eternal youth bless and beautify the world.

The experience is lost, however, the moment Hyperion engages in reflection:

On this height I often stand, my Bellarmin! But an instant of reflection hurls me down. I reflect, and I find myself as I was before – alone, with all the griefs of mortality; and my heart's refuge, the world in its eternal oneness, is gone. Nature closes her arms, and I stand like an alien before her and understand her not.

Everyday, 'Apollonian' rationality is what destroys unity by introducing a fissure between nature and knowing subject:

Ah! Had I not gone to your schools! ... Knowledge has corrupted everything for me. Among you I became so truly reasonable, learnt so thoroughly to distinguish myself from what surrounds me, that now I am solitary in the beautiful world, an outcast from the garden of nature in which I grew and flowered, drying up under the noonday sun.

Following the biblical narrative of paradise, fall, and redemption, *Hyperion* ends with a vision of recovered oneness:

Oh thou ... Nature! ... Men fall from thee like rotten fruits, oh let them perish, for thus they return to thy root; so may I, too, O tree of life, that I may grow green again with thee ... Like lovers' quarrels are the dissonances of the world. Reconciliation is there, even in the midst of strife, and all things that are parted find one another again in the end ... all is one eternal glowing life.[73]

Nietzsche says of *Hyperion* – at the same time evidently disclosing his own state of mind – that

although it radiates with a transfiguring shimmer, everything is dissatisfaction and lack of fulfilment; the forms the poet conjures up are 'airy images, which, in sounds, awaken home-sickness, delighting us, but also awaken dissatisfied yearning'. Nowhere does the yearning for Greece reveal itself in purer tones than here; nowhere is Hölderlin's spiritual relatedness to Schiller and Hegel, his intimate friend, clearer than here.

Yearning for the paradise of ancient Greece expresses, of course, not only teenage angst but also Pforta's communal dream.

* * *

Empedocles was a Greek poet, prophet, mystic and scientist who lived in the early fifth century BC. In one of his poems he represents himself as a 'deathless god, no longer mortal' surrounded by crowds asking for the 'healing word' to cure them of disease. According to legend, he possessed the power to raise the dead and, as already noted, died his own mortal death by throwing himself into Etna's crater. Of Hölderlin's *The Death of Empedocles* – a work which inspired him to attempt his own version of the myth – Fritz writes,

In the unfinished tragedy 'Empedocles', the poet discloses for us his own nature. Empedocles's death is died out of a god's pride, scorn for humanity, satiation with the earth, and
pantheism. Whenever I read it the whole work shakes me to the foundations in a quite
unique way. In this Empedocles dwells a divine majesty.

Here, again, there appears the idea of transcending the mortality of human individuality:
Empedocles is able to cast off the mortal coil because he is, or has become, an immortal. But
what is the relevance of 'pantheism'? I think the answer is that the experience of merging
into 'the One' must be, above all, a *redemptive* experience, an experience in which all sorrows
are washed away. Schopenhauer, criticising Spinoza's pantheism, claimed that the One is
'not divine but demonic'. But if that were the case then the idea of merging with the One
would repulse rather than attract. To attract, to redeem, to be the source of joyful ecstasy,
the totality of things must be experienced as divine.

* * *

Nietzsche's early experience of Hölderlin, as expressed in this eulogy on his 'favourite poet',
provides, I shall suggest, the hidden vision that shaped the deepest regions of his final
philosophy. For a time Schopenhauer obscured the vision and led him away from Hölderlin.
But from *Zarathustra* onwards, his philosophy is a long return. It is hard, therefore, to over-
emphasise the essay's importance. His teacher, Professor Koberstein, was unenthusiastic,
however. Giving it a mark of II/IIa (about a B+), he commented, 'I should like to give
the author a piece of friendly advice: to concern himself with a poet who is healthier, more
lucid and more German'. By repeating, exactly, the sentiments of the 'imaginary friend', he
proved that the entire essay was, for him, water off a rather dense duck's back.

Morality and Politics

Much of the already-mentioned *Germania* lecture, 'Fate and History',[74] has little to
do with either fate or history. In particular, it contains a number of remarks about
morality.

'As custom (*Sitte*), the product of a particular people at a particular time, represents a
particular direction of the spirit', Nietzsche writes, 'so morality (*Moral*) is the product of a
universal development of humanity, the sum of all truths for our world'. It is not entirely
clear what this means, but it bears on a paradox in Nietzsche's mature philosophy. The
paradox is that although in general an 'ethical relativist' (there are no culture-independent
moral truths, moral values are at most valid for a particular culture at a particular time)
Nietzsche also seems to offer his own particular set of values – strength, self-discipline, and
self-development – as absolute values. Possibly this early remark provides a clue to resolving
the paradox: as opposed to 'customary' values, Nietzsche's own, very abstract values are what
flourishing human beings always have, and always will, exemplify.

Another interesting remark in this early work is 'the good is only the most subtle development of evil'. What lies behind the remark there is no way of knowing. But it is an
interesting one since the sublimation of 'evil' into 'good' is, we shall see, a major theme in
Nietzsche's mature philosophy: we must not seek to 'castrate' the evil in man, he holds,
because all that is good in him is, in reality, sublimated evil.

A third theme central to the mature philosophy which receives an airing in 'Fate and
History' concerns the tension between individual and community:

the struggle between the individual and the general will: here is indicated that eternally crucial problem, the question of the justification of the individual to the people, the people to humanity at large, and humanity to the world.

The most common understanding of Nietzsche's mature philosophy is, in a slogan, that 'only the superman counts'. Only the exceptional individual is of any value; the rest of society, 'the herd' (particularly its female contingent), is usually an impediment to the appearance of the great individual and at best his footstool. Later we shall investigate the accuracy of this representation. What can be said of this early thinking, however, is that it is precisely the opposite of this view: as a people must find its justification to humanity and the world at large, so the individual must find his justification in his contribution to his people.

Before leaving the topic of Nietzsche's early views on morality, a word on moral education. In his mature philosophy, especially in *On the Uses and Disadvantages of History for Life*, Nietzsche repeatedly focuses, in a characteristically nineteenth-century way, on the centrality of 'monumental' figures or 'educators' (roughly speaking, 'role models') to moral education. This idea is already strongly prefigured in the Pforta writings. So, for example, in an essay discussion in March 1864 of the proverb that one should 'only speak good of the dead', Fritz says that, while obviously false if one is interested in history as an objective science, nonetheless, when it comes to history as an *art* that is devoted to the 'clarification of life', the saying possesses merit since, in this context, we are interested not in accuracy but in moral guidance. The important element of truth in the saying is that what we really honour in the dead is not the individual but rather 'the eternal truth he embodies'.[75]

The same anticipation of *The Uses and Disadvantages of History* is found, in January of the same year, in what looks to be a school essay entitled 'On the Attractive, Educational and Instructive that Lies for the Young in the Study of the History of the Fatherland'. The great deeds of our ancestors, he writes, affect us because they are seen as our *own* deeds. The history of other peoples can affect us to a degree, but not nearly as powerfully as that of our own, because with their heroes we lack a comparable identification. The value of identification with the heroes of national history is that 'grasping the Fatherland as a whole warns us to be true to its virtues'. 'In the enchanted pictures of national history', Fritz concludes, 'we become clear as to which destiny our people must fulfil, what the task is that is given to it'.[76]

* * *

True to his upbringing, Fritz began his Pforta years a monarchist. Monarchy represents the best form of government, he writes, in mid-1861, particularly in times of war. As already noted, the power of the Persians he claims to have depended 'not on the cleverness of the people but on their holding their monarchy more in honour than others'.[77] Soon, however, monarchism becomes modified by a good dose of Pforta liberalism. Developing an enthusiasm for Napoleon III,* he made him the subject of a *Germania* lecture in early 1862.

Napoleon III, though feared and loathed by the Germans (including the *Germania* audience, which received the lecture very badly), was a man of intelligence and culture.

---

* Napoleon III, Bonaparte's nephew, was elected President of the French Republic in 1848 and assumed the title of Emperor in 1852. Following his disastrous loss of the Franco-Prussian war, he was exiled to England in 1871 and spent the remainder of his days in Chislehurst, in Kent. *Quel dommage!*

Starry-eyed with enthusiasm, Fritz calls him a 'genius' (the ancestor-concept of *Zarathustra*'s 'superman'). What he admires, however, is, as he sees it, the 'unbelievable moderation' of his advance to power; 'the fact that he was elected president by the parliamentary representatives of the people and then Emperor by a popular vote of six million' and so always represented 'the will of the whole people'. At every stage, therefore, Napoleon was supported by, and expressed, the popular will. This the 'genius' must always do, for otherwise his government will contain the 'seeds of its own corruption'. The ideal of a 'free state' is, in other words, 'a president approved by the representatives of the people'.[78]

This very English-sounding approval of parliamentary democracy is echoed in Fritz's 'Whiggish' comments of the same year on English history itself. The Revolution of 1642 succeeded, he holds, because Charles I attempted an 'absolute monarchy', an 'aggressive despotism'. His death is a strong reminder of the force of public opinion: the 'spirit of the people' would not stand for its freedoms being attacked and its authority being flouted, although Charles's execution was unnecessary and exceeded their demands.[79] Further signs of English-sounding liberalism are to be found in the notes from late 1862, which observe that human rights, in particular the right to freedom from slavery, derive not from the state but from the 'godly worth' of each human individual.[80]

In spite of such liberalism,[81] however, Fritz retains his belief in a social hierarchy under the strong leadership of the political 'genius'. And he believes the genius must be allowed special privileges. As he puts it in the Napoleon III lecture, 'the genius is dependent on other and higher laws than are ordinary people'. This creates a paradox which is, however, only apparent:

> The genius is dependent on other and higher laws than are ordinary men, on laws that often seem to contradict the fundamental laws of morality and justice. Fundamentally, however, these laws are the same when grasped in the widest perspective ... The genius represents the peak of a natural and spiritual harmony ...[82]

This is an important passage, for it deals with a theme that runs through Nietzsche's mature philosophy and is often misunderstood as 'immoralism'. The mature Nietzsche regularly attacks moral universalism – 'those who say "good for all, evil for all"', as *Zarathustra* puts it. Though this is often taken to be a manifestation of the supposed 'only-the-well-being-of-the-superman-counts' thesis it is in fact, as here, a manifestation of something quite different. Partly the rejection of universalism reflects Nietzsche's conviction that different values are appropriate to different cultures at different times. The 1862 notes, for example, argue that the mistake made by communism is that of supposing the same form of government to fit all peoples equally well, which it does not, since they all experience the world differently.[83] But Nietzsche also rejects universalism on an intra-social level. This is because he holds what I shall call his 'stratification of the virtues' thesis: what is virtuous for me depends on my station in life, on the role I play within the social totality. Virtues, that is, are specialised because that is the way in which individuals best contribute to the communal good. So if I am either a political or a spiritual leader, privileges indeed accrue to me which do not accrue to those called by nature to a humbler role in society. But this is not because only my well-being counts but rather because the communal good is best served by my having those privileges. Not just Goethe but the community as a whole suffers if it is deprived of his poems because he needs to earn a living.

Homeland versus World Citizenship

We have seen, in Fritz's early poetry and recollections of childhood, a deep yearning for rootedness in 'blood and earth', in homeland. But after he made the transition to Pforta, signs of a different perspective on *Heimat* (homeland) began to appear. In August 1859 he composed the following:

> *Fleet horses bear*
> *Me without fear or dismay*
> *Through distant places.*
> *And whoever sees me, knows me*
> *And whoever knows me calls me:*
> *The homeless man...*
> *No one dares*
> *To ask me*
> *Where my homeland is:*
> *Perhaps I have never been fettered*
> *To space and the fleeting hours,*
> *I am free as an eagle...*[84]

Here he seems to be discovering the upside of 'homelessness', facilitated, perhaps, by having settled somewhat into boarding-school life (though he might, on the other hand, simply be putting a good face on having been uprooted from his home.) A similar thought is expressed at about the same time in the fragment *Capri and Heligoland*: 'we are pilgrims in this world – we are citizens of the world' he writes.[85] In later life, following a decisive turn against Prussian nationalism, Nietzsche called himself a 'good European' and hoped that European culture would become globalised into *the* world culture. Such 'cosmopolitanism' seems to be anticipated here. In 1864, however, in the reflections on the importance of national history discussed above (p. 47), one of the advantages of national history is said to be that it prevents us from wandering away into 'dreams of world-citizenry'. Yet only a month later, in a school essay on the question of whether exile was a more severe punishment in the ancient than in the modern world[86] (the English shipping their criminals to Australia is cited as a modern version of exile), he chastises Ovid's lament at his exile from Rome as 'unmanly'. Suggesting that we enlightened moderns have overcome antiquity's excessive attachment to homeland just as we have overcome its xenophobia, he asserts that we have learnt not to be constricted by the customs into which we are born. And because, above and beyond the homeland, stands 'a man's inner conviction, his honour, indeed his whole spiritual world', in short a 'spiritual homeland', we can even, he suggests, find a new homeland in what was previously foreign.

All this, in contrast to the previous month's dismissal of 'world-citizenship', looks to be a (perhaps not wholly coherent) affirmation of it. What we must say, I think, is that during the Pforta years there exists an unresolved tension between homeland and cosmopolitanism, with Fritz pulled sometimes one way and sometimes the other. One of the major achievements of his mature thought, I shall suggest, is to produce a genuine resolution to the conflict.

Fate and Freedom

The *Germania* lecture of 1862, 'Fate and History', covers, we have seen, a number of topics that have little to do with its title. But now, finally, we come to the topic the title announces, the question of the relation between causal determinism – 'fate' – and the freedom of the human will; Fritz thinks of 'history' as a record of free human action.

The question he confronts – a problem so difficult that some contemporary philosophers believe its solution to be, in principle, beyond the human mind – is whether human freedom, the apparent presupposition of the moral and existential concerns we have as human beings, is compatible with the principle that every event has a cause, the heart of the scientific outlook on the world. The supplementary question is: if they are not compatible, which of the two should be abandoned? It cannot be said that Fritz solves the problem. Indeed the discussion is thoroughly confused, as one might expect from a seventeen-year-old philosophical novice.

One matter Fritz is not confused about is the consequences of universal causal determinism: 'were it to be the only fundamental truth, man would then be the plaything of dark, causal forces, without responsibility for his mistakes, completely free from moral distinctions, nothing but a necessary link in a chain'. If it were true, he says, the best thing would be not to know it, for the knowledge of such a truth would cause unbearable rage, would cause a man 'convulsively to struggle in the bonds that hold him', create in him a 'mad lust to upset the mechanism of the world'.

As to whether fate or freedom represents the truth of the matter, the essay is completely indecisive. 'Perhaps freedom is the highest potentiality of fate' it opines vaguely – the idea being, possibly, that world-history at a certain point causes the emergence of causally undetermined entities. But as to why we should think it true that fate, at a certain evolutionary point, as it were, bows out of the picture, it has nothing to say.

As if realising he has not done justice to the question of freedom, Fritz returns to the topic a few weeks later in 'Freedom of the Will and Fate'.[87] Now his impulse is to have his cake and eat it, to show fate and freedom to be compatible. The actions of an individual begin, he argues, not with his birth but in the embryo and perhaps in his parents and ancestors. Our actions, in other words, are wholly, it seems, determined by our genetic inheritance. So determinism is true. But 'free will…means the ability to act consciously, while fate is the principle that determines us unconsciously'. What follows is that 'the strict difference between fate and freedom disappears'. They are, in other words, compatible, each necessary to a proper conception of the human individual: '*fatum*-less, absolute freedom of the will would make man a god, the fatalist principle would make him a robot'. This has a fine rhetorical ring, but is of little intellectual value. For if freedom is just *consciousness* of choice, those choices being one and all completely determined by forces which are beyond our control and of which we are unconscious, the problem of how we can possibly attribute freedom and responsibility to people remains unresolved. *The Manchurian Candidate*'s would-be assassin, brainwashed into wishing to kill the President, is certainly conscious of his choice to do so. But he is, in fact, nothing but the brainwashers' robot. As we shall see, Nietzsche wrestled with the problem of freedom and determinism all his life.

3

Bonn

NIETZSCHE PASSED through the Pforta gateway, for the last time as a pupil, on September 7, 1864. Surrounded by a crowd of schoolboys, assembled to give the school-leavers a ceremonial send-off, he and eight others mounted a garlanded carriage escorted on both sides by festively clad postillions. The future lay in Bonn, at whose famous university he had decided to enrol, mainly because of its distinguished philologists, Otto Jahn (en passant, a renowned Mozart biographer) and Friedrich Ritschl (see Plate 6), but also because he would have a friend there: born and brought up in the Rhineland, Paul Deussen (see Plate 7) planned to attend his home university. In the meantime, the two young men had five free weeks before the beginning of the university year.

Free at Last

The first two weeks were spent in Naumburg, where Deussen made a very good impression on the Nietzsche family. Then, on September 23, the two friends set off on a slow meander westwards towards Bonn.

'One must', Nietzsche wrote to a friend still at Pforta, 'experience constraint in order to be able to savour freedom'.[1] After six years of intense study, cooped up in a quasi-monastic institution which located the real world a couple of millennia in the past, Nietzsche, on his Rhineland trip, experienced the charms of first freedom to an intense degree. His letters sparkle with the excitement of being able to do just what he wants, and with the fascination of a new world (he had never before been out of eastern Germany) whose every detail is vibrant and important: 'I take note of everything, the distinctive characteristics of the food, activity, agriculture and so on', he writes home.[2]

The westward meander was punctuated by three stops. The first was at Elberfeld, near the Rhine, east of Düsseldorf, Nietzsche's first encounter with Catholic Germany. Here they spent the night with one of Deussen's aunts:

> We refreshed ourselves with wine and bread – around here, everywhere you go you get lovely cakes and slices of pumpernickel ... the town is extremely commercial, the houses

mostly clad in slate. Among the women that one sees, I noticed a strong predilection for a pious hanging of the head. The young women are very elegant wearing coats with extremely narrow waists...After visiting several cafés on Sunday afternoon we drank a fine Moselle wine in the evening...my piano improvisations achieved considerable effect...everything is completely – as Lisabeth would say – 'enchanting'.³

The friends then proceeded to Königswater, a few kilometres downstream from Bonn, on the opposite bank. Here they engaged in the boyish high jinks one would expect from young men on first release from boarding school. Deussen's madcap cousin, Ernst Schnabel, persuaded them to take a horse ride about which Nietzsche remained wisely silent in his letters home, but which Deussen describes in his memoirs:

Intoxicated with wine and camaraderie, we allowed ourselves, in spite of having very little money, to be persuaded into hiring horses to ride up the Drachenfels ['Dragon Rocks', a famous tourist sight along the Rhine, visible from Bonn]. It is the only time I have ever seen Nietzsche on horseback. He was in a mood to interest himself less in the beauty of the scenery than in the ears of his horse. He kept trying to measure them and make up his mind whether he was riding a donkey or a horse. In the evening we acted still more insanely. The three of us were wandering through the streets of the little town making overtures to the girls we assumed to be concealed behind the windows. Nietzsche whistled and cooed 'Pretty darling, pretty darling'. Schnabel was talking all kinds of nonsense, making out that he was a poor Rhineland boy, begging for a night's shelter.⁴

Though one dreads to think how the boys felt the next morning, the matter of the ears lends a certain Midsummer-Night's-Dream charm to this escapade.

The friends' third and longest stop was with Deussen's parents in Oberdreis, near Koblenz, again close to the Rhine. Here Nietzsche found Deussen's father (like his own, a Lutheran pastor) 'a good and great man who, however, doesn't always stick to the point', and his mother, the 'Frau Pastorin', a woman 'of such education, delicacy of feeling and expression, and of such capacity for hard work, as to be almost unique'. His main interest however was reserved for Deussen's sister, Marie ('sometimes she reminds me of you, so I cannot withhold my especial favour',⁵ he wrote Elizabeth), to whom, as with Anna Redtel, he expressed his affection with a musical dedication.

On October 15, 1864, Fritz and Frau Deussen celebrated their joint birthday:

Early in the morning we sang a four-part chorale 'Praise the Lord, oh my Soul' outside Frau Pastor Deussen's bedroom...In the evening we played party games on the grass and did some dancing...Early the next morning we travelled six hours to Neuwied, having taken a moving farewell. We were a little tired when we got to the steamship [to travel down the Rhine] and arrived in Bonn at about 4 o'clock.⁶

* * *

Bonn was an expensive place and because of Franziska's straitened circumstances – she could afford him only twenty talers a month, whereas he needed at least thirty – Nietzsche was constantly short of cash. His letters home are full – eventually to his own embarrassment – of 'the old complaint', a plea for more money. He was so hard up that it took him two weeks just to raise the seven talers needed to enrol in the university. Eventually he did enrol, for his mother's sake as a theology student, though he intended to focus primarily on classics.

Nietzsche found a room on the second floor of a house, Bonngasse 518, whose relative comfort – 'spacious, with three large windows, everything very elegant and clean, and with a sofa'[7] – delighted him as the height of luxury after six Spartan years at Pforta. Impoverished though he was, he could not resist renting a pianino (piccolo piano), over which he hung a portrait of his father.

In spite of – and of course, adding to – his poverty, Nietzsche's time in Bonn was filled with student parties on Rhine steamers, copious quantities of Rhineland wine, many beery evenings in the *Kneipe* [pub], and trips up the river to nearby Cologne. The principal occasion of this dissolute life-style was the fact that on arrival in Bonn, Nietzsche decided to join a student fraternity – the Franconia.

Beer-Drinking on the Rhine

Fraternities, *Burschenschaften*, or *Corps* were (and to a considerable extent still are) a dominant feature of student life in Germany. Established in 1815 by young Germans recently returned from the 'wars of liberation' against Napoleon's armies of occupation, their original aim was to promote a united, generally liberal, Germany. By 1860, however, they had degenerated into little more than social clubs devoted to beer and duelling, the point of the latter being to acquire a duelling scar. Membership usually had (and still has), however, a serious, ulterior purpose: establishing connexions with future leaders of industry and politics that would be useful in later life – 'networking', in short. To his mother, unimpressed by the fraternity phenomenon, Nietzsche put this in more elevated terms: the fraternities were, he wrote, 'the future of Germany and the nursery of German parliaments'.[8]

Nietzsche's own motives for joining Franconia were mixed. He admired the original idealism of the fraternity movement, describing it, in the 1872 *On the Origins of Our Educational Institutions*, as 'the inner summoning and renewal of the purest ethical forces'. But of course he knew full well that the fraternities of 1860 had degenerated into drinking clubs. Partly, I think, he joined for company – Franconia had a large Pforta contingent whom he already knew, including Deussen. But also, I think, as an ambitious boy from a poor background, he was not above wishing to plug into a network of power and influence that might give him a leg up in his future life.

Writing as a law student from Göttingen (where, following family tradition, he had joined the Saxonia fraternity), Nietzsche's artistic and sensitive friend Carl von Gersdorff complained that, though he had made good friends in the fraternity, only family pressure kept him from resigning on account of the 'disgusting, barbaric beer-drinking'.[9] Nietzsche, however, replied that 'whoever, as a student, wants to get to know his age and his people, must sport a fraternity's colours. The connexions and their directions represent, in the sharpest possible way, the type of the next generation of men'. Admittedly, he continues, the 'beer-materialism [*Biermaterialismus*]' of some of the members is intolerable but it just had to be endured'.[10] Though this might remind one of Prince Hal's carousing with lowlife Falstaff so that, as king, he would know his people, Nietzsche's pose of sociological detachment is surely disingenuous. What he is saying, in code, is that one needs to be in a fraternity in order to network.

On another occasion Nietzsche refers to his desire to experience the life of a 'fast-living student'.[11] Ronald Hayman, ever keen to get the subject of his biography onto the psychoanalyst's couch, suggests that the shy 'introvert' from Pforta was engaged in a conscious programme of turning himself into a gregarious 'extrovert'.[12] But this seems to me unnecessarily esoteric. The fact is, surely, that after six years cooped up in boarding school, giving the hormones a run, giving oneself a good blast of wine, women and song, is normal, even *standard*, behaviour. Like the ride on the Drachenfels, beer drinking on the Rhine comes under the rubric 'tasting the first delights of freedom'.

* * *

Writing to his mother to announce his membership in Franconia, Nietzsche says defensively 'I can see you shaking your head' and tries to put an elevated gloss on things: 'seven Pforta alumni joined at virtually the same time … most are philologists and all are lovers of music'.[13] To Pinder he represents himself and his fellow Pforta alumni as the authentically cultured members of the Fraternity, trying to turn the (in a later slang) jocks in a 'more spiritual direction'.[14] This is probably true. Nonetheless, there can be no doubt that Nietzsche himself fully indulged in 'beer-materialism'. For one thing he admits to frequent excursions to fun fairs, dances, nights in the pub and to developing a beer belly.[15] And for another, he admits, with a combination of shame and bravado, to a hangover (not, it should be said, to his mother, but to Elizabeth, who could be relied upon, in the end, to smile indulgently on even the worst foibles of her big brother):

> Having just wrenched myself out of bed, I am writing this morning in direct refutation of the opinion that I have a hangover [*Kater*, which also means 'tom-cat']. You will not know this hairy-tailed animal. Yesterday evening we had a great assembly, ceremonially singing 'Father of the People' and endlessly drinking punch … We were forty people in all, the pub was splendidly decorated … yesterday's *Gemütlichkeit* (warm togetherness) was heavenly …[16]

Not only did Nietzsche get drunk, he also became enough of a jock to indulge in a duel. As reported by Deussen, walking one day in the marketplace, he struck up an acquaintance with a lad from another fraternity. They had a pleasant chat about art and literature and then Nietzsche asked him, in the politest possible way, if he would engage in a duel. The other agreed, and though Deussen was extremely worried for his myopic and by now fattish friend (von Gersdorff's cousin had almost died from a duelling wound),[17] there was nothing he could do about it.

> They locked swords, and the glinting blades danced around their unprotected heads. It lasted scarcely three minutes, and Nietzsche's opponent managed to cut in low *carte* at the bridge of his nose, hitting the exact spot where his spectacles, pressing down too heavily, had left a red mark. Blood trickled to the ground, and the experts agreed that past events had been satisfactorily expiated. I packed my well-bandaged friend into a carriage, took him home to bed, assiduously comforted him, forbade him visits and alcohol. Within two or three days our hero had fully recovered, except for a small slanting scar across the bridge of his nose, which remained there throughout his life and did not look at all bad on him.[18]

(The last sentence is mistaken; later photographs show no sign of a scar. Deussen delicately omits mention of the fact that, whether through squeamishness or incompetence, Nietzsche failed to inflict the desired scar on his opponent.)

The Cologne Brothel

The other important activity of the Franconians was chasing girls. Deussen and Elizabeth have combined to create a picture of Nietzsche as someone who had nothing to do with such activity, as having virtually no sex drive. Elizabeth writes that 'his love never exceeded a rather moderate and poetical attachment . . . throughout his life he never once fell into the clutches of a great passion or a vulgar love',[19] while Deussen claims that 'according to all that I know of Nietzsche I think that the words *mulierem nunquam attigit* (he never touched a woman) apply'.[20] Both these claims are highly suspect. Elizabeth's biography, rushed into print after Nietzsche's collapse into insanity at the end of 1888, attempted to portray his life as that of a Christian saint, and in particular to rebut the claim that his madness was due to syphilis, while Deussen had no personal contact with Nietzsche at all between 1873 and 1887.

Nietzsche certainly lived a life that was, in the main, chaste. But he also wrote poems such as the following, which appears in a section of *Zarathustra* entitled 'Among the Daughters of the Desert':

> You desert maidens,
> At whose feet I,
> For the first time
> A European under palm-trees,
> Am permitted to sit . . .
> Beside the desert,
> And in no way devastated:
> For I am swallowed down
> By this smallest oasis:
> – it simply opened, yawning,
> Its sweetest mouth,
> The sweetest-smelling of all little mouths:
> Then I fell in,
> Down, straight through – among you,
> Dearest maidens . . .
> Here I now sit
> In this small oasis . . .
> Longing for a girl's rounded mouth

and so on.[21] That this could have been written by someone who never experienced 'vulgar' lust is inconceivable. More concretely, the no-sex-drive thesis (together with the hypothesis that he was gay, a hypothesis difficult, though admittedly not impossible, to reconcile with the above poem) is cast into severe doubt by his various admissions to have visited brothels in Leipzig and Naples (see below pp. 234, 240).

In any case, what is not in doubt is that Nietzsche did visit a brothel in Cologne, half an hour up the Rhine from Bonn. Cologne dazzled, fascinated, and appalled small-town Nietzsche. 'It makes the impact of a world city', he wrote Elizabeth, 'an unending variety of languages and a motley of costumes [the city in *Thus Spoke Zarathustra* is called 'The

Motley Cow'] – unbelievably many pickpockets and other kinds of tricksters'.[22] One day in February 1865, according to Deussen's account of what Nietzsche told him,

> he travelled alone to Cologne, and then had himself taken round the local tourist sights by a servant, and finally asked to be taken to a restaurant. The servant, however, took him to a house of ill-repute. 'I found myself', Nietzsche told me the next day, '"suddenly surrounded by half a dozen apparitions in tinsel and gauze, looking at me expectantly. For a short space of time I was speechless. Then I made instinctively for the piano as being the only soulful thing present. I struck a few chords, which freed me from my paralysis and I escaped"'.[23]

Generations of biographers have taken this story at face value, and it is, indeed, likely that it accurately reports what Nietzsche *told* his somewhat prim friend. But observe its intrinsic implausibility. 'Take me to a *Restaurant!*' sounds nothing like 'Take me to a *Bordell!*' – although rushing to the piano has the ring of truth to it, suggesting the virgin schoolboy's terror before the ultimate mystery of the 'eternal feminine'. Probably he gave instructions to his guide using some vague term accompanied by a nudge and a wink. Nietzsche was, remember, on his own showing, trying to be a 'fast-living student' at the time. What is most likely is that having arrived in the bordello with the intention of being relieved of his virginity, he lost his nerve. Thomas Mann uses this incident in his novel *Doctor Faustus*, making his hero think so much about the snub-nosed girl who had brushed his arm that he goes back. Later he wrote an essay suggesting that this is what Nietzsche in fact did.[24] This seems to me by no means improbable. One might even speculate that the poem about the 'daughters of the desert' quoted above is a recollection of the daughters of the moral 'desert' of Cologne.

David Strauss and the Critique of Christianity

Student life, of course, is not just beer and skittles. It requires a certain amount of study. Having enrolled as a theology student, Nietzsche was required to study some theology. Later, he said his only interest had been 'critique of sources', by which he meant the transfer of the techniques of textual criticism from Greek philology to the Bible. Primarily what he had in mind was his reading of David Strauss's *Life of Jesus*.

First published in 1835–6 in two volumes under the title *The Life of Jesus Critically Examined*, Strauss's work caused a storm of controversy. (It had a profound impact on George Eliot, causing her to abandon her faith and, in 1846, to translate it into English under her real name of Marian Evans.) In 1864 he brought out a shortened version under the title *The Life of Jesus Examined for the German People*, which is the version Nietzsche possessed and read with avid attention.[25]

Strauss's interest is in the way Jesus's life had been presented by his disciples. Far from being accurate historical chronicles, he maintains, the gospels are exercises in myth-making, partly conscious and partly unconscious, the purpose of which is to elevate and inspire. The myths of the immaculate conception and of Jesus' death and resurrection are parts of an inspirational narrative. Contrary to common belief, none of the gospels were eye-witness reports but were composed many years later. There are, moreover, many inconsistencies between the authors of the gospels and between them and Paul, an aspect of Strauss's critique Nietzsche records in his notebooks for March 1865.[26] Deeply anticlerical, Strauss states in his preface that 'what we must recognise is that if Christianity ceases to be a miracle, the ecclesiastics will no longer be able to pass themselves off as the agents of the miracle they like to serve'. Christian metaphysics, in other words, is a priestly confidence trick designed to increase their prestige and power.

* * *

Unsurprisingly, given the time spent drinking, the work Nietzsche produced in Bonn was sparse – he never actually turned in a single finished essay during the entire year. Nonetheless he did produce some writings on religious themes which, though fragmentary, show how strongly his thinking was influenced by Strauss. Although produced by a theology student, the standpoint of these fragments is not that of a believer but of an external, indeed hostile, observer.

One fragment, for example, describes 'the worldview of the Catholic middle ages' as essentially 'super-naturalistic'; heaven is located above the seven spheres of the planets and hell in the centre of the earth. The essence of this view is, he says, 'a dualism between spirit and nature'. Protestant orthodoxy, Nietzsche continues, took over this worldview. The consequence is that for it, too,

> the earth is a place of exile, the body is a prison. We must be filled with hate and disgust towards life. Man experiences a terrible urge to self-destruction. The earth and all its concerns are the absolute opposite of all that is heavenly.[27]

And in another fragment from the same year – the title 'On the Life of Jesus' makes it clear that he is précising Strauss – he writes that

> according to the view of believers, God, as the ground of life and the preserver of world-history, is justified, indeed required, to intervene in its progress. This view de-divinises the world...Is such a separation of God and world really capable of philosophical justification?[28]

Fragments such as these show that Nietzsche's efforts as a theology student, far from preparing him for the life of a priest, were pushing him in quite the opposite direction. Not only has he lost his faith, he now, under Strauss's guidance, begins to see Christianity as a positively pernicious phenomenon, so that the loss of faith no longer seems a matter of regret but the beginning, rather, of a new, spiritually healthier existence. Here, therefore, are the beginnings of the critique of Christianity that will appear in Nietzsche's mature philosophy. Christianity, by making the supernatural world the locus of all that is holy and blessed, 'de-divinises' the natural world, deprives it of the holiness it had possessed in pre-Christian times, transforms it, indeed, into a place of pain and exile. And, following the kind of immanent religiosity Strauss takes over from Hegel, we also see the beginning of the idea that any God worth worshipping must be an *immanent* god, a god who is not 'above' but rather *is* the world – the pantheistic notion towards which Nietzsche's engagement with Hölderlin's poetry had already provided an impetus.

Matching Strauss's anticlericalism, the Bonn fragments also reveal the beginning of Nietzsche's identification of priests as evil-minded propagators of a pernicious worldview. The missionaries to Africa, for example (those same missionaries to whom, as children, he and Elizabeth had donated toys), 'confus[ing] the concepts of theism and morality', pretend that there is an obligation to convert the barbaric 'heathens' to the true faith. But lacking the ability to prove the existence of their God, they are reduced to 'threats and bribes'. 'In short', Nietzsche concludes, 'the Christian priesthood suffers under the same fanaticism as all priests'.[29] Given remarks such as these, it is clear that the idea of following his father into the priesthood is, by now, dead as a dodo.

* * *

Unsurprisingly, letters from home during the Bonn year reveal increasing anxiety about Nietzsche's spiritual direction:

> All good wishes from your mother on your birthday. God alone knows how I bear you in my heart. Take the Lord God as your leader on your new life path and for the new year of your life; if you do he will bless you and protect you so as to continue the joy of your dear, blessed father and me and Lieschen.[30]

And, reinforcing the family pressure to remain on the straight and narrow, Elizabeth joins in, even parroting her mother's phraseology: 'Happy birthday…and now I write quite simply that my innermost prayer to God is that, in this new year of your life and on this new life path, he will protect you so that you will remain as dear and good as in the past'.[31]

All to no avail. Returning home for the Easter holidays of 1865, fatter and given to talking in the boorish manner of fraternity drinking evenings, he abruptly announced his decision to abandon theology for philology, brandishing Strauss's book before the horrified faces of his mother and sister. And he refused to accompany his mother to Sunday service and Holy Communion. According to Elizabeth, a stormy scene ensued which reduced Franziska to tears and only ended when Aunt Rosalie – the family's theological expert – explained sagely that 'in the life of every great theologian there had been moments of doubt and that it was much better at such moments to avoid all discussion'. Eventually Franziska agreed, and agreed, too, that Fritz should never be forced to do anything against his conscience.[32] From now on, however, religious subjects became taboo between mother and son. Though he remained her most dearly beloved child for the rest of his life, she withdrew into the castle of her faith and he into the castle of his denial. 'Actually', she wrote to her brother Edmund, 'I don't think philosophy is a subject for women; we lose the ground from under our feet'.[33]

Meanwhile the conflict had thrown Elizabeth into a spiritual crisis of her own, a battle between small-town conventionality and hero-worship of her brother. Though she tried to make peace between mother and son, she was always ultimately on Fritz's side, party to a secret alliance against parental oppression. All his life she was 'there' for Fritz. She worshipped a picture of him she had constructed and, as Nietzsche's wonderful Swiss-German biographer, Curt Paul Janz,* comments, woe betide anyone – *including Nietzsche himself* – who tried to disturb it.

---

* J I pp. 148–9. Curt Paul Janz, forty-six years a viola player in the Basel Symphony Orchestra, became interested in Nietzsche via the latter's relationship with Richard Wagner. Running to 1,980 closely packed pages in three volumes, his biography – devoted to Nietzsche's life, not his works – is not only comprehensive but full of shrewd human insight. Though he is now (2009) in his ninety-eighth year, I have profited from an illuminating correspondence with him during the writing of this book.

In May 1865 Elizabeth wrote Fritz that she was going to visit their uncle Edmund to try to resolve her crisis – she probably chose Edmund because, as we have seen (footnote on p. 5 above), he himself had been through a period of religious doubt and had emerged on the other side, his faith more or less intact. 'With your views', she wrote Fritz,

> – which are actually depressing – you have found a too-willing student. As Mamma says, I too have become overly clever, but since I can't forget my lama- [conformist] nature I am full of confusion . . . This however is certain: it is much easier not to believe than the opposite, and the difficult is likely to be the right course to take . . . Anyway I really regret your bringing the unhappy Strauss with you on holiday, and that I've heard so much about him from you. For to hear that it is possible to doubt and criticise what are (at least to believers) the loftiest things is the first step towards a new belief or unbelief. And when that happens, it is for me as though the firm protective wall has fallen, and one now stands before a broad, map-less, confusing, mist-enshrouded desert where there is nothing firm, with only our own poor, miserable, and so often fallible spirit to guide us.[34]

This clearly made an impact on Nietzsche – the 'desert' image recurs throughout his work to describe the desolation of Godlessness – and, for the first and almost last time in his life, he treats Elizabeth as deserving an intellectually serious reply:

> This time you have provided me with rich material which I enjoy very much 'chewing over' in an intellectual sense.
>
> In the first place, however, I must refer to a passage in your letter which was written with as much pastor-colouration as with a lama's heart. Don't worry, dear Lizbeth. If your will is as good and resolute as you say our dear uncle won't have too much trouble. Concerning your basic principle, that truth is always to be found on the side of the more difficult, I agree in part. However, it is difficult to believe that 2 × 2 does not equal 4. Does that make it therefore truer?
>
> On the other hand, is it really so difficult simply to accept as true everything we have been taught, and which has gradually taken firm root in us, and is thought true by the circle of our relatives and many good people, and which, moreover, really does comfort and elevate men? Is that more difficult than to venture on new paths, at odds with custom, in the insecurity that attends independence, experiencing many mood-swings and even troubles of conscience, often disconsolate, but always with the true, the beautiful and the good as our goal?
>
> Is the most important thing to arrive at that view of God, world and reconciliation which makes us feel most comfortable? Is not the true inquirer totally indifferent to what the result of his inquiries might be? When we inquire, are we seeking for rest, peace, happiness? Not so; we seek only truth even though it be in the highest degree ugly and repellent.
>
> Still one final question: if we had believed from our youth onwards that all salvation issued from someone other than Jesus, from Mohammed for example, is it not certain that we should have experienced the same blessings? It is the faith that makes blessed, not the objective reality that stands behind the faith. I write this to you, dear Lisbeth, simply with the view of meeting the line of proof usually adopted by religious people, who appeal to their inner experiences to demonstrate the infallibility of their faith. Every true faith is

infallible, it accomplishes what the person holding the faith hopes to find in it, but that does not offer the slightest support for a proof of its objective truth.

Here the ways of men divide: if you wish to strive for peace of soul and happiness, then believe; if you wish to be a disciple of truth, then inquire.[35]

Two themes which will come to dominate Nietzsche's mature philosophy receive an important airing here. First, the posing of a stark choice between often bitter truth and often happy illusion and, second, Nietzsche's – the 'free spirit's', as he will later say – binding himself heroically to the mast of truth.

It is important to recognise that for Nietzsche this is no merely academic choice. As he says to Elizabeth, Christian faith really does 'comfort and elevate'. He appreciates all too well the security and warmth provided him by his extended, always Christian, family. And as the musician who believes that 'without music life would be an error', he continues to treasure the musical heritage of Lutheranism; in June 1865, as a member of the six hundred strong Bonn Municipal Choral Society, he sings 'with incomparable enthusiasm' in Handel's 'Israel in Egypt' during the three-day Cologne music festival.[36] Though he objects to the 'bigoted Catholicism' of the Rhineland[37] and to the influence within the university of Jesuits dedicated to 'eradicating Protestantism',[38] he does so not as an atheist but out of identification with his Protestant homeland, an identification that leads him to become an active member of the Gustav Adolphus Society, an anti-Catholic club for the Protestant diaspora.[39] To Aunt Rosalie he complains that the local preachers are all inferior to those of Naumburg and that local festivals are all offensively Catholic in character.[40]

In Bonn, Nietzsche continued to be intensely nostalgic for the boyhood magic of Christmas. Unable to afford the fare home for the Christmas of 1864, he wrote to his mother and sister,

> I do hope you will have a Christmas tree with lights…We will light a tree in the tavern but naturally that's only a pale reflection of how we celebrate at home, for the main thing, the family and circle of relatives, is missing…Do you remember what wonderful Christmases we had in Gorenzen [where Uncle Edmund was pastor]?…It was so lovely; the house and the village in the snow, the evening service, my head full of melodies, the togetherness…and me in my nightshirt, the cold, and many merry and serious things. All together a delightful atmosphere. When I play my 'New Year's Eve'* it is this that I hear in the sounds.[41]

Emotionally, then, Nietzsche remained a Christian, specifically a Lutheran Protestant. And he remained deeply dependent on the contemplative distance from daily life occasioned by the festivals of his youth.[42] 'I love New Year's Eve and birthdays', he writes,

> for they allow us hours – which admittedly we can often create for ourselves, but seldom do – in which the soul can stand still and review a phase of its own development. Crucial [e.g., New Year's] resolutions are born in such moments. I am accustomed on these occasions to bring out the manuscripts and letters of past years and to make notes. For a few hours one is raised above time and almost steps outside one's own development. One

---

* 'A New Year's Eve' [*Eine Sylvesternacht*], a piece for piano and violin written in 1864 (track 13 on the Web site for this book).

secures and documents the past and receives the courage and resoluteness to resume travelling along one's path. It's lovely when the blessings and wishes of the relatives fall like a mild rain on these resolutions and decisions, the first seeds of the future.[43]

That his intellect tells him that the Christian God is mere superstition is indeed, therefore, as he says in the letter to Elizabeth, a deeply 'ugly' truth. For him, as much as for her, the effect of his intellect (or that of David Strauss) is to cast him into a 'desert' of which there can be no 'map'. In quoting to Raimund Granier (his companion in teenage rebellion) from Byron's *Manfred* –

> *But grief should be the instructor of the wise;*
> *Sorrow is knowledge: they who know the most*
> *Must mourn the deepest o'er the fatal truth.*
> *The tree of knowledge is not that of life.*[44]

– he is expressing his own divided and troubled spirit, the conflict between the view from his head and the needs of his heart.

Given, then, the emotional desolation it entails, it is worth asking what it was that impelled Nietzsche to commit himself, so unconditionally, to truth. One answer is that he had no option. Having once apprehended the devastating impact of Straussian (not to mention Darwinian) 'science', there could be no forgetting what he had learnt. Once the Pandora's box of knowledge had been opened there was no shutting the lid. Yet the question remains as to what *justification* Nietzsche gave himself for becoming a knight of truth.

As we saw in the last chapter, Nietzsche regards supernaturalist religious belief as belonging to the 'childhood of peoples' (p. 33 above). So overcoming primitive superstition is a matter of becoming an intellectual *adult*. Still, one might press the question: just what is so important about becoming an adult? Zarathustra says that his fundamental message is 'become who you are'[45], an abbreviation of the Greek poet Pindar's injunction to 'become who you are, having learnt what that is', which would certainly have impressed itself on Nietzsche's mind in the course of his classical studies at Pforta. Life, in other words, is about the realization of potential, about growing and maturing into a fully realized adult in the way in which an acorn, given the right conditions, grows and matures into an oak. Still, the annoyingly persistent questioner might demand, why *should* we do that? What is so bad about being an 'acorn'? The only answer one can readily think of is that it is part of the intention underlying divine creation that each thing should realise its potential. It is, therefore, with good reason that, in 1887, in *The Gay Science*, Nietzsche finally asks whether we knights of truth are not still 'too pious'.[46] Nietzsche never abandons his commitment to truth. But a major task of his mature philosophy is to find a non-'pious' justification for it.

Leaving Bonn

By February 1865 Nietzsche was fifty-five talers in debt (roughly a year's rent for his room in the Bonngasse) and it was clear, Bonn being far more expensive than other university towns, that he could stay there no more than a year.

In the philology department at Bonn, the two giants, Otto Jahn and Friedrich Ritschl, had become involved in one of those feuds (typical of academia both then and now) the origin of which no one can remember. The result was Ritschl's accepting a chair in Leipzig (responding to a 'call', as the Germans say). By May – yearning in any case to return to the Protestant heartland (Leipzig is only sixty kilometres from Naumburg) – Nietzsche had decided to follow him. An added incentive was that von Gersdorff had decided to give up the tedious study of law at Göttingen and move to Leipzig to study German literature.

Nietzsche's final weeks in Bonn were marred by rheumatic pains and splitting headaches, aggravated by torrential downpours of rain and by the Rhine Valley's enclosed, humid climate. Probably, too, there was a psychosomatic element: increasingly, we shall see, transitions in Nietzsche's life were accompanied by attacks of ill health.

The evening of his departure by Rhine-steamer on August 9, he was accompanied to the pier by Deussen and his new friend and fellow Franconian Hermann Mushacke.* Three weeks later he wrote to Mushacke from Naumburg attempting to sum up his time in the Rhineland. Bonn, he wrote, had left a nasty taste in the mouth. For while he hoped, eventually, to 'look back on it as a necessary link in his development',

> at the moment this is not possible. It still seems to me that in many respects I have culpably wasted the year. My time with the Fraternity seems to me, to be frank, a faux pas, in particular the last summer semester. In doing so I transgressed my principle of devoting no more time to things and people than is necessary to learning them ... I'm annoyed with myself ... I am by no means an unqualified fan of Franconia. To be sure, I think back on good comradeship. But I find its political judgment minimal, only active in a few heads. I find the face they present to the world plebeian and repulsive, and not being able to keep my disapproval to myself have made my relations with the others uneasy ... With my studies I must also be fundamentally dissatisfied, even though much of the blame must be ascribed to the Fraternity, which thwarted my best intentions. Right now, I am aware of what wholesome relief and human elevation is to be found in continuous, urgent work ... I am ashamed of the work I did there ... It's junk. Every single piece of school work I did was better.[47]

Notable here, after a relatively dissolute year, is the reassertion of the Pforta-Protestant work-ethic which would never again desert him. ('What do I care for happiness? ... I have my work', says Nietzsche's alter ego, Zarathustra.) Notable, too, is the equally Prussian-Protestant necessity to construe one's life as a narrative of self-development, a pilgrim's progress towards self-perfection. On both counts Nietzsche is ashamed of the Bonn year and on both counts he puts the blame on his association with the Fraternity. It is no surprise, therefore, that, in October 1865, during his first semester at Leipzig, he posted a letter of resignation (without it he would have been a member for life):

> I do not cease [he wrote] to value the idea of the Fraternity highly. I will simply confess that to me its contemporary manifestation is something I am dissatisfied with. It was hard for me to bear a full year as a member of Franconia. But I held it to be my duty to get to know it. Now nothing binds me to it. So I say farewell. May Franconia soon overcome the stage of development in which it finds itself at present.[48]

---

* A Berliner, Mushacke accompanied Nietzsche to Leipzig, where he remained, however, for only one semester. He fought in the Franco-Prussian war and was awarded the Iron Cross. He then completed his studies in Rostock and became a high school teacher like his father before him. Nietzsche lost contact with him after moving to Basel in 1869.

4

Leipzig

Getting Settled

LEAVING BONN, Nietzsche returned to Naumburg, where he spent the rest of August 1865, recovering from the ailments that afflicted his last weeks in the Rhineland. This was followed by two happy weeks staying with the Mushacke family in Berlin and seeing the sights. He got on so well with Hermann's father, Eduard, that the latter, in spite of the age difference, proposed they should address each other with the familiar *du*.[1] And then the two friends travelled to Leipzig, where they arrived at the Berlin railway station on October 17. 'First of all', Nietzsche recalls,

> we wandered about the city centre quite aimlessly, enjoying the sight of the lofty houses, lively streets and constant activity. Then we adjourned for a little rest about midday to the Reisse Restaurant . . . It was on this occasion that I first read the newspaper at midday, which thereafter became a regular habit. But all we did that morning was to note down the various advertisements for 'respectable' or even 'elegant' rooms, 'with bedroom' etc.[2]

After a depressing afternoon traipsing up and down smelly staircases to view far from 'elegant' rooms, they found their way into a secluded side street, the Blumengasse (now Scherlstrasse), within easy walking distance of the university. Here Nietzsche found a room at number 4 above an antiquarian bookshop owned by his landlord, Herr Rohn, while Mushacke found lodgings next door. (In April of the following year Nietzsche moved to 7 Elisenstrasse, driven out by the noise of children.)

The next day the two new arrivals presented themselves for enrolment at the university – by chance, exactly a hundred years to the day since Goethe's enrolment. Nietzsche took this as a splendid omen, though, to the barely suppressed laughter of the assembled freshmen, the Rector delivered a speech explaining that 'a genius often chooses extraordinary paths to his goal', so that they should in no way take Goethe's student life as a model for their own.[3] (Forced by his father to study law, which he found a bore, Goethe spent most of his time at Leipzig carousing and chasing girls.)

The next salient event was Ritschl's inaugural public lecture following his own recent arrival from Bonn:

> Everybody was in a great state of excitement [Nietzsche records] at the appearance of the famous man whose behaviour in the affair at Bonn had brought his name into every paper and home. The hall was thus packed...Suddenly Ritschl made his way into the hall in his large felt slippers, though otherwise he was faultlessly attired in evening dress, with a white tie. He looked with good-humoured cheer at the new world before him, and soon discovered faces which were not strange. While going from group to group at the back of the hall he suddenly cried, 'Hallo! There is Herr Nietzsche, too!' and he waved his hand gleefully to me.[4]

About a month after he arrived in Leipzig, there occurred the most important philosophical encounter of Nietzsche's life: in his landlord's bookshop he discovered a second-hand copy of Arthur Schopenhauer's masterpiece, *The World as Will and Representation*, bought it, read it cover to cover, and was bowled over. (Richard Wagner had had a similar 'conversion experience' eleven years earlier.) He immediately declared himself a 'Schopenhauerian', as he would continue to do for the next decade. What exactly he meant by this I shall discuss in the next chapter.

Happy Times

Nietzsche's student years in Leipzig were the happiest of his life. Apart from his sister, who remarks on the unmistakably cheerful tone of his Leipzig recollections,[5] biographers have missed the happiness of the Leipzig years. Determined to press their subject into the romantic stereotype of the misfit loner crippled by ill health, they fail to recognise that, though he certainly ended up that way, it is not how he always was. Even Nietzsche himself, much given to presenting himself as a romantic loner, admits that the stereotype does not fit the Leipzig years. 'The last year in Leipzig', he wrote von Gersdorff in October 1866,

> has been very dear to me. Whereas in Bonn I had to accommodate myself to rules and forms I didn't understand, had pleasures forced on me that I couldn't bear, and lived a life without work among crude people [in the Franconia Fraternity] who put me into a deep, bad mood, Leipzig has unexpectedly reversed all that. Delightful, dear friendships, unearned favours from Ritschl, numerous co-workers among my student colleagues, good taverns, good concerts, etc. Truly they all combined to make Leipzig a very dear place to me.[6]

Let us review the grounds of Nietzsche's happiness during the Leipzig years. First, the period was a time of excellent health. (This was, perhaps, as much an effect as a cause of happiness.) The terrible headaches, vomiting, gastric troubles, and insomnia that would plague his later years made virtually no appearance in Leipzig. And second, always intensely in need of friends, Nietzsche had, in the Leipzig years, a group of close friends, either on the spot or in regular contact by letter. Foremost among them was Erwin Rohde (see Plate 13), a gifted fellow student of Ritschl, followed by von Gersdorff, and, some distance behind, by Deussen and Mushacke.

The friendship with Rohde* embraced all aspects of their lives. They read Schopenhauer together, took lessons in riding and in pistol shooting, and in the summer of 1867 took off on a battery-recharging two-week walking holiday in the Bohemia forest. (During this trip they located the village of Klingenbrunn, to which Nietzsche would return, in dramatic circumstances, in 1876.) 'This last summer', Nietzsche wrote to von Gersdorff at the end of 1867, he and Rohde 'did almost everything together'.[7]

* * *

A third source of Nietzsche's happiness was the fact that, in Ritschl, the bestower of 'unearned favours', he had found the dream professor – the opposite of the usual German 'God-professor', to whom one had (and has) to apply, in writing, a month in advance, in order to obtain a ten-minute interview. Brilliant, eccentric, amusing, obsessed by his subject, Ritschl made himself above all a father to his favourite students, committed to caring for all aspects of their lives and careers. (Behind his back Nietzsche indeed called him, affectionately, 'Father Ritschl'.) And Nietzsche had the good fortune to be his all-time favourite student.

Nietzsche first caught Ritschl's eye for exceptional talent when, having written another essay on Theognis (the obscure Greek poet about whom he had written at Pforta), he plucked up the courage to show it to Ritschl. A few days later he was summoned to a meeting. Saying he had never seen such impressive work from a student, Ritschl commissioned him to expand it for publication in the *Rheinisches Museum für Philologie*, the (still flourishing) scholarly classics journal of which he was the editor. From this day on, Nietzsche recollects, an intimacy rapidly developed:

I went twice almost every week to see him at lunchtime and on every occasion found him ready to indulge in serious or frivolous conversation. As a rule he sat in his armchair and had the Cologne newspaper in front of him, which, together with the Bonn newspaper, he had long been accustomed to read. As a rule, amid the vast medley of papers, there stood a glass of red wine. When he was at work he always used a chair which he had upholstered himself...In his talk he showed no inhibitions; his anger with his friends, his discontent with existing conditions, the faults of the university, the eccentricities of the professors were all expressed...He likewise poked fun at himself, at his elementary idea of managing his affairs, and would tell, for instance, how, formerly, he had been in the habit of concealing the

---

* Erwin Rohde (1845–98), the son of a Hamburg doctor, had also followed Ritschl from Bonn to Leipzig. Towards the end of 1867 he moved to Kiel, where he completed his doctorate in 1869 and, in 1872, finally obtained an assistant professorship. Under Nietzsche's influence, he became both a Schopenhauerian and a Wagnerian. Thus, with Nietzsche's turn, in 1876, against both Schopenhauer and Wagner, their friendship cooled dramatically, particularly on Rohde's side. Rohde married in 1877 and produced four children. He held professorial chairs at Jena, Tübingen, Leipzig and Heidelberg, becoming one of the greatest classical scholars of the nineteenth century. His book *Psyche* remains, to this day, a standard work on Greek cults and beliefs about the soul. In 1886 there occurred a final and unsatisfactory meeting between the erstwhile friends. Following Nietzsche's mental collapse, he was approached by Elizabeth in 1894 to advise on publication of the manuscript remains. His judgment of their quality was uniformly negative and he advised (unsuccessfully) against all further publication. This occasion was the last time he saw Nietzsche, who, however, was unable to recognise him.

money he received in notes of ten, twenty, fifty or a hundred talers in books so as to enjoy the surprise of their discovery later on ... His eagerness to help others was simply splendid; and for this reason many young philologists, in addition to being indebted to him for their advances in scientific knowledge, also felt themselves bound to him by an intimate and personal debt of gratitude.[8]

Not only was Ritschl the dream professor, he also had a delightful wife. Sophie Ritschl was fourteen years younger than her husband, Jewish,* a sparkling wit and a music lover. As we shall see, it was she who, through her friendship with Ottilie Brockhaus, the sister of Richard Wagner, facilitated Nietzsche's first meeting with the great man. Nietzsche spent a considerable amount of time in Sophie Ritschl's drawing room. Following the standard romantic model of impossible love (both Rousseau's St-Preux and Goethe's Werther were in love with the wives of exemplary men), Nietzsche of course fell in love with Sophie, as he would soon fall in love with Cosima Wagner. In a letter to Rohde, he calls her his 'intimate friend' and speaks of mysterious 'feminine influences' on his life.[9] Elizabeth was thus right in referring to a 'poetic' element in Nietzsche's relations with the opposite sex (p. 55 above) even though, as we have seen, she was completely wrong in claiming that *only* 'poetry' was involved.

A further important element in the happiness of the Leipzig years was the Philological Club which, at Ritschl's suggestion, Nietzsche and two fellow émigrés from Bonn founded in early 1866, subsequently inviting seven further students to join. The club met on a weekly basis to hear lectures from one member or another, which must often have been of a high standard, since only the best students had been invited to join. But it clearly had a social as well as intellectual aspect, since it met in such places as the Deutsche Bierstube (German Alehouse), the Lion Tavern, or Mahn's restaurant. As we saw, in his itemization of the delights of Leipzig, Nietzsche mentions 'numerous co-workers among my student colleagues' and 'good taverns' in the same breath.

In the previous chapter I mentioned Nietzsche's lifelong attempt to form circles of exceptional people devoted to elevated, cultural ends. The *Germania* Society was the first attempt, the vague notion of returning the Franconia fraternity to its noble roots a second, and now the Philological Society was a third. The most important circle of his Leipzig years, however, was that which he created by persuading, even bullying, his friends and acquaintances into becoming, like himself, 'Schopenhauerians'. As promised, the meaning and significance of being a 'Schopenhauerian' will be discussed in Chapter 5.

* * *

In Leipzig, then, Nietzsche enjoyed good health, intimate friends, a dream professor who provided the substitute father he always sought, a circle of philological colleagues, and a circle of fellow Schopenhauerians. In addition to all these gifts of fortune, Leipzig was also a splendid place for culture – first of all, for music. One of the great centres of German music, Leipzig had been Bach's workplace in the eighteenth century and Schumann's and Mendelssohn's a couple of decades before Nietzsche's arrival in the nineteenth. It was

---

* Though *anti*-anti-Semitism is one of the most salient aspects of Nietzsche's mature thought, his correspondence at this time, particularly when he was writing home or to von Gersdorff, contains occasional anti-Semitic remarks of a routine and not very deep character. He did, however, find it offensive when a fat student sat on a chair of Sophie Ritschl's and described it as 'not very kosher' (KGW 1.4 60 [1]).

also the birthplace of Richard Wagner. In addition to offering a rich concert life centred on the famous Gewandhaus Orchestra, it was also a centre of – usually vigorously polemical – theorising for and against 'modern music'. Founded by Schumann in 1834, the *Neue Zeitschrift für Musik* (to which the *Germania* Society had subscribed (p. 27 above)) was published in Leipzig and had become dedicated to the defence of 'modern', that is to say Wagnerian, music. It was in the *Neue Zeitschrift* that the great conductor Hans von Bülow published some of his fiercest articles in defence of *Tannhäuser* and other Wagner operas, thereby arousing counterblasts from another Leipzig publication, *Die Grenzboten*, which the novelist Gustav Freytag had turned into a bastion of anti-Wagnerian polemics.

Nietzsche regularly attended concerts, often in the company of Karl Franz Brendel, Schumann's successor as editor of the *Neue Zeitschrift*. He also sang in Beethoven's *Missa Solemnis*, though not taking part in the actual performance on account of a cold, a performance which he describes as 'one of [his most] wonderful musical experiences ever'.[10] And theatre, too, he often attended, fancying himself in love with various actresses. To one of these, the glamorous 'blond angel', Hedwig Raabe, he sent flowers accompanied by an expression of undying devotion.

Nietzsche's time in Leipzig was, then, full of the fun and sociability one expects of student life. Of course it was not just that. What distinguished it from life in Bonn and provided it with the necessary 'backbone' ('a profession is the backbone of a life', he once wrote)[11] was that he was also working hard and successfully. This satisfied his Prussian-Protestant conscience, the already noted need to see his life as diligent and constant self-improvement. 'Religious people', he wrote von Gersdorff early in 1867,

> believe that all the sorrows and accidents which befall us are calculated with the precise intention of...enlightening them. We lack the presuppositions for such a faith. It does however lie in our power to use every event, every small and large accident, for our improvement and proficiency, to derive benefit from them. The intentional character of the fate of the individual is no fable if we understand it as such. It is up to us to make purposeful use of fate: for in themselves events are empty shells. It depends on our disposition: the worth that we attach to an event is the worth it has for us.[12]

(This is what, in his mature philosophy, he calls projecting a 'personal providence' into one's life: interpreting it so that everything that happens is 'for the best'.[13] Doing this, we shall see, is the key to 'willing the eternal return'.)

The Study of Classics

Nietzsche's student days were, then, happy days. This does not imply, of course, that they were devoid of worries and dissatisfactions. The principal dissatisfaction (as yet no bigger than a man's hand but destined, over the next decade, to assume major proportions) was with the current practice of his chosen discipline (or 'science') of classical philology, a dissatisfaction reinforcing, and reinforced by, his growing attachment to philosophy in general, and to Schopenhauer in particular. 'The next generation of philologists', Nietzsche writes in his notebooks, must give up the endless 'chewing the cud' all too characteristic of the present generation.[14] 'Academic ruminants' (as he calls them in *Zarathustra*) are mere parasites, endlessly chewing over the great creative thoughts of the past but creating nothing themselves. Disciplines, he writes, sometimes grow 'senile', in which condition their practitioners, 'those emaciated bodies with dried up veins and withered mouths, search out and, like vampires, suck up the blood of younger and more flourishing natures'.[15] Contributing to this effect is the fragmentation of contemporary philological research into ever more minute areas of expertise, a process that has become so intense that its practitioners have been reduced to the role of assembly-line 'factory workers'. What today's scholars lack is the synoptic vision, the 'large-scale thinking', which would enable them to see not just the trees but also the forest. Future philologists must, that is, 'learn to judge on a larger scale so that they can exchange the minutiae of particular matters for the great considerations of philosophy'.[16]

If we ask why philology must deal in 'the universal-human … shaped by the moulding hands of philosophy',[17] the answer – one that will become central to Nietzsche's mature philosophy – is that 'history' in general and classical philology in particular are valueless unless 'some kind of large cultural purpose lies on their horizon',[18] unless, that is, we can gain 'insights that have an essential influence upon ourselves'.[19] Later on, Nietzsche answers the fundamental question, 'What is the point of classical philology?' by saying that the study of the Greeks is justified to, but only to, the extent that it provides a 'polished mirror' in which we can view *ourselves*.[20]

The essence of this critique of the mid-nineteenth-century study of classics is the demand that any worthwhile discipline must be existentially 'relevant' – relevant to life, to *our* life. The complaint is that no academic study, particularly not the study of the dead texts of the past, can be an end in itself. Practiced as such, it becomes a 'vampire' that sucks the life-blood out of those it has seduced into its precincts, turns them into desiccated scholars with bad digestions, condemned to live useless, and so meaningless, lives.

It is important to emphasise that, at this stage, Nietzsche has by no means given up on classical philology. He does not condemn the discipline as such but speaks, rather, as a 'young Turk', a spokesman for the coming generation which demands radical reform, the nature of which, we may assume, was a hot topic, over a beer, in the evening discussions of the Philological Society. Given their training and talents, he writes Rohde, they themselves have no alternative but to become academics:

> We have no other way of being useful to our fellow men. In the final analysis one cannot live just for oneself. Let us [however] play our part in bringing it about that young philologists acquire the necessary scepticism, are free from pedantry and from the overestimation of their discipline, so as to be true promoters of humanistic studies.[21]

And, reflecting on what his own future pedagogical practice should be, he writes,

> The aim that lies before me is to become a really practical teacher and to be able to awaken the necessary reflection and self-examination in young people which will enable them always to keep the why, the what, and the how [but particularly 'the why'] of their discipline ever before their eyes.[22]

Nonetheless, though Nietzsche speaks as a reformer rather than an enemy of classical philology, with the advantage of hindsight one can see in this critique portents of the future divorce between himself and the discipline. Given, that is, the entrenched conservatism of academic institutions, and given that Nietzsche would soon raise his young Turk's head above the parapet with his first book, *The Birth of Tragedy*, it was inevitable that someone – his name was Wilamowitz-Möllendorff – would shoot at it.

In the critique, one can see, too, the foundations being laid of what would eventually become a breach (though never an absolute one) between Nietzsche and his beloved teacher Ritschl. For all his admiration and affection for him, quite early in their acquaintance, Nietzsche has to admit that Ritschl 'greatly over-estimated his special subject and therefore showed some disapproval of philologists approaching philosophy too closely'[23] – of their relating the study of antiquity to the great existential themes of death, pain, and meaning, precisely, we shall see, the central topics of Schopenhauer's philosophy.

Another dangerous element in Nietzsche's attachment to Schopenhauer lay in the latter's vitriolic contempt for the 'professors of philosophy'. Independently wealthy, Schopenhauer scorned those who lived 'from' rather than 'for' philosophy: since he who pays the piper calls the tune, independence of thought, he held, requires independence of means.

A final reservation about life as a philologist lay in Nietzsche's desire to unify the artistic and scholarly sides of his nature; to write, as he wrote von Gersdorff in April 1867, with style and grace 'according to the Schopenhauerian model'. He wished to get away from writing 'as stiffly and dryly, as confined by the corset of logic, as I wrote in, for example, my Theognis essay',[24] the style approved by the then current mores of philology.

For all this, Nietzsche would be in his seventh heaven when, out of the blue, he was offered a professorship in classical philology. Thus, while his reservations about his chosen profession are important as portents of the future, none of them did anything to seriously darken the happy skies of Leipzig.

War and Politics

Other skies, however, were getting very dark indeed. Bismarck was conjuring up the thunderclouds of war.

In the wake of Napoleon's defeat at the battle of Waterloo in 1815, the German Confederation had been established, a loose collection of thirty-nine independent German-speaking states, most of them still run on quasi-feudal lines, under the leadership of Austria. Bismarck, who became Prime Minister of Prussia in 1862, was convinced that the German states could be united under Prussian leadership only after Austria had been defeated. (At the time Nietzsche agreed, quoting to von Gersdorff Napoleon's remark that 'only on the rubble of Austria can a German future be built'.)[25] Accordingly, while cunningly manoeuvring Austria into the position of apparent aggressor, he prepared for war.

The formal cause was control of the northwestern duchy of Schleswig-Holstein. (The British Prime Minister, Lord Palmerston, claimed that only three people had ever understood 'the Schleswig-Holstein question', but that one was dead, another in an asylum, while he himself had forgotten the answer.) On June 14, 1866, the Austrians persuaded the confederate parliament in Frankfurt to mobilise against Prussia, precipitating the latter's declaration that the Confederation no longer existed. On the following day, under cover of darkness, Prussian armies invaded Saxony, Hanover and Hesse, and hostilities began on several widely scattered fronts.

For Germans, this civil war – a war that, to some degree, ranged the Protestant North against the Catholic South – involved some of the same fratricidal stresses as the nearly contemporaneous American Civil War. Deussen, for instance, isolated in Tübingen, would have faced internment as an enemy alien had he been called up by the Prussians. Though much less bloody than the American war, the bitter feelings it aroused have been handed down from generation to generation. (Bavarians are still liable to describe Berliners as 'Prussians', fancying thereby to deliver an insult, while the latter protest that Prussia does not exist.)

In Saxony, the nominal ruler was King Johann I, a scholar-poet who had translated Dante into German. But the power behind the throne was the anti-Prussian Count Beust – one of Nietzsche's *bêtes noires* – who had unwisely allied his mainly Protestant country with Catholic Austria and Bavaria.

As Bismarck knew, the southern armies were no match for the partly professionalized, highly trained and motivated Prussians, equipped with a devastating new weapon, the rapid-firing rifle known as the *Zundnadelgewehr* [needle-igniting gun]. Nor were they any match for the Prussian general staff, led by the brilliant Helmuth von Moltke, who used trains to deploy the Prussian armies at a speed never before seen in warfare. On July 3, 1866, the Austrians suffered a major defeat at Königgrätz (Sadowa) in northern Bohemia. The following year, having annexed Schleswig-Holstein, Hanover, Hesse, Nassau and the formerly free city of Frankfurt, Prussia created the North German Federation with the Prussian King as head and Bismarck as the power behind the throne. This was the nucleus of what, five years later, would become the German Reich, with the Prussian King as its Emperor and Bismarck as Chancellor.

At the end of June, 1866, the Duke of Mecklenburg's Prussian soldiers made a triumphal entry into Leipzig without a shot being fired. Though Saxony avoided outright annexation and was allowed, like Bavaria, to keep its king, it was now (all of it) a de facto Prussian vassal. Local reaction was divided. Many houses flew the black, white and red flag of German nationalism; others sported the white and green of Saxony. Nietzsche and his friends gathered at Kintschy's coffee house, transformed overnight into a pro-Prussian camp. Mahn's restaurant, on the other hand, which, formerly, he had often patronised, remained sullenly Saxon.

Nietzsche, at this time an ardent supporter of both Bismarck and the Prussians, was jubilant. To his mother, a few days before the result of Königgrätz became known, he wrote, 'I am as much a committed Prussian as for example my cousin [Rudolf Schenkel] is a Saxon'.[26] And then, after hearing the result of Königgrätz, he rhapsodised to Mushacke (living in the Prussian capital, Berlin):

> Who wouldn't be proud to be a Prussian in these times. One has the feeling that an earthquake is making the earth – which one had thought immovable – uncertain, as though history, which had been stopped for many years, were suddenly in motion again.[27]

Writing to Pinder, also in Berlin, he referred to Bismarck as 'this so gifted and active minister' whom the French rightly called a 'revolutionary'.[28] And to von Gersdorff, on active service in the field, he wrote: 'For me, too – frankly – it's an unusual and quite new pleasure to find myself for once in agreement with the current government'.[29] A little later he tells him of the immeasurable pleasure Bismarck gives me. I read his speeches [in the newspapers, presumably] as though drinking strong wine – I make the tongue pause so that it doesn't drink too fast, allowing me to savour the pleasure for a long time.[30]

To anyone acquainted with the mature Nietzsche's loathing of Bismarck (the effective ruler of Germany his entire adult life), of Prussia, and of all forms of nationalism, these must appear strange sentiments. The question arises, therefore, as to what it was which, at the time, made him so passionately a Prussian.

One point, to which I shall return shortly, is simply that he liked war, saw it as an heroic boys' own adventure. Recall his tin soldiers, his fascination with the siege of Sebastopol, and the elaborate war-games of his childhood (pp. 14–15 above). But even if he had not thought war glamorous, he would still have supported Prussia because he agreed with Bismarck's war aims – with, at least, what he *took* to be those aims. Nietzsche was, that is, an enthusiastic supporter of German unification, the reason being that he saw it as the only way of abolishing the petty dynastic houses that ruled the multitude of German states. 'If the German people become one', he wrote, then 'Herr v. Beust together with all the princes of the middle-sized states can be embalmed'[31] as relics of the past. And he supported the Prussian war-effort because 'in the end, this Prussian way of getting rid of princes is the most comfortable for all concerned'.[32]

The reason he wanted to get rid of the princely rulers of the petty German states was that he saw their quasi-feudal absolutism as oppressive. At this early stage in his life, that is to say, he remained true to the liberalism which Pforta had seen as part of a genuine humanism. To von Gersdorff he wrote,

> All the political parties [of Prussia] are really liberals . . . It does no harm that our government is called 'conservative' since for the king it's a form of disguise . . . that allows him to proceed along his free-thinking way.[33]

And, as we shall see (p. 78 below), in recommending him for his first job, Ritschl, with whom he must have discussed politics at length, describes him as supporting German unification on liberal grounds. At this stage in his life, therefore, Nietzsche (who in his maturity would become an implacable opponent of liberalism) retained a commitment to the liberal freedoms of speech, association, religion, property ownership and immunity to arbitrary arrest. His generally positive references to the institution of parliament suggest[34] that he was also in favour of some kind of parliamentary democracy, probably on the British model (again a position that would be reversed in his mature thought).

Getting rid of petty princes was, then, the ground of Nietzsche's support of Bismarck's war aims. And he would soon support a war against France, believing, again with Bismarck, that only such a war could create an 'emotional commitment to unification' of sufficient power to be effective, and that 'in Europe as a whole, the older order will remain as long as Paris remains the centre [of power]'.[35]

These remarks show a certain consistency between what, in 1866, Nietzsche admired in Bismarck and what, in his maturity, he came to admire in Napoleon. He saw him, that is to say, as a 'good European', a statesman of ultimately cosmopolitan convictions engaged in a 'grand politics' of German and eventually European unification. This is why he called Bismarck a 'revolutionary' and is what he was referring to in speaking, à la Hegel, of 'history' as 'starting again'. In short, he took Bismarck to be, in the final analysis, an anti-nationalist. When he turned against him it was because the scales had fallen from his eyes. He realised that the Machiavellian Bismarck had completely fooled him (along with most other people) and that, far from being a 'good European', he was, in fact, a dangerously power-crazed Prussian nationalist, committed to nothing save the interests of the Prussian Junker class from which he arose.

* * *

Such enlightenment, however, did not occur until well into the 1870s. In 1866 Nietzsche's support for the war against Austria was absolute. It should also be recorded, however, that another side of his nature was beginning to at least register the appalling human cost of Bismarck's policies of 'iron and blood'. Hearing of the death, on the battlefield of Königgrätz, of Oscar Krämer, the kind-hearted prefect who had looked after him at Pforta (p. 24 above), he wrote home that no number of Austrian deaths could compensate for the loss of this fine person. And in the same letter he recorded the death of the twin brother of his landlord on the same battlefield, and that von Gersdorff's eldest brother, Ernst, had received a severe sabre wound to the head.[36]

In January 1867, von Gersdorff wrote Nietzsche that Ernst had finally died of the wound, aged twenty-seven:

> for twelve hours, unconscious, he fought with death … the battle must have been a terrible one; his face unrecognisable, rolling eyes, spasms in all his muscles, then a scream, the expulsion of air from the lungs, then another one, then all was still. The face was again as it had been, the expression noble and reposed as in life.[37]

Nietzsche replied by comparing his Aunt Rosalie's recent death, the end of a life brought to 'completeness', with this appalling waste of young talent – 'what such powers might have achieved!' He concluded by referring his suffering friend to Schopenhauer's doctrine that suffering is a path to 'denial of the will', to the insight (of which more in the next chapter) that the end of life is something to be welcomed rather than regretted.[38]

The war deaths of 1866 began, therefore, to touch Nietzsche as something more than numbers in a newspaper. To be sure, none of this human cost turned him as yet against either war or Bismarck. A characteristic of Nietzsche's (in his own language) 'slow-willed' personality is that it took a long time for experiences to 'sink in' far enough to cause him to change his mind. But the deaths of 1866 represent the beginning of a ledger – the deaths of 1871 would crucially add to it – that eventually made the abolition of war a central goal of his thinking.

Military Service

Bismarck's Prussia was, through and through, a militarised society.[39] The army itself, first of all, was (like Pforta) a 'total' institution. Conscripts were isolated from the external world for the first four to six weeks in order to be 'broken in'. They entered an alien and highly disciplined world of arcane rules and had drilled into them the virtue of unquestioning obedience to authority. The army worked on the bodies of its conscripts through physical exercise and drill (in his military training Nietzsche had to relearn horse-riding, learning to do it in a more 'regimental' manner), thus changing their whole appearance. People were often able to identify ex-soldiers by their ramrod-straight bearing and brisk movements; in later life, Nietzsche was often taken for a retired army officer.

Aware of the effect the army had on its conscripts, the state used it to indoctrinate its citizens, so that it came to be known as the 'school of the nation'. The men were supposed not only to become good soldiers but also to acquire 'transferable skills' such as discipline, cleanliness, and the 'right' political attitude: love of king and fatherland and obedience to authority. Such 'right' attitudes make frequent appearances in both von Gersdorff's and Nietzsche's letters. In his valediction for his dead brother, Ernst, for instance, von Gersdorff writes admiringly that 'his duty was his will'. And Nietzsche talks about 'personal, *that is*, fatherlandish [*vaterländisches*] interest'.[40]

Given the still-living memory of humiliation and occupation by Napoleon's armies, the newly effective army possessed enormous prestige within society at large, prestige which, as a conscious exercise in public relations, it sought to improve through carefully choreographed marches and parades designed to display its strength and efficiency. And even though it had long been realized that bright colours made easy targets on the battlefield, it was reluctant to change into grey, recognizing the attraction of a spectacular military appearance. While ordinary civilians walked around in dull, dark suits, the soldiers' uniforms emphasised their slim waists, broad shoulders, and upright bearing. The sabre at their side added the glamour of a 'licence to kill'. Boys wore navy uniforms, tin soldiers were favourite toys, and – as with Nietzsche – soldierly themes pervaded children's games. Nietzsche refers to Elizabeth's love of military uniforms[41] and had himself photographed in full military regalia, plus sabre (see Plate 8).

In such an atmosphere, risking life and limb for the Fatherland became the ultimate virtue, not only in official rhetoric but also in personal war memoirs:

> Things might be rough in war [one soldier recalled] but, nevertheless, no other time is marked by such noble and truly grand virtues . . . It produces strong enthusiasm, audacious courage, preparedness for sacrifice, a wholly altruistic sense of duty, proud nationalism and an unshakable love for king and fatherland. In short it produces men.[42]

Given this social climate, a climate that encouraged martial rituals such as the fraternity duel, many young men wanted to become officers. While Prussian lieutenants were regarded as 'young gods', as the historian Friedrich Meinecke records from personal experience, even non-commissioned officers could reach the status of demigods.[43]

Nietzsche was fully absorbed by the culture of his time and place. 'Our situation is simple', he wrote home just before the result of Königgrätz became known:

> When a house is on fire, one doesn't ask who was responsible for starting it. Rather one extinguishes it. Prussia is on fire. Now it must be saved . . . I am a committed Prussian . . . It is dishonourable to sit at home when the Fatherland begins a war of life and death.[44]

It is thus no surprise that on two occasions he attempted to volunteer for the army,[45] only to be rejected each time on account of his short-sightedness.

In September 1867, however, with the threat of renewed warfare never far away, his number eight glasses (which, according to Elizabeth, were actually far too weak) were no longer deemed an objection and he was declared fit for service. Unable to join the guards in Berlin, he ended up in Naumburg for a year's military service in the less glamorous mounted artillery. This had at least the advantage that he could live at home and continue his philological studies in the evenings. As well as an essay on Democritus (the inventor of atomism), he also had another – one might well think incredibly tedious – commission from Ritschl to work on, the completion of an index of the *Rheinisches Museum*. He must, though, have been encouraged on hearing that the essay Ritschl had encouraged him to write on Diogenes Laertius's sources had won a major University prize.

* * *

Life in the barracks could scarcely have presented a starker contrast to his comfortable former life as a student: endless mucking out of stables and grooming of horses. He had also, as already mentioned, to learn to ride in a new, military style. And drill, drill, and more drill. If one drilled philologists with equal thoroughness, he joked to Rohde, all philological problems would be solved in ten years.[46] With, however, his usual determination to make the best of things (to 'love fate', as his mature philosophy puts it), Nietzsche judged his changed existence a useful 'intermediate dish' since, he asserted (endorsing Prussian ideology), the rigours of military life make a man of one.[47] And he was extremely proud to be accounted the best rider among the thirty new recruits.

Then, in March of 1868, he missed his mount and damaged his chest on the pommel of the saddle. This was no doubt due to the myopia that should really have disqualified him from military service once again. (Elizabeth comments that short-sightedness made it hard for him to measure distances, with the result that he often strained an ankle.)[48] The chest wound became infected, putting him in bed for ten days, in great pain and taking morphine every morning. Eventually bits of bone began to come out with the pus. An operation was contemplated, resulting in his being sent to a celebrated surgeon in Halle, Richard von Volkmann, who in the end dealt with the problem simply by painting the wound with iodine. Nietzsche was out of military action for five months, during which time he was promoted to lance-corporal; 'I've become a *Gefreiter* [lance-corporal], oh that I was a *Befreiter* [freed person]', he punned gloomily to Rohde.[49]

On October 15, 1868, his twenty-fourth birthday, his wish was granted: he was officially declared 'temporarily unfit for military service'. Since, however, he saw that war against France would happen sooner rather than later, and since he wished to participate as a commissioned rather than non-commissioned artillery officer, he arranged to do another month's service in the following spring, during which he acquired the necessary knowledge of gun-hauling.

Return to Leipzig: First Meeting with Wagner

On being discharged from the military, Nietzsche immediately returned to Leipzig. Feeling himself to have outgrown the student life – military life had made a 'man' of him – he looked for somewhere more comfortable to live than the student digs of the past. This he found by becoming a paying guest in one of the finest houses in the city, Lessingstrasse 22, the home of Professor Friedrich Biedermann, a former member of the local parliament and editor of the *Deutsche Allgemeine Zeitung* newspaper. Here Nietzsche arranged to eat all his meals; 'thank goodness to get away from the smell of fat and the many Jews' that belonged to his former restaurant existence, he wrote home.[50]

Life at the Biedermanns' certainly was comfortable:

> Old Biedermann [he wrote Rohde] is a man true to his name ['*bieder*' means 'smug', 'respectable', 'conventional', 'conservative', 'bourgeois'], a good father and husband – in sum, everything one usually puts in an obituary. His wife is a *Biederfrau* ['smug', etc., woman], which really says everything. And so we pass on to the two *Biederfräulein* ['smug', etc., girls], *Biederfräulein* I and *Biederfräulein* II.[51]

Biedermann arranged for Nietzsche to do the opera and some of the book reviewing for his paper. And in the Biedermanns' drawing-room he met many of the leading politicians, artists, and actresses of the time. Thus, without really trying, he found himself at the urbane heart of Leipzig's cultural and social life.

* * *

As we have seen, Nietzsche had been fascinated by the phenomenon of Richard Wagner ever since Krug had persuaded *Germania* to subscribe to the *Neue Zeitschrift für Musik* and since the two of them had explored the piano reduction of *Tristan und Isolde* together in 1862 (pp. 27–8 above). After his return to Leipzig he made a deliberate attempt to get to know Wagner's sister, Ottilie,[52] wife of the orientalist Professor Hermann Brockhaus, a task which was easy to achieve: first, because Sophie Ritschl and Ottilie were best friends, and, second, because Nietzsche was friendly with Ernst Windisch, a favourite student of Brockhaus who was branching out from classical philology into Sanskrit studies.

Though fascinated, Nietzsche was, at the beginning of the Leipzig years, not yet a complete Wagnerite. In October 1866 he wrote to von Gersdorff that he had the score of *Die Walküre* to which, he reports, 'my reactions are very mixed, so that I can't really make a judgment about it. The great beauties and virtues are permeated by great uglinesses and failings'.[53] By October 1868, however, he was much more enthusiastic. Referring to *Tannhäuser* and *Lohengrin*, he wrote Rohde that what particularly affected him was the 'sphere of feeling', the 'ethical air, the Faustian perfume, cross, death and grave'.[54] A few days later he wrote him that he had been attending concerts in his capacity as the *Deutsche Allgemeine*'s music critic – he was accustomed to sitting with three other music critics, including one from Brendel's *Neue Zeitschrift*, the four of them constituting a 'sharp corner' of expertise – and had been completely conquered by both the prelude to *Tristan* and the overture to *Die Meistersinger von Nürnberg*:

> I cannot bring myself to preserve critical detachment towards this music. It sends a thrill through every fibre, every nerve; and so prolonged a feeling of ecstasy as that produced by the last-named overture I have not experienced for a very long time.[55]

The following February he attended the first Dresden performance of the *Die Meistersinger* (it had been premiered in Munich in June 1868, with Wagner sitting next to King Ludwig of Bavaria in the royal box), where he reported experiencing 'the strongest feeling of a quite sudden homecoming and of being at home (*heimisch*)'.[56] (Since the opera's first act starts with the music of his homeland, a Lutheran chorale, Nietzsche had a special reason to feel *heimisch*. But his reaction was, I think, quite typical, even among those sceptical of Wagner's other works. What is immensely reassuring about the opera is that the startlingly new music of Walther von Stolzing's prize song, after many trials and tribulations, is ultimately accepted by the mastersingers' guild, thus demonstrating the power of tradition to bend without breaking, to absorb the novel energy of (in Nietzsche's later terminology) the 'free spirit' while yet preserving the integrity of tradition. And presiding over the entire work is the wisdom of Hans Sachs, who, though given to melancholy, is, nonetheless, surely the most reassuring father figure in the whole of opera.)

* * *

Wagner was born in Leipzig in 1813. In 1849, however, he was in Dresden, where, though director of music at the King of Saxony's court, he helped his Russian anarchist friend Mikhail Bakunin organize an abortive workers' uprising in the city. As a disciple of Proudhon, who held that 'property is theft', and of Feuerbach, who held that 'no one without the courage to be absolutely negative has the strength to create anything new', Wagner was involved in grenade manufacture and in trying to persuade the local militia to join the side of the workers. As a result he was forced, after the failure of the revolution, to flee to Switzerland, where he spent the next twelve years in exile. In December 1851, however, appalled at the success of Napoleon III's *coup d'état*, which resulted in the abolition of the French parliament, he abandoned not only his commitment to his anarchist version of socialism but also political action as such, a retreat which, we shall see, was cemented by his discovery of Schopenhauer's 'world-denying' transcendentalism three years later.

Given his history (his abandonment of revolutionary politics was not widely known) and his reputation for an exotic love life, the Wagner who visited his sister in Leipzig in November 1868 was a controversial, even scandalous figure, a scandal given a local dimension by his suggestion that the Leipzig music conservatory should be moved to Dresden and by his attack on, among others, the local hero, Felix Mendelssohn, in '*Das Judentum in der Musik* [Judaism in Music]'.* Unsurprisingly, therefore, his visit to Leipzig was supposed to be kept secret, particularly from the local press.

To the fact that Rohde was sick we owe a long letter[57] in which Nietzsche amusingly dramatises his first meeting with Wagner. Returning to his lodgings from a meeting with Ritschl on the afternoon of November 6, 1868, he reports that he found a note from his friend Windisch: 'If you would like to meet Richard Wagner, come to the Café Theatre at 3.45 pm'. He rushed off to keep this cloak-and-dagger appointment, where he was informed, *sotto voce*, that Wagner was staying with the Brockhauses; furthermore, that he had played Walter's prize song from the *Die Meistersinger* in the presence of Sophie Ritschl, who had said she already knew it through her husband's student. 'Joy and amazement on Wagner's part. He expresses a strong desire to meet me incognito'. Nietzsche and Windisch then rushed off to the Brockhauses' house, only to discover that Wagner has gone out 'wearing an enormous hat' – presumably with the brim well down over the eyes to disguise his identity. (Since Wagner was extremely short (about 5′ 4″) this cannot have been all that easy.) Alleviating their disappointment, however, the two young men received an invitation to return the following evening, a Sunday.

---

* This anti-Semitic tract had been published in Brendel's *Neue Zeitschrift für Musik* in 1850, and had led to a petition being signed by Brendel's professorial colleagues, many of whom were Jewish, demanding his dismissal from his position at the Leipzig music conservatory.

Assuming the meeting would be a large, formal occasion, Nietzsche – always something of a dandy – was happy that, serendipitously, he had an evening suit on order from a tailor and promised for that very Sunday. The suit was not quite finished when he called at the shop, but it was promised in three-quarters of an hour. When he returned it was still not finished. Finally, at about six-thirty, a 'little old man' arrived at the Biedermanns' house with a package and a bill:

> I take it politely: he wants cash on delivery [which Nietzsche did not have to hand and likely not at all]. Flabbergasted, I explain that I wanted no dealings with him, my tailor's employee, but only with the tailor himself, from whom I ordered the suit. The man puts more pressure on me; the time puts more pressure on me. I seize the things and begin to put them on. Force on my side versus force on his. Imagine the scene: I am fighting in my shirt because I want to step into the new trousers.

The little old man, however, won the battle. He went off with the suit, leaving Nietzsche sitting on the sofa in his shirt, swearing dreadful revenge against the tailor, and wondering whether his old black jacket was good enough for an evening with Richard Wagner. He then stormed out into, as it happened, a rainstorm, fearful of being late for the appointment, hoping his old clothes would do. But as it turned out there was no formal gathering at all, only the Brockhaus family, Nietzsche, Windisch and Wagner.

What followed was one of Wagner's bravura performances:

> I was introduced to Richard and spoke some words of appreciation. He inquired very precisely how I had got to know his music, abused terribly all the performances of his operas, except the famous Munich one [of *Die Meistersinger*], and made fun of the conductors who call out to their orchestra in a comfortable tone of voice, 'Now gentlemen, some passion', 'My dear fellows, a bit more passion'. Wagner likes very much to imitate the Leipzig accent... Before and after dinner he played [the piano] and included all the important sections of *Meistersinger*, imitating all the vocal parts and growing very exuberant. He is a wonderfully lively and animated man who speaks extremely fast, is very witty and makes a gathering of this private sort very cheerful. In between times, I had a longish talk with him about Schopenhauer and you can imagine what joy it was for me to hear him speak of Schopenhauer with a quite indescribable warmth, saying how much he owed to him and how he was the only philosopher who understood the nature of music. Then he asked how the professors felt about him these days and laughed a lot about...the 'philosophical timeservers' [Schopenhauer's 'professors of philosophy']. Afterwards he read a portion of the autobiography he is now writing, an extremely amusing scene from his Leipzig student days, which I still can't think about without laughing... At the end of the evening as we two were about to leave he pressed my hand very warmly and invited me most cordially to visit him in order to discuss music and philosophy. He also commissioned me to make his sister and relatives familiar with his music – which I solemnly agreed to do.

Nietzsche was dazzled, completely won over. The fact that he refers to Wagner as 'Richard' only two days after first meeting him indicates the instant warmth and connectedness he felt towards the man who was exactly the age his father would have been.

The immediate effect of the encounter was the setting of Wagner alongside Schopenhauer as the guiding hero of his life. He wrote to Rohde,

> Wagner whom I now know from his music, his poetry, his writings on aesthetics and, not least, from happy personal acquaintance with him, is the most vivid illustration of what Schopenhauer calls a 'genius'; the similarity in all particulars springs immediately to the eye. I wish I could tell you all the details of his life which I mostly know through his sister. How I wish we [Nietzsche and Rohde] could be together...to allow ourselves to be swept away in this Schopenhauerian sea of sound, in whose most secret breaking of the waves...one experiences an astonishing discovery of oneself.[58]

'Fairy-Tale-Like and Seven-League-Bootish'

At the beginning of 1869 the chair of classical philology at the University of Basel fell vacant. The departing incumbent, Adolf Kiessling, wrote to his former teacher, Ritschl, asking about Nietzsche, whose work he had read in the *Rheinishes Museum*. In the reference he sent in reply, Ritschl wrote that in his thirty-nine years of teaching he had '*never* known a young man who has matured so early'. He called him the leader of all the young philologists in Leipzig and prophesied that he would become one of the foremost German classicists. Kiessling passed this information on to Professor Wilhelm Vischer-Bilfinger, a philologist who headed the city of Basel's education committee and the university council, and who then approached Ritschl for further information. In reply Ritschl described his star pupil as

> without private means...possessing no particularly political nature. Though he has a general sympathy for German unification, he has no sympathy for Prussianness – as little as I have; on the contrary he has a lively sensibility for free civic and cultural development.[59]

(Ritschl's representation of Nietzsche as anti-Prussian may have been calculated to appeal to Swiss republicanism, may have been Ritschl's projection of his own politics onto Nietzsche, or may have been the result of Nietzsche's trimming his sails to match his patron's sensibilities. It is, in any case, as we have seen, false. His turn against Prussia was still several years down the track.)

The result of this academic networking was that on February 12, 1869, Nietzsche was appointed to the position. On March 23 he was awarded his doctorate, without examination, on the basis of the work published in the *Rheinisches Museum*. He never did a *Habilitation*, the second Ph.D., which, in the German system, is normally the prerequisite of any academic post.

So, at the age of twenty-four, unlike Rohde and Deussen, who would have to wait years to obtain academic positions, Nietzsche suddenly found himself an assistant professor with a salary of 3,000 Swiss francs (about 800 talers or 2,540 marks) per year, a comfortable income for a single man, though inadequate to sustain a married couple. In addition to university lecturing, the position also required six hours a week teaching at the local Pädagogium, the grammar school that had once been part of the university. The following year Nietzsche was promoted to full professor. As he wrote von Gersdorff, there was 'something fairy-tale-like and seven-league-bootish'[60] about the ease with which, thanks to Ritschl, he strode through – or rather past – the normal hoops of an academic career.

Nietzsche was so overcome by his good fortune that he spent an entire afternoon walking up and down the Leipzig promenade humming tunes from *Tannhäuser* – appropriately, since one of the great attractions of Basel was that it was only a stone's throw from Tribschen, Wagner's place of exile. Then he announced the good news by penning a series of short notes on a dozen visiting cards which he sent to friends and acquaintances, adding, underneath his printed name, 'Professor extraord[inary] of Classical Philology at Basel University'. His mother burst into tears of bewildered happiness. Momentarily he seems to have been overcome by his own grandeur, sending a letter terminating his friendship with Deussen (an edict later rescinded), who, he felt, had not been sufficiently sensible of the honour of being able to call a proper professor his friend.[61]

Nietzsche's original plan had been to take 'time out' after completing his university studies. He had planned a year's 'overseas experience' with Rohde in Paris, in order, as he wrote wistfully to Rohde after he knew the trip was off,

> to taste the life of a wanderer, ... to be an onlooker not a player. I saw the two of us with serious eyes and smiling lips striding through the Paris crowds, a couple of philosophical flâneurs,

sight-seers with a particular interest in the great museums and libraries of Paris.[62] Since, however, the Nietzsches were genuinely poor – his mother had almost nothing to live on save her meagre widow's pension – this had always been, as Rohde pointed out, 'a pipe dream'.[63]

Nietzsche's final days before leaving for Basel were a little melancholy. Apart from farewelling the dream of Paris, he had also to farewell his youth. To von Gersdorff he wrote from Naumburg on April 11,

> Time is up, this is my last evening in the homeland; tomorrow I'm off into the wide world, into a new and unfamiliar profession, into the heavy and oppressive atmosphere of duty and work. Again I must say farewell: the golden time of free, unconstrained activity, the care-freeness of [living in] the present, of enjoying art and the world as a disengaged, or at least only mildly engaged, observer – this time is now past and beyond recovery. Now the strict goddess of daily duty rules ... I must now myself become a philistine ... One pays a price for office and status – the only question is whether the bonds are of iron or thread ... A herd man – may Zeus and all the muses protect me from that. I have indeed moved nearer to belonging to the species 'cog in the machine [*Fachmensch*]'.[64]

The job offer was, of course, one Nietzsche could not refuse. These sentiments are nonetheless genuine. What lies at their root is partly the Schopenhauerian perspective on the life of a professor, but more specifically Nietzsche's increased attraction towards philosophy and consequently away from philology. In his last months in Leipzig he had even started to make notes for a contemplated doctoral thesis in philosophy – on the concept of teleology since Kant.

Nonetheless he put a brave face on things and on April 13 left his home town and his youth behind him. From Naumburg he travelled in leisurely stages via Bonn and Cologne, arriving in Basel on April 19, 1869. The university required him to give up his Prussian nationality so that they would not lose him to military service, but since he had not yet acquired Swiss nationality, he became, in the language of Swiss bureaucratese, '*heimatslos* [homeless]'. And since he never actually took out Swiss nationality, 'homelessness' – a major theme in his poetry – became his official status for the rest of his life. His later description of himself as a 'European' was, in fact, the literal truth.

5

Schopenhauer

ONE DAY, towards the middle of November 1865, shortly after arriving in Leipzig, Nietzsche succumbed, in spite of his straitened student means, to a sudden impulse:

> I came across this book in old Rohn's second-hand bookshop, and taking it up very gingerly I turned over its pages. I know not what demon whispered to me: 'Take this book home with you'. At all events, contrary to my habit of not being hasty in the purchase of books, I took it home. Back in my room I threw myself into the corner of the sofa with my booty, and began to allow that energetic and gloomy genius to work upon my mind. In this book, in which every line cried out renunciation, denial and resignation, I saw a mirror in which I espied the whole world, life, and my own mind depicted in frightful grandeur.[1]

The 'gloomy genius' was Schopenhauer and the book *The World as Will and Representation*. (Since it had been published in Leipzig but sold extremely badly, numerous copies were probably still to be found in local second-hand bookshops.) As noted in the previous chapter, Nietzsche immediately became a 'Schopenhauerian'. What, we must now ask, did that entail?

The World as Will and Representation

ARTHUR SCHOPENHAUER (1788–1860) had private means, which he cultivated astutely. He had inherited from his father, who (before jumping to his death from the attic of his house) had been a successful Hamburg businessman. Schopenhauer scorned the 'professors of philosophy', partly out of snobbishness towards people who had to work for a living, but mainly, as already noted, on the ground that independence of means is a precondition of independence of thought. (He was basically right about nineteenth-century German universities. Since they were almost always funded by kings and princes, the legitimacy of whose rule rested mainly on the claim that they had been appointed to it by God – the doctrine of the 'divine right of kings' – philosophers such as Kant and Hegel found the outright denial of God's existence a virtual impossibility.) Accordingly, Schopenhauer never held a paid university post, living, in the felicitous German phrase, as a *freier Schriftsteller*, a 'free writer' or, as the English say, a 'freelance'. The last twenty-seven years of his life he lived alone in Frankfurt. In his study he had, on the wall, a portrait of Kant, on his desk, a statue of the Buddha, and, at his feet, a poodle. He loved opera, preferred animals to humans, and played the flute. His views on women are unprintable.

The World as Will and Representation, first published in 1818 but extensively revised and doubled in size in 1844, was Schopenhauer's only major work of systematic philosophy.[2] It is divided into four books.

In the first book, following his admired (though at times criticised) predecessor, Immanuel Kant, Schopenhauer asserts that, as its first sentence puts it, 'The world is my representation'. Space and time, substantiality (thing-ness) and causal connectedness, that is to say, are not 'out there', independent of us. Rather, they are the 'forms' and 'categories' which the human mind imposes on everything that arrives in consciousness – in the same way in which, for example, green sunglasses impose greenness on everything seen through them, or a word-processing programme with the font set to 'New Roman' imposes 'New-Romanness' on everything that appears on the computer screen. 'Nature', that is to say, the world of both everyday experience and natural science, is our own creation, a world of mere 'appearances' or 'phenomena'. In the last analysis it is a fiction; ultimately, as Schopenhauer puts it, a 'dream'.[3] This, in philosophical jargon, is Schopenhauer's Kant-inspired 'idealism' (a confusing term, better thought of in connexion with 'idea' than with 'ideal').

Beyond the 'dream', on the other side of the 'veil' created by our minds, is the real world; in Kant's language, the 'thing in itself'. Following his affinity with Indian thought, Schopenhauer often speaks of that which is interposed between us and the thing in itself as the 'veil of Maya'.

What is this real world like? Kant's – to Schopenhauer and nearly all his contemporaries – intensely frustrating answer is: we can never know. Since we can never step outside our own minds, we can never step outside the form they impose on our experience. And so, since we can never have 'veil'-free experience, since we see at best only through a glass, darkly, we have to reconcile ourselves to the fact that ultimate reality lies forever beyond the reach of human cognition.

* * *

In the second book of the masterwork – in, at least, the earlier edition – Schopenhauer appears to reject Kant's frustrating conclusion. If we attend, first, to our own bodies, and if we look inwards rather than outwards, he suggests, we find a kind of experience that is veil-free. And what we find in this experience is, in a word, 'will'. That which presents itself to outer perception as bodily action presents itself, in introspection, as 'will' (feeling, emotion, desire and decision). This provides the vital clue to the nature of reality in general. That which, from the outer perspective, appears as a physical body is, Schopenhauer announces, in its inner reality, will. So the Kantian problem is solved. Take away the veils and what is left, as the thing in itself, is will:

> What Kant opposed as *thing in itself* to mere *appearance*, this *thing in itself*, this substratum of all phenomena and therefore of the whole of nature, is nothing but what we know directly and intimately and find within ourselves as *the will*.[4]

Though a major philosophical breakthrough, in another respect, Schopenhauer thinks, this is not a happy discovery. For the fact that the essence of everything is 'will' means that the essence of life is suffering. This is the 'pessimism' for which Schopenhauer is famous. Life contains many pains and few pleasures; its overall and overwhelmingly dominant character is suffering. For this conclusion he presents a number of converging arguments.

Surveying the animal world, we see that the will – the 'will to live' – of one creature has no option but to hunt and kill another. Red in tooth and claw, nature is a place where only the fit and murderous survive (Schopenhauer anticipates important aspects of Darwinism by some forty years). Hence fear, pain and death are by no means accidental malfunctions of a generally benevolent nature but belong, rather, to its essence.

Turning to the human world, we find the will to be equally a curse. Schopenhauer gives several reasons for this. One argument points out that the viciously competitive life of non-human animals is merely ameliorated, not removed, by human civilization. Though we do not often kill each other, the pursuit of one individual's desires typically and knowingly harms those of another. As the ancients knew, '*Homo homini lupus*', 'man is a wolf to man'.[5]

The most intriguing of Schopenhauer's arguments for pessimism, however – I shall call it the 'stress or boredom argument' – argues that even if we were *never* caused to suffer by other human beings, suffering would still constitute the overwhelming character of our lives. Briefly, the argument runs as follows. The will that is the essence of humanity as of everything else is either satisfied or not. If my will is not satisfied then I suffer. If, for example, I will food or sex but none is available, then I suffer the pain of hunger or of sexual frustration. But if, on the other hand, I achieve what I will, then very soon I experience an even worse form of suffering – boredom. If I achieve sex, Schopenhauer thinks (though he never married he was known to actresses), then almost immediately I suffer post-coital *tristesse*: 'Everyone who is in love will experience an extraordinary disillusionment after the pleasure he finally attains'.[6] If (to think Schopenhauer's argument in terms of contemporary consumerism) I lust after a shiny new Mercedes sports car and finally acquire one, I may experience a couple of weeks of shallow pleasure. After that, however, it slumps into the invisibility of being just 'the car'. Hence, Schopenhauer concludes, life 'swings like a pendulum' between the two 'poles' of suffering – lack and boredom.[7]

* * *

Having diagnosed the sickness of the world in general, and of the human condition in particular, in the first two books, *The World as Will*'s third book turns to the question of cure, to avenues of escape from the suffering that is life.

In the aesthetic contemplation of art or nature, Schopenhauer observes, the will is, for a moment, silenced. In routine, everyday experience everything is perceived in terms of our practical interests, 'in relation to the will'. The hillside shows up as a 'nice piece of real estate' ripe for 'development', or as a valuable bauxite deposit ready for mining. In its aesthetic contemplation, on the other hand, perception becomes 'disinterested' (a term Schopenhauer takes over from Kant and which is not to be confused with 'uninterested'). Absorbed, for a moment, in aesthetic contemplation of the hillside (the breathtaking sight, perhaps, of Cézanne's Mont Sainte-Victoire dissolving into the mysterious blue of the Mediterranean sky), we are, as we indeed say, 'taken out of ourselves': we become oblivious to our individual selves and so to our wills. For a moment we become 'the pure, will-less, ... timeless subject'[8] of disinterested perception. And when this happens we achieve a brief escape from the anxiety and pain that is inseparable from all willing. For a brief moment – Schopenhauer sings here a kind of hymn to art – we experience

> the peace always sought but always escaping us on the … path of willing … the painless state, prized by Epicurus as the highest good and as the state of the gods; for that moment we are delivered from the miserable pressure of the will. We celebrate the Sabbath of the penal servitude of willing; the wheel of Ixion stands still.[9]

The essence of almost all the arts, then, is that they give us a purified, will-free perception of the world – the *visible* world, of course, the world of 'appearance'. Music, however, is different since, quite evidently, Schopenhauer observes, it does not represent the visible world. (Representations of bird-song and battle-scenes he regards as trivialisations of music.) This leaves two options. The first is to adopt what we might call the 'formalist' view, the view that music represents nothing, but pleases simply as a harmonious pattern of meaning-less sounds in the way in which abstract painting pleases as a harmonious pattern of meaning-less colours. This was the opinion of Leibniz, who, Schopenhauer reports, described music as 'An unconscious exercise in arithmetic in which the mind does not know it is counting'.[10] The second is to adopt what we might call the 'deep representation' view, the view that music *does* represent, not the world of appearance but rather the 'thing in itself'. Schopenhauer rejects the formalist view on the grounds that it cannot explain the profound significance we ascribe to music and concludes that, unique among the arts, music gives us 'veil'-free access to reality in itself. This makes music the highest of the arts, an 'unconscious exercise [not in arithmetic but rather] in metaphysics in which the mind does not know it is philosophising'.*,[11]

The fourth and final book of *The World as Will* begins with an account of moral virtue. Since the only will, the only locus of sensitivity to pain and pleasure, with which we are directly acquainted is our own, since only our own pain and pleasure is 'real' to us, mostly, says Schopenhauer, we are 'egoists'. Our own interests count for everything, those of others not at all, since, experientially, our own are the only interests that *exist*. But actually, based as it is on the assumed reality of a world of individuals, egoism is an expression of metaphysical delusion. Schopenhauer argues for this as follows. Space and time, as Kant has taught us, exist only in the apparent world. But individuality depends on space and time: one can only discriminate things as distinct objects if they occupy different parts of space, or, if they occupy the same space, do so at different times. It follows that the thing in itself must be 'beyond individuality', be, in fact, an undifferentiated unity, 'One'.

In contrast to the selfish egoist, the virtuous person is someone who has insight into this metaphysical truth. Intuitively, she understands the ultimately illusory character of division and difference. (Schopenhauer thinks that women are generally better at this than men – his one nice remark about women.) Unconsciously she realises the wisdom contained in the formula of the *Upanishads*, '*tat tvam asi* (this art thou)'. So she takes the other's pain as her own. Virtue is thus simply altruism, the essence of which is identification with

---

* After discovering Schopenhauer, Richard Wagner adopted the deep representation view. His opponent, the Viennese music critic and self-appointed Brahms protagonist Eduard Hanslick, defended the formalist view. Formalism versus deep representation dominated late-nineteenth-century musical polemics.

others. Schopenhauer's word for such identification is 'sympathy'. But since life is suffering, since there are few joys and many sorrows with which to identify, it is, more specifically, 'compassion'.

There are different degrees of insight into the Oneness of all life, but the highest degree belongs to the Christ-like saint who takes as his own the sufferings of the entire world. When, however, altruism reaches a pitch such as this, a profound transformation, a radical 'gestalt switch', occurs. For the saint suddenly realises that altruism is *futile*; that efforts to alleviate the suffering of others, the works of love, at best only change the form of suffering (from stress to boredom or vice versa), but can never diminish its quantity. 'If', writes Schopenhauer,

> we compare life to a circular path of red-hot coals having a few cool places, a path we have to run over incessantly, then the man ensnared in delusion [i.e., the egoist] is comforted by the cool place on which he is just now standing or which he sees near him and sets out to run over the path.

The saint, by contrast, having completely seen through the illusion of individuality,

> sees himself at all places simultaneously and withdraws ... In other words, it is no longer enough for him to love others as himself and to do as much for them as for himself.[12]

With, that is, the intuitive realisation that life as such is, was, and always will be suffering comes a revulsion, a rejection of the will and the world which Schopenhauer calls 'denial of the will'. Ultimate insight expresses itself as a 'transition from virtue to asceticism'.[13]

Asceticism represents a kind of 'salvation' from this world of pain: as the Stoics saw, if willing is the source of suffering, then the reduction of willing is a reduction of suffering. But Stoicism, lacking a 'transcendent end',[14] is not true salvation: that comes only with death. With death this dream – more exactly, nightmare – of life comes to an end. As to what replaces it we cannot say. Since language and conceptual thought are confined to the world of appearance, that which is beyond the dream is, to us, 'nothing'.* Yet we have only to attend to the beatitude of the mystics, to

> that ocean-like calmness of the spirit, that deep tranquillity, that unshakable confidence and serenity whose mere reflection in the countenance as depicted by Raphael and Correggio, is a complete and certain gospel ... [in order to] banish the dark impression of that nothingness, which, as the final goal, hovers behind all virtue and holiness and which we fear [in Francis Bacon's borrowed simile] as children fear the dark.[15]

Attention to the testimony of the mystics, in other words, testimony which is brought to us and 'vouched for with the stamp of truth by art',[16] establishes that the nothing-to-us is

---

* How, the reader may feel inclined to protest, can the reality beyond the 'dream' of life be 'nothing' intelligible to us when Schopenhauer has just got through revealing to us his great discovery that reality in itself is 'will'? This question will be addressed shortly.

a *heavenly* nothing, a realm of bliss. What those few spirits who have had direct encounters with the transcendent know is not only that the Ultimate is 'One' but also that it is a *divine* 'One'. 'Pantheistic consciousness', writes Schopenhauer, 'is essential to all mysticism', as exemplified by Meister Eckhardt's spiritual daughter who cries out after her epiphany, 'Sir, rejoice with me, I have become God'.[17]

Nietzsche's Conversion

Thus, in brief, the extraordinary doctrine that, virtually overnight, converted Nietzsche into a 'Schopenhauerian'. But just what was it about Schopenhauer's philosophy, we need now to ask, which had such a profound effect?

Nietzsche was by no means alone in falling under Schopenhauer's spell. On the contrary, after a lifetime of obscurity, he had, within a decade of his death in 1860, become, as Nietzsche later notes,[18] the most celebrated nineteenth-century German philosopher. Nietzsche is, therefore, something of a representative figure: in asking what it was about Schopenhauer's philosophy that appealed to him, we are also asking what it was that appealed to considerable numbers of educated people in the second half of the nineteenth and even in the twentieth century.

Albert Camus begins *The Myth of Sisyphus* with the famous assertion that 'there is but one truly serious philosophical problem and that is suicide. Judging whether life is or is not worth living amounts to answering the fundamental question of philosophy'. With this raising of the question concerning the value (and inevitably, too, the meaning) of life, a new kind of philosophy is born: 'Existentialism', a philosophy that, rather than puzzling over abstruse matters of theory interesting (indeed intelligible) only to a narrow clique of professionals, attends to the deep, worrying, and very difficult questions that lurk in the consciousness of every human 'existence'. The person, however, who first put Camus's question on the table (and also, as it were, presented the case for the prosecution) was Schopenhauer. In this sense of the term, therefore, he was the first 'Existentialist', the first philosopher (since antiquity) to take philosophy out of libraries and lecture halls and into people's lives.

And he did so in prose of masterly clarity, elegance, wit and incandescent fury (directed mainly against Hegel's cheap optimism and 'brain-rotting' obscurity), and with a capacity for the concrete, telling example that is worth a thousand windy words. Schopenhauer not only speaks to *us* as opposed to a narrow clique of desiccated scholars, he also speaks in a way we can easily understand. (Nietzsche's critique of the then-current practice of philology, let us recall, objected precisely to its desiccated, introverted professionalism and lack of existential relevance.) The question remains, however, as to what it was about – specifically, the *content* of Schopenhauer's philosophy that seemed to Nietzsche and his circle to be of such vital importance.

Nietzsche's student years were, I have emphasised, happy years, the happiest of his entire life. Yet something was missing. Though he had entered the university of Bonn with the formal intention of studying for the priesthood, we know that even before leaving Pforta, he had, in fact, 'lost his faith'. Christian metaphysics ('theological astronomy' he later calls it),[19] God, heaven, and the immortal soul had been rendered unbelievable by the natural and human sciences of modernity. Later on, in *The Gay Science*, he records, in a strongly autobiographical way, the agonising loss of a spiritual homeland that results from the 'death of God'. 'Where is God?' he cries:

> 'I'll tell you! *We have killed him* – you and I! We [we modern thinkers] are all his murderers. But…what were we doing when we [we 'Copernicans'] unchained this earth from its sun? Where is it moving to now? Where are we moving to? Away from all suns? Are we not continually falling? And backwards, sidewards, forwards in all directions? Is there still an up and a down?[20]

What had Nietzsche lost in losing the faith of his family? What was it the religion of his childhood had provided him with? In essence, three things: an account of how one should live, the ethics of Christian love; an antidote to fear of death, the doctrine of the immortality of the soul; and an account of the meaning of life as 'salvation', the attainment, through virtue, of eternal, heavenly bliss. The loss of this framework for living is what *The Gay Science* identifies as the 'directionless' character of post-Christian existence. Such a framework, however, is precisely what Nietzsche believed he had rediscovered in Schopenhauer's philosophy. Hence the ecstasy of his first response. The young man who entered Rohn's bookshop was, he tells us, 'devoid of fundamental principles'. But what he rediscovered in Schopenhauer – the language is explicitly religious – was, he tells us, 'sickness and recovery, banishment and refuge, hell and heaven'.[21] What he discovered in Schopenhauer was, he believed, a recasting of the essence of the Christianity of his childhood in a form fit for adults.

Schopenhauer himself took his philosophy to have this character.[22] And one can see why, since Christianity (the Lutheranism of Nietzsche's childhood, at least) agrees with him on the following fundamental doctrines. First, that this world is a 'vale of tears', a place of sin and suffering. Second, that one should 'love one's neighbour as oneself', that love, compassion for suffering, is the proper ethical stance towards others. Third, that death is not to be feared, since it is merely a transition to another realm of being. And fourth, that one's post-mortem existence is the goal and meaning of life since (for the virtuous, at least) it is a realm of eternal bliss.

In a word, then, Nietzsche's discovery of Schopenhauer had the character of a 'conversion', almost 'born-again', experience: it was the rediscovery of religion, a recasting of the old religion in a new form.

This explains the religious colour of his response to reading *The World as Will*. Almost immediately he began to speak of Schopenhauer as 'my master', a kind of high priest whose 'disciple' he was. And he began to practise bodily penances such as allowing himself only four hours sleep a night, following Schopenhauer's recommended path through asceticism to 'salvation'.[23] He became, moreover, an evangelist for the new faith, began, as he put it, to 'make propaganda on [Schopenhauer's] behalf and lead various people by the nose to him'.[24] Being a 'co-religionist' became a virtual precondition of friendship with Nietzsche. Over his friendship with Rohde, he wrote, 'the genius of…Schopenhauer of course presides',[25] as it did over the friendships with Mushacke and von Gersdorff. Only Deussen proved resistant to the new faith, forcing Nietzsche effectively to threaten to break off the friendship if he did not see the light.[26],* And over the fateful future friendship with Wagner Schopenhauer would preside as well.

Nietzsche records that every fortnight he, von Gersdorff, and Mushacke met with the Naumburg pastor Friedrich Wenkel, 'an inexhaustible researcher and protagonist for Schopenhauer's teaching',[27] in Café Kintschy, in order to 'schopenhauerianize'.[28] Within the network of Schopenhauer-disciples, both in Leipzig and in other parts of Germany, the 'master' was elevated to an almost Christ-like status: on one occasion that involved the drinking of wine Nietzsche compares the gathering of 'friends of Schopenhauer' to a gathering of the first Christians.[29]

As with any group of devotees, the disciples became desperate to obtain a visual image of their guru. Eventually von Gersdorff tracked down the owner of a portrait by Jules Luntenschütz (see Plate 9) belonging to a former acquaintance of Schopenhauer. Breathlessly, he reports that the owner of the icon

took us to his study and here I saw the heavenly picture of our master, before which one could stand for hours, in order to look into his clear eyes. A god-like brow that appears to rise to infinity, framed by beautiful white hair under white eyebrows like those of the Olympian Zeus, two eyes of clarity and depth from which one cannot tear oneself away, once one has become accustomed to the gaze which at first seems to dazzle one. The mouth is broad but has the friendly, mild expression of inner peace, though one cannot miss his capacity for cascades of bitter, satirical scorn,[30]

and so rhapsodically on. Nietzsche replies, equally breathlessly, that he has passed this precious description on to 'two other disciples of our master, namely Rohde ... and Wenkel'.[31]

Above all what appealed to Nietzsche was Schopenhauer's doctrine of 'salvation'. Describing his stance to Christianity in 1866, he writes,

If Christianity means 'faith in an historical event and an historical person' I have nothing to do with this Christianity. But if it means a need for salvation then I value it highly ... Oh, if only all philosophers were disciples of Schopenhauer.

And he confesses to still experiencing 'the metaphysical need' which he holds to be universal to all human beings.[32]

'Metaphysical need' refers to the title of the chapter of *The World as Will* – 'On Man's Need for Metaphysics'[33] – which contains Schopenhauer's principal discussion of religion. Human beings are unique, he argues, in living in the consciousness of mortality. Only they live in the light of 'the nothing [*das Nichts*]' which they must one day become and which (particularly in a post-Christian age) they suspect to be an 'absolute' or 'empty' nothing.[34] Fear of death is innate and universal, simply the obverse of our biologically programmed 'will to live'. Assurance of the non-finality of death is the true heart of any great

* There is irony in this, since, when he eventually did convert, unlike Nietzsche, who would become an apostate, Deussen remained faithful for life, founding the Schopenhauer Society in Frankfurt and becoming the first editor of its *Jahrbuch* [Yearbook] (to which the present author has contributed a number of essays).

religion: no religion has ever achieved the status of a world religion without a doctrine of immortality.

And providing an 'antidote' to fear of death, providing a 'consolation' for its inevitability, is also, Schopenhauer holds, the principal task of philosophy, which is why Socrates defined philosophy as a 'preparation for death'.[35] This becomes even more true in the modern world: since, for educated people, Christian metaphysics is no longer believable, only in philosophy, if anywhere, is any kind of consolation to be found.

As I have already suggested, Schopenhauer's doctrine of salvation, indeed his whole philosophy, is really an interpretation of death. Its foundation is idealism. According to Schopenhauer's idealism, death is simply the termination of the 'dream' of life. A dream, however, demands a dreamer, a dreamer who must stand outside the dream. It follows from idealism, therefore, that our real self is completely untouched by death. This is why Schopenhauer says that idealism is 'the most complete answer'[36] to the question of immortality, proving, as it does, the 'indestructibility of our inner [true] nature' by death.[37] Most of the time, of course, we use the 'equivocal' word 'I'[38] to refer to our everyday, embodied, 'empirical' self, and that does indeed terminate with death. Metaphysical insight, however, leads us to see that the true referent of the 'I' is the 'transcendent' self, the self that lies beyond time, and so beyond both birth and death.

This, then, is the heart of what Nietzsche takes over from Schopenhauer. His 'metaphysical need' to know the non-finality of death, no longer able to be satisfied by Christianity, finds a new satisfaction in the implications of Schopenhauerian idealism.

The Impact of Kant and Lange

About nine months after discovering Schopenhauer, Nietzsche became engrossed in another book: Friedrich Lange's *History of Materialism and Critique of Its Significance for the Present*. This work, which he read when it first appeared in 1866, provided him with something of a grasp of Kant's philosophy, a grasp he increased during late 1867 and early 1868 by reading Kant's *Critique of Judgment* and Kuno Fischer's recently appeared two-volume study of Kant.[39]

Lange's book is divided into two parts. The first contains a history of materialism from the ancient Greeks to Kant, the second a critical discussion of materialism from Kant to the mid-nineteenth century.

Lange represented the beginning of Neo-Kantianism, an abandonment of the metaphysical excesses of 'German Idealists' such as Fichte and Hegel and a return to Kant's epistemological modesty. Impressed by the advance of natural science in the nineteenth century, he was at the same time – like Kant – intensely worried by it. More exactly, he was worried, not by science as such, an estimable and vital enterprise, but rather by science turned into metaphysics – the metaphysical thesis of materialism, the thesis that ultimate reality consists of matter in motion and nothing else. Like Kant, who said that the aim of his *Critique of Pure Reason* was to 'sever at the root' the triple evils of 'materialism, fatalism and atheism',[40] he was intensely disturbed by the existential implications of this doctrine, its threat to religion and morality.

Lange's solution is a return to Kant's idealism together with his doctrine of the unknowability of the thing in itself. Science can and must explore the world of material nature, but ultimately that is merely a 'phenomenal' or 'apparent' world. It follows that, with respect to knowledge of ultimate reality, properly understood, science has nothing to say.

Lange's original contribution to the Kantian position is to show that metaphysical materialism is self-undermining in that *it itself* leads to the conclusion that it can speak only of an apparent world: fully thought out, the 'consistent, materialistic view...changes around...into a consistent, idealistic view'.[41] Thus science itself, in particular the physiology of perception, shows that our consciousness of, for example, colours, is not consciousness of something 'out there' in the world but is merely the brain's subjective response to light waves impinging on the retina. Science itself holds that the noisy, colourful, tasty, smelly entities of human experience are simply our own invention. But if that is so then, equally, the entities it itself postulates, the human brain, retinas, light waves and the like, must be human inventions, too. Science thus demonstrates its own ignorance of ultimate reality. Space, for example, Lange claims, might, in reality, have four rather than three dimensions without that making any difference to the character of our experience.[42] The moral, then, is that by quite properly showing that the mind constructs its world, science limits its own competence to the world of appearances. To human beings, laymen and scientists alike, ultimate reality is an 'inconceivable order of things'.[43]

* * *

Nietzsche writes to von Gersdorff recommending Lange as 'the best account' of 'the materialist movement of our times, of natural science and its Darwinian theories'. Yet in fact, he continues, it contains much more than that, offering 'infinitely more than its title promises'.[44] It does so since, far from being himself a materialist, Lange is actually, Nietzsche correctly observes, a 'highly enlightened Kantian'.[45]

Lange's own position, Nietzsche continues (here he is actually quoting Lange's own self-summary[46] without making it clear that that is what he is doing), can be summarised in the following three sentences:

(1) The sensible world is the product of our own faculty of organization.
(2) Our visible (bodily) organs are, like all other parts of the world of appearance, only pictures of an unknown object.
(3) What our faculty of organization [the 'self in itself'] really is, therefore, is just as unknown as the real outer object [the 'thing in itself']. In each case we experience only their products.

So, Nietzsche concludes in his own words, 'the true essence of things, the thing in itself, is...unknown to us'.[47]

Criticising Schopenhauer

Sometime in late 1867 or early 1868, about a year after penning the above synopsis, Nietzsche applies Lange's 'enlightened Kantianism' to Schopenhauer's philosophy in an extended critique of the latter. The focus of the critique is Schopenhauer's claim, made more than thirty times in Book II of the first edition of *The World as Will*, to have cracked the problem of the nature of the thing in itself, to have discovered it to be 'will'.

'The attempt to explain the world according to a single factor', Nietzsche writes in his notebooks, 'is a failure':

> The question all metaphysicians yearn to answer...as to whether nature can finally be fathomed, is answered by Schopenhauer with a definite 'Yes'...The solution to the last and most important riddle of the world is...the groundless, knowledge-less will...But this is a dubious discovery. The first objection...is that the concept of a thing in itself is merely a hidden category. In the place of the Kantian X he places the will, but only with the help of a poetic intuition, for the attempted logical proof can satisfy neither Schopenhauer nor us. In Schopenhauer's favour,...there *can* be a thing in itself though only in the sense that everything that can be thought up by a philosophical head is possible in the domain of the transcendent. And this possible thing in itself *can* be the will but...that is a mere guess...The world will not fit as comfortably into his system as Schopenhauer had hoped in the intoxication of first discovery. In his old age he complained that the most difficult problems of philosophy are not solved even by his own philosophy, by which he meant the question of the limits of individuation...His system is permeated by contradictions. Schopenhauer says that, as thing in itself, the will is free of all the forms of its appearance...It is, he says, "never an object, since everything that is an object is mere appearance...But he demands that what is never an object can be objectively thought...he decorates it with predicates, like bright clothes, drawn from the world of appearances...thus the [real, Kantian] concept 'thing in itself' is quietly abandoned and another secretly substituted.[48]

In a word, then, Lange's central impact on Nietzsche is to make him reject what appears to be the most central and distinctive claim of Schopenhauer's philosophy, its identification of ultimate reality as 'will'. What is puzzling, however, is that this rejection diminishes Nietzsche's dedication to the 'master' not a jot. On the contrary, it increases it: 'You will see that from Lange's "strict, critical standpoint"', he concludes his letter to von Gersdorff, 'our Schopenhauer remains to us, indeed becomes even more to us'.[49] And that his spell did indeed remain and increase is proved by, as we shall see, the intensely Schopenhauerian character not only of the friendship with Wagner but also of Nietzsche's first book, *The Birth of Tragedy*, which grew out of it. But how on earth could it have happened that the reading of Lange and consequent critique of Schopenhauer intensified rather than diminished his devotion to the master?

Reconstructing Schopenhauer

Nietzsche's observation that *The World as Will* is 'permeated by contradictions' is entirely just. The most fundamental contradiction is the following.

Schopenhauer's doctrine of 'salvation', as we have noted, is really the provision of a 'consolation' for death. Its foundation lies in the evident consequence of idealism that the true self, the dreamer of the 'dream' of life, is untouched by death. The question, though, is whether this doctrine is really consoling at all. For if the claim that the thing in itself is the 'will' is true, the claim repeated many times in Book II, then the real self has to *be* the will, the one and only ultimately real entity. But, Schopenhauer holds, the will is both the 'bearer'[50] of all the world's pains, past, present and future, and also their *source*: as the only reality, it has to be the source of everything and is therefore responsible for the fact that life is suffering; for the fact that the world is the '*worst* of all possible worlds',[51] possessing as it does the character of a concentration camp. The world will is, therefore, fundamentally *evil*: at bottom, Schopenhauer says, 'nature is not divine but demonic', 'devilish'.[52] There is thus an 'eternal justice' in the world; an exact balance between the wickedness of its essence and the wretchedness of its fate.[53]

But if *that* is what our true self is then, far from receiving 'consolation' in the face of death, to realise the character of one's true self is to descend into a realm of cosmic self-disgust. Acceptance of Schopenhauer's philosophy then becomes a descent into a terrible kind of madness. Life is suffering and so not worth living. But suicide is not worth contemplating either, since death merely transforms personal into cosmic suffering – which one thoroughly deserves on account of being fundamentally evil. So one's choice is between hell and – hell. In short, if the will is the thing in itself then there can be *no* doctrine of 'salvation' in Schopenhauer's philosophy.

But, of course, there *is* such a doctrine. The mystics, we have seen (pp. 85–6 above), know about it, know that the reality beyond the 'dream' is 'divine', the object of ecstatic, 'pantheistic consciousness'. So Nietzsche is absolutely right: at the heart of *The World as Will* is a crippling contradiction, a contradiction between the conclusion of Book II and the conclusion of Book IV. At the end of Book II reality is at bottom 'demonic'. At the end of Book IV it is at bottom 'divine'. Only the fact that several hundred pages separate the two conclusions makes it possible to miss this contradiction.

Nietzsche, as we saw, reports that in old age Schopenhauer admitted that his philosophy had not solved 'the most difficult problems of philosophy' (p. 91 above). This is correct. What Nietzsche is referring to is the fact that in the later, expanded 1844 edition of the masterwork, Schopenhauer begins to severely qualify the earlier, bald assertion, made in the 'intoxication' of youth, that the will is the thing in itself: he now begins to insert into the work's new, second volume remarks like 'the question of what that will which manifests itself in the world and as the world is ultimately and absolutely in itself…can never be answered'.[54] But given the avidity with which Nietzsche and his fellow disciples pounced upon any scrap of information they could discover about 'the master', they may also have known of a letter Schopenhauer wrote to his literary executor, Julius Frauenstädt, eight years before his death, in which he says that his philosophy seeks to describe the thing in itself only 'in relation to [i.e., as] appearance'. 'What the thing in itself is apart from that relation' Schopenhauer continues, he does not say 'because I do not know what it is'.[55] The effect of this is to withdraw 'will' to the appearance side of the appearance/reality dichotomy. Though 'will' provides a deep*er* account of the world than its description in terms of material bodies, the world it describes remains in the realm of appearance. 'Will' is, then, as one might loosely put it, a description of penultimate rather than of ultimate reality. In the final analysis, the will – *as* will – belongs to the 'dream'.

In the end, then, Schopenhauer reaffirms Kant's position that the thing in itself is, to philosophy at least, unknowable. And this resolves the contradiction in his thinking, makes genuine room for the doctrine of salvation. (It is, perhaps, not without significance that he did this towards the end of his life; at a time, that is, when he himself would have been in increasing need of 'consolation' in the face of death.) And it is this position which, under

Lange's influence, Nietzsche endorsed – happily endorsed, since it allowed him to find in Schopenhauer, after all, what he could no longer find in Christianity, the satisfaction of his 'metaphysical need' for comfort in the face of death.

* * *

Of course, to say, with Kant, Lange, with the older Schopenhauer and with Nietzsche, that the reality standing behind the world of appearance transcends the limits of rational, philosophical thought and knowledge cuts two ways. On the one hand, it disqualifies the claim to know ultimate reality to be the demonic will. Equally, however, it disqualifies the claim to know that it is divine. If reality in itself is simply *terra incognita* then it can no more be known to be divine than it can be known to be demonic, and the doctrine of salvation gets no purchase. The question remains, therefore, as to why Nietzsche should say that Lange's 'strict, critical standpoint' actually intensifies his devotion to Schopenhauer (p. 91 above).

In trying to find an answer to this question,[56] a good starting-point is Kant, and in particular his famous remark that the task of the *Critique of Pure Reason* is to 'deny [rational] *knowledge* in order to make room for [religious] *faith*'.[57]

Returning to the older (and wiser) Schopenhauer, we see him, while agreeing with Kant in denying rational knowledge of the transcendent, offering, in a positive assessment of the knowledge-claims of mysticism, something more than mere 'faith' that transcendence is salvation. Philosophy, he says, being essentially 'rationalism', runs up against its limits, as against the walls of a prison,[58] when it tries to discuss the transcendent. It can point to a domain of 'illuminism' or 'higher consciousness' but cannot 'set even one foot thereon'.[59] Hence, his own philosophy, he says, at its highest point, is forced to assume a 'negative character'. It can speak of what is abandoned in 'denial of the will' but not of what is gained. Where philosophy comes to an end, however, mysticism 'proceeds positively'.[60] And when we reflect that all mystics, even though they come from widely different ages and cultures, report (according to Schopenhauer) the same experience, the merging of oneself with the divine, we can reasonably conclude that whatever it is they 'see' is both wonderful and real.[61] This conclusion, as we saw, is reinforced, according to Schopenhauer, by great art's 'stamp of truth':[62] to see 'the peace that is higher than all reason, that ocean-like calmness of the spirit, that deep tranquillity, that unshakeable confidence and serenity, as depicted by Raphael or Correggio, is to receive 'a complete and certain gospel: only knowledge remains, the will has vanished'.[63]

The colon in this last remark (equivalent to 'since') indicates that in order to validate mystical beatitude, Schopenhauer is appealing to the doctrine of aesthetic veracity expounded in *The World as Will*'s third book: since it is the will – practical interest – which manipulates and distorts perception, it follows that when we escape the will, as do authentic mystics, we become a 'clear mirror' of reality, completely 'objective'.[64] On a mind that is pure receptivity, reality impresses itself just as, in itself, it is. This is the doctrine followed by the youthful Nietzsche in his attempt to validate the reality of Schopenhauerian salvation. Commenting on his reading of Lange, he writes to von Gersdorff that the consequence of ultimate reality's inaccessibility to the rational mind is that 'art is free'. What he means is that intimations of the transcendent in art are free of the possibility of assessment, and so of contradiction, by reason: 'Who', he asks rhetorically, after assimilating Lange's Kantianism, 'would seek to refute a work of Beethoven or to find an error in Raphael's Madonna?'[65]

Under what I call 'intimations of the transcendent', Nietzsche has in mind, first and foremost, I think, what one (or at least he) 'grasps' through music. Schubert's famous 1817 hymn 'To Music' reads in part, 'Oh blessed art, in how many grey hours,/ When life's fierce orbit encompasses me,/ Hast thou...transported me to a better world'. This kind of 'salvation through music', we have seen on several occasions, was Nietzsche's repeated experience of the 'blessed art'. At fourteen, the Hallelujah Chorus made him feel part of the 'joyful singing of angels, on whose billows of sound Jesus ascended to heaven', leading him to decide that the sole valid purpose of music is to 'lead us upwards' (p. 4 above). Even after the loss of his Christian faith, the link remains between music and the divine: 'the communication of the daemonic', that is to say, 'a dim intimation of the divine...a feeling from out of which heaven suddenly shines forth' is the effect of great music (p. 38 above). (One might think here of the finale of Gustav Mahler's 'Resurrection' Symphony.) Nietzsche's experience and conception of music, as I have remarked, was, and up until the end of his sanity remained, fundamentally religious.

The question, though, that needs to be asked about this doctrine of 'salvation through music', or through art in general, is whether Nietzsche takes himself to be adopting a Kantian or a Schopenhauerian position. If he is following Kant, aesthetic intimations of transcendent salvation can only have the status of 'faith', can only provide subjective conviction with respect to the objectively unknowable. If he follows Schopenhauer, on the other hand, aesthetic, and above all musical, intimations are accorded the status of (non-rational) knowledge of the transcendent.

Two factors support the view that, in fact, the youthful Nietzsche follows Schopenhauer rather than Kant. The first is a letter of October 1868 to Paul Deussen in which he says that the latter's call for a 'critique of [Schopenhauer's] system' is, he supposes, acceptable if it means pointing out the various 'failed proofs and cases of tactical clumsiness' it contains – he had, after all, produced his own Schopenhauer-critique a year earlier. But, he continues, such a critique is entirely unacceptable if it means criticism of Schopenhauer's 'worldview'. The latter is beyond criticism since (he is here implicitly accusing the often-patronized Deussen* of spiritual denseness) it is

something one either grasps or does not. A third standpoint is inconceivable. Someone who does not smell a rose cannot truly criticise it. And if he does smell it then – *à la bonheur*! After that he loses the desire to criticise.[66]

What he must be referring to here under the rubric 'worldview' is the ultimate goal and final point of Schopenhauer's philosophy, the 'happiness [*bonheur*]'-creating doctrine of transcendent salvation. It is this, together with our 'metaphysical need' for it, that is beyond criticism. And what he seems to be doing is setting up intimations of the transcendent through art – or through philosophy considered, as he now thinks it should be, as a form of art[67] – as analogues of the information provided by the physical senses, in other words as modes of *seeing*.

* In his memoirs Deussen notes the unmistakable fact that 'Nietzsche's tendency always to correct me, to schoolmaster me and sometimes really to torment me, . . . will be clear from our on-going correspondence after the Bonn year' (J I p. 161). Nietzsche never granted Deussen the intellectual equality he accorded, for instance, Rohde or von Gersdorff.

A second reason for taking Nietzsche to be treating art as a mode of transcendent cognition is the character of the self-criticism that follows, a decade later, after his turn to 'positivism' and against the Schopenhauer-Wagner worldview. People suffering from 'religious after-pains', he says in *Human, All-Too-Human*, speak (with Schopenhauer) of 'the complete and certain gospel in the glance of Raphael's Madonna'.[68] Or at a certain point in the last movement of Beethoven's Ninth Symphony such a person is liable to 'feel he is hovering above the earth in a dome of stars with the dream of *immortality* in his heart: all the stars seem to flitter around him and the earth seems to sink further and further away'.[69] Beautiful though this is, Nietzsche is by now bent on debunking such 'deification' of art as indulged in by both Schopenhauer and his own former self. We have, he says, 'profound feelings' which seem to take us 'deep into the interior, close to the heart of nature'. 'But such feelings', he then adds, in a passage of insightful self-deconstruction,

> are profound only insofar as when they occur certain complex groups of thoughts which we call profound are, scarcely perceptibly, regularly aroused with them; a feeling is profound because we regard the thoughts that accompany it as profound. But a profound thought can nonetheless be very distant from the truth... If one deducts from the profound feeling the element of thought... what remains is the *strong* feeling, and this has nothing to do with knowledge.[70]

That this is *self*-criticism, that the paradigm victim of 'religious after-pains' is his own former self, is made explicit in *Ecce Homo*. In *Human, All-Too-Human*, he writes, choosing his words carefully, 'I liberated myself from that in my nature *which did not belong to me*'.[71] Deconstructing the thought that music takes one to the 'heart' of things is overcoming something that he once believed and so lies *in his nature*, though it is now a part of that nature he rejects and believes he has overcome. Such a rejection, however, lay far in the future. In 1868 Nietzsche possessed both a religious devotion to Schopenhauer that reduced to insignificance his various criticisms of 'the master' and a conviction that great music provides us with genuine knowledge of final salvation. Since Richard Wagner was equally besotted with both Schopenhauer and the idea of 'salvation through music', the two were thus fated to the immediate bonding that occurred in the drawing-room of Ottolie Brockhaus.

PART TWO

The Reluctant Professor

6

Basel

Basel in 1870

NIETZSCHE ARRIVED at Basel's central railway station on April 19, 1869, to take up his new position at the university. The city that greeted him was in the slow, and somewhat reluctant, process of opening itself up to the modern world by demolishing its medieval wall. In 1844 a new gate had been cut into the wall to allow a railway connexion to Strasbourg – Switzerland's first railway line. But it was closed at night so that, as the city council put it, free of the judder of trains, 'the citizens could continue to sleep the sleep of the just'. Further gates were cut over the next twenty years to allow more rail connexions, but they remained closed at night and were manned by police during the day. In 1868, however, over the protests of small businessmen who feared that an open city would ruin their business, the demolition of the entire wall began, until only three of the medieval gatehouses remained, preserved as memorials.

With 30,000 as opposed to Leipzig's 100,000 inhabitants, Basel must have struck Nietzsche as a small town, which would have pleased him given his preference for small, medieval towns over large, modern cities. And even though Basel was in the process of modernising, the medieval town was still very much in evidence. Elizabeth reports:

> My brother always expressed his delight at having known good old Basel; he declared that by this means he had been afforded a deeper insight into the Middle Ages. The whole community at Basel, with its deeply rooted customs and usages, was particularly pleasing to us Prussians ... Basel's magnificent ancient houses ... its staunchly united families who all paraded to church on the best of terms on Sundays; its old servants who worked in the same family from one generation to another; the old fashioned way in which its inhabitants greeted one another in their low-German dialect – all this struck us as belonging to an age long since buried in oblivion.[1]

Nietzsche spent his first weeks in the 'fairly horrible' Spalentorweg 2 near the Spalentor, the largest of the remaining gatehouses. The lodgings were, however, compensated for by the quality of the food at the central station, which was (as Swiss-German food remains to this day) like German food, only better.² After ten weeks he thankfully moved to permanent lodgings in the nearby Schützengraben (defensive trench). Number 45 (today number 47) was a four-storey terrace house at the then edge of the town, close to fields and gardens, and with an open view across the Rhine to Germany and the Black Forest beyond, yet at the same time only fifteen minutes' walk from the university.

Though to the English, Basel would have seemed very German, to Nietzsche, who had never before been outside Germany, it would have seemed very foreign. What he would chiefly have noticed, in contrast to Prussia, was the absence of the self-assertive state. There was no king – the rector of the university was elected by the professors rather than being a royal appointment – no aristocracy, and no cult of the military. Military parades, such a feature of Prussian life, were unknown. And in contrast to Germany, there was no national ecclesiastical hierarchy to which local clergy were subordinate.

The city council of what was, in effect, a city-state was run by members of the old Basel families. Nietzsche wrote to Ritschl shortly after arriving that 'here one can be cured of republicanism',³ making the point that rule by the haut bourgeoisie is likely to be no more democratic than rule by royalty. Basel's old patrician families derived their wealth from manufacturing. But they were also highly cultured: both Nietzsche's head of department, Wilhelm Vischer, and his hero, the great historian Jacob Burckhardt, came from such families. And they were genuinely concerned to maintain a high level of culture in the citizenry at large, something Nietzsche greatly respected:

> I am quite well aware of what kind of place this is . . . a city which endeavours to promote the culture and education of its citizens in a manner so lavish as to be quite out of proportion to its size. It thus represents a comparison that is a shameful rebuke to much larger cities . . . so much more is *done* for these things here than elsewhere.⁴

In general, Nietzsche's Basel exhibited a tight interconnection of political, economic, and intellectual leadership that must sometimes have called to mind the ideal city-state of Plato's *Republic*.

Since Basel's patrician families were determined to avoid cultural provinciality, to keep their city at the forefront of European cultural and intellectual life, their focus was the university. Its function was to be not just an institute for technical training but also, as the city council put it, 'the hearth of the cultural-spiritual [*geistige*] enlivenment of the citizenry'. Its single building was situated a short walk from the red-sandstone cathedral on the Rheinsprung (Rhine-leap), a steep street leading down to the old wooden bridge (with a chapel in the middle) which at the time was Basel's only means of crossing the 100-metre-wide Rhine. Founded in 1460, the university, in 1870, had fallen on hard times. This was due partly to a decline in the price of silk ribbon, the mainstay of the Basel economy, partly to the diversion of two-thirds of the income of the Canton of Basel to its rural regions, and partly to the fact that the new universities in Zurich and Bern were making it difficult to attract students: in Nietzsche's time, the total number never reached 200. Dedicated supporters, however, kept the university going. A 'Voluntary Academic Association' was founded with the aim of raising money to restore the university to its former glory and, by means of the regular offering of public lectures, to root its well-being in civic pride. As we shall see, a number of Nietzsche's first seriously philosophical essays were given as public lectures under the Association's auspices. This determination to preserve a tight bond between town and gown was the origin of the requirement, unique to Basel, that university professors should teach the higher classes in the Pädegogium, the local grammar school. In Nietzsche's case this almost doubled his teaching load.

University Life

In the beginning, Nietzsche affected to despise life in Basel. Particularly in letters to Sophie Ritschl, he describes Swiss women as boring, Swiss cheese as inedible, Swiss culture as provincial, and Swiss patriotism as something 'which, like Swiss cheese, comes from sheep and looks just as jaundiced'. Even Jacob Burckhardt, whom he would come to revere more than any other living person, he presented as living a low kind of existence, drinking beer night after night with bores in the pub.[5]

It needs to be remembered, however – Sophie Ritschl being his impossible love – that as well as expressing genuine homesickness, these remarks were mainly intended as an indirect way of saying he missed her. Soon, in fact, Nietzsche became proud to designate himself a 'free Swiss'. He had legitimate complaints about Basel: the fact that his salary, being paid six months in arrears, left him penniless for his first half-year, the fact that even when it arrived – Swiss prices being higher than anticipated – he found it difficult to afford holidays, and the fact of his enormous teaching load. But that he remained in Basel for a decade, the longest settled period in his entire life, and in 1873 turned down the offer of a chair back in Germany, in Greifswald, speaks importantly of his overall commitment to the place.

***

On May 28, 1869, Nietzsche gave his inaugural university lecture, 'Homer and Classical Philology', a lecture in which he repeated the critique he had been developing in Leipzig of the current state of classics. Properly practised, he asserted, philology should be a mixture of science and art with all its activity 'embedded in a philosophical worldview so that individual, isolated details evaporate as things that can be cast away, leaving only the whole, the coherent' – a preview of just what he would set out to provide in *The Birth of Tragedy*. Though he suspected that Leipzig had been scandalized when word of the lecture filtered back, it was well attended and well received in Basel. A fortnight after the lecture he wrote home that 'the people here were convinced of a good many things . . . and I now see clearly that my position here has been rendered secure by means of it'.[6]

Nietzsche held classes from seven to eight o'clock every weekday morning, with a total of eight student-contact hours a week. In addition, he taught six hours a week at the Pädegogium. In his first few semesters, his university lectures covered the history of Greek literature and pre-Socratic philosophy, Greek and Roman rhetoric, ancient Greek religion, Plato's life and teachings, Aeschylus's *Libation Bearers*, Sophocles's *Oedipus the King*, and Hesiod's *Works and Days*. At the Pädegogium he taught Plato's *Apology*, *Phaedo*, *Phaedrus*, *Symposium*, *Republic*, and *Protagoras*, selected books from Homer's *Iliad*, Aeschylus's *Prometheus Bound*, and Sophocles's *Electra*. On top of teaching duties, he had university council, faculty, and library committee meetings to attend, and while his election as dean of humanities in 1874 testifies to the respect in which he was held by his colleagues, it must have increased this enormous work-load still further. On top of all this, he frequently took over the classes of indisposed colleagues and gave numerous public lectures in order to raise the public profile of the university. And, of course, his Prussian conscience made it impossible for him to put less than a hundred-and-fifty-per-cent effort into every class he taught. It is little wonder that after only one year's service he was promoted to full professor – at the age of twenty-five.

As a teacher Nietzsche was both exciting and demanding. He treated his sixth form pupils as if they were already university students, demanding a great deal of independent research. The best of them he passed on to his alma mater in Leipzig. He also formed a social bond with them, putting on five-course dinners at the ends of the semesters.[7] Nietzsche was one of those teachers with an instinctive and effortless command of discipline. In a sketch for *Ecce Homo* (only part of which appears in the work itself), he recalls that

> at bottom I belong among those involuntary educators who neither need nor possess ped-agogical principles. The sole fact that in seven years of teaching the senior class at the Basel Pädegogium I did not have occasion to mete out a single punishment, along with the fact that, as I was later assured, even the laziest pupils worked hard when they were in my classes, gives some indication of this. A clever little stratagem from my teaching days remains in my memory: whenever a pupil failed to recite adequately the topic of the previous class, pub-licly I always blamed myself – I said for example that everyone had a right to demand of me further elucidation and commentary if what I had said was too cursory or vague. A teacher has an obligation to make himself accessible to *every* level of intelligence…I've been told that this little stratagem was more effective than any sort of scolding. – In my dealings with my grammar school pupils and university students I never had any real difficulty.[8]

Some of Nietzsche's claims in *Ecce Homo* are, we shall see, more than a little fanciful. But that this is not one of them is confirmed by students' recollections. One Pädegogium student, for instance, recalls that 'not one of our schoolboy tricks passed unnoticed by him', and reports an occasion when

> one of us (now discharging his duties as a highly respected principal of a training college) who had not prepared his work well was called upon shortly before the end of the lesson to construe a certain sentence. Standing up, and with an apparent eagerness for the task, he recited the Greek text which he had to construe, as slowly as he could until the bell rang. With a view to making assurance doubly sure, he read one more sentence, then confid-ently stopped. Nietzsche did not move. Our schoolboy's brow grew wet with perspiration. 'Professor', he stammered, 'have you not perhaps overlooked the bell that has just rung?' Nietzsche looked straight at him for a moment, and then, without moving a muscle, cor-rected him by saying: 'You mean to say, I did not *hear* it', and then left the room. On the following day he began his lesson by turning to the same pupil and saying smartly, 'Now sir, you construe'.[9]

In sum, Nietzsche was one of those rare teachers able to inspire and shape an entire life, a true 'educator' in, as we shall see, his own rich sense of the word.

One of his students recalls not only Nietzsche's quality as a teacher – 'he treated us more as comrades than as the mischievous wild urchins that we actually were' – but also his appearance: 'Physically he was of a delicate and refined build, with a rather feminine way about him, in stark contrast to his martial moustache, which seemed to overcompensate for the rest of his features'.[10] Nietzsche's appearance excited frequent comment because of an evident attention to it amounting, almost, to dandyism. In accordance with the style of the day (the opposite of today's death-evading cult of youth) he took great pains, as Elizabeth records, to select 'only those styles and materials which would give him an elderly appearance; he absolutely repudiated anything in the way of a youthful or smart cut, and he approved only of those clothes, fashions and hats which were patronised by elderly men'.[11] The famous moustache, of course, already of sizeable proportions, added to the elderly effect.

Colleagues and Friends

For the most part, Nietzsche's colleagues at the university showed him an amiability unusual in academia. During his first year, indeed, he complained of being overwhelmed by dinner invitations. The colleagues who were most important to him were Wilhelm Vischer-Bilfinger, Johann Jacob Bachofen, Ludwig Rütimeyer, and, most important of all, Jacob Burckhardt.

Vischer-Bilfinger was a major force in university administration. A classicist himself, he had refounded the classics department in 1861. Always sympathetic to Nietzsche – it was he, as we saw, who arranged his appointment – he did his best to smooth his protégé's path throughout the decade in Basel. Bachofen, like Vischer-Bilfinger a member of one of Basel's patrician families, was a maverick ethnologist interested in the communal origins of early humanity. Like Nietzsche, he rejected the dry-as-dust, speculation-shy, detail-obsessed 'scientific' study of the past. His fundamentally Christian outlook prevented a deep intimacy between himself and Nietzsche, though the latter was predictably attracted to his wife, who was thirty years younger than her husband but only one year younger than Nietzsche. Rütimeyer was a professor of anatomy and zoology who nourished the scientific side of Nietzsche's nature by, in particular, introducing him to critiques of Darwin's theory of evolution.

Burckhardt

With Jacob Burckhardt (1818–97) Nietzsche developed much closer and longer-lasting relations than with the other three. Born into one of the most patrician of Basel families, he was of the same generation as Wagner and Nietzsche's father. Like Nietzsche he was multi-talented, a gifted poet, artist, playwright (for puppet theatres), and musician. Nietzsche came to worship him, not only as a towering intellect but also as a great teacher and great human being. As he was going mad in January, 1889, he wrote to Burckhardt: 'you (*Sie*) are – you (*du*) are – our great, greatest teacher'.[12] The switch from the formal to the familiar 'you', here, is revealing: losing touch with reality, Nietzsche claimed an intimacy which, though he yearned for and sometimes claimed to be approaching it,[13] he never truly possessed.

The reason lay not merely in the differences in age and taste – Burckhardt always disliked the Wagner phenomenon, with which Nietzsche was becoming ever more enamoured – but also in Burckhardt's fragile, retiring, asocial personality. Though a charismatic teacher, he was a depressive who feared his own collapse into terminal despair. A note from the summer of 1875 – 'those who are repressed out of desperation, like Jacob Burckhardt'[14] – shows that Nietzsche had, in fact, some grasp of this. Burckhardt, of course, understood Nietzsche's intellectual brilliance and appreciated him as a tremendous asset to the university. Often he engaged in intense, extended conversations with the young philologist. But friendship, as opposed to collegiality, he never granted Nietzsche – or anyone much.

Burckhardt is best known for *The Culture of the Renaissance in Italy*, a work which exercised a profound influence on Nietzsche's mature thought. It appeared in 1860 and has never gone out of print. It was this work, more than any other, which established the concept of the Italian fourteenth and fifteenth centuries as a decisive rupture with the medieval past that constituted the birth of modernity. The work emphasises the Italian Renaissance as the first emergence of powerful, self-conscious individualism, which Burckhardt saw as a Janus-faced phenomenon: on the one hand, it produced an outbreak of ferocious sensuality, violence, and warfare; on the other, the art of Raphael, Leonardo, and Michelangelo. (Given the Swiss connection, Burckhardt's account of the Renaissance is probably the more or less remote origin of the famous lines

Italy for thirty years under the Borgias had warfare, terror, murder, bloodshed, but produced Michelangelo, da Vinci, and the Renaissance. And Switzerland had brotherly love and five hundred years of democracy and peace. And what did they produce? The cuckoo clock.)*

Overbeck

Nietzsche desperately missed his friend Rohde, who, during the first Basel year, was on an extended tour of Italy. He writes to him with a loving affection that might raise a few modern eyebrows:

Think of staying a time with me on your return trip [from Italy]: it might be the last chance for a long time. I miss you quite unspeakably . . . It's a quite new feeling to have no one on the spot with whom one can speak of the best and the worst in life . . . my friendship . . . is really becoming somewhat pathological: I beg you like a sick man: come to Basel.[15]

But since he also writes to his prudish mother in the same vein – 'I wish my friend Rohde were here – it's troublesome to have to find an intimate friend again'[16] – it is evident he had nothing to hide. In 1871 he applied for a chair in philosophy partly to align his profession with where he found his heart increasingly to be, but, even more pressingly, to get Rohde to Basel as his successor to the chair of philology. (As we shall see, the application came to nothing.)

In April 1870, however – again as a result of the recruitment efforts of Vischer-Bilfinger – a young theologian who did a great deal to alleviate Nietzsche's desire for a soul brother joined the university. Franz Overbeck (see Plate 10) came to share number 45

---

* The lines are from the 1949 movie *The Third Man* and were invented either by Graham Greene, who adapted the script from his own novel, or by Orson Welles, who spoke the lines in the character of Harry Lime. The director was Carol Reed.

Schützengraben. The two of them christened their house the *Gifthütte* (poison cottage) after a tavern with the forbidding name of *Das Gifthüttli** ('poison cottage' in Swiss dialect), about the half-way point of the short walk from home to university. Overbeck and Nietzsche were to dine together virtually every evening for the next five years.

Overbeck was seven years older than Nietzsche. Though German, his father had become a naturalized Briton, and as a young man Franz carried a British passport. His mother was French and he himself grew up in St. Petersburg. He spoke English, French, and Russian at home, and first learnt German when he arrived in Germany to attend school in Dresden at the age of eleven. Overbeck's inaugural lecture was titled 'On the Origin and Right of a Purely Historical Approach to the New Testament'. Having lost his faith (without it being the trauma it was for Nietzsche), he approached the Bible not as a believer but as a philologist studying an historical document. In 1873 he openly declared that he and his wife no longer regarded themselves as belonging to the Christian church – to the delight of Nietzsche, who gleefully declared that 'Some day our house [the poison cottage] will be one of ill-repute'.[17] Though Overbeck's apostasy precluded him from ever gaining a position in a German university – he remained in Basel the rest of his professional life – that no one tried to sack him testifies to the tolerance of the Basel elders.

Overbeck became the one friend who remained faithful to Nietzsche his entire life. He was also the one friend with whom Nietzsche never quarrelled: 'Our friendship was without shadows', Overbeck recorded. Nietzsche wrote in turn,

> Overbeck is the most serious, candid, personally lovable, and least complicated person and researcher that one could wish for as a friend. At the same time he has that radical quality I need to have in all the people with whom I associate.[18]

In 1879, at the lowest point in his health, Nietzsche would confess that Overbeck's loyalty and friendship had saved his life: 'In the midst of life I was "surrounded" by my good Overbeck – otherwise that other companion would have perhaps have risen up to greet me: *Mors*'.[19] Ten years later, as we shall see, Overbeck literally saved Nietzsche's life.

Isle of the Blessed

In spite of his diligence in discharging his duties, Nietzsche was never comfortable inside the skin of a university professor. In the first place, there were the reservations about classical philology and the increasing vulnerability to the seductions of philosophy he had brought with him from Leipzig. But even if he had been successful in his application for the chair of philosophy, he would still have felt uncomfortable. For what really bothered him was the repression of individuality, the necessity to conform to the expectations placed on a professor, to become a cog in the academic machine. 'I have become', he wrote Sophie Ritschl in self-disgust, 'the model of the German professor', covered in (chalk) 'dust', an 'educated mole'.[20] To Rohde he wrote in early 1870 that he doubted he could ever be a 'proper philologist' and envied his friend roaming through Italy, 'free as a desert animal'.

---

* Possibly the name derived from an ancient joke about the quality of the beer; possibly there had once been an arsenic mine on the spot.

(Rohde, on the other hand, almost certainly envied Nietzsche's academic success and financial security.) The heaviest burden, Nietzsche continues, is 'always having to represent to people the role of the teacher, the philologist, and that I have to prove myself as such to everyone I meet'. This noble profession, he continues, 'has something aggressive about it',[21] aggressive towards the expression of free individuality.

In fact, however, Nietzsche was able on a regular basis to escape the life of an 'educated mole'. He discovered a 'refuge beyond price'[22] in a place called Tribschen, about three hours away by (invariably punctual) train.

Tribschen is a lakeside promontory twenty minutes' walk along the lake from the centre of Lucerne. (Tolstoy could not stand Lucerne because, then as now, it was overrun by tourists, in the nineteenth century usually English.) It was here that, with money supplied by King Ludwig of Bavaria, Wagner had rented a large, square, four-storey, early-nineteenth-century house (see Plate 11), which he had a Paris interior designer decorate in a rococo style. This, as Elizabeth tactfully puts it, for a soberly Swiss house, was 'somewhat lavish in the use of pink satin and little cupids'.[23] Situated on a knoll above the lake and surrounded by tree-filled parkland grazed by cows and sheep, it commanded a spectacular view across the waters of Lake Lucerne: to the east, visible from the windows of the drawing-room, were the summits of the 2,000-metre Rigi and the three knuckles of the Bürgenstock, while to the southwest lay the often cloud-wreathed Pilatus. (J. M. W. Turner's many paintings of both the Rigi and the Pilatus had helped make Lucerne a favourite destination for English tourists in search of 'the romantic'.)

Wagner, exiled from Germany, had moved to Switzerland in 1849 and to Tribschen in 1866. By 1870 he was at the height of his musical powers, having completed the first two operas of the *Ring* cycle, *Das Rheingold* and *Die Walküre*, as well as *Die Meistersinger* and *Tristan und Isolde*, and was hard at work on *Siegfried*, the third part of the *Ring*. He was happier in Tribschen than he had been anywhere else. And the same was true of Nietzsche. At the end of his life, looking back through the pain and recrimination of a broken friendship, Nietzsche remembered Tribschen as 'a distant isle of the blessed'.[24] (Though, to be prosaic, it is more like a peninsula.)

Living with Wagner in Tribschen was the Frau Baronin Cosima von Bülow (see Plate 12). Born in 1837 (the same year as Overbeck), she was twenty-four years younger than Richard and only seven years older than Nietzsche. The illegitimate daughter of the great pianist-composer Franz Liszt and the formidable, but maternally negligent, Countess Marie d'Agoult, she was the estranged wife of Liszt's favourite pupil and Wagner's conductor, Hans von Bülow.* Also living at Tribschen were Cosima's four daughters, Daniela, Blandine, Isolde, and Eva, the former two fathered by von Bülow, the latter two by Wagner. It says a great deal for the tolerance of the largely Catholic Lucerners that they allowed this scandalously bohemian couple to live in their midst.

In addition to the Wagner–Bülow composite family, the extended household contained a governess, a nurse, five servants, two dogs, several cats, a peacock and a peahen (who obviously squabbled a lot, since they were called Wotan and Fricka), a horse gifted by King Ludwig, called Grane (otherwise, Brunhilde's steed in the 'Ride of the Valkyries'), and

---

* Von Bülow conducted the first performances of *Tristan* in 1865 and of *Die Meistersinger* in 1868. In 1875, in Boston, he conducted the world premiere of Tchaikovsky's first piano concerto. Though Cosima left him for Wagner in 1868, he never seemed to bear a grudge, continuing to champion Wagner's music, as well as Brahms's, until the end of his career.

numerous cows, chickens and sheep. Presumably to harmonise with the rococo decor of the house, Wagner frequently dressed up in his famous seventeenth-century Flemish painter's outfit – black velvet coat, black satin breeches, black silk stockings, a large, black floppy hat pulled down like a beret over one ear, and a satin cravat tied in a large bow over his lace and linen shirt. In general the household constituted, as Cosima puts it, 'the usual confusion of genius-creating, children-confusion, people relaxing noisily, animal-idolatry, etc'.[25]

Nietzsche had been in Basel only a month when he decided to take up the invitation to visit Wagner had issued in Leipzig. On Saturday, May 15, 1869, interrupting a paddle-steamer trip round the lake, he alighted at the Tribschen pier and arrived unannounced at the Wagners' villa. He stood irresolute outside the house for some time listening to the insistent repetition of a plaintive chord on the piano – it later proved to be from the third act of *Siegfried*, on which Wagner was working. He eventually plucked up courage to knock on the door, only to be told that the master was working and could be interrupted by no one, not even Cosima. He was, however, invited to return for dinner two days later on Whit Monday.[26] This second visit must have been a great success, since the young professor was then invited to return for the celebration of Wagner's fifty-sixth birthday on May 22. Teaching commitments made this impossible, but Nietzsche was back at Tribschen for the weekend of June 5–7, and was thus present when Cosima gave birth to the Wagners' first and only son, Siegfried, on the sixth (an event legitimised post facto when Richard and Cosima finally married in August 1870). From then on he had an open invitation to visit whenever he wished, and in the three years between his first visit and the Wagners' departure for Bayreuth in the spring of 1872 did so on twenty-three occasions. He was given his own bedroom, often put in charge of the children, treated, in effect, as 'family'. (On one occasion Wagner asked him if he would be Siegfried's guardian should anything happen to him.) Nietzsche, too, felt himself a member of the family, referring collectively to himself and the entire Wagner menagerie as 'we Tribscheners'.[27]

As well as being present for Siegfried's birth, Nietzsche was also present on Christmas Day 1870 for the celebration of Cosima's – and of course another's – birthday. (Cosima had been born during the night of December 24–5.) About half-past seven in the morning, fifteen musicians, together with the extended family that included Nietzsche, gathered quietly on the stairwell of the house. What happened then Cosima recorded in her diary:

> As I awoke, a swelling sound came to my ear, ever louder. I could no longer imagine it a dream, it was music sounding, and what music! As it sounded out Richard came into the room with the five children and gave me the score of the 'symphonic birthday greeting'. I was in tears but so was the entire household.[28]

The music that received its first performance – Nietzsche had also attended the dress rehearsal held in secret in Lucerne the previous day – was known within the family as the 'Tribschen' or 'Stairwell Idyll' and to the world as the 'Siegfried Idyll'. During the morning, Christmas presents were exchanged. Nietzsche received a special copy of Wagner's 'Beethoven' essay, and a splendid edition of the complete works of Montaigne, of whom he was known to be a fan. In return he gave Richard what he had asked for, a print of Dürer's 'Knight, Death and the Devil', and Cosima a copy of his 'The Origin of Tragic Thought', a preparatory essay for *The Birth of Tragedy*. In the afternoon there was another private concert: first a repeat of the Siegfried Idyll, then a Beethoven septet, and finally the Siegfried Idyll once again, after which the musicians were released to travel home to Zurich.

***

Nietzsche accorded Wagner the same quasi-religious reverence he accorded Schopenhauer. Shortly after his first visit to Tribschen he wrote Wagner,

> The best and most elevated moments of my life are bound to your name, and I know only one other man, and that is your spiritual brother, Arthur Schopenhauer, for whom I have a similar reverence – yea, even more as *religione quadam*... At a time when the masses stand and freeze in cold fog it is a great privilege to be able to warm oneself at the light of genius.[29]

The letter is signed by 'your truest and most devoted disciple and admirer'. Three months later he wrote to von Gersdorff,

> I have found a man who reveals to me as no other the image of what Schopenhauer calls 'the genius' and who is quite possessed by that [Schopenhauer's] wonderfully intense philosophy. He is none other than Richard Wagner, about whom you should believe none of the judgments to be found in the press, the writings of musical scholars, etc. *No one* knows him and is capable of judging him because all the world stands on a different footing to him and is not at home in his atmosphere. There dwells in him such uncompromising idealism, such deep and affecting humanity, such exalted seriousness of purpose that when I am near him I feel as if I am near the divine.[30]

At the end of May 1870, Rohde, who had not seen his friend for nearly three years, visited Basel and was of course taken to Tribschen. After the visit Nietzsche wrote Cosima,

> Rohde confessed to me that he had experienced [in Tribschen] the high point of his fifteen-month journey 'into the blue': he experienced wonder and reverence for the total existence there which was permeated by something religious. I understand how the Athenians could have erected altars to Aeschylus and Sophocles, and how they gave Sophocles the heroic name 'Dexion' [receiver of the gods] since he had taken the gods into his home as guests. The presence of the gods in the house of the genius is what awakens the religious atmosphere I have reported.[31]

Soon after first visiting Tribschen he began to address Wagner as 'master' and to see his own career as taking second place to the composer's: on more than one occasion he offered to take leave from, even to abandon, his own career in order to dedicate himself full time to the amazingly ambitious project of building an opera house in Bayreuth custom-designed for the sole purpose of performing Wagner's operas. That Wagner never showed any interest in taking up these offers was due to the fact that, since Wagner thought of his music-dramas as the rebirth of Greek tragedy, Nietzsche was of most use to him as a respected professor of Greek who could certify that they were indeed such a rebirth.

Given this conception of himself as a satellite orbiting the Wagnerian sun, it is little wonder that Nietzsche developed a chatty and intimate relation with his fellow satellite,

Cosima, who was, in any case, nearly his own age. (The chat sometimes took on an anti-Semitic flavour with Nietzsche responding in kind to Cosima's violent anti-Semitism.) The intimacy led to Nietzsche's usual habit of developing an impossible love, one he would carry with him for the rest of his life. As he was going mad he began to refer to Cosima as his true love, 'Ariadne', and to himself as 'Dionysus', and to suggest that her relations with Wagner were 'in the nature of adultery'.

In *The Gay Science* Nietzsche outlines his conception of gender relations. Women, he says, find true satisfaction, exercise a 'surplus of strength and pleasure', in becoming the 'function' of a man.[32] (Since he had adopted just this 'feminine' role in relation to Wagner he was in a way, perhaps unconsciously, speaking from personal experience.) They do this, he continues, by, for example, becoming a man's 'sociability'. This perfectly describes – and was probably based on observation of – Cosima's relations with Wagner. For every letter Wagner writes Nietzsche she writes ten, and whereas Wagner's are usually short, even telegrammatic, hers, to her 'Dear, Dear Professor Nietzsche', often run on for five or six pages. And since Nietzsche had also adopted the role of a 'function' she had no compunction in setting him numerous tasks. He was commissioned, for example, to track down a lost picture of an uncle of Richard's, and was often sent on shopping expeditions in Basel for things unobtainable in Lucerne, for items such as silk underwear for Richard and puppets and a puppet theatre for the children. According to Elizabeth, however, in spite of his massive workload at the university, Nietzsche undertook these tasks willingly and with close attention to detail. Drawing on his own childhood expertise in the realm of puppet theatre, he complained to a shopkeeper that a puppet devil was not black enough and a king not sufficiently realistic. On top of these commissions, Wagner chimed in by delegating to Nietzsche the dogsbody task of overseeing the printing of *My Life*, the autobiography he had written at the request of King Ludwig.

What did the Wagners think of their young professor? Clearly they had no doubts about his intellectual brilliance, and in their long, three-sided evening discussions of culture, art, and philosophy, they deferred to him absolutely on all matters Greek – which Wagner could read hardly at all. And they really did enjoy, as well as finding it useful, having him as a member of the family.

On the other hand, they did not think much of something close to Nietzsche's heart and self-conception, his musical compositions. Invited to spend Christmas of 1871 once again at Tribschen, Nietzsche declined, ostensibly because he needed to work on his lecture series, *The Future of our Educational Institutions*. The real reason, however, was that, attempting to match the spirit of Wagner's birthday gift of the *Siegfried Idyll* the year before, he had left under the Christmas tree the score of his 'Memories of a New Year's Eve', a four-handed piano work (that expands on the theme of the earlier 'A New Year's Eve', track 13 on the Web site for this book). Cosima and Nietzsche had often played together, but in his absence, Hans Richter* took his place at the piano. While they were playing, a servant remarked that 'it didn't sound very good', upon which, finding her own thoughts articulated, Cosima

---

* Richter conducted the first complete performance of the *Ring* at Bayreuth in 1876, and later became conductor of the Hallé Orchestra and then the London Symphony Orchestra in England, to which he brought a hitherto unknown thoroughness of preparation. In his later years he became a keen promoter of the music of Edward Elgar. As a conductor he was monumental rather than mercurial in approach, focusing on the overall structure rather than the expressive detail of major works, a style, as we shall see, that Nietzsche came strongly to endorse.

broke down in a fit of giggles. Wagner left the room not, as they had at first assumed, in anger, but rather to control his own giggles.³³ (In Nietzsche's defence, however, it should be mentioned that neither Liszt nor Richard Strauss thought him too bad as a composer.)

The End of an Idyll

Tribschen was the place where Nietzsche felt more at home than anywhere else in his entire life. In the large-spirited, warm, funny, flawed, overflowing and overwhelming genius that was Richard Wagner, he found a father whom he could worship. As we shall see in the next chapter, Wagner was an intellectual father to Nietzsche, exerting a profound influence over *The Birth of Tragedy*. But he was also personally and emotionally a father, persuading him, for example, to give up the vegetarianism which, following von Gersdorff, he had for a short time adopted. In Cosima Nietzsche found a mother, fantasy lover, confidant, and friend whom he could look up to as an ideal of womanhood. (Literally look up: beaky-nosed Cosima towered over the severely vertically challenged Wagner – photographs of the pair (such as Plate 12) required her to sit – and she towered over the mildly vertically challenged Nietzsche.) And in the Wagners collectively he found an adopted family that breathed the air of high European culture and was, unlike his own, free of the stifling constraints of petit bourgeois morality: as he put it in a letter, 'In Wagner's villa…at the foot of the Pilatus in a magic lake-and-mountain solitude, we live together in the most exciting conversations, in the most lovely family circle, quite removed from the usual social trivialities'.³⁴ What made the conversation exciting was the sense of Tribschen as a world-historical pivot, the sense of the Bayreuth project as a new beginning for Germany, for European culture, and perhaps for humanity as a whole. Elizabeth, who visited Tribschen in July 1870 and again in the spring of 1871, has left a record of the atmosphere:

> I can still remember the last evening I spent there. The sun was just setting but the moon already stood full and bright over the luminous snowfields of Mount Titlis.* And, as the light of the sun gradually waned and surrendered the earth to the pallid glow of the moon, and the lake and the picturesquely shaped mountains grew ever more delicate, more diaphanous,…our animated conversation gradually subsided, and we all sank into dreamy silence. We four (really five) were wandering along the so-called *Räuberweg* [robbers' path] close to the lake. In front walked Frau Cosima and my brother – the former dressed in a pink cashmere gown with broad revers of real lace which reached down to the hem of the garment; on her arm there hung a large Tuscan hat trimmed with a crown of pink roses, and behind her paced a dignified, heavy and gigantic coal-black Newfoundland dog, 'Russ'. Then followed Wagner and myself – Wagner being attired in a Flemish painter's costume…I can still remember quite vividly how the shafts of light coming through the trees caught each of us in turn, as we walked silently along, looking out across the silvery lake. We listened to the soft murmur as the diminutive breakers lapped against the bank.³⁵

But the enchanted mood was not to last. From about the middle of 1870 Wagner began to speak of the need to move to Bayreuth. Faced with the collapse of his ideal world, Nietzsche

* 3,020 metres high, about 30 minutes by (modern) train south of Lucerne.

wrote to Cosima on June 19 that if they moved, he would like to take several years leave from the university and move to Bayreuth himself, where he would devote himself entirely to Wagner's project.[36] Two days later, he sprained an ankle and was laid up in bed for two weeks – sickness being, as Curt Janz observes,[37] his usual response to psychological trauma.

Wagner finally abandoned Tribschen on May 22, 1872. When Nietzsche arrived on the twenty-fifth only Cosima, the children, and the servants remained. Cosima was as sad at leaving their 'isle of the blessed' as he was, so he tried to cheer her up by playing the piano. To Rohde he wrote: 'Tribschen is no more. I was there for a few days – melancholy days – and walking as if among ruins'.[38] And to von Gersdorff,

> Last Saturday we bid a sad and deeply moving farewell to Tribschen. Tribschen has now ceased: we wandered around as if among sheer rubble, the feeling of sadness was everywhere; in the air, in the clouds. The dog wouldn't eat. If one addressed them one found the servant-families constantly sobbing. We packed up the manuscripts, letters and books – oh it was so miserable! These three years I have spent near to Tribschen, which I have visited 23 times – what they mean to me! Without them what would I have been! I am happy that I have at least engraved in stone the world of Tribschen in my book [*The Birth of Tragedy*].[39]

The Wagners' departure left Nietzsche bereft. At the end of his life, despite the hundreds of polemical pages he had by this time written against the great 'sorcerer', Tribschen still remains, in *Ecce Homo*, an enchanted dream:

> That which has refreshed me by far the most profoundly and cordially [was]...without a doubt my intimate association with Richard Wagner. I offer all my other human relationships cheap, but at no price would I relinquish from my life the Tribschen days, those days of mutual confidences, of cheerfulness, of sublime incidents – of profound moments...I do not know what others may have experienced with Wagner: over our sky no cloud ever passed.[40]

Nietzsche never took to Bayreuth. Though Wagner's grand house there was called *Wahnfried* – roughly, 'place of peaceful escape from the world's crazy delusions' (see Plate 14) – Nietzsche found it all-too-crazy. Though he soldiered on in Wagner's cause for another four years – with increasing degrees of doubt and increasing moments of friction with the 'master' – the old, sublime intimacy was never recaptured. It is hard to resist the conclusion that, emotionally, Nietzsche experienced the move from Tribschen to Bayreuth as a betrayal, as his second 'abandonment' by a father. Returning on a hiking trip to the Rigi in 1874, he revisited Tribschen several times. 'I missed much, much', he wrote Rohde, 'completely "disinherited"'.[41] If the Wagners had remained in Tribschen, *Human, All-Too-Human, The Wagner Case*, and *Nietzsche contra Wagner*, not to mention the rest of Nietzsche's mature philosophy, might never have been written.

7

Richard Wagner and the Birth of The Birth of Tragedy

OR THREE years, we saw in the previous chapter, Nietzsche was regarded by all concerned as a member of the Tribschen household. Along with emotional warmth and sublime music, Tribschen also provided him with an intensely stimulating philosophical environment, presided over by the spirit of Arthur Schopenhauer. To his 'wonderfully deep philosophy'[1] Wagner and Nietzsche were, as we have seen, equally devoted. Nietzsche sent his essays and lectures to the Wagners for discussion and scrutiny and thanked Wagner for the 'many purely scientific problems' that resolved themselves through their discussions.[2] And Wagner sent Nietzsche the completed 'Beethoven' essay, to which the latter replied, 'I can make clear to you how much there is for me there by way of learning your philosophy of music – that is, *the* philosophy of music – in an essay I wrote this summer entitled "The Dionysian Worldview"'[3] – a preliminary airing of the central themes of Nietzsche's first book. As noted, Cosima was no mere onlooker but rather an active contributor to the intellectual life of Tribschen. A woman of considerable education and perspicacity, she regularly bombarded Nietzsche with salvoes of often searching questions about his philosophical work. In dedicating his *Five Prefaces to Five Unwritten Books* to her in 1872, he wrote, 'in deeply felt respect and as an answer to questions raised both by letter and in conversation'.[4]

The product of this emotional and intellectual intimacy was *The Birth of Tragedy*. The Preface dedicates the work to Wagner, describing it as the continuation of a 'conversation' with him, a conversation he could have had with no other person. What made this 'conversation' possible was the fact that as well as being a composer, conductor, and poet of genius, Wagner was also a serious intellectual with a developed and distinctive worldview. Nietzsche scholars and enthusiasts have almost universally sought to deny Nietzsche's debt to this view,[5] on account of its undoubtedly unpleasant elements: anti-Semitism and, later on, German chauvinism. There is, however, no getting away from it: to really understand Nietzsche's book, one needs to understand 'the Bayreuth horizon',[6] as his notebooks describe it, within which it was developed, the 'Wagnerian spectacles', in the words of a contemporary reviewer,[7] through which it views the world.

The Wagnerian Worldview

Wagner's philosophical thinking focuses on four interconnected topics: society, politics, art and religion. I shall begin with 'society', with Wagner's *Kulturkritik*, his critique of the cultural condition of Western modernity. The critique focuses on two things: on Christianity and on the effects of industrialization and bureaucratisation.

Wagner was aware that, for most educated people of his time, Christianity no longer compelled belief. Nonetheless, he argues, it has left behind a pernicious legacy. Whereas the Greeks conceived happiness to be the normal human condition, the Christian worldview condemns us to life in a 'loathsome dungeon'.[8] Christianity teaches us to despise all things earthly – while contradicting itself by simultaneously preaching universal brotherly love.[9] Not that this was Jesus' doing. The Galilean carpenter himself was a kind of revolutionary socialist, a man of the working classes who really did practice the universal love he preached. Not he but rather the Roman Church (this will become a key theme in Nietzsche's later work) invented the other-worldly metaphysics that leads to contempt for this world.[10] In general, then, Christianity has been a destructive force that has left us a legacy of self-contempt.

And it has, moreover, prepared the way for the inhuman character of modern economic life. If man is a worthless being, then there is no reason not to treat him, as modern industrialised society does, as 'mere steam-power for its machinery'.[11] In modern society, that is to say, work has become nothing but wearying, dehumanizing 'toil'. Men have been turned into slaves of the machine, have, indeed, become machines themselves.[12]

This has had a terrible effect on human well-being. Since the masses are trained to be nothing but machine-parts, and are in any case exhausted by work, they are capable of nothing but cheap, mindless pleasures in the moments of leisure allowed them. But since cheap consumerism produces ever-diminishing returns, *boredom* becomes the salient mood of modernity. In the consumer society people are 'bored to death by pleasure'.[13] Part of Wagner's anti-Semitism consists in seeing Jews as particularly productive of, and given to, consumerism, though in his later writings he points the finger at the French: that which is engulfing modernity is 'French materialism'.

The decay of modern society has had a particularly deleterious effect on art. The mechanical reproduction of artworks and consequent 'democratization' of taste means that even the meanest among us can put the noblest types of art on his mantelpiece[14] – which numbs our ability to reverence great art. Casual familiarity, in other words, breeds contempt. When it comes to music and the theatre, all the work-weary audience wants and is capable of is 'distraction and entertainment'. The result is that modernity is no longer capable of the *Gesamtkunstwerk*, the 'collective artwork', that was the glory of Greece. Rather than being gathered together, as in Greek tragedy, with each art-form playing a vital role in the total artwork, the arts are now essentially separate, with each catering to a particular niche-demand for pleasure. Thus opera, and in particular French and Italian opera, panders to an audience interested only in music – music for easy listening. The plots are a joke, one talks through the longueurs between the big arias, and when they finally arrive one demands 'six encores' – destroying, of course, any possibility of dramatic continuity and reducing the occasion to 'a chaos of trivial sensations'.[15]

Turning to the literary aspect of modern life, Wagner observes that we live in a 'paper' culture. We suffer from 'lexicomania', from (in my own rather than Wagner's language) 'information overload'. This means that the character of our age is essentially 'critical', critical in a way that stifles creativity. Overwhelmed by 'cultural history', we succumb to the sense that 'it's all been done before' and are reduced to recombining past artistic styles.[16] (We might refer to this as Wagner's anticipation of 'postmodern nihilism'.)

Wagner's final major criticism of modernity concerns social atomisation. Whereas, in the past, we were bound together by the fellowship of a common purpose – he thinks, here, of the world celebrated in *Die Meistersinger*, the world of artists and craftsmen working together to produce the medieval cathedral – modern society is a society of 'absolute egoism'. Everyone pursues his own, selfish goals, the only cohesive force being the state. But the modern, bureaucratic – 'red tape' – state is worse than uncontained egoism. Aided by religious dogma and the press, it says to individuals, 'so shall you think and no other', mind-controls them into robotic instruments of its pernicious, militaristic aims.

* * *

So much for diagnosis of our parlous condition; what now of remedy? The key is Greece and above all Greek tragedy. Not, Wagner hastens to add, that we should seek a slavish restoration of the Greek through a 'sham-Greek mode of art' (the Victorian bank disguised as a Greek temple). Insofar as we admire the Greek, we should recreate it as a contemporary reality rather than as a fossilised relic of the past. And by no means should we admire everything Hellenic – in particular, not the 'dishonourable slave yoke' on which Greek economic life was based. Precisely the main goal should be to replace the quasi-slavery, the 'universal journeymanhood, with its sickly money soul' of modern society, with a 'strong' and 'free manhood'.[17] Nonetheless, says Wagner, it is the Athenian theatre which provides 'the typical model of that ideal relation, dreamt of by me, between theatre and public'.[18] How so? What, for Wagner, was Greek tragedy, and what distinguished it from the sick theatre of the present age?

* * *

First of all, Greek tragedy was not 'entertainment'. It occurred

> on none but special, sacred feast days, where the taste for art was coupled with the celebration of a religious rite, in which the most illustrious members of the state themselves took part as poets and performers, to appear like priests before the assembled populace of field and city; a populace filled with such high expectations from the sublimity of the artwork to be set before it, that a Sophocles, an Aeschylus, could set before the *Volk* (people) the deepest-meaning of all poems, assured of their understanding.[19]

Second, it was a 'collective [*Gesamt*] artwork [*kunstwerk*]'. It collected, or gathered, in two senses. First and most obviously, it collected all the arts, in particular words and music, together into a single artwork. (Though the music is lost, leading us to think of Aeschylus or Sophocles as purely literary works, to think this way, Nietzsche remarks in his notebooks, is like thinking of *Tannhäuser* as just words.)[20] Second, it collected the whole community together and so created and preserved it *as* community. In contrast to fragmented modernity, in Greece

> all division…all scattering of forces concentrated on this *one* point…all division of elements into separate channels must needs have been as hurtful to this *unique* and noble artwork as to the like-formed state itself; and thus it could only mature but never change its nature. Thus art was conservative…[21]

Notice that 'collection' in the first sense is taken to require 'collection' in the second sense, that the artwork can only gather the community if it also gathers the arts. If it fails to gather the arts, then the audience fragments into niche audiences for the individual arts. Fragmentation of the arts, Wagner believes, entails fragmentation of the community – a thesis that receives some support from the way in which, in contemporary society, different kinds of music operate as 'badges' identifying different, mutually exclusive subcultures.

How does the *Gesamtkunstwerk* gather – create and conserve – community? (Notice that, given that Greek tragedy is the 'model' of the 'ideal relation between theatre and public', in describing the Greek artwork Wagner is simultaneously designing the 'artwork of the future', the model of what his own music dramas are intended to be.) Fellowship and community that extend beyond the merely biological fellowship of common ancestry, writes Wagner, can only flourish where religion and myth flourish. The 'Hellenic races'

> solemnized the joint memorial celebration of their common descent [and so became *Greeks*] in their religious feasts, that is, in the glorification and adoration of the god or hero in whose being they felt themselves included as one common whole...they materialized their national traditions in their art, and most directly in the fully-fledged work of art, the tragedy.[22]

Tragedy, in other words, was a religious act, an act in which the 'national tradition' – the ethos of a people, their conception of the proper way to live – was articulated in the form of myth. Indeed, continues Wagner, as the rites of the temple descended into soulless convention (mirrored by the decline of the Church in the nineteenth century), the amphitheatre became *the* place where the essence of religion, 'religio-social convention', received its articulation.[23] The 'perfect work of art' that was Greek tragedy became

> the abstract and epitome of all that was expressible in the Grecian nature. It was the nation itself – in intimate connexion with its own history – that stood mirrored in its artwork, that communed with itself and, within the span of a few hours, feasted its eyes with its own noblest essence.[24]

It was able to do this because its content was myth, myth being a clarification and 'condensation' of 'the view-in-common of the essence of things', a view of 'nature...men and morals'.[25] In myths, that is to say (be they Greek myths or the Norse-derived myths of Wagner's own music-dramas), are incorporated the essential laws of what is and what ought to be: men should know they are not gods (witness the fate of Oedipus) and that power corrupts (witness the devastation wrought by Wotan's quest for the ring of the Nibelung). Greek tragedy, in other words, was essentially *didactic* (a quality that Brecht, who, like the Greeks, used both masks and music, attempted to recapture).

Since it is the essence of the *Volk* [people] itself that comes to presence in the artwork, in a certain sense it, rather than any individual, is the 'creator' of the artwork. The individual playwright is merely the clarifying articulator of communal ethos. The communal artwork flourished 'just so long as it was inspired by the spirit of the *Volk*...that is, a *communal* spirit'. When aesthetic 'egoism' raised its head in fourth-century Greece 'the people's artwork ceased'.[26]

Community or *Volk*, as Wagner conceives it, is what we might call a uni-cultural society; a society in which, whatever lower-level varieties of life-style there may be, everyone agrees on a fundamental conception of the good life – on fundamental 'values' – independent of those values being enforced by the state. It needs to be asked, therefore, why we should value the uni-cultural society. (Since this conception is the direct opposite of the twentieth century's ideology of 'multiculturalism', which now finds itself in such serious difficulties, Wagner's thoughts about community have considerable contemporary relevance.)

A *Volk*, writes Wagner, consists of all those who feel 'a common and collective want'. Authentic members are those who 'recognise their individual want as a collective want, or find it based thereon'. Within a *Volk*, collective need provides a basis, the only basis, for 'necessary action'. In other words, it gives life a goal and meaning. Where there is no necessary action there is only 'caprice'. All that remains, in other words, is the pursuit of wants that are not only 'egoistic' but also 'artificial', and therefore meaningless – the state of modern society. The communal artwork of the future, says Wagner, will reawaken 'holy necessity' so that life will reacquire meaning.[27] More specifically, *work* will become meaningful again and thus satisfying. In 'On State and Religion', Wagner explains that he parted company with the socialism of his youth when he realised that socialist politicians just wanted to rearrange the world of 'toil', whereas for him the point was to *abolish* toil, to reform work practices so that, as with medieval husbandry, they would once more constitute a 'beautiful life'; a life in harmony with nature and the seasons, punctuated by frequent 'recreations and festivities'[28] (the life, to make the point once again, that is celebrated in *Die Meistersinger*). Moreover, since necessary action addresses collective want, it will abolish classes – though not differences. Everyone, according to his or her own station, will work towards the communal goal. By becoming members of a team (or, one should perhaps say, choir), alienation between one human being and another will be overcome.

* * *

Central to the above thinking, very clearly, is the notion of *Volk*. The *Volk* creates and is conserved by the artwork; the individual finds meaning and community within the *Volk*. This raises the question of where Wagner stands on the issue of nationalism versus internationalism, localism versus cosmopolitanism.

Wagner observes that while the Roman Empire abolished the reality of *Volk*, and Medieval Christianity, by recognising only '*Christian* man', abolished the very concept, he wishes to revive the concept and reinvigorate the reality.[29] Yet – this is the socialist strain in his thinking – the importance of a flourishing *Volk* is not to exclude concern for universal humanity. Whereas

> the Grecian artwork embraces the spirit of a fair and noble nation, the artwork of the future must embrace the spirit of a free mankind, delivered from every shackle of hampering nationality: its racial imprint must be no more than an embellishment, the individual charm of manifold diversity, not a hampering barrier ... We must love all men before we can rightly love ourselves.*,[30]

* Even, one might ask rhetorically, the Jews? Theoretically, at least, we must. In the infamous 'On Judaism in Music', Wagner at least has the grace to place the blame for the status of the Jews as malign outsiders on Christianity's refusal to assimilate them. Logically speaking, the solution to 'the Jewish question' is thus assimilation (WMD pp. 51–9). What makes such paranoia so dangerous,

Wagner's cosmopolitanism reveals itself, too, in the insistence that the content of myth is both inexhaustible and true for all times and cultures, the only task of the poet being to 'expound' it in a particular way to a particular audience.[31] In 'On State and Religion' he rather surprisingly attacks 'patriotism' as a harmful delusion [*Wahn*].* It is harmful because it is simply an enlarged egoism which, fanned by the press, is responsible for the state of permanent – actual or incipient – warfare in which the modern world exists. (Patriotism, in other words, is the last refuge of demagogic scoundrels.) From this he concludes the necessity of monarchy, with the king's job being to stand above national politics, to be concerned for 'human interests far above mere patriotism'.[32]

How can Wagner consistently be both a nationalist and an internationalist? The remarks concerning the 'charm of diversity' and 'inexhaustibility of universal myth' suggest a synthesis between multi-culturalism and uni-culturalism – 'multiplicity in unity'[33] as Nietzsche later puts it – somewhat in the way in which 'the medieval cathedral' encompassed a host of regionally, temporally, and stylistically diverse manifestations, or a single language encompasses a host of regional dialects. Or we might think of a Beethoven symphony – with its inherent possibility of yielding infinitely diverse, but equally valid, interpretations – as a model on which to understand the idea of universal myth as susceptible to indefinitely many different interpretations within the different, as it were, dialects of different cultures.

In later life Wagner's nationalism took a different and much less palatable form. As Nietzsche put it in 1888, explaining his turn against Wagner, the middle-aged Wagner lost the 'cosmopolitan taste' of his youth, becoming instead *reichsdeutsch*, a Bismarckian jingoist.[34] Yet still, at least in theory, the older Wagner sought to reconcile his position with ultimately international concerns, writing, three years before the outbreak of the Franco-Prussian war, that

> to extricate ourselves from the tyranny of [France's] materialistic civilization … is precisely the mission of Germany; because Germany, of all continental countries, alone possesses the needful qualities and forces of mind and spirit to bring about a nobler culture'.[35]

German 'inwardness' must, that is, be extended – by force of arms if necessary – to save from itself a civilisation dominated by French decadence. (The perniciousness of this appeal to a God-given German 'mission' is revealed by the fact that precisely the same appeal to a unique national mission was used by right-wing intellectuals to justify Germany's entry into the First World War and by right-wing, German-philosophy-inspired intellectuals to justify the younger Bush's invasion of Iraq.)

however, is that, once Jews are cast in the role of a fifth column in the midst of the *Volk*, elimination presents itself as a ready alternative to assimilation.

* *Wahn* is a word Wagner uses with great frequency. It is hard to translate – Ashton Ellis wisely leaves it untranslated – because he distinguishes both harmful and beneficial forms of *Wahn* (religion is a beneficial form) in somewhat the way in which Plato, in the *Phaedrus*, distinguishes good and bad forms of 'madness'. ('Divine' madness, for Plato, is the inspiration essential to both great poetry and true love.) In itself, it seems to me, *Wahn*, as Wagner uses it, is a neutral term meaning something like 'set of beliefs that exceed any possible evidence we could have for their truth'. Nietzsche's notebooks of the Tribschen period are full of this use of *Wahn*, for which *Illusion* is used as a frequent synonym that is similarly ambiguous. Later on he will use 'error' in a similar way.

The Artwork of the Future

In Wagner's view, we have seen, modernity is sick. The heart of his remedy lies in the restoration of the collective artwork, the 'model' for which is provided by Greek tragedy. But what exactly will this redeeming artwork be like, this 'artwork of the future'; an artwork, that is to say, which 'presages th[e] life of the future and longs to be contained therein'?[36] What, in other words, is the theoretical template which Wagner the artist – this most theory-driven of all great composers – tries to realise?

It will be, we know, a work that 'collects' in the double sense of gathering the individual arts into a single work and of gathering the community into a clarifying affirmation of itself. But what about the internal structure of the work? What exactly is the relationship between the constituent elements, between, in particular, the principal players, music and words? There is no univocal answer to this question, since the answer given by the later Wagner is quite different from that given in his youth. I shall present, first, Wagner's early account and then his revised account, a revision that exemplifies the familiar parabola leading from the idealism of youth to the resignation of age but which was also crucially shaped by Wagner's discovery of Schopenhauer.

* * *

The younger Wagner emphasises, first of all, the need to restore 'organic unity' to the artwork. What must be overcome is the 'chaos' of disconnected bits that is Franco-Italian opera. (Nietzsche's 1888 description of Wagner as a gifted 'miniaturist' who lacked the capacity to construct genuinely unified wholes[37] is thus a particularly deadly insult.) There must be no 'ritornellos', no 'self-glorifying' musical interludes, no big arias, that disrupt the dramatic continuity of the work.[38] What is required between poet and musician is not competition but rather the 'spirit of community'. They should be like two travellers, one of whom (the poet) describes the land, the other the sea, but who then visit each other's territory and become one.[39] They are to collaborate in the following way. When words lose elevation (when, for example, they merely expedite the plot) the orchestra comes to the fore, conveying a feeling of foreboding or remembrance which underlies the drama – one might think here of film music. But where speech ascends the heights of poetic passion, the orchestra recedes into the background.[40]

Though this early account of the relation between music and words *sounds* very egalitarian, it is actually not so at all. For Wagner makes clear that the real threat to the unity of the artwork comes from musical caprice, from the composer's pandering to the desire of lazy listeners for easy melody – 'Nessun Dorma', 'One Fine Day', and so forth – the aria designed to receive 'six encores'. Ultimately, the dominant element in the work must be the words: passages in which the orchestra comes to prominence 'are never to be determined *by the caprice of the musician*, as a random tricking out of sound, but *only by the poet's aim*'.[41] And this, in fact, is the natural relation between music and words, a relation reflecting the origin of music in passionate speech: 'Song is just talk aroused to the highest passion: music is the speech of passion'.[42]

Wagner is not very explicit as to just why music must be ultimately subordinate to words. The ground *cannot* be that only words can produce unity, since there obviously exists musical as well as dramatic unity, the unity possessed by 'absolute' (purely instrumental) music when it is good music. It is, however, pretty obvious why words must be the dominant element of the collective artwork. If its function is to gather the community in a clarifying affirmation of its fundamental ethos, then the most crucial demand on the artwork is that *it should articulate that ethos*. And that is something only words can do. As Martin Heidegger puts it in the first volume of his monumental Nietzsche-study, 'a solidly grounded and articulated position in the midst of beings' is 'the kind of thing only great poetry and thought can create'.[43] If we are to renew our shared understanding of the good life then, in terms of Wagner's metaphor, 'land' has to take precedence over 'sea', for one cannot take one's bearings when one is, as we indeed put it, 'all at sea'.

The Impact of Schopenhauer

The philosophical works that roused Nietzsche to ecstasy during the Tribschen period were the 'magnificent'[44] 'Beethoven' essay of 1870 – Beethoven was important to Wagner because he regarded himself as, in Cosima's words, 'Beethoven's only son'[45] – and 'On State and Religion' of 1864–5. The latter, Nietzsche wrote von Gersdorff, alluding to the fact that the essay takes the form of a letter to Wagner's patron, Ludwig II of Bavaria,

> is a great and deep essay in which he explains to his 'young friend', the little king of Bavaria, his inner stance towards state and religion. Never has a king been spoken to in a more worthy or philosophical manner;* I was completely elevated and at the same time shaken by its idealism.[46]

These works were, however, written under the influence of Schopenhauer's *World as Will and Representation*, which Wagner discovered in 1854 and immediately reread four times. As Nietzsche observes to von Gersdorff, 'On State and Religion' 'seems at every point to spring from the genius of Schopenhauer'.[47]

What did Schopenhauer mean to Wagner? What effect did his *The World as Will* produce on the composer? It produced, or at least powerfully reinforced, a sea-change in, on the one hand, his views on society, politics, and redemption, and on the other, his views on the proper nature and significance of music. As we shall see, these U-turns are intimately connected.

Speaking with particular reference to *Tristan und Isolde*, the first of his operas to be entirely created after his discovery of Schopenhauer, Wagner wrote Franz Liszt in December 1854 that Schopenhauer's philosophy came to him 'like a gift from heaven'. Its chief idea, he explains,

> the final negation of the desire for life, is terribly serious, but it shows the only salvation possible. To me of course that thought was not new, and it can indeed be conceived by no one in whom it did not pre-exist, but this philosopher was the first to place it clearly before me...longing for death, for absolute unconsciousness, total non-existence...[f]reedom from all dreams is our only final salvation.[48]

---

* The competition is provided by Plato's attempt to persuade the Tyrant of Syracuse to govern according to the principles of his *Republic*.

And in *Tristan* itself the star-crossed lovers sing at length of their longing for 'oblivion':

> *In the surging swell,*
> *In the ringing sound,*
> *In the world-breath*
> *In the waves of the All*
> *To drown,*
> *To sink down –*
> *Unconscious –*
> *Supreme bliss –*

are Isolde's final words as she sinks 'as if transfigured' onto Tristan's lifeless body, thereby bringing both her earthly life and the opera to a close.

As Wagner says in the letter to Liszt, the thought that the solution to the problem of life lies in its 'negation' 'pre-existed' in his mind before he found it articulated by the great pessimist. Writing, in 'On State and Religion', to Ludwig, who had asked him (apprehensively, one assumes) if he still held the revolutionary doctrines of his youth, Wagner says that having discovered socialism to aim not at overcoming but simply at reorganizing the dehumanized workplace of industrial modernity, he decided, 'as it were, that "my kingdom is not of this world"', and that 'world-improvers' of whatever kind were in fact 'victims of a fundamental error, and demanded from the world itself a thing it cannot give'.[49] What this means for the king, his self-appointed tutor continues, is that he must become a kind of religious role model, a saint-like figure embodying the nature of 'true religion'. Recognising the irremediable 'unblessedness of human being', the 'innermost kernel' of religion is, continues Wagner,

> denial of the world – that is, recognition of the world as a fleeting and dreamlike state of mind reposing merely on illusion – and struggle for redemption from it, prepared for by renunciation, attained by faith.[50]

Redemption from, the 'Beethoven' essay adds, the '*Wahn* of individuality' and the 'hell of [an] existence filled with terrible discord'. Wagner concludes, with Schopenhauer, that redemption consists in transcending the illusion of plurality, in recognising that true reality is an indissoluble unity, an undifferentiated 'Oneness' which abolishes the very possibility of discord.[51] Religion, that is, points us to a self- and world-transcendence in which we experience the 'inner happiness' of the saint, sure in the knowledge of his other-worldly redemption; or the happiness of the martyr – the king, Wagner writes prophetically to Ludwig, is a 'tragic' figure. This tells us the task of great – that is to say, religious – art. Its task, Wagner continues (above all one thinks, here, of *Tristan*),

> is to lift us up above life and show it as itself a game of play: a game that, take it ne'er so terrible and earnest an appearance, yet is here again shown to us as a mere *Wahn* picture, so that in this way it comforts us and wafts us from the common truth of our distress.[52]

Three things are going on here. First, the affirmation of Schopenhauerian pessimism: life is suffering; remedial human endeavour can change its form but never its quantity and is therefore futile. So the optimism that is presupposed by schemes of world-improvement such as the socialism of Wagner's youth is based on delusion. More generally, politics is delusion, *Wahn*: moving from Tribschen to Bayreuth, as we saw, Wagner inscribed above the front door of the new house, 'here where my delusions have found peace, I name this house *Wahnfried* (delusion-peace)' (see Plate 14).

Second, the passage no longer affirms socialist materialism but rather Schopenhauerian idealism: nature, the everyday world, is but a 'dream' and so life is nothing but a 'game'.[53] This is what makes the third element in Wagner's later philosophy possible, an affirmation of the possibility of 'salvation' from this world of pain, salvation through transcendence to 'another world'.[54] Salvation, Wagner holds, will 'redeem us from the curse of appearances', from discord and pain. Of course we cannot provide a rational proof that there is a redemptive other world. Religious other-worldliness is in that sense *Wahn*, too, a matter of faith rather than reason. But it is healing rather than diseased *Wahn*.[55]

But how can we access this faith? How can we acquire the phenomenological experience of the reality of this world beyond plurality and so beyond pain? The key is music, music understood in the light of Schopenhauer's revelation of its true nature.

* * *

As we saw (p. 84 above) Schopenhauer held that while, along with language and conceptual thought, all the other arts deal with the visible world of appearance, music, in a non-conceptual manner, discloses to us the nature of ultimate reality, the 'thing in itself'. In the 'Beethoven' essay, Wagner says that it was Schopenhauer who first properly defined the position of music in relation to the other arts, indicating thereby his acceptance of this high, metaphysical claim for music. Being a layman, Wagner continues, Schopenhauer could not properly demonstrate his claim, but attention to Beethoven's musical development from his beginning as a showy and relatively superficial piano virtuoso to the profound unworldliness for which he is remembered shows that Schopenhauer was right.[56]

Failing to recognise Schopenhauer's great discovery of the uniqueness of music, Wagner writes, some people (foremost in his mind, here, is the musical formalist Eduard Hanslick) have applied the criteria of the plastic arts quite inappropriately to music, judging it in terms of the beautiful, our 'pleasure in beautiful forms'.[57] This was the position from which Beethoven, following the tradition of Haydn and Mozart, started. In his maturity, however, he showed us that the proper category for assessing the greatness of great music is not the beautiful but rather *the sublime*. When great music 'engrosses us, she transports us to the highest ecstasy (*extase*) of consciousness of our infinitude'. The highest music is, therefore, 'religious' in character. In communicating a 'holy', that is, redemptive, state, it is religion purged of 'dogmatic fictions'.[58]

This is the character of Beethoven's great music. It speaks the 'highest wisdom' in a language not understood by the reason of this most unreflective of geniuses. As the deafness of which he never complained overtook him he became, as it were, the 'blind seer'. (According to Greek mythology, Tiresias was struck blind by Hera, acquiring thereby the gift of second sight.) His wisdom brings us the 'highest comfort'. Who, Wagner asks rhetorically, on listening to the 'Pastoral' Symphony, has failed to hear the redeemer's words 'today thou shalt be with me in paradise'?* Beethoven gives us an 'immediate experience [of redemption] of

---

* Certainly Walt Disney hears these words, his classic *Fantasia* allowing a day in the life of Arcadia to grow out of Beethoven's music.

transparent comprehensibility'. His renowned cheerfulness is the 'world-creating Brahma' laughing at himself. Beethoven's Pastoral[59] and Seventh symphonies deliver us from all earthly guilt so that the after-effect, when we return to the everyday world of 'semblances', is the feeling of having 'forfeited paradise'.[60]

This elevation of music to the status of religion confirms, of course, Schopenhauer's claim that music is superior to all the other arts. In particular, it is superior to poetry. 'Poetry', Wagner now writes, 'must always be subordinate to music'. Schiller's words in Beethoven's 'Choral' Symphony are, as words, unimportant – it is significant that, in the final movement, the melody to which they are set precedes them as purely instrumental music. At most they help intensify the mood that belongs to the music. And in the *Missa Solemnis* the voices (aided, of course, by the fact that they sing in Latin) function as pure, musical sounds. Wagner here echoes Schopenhauer's remark that since the superficiality of words can but be a distraction from the deep metaphysical significance of music, the mass is superior to opera – superior because, through constant repetition, its words have become a mere 'solfeggio', meaning-free sounds.[61]

Wagner's reversal of his earlier theory of the relative significance of music and words is mirrored in his post-Schopenhauerian compositions. The discovery of *The World as Will* took place in the middle of his writing the *Ring* cycle (the libretto for the whole work had been completed much earlier) and came to have a profound impact on the character of the work. Whereas in the earlier part of the *Ring* – specifically, *Das Rheingold* and the first act of *Die Walküre* – the music is strictly subordinate to the drama, in the post-Schopenhauerian part of the cycle the orchestra becomes more and more dominant. In the second and third acts of *Die Walküre* and in *Siegfried* and *Götterdämmerung* there are long passages in which the words come close to being pure, Schopenhauerian solfeggio. In *Tristan* the drama is so slow and the music so long that the work is sometimes referred to as the opera without action. Nietzsche suggests that it can, in fact, be experienced as a purely instrumental work, a vast 'symphony',[62] while my own experience of (James Levine's version of) Wagner's last opera, *Parsifal*, is of a single, five-and-a-half-hour-long adagio movement. It may be this approximation of the later works to 'absolute'[63] music – had he lived Wagner planned to write only symphonies, after *Parsifal* – that leads Nietzsche to suggest in his notebooks that the term 'music-*drama*' is actually a bad one.[64]

Not only is music more important than words, it actually – again Wagner directly reverses his earlier position – gives rise to them: the music of a great artwork 'contains the drama in itself'.[65] What lies behind this idea, I believe, is Schopenhauer's analysis of emotion into a distinct phenomenological feeling plus an emotional object, together with the (in my judgment, correct) idea that music allows one to experience the universal 'inner nature' of an emotion divorced from its object.[66] So, for example, a real experience of sadness consists in the feeling of sadness plus the object or occasion of the emotion – the death of one's grandmother, perhaps. What 'sad', purely instrumental, music gives us, however, is 'objectless sadness'; it gives us the experience of sadness but without offering anything to be sad about. This, Schopenhauer says, makes it possible to supply a piece of absolute music with an official or unofficial text, which stands to universal feeling in the relation of an 'example'.[67] Hence, for example, the 'Pastoral' Symphony and the 'Moonlight' Sonata, neither of which titles were supplied by Beethoven. (The text may, of course, be visual, as in Walt Disney's *Fantasia*.)

All great art, claims Wagner, is in fact created out of, if not literal music, at least 'the spirit of music': Greek culture was so created, as was the art of the Italian Renaissance.*,[68]

* * *

In summary, then, Wagner's post-Schopenhauerian thought contains two fundamental reversals of earlier positions. First, anarchist-socialist optimism is replaced by pessimism about the human condition, with the result that 'salvation' is to happen no longer in a future state of *this* world but in, rather, *another* world. 'Salvation', as one might put it, is no longer redemption *of* the world but rather redemption *from* the world. And second, instead of music being the servant of words and drama, it now assumes priority over the words, which threaten to become, indeed, entirely functionless in the artwork. These changes are of course connected. For if, as in the early theory, the point is to improve the world, to revive community through the community-'collecting' artwork, then, evidently, the artwork has to be *about the world*. In other words, ethos-expounding myth, which only words can articulate, becomes the crucial element in the artwork. On the other hand, if, as in the later theory, one has abandoned 'world-improvement' as futile, then what one wants from a 'redemptive' artwork is something which allows one to *transcend the world*. Since, on Schopenhauer's account, this is precisely what great music does, music becomes the crucial element in the artwork.

Unfortunately for the clarity of his position, Wagner never clearly announces the abandonment of his early philosophy of life and art for this new, and diametrically opposed, one. He never clearly states that he has given up on the ideal of the artwork as an agent of *social* redemption, never clearly states that, according to his later thought, 'redemption' has become a purely *individual* notion. Even a reader as acute as Martin Heidegger missed this point. Heidegger writes that what Wagner wanted was that 'the artwork should be a celebration of national community . . . should be *the* religion' of the people. But, he continues, Wagner's 'attempt had to fail'. For he made music, and, in particular, a kind of music that launches us into 'sheer indeterminacy, total dissolution, sheer feeling' preeminent, whereas (to repeat the quotation) 'only great poetry and thought' – in short, words (assisted, perhaps, by action) – can 'create a solidly grounded and articulated position in the midst of beings'.[69] This misses the point, since by the time Wagner came to allow 'dissolving' or, in his own language, 'sea-of-feeling' music to dominate his works, he had, in reality, given up on the national community, together with all things worldly.

But Heidegger can be excused, since Wagner himself never properly resolved the inconsistency between his earlier and later positions. In the 'Beethoven' essay, written sixteen years after his Schopenhauerian 'turn', he still speaks of the 'redemption *of* modern civilization'[70] as a task for the 'German spirit',[71] and in 'On State and Religion', mixed in with the idea of the king as a role model of the religious turn to other-worldliness, is the idea, preserved unmodified from the socialism of the 1840s, of the king as the protector of the deprived classes and of universal 'human interests' as such – the best protector because he is above the clash of powerful vested interests, the nature of day-to-day politics.[72] Moreover, Wagner continues to celebrate the creation of 'national community'

---

* The full title of Nietzsche's book is *The Birth of Tragedy out of the Spirit of Music*. 'Spirit of music' indicated the depth of the work's debt to Wagner since it was coined in the latter's 'Beethoven' essay, which had preceded it into print by two years.

through art in *Die Meistersinger*, another wholly post-Schopenhauerian work. And the whole Bayreuth project that was the obsession of the last decades of his life was an attempt to create, as he explained on the occasion of the laying of the foundation stone in 1872, a 'German national theatre'.[73]

* * *

Nietzsche's first attempt to have *The Birth* appear in print consisted in a letter to the Leipzig publisher Wilhelm Engelmann. (The attempt was unsuccessful, the book eventually finding a home with Ernst Fritzsch, the Leipzig publisher of many of Wagner's own theoretical writings.) The letter says that although the work has something new to offer Greek philology (what Nietzsche was *supposed* to be doing as a professor of Greek) its 'real task is to elucidate the strange puzzle [or 'riddle', *Rätsel*] of our times, Richard Wagner in his relation to Greek tragedy'. He goes on to say that the work bears on issues recently aired by Eduard Hanslick (Wagner's opponent) and should therefore be of considerable interest to the musical world and to the thinking public in general.[74] We need not, I think, take 'real task' too seriously. Throughout his life Wagner continued to be a 'hot' topic, so that Nietzsche's books, as he knew, always found a publisher more easily when he could stress a Wagnerian connexion. Nonetheless the letter does, I think, indicate that at least *one* important element in *The Birth* will be the resolution of some 'puzzle' concerning Wagner's relation to Greek tragedy.

It is by now, I think, plain as a pikestaff what it is that constitutes the puzzle in question: it is the apparent contradiction between Wagner's pre- and post-Schopenhauerian conceptions of the artwork. This, as we shall see, is identified in *The Wagner Case* of 1888 as the fundamental reversal in both Wagner's theory and his practice.[75] Or perhaps, given Wagner's retention of many of his earlier ideas in his later thought, one should speak not diachronically about 'early' and 'late' Wagner but rather synchronically about a split personality, about the contradiction between the 'socialist Wagner' and the 'Schopenhauerian Wagner'. What we can expect, therefore, is that, *inter alia*, *The Birth*, to which I now turn, will provide a resolution of this apparent contradiction.

The Wisdom of Silenus

*T*he Birth of Tragedy* was written, I have emphasised, under the influence of Richard Wagner. But it was also written under the equally powerful influence of, as Nietzsche calls him, Wagner's 'brother in spirit',[76] Arthur Schopenhauer. While dedicated to Wagner, the work is also written, as he puts it at one place, 'in [Schopenhauer's] spirit and to his honour'.[77] This latter allegiance entails two crucial commitments. First, in company with (the later) Wagner, *The Birth* subscribes to Schopenhauer's idealism: the everyday world, the world of, in Schopenhauer's phrase, the *principium individuationis*, the world of individuality and plurality, of *things*, is mere 'appearance'; ultimately, as we saw, just a 'dream'. And second, again with Wagner, it subscribes to Schopenhauer's pessimism. Life, ultimately, is not worth living, since its dominant character is suffering.

Influenced by Wagner, I think, Nietzsche connects pessimism with individuality in a more explicit manner than does Schopenhauer. 'Individuality', he writes, 'the curse of individuality', 'is the primal cause of all suffering'.[78] Suffering is thus a *structural* feature of life as a human individual. As individuals, we are first of all condemned to death – in contradiction to the human essence, which is, in Schopenhauer's phrase, the 'will to live'. Nietzsche calls this the 'absurdity', the tragic yet 'comic' character of human existence:[79] whatever bubble of a life we blow up will inevitably be punctured by time and death. And second, as individuals sharing the world with a plurality of other individuals, we are condemned – in part for Darwin's kind of reasons – to disharmony, conflict, and pain. Pain and absurdity add up to what Nietzsche calls the 'nauseous' character of existence.[80]

Albert Camus said, to repeat, that the only serious problem of philosophy is 'the question of suicide'; the question of whether or not life is worth living. Nietzschean–Wagnerian–Schopenhauerian pessimism holds that it is not. Nonetheless, Nietzsche would say, Camus's equation is a misleading one since, for us, suicide is not an option. The non-rational but inescapable (biologically programmed) 'will to live' – the abhorrence of death as the *summum malum* – means that (with only the very occasional, biologically malfunctioning exception) we will choose existence 'at any price' over non-existence.[81] We have no option but to live. This transforms the problem. The relevant question is not whether or not life is worth living but rather, given that we *must* live, how to make it bearable, how to make the best of a bad job. This is where Greece, and in particular Greek art, becomes relevant.

The Greeks, Nietzsche suggests, were really Schopenhauerians. Their 'exquisite' sensitivity to the 'terrors and horrors' of human life is captured in their myths; in the fate of Oedipus, the wisest man on earth, condemned unknowingly to murder his father and sleep with his mother, of Prometheus, condemned on account of his love of man to have an eagle feed on his liver through all eternity, but most directly in the 'wisdom of Silenus'. Captured by King Midas and forced to divulge his wisdom, the companion of Dionysus declares 'with a scornful cackle',

> whoever is man can never achieve the most to-be-desired, can have no part of the best. For mankind, for man and woman, collectively and separately, the most preferable would be never to have been born. The next best, however – having been born – would be to die soon.[82]

In spite of such knowledge, however, the Greeks survived and thrived: though massively outnumbered, they defeated Darius's Persians and, *en passant*, as it were, created Western civilisation and brought it to a greatness never since matched.

How did they manage this? How did they manage to conquer the 'nauseous' character of life? Through, Nietzsche asserts, their art. This is where they become relevant to us: already in Leipzig, as we have seen, rejecting the blinkered professionalism that treated philology as an end in itself, Nietzsche had adopted the view that the *only* serious point of studying history, and in particular ancient history, is to use it as a 'polished mirror' in which to view ourselves.[83] We want to learn about Greek art because, through a 'rebirth' of the Greek artwork, we can hope to overcome our own 'nausea'.

Nietzsche analyses Greek art in terms of a celebrated duality which, as noted, was probably inspired by the 'favourite poet' of his schooldays, Friedrich Hölderlin (see p. 42 above): the duality between the 'Apollonian' and the 'Dionysian'. He distinguishes two principal types of Greek art, the Apollonian art of, above all, Homer, and the Dionysian art of Greek tragedy, of Aeschylus and Sophocles. I shall discuss these in turn.

Homer's Art

One of the confusing things about *The Birth* is that it uses 'Apollonian' in two senses. In the first it just means the everyday world, the world governed by Schopenhauer's *principium individuationis*. Since Apollo is the god of the boundary-drawing that creates individuality (as well as justice),[84] the everyday world is 'Apollonian' simply in virtue of being a world of individual *things*. In terms of the capacities of the human mind which generate that world, the Apollonian is the domain of the conceptual, the linguistic, the rational (of the left hemisphere, in terms of popular neurology).

In the second sense, 'Apollonian' refers to this world raised to a state of glory in Homeric art, its 'perfection', 'apotheosis', 'transfiguration'.[85] Whereas Christian art erects a non- and indeed anti-human ideal – none of us can have a virgin birth or escape sexual lust – Apollonian art, in its portrait of gods and heroes, does exactly the opposite. It 'deifies everything [human], whether good or evil'.[86] It was a radiant portrait of *themselves* the Greeks constructed in Apollonian art, the 'ideal image of their own existence'. Thus, concludes Nietzsche – making explicit that Homeric art is a religion, a 'religion of life not of duty or asceticism'[87] – do the gods 'justify the life of man by living it themselves – the only satisfying theodicy!' In this way the Greeks of the eighth century 'overcame ... or at any rate veiled' the 'terrors and horrors' of existence, seduced themselves into continued existence. 'Existence under the bright sunshine of such gods is regarded as desirable in itself'.[88]

What exactly is the character of this 'transfiguration' of human life? Frequently Nietzsche speaks of 'illusions' and 'lies',[89] conjuring up the idea of falsification, of sentimentalisation, a view of life with the unpleasant bits covered over. In fact, though, this cannot be his view, first because Homer's stories are *war* stories, packed with danger, death, and destruction, and second because, as he explicitly says, in Homer 'all things whether good *or evil* are deified'.[90] So *concealing* the 'terrors and horrors' of life cannot be the intended account of transfiguration.

Nietzsche speaks of Apollonian art as 'transform[ing] the most terrible things by joy in mere appearance and redemption through mere appearance'.[91] And he speaks of the Apollonian artist as one who – unlike the scientist, who always wants to 'uncover', to get to the bottom of things – 'cling[s] with rapt gaze on what remains even after such uncovering'.[92] Even after the uncovering of unpleasant truth, the Apollonian artist takes delight in the beautiful, delight in 'beautiful forms'.[93]

This suggests that the art of the Homeric epic – and the corresponding attitude to life – is a matter not of elimination but rather of focus. It suggests an attitude in which one is inclined to describe life as 'terrible but magnificent'. In Uccello's *Battle of San Romano*, for example, the ground is littered with bodies and body parts. But what captures one's attention is the magnificence of the horses, the athleticism of the combatants, the sheen on the armour and the proud flutter of the pennants streaming in the breeze. (This is an apposite comparison since Nietzsche compares human existence to that of soldiers in an oil painting of a battle scene.)[94] Were one to look for a modern instance of Apollonian art, what might come to mind is the Western: death and destruction are all about, but what one focuses on is the cool courage and the sheer 'style' of its heroes. On a more debased level, the same phenomenon is exhibited by the 'women's' magazine. Terrible things – drunkenness, disease, divorce and death – happen to its gods and goddesses (minor royals, film stars, rock musicians and football players), but through it all the glamour remains, their stardom shines on.

* * *

The Apollonian outlook on life – in the Preface to *The Gay Science* Nietzsche calls it 'being superficial – *out of profundity*' – requires a strongly external approach to both others and ourselves. It requires that death be, as it is in the Western, bloodless and painless. It requires a kind of inner anaesthesia. This, I think, is why Nietzsche associates it with 'illusion': it represents, as it were, a three-dimensional object as two-dimensional. Though there is no censorship of *facts* there is censorship – censorship of *perspectives*. Subjectivity, the inner perspective, how it feels to be on the *inside* of loss, injury and mortality, is not allowed to be shown. But the Greeks *knew* about the inside of things. They had an 'exquisite' sensitivity to the 'terror and horror' of existence. This is why Nietzsche calls the Apollonian attitude (in an entirely non-judgmental way) a 'lie'. It is a form of self-deception.

This makes the Apollonian outlook seem a somewhat fragile 'prophylactic'[95] against nihilism, against 'nausea' and despair. The pain of things has a way of forcing itself on one, no matter how 'superficially' one lives. One thinks, perhaps, of the tragic imprisonment, decay, and death of the brilliant Oscar Wilde, Nietzsche's contemporary and in many ways someone who attempted to personify the Apollonian stance. Or one thinks of the impossibility of maintaining such a stance in the face of the death of one's child. Or of one's own death. Or, in Nietzsche's case, approaching madness.

It is on account of this fragility, I think, that, while the Apollonian solution to nausea and nihilism receives honourable mention, Nietzsche's preference is for the 'Dionysian' solution that is embodied in Greek tragedy, a solution which he describes as the 'more profound'[96] of the two. With Greek tragedy, he says, art attains 'the highest goal . . . of all art',[97] is, that is to say, of the highest service to life.[98]

Greek Tragedy

Nietzsche's key term for the Apollonian is 'dream'. This word does triple duty, indicating, first, that Apollonian consciousness deals in images, second, that its world of the *principium individuationis* is metaphysically ideal, a *mere* dream, and, third, that in Apollonian art this world has been raised to a state of beauty. It serves the last function because, for Nietzsche, the essence of the classical ideal of beauty is economy of 'essential' form and because 'in our dreams . . . all forms speak to us; nothing is superfluous or unnecessary'.[99] Irrelevant details such as the licence-plate number of the articulated truck bearing down on one are simply omitted by the artistry of dreams.

On the surface, the tragic art of the fifth century is no different in kind from the Homeric art of the eighth. The same cast of gods and heroes appears in both. What is different, however, is that beneath the beautiful surface of the 'Apollonian dream'[100] common to both, tragedy possesses a 'Dionysian' depth unknown to Homer.

Whereas 'dream' stands for the Apollonian, Nietzsche's word for the Dionysian is *Rausch*: intoxication (Dionysus, Bacchus, is of course the god of wine) or, better, 'ecstasy', a 'standing out of oneself [*ex-stasis*]', out of everyday consciousness.[101] In Schopenhauerian terms, the Dionysian state is one in which one overcomes the *principium individuationis*, the illusion of individuality and plurality, to realise, intuitively, one's identity with the one true being which everything is. In Dionysian ecstasy, preserved in the medieval carnivals of St. John and St. Vitus,[102] in 'Beethoven's jubilant "Ode to Joy"' (and still, to some degree, in the modern rock concert and football stadium),

> not only is the bond between human beings renewed … but nature, alienated, inimical, or subjugated, celebrates once more her festival of reconciliation with her lost son, mankind. Freely the earth offers up her gifts, and the beasts of prey from mountain and desert approach in peace. The chariot of Dionysus is laden with flowers and wreaths; beneath its yoke stride panther and tiger … Now all the rigid, hostile barriers which [Apollonian] necessity, caprice or 'impudent fashion'[103] have established between man and man break asunder. Now, hearing this gospel of universal harmony, each person feels himself to be not simply united, reconciled or merged with his neighbour, but quite literally one with him, as if [in Schopenhauer's language] the veil of Maya had been torn apart, so that mere shreds of it flutter before the mysterious primordial unity. Singing and dancing, man expresses his sense of belonging to a higher community, has forgotten how to walk and talk … [104]

In terms of the capacities of the human mind, the Dionysian is that which transcends concepts, which cannot properly be articulated in language. And in aesthetic terms it is music, more exactly 'dithyrambic' music, music which, like Wagner's, dissolves everything into a 'sea of feeling'. In the terminology Wagner uses, Dionysian music is 'sublime' rather than 'beautiful' (p. 121 above). It is music which abolishes the illusion of division and absorbs us into the unitary heart of being.

The origin of Greek tragedy, Nietzsche argues, lay in the Dionysian festival,* in the 'dithyrambic' chanting of hymns in honour of Dionysus. Later on, actors and action were added to the chanting – the music 'gave birth' to the drama – and still later a formal division came into being between chorus and audience. Yet the spectators, in the great period of Greek tragedy, carrying with them the memory that, originally, everyone was part of a unitary congregation of worshippers, still felt themselves to be part of the chorus: 'The audience of Attic tragedy identified itself with the chorus on the *orchestra* [the semi-circular area in front of the stage], so that there was fundamentally no opposition between public and chorus'; 'the whole [was] just one sublime chorus'.[105]

This identification enables Nietzsche to give an account of the 'tragic effect', of the seeming paradox of our deriving satisfaction from witnessing the destruction of figures who, in most ways, represent what is finest and wisest among us. As members of the Greek audience we partially empathise with the hero in his inexorable march to destruction. But because our primary identification is with the chorus, we find ourselves transported by its hypnotic singing into the Dionysian state. In this condition we experience, says Nietzsche, a 'metaphysical comfort' for the nauseous character of human existence. This happens because the world of individuals becomes 'unreal' for us,[106] a 'game of play' in Wagner's language (p. 120 above): individuals, including our own normal selves, become like soldiers in a painting of

---

* This, presumably, is *The Birth*'s contribution to Greek philology, which the letter to Engelmann (p. 124 above) claims it makes. It is an important and genuine contribution still widely accepted by classical scholars.

a battle scene.[107] Instead of identifying with anything *in* the world of appearances, 'for a brief moment', we become

> the primordial being itself and we feel its unbounded greed and lust for being: the struggle, the agony, the destruction of appearances, all this now seems to us to be necessary given the uncountable excess of forms of existence thrusting and pushing themselves into life, given the exuberant fertility of the world-will[108]

that we are. This is the only perspective from which we can justify the nauseous in life: 'only as aesthetic phenomena' – only, that is, from *outside* the world of human individuality – 'do existence and the world appear justified'. Only from this perspective can we apprehend the 'ugly and disharmonious' (which from the inside render human existence unbearably 'nauseous') as nothing more than parts of an 'artistic game' which the primal unity plays with itself.[109]

This, then, is the 'solace' brought by the great artwork. For a brief moment I overcome prosaic, everyday realism and realise the truth of Schopenhauerian idealism. The absurd and nauseous character of life and the world, I realise, is not *my* problem since death and pain only exist in the epic movie in which I am no longer a participant. Rather – given my identity with the 'world-building force' that 'the dark Heraclitus' compared to a child building sandcastles and then knocking them over again[110] – I am its 'sole author and spectator'.[111] Pain and death, I see, are not just parts but rather *necessary* parts of the world-movie since (as Margaret Atwood once ruefully observed) there is no narrative without conflict, no encompassing of the new without destruction of the old.

* * *

Nietzsche observes that the Dionysian state is accompanied by a 'dwindling of the political instinct', by indifference, even hostility, towards 'the state and the sense of homeland'.[112] This is why, unless it is modified and controlled in some way, the 'ecstatic brooding' of Dionysianism 'leads a people ... along the [Schopenhauerian] road to Indian Buddhism', engenders 'apathy' towards 'worldly affairs' and a 'Buddhistic longing for nothingness'.[113] State and homeland, that is to say, are Apollonian entities: the state requires structure and hierarchy, homeland requires the drawing of a boundary between 'home' and 'abroad', between where I belong and where 'the other' begins. So if I have ascended to the 'higher community' which comes from the abolition of all difference and division, I will find the idea of return to the world of individuation – individuation being, recall, 'the primal cause of all suffering' – nauseating:

> As soon as everyday reality re-enters consciousness it is found to be nauseous: an ascetic, will-denying mood is the product of this condition. The Dionysian is set against the meanness and commonness [of the everyday] as a higher order. The Greek now wants absolute escape from this world of guilt and fate[114] ... In the consciousness that comes with the awaking from intoxication, he sees everywhere the horror or absurdity of human existence; it nauseates him. Now he understands the wisdom of the forest god,[115]

the wisdom, that is, of Dionysus's intimate companion, Silenus.

This, of course, is also the 'wisdom' of the later Wagner, the Wagner who affirms that 'my kingdom is not of this world' and longs for 'death, for absolute unconsciousness, total non-existence' (p. 119 above). And it is the potential effect of Wagner's later music-dramas: no one, writes Nietzsche, could listen to the final act of Wagner's dithyrambic *Tristan* as absolute music, 'purely as a vast symphonic movement', without 'suffocating as their soul attempted convulsively to spread its wings'.[116] (The allusion is to Plato's *Phaedrus*, to the soul's regrowing its wings in preparation for its upward flight from earthly exile to its true homeland on the 'rim of the heavens'.)

But of course *Tristan* is *not* (quite) pure music and neither was Greek tragedy. They both contain words and action, the Apollonian element. This, says Nietzsche, shields us from the full force of the Dionysian effect, 'restores the almost shattered individual with the healing balm of illusion'. We are subjected to the 'noble deception' that the tragedy is a purely Apollonian affair, that it concerns nothing but the fate of an individual in the only world there is, the world of individuals. Even the playwright succumbs to the 'deception', fails to grasp the deep meaning of his own work. The result is that we return, rubbing our eyes, to everyday life 'strangely comforted' yet 'relieved of the burden' of understanding the nature of the comfort. Relieved of the burden of Dionysian insight, we are able, once more, to act.[117] This is the true and profound meaning of Hamlet's paralysis: his insight is that 'knowledge kills action; action requires . . . the veil of [Apollonian] illusion'.[118] And, in the end, this illusion is the parting gift of the great artwork, whether it be Greek tragedy or the Wagnerian music-drama. Like a fairy godmother, Lethe draws a veil of forgetfulness over our moment of world-negating, redemptive insight. We can carry on, notwithstanding.

The Role of Myth

Thus far, Nietzsche's analysis appears to leave only a rather attenuated role to the Apollonian element in Greek tragedy: its sole task seems to be to act as a veil of illusion that enables us to recover from Dionysian insight. In the closing pages of *The Birth*, however, Nietzsche sets out to correct this impression.

Whereas the music constituted the Dionysian element in Greek tragedy, the heart of the Apollonian element is the poetic text, the words. Specifically, it is the mythic content of the work, the religious content – Sophocles, Nietzsche emphasises, was a 'religious' writer.[119] Closely echoing Wagner's talk of myth as a 'condensation' that is true for all ages and cultures (p. 119 above), Nietzsche says that the mythic figures of Greek tragedy are 'contracted' images which 'abbreviate appearances'. He adds that they are human *types* rather than individuals (the effect of the actors' masks), which endows them with universal significance.[120]

What is the importance of religious myth? Again repeating Wagner almost verbatim, Nietzsche says that 'only a mythic horizon unifies a culture'. Only myth provides it with 'a secure and sacred place of origin'. The images of myth, he continues,

> must be the unnoticed but ever-present daemonic guardians under whose tutelage young souls grow up and by whose signs the grown man interprets his life and his struggles; even the state knows of no more powerful unwritten laws than the mythical fundament which guarantees its connection with religion and its emergence from out of mythic representations.

'Art and *Volk* [people], myth and morality', he concludes, are 'necessarily . . . entwined'. A people is only properly a people if it can impose a mythic, 'eternal' view on its experience.

Neither a people nor an individual human being can thrive without there being 'gods of the hearth' to constitute its 'mythical homeland'.[121]

In a word, then, the mythic content of tragedy articulates, in allegorical form, the ethos of a community. In doing so it is a 'collective artwork' in the double sense of being a 'festive reunification of the [individual] Greek arts'[122] and in the sense of gathering the community, and thereby creating and preserving it *as* community. Whereas the mystery plays of medieval Germany had the function of allowing the individual to *separate* himself from the community in private meditation, 'the Greeks viewed the ancient tragedies in order to collect [*sich sammeln*] themselves'.[123]

Solution to the Riddle of Wagner's Relation to the Greeks

We are now in a position to return to Nietzsche's claim in the letter to Engelmann (p. 124 above) that *The Birth* provides a resolution of 'the riddle of Wagner's relation to Greek tragedy'. The enigma was, let us recall, the apparent contradiction between Wagner's early or 'socialist' conception of the great artwork and his later or 'Schopenhauerian' conception. According to the first, 'world-improving' conception, the point of the work is to find a *this-worldly* 'salvation' of humanity through the reestablishment of (socialist-anarchist) community and hence of meaning in the lives of individuals. And according to this conception, too, the words – in Nietzsche's terminology, the Apollonian element in the artwork – have to be the dominant element. The work, as we might put it, has to be a music-*drama*. According to the second, world-rejecting conception, however, there is no hope of this-worldly redemption, so that the only function of the artwork is to intimate the existence of an *other-worldly* redemption. According to this conception it is the musical – Dionysian – element in the artwork that has to be dominant; the words, indeed, threaten to drop out altogether as at best irrelevant and at worst a distraction. The work has to be a *music*-drama.

One would think that the only possible resolution of the Wagnerian contradiction would be to abandon either the early, Apollonian, or the later, Dionysian, theory of the artwork. However, it now becomes clear that Nietzsche's – intellectually stunning – solution to the seeming contradiction is to show how the artwork can be *both* Apollonian *and* Dionysian: how it can *both* comfort the individual in the face of the nauseous character of human existence *and* promote the flourishing of community by gathering it in a celebration and affirmation of its fundamental understanding of how human existence is and ought to be. Though the 'metaphysical comfort' brought by Dionysian insight brings with it the *threat* of 'Buddhistic negation of the will', of Hamlet-like paralysis, the 'noble deception' worked by Apollonian illusion blocks that path to nihilism and allows the artwork to carry out its world-affirming work of communal gathering. And as for the question of precedence between words and music (the topic of an entire opera, Richard Strauss's *Capriccio*) the answer is that neither is superior to the other. Since words and music perform different but equally vital tasks, there is genuine equality between Apollo and Dionysus, a genuinely 'fraternal union'.[124]

This is an intellectual tour de force, a sorting out of Wagner's contradictory position for which the fecund but muddled composer ought to have been profoundly grateful.[125] One can imagine an enlightened Wagner replying to requests for a statement of what he really thought about Greek tragedy with 'I don't know: ask Nietzsche what I think'. (As a matter of fact Wagner *did* say precisely this on reading the second of the *Untimely Meditations* of 1874: 'I am proud and delighted to announce', he wrote Nietzsche, 'that I need to say nothing more and can leave all further discussion to you'.)¹²⁶

Socrates and the Death of Tragedy

Eccentrically, Nietzsche thinks, with Wagner, that Greek tragedy died in the hands of Euripides. Even more eccentrically, he thinks that the *éminence grise* behind this murderous act was Socrates. Essentially, Euripides did two things. First, by 'putting the spectator on the stage', in other words, by turning tragedy into a representation of everyday life, he killed the universal archetypes that raised it to the level of myth. And second, he killed the chorus. Influenced by Socrates's view that 'reason [is] the root of all enjoyment and creation', he was perturbed by the 'puzzling depth', the 'comet's tail' of significance, trailed after them by the characters of his predecessors, Aeschylus and Sophocles. Since it was the mysterious, dithyrambic chanting of the chorus that was the source of this incomprehensible meaning, he eliminated the chorus. This was done in the spirit of 'aesthetic Socratism', the conviction that to be beautiful is to be 'rational'.¹²⁷

'Socratism' as such Nietzsche identifies with reason's joy in 'unveiling', in getting beneath the surface of things to uncover their hidden mechanism. 'Socratic man' (also 'Alexandrian man' and 'theoretical man') is one who, like the historical Socrates, has the 'imperturbable belief that thought, following the thread of causality, reaches down into the deepest abysses of being, and that it is capable not simply of understanding existence but even of *correcting* it'.¹²⁸ Socratism is, in other words, the faith that science together with its offspring, technology, has the capacity to solve every human problem. This makes it an 'optimistic' doctrine that believes in the possibility of 'earthly happiness for all'.¹²⁹ It is thus not difficult to see why, from the 'Socratic' point of view, Dionysian tragedy had to go. It undermines faith in reason, the key to human happiness.

Nietzsche makes two claims about Socratism. First, that it is *false*, an 'illusion'. Thanks to 'the extraordinary courage and wisdom of Kant and Schopenhauer', thanks in other words to metaphysical idealism's confinement of causality to the dream-world of appearances, we know that ultimate reality is *not* accessible to, and hence not 'correctible' by, science.¹³⁰ Socratism is thus a form of hubris on account of which a Socratic culture is liable to catastrophic and totally unanticipated traumas as the 'child-god' smashes one of its sandcastles (see p. 129 above). Nietzsche's second claim is that Socratism is the way we, the post-Enlightenment West, are now. (So we might think of 9/11 or of global warming as just such a trauma.) *Modern* man is Socratic man. To these claims Nietzsche adds a third: Socratic culture is *degenerate* culture. How so?

What Is Wrong with The Way We Are Now?

Nietzsche identifies two things as wrong with modern culture. First, through the dominion of scientistic materialism and the consequent loss of the Dionysian, we have lost that 'metaphysical comfort' which saved us from becoming 'rigid with fear' in the face of the 'horrors of individual existence', in the face, above all, of our inevitable 'destruction', death.[131] In *Wagner in Bayreuth* Nietzsche writes that 'the individual must be freed from the terrible anxiety which death and time evoke'.[132] This, however, our post-Christian, post-metaphysical culture cannot do for us. It follows that a Socratic culture must be haunted by anxiety, evasion, and ultimately terror, in the face of death.

The second thing wrong with our Socratic culture, according to Nietzsche, is that we have lost myth. Modern man is 'mythless man'.[133] The reason has to do with the role of art in modernity.

Myth, we know, whether in Homeric or tragic art, belongs to the Apollonian. The central effect of Apollonian art is, we have seen, to 'transfigure', to 'glorify', to 'perfect'. By using the techniques of the trade – highlighting the attractive, pushing the not-so-attractive into shade or soft focus, and so forth – it raises its figures from the mundane to the glorious. It makes them *shine*,[134] thereby endowing them with charismatic authority. They become 'heroes', figures we 'esteem' and hence seek to emulate.[135] They become, in a crude and not entirely accurate nutshell, 'role models'.

It would be foolish to deny that things 'shine' in modernity. Our culture is full of shiny things, of 'gods' and 'heroes': Princess Di (as immortal as any of the Olympians), Madonna, the Beckhams, the winner of the latest Oscar or reality TV show and so on. All of them are made to shine by Apollonian art (otherwise known as 'the media'). The problem, in fact, is that *too many* things shine in modernity, and that their shine rubs off too soon.

This is anticipated with great prescience by Nietzsche. 'Only by myth', he writes, 'can all the energies of fantasy and Apollonian dream be saved from aimless meandering'.[136] 'Aimless meandering' seems to me to capture precisely the fickle flicker of celebrity – the 'Apollonian dream' of the present age. And what this means, for Nietzsche, is that the 'Apollonian art' of Western modernity is devoid of 'mythic' content.

The important thing to notice here is that, for Nietzsche, 'myth' means something like 'unified, comprehensive, and consistent myth'. For him a myth is something that can constitute 'the unity [*Einsein*] of *Volk* and culture', something that can constitute 'the noble core of [a] ... people's character [*Volkscharakter*]'; something that could count as, for example, '*the* German myth'.[137,*] So, for example, the entire panoply of Greek gods and heroes constitutes a *single* myth, the entire range of Christian divinities and saints another. 'Myth' for Nietzsche means, in short, just what it means for Wagner – a 'view in common of the essence of things' which constitutes 'the nation itself' (p. 115 above). From this point of view the problem with modernity is that all we have is an incoherent and constantly changing chaos of myth-*fragments*, a 'pandemonium of myths ... thrown into a disorderly heap'.[138] We live, as *Zarathustra* will put it, in a 'motley' town.

What is wrong with the mythless 'motleyness' of modernity? In pointing to the specific symptoms of this, Nietzsche develops a 'cultural criticism' which is deeply indebted to Wagner's and which persists with remarkable consistency throughout his career.

The first symptom is loss of unity. Since the unity of a community, of a 'people', can only exist when individuals are gathered into the 'maternal womb' of a unified myth, there is, in modernity, no community, no homeland. Instead, all we have is a 'wilderness of thought,

---

* Sounding much like Sachs at the very end of *Die Meistersinger*, Nietzsche calls, in the closing pages of *The Birth*, for a '*rebirth of German myth*' (BT 23; Nietzsche's emphasis). As soon as he had recovered from his infatuation with Wagner, such nationalist sentiments disappear from his thought – become, indeed, anathema to it. What never disappears, however, we shall see, is his commitment to the vital importance of communal myth, *supra-national* communal myth.

morals, and action', a 'homeless wandering about'.[139] Modern society has become the atomized world of, in Wagner's phrase, 'absolute egoism', with the only unity being the artificial and oppressive one of the state. As a consequence, communally and so individually, life becomes meaningless.

The second symptom is a 'greedy scramble to grab a place at the table of others', the search for meaning in the supermarket of foreign religions and cultures.[140] One might think here not only of the thriving 'Eastern-guru' business but also of so-called postmodern architecture, the raiding of past and alien styles as an expression of the hollowed-out emptiness of our own culture, which, Nietzsche points out, is not really 'post' modernity at all.

The final symptom is modernity's 'feverish agitation'. The loss of the eternal, mythical perspective on things, the loss of a meaning of life, leads to an 'enormous growth in worldliness', a 'frivolous deification of the present ... of the "here and now"'.[141] This is what modern German sociologists call the *Erlebnisgesellschaft* – the society driven by the frenzied quest for 'experiences', cheap thrills; for sex, drugs, rock and roll and 'extreme' sports. It is the society described by Wagner as 'bored to death by pleasure'. Without a communal ethos to give aspiration and meaning to one's life, the only way of keeping boredom at bay is the frenzied search for cheap thrills. What Nietzsche and Wagner both have in mind, I think, is Schopenhauer's stress-or-boredom observation (p. 83 above). Without the (healthy) stress provided by an identity-defining ideal, one can only try to preserve oneself from boredom through the ever-diminishing returns of ever more exotic thrills.

* * *

In *The Birth of Tragedy*, Nietzsche calls for the living of Greek history in reverse.[142] So what he calls for is something that will play, in modern life, the role that was played by the tragic festival in the lives of our 'radiant leaders', the Greeks, at the highest point of their culture.[143] With Wagner, therefore, what he calls for is the rebirth of Greek tragedy in the 'artwork of the future'. The overridingly central message of *The Birth* – its raison d'être – is thus the call for the birth of the Bayreuth Festival.

8

War and Aftermath

THE PREPARATIONS for *The Birth of Tragedy* were interrupted by an event on the world-stage which produced profound and permanent effects on Nietzsche's thinking. Halfway through writing a letter begun on July 16, 1870, telling Rohde what a good impression he had made on the Wagners during his May visit to Tribschen, he heard the news:

> Here is a fearful thunder-clap: the Franco-German war has been declared and our whole threadbare culture is toppling over with the terrible demon at its throat...We may already be at the beginning of the end. What a wasteland! We will need monasteries once again. And we will be the first brothers. – Your true Swiss.[1]

This reveals something of Nietzsche's initially confused and ambiguous response to the July 19 declaration of war. On the one hand he is horrified that European culture has failed to prevent the outbreak of war, that it is lapsing into barbarism. But on the other, already perceiving Europe to be a culture in need of regeneration, he sees the possibility of cells of regeneration – 'monasteries' – growing up on the 'wasteland' left by the perhaps cleansing fire of war. (The 'monastery' – or sometimes 'colony' – 'for free spirits' will soon become a major theme.) That he signs the letter 'Your true Swiss' suggests that, taking advantage of Swiss neutrality, he plans to sit the whole thing out. At virtually the same time, however, he wrote to his mother, 'Really, I'm depressed about being a Swiss. It's about our culture! And for that no sacrifice is too great! This damned French tiger'.[2] And a couple of days later he wrote Sophie Ritschl that he felt ashamed of having to remain inactive when the time had finally arrived for which his military training had prepared him.[3]

At first, Nietzsche made no move to involve himself in the war. Instead he took Elizabeth, who was staying in Basel, for her first visit to Tribschen, and then, on July 30, to the Maderanertal, a wildly romantic valley 1,300 metres above sea level, where they stayed at the hotel Alpenklub. Here he wrote 'The Dionysian Worldview'[4] (the work in which the Apollonian/Dionysian duality first comes to prominence in his analysis of Greek tragedy). Staying in the same hotel was a Hamburg landscape painter, Adolf Mosengel, whom they had already met en route. Intense conversations with Mosengel, as well as news of German victories – though with heavy losses – at Weissenburg and Wörth, galvanised Nietzsche into emerging from the shelter of Swiss neutrality. On August 8 he wrote to his head of department, Wilhelm Vischer, requesting leave from the university in order to fulfil his '*German* duty' to the Prussian 'fatherland' either as a soldier or as a medical orderly.[5]

He communicated his intentions to Cosima. In spite of her French connexions – she was related through her mother, Marie d'Agoult, to the French war minister – both the Wagners were passionate supporters of the German cause. They thought, nonetheless, that people of culture and intellect had better things to do than to get shot. Cosima tried to dissuade Nietzsche from active service, suggesting that, in the well-organized medical service, his amateurish efforts would be more of a hindrance than a help, and that he could better contribute to the war effort by sending a hundred cigarettes to the front.

In the event, the university granted Nietzsche leave of absence but, in view of Swiss neutrality, only to act as a medical orderly. Accordingly, accompanied by Mosengel and Elizabeth (who was having trouble getting back to Germany, most trains having been requisitioned as troop transports), he made the tortuous journey from the Maderanertal, via Lindau on Lake Constance, to Erlangen, in Bavaria, where he arrived on August 13. During the journey, as Elizabeth reports, they had been in high spirits and had sung jolly songs, but, seeing the wounded all around them on their arrival, became ashamed of their previous 'childish frivolity'.[6] In Erlangen Nietzsche underwent training to become a medical orderly in the *Felddiakonie* [Field Service], an arm of the Red Cross.

The Franco-Prussian War

The official declaration of war came from the French parliament acting on the instructions of the Emperor Napoleon III (the nephew of Napoleon Bonaparte, whom Nietzsche had so admired as a schoolboy (pp. 47–8 above)). Though the formal cause was the possible accession of a German candidate to the Spanish throne, the outbreak of war had to a large degree been engineered by Bismarck. Playing on French fear of rising Prussian power and on Napoleon's vanity, he saw the war as the necessary means of persuading the southern German states to join the North German Federation in what, at the conclusion of the war in 1871, became a united Germany, the Second* German Reich.

Though the war lasted a bare six months, it was a bloodbath, in many ways a dress rehearsal for the horrors of the First World War. On top of a large but unknown number of civilian casualties, there were something approaching half a million military casualties – dead or wounded – three-quarters of the deaths, 156,000, being on the French side. The French deployed, for the first time, a machine gun, the *mitrailleuse*, but far more deadly was the new breech-loading rifle, the *chassepot*, with twice the range of the German 'needle gun'. The Germans, on the other hand, had new, breech-loading artillery constructed out of steel, decisively superior to the French artillery. Even more importantly, the Prussians had compulsory military service and a population hardened into a militarized, nationalistic, and Francophobic whole by the 'War of Liberation' (from Napoleon's occupying army) of

---

* The Holy Roman Empire (which, famously, was neither holy, nor Roman, nor an empire) was the first. The third, of course, was Hitler.

1813–14, which regarded dying for the 'fatherland' in battle as a glorious act. Another vital advantage was the existence of the first permanent general staff devoted to full-time planning for possible and actual warfare, and in Field-Marshall Helmuth von Moltke a military strategist of genius. As he had against the Austrians five years earlier, von Moltke used the railways to deploy troops with a speed that bemused the French.

Winning a series of battles, though often at a severe cost – Wissenburg, Spicheren, Wörth, Mars-la-Tour, Gravelotte, Metz – the Germans advanced through Alsace and deep into France, until finally Napoleon surrendered at Sedan, together with 104,000 men, on September 2, 1870. The Germans then advanced on Paris, which they besieged from September 19 until finally it fell on January 28, 1871. An armistice was signed on that day, Wilhelm I of Prussia having been proclaimed Emperor of a united Germany ten days earlier. This was followed by a peace treaty signed at Versailles on February 28 which, however, the Paris workers and home guard refused to accept, seizing control of the capital on March 18 and setting up the Paris Commune. With tacit Prussian approval, the French army re-conquered Paris and executed tens of thousands of workers and revolutionaries in the 'Bloody Week' of May 21–28. The war resulted in the ceding of Alsace-Lorraine to Germany, further fuelling the Franco-German bitterness that would explode, forty-three years later, into the First World War.

Nietzsche's War

N ietzsche's medical training in Erlangen lasted ten days. Every morning the trainees were taught how to dress and bandage wounds, practicing largely on wounded men returned from the front. Obviously pressed for time but finding it necessary to record his part in world history, Nietzsche kept a fragmentary diary for the period:

> Today, Saturday [August 20, 1870]…we just chloroformed a Frenchman for a plaster-of-Paris cast (the hand is shattered; under the anaesthetic he called out '*Mon Dieu mon Dieu je vien*' [My God, I am coming]). Before that a girl of eleven, to save her leg from amputation. A few days earlier in a house, a boy with a huge head wound, chloroformed; very difficult. Yesterday a Prussian died in the hospital, shot in the lung, today a second. A Prussian, Liebig, in a good state; healthy appetite, a good night's sleep, but little hope, arm-bone shattered, not possible to do a cast.[7]

Leaving for the front at Wörth on August 23, Nietzsche, as Elizabeth records (in her characteristically saccharine manner), was put in charge of a medical unit as well as being

> entrusted with large sums of money and a whole host of personal messages, and thus he had to find his way across the battle-fields from [field] hospital to hospital and from ambulance to ambulance, in order to comfort the wounded and the dying, and to take the last words of farewell and remembrance from dying lips.[8]

On August 28 he wrote his mother that 'with this letter comes a memory of the fearfully devastated battlefield [of Wörth] covered everywhere with indescribably sad human body parts and stinking corpses'.[9]

On September 2 Nietzsche and Mosengel, who had been together all this time, were put on a hospital train in Ars-sur-Moselle to accompany the wounded to hospital in Karlsruhe. Since the weather was atrocious the wagons had to be kept shut the entire journey. Nietzsche described the journey in a letter to Wagner:

> with these three days and three nights[10] in the midst of seriously wounded men, we reached the uttermost limits of our exertions. I had a ghastly cattle-truck in which lay six severely wounded men, and I was the only person there to give them their food, to bandage their wounds and to see to them generally. [To von Gersdorff he adds the detail that he had to attend to their 'human needs'.[11]] All of them had broken bones, many had four wounds, and in addition I observed that two had hospital gangrene. That I was able to endure this disease-ridden air, and could even sleep and eat, now seems to me quite miraculous.[12]

Though he endured the journey, he did not emerge unscathed. By the time the train arrived in Karlsruhe, he was feeling very ill. With difficulty he carried on to Erlangen, where he was confined to bed. A doctor diagnosed severe dysentery, together with diphtheria, both of which Nietzsche had observed in the cattle-truck.[13] Mosengel, he wrote von Gersdorff,

> has the task of looking after me. And that was no mean task, given the character of the diseases. After I had been treated for several days with opium and tannic acid [enemas] and silver nitrate the danger passed. After a week I was allowed to travel to Naumburg, but I'm still not properly recovered. On top of all this the atmosphere of the experience has surrounded me with a gloomy fog – for a long time I had a plaintive ringing in the ears that wouldn't stop.[14]

Another effect of his war service was that, since the training in Erlangen had given him an elementary knowledge of drugs, Nietzsche now felt himself qualified to self-prescribe – which he did for the rest of his life with, almost certainly, largely deleterious results.

Nietzsche remained in bed in the Hotel Wallfisch (Whale) in Erlangen until mid-September, after which he spent a month recuperating in his mother's house in Naumburg, where the above letter was written. On October 21 he set off to return to work in Basel, arriving, frozen, for an overnight stop in Frankfurt on the twenty-second. On the twenty-third he arrived in Basel, having struggled with nausea the entire journey.[15]

The Aftermath

Though more or less recovered physically, Nietzsche's war experiences, even though they lasted barely a month, together with his anxieties for von Gersdorff (who remained at the front until the bitter end) and the knowledge that sixteen of his Pforta contemporaries had been killed in battle,[16] left him psychologically damaged. To Vischer he wrote that he was burying himself in philological work to try to escape the 'terrible images' engraved in his memory, but still suffered from 'nervous trouble and sudden weakness'.[17] And Elizabeth reports that even several years later, when Rohde (a non-participant) complained he had heard very little of Nietzsche's war experiences, 'my brother ejaculated painfully: "I cannot speak of such things, it is impossible; one must endeavour to banish such memories from one's mind.' [18] There can be little doubt that these symptoms – the recurrence of flashback images long after the event – describe what would now be diagnosed as 'post-traumatic stress disorder'.

The effect of this condition was to produce in Nietzsche a transformation not unlike that experienced by the First World War poets on both sides. As we saw, Nietzsche had been, throughout his early manhood, a passionate Prussian eager to serve the 'Fatherland' on the battlefield and if necessary die for it. Since boyhood, moreover, war of any sort had been, for him as for Prussian children in general, a glamorous activity, radiant with (in the language of *The Birth of Tragedy*) 'Apollonian' splendour. As Elizabeth records, he went off to war in high good spirits. But the unglamorous reality of stinking body parts (a reality to which he was, in fact, more exposed than had he served with the relative remoteness of an artillery officer), and the deaths of his schoolfellows, barely out of their teens, stripped away the Apollonian glamour by exposing him in the most direct way possible to the 'terrors and horrors' of life. (There is, one may suspect, a biographical basis to *The Birth*'s awareness of the fragility of the Apollonian 'lie'.)

To be sure, Nietzsche did not become, overnight, a pacifist. In September 1873 he was still capable of writing Wagner that 'the one good thing is the German soldier'. [19] As with most experiences, it took Nietzsche a long time to digest his war experiences, for their full effects to become manifest. Nonetheless, the post-traumatic stress he suffered in 1870 is, in my judgment, the decisive event which produced two fundamental changes in his thought. The first is an intense focus on the problem of human violence that comes to the fore for the first time in his post-war writings. And the second is a newly critical focus on Bismarck's Prussia, the true instigator of the war.

Violence

Nietzsche grew up in a time of continual – actual or immanent – war. His first response to the outbreak of the Franco-Prussian war, as we have seen, was to see it as a failure of 'culture': the collapse of a 'threadbare culture', the 'winter sleep of culture'. [20] This makes it clear that whatever exactly 'culture' is, if something is to be worthy of the name it must contain some technique for dealing with the problem of violence.

As in the case of almost every other human problem, Nietzsche turns to antiquity, and in particular the Greeks, for a solution. Though he touches upon it in *The Birth of Tragedy*, the most sustained consideration of the problem of violence in his early philosophy is 'Homer's Competition', [21] one of the *Five Prefaces to Five Unwritten Books* presented to Cosima as a birthday present at Christmas, 1872. Though never published, this is an important work in which several of the key themes of his mature philosophy become visible for the first time.

The 'humane', that which elevates humanity above the animals, reached its highest development in the Greeks. Yet at the same time, Nietzsche writes, the Greeks had, at the root of their nature, a 'wanton cruelty', a 'tiger-like pleasure in destruction': Alexander's and Achilles's habit of trailing the bodies of defeated enemies behind their chariots is a case in point. (He is writing, here, in conscious opposition to the eighteenth-century portrait of the Greeks as *serenely and effortlessly* humane.)

The Greeks, as we know, are the 'polished mirror' (pp. 68, 125 above) in which we can view ourselves. If the most humane of all species of humanity were not free of the disposition to violence, no species is. The disposition to cruelty, aggression, violence (later, Nietzsche will speak of the 'will to power') is innate to human beings, 'hard-wired' into our constitutions. There can be, therefore, no question of *eliminating* the disposition to violence. The only possibility is that culture can somehow *contain or redirect* it. This is a fundamental and very difficult insight on Nietzsche's part, requiring a radical break with traditional European morality. Since the Christian ideal of selfless love, the injunction that one *ought* to love even one's enemies, presupposes that one *can* love even one's enemies, that, in principle, violence can be eliminated from the human psyche, Nietzsche's insight into its ineliminability is only accessible to someone who has abandoned the psychological presuppositions of Christian morality.

Given the recognition of the ineliminability of violence, Nietzsche continues, the ancient world exhibited three responses. The first was to despair of human nature, as did the followers of the Orphic cult: exposure to a world of combat and cruelty led to 'nausea at existence', to the view that 'a life rooted in such an impulse was not worth living'.[22] The second response was to give the impulse free rein. This is what characterised the 'barbarian' world, in which the 'statutes' of civilised life were regularly swept away by the 'witches brew' of 'sensuality and cruelty'.[23]

The third response was that of the Greeks. The first important fact about them is that they 'acknowledged' the 'impulse . . . to combat and the pleasure of victory'.[24] Their moral judgments, that is, had a different 'colouration' from ours: there was nothing 'sinful' about aggression and cruelty, no wilful contravention of God's laws, it was just *there*, a brute fact about the way things are. On the other hand, they recognised that naked aggression was harmful; though not 'sinful', it is, in Nietzsche's later language, 'stupid'. And so their task was to find for it a non-destructive, indeed positively productive, form of expression. Their greatness was that they succeeded: they learnt to 'purify' the will to violence, to transform the 'terrible' into the 'noble', the 'damaging into the useful'.[25] They did this by learning how to 'spiritualise' violence,[26] how to find for it a surrogate form of expression. In the language Freud used to describe a notion he almost certainly took over (without acknowledgment) from Nietzsche, they learnt to 'sublimate' violence.

One of the ways in which they did this was through art. Hence their pleasure in Homer's vicious war stories and later on in Greek tragedy. Whereas the Dionysian festivals of the barbarians turned into orgies of sex and violence that often included human sacrifice, in the Dionysian festival of the Greeks, the tragic festival, they 'killed' their heroes not in life but, as Nietzsche would later put it, 'in effigy'.[27] A more productive way in which they sublimated violence, however, was through 'competition'.

In acknowledging human life as essentially 'combat and victory', the Greeks acknowledged it as the domain of the goddess Eris, the goddess of 'envy', trouble and strife. The Greek concept of envy was, however, quite unlike ours. For they acknowledged, in fact, *two* goddesses – a 'bad' Eris but also a 'good' one. Bad Eris created war (she started the Trojan War by throwing her golden apple, an object of universal lust, among the guests at the wedding of Peleus and Thetis) but, as we learn from Hesiod's *Works and Days*, Zeus also created good Eris in order to drive men to work and prosperity. The difference between the two is that while the dominance of bad Eris leads to the 'struggle to the death', good Eris leads to 'competition': as Hesiod puts it, she drives even the unskilled man to work: and if someone who lacks property sees someone else who is rich, he likewise hurries off to sow and plant.... Even potters harbour grudges against potters, carpenters against carpenters, beggars envy beggars and minstrels envy minstrels.

As Hesiod indicates, competition, *agon*, dominated Greek life; Greek culture was essentially 'agonistic' and was prized as such. Education was agonistic: striving for preeminence, 'selfishness' in modern language, Nietzsche suggests, was encouraged as contributing to the good of the community as a whole. The great playwrights of the fifth century competed with each other; they even, Aristotle records with amazement, competed with the dead, above all with Homer. Plato invented the dialogues in order to demonstrate that he could outdo the Sophists in dialectical 'combat'. And of course, the Greeks competed with each other at the Olympic games. Sublimated aggression was thus what created and fuelled the culture of the Greeks.

The enduring lesson Nietzsche draws from his reflections on the Greeks is not merely that it is impossible to eliminate the cruel and violent from human nature but also that one *should not wish to do so*, since 'man's ... terrible potentialities which are regarded as inhuman are ... in fact the fruitful soil from which alone everything humane, in feelings, deeds, and works can grow forth'.[28] The 'noble' and 'humane', Nietzsche will emphasise in his mature philosophy, is not something injected into the natural order by a supernatural agency, but is, rather, a redirection by culture of the 'blond beast' in us. We need to conserve our 'evil' potentialities for the sake of the 'good'.

Prussia

After his return from the Franco-Prussian battlefield, Nietzsche's letters begin to evince sentiments in stark contrast to the passionate Prussianism of his youth. He begins to have serious doubts as to whether Prussia's emergence as the preeminent power in continental Europe is good either for Prussia or for Europe. 'Let us hope', he writes von Gersdorff in November 1870,

> that we don't have to pay too dearly for the tremendous national success [in the war] in an area where, in my view, no loss at all can be sustained. In confidence: I hold the Prussia of today to be a highly dangerous power for culture. Sometime in the future I shall publicly expose the nature of the educational system.

'We must', he adds, 'be philosophers enough not to be carried away by the general euphoria of victory'.[29] The following month he describes the culture – or as he prefers to call it, 'barbarism' – of Bismarck's Prussia as the 'enemy that grows now on the bloody ground of this war'. And he adds that 'Our battle stands before us ... the bullet that will kill us will not come from guns and cannons'. The situation must be redeemed, he continues, by 'a new spirit in the scientific and ethical education [*Erziehung*] of our nation' that is to be promoted by 'a new force in classical studies'.[30]

To understand what he takes to be wrong with Bismarck's Germany, what he means by 'a new spirit in scientific and ethical education' and how he envisages such a spirit redeeming

German culture from its quasi-'barbaric' condition, we need to turn to the series of public lectures on education, delivered between January and March 1872, in which he carried out his threat to 'expose the nature of the Prussian educational system'.

On the Future of Our Educational Institutions

Nietzsche delivered his lectures on education under the auspices of the 'Voluntary Academic Association', the association formed, as we saw, to root the university in civic pride, engender productive interaction between town and gown, and alleviate the university's perpetual shortage of funds.

The discussion begins with a critique of current trends in Prussian education, which widens into a critique of Prussian society at large. Its focus is the 'gymnasium', the 'high', 'secondary', or 'grammar' school. Nietzsche's critique is conducted from an essentially conservative point of view. His general view is that German education was set on the right path in the 'wonderful, deeply thoughtful, exciting times of the Reformation' and carried further along that path in the time of Schiller and Goethe,[31] but that in modern Prussia, a dreadful perversion of this noble model has taken place. (Since, as we saw, Nietzsche's own school was a Reformation foundation and was grounded in the 'Weimar classicism' of Goethe and Schiller, Pforta appears to be functioning, here, as the gold standard.)

To understand why Nietzsche takes the late-nineteenth-century Prussian gymnasium to be the perversion of a noble ideal, one needs to understand that German education has traditionally divided secondary schools into the realschule, devoted to training people destined for the trades and professions, and the gymnasium, devoted to the education of a small, academically gifted elite. To get the point of Nietzsche's critique, one needs to think of a traditional gymnasium as more like a modern liberal arts college than an Anglo-Saxon high school. The teachers did research, and, as we saw in the case of Pforta, often moved back and forth between gymnasium and university. The students usually remained at the gymnasium until their nineteenth or even, as in Nietzsche's case, twentieth year, and, by the time they completed the school-leaving examination, were, in fact, ready to begin graduate study. That the gymnasium was so much like the modern university gives Nietzsche's critique a sometimes startling application to the latter.

* * *

Nietzsche identifies two developing trends in Prussia's newly centralized educational system as 'ruinous': a 'broadening' of education and a corresponding 'weakening'.[32] Education, he says, has become democratised, has become education for the ' broad masses'.[33] The consequence is an ever-widening gap between the demand for teachers and the supply of those with genuine ability and vocation. This has the 'weakening' effect of lowering the general level of education: dumbing down damages the genuinely gifted among both teachers and students. Since 'like delights in like',[34] mediocre teachers appoint further mediocre teachers and ever-increasing mediocrity becomes the character of the institution. This is fine for the mediocre. Finding a certain 'harmonious proportion' between their abilities and the spirit of the institution, these mediocre time-servers feel themselves 'justified'.[35] The teacher of genuine ability, on the other hand, feels increasingly alienated, while the student of ability finds the institution to have less and less to offer.

As to the cause of this ruinous condition, Nietzsche refers in part to a 'prevailing ethic' in the population at large, the 'economic dogma' that demands 'as much knowledge and education as possible – consequently as much production and demand as possible – consequently as much happiness as possible'. (The 'knowledge economy'!) This reduction of the good life to happiness and happiness to money makes the production of 'current' human beings – those with up-to-date skills that lead to the acquisition of wealth – both the goal of and the motive for seeking education.[36]

More emphatically, however, Nietzsche highlights the Prussian state as a cause of the current condition of education. His reflections on Prussia he takes to have a more than parochial significance since, on account of its military power, Prussia is being increasingly admired and imitated by other states.[37]

Prussia, he says, has become, in the jargon of the age, a 'culture-state [*Kulturstaat*]'.[38] It has taken upon itself the tasks of financing, determining the content, and examining the end-product of education and hence the task of determining the culture of society in general.[39] On the mass of its people it makes the demand: 'Be awake, be conscious! Be clever'.[40] The means it employs to create mass education are to make gymnasium (and, in most cases, university) education the prerequisite for admission to good positions in the army and the civil service. This has the effect that the gymnasium comes to be seen as nothing but a 'rung on the ladder of honour' to socially prestigious employment.[41]

A more subtle means is the use of Hegelian philosophy as propaganda – particularly in the schools themselves. Since Hegel glorifies the state as (according to Nietzsche) 'the absolutely complete ethical organism', it follows that the meaning of life lies in service to, in sacrifice – perhaps the ultimate sacrifice – for the state. From this it follows that 'the task of education is for each of us to find out the place and position where he can be of most useful service to the state'.[42]

The state's aim is simple: to achieve 'omnipotence', in other words, total power in relation to other states, global dominion. So the schools, with the Hegelian 'state culture' propagated within them, become the parallel of that other Prussian innovation, universal military service.[43] What Nietzsche is working towards, here, I think, is the concept of the 'total' society discussed in Chapter 4 (pp. 72–3 above): more specifically that of the 'totally mobilized society' articulated half a century later by Nietzsche's admirer Ernst Jünger – a society which is 'totalitarian' in the sense that all aspects of social life are drawn into, and governed by, the aim of the state, which is, essentially, conquest and expansion through the exercise of power.

* * *

Nietzsche sees the Prussian state as personifying the spirit of the new 'rolling age', the mechanized age of 'dizzying haste'.*,[44] The 'mechanization' of education is an aspect of the mechanization of life in general. Nietzsche's critique of education is addressed to those 'few human beings' who, like himself, feel out of step with the rolling age, those who 'still do not feel an idolatrous pleasure in being crushed by its wheels'.[45] It is addressed to those who are prepared to work towards an alternative model of higher education and thereby a revival of society in general. This model is offered not as a radical break with the past but rather as a recovery of the noble essence of the traditional German conception of the gymnasium. According to Nietzsche's model, the mission of the gymnasium is *not* education towards becoming a useful functionary of the state, but rather 'education [*Erziehung*] towards culture [*Bildung*]'.[46] (Since Nietzsche identifies 'true education' with this latter, regarding the

---

* 'Rolling' of course refers to the railways, still a technological marvel in the 1870s. To get a sense of their radical impact on human life, it is worth noting that the proportional increase of speed of travel they represented was greater than that introduced by either the automobile or the aeroplane.

former as mere 'instruction' or 'training', his thesis can be expressed as a tautology: the proper aim of education is education.)

Nietzsche's use of *Bildung* is not easy to grasp. The clue is to realise how heavily indebted it is to Schopenhauer's account of the aesthetic state as an escape from the will into 'disinterestedness' (pp. 83–4 above). First of all, says Nietzsche, education to culture, true education, has nothing to do with the 'struggle for existence', nothing to do with mere 'bread-winning': 'true education disdains polluting itself with the needing and desiring individual'. It aims rather to produce elevation to what Schopenhauer calls the point of view of 'the pure, will-less . . . timeless subject of knowledge' (p. 83 above). To this end education should be careful to preserve the adolescent's natural affinity with nature, since in

> recognis[ing] himself again as if in countless dispersed reflections and mirages in the colourful whirl of changing appearances . . . he will unconsciously have a feeling for the metaphysical oneness of all things in the great likeness of nature, and at the same time calm himself in its eternal persistence and necessity.[47]

Communing with nature liberates one from the 'egoistic'[48] will and elevates one to the 'eternal' point of view that belongs to *The Birth*'s 'primal unity', an elevation which has a 'calming' effect since it allows one to realise that, *as* the primal unity, one is beyond time, change, and death. But it also raises one to a condition of knowledge since, elevated above the flux of fashionable opinion, one is free to become 'the clear mirror of the eternal and unchanging essence' of things.[49]

The capacity for prolonged habitation of this state is what Schopenhauer calls 'genius'.[50] And so, too, does Nietzsche. In his description of how the education of genius is to proceed, however, the notion acquires various un-Schopenhauerian features.

The aim of education towards *Bildung*, Nietzsche tells his audience, is that of 'prepar[ing] the birth of the genius and the begetting of his work'.[51] The focus of such education is the study of German language and literature but, even more importantly, that of classical antiquity, to which the 'German essence' stands in a bond which, though crucial, is 'full of secrets and difficult to grasp'.[52] The student must become familiar with the mountain-peaks of the true 'German spirit', men of authentic 'genius' such as Goethe and Winkelmann, and through these 'high priests of classical education' become intimate with Greek antiquity itself, 'the right and sole home of education'.[53] Education, that is, must restore us to our 'Greek homeland'. 'The Hellenic, infinitely distant and enclosed with diamond ramparts',[54] must become 'the place of pilgrimage for the best and most gifted human beings'.[55]

What makes this un-Schopenhauerian is that whereas Schopenhauer discusses genius only in the context of art, what Nietzsche is contemplating here is very clearly *moral* development – as he calls it in the letter to von Gersdorff, an 'ethical education' (p. 141 above). Nietzsche's aim, that is to say, is that the reformed gymnasium will produce a 'small troop'[56] who will combat the 'barbarity' of the present by becoming the instigators and avant garde of a regeneration of culture in general. But to do that, to instigate a society-wide commitment to the Germano-Greek content of the authentic German 'spirit', the alumni of the gymnasium must themselves burn with a 'consuming longing for the Greek',[57] a longing to realise the moral excellences of the Greeks in their own lives. This means that the study of antiquity – here Nietzsche returns to his long-harboured plans for a reform of classical philology – is not a merely 'scientific' exercise but is, rather, the acquiring of reverence for the exemplary figures on whom we are to model our lives. As he puts it in his notebooks, 'The Hellenic has for us [in the true gymnasium] that status which the saints have for Catholics'.[58] In the true gymnasium the Greeks become the 'polished mirror' in which to view ourselves – not so much as we *are* but rather as we *aspire* to be.

* * *

But how exactly are these pathfinders to carry out their task of social regeneration? Once brought to maturity, what, actually, is the task of 'genius'? What exactly, indeed, given that it is not simply a carbon copy of Schopenhauer's conception, is Nietzsche's conception of genius?

Inescapably connected to the idea of genius is the notion of creation, origination, 'originality': the Greek origin of the word, *gignesthai*, is connected to the idea of giving birth. In the eighteenth century the originality of genius was conceived as that which escapes capture by traditional rules. As Kant puts it, genius is something 'for which no definite rule can be given . . . which cannot be learnt by a rule'.[59]

There are, however, two different conceptions of originality and of the kind of rules in question. One is originality of *expression*, the other originality of *content*. Alexander Pope emphasised the first, speaking of the works of genius as 'what oft was thought but ne'er so well expressed'. Schopenhauer, on the other hand, emphasised the latter. Whereas, he says, 'the person endowed with talent thinks more rapidly and accurately than do the rest, the genius perceives a different world from the one they see; talent is like the marksman who hits a target which others cannot reach; genius is like the marksman who hits a target . . . others cannot even see'.[60] Nietzsche's crucial departure from Schopenhauer's notion of genius is, it seems to me, that at this stage of his career, at least, he thinks of the originality of genius in terms of expression rather than content.

In accordance with 'the aristocratic nature of the spirit', the 'natural order of rank', Nietzsche tells his audience, the proper order of society is 'the mastery of great individuals', the 'servitude of the mass . . . under the sceptre of genius'.[61] Though this is evidently inspired by Plato's pyramidal *Republic* – the mass of craftsmen at the bottom, the military and civil service in the middle, and the 'philosopher king' at the top – what Nietzsche is talking about here is not, in fact, the state, but rather civil society (the *Volk* [people], as he calls it) of which the state *ought* to be the servant. What is important to him is not that the genius should assume political leadership of the state but rather that he should provide 'spiritual leadership' in 'the empire of the intellect',[62] cultural leadership in the realm of civil society.

But just how is this spiritual leadership to operate? Nietzsche says (repeating Wagner's thesis of the *Volk* as the true creator of art (p. 116 above)) that the

> highest and noblest cultural forces . . . burst forth out of the unconsciousness of the people, [and] . . . have their motherly vocation in the begetting of genius and then in the proper education and cultivation of the same.[63]

The 'genius' to whom the people give birth has, then, the task – here we come to the *expressive* conception of the originality of genius – of 'allowing to step into appearance, to rise forth, the highest destiny of a people . . . in an eternal work, thereby anchoring its people in the eternal, and redeeming it from the changing sphere of the momentary',[64] from the flux of fad and fashion. The genius, that is to say, is to bring about what can indeed be called an 'education of the people'. This, however, is something which cannot be achieved directly; it cannot be achieved by, for example, the introduction of universal compulsory education by the state. Rather,

> the authentic, deeper regions in which the great masses generally meet with culture, regions where the *Volk* nourishes its religious instincts, where it further poeticises in its mythical images, where it keeps up its faith in its customary morality, its right, the soil of its homeland, its language,[65]

can only be reached through the work of genius, the task of which is to articulate that 'customary morality', spiritual 'homeland' – in other words, to allow the 'highest destiny of a people' to 'rise forth'.

What is clear from this is that we are back with Greek tragedy, with the 'collective artwork' that 'collects' the *Volk* in clarifying affirmation of its fundamental ethos. What is clear, in other words, is that the paradigms of 'genius' are Sophocles and Aeschylus – and Richard Wagner. The ultimate reason, then, that 'education to culture' is important is that only by giving birth to, and nurturing, the genius and his works can a community recall itself from a 'fallen' and 'barbarous' condition to those 'eternal', but 'infinitely distant', values which make it the community that it is. Only, to speak specifically to Germans, through the cultivation of genius in the classics-focussed gymnasium can we be restored to our 'Greek homeland'.

* * *

I should like to end with three comments on this perhaps not entirely convincing argument.* The first consists in noting that Nietzsche's call for a return to an 'education towards *Bildung*' is, in essence, the call for a return to the conception of the humanistic gymnasium worked out in the early nineteenth century by the celebrated geographer, linguist, diplomat and educationalist Alexander von Humboldt – whom Nietzsche never mentions. The difference, however, is that whereas, for Humboldt, *Bildung* was an end in itself, the essence of becoming a fine human being, for Nietzsche it is, additionally and ultimately more importantly, a matter of social utility, of producing a flourishing community through 'spiritual leadership'. As he puts it in his notebooks, 'The eternal task of *Bildung* [is] the organization of an intellectual caste that is independent of church and state',[66] such that every member of this caste will 'live and act in the noblest strivings of its *Volk* or of mankind … in order to free his people from crooked paths, with his picture of the ideal before his eyes'.[67] As we shall see, this idea of the responsibility of the exceptional person to his community, his responsibility to become, in one way or another, a 'spiritual leader of the people', stays with Nietzsche until the end of his career.

A second and related comment consists in drawing attention to the essential 'Prussianness' of Nietzsche's reform plans. According to the 'Hegelian' philosophy that Nietzsche rejects, the proper, meaningful life for the individual consists in commitment and service – in accordance with one's abilities – to the ultimate 'ethical organism', the 'state'. Yet he himself thinks in equally 'organic' terms. His ideal society, that is to say, is the 'orchestra',

---

* A critical questioner might wonder why there is such an exclusive link between the German and the Greek, why the Judeo-Christian fails to receive a mention, and why only artworks count as works of 'genius'.

an orchestra directed by a conductor of genius so that every movement of every individual is harmoniously – and freely – coordinated with that of every other individual.[68] It is in membership of, and service to, an 'orchestral' society that the individual finds a meaningful life. Nietzsche's objection to the 'Hegelian', Bismarckian, state is, then, in no way an affirmation of the liberal-democratic notion of the primacy of the individual, of the idea that the function of the state is to create a space in which individuals live their own atomic lives, uncoordinated with the lives of others. Rather, his objection is simply that the true 'ethical organism' is not the state but rather 'the people' and its culture. The state should not, he says, be 'the border guard, regulator, or overseer' of the people and its culture. Rather, it should be 'the robust, muscular comrade, ready for battle, and a companion on the way, who gives the admired, nobler...friend safe conduct through the harsh realities'.[69] Bismarck's Prussian *Kulturstaat* has, then, got things precisely the wrong way round. Rather than the culture of civil society being controlled by, and subordinate to, the aims of the state, the state should be subordinate to, an expression of, the ethos of civil society. And this means that the genius, the articulator of the authentic nature of civil society and thereby its spiritual leader, is ultimately the superior of the leader of the state. When Martin Heidegger explained that he joined the Nazi party in order *'den Führer zu führen'*, to lead the leader, he was in fact tuning in to a long German tradition concerning the relation between politics and culture, between the state and the life of the spirit, to which Nietzsche was an earlier subscriber.

A final comment consists in calling attention to the continuity between *Educational Institutions* and *The Birth of Tragedy*. The latter work calls for the rebirth of the collective artwork, the former addresses the question of what we should do to promote the birth of such a work. Though at first glance *Educational Institutions* looks to have moved on to quite different territory, the worldview to which it subscribes is, in fact, identical with the Wagnerian worldview subscribed to by *The Birth*.

9

Anal Philology

NIETZSCHE RETURNED to Basel from his war service at the end of October 1870, in time to begin teaching for the winter term. He was suffering, as we saw, not only from the after-effects of dysentery but also from post-traumatic stress. To the former he attributed continuing digestive problems and stomach aches; to the latter we can probably attribute the insomnia, exhaustion, and depression which afflicted him for the next six months. On top of everything else, he was suffering from haemorrhoids. The resumption of lecturing convinced him that the tension between profession and calling, philology and philosophy, was only making his health worse. This moved him to write to Rohde that he planned soon to exit the university completely in order to create a 'new Greek academy' allied to the Bayreuth cause.[1] By the end of the year, however, he had another idea: he would apply for the recently vacated chair of philosophy, with Rohde taking over his old position in philology.

By February 1871 Nietzsche's health was so bad he was forced to take sick leave and retreat, with Elizabeth in attendance, to the Hôtel du Parc in Lugano for six weeks' recuperation. On returning to Basel he found that his application for the philosophy chair had been rejected. He claimed to have been victimised on account of his Schopenhauerian allegiances but the rejection was, in fact, fully justified, since he lacked not only training in philosophical method but also – a gap he never filled – a basic knowledge of the history of the subject. Apart from the *Rhetoric*, he knew none of Aristotle's major works, knew nothing of the medieval scholastics, the continental rationalists or the British empiricists. And though he did read Kant's *Critique of Judgment*, he almost certainly knew the *Critique of Pure Reason* only from secondary sources. (In the half-page summary of the history of Western philosophy in *Twilight of the Idols* called 'How the True World Became a Fable', it is notable that no philosopher inhabiting the two-millennia gap between Plato and Kant receives a mention.) Nietzsche would, therefore, have been quite incapable of meeting the teaching needs of a small department.

By September 1871, however, he seems to have recovered from his depression and from the disappointment of his rejected application: 'Basel is great', he wrote von Gersdorff, 'my friends like Basel and Basel likes my friends'.[2] This was the mood in which, at the beginning of 1872, he received the offer of a chair at the University of Greifswald, situated on the Baltic coast in northeast Germany. He quickly rejected it, in spite of Greifswald's proximity to Kiel, where Rohde had settled as *Privatdozent*, an unpaid lecturer. But he also, with some embarrassment, rejected the torchlight procession the Basel students proposed in honour of what they took to be his loyalty to their city. He rejected the procession because the students – and the university, too, which increased his salary – had to some degree misperceived his motives.

To his mother he explained that one should not be looking for a new kind of happiness when one already had, as he had in Basel, 'good friends and a good reputation'. But he added that the real ground of his rejecting the offer was his lack of ambition for an 'academic career'.[3] This was a diplomatic understatement, since he was again entertaining the idea of abandoning academia and its secure income completely, a step he knew would appal his mother. His latest fantasy was that the still chair-less Rohde would succeed him in Basel, leaving him free to work full time for the Wagner cause. His idea was to become a peripatetic lecturer visiting the various Wagner societies that had sprung up all over Germany, with the aim of raising the money for the completion of the Bayreuth opera house. (That he would only be preaching to the converted, and that a cash-strapped project would hardly be helped by having to pay him a salary, is symptomatic of Nietzsche's always tenuous grasp of financial reality.) Wagner, as already noted, rejected the offer, but Nietzsche was still dreaming about the double coup in April of 1872.[4]

The fact is that Nietzsche was gripped by Eris – 'good' Eris. He wanted to go to war – war on behalf of Wagnerian regeneration and against the 'vandalized' culture of modernity. *The Birth of Tragedy* had explained the urgency of the war; now he wanted to put his life behind his words. The desire for cultural 'warfare' is quite explicit. Responding to the now demobilized von Gersdorff's affirmation of his commitment to the Wagnerian cause, he writes in November 1871,

> It's as though you are still a soldier and now strive to prove your military disposition in the field of philosophy and art. And that's right: particularly in these times, it is only as fighters we have a right to exist, only as the advanced guard of a coming age of whose outlines we have, in our best moments, a dim intimation.[5]

And then a couple of months later,

> Whatever you do, always remember that we two are called to fight and work in the vanguard of a cultural movement in which – perhaps in the next generation, perhaps later – the great mass will take part. This shall be our pride, this shall stiffen our sinews. And I have, incidentally, the belief that we are born, not to be happy, but rather to do our duty: and we will regard ourselves as blessed if we know where our duty lies.[6]

And Rohde, too, he regards as a fellow 'warrior', addressing him, on various occasions, as his 'comrade in arms'.

The year 1872 began with the appearance of *The Birth of Tragedy*, Nietzsche's war-'manifesto',[7] on January 2. From then on, Nietzsche organized his life as a military campaign. Having, as he wrote Rohde, 'concluded an alliance' with Wagner,[8] he subordinated everything to his battle plan. Between January and March he delivered the already-discussed lectures *On the Future of our Educational Institutions*, which even the Wagners found over-done in their strident tone. In March he was invited on a trip to Greece by the son of Felix Mendelssohn. And though he was awed and delighted by the connexion with the revered composer who had been the focus of musical life in Leipzig and a friend of Gustav Krug's father, he nonetheless declined the invitation for fear of running afoul of Wagner's anti-Semitism. (It is notable that the thoughtless anti-Semitic rhetoric that sometimes mars his early letters increases markedly during the Tribschen period.)

In the same month Nietzsche insisted on Rohde's presence at the festival celebrating the laying of the foundation stone of the Bayreuth opera house, the 'Festival theatre [Festspiel-haus]' (see Plate 15), on May 22, 1872: 'the two "Wagnerian" professors', he wrote (the previous month Rohde had finally obtained a junior professorship in Kiel), 'must not be absent'.[9] They both duly attended along with, among others, Gustav Krug, the friend who had first infected Nietzsche with the Wagner bug, and the starry-eyed and determinedly idealistic Wagnerian Malwida von Meysenbug (see Plate 16), who would soon begin to play an important role in Nietzsche's life. Though the foundation stone was laid in pouring rain – the 'Green Hill' above the town must have been a sea of mud – there was a mag-nificent performance of Beethoven's Ninth Symphony in the Margrave's rococo theatre in the town with a chorus of three hundred singers for the last movement. Cosima noted in her diary that the evening was 'quite magnificent' and (in the spirit of Schopenhauer) that everyone 'felt free of the burden of mortal existence'. Rohde returned to Kiel feeling that he had just said goodbye to his true home, and that it was, more than ever, his duty to add his 'weaker strength' to his friend and fellow warrior 'in this battle for the highest good'.

Rohde's 'Higher Advertising'

Predictably, the Wagnerians greeted the appearance of *The Birth of Tragedy* (published, as we know, by Wagner's own publisher, Fritzsch) with high enthusiasm. There were letters of warm appreciation from Wagner himself, from Liszt, and from Hans von Bülow. But as far as the rest of the world was concerned, and, in particular, as far as the philological world was concerned (the work did, after all, make important historical claims about both the birth and the death of Greek tragedy), it was greeted by an ominous silence. Nietzsche had, however, brought *The Birth* into the orbit of his military planning prior to its appearance. Anticipating that the philologists would do their best to ignore it, he had suggested to Rohde at the end of the previous year that he should 'personally take the philologists in hand, perhaps in the form of a letter to the editor of the *Rheinisches Museum* or in a[n open] letter to me. In brief, what I'm in need of is "higher advertising"'.[10] Rhode complied with an extended review of *The Birth*. Rejected by the *Literarisches Zentralblatt*, it appeared, in a revised form, in the less scholarly, but strongly pro-Wagner, *Norddeutsche Allgemeine Zeitung*, Berlin's leading daily newspaper, where it could not but create a stir. Rohde had hoped his review would appear before the foundation-stone festival, but in the event it appeared four days later, on May 26.

Rohde's review was an act of genuine courage. Occupying only a junior position in the academic hierarchy, he risked irreparable harm to his reputation and career through alienation of the philological establishment. (Fortunately the damage turned out to be only temporary.) In the review, Rohde identifies Nietzsche as, like himself, a disciple of

Schopenhauer and as a prophet of the new music. Schopenhauer, he argues, is significant as the person who finally overcame Christian metaphysics, Wagner as the person who
overcame the classical tradition in art. From this new, 'modern' standpoint, Nietzsche, he
suggests, offers a radically new interpretation of the Greeks in which the previous 'scientific',
value-free conception of philological method plays a much reduced role. Sidestepping the
issue of whether or not one should be entitled to expect a 'scientific' work from a professor
of philology, Rohde calls Nietzsche's approach a 'philosophical-artistic mode of observation' that provides a much needed corrective to Hegelian, scientific optimism. 'Socratism',
the overvaluing of reason and science, he continues, destroyed Greek mythology and constitutes our greatest danger in the present age, for 'how can a sovereign logic which, in
its cheerful self-confidence, must regard the resolving of all world-riddles as in principle
attainable, have any place left for art save that of a charming diversion for those hours when
we are exhausted by the work of abstract thought?' Science had indeed made great progress,
so it is no wonder that it is 'gradually declaring all regions of the earth and the human mind
to be its possession'. But such arrogance is deadly. Humanity has an essential need for myth.
The old myths are indeed dead. But – Rohde concludes on an optimistic note – 'in noble
art there still lives the ability, in mythical re-reflection, to place the hidden features of the
great world-goddess [Gaia, presumably] before the enchanted eye'.[11]

Wilamowitz's Counterblast

Though Cosima would have preferred Rohde's review to have been more accessible to
the general public, Nietzsche thought it terrific. 'Friend, friend, what an achievement!'
he enthused the next day, ending his testosterone-filled letter with 'fight, fight, fight! I need
war'.[12] And he asked Fritzsch to make fifty copies, and had him send a copy to his head of
department, Vischer – without informing the latter that its author, 'Prof. Rohde in Kiel',
was his best friend! Four days later, however, a quite different view of *The Birth* appeared in a
pamphlet full of vicious invective entitled 'Philology of the Future – a Rejoinder' – a pun on
Wagner's 'music of the future'. The author was one 'Ulrich von Wilamowitz-Möllendorff,
Dr. phil.'

Wilamowitz – who eventually became, and remains, a giant of classical studies and, in
later life, regretted his pamphlet – was also a Pforta alumnus. Nietzsche, though he was four
years older, knew him slightly. (Erdmann von Wilamowitz-Möllendorff, Ulrich's great-
grandnephew – ironically, the custodian of the collection of Nietzsche's personal library
in the Anna Amalia Library in Weimar – gleefully claimed to me in conversation that
his great-granduncle's animus towards Nietzsche began at school where Nietzsche, then a
prefect, had reported him for smoking, and had been exacerbated when his marks in the
school-leaving exam failed quite to match up to Nietzsche's stellar performance.) Wilamowitz, who had yet to find an academic position, was a young, aggressive and gifted man
on the make. Whether or not it entered into his conscious calculations, it was obviously in
his interest to present himself as the champion of the establishment views in the world of
Greek philology.

Wilamowitz begins his review by saying (with an unmistakable sneer) that with
Nietzsche 'the metaphysician, the [Wagnerian] apostle, and Dionysian prophet' he will
have nothing to do. But since the author of *The Birth* is also a professor of classical

philology – Nietzsche presents himself as 'Full Professor of Classical Philology at the University of Basel' on the title page – it is incumbent on him to satisfy at least minimal professional standards. But he does not do so. His 'world-shaking' new interpretations of the texts of Archilochus, Euripides, et al. are products of 'ignorance and a lack of intellectual integrity'. Nietzsche lacks the scientific objectivity to understand the Greek texts in relation to their historical situation, and gives them ridiculous interpretations in order to produce Wagnerian–Schopenhauerian propaganda. He is ignorant of Winkelmann's* authoritative work, of the archaeological evidence, and is wildly wrong in the assigning of dates. (He refers, here, to Nietzsche's bad results in mathematics in his school-leaving exam, which supports the idea of an animus begun at Pforta.) As an example of Nietzsche's 'scientific' incompetence – or dishonesty – Wilamowitz mentions his failure to discuss Aeschylus's Lycurgean trilogy, in which Orpheus led the followers of Apollo in a clash with the devotees of Dionysus, a (fragmentary) text which, he suggests, makes the idea of an Apollonian–Dionysian 'brotherhood' ridiculous. Nietzsche also fails to mention the fact that the *Hippolytus* of Euripides contains an attack on Socrates which makes the idea that the latter inspired the former absurd. Wilamowitz ends his diatribe by saying that Nietzsche's

> religious gospel I am happy to ignore. My weapons do not touch it. Admittedly I am no mystic, no 'tragic man'…to me that will always be a drunken dream…One thing however I demand; that Herr Nietzsche practices what he preaches, grasps the thyrsos [a staff wound round with vines that symbolizes Dionysus]…and resigns the chair from which he is supposed to be teaching science; he must gather his tigers and panthers[†] to his knee, or whatever, but no longer seek to teach Germany's philological youth who must learn to study in ascetic self-denial.[‡,13]

Alienation of Ritschl

Wilamowitz's pamphlet was not, obviously, the response to *The Birth* Nietzsche had hoped for. Much more painful, however, was the reaction of his old teacher, mentor and friend, Friedrich Ritschl.

After the book appeared, Nietzsche waited with bated breath for, above all, Ritschl's reaction. But none came. Eventually, on January 30, 1872, he wrote Ritschl that he was astonished not to have heard from him, the book being a 'manifesto' to which silence was not a permitted response, least of all from his 'revered teacher'. The book, he added, was

> full of hope for our science of antiquity, for the German essence, even if a number of individuals will have to go under…The practical consequence of my views [i.e., the introduction of a new way of doing philology]…you'll be able to guess, partially, when I say that here [in Basel] I'm delivering public lectures 'On the Future of Our Educational Institutions'.[14]

---

* Johann Joachim Winkelmann (1717–68), the art historian who began the obsession with Greece that dominated German intellectual life at least until the mid-twentieth century.
† *The Birth*'s evocation of Dionysian ecstasy has Dionysus approaching in a flower-strewn chariot drawn by a tiger and a panther (see p. 128 above).
‡ The last sentence is probably intended to bring to mind the charge of corrupting the city's youth brought against Socrates by the Athenian court, a charge which led to his enforced suicide.

Forced to do so, Ritschl finally reacted in mid-February. At sixty-five, he said, he was too old to properly explore new 'spiritual worlds'. And he lacked the background in Schopenhauer to judge that aspect of the work – which did not deter him from remarking (apropos Schopenhauerian salvation) that 'we can as little overcome individuality as the individual leaves and blossoms of an individual plant can return to their roots'. Nonetheless, he continued, if he was compelled to comment he wanted to make the point that 'you can hardly expect an "Alexandrian" [i.e., "Socratic" type] and scholar' such as himself 'to condemn knowledge and allow the power to liberate and transform the world to be found only in art'. And, as 'an old pedagogue', he really had to wonder whether Nietzsche's plans for a reformed education would not, in fact, lead to a 'juvenile scorn for science without gaining thereby an increased feeling for art', thus opening the door to 'not poetry but rather general dilettantism'.[15]

There was too much affection between Nietzsche and Ritschl for either to allow the strained relationship to break entirely. Their correspondence continued and Nietzsche pleased Ritschl by returning to philological work. He produced a suitably 'scientific' article entitled 'The Florentine Treatise Concerning Homer and Hesiod' which appeared in Ritschl's *Rheinisches Museum* in February 1873 and he continued to send good students to Leipzig. Nonetheless, a breach had opened up that never properly healed, and Ritschl remained always defensive about his profession. In July, while agreeing that Wilamowitz's pamphlet itself failed to satisfy 'scientific' standards, he asserted that 'I can never agree with you that only art and philosophy can teach mankind. For me history does so too, in particular the philological branch of the same'.[16] And that he was still angry with Nietzsche in February of the following year is clear from a letter to Vischer:

> But our Nietzsche yes, that's really a sad story...It is remarkable how in that single man two souls live side by side. On the one hand the most rigorous methodology of schooled, scientific research...on the other, this fantastic-exaggerated, overly clever reaching into the incomprehensible, Wagnerian-Schopenhauerian-art-mysticism-rhapsodizing! What annoys me most is his impiety against his true mother who has suckled him at her breast: philology.[17]

Wagner's Intervention

Twelve days after the appearance of Wilamowitz's pamphlet, Wagner raised the temperature still further by publishing an open letter to his 'esteemed friend' Friedrich Nietzsche. It appeared on June 23, 1872, in the same pro-Wagnerian newspaper, the *Norddeutsche Allgemeine Zeitung*, that had published Rohde's review. Emphasising that the Wilamowitz pamphlet is by a mere 'Dr. phil.' – i.e., that it is the work of a jobless upstart attacking a full professor – he reports that, as a schoolboy, his initial passion for philology had been killed by the dry-as-(chalk)-dust approach to philology exemplified by Wilamowitz's small-minded logic-chopping. And then he raises the key question: what is the use of classical philology? Since Wilamowitz emphasises its 'scientific' character, one would suppose, he says, that it would be found useful by the other human sciences. Yet theologians, jurists, physicians et cetera exhibit no interest at all in philology as currently practised. Hence 'philologists must instruct each other, presumably with the sole object of turning out philologists, i.e., high-school teachers and university professors who will then "bake" a fresh batch of high-school teachers and university professors' ad infinitum. As currently practised, in other words, philology is an hermetically closed circle which serves only itself and contributes nothing at all to the community that pays its 'hefty salaries'. What we need, therefore, is a new kind of philologist, one who will make the discipline 'relevant' to non-philologists – Wagner is here accepting and endorsing the implication of Wilamowitz's title that Nietzsche is concerned to establish a new kind of 'Philology of the Future'. What we need is a philologist who 'speaks to us and not to his colleagues' and who 'transfuses life into the purely philological profession from those fountains of human knowledge which have waited hitherto in vain for fertilising by philology'.[18]

As usual, Wagner bludgeons his way to the heart of the matter. ('Every time Wagner insults someone he raises a deep problem', Nietzsche remarks in his notebooks.)[19] But in the profession it only increased Nietzsche's bad odour. Hermann Usener, Ritschl's successor in Bonn, called *The Birth* 'sheer nonsense' and, donning the black cap as it were, pronounced that 'scientifically, Nietzsche is dead'. As indeed he was. Philology students were advised to avoid Basel, and for the winter semester of 1872–3 Nietzsche had a total of two students, neither of whom was a philology major. At a time when Burckhardt was attracting an audience of fifty-three for Greek cultural history, and Nietzsche's friend Heinrich Romundt – an unpaid junior lecturer – twenty for his philosophy course, Nietzsche's teaching was essentially confined to the grammar school.

Von Bülow and the 'Manfred Meditation'

U nsurprisingly, given the Wilamowitz fracas, Nietzsche fell ill with stomach and bowel problems in June. But, though distressed at the damage to his university, he was soon able to exhibit a certain amount of grace under fire. Though insisting that Wilamowitz must be 'slaughtered' and providing Rohde with the ammunition to do so, he came to view the whole affair with slightly indulgent humour, suggesting that the cheeky 'lad' had probably been egged on by establishment figures:[20] writing to Krug, he asked him whether he had seen the recent pamphlet by – a rather good pun – 'Wilam-ohne-witz [William-without-wit]'.[21]

In July, however, he received a further blow. Encouraged by Hans von Bülow's enthusiastic response to *The Birth* – they had met the previous May at the laying of the Bayreuth foundation stone – Nietzsche sent him his 'Manfred Meditation', a piano work (composed in April 1872), which tries to imitate the *Zukunftsmusik* style of *Tristan* (track 15 on the Web site for this book). Von Bülow, famously tactless (he once told the tenor he was conducting as the 'Knight of the Swan' in Wagner's *Lohengrin* that he was the 'Knight of the Swine'), pulled no punches. The piece, he wrote Nietzsche, was

> the most extreme piece of fantastic extravagance, the least uplifting and most anti-musical set of marks on manuscript-paper I have come across in a long time. Frequently I had to ask myself: is the whole thing a joke; perhaps you intended a parody of the so-called music of the future?[22]

Responding to this blow, Nietzsche again displayed grace under fire. He thanked von Bülow for his frankness, admitted his poor musical taste and that he did not properly understand the syntax of music, and assured him that 'I will certainly never forget your advice. I say, as children do when they have done something stupid, "I promise I won't do it again"'.[23] And, true to his word, the 'Manfred Meditation' marked almost the end of his attempts at musical composition.

Nietzsche scholars generally take the view that von Bülow's judgment represented nothing more than the obvious truth about Nietzsche's talents as a composer. But this ignores the fact that Liszt was happy to play his 'Memories of a New Year's Eve' (see p. 109 above) in Bayreuth, later on in 1872, and, when told of von Bülow's judgment, commented, with a sad shake of the head, that it was 'way over the top' [*sehr desperat*].[24] And indeed it seems possible that more than musical objectivity may have been behind von Bülow's judgment. For the fact is that he himself had tried to be a composer of *Zukunftsmusik* and had failed dismally. This, indeed, may have been one of the reasons Cosima left him for Wagner. Wanting, rather like Alma Mahler, to be always at the side of creative genius, and seeing that von Bülow had no original talent as a composer, it is suggested, she jumped ship.[25]

Nietzsche, to venture my own opinion, was not a bad composer. And he was, of course, a terrific pianist. But he had two failings. First, he lacked command of large-scale structure. (One might, indeed, say the same of his philosophical writings: that the structureless, aphoristic style of many of his mature works stemmed more from necessity than from virtue.) Nearly all of his musical compositions last less than five minutes, and when he attempts a longer work he is unable to provide it with genuine unity. The 'New Year's Eve' music, for example (track 13 on the Web site for this book), after a lovely opening, degenerates into vague meanderings. His second failing was that he was never able to find an original voice. Everything he wrote sounds like someone else: Schumann or Liszt on a bad day, for example. Since imitation is the time-honoured method of learning, another way of saying this is that, as a composer, Nietzsche never developed beyond the student stage.

Retreat to the Mountains

Breaking through the storm clouds of mid-1872 were two rays of sunlight. First, Nietzsche's friend from Leipzig days, Heinrich Romundt, a philosopher who was writing a doctoral thesis on Kant's *Critique of Pure Reason*, finally agreed to move to Basel. Second, on June 28, together with von Gersdorff, he travelled to Munich to attend his first performance of *Tristan* (a decade after he and Krug had first studied the score). Nietzsche was so overcome by the experience (as one is) that, even a week later, he wrote Rohde that 'about *Tristan* I cannot speak'.[26] Only on July 25 could he confess that 'it is the most tremendous, the purest and the most unexpected thing I know. One swims in sublimity and happiness'.[27]

But one *Tristan* does not make a summer. So at the end of September Nietzsche set off for the mountains to lick his wounds. Intending to travel all the way to Italy, he arrived by post-coach at the tiny village of Splügen, set in a valley, five thousand feet above sea level, near the Swiss–Italian border. 'It was as if I had never known Switzerland…this is my nature' he wrote of the coach ride along the dramatic Via Mala. His letter to his mother continues,

As we approached Splügen I was overcome by the desire to remain here. I found a good hotel, with a quite simple little room. But it has a balcony with the most beautiful view. This high alpine valley…is just what I want. There are pure, strong gusts of air, hills and boulders of all shapes, and, surrounding everything, mighty snow-covered mountains. But what pleases me most are the splendid highroads over which I walk for hours ... At noon when the post-coach arrives I eat with strangers. I don't need to speak, nobody knows me ... In my little room I work with fresh vigour ... on my current main theme, 'The future of our Educational Institutions'. [At this stage he intended turning the lectures into a book.] ... Now I know a corner of the earth where I can live powerfully and with fresh activity, but entirely free of company. Human beings, here, are like shadow-pictures.[28]

In the end, Nietzsche came to settle on another, even higher, valley in the same southeast corner of Switzerland, the Engadine. But already we see the emergence of what will become an ever more prominent theme: Nietzsche's need to be alone with his thoughts.

Anal-Compulsive Philology

In mid-October, Nietzsche returned to Basel in time to catch Rohde's counter-attack on Wilamowitz, which appeared on October 15, 1872 (Nietzsche's twenty-eighth birthday). Descending to Wilamowitz's level of invective, if not lower, Rohde's pamphlet – at forty-eight pages a third longer than Wilamowitz's – was entitled *Afterphilologie*. As well as meaning 'pseudo', *After* also means 'anus'. A free but felicitous translation of his title might be 'Anal-Compulsive Philology'.[29]

In the pamphlet, Rohde tries to hoist Wilamowitz with his own petard, pointing to misquotations in order to suggest that he fails to live up to his own 'scientific' standards. He continues by noting that though Wilamowitz takes the part of 'Socratic man', who, according to *The Birth*, is the myth-destroying opponent of an 'artistic culture', he has, in reality, as much to do with Socrates – whom Nietzsche respects as well as criticises – 'as an ape with Hercules'. Rohde ends by suggesting that the jobless Wilamowitz's call for Nietzsche to step down from his chair causes one to 'smile at the ingenuousness with which the actual motive of the denunciatory zeal of this ambitious doctor of philology stands revealed'.[30]

Existential Philology

What was all this sound and fury really about? The curious fact is that while all participants in the fracas – including Nietzsche – agree that the issue is, as Wilamowitz's title puts it, the 'future of philology', philology is never mentioned in *The Birth*. So what is at issue is not so much what is *said* in the book but rather what it *exemplifies* and *implies*.

As he had already demanded of philology in his Leipzig days, in *The Birth* Nietzsche assimilates, and ultimately subordinates, his discussion of the Greeks to the 'great considerations of philosophy' (see p. 68 above). Because he conceived the philosopher as the 'physician of culture',[31] of *our* culture, it follows, as he puts it in the notes for the unfinished 'We Philologists', that 'the task of the philologist is that of understanding *his own age* better by means of the classical world'.[32] What, then, *The Birth* exemplifies, and implicitly holds up as a model for the future of the discipline, is what we might call 'existential philology'. Rohde refers to this in his original review of the book by suggesting that it provides 'an explanation and justification of the appearances'[33] – provides *us* with an explanation, explains to *us*, in what way, and in what sense, life is worth living. This, too, is what Wagner demands: a philology not just for philologists but one that is 'relevant' to the fundamental existential issues of humanity at large.

But this caused offence to the philological establishment for at least two reasons. First, it demanded a synoptic view of antiquity and hence offended the 'factory worker', the academic 'mole' (p. 105 above) burrowing away in his narrow speciality. And second, by suggesting that only a 'relevant' philology could justify its keep, it undermined the moral credentials of the nineteenth-century philologist's complaisant assumption that his discipline was an end in itself.

A further way in which *The Birth* offended the philological establishment was by undermining the perceived view of the Greeks as 'serenely rational'. By emphasising the irrational, Dionysian element in Greek life, by emphasising that Greek 'rationality' was an *achievement* rather than a birthright – the work's lasting, historical merit, it seems to me – Nietzsche undermined the Winkelmann–Goethe–Schiller classicism to which the establishment was still wedded.

A final and perhaps supreme offence was committed by the portrait of 'theoretical', scientific man as – so, at least, it could be read – an anal-retentive control freak, terrified of the mystery of life and out of touch with an ultimate reality accessible not to science but only to the artist in a state of Dionysian ecstasy. Since, as we saw, the likes of Wilamowitz conceived of themselves as, precisely, scientific men par excellence, they took the portrait of 'theoretical' or 'Alexandrian' man' – Ritschl explicitly did this (p. 153 above) – as an insulting portrayal of themselves. As von Gersdorff put it, Wilamowitz's pamphlet represented 'the cry of rage of theoretical man who sees a reflection of his true features for the first time and wants to smash the mirror'.[34]

Wilamowitz's review did not, as he had hoped, run Nietzsche out of the profession. His student numbers eventually recovered and, in the event, he had another seven years to go as a professor of philology – though the 1873 article on Homer and Hesiod (p. 153 above) was the last of his philological publications. Wilamowitz did, however, set the scholarly (some would say dry-as-dust), anti-speculative tone that dominated the study of classics throughout the following century. Looking back in the light of the near-death of classical philology, on the fact that it is now nearly impossible to study Greek in secondary school, one might well come to the conclusion that Nietzsche was right in his perception that the discipline was in need of a radical reform that would direct it towards 'relevance'. Nonetheless, the publication of *The Birth* and the events surrounding it cost him dearly. He lost the respect of the profession and never really recovered the old intimacy with Ritschl. One of Elizabeth's – very rare – insights is that the publication of *The Birth* established a pattern that would be repeated by almost every subsequent book: those who thought they knew him discovered in it a new Nietzsche from whom they felt estranged. Every step forward in his spiritual development, she observes, was accompanied by loss, suffering, and loneliness.[35]

Relations with the Wagners

At the end of November 1872 Nietzsche spent three days with the Wagners in Strasbourg, where they were trying to find singers to perform the *Ring* cycle. They invited him to spend Christmas in the new house in Bayreuth. Pleading 'exhaustion', however, he decided to spend Christmas in Naumburg, the first time for four years. After a stressful year it was probably true that he needed a dose of motherly comfort.

Wagner was not pleased by the non-appearance at the first Christmas in the new house of the person whom he had told, the previous June, he regarded as a son.[36] And since the journey from Basel to Naumburg was much longer than to Bayreuth, he was not impressed by the 'exhaustion' excuse. Insult was added to injury by the fact that there was neither the usual Christmas present nor a card announcing that one would be on the way. Nietzsche was simply absent. Only at the beginning of January did the *Five Prefaces to Five Unwritten Books* arrive with a dedication to Cosima. In February 1873, Cosima wrote Nietzsche that Wagner had been offended by the 'slight' but that all was now forgiven. The following month Nietzsche wrote von Gersdorff,

> I hadn't known that W[agner] was much offended by my non-appearance. God knows, by the way, how often I have offended the Master: each time I'm amazed and can't ever quite get to the cause of it.

But then he shows he really *does* know the cause:

> Please give me your opinion concerning my repeated offences. I can't conceive how anyone can be, in fundamental matters, more true or more deeply committed than I am: if I could think how, I'd be even more so. But in little, subordinate side-issues, and in a certain, almost 'sanitary', distancing from personal cohabitation that I find necessary, I must grant myself a freedom, really only to be able to preserve my loyalty in a higher sense.[37]

This is the first suggestion in Nietzsche's letters of any cloud in the Wagner–Nietzsche sky. And though not much bigger than a man's hand, it indicates both the beginnings and the character of the storm to come. Nietzsche needed the 'space' to be his own man, to escape from the overpowering presence of 'the Master' – and from the constant, time-consuming errand-running demanded by Cosima. The rudeness surrounding his Christmas non-appearance was probably a somewhat adolescent attempt to establish that space. The other highly significant feature of the letter to von Gersdorff is the distinction between Wagner *the man*, from whom Nietzsche requires a certain 'distance', and the 'fundamental matters' of Wagnerianism, to which he remains utterly committed. This distinction will be developed in the 1876 *Wagner at Bayreuth* into a division between the 'higher' and 'lower' Wagner. And later on it will develop into a complete rejection of Wagner the man and composer combined with, so I shall suggest, a never-to-be-relinquished commitment to Wagner the cultural critic, the constructive social theorist, and the philosopher of art.

Five Prefaces to Five Unwritten Books

The *Five Prefaces to Five Unwritten Books*[38] were not only late as a Christmas present but also somewhat ungraciously given. Bound together in an ugly brown leather cover, they were not well received. 'Prof. Nietzsche's manuscript does not restore our spirits', Cosima confided to her diary. And she complained to Malwida von Meysenbug of the 'clumsy abruptness' that sometimes accompanies the 'deep insights' in his work, adding 'we wished he would stick, in the main, to Greek themes'.[39]

Quite apart from the fact that the collection contained elements which were, as we shall see, incompatible with some of Wagner's deepest beliefs, Cosima was, I think, right to be disgruntled with the assemblage. Realising that he needed to give *something* by way of a Christmas present, it seems to me likely that Nietzsche simply threw together a hasty assemblage of fragments he had lying around. The result is of varying quality and, due to the fact that the fragments were written at different times, internally inconsistent. All in all, a non-unity that should not have become a Christmas present.

* * *

The first of the *Prefaces*, 'On the Pathos of Truth', is an early version of 'On Truth and Lies in a Non-moral Sense'[40] (unjustly celebrated as a work of profound insight by Nietzsche's postmodernist admirers), which was completed in the summer of 1873. I shall take the opportunity to discuss both works together.

The great philosophers, observes 'The Pathos of Truth', think they have *the* truth, a truth that will last for all time. But – this is what makes them tragic figures – there is no truth. The idea of absolute truth is merely the 'delusion (*Wahn*) of a god'. 'On Truth and Lies' (which begins by repeating the antepenultimate paragraph of 'The Pathos of Truth') seeks to explain why this is so.

It offers three arguments. First, though we think that the way the world appears to our intellect is *the* way it is, a midge or a bee, if it could contemplate the question, would have exactly the same 'puffed up pride' with respect to the entirely different way it appears to them. 'For the plant, the whole world is plant, for us human' reads a note from this period.[41] So 'truths are illusions we have forgotten to be such'.

Second, the possibility of anything being either true or false depends on language. But words are simply conventionally agreed responses to particular 'nervous stimulations', as arbitrary as the gender of nouns. (In German, every noun is either masculine, feminine, or neuter.) Hence (presumably because other languages apply entirely different words to the same nervous stimulations) there is no way things which count as true in our language can be held to be true in the sense of corresponding to the way the world really is.

Third, the concepts ('dog', for example) we deploy in language are abstract: they gather individual things together as 'the same'. But this is to 'make equivalent what are not equivalent'. Hence, once again, anyone who thinks they possess even a single truth about the real world is pathetically deluded.

The quality of this discussion is low and reveals another justification for the Basel philosophers' rejection of Nietzsche's application for the philosophy chair. What the discussion reveals more than anything is – brilliant though he was – Nietzsche's lack of training in the *craft* of technical philosophical thinking. Had he been schooled in Aristotle and medieval scholasticism – had he, for instance, like Heidegger, attended a Catholic seminary – he would have produced none of these slipshod arguments.

Let us observe, first of all, that, were the conclusion that 'truth is an illusion' to be true, a serious puzzle would be raised as to how the 'clever animal' that is man has been able to survive in a competitive environment. Nietzsche makes no attempt in 'Truth and Lies' to address the fact that human survival presents a prima facie case that, at least mostly, our beliefs about the world are true.

The second observation concerning Nietzsche's conclusion is that he contradicts himself. It is a good thing our supposed truths are illusions, he says both in 'Truth and Lies' and in 'The Pathos of Truth', since truth is terrible: if anyone were (*per impossible*) to peer through a crack in the chamber of consciousness he would see that 'humanity, in the indifference of its ignorance, rests on the pitiless, the greedy, the insatiable, the murderous'. Humanity 'clings to dreams, as it were, on the back of a tiger'. So, it seems, there *is*, after all, the possibility of knowing the truth about the world – of at least a *philosopher's* knowing that truth. *Nietzsche* knows that behind the veneer of civilisation the human animal is a wild beast. So truth is an illusion and Nietzsche knows the truth. A contradiction.

Turning to the first of the arguments summarised above, the fact that the midge sees the world differently from us does not, in reality, mean that our beliefs are *false*, since we and the midge *may both be right*. We see a rotten apple, the midge sees an egg-laying site. We are *both* right.* The second argument – the argument about different languages applying different signs to 'nerve stimulations' – confuses sentences and statements, a fallacy exposed in every 'Critical Thinking 101' course. 'Grass is green' is a different sentence from (the German) '*Gras ist grün*'. But they both mean the same, make the same 'statement'. And what they both say is *true*. The things that are true or false, that is to say, are, strictly speaking, not sentences, but statements. So the fact that different languages apply different signs to the same nerve stimulations has no tendency at all to show that truths can never be expressed in those languages.

The final argument is weakest of all, embarrassingly bad. That collies, dachshunds, terriers and German shepherds are all classified as 'dogs' does not claim them to be *completely the same* – 'equivalent'. It merely claims them to be the same *in a certain respect*.

With the line of thought being developed in the first *Preface* Cosima was, then, right to be thoroughly dissatisfied. The second, 'Thoughts Concerning the Future of Our Educational Institutions', is virtually identical with the preface to the eponymous lecture series (pp. 142–7 above) and so needs no further discussion.

The third *Preface*, 'The Greek State',[42] was actually written in the first weeks of 1871[43] and had originally been intended as a chapter for *The Birth*. Wagner would have found it positively offensive since it praises both war and slavery; the first he wished to overcome and the second he considered an abomination.

The essay's tone is that of overcoming the squeamishness, the 'excessive sensitivity of modern man', of unflinchingly facing up to some hard, 'cruel-sounding' truths. The argument is as follows. Culture is the highest goal since only through it does nature achieve her 'salvation in appearance, in the mirror of genius'.[44] This demands two things. First the state, necessary to overcoming the 'war of all against all' that precedes it and thereby to produce the conditions of security in which alone art can flourish. And second, within the state, slavery, so as to create the conditions of leisure necessary for the 'genius' to produce art. (This he adds, a further remark liable to have offended Wagner, is why socialists have always hated art.) The state thus has to be the 'broad based pyramid' outlined in Plato's *Republic*; in fact, the right order of the state is precisely that outlined by Plato save for the substitution of the 'genius in the most general sense' for Plato's 'genius of wisdom and knowledge',[45] the

---

* The idea that different perspectives may reveal different, but complementary, truths about reality is a doctrine I call 'plural realism'. In Chapter 23 (pp. 474–6 below) I shall suggest that it is, in fact, plural realism that constitutes the mature Nietzsche's account of truth and reality.

'philosopher-king'. What we need, in other words, is a state ruled by Sophocles rather than Socrates. But the state can only flourish under conditions of (actual or threatened) war: in times of peace, the 'iron grip' of the state loosens and decays. Hence war is necessary for culture.

The standard of argument in this *Preface* is again low. It suffers, in a way in which Wagner's writings never suffer, from a misuse of history, from supposing that every aspect of an admired period in the past must be reproduced to reproduce those features which make it admirable. Fairly obviously, the argument that only societies that reduce the majority to – at least economic – 'slavery' can produce art is refuted by the washing-machine: art indeed requires the artist to be freed from the necessity of life-sustaining work, but since machines can generate such freedom there is no need for human 'slavery'. And even granted that the state needs an external threat to ensure its authority, such a threat may consist in economic, artistic, or even sporting competition rather than the threat of violence. As Nietzsche realises in *Thus Spoke Zarathustra*, a nation may seek to dominate its neighbours through cultural 'shining' rather than military conquest.[46]

Another weakness – a weakness that runs through much of his early thinking – is an unclarity concerning the condition of the 'slave'. On the one hand there is what we may call the 'aesthetic fascism' view. The 'world of art' that belongs to a small number of 'Olympian men' requires the 'misery of men living a life of toil'.[47] The 'pyramidal' society offers nothing but exploitation and misery to the slave, but that does not matter since only the life of the genius – through whom nature reaches her highest goal – is of any value.* But on the other hand, Nietzsche asks us to observe

> what an elevating effect on us is produced by the sight of a medieval serf, whose legal and ethical relationship with his superior was internally sturdy and sensitive, whose narrow existence was profoundly cocooned – how elevating and how reproachful.[48]

This makes it look as though, after all, Nietzsche cares about the well-being of the slaves, but wishes to argue that slavery is in the best interest of the slave type of person since he is, first, protected by 'sensitive' legal requirements from unlimited exploitation and, second, lives a life not of 'misery' but rather of enviable security.

The fourth *Preface*, 'On the Relation of Schopenhauer's Philosophy to a German Culture', argues the need for a general 'public education' as opposed to the mere 'public opinion' manufactured by newspapers. And it attacks the so-called educated classes of the present age as suffering from 'philistine complacency [*Gemütlichkeit*]'. What creates complacency, Nietzsche says, is 'historical consciousness'. Such consciousness kills enthusiasm. When everything is historically grasped we enter a spirit of '*nihil admirari*'. So, for example, to become aware of our moral values as just one item on a vast historical menu of alternative sets of values destroys our commitment to our own values, since we can find no ground for preferring them to any of the alternatives on display, and lapse – there are strong echoes of Wagner's critique of 'cultural history' (p. 113–14 above) here – into ('postmodern') nihilism. Action, commitment, passion, Nietzsche is suggesting, require a certain chauvinism, a sense

---

* This is what I called the 'only-the-superman-counts' view. For many interpreters, this is not merely something half-suggested in some of Nietzsche's youthful works, but the heart of his mature philosophy. I shall be concerned to reject this interpretation.

of one's own values as the only *possible* values. (In the 1887 *Genealogy of Morals* he will deploy 'historical consciousness' to, as he sees it, the benevolent end of deconstructing Christian morality.)

The final *Preface*, 'Homer's Competition', is by far the best and most important of the set. But I shall discuss it no further, since it was examined at length in the previous chapter (pp. 139–41 above). Suffice it to say that, written nearly two years after 'The Greek State', by pointing to the existence of 'good' as well as 'bad' Eris, it completely undercuts the earlier work's argument for the necessity of war. Since 'competition' exists as an alternative to physical violence, there is no reason that the 'agonistic' relation of sublimated violence that obtains *within*, and fuels the life of, a healthy state should not also obtain *between* states.

In sum, then, the *Five Prefaces* add up to a collection of highly variable quality in which some parts contradict others. Truly, as Cosima suggests, a curate's egg.

10

Untimely Meditations

Nietzsche's 1873 was marked by two tensions. The first was between his role as a professor of classical philology and his ever-increasing absorption in philosophy, between his *Beruf* [profession] and his *Berufung* [vocation], as he elegantly describes it.[1] The second was between, on the one hand, his still total commitment to viewing the world from within the 'Bayreuth Horizon' (p. 112 above) and to doing whatever he could for the Bayreuth cause and, on the other, his growing need to escape the gigantic shadow cast by Wagner's personality and intellect, to find a place in the sun in which he could grow into his own man. (The composer Peter Cornelius, notwithstanding his absolute devotion to Wagner, experienced exactly the same problem.) The first of these dilemmas he attempted to resolve by teaching and writing about those classical texts which were susceptible to philosophical treatment. Thus, though he would never again, after 1872, publish a book devoted to a classical text, 1873–4 did see a substantial, unpublished study of the pre-Platonic Greek philosophers, *Philosophy in the Tragic Age of the Greeks*. The second tension he attempted to resolve by, on the one hand, writing furious polemics on Wagner's behalf and at his behest while, on the other, confining his personal interaction with the Wagners to the 'virtual' interaction of letters (Cornelius adopted the same strategy), gaining thereby their disappointment and disapproval. Given these troubled waters, it is no surprise that Nietzsche's health suffered once again: 1873 was plagued by viral infections, eye-trouble and intestinal problems, the latter probably still the result of the dysentery contracted during his war service. In terms of health, 1873 set the pattern for the rest of Nietzsche's life: from now on, up until his final three months of sanity, he will never be free of such troubles for more than a few weeks at a time.

Fun in Basel

The year began well. Nietzsche was asked to judge a competition for the best essay on the poetry of Wagner's *Ring* cycle by the *Allgemeine Deutsche Musikverein* (All-Germany Music Society). He was quite proud of this, announcing his appointment in several letters – proud, presumably, because the invitation suggested that he was achieving a certain status and success with respect to his life-defining goal, Bayreuth.

He was also extremely happy to have two close friends in Basel: 'Overbeck and Romundt, my table-, house- and thought-friends', he wrote to Rohde, 'are the most excellent company in the world'.*,2 Romundt, who was now writing an *Habilitation* (second Ph.D.) on the theory of knowledge, he admired as a teacher of radical philosophical views who was able to excite his students. Overbeck he loved for his simple good-heartedness and admired for his 'radicalism' (p. 105 above).

In April we learn something of the character of Overbeck's 'radicalism':

> In my house [he writes Malwida von Meysenbug] something very notable is coming about: a characterisation of our current theology with respect to its *Christianity*. My friend and brother in spirit, Prof. Overbeck, to the best of my knowledge the most free-thinking theologian alive and the possessor of an enormous knowledge of Church history, works now on this characterisation and will ... make known a startling truth.[3]

'Our house', he writes, alluding to his own and Overbeck's radical dissection of current sacred cows, 'will one day become notorious'.[4]

Overbeck's book, *How Christian Is Our Present-day Theology?* was published in November 1873 by Fritzsch, three months after the first of Nietzsche's *Untimely Meditations* appeared with the same publisher. It argued that original Christianity was a matter of practice rather than theory, of the heart rather than the head, with the result that 'Christian theology' is in fact an oxymoron – ideas which appear in Nietzsche's *Antichrist* and which, sixty years later, influenced Martin Heidegger's attack on 'the God of the theologians'. In Overbeck's copy of the first *Untimely Meditation* – an assault on a sacred cow that was as radical, as we shall see, as Overbeck's – Nietzsche inscribed:

> A pair of twins from one house/Go forth bravely into the world/To tear world-dragons limb from limb/Friendship is what it's called/The one father to the other.

* * *

At the beginning of 1873, as we saw, only two students enrolled for Nietzsche's course on Greek and Roman rhetoric. He decided, therefore, that the class should meet in his apartment in the *Gifthütte*. Sometimes beer was provided. He also often entertained his grammar-school students there. One of these, Louis Kelterborn, has left a description of Nietzsche at home:

> One is immediately impressed by the combination of exceptional courtesy and refinement in manner and behaviour with the most charming and natural kindliness, so that one soon feels elevated directly and automatically to a finer and nobler, cleaner and higher, spiritual atmosphere ... In complete harmony with the tastefulness of his demeanour and clothing, and with his almost military precision, are all the furnishings of the apartment in the pleasant, middle-class house. In light-coloured breeches and a brown frock-coat or jacket, and, out of doors, wearing a top-hat [quaintly old-fashioned, even then] – this is how he lives in

---

* This makes it sound as though Romundt had actually moved into the *Gifthütte*. But since Nietzsche writes on April 1, 1874, that 'Romundt has been our housemate since yesterday', he must just mean that he visited frequently.

my memory. On hot summer days [Basel can become extremely humid] he tried to lower the temperature in his room with blocks of ice.[5]

The happiness of Nietzsche's home life was increased when a Frau Baumann, a true house mother, took over the ownership of the Schützgraben house in June. This led to the *Gifthütte* being rechristened *Baumannshöhle* [Baumann's cave] and to frequent references to its inhabitants (including Romundt from April 1874) as 'cave bears'. The 'cave' must have possessed a samovar (perhaps on account of Overbeck's Russian background) since, years later, Nietzsche sent Overbeck a postcard reminding him of their time together there:

> Verses from Baumann's Cave
> Wisdom speaks: there where thoughts are absent
> There the tea [*Tee*] arrives at the right time
> A god still unknown to the souls of the Greeks
> 'Machine god' [*Maschinentheos*] – lets us become wise!
> (Thus spoke one of the cave-bears to the other as he learnt how to drink tea from him.)[6]

As well as being happy in his cave, Nietzsche also enjoyed a vibrant social life. He was regularly to be found in the homes of colleagues and in Basel's best patrician houses – often overlapping categories since, as noted, many of the professors came from the best families. In March he wrote home that

> There have been several festivities e.g. at the Vischers, to celebrate two engagements ... a ball at the Vischer-Bischoffs, a hundred people were there; before that Sally, Frau Walter, and some men put on an operetta. Then I was one evening with the good Siebers, with Socin and Jacob Burckhardt.[7]

The Penguin translation of *Ecce Homo* has, on the cover, a Caspar David Friedrich portrait of a man, seen from the rear – Nietzsche, we are encouraged to believe – standing alone on a mountain-top, gazing down into the mist-filled valleys below. This promotes the image of Nietzsche as a misanthropic social misfit. We know already, however, from his busy social life in Leipzig, that this romantic stereotype is actually a myth. (The isolation of his later years, we shall see, was the product not of misanthropy or social incompetence but of appalling health and a workaholic nature.) In Basel the sociability of his Leipzig years continued and even intensified. Here, for example, is Frau Ida Miaskowski's memory of him in 1874:

> In winter we founded a small social group which every two weeks met in the evenings. On one of these evenings there was, for Nietzsche's benefit, a charming performance ... a tableau vivant from the *Die Meistersinger* ... When all the guests were assembled, I asked Nietzsche to play the prize song and opened the door to the dining room, in which the charming tableau was set up ... Everyone was delighted and Nietzsche, in fact, greatly moved. He took my two hands and pressed them again and again, in thanks for the charming surprise ... my Emmy, she had never been in such a circle of innocent fun. The strange thing was that the two chief sources of merriment, Overbeck and Nietzsche, were known throughout Germany as terrible pessimists and Schopenhauerians! Last Thursday we did a lot of music. Nietzsche improvised entrancingly and Overbeck brought four-handed pieces by Schubert.

On another occasion she wrote,

> This evening is our Tuesday group. Nietzsche says he's got a funny book to read aloud [it was a collection of humorous stories by Mark Twain]. Last time it was great fun, we read, played, and jumped about until half past twelve.

And she records that during the winter Nietzsche came regularly on Fridays to accompany her while she sang.[8]

Gloom in Bayreuth

In March 1873 – showing that his impulse to compose had not been entirely squashed by von Bülow's savage judgment – Nietzsche composed a 'Monodie à deux', a four-handed piano work for the wedding of a Herr Monod (track 16 on the Web site for this book);* since a 'monody' is a work that has a single melodic line (as well as being a pun on its recipient's name), the piece was, he pointed out, 'highly symbolic for a wedding'.[9] The following month he finally made his first visit to Bayreuth, accompanied by Rohde, to spend the week of Easter (April 6–12) with the Wagners in their new, but far from finished, house, *Wahnfried*.

He caught them at a bad moment. Of the thousand sponsorship certificates that needed to be sold before work on the Festspielhaus could even begin, only two hundred had actually been sold. Wagner was thus in a grumpy mood – most unusually, he said at one point that he couldn't stand the 'continual chatter' in the house – secretly regretting (with Nietzsche) that he had ever left Tribschen. Harassed by the need to deal with communications from the Wagner societies all over Germany and to engage in promotional activity with the hated press (and so more than usually anti-Semitic), he loathed the distraction from the chief task of completing the orchestration of *Götterdämmerung*. When Nietzsche tried to cheer them up by playing one of his own compositions – probably a reduced version of the 'Monodie à deux' – he failed: 'we were irritated by our friend's music-making hobby', Cosima wrote patronizingly in her diary. Nietzsche was, however, allowed to read from his work-in-progress, *Philosophy in the Tragic Age of the Greeks*, on three evenings, which indicates that it at least was treated with more respect than his music.

* * *

This work is chiefly notable for its close identification with Heraclitus, an identification Nietzsche retained throughout his life. Anaximander, in the oldest known fragment of Western philosophy, wrote,

> Whence things have their coming into being there they must also perish according to necessity: for they must pay a penalty and be judged for their injustice, according to the ordinances of time.

All that is born is condemned to death. For Anaximander, existence is a kind of punishment for some mysterious guilt, some kind of 'original sin'. With Heraclitus, however, Nietzsche argues, we learn how to overcome Anaximander's pessimism. Unlike Parmenides, who held that 'becoming' (change) is an illusion, Heraclitus agrees with Anaximander that becoming

---

* Gabriel Monod married Olga Herzen, daughter of Alexander Herzen, the Russian socialist revolutionary, and foster daughter of Malwida von Meysenbug, who had kept Herzen's house for him in London (see further p. 231 below).

is real. Indeed there is *nothing but* becoming – it is Parmenides's 'being' which is an illusion. Heraclitus's achievement, Nietzsche continues, was to transfigure Hesiod's 'good' Eris into a cosmic principle. Unlike the frozen world of Parmenides, Heraclitus's world consists in eternal 'competition', innumerable pairs of opposites 'wrestling in joyous combat'.

But does this not involve guilt and suffering, as Anaximander says? 'Yes', Nietzsche reports Heraclitus as saying, 'but only for the limited human being who sees divergently not convergently'. To the 'aesthetic man' or the 'child-artist' (*The Birth of Tragedy*'s hero), it is all innocent play.¹⁰

In a note written slightly earlier, Nietzsche says that

> The Greek nature knew how to make use of all the *terrible* features [of the world]…the use of the harmful for the sake of the useful is idealised in the world view of Heraclitus.¹¹

This explains the meaning of 'convergent'. Heraclitus, Nietzsche holds, achieves a view according to which the world can be joyously affirmed, since the harmful ultimately leads to the beneficial – but only in the eyes of someone who ascends from the point of view of the human individual to that of the world-creating child-god-artist. As in *The Birth*, therefore, overcoming Anaximander's 'nausea' consists, for a Heraclitean, in a transcendence of human individuality.

Though Cosima found the readings from *Philosophy in the Tragic Age* 'new and interesting' she records no comment from Wagner, who likely found the work (which mentions neither music nor drama) tangential to his own, pressing concerns.

* * *

Four days after returning from Bayreuth to Basel, Nietzsche humbly wrote to Wagner about the visit:

> If you seemed not satisfied with my presence I understand it only too well, without being able to do anything about it, for I learn and perceive only very slowly. And every moment with you I experience something I had never thought before and which I wish to impress on my mind. I know very well, dearest Master, that such a visit can be no relaxation for you, must indeed be virtually unbearable. I have often wished to give at least the appearance of greater freedom and independence, but in vain. Enough. I ask you simply to take me as your pupil…It is true that I become each day more melancholy when I feel so deeply how much I'd like to be useful to you in some way or other, and how completely unsuited I am for that, so that I can do nothing to alleviate your distraction or cheer you up.¹²

The letters of the Tribschen period exhibit *reverence* for 'the Master'. But with its echoes of a Christian confession of inalienable sinfulness, this letter can only be described as *grovelling*. The most revealing line, however, is the reference to the need for 'greater freedom and independence'. Nietzsche is here trying in the most delicate manner to tell the Master to his face what he told von Gersdorff in the letter quoted in the previous chapter: that he needs a 'sanitary' distance from 'personal cohabitation' with Wagner, needs to be free of his overpowering personal presence in order to be 'true to him in a higher sense' (p. 158 above).

Nietzsche's technique for gaining that distance was to replace 'personal cohabitation' with letters of this grovelling character. Even after Wagner had replied in his bluff, good-humoured way that 'you must come and "burden" me more often' and that the children (missing him as much as their father, presumably) have been playing 'Nietzsche and

Rohde',[13] Nietzsche continues in his grovelling vein, writing Wagner in May that he is 'sensible every moment', that without him he would be 'a still-born creature'.[14] But while the letters grovel, his personal attendance at Bayreuth dwindles to almost nothing. In contrast to the twenty-three visits to Tribschen between 1869 and 1872, from 1872 to 1874 he paid only four visits to Bayreuth, and none at all in 1875.

Scholars often suggest that this distancing of himself from Wagner, the man, was also a distancing from Wagner, the artist and thinker. But this is not so. Throughout 1873 his private notebooks reveal *not the slightest* hint of a departure from Wagner's worldview and not the slightest reservation about either his music or his philosophy. Indeed they continue to affirm that Nietzsche's thoughts are all 'Bayreuth-horizon observations'.[15] And they contain a great deal of Wagner admiration in a context where flattery has no point: the already quoted 'Every time Wagner insults he touches on a deep problem', for example.[16]

First Untimely Meditation: David Strauss, the Confessor and the Writer

In the first of the 'grovelling' letters quoted above, Nietzsche, having lamented his inability to cheer Wagner up, continues,

> But perhaps after all I can [cheer you up], when I've completed what I'm working on, namely a piece against the famous writer David Strauss. I have read through his *Old and New Faith* and have been amazed at its obtuseness and vulgarity.[17]

To this, in his 'please-be-a-burden-again' letter, Wagner responds, 'with regard to the Straussiana, the only thing that causes me pain is that I can't wait for it. So – out with it!'[18]

In 1868 Wagner had been involved in a public squabble with Strauss and had directed three satirical sonnets against him. When Strauss's *Old and New Faith* appeared in 1872, Wagner had found it, as Cosima records, 'deeply superficial'. Nietzsche knew, therefore, that the attack on Strauss would please Wagner. Back in Basel at the beginning of May 1873, he wrote to Rohde that he had again 'spewed forth some lava'. He had come back from Bayreuth, he says, 'in such a prolonged melancholy, that holy fury became the only way to get out of it'.[19] This was the first sketch of, as von Gersdorff would christen it, the *Straussiade* (sometimes *AntiStraussiade*), warrior-Nietzsche's 'cannonade' against Wagner's enemy. The work was written at lightning speed. It was finished in May and (publishers, like postal services, being much more efficient then than now) appeared with Fritzsch in July.

Why, however, Strauss? Of all the many figures both he and Wagner disapproved of, why did Nietzsche select the author of *The Old and New Faith*, in particular, as an object on which to vent his bottled-up fury?

Initially Nietzsche thought of calling the *First Meditation*, indeed his whole projected series of *Meditations*, 'the philosopher as physician of culture'.[20] But in fact, as he recognises in *Ecce Homo*, a metaphor of violence is more appropriate to the work's 'warlike' character. It is, he says, an 'assassination [*Attentat*]'.[21] Yet as *Ecce Homo* also says, the real object of attack is not Strauss in particular but rather 'German culture' in general.[22] So the attack is in a sense impersonal – Strauss is of interest only as a paradigm of what is wrong with the character of the (non-)culture of Bismarck's Germany.

As we saw, together with George Eliot, Nietzsche had once admired Strauss: Strauss's *Life of Jesus* played a crucial role in his own liberation from Christian faith (pp. 56–7 above). At twenty, he recalls in 1888, he took great pleasure in its deconstruction of the Bible.[23] In the *Meditation* itself he acknowledges that Strauss had *once* been a fine scholar. The figure he attacks, however, is the aged, soft-minded Strauss who reintroduces by the back door the religion which, in his days of tough-minded vigour, he had kicked out of the front. The author of *The Old and New Faith* offers, Nietzsche notes, a version of Hegelian optimism – a kind of evolutionary pantheism – as an alternative religion. He offers 'the rationality of the real'[24] as leading to a 'heaven on earth'.[25] Nietzsche offers three lines of criticism.

First, it is a stupid 'ease and contentment doctrine'. Like Hegelianism in general, it is merely a 'deification of success', an 'apotheosis of the commonplace'.[26] In his notebooks, Nietzsche repeats Schopenhauer's claim that 'the Hegelian "world-process" ends in a fat Prussian state with good police'.[27] As Nietzsche sees it, that is, the Hegelians of the 1870s take Prussia's triumph over France to be the final coincidence of 'the rational' (i.e., the good) with the real; the 'end of history'. His objection is that this is nothing more than a contemptible pandering to Strauss's self-satisfied, bourgeois audience, the complacent 'we',[28] as whose spokesman he appoints himself. Already in its fourth edition after less than a year in print, Strauss's *Old and New Faith* was a blockbuster. 'We have a low opinion', Nietzsche writes to Cosima, 'of what finds immediate success and acceptance in these desolate times'.[29] Such pandering might have *something* to be said for it were there anything to admire about Bismarck's Germany. But, in fact, nothing is admirable about a bourgeois 'philistinism' which, like a worm, conceived of heaven as nothing higher than a 'fat carcass'.[30]

As we have seen, what Nietzsche loathes about Wilhelminian Germany is the mood of triumphalism (mirrored in Strauss's Hegelian triumphalism), the assumption that military victory over France was somehow a proof of the superiority of German culture. (The equally disastrous mood of America's 'neo-cons' after the collapse of the Soviet Union provides a parallel.) Nietzsche makes the obvious point that the victory over France had nothing to do with cultural superiority. It was due, rather, to 'strict military training, superiority in the science of warfare among the leaders' and 'unity and obedience among the led'. 'One more victory like this', he adds, 'and while the German Reich will survive, the German will be destroyed'.[31] Of course, the fact that the Bayreuth project – the one hope of reviving 'the German' – appeared to be foundering through lack of funds merely confirmed Nietzsche's assessment of imperial Germany as a society engulfed by 'barbarism'. 'War-triumphalism', he notes, is a greater danger to 'the secretly growing fruit'* than military defeat would have been.

* KSA 7 19 [314]. This Hölderlin-like phrase is illuminated by a note which reads, 'Hölderlin on Germany: "Now you tarry and keep silent, ponder a joyful work/The only thing, like yourself, that is/Born out of love and is good, as you are./Where is your Delos, where your Olympia,/So that we can all find ourselves in the highest festival?/But how will your son guess, what you, immortal one, have long prepared for yourselves?"' (KSA 7 27 [69]). For Hölderlin, as for Nietzsche and Wagner, the redemption of German life depends on the return of the Greek 'festival'. What this note indicates, I think, is that in the 1870s (and, in fact, all his life) Nietzsche identifies his stance towards the Germans with that of his 'favourite poet' (pp. 42–4 above): the stance of 'tough love', the love that speaks the hard truths that need to be spoken, but never gives up hope that the Germans will one day redeem themselves.

Nietzsche's second criticism is directed against Strauss's pantheism. Even if there is, as Strauss claims, a primordial source of everything, how, he asks, can it possibly be called 'God' and made an object of religious veneration given that, as the source of everything, it is also the source of all *evil*?[32] As we have seen, Nietzsche himself is concerned with this problem of evil, with attaining the Heraclitean view that sees evil as justified by its contribution to a greater good (p. 167 above). Thus the criticism here, one may assume, is not so much of pantheism itself as of the fact that Strauss has not seen the problem, has made no intellectual effort to overcome what, *on the face of things*, is a crushing objection to pantheism.

Nietzsche's third criticism amounts to the claim that, in the language of *The Birth of Tragedy*, Strauss is a 'Socratist', that he is the 'theoretical man' who believes that science can achieve absolute mastery over nature and thereby solve every human problem. The *Meditation* raises two objections to the Socratism which, remember, Nietzsche takes to be the dominant outlook of the present age. First he repeats the claim of *The Birth* that Socratism is shown to be false by Kantian philosophy. Strauss, he says, is one of those people who cannot understand Kant. That he subscribes to 'the crudest sort of realism' shows that he has no understanding of

> Kant's critique of reason . . . no notion of the fundamental antinomies of idealism [Nietzsche means 'antinomies that are *resolved by* idealism] or of the extreme relativity of all science and reason. Or: it is precisely reason that ought to tell him how little of the in-itself [*Ansich*] of things is determined by reason.[33]

So, since it cannot know reality, science cannot control it, is powerless in the face of the traumas created by the creator-child-artist's decision to smash one of its sandcastles. (Of course, even if it could control the world, Nietzsche believes, that would not solve our most essential problems. Man cannot live without the idealism of inspirational myth and Socratism, as we know, kills myth. Strauss, he observes, would put a visionary such as Jesus in a madhouse and has nothing to say about the mythic significance of the resurrection other than that it is 'humbug'.)[34]

Nietzsche's second objection to Strauss's Socratism is that it is 'consciously dishonest'. The great dragon-killer pulls his punches for fear of disturbing the complaisant sleep of his audience. On the one hand he claims to accept Darwin's theory of evolution. But, on the other, he tells one to 'remember you are a man not a mere creature of nature'. In other words, rather than seeing that this revolutionary new metaphysical material-ism demands a revolutionary new morality based on acceptance of the 'war of all against all', Strauss tells us we can go on just as before. Instead of saying 'I have liberated you from a helpful and merciful God, the universe is only a rigid machine, take care you are not mangled in its wheels',[35] Strauss pretends that everything can carry on in the same old way.

* * *

Wagner loved the first *Meditation*, writing to Nietzsche, 'I have re-read it and swear to God that you are the only one who knows what I want'.[36] Liszt noted that he was full of 'sympathetic wonder' at the work.[37] And though Cosima was less impressed, she was moved, by some disparaging remarks about Nietzsche by Wagner's sister, Ottilie Brockhaus, to defend him as someone who 'had put his whole career in jeopardy for her [Ottilie's] brother' and was his 'truest follower'.[38] Gottfried Keller (the Swiss author of the novel *Green Henry*, which Nietzsche greatly admired) on the other hand thought it a 'juvenile' product of someone overeager to be a 'big man'.[39] Karl Hillebrand, the distinguished man of letters, however, called it a 'witty' work and observed, shrewdly, that it was a 'sign of a return to the German [moral] idealism that our grandparents aspired to'.[40] In Basel, the *Straussiade* did Nietzsche no harm at all. The God-fearing were delighted by the attack on the notorious 'atheist'; the remainder found it amusing. It was, in fact, shortly after the appearance of the *Meditation* that his colleagues elected him dean of the faculty for the following year. Strauss himself was bemused; 'how can one be so furious', he wondered, 'with someone who has never crossed his path?',[41] a question the answer to which should now be clear enough. When, however, Strauss died in February of the following year, Nietzsche had an attack of remorse: 'I hope I didn't make the last years difficult to bear and that he died without knowing anything of me', he wrote von Gersdorff.[42]

Rest Cure in Flims

The final pages of the first *Meditation* were completed by dictation. In May 1873, there was a dramatic deterioration in Nietzsche's eyesight. He experienced agonizing pain in the eyes and by the time his sister came to visit on June 5 he could no longer read or write. He was forced to wear dark glasses whenever he ventured out of doors and in fact spend most of the time indoors behind drawn curtains. Fortunately, von Gersdorff, newly returned from Italy, was on hand for Nietzsche to dictate the *Meditation* to him and to prepare the final, print-ready manuscript. In spite of his own ill health, von Gersdorff altered his plans and stayed at Nietzsche's side as amanuensis until September – my 'left eye' as well as my 'right hand', Nietzsche describes him to Wagner.[43] (That von Gersdorff and soon others would perform this service indicates that those who knew Nietzsche sensed already that they were dealing with a person of exceptional importance.)

By early July, Nietzsche's condition had deteriorated so rapidly that his medical friend, Dr. Immermann, told him that he would have to cancel his grammar-school teaching before the end of the school year and undergo a rest cure in some secluded mountain village. Evidently Immermann felt there was a psychosomatic factor contributing to Nietzsche's condition: he diagnosed over-stimulated nerves and offered, by way of remedy, the instruction: 'be more stupid and you will feel better'.[44]

Taking Immermann's advice, in a manner of speaking, Nietzsche and von Gersdorff left Basel on July 7 for Flims, a thousand metres above sea level to the west of Chur, where they stayed, until they returned to Basel in the middle of August, in a chalet-pension above the village, overlooking Lake Caumau. Later Romundt joined them. Von Gersdorff describes the holiday in a letter to Elizabeth:

we are thoroughly satisfied...the region is heavenly...the house is on the high road and is very new and clean. The beds are excellent the food substantial...excellent home-cooking...one can undergo a milk cure. Fritz does so. At five-thirty in the morning and five in the evening a large glass...In the mornings, we have so far walked in the forest beneath larches and firs [shade for Nietzsche's eyes]; in the sight of sublime mountains we have read *Walküre*, *Siegfried*, and *Twilight of the Gods*. This is the right place to experience 'twilight'. After lunch we pull Plutarch apart, after which we have a siesta lying on the moss or the grass. Five-thirty we go swimming. At seven the evening meal, always a hot one. And so our time flows by, well used, as the Dresden songbook puts it, to all eternity. Just now Fritz received a unusual visit. Dr Vetter, a grammar school teacher from Chur, disclosed himself as the winner of the 300 talers [for the essay competition on the *Ring* for which Nietzsche had been a judge].[45]

On August 8th, the first bound copies of the *Straussiade* arrived in Flims by post. Von Gersdorff takes up the story in a letter to Rohde:

At half-past three we made our way down to the green Lake Caumau. We engraved the initials U. B. I. F. N. 8./8. 1873* on a sloping slab of marble. Then we swam out to a rock that rose up out of the green waters in the middle of the lake. Here we surreptitiously inscribed U. B. F. N. C. G. H. R. 8./8. 1873,[†] after which we tarried a while on the delightful Rheingold rock. The sun...smiled down on the earth out of whose dark depths the rock rose up. After the swim we blessed the first stone and its inscription with wine...In the evening it was divinely pure and clear. This is how we celebrated the *Antistraussiade*.[46]

The Rosalie Nielsen Affair

Rosalie Nielsen may well have been the first, as one might describe it, left-wing Nietzschean. The Nielsen affair started shortly after the appearance of *The Birth of Tragedy*. A wildly enthusiastic fan, this somewhat elderly, ugly widow, who imagined herself to be the female incarnation of Dionysus, developed a long-distance infatuation with the book's author and began to bombard him with letters accompanied by photographs of a symbolic nature. In the summer of 1873 she began to visit him, visits which he received – perhaps unfortunately – with his usual quiet courtesy. After returning to Leipzig it appears that she made an attempt to buy Fritzsch, the Wagnerians' house publisher, in order, so she claimed to Nietzsche, to ensure that their writings were well cared for. Fritzsch, afflicted with strikes by left-wing trades unions and in financial difficulties, was indeed ripe for a takeover. Since Nielsen appeared to have connexions with Mazzini and the Italian Marxists, October found Nietzsche fearing an international conspiracy to take control of Wagner's publisher with the aim of sweeping this renegade socialist off the stage.[47] Though Fritzsch was indeed in trouble, it appears that the conspiracy existed entirely in Nietzsche's, or perhaps Nielsen's, head. In any case he was soon able to laugh at the whole affair, but not as heartily as Wagner, who composed nine verses of doggerel to express his gratitude for Nietzsche's concern for (even imaginary) threats to Enterprise Bayreuth. One reads as follows (the end of every line save the last rhymes):

* '*Unzeitgemässe Betrachtung I* [*Untimely Meditation I*], Friedrich Nietzsche, 8.8.1873'.
† '*Unzeitgemässe Betrachtung* Friedrich Nietzsche, Carl Gersdorff, Heinrich Romundt, 8.8.1873'.

Schwert, Stock und Pritzsche
kurz, was im Verlag von Fritzsche
schrei', lärm' or quietzsche
das schenk ich meinem Nietzsche,–
wär's ihm zu was nützen.
Sword, stick and fool's wand
in short, whatever in Fritzsch's firm
shrieks, dins or squeaks
I give to my Nietzsche, –
May he find it useful.

Vaguely comical though the episode is, it does reveal Nietzsche's already well-developed hostility to socialism and organized labour, attitudes reinforced in the patrician houses of Basel, whose owners were themselves having trouble with union activism. In a note of the period he writes that he has 'a few pious wishes: removal of the universal right to vote, retention of the death penalty, and restriction of the right to strike'.[48] The ground of his hostility is of course the view outlined in 'The Greek State' that since art requires the leisure of the few created by the toil of the many, art and socialism are sworn enemies (see p. 160 above). (Since Wagner saw through this spurious opposition, he was able to take a less paranoid attitude to socialism and hence took the Nielsen affair more lightly.)

Summons to the Germans

The financial situation of the Bayreuth project, bad at the time of Nietzsche's Easter visit, had deteriorated still further over the summer, so that by August it was decided that there should be a new public appeal for funds. Wagner suggested that Nietzsche should write a manifesto to be presented for approval at the meeting of the combined German Wagner societies (i.e., Wagner's financial sponsors) to take place in Bayreuth on October 31. Nietzsche agreed but found the manifesto difficult to write, not least because, on account of his eyes, he had to dictate the whole thing to Romundt. The draft was posted to Wagner on October 25.

The 'Summons' begins by warning 'the Germans' that the eyes of the world are upon them to see whether they will measure up to the Bayreuth artwork, an artwork which, separating itself from the 'disgraceful' triviality of the current German theatre, will for the first time constitute a 'site for the national spirit'. Do you not, Nietzsche demands of his audience, feel compelled to help in this re-creation of the German nation through the 'artwork of the future'? Can you stand idly by while this crucial attempt is being made? The Germans are reputed to be 'the people of thinkers'. But perhaps – the rest of the world is wondering – they have come to the end of their thinking. That, certainly, is what the repeated attacks on Wagner's project suggest. The 'Bayreuth Event of May 1872' (the laying of the foundation stone) was not, Nietzsche continues, the gathering of a musical sect. It was rather the coming together of the nation and a purification of dramatic art of world-wide significance. The Wagnerian artwork is 'the nation's drama', a drama which constitutes the most important possibility of recovering an 'original', authentically German, way of living. Those who are 'unselfish and prepared for sacrifice' will commit themselves to this project, and when this happens Germany will cut a new kind of figure on the world-stage:

> The German will appear honourable and the bringer of healing only when he has shown that he is to be feared and yet *through the straining of his highest and noblest artistic and cultural powers will make it forgotten that he was fear-inspiring.*

We must, Nietzsche concludes, 'support with all our powers a great art-deed of the German genius', this 'purification and dedication through the sublime magic and terror of authentic German art'; otherwise the 'powerfully aroused drives of political and nationalistic passions... will force our successors to conclude that we Germans have lost ourselves just as we had rediscovered ourselves'.[49]

Throughout the eighteenth and nineteenth centuries, the Germans were known, and came to know themselves, as *Das Volk von Dichten und Denken*, 'the people of poetry and thought'. In contrast to the commercial drive and military might of imperial Britain, the Germans were thought of as peaceful, somewhat dreamy people who preferred writing poems to acquiring colonies. This is the sense of the Germans Nietzsche conjures up with the phrase 'people of thinkers'. Though he is not opposed to a militarily strong and politically united Germany, 'poetry and thought' is the more essential, 'original' nature to which he refers, the German 'soul' that is threatened with destruction by the greedy materialism and lust for power of the Bismarckian present. Nietzsche's 'Summons' does not abandon nationalistic passions; rather it redirects them. Instead of being feared as the preeminent military power in Europe, the Germans should strive to 'shine'[50] through cultural preeminence. 'Bad' Eris must be transformed into 'good' Eris ('hard' into 'soft' power). This is the sense of the following note from early 1874:

> It is quite false to say that previously the Germans were aesthetic, now they are political. The Germans sought an ideal in their Luther; German music, higher than anything else we know as culture. The quest for that should stop because they have power? Precisely power (on account of its evil nature) should direct them there more strongly than ever. He [sic] must apply his power to his higher cultural goal... The glorification of the modern state can lead to the destruction of all culture.[51]

* * *

Nietzsche tried out a draft of the 'Summons' on Rohde, who said that, though 'spoken from the heart', given that it was supposed to address the unconverted rather than the converted, to win over those previously opposed to Bayreuth, its coercive rhetoric ('the eyes of the world are upon you', etc.) was unlikely to be effective.[52] And though Wagner liked it and Cosima thought it 'very beautiful' and that speaking with 'faith and truth' rather than mere 'cleverness'[53] was just what was required, the committee of sponsors agreed with Rohde. It was rejected as 'too sharp' and replaced by a more innocuous pamphlet by a Professor Stern from Dresden. Nietzsche took the rejection with his usual grace in adversity, admitting to Rohde without rancour that all along his had been the 'right response' to the 'Summons'.[54]

Second Untimely Meditation: *The Uses and Disadvantages of History for Life*

Nietzsche was philosophical about the rejection, perhaps because he had a more important fish to fry. Throughout the year he had been meditating in his notes on a question of great moment to both himself and Wagner, the question of whether historical knowledge is a good or bad thing. These ruminations culminated, in about November, in the idea of devoting a second *Meditation* to the topic. For Nietzsche, of course, 'history' is above all Greek history, so that the *Meditation* on the 'uses and abuses of history' (the notebooks, at one point, contemplate this as a possible title) are, once again, to a large degree, a meditation on his own profession, on the uses and abuses of classical philology. The work was completed by Christmas, again with extensive secretarial help from Romundt and Overbeck, and appeared, once more with Fritzsch, in February 1874.

The second *Meditation* is a major work, on a different level to its, ultimately somewhat journalistic, predecessor. As the title indicates, it is about the uses and misuses of history, where 'history' means not 'the past' but rather 'representations of the past', historiography. The general argument is that while history of the right sort is essential 'for life', history of the wrong sort kills it. By 'life', here, Nietzsche means something like 'health', that is to say, 'growth': good history is essential to the growth of a living thing 'whether this living thing be a man or a people or a culture',[55] bad history stunts it. Nietzsche distinguishes three types of history that can promote growth.

* * *

Monumental History. Representations of the past, writes Nietzsche, function 'monumentally' – are placed, as it were, on a 'pedestal' – when they are used to present us with figures that are 'exemplary and worthy of imitation',[56] models of self-'transfiguration'.[57] Such 'mythic' figures promote 'greatness' by inspiring imitation. They are the objects of celebration at 'popular festivals' – in the Greek temple or medieval cathedral, for example. Through the 'eternalizing power of art and religion', their power to invest figures with 'pious illusion', with charismatic authority,[58] they 'bestow upon existence the character of the eternal and stable'.[59] What Nietzsche is talking about here is moral education. 'Monumental' figures – 'role-' or, less crudely, 'life-models' – are the reappearance of the 'images of myth' which, according to *The Birth*, 'must be the unnoticed but ever-present daemonic guardians under whose tutelage young souls grow up and by whose signs the grown man interprets his life and his struggles' (p. 130 above).

Antiquarian History. A person – and historian – with an 'antiquarian' stance to the past is 'the preserving and revering soul' who

> wants to preserve for those who ... come after him the conditions under which he himself came into existence. An antiquarian person reveres the past *in toto*; his soul is, indeed, constituted by the totality of the past.[60]

This kind of personality – someone who wants everything to remain eternally the same – can be of great value as a limit on the excesses of monumental history. While role models always need a certain amount of re-creation, 'poetic invention', to make sense in the current context – the Italians of the Renaissance were inspired by Greek models, but that did not mean donning togas and sandals – this can easily get out of hand, leading to figures which, as 'free poetic inventions', have no genuine connexion with the past at all. This can cause great harm to the continuity of a culture, indeed destroy it. Revolutions typically happen through the glamorization of monumental figures that have no authentic roots in history at all (Stalin, Hitler or Mao, for example). The antiquarian spirit is a vital safeguard against the worshiping of false idols such as these.[61]

The downside of the antiquarian soul, however, consists in the fact that it reveres *everything* that is past: even 'the trivial, circumscribed, decaying and obsolete acquire their own dignity and inviolability through the fact that...the soul of the antiquarian man has emigrated into them and there made its home'. This makes it blind to the need for *any* kind of change. And this refusal to recognise the need to do away with the 'decaying and obsolete' can lead to a 'mummification' of the spirit which can cause great harm to both individual and community.[62] This is the point at which 'critical' history becomes important.

Critical History. Only monumental history, writes Nietzsche, can be creative. It alone can embody a vision of the future, inspire 'architects of the future'.[63] Pure antiquarianism, on the other hand, paralyses creation. Here it becomes clear, he says, that 'critical' history is also necessary 'in the service of life'. To flourish, 'man must possess and from time to time employ the strength to break up and dissolve a part of the past', and this is what the readiness to condemn aspects of the past achieves. But how does the critical spirit judge which aspects of the past need to be abandoned? On the basis of 'life', says Nietzsche. The critical historian determines which aspects of tradition, as impediments to the health and growth of society, need to be abandoned.[64]

Nietzsche says that all three of the above types of historiography, provided they interact in the right way, 'serve life'. Monumental history inspires cultural change, change which, through continuity with the past, preserves the identity of a culture. The antiquarian spirit, on the other hand, by placing a brake on the wilder uses of the 'monument', helps to ensure that cultural change really is identity-preserving, that it takes the shape of reform rather than 'revolution'.[65] The critical spirit makes the whole process possible. By counteracting the ossifying effects of pure antiquarianism, it creates the ground on which it becomes possible to erect effective monuments.

* * *

History Not in the Service of Life. Repeating a line from the first *Meditation*, Nietzsche defines 'culture' as 'unity of artistic style in all the expressions of the life of a people':[66] the life of *all* the people, with no division into cultivated and uncouth, he emphasises, echoing, if not Wagner's socialism, at least his communitarianism.[67]

The use of 'style' here might, disconcertingly, seem to make 'culture' a matter of form rather than content, but, in fact, that is not Nietzsche's intention. 'Style' is not *opposed* to substance; rather (as in our use of 'life-style') it embraces it. This is clear from the fact that Nietzsche goes on to define culture as 'unity of feeling among a people'.[68]

As we know from *The Birth of Tragedy* (pp. 130–1 above), 'unity of feeling' is created by the possession of gods who provide a 'mythical homeland' for a community as a whole. It is created, in other words, by a pantheon of 'monumental' figures who collectively embody communal ethos.

Repeating Wagner's cultural criticism and that of his own earlier works, Nietzsche says that, by the above standards, modernity fails to count as a 'culture', that it is merely a collection of atomic individuals held together by that artificial entity, the state. 'We have no culture, only civilisation', he writes in his notebooks of the period;[69] no culture, merely plumbing and the police. The reason for this is that modernity has become a 'fairground motley', a 'chaotic jumble' of different life-styles,[70] a mere 'encyclopaedia' of scraps of past and foreign cultures.[71] (This is what I called the 'motley critique' of modernity.) And the principal cause of this is the misuse of history, the use of history in a life-*damaging* way.

Used in a healthy way, Nietzsche emphasises, history is an *art*. One does not approach the past omnivorously but selects one's points of focus on the basis of the values they embody and how instructive they are with respect to those values. (The 'Whig' view of British history or, for that matter, presumably, the 'Hegelian' view of German history would count as 'artistic' forms of historiography.) And the healthy telling of history must be 'artistic' in that it must be done in a way that surrounds its heroes with the 'pious illusion' discussed above, without which they cannot motivate: 'only if history can endure being transformed into a work of art will it perhaps be able to preserve instincts or even evoke them'.[72] Note that this is just a reaffirmation of the inspirationally didactic approach to history and philology outlined in *On the Future of our Educational Institutions* (pp. 144–5 above).

This healthy practice of history is, however, destroyed by the modern conception of historiography as value-free 'science'. In two ways. First, history as science is history reduced to statistics and historical laws. But these only show man as a 'herd animal'. The individual, and in particular the great, inspirational individual, disappears into the mass.[73] And second, through indiscriminate reproduction of the past, scientific history reveals our own set of values as just one set on a smorgasbord of alternatives. This produces, as Nietzsche says in the fourth of the *Five Introductions to Five Unwritten Books*, the spirit of '*nihil admirari*' (see p. 161 above). In setting 'our' ethos side by side with a myriad of other options, history (and 'cultural studies' in general, one might add) 'deconstructs' it, deprives it of its unconditional authority over us. As in the Roman Empire, modernity's 'cosmopolitan carnival of gods' turns modern man into 'a strolling spectator', his mood one of cynical 'senility'.[74] Deprived of naive confidence in our inherited conception of the proper life, we come to 'distrust our instincts' and become incapable of committed action. Postmodern nihilism has arrived.

Notes from the Underground

Stylistically, Nietzsche's published works before 1876 belong firmly to the German nineteenth century. Whether he is deploying the poetic, dithyrambic style of *The Birth* or the polemical style of the *Straussiade*, the vocabulary is florid and hyperbolic, the sentences long and heavy. As Nietzsche himself observed in 1886, *The Birth* is (to a modern sensibility)

> badly written, clumsy, embarrassing, with a rage for imagery and confused in its imagery, emotional, here and there sugary to the point of effeminacy, uneven in pace, lacking in the will to logical cleanliness ... ponderous.[75]

There is no wit (as opposed to bombast) in *The Birth*, or in any of the early published works. Beneath the public surface, however, in the privacy of his notebooks, beginning in the summer of 1873, a new Nietzsche is starting to take shape: a Nietzsche of short, dancing sentences, witty epigrams, more French than German in feeling. Though he will not make his first public flight until 1878, in the notebooks, Nietzsche the aphorist is growing his wings; often by recording the aphorisms of others, Goethe, Luther, Lichtenberg, but also by crafting his own. Some even contain a faint echo of his contemporary Oscar Wilde. Here are some examples: 'If happiness were the goal, the animals would be on top. Their cynicism consists in forgetting: that is the quickest route to happiness, even if it's one that's not worth much'.[76] 'He speaks more clearly than he thinks'.[77] 'Luther: "If God had thought about the heavy guns he wouldn't have created the world"'. 'Forgetfulness belongs to all creation'.[78] 'Paraphrase of culture – a temperature and mood which allows many originally hostile forces to play a single melody'.[79] 'If philosophers would dream up a *polis* [city-state] today it would certainly not be Plato's *polis* but rather an *apragopolis* (town of strolling spectators)'.[80] And so on.

It is not, however, merely the beginnings of wit that makes the notebooks of the early 1870s worth reading. What also recommends them is the fact that they deal with matters touched on in the published works of the period either only lightly or not at all. I shall briefly present some of these notebook discussions arranged according to topic.

Idealism versus Realism. Idealism, Nietzsche writes, indicating that he is still convinced by Kant and Schopenhauer's arguments, is not an hypothesis but a fact. One speaks of natural things and processes but they are all contained in the representation of the subject. The brain does not think: rather we (the world-transcendent subject) think the brain.[81] Again, sensations are not the work of our sense organs. Rather, sense organs are entities we create on the basis of sensations.[82] For all this, Nietzsche continues, one could still observe, against Kant, that, even granted all his arguments for idealism, the world might still be exactly as it appears. By a happy coincidence, in other words, the world-story the human mind constructs might just happen to exactly match the way reality 'in itself' is. But actually, Nietzsche adds, it would not be a *happy* coincidence at all. For one could not live with such 'scepticism'.[83] We *need* there to be another world and for it to have a quite different character from this world. We need some kind of other-worldly 'salvation', if not of a Christian, then at least of a Schopenhauerian kind.

The Limits of Science. Early in 1873, Nietzsche began to make up for the absence of natural science from his Pforta education. From the Basel university library he borrowed a considerable number of books on physics, chemistry and astronomy. (The most important of these, the *Philosophiae naturalis Theoria* by the Croatian Jesuit Roger Boscovich, developed an atomic theory in which atomic 'puncta' are extensionless points in space from which causal forces are exerted – an anticipation of the 'force fields' of modern science.) It would be a mistake, however, to see interest in natural science as representing a turn to the world-view of scientific materialism. The truth is rather the opposite. The notes of 1872–3 are dominated by remarks concerning the limitations of science and of 'scientific man'. The latter, for example, is said to be one who, surrounded by the most terrible existential problems, plucks a flower to count the number of cell-threads it contains. But as (according to Nietzsche) Pascal pointed out, he does so evasively. His motive is to escape the existential questions of 'why?' and 'where to?' – questions which make him shudder and to which he has no answer.[84]

The proper stance towards science on the part of philosophy, however, is not to destroy but rather to 'control' it, place it in perspective by attending to its philosophical presuppositions.[85] This is what Kant did. When he wrote in the introduction to the *Critique of Pure*

Reason, 'I must beat back knowledge in order to make room for faith', he said something 'very significant', something that answered to a 'cultural need'.[86]

Nietzsche writes that though it has terrible consequences for art, religion, and morality (the consequences Strauss refused to confront), Darwin's theory of evolution is something 'I hold to be true'.[87] Is this not inconsistent with his endorsement of Kantian idealism? Not so: 'One speaks of geological and Darwinian processes ... but it is completely impossible to think the (world-creating) subject away'.[88] Darwinism, in other words, is true all right, but only *within* a certain – human – perspective. That reality 'in itself' is Darwinian (or even spatial or temporal) we have no right to assume since reality in itself is terra incognita.

The genius. In all its phases, Nietzsche's philosophy attaches extreme importance to the exceptional individual, referred to, at different times, as 'the genius', 'the free spirit', 'the higher type', 'the philosopher of the future', and 'the superman'. As already intimated, a fundamental interpretative issue is this: does Nietzsche take the outstanding individual to exist ultimately for the sake of the entire community, or, conversely, does he suppose the community to exist for the sake of the outstanding individual? In the 1873 notes, picking up on the 'necessity of slavery' theme, Nietzsche says that talk of the subordination of the individual to 'the wellbeing of the whole' is often misunderstood: he should be subordinate not to the state or to powerful individuals but to the highest individual, the 'highest exemplar'; not to the 'strongest' but to the 'best'. These highest types are 'the creative men, whether they be the best morally or useful in some other, large sense; in other words, the purest types and improvers of humanity'.[89] This emphasis on utility implies that the community as a whole indeed derives some kind of contribution to its well-being from the privileged existence it grants to the genius (for example, by raising huge sums of money for Bayreuth).

In discussing *The Future of Our Educational Institutions*, we saw the nature of the benefit the community derives from the genius. The paradigmatic geniuses are Sophocles and Wagner (p. 146 above), and what these 'spiritual leaders' do is to articulate through the great artwork that fundamental ethos without which the community cannot *be* a community. This thought seems to be repeated in the remark in the notes that it is in the work of genius that 'the ethical powers of a nation show themselves'.[90]

In the notes, however, another kind of justification of the genius can be obscurely felt. Nietzsche quotes Goethe as saying that the 'final cause', the ultimate purpose, of the world is dramatic poetry.[91] Other notes suggest the idea lying behind this. 'In the great genius ... the will reaches its salvation'.[92] It does so, the notes sometimes suggest, because the purpose of the world, that is, the 'primal unity's' purpose in creating it, is its own aesthetic perception, and this it achieves through and only through the vision of the artistic genius.[93] It is not clear how seriously Nietzsche takes this idea and how much he is simply playing around with the Schopenhauerian metaphysics of *The Birth*. But whatever its status, this kind of justification of the genius – a justification which makes it the community's business to serve the genius (who in turn serves the primal unity) rather than vice versa – is entirely dependent on Schopenhauerian metaphysics. Once Nietzsche abandons that metaphysics, I shall (as already promised) argue, he is entirely clear that communal interests are prior to those of the exceptional individual.

Nationalism versus Cosmopolitanism. For much of his youth, we know, Nietzsche was a proud and passionate Prussian, an ardent nationalist. But in his mature works, we shall see, he prides himself on his *anti*-nationalism, on being not a German but a 'good European'. In the notes of 1873 we can, I think, identify the moment of transition from nationalism to cosmopolitanism.

The notebooks covering the period from the end of 1872 to the beginning of 1873 find Nietzsche regularly complaining about the subservience of the Germans to French cultural practices.[94] In the notes running from the spring to the summer of 1873 we still find Nietzsche deploring 'the abstract European' man, 'a man who imitates everything badly'.[95] Yet by the autumn of that year we find him saying that

> fundamentally, cosmopolitanism must spread out. The arbitrary boundaries of the nation state gradually lose their mystery and appear, much more, as terrible and bad. The antagonisms become sharper in a way that cannot be overcome. Fever produces death.[96]

One should not over-emphasise this reflection – Nietzsche's notes are always experiments in thought rather than enunciations of doctrine. Yet the note is significant as the first occasion on which Nietzsche sees that there is something, perhaps, to be said *in favour of* cosmopolitanism, namely, that it helps overcome war.

Why Philosophy? Reflecting on the 'Pre-Platonic' philosophers, Nietzsche observes that none of them created a mass following. What then, he asks, is the use of philosophy judged against the ultimate good, the cultural health of the community? Philosophy can do various things: it can 'subdue the mythical' by strengthening the sense of scientific 'truth', as did Thales and Democritus, or do the reverse, as did Heraclitus. And it can smash every kind of dogmatism, as did Socrates.[97] The judicious philosopher thus needs to be the 'physician of culture': to diagnose the cultural needs of his times and prescribe accordingly. For us, Nietzsche continues, the task of the philosopher is to combat 'worldliness' (materialism), to 'limit the barbarising effect of the drive to knowledge'. The cultural physician of today must be guided by the knowledge that 'culture can only ever proceed from the centralising significance of an art or an artwork'. His fundamental task is to prepare the way for such an artwork[98] – for, in other words, Bayreuth.

And should such an artwork and culture one day return, what would then be the task of the philosopher?

> The philosopher of the future? He must be the higher tribunal of an artistic culture; like the security force opposed to all stepping out of line.[99]

In a healthy culture, where there is no longer any need for the cultural 'physician', the philosopher's task is to be a cultural *guardian* who preserves that health for as long as possible (a theme which will reappear at the end of Nietzsche's career in *The Antichrist*).

The Future of Religion. 'With regard to religion one notices an exhaustion – one is finally tired of the old important symbols . . . it is time for the invention of something new',[100] a new religion. This we know already. Because, as *The Birth of Tragedy* emphasises, a great, artistic culture such as that of the Greeks is at the same time a religious one, the return of an 'artistic culture' is *a fortiori* the return of a religious one. But what will this new religion be like? From Schopenhauer, we know 'how deep the new religion must be'. For it must be such that

(1) both the immortality theme and the fear of death disappear [it must, as the Schopenhauerian worldview does, overcome fear of death *without* postulating personal immortality] (2) the separation of body from soul disappears (3) it contains the insight that the suffering of existence cannot be overcome by corrective measures of a palliative sort [it must overcome Socratism] (4) that the relationship to a God is past (5) [it must enjoin] compassion (not love of self but the oneness of all that lives and suffers).

Nietzsche adds that the 'counter-image to culture' occurs 'when religion is no longer possible'.[101] This concluding remark is very important since, I shall suggest, Nietzsche's whole life and philosophy is, above all else, a struggle to find a new religious outlook that will re-found 'culture'.

11

Aimez-vous Brahms?

NIETZSCHE SPENT the Christmas and New Year of 1873–4 in Naumburg. Despite being sick with 'the usual litany', he was as thrilled as ever by his Christmas presents, itemising them in a letter to von Gersdorff with boyish glee: among others, a gilt photo album for large photographs, a wooden letter holder with a carved floral design from Elizabeth, items made of Russian leather from Princess Therese of Altenburg (his father's former pupil), and a large Raphael reproduction.[1] From Naumburg he made a side trip to Leipzig to check up on how the second *Untimely Meditation* was going with Fritzsch and to visit Ritschl, who subjected him to 'a verbal barrage' concerning the awfulness of Wagner's poetry, Overbeck's book, and Nietzsche's supposedly pro-French stance[2] (a supposition based, presumably, on his critique of Wilhelminian Germany).

Back in Basel at the beginning of January, he was sick most of the time through to the beginning of April with the usual intestinal troubles and nausea. And his eyesight was as bad as ever. Fortunately, however, his high-school pupil, Adolf Baumgartner, whom he found both talented and sympathetic,[3] offered his services as amanuensis. Son of a now-deceased Alsatian industrialist, Adolf introduced Nietzsche to his mother, Marie, with whom, we shall see, he formed a warm friendship.

Depression, Marriage, and Dropping Out

For much of the first half of 1874 Nietzsche was again depressed. At the beginning of April he reports that though his physical health is now 'excellent' he is very 'dissatisfied' with life.[4] The following month he writes that he is 'conscious of a deep melancholy underlying all [his] . . . cheerfulness'.[5] (Cheerfulness remained at least the outer character of his life, his Basel social calendar being as full as ever.)

The 'gallows humour'[6] pervading Nietzsche's letters allowed Bayreuth to get wind of his depression. Worried, they discussed his condition within their circle of friends. Cosima wrote to Malwida von Meysenbug that she feared he would follow Hölderlin into madness, an idea she got from von Gersdorff, who put it to Nietzsche directly that he had 'an element of Hölderlin's nature' in him.[7]

The meditations on what to do about Nietzsche's state of mind culminated in Wagner's writing to him on April 14 putting his own, crudely vulgar, gloss on the consensus diagnosis:

> Among other things I think that the masculine life you live in Basel in the evenings [with Overbeck and Romundt] is something I never led... it seems that you young men lack women: that is to say... why take and not steal? In an emergency one can always steal. What I mean is, you must marry or compose an opera... Oh God, marry a rich woman! Why is only von Gersdorff a proper male!... compose your opera, but it will be damned difficult to get it performed. – What kind of devil made you just a pedagogue!... I bathe now every day because I can't bear my belly. Do the same! And eat meat! [Nietzsche and von Gersdorff had been flirting with vegetarianism.][8]

As a follow-up to this letter, von Gersdorff (whose letters, since the previous year, often seem more sympathetic to the Wagners than to their errant 'son') wrote that he fully supported the advice to marry which he had discussed with the Wagners. 'There are plenty of women around', he wrote, adding – generously – that 'finding the right one is your business'.[9] Nietzsche was amused. Though, he wrote von Gersdorff, he found the idea of 'you and the Bayreuthers sitting together in a marriage-advisory-commission' deciding what to do about his status 'truly heavenly', he did not quite see himself setting out on a ' crusade' to reach such a 'promised land'. And anyway, he pointed out, von Gersdorff was no more advanced in that direction than he was.[10]

Wagner's letter, as well as being vulgar, demonstrates precisely why Nietzsche needed to distance himself from, as he would call it, Wagner's 'tyrannical' nature that recognised no personality other than his own (p. 186 below). Because he, Wagner, is highly sexed (*Tristan und Isolde*'s 'Liebestod' is surely the most explicit evocation of sexual orgasm in the history of music) so must Nietzsche be. But he has no outlet given that all his intimate relations are with men, and is liable, Wagner clearly hints, to find the sexual urge diverted into perverted channels. In fact, however, sex is entirely beside the point. The only sensible advice Wagner gives is that he should marry a *rich* wife to relieve him of the burden of teaching. For this was, in fact, the root of the problem.

At the beginning of May 1874, Nietzsche wrote to von Gersdorff that he was 'in a very good state' and that 'any kind of depression or melancholy is far and deep beneath me'. He adds that he is now making very good progress on his third *Untimely Meditation*.[11] Whether or not the report is accurate, the conjunction is significant. For what really got Nietzsche down were the multiple distractions, inseparable from the life of a university and grammar-school teacher, that prevented him getting on with his 'real' work. The source of his depression was the conflict between, on the one hand, his membership in an academic world which, according to his education-critique, had sold out on the task of true education, and, on the other, the vocation to be, in every sense, a free writer of explosive philosophical books, a vocation in terms of which, increasingly, he defined his true being. In other words, the source of his depression was the sense of failing to be his true self, his failure to follow his own demand that one should 'become who one is'.

Writing to Malwida von Meysenbug on the completion of the third *Meditation* in October, Nietzsche observes that 'a tremendous happiness lies in making progress, stepwise, with one's task – and now I have completed three of the [as he planned at this time] thirteen *Meditations*.[12] Ingrained into Nietzsche, to repeat, was the work ethic of his Protestant homeland. Happiness, 'sky-blue' happiness, he observes in *Zarathustra*, *is* (meaningful, life-defining) work. More exactly, it is *production*, the only sure proof of work. 'Without productivity', he confides to his notebooks, 'life is worthless and unbearable'.[13] And to Rohde he wrote at the beginning of June: 'I'm in a reasonably productive mood and hence cheerful, have my sister here, in brief I resemble a happy person insofar as I know what happiness is'.[14]

In fact, though, production sufficient to satisfy Nietzsche's driven, Protestant conscience was impossible so long as he remained a professor:

> You can guess [he wrote von Gersdorff in April] how fundamentally melancholy and despondent I am, as a productive being! All I ask is some freedom, some real air to live and defend myself. I become outraged at the many, uncountably many, unfreedoms that hold me imprisoned. There can be no question of a real productivity when one emerges so little from unfreedom, from the suffering and burdensomeness of imprisonment.[15]

And Nietzsche was speaking no more than the obvious truth: on top of teaching thirteen hours a week, six at the university and seven at the Pädegogium,[16] a truly appalling load for any academic let alone one who was half-blind, he had been responsible, since the beginning of 1874, for all the administrative duties associated with being a dean. 'Now a new office on my back – I've had enough', he wrote, exasperatedly, to von Gersdorff.

One of the recurrent symptoms of Nietzsche's depression is the repeatedly expressed desire to 'drop out', a desire which always centres round the need to resolve the conflict between profession and vocation in favour of the latter. At the beginning of February 1874, he writes his mother, 'I'd love so much to have a tiny farm and then I'd hang my professorship on the nail. I've now been a professor for 5 years, I think that's enough'.[17] The following month he reports that 'my sister is visiting me and day by day we forge the most beautiful plans for an idyllic and simple future life filled with work'.[18] And to Wagner he writes that he hopes the Master will not be upset if 'one day I am not able to stand the university with its peculiar scholarly air any more. I think each summer about "becoming independent" in the most modest of circumstances (under which I'm proud to say that I can live)'.[19]

Though he spoke to his mother of a farm, by May the setting for his retreat has changed to a more urban setting:

> I've chosen Rothenburg-ob-der-Tauber as my private fortress and hermitage...There it's at least all traditionally German [*altdeutsch*]. I hate the characterless, mixed [i.e., 'motley'] cities [of modernity] that have lost their wholeness. There I can work out my thoughts, I hope, and make plans for decades ahead and bring them to completion.[20]

(This passage reveals more than Nietzsche's desire to be a full-time writer. Rothenburg was – and still is – a small, medieval town near Nuremberg in Franconia, visually untouched by modernity. Like Nietzsche's Naumburg entirely circumscribed by an ancient wall, it is very much like the Nuremberg celebrated in Wagner's *Die Meistersinger* as a place of cultural unity, continuity and security. When Nietzsche remarks in his notes that 'Wagner's cheerfulness [in *Die Meistersinger*] is the feeling of security that belongs to someone who has returned from the greatest dangers and excesses into the boundedness of the home-land',[21] he is expressing his own, as well as Wagner's, nostalgia for the community of the past: a community which, as such, needs to be 'walled', because, as Heidegger remarks, a boundary is where something starts as well as where it stops.)

Wagner in the Balance

Nietzsche's creative genius was, then, becoming increasingly alienated from life in Basel. He was alienated, in particular, from the burdens of university life which were only increased by his inability to discharge his duties with anything less than hundred-percent Prussian conscientiousness. Alienation from the university was increased by the death, in July 1874, of his fatherly friend Vischer-Bilfinger, who had been responsible for his original appointment and stuck by him through thick and thin:

> Our good old Vischer is dying [he wrote Rohde]. He is without doubt of all Baselers the one who gave me the most significant and deepest trust . . . I lose a great deal and will become even more alienated from the university than I already am.[22]

A potentially even more traumatic alienation, however, was occurring, from the beginning of 1874, in the notebooks: alienation from Wagner, alienation, at least, from certain aspects of that titanic figure, an alienation that provided some of the material which eventually gave rise to the fourth of the *Untimely Meditations*, *Richard Wagner in Bayreuth*.[23]

I emphasised in the previous chapter that throughout 1873 Nietzsche's notebooks contain not a breath of criticism of Wagner. Private reflections on 'the Master' are as reverential as public pronouncements. So it comes as a bolt out of the blue when, from the beginning of 1874, one begins regularly to stumble upon remarks of the order of 'none of our great composers was, at twenty-eight, still so bad a composer as Wagner',[24] or 'From Bach or Beethoven there shines out a pure nature. Wagner's ecstasies are often violent and not naive enough'.[25] What really startles about such remarks is not that they are overwhelmingly critical, which they are not, but that they are critical at all. Wagner, that is to say, has ceased to be 'the Master', an object of quasi-religious reverence, and has become a mere mortal possessing many of the frailties that go with that condition. He has, in short, been relegated from the league of the gods to that of the human, indeed all-too-human.

A letter written to Rohde in February explains what it was that led Nietzsche to turn Wagner into an object of critical appraisal. Referring to rumours of a 'miracle' (the 100,000 talers donated by Ludwig of Bavaria at the end of the following month without which the entire Bayreuth project would have collapsed), Nietzsche says,

> Let us hope it's true. Since the beginning of new year it has been a dismal outlook [for Bayreuth] in the face of which I was finally able to rescue myself in the weirdest manner: I began, with the greatest coldness of observation, to investigate why the project might fail. In doing so I have learnt a lot and believe I understand Wagner much better than before. If the 'miracle' is true then the results of my analysis won't upset anything. Rather, we shall want to celebrate and have a party.[26]

What Nietzsche is doing here is indeed, as he says, deeply 'weird'. Fearing the collapse of the Bayreuth project, which up to now has been the meaning of his life, he decides to analyse the reasons for its likely failure – while simultaneously hoping against hope that it will *not* fail. It is as if a fanatical supporter of a football team, losing confidence in his team on the eve of the big match, set out to explain the causes of its defeat, while still hoping against hope that it will triumph on the day.

Nietzsche's examination of the Wagner phenomenon, it should be said, although indeed 'coldly' forensic, is nothing like the 'assassination' of Strauss – or the 'assassinations' of Wagner that would come later. It is not an assassination-attempt, first, because he attributes much of the trouble with the Bayreuth project not to Wagner but rather to the audience and culture he is forced to work with and within, and, second, because while itemising Wagner's weaknesses, he also gives due weight to his strengths. The overall character of the discussion is that of a balance sheet. And on balance, Nietzsche finds the weaknesses to be pretty much equal to the strengths.

The criticisms coalesce, it seems to me, around four main points. The first is that Wagner is at the root of his nature an *actor*.[27] Rather than allowing the audience to overhear, as it were, something arising from inner necessity, Wagner is at every moment conscious of his audience, always calculating how to produce the maximum 'effect'. His music, that is to say, is a kind of 'affect-painting' aimed at casting the audience into an 'intoxication of sensory ecstasy'; its aim is to *move* – at any price.[28] (Is the prudish pastor's son shocked, one wonders, by *Tristan*'s overt sexuality, and by his own responsiveness to it?)

The second criticism is that not only is Wagner an 'actor', he is an actor of a particularly 'tyrannical' nature. This explains the fact that his works are in every respect 'colossal'[29] – *Parsifal* lasts five-and-a-half hours, the *Ring* cycle seventeen hours (minus intervals), and the need for a new opera house was generated by Wagner's demand for orchestral and stage resources on a scale no previous composer had even dreamed of. Wagner aims not just to move but to *overwhelm*, to 'intimidate' by the sheer scale of his works.[30] He is, in Nietzsche's later terminology, the 'will to power' incarnate. Wagner's tyrannical nature (we must be thankful, Nietzsche reflects, that he has no *political* power)[31] affects both his response to other composers and his social thinking:

> The tyrannical [in him] allows validity to no other individuality save his own and that of his intimates [i.e., clones]. The danger for Wagner is great, when he does not allow Brahms to be valid. Or the Jews.[32]

Or Nietzsche – hence the need for 'distance'. This is an important note for two reasons. First, because of the reference to Brahms, shortly to become, as we shall see, the topic of a painful encounter between Wagner and 'son', and second, because of the reference to the Jews. The note represents the first occasion on which the unpleasant but mind-less anti-Semitism that mars Nietzsche's early correspondence is replaced by an explicitly anti-anti-Semitic remark. It shows, in other words, that the beginning of Nietzsche's questioning of German anti-Semitism lay in his questioning of the Wagner phenomenon.

Johannes Brahms, supported by the Wagner-hating Viennese music critic Eduard Hanslick, was regarded in the late nineteenth century as the flag-bearer for 'classicism' – for classical 'restraint' as opposed to the romantic 'excess' of Bayreuth. This introduces the third of Nietzsche's criticisms, a criticism in which he returns to his own innate musical conservatism: Wagner, all too often, lacks 'measure' and 'limit', though it has to be said to his credit that, at times, in parts of the *Ring* and in *Die Meistersinger*, he recovers it.[33] With Wagner, that is, one often struggles in vain to find bar-lines and hence rhythmic order in his music. This lack of 'measure', Nietzsche continues, evokes the wandering 'infinity' of the sea[34] (an effect, we know, Wagner consciously sought to produce). The only age in which Wagner, the thinker, finds no echo of himself is the age of classical revival, the Renaissance.[35] This lack of a classical sensibility might be portrayed as authentic, honest, rugged German 'crudeness', but to do so would mistake the German musical tradition. For German music is by no means mere 'peasant burping' – it was saved from that by importing refinement of form from Italy.[36] Yet all that acquired 'grace and delicacy' (Mozart) and 'dialectical precision' (Bach) is lacking in Wagner.[37]

Translated into the language of *The Birth of Tragedy*, this criticism of Wagner's lack of the classical boils down to the criticism that it lacks 'Apollonian' structure, is a kind of pure, 'sea'-like 'Dionysianism'. In other words, a great deal of Wagner's music is unmediated Dionysianism. This connects with Nietzsche's fourth and final criticism: Wagner's art 'transcends' rather than 'transfigures' the world. It is a Schopenhauerian art of 'flight', of world-denial. But of what use is such an art, an art in which the 'will to life' finds no expression? It is an art that can have no 'moral effect' other than 'quietism', which, Nietzsche implies, does not count as a properly moral effect at all.[38]

This criticism repeats *The Birth of Tragedy*'s point that only the Apollonian, conceptual element in the artwork can perform the life-affirming function of 'collecting' the community in clarifying affirmation of its fundamental ethos; only an Apollonian, 'classical' artwork (as Wagner's earlier conception of the artwork affirmed) can have 'moral' significance. Thus, to the extent that Wagner's later works, *Tristan* and the yet-to-be-composed *Parsifal*, become, in both theory and practice, almost purely Dionysian, they cannot perform the community-creating function which, so it seemed, was the whole point of the Bayreuth project. There is, therefore, a fatal contradiction between the avowed purpose of the Bayreuth project, that of creating a national theatre, and the character of the artwork that will be presented there.

The question these reflections present is this: what has happened to *The Birth*'s, as I called it, tour de force, its demonstration of the *compatibility* of the world-improving and world-denying Wagner, the demonstration that the collective artwork could *both* gather community *and* provide a Dionysian 'comfort' in the face of pain and death (pp. 131–2 above)? It is hard to say. Perhaps it is a matter of which opera one attends to, which is uppermost in Nietzsche's mind. If one thinks of *Tannhaüser*, *The Flying Dutchman*, the first half of the *Ring*, or, certainly, of *Die Meistersinger*, the 'collecting', Apollonian myth is without question more than adequately present. It is perhaps relevant, however, to recall that fairly recently Nietzsche has witnessed his first, profoundly affecting performance of *Tristan* (p. 155 above), the drama-less 'music-drama' that threatens one with 'expiring in a spasmodic unharnessing of all the wings of the soul'.[39] Perhaps Nietzsche sees, in *Tristan*, the future direction of Wagner's art and sees, therefore, that the work of reconciliation undertaken in *The Birth* has become redundant.

* * *

Though the above remarks represent serious criticisms, other notes mitigate their force. One of the ways in which they do this is by putting a different 'spin' on the same phenomena that were objects of criticism. Thus, approaching the question of Wagner's lack of 'classical' refinement, his 'crudeness', from another perspective, one note observes that it is

> not to be forgotten: . . . Wagner's art speaks the language of the people and that means that, unavoidably, even the noblest things undergo a marked coarsening. It is intended to work at a distance and to knit together the chaos within the community. E.G. the 'Imperial March' [*Kaisermarsch*].⁴⁰

(There is an unspoken allusion here, I think, to Greek tragedy: because the actors spoke in the open air before an audience often numbering thirty thousand, they had to *shout* their lines.) Turning to the mainly pejorative description of Wagner as an 'actor', Nietzsche observes that an actor's rhetoric is more honest than so-called objective art because (like a conjurer) it makes no attempt to disguise its intention, to hoodwink.⁴¹

The principal line of mitigation, however, consists in highlighting the unhelpful conditions under which Wagner has to work. We live, that is to say, in the age and place of 'anti-art'.⁴² Theatre, in particular, is something Wagner cannot persuade the Germans to take seriously.⁴³ What he attempts is to mobilise the 'mass' of theatre-goers so that society as a whole becomes a 'theatocracy [*Theatrokratrie*]'. If he had been an Italian (where they are serious about opera) he would unquestionably have succeeded in bringing about the social transformation he sought. But Germans have no respect for opera, viewing it as imported and 'un-German'.⁴⁴ Wagner, that is to say, makes huge claims for the significance of art for society: he is a 'Luther figure', who seeks to produce a new 'Reformation' of the whole community. But the Germans of today find such aims 'immodest', are not attuned to greatness.⁴⁵ Wagner, it is true, has his followers. But they are far from being the genuine 'reformers' he needs. Rather, they are musicians interested only in novel effects, singers with not-very-good voices, worshippers mesmerised by the cult of genius, or listeners bored with the old art and with life in general, interested only in 'intoxication'.⁴⁶ All in all, the times are entirely unripe for a second 'Reformation'.

* * *

Nietzsche's account of Wagner's positive virtues boil down to one, for Nietzsche supremely important, word: *unity*.

> The music isn't much good, nor the poetry, nor the plot nor the acting which is often mere rhetoric. But it's all, as a whole, a unity, and all at the same level. Wagner as a thinker is on exactly the same level as Wagner the musician and poet.⁴⁷

Wagner's 'strongest power', in fact, is his feeling for

> unity in difference, outside himself as an artist and within himself as an individual. He has an innate capacity to perceive the relation of the arts to each other and the connexion of state and society to art.⁴⁸

Wagner's feeling for unity in difference makes him a genuine 'bearer of culture'.⁴⁹ So that actually (a moment of optimism),

> It is seriously possible that Wagner can wean the Germans from their obsession with the individual, isolated arts. Perhaps it will even be possible to derive from his aftermath the

picture of a unified culture [*Bildung*] that can never be achieved through the mere addition of individual skills and regions of knowledge to each other.[50]

In other words, for all Wagner's faults, and for all that the excessive dominance of his 'sea'-like, Dionysian music often confuses and contradicts the Bayreuth ideal, we can still hope that from the after-effect of his work will grow something that really is a 'Reformation' of the community as a whole.

That, in any case, is the note on which Nietzsche concluded his reappraisal of the Wagner phenomenon. Writing to the Wagnerian Carl Fuchs* at the end of April, he suggests that

later, after a few years, we shall think together about our kind of "culture-war [*Kulturkampf*]"† (as the cursed phrase has it) to found a public theatre – later when we have a few more names and are not so thin on the ground. Until then we must all fight alone – I have forged a good weapon with my…Untimely Meditations with which I hit people over the head until something comes out.[51]

In sum, then, at the conclusion of his meditations on Wagner, Nietzsche remains, in spite of serious reservations about the man, thinker, and artist, as committed as ever to the Bayreuth ideal, to the rebirth of the community-gathering theatre of the 'collective artwork'. The split that begins to appear, here, between Wagner, on the one hand, and what we may call the 'Wagnerian ideal', on the other, remains with Nietzsche until the end of his career. Though his reservations about the former continue to increase, the latter, so I have promised to argue, remain with Nietzsche until the end.

The Home Front, a New Publisher, Women

Meanwhile, on the home front, Romundt was becoming something of a worry. He failed in January 1874 to get a permanent position in philosophy at Basel and his whole professional future began to look extremely bleak. (The position went, instead, to Max Heinze, Nietzsche's former tutor at Pforta. Though he retained cordial personal relations with Heinze, he regarded him as an intellectual 'flathead'.)[52] Nietzsche attributed

---

* Fuchs represented another friendship that grew out of the Bayreuth circle and which, though Nietzsche often placed it under stress, endured until his final collapse. Fuchs was a former student of von Bülow, an organist and pianist and a well-known publicist on aesthetic questions who had written a Ph.D. thesis on Schopenhauer's philosophy of music. For many years he was musical director for the city of Danzig (Gdansk). In 1900, the year of Nietzsche's death, he was responsible, along with the concert pianist Walther Lampe, for erecting a memorial to Nietzsche on the Chasté peninsula in Lake Sils near Sils Maria (see Plate 26), a favourite spot of Nietzsche's. The friendship was conducted mainly by letter: the two met only three times.

† *Kulturkampf* was the phrase coined in 1873 to describe Bismarck's attempts to eliminate the Catholic Church as a rival source of power within Germany by bringing its functions, such as marriage and education, under the control of the state. Though no friend of the Catholic priesthood, Nietzsche viewed Bismarck's anti-Catholicism with a jaundiced eye, regarding it as part of his attempt to construct a *Kulturstaat* (p. 147 above), a quasi-totalitarian state.

the failure, as he did his own failure to gain the chair of philosophy, to 'fear of Schopen-hauer'.[53] Given, however, that he reported in February that he and Overbeck were worried about 'the excellent Romundt [since] he has become a joyless mystic...clarity was never his thing, experience of life also not, and now he is developing a weird hatred of all culture',[54] there may have been other causes.

At the end of March Elizabeth arrived (see Plate 17) to spend the summer keeping house in the 'poison cottage', now 'Baumann's Cave'. Her practice since 1870 had been to spend the summers in Basel and the winters in Naumburg, though Franziska's possessiveness required diplomacy on Fritz's part to preserve the arrangement. The struggle between himself and his mother, Elizabeth reports him as saying, resembled 'the fight for Helen between the Trojans and Danaans'.[55]

In May, brother and sister spent a holiday in a five-star hotel next to the Rhine Falls near Schaffhausen (the largest waterfalls in Europe) where, Elizabeth records, they laughed a lot, a merriment which enabled Fritz to 're-establish the equilibrium between reality and concentrated thinking'. Amusingly, she recalls that Fritz would have nothing to do with any *table d'hôte*, calling it 'the grazing of herds'. Responding to an exorbitant bill, he declared with a solemn pun (it is not entirely clear that Elizabeth got it) that 'one always has to pay dearly for grazing away from the herd'.[56]

* * *

On July 9 Nietzsche received what was effectively a 'headhunting' letter from Ernst Schmeitzner in Chemnitz. Schmeitzner wrote that he proposed to set up a new publishing house specialising in 'the best' in German philosophy, literature, and aesthetics, and asked for a work from Nietzsche's pen.[57] Because Fritzsch had been unable to pay the honorariums for the last two publications, Nietzsche responded favourably. On July 18 he sent him a draft of the third *Untimely Meditation* and asked him to take over its two predecessors from the troubled Fritzsch which, by the end of the year, Schmeitzner did. Of course, this separation from the Wagnerians' 'house publisher' marked a further widening of the distance between Nietzsche and the Wagners, particularly because Schmeitzner was, as we shall see, from their point of view, politically suspect.

* * *

The year 1874 saw two new women friends enter Nietzsche's life. In addition to his continuing exchange of letters with Malwida von Meysenbug, he developed a short but beautiful 'letter-friendship' with an Italian noblewoman, Emma Guerrieri-Gonsaga, who had been greatly impressed by the second *Untimely Meditation*. Agreeing with Nietzsche that the old religion was dead, and was in any case unacceptable on account of its 'lies' exposed by David Strauss, her quest, she wrote, was for a 'future religion built on completely philosophical foundations'.[58] Asked whether he agreed, Nietzsche replied that his answer would be found in his third *Untimely Meditation*[59] (to which we shall turn shortly).

A further friendship developed with Marie Baumgartner, the mother of his pupil and amanuensis, Adolf, whom he started to visit in Lörrach near to Basel, just over the border in Germany. Highly educated and liberal-minded, Marie, though now officially German as a result of her remarriage to a Herr Köchlin, was a loyal Alsatian, originally from Mulhausen. Identifying far more with French than with German culture – she translated Nietzsche's third *Untimely Meditation* into French – she hated the German annexation of Alsace at the end of the Franco-Prussian war and published tracts against it.[60] In that vein, she responded strongly to Nietzsche's remark, in the introduction to the first *Meditation*, that German post-war triumphalism threatens to be 'the destruction of the German spirit for the sake of the German Reich',[61] seeing an affinity between a German and an Alsatian protest against the arrogance of German imperialism.

Marie's letters to Nietzsche reveal a more-than-motherly interest – she writes that she dreams of him – though neither would for a moment have contemplated transgressing bourgeois conventions. Thirteen years older than Nietzsche, the relationship resembled that between him and Cosima, of whom she was jealous. A keen idealist and Schopenhauerian, she was one of the many friends who were greatly upset by Nietzsche's 'positivist' turn in 1876, writing to him, with reference to *Human, All-Too-Human* (the first public manifestation of the 'turn'), that

> this new book seems at many places designed to shock, to block any [human] closeness – and yet your whole being and doing is such that one must love you ... I shall never give up my belief in human goodness ... what kind of happiness can there be if this is exterminated?[62]

In spite of the spiritual gulf opened up by *Human, All-Too-Human*, when Nietzsche left Basel in 1879, she was moved to tears.

The roles in which Nietzsche cast his women friends took several forms: the pure mother, Malwida von Meysenbug, the sister-lover, Cosima, the mother-lover, Marie, the pure friend, Meta von Salis, the pure lover, Lou Salomé, and the pure sister, Elizabeth. What nearly all his women friends (Elizabeth excepted) have in common, however, is that they were intelligent, highly educated, and widely read. Biographically, therefore, it is no surprise that when the application of a Fräulein Rubinstein from Leipzig to enrol for a Ph.D. programme brought the question of admitting women to the university before the committee of Basel's combined faculties on July 10, 1874, Nietzsche was among the four members who voted *for* their admission. Because, after a two-hour discussion, six faculty members (including Burckhardt) voted against admission, the motion was lost. But Nietzsche and the other three supporters of the motion must have been upset by the result, because they requested that their dissenting view be explicitly recorded.[63] Nietzsche's mature writings are famously anti-feminist, even misogynistic. Later on we shall have to ask what happened to this early, at least partial support for emancipationist demands.

Bergün

On July 17, the summer holidays having started, Nietzsche travelled with Romundt to Bergün. On the way he stopped at Chur where, so he wrote Elizabeth, he 'almost decided to marry' a Fräulein Berta Rohr, whom they had met the previous year in Flims.[64] Elizabeth's disapproval called Fritz's family-diplomacy into play once again, as he assured her that he was just joking.[65] But because he told von Gersdorff at the same time that he had been reluctant to leave Chur on Berta's account,[66] one suspects this was not entirely true. Indeed, as a rival to the theory that Nietzsche was really gay, one might suggest that it was the obsessive, quasi-incestuous jealousy Elizabeth displayed towards any women who threatened to become closer to Fritz than herself, rather than the love that dare not speak its name, that proved the major impediment to his following the instructions of the 'Bayreuth marriage-commission' to find a wife.

Bergün lies 1,400 metres high in the Albula Valley (*Albulatal*), near to Splürgen and to Nietzsche's eventual summer home, Sils Maria. Here they stayed in the Hotel Piz Aela. Nietzsche describes the holiday to von Gersdorff:

Here (in Bergün, take a look at Baedecker)…we are the sole guests in a hotel that hundreds of travellers pass by every day on their way to or from St. Moritz. Of course, we do not have a lake here like the one we had in Flims: recently we found one about three hours up the mountain at about 6,000 feet, bathing and swimming in it until we almost froze, emerging red as lobsters (*feuerrot*).[67]

And to Overbeck:

Here we are living in a fine hotel, where we are well taken care of and not overcharged…Up to now we have seen a cliff near the Albula bridge, which connects and overlooks two lonely valleys in the high mountains – a place where I would like to build myself a tower – and a sulphur spring in one of the side valleys: we brought some of the water home with us in bottles in order to get rid of some minor constipation caused by [a characteristically extraordinary diagnosis] our consumption of Veltliner wine.[68]

Towards the end of July the mist and rain closed in, as so often happens in the high Alpine valleys:

terrible rain the last several days, everyone's suffering cabin fever [*sehr ungeduldig*] – that is the way it is in this isolated place. Only I don't share it since I am busy thinking about and finishing my new work [the third *Untimely Meditation*]. Engaged in that, one lives in a different place where one doesn't have anything to do with rain any more.[69]

Brahms Banned in Bayreuth

Save for the knowledge that he was persona non grata in the Wagner camp, Brahms had never risen above Nietzsche's musical horizon before the middle of 1874. He was, until then, terra incognita. In June, however, all that changed. Nietzsche wrote to Rohde from Basel:

Your countryman [both Rohde and Brahms were born in Hamburg] was here recently and I've heard much of his music, above all his *Triumphlied* [Triumphal Song] which he himself conducted. To me it was the most difficult problem of aesthetic conscience to come to terms with Brahms.[70]

So taken with the *Triumphlied* was Nietzsche that he travelled to Zurich to hear it again on July 12. (Given that, of the works for which Brahms is famous, only the *German Requiem* had been completed to date, the choice is not as weird as it seems.)

Brahms composed the *Lied* to celebrate victory in the Franco-Prussian war. Wagner had composed his *Kaisermarsch* [March Imperial] for the same purpose. But whereas Wagner had no real affection for the Hohenzollern dynasty and composed the Imperial March only in an (unsuccessful) attempt to drag the Emperor into the project of making Bayreuth a *national* German theatre, Brahms was genuinely devoted to the Emperor and proud of the Reich.

Travelling from Bergrün, Nietzsche arrived in Bayreuth on August 5 with the score of the *Triumphlied* ticking away like a bomb in his suitcase. Sick as usual after travel, he booked himself into the *Sonne* [Sun] Hotel. Wagner, however, on hearing of his arrival, rushed over and insisted he stay in the now nearly completed *Wahnfried*. Nietzsche quickly recovered and their first evening together went off well. The following evening, however, matters took a different turn.

Things must have got off to a bad start because, as Cosima records in her diary, Nietzsche told them he and Overbeck had accepted an offer from Schmeitzner to publish with him. They were thus forced to 'serve the Social Democratic [socialist] Party' because that was their only way of getting published.[71] By this time, of course, there was no love lost between Wagner and the socialists.

After dinner, gathered in the huge drawing-room stuffed to overflowing with Victorian objects – Richard's piano, his big writing-desk, Cosima's smaller writing-desk, pictures, busts, books, souvenirs and potted palms – Richard entertained the guests, who included the concert pianist Paul Klindworth and, according to Nietzsche, the great Wagnerian soprano Lilli Lehmann, by playing a piano reduction of the Rhine-maidens scene from the end of *Götterdämmerung*.* As soon as he had finished, Cosima records, Nietzsche 'burst forth' with the score of Brahms' *Triumphlied*.

Let us recall, here, Nietzsche's private reflections on Wagner's 'tyrannical' nature; that 'the danger for Wagner is great, when he does not allow Brahms to be valid. Or the Jews' (p. 186 above). 'Danger' means, here, something like 'danger that all the promise will be crushed out of the Wagnerian enterprise by a tyrannical nature that refuses to allow anyone else to breathe'. So what, it seems, Nietzsche was trying to do was to reform Wagner's character – a presumptuous enterprise given that, at sixty-one, Wagner was thirty-one years his senior. Or else he was trying to provoke a final breach in the event of failing to persuade Wagner at least to give Brahms a fair hearing. He was, it seems, offering something like an ultimatum: stop being such a tyrant or else I'm off. Of course what really mattered was Wagner's perceived 'tyranny' towards *Nietzsche*: Brahms, one may suspect, was a surrogate for himself. In any case the effort came to nothing because, Cosima records, 'R[ichard] laughed loudly at the idea of setting the word *Gerechtigkeit* [justice] to music'.[72]

On the following afternoon, someone, it is unclear who, sat down at the piano and played the offending piece. Wagner became furious, lamenting, writes Cosima, 'the dismal character of the composition which … friend Nietzsche had praised'. It was, he claimed, derivative from Handel, Mendelssohn, and Schumann, and lacked both Liszt's spirituality and authentic emotion.[73] The remainder of the day saw no further talk of Brahms. In the evening, after playing some pieces from operas by Auber, Wagner finally formally buried Brahms's piece of jingoism by playing his own, by implication, infinitely superior version of the same thing, the *Kaisermarsch*.

---

* The opera and with it the entire *Ring* cycle would be finally completed three months later on November 21, twenty-six years after Wagner's first thoughts on the subject.

Wagner's perception of the traumatic occasion is recorded by Elizabeth. Wagner told her, she writes, that

> Your brother laid the red book [containing the *Triumphlied*] on the grand piano, and whenever I came down to the drawing-room this red object stared right at me – it literally inflamed me, just as a red rag does a bull. I could very well see that, by means of it, Nietzsche wished tacitly to say, 'Just look! here is someone who has done good work too!' Well, the end of it was that one evening I simply fell into a passion, and fell almost to bits as well! 'But what did my brother say?' I demanded anxiously. 'He said nothing', Wagner replied, 'he simply blushed and gazed at me with mingled surprise and calm dignity'. I would give a hundred thousand marks for a bearing such as Nietzsche's – always distinguished, always dignified![74]

Nietzsche never mentioned the Brahms incident in any letter. Elizabeth recalls that when, sitting with him on a bench in a park in Baden-Baden, she asked him why he had never told her the story of Brahms's *Triumphlied* he replied 'Lizzie, on that occasion Wagner was not great'.[75]

Wagner also gave an account of the incident to his friend Hans von Wolzogen. Wagner told him, Wolzogen recollects, that

> Nietzsche said that I *had* to get to know the music in order to have a proper opinion about it. I refused, but he kept on at me. In the end I became furious with him (you know how I am when I get angry – my poor Cosima has had to suffer from it often enough). I became crude – my God I did ! – Nietzsche flew out of the door. Yes, that's the way I am – *and he never came back*! And now…I'm supposed to love Brahms on whose account I've lost my Nietzsche![76]

Nietzsche remained in Bayreuth until August 15, Cosima's diplomacy preventing an open breach. But clearly relations between the once-revered Master and the once-revering guest were now under great strain. Nietzsche caused Wagner 'many difficult hours', Cosima records. 'Among other things, he [Nietzsche] maintained that the German language gave him no pleasure, and that he would rather talk in Latin, etc.' – another deliberate provocation of the nationalistic Wagner.[77]

Wagner is right that he 'lost' Nietzsche on this occasion. Though Nietzsche continued to support the Bayreuth cause, though the Wagners continued to be enthusiastic about Nietzsche's publications for another year, and though sporadic letter exchanges continued (in 1875 Nietzsche wrote a total of five letters to the Wagner household), the old intimacy never returned. The Brahms occasion was the last time Nietzsche would ever stay as a guest in Wagner's home. From now on, until open warfare was declared, the relationship was political rather than personal.

* * *

Compounding the disaster of the visit to Bayreuth, on the return journey to Basel, Nietzsche had his bag stolen at Würzburg railway station. It contained, among other things, a signed copy of the libretto of the *Ring* cycle. Writing as if making a major discovery about human nature, he concludes his account of the incident to von Gersdorff with 'Moral: one shouldn't leave one's suitcase unattended on railway stations, otherwise there will be some horrible, cunning brute waiting there, on the lookout for suitcases'.[78] Nietzsche was, as Elizabeth remarks apropos this incident, somewhat naive regarding the ways of the world.

Third Untimely Meditation: Schopenhauer as Educator

The completed third *Untimely Meditation* was sent to Schmeitzner on August 19 and appeared on October 15, 1874 (Nietzsche's thirtieth birthday). Nietzsche had complimentary copies sent to Wagner, von Bülow, Malwida von Meysenbug, Marie Baumgartner, Emma Guerrieri-Gonzaga, Krug (but not Pinder), Rohde, von Gersdorff, and a couple of others. This list is of some significance given Nietzsche's remark that 'only the reactions of six or seven readers are of any significance'.[79] (That he writes only for 'the few', or even 'no one', becomes, we shall see, an important theme in his mature work.)

Nietzsche always regarded the third *Meditation* as a crucial work. In 1882 he recommended it to Lou Salomé as presenting his 'fundamental attitude' – to everything, presumably.[80] Its topic is what, fifty years later, Heidegger would call 'authenticity'. It is about overcoming the 'laziness' that makes human beings seem like 'factory products . . . pseudo-men dominated by public opinion'. Though most of us inhabit that condition, none of us (none, at least, of Nietzsche's proper readers) is really comfortable with being merely a 'herd' type. It is, moreover, a condition we can escape: 'The man who does not wish to belong to the masses needs only to . . . follow his conscience, which calls to him: "Be yourself! All you are now doing, thinking, desiring, is not you yourself"'.[81] But how is one to discover this 'self' one is to become?

Post-Freudian psychotherapy typically thinks of the 'true' self or 'ego' as a kind of drive or pressure buried within each unique individual, struggling to burst through the lid of social repression. Nietzsche dismisses this picture completely: 'your true nature lies, not concealed deep within you but immeasurably high above you, or at least above that which you usually take yourself to be'.[82] The true self is a 'task' to be performed rather than a pressure to be released. And to discover one's task one needs to ask what one has 'truly loved up to now'; what it is, in other words, 'which has drawn [one's] . . . soul aloft?'[83] But how is one to discover that?

At this point, the considerations of the third *Meditation* begin to converge with those of the second. To discover one's true love and task one is to seek out a 'revered object' which supplies one with the 'fundamental law of [one's] . . . own true self'. In the second *Meditation* such heroes were described as 'monumental' figures. Here they are described as 'educators'.[84] Nietzsche's point is not difficult to grasp. What he is talking about, once again, is the 'role model'. Christians, for example, often treat Jesus in this way. Pondering, in a difficult situation, how to act in accordance with their innermost conscience, they often ask themselves: 'What would Jesus do in this situation?' To do this is to take Jesus as, in Nietzsche's sense, an 'educator'.

Nietzsche now turns to the possibility of the philosopher as 'educator'. He makes clear that by 'philosopher' he means someone whose thought is embodied in their life, so that they can provide an 'example' one can follow. Kant was a great thinker but, in this sense, no 'philosopher', because, for all the call to moral courage contained in his theorising, in life, he cravenly submitted to petty conventions of academic life and pretended (for the sake of his job) to a religious belief he did not have.[85]

Because the function of the 'educator' is to enable us to stand out against 'public opinion' and become our individual selves, he must above all *himself* stand out against public opinion. This is particularly true in the destitute times of modernity marked, as they are, by (a) loss of community – we live in 'an age of atoms, of atomistic chaos', (b) low materialism, 'greed for money', (c) egoism, 'all men feel in themselves only the self-seeking worm', (d) the reduction of individuals to media-controlled 'automata', (e) a moral vacuum – Christianity destroyed the 'natural' values of antiquity but has now, itself, lost the power to direct people's lives – and (f) 'haste and hurry', so that, even if we knew what they were, we would have no time to allow 'eternal' values to govern our lives, no time for moral equanimity.[86] In the morally vacuous age of the mechanized, atomized, harried, consumer society, the educator must be, above all, out of step with the spirit of the age: 'untimely'.

And here we come, finally, to Schopenhauer, whom, even after his turn against him in 1876, Nietzsche continues to describe as 'my first and only educator'.[87] We come, that is, to 'Schopenhauer' not as a collection of writings but rather as a 'living man', because, of course, only the living man can provide a 'model' *for life*.[88]

Schopenhauer's most salient character trait, Nietzsche suggests, is precisely his ruggedly courageous 'untimeliness'. Unlike Kant, he scorned the scholarly clique of professors who might otherwise have given him a job, and, in an age dominated by Hegel's triumphalist optimism, did not hesitate to propound his inevitably unpopular philosophical pessimism. Displaying the 'heroism of truthfulness', Schopenhauer acknowledged the fact that a happy life is impossible, that the highest form of humanity is the 'heroic life'; a life that accepts 'the suffering involved in being truthful'[89] – in being a kind of existential whistle-blower.

For other swimmers against the tide the social ostracism to which they condemned themselves proved too much. Hölderlin went mad and Kleist committed suicide. But, like Wagner, Schopenhauer possessed the 'iron constitution' which enabled him to withstand the 'solitude' to which he was condemned.[90]

Nietzsche now asks what 'circle of duties' can be drawn from this ideal. How can we show that it points towards 'practical activity', that is to say, 'educates' our *lives*?[91] Schopenhauer himself was neither a critic of *current* society nor a social reformer. He did not think modernity was any better or worse than any other age because he thought that *all* human life in *all* ages was equally painful and worthless. Thus it comes as no surprise when Nietzsche acknowledges that it is a 'hard … task' to show that *anything* practical follows from the 'loftiness' of 'Schopenhauerian man', that one might well take from him the rejection of 'any participation in the world of action'.[92] Nonetheless, in a startling passage of thought, he manages to extract practical duties from the adoption of Schopenhauer as role model.* The duties that derive from the model are not, he says,

> the duties of a solitary: on the contrary they set one in the midst of a mighty community held together not by external forms but by a fundamental idea. It is the fundamental idea of *culture*, insofar as it sets for each one of us but one task: *to promote the production of the philosopher, the artist and the saint within us and without us and thereby to work at the perfecting of nature.*[93]

* As we have seen, Schopenhauer *does* reject 'participation in action'. The highest insight into the nature and value of life is embodied in the 'transition from virtue to asceticism' (p. 85 above). What Nietzsche is suggesting is that he understands Schopenhauer's system better than Schopenhauer himself, that its implications are actually different from what Schopenhauer takes them to be.

In support of this startling leap of thought Nietzsche says that 'nature' needs both the philosopher and artist to achieve its 'metaphysical goal . . . of its own self-enlightenment'; and here he repeats Goethe's remark that dramatic poetry is the *causa finalis* [ultimate purpose] of the world. And Nature needs the 'saint' (as conceived by Schopenhauer) because only through him can nature achieve final 'redemption from itself'.[94]

As with the earlier reference to Goethe's remark (p. 179 above), this strange passage of thought takes us back to the version of Schopenhauer's metaphysics presented in *The Birth of Tragedy*. We are all, he suggests there, nothing but figures in, as it were, a painting of a battle-scene[95] constructed by and for the only real being, the 'Primal Unity' or 'Will' – or 'Nature', as it is now called. It follows that because we are the 'Primal Unity's' creatures it is our duty to collaborate in allowing this world-creating child-artist to see his own nature reflected in the purified world-picture painted by the philosopher and the artist. And it follows, too, that we must collaborate in the appearance of the saint: for only by experiencing, through the saint's insight, the necessity for 'denial of the will' can Primal Will see the need for its own, and man's, redemption through the 'abolition' of the world of pain it has constructed. Only through the insight (or perhaps one should say 'rapture') of the saint can we hope that one day the world will come to an end.

This barely intelligible passage has very little to be said for it, lost, as it is, in the darkest and most self-contradictory regions of Schopenhauer's metaphysics. The unanswerable question is: Why on earth should we have any 'duty' to the world's creator, particularly one of so questionable a character as *The Birth*'s 'Primal Unity'? Thankfully, however, Nietzsche will soon make his turn against Schopenhauerian metaphysics, and when he does, as already noted, the idea of art as 'Nature's' *causa finalis* will disappear without trace.

There is, however, a quite different line of thought by which Nietzsche seeks to arrive at approximately the same conclusion, one that will become more and more salient as his philosophy matures. 'Mankind', he says, 'must work continually at the production of individual great men – that and nothing else is its task'.[96] (Because he conceives of 'greatness' as accentuating the difference between humans and animals to the maximum degree,[97] the 'great' individual will have to be a *geistige* [spiritual-intellectual] figure, approximately, in other words, a philosopher, artist or saint.) In explaining why this is our overriding task, Nietzsche appeals, not, this time, to high-flown metaphysics, but rather to biology:

> How much one would like to apply to society and its goals something that can be learnt from observation of any species of the animal or plant world: that its only concern is the individual higher exemplar, the more uncommon, more powerful, more complex, more fruitful – how much one would like to do this if inculcated fancies as to the goal of society did not offer such tough resistance! We ought really to have no difficulty in seeing that, when a species has arrived at its limits and is about to go over into a higher species, the goal of its evolution lies, not in the mass of its exemplars and their well-being . . . but rather in those apparently scattered and chance existences which favourable conditions have here and there produced.

So, concludes Nietzsche, mankind ought to seek out and create the 'favourable conditions' under which those great men can come into existence. And for the rest of us, our lives acquire their 'highest value' when we live 'for the good of the rarest and most valuable exemplars'.[98]

Nietzsche here is appealing to a version of (social) Darwinism – remember that he had decided by the beginning of 1873 that Darwin's theory of evolution was 'true'.[99] And what he is appealing to, in particular, is the value of, in Darwinian language, the 'random mutation'. According to evolution theory, he is observing, a species evolves into a 'higher' species when it produces a mutation which is better adapted to the current state of the environment. Because the mutations breed successfully whereas the remainder tend to die out before doing so, gradually the species evolves into a new species better adapted to thriving in the current environment. Because human beings and human societies belong, just like plants and animals, to the realm of biology, Nietzsche concludes, we ought to apply this same principle to society and so do everything possible to promote the appearance of 'chance existences', random mutations. (This idea may have developed in conversation with Wagner because it appears in metaphorical form in *Die Meistersinger*: as Hans Sachs eventually convinces them, the mastersingers must accept the wild novelty of Walter's prize song, must admit Walter into their guild, because the law of life is: change or die.)

As I have mentioned before, the most common interpretation of Nietzsche represents him as an 'aristocratic individualist': only the 'great' individual, the 'superman', is of value; the rest of us must be his slaves. It is important to notice, therefore, that on neither of the above lines of argument does the exceptional individual possess *ultimate* value. On the Schopenhauerian line of argument the great individual is a *means* to the self-understanding and consequent self-transformation of the 'Primal Unity', so that the ultimate value is something like the well-being of 'being' as a whole. On the Darwinian line of argument the great individual is again valuable only as a *means*, this time a means to the evolution of *society as a whole* to a 'higher' condition.[100] Even though, therefore, the third *Meditation* places great stress on the importance of the great individual, it at no point offers him as an end in himself, at no point propounds the 'only the superman counts' doctrine. This pattern, as we will discover, runs throughout all of Nietzsche's mature philosophy. The great individual is crucially important but only ever as a means.

* * *

Our 'sole task' is, then, to 'promote' the production of 'individual great men', of 'geniuses'. The only remaining question is *how* the non-geniuses among us are to do this. Are we all consigned to slavery to create his 'freedom from the necessity of earning a living'?[101] Should all non-geniuses become coal-miners or sock-darners? Not so. Even 'second and third rate talents' can contribute to the task by preparing both 'within' and 'without' for the appearance of genius.[102] Presumably the idea here is that the higher the general level of culture the more favourable are the conditions for the appearance of genius. The inspiring teacher who is not himself a genius can turn the potential genius into an actual one. Presumably, however, *fourth*-rate talents *are* confined to coal-mining and sock-darning.

* * *

Karl Hillebrand had given the first *Meditation* a good review, earning thereby Nietzsche's undying gratitude (in *Ecce Homo*, he calls him 'the last *humane* German who knew how to wield the pen').[103] But his response to the third was distinctly critical. 'Herr Nietzsche', he wrote (with considerable justice) in Augsburg's *Allgemeine Zeitung*,

> tells us perhaps in too great detail but at the same time not quite precisely enough how the acquaintance with Schopenhauer, that he has had for about nine years, has affected him and how it could affect other young men. He focuses on the philosopher as educator, but I confess that I can't always follow him.[104]

Cosima, on the other hand, claimed to experience no such difficulty and attributed Hillebrand's difficulties to 'a completely Hegelized brain'.[105] She began a five-page letter of appreciation with the words 'this is *my* Untimely [Meditation]', particularly liking the call to authentic individuality in the first section and 'the intoxicating fire with which the whole thing glows'. The work, she suggests, will become the Bible of all those who have spent their lives struggling and suffering for a 'great idea'.[106] And Wagner himself sent four telegrammatic lines of appreciation:

> Deep and great. Most audacious and new the presentation of Kant [as, unlike Schopenhauer, not truly a 'philosopher']. Truly comprehensible only for the possessed … May you cast long and deep shadows into the sunny land of these bonny times![107]

Von Bülow loved the work and was particularly impressed by the correlation between (subservience to) 'public opinion' and 'private laziness'.[108] Malwida von Meysenbug wrote that the work 'is always with me; it has become my Bible. Never has anyone defined the object of culture more beautifully', and Elizabeth, too, was deeply moved.[109]

What these reactions make clear is that what the – particularly female – fans of the third *Meditation* responded to was its quasi-religious rhetoric of authenticity: the appeal to the reader to step outside lazy conformism to 'the herd' (to escape what Heidegger would call 'the dictatorship of the They' and Sartre 'bad faith'), to sacrifice all for the sake of some great, world-redeeming ideal. The only one of Nietzsche's acquaintances who did not respond in this way – which suggests she must have been an interesting woman – was Emma Guerrieri-Gonzaga, who, although putting her finger on the appeal of the work, its passionate 'yearning to escape a terrible world' and to attain a 'higher realm of truth, beauty and love', notes that it fails to address the fact that 'nature had given us no wings' to reach such a realm, so that the overall effect of the work is depressing.[110]

The most amusing response to the *Meditation* came in the form of an anonymous telegram which read: 'You are like the spirit that you can understand, but you are not like me. [signed] Schopenhauer'.[111] (Schopenhauer had already been dead fifteen years.) This was Nietzsche's own final assessment of the work. In *Ecce Homo* he says that, really, it only uses Schopenhauer as a 'semiotic' for himself, that what he is really talking about is '*Nietzsche* as educator'.[112]

Or rather as *future* educator. For what is really salient about the work is the gulf between its high idealism and Nietzsche's actual life. In the work, as we saw, Kant fails to count as an authentic 'philosopher' because, although preaching moral courage, in practice he 'clung to his university, submitted himself to its regulations … endured to live among colleagues and students',[113] as well as professing a religious faith he did not have. In contrast to the courageous Schopenhauer, Kant never properly became the 'self' that he potentially was. But another thinker who 'clung to his university' (the passage is almost overtly autobiographical) when his true 'self' demanded he do something quite different was Nietzsche. Thus when Elizabeth put it to him that he was himself the 'educating philosopher described in the essay' he quite correctly replied that she was (as usual) talking 'nonsense'.[114] For as he confessed to von Gersdorff at the end of 1874, with the burdens of university life it had for a long time been impossible for him to think about 'untimely things'.[115] The call of 'conscience', in other words, has been overruled by the mechanized slavery, the 'haste and hurry', of university life. Nonetheless, the fact that it was articulated so clearly in the work must have provided Nietzsche with at least a further impulse towards practising what he preached.

Christmas at Home and the 'Hymn to Friendship'

The writing of the third *Meditation*, which Nietzsche had found particularly difficult, had cost him a great deal of nervous energy. With it out of the way, and with its, on balance, highly favourable reception, he was able to relax when he returned to Naumburg for a white Christmas (again turning down an invitation to spend Christmas in Bayreuth). Taking a break from philosophical work, he was able finally to complete the 'Hymn to Friendship' in both a piano solo and four-handed version. (The melody of this work was recycled in the 'Prayer to Life', music track 17 on the Web site for this book.) Though a purely instrumental work, it has a programme which he describes to Malwida:

> First verse: prelude – hymn for the procession of the friends to the temple of friendship.
> Intermezzo: – as if in sad-happy recollection.
> Second verse: hymn.
> Intermezzo: like a prophesy of the future, a glance into the furthest distance.
> Third and final verse: finale – song of the friends.[116]

Nietzsche was very pleased with the piece, regarding it as 'a clear proof' of the purely subjective nature of time: though it lasts only fifteen minutes one 'forgets one's [everyday] time' because a whole lifetime is traversed in the piece.[117] (One can think of the imminent car-crash experience in which 'one's whole life flashes before one's eyes' to get his point.)

While in Naumburg Nietzsche met the new wives of both Pinder and Krug, encounters which made it clear that he was growing away from these intimates of his youth. 'I saw a lot of Krug and Pinder at Christmas', he wrote Rohde. 'I tell you: you and I have an eternal youth of love, in contrast with these thirty-year-old greybeards'.[118] On January 3 he travelled back to Basel through heavy snow and intense cold.

12

Auf Wiedersehen Bayreuth

Returning to Basel on January 4, 1875, Nietzsche felt more oppressed than ever by the mountain of work facing him. In addition to the appalling burden of his university and Pädegogium teaching, he had foolishly promised Schmeitzner a further ten *Untimely Meditations* over the next five years. But those – his 'real' work of cleaning up the 'soul' of the age – he could only produce, he told von Bülow, during holidays and periods of sick leave. 'Thank God', he wrote, with the false hope of the chronically sick, that, apart from the ongoing eye problems, for once 'there is no illness in sight, and the daily cold baths I take makes it extremely unlikely I will ever be sick again'.[1] This was in January! Like his alter ego, Zarathustra, Elizabeth comments, Nietzsche liked to 'mock the winter'.[2] To Malwida von Meysenbug he wrote that he had so many professional duties that he stumbled from one day to the next in a 'drugged' condition. He envied, he wrote, the dead, but had resolved to grow old, not out of pleasure in life, but in order to complete his 'task'.[3]

By February, however, he had brightened up, somewhat. 'It is a gift of Tyche' (the goddess of luck), he wrote Rohde, 'to live in these Bayreuth years'. Though the Bayreuth Festival would not take place until the following year, Wagner had planned an elaborate series of rehearsals for 1875. Since the music was incredibly new and different, it was universally agreed that one needed to attend the rehearsals (now we would listen to recordings) to prepare oneself for the actual performances. Apprehensively, however, Nietzsche added that his expectations were so high that he was likely preparing himself for a fall.[4] Life is 'dangerous', he wrote; one 'trembles before the future'.[5]

Several of Nietzsche's university students have recorded memories of him in this phase of his life. Jakob Wackernagel recalls that although Nietzsche took his seminars for advanced students very seriously,

> his lectures were not much appreciated by us [undergraduate] students. From Jacob Burckhardt we had come to expect a high standard of lecturing. But Nietzsche's lectures were delivered in an extremely dry and factual manner, with only the occasionally memorable phrase. So, for example, we found his 'Introduction to Plato' particularly boring.

On the human level, however, Wackernagel continues,

> one took great pleasure in his company. In the first years of his being here [in Basel] he had a rich social life that included dance-evenings. The young women were enchanted by him. We students listened eagerly to their accounts of conversations with him. One of them once told me, for instance, he had told her he had dreamt he was a camellia.[6]

Another student, Ludwig von Scheffler, records a more favourable impression of Nietzsche's lectures:

> I found that the challenging tone in writings did not correspond to his behaviour as a private person. To discover him to possess such modesty, almost humility, of manner was a surprise. He was short rather than of medium height, the head sunk deep into the shoulders of the compact, yet delicate, body. And behind the iridescent spectacles and the long, drooping moustache the face had that spiritual look which often lends an impressive presence to short men…a heavy, almost tired, walk to the lectern…he did not have the stentorian voice of the orator, nor the sharply articulated but fundamentally ineffective modulation typical of the pathos of many university lecturers. Nietzsche's delivery was soft and natural, as it escaped his lips. It had only one thing to be said for it: it was spoken directly from the soul, which attracted one's immediate sympathy.[7]

There probably was, however, something in the less favourable description, since Nietzsche admitted to Rohde during this period that to preserve his health and strength for his 'real' work, he had given his students 'a couple of venerable old warhorses' he could 'ride in his sleep'.[8]

* * *

February brought the annual torment of the Basel *Fastnacht* [carnival]. Most intolerable of all were the drums, which played continuously from seven in the morning until well into the evening. So Nietzsche fled to Lucerne for the weekend of February 14–15: 'I found deep snow and a heavenly silence', he wrote home. 'It was like a huge general pause in a loud piece of music; one heard the silence'.[9] The best thing about Lucerne, however, was walking up Mount Pilatus. It had, he wrote von Gersdorff, a particularly personal meaning for him,[10] a meaning that becomes clear in a letter to Rohde written shortly after his return to Basel: 'it seems to me that I want to become a mountain man; my way of life will gradually become as fortified and inwardly independent as a mountain man's'.[11] A 'mountain man' is, we shall see, just what, in a few years, Nietzsche did become. The retreat from the noise of Basel to the silent solitude of the mountains was, as he anticipated, a pre-echo of his future life.

While Fritz was in Lucerne, Elizabeth arrived in Bayreuth to run the Wagner household for the six weeks they were away for concerts in Vienna and Budapest. Franziska had been thoroughly opposed to the idea. To her, Wagner was a scandalous figure, whom she always refused to meet. But Nietzsche was delighted by the intimacy that grew up between Elizabeth and Cosima – they soon began to use the familiar *du* with each other – because, it seems clear, it allowed him to preserve the relationship with the Wagners by proxy, and so avoid Wagner's suffocating presence.

By March, pressure of work led to an almost complete withdrawal from Basel's social life.[12] 'Why on earth does anyone become a professor at twenty-four!' Nietzsche lamented a few months later. 'I have been bowed down by work the last six years'[13] – the entirety of his life as a professor, in other words.

We Philologists

In March, suffering his usual eye trouble, Nietzsche began to dictate to the visiting von Gersdorff a prospective fourth *Untimely Meditation*, to be called 'We Philologists'. In the notes for this project he returns once again to the question of what if anything justified the unique status of 'the Greek': the idea that ancient Greece was the acme of Western civilization, so that all our efforts should be directed to recreating this cultural ideal. This notion had been unchallenged in Germany since Goethe and Winkelmann in the eighteenth century, and justified, of course, the preeminent position occupied by Greek philology in German education.

What, Nietzsche ponders, justifies this supposedly exemplary status of the Greeks? Why should we treat them as role models? What is supposed to be so special about them? Given an interest in the ancient world, should we not attend at least equally to the ancient Jews, Egyptians or Persians? In the main, Nietzsche reflects, the preeminence of the Greeks comes from a combination of false idealization, flight from the realities of the present to a sentimental dream, hostility to Christianity, and repetition of the cultural cringe of the Romans. So surely the imitation of the Greeks is a 'refuted principle'?[14] Actually not, Nietzsche eventually decides. What is crucially important about the Greeks is that although they share in the universal nature common to all humanity, their child-like innocence, their 'naivety', allows important human phenomena – state, education, sex and art – to show up with a unique clarity: 'a Greek cook is more of a cook than any other'.[15] The Greeks were open, candid people because, unlike Christian and post-Christian humanity, they were shameless:

> If I say that the Greeks were, collectively, more ethical than modern humanity what does this mean? The whole visibility of their soul in action shows that they were without shame. They did not know the bad conscience. They were more open, more passionate, as artists are; they carried with them a kind of childlike naivety, and so all the bad things they did carried with them a kind of purity, something approaching the holy.[16]

(Albert Camus celebrates Greek 'naivety' in a similar way, associating it, in particular, with the nakedness of their athletes.) So the Greeks are, after all, worthy of special attention. Nonetheless attention must be paid to the *real* Greeks, not to the sentimentalized, 'gold-paper-wrapped',[17] 'castrated'[18] image of them that has been dominant since the eighteenth century. We must recognise the 'human, *all-too*-human'[19] in Greek – and so in human – nature: we must '*bring to light the irrational in human affairs, without any trace of shame*'. Only when that is done 'will one be able to distinguish what is fundamental and incapable of improvement from what can be improved'.[20] Moreover, only when we frankly acknowledge the all-too-human will we be able to deal with it in a sensible way. Like the Greeks themselves, we must acknowledge

> the lust for intoxication, for trickery, for revenge, for bearing a grudge, for vilification as human, and so be able to integrate them in the building of society and ethics. The wisdom

of [Greek] institutions lay in that absence of a separation between good and evil, black and white. The nature which thus showed itself was not denied but only integrated, restricted to particular cults and days. That is the root of all the free-spiritedness [*Freisinnigkeit*] of the ancients: one sought, for natural forces a moderate discharge, not destruction and denial.[21]

This is an important anticipation of Nietzsche's later critique of Christianity's treatment of 'evil'. More locally it is, I think, a protest against hypocritical, Victorian prudery which, for instance, banished sex to backstreet brothels.

'My goal', Nietzsche writes, is '*enmity* between our contemporary "culture" and that of [authentically apprehended] antiquity. Whoever serves the former must hate the latter'.[22] The trouble, however, with philology as currently practised is that it uses its representation of the Greeks in an entirely unproductive way in order to *justify* the current state of culture. The Greeks, that is to say, did not simply 'decorate and polish' like the Romans. For them culture belonged to the roots of life.[23] Modernity, which views 'culture' as mere icing on the cake, a thin veneer of cultivation laid over a reality of crass commercialism, congratulates itself that it is repeating the best of Greece. But, in fact, the concept of culture as 'decoration' comes from the Alexandrian–Roman period which already represents a decline from the greatness of Greece.[24] Nietzsche's protest, here, is against the nineteenth century's taste for facades – for laying a veneer of either classical or gothic ornamentation over otherwise identical buildings. His critique is not unrelated to that of the Bauhaus.

At one in his enmity with his mentor, Schopenhauer, Nietzsche attributes this use of history as a form of self-congratulation above all to Hegel. All modern historians write from the 'standpoint of success'. They assume that we live in the best of all possible worlds and so read our life back into that of the Greeks, and then read their (mis-)interpreted life back into our own, thereby congratulating both them and us. Modern historians, in other words, are closet theologians.[25] Nietzsche sees only one exception to this viciously unproductive circle – his colleague Jacob Burckhardt.[26]

* * *

Burckhardt was, like Nietzsche (but unlike Nietzsche remained), a Schopenhauerian. With Schopenhauer – whose personality he in many ways shared – he sees the basic human condition as one of misery. And, again with Schopenhauer, he sees history as eternal repetition of the same patterns of violence and irrationality. This is why Nietzsche identifies him as the one significant exception to nineteenth-century historians' Hegelian determination to tell history as the ever-greater triumph of reason, truth, and justice. Burckhardt is most famous for applying this view to the Renaissance (p. 104 above). But he also applied it to the Greeks, devoting his historical acumen to deconstructing the serenely-rational-and-happy portrait of them painted by eighteenth-century classicism, to uncovering the violent and irrational underbelly of Greek life and art.

Of course, Nietzsche, too, had been independently engaged in deconstructing the eighteenth-century view of the Greeks in *The Birth of Tragedy*, in emphasising that they were by no means immune to the destructive side of the Dionysian. Yet *The Birth* was itself, in at least one respect, triumphalist: unlike the 'barbarians', the Greeks had *succeeded* in sublimating the dangers of the Dionysian by means of the tragic festival. The notes for 'We Philologists', on the other hand, insist far more emphatically on the dark underbelly still existing in Greek life, insist that 'someone who fails to grasp how brutal and meaningless history is will have no chance of understanding the drive to give it sense'.[27]

Nietzsche had attended Burckhardt's lectures on Greek cultural history in 1872 and together they had long and intense discussions about their common interest. It is likely, therefore, that Burckhardt's influence is at work in 'We Philologists'. In one respect, however, Nietzsche thought that even Burckhardt had failed to look unflinchingly enough into the Greek darkness. Writing to Rohde in May 1876, he complains that in Rohde's work on the Greeks he evades the 'pederastic relationship' in Greek life, a particularly glaring omission, since both the education of Greek youth and the Greek concept of Eros were based on it: the Greeks' conception of heterosexual love was, Nietzsche claims, based on the model of the older man's love for the boy. Burckhardt, he adds, engages in the same evasion. In his lectures he never mentions the subject.[28]

'We Philologists' was never published, indeed never evolved beyond the stage of notes. In May of 1875 Nietzsche complains that though he has written forty pages the work would not 'flow'.[29] It is unclear what the problem was. But the most likely explanation is that, having already spiritually disengaged from his profession, he no longer had sufficient energy to attack its current practice yet again. It is notable that in spite of the prospective title of the work, the notes, while saying a great deal about the Greeks, have very little to say about the current state of philology.

A Review, a Farewell to Romundt, a Birthday Greeting to Wagner and a Health Crisis

On April 1, 1875, a long review of the first three *Untimely Meditations* appeared in London's *Westminster Review*. Founded by Bentham and Mill with editorial contributions from George Eliot and later Thomas Huxley (who first coined the term 'Darwinism' in its pages), this important journal had discovered Schopenhauer in 1853 at a time when he was still unknown in Germany. Noting Nietzsche's devotion to Schopenhauer, the anonymous reviewer, though acknowledging the latter's humour and sharp observations on human nature, still castigates him as one of the worst of Germany's 'ontological card-castle' builders. And, turning to Nietzsche, the reviewer hopes that 'positive thought in some form will...triumph in the end over the barren and bewildering metaphysics of Germany'.[30] Nietzsche heard that the reviewer was somewhat 'cross' but was delighted to be gaining serious attention in England.[31] The review is important, for it stresses how out of tune with the scientific, materialist outlook of the age Nietzsche and Wagner's resurrection of Schopenhauer's idealist metaphysics was. And it is prescient in that, very shortly, 'positive thought' will indeed triumph over metaphysical 'houses of cards' in Nietzsche's thought.

* * *

In February, Heinrich Romundt, always more absorbed by the world-denying aspects of Schopenhauer than Nietzsche, announced to his flat-mates in Baumann's Cave that, having failed to gain a philosophy post at the university, he was going to become a Catholic priest. Nietzsche regarded this as a personal betrayal, as did Overbeck, not merely on account of the retreat from reason to faith but because of the *type* of faith:

Oh our good Protestant air! I have never been more aware of my innermost dependence on the spirit of Luther – and now this unhappy man wants to turn his back on everything that comes from this liberating genius. I ask myself whether he has lost his reason and whether he isn't best treated with cold baths.[32]

Most people of a Protestant upbringing have a disposition to experience Catholicism's dark interiors, incense, candles, sacred hearts, and gilded statues of the Virgin as cheap theatre for illiterate peasants. Most Protestants are idol-smashers at heart. This, I think, is what Nietzsche means by 'Protestant air' – aesthetic austerity, freedom from idols.

On April 10 Romundt finally departed from Basel in a Charlie-Chaplinesque manner that epitomised his whole being:

> Overbeck and I were attending to his [travel] needs more than he himself – he kept drifting off into indifference. The complete indecisiveness of his nature came to a comical head when, an hour before his departure, he decided he didn't want to go. He didn't give any reasons so we made sure he would be departing that evening. He became passionately miserable and kept repeating that what was best and good in his life was now at an end. In tears, he kept begging for forgiveness; he didn't know how to deal with his misery. A characteristic disaster happened at the last moment. The conductor closed the doors [of the train about to depart] and Romundt, wanting to say something more to us, tried to lower the glass window of the carriage. This, however, put up resistance. He tried again and again, all the while, as he was thus tormenting himself, attempting to make himself understood to us – but without success. The train pulled slowly out of the station...the ghastly symbolism of the whole scene lay heavily on [our]...spirits.[33]

The next day Nietzsche retired to bed with a 'thirty-hour headache and much vomiting of bile' – which once again shows how stress activated his underlying health problems. To his relief, Romundt soon abandoned his intention of 'going over to Rome'. He ended up a high-school teacher in Oldenburg and writer of occasional philosophical essays.

* * *

On May 24 Nietzsche sent his usual birthday greetings to Wagner (two days late). It is one of the deepest letters he wrote anyone and indicates, I think, that the level at which he communicated with Wagner was deeper than with anyone else (except, as we shall see, Lou Salomé). 'When I think of your life', Nietzsche writes,

> I have the feeling of a dramatic course to it: as though you are too much a dramatist to live in any other form and, in any case, can only die at the conclusion of the fifth act. When everything drives and storms towards a single goal, accidents, it seems, disappear, are afraid to appear. On account of the powerful thrust everything becomes necessity and iron.

This is an early appearance of one of the central themes in Nietzsche's mature philosophy: that in order to lead satisfying, meaningful lives we must create our lives as artworks, aesthetic unities which incorporate all that has happened, so that nothing appears any longer as 'accidental'.

Nietzsche continues the letter by telling Wagner of a 'strangely beautiful prophesy' he had found among the poems of 'poor Hölderlin, with whom things didn't go as well as with me and who only had an intimation of that in which we trust and will come to see'. And then, as a birthday gift, he quotes the poem in full. It reads,

Oh holy heart of the Volk, *Oh Fatherland!*
All patient like the silent mother earth
And all-knowing, even though from out of your
Depth the alien has its best.
They harvest your thoughts, your spirit,
They happily pluck your grapes, you they scorn
You untended vine, so that you
Wander in wild confusion over the earth.
Thou Land of high, most serious genius!
Thou Land of love! I am yours already,
[But] often I weep angrily, that you so often
Stupidly deny your own soul.
Now you tarry and remain silent, intending a joyful work
That which you create, intends a new figure,
The only thing that, like you yourself, is born
out of love and is good like you.
*Where is your Delos,** *where your Olympia,*
So that we can find ourselves in the highest festival?
But how can your son guess what you
O immortal one, have long prepared for yours?[34]

Nietzsche quotes this poem to validate, once more, Wagner's project of bringing about the rebirth of Greek tragedy – 'the highest festival'. With luck, he is suggesting, the Bayreuth project will be in harmony with the heart of the German *Volk*. And perhaps he wishes to remind Wagner that the rebirth of 'the Greek' *is* his project, one he should not allow himself to be distracted from.

One of Hölderlin's favourite stances is that of 'holy mourning' – mourning the soul of the *Volk* which has not yet recovered itself. It finds expression, here, in the poet's 'angry weeping' over the fact that the German *Volk* has strayed so far from its true self. Nietzsche's reverence for Hölderlin explains, I believe, the form taken by his, as we are about to see, disaffected behaviour at the first Bayreuth Festival: he took himself to be inhabiting the stance of 'holy mourning', mourning for what might have been but is not yet. Hölderlin, as it were, scripted Nietzsche's response to the Festival.

Wagner, it appears, never replied to this letter.

* * *

On May 14, Nietzsche received from Schmeitzner a friendly reminder of his commitment to produce ten more *Untimely Meditations*, and a request for the manuscript of the fourth, so that he could start printing in June. Probably as a result, Nietzsche's health entered a steep decline. For the next six weeks, despite the consoling presence of Elizabeth, he suffered acute eye-aches, headaches and terrible stomach convulsions, some of them so violent that blood came up with the vomit. His friend and doctor, Professor Immermann, at his wits' end, tried him first on a solution of silver nitrate (used, these days, to prepare photographic paper, darken hair, and remove warts), and when that produced no improvement, very high doses of quinine. On June 28, von Gersdorff wrote to his friend in Basel, 'I don't want to

---

* In Greek mythology, an island sanctuary that was the birthplace of Apollo.

shake your confidence in the medical treatment but it nonetheless sounds to me as though I[mmernann] has been making dubious experiments on your poor stomach'.[35]

Meanwhile, in spite of knowing his condition, Cosima sent him one of her usual shopping lists. Could he please acquire, from Strasburg (a significant distance from Basel), she wrote in July, 'a few pounds of caramel sweets, ditto pâté d'abrocots, a bag of fruit confits (not in bottles of syrup but rather glacéd), a bag of orange glacées',[36] as if Nietzsche had nothing better to do than act as a domestic servant of the Wagner household. In *Assorted Opinions and Maxims* he records, under a veil of impersonality, the response this kind of treatment eventually produced:

> *Bitterest Error*: – It offends us beyond forgiving when we discover that, where we were convinced we were loved, we were in fact regarded only as a piece of household furniture and room decoration for the master of the house to exercise his vanity upon before his guests.[37]

Nietzsche bore his health troubles with his usual fortitude, not entirely unhappy, perhaps, that they would provide a valid excuse not to attend the Bayreuth rehearsals, due to start in August. Echoing his youthful determination to inhabit the religious faith that everything, no matter how seemingly terrible, contributes to a greater good and anticipating his coming theme of life as an artwork, he wrote Marie Baumgartner that he was attempting to understand his life as

> an artwork in which this existence and my personal circumstances [his health, the fact that his profession left him no time to write] are connected in such a way that they are not harmful but are even useful. Every project rests on that. This means then: rejecting many things [e.g., friendship with Wagner] in order not to have to reject the main thing. You see: I am not without courage.[38]

'Cure' in Steinabad

In spite of – or because of – Immermann's treatment, Nietzsche's condition grew steadily worse. In desperation his doctor friend told him to give up all plans of going to the Bayreuth rehearsals and undergo instead a 'cure'. Accordingly, Nietzsche set off on July 15 for four weeks in the thermal resort of Steinabad, near Bonndorf, just over the German border in the Black Forest. The clinic was run by a gastric specialist, a Dr. Joseph Wiel, who had an international reputation as the author of a cookbook detailing a regimen of health through diet. Nietzsche had great respect for him: himself a believer in dieting one's way to health, he called Wiel a 'medical revolutionary'.[39] 'Quack', however, even by the standards of the time, would be more appropriate – as the chronically sick do, Nietzsche was forever grasping at straws. Wiel prescribed cold-water enemas first thing every morning and four small meals a day composed almost entirely of meat, preceded in the morning by some Carlsbad fruit salts and accompanied, at midday and in the evening, by a glass of claret. As Nietzsche wrote Marie Baumgartner three days after his arrival, 'no water, no soup, no vegetables, no bread'. Finally, he suffered, as he had in boarding school, the application of leeches to his ears.⁴⁰ And, when he left Steinabad, Wiel's parting advice was to have his food cooked only in enamelled pots (which, as one knows, always become chipped).⁴¹

Wiel diagnosed 'chronic stomach catarrh accompanied by significant widening of the stomach'.⁴² 'Catarrh' postulated an inflammation of the lining of the stomach, and 'widening' was postulated in order to account for the patient's headaches: the 'theory' was that the widening of the stomach interfered with the circulation of the blood so that not enough reached the brain.⁴³

* * *

What, apart from the congenital near-blindness in his right eye, was really wrong with Nietzsche at this stage in his life? As von Gersdorff recognised,⁴⁴ Nietzsche clearly suffered from symptoms indistinguishable from those of migraine. Nausea and vomiting, sensitivity to light, and fatigue are classical migraine symptoms, while the things that affected Nietzsche, emotional stress, bright light and loud noise (the Basel carnival drums) are classical triggers. But what about his intestinal problems? Immermann suggested a stomach ulcer.⁴⁵ The pain of a stomach ulcer, however, is typically relieved by drinking milk, and though Nietzsche drank plenty of milk, and occasionally thought it might be helping,⁴⁶ there is no real evidence that it did. Another difficulty with the stomach-ulcer hypothesis is that while, typically, ulcers either go away by themselves or else lead to serious complications such as death, Nietzsche suffered intermittent stomach pain all his life, but certainly did not die of a stomach ailment. This suggests that, insofar as it is one, 'irritable bowel syndrome' (IBS) is a more plausible diagnosis of the stomach-pain side of Nietzsche's complex medical condition. The history of his stomach problems – periods of intense pain followed by periods of complete freedom from pain, the alternation of constipation with diarrhoea, frequent fatigue and the perceived need for bed-rest, the lack of any successful dietary remedy and the frequency with which emotional stress triggered an attack – are all consistent with IBS.

* * *

By the beginning of August Wiel thought he noticed a lessening of the 'stomach widening', but since the patient showed no improvement, he abandoned his diagnosis in favour of Immermann's suggested stomach ulcer.⁴⁷ Yet since he did not change the treatment Nietzsche's condition, unsurprisingly, did not improve, allowing him only a few 'good' days among the many bad ones.⁴⁸

One of few advantages of the Steinabad institution was its swimming pool: too cold for ordinary mortals (lacking Pforta conditioning), Nietzsche reports that he was able to have it to himself at six o'clock every morning.⁴⁹ Another advantage was the surrounding pine forest, where he could walk in the dim lighting that protected him from eye-pain and headaches. His former student Louis Kelterborn remembers visiting Nietzsche in Steinabad:

> It was a bright, warm July Sunday and nature was showing herself off in her finest jewellery…But rather than enjoying nature, the greatest joy for me was to meet once again my welcoming friend. Certainly one saw in his face and colour that he was sick, and he described in detail how he was doing, as well as the details of his treatment, of which he had great hopes. He showed me all around the thermal establishment and the park surrounding it, wanted me to take a swim, which I declined, and after lunch we went for a hike of several hours through the wonderful surrounding forest. Nietzsche had always been a lusty hiker and the powerful, regular bodily movement of brisk walking always seemed to

do him good. Here, one was able to breathe the full, spicy smell of the wonderful fir-trees. At each new turning the path passed through new beauties...above all one experienced the all-embracing, deep silence as a true blessing. We met very few other hikers and our path took us through no villages...And so we felt ourselves far away from all human bustle and noise, and in this mood of deep satisfaction and repose of the spirit I enjoyed twice as much the always so unusual, elevated and exciting conversation.[50]

What might they have talked about? Health and the link between health and dietary and other personal habits would have been a likely topic. 'I won't be healthy until I earn it' he writes von Gersdorff.[51] In another letter he suggests that it is 'the machinist' rather than 'the machine' that is sick,[52] culpably or 'morally' sick, sick on account of 'dwelling on the evils of the world too much'.[53] In the birthday letter to Wagner mentioned earlier, he writes,

I wish us both happiness and I wish us both health...What I really want to say is: egoism lurks within illness, whereby that illness is forced to think always of itself: while genius, in the fullness of its health, always thinks only of the other, involuntarily blessing and healing merely by laying on his hand. A sick man is always a scoundrel...[54]

These remarks are not entirely consistent with each other. The main thrust, however, consists of three ideas. First, that physical disease is caused by psychological disease and, conversely, physical health by psychological health. Second, that, therefore, the cure for physical disease is always psychological – as we say, 'getting one's head in order', 'mind over matter'. And third, that psychological disease is always the product of 'moral' disease (vice) and psychological health the product of moral health (virtue). The diseased are always 'egoists' who *subtract* from the general good, the healthy are always altruists who *add* to it.

The correlation between health and virtue is, we shall see, a central theme in Nietzsche's mature philosophy. Importantly, however, the order of causation is reversed. Whereas, here, Nietzsche's main tendency is to make psychological and so physical health the product of virtue (conceived as altruism), in his maturity he makes virtue the product of psychological health.

Nietzsche had good reason to abandon this view, which makes one's physical health a barometer of one's moral health. For not only is the view that all physical disease is psychosomatic ridiculous quackery ('Death is a failure of positive thinking', and so on), it also embodies a vicious, closet theology to which the chronically sick brought up within a Christian culture are particularly vulnerable: my sickness *must* be my own fault, a punishment for my wickedness, since – this premise is spoken only *sotto voce* – there is an all-powerful, wholly good God and he *could not* allow unmerited suffering to occur.

* * *

Another topic of conversation must, of course, have been Bayreuth. Deeply uncomfortable that all his friends (whom *he* had persuaded to become Wagnerians) were in Bayreuth for the beginning of the rehearsals of this radically new musical experience, Nietzsche knew that he was not merely absent but that his friends would experience his absence as a Sartrean absence. (I go into a bar for an urgent meeting with my friend Pierre, but he is not there. What I am aware of, Sartre suggests, is neither the bottles behind the bar, nor the barmaid, nor the drinkers, but simply and solely *the absence of Pierre*.) Trying to excuse himself to

Rohde, Nietzsche writes from Steinabad that he is in Bayreuth 'more than three-quarters of the day in spirit, and hovers above it like a ghost'.[55] And to Overbeck on his last day at the spa,

> whenever I get a letter from Bayreuth I experience a half-hour spasm: it's as though I must jump up, throw everything aside and rush to join you all. Like a wondrous temptation, I often hear on my walks something of the "liquid gold" of that orchestral sound, and then I feel boundlessly deprived. To know that you are there – it could so easily have happened that none of us were…[56]

The 'us', here, points to another topic that was on Nietzsche's mind in Steinabad: the formation of a commune of 'untimely' thinkers or, as he was beginning to call them, 'free spirits'.[57] To von Gersdorff he writes that

> We must still make use of our youth to learn many things. And gradually it will come to a communal existence of living and learning. There is always someone new who wants to join this company, as, for example, a very gifted and early-maturing (though early-suffering) pupil, the [Basel] law student [Albert] Brenner.[58]

As we shall see in the next chapter, Brenner did in fact join Nietzsche the following year in Sorrento, in what the latter described as a 'monastery for free spirits'.

Another topic Nietzsche might have discussed with Kelterborn was his, Nietzsche's, own future. Writing to Carl Fuchs, who complained about his lack of success as a musician, Nietzsche reminds him of Liszt's remark that many are robbed of success through being in a hurry, through a 'not-wanting-to-wait'. For himself, he continues, quoting Shakespeare (*Hamlet*), 'readiness is all':

> One shouldn't allow fate to see what it is one wants…It is my innermost disposition to harbour something for years, and not allow myself to recognise it, but then when it grips me, to embrace it; I was 'ready'.[59]

Curt Paul Janz finds an unacceptable gulf between the high idealism of the *Untimely Meditations*, the demand that one becomes the 'true self' lying 'immeasurably high above' one, and Nietzsche's reluctance to abandon the university. But, quite apart from the fact that he had virtually no means of support other than his salary, and that he also needed to help support his mother, Nietzsche was, I think, not so much *evading* the decision that needed to be made as *attentively waiting*, holding himself alert and at the 'ready' for the right moment to arrive. To Marie Baumgartner he writes from Steinabad,

> Various things are now growing in me and from month to month I see some things about my life's mission more definitely, without having the courage to tell anyone. A quiet, but quite decisive progress from step to step. That is what vouchsafes to me that I will go fairly far. I seem to myself to be a mountain climber – see how proudly I can speak.[60]

* * *

Nietzsche found no interesting company among his fellow convalescents in Steinabad and spent most of his time alone. He did, however, do a little communal sightseeing: a walk to Rothaus to visit what was said to be the largest brewery in Germany, and visits to a cheese-making factory and a pig farm.[61] He left on August 12.

A New Apartment and New Friends: Paul Rée and Heinrich Köselitz

Meanwhile, back in Basel, Elizabeth had taken over a new apartment for them both at 48 Spalentorweg, a couple of minutes walk from Baumann's Cave. Quasi-marital existence suited them both: Elizabeth because she had always been half in love with her brother, Fritz because the 'cure' in Steinabad had been no cure at all, so that, on returning to Basel, he needed something other than his previous bachelor existence and Frau Baumann's cooking. His very survival depended on it, he wrote Overbeck.[62] The apartment at number 48 allowed Nietzsche an entire floor to himself, while Elizabeth had part of an upper floor. In all there were six rooms partly filled with furniture sent from Naumburg, as well as a kitchen, a cellar, and a housemaid-cook. Though it was probably beyond his means – he had to borrow a hundred talers from von Gersdorff[63] – Nietzsche found the new home comforts very satisfactory: 'Everything round me is completely Nietzschean and strangely comforting', he reported.[64]

The remainder of the year was punctuated by frequent attacks of all the usual troubles. Often he could not read or write, so that Elizabeth entertained him by reading aloud the novels of Sir Walter 'Skott' (sic)[65] – all of them, she believed. By December Nietzsche calculated that in every two-to-three-week period he was spending thirty-six hours in bed.[66] Christmas was particularly bad, marked by a massive collapse of, as he habitually called it, 'the machine'. This led him to a new self-diagnosis. The single source of all his problems was an 'inflammation of the brain': his father had died at thirty-six and he would quite possibly die even sooner.[67] By January of the following year his health required that he give up the high-school teaching and, the next month, he had temporarily to suspend his university courses, too.

* * *

In spite of his condition, the autumn of 1875 marked the beginning of, after Wagner, the two most philosophically important friendships of Nietzsche's life: the first, with Paul Rée, intimate and ultimately traumatic; the second, with Heinrich Köselitz, less intimate but longer lasting.

Paul Rée, five years younger than Nietzsche, was of part Huguenot but mainly Jewish origin (see Plate 18). Philosophically disposed, he began, like Nietzsche, as a Schopenhauerian. He had, however, come to reject the latter's idealist metaphysics and adopted a thoroughly scientific, 'positivist' outlook. Anyone who rejected Darwin, he wrote, need not read his (Rée's) works.

In 1875 he published his *Psychological Observations* as well as completing a Ph.D. thesis on 'The Noble in Aristotle' at Halle. In 1877 his *The Origins of the Moral Sentiments* appeared, and in 1885 both *The Genesis of Conscience* and *The Illusion of Freedom of the Will: Its Causes and Consequences*. But then, failing to find an academic post, he abandoned philosophy for medicine and, in 1890, qualified as a doctor. After ten years of selflessly caring for the peasants on his brother's estate in East Prussia, he moved to Celerina, in the upper Engadine Valley, near St. Moritz, where he cared for the mountain people, who came to regard him as a near-saint. In 1901, a short distance away, he slid on some ice and drowned in the river Inn. Ironically, in that he and Nietzsche had parted amidst violent recriminations (see Chapter 18), this was but a stone's throw from Sils Maria, where, twenty years earlier, Nietzsche had found his spiritual home. It is possible that Rée's death was suicide. Though of a gentle and upright disposition and given to self-deprecating humour, while rejecting Schopenhauer's metaphysics, he continued to share Schopenhauer's low opinion of the value and virtue of human existence. Moreover, though himself Jewish, those who knew him well, such as Lou Salomé and the sociologist Ferdinand Tönnies, agree that he was anti-Semitic.

Following the victory in the Franco-Prussian war, a wave of anti-Semitism arose in tandem with the German racial chauvinism Nietzsche loathed. The term 'anti-Semitism' was first coined by Wilhelm Marr in 1879 to describe the political opposition to Jewish emancipation he was helping to foment. (Cosima Wagner, as we have seen, was particularly badly infected, and recorded in her diary on first meeting Rée in 1876, 'Cold and precise character, does not appeal to us; on closer inspection we came to the conclusion he must be an Israelite'.)[68] Theodor Lessing discusses Rée in his book *Jewish Self-Hatred* as an example of someone who absorbed the anti-Semitism of his environment and turned it into a powerful inner drive to self-hatred. Lou Salomé, who eventually became a psychoanalyst and a member of Freud's inner circle, drew a connection between Rée's self-hatred and his altruism: in losing himself in selfless devotion to others, she suggests, he experienced as a 'happy deliverance' from himself.[69] It is also possible, though not certain, that Rée was tormented by homosexual inclinations.

In October, Nietzsche wrote Rée, whom he had briefly met through Romundt in May 1873, his first letter, to tell him how much he had enjoyed the anonymously published *Psychological Observations* and that he had instantly penetrated the incognito.[70] Rée replied from Paris that he'd always admired Nietzsche from afar and that he would like to be able now to think of him as a friend.[71] Rée visited Nietzsche in February of the following year, and the next month Nietzsche wrote his 'new-won friend' of his delight in knowing someone quite different from anyone he knew in Basel, someone with whom he could talk about 'humanity'. 'Shall we', he wrote,

> make this shared need the basis of our friendship and hope to meet often? It would be a great joy and profit to me if you say 'Yes'. Let us see, then, how much personal openness a friendship founded on this basis can bear! I do not find it so easy to promise this … But I wish from the heart to deserve your openness … [72]

What seems to be contemplated, here, is a friendship founded on two things: a 'scientific' interest in 'humanity', and an, as it were, 'encounter-group' commitment to personal openness, soul-to-soul disclosure.

A letter to Rohde elaborates on what Nietzsche means by 'talking about humanity'. Rée's *Psychological Observations*, he writes, is the work of a '"moralist" of the sharpest sight, a talent very rare among the Germans'[73] (precisely the 'cold precision' which Cosima, who preferred to see things softened by clouds of Catholic incense, disliked about him). Rée's *Psychological Observations*, probably influenced in form and content by Schopenhauer's often sardonic *Aphorisms on Life's Wisdom*, as well as by the seventeenth-century French aphorist La Rochefoucauld (whom Schopenhauer also admired), is, as Nietzsche explains, the work of a 'skilful marksman who again and again hits the bullseye – but it is the black of human nature'.[74] It is, in other words, an exercise in the 'hermeneutics of suspicion'. Following La Rochefoucauld's observation that 'Self-esteem is cleverer than the cleverest man of the world' (which Schopenhauer quotes)[75] and causes us constantly to deceive ourselves as to the true motives for our actions, Rée's book is composed of *amour-propre*-puncturing aphorisms such as 'Speakers and authors generally convince only those who were already convinced', 'If vanity did not exist nearly all the sciences would still be in the cradle', 'We regard only those critics as competent who praise our achievements', 'When one can no longer love one thinks of marriage', and so on.

An important question is; how does Nietzsche's fascination with Rée's book, a fascination that soon led him to attempt aphorisms on similar lines of his own, fit with the high moral idealism of the three completed *Untimely Meditations* and of the still to be completed fourth one? Although one might anticipate that a preoccupation with the 'seamy' side of the psyche would lead to a rejection of the *Meditations'* idealism as unrealistic, Nietzsche's thinking did not, in fact, lead him in that direction. Though he was about to reject the *metaphysical* idealism of Kant and Schopenhauer ('The world is [nothing but] my representation') in favour of realism – or 'réealism'[76] as he calls it, acknowledging his friend's influence – *moral* idealism, we shall see, remained with him all his life. As he says in the 'We Philologists' notes, however, a useful idealism must be based on warts-and-all realism about human nature, not on 'gold-paper-wrapped' (p. 203 above) sentimentality. Only realism, réealism, about human nature can hope to discriminate between what is unalterable ('hardwired') in it and what can be changed. Only realism, therefore, can discriminate between futile and useful kinds of idealism. As he was to put it seven years later:

> How many people know how to observe something? Of the few who do, how many observe themselves? 'Everybody is furthest away from himself...We want to become who we [truly] are...to this end we must become the discoverers of all lawfulness and necessity in the world. We must become *physicists* to become in this sense *creators* – while up to now all value-estimations and all ideals were based on ignorance of physics or [as in the case of Christianity] built to contradict it. Therefore, long live physics! And even more, that which compels us to it – our [La Rochefoucauldian–Schopenhauerian–Réeian] honesty![77]

Notice that since the notes for 'We Philologists' were written *before* Nietzsche read Rée's *Psychological Observations*, we should think in terms of a convergence of interest in 'humanity' rather than Rée's turning Nietzsche in an entirely new direction.

* * *

Heinrich Köselitz (see Plate 19), known to generations of Nietzsche-readers as 'Peter Gast',* nine years Nietzsche's junior, knew him for a longer period, and with fewer interruptions, than any other friend save Overbeck. He proved invaluable as an amanuensis – towards the end, he was the only person who could read Nietzsche's writing – but Nietzsche never really granted him either the respect or intimacy he gave to other friends, never accorded him the use of the familiar *du*. Basically, the relationship always remained that of

---

* Nietzsche invented this pseudonym thinking it would further Köselitz's career as a composer and persuaded him to adopt it. '*Gast*', in German, means 'guest', and 'Peter' derives from the Latin '*petra*', meaning 'stone'. So (a point I owe to Robin Small) the name seems to contain a joking reference to the 'stone guest' who carries the Don off to hell at the end of Mozart's *Don Giovanni*. Nietzsche regarded Köselitz as 'the new Mozart', which increases the plausibility of this etymology.

professor to student. The son of a patrician Saxon industrialist, Köselitz studied music in Leipzig and aspired – unsuccessfully – to be an opera composer. A fan, initially, of Wagner and Schopenhauer, he was tremendously impressed by *The Birth of Tragedy*, which he accurately described as 'a tremendous protest against the enervating, instinct-dissolving effects of our Alexandrian culture'.[78] He was also deeply impressed by the first two *Untimely Meditations*. Encouraged by Schmeitzner, whom he knew, he and his friend Paul Widemann decided to transfer from Leipzig to Basel University in October 1875, in order to attend Nietzsche's lectures.

'When we first met him', Köselitz recollects in an extended record of his first acquaintance with Nietzsche,

> we were astounded by his appearance. A military officer! not a 'scholar' at all … The impression was of eminent self-control [the Pforta/Prussian look]. Strict towards himself, strict in matters of principle, he was, by contrast, in his judgments of other people, extremely generous.

About this time, Nietzsche composed a *Hymn to Solitude*,* a work, Köselitz reports, 'full of harsh heroism inextricably mixed with soft and *dolce* passages which are yet resisted with defiance'. Köselitz heard him play the work (the score of which has been lost) on the piano: 'Nietzsche's touch was of great intensity without being hard, his playing evocative, polyphonic and many-layered, so that from the orchestral sound he brought out here the flutes and violins and there the trombones'.

A closer relation, Köselitz continues, began at the end of April 1876 when he learnt of the existence of an unfinished fourth *Untimely Meditation* that was concerned with Richard Wagner. He persuaded Nietzsche, 'who held it to be too personal and therefore unpublishable', to add the three final chapters and himself undertook to produce a print-ready copy. Originally intended as a private gift for Wagner's birthday, it ended up as a work designed to be a part of the first Bayreuth Festival.[79]

Veytaux, Geneva and a Marriage Proposal

March of 1876 brought with it the annual torment of the Basel *Fastnacht*. Perhaps with *The Birth of Tragedy*'s distinction between 'barbarian' and Greek manifestations of the Dionysian in mind, Köselitz described the carnival as 'less *joyful* than barbaric and brutal, the expression of which is the incessant drumming'.[80] This time Nietzsche found refuge by travelling with von Gersdorff to Veytaux, near Montreux on Lake Geneva, where he remained a full month from March 6 until April 6, walking six hours a day through generally wet and wintry conditions. He was thrilled to visit nearby Castle Chillon, made famous by Byron's poem *The Prisoner of Chillon*, the work of his boyhood hero.

Considerably restored, Nietzsche travelled from Veytaux to Geneva, where he wanted to pay homage at the house in which Voltaire had spent his exile – he refers to this paradigm 'Socratist' as 'my highest hero', a symptom of the sea-change occurring, at this time, in

---

* At the same time he was reading the Buddhist text the *Sutta Nipata*. He particularly liked the line 'I wander lonely as a rhinoceros' (KGB II.5 495) – an interesting variant on Wordsworth's 'cloud'.

his spiritual-intellectual outlook.[81] He also wanted to meet a Countess Diodati, who was supposed to have finished a French translation of *The Birth of Tragedy*, and catch up with Hugo von Senger, musical director of the Geneva symphony orchestra and an enthusiast for Wagner and Berlioz. (During Nietzsche's stay he conducted Berlioz's Overture to Benvenuto Cellini at his guest's request.)

The countess, however, turned out to be confined to a lunatic asylum, having lost her mind. Von Senger, whom Nietzsche had first met in 1872, was a fan of *The Birth* and had visited Nietzsche in Basel the previous February. He was somewhat neurotic and, as the Germans say, a 'skirt-hunter'. After he kissed his English piano pupil Eliza Vaughan during a lesson she, a woman of character, forced him into an unhappy marriage. Among his current piano students was the slim, blond and beautiful Mathilde Trampedach (see Plate 20), who was secretly in love with him and who would eventually become his third wife.

One morning von Senger turned up with Nietzsche in tow at the Geneva pension where Mathilde was staying together with her sister. 'Unfortunately', Mathilde recalls, 'we couldn't see the famous man since, in spite of the dim light, he held a thickly lined green sun-shade over his head [thus casting his face into shadow], undoubtedly on account of his weak eyes'. A few days later von Senger invited the two girls to join him and Nietzsche for a carriage drive. Mathilde joined in the conversation about poetry and poets, asking Nietzsche if he knew Longfellow's *Excelsior*. When he confessed his ignorance she offered to produce a German translation. Mathilde continues,

> The two men were deep in conversation about the freedom of peoples, at which point I couldn't stop myself interjecting that it was astonishing that people desperate for outer liberty scarcely noted how limited and constricted they were inwardly, and that liberation from the weight of human weaknesses demanded the greatest degree of energy … as I looked up I caught Nietzsche's intense eyes fixed on me.

Mathilde met Nietzsche a third and final time:

> He came to say goodbye and was led into the reception hall where he greeted us with a solemn bow. Then he turned to the piano [as in the Cologne brothel] and began to play with increasing waves of stormy feeling until these subsided into solemn harmonies, finally disappearing into a *pianissimo*. Shortly after, we parted without a word being uttered. The only gesture was a deep bow.[82]

A couple of days later Mathilde received a letter from Nietzsche (which, of course, she preserved):

> *Mein Fräulein* … gather all the courage in your heart in order not to be terrified by the question I now ask you: will you marry me? I love you and it seems to me you already belong to me. Not a word about the suddenness of my affection … What I want to know is whether you don't feel as I do – that we were never strangers to each other. Don't you think that binding ourselves together would make both of us freer and better than we could

manage alone – in other words excelsior?* Will you dare to travel with me, with someone who strives most sincerely to become freer and better? On all the paths of life and thought? Please cast aside all inhibitions and let your heart be free. No one knows of this letter apart from our common friend Herr von Senger.[83]

Apart from Mathilde's beauty and intelligence, and the fact that Overbeck had recently announced his engagement to the wonderful Ida Rothpetz, thereby making the issue of marriage a pressing one for Nietzsche, the clue to this extraordinary offer probably lies in the repeated appeal to 'freedom'. Mathilde's temerity in intervening in a man's conversation led Nietzsche to suppose she was a new kind of liberated bohemian, a woman who was already the convention-defying 'free spirit' he would like to be and with whom he could therefore bypass normal social conventions. Of course, he could not. Mathilde gracefully turned him down. Quite apart from the fact she was already in love with von Senger, if there is any truth in the 'selfish-gene' theory, what women seek in a marriage partner is a good provider. And that, quite evidently, Nietzsche would never be.

The foregoing hypothesis about Nietzsche's motivation is confirmed by a letter he wrote the following month to von Gersdorff:

> I won't marry; in the end, I hate the restrictions and being enmeshed in the whole 'civilized' ['bourgeois', 'suburban'] order of things. Hardly any woman will be free-spirited enough to follow [sic] me – ever-increasingly, the [bachelor] Greek philosophers seem to me to provide the model of the desirable way to live.[84]

Back in Basel on April 12, sun-tanned, temporarily in reasonable health, and carrying no visible scar from Mathilde's rejection, Nietzsche received a proposal from Malwida von Meysenbug that, for the sake of his health, he should spend the following winter and spring with her under the mild Italian sky. (A 'change of air' was the remedy for ill health the Victorians prescribed more frequently than any other.) In June he was granted a year's sabbatical leave for which, after seven years employment, he was due, and this made it possible for him to take her suggestion seriously.

Wagner in Bayreuth

Meanwhile Nietzsche had been hard at work on the fourth *Untimely Meditation*, *Wagner in Bayreuth*, which appeared with Schmeitzner on July 10, 1876. He asked that complimentary copies be sent to the Wagners (two), von Gersdorff, Rohde, Rée, Malwida von Meysenbug, Romundt, his mother, Fuchs, Sophie Ritschl, Krug (but again not Pinder), von Senger, Hillebrand, Marie and Adolf Baumgartner, and four others[85] – the 'few' for whom he wrote.

---

* The translation of the Latin title of Longfellow's poem is 'ever higher' or, more loosely, 'onwards and upwards'. The poem describes a young man who passes through an alpine village bearing a banner on which 'Excelsior' is inscribed. Ignoring all warnings, he climbs higher and higher until, inevitably, 'lifeless but beautiful', he is discovered lying half-buried in the snow.

The work was timed to coincide with the first Bayreuth Festival, due to start the following month. The idea was to explain the significance and importance of the event, in other words, to produce a work of the same character as *The Birth of Tragedy*, though now, like the *Summons to the Germans*, with the focus exclusively on Wagner. Nietzsche wrote the work with difficulty.[86] A major reason was that by the time he came to write it his attitude toward Wagner had changed from adulation to ambivalence. As we saw in the last chapter, personal difficulties with Wagner are accompanied in the notebooks of the period by many of the criticisms of the artist (that he is an 'actor', a 'tyrannical' producer of cheap effects, that his music 'denies' rather than 'affirms' life) which, in later life, would form the basis of the 'case against Wagner' Nietzsche would prosecute with great ferocity.

The diplomatically ingenious device Nietzsche adopted to reconcile public commitment with private reservation was to borrow the narrative structure of Wagner's own 'Beethoven' essay (p. 121 above) to compose an idealised biography in which Wagner's 'higher' self eventually triumphs over the errors and weaknesses of his 'lower' self. This enabled him to combine the need for hagiography with the requirements of his own integrity, by offering a veiled warning to Wagner to remain true to his highest ideal.

Retrospectively, in *Ecce Homo*, Nietzsche indicates that, in reality, he had already given up hope that either Wagner or Bayreuth would live up to that ideal: in the essay, he says, 'at every psychologically decisive point I am only talking about myself, – you can put my name, or the word "Zarathustra", without hesitation wherever the text has the word "Wagner" . . . it does not come into contact with Wagnerian reality even for a moment'.[87] The result is that, like *Schopenhauer as Educator*, the essay 'basically only talk[s] about me . . . is a vision of *my* future'.[88] In other words, Wagner's 'higher' self and ideal is really not *his* ideal at all but rather *Nietzsche's*. From our point of view, however, this makes the essay even more important. For what these remarks tell us is that the at least quasi-Wagnerian ideal sketched in 1876 *remains* Nietzsche's ideal at the very end of his path of thinking, in 1888.

* * *

The *Meditation* begins by deploring the state of modern theatre, a place of 'luxury art',[89] cheap, escapist thrills for a bored and work-weary audience. The modern world is, however, so interconnected that to change one element in it would be to change the totality: to reform the theatre, to produce 'a higher, purer art', would be to transform morality, politics and civil society. It would, Nietzsche claims, abolish the sickness of 'modern man' and create a new and healthier culture.[90] (One might make this claim less far-fetched than it sounds by thinking about television. To produce 'a higher, purer' television might indeed, as Lord Reith of the BBC believed, produce a profoundly different society.)

Initially, Wagner – the 'lower' Wagner – was himself ensnared by the decadence of modern culture, was just another composer of grand opera. His immense ambition meant that, in the beginning, he sought to outdo competitors such as Meyerbeer in the production of empty 'artifices' and cheap, 'hypnotic' 'effects' designed to 'wrest a success from the public' (a low version of the Greek *agon*, presumably). Never, Nietzsche comments, can a great artist have started out so deeply involved in error, or in a more 'revolting' form of his art.[91] (Recall the note quoted in the last chapter that no great composer was so bad at twenty-eight as Wagner (p. 185 above).) But then he became a socialist revolutionary and shuddered at his former life as the lackey of a corrupt society. His music now becomes the voice of the people, his aim the replacement of oppressive capitalism, with its reduction of human beings to mere 'workers', with a real, human community, an authentic *Volk*.

The failure of the 1848 revolution shattered his expectations and for a time he entered the Schopenhauerian spirit of world-denial. In *Tristan*, his '*opus metaphysicum*', a broken man longs for the mysteries of night and death. Then, however, a new optimism took hold. This expressed itself in the 'miracle' of *Die Meistersinger*, a work in which, though older and wiser than in his revolutionary days, Wagner once again affirms life and seeks to discover 'the germ and first source of the life of a truly human community to be perfected at some point in the future'.* In his full maturity, that is, Wagner finally becomes his 'true' self, the 'dithyrambic dramatist', the dramatist who, by cleaning up the Augean stables of modern theatre, offers the possibility of a new order of things in which human beings can once more flourish.[92]

Alone, of course, he could not do this. But Wagner is not alone. 'Friends' (the members of the Wagner societies) came to him – this was the cause of *Die Meistersinger*'s new optimism – a band of self-sacrificing idealists. This is the 'germ' of Wagner's 'truly human community' of the future which the collective artwork will collect together in Bayreuth. All who attend will be 'untimely' men, far removed from the so-called 'cultivated persons' (the diamonds-and-tiara crowd) of the present age.[93]

Courageous action is impossible without a dream, an ideal vision.[94] Not that Wagner is a utopian; he believes in no 'final order of things'. But he does believe in the future, because he believes that some of the present traits of Western man do not belong to the 'bone structure' of human nature and as a result are capable of being changed.[95] The 'vague lineaments' of this better future can be inferred from a proper apprehension of our present 'need'.[96] What then is the 'need'?

Language, Nietzsche observes (closely following Wagner's *Opera and Drama*), is sick. By being required, in a machine society, to become the abstract, conceptual tool of 'theoretical man', it has lost its original purpose, the capacity to express feeling, to speak 'naively'. Rather than being an instrument of authentic, soul-to-soul communication, language as we now know it renders us inarticulate, alienated one from another. (Recall Nietzsche and Rée's yearning to be completely 'candid' with each other.) Faust, the man of science, theoretical man *par excellence*, who yearns to experience real life and love, personifies our predicament. Wagner's 'dithyrambic' (i.e., Dionysian) music, however, provides an antidote. When we 'swim' in its 'enigmatic, fiery element … we no longer possess any standard of ['theoretical'] measurement, everything fixed and rigid begins to grow fluid', a fluidity which overcomes 'all artificial alienation and incomprehension between man and man'. This, says Nietzsche, touching on Rousseau's theme of the 'noble savage', returns us to 'nature', nature, however, '*transformed into love*'. Thus returned, we recover 'supra-personal joy', that is to say, 'right feeling'.

'Right' – in other words Dionysian – 'feeling' is not, however, *mere* feeling. It seeks out a 'corresponding necessary shape in the world'. It seeks out, that is to say, expression in a communal structure, a state. As *The Birth of Tragedy* thinks of tragic drama as 'born' out of, in the words of its subtitle, 'the spirit of music', so Nietzsche now thinks of an entire community as thus born. With extraordinary ambition, he suggests, in effect, that Wagner's music offers us the possibility of *a state founded on music*.[97]

---

* Notice how Nietzsche's narrative requires the fiction that *Die Meistersinger* is the crown and terminus of Wagner's output. Since, as we have seen, the essay really expresses *Nietzsche's* ideal, this suggests the idea that *Die Meistersinger* is the artistic expression of the crown and terminus of *Nietzsche's* philosophy.

What he is doing here, essentially, is repeating the 'universal brotherhood' passage from the beginning of *The Birth of Tragedy* (p. 128 above). Under the 'magic' of Dionysus, he says there, 'all the rigid, hostile barriers' between man and man are abolished, so that each person, 'singing and dancing', feels himself 'merged' with his neighbour into a 'higher community'. The 'football-crowd' feeling, as I called it. There, too, he anticipated the idea of a state founded on music by asking us to imagine 'Beethoven's jubilant "Ode to Joy" translated into visible form'. (Notice, incidentally, that it is the idea of a state founded on music that explains his otherwise peculiar taste for quasi-political pieces of music such as Brahms's *Triumphlied* and Wagner's *Kaisermarsch* (pp. 192–3 above). Had he been English and of a later generation he would have enthused about Elgar's *Pomp and Circumstance* marches.)

Of course, a community or state cannot be founded on 'right', in other words communal, 'feeling' alone. This is where the 'drama', the 'Apollonian' side of the 'dithyrambic drama', comes into play. Though 'art is, to be sure, no instructor or educator in direct action', Wagner's works do provide a framework of action, for they represent, says Nietzsche, 'the most moral music I know'.[98] ('Morality', says a memorable note from this period, 'is the grammar of life'.)[99] His characters, that is, provide an inspirational 'abbreviation of the endlessly complex calculus of human action and desire'. Wotan, Sachs, Brunhilde, Elizabeth, and Senta are tremendously elevating role models who draw us time after time to the triumph of love over power and greed. The *Ring* cycle, in short, is 'a tremendous system of [moral] thought', one that is expressed, however, not through concepts but through myth. Because it is addressed not to theoretical man but to his 'antithesis', the *Volk*, it 'thinks mythologically' as the *Volk* has always done. Its morally inspirational content, as one might put it, is *shown* rather than *said*.[100]

One 'need', then, to which the Wagnerian music-drama responds is the need for community. But as in *The Birth*, Nietzsche sees it as responding, too, to the individual's need to overcome suffering and death. We need, he says, to be delivered from 'the terrible anxiety which time and death evoke' and from the 'serious and stressful' in life. To do this 'the individual needs to be consecrated to [i.e., to identify himself with] something higher than himself – that is the meaning of tragedy'.[101] This is part and parcel of the Dionysian feeling that merges us with our neighbour. When we 'swim' in the 'enigmatic fiery element' (*Tristan*'s *Liebestod*) that dissolves everything 'fixed and rigid' we 'no longer know ourselves', and so are released from the suffering and mortality that is the penalty of individuality:

> for a few hours, at least, … we fancy we have returned to free nature, to the realm of freedom. From this vantage point we behold, as though in immense air-reflections, the struggles, victories and defeats of us and our kind as something sublime.

The previously fearful and stressful now appear more like 'strangely isolated fragments in the total experience'. Even death itself now appears as 'the supreme stimulus to life'. When we return to everyday life we bring with us a new kind of equanimity: 'transformed into tragic men we return to life in a strangely consoled mood, with a new feeling of security'.[102]

As in *The Birth*, Nietzsche appeals here to self-transcendence as the key to the 'tragic effect'. Dionysian music raises us from an individual to a universal, 'supra-personal' viewpoint. From this perspective, that of the 'primal unity', stress and pain lose their sting because they are not *our* stress and pain, death is no threat because it is not *we* who die. And indeed, since there is no gain without pain, since the destruction of the old is necessary to the birth of the new, we see that life *demands* pain and death in order to be the developing, ever-changing phenomenon of Heraclitean fascination that it is. From the Dionysian point of view we *welcome* the appearance of death in life.

Thus far, *Wagner in Bayreuth* is a recognisable continuation of the interpretation of Bayreuth offered in *The Birth*. However, in October 1875, Nietzsche wrote to Rohde as follows:

> My observations under the title *Richard W[agner] in Bayreuth* . . . are almost finished. It is, however, way below the standard I demand of myself. It has therefore, for me, only the value of a new orientation to the most difficult point in our experience to date. But I'm not in complete command of it and see that it is not completely achieved.[103]

This indicates, first, that *Wagner in Bayreuth* attempts to view Bayreuth from a radically new vantage point and, second, that the attempt is, in Nietzsche's judgment, not entirely successful. What, then, is the 'new orientation' and why is it not an entire success?

My hypothesis is that the key is to be found in the use of the word 'fancy', in the claim that in the Dionysian state 'we fancy (*wähnen*) we have returned to free nature', to (the language echoes Kant's talk of 'intelligible' or 'noumenal' freedom) the 'realm of freedom' (p. 220 above). Nietzsche's *wähnen* is derived from Wagner's word *Wahn*, which, we know, has, as the most obvious of its several meanings, 'delusion' and 'illusion'. The suggestion contained in the use of the word is that whatever the psychological benefit of the Dionysian 'high', the ascent to the 'highest rungs of sensibility',[104] the experience is actually an illusion since there is, in fact, *no* 'realm of freedom', no metaphysical domain beyond the everyday world of individuals. In *The Birth of Tragedy*, of course, Nietzsche could never have used such a word since, subscribing as the work does to Kantian–Schopenhauerian idealism, the 'primal unity' with whom one identifies in Dionysian experience is absolutely real. It is, indeed, the *only* real being, it being the everyday world that is illusory, merely a 'dream'. In *The Birth*, in short, it is the *everyday world of individuals* that is *Wahn*. Here, however, the 'antithesis' is reversed. Although it may sometimes seem to the composer of *Tristan* that 'the dream is almost more real than waking actuality', the fact of the matter is that the Dionysian dream is *just* a dream.[105]

What this indicates is that a profound shift in Nietzsche's thinking has occurred before, or during, the writing of the fourth *Meditation*. He has abandoned metaphysical idealism in favour of realism – naturalism or, in a broad sense, 'materialism' – the shift to the 'positive thought' the reviewer in the *Westminster Review* hoped Nietzsche would eventually find his way to (p. 205 above). This is confirmed in a letter of 1878: prior to attending the Bayreuth Festival (and so prior to the publication of *Wagner in Bayreuth*), he says, he had undergone a 'transformation and crisis' (accelerated, surely, by discussions with Rée) that consisted in 'the battle of reason against all metaphysical mystification of truth and simplicity, against that [so-called] reason which sees in everything a miracle and absurdity'.[106] In spite of this turn to positivism, however, he remains convinced of the value of the Dionysian state and personally addicted to the 'liquid gold' of Wagner's music. The 'new orientation', I suggest, therefore, consists in the attempt to produce a new synthesis, to combine a commitment to the significance of Wagner's Dionysian music with a new, un-metaphysical, even anti-'metaphysical', outlook, a new philosophical worldview. The attempt, in a word, is to produce a *Dionysianism without metaphysics*.

Why did he feel not completely 'in command' of the new synthesis between Dionysian-ism and naturalism? Why did he have the sense that something was not quite right about it without – as often happens in philosophy – being quite able to put his finger on the problem? Why, if he has not been persuaded otherwise by Köselitz, would he have left the work unfinished and unpublished?

What worried him was perhaps the following. The essay suggests that two things are true of the state into which we are transported by Wagner's music: that it is psychologically beneficial and that it is a delusion. That, of itself, is no problem, since delusory states can often have beneficial effects: believing in the fidelity of one's actually unfaithful spouse is, in most cases, an example. The trouble, though, is that the publication and comprehension of Nietzsche's essay *would have the effect of destroying the illusion*. Even more to the point, the content of the essay destroys the illusion *for Nietzsche*. If I know, if Nietzsche knows, that the sense I have had of universal brotherhood and of my immunity to death and suffering is nothing more than a 'drug'-induced hallucination, a cheap trick produced by, as the *Meditation* indeed calls him, the great 'sorcerer',[107] anything more than a momentary benefit is destroyed. In a word, then, Nietzsche believed the new synthesis to be a failure. A genuine reconciliation between Dionysianism and naturalism must be illusion-free and so requires the possibility of an overcoming of individuality without the 'dream' of a supra-natural identity to which one transcends. Later on, in his mature thought, I shall suggest, Nietzsche does achieve a genuine synthesis between Dionysianism and naturalism, does show how there can be Dionysianism without 'metaphysics'. But that lies well in the future: a great deal of water will need to flow under the bridge before it arrives. The fourth *Meditation* rests, it seems to me, on the insight that there ought to be a reconciliation. But as yet, Nietzsche is 'not in command' of the insight because he is unable to perform the reconciliation.

* * *

Given the implied criticism contained in *Wagner at Bayreuth*'s narrative of its subject's progression from producer of cheap, 'tyrannical' effects to 'dithyrambic dramatist', it is no surprise that Nietzsche was extremely nervous about the reception it would receive in Bayreuth. He made at least four attempts to draft the letter to the Wagners that would accompany their complimentary copies.[108] To Cosima he wrote that he could not restrain himself from expressing from afar his great joy in the 'great and portentous event' about to occur. To Wagner he wrote that, after completing the work, he felt like the rider of Swabian legend who traversed the *Bodensee* (Lake Constance) in winter but only after arriving on the other side (since the ice was covered with snow) realized, with terror, what he had done. He added that only Wagner's stated commitment to 'German freedom' gave him the courage to produce the work, the content of which he had carried within him since his fourteenth year. And with nervous prescience he observes: 'My writing brings me the unpleasant consequence that every time I publish a work something in my personal relationships is called into question and has to be put right through the expenditure of human sympathy'.[109] (The difficulty, of course, in friendships based too strongly on shared commitments, is that they cannot accommodate changes of mind.)

Wagner's reply, however, seemed reassuring: 'Friend! Your book is terrific! – Where did you get such knowledge of me?[110] – Come soon and acclimatize yourself to the impact [of the music] in the rehearsals'.[111] And he sent a copy of Nietzsche's work to King Ludwig.

Cosima replied with four anodyne lines, so that between them the Wagners responded to the gifts with a total of eight lines. They were, of course, incredibly busy with last-minute preparations for the Festival. Still, eight lines indicates that Nietzsche was no longer the quasi-son whom Wagner had once wanted to become Siegfried's guardian.

Other reactions to the work, at least among Wagnerians, were extremely favourable. Malwida von Meysenbug wrote him that, along with Wagner, he was 'showing mankind its holy goal as no other, not even Schopenhauer, has done' and asked to be granted the right to look on him 'with the happy pride as only a mother can have towards her beloved son'.[112] Romundt wrote that he read the work at a sitting, unable to put it down, and that it opened up a wonderful 'new world' and 'awakes the conviction that its hour must come'.[113] Rohde wrote that he was reading the work to his fiancée, adding, paternalistically, 'she is still very young and I need and want to educate her'.[114]

The First Bayreuth Festival

The programme for the first Bayreuth Festival was as follows:

29 July–4 August (1876) third cycle of rehearsals.
6 August: dress rehearsal for *das Rheingold*.
7 August: dress rehearsal for *die Walküre*.
8 August: dress rehearsal for *Siegfried*.
9 August: dress rehearsal for *Götterdämmerung*.
13, 14, 16, 17 August: first performance of the *Ring* cycle (i.e., the above four operas).
20–23 August: second performance of the *Ring* cycle.
27–30 August: third performance of the *Ring* cycle.

In spite of ill health, Nietzsche arrived on July 22 and remained in Bayreuth until August 27, apart from an interlude in Klingenbrunn from August 4 to 12. Edouard Schuré (French music critic, writer on the occult, Wagnerian, Nietzsche-admirer, and, later, anthroposophist and friend of Rudolf Steiner) has left a description of Nietzsche in Bayreuth:

I was impressed by both his intellectual-spiritual superiority and his strange physiognomy. The high forehead, the short brush-cut hair and the prominent, Slavic cheekbones. The thickly drooping moustache as well as the sharp facial features seemed to lend him the appearance of a cavalry officer, had it not been for an immediately apparent expression of simultaneous shyness and superciliousness. The musical voice, the slow manner of speaking, pointed to his artist's nature. His cautious, thoughtful walk was that of a philosopher. Nothing was more misleading than the apparent repose of his facial expression. The fixed, immobile eyes betrayed painful thought-processes. The eyes were simultaneously those of a sharp observer and a fantastical visionary . . . In passionate moments his eyes would become moist, lost in dreaminess, only to become aggressive once again. Nietzsche's whole presence revealed his distance, the scarcely concealed scorn that frequently marks the spiritual aristocrat. During the dress-rehearsal and the three first performances of the tetralogy [i.e., the *Ring* cycle] Nietzsche appeared sad and oppressed . . . In the presence of Richard Wagner he was shy,* inhibited, and almost always silent. When we left the performances together he uttered not one word of criticism; he showed much more the resigned sadness of someone who had lost something.[115]

Schuré was right. Nietzsche was melancholic, inhabiting, as I suggested, Hölderlin's stance of 'holy mourning' (p. 207 above). When people asked him about *Wagner in Bayreuth* he replied that he did not want to discuss that 'old stuff', and when it was pointed out it had only appeared five weeks previously he replied that it seemed more like five years.[116] On July 24 he walked out of a rehearsal of *Götterdammerung* saying he could not bear it[117] – could not bear the 'liquid gold' he had imagined in Steinabad! Though he managed to enjoy it better a few days later,[118] he still wrote to Elizabeth on the following day that he 'almost regrets' coming to Bayreuth. (The German he uses for 'regret' is *'Bereut'*, a pun on *'Bayreuth'*.)[119] Eventually, on August 4, he could bear Bayreuth no more, attempted to give away his tickets, and left for the mountain village of Klingenbrunn ('tinkling fountain'), near Spiegelau, a six-hour train journey away, in the Bohemian Forest, on the Czech border.

Why was Nietzsche so depressed? Why did he feel he had 'lost something'?

To start with, the weather was 'insanely hot' and humid, something he always hated. And he hated the low-ceilinged apartment he had rented in the centre of the overcrowded town. These problems, however, he remedied by spending his days with Malwida von Meysenbug, whose rented house had 'a lovely cool garden'.[120] He was, of course, in less than ideal health. But he himself later admitted that his flight from Bayreuth was caused by not a physical but by a spiritual 'crisis' which he disguised under the polite fiction of ill health.[121] And as we shall shortly see, he made a remarkably quick recovery from his supposed ailments. What, then, was the character of this 'crisis'?

Curt Paul Janz suggests that with half the nobility of Europe gathered in Bayreuth, no one, especially not Wagner, paid any attention to an obscure professor, with the result that Nietzsche suffered a fit of pique. But this is most implausible. Wagner did not ignore him; on the contrary, it was Nietzsche who refused all social invitations, including those from the Wagners.[122] Elizabeth reports that 'Wagner never lost an opportunity of honouring and distinguishing' Nietzsche but that Fritz 'escaped these flattering attentions whenever he could for he disliked Wagner's boisterous praise'.[123] Nietzsche himself later wrote that the 'bitter disappointment' of Bayreuth was caused by the enormous gap between the ideal he carried with him to Bayreuth and the reality he experienced.[124] Confronted with reality, the ideal (as he had long suspected it would, but hoped against hope to be proved wrong) turned out to be, as he later put it, a *'fata morgana'*, a mirage.[125] How so?

To start with, the audience was (as it has remained) quite other than the band of idealistic, 'untimely' men of talent *Wagner in Bayreuth* had envisaged. Rather than these, it was dominated by high society, a constant procession of dukes and princes. Regular guests at Wahnfried, for example, included the Baroness von Schleinitz, the Baroness von Meyendorf, the Countess Usedom, and the wife of the Italian cabinet minister, Minghetti, who liked the 'democratic' feeling of mingling with the odd painter or doctor in the

---

* 'Moralists are always shy because they know that as soon as people notice their inclinations they will be taken for traitors and spies' (AOM 72).

Wagner household and in a nearby alehouse.[126] Ludwig of Bavaria was present, of course, though only for the dress rehearsals, which, in the case of *Rheingold*, he insisted on seeing alone.* For the first performance proper of the *Ring*, the German Emperor arrived and embraced Wagner (even though he actually disliked his music). The Emperor of Brazil attended, as did the Grand Duke of Weimar, who was greeted with great pomp at the railway station by Franz Liszt. In short, the audience was neither Wagner's 'people' nor Nietzsche's select group of avant-garde artists, social reformers, and dedicated 'friends'. With a few exceptions, rather, it was, as Nietzsche later put it, the 'loafing riff raff of Europe'.

As Elizabeth observes, what was supposed to initiate a radical reformation of the theatre turned out to be just another festival of grand opera.[127] But, of course, the cost of the whole exercise ensured, from the start, that this would be so. When Nietzsche tried to get rid of eight tickets (i.e., one *Ring* cycle for two people), he offered them to his friends the Baumgartners at 100 talers. But even that, presumably a discounted rate, would be something like 6,000 U.S. dollars in today's money, a price only the social elite could afford. Thinking about the whole enterprise hard-headedly, one could easily have predicted from the start, on financial grounds alone, that the new 'Reformation' was doomed to failure.

The audience, then, fell dramatically short of Nietzsche's idealistic vision. What, however, of the artist? What of Wagner himself?

One difficulty many found during the Festival was the preservation of a suitable solemnity on what was supposed to be a quasi-religious occasion. The problem consisted in the many faults of staging – to this day a constant hazard for non-minimalist productions. In one performance, *Rheingold*'s Rhine maidens started whirling round and round as if sitting on horses on a fun fair merry-go-round, while *Siegfried*'s terrifying dragon, Fafner, appeared with a head and body but no neck. The neck, it appears, had been sent by the dragon's London manufacturers not to *Bayreuth* but rather to *Beirut*.[128] This, however, is not what disappointed Nietzsche. Rather, it was Wagner's highly naturalistic conception of the staging. 'I utterly disagree with those who were dissatisfied with the decorations, the scenery and the mechanical contrivances at Bayreuth', he later wrote. The problem, rather, was that 'far too much industry and ingenuity were applied to the task of chaining the imagination to matters which ... belied their epic origin',[129] a mode of production, in other words, which killed the mythic potential of the works. (Nietzsche would likely have approved of the minimalist productions designed by Wagner's grandson, Wieland, during the 1950s and '60s.)

In *The Birth of Tragedy* and in the second *Untimely Meditation*,[130] as we saw, Nietzsche insists that genuinely mythic figures need to be, like the masked figures of Greek tragedy, abstract rather than naturalistically detailed. An abstract, 'Brechtian' production requires each individual to recreate figures and their environment in terms of his own imagination and so allows diversely constituted individuals to be collected together in a shared 'agreement'. It follows that minimalist productions are what is required, not the naturalism of 'special effects'. (As someone wisely remarked, special effects are the death of film.) But

---

* When the sound proved too hollow without an audience, Elizabeth reports, a bunch of ordinary townspeople were gathered together for *Walküre* – quite the wrong audience, a 'motley' bunch of 'philistines', she complains (YN p. 378), demonstrating thereby not merely her lower-middle-class snobbery but also her ignorance of Wagner's conception of the Festival as being of and for 'the people'.

Wagner clearly revelled in 'special effects'. In *Wagner in Bayreuth* Nietzsche had argued for Bayreuth on the grounds that it was essential for Wagner to leave behind, by example, a tradition of the proper performance of his works. But here he was, Spielbergising, as one might say, his own works. This shows how far he had departed from the 'rebirth of Greek tragedy' ideal, how far the producer of cheap effects – his supposedly 'lower' self – had, in fact, the upper hand. Hölderlin's questions, 'Where is your Delos, where your Olympia', where your 'highest festival?' quoted in his birthday letter to Wagner (p. 207 above), receive the sad answer: 'nowhere'.[131]

The same letter, however, mentions another cause of his despair at Bayreuth: the positivist turn against the 'metaphysical mystification of all truth and simplicity' (p. 221 above) that had occurred prior to his arrival; the turn against Schopenhauerian-Wagnerian metaphysics and towards naturalism. In *Wagner in Bayreuth* he had attempted a synthesis between Wagner's Dionysian music and his new naturalism. But this had proved as unsatisfactory as had Bayreuth. It was, then, time to give up trying to incorporate Wagner into his new outlook. It was time for the warrior, Nietzsche, to take sides for 'reason' and against Wagner. And so he left for Klingenbrunn to gather his strength.

Return to Bayreuth and a Flirtation

During his week in Klingenbrunn, after a day in bed to recover from the tortuous journey, Nietzsche wrote, with astonishing speed, a third of what would become the defining work of his 'positivist' period, *Human, All-Too-Human*. The provisional title was *The Ploughshare* – a ploughshare being that which ploughs up the old ground in preparation for a new planting. In this work the metaphysics of the 'Bayreuth horizon' is finally and fully replaced by its opposite: the new, materialistic, scientific, realistic, anti-metaphysical, anti-Schopenhauerian 'horizon' that brought Nietzsche into line with the mainstream of late-nineteenth-century educated thought. It was, therefore, during, though sequestered from, the Bayreuth Festival that the 'new' Nietzsche emerged into light of day. Yet at the end of the week he went back to Bayreuth. Though he had enjoyed the 'pure air' of the mountains, he went down, once again (as would his alter ego, Zarathustra), into the 'fumes' of the valley. The puzzle is why he should have done so.

One reason is that, as Elizabeth observes, he needed the music as an addict needs a drug. 'The silkworm', she quotes him as saying, 'drags its old prison along with it for some time after it first emerges from the chrysalis'.[132] And though the ostensible subject is Beethoven, he refers to the same thing in a section of *Human, All-Too-Human* (its beauty and significance allow it to be requoted) entitled 'Art makes the thinker's heart heavy':

> How strong the metaphysical need is, and how hard nature makes it to bid it a final farewell, can be seen from the fact that even when the free spirit has divested himself of everything metaphysical, the highest effects of art can easily set the metaphysical strings, which have long been silent or indeed snapped apart, vibrating in sympathy; so it can happen, for example, that a passage in Beethoven's Ninth Symphony [in the last movement] will make him feel he is hovering above the earth in a dome of stars with the dream of *immortality* in his heart: all the stars seem to glitter around him and the earth seems to sink further and further away. If he becomes aware of being in this condition he feels a profound stab in the

heart and sighs for the man [Wagner] who will lead him back to his lost love, whether she be called religion or metaphysics.[133]

Though in *Human, All-Too-Human* Nietzsche calls upon the thinker's 'intellectual probity' to resist the siren call of his 'lost love', in Klingenbrunn, if Elizabeth is correct, he succumbed. He succumbed, that is to say, to his continuing need for Dionysian transport.

Emotionally, then, Nietzsche was still attached to Wagner's music. And emotionally he was still attached to the person and the project that had been the meaning of his life for over a decade: 'I was sick', he recalls later, because 'my task had been withdrawn from me'.[134] In retrospect, Nietzsche simplified the sequence of events in Bayreuth to the point of falsification. The way he tells it in *Ecce Homo*, he left Bayreuth for Klingenbrunn, his mind clearly made up, and never returned.[135] In reality, however, he was in a terrible state of confusion, lost in a terrible conflict between heart and head. As a thinker he had decided that the Bayreuth project was a worthless failure. But as a man, virtually all of whose friends *he* had converted to Wagnerianism, he remained emotionally bound to the project. When he first arrived in Bayreuth he wrote anxiously to his sister, 'you are not to tell anyone, but only half the tickets are sold for the second cycle and for the third scarcely a third'.[136] And Elizabeth recalls that when he finally left he sighed, 'Oh Lisbeth, so that was Bayreuth!' with tears in his eyes.[137]

Thus, the human reality was that Nietzsche was impossibly conflicted. He knew Wagner's art had no real cultural importance, that all his early hopes for it were a '*fata morgana*'. Yet at the same time he had desperately wanted it to succeed.

* * *

Back in Bayreuth love was in the air. Emboldened, perhaps, by the eroticism implicit in the convention-abolishing Dionysianism of Wagner's music, Rohde, in spite of his recent betrothal,[138] paid compliments to every woman he met. (The previous September he had seen *Tristan* in Munich which, he wrote, 'shook me in a very personal way...I felt the pulse-beat of the yearning passion absolutely directly'.)[139] And von Gersdorff, for his part, fell madly in love with an Italian countess. Nietzsche, having perhaps decided that since the occasion was not the momentous, sacred event he had hoped for he might as well enjoy himself, fell for a beautiful blond called Louise Ott who was also a gifted singer and passionate Wagnerian. A native of Alsace, she had married and moved to Paris.

Louise left Bayreuth before Nietzsche. (The claim in *Ecce Homo* that he left first despite the attempts of a 'charming Parisienne' to detain him[140] is pure fiction.) After she had gone Nietzsche wrote her that 'it was dark around me when you left Bayreuth, it was as if someone had taken away the light', and went on to say that 'I think of you with such brotherly warmth that I will love your husband because he is your husband'.[141] Louise's reply exceeded the bounds of propriety:

> How good it is that a true, healthy friendship can exist between us so that we can think of each other from the heart without our consciences forbidding it...I can't however think of your eyes: I still feel your dear, deep look on me as it was back then...Everything that has happened between us must be kept secret.[142]

By early September propriety is trying to assert itself in the correspondence – Louise lets him know she is a Christian and asks him if he believes in the immortality of the soul.[143] (The answer is that he does not since a notebook entry of the previous year says that *no one* in their senses does so any more.)[144] But at the end of September Nietzsche still has Louise on his mind, writing her that the new friendship was 'a little dangerous, like new wine'.[145] There is genuine eroticism in the fallout from this, as it were, shipboard romance – a *Brief Encounter* kind of eroticism where 'decency' means that love never really has a chance.

13

Sorrento

NIETZSCHE ARRIVED back in Basel from Bayreuth on August 27, 1876, and continued working on the notes that would eventually become *Human, All-Too-Human*. Since Elizabeth, after a year as his housekeeper, had gone back to Naumburg, he returned to his old, bachelor digs in Baumann's Cave. Overbeck was in Dresden with his new wife, Ida, and so Nietzsche's favourite student, Adolf Baumgartner, took over the rooms he had vacated. And Rée took his place in lunchtime conversations.

In Bayreuth, Malwida von Meysenbug had renewed her suggestion that, for his health, Nietzsche should join her in Italy. Nietzsche had applied for sabbatical leave the previous May, stressing (as one does) the 'academic' character of his proposed visit to the South[1] – to the homeland of classical civilisation. The leave approved, he accepted Malwida's invitation and arranged to be accompanied by a favourite former pupil, the delicate Albert Brenner (who had, in fact, barely eighteen months to live). On September 26 he asked Malwida if he could bring Rée, as well, since he 'took great delight in his utterly clear head as well as his considerate, truly friendly soul'.[2]

Shortly before leaving for Sorrento he received a telegram from Wagner, who, suffering from the stresses of the Festival, had also decided on Italy as a place of recuperation. It must have been difficult for Nietzsche not to find it insulting:

> Please send two pairs of silk vests and underpants made in Basel on Wednesday to Bologna Hotel Italy. Until then Venice Hotel Europa. Richard Wagner.[3]

This was either emotionally dense or else a crude attempt to reassert the old 'Master'–servant relationship – precisely what Nietzsche had found it imperative to escape. Yet, ever anxious to prevent his newly critical stance to Wagner developing into an overt personal breach, Nietzsche replied that the task delighted him since it reminded him of the old Tribschen days. He reports in the same letter that he spends most of his time in a darkened room undergoing an atropine (deadly nightshade) treatment for his eyes (prescribed by his Basel ophthalmologist, Dr. Schiess) and that he plans to become healthy in Italy or else die. For good measure he ends his letter by pandering to Wagner's anti-Semitism: 'please greet my "noblest friend" your revered wife, to use one of the most impermissible Germanisms of the Jew, Bernays'.[4]

Going South

On October 1 Nietzsche set off to pick up Rée from Montreux, where he had been visiting his affluent mother in her holiday resort. From there they went to nearby Bex, southeast of Lake Geneva. After two delightful autumn weeks amidst the golden leaves of this wine-growing region, a time Rée described as 'the honeymoon of our friendship', they continued on to Geneva to pick up Brenner. From there they took the evening train through the new Mont Cernis tunnel to Turin and thence to Genoa.

In the first-class compartment (one supposes Rée and Brenner were asleep) Nietzsche struck up a conversation – over blowing up her air-cushion – with a remarkable young woman, Isabella von Prahlen (later Baroness von Ungern-Sternberg), and her slightly older companion, Baroness Claudine von Brevern. They talked flirtatiously through the night – a travellers' romance – enjoying what Isabella recalls as 'an orgy of thoughts'. Nietzsche posed the suggestive question 'Are you a free spirit too?' to which Isabella replied, equally suggestively, that she would like to be.[5] From Genoa, Nietzsche and company boarded the steamer for the three-day trip down Italy's western coast to Naples. On a sightseeing stopover in Pisa Isabella and Nietzsche caught up with each other again, where, she recalls, they agreed that egoism was the highest form of culture – refined egoism, however, not crude self-indulgence. She also recalls that Rée appeared jealous of the time Nietzsche spent with her: 'he took me aside and went on and on about his displeasure over the fact that I, in spite of his efforts to the contrary, had got Nietzsche dangerously excited', when what he needed was 'great quietness and solitude on account of a serious nervous condition'.[6] (One thinks, here, of the suggestion that Rée was given to homosexual inclinations.)

In Naples they were collected by Malwida von Meysenbug and the next day, October 27, they arrived in Sorrento to take up residence in a modest pension, the Villa Rubinacci (now unrecognisably transformed into the Hotel Eden), off the Via Correale, where she had rented the second and third floors. The Wagners had arrived in Sorrento before them and were recovering from the Festival, in typically Wagnerian style, in the best hotel in town: set amid five acres of citrus groves, manicured lawns, palm-lined avenues, and exotic flowerbeds, the Grand Hotel Excelsior Vittoria, atop a cliff with a sheer two-hundred-foot drop into the sea, commands a panoramic view of the entire Gulf of Naples towards Vesuvius in the distance. Since the pension was less than five minutes walk from the hotel, they called on the Wagners as soon as they arrived.

Malwida von Meysenbug

Malwida, twenty-eight years older than Nietzsche, was a remarkable woman who, though he must have tried her patience many times, remained faithful to him even when, in the process of going mad, he abused her fearfully. She also remained true, her whole life, both to Wagner, to whose inner circle she belonged, and to Schopenhauer – in other words, to the worldview that Nietzsche and Rée, in Sorrento, set out to abolish. In spite of this, as well as appreciating her substitute mothering, Nietzsche had great respect for her character, reading and re-reading her autobiography, *Memoirs of a Female Idealist*,[7] and recommending it enthusiastically to his friends. She had considerable influence on him – his famous remark that 'without music life would be an error' seems to derive from her remark, apropos Wagner, that 'without music life would be a desolation'.[8] Their friendship was aided, I think, by certain similarities in their natures and life-histories, the most evident being their shared love of the South, the South as a physical place but also as a spiritual vision, the vision of, among others, Hölderlin and Claude Lorraine.

As she recounts in her *Memoirs*,[9] Malwida was born into a family of minor north German nobility. As a child, she was, like Nietzsche, ultra-pious. She also lost a small brother. Like Nietzsche she abandoned Christian metaphysics during adolescence, along with Christian asceticism: 'the senses', she wrote, 'are the instruments, not the enemies, of the spirit'. Unlike Nietzsche, however, she preserved an uncompromising, that is to say an 'idealist's', commitment to Christian – i.e., Schopenhauerian – ethics: 'compassion', she wrote, is the 'true essence' of the ethical life. 'To be good is my ideal', she continued, so that eventually 'compassion vanquished the last traces of selfishness in me'. Part of what Nietzsche admired in her was the absolute 'purity' of her commitment to her 'ideal'.[10]

Though Malwida had rejected the Christian God, she retained a Spinoza-like, pantheistic religiosity: awe before the mystery. 'God', she records, became 'no longer individual to me but rather filled the universe, now at one with the strict laws governing the world'. Like Nietzsche, Malwida rejected personal immortality. The demand for it she regarded as 'a personal selfishness...[an] arrogance of the ego'. Immortality, she concluded, can only consist in a transcendence of personality: 'only the spirit freed of all individuality is immortal'.[11] And she records her own experience of such freedom, of experiencing her 'consciousness of unity with all that is'.[12] Though, in the Sorrento period, Nietzsche would not have countenanced this account of immortality as mystical absorption into a pantheistic All, by the time of *Zarathustra* it became, as we shall see, a central idea – a fact that may be partially attributable to Malwida's delayed influence.

Malwida's autobiography is a story of personal liberation, of a free spirit trying to realise her freedom – to 'become who she was'. A hero of the early feminist movement – the *Memoirs* became compulsory reading for the next generation of emancipationists – she broke with her ultra-conservative family over her support for the 1848 workers' uprising. She became, that is, a radical democrat and socialist, which is what attracted her to the early Wagner. (They quarrelled over his abandonment of socialism.) The focus of her free-spiritedness was female emancipation – workers' and women's rights were, for her, the same cause. Emancipation, she saw, demanded financial independence, which in turn demanded education. Accordingly, she became involved in setting up an embryonic university for women in Hamburg before being forced, as a political revolutionary, to flee to London. Here she became a close friend and governess to the children of the exiled Russian anarchist-socialist Alexander Herzen, whose daughter, Olga, she eventually adopted as her own. (It was Olga's marriage to Gabriel Monod for whom Nietzsche wrote the 'Monodie à deux' (p. 166 above). Malwida clearly had a great need to mother people – not just Nietzsche but, it sometimes seems, every young feminist in Europe. After Nietzsche's collapse she adopted a similarly motherly relationship with the future Nobel laureate Romain Rolland.

The Villa Rubinacci

The apartment in the Villa Rubinacci (that Malwida had rented from the Attanasio family) had two floors, and was to be Nietzsche's home for the six months from October 27, 1876, until May 7, 1877. The less luxurious upper floor was occupied by the self-sacrificing Malwida and her loyal and efficient housemaid-cook, Trina (who taught Nietzsche to cook risotto). The lower floor consisted of a large dining room and living room for communal gatherings, as well as bedrooms for, as Wagner called them, the 'three boys'. The villa occupied an elevated site surrounded by groves of oranges and lemons that were (and still are) used to make the delicious *limoncello* liqueur. These were interspersed with olive groves and vineyards, intensive cultivation being possible in the rich volcanic soil provided by Vesuvius. Nietzsche loved to take long, thoughtful walks in the shade of the lemon trees. There was a particular tree, he told Malwida, in whose shade new thoughts were guaranteed to come to him. The villa was backed by pine-covered hills – 'pines which listen, deepening further … the southern stillness and the midday quiet'[13] – beyond which lay the beautiful Gulf of Sorrento. From the front balconies, overlooking the Gulf of Naples, were views to Capri in the west and Vesuvius in the northeast, active as Nietzsche arrived in Sorrento. Some of these land- and seascapes reappear in *Zarathustra*.

The day of Malwida's 'small colony' (as she described it) began when everyone rose at 6.30 and went – at Nietzsche's insistence – for a brisk walk. 'One can do things in a "barracks"', Brenner wrote home, 'that would be unbearable if one were alone'. (Since he was an insomniac, Nietzsche's day often began much earlier – he kept a slate tablet at his bedside to record thoughts that came to him during the night.) Breakfast was taken communally at 7.30. From 9.00 until 10.00 Nietzsche would dictate to Brenner – his eyesight was so bad at this time that his normally voluminous letter-output was reduced to a few postcards. After a communal lunch, there would be more walks and excursions in the surrounding area. Sometimes they wound their way up the hills behind the house to farmhouses where, Malwida recollects, 'comely girls' danced the tarantella. Sometimes they rode on donkeys, occasions on which Brenner's poor riding and long legs scraping the ground caused general merriment.[14] Sometimes there would be longer excursions: three-hour walks over the hills to the Gulf of Sorrento or excursions to Pompeii ('inoffensive vulgarity', Nietzsche calls it in *The Gay Science*, referring to its Roman inhabitants rather than modern visitors).[15] Or they would take a boat to Capri or Ischia. After dinner, the evening would be devoted to discussing the 'colonists'' various projects or to readings from, *inter alia*, Voltaire, Montaigne, Diderot, Burckhardt, Ranke, Thucydides, Herodotus, Calderon, Cervantes, Michelet, Turgenev, Renan, the Bible, La Rochefoucauld, Stendhal, Plato's *Laws* or from Adolf Baumgartner's notes taken from Burckhardt's lectures on the Greeks, on which Nietzsche, as the resident classicist, would then give a commentary. (The murderer of evenings such as this, television has a lot to answer for.) On Christmas Eve the communal sitting room was transformed into a garden with lighted orange trees (in pots, presumably), piles of roses and camellias, and the ceiling hung with Chinese lanterns. As presents, Rée received a mirror – a reference to his emphasis on vanity as a factor in human motivation – Brenner a silk umbrella, and Nietzsche a Sorrentine house-cap, which he mistook for a Turkish fez.

Nietzsche was working on the material that would become *Human All-Too-Human* – by the time he arrived it had mutated from being *The Ploughshare* to being planned as a fifth

Untimely Meditation under that new title – and Rée was working on his *Origin of the Moral Sentiments*, which would appear the following year. In Nietzsche's presentation copy he inscribed a dedication calling himself the work's father and Nietzsche its mother. Nietzsche recommended the manuscript to his own publisher, Schmeitzner, saying that it employed 'so new and thoroughly rigorous a method, that it will probably represent a turning point in the history of moral philosophy'.[16] Alfred Brenner was working on a novella, *The Flaming Heart*, and Malwida on her novel *Phaedra*, as well as a collection of essays, *Mood-Pictures from the Legacy of an Old Woman*.

Given their different outlooks, that they got on so well is a tribute to everyone's capacity to separate friendship from opinion. There must, nonetheless, have sometimes been sharp disagreements in the evening discussions. Whereas both Rée and Nietzsche thought they were employing a new method of inquiry which they called 'historical philosophy' and which they believed turned philosophy into a branch of the 'natural sciences',[17] Malwida, in *Mood-Pictures*, repeats Schopenhauer's observation that scientific method, even within its paradigm field of inquiry, physics, cannot account for its own foundations – cannot explain the nature of fundamental forces such as gravity and magnetism – let alone encompass phenomena such as love, spirituality, and artistic genius.[18] Consistent with this, she believed that Nietzsche was over-impressed by Rée's novel way of addressing philosophical questions:

> Dr. Rée's strict scientific and realistic outlook was something almost completely new in relation to his [Nietzsche's] creative output that had, until then, been permeated by an inner poetic and musical element. It gave him an almost childishly astonished pleasure. I often noticed this and gave him a humorous warning that I did not share Rée's outlook, despite my high respect for his personality and recognition of his good nature, which showed itself particularly in his self-sacrificing friendship for Nietzsche.[19]

Later on she remarked, to Lou Salomé, apropos what she (wrongly) took to be Rée's defence of egoism, that his own character was 'the most shining refutation of his own theories'. Concerning the aphorisms in the style of Rée and his French models that Nietzsche was now producing, Malwida felt that though some were brilliant, many, which made clear the dismaying transformation of his worldview, were distinctly unpleasant.[20] Of those preserved in his notebooks of the period, one can guess that she appreciated neither 'Schopenhauer is to the world as a blind man to writing'[21] nor

> Fear dwells in the heart of human fantasy. The last form of the religious consists in affirming the completely dark, inexplicable region; in this … one thinks, the world-riddle must be concealed,[22]

a direct critique of her own religious mysticism. On the other hand, she would have been delighted by 'Socialism rests on the decision to recognise all men as equals and to be just to all of them: it is the highest form of morality'.[23] In Nietzsche's entire career, the only remarks that are anything other than rampantly hostile to socialism come from this period, and must reflect the temporarily moderating influence of Malwida. The remark that 'The wise person knows no custom save that which takes its law from himself'[24] would have appealed to her as validating her own struggle to free herself from the conventions of her family and class, as would have the idealism of 'The free spirit lives for the future of mankind so that he invents new life-possibilities to weigh against the old ones'.[25] The fundamental agreement between Malwida and Nietzsche was the need to discover a new form of culture. Their fundamental disagreement concerned its character.

* * *

Since the Wagners were just two minutes round the corner for the first ten days of the Sorrento idyll, there were regular visits. Malwida, devoted to two men now in a state of spiritual enmity, found that though Nietzsche never objected to the visits, his demeanour in company with the Wagners exhibited 'a certain forced naturalness and cheerfulness, that was otherwise quite foreign to him'.[26] On November 5 there occurred what was to prove to be the last meeting between the two, two people who had experienced perhaps the greatest and most productive artist–philosopher friendship – a 'star friendship', Nietzsche called it[27] – there has been. Wagner needed to return to Bayreuth to work on his final opera, *Parsifal*, and would soon be off to London to give a series of eight concerts in the Royal Albert Hall. (Here Cosima struck up a warm relationship with George Eliot, most surprising, given her anti-Semitism and Eliot's passionate anti-anti-Semitism.)

Nietzsche, though needing to escape the overpowering presence of the 'Master', was, as ever, concerned to avoid an open breach and continued to try to preserve the relationship by letter. The month after the Wagners' departure he sent a chatty letter to Cosima confessing, however, to a growing 'difference' with Schopenhauer and standing on the side of 'reason' against all the 'dogmatic' fundamental principles of his philosophy.[28] Cosima wrote a long and friendly reply in which, however, she says, somewhat ominously, that she would be interested to hear what objections he has to 'our philosopher'.[29] This was not quite her last letter to him. That was written on October 22 of the following year, a letter in which she thanked him for sending her an exegesis of the *Ring* cycle by a Doctor Otto Eiser – of whom more shortly.

A few days after his last meeting with Wagner, Nietzsche heard of the death of Ritschl, 'the last great philologist'.[30] In less than a week he had lost two fathers.

* * *

The beginning of 1877 saw Nietzsche often confined to bed with the familiar combination of blinding headaches and vomiting. Desperate, and after consulting with his Basel ophthalmologist, Dr. Schiess, he arranged to be examined by a Professor Schrön at the university clinic in Naples. Schrön dismissed the idea of a brain tumour, spoke of neuralgia, and said that the condition could last several years and then suddenly disappear. What he suggested by way of treatment is unknown, save for the fact that he recommended sexual release, which, apparently, Nietzsche achieved with several visits to Naples brothels.[31]

At the beginning of April, Rée left for Jena, where he felt that his Darwinian convictions would be more acceptable than in conservative Basel, and Brenner returned to Basel for the beginning of the university's summer semester. Nietzsche missed Rée badly: 'nothing is more desolate than Rée's room without Rée...don't let me ever lose you again', he wrote his absent friend.[32] Left now alone with Malwida, the conversation returned once again to marriage plans. Malwida proposed various candidates as, by letter, did Elizabeth – Olga Herzen's sister Natalie came under consideration. The ostensible reason was to make Nietzsche financially independent of his job in Basel – the successful candidate must be both 'good and rich', as Malwida succinctly put it. But given Schrön's advice, Nietzsche may have had 'medical' reasons for becoming quite desperate about the project – by July, he is writing that he *must* marry before the autumn even if he has to pick someone up off the street.[33] That 'medical' considerations supplied a motive is supported by his repeated, frank declaration in *Human, All-Too-Human* that a man needs regular sexual outlet – from which he concludes that since a good marriage must be based on friendship rather than sexual attraction (which in any case inevitably wanes), it must tolerate 'exceptions', 'mistresses'.[34] As usual, however, all the marriage plans turned to dust.

Perhaps another motive Nietzsche had for wanting to marry was a sense of increasing isolation, of growing more and more distant from his oldest and most intimate friends. Overbeck was now married and, during the Sorrento period, Nietzsche had no communication at all with either Rohde or von Gersdorff. His first letter to the latter since July 1876, in fact, was written at the end of December 1887 – and then it was only to tell von Gersdorff to stop sending abusive letters to Malwida.[35] (Von Gersdorff blamed her for the unhappy course of his love affair with an Italian girl.) Nietzsche did receive a letter from Paul Deussen together with a copy of his new Schopenhauer book, *Elements of Metaphysics*. In thanking him Nietzsche praised the book for its clear and comprehensive presentation of Schopenhauer's philosophy. He added, however, that he wished he had such a book much earlier, since 'your book is *an able collection of everything that I no longer hold to be true*', and concluded the letter by saying that he would say no more 'in order not to cause you pain on account of the difference in our judgments'.[36] Deussen received no further communication until a scribbled note in March 1883. The loss of these friendships was a serious matter since it was the loss of almost everyone with whom he used the familiar '*du*' – in spite of their relative intimacy he and Rée never progressed beyond the '*Sie*'.

Rée's absence was, however, partially compensated for by a growing friendship with his admirer, the writer and painter Baron Reinhart von Seydlitz, *inter alia*, president of the Wagner Society in Munich. Nietzsche had lured him and his attractive Hungarian wife south to Sorrento with lyrical descriptions of the 'well-covered walks between orange groves where there is no wind at all, so that only from the stormy movements of the pines above can one see how the world storms outside (the reality and image of our life here – true in both respects)'[37] – the effect of this parenthetical remark must be to report both physical windlessness and psychological equanimity.

Rosenlaui: Nietzsche and Sherlock Holmes

By the beginning of May 1877, Nietzsche was spending one day in three in bed with awful headaches. And since he believed that extremes of temperature exacerbated his health problems, the approach of summer made departure inevitable. On May 8 the von Seydlitzs accompanied him to Naples to board the ship to Genoa and saw that his bags and books were safely stowed. The journey northwards was rough, so that, in addition to terrible headaches, Nietzsche suffered violent seasickness; eight times during the three-day voyage he had to change his place on the boat to avoid nauseating odours and the sight of other passengers 'tucking in' with horrible gusto. From Genoa, his first stop on the slow journey back to Basel was in Bad Ragaz, in the Swiss province of St. Gallen, near the border with Liechtenstein. Since the hoped-for improvement in health which had been the main reason for the stay in Sorrento had not occurred, he intended to try yet another thermal 'cure' in this spa resort. During his three-and-a-half-week stay Nietzsche more or less decided to give up his professorship – provided he could marry a rich woman – until a visit from the ever-practical Overbeck persuaded him to postpone the decision.

Bad Ragaz having produced no improvement in his health, Nietzsche decided he needed cooler, and so higher, air. On June 11 he moved to another spa town, Rosenlaui (literally 'avalanche of roses'), in an alpine valley above Meiringen, 1,300 metres above sea level. Apart from a two-week interruption near Zug with his sister, he spent the remaining three-and-a-half months of his sabbatical in Rosenlaui. With the surrounding Alps and thick pine forest in the valley it was, he wrote, 'my kind of nature'. And it seems that he did experience in Rosenlaui an at least momentary improvement in health. When he had a relapse he felt he should be still higher.[38]

Since the ski season was over, Nietzsche found himself at first the only guest in the Hotel Rosenlaui and obtained a cheap rate. He economised even more by avoiding the set meal at the *table d'hôtel*. He ate, in fact, only two meals a day, claiming to Malwida that he needed less food than other people.[39]

From Rosenlaui he wrote Overbeck that the work on *Human, All-Too-Human* was going well: 'I walk six to eight hours a day and think out the material which I afterwards throw down on paper, quickly and with complete certainty'.[40] This manner of working – long thoughtful walks, accompanied always by a notebook, followed by short periods of intense writing – became the modus operandi for the rest of his life. His eyes, he thought, demanded it: 'I have eyesight for about one-and-a-half hours a day . . . If I read or write longer a bad attack of pain follows the same day'.[41] The aphoristic style of nearly all his mature works – he once said he approached philosophical problems like cold baths, fast in and fast out[42] – was thus not merely a literary choice: it was demanded by the condition of his eyes. Or, more accurately, demanded by what he *believed* about his eyes. For he had already been advised by two doctors, Schiess in Basel and Schrön in Naples, and would shortly be advised by a third, that the more he used his eyes the closer he would come to complete blindness. Though the advice was, in fact, quite wrong, it may well have persuaded him to believe that he *ought* to feel pain if he used his eyes for more than an hour and a half, and so caused, or at least contributed to, his actually feeling such pain – a reverse-placebo effect, as one might put it.

Since input always delays output, the speed with which Nietzsche worked on *Human, All-Too-Human* was probably aided by the fact that he had only three books with him: a new book by Mark Twain – 'I love his craziness more than German cleverness' he wrote Rée – Plato's *Laws*, and Rée's just-appeared *Origin of the Moral Sentiments*. 'I am certainly the first to read you next to a glacier', he wrote his friend, 'the right place to read a book which surveys human nature with a kind of contempt and scorn (oneself very much included) mixed with compassion for the multiple torments of life'.[43]

In Rosenlaui Nietzsche returned to his usual voluminous level of correspondence. Some letters concern his desperate desire to give up the job. He dreads, he writes Marie Baumgartner, returning to the 'twilight of my Basel existence'. He is certain he has a 'higher destiny', a 'higher task', than being a philologist, yearns to emerge from his inauthentic life as an academic. 'I lust after myself', he tells her.[44] As ever, however, 'becoming himself' is linked to the marriage project. Yet, with something like desperation, he realises that all the candidates so far considered have been pipe dreams. Natalie Herzen, in particular, had made it quite explicit that she was a non-starter.

Though she was obviously not a marriage-candidate, Nietzsche still carried a candle for Louise Ott. On hearing she had become pregnant he wrote to her that

> recently [i.e., in imagination] I looked into the darkness of your eyes. – 'Why does no one look at me with such eyes?' I cry out full of bitterness. Oh it is so awful!- Why have I never heard you sing? . . . Somewhere in the world there must be a voice for me.[45]

(The eroticism of this letter finds its way into *Zarathustra*'s personification of 'life' as a woman to whom Zarathustra sings, 'Into your eyes I looked of late, O life, and into the unfathomable I seemed then to be sinking'.)[46]

* * *

While in Rosenlaui Nietzsche received a copy of a poem, 'Prometheus Unbound', from a Jewish admirer, Siegfried Lipiner, a member of a small circle of Nietzsche-admirers in Vienna (whose enthusiasm would eventually filter through to Freud). The poem is concerned with salvation through suffering. (Lipiner later became a close friend of Gustav Mahler and, partly by transmitting *The Birth*'s ideas on tragedy, had a significant influence on the text of the latter's works – the Third Symphony contains a setting of *Zarathustra*'s 'Intoxicated Song' (see Plate 26).) Nietzsche knew Lipiner was Jewish from some anti-Semitic descriptions of him by Rée and Rohde: Rée described him as 'a not particularly appetizing man', while Rohde described him as 'one of the most bow-legged of all Jews, though with a not unsympathetic, shy, sensitive expression in his ghoulish, Semitic face'.[47] Nietzsche thought the poem terrific, writing Rohde that 'if the poet is not a veritable "genius" I don't know what one is any more . . . all of it is wonderful and it's as if I meet in it my own self elevated to a state of divinity'.[48] To Lipiner himself he wrote at the end of August, 'tell me quite frankly whether in the matter of ancestry you stand in any kind of relation to the Jews. I have recently had so many experiences which have roused in me a very great hope for youths of this ancestry.[49]

This, I think, is the decisive moment at which Nietzsche finally completes his rejection of anti-Semitism. When one notes that, a year earlier, he had still been prepared to pander to Wagner's anti-Semitism, we can see that the friendship with Rée and his admiration for Lipiner, together with the fact he no longer felt the need to think exactly what Wagner thought, had finally brought about a clear rejection of the movement gathering around him as a political force. This prepared the way for a breach with his sister, who, as we shall see, would marry one of the worst anti-Semites of all.

* * *

The Rosenlaui Valley, with its historic hotel, in which Goethe had stayed in the 1780s, and with its wonderful waterfalls, walks, and amazing views towards the Eiger, Mönch, and Jungfrau mountains, was much favoured by English tourists. One of them was Sir Arthur Conan Doyle, who was so impressed by the drama of the nearby Reichenbach Falls that in 'The Final Problem' (1891) he sent Sherlock Holmes over them, locked in deathly embrace with his arch-enemy, Professor Moriarty (only to resurrect him later in response to popular demand). Nietzsche did not meet Doyle, but he did meet George Croom Robertson, professor of philosophy at University College, London, and editor of the (to this day) prestigious philosophy journal *Mind*. He found Croom Robertson 'extremely sympathetic' and

was deeply impressed by what he took to be the state of English philosophy: *Mind*, he wrote
Rée,

> has all the great Englishmen as contributors, Darwin (who contributed a charming essay
> 'Biographical Sketch of an Infant' in Number VII) Spencer Taylor and so on. As you know,
> we in Germany have nothing similar or as good.[50]

Nietzsche adds that he had persuaded Croom Robertson to read Rée's new book and discuss it in his journal – a promise the editor kept by writing a short review. Back home,
Croom Robertson wrote Nietzsche that his *Untimely Meditations* were mentioned in a survey of recent German philosophy by Wilhelm Wundt that was about to appear in *Mind*.
Wundt, not having caught up with the sea-change in Nietzsche's outlook, wrote the following:

> A prominent representative of the pessimistic strain in our literature is Professor Friedrich
> Nietzsche of Basel, the successive parts of whose *Untimely Meditations* have drawn much
> notice. In the writings of Nietzsche and others of his stamp, the pessimistic mood is com-
> bined in a very peculiar way with an enthusiastic devotion to certain ideas closely related
> to religious mysticism. Richard Wagner and his music are ardently worshipped by this sect
> of pessimists. The great composer himself is won over to Schopenhauer by the philos-
> opher's profound views of the nature of music, and his [Wagner's, presumably] enthusiastic
> admirers declare that the Will has been revealed as cosmological principle in the [Ring of
> the] Nibelungen.[51]

Back in Basel

The beginning of September 1877 found Nietzsche back in Basel dreading the thought
of returning to lecturing – 'the greatest curse of my life'[52] – and greatly afraid that
the philosophical 'booty'[53] of his sabbatical would go cold on him. His mental and physical condition had deteriorated very badly during his sabbatical year: Ida Miaskowski
hardly recognised the cheerful fellow who had been her music and dancing partner in his
early Basel days (pp. 165–6 above). With Elizabeth once more in attendance, he moved
into a new apartment in 22 Gellerstrasse. Though he hated the idea of teaching again
he was, in a way, happy to be back in Switzerland. He had thought, he wrote Malwida, of seeing whether he could live in Italy, on Capri, but regretfully saw that 'Italy
drains away my courage, enervated me ... In Switzerland I am more "I", and since I build
ethics on the development of the "I" and not on its evaporation, it follows that – In
the Alps I am unconquerable, that is, when I am alone and have no enemy other than
myself'.[54]

Nietzsche's fears that the onset of teaching would mean loss of contact with the work on
Human, All-Too-Human proved unfounded. With Köselitz on hand to act as both amanuensis and general raiser of spirits, the two of them worked hard assembling the 'booty' of
the Sorrento period into publishable form. Work proceeded apace and by the end of the
year it was almost finished.

The Shocking Incident of the Friendly Doctor
and the Doctoring Friend

During his stay in Rosenlaui Nietzsche had met, and been impressed by, a keen admirer of both Wagner and himself, a Frankfurt doctor named Otto Eiser. Eiser gave him some medical advice but pressed him to come to Frankfurt for a thorough examination, which Nietzsche did during the first week in October. Here he was examined not only by Eiser but also by an ophthalmologist, Dr. Gustav Krüger. The gist of the combined diagnoses was that Nietzsche's headaches and convulsive attacks were caused partly by damage of unknown origin to the retinas of both eyes and partly by 'a predisposition in the irritability of the central organ' (i.e., the brain) originating in 'excessive mental activity'.[55] (This latter piece of pseudo-science was a repetition of the 'be more stupid and you will feel better' advice given to him by Immermann in Basel.) Eiser ruled out the possibility of any kind of a brain tumour[56] – Nietzsche's constant fear was that he had inherited his father's 'softening of the brain' – which, in the absence of modern scanning technology, he was actually in no position to do. Nietzsche's condition, Eiser suggested, was incurable but manageable. Blue lens spectacles, refraining from spicy food, wine, coffee, and tea, a quiet life, and (Eiser's one and only piece of sensible advice) abandoning all 'heroic remedies' such as cold baths in winter were recommended. The killer blow, however, was, once again, the prescription that, to avoid blindness, Nietzsche should give up all reading and writing for several years.

On October 10 Nietzsche wrote the already-mentioned letter to Cosima recommending the ubiquitous Eiser's interpretive essay on the *Ring* (it was published in the *Bayreuther Blätter*, Wagner's house magazine, in the following year). He continues the letter by saying that three doctors (Schiess, Schrön and Krüger) have now told him that 'blindness is inevitable – unless I submit to the hard judgment of the doctors: for several years absolutely no reading or writing'. He adds that a 'terrible decision' has to be made but that he does not lack the courage to make it – implying that he will continue with his work.[57]

On hearing from Cosima of Nietzsche's predicament, Wagner worked out that Eiser must be one of the doctors instrumental in providing the dismal diagnosis. He then took it upon himself, on October 23, to write to Eiser with his own diagnosis of the root cause of Nietzsche's troubles, telling him that the patient 'will more likely listen to the advice of a friendly doctor than a doctoring friend'. The cause of Nietzsche's troubles, asserted Wagner, was 'masturbation' (the old belief, now a joke, that masturbation makes you blind) and Nietzsche's 'altered mode of thought' was due to 'unnatural debauchery with indications of pederasty'.[58] Nietzsche should get married without delay. This latter 'diagnosis' harks back to Nietzsche's warning from Wagner that he was too intimate with his men friends, something of which Wagner had never been guilty. Wagner once wrote to a friend,

> Love in its most perfect reality is possible only between the sexes; it is only as man and woman that human beings can truly love ... it is an error to look upon this as only one of the forms of love, as if there were other forms co-equal with it ... it is only in the union of man and woman (sensuous and super-sensuous) that the human being exists'.[59]

True love is inseparable from sex. Nietzsche loved his men friends. Ergo, Nietzsche was a pervert.

Patient confidentiality counting, evidently, for nothing, Eiser replied to Wagner at length:

> Concerning your hypothesis [of unnatural debauchery] I found in my investigation no direct ground for this kind of assumption, though I am far from dismissing your observations. *Against* the presence of masturbatory influences the statements of the patient himself seem to speak. At the mention of his sexual condition Nietzsche assured me that he had never been syphilitic but he also denied my suggestion of strong sexual excitement and abnormal satisfactions...Relevant seems to me the fact that he...reported gonorrhoea infections from his student years – and then he also reported that, on medical advice, he had recently engaged in intercourse in Italy. The truth of these assertions is not to be doubted and they prove at least that the patient has the capacity for normal sexual satisfaction...also in relation to marriage...he seems dedicated to the idea of it in a way that an inveterate masturbator would not be.[60]

Since Nietzsche, as we have seen, had a very strong aversion to telling anything other than the strict truth, and since Eiser, as a Wagner-idolater would rather have endorsed the latter's diagnosis than contradict it, this report is almost certainly true. (Notice that though the visits to brothels might seem to tell in favour of the traditional story that the madness into which Nietzsche lapsed in 1889 was caused by end-stage syphilis, the fact that he explicitly confronts and rejects the possibility of syphilitic infection tells against it.)

In a further offence against patient confidentiality, both the existence and the contents of the Wagner–Eiser correspondence were somehow leaked soon after it occurred. At the second Bayreuth Festival, in 1878, the gossip was all about the absent Nietzsche – about how he was going blind through masturbation, had been picking up prostitutes in Italy, had had venereal disease as a student – and somehow the gossip came to Nietzsche's ears. In February 1883, on hearing of Wagner's death, he wrote Overbeck, 'Wagner was by far the fullest man I have known and in this sense I have suffered terribly from his absence these six years. But something like a deadly insult came between us'.[61] Later he called it 'an *abysmal* treachery of revenge'. What he was referring to is explained in a letter written to Köselitz in April 1883: 'Wagner', he wrote, 'is full of malicious ideas – but what do you say to the fact that he exchanged letters (even with my doctors) to voice his *belief* that my altered way of thinking was a consequence of unnatural debauchery, with indications of pederasty?'[62] The final years of Nietzsche's sanity, we shall see, were filled with obsessively vitriolic attacks on Wagner. There can be little doubt that the appalling incident of the friendly doctor and the doctoring friend contributed to both the strength and the quality of these attacks.

14

Human, All-Too-Human

ON NEW Year's Day, 1878, Nietzsche gifted his autographed copy of the score of *Tristan* to Köselitz and of *Die Meistersinger* to Köselitz's friend and his own sometime student, Paul Widemann. If he had thought to clear the decks of Wagneriana, however, he failed since the next day he received from Wagner a copy of the completed libretto of his final opera, *Parsifal*. To von Seydlitz Nietzsche wrote,

> Impression on first reading: more Liszt [a Catholic] than Wagner, spirit of the Counter-Reformation. To me, accustomed as I am to the Greek, the universally human, it's all too limited to the Christian era. Pure psychological fantasy, no flesh and much too much blood...The language reads like a translation from a foreign language.[1]

One might think of El Greco's boneless, fleshless, ghostly, already-almost-ascended-to-heaven saints and martyrs to get the point about Liszt and the Counter-Reformation. Wagner had anticipated this reaction by signing the copy 'for his dear friend, Friedrich Nietzsche, Richard Wagner, Church Councillor', a self-deprecating joke that Nietzsche stubbornly refused to get. 'Incredible', he comments retrospectively in *Ecce Homo*, 'Wagner had become pious'.[2]

A few days later, *Human, All-Too-Human* was finally completed and sent off to Schmeitzner. It was planned to appear in May, timed to commemorate the hundredth anniversary of the death of Voltaire, Nietzsche's temporary hero, to whom the first edition of the work was dedicated. He was extremely nervous about the work's reception. For 'personal reasons' – the desire not to upset the Wagners and his Wagnerian friends – he wanted it to appear under a pseudonym (as had Rée's *Psychological Observations*),[3] a silly idea which Schmeitzner rejected on the ground that the name of an established author was a commercial asset. Nietzsche caved in but still insisted that the preparation of the publication be kept secret. Even Rée was not to be forewarned.[4] Since the appearance of the work without *any* forewarning would surely have the effect of creating *more* of a bombshell, Nietzsche seems to have had mixed motives, seems to have both not wanted and wanted to shock the world. Above all, he seems to have both not wanted and wanted to shock the

Wagners. At the beginning of the year, when he was still planning for the work to appear under a pseudonym, he sketched a letter to accompany Wagner's complimentary copy, a letter which in the event was never sent:

> in that I send [this new work] I lay my secret trustingly into your and your noble wife's hands and assume that you will now keep it as your secret. The book is by me: I have brought to light my innermost feelings about men and things and for the first time circumscribed the periphery of my thinking. In times of paroxysms and torments this book was my comfort. It must have a pseudonym because I don't want to disturb the effect of my earlier works, because I want to prevent the public and private abuse of my person (my health won't stand it), and finally because I want a *sober discussion* to be possible in which my intelligent friends can take part without personal feelings of tenderness standing in the way...I feel like an officer who has stormed a fortress, wounded indeed, but he is up there and has unfurled his flag...Although I know no one who is of a like mind with me, I conceive of myself as having thought collectively rather than individually – that strange feeling of being both alone and one of many – a herald gone on ahead who doesn't exactly know whether the company of knights is following or whether it even exists.[5]

With the usual efficiency of nineteenth-century publishers the book appeared, on time, on May 7 with, significantly, no reference to its author's academic position on the title page. Complimentary copies were sent to Köselitz, Paul Widemann, Rohde, Rée, von Seydlitz, Malwida, Lipiner, Romundt, Mathilde Maier (whom Wagner once thought of marrying),[6] Marie Baumgartner, Carl Fuchs, Hillebrand, Croom Robertson, Eiser, Deussen, von Bülow, Burckhardt, Overbeck, Gabriel Monod, Elizabeth, the Wagners (one copy each), the Basel University library, and six others.

The Turn to Positivism

As we have seen, Nietzsche underwent a 'transformation and crisis' of which he first became 'fully conscious' during the summer of 1876, shortly before the first Bayreuth Festival (pp. 221 above). The consequence of this transformation was a commitment to 'the battle of reason' against 'all metaphysical mystification of truth and simplicity'.[7] Later on, he described this as a turn to 'positivism'.[8] *Human, All-Too-Human* is the product and record of this turn.

Schopenhauer's (and Wagner's) version of Kant's metaphysical idealism entails the existence of a meta-physical, supra-natural world 'beyond' or 'behind' the 'dream'-world of nature; beyond, as Schopenhauer puts it, 'the phenomenal appearance of things'.[9] Nietzsche's turn to positivism is, above all, a turn away from metaphysical idealism. It is the 'abolition' of the metaphysical word.[10] Above all, his positivism is a turn to metaphysical realism – or 'réealism'.[11] *Nothing* exists 'behind' nature, nothing exists *but* nature. Hence, positivism concludes, nothing is beyond the reach of natural science, nothing is knowable save that which is, in principle, knowable by science. Why did Nietzsche make this turn from metaphysics to materialism, to naturalism?

One important fact is that the 'romanticism', as Nietzsche came to call it, of Schopenhauer, Wagner, and *The Birth of Tragedy* was always a *neo*-romanticism. The real romantic movement had more or less finished in the early nineteenth century, to be replaced by the spirit of science and technology, by Darwin, railways, and global electronic communication: *The Origin of Species* appeared in 1859, Basel got its first railway connexion in 1844, Naumburg in 1849, the telegraph was invented in 1832, the telephone in 1876. Auguste Comte had invented the 'philosophy of positivism' in the 1830s* and positivism had become the dominant outlook of the educated classes. Viewing history, à la Hegel, as a story of humanity's development from infancy to maturity, Comte distinguished three 'ages of man': the religious, the metaphysical, and the scientific, that is to say, 'positive'. With positivism humanity reaches its highest development and full maturity.

Positivism, roughly speaking the 'Socratism' attacked in *The Birth of Tragedy*, is what, in his early period, Nietzsche was reacting *against*. With Wagner, he was, as we have seen, self-consciously 'untimely', a swimmer against the tide of current, educated opinion: against, for instance, the complaisant materialism of David Strauss. But in *Human, All-Too-Human* he has given up the fight, given up, at least, *this* kind of 'untimeliness'.

Looking back, in 1888, on the 1876–8 turn to positivism and reconstructing his state of mind at the time, Nietzsche writes, 'the true world (i.e., the Kant–Schopenhauer 'thing in itself') [is] now a...superfluous idea – *consequently*...let us abolish it'.[12] Notice that there is, here, no talk of *proof*. At no point does Nietzsche claim that metaphysical idealism has been *refuted*, that naturalism has been *proved*. The turn to positivism is rather a matter of *decision*, the decision to adopt a new 'research programme' with naturalism and the potential omniscience of science as its defining presupposition. What Nietzsche is doing in *Human, All-Too-Human* is trying on for size the spirit of the Darwinian age, trying to determine whether we cannot see our way to a better society by adopting that outlook not fifty but rather a hundred and fifty percent: as we shall see, Nietzsche perceives that beneath the surface of the positivist outlook a great deal of the previous metaphysico-religious outlook remains, disguised but not eliminated.

So, in *Human*, Nietzsche has decided to trade in the Schopenhauerian for a réealist 'horizon' – on, I suggest, the provisional basis he sees as demanded by true science: 'men of convictions', he writes, are not 'men of science'; the 'scientific spirit' always brings with it a 'cautious reserve' with respect to all convictions – including, consistency demands, naturalism itself.[13] (The move from positivism to Nietzsche's mature philosophy is, once again, I shall suggest, a shift of 'horizons' – a matter of synthesising the romantic and positivist horizons into a third. Thomas Kuhn's account of the history of science as a matter of 'paradigm shifts' fits Nietzsche's intellectual career very well.)

Nietzsche's paradigm shift to positivism explains *Human, All-Too-Human*'s title. As we shall see, its main topics are religion, art, and morality, phenomena which, in the Kant–Schopenhauer tradition, are taken to demand a metaphysical explanation. Nietzsche's strategy is to show that in fact none of them do, that they are all capable of an entirely 'human' explanation. As *Ecce Homo* puts it, 'the title says: "where you see ideal [i.e., non-natural] things, *I* see human, alas all-too-human things"'.[14]

As observed, Nietzsche's strategy is not to *refute* metaphysics but to show that the metaphysical world is a 'superfluous' hypothesis. Consider, by way of illustration, Freud. Why do people believe in God? One explanation might be: for the same reason they believe in the

---

* In *Dawn* Nietzsche calls Comte 'that great and honest Frenchman beside whom the Germans and English of this century can place no rival' (D 542).

sun – there is a God and people experience his presence. But Freud's explanation is: because people have a need for a father figure, they invent him. Freud's explanation is thus 'alas all-too-human' for religion because it shows, if true, that we do not *need* the 'God hypothesis' to explain religious belief. In a similar way Darwin's 'dangerous idea' is 'all-too-natural' for religion: by explaining the appearance of 'intelligent design' in the world in terms of the purely natural mechanism of natural selection it demonstrates another way in which the God hypothesis is redundant.

The Free Spirit: Nietzsche and the Life-Reform Movement

Thus the title of the work. Almost more interesting, however, is the subtitle: *A Book for Free Spirits*. At one stage Nietzsche had thought of *The Free Spirit* as the book's main title.

Books, – at least his books – Nietzsche believes, are, in the wrong hands, 'dangerous'. And so, as noted, he always writes for a very select audience, for the 'very few'.[15] In defence of the 'obscurity' of which he accuses himself, he says that he has no desire to corrupt 'old maids of both sexes' who have nothing to keep them going but their 'innocence'. And so he writes in a manner only his 'friends' will understand.[16] As we shall see, he often *begged* various 'old maids' – whom he loved dearly – not to read his books. So one function of the subtitle is to constitute, as it were, a health warning: 'for free spirits' *alone* – for, at least, *potential* free spirits alone. The subtitle is, as it were, a 'restricted audience only' sticker.

What effect is the book supposed to have on the potential free spirit? Most people write books for money. Or, if they are academics, to gain tenure, or promotion. Or, in the best instance, to interest and instruct. But not Nietzsche. He wrote, as the perceptive Lou Salomé put it, 'not to *teach* but to *convert* [*Er will nicht* lehren *sondern* bekehren]'.[17] All his books, as he put it in a letter to Rohde, are 'bait and seductive voices'[18] designed to recruit suitable individuals to his cause. To Reinhart von Seydlitz, whom he hoped to seduce away from Wagner, he presented himself quite openly as a 'pirate … always, like any other corsair, seeking to steal human beings, not to sell them into slavery but, around me, into freedom.[19]

In his early period the cause had been Wagner's programme of cultural regeneration. Now it is regeneration through positivism. The cause is different but the desire to convert remains unaltered. Who, however, are these potential 'free spirits' he hopes will join his new cause? What *is* a free spirit?

* * *

Nietzsche writes, 'A free spirit thinks differently from what, on the basis of their origin, environment, class and profession, or on the basis of the dominant view of the age, would have been expected'.[20] So a free spirit is someone who thinks – and so acts – differently from the 'fettered spirit',[21] from what Nietzsche will later call the 'herd-type'. The free spirit thus swims against the current of his times, is, in other words, 'untimely'. 'Free spirit' is the successor concept to 'untimely spirit'.

'Free-spiritedness' was in the air during the closing decades of the nineteenth century. Thoughtful people were fed up with the stuffy and often hypocritical conventions of Victorian, Wilhelmian society. In 1898 the term '*Lebensreform Bewegung*', 'Life-Reform Movement', was coined to describe the counter-culture that had been developing for some time in German-speaking countries.

Life reformers were *against* – sought 'freedom' from – some subset of: the big city which isolates individuals into anonymous, lonely 'atoms'; modern industrial technology which reduces human beings to mere tools ('human resources', as we now say) and speeds up life to an inhuman pace; the 'totalizing' bureaucratic state which absorbs all aspects of life into itself; established religion (life reformers were 'free-thinkers'); alcohol; middle class 'materialism' (consumerism); and 'Victorian' morality in all its forms, especially its repression of emotion, sex, and women. Life reformers were *for*: the communal solidarity of traditional village life (in many African villages it is still the case that if anyone starves everyone does); the 'unalienated' character of traditional work practices (Nietzsche observes that in the traditional craft economy, purchasing an artefact was a 'bestowing of distinction' akin to that which we now bestow in buying a painting);²² living in nature and in harmony with its rhythms; natural healing and meditation; nudism (the *F[reie]K[örperliche] K[ultur]* (Free Bodily Culture) was part of the movement); loose, flowing clothing; sunbathing; vegetarianism; a new religious spirituality tending in pantheistic and/or pagan directions; dance; peace; 'free love'; and female emancipation. And *youth*; whereas up to the middle of the century young people had sought to look older than they were, had dressed like their fathers and grandfathers (Nietzsche carried the practice on longer), life-reformers started to celebrate youth as the time of life in which one is least affected by, most in a position to liberate oneself from, the fetters of an unhealthy, life-repressing culture. A trend-setting, cultural weekly, simply called *Jugend* (youth), gave its name to the new design style of *Jugendstil*, the German name for art nouveau. One important strand in the life-reform movement was the *Jugendbewegung* (Youth Movement), which grew out of the *Wandervogel* –'Free as a Bird' – movement. Somewhat like the Boy Scouts, *Wandervogel* youths would go on weekend trips into the forest, where they would light campfires and sing songs about the joys of escaping the grey and grimy city. (Later, they found themselves hijacked by the *Hitlerjugend*.) Above all, life-reformers were dedicated to *life* in the 'get-a-life' sense that implies *joy*: they wanted more *Lebensfreude*, joie de vivre, than was offered by the grim repression of the Dickensian city.

To escape the atomized life of the urban mainstream, life-reformers often sought to, as we now say, 'drop out', to recover a sense of community by creating various kinds of communes in rural settings. The idea of the commune became a focal part of the life-reform movement. African Spir (1837–90), for example, a Russian philosopher Nietzsche admired, drew up a plan for a 'community of rational living', which he published in the hope of gaining recruits.* Among the twenty-two statutes of his proposed constitution one finds, for example, the rule that everyone will address each other with the familiar *du*, that there will be no alcohol or gambling, and that eating will be communal, as will be evenings dedicated to discussions, lectures, music, or games (as, for instance, in Sorrento).²³ Often the life-reform impulse towards a new mode of communal living led to emigration – to South Africa or South America. Elizabeth's ill-fated attempt, in 1886, to create the colony *Nueva Germania* in Paraguay was in part, I think, a disastrous and corrupt version of the life-reform impulse.

The most famous *Lebensreform* commune was Monte Verità in Ascona, on the shore of Lake Maggiore, which was established in 1900 with Tolstoy and Nietzsche as its heroes. It became a focal point for counter-cultural, 'free-spirited' figures in the first decades of the

---

* Like his friend Tolstoy, with whom he had fought in the Crimean war, Spir freed the serfs on his estate as soon as it was allowed. Nietzsche read and admired the exposition of his theoretical philosophy in *Thought and Reality*, though it is not certain he knew of Spir's plans for a commune.

twentieth century, *inter alios*, D. H. Lawrence, Carl Jung, Isadora Duncan, Max Weber, Martin Buber, Stefan George, James Joyce, Walter Gropius and Hermann Hesse. It is to the life-reform movement that the 'hippie' movement of the 1960s traces its ancestry, as do today's Greens.

Though Nietzsche was no 'hippie' – as observed, his upright bearing and famous moustache, plus his enthusiasm for self-discipline, cold baths and brisk walks, led to his being mistaken for a Prussian cavalry officer – he had, nonetheless, many affinities with the life-reformers. So, for example, he polemicized against alcohol[24] and tobacco, experimented with vegetarianism, and was an enthusiast for 'alternative' medicine. He hated the 'harried',[25] atomized life of the big, industrialised city – *Human, All-Too-Human* complains that in modern life we see everything 'as if from a railway-carriage window'[26] – and hated the totalizing, bureaucratic, Bismarckian state.

Brought up in rural Naumburg, moreover, Nietzsche was always, at heart, a 'small-town boy': 'we wish to live in a small town' he declared flatly.[27] The closest he came to a home in later life was Sils Maria, a tiny peasant village in the Swiss Alps. Even when he felt that the climate that suited his health required him to live part of the year in cities, he sought out village-like parts of them (his, to this day, quiet backwater of Genoa, for example) and praised those of their features that they shared with small towns (the stylistic homogeneity of Turin, for example). In contrast to the harried life of the city he believed that one should live close to, and in harmony with, nature, that one should possess a '*country sensibility*':

> If a man has not drawn firm, restful lines along the horizon of his life, like the lines drawn by mountain and forest, his innermost will itself grows restless, distracted and covetous, as is the nature of the city-dweller: he has no happiness himself and [consequently] bestows none on others.[28]

Nietzsche chose to live among the lakes and the forests of some of the most beautiful places in the world: 'he possessed', wrote his friend Meta von Salis, 'the most conspicuously developed talent for discovering the privileged places on earth'. Paradise, he wrote, in a passage entitled '*et in arcadia ego*', is a Poussin landscape – populated by Greek heroes.[29]

Nietzsche believed, too, at least in theory, in 'free love'. He was against marriage (except as a last, financial resort), told the beautiful but married Louise Ott that, as a 'free spirit', he was, like wine, highly 'dangerous' to her,[30] and, as we shall see, wanted to live in a 'wild' ('de facto') marriage with Lou Salomé. Like his admirer Isadora Duncan, he believed in dance (recall how much he enjoyed balls in his early Basel days) – literal dance, but also the spiritual 'dance' that, in *Thus Spoke Zarathustra*, triumphs over 'the spirit of gravity'. And he believed in *youth*: my works are always for 'the youth', he writes.[31] He was, moreover, until a dramatic change of mind in 1882, in favour of female emancipation and had, remember, fought hard to gain admittance for women to Basel University. Finally, and above all, Nietzsche believed in *joy*, in 'life' in the sense of living it to a joyful fullness: the entire point of his philosophy, he writes, is to recover that ability to 'rejoice' possessed by the ancients but destroyed by Christianity, to lay the foundations for a new 'temple of joy'.[32]

Nietzsche can, then, be seen as belonging to the life-reform movement and as speaking on behalf of the counter-culture it represented: recall the remark in the letter to Wagner that he thinks of himself as 'having thought collectively rather than individually' (p. 242 above). As he saw it, I believe, the formulation of the concept of the free spirit in *Human, All-Too-Human* is an attempt to articulate the spirit of the life-reform movement.

The movement, of course, did not consist in a set of articles to which one either signed up or did not. It was, rather, a loose assembly of beliefs and ideals such that a given individual would subscribe to some but by no means all. Different individuals, that is, would give different 'spins' to the movement. *Human, All-Too-Human*'s particular 'spin' is positivism, as its dedication to the Enlightenment hero Voltaire, that 'great liberator of the spirit', makes clear.[33] Life-reform is going to be carried out, not through anything 'soft-headed' such as Wagnerian music, prayer, astrology, spiritualism or the power of crystals, but through the remorseless wielding of 'hard-headed' scientific enlightenment to clear away every ancient superstition unable to justify itself before the court of reason. As Nietzsche writes in his notebooks, he dreams of

> a fellowship of men who want to be unconditioned, who give no quarter and want to be known as destroyers. They subject everything to their critique and sacrifice themselves for the truth. The bad and false are exposed to the light of day.[34]

* * *

This talk of the Nietzschean hero as a 'destroyer' raises the question of whether the concept of the free spirit is an entirely 'negative' one. Effectively, *Human, All-Too-Human* administered the coup de grâce to the friendship with Rohde. He hated the book and could not recognise his friend in it. The idea of the free spirit was, he thought, a 'purely negative, unfruitful concept'.[35] Michel Foucault, taking much of his inspiration from the work, seems to have thought the same. But both are wrong.

A key sentence in *The Gay Science* (its first four books are still proximate to Nietzsche's positivist period) is 'Only as creators can we destroy'.[36] And in the 1886 introduction to the second edition of *Human*, Nietzsche describes the free spirit who just wants to 'prowl around' in the 'desert' he has created by destroying all the old certainties as suffering from a 'sickness'.[37] Destruction, for Nietzsche, is *always* a prelude to construction – apart from reading him as a Nazi, reading him as a pure 'deconstructionist' is the most serious misreading possible.

Writing to Romundt in April 1876, he says 'Let us swim onwards against the current … I honour only one thing: moral freedom and insubordination'. But then he immediately adds, 'I hate all feebleness and scepticism. Through the daily need to raise oneself and others higher, with the idea of purity before one's eyes – always as an excelsior – so I wish myself and my friends to live'.[38] 'Excelsior', 'ever higher', we saw, is the title of the poem to which he referred in proposing marriage to Mathilde Trampedach, a proposal in which he describes himself as, like Longfellow's mountain climber, someone who 'strives most sincerely to become freer and better' (see pp. 216–17 above). And the point is, of course, that one cannot strive to become 'better' without some conception of what it is that constitutes 'betterness'.

So the Nietzschean free spirit wants to deconstruct the old 'faiths', to become 'free' *from* them. But only in order to be free *for* some positive ideal. A prime task, therefore, in examining *Human, All-Too-Human* will consist in asking what the positive ideal is in the name of which the metaphysical superstitions of the old culture are being destroyed.

The Monastery for Free Spirits

Human, All-Too-Human, we have seen, is a consciousness-raising exercise. It is 'bait' intended to 'seduce' those with the potential to think as Nietzsche does away from mainstream culture, or from other versions of life-reform, to his own particular version of the movement. In addition, however, Nietzsche has something more specific in mind. As well as general consciousness-raising he wants, like African Spir, to found a commune based on 'rational' living – ultimately, I think, a family of communes.

He wants to create, that is, what he variously calls a 'monastery for free spirits', 'the school of the Educator',[39] an 'ideal colony', a 'modern monastery'. The life he shared with Malwida, Rée, and Brenner in Sorrento he thought of as the prototype of such a commune.[40] Malwida reports having discussed the commune idea in Sorrento. Their evenings together were so peaceful and harmonious, she reports, that she suggested, jokingly, that the Sorrento ménage 'represented an ideal family'. This, she continues, led them to develop a plan to found

> a kind of mission house for adults of both sexes to have a free development of the noblest spiritual life so that they could then go forth into the world to sow the seeds of a new spiritualized culture... Nietzsche and Rée immediately offered their services as teachers. I was convinced I could attract many women students... in order to develop them into the noblest representatives of the emancipation of women.[41]

Already, in his early period, Nietzsche had had the idea of an organized, communal gathering of 'untimely', Bayreuth-inspired spirits. Writing to Rohde in 1870, he says that the point of their writings is to draw people away from mainstream educational institutions and into a new kind of 'monastery' that would constitute a 'new Greek academy'.[42] As we have seen, Nietzsche had a profound belief in the power of education either to ossify people into clones of the status quo or to liberate them to new and healthier cultural horizons. So the idea of a new academy, a kind of residential 'free university',[43] is the idea of a cell of resistance to the prevailing culture which cultivates the seeds of a new one.

Nietzsche uses the term 'monastery' more frequently than any other to refer to his proposed commune because it effectively comprehends all the strands in his thinking. First, it is to be a place where people 'free' themselves – 'drop out', sequester themselves – from current society. Like the Christian monastery, it is to be a place for those 'who wish to have nothing more to do with the world' in its present condition.[44] Second, it is to be a place where, as in the Christian monastery, people live *ascetically*, 'in great simplicity'.[45] They reject the materialism of the modern, middle-class mainstream. Third, the 'monastery' will be a place of *learning* – in the Middle Ages almost all scholars were monks. The life of the mind will provide the focus of 'monastic' life: 'work' will principally be reading, discussing, and producing works of literature, art, science and philosophy.* And fourth, as the Christian monastery sought, through prayer, sacrifice and example, to work for the redemption of mankind, so Nietzsche's monastery, too, is to work (through Reason rather than God, of course) for the 'redemption' of mankind: its members are to become the 'leader(s) and educator(s) of mankind'.[46] As we know from the *Untimely Meditations*, an 'educator' is an exemplary figure, a role model. So the commune of free spirits will lead, at least in part,

---

* A note from the summer of 1875 reads: 'Statute of the Society of the Untimely. Each quarter, everyone will present a written report on his activities. O.R.G.B.N.' (KSA 8 5 [97]). The initials stand for an envisaged core membership; almost certainly, Overbeck, Rohde, von Gersdorff, either Brenner or Baumgartner, and Nietzsche himself. A partial prototype of such a society was, of course, the *Germania* Society of Nietzsche's boyhood.

by example: they will lead by modelling the kind of life they hope will eventually 'redeem' society at large, 'signpost' its way out of its current desolation into a new and 'higher' culture. Occasionally the monastery ideal finds its way into the published works. Here is how Nietzsche described it in 1879:

> Lectures and hours of meditation for adults, and these daily, without compulsion but attended by everyone as a command of custom: the churches as the worthiest venues for them because richest in memories: every day, as it were, a festival of attained and attainable dignity of human reason: a new and fuller efflorescence of the ideal of the teacher, in which the priest, the artist and the physician, the man of knowledge and the man of wisdom [i.e., Nietzsche] are fused with one another . . . this is my vision: it returns to me again and again, and I firmly believe that it lifts a corner of the veil of the future.[47]

Human, All-Too-Human: The Attack on Metaphysics

The fundamental aim of *Human*, we have seen, is to hunt down and destroy belief in a metaphysical world, in both its overt and covert forms, as a preliminary to constructing a new, post-metaphysical, 'rational' culture. As noted, Nietzsche identifies three fundamental areas in which belief in the metaphysical occurs – religion, art and morality – and sets out to show, in each case, that the origins, the *causes*, of metaphysical belief are anything but *reasons* for such belief. This is what he calls his 'historical' (later 'genealogical') method of philosophising.[48] Since a *rationally justified* belief must be based on good reasons, to show a particular belief not to be so based is to 'refute' it – not in the sense of conclusively showing it to be false, but rather in the sense of showing that a rational being, Nietzsche's target reader, must expel that belief from the set of beliefs he subscribes to. The 'historical' method Nietzsche and Rée worked out between them is, I think, their ingenious and influential answer to the following problem: given that one cannot *prove* them to be false, how can one construct a rational critique of metaphysical beliefs?

Religion. Why do people believe in the world of religious metaphysics? Nietzsche's approach is that of the picador rather than matador: rather than delivering a single, killer thrust, he identifies a large number of causes that contribute to religious belief and patiently shows, one by one, that they are all disreputable. He observes, for example, that though religious belief may make one happier, this in no way entails the truth of the belief.[49] This might seem too obvious to be worth saying anywhere past a Critical Thinking 101 course, but in fact Nietzsche is entirely right in observing that an 'all-too-human' and all-too-common failing is the unconscious inference from happiness to truth. As he points out, people ruthlessly logical and rigorously rational when dealing with most things in daily life – financial investment, for instance – suddenly switch the rational brain into neutral when it comes to the 'big', existential questions. The desire to find a profound and comforting meaning in life leads to wishful thinking, to belief in, for example, astrology, reincarnation, karma, aliens or the Christian heaven.[50]

Then again, Nietzsche suggests, Christianity 'burden[s] the heart so as afterwards to be able to lighten it'.[51] Our Christian belief in our own 'original sinfulness' is the result of ecclesiastical indoctrination aimed not at imparting a truth but at increasing priestly power. We are victims of a kind of confidence trick. The same is true of the ascetic practices of saints and mystics: we are easily convinced that they must possess some vital piece of knowledge to practise such extremes of self-denial. But actually they have no such knowledge. The all-too-human origin of such practices is, once again, the lust for status and power.[52] (Here we see the first glimmering of a concept central to Nietzsche's mature philosophy: the 'will to power'.) Another disreputable origin of religious belief is the misinterpretation of pathological conditions.[53] For example (Nietzsche's aphorisms are often invitations to construct, as I do here, one's own examples), the man who says that 'God speaks to him every day' is likely suffering from an over-active 'super-ego'. Then again, the metaphysical-ethical system of Christianity can function to alleviate boredom: the battle against the 'inner enemy' of, in particular, sexual lust, makes life more interesting. In a world offering fewer outlets for human aggression, Christianity invented a new form of warfare.[54] But, of course, there is no more a valid route from boredom-alleviation to truth than there is from happiness.

Another kind of tracking down of disreputable origins of religious belief involves a form of speculative anthropology. The prehistoric origins of religion lie in primitive humanity's attempt to understand the workings of nature. Originally, Nietzsche suggests, human beings had no conception of *natural* causality. Everything was understood anthropomorphically: the storm was a god's anger, spring rain a god's benevolence. The way one seeks to control the behaviour of people is to perform services for them, offer them gifts. And so primitive man offered the gods things they could be expected to enjoy: sacrifices and entertaining spectacles of sex and violence, warfare, in other words. Hence the origin of 'the religious cult' lies in a primitive attempt to bring order into nature.[55] Of course, we are no longer animists. Yet the preservation of belief in gods, passed down unthinkingly from generation to generation, suggests that 'a piece of primitive humanity continues to exercise itself' in us.[56] To the extent we still believe in gods we are likely to be unconsciously adhering to a piece of primitive – i.e., superseded – science.

A final point. Nietzsche concedes that there *could* be a 'metaphysical world'. Since 'we behold all things through the human head and cannot cut off this head', we cannot rule this out as a possibility. Since we cannot remove the Kantian 'sunglasses' of the human mind we have no certain idea of how reality 'in itself' is. Nonetheless, he continues, 'only passion, error and self-deception' have made the metaphysical world 'valuable, terrible, delightful', have populated it with God, the angels, and the souls of the departed. When one has exposed these disreputable origins of these beliefs, he says, 'one had refuted them' – shown them to be, to repeat, not *false*, but rather unworthy of rational belief, devoid of rational *justification*.[57]

* * *

Art. The first thing that needs to be said is that, contrary to appearances, when Nietzsche attacks 'art' he does not mean to attack all art. As we shall see, there is actually an important place for some kinds of art in the new world *Human* is intent on constructing. What Nietzsche attacks, rather, is 'romantic' art, metaphysical art, art that deals in world-transcendence. In other words, though he is never mentioned by name, Wagner's art. Essentially what Nietzsche now wants to abandon – banish – is what, in *The Birth of Tragedy*, he had called 'Dionysian' art, the art of 'metaphysical comfort'. What he wants to retain is 'Apollonian' art, the art that 'teaches us to seek joy [not 'behind' but rather] in the appearances'.[58]

'Art' (metaphysical art), says Nietzsche, 'raises its head when religions relax their hold'. In a post-Enlightenment world in which educated people would be embarrassed to affirm the dogmas of Christian metaphysics, they can continue to enjoy religious feelings and moods in art. 'Art', as one might put it, offers religious feeling without doctrinal responsibility. What kinds of feeling? 'People' (i.e., Schopenhauer; see p. 85 above) talk, Nietzsche observes, of the certainty of redemption as revealed in 'the whole sure gospel in the glance of Raphael's Madonna'. But even more strongly they derive the same feeling from music: 'it can happen', as we know (p. 95 above), that a passage in Beethoven's Ninth Symphony will make [a person] feel he is hovering above the earth in a dome of stars with the dream of *immortality* in his heart'.[59]

The subject of this passage is, of course, Nietzsche himself, Nietzsche as representative of the spiritual condition of his age. Recall that, at nineteen, even though he had lost his Christian faith, he still regarded all great music as religious in character, as generating a feeling 'out of which heaven suddenly shines forth', 'a dim intimation of the divine' (p. 38 above). And notice that 'the passage in Beethoven's Ninth Symphony' is evidently the 'Ode to Joy' in the last movement – precisely what the opening of *The Birth of Tragedy* had identified as the moment of Dionysian transcendence.

What have these accurate and autobiographical observations to do with demolishing metaphysics? Nietzsche says that experiences such as these show how easy it is for the free spirit once again to 'sigh for his lost love whether she be called religion or metaphysics'. They show the continuing strength of 'the metaphysical need'.[60] The reference, as observed earlier, is to Schopenhauer's chapter entitled 'On Man's Need for Metaphysics',[61] a chapter in which he argues that the primary function of religion and metaphysics is to overcome pain and death, to address the universal human need for the assurance of an immortality that will compensate for the suffering of mortal existence. Nietzsche's point is that insofar as we have these experiences and base half-beliefs upon them we are backsliders, not really, or not yet, fully free spirits. At the very least, our 'intellectual probity' is put to the test.[62]

In a related passage, Nietzsche provides the brisk, 'historical' deconstruction of metaphysical beliefs based on musical feeling we have already discussed (p. 95 above). We have 'profound feelings' which not only seem to carry one into the heart of ultimate reality but also seem to be somehow self-certifying. But, he observes, such feelings only seem profound because, imperceptibly, they arouse certain groups of thoughts which we regard as profound – thoughts about death, judgment, heaven and hell, the 'first and last things' (the title of Part I of *Human*) that Christians are supposed to meditate upon. Yet, he continues, 'a profound thought can nonetheless be very far from the truth as, for example, every metaphysical thought is'. And when we deduct the thought from the feeling 'all we are left with is *strong* feeling, and this has nothing at all to do with *knowledge*'.[63]

Another line of attack presents the metaphysical artist as something of a con artist. (As Lou Salomé points out, the Wagner cult is the unnamed target here.)[64] Artists of this ilk encourage the romantic notion and cult of 'genius'; the idea of the great artist as someone who is able to see through 'as it were, a hole in the cloak of appearance' so that he is 'able to communicate something conclusive and decisive about man and the world'.[65] Though they seem to be fighting for an element of the divine in human nature, they are actually fighting to generate the maximum prestige for their art (so as, for example, to raise money for Bayreuth).

One of the techniques used to boost the cult of genius is to disguise all signs of 'becoming' in the artwork so as to give it the appearance of a casually improvised perfection that only a god could have achieved. One has this feeling before, for instance, the temple at Paestum (Nietzsche visited it on one of his excursions from Sorrento), the feeling that 'a god must one morning playfully have constructed his dwelling'.* In fact, however, the briefest of glances into Beethoven's notebooks shows that not a gift from heaven, not the inspiration of the 'muses' (the origin of 'music'), but rather hard work and good taste are what make a great artist: 'All great artists have been great workers, inexhaustible not only in invention [of material] but also in rejecting, sifting, transforming, ordering'.[66] In a word, so-called 'genius' is nine-tenths perspiration and at most one-tenth inspiration.

Not only do artists promote the cult of genius, but also we, the audience, connive with them – out of the all-too-human motive of vanity. Because we ourselves cannot write a Shakespeare play, we deceive ourselves into thinking they must be of miraculous origin. This rescues our vanity since, in Goethe's words, 'the stars we do not covet'. Thus, when we treat someone as divine (when we call the singer a 'diva' or the composer *Maestro* – or 'Master'), what we really mean is 'here there is no need to compete'.[67]

* * *

Morality. Christian morality as articulated by Kant, and more particularly by Schopenhauer, is based on two ideas. The first is that virtue consists in altruism – 'unegoism' as Nietzsche calls it. The ideal against which we are to measure ourselves is Jesus, that paradigm of pure, selfless, universal love. The second idea is that of freedom and responsibility. According to Christian moralists, the actions we perform are our own free choice: in every case, we could have acted otherwise than we did. It follows that we are responsible, 'accountable', for all our actions. Combined, Nietzsche believes, these ideas are disastrous for human psychological health. Because we feel we *ought* to be 'unegoistic', and believe, moreover, that we *can* be unegoistic, yet know that, at least most of the time, we are not, we suffer from *guilt*, low self-esteem.[68] It thus becomes central to Nietzsche's life-mission to liberate us from the grips of Christian morality.

So far, this has nothing to do with metaphysics. But in Schopenhauer's hands Christian morality quickly acquires metaphysical baggage. Like Kant, Schopenhauer believes that events in the natural world are, without exception, subject to causal laws. If nature were all there was there could be no freedom. But in fact, thanks to metaphysical idealism, we know that nature is mere 'appearance', behind which is the 'intelligible' world of the 'thing in itself'. And here we find the ground of freedom: since, as Kant shows, causality is nothing more than a 'form' of appearances, the self 'in itself' has to be undetermined, free. Hence, in spite of exceptionless causal determinism throughout nature, the responsibility we feel for our actions and the guilt we feel when they are not up to the moral mark are entirely justified.

Thus far, Schopenhauer merely repeats Kant:[69] though as natural beings we are fully determined, as 'intelligible' beings we are free. But, as he justly observes, the details of how this scheme of things could work are left by Kant in a state of deep mystery. His own contribution is to provide those details. It works like this. The 'apparent' world of nature is like a train system: where the trains go is entirely beyond my control. But which train I

* Mozart's 'Jupiter Symphony' is a better illustration of Nietzsche's point. It was so called because, it was felt, only a god could have created such effortless perfection. Or rather, that is how one was *supposed* to feel. The nickname came not from Mozart but rather from someone interested in selling the product, the musical impresario Johann Solomon.

step into is entirely up to me. I am born, that is to say, with a particular character which functions just like the character or nature of any other natural being. Just as the rock's behaviour is completely determined by its nature plus the circumstances it finds itself in (if thrown into water it will sink rather than float), so my behaviour is completely determined by my character plus the circumstances I find myself in. If I am a kleptomaniac and see something nice I will steal it. *What character I have, however – what character I have 'stepped into' – is entirely up to the 'intelligible' me,* the result of an 'intelligible' act of free choice by my real self. Hence, although all my actions are causally determined, I am at the same time both free and responsible.[70]

The second way in which morality, in Schopenhauer's hands, acquires metaphysical baggage concerns the possibility of altruism. As we saw (p. 84 above), the norm of human behaviour is, for Schopenhauer, egoism. This is rooted in the fact that the only pain and pleasure I feel are my own, that in terms of one's naive and natural experience of the world, others are no different from feelingless robots. If, then, the natural world of individuals were absolutely real, altruism would find neither explanation nor justification. But, though rare, altruism does occur. And the only possible explanation of this is that the altruistic person has the metaphysical insight that behind the 'veil of Maya' all is One. Given this insight, another's suffering becomes just as much 'mine' as my own. In this way, moral virtue becomes, for Schopenhauer, just like art, a matter of 'genius'; a matter, once again, of 'seeing through a hole in the cloak of appearance' (p. 251 above).

In two ways, then, Nietzsche observes, metaphysical notions, 'mythological monsters', are called upon to 'buttress' morality.*,[71] Schematically put, Schopenhauer's argument is the following. (1) We have the freedom to act altruistically and ought so to act. (2) For two reasons, this is not possible if there is only a natural world. So (3) there must be a supernatural, metaphysical world. Nietzsche's deconstruction of this route to the metaphysical takes the form of attacking (1). The attack is two-pronged. First he argues that there is no reason to believe in freedom of any kind. And second, he argues that, in particular, we are not free to be altruistic.

* * *

Nietzsche's critique of freedom is simple: since universal causal determinism is true, everything, and in particular every human action, is a necessary, 'mathematically calculable' consequence of past events. If one were all-knowing one would be able to predict from the present state of the world every future action.[72] From universal causation Nietzsche derives immediately the absence of free will.[73] (Notice that, here, Nietzsche has no time for the idea that there might be an important kind of freedom that is *compatible with* universal causal determinism. In his later works, he will change his mind on this.)

---

* In deconstructing the route to the metaphysical through art, Nietzsche is attacking a tendency that most of us can, if not share, at least empathise with. But in criticising the route through morality he is attacking a route shared only by those immersed in the philosophy of Kant and Schopenhauer. Lest it be thought that Nietzsche really should not be bothering with routes liable to be taken only by those with that very special background, it needs to be once again remembered that he writes, in the first instance, for a particular audience: first for himself – *Human* is the work in which 'I liberated myself from that in my nature *which did not belong to me*' (EH III HH 1) – and second for Germans of the late nineteenth century with backgrounds very like his own. For his chosen, primary audience it would be almost certain that they, too, were, or had been, immersed in the Wagner–Schopenhauer worldview.

Why should we believe in universal causal determinism? Nietzsche provides no direct argument for its truth. It is, rather, a fundamental axiom of the scientific research programme to which *Human* is committed. Instead, he defends the principle indirectly by attacking what (Newtonian rather than quantum mechanics being the order of the day) he takes to be the only possible objection to the principle – the alleged existence of human freedom.

Originally, suggests Nietzsche, it was thought that *everything* happens on account of a free will: hunger, for example, just happened – on its own account. Because primeval man could not see a cause, he assumed none existed and that everything happened of its own free will. We have now dispensed with this piece of pre-history – except in the case of ourselves. But now it is time to divest ourselves of this last relic of primeval thought, to take the final step from humanity's childhood and into intellectual adulthood. We should no more call a human being immoral for his harmful actions than we call the thunderstorm immoral for making us wet. [74]

What, however, is it which has prevented us taking this step to *complete* scientific naturalism? Nothing other than Christianity's cultural indoctrination designed not for our benefit but to promote its own power.[75] Free will is an invention of the priests designed to make us dependent on them. (I shall return to this claim shortly.) Belief in free will thus has a thoroughly disreputable provenance and should be abandoned by any rational being. And so there is no need for Schopenhauer's exotic metaphysics. The ethics it was designed to explain and justify was a 'false ethics'.[76]

* * *

I turn now to Nietzsche's attack on the morality of altruism, the Christian ethic of, as *Zarathustra* will call it, 'neighbour love' articulated in Schopenhauer's moral philosophy. As we have seen, Schopenhauer's route from virtue to the metaphysical is, in a nutshell, the following argument. Were naturalism to be true, all action would be egoistic. But, though rare, there are occasional cases of genuine altruism. Therefore, naturalism cannot be true; there must be a metaphysical world. An obvious way, therefore, of blocking this route to the metaphysical would be to deny that there are any exceptions to the norm of egoism.* This is Nietzsche's strategy. Egoism is not merely the norm, it is the universal rule. The strategy, in other words, is to argue for 'psychological egoism' – the doctrine that *all* human action is motivated by self-interest.[77]

Actually, Nietzsche affirms a particular form of psychological egoism – psychological hedonism. This is the view (one that, later, he will emphatically reject) that all actions are motivated by self-interest *plus* a particular view of self-interest: that the only interests we have are in experiencing pleasure and avoiding pain: 'in every case', Nietzsche writes, 'the sole desire that satisfies itself is the desire for my own pleasure'.[78]

So far as arguing for the thesis goes, Nietzsche's technique is to explain away *apparent* cases of altruistic action or feeling. Thus, for example, 'pity' is really an exercise in feeling powerful.[79] If I give the 200 dollars I have just taken out of the ATM machine to the beggar on the pavement my motive is to enjoy the experience of my own superior position in life. And truthfulness, far from being an exercise in honesty or justice, is generally explained

---

* A more successful way would be to point out that Schopenhauer's account of virtue as insight into the truth that one's own true, metaphysical self is identical with all other metaphysical selves reduced phenomenal altruism to metaphysical egoism. If, then, phenomenal egoism had no 'moral worth' neither should metaphysical egoism.

by the fact that lying requires high intelligence and a good memory, so that the motive people generally have for being truthful is fear of being found out.[80] And so on, through many other detailed analyses disclosing the all-too-human motives underlying apparent altruism.

The problem, however, with the assembly of such cases is that, at best, they add up only to the position, already admitted by Schopenhauer, that egoism is the *general* rule of human behaviour. No assemblage of cases can establish that it is the universal rule. And indeed common sense tells us that the universal rule is false. People sacrifice themselves in war without, sometimes, any belief in an afterlife or any fear of social retribution if they do not. And people do things because they think it their duty. Of course, Nietzsche can claim that, given time, he can discover an egoistic motive in these cases, too, but the question is: how does he know? The claim that there *must* be such a motive to discover is no more than ungrounded, indeed *irrational*, dogmatism – precisely what the Enlightenment, scientific outlook is supposed to be overcoming. Rohde particularly disliked what he saw as the dogmatism of Nietzsche's book.

Recognising this, perhaps, Nietzsche tries to redeem the situation via the desperate move of producing an *a priori*, conceptual argument for psychological egoism:

> No one has ever done anything that was done wholly for others and with no personal motivation whatsoever. How indeed should a man be *able* to do something that had no reference to himself, that is to say, lacked all inner compulsion…How could the ego act without the ego?[81]

The argument gestured towards, here, is this: an action is a bodily movement caused by a desire or want, 'an inner compulsion'; in other words, a preference. So every act I perform satisfies some preference of mine. My self-interest is composed of my preferences. Therefore, every act is self-interested. But, as already pointed out, it seems simply false to suppose that all preferences are self-interested. The man who dies in battle *sacrifices* self-interest to love of country. Lacking a philosophical training, technical logic-chopping was not Nietzsche's strong suit.

Why Deconstruct Metaphysics?

Nietzsche acknowledges a serious downside to his deconstruction of metaphysics, the survey of which we have now completed. The loss of Christianity, in particular – a process which is happening anyway, but which *Human*'s deconstructive programme aims to expedite – has a tragic side to it. For Christianity has, in fact, been responsible for the finest products of Western civilisation – likely, Nietzsche is thinking here, *inter alios*, of his fellow Saxons, Bach and Handel.[82] And moreover, the 'slow-breathing repose' of a past in which one was able to view oneself from the perspective of eternity contrasts sharply with the 'agitated ephemeral existence of the present age'.[83] The question presents itself, therefore, as to what the point is of demolishing faith in the metaphysical world. What, if anything, makes the enterprise worthwhile?

Nietzsche himself raises this question: 'will our philosophy…become a tragedy? Will truth not become inimical to life, to the better man?'[84] He worried about this in the notebooks. The worry concerns, in particular, the programme of 'psychological observa-tions' designed, at least on Nietzsche's part, to demolish the idea of human altruism. La Rochefoucauld and 'the author of the *Psychological Observations*' (i.e., Rée) are, he observes, 'skilful marksmen who always hit the *Schwarze*'. *Schwarze* means 'bullseye'. But it also means 'the black'. So, here, he is making two points at once: Rée's aphoristic 'observations' on human nature are always dead on target. But equally, they always highlight the black side of human nature – offer, in Heine's phrase, a 'night view' of humanity. The same is true of his own 'observations'. A couple of examples: 'One is twice as glad to leap after a man who has fallen into the water where there are people present who dare not do so'.[85] 'There are few who, when they are in want of matter for conversation, do not reveal the more secret affairs of their friends'.[86] Aphorisms such as these have an 'ouch' factor. As Nietzsche says, they put us on the 'moral dissecting table' where 'knives and forceps' are applied in a way that is not only precise but also 'cruel'.[87]

The notebooks worry about the effect of such 'cruelty'.* 'Belief in the good', in 'unegoistic actions', he observes, has increased social trust. But belief in the opposite will make human society 'weaker, more mistrustful'. To be sure, one can admire the skill of the marksmen, yet 'in the interests of human wellbeing one could wish they did not have the intention of belittling and creating suspicion'.[88] So would we not be better off without them? (Notice the passing of a shadow over the relationship with Rée. Nietzsche places, here, a question mark against both Rée's character and his influence on Nietzsche's own work.)

Nietzsche's method of rejecting this doubt is not entirely consistent – due, I suspect, to a subterranean struggle between his own, fundamentally constructive, life-affirming impulse and Rée's disposition to world-denying nihilism. He has, that is, two different ways of responding to the doubt.

The first response observes that although his programme of deconstruction is essential to killing off the 'mythical monsters' invented by Christianity, 'whether psychological obser-vation is more advantageous or disadvantageous to man may remain undecided'. What is certain, however, he continues, is that it must carry on since science, 'which knows no regard for final objectives' to do with human well-being, 'cannot dispense with it'.[89] This raises the obvious question: why science? Why the will to truth whatever the cost?

In a discussion of this same issue – truth versus human happiness – in connection with religion, Nietzsche decides that, at least in the short term, the destruction of religion *will* make human beings more miserable since science can offer nothing by way of an equivalent comfort. So, as Byron puts it in his poem *Manfred* (the inspiration for Nietzsche's ill-fated *Manfred Meditation* (p. 154 above)),

> *sorrow is knowledge: those who know the most*
> *must mourn the deepest o'er the fatal truth,*
> *the tree of knowledge is not that of life.*

Nonetheless, he continues, one has to hold fast to the work of deconstruction since 'one can no longer have any association with [Christianity] without incurably dirtying one's intellectual conscience and prostituting oneself before oneself and others'.[90]

---

* They also worry that it can be overdone. 'You have', Nietzsche writes, initiating a line of self-criticism, 'developed the art of finding a shameful origin to such an extent one would find a dis-cussion of…tooth-brushing demeaning' (KSA 8 42 [29]). 'Sometimes', as Freud probably did not say, but Bill Clinton might have, 'a cigar is just a cigar'.

This, as we might call it, 'macho morality', is the typical companion of positivism. The same morality appears in another positivist work, Albert Camus's *The Myth of Sisyphus*; in Camus's attack on Kierkegaard's 'leap of faith' as 'philosophical suicide', a 'mutilation of the soul' that is a burning insult to 'human pride'. Real men, 'knights of truth',* do not go snivelling back to religion or religious substitutes such as Wagner's music because, like Sisyphus pushing his rock up the mountain throughout all eternity, they can stand the pain.

In some passages Nietzsche presents a kind of argument for 'macho morality'. Since the definition of 'man' is 'rational animal', since reason is the 'human essence', it follows that the ascent of man through the superstitions embodied in religion and art to the scientific outlook of Enlightenment rationality represents his 'progressive humanisation'. The cultivation of 'reason and science, the highest powers of man' represents, that is to say, humanity's (Hegelian or Comtean) progress from infancy to full maturity, to the full realization of its distinctive powers.[91]

The argument, here, seems to be this. The human essence is rationality. Hence the unconditional pursuit of truth (i.e., being a completely rational being) is the fullest development of the human essence. Therefore, one ought to pursue truth at any price. However, once the argument is set out like this its weaknesses become obvious. First, though venerable, the definition of man as 'rational animal' is actually quite arbitrary. For even if rationality is, within the animal world, unique to humans, so are, for instance, religion, art, politics and laughter. So one might equally well define 'man' as 'artistic animal', 'religious animal', 'political animal', or 'animal with a sense of humour'. Laying this aside, however, the argument contains a bad mistake concerning rationality. If, that is, rationality is viewed (actually implausibly) as a capacity that sets us apart from other animals then what must be meant is *instrumental* rationality, the calculation of efficient means to desired ends. But being rational in this sense does *not* entail a commitment to truth at any price. If, for example, the loss of religion really would make us, even in the long run, more miserable than we are, then, if possible, we ought to try to preserve it. Nietzsche has missed this point because he has confused *complete* rationality with *pure* rationality, where a purely rational being is conceived as a pure thinker with no desires other than the desire to know. As it were, a brain without a body. But human beings are not like that.

* * *

Really, however, Nietzsche's dalliance with 'macho morality' is no more than a dalliance. For his main – certainly his best – thrust consists in arguing, first, that, on balance, the old, metaphysical culture has been seriously damaging to human well-being, and, second, that, *at least in the medium to long term*, Enlightenment reason and science, properly deployed, will make us better off, will produce a 'higher' culture in which human beings can live far more flourishing lives than in the old culture. He has, it seems to me, three basic lines of argument to demonstrate that the old, Christian culture has been seriously damaging to human health. The first has to do with its promotion of self-hatred, the second with its failure to address the real causes of suffering, the third with the incapacity of Christian ethics to promote social well-being.

Self-hatred. Christianity, says Nietzsche, 'serves the end of not merely casting suspicion on everything human but of oppressing, scourging and crucifying it'. Above all, of course,

---

* In *The Birth of Tragedy* Nietzsche praises Schopenhauer for his frank acknowledgment of the misery of human existence, referring to him as, 'after the manner of Dürer', a 'knight of . . . truth' (BT 20). The reference is to Dürer's *Knight, Death and Devil*, a print of which Nietzsche possessed and which, as he told Malwida, affected him deeply (KGB II.5 436).

it crucifies sex. (Lack of sexual release, he observes, generates sexual fantasy, so that the Christian saints suffered from many 'dirty' fantasies which they had to confess and then scourge themselves all the more.) The moral demands Christianity places on us are, *by design*, impossible to fulfil, the point being to make us feel '*as sinful as possible*' – and hence dependent on the Church's power of absolution, and hence, of course, on the priests. Christianity, to repeat, 'burden[s] the heart so as . . . to be able [partially] to relieve it'. The principal means of doing this is by creating role models it is impossible to live up to. (None of us can, in Jimmy Carter's words, avoid 'adultery in the heart', none of us can survive without killing at least small things.) The Christian compares himself with God (or Jesus) so that, even after the idea of God dies away, one is left with a 'feeling of depression' caused by 'the pang of conscience . . . the feeling of guilt'. The Christian is like Don Quixote, who underestimates his own courage because his head is filled with the 'miraculous deeds' of the heroes of medieval chivalry.[92]

Of course, this strategy of making us feel unspeakably sinful demands that we have free will – otherwise our sinfulness would be the creator's fault, not ours. This is why the denial of free will, and so of moral responsibility, is so important to Nietzsche: the real payoff is the denial of *guilt*. The abolition of free will is thus, in a way that curiously mimics Christianity itself, *redemptive*. 'The dismal, fear-inspiring dream' disappears (recall Fritz's terror before the statue of the knight in his father's church (p. 8 above)) and when one opens one's eyes one is once more in 'paradise'.[93] Discarding the myth of free will, humanity recovers its lost 'innocence'.[94]

Causes of Suffering. Given some form of suffering, Nietzsche observes, one can either 'alter its effects on our sensibility' or remove its cause. Christianity does the former – your worldly misfortune is God's chastising you but thereby revealing that he has you in the forefront of his mind, that you are the object of his (tough) love. Christianity 'narcoticises' (is, as Marx observed, 'the opium of the masses'), but in doing so it distracts one from seeking to remove the cause of suffering. If one takes a pain-killer the impetus to go to the dentist is weakened.[95] In the same vein, Nietzsche observes that education (he is thinking here of technical education) will be taken seriously only after belief in God has disappeared, just as medicine can only flourish as a science when one gives up belief in miracles.[96] Self-help will only flourish after we give up the idea of divine help.

One might, of course, object that many of the things that cause us to suffer – the certainty of death, the competitive structure of life – *cannot* have their causes removed by science, so that an 'altering of our sensibility' by a religion of some sort will always be necessary to a flourishing existence. Sensing this weakness in his position, Nietzsche prevaricates. On the one hand, he writes that due to the advance of science, 'the realm of implacable destiny is growing narrower and narrower – a bad outlook for priests and writers of tragedy',[97] which might be suggesting that the ultimate aim of science is human immortality. But on the other hand, he suggests that the aim of science is more modest: 'as little pain as possible, as long a life as possible, thus a kind of eternal bliss'.[98] But of course 'longer' life is no kind of 'eternal' life at all, so that the problem of death remains. As Nietzsche recognises in his mature philosophy, his position here is unsatisfactory. Something deep and serious needs to be said about death – as it had been in *The Birth of Tragedy*.

Ethics. Before Christianity appeared, Nietzsche writes, the standard of 'good' and 'evil' was custom, and custom was based on social utility. That was the standard, not the question of whether one's motives were 'egoistic' or 'unegoistic'. Provided one habitually submitted to custom one was a 'good' person; the question of whether one did so willingly or unwillingly was irrelevant. So pre-Christian moral judgments were based on the consequences of actions. If they were beneficial no one was interested in examining your motives. (Kant says that the shopkeeper who is honest because he believes honesty the best business policy deserves no moral credit, that only if he is honest because he sees it to be his *duty* is he morally admirable. If Nietzsche is right, a pre-Christian would see no moral difference between the two.)

Social utility is really the only rational basis for morals. And the fact is, Nietzsche argues, that the well-being of society at large is much better promoted by everyone pursuing his own 'highest good' than by 'pity-filled agitations and actions for the sake of others'. Of course crude individuals will have a crude understanding of their own good that will by no means promote general well-being. What we need is a cultivated understanding of our own 'highest advantage'.⁹⁹ As well as affirming psychological egoism, therefore, Nietzsche also affirms a form of 'ethical egoism': not only *are* we, we also *ought* to be, 'enlightened egoists' – as Nietzsche and Isabella von Prahlen agreed while sightseeing in Pisa (p. 230 above). We ought to pursue that which best promotes our happiness – not that which seems to, but that which *really does* promote it.

It is not, then, Christian altruism but rather enlightened egoism, Nietzsche claims, which best promotes the welfare of society as a whole. Why does he believe this? The only clues are his identification of pursuing one's 'highest good' with 'cultivating the personal in us', 'mak[ing] oneself a complete *person*'.¹⁰⁰ To find out what he has in mind, here, some fishing around in other texts is called for.

Through all phases of his career, Nietzsche speaks repeatedly of one's *Aufgabe*, one's 'task' or 'mission'. In *Schopenhauer as Educator* one's 'true self' is identified as a 'task' set 'high above' one (p. 195 above). In *Zarathustra* the eponymous hero says 'what does happiness matter to me . . . I am striving after my work', to which his animals reply, 'but you are basking in a sky-blue lake of happiness', which forces him to admit that they know him as well as he knows himself.¹⁰¹ Part of what is involved, here, is the so-called 'paradox of happiness': just as playing the piano or typing goes better if one avoids thinking about where the fingers are going, so happiness is best achieved not by aiming directly at it but rather by absorbing oneself in commitment to some task *other than* the achievement of one's own happiness.

Nietzsche writes to Malwida, on his way back to Basel from Sorrento in July 1877, that in spite of his alienation from the life of a professor and dread of once more having to lecture, he is going back because he 'can't stand it not to have the feeling of being useful; and the Baselers are the only ones who allow me to feel that I am'.¹⁰² (Soon he will change his mind, deciding that he is more useful to humanity as a 'free' writer.) This is a fundamental (and to my mind correct) theme in all of Nietzsche's writing: to cultivate oneself fully, as an integrated person, one needs a life-unifying 'task' – in Sartre's language a 'fundamental project' – that gives unity and coherence to all one's lesser projects. Moreover, this task has to be *other*-regarding, other-benefiting. We might put his point by saying that living a truly satisfying human life is a matter of being, as it were, a 'professional'. One cannot be an actor without an audience, a doctor without patients, or a lawyer without clients. And one cannot be fulfilled as an actor or doctor without feeling one is doing a good job, benefiting one's audience or patients. In a similar way, Nietzsche holds, I think, that genuine happiness is a matter of having an other-directed, life-defining task – a life 'meaning' – and feeling you are making a good job of it; making, as we say, 'a contribution'. It is, then, truly enlightened egoism, rather than sighing with ineffectual, Christian pity or gritting one's teeth with Kantian dutifulness, that produces productive commitment to the welfare of one's community at large.

Nietzsche's Higher Culture

We come now to, ultimately, the most important, the constructive, side of *Human*. We need, Nietzsche has argued, to develop a new, 'enlightened', *thoroughly* post-Christian society, a 'higher' culture based on 'reason'. What will it look like?

We live, he says, in the 'age of comparisons'. With the new technologies of travel and communication – railways, the telegraph and the prospect of airships[103] – we are no longer prisoners of the enclosed, hermetically sealed national cultures of the past. We live, rather, in Wagner's 'paper culture', amidst a whole 'polyphony' of fragments of past and different cultures. Earlier, we saw, Nietzsche deplored this 'fairground motley' of modern culture, but here he looks on its bright side. The (as we now say) 'multicultural' character of modernity gives us the opportunity of consciously *choosing* a new culture on the basis of comparison, of mixing and matching.[104] What, then, should we choose?

First, the new culture should be purged, of course, of all the deplorable features of modernity. It will, for example, avoid the 'comedy' of unreason whereby (as in Goethe's fable of the Sorcerer's Apprentice) human beings invent machines to make their lives easier but end up as industrial (or electronic) slaves of their own technology, mere 'material for heating up the great machine', which then becomes an 'end in itself'.[105] Second, the new age will be one in which culture is not threatened by the 'means to culture'.[106] Nietzsche is expressing, here, his opposition to the 'big', all-controlling state, whether it be Bismarck's Prussia or the 'totalising' state he thinks would arrive were socialism to have its way. Influenced by Burckhardt's account of the Italian Renaissance,[107] Nietzsche sees a degree of social anarchy as necessary to the emergence of the exceptional individual. An all-controlling state produces mere 'herd' types, robotic, Orwellian conformists: 'The state is a prudent institution for the protection of individuals from one another: if it is completed and perfected too far it will in the end enfeeble the individual and, indeed, dissolve him – that is, thwart the original purpose of the state'.[108]

Then again, in contrast to at least Prussian modernity, there will be no conscript army, since conscription is a guaranteed way of killing off the bravest and the best, precisely those whom society needs for 'a good and abundant posterity'. It kills them off because they naturally gravitate to the most dangerous leadership positions.[109] Nietzsche mentions the Greeks in this connexion, but is surely thinking, too, of the Pforta alumni who died on Bismarck's battlefields. (Shortly, we shall see, he decides that standing, national armies should be abolished altogether.)

Then again, in contrast to the frenetic pace of modernity and to its obsession with activity and production ('outputs', as we say in the modern university), the new culture will place a high value on 'idleness', will make a great deal of space for the '*vita contemplativa*'. Active men are 'generic creatures', herd types: since they act rather than think, they have no chance of thinking, in particular, that there might be something wrong with the culture which they inhabit and which shapes their actions. Only thinkers have a chance of challenging the status quo, of becoming unique individuals – 'free spirits', in other words.[110]

The Theory of Cultural Evolution

Nietzsche's defence of 'idleness' raises the question of the importance of free spirits. Why, exactly, does he value them so highly? *Human*'s fundamental aim, we have seen, is a second 'Reformation', a paradigm shift to a new culture.[111] It is, moreover, a book 'for free spirits'. Evidently, therefore, free spirits are the key element in bringing about this paradigm shift. But how and why should this be so?

Nietzsche observes that 'fettered' spirits act out of habit rather than reason. One does not become a Christian as the result of a reflective choice following a course in comparative religion, but rather in the way in which those born in wine-drinking countries become wine-drinkers.[112] (The geographical clustering of religions shows that Nietzsche is, in general, right.) Fettered spirits, he continues, regard free spirits as dangerous because they assume that their established 'faith' is what best promotes communal utility. But precisely because their traditional practices are based on faith rather than reason, they are sometimes wrong. In a metaphor, the community may find itself in a forest and unable to find its way out. This is where the free spirit may be useful – or the 'genius', a word now to be understood 'without any flavour of the mythological or religious': the free spirit or genius is 'original' in that sometimes he 'discovers a new path which no one else knows'. [113]

Somewhat perversely, Nietzsche speaks of this process as 'progress' to a 'higher culture' through 'degeneration'. 'History', he writes,

> teaches us that the branch of a people [*Volk*] that preserves itself best is that in which most people have, as a consequence of the sameness of their shared habitual and undiscussable principles, that is to say, as a consequence of their shared faith, a living sense of community.[114]

Hence the preservation of a community demands that fettered spirits are always the 'rule', free spirits the 'exception'.[115] However,

> the danger facing these strong communities founded on similarly constituted, firm-charactered individuals is that of the gradually increasing inherited stupidity that haunts all stability like its shadow. It is the more unfettered, uncertain and [according to the prevailing morality] morally weaker individuals upon whom *spiritual progress* depends in such communities: it depends on the men who attempt new things and, in general, many things. Countless numbers of this kind perish on account of their weakness without producing any visible effect; but in general, and especially when they leave posterity, they effect a loosening up and from time to time inflict an injury on the stable element of a community. It is precisely at this injured and weakened spot that the whole body is, as it were, *inoculated* with something new; its strength must, however, be, as a whole, sufficient to receive this new thing into its blood and to assimilate it. Degenerate natures are of the highest significance wherever progress is to be effected. Every progress of the whole has to be preceded by a partial weakening. The strongest natures *preserve* the type, the weaker help it to *evolve*.

To make clear that, as *types*, the fettered and free spirits are of *equal* value, Nietzsche ends the passage by saying that 'only when there is securely founded and guaranteed long duration is a steady evolution and ennobling inoculation at all possible: though the dangerous companion of all duration, established authority, will, to be sure, usually resist it'.[116] Oppression and resistance, reaction and reform, represent, therefore, not isolated periods of turbulence but rather a permanent ('agonistic') tension in, the permanent dynamic of, a healthy society.

Given this account of cultural evolution, which, as we saw, made its first, embryonic, appearance in the third *Untimely Meditation* (pp. 197–8 above), it becomes very natural to describe the free spirit as the 'random mutation' – Nietzsche uses the word 'mutilation'.[117] As we know from *The Birth of Tragedy*, a community can only thrive, can only exist as a community, through possession of a shared communal 'faith'. But such a faith can become a 'stupidity' when it disables the community from meeting the challenges presented by an ever-changing environment. (Some people argue, for example, that the 'faith' that is Western democracy is incapable of meeting the challenge of global warming.) Hence a healthy society needs pathfinders, those who reject the established way of doing things and herald a new form of life, 'invent new life-possibilities to weigh against the old ones'.[118]

This account of social evolution is pure (social) Darwinism. Strangely, though, and this is the perverse element in the discussion, Nietzsche offers it as an *objection* to Darwinism – which, remember, five years earlier, in 1873, he had held to be 'true'.[119] Since it is 'precisely the weaker natures' that contribute to social evolution, he claims, 'the celebrated struggle for existence does not seem to me the only theory by which the progress or strengthening of a ... race can be explained ... A people that becomes somewhat weak and fragile but as a whole is still strong and healthy' is most successful.[120] This is a really very weak objection and confirms the suspicion that Nietzsche only knew Darwin from second-hand sources. Darwinism holds merely that the *most adaptive* species survive best. It is not at all committed to the 'survival of the fittest', where the fittest or strongest species is identified as that which best preserves its system of internal organisation.

Rational Living: Slavery, Punishment, Euthanasia, Eugenics, Conservation

What the 'idleness' of the reflective free spirit – to whom the future direction of society is entrusted – means is freedom from the need to earn a living. And this, of course, comes at a cost. If some are to be 'idle' others must support them. So a rational society will be *hierarchical*. Such a hierarchy, however, is not exploitation but merely the delegation of manual labour to those who suffer least from it.[121] This suggests that Nietzsche endorses a benevolent kind of slavery: the ancient slave (Diogenes was one), he points out, probably correctly, worked less hard and lived more happily and securely on the whole than the nineteenth-century industrial worker, ruthlessly exploited in the Dickensian world of the machine society.[122]

As I pointed out earlier, the need-for-slavery argument seems to be refuted by the washing machine. But actually, by 1877, Nietzsche has realised this, since in the notebooks he says that there will always have to be people to do the 'hard and rough work *so long as they cannot be relieved of it by machines*'.[123] It would seem then that slavery is not, after all, an absolutely necessary feature of Nietzsche's 'utopia'.[124] Given that he abhors industrial slavery, warns against our becoming 'slaves of the machine', it would seem that in the

Human period he defends 'slavery' as at most a contingent and temporary necessity. (Later on, he will change his mind, discovering a different ground for defending 'slavery in some sense'.)

* * *

Since there is no free will, 'our crime against criminals is that we treat them as scoundrels'.[125] Since there is, that is to say, no 'guilt' in the criminal, since his action is the necessary consequence of his environment and heredity, there should be no element of retribution, of delivering 'just desserts' to the offender. The sole function of punishment is to deter – though the inclusion of capital punishment in the armoury of deterrents can never be justified.[126]

Self-chosen euthanasia will be sanctioned by the rational society, as it was in the ancient world. Since we have given up religious prohibitions, taking the path of the 'free death'[127] rather than waiting for the utter collapse of the bodily 'machine' represents a 'victory of reason'.[128]

Then again there will be a whole range of more rational choices concerning 'the propagation of men' (eugenics), nutrition, and education.* And we will learn 'to manage the earth as a whole [more] economically'.[129] (Already Nietzsche sees the need for environmental conservation. Amazingly, in the notebooks of 1882, he anticipates global warming: 'One should preserve . . . forests. It is true: through the clearing and cutting down of the forest the earth is becoming warmer'.)[130] In general, then, in Nietzsche's 'new, conscious culture', reason will triumph over tradition. Given, in addition to these 'rational' reforms, Nietzsche's unwavering support for brothels, one senses, in these prescriptions, much of the spirit of twentieth-century Holland and Scandinavia.

Religion and Art in a Higher Culture

Though Nietzsche's rhetoric gives the impression that *Human* is an assault on all forms of religion and art, this impression is misleading. In reality, it is only *metaphysical* forms that are shown the door.

Nietzsche writes – surprisingly in view of his new enthusiasm for science – that after the joy of first discovery, science does not, in fact, add pleasure to life, indeed 'deprives us of more and more pleasure through casting suspicion on metaphysics, religion and art, sources of joy to which mankind owes almost all of its humanity'. For this reason 'a higher culture must give man a double-brain, as it were a brain with two chambers, one for the reception of science, the other for that of non-science'. This, he says, is a requirement of 'health'. If it is not done, 'illusion, error and fantasy, because they give pleasure, will return and drive out the scientific interest in truth'.[131] It is, he continues, a sign of 'strength and flexibility' to be able to 'dance' between the scientific and the artistic-religious perspectives.[132] A higher culture must, then, construct 'so large a hall of culture' that both science and non-science

---

* As argued in *The Future of Our Educational Institutions* (pp. 142–7 above), the dumbing down of higher education for the masses will cease; high schools will be genuinely *high* schools, 'elitist' (or 'meritocratic') institutions reserved for the cultivation of the creative free spirits our cultural health demands. It should by now be clear that Nietzsche's theory of cultural evolution and his educational 'elitism' are mutually reinforcing.

'can be accommodated within it, even if at opposite ends'.*,¹³³ It seems, then, that, after all, both religion and art will have a role to play in the 'rational' society. What are these roles? A clue is provided by the remark in the notebooks that though science can discover means it cannot determine goals.¹³⁴ I shall discuss first religion and then art.

In discussing the origin of 'the religious cult' Nietzsche says, it will be remembered, that prehistoric humanity turned to animism because it had no conception of natural causation, of an order in nature independent of the free wills of human or super-human beings. Terrified by the power of natural forces, it attempted to propitiate them in the way one propitiates powerful human beings. Yet at the end of the discussion he says that Greek religion, the religion of the Olympians, was different from this, was of a more 'noble' origin, not being born out of fear. The Homeric Greeks had no need to propitiate animist gods since they had the conception of *moira*, fate, the conception of a causal order independent of, and above, even the gods.¹³⁵ (Wagner embodies this idea in the *Ring*: the 'fate'-weaving Norns are beyond even Wotan's control.)

Pursuing the theme of the 'nobility' of Greek religion, Nietzsche explains that the Greeks saw their gods not, on the Jewish or Christian model, as masters, but 'only [as] the reflection, as it were, of the most successful exemplars of their own caste'. They saw them as relatives (he could have pointed out that they often interbred with mortals), as an aristocracy that represented 'an ideal, not an antithesis to their own natures'.¹³⁶ The Greeks saw themselves and the gods as 'two castes, living side by side, one nobler and mightier, and one less noble; but both somehow belong together in their origins and are of *one* species; they have no need to be ashamed of one another'.¹³⁷ This is how Greek sculpture is to be understood: the statue in the temple honours man and god together, honours, as we might put it, *man as god.*¹³⁸ Greek religion is, then, a 'humanistic' religion; it is the religion of Michelangelo's big-muscled (as opposed to El Greco's non-muscled) heroes, the religion of the Soviet glorifications of soldiers and workers.

Notice that Olympian religion is un-'metaphysical'. The gods do not inhabit a supernatural world but live 'side by side' with us in one world. In *The Birth of Tragedy* Nietzsche claims that 'the foundations of art and community, myth and morality, are necessarily and inseparably intertwined', adding that religious myth is what 'constitutes the unity of a community and culture', 'the noble core of [a] ... people's character.'¹³⁹ The Olympian myth, by comprising a pantheon of role models (models whose all-too-human qualities allow one to identify with, rather than being intimidated by, them), showed the Greeks what it was to be a proper Greek, what was the right way to live.

This – Wagnerian – theme is reaffirmed in *Human*. Without the shared religion first articulated by Homer, there would have been no Greece:

> The greatest fact in the cultivation of Greece remains that Homer became pan-Hellenic so early ... For Homer, by centralising, made everything level and dissolved the more serious instincts for independence ... All great spiritual forces exercise ... a repressive effect; but it makes a difference whether it is Homer or the Bible ... that tyrannises over mankind.¹⁴⁰

---

* It is temptingly neat to represent Nietzsche's turn to positivism as an affirmation of precisely the 'Socratism' condemned in *The Birth of Tragedy*. But this, it can now be seen, is an oversimplification. For whereas Socratism affirms the adequacy of science to satisfy every human need – it can know 'and even correct being' (p. 132 above) – Nietzsche's positivism rejects that. Nietzsche's positivism is not scientism.

Nietzsche argued in *The Birth* that 'Socratism' – the view that nothing other than science is needed for a flourishing life – killed myth in ancient Greece and is doing so again in modernity. Since community can exist only through shared, religious myth, Socratism is the cause of modernity's loss of community. In *Human*, as we have seen, Nietzsche continues to value 'a living sense of community'[141] as much as he did in *The Birth*, continues to view the 'motley' cultural chaos of modernity as something to be overcome. Given this, as well as his unswerving admiration of the Greeks, it is clear that what he wants in his higher culture is something modelled on the religion of the Greeks – a religion that, though unmetaphysical, performs the task he believes only religion can perform: that of creating and preserving community. It is worth observing that Nietzsche's conception of what a religion should do exactly matches the sociologist Emile Durkheim's conception of what a religion *is*. Durkheim defines 'religion' as 'a unified system of beliefs and practices relative to sacred things...which unite in one single moral community...all those who adhere to them'.[142] For Nietzsche, too, 'moral community' is precisely what religion is concerned with.

* * *

Nietzsche writes, 'art has taught us for thousands of years to look upon life in any of its forms with interest and pleasure, and to educate our sensibilities so that we at last cry [in Goethe's words] "life, however it may be, is good"'.[143] What he has in mind, here, is 'Apollonian' art, art which teaches us to find joy not 'behind' but rather *in* the natural world. This suggests that although metaphysical art is expelled from the higher culture, Apollonian art remains.

This, indeed, is really *demanded*, if a 'Greek' form of religion is to be preserved. For as both history and, as we have seen, *The Birth* tell us, art and religion are 'necessarily and inseparably intertwined'. Nietzsche makes this clear the following year in *Assorted Opinions and Maxims*, published as an 'appendix' to *Human, All-Too-Human*. Art, he says, ought to be dedicated to 'signposting the future'. The artist is not required to draw up a blueprint for 'a world in which nations and societies would prosper better' – that is the thinker's, Nietzsche's, task. Rather, he will

> emulate the artists of earlier [Greek] times who imaginatively developed the existing images of the gods and *imaginatively develop* a beautiful image of man; he will scent out those cases in which, in the *midst* of our modern world and reality and without any artificial withdrawal from or warding off of this world, the great and beautiful soul is still possible, still able to embody itself in the harmonious and well-proportioned, thus acquiring visibility, duration and the status of a model, and in so doing through the excitation of envy and emulation, help create the future.[144]

The 'good poet' of the future will, Nietzsche adds, depict '*only reality*', he will avoid those 'superstitious, half-mendacious, faded subjects' – *metaphysical* subjects, in other words – favoured by poets of the past. But he will depict 'by no means every reality! – He will depict a select reality!'[145] The creation of role models – the 'monumental' figures of the second *Untimely Meditation* – requires, in a word, the 'illusionistic' powers of Apollonian art, the simultaneous highlighting of the noble and veiling of the ignoble ('lying' in the interests of a higher truth).

This – right in the midst of the positivist revolt against Wagnerian romanticism – returns us to Wagner; to the community-'collecting' artwork of the early Wagner, of the 'ideal' Wagner as represented in *Wagner at Bayreuth*. In the notebooks of the period, Nietzsche is quite explicit that his break with Wagner is by no means absolute: 'One should never forget', he writes, 'that in the second half of the nineteenth century – admittedly not precisely in the way of good and insightful people – Wagner brought art into consciousness as an important and magnificent phenomenon'.[146] And again: 'If only Wagner would think otherwise about things: as it is, it is up to us to be better Wagnerians than Wagner'.[147]

Globalization

Nietzsche observes, with his often startling insight into the future, that though princely dynasties and their allies seek to artificially preserve national hostilities, transport and information technology is slowly but inexorably abolishing national differences, is producing a mixed 'European man'. We should, he says, welcome this process and 'not be afraid to proclaim oneself simply *a good European*'.* Not merely welcome, but be prepared to extend the process to global proportions: we must 'prepare the way for that still distant state of things in which the good Europeans will come into possession of their great task: the direction and supervision of the total culture of the earth'.[148] Why do we need, first, the coming into being of a unitary European culture and, second, the globalization of that culture so that the European community becomes a global community?

One consideration concerns economic activity. Since the (now as then) fashionable theory of 'free trade' is 'naïve', a degree of planning of world economic activity, the setting of 'ecumenical goals', is necessary to best contribute to the 'requirements of mankind'.[149] (One can extend the thought to global warming, not to mention the financial meltdown of 2008–9. Since the problem is global, only global co-operation can solve it.) Nietzsche's overriding concern, however, is the abolition of war.

The dream of enduring global peace goes back at least to the Roman Empire, to the *Pax Romana*. Kant dreamt of it in a pamphlet designed to show the way to a 'Perpetual Peace among Nations', the British Empire dreamt of a *Pax Britannica*, and after the First World War (supposedly 'the war to end all wars') the dream would lead to the creation of the League of Nations and then the United Nations.

Intensified by his experiences on the killing-fields of the Franco-Prussian war, Nietzsche shares this dream of world peace – an affinity with Christianity, and in particular with the spirit of Christmas, which, we noted, he never lost: the yearning for a time when '*all* men are to share the experience of those shepherds who saw the heavens brighten above them and heard the words: "on earth peace, good will toward men"'. Such a time has not yet come, he adds, because 'it is still *the age of the individual*', of individual people and nations.[150]

---

* HH 475. Nietzsche always speaks of 'the European' as the object of his focal concern, but he means what we now mean by 'the West'. He writes, 'Europe comprises much more territory than geographical Europe...America especially belongs to it, insofar as it is the daughter-land of our culture. On the other hand the cultural concept 'Europe' does not include all of geographical Europe. It includes only those peoples and ethnic minorities who possess Greek, Roman, Jewish and Christian culture as their common past' (WS 215).

Why does the dream of perpetual peace require global community, a unified global culture? Because, Nietzsche seems to argue, leaving aside imperialism (which *a fortiori* will come to an end if Europe takes over the direction of the 'total culture of the earth'), the ground of warfare is militarization, which is based on paranoia between nations, which in turn presupposes an absolute distinction between 'them' and 'us'. Warfare is fundamentally, Nietzsche seems to say, a 'clash of civilizations'. Therefore, only a global culture expressing itself in some form of world government can offer a hope of demilitarization, which is the only possible 'means to real peace'.[151]

Of course, if world peace did break out, there would be a problem of what to do with humanity's innate aggression and its need for those 'earthquake shuddering[s] of the soul', the thrills, excitements and sublime experiences of warfare. This is a problem for culture – warfare always represents the 'hibernation of culture'.[152] The cultural solution, as we know, is the sublimation of bad into good Eris, warfare into 'competition' (pp. 140–1 above). This can take more or less productive forms. Under the *Pax Romana* the Romans took up 'animal baiting, gladiatorial combat and the persecution of Christians', whereas present-day Englishmen, 'who seem on the whole to have given up warfare', go in for 'perilous journeys of discovery, navigations, mountain climbing' – extreme sports.[153]

The Problem of Free Will

Is Nietzsche's 'higher' culture really higher? Is it one in which we really would live more flourishing lives than we do now? In many respects I think we would. Two crucial issues, however, need to be raised. Can human life really flourish without the belief in free will, and can it flourish without belief in some kind of metaphysics, or as I prefer to say, 'transcendence'?

What would life be like without the belief in free will, without the belief that we possess freedom, in the radical sense Nietzsche discusses? Nietzsche suggests that free will is nothing more than a piece of bad propaganda, a fiction invented by priests in order to be able to make us feel sinful. But while this may be one route to the idea, it is hardly the only one. Jean-Paul Sartre makes radical freedom the heart of his 'phenomenological' description of the 'life-world', the world-understanding in which human beings live and move and have their everyday being, and he is far from being a priestly type. Sartre sums up his view of the centrality of radical freedom in the slogan-definition of 'Existentialism': 'existence before essence'. We come into existence with no predetermined 'essence' or character. Within the limits imposed by biology and history (I cannot choose to be a pro basketball player if I am five foot five or an astronaut if I am born into the thirteenth century), what our character will be is entirely dependent on our own, undetermined choice. And one might well feel that Sartre is right: that existence without at least the possibility of radical self-determination would be unbearable, that a life condemned, from the beginning, to imprisonment in a predetermined character would not be worth living. The fact that, even in this postreligious age, we cling so strongly to the – for Nietzsche – 'illusion' of freedom suggests this to be so.

Nietzsche addresses this problem in *The Wanderer and His Shadow* (destined to be incorporated into an expanded *Human, All-Too-Human* in 1886). Only confused thinking, he suggests, renders the abandonment of free will threatening. People find it so because they fall into 'Islamic fatalism', the reification of fate as a power against which we may struggle but which will always be too powerful for us. From this they derive the demoralising conclusion that all action is futile since how the future will be is already set in concrete. Correctly, Nietzsche points out that this is an error. It is an error because

> you yourself, poor fearful man, are the implacable *moira* [fate] enthroned even above the gods that govern all that happens; you are the blessing and the curse and in any event the fetters in which the strongest lies captive; in you the whole future of man is predetermined: it is of no use for you to shudder when you look at yourself.[154]

Determinism, in other words, does not render one's actions futile since those actions *belong to* the process that creates the future. We cannot be oppressed by fate as an external force because we are, as it were, on the inside of fate. The question arises, however, as to who 'we' are. If I am 'fate', then, rather than identifying myself with a brief temporal span as I normally do, I have to identify myself with the entire history of the universe and with its entire future. The abandonment of free will does not necessarily render life worthless. But it does require a radically new understanding of personal identity – a transcendence of the normal understanding of the ego. As we shall see, the mature Nietzsche accepts and celebrates this new understanding.

On Man's Need for Metaphysics

As Nietzsche recognises in discussing the 'dream of immortality' evoked by Beethoven's music (p. 251 above), the 'metaphysical need' is above all the need for some kind of comfort in the face of our primal terror, death. The assurance of death's non-finality, of continued existence in some metaphysical realm, is the solution to the problem offered by almost all religions. Nietzsche thus confronts a pressing problem: how is the 'rational', post-metaphysical society to deal with our need for comfort in the face of death?

Nietzsche's treatment of this problem is unsatisfactory. One strategy is to ignore – evade – the topic as far as possible. Unlike *The Birth of Tragedy*, which faced the question of death head-on, one has to look hard to find the topic even mentioned in *Human*. When it is touched on, the treatment is generally brief, shallow, and evasive (as in, for example, the discussion of euthanasia above).

Only superstition, Nietzsche claims, leads us to think of death as 'a very important thing' (in a letter to von Gersdorff he calls it 'the greatest triviality in the world'),[155] as the crossing of a bridge of tremendous significance.[156] But this suggestion that the only reason we find death important is that we believe it the crossing of a bridge from one world to another is quite wrong. Whether or not we believe in an afterlife, death is of tremendous importance *because it is the end of life and because our most fundamental, biologically programmed, impulse is the will to life*. Death is, therefore, the denial of our most fundamental desire. Without some comfort in the face of its inescapability, without learning, somehow, to die what Martin Heidegger calls 'the good death', our lives (as, in the period of the *Untimely Meditations*, Nietzsche was willing to admit) will be filled with repressed anxiety in the face of which they cannot fully flourish. As observed earlier, Nietzsche thinks that religion 'alters our sensibility' with respect to human anguish, whereas what we should be doing is removing its cause (p. 258 above). The needs catered for by religion, he claims, are 'not immutable: they can be *weakened* and *exterminated*'.[157] But not death. Death, and our abhorrence of it, *is* 'immutable'. It is, therefore, *essential* to alter our primal sensibility towards it in some way. What *Human* should have done was to search for a *non-metaphysical* mode of alteration. That it does not is a deficiency, one that will be remedied in later works.

PART THREE

The Nomad

15

The Wanderer and His Shadow

THE APPEARANCE of *Human, All-Too-Human* in May 1878 coincided with a yet further deterioration of Nietzsche's health which, the previous March, had reached such a state that he was finally released from all teaching obligations to the grammar school. His health cannot have been improved by a weird letter from the formerly admired Siegfried Lipiner (p. 237 above) virtually demanding to run the life of his 'dearly beloved',[1] which Nietzsche rightly described as an 'unbelievable impertinence'.[2] Neither can his health have been improved by the reactions to his radically new line of thinking.

Reception of *Human, All-Too-Human*

Nietzsche's nervousness concerning the book's reception was entirely justified. About the only positive response came from Burckhardt, who, delighted that Nietzsche was 'healed' of Wagner, who had always offended his classical taste, called the work a 'sublime book'.[3] In Russia the book was banned outright. Much more serious, however, was the Bayreuth reaction, about which he had been most nervous.

Schmeitzner reported that Wagner claimed to have read only a few pages 'in order not to upset the delightful impression left by [Nietzsche's] earlier works'.[4] But this did not stop him issuing a counterblast in the September edition of the *Bayreuther Blätter*: though Nietzsche is not mentioned by name, Wagner's article, entitled 'The Public and Popularity', held up to ridicule a book supposedly called *Menschliches und Unmenschliches* [The Human and Inhuman]. Cosima's reaction was more vicious: she blamed Rée – 'A thumbing through a few significant sentences was enough and I laid the book aside…Much accounts for the sad book! Finally Israel came into it in the form of Dr. Rée, very smooth, very cool, simultaneously captivated and subjugated by Nietzsche, in truth, however, outsmarting him, a microcosm of the relation of Judea and Germany'. Elizabeth notes that Cosima's reaction was representative of the Wagner circle: 'the anti-Semites started the theory that Rée was the evil Semitic principle which had diverted Nietzsche, the honest Aryan visionary, into verbal hair-splitting'. And then she adds, in one of her occasional flashes of insight, insight into the fundamentally constructive nature of the book, that 'people entirely overlooked the warm under-current of humanity in the book' – a current directly opposed, as Elizabeth sees it, to Rée's arid views.⁵

Even those not given to anti-Semitism saw the work as the product of Rée's baleful influence. Reinhardt von Seydlitz complained to Nietzsche that 'everything is much too réeal' in the book (this is the probable origin of the term 'réealism'),⁶ and Rohde complained that he felt transported from a hot bath (the 'heat' of Nietzsche's romantic period) into an ice-room. He complained that Nietzsche's soul had been replaced by Rée's and went on to assert that the lack of 'accountability' Nietzsche proposes implied moral complacency, and that egoism is something Nietzsche himself strives against and so cannot genuinely endorse.⁷ Even Nietzsche's formerly devoted student Adolf Baumgartner, son of his good friend Marie, loathed the book, loathed, as he saw it, its attempt to reduce the complexity of the human heart to 'a few formulas'.

Malwida von Meysenbug did not like the book either, but expressed her dislike in a deep and prophetic way: 'You will go through many phases in your philosophy', she wrote, since

> unlike Rée, you are not born to analysis: you need to create artistically and though you strain against it, your genius will lead you to the same thing as *The Birth of Tragedy*, only with no more metaphysics...Unlike Rée you cannot use the scalpel to lay apart legs and arms and say, thus is the human being put together.⁸

Malwida's prediction, I shall argue, is precisely where Nietzsche's philosophy ends – the fundamental position of *The Birth of Tragedy*, minus metaphysics. Malwida, however, shared in the universal sense that *Human* was excessively influenced by Rée. Nietzsche tried to pass off the accusation with a joke, writing to Rée to congratulate him on his 'new authorship'.⁹ In fact, though, as I (and Elizabeth) have suggested, there is a constructive spirit in the work that is in fundamental contrast to Rée's, as it seems to me, negative cast of mind. Lou Salomé, who, as we shall see, was in a better position to compare Rée with Nietzsche than anyone else, makes essentially this judgment, too. Rée, she says, was a 'cold, undeviating, lucidly logical, scientific thinker' whose 'brusque one-sidedness' was the opposite of 'Nietzsche's artistic, philosophical and religious wealth of spirit'. (Interestingly, she adds that Rée had the 'keener mind' of the two, which is probably correct: technical philosophical analysis, I have already observed, was not Nietzsche's strong suit.)¹⁰

* * *

As soon as the semester ended, Nietzsche left Basel's heat and humidity for Grindelwald, high in the Berner Oberland at the foot of the Eiger and Wetterhorn. He desperately needed to recover from the appalling strain of trying to lecture amidst repeated attacks of headaches, eye pain, and vomiting together with the anguish of not being able to do his 'real' work. 'I am off', he wrote Marie Baumgartner at the end of July 1878, 'to the mountains, to the highest solitude, off, I'd like to say, to myself'¹¹ – off, in other words, to the 'real' task that constituted his 'real' self. Unfortunately the three weeks in Grindelwald did nothing for his health. Writing home to express his delight that his mother had finally been able to buy the Naumburg house she had been renting, 18 Weingarten, he observed that being seven thousand feet above sea level had done nothing for his health, so that he had become 'almost suspicious' of mountain air.[12] Evidently he had been testing some theory to the effect that thin mountain air would improve his condition. Since it had not worked, he descended to Interlaken, a mere fifteen hundred feet above sea level, where he remained for several weeks.

Back in Basel in mid-September for what would prove to be the final semester of his academic life, Nietzsche moved to a new apartment, 11 Bachletten Strasse, in an unfashionable, semi-rural suburb right on the outskirts of town, which he chose in order to maintain his 'medicinal' regimen of long, solitary walks. It was here that he completed the first of the two works he eventually published as Volume II of *Human, All-Too-Human*.

Assorted Opinions and Maxims

Finished at the end of December 1878, this 'appendix' to the work 'for free spirits' appeared in March of the following year. As suggested by the rather weak title and by the fact that it was published as an addendum to *Human, All-Too-Human*, this is a fairly random collection of bits and pieces that did not find their way into the main work. Since I have already discussed many of the more important sections of the work I shall be brief.

In general terms *Assorted Opinions* shares the same Theoretical outlook as the main work: rejection of the 'metaphysical', naturalism and universal causal determinism with the consequent understanding of the individual as, in a striking image, nothing but a 'poor wave in the necessary wave-play of becoming',[13] a mere ripple in the great ocean of causes and effects. Hence, as before, free will is rejected – only vanity prevents us acknowledging the 'unfreedom of the will'[14] – and, with it, moral responsibility: if anything were to be accounted a 'sinner' it would have to be not the 'wave' but rather the entire 'wave-play of becoming'.[15] As before, Nietzsche appears still to affirm psychological hedonism – a virtue, he says, becomes fixed in our character only to the extent that its exercise is experienced as pleasurable.[16]

Within this framework Nietzsche offers a miscellany of observations, many of which represent advice on how to cultivate free-spiritedness. For example: don't believe *anything* you read in the papers,[17] it is best if one has an 'inner fire' that renders both art and wine unnecessary,[18] the individual who follows conventional morality 'outvotes himself',[19] and so on. Some of the aphorisms have an autobiographical flavour: as already noted, the remark that psychological observers are bashful because they know that as soon as people notice their inclination they will be taken for 'spies and traitors' provides insight into his own social reserve, commented on by many acquaintances.

One significant change in *Assorted Opinions* is the disappearance of what I called the 'macho morality' of affirming the value of the 'scientific' observation of human nature, whatever its consequences for human life. Nietzsche now says that the utility of the 'unconditional search for truth' is so clear that we are obliged to accept the minor harm it occasionally causes.[20] In other words, though he is still advocating that truth be pursued unconditionally, the reason seems to be that, as a *general policy*, it best promotes the flourishing of human life. Nietzsche now appears, therefore, to reject the idea that 'truth' is a higher value than 'life', to accept that the quest for knowledge must justify itself in the court of life.

Another departure from *Human* is the observation that it is a mistake to take 'psychological observations' as absolute, since they are in fact only approximately true and often valid for only a decade.[21] As, I suspect, does the departure from 'macho morality', this appears to mark the beginning of Nietzsche's distancing himself, intellectually speaking, from Rée. Whereas the latter, with his bleakly Schopenhauerian outlook, presents his 'black' observations on human nature as eternally valid, Nietzsche's constructive and more optimistic spirit holds out the possibility of the removal, or at least transfiguration, of the dark side of humanity.

Leaving Basel

As 1878 drew to a close, Nietzsche's health became so bad that for the first time in his career he began to cancel university lectures. And not at all beneficial to his physical condition was the fact that, by now, the tension between profession and calling, between 'taskmaster' and 'goddess and lover', was constantly at the front of his mind.[22] On top of everything else, he fell on some black ice and developed an infected finger, which proved difficult to heal.

The beginning of the following year saw repeated attacks of headaches and vomiting, one attack lasting nine days, with his eyes reduced to a condition of near-uselessness. As a result, he developed a violent, as he called it, 'Baselophobia'.[23] With its alternation between freezing cold and humid heat, it was Basel, he decided, that had deprived him of his health and would, if he stayed there much longer, claim his life.[24]

In March, too scared to make his usual move to the high Alps – 'they looked like a snow-covered grave', he scribbled on a postcard to Overbeck[25] – he attempted a spa 'cure' in Geneva. But there was no improvement. Elizabeth saw him when he returned to Basel and recalls a brother she hardly recognised, 'a weary man, prematurely aged'. With solid common sense, she attributed his condition not to the Basel climate but to his dietary asceticism: 'he lived entirely on fruit, rusks [*Zwieback*], vegetable soups specially made for invalids, and cold roast meat, prepared for him each day by a delicatessen. There is no doubt my brother was trying at this time to imitate Diogenes...he wanted to find out the minimum required to satisfy a philosopher's wants'.[26] (Recall Nietzsche's claim that he needed less food than other people (p. 236 above).)

In these circumstances, depressed and feeling able to use his eyes only twenty minutes a day, he finally decided he had to resign his professorship. Basel and the job were killing him: '*Ergo: Academia derelinquenda est*'.[27] Accordingly, on May 2, 1879, he dictated a letter to the chairman of the university's governing council asking to be relieved of all further academic responsibilities. The request was supported by his ophthalmologist, Professor Schiess, and by a Professor Massini, a pathologist, both certifying him as incapable of continuing in his position. The request was granted and, with the unwavering generosity Basel had shown him through thick and thin, he was granted a pension of one thousand francs per annum. This would soon be supplemented by the city's Voluntary Academic Association (for which, recall, he had delivered, *inter alia*, the *Future of Our Educational Institutions* lectures). Both pensions were to run for an initial period of six years, which guaranteed him two-thirds of his regular university salary. For the rest of his sane life, the pensions (later extended beyond the six years) would be administered for him, in Basel, by the faithful Overbeck.

St. Moritz

Armed with his pension, just adequate for his meagre needs, Nietzsche put into effect the long-harboured plan of removing to the spa and 'cure' resort of St. Moritz, at the northeastern end of the Engadine Valley, where he stayed from June 21 to September 16. With a chain of lakes strung along its length, the Engadine is, at 2,000 metres, the highest of Switzerland's alpine valleys. The town itself was, however (then as now), too crowded and too expensive, so he took a room in a private house about an hour's walk from the town centre.

Nietzsche immediately felt in tune with the valley which, from now until his final collapse, would be the nearest he would ever come to a homeland. 'I have now taken possession of the Engadine', he wrote Overbeck on arrival, 'and am, as it were, in *my* element, quite wondrous. I am related to this landscape'.[28] He loved the walking tracks through the forests – 'as if laid out specially for my almost-blind self' – and called the air (probably correctly) 'the best in Europe'.[29] He continued to follow the self-doctoring, ascetic practices of the ancient philosophers, as Elizabeth had observed him doing in Basel: 'My regulation of the day and way of living and eating', he wrote Overbeck in July, 'would not shame the sages of antiquity: everything very simple yet a system of 50 often very delicate considerations'. But to no avail: 'I am just as sick here as everywhere else and have been in bed for the past eight days'. He was convinced, nonetheless, that 'St. Moritz is the right place for me'.[30]

Health and Epicurus

It was in St. Moritz that Nietzsche completed *The Wanderer and His Shadow* (the title derives from the fact that the work begins and ends with a dialogue between 'The Wanderer' and 'The Shadow'). One projected title was indeed 'Passages of Thought in St. Moritz, 1879'.[31] Virtually all of it was written in pencil in six pocket-sized notebooks which he took with him on his walks. On September 11 the manuscript was sent to Venice for Köselitz to make a print-ready copy, and it appeared with Schmeitzner on December 18.

It is important to note that when it first appeared it was not presented as in any way connected to *Human, All-Too-Human*. Unlike *Assorted Opinions and Maxims*, which had *Human, All-Too-Human* as the main title on its title page and billed itself as an 'appendix', *Wanderer* was presented as an entirely independent work. Only in 1886 was it combined with *Assorted Opinions* to form Volume II of the expanded second edition of *Human*. What the 1886 inclusion indicates is that *Wanderer* is a 'positivist' work sharing the same anti-metaphysical, naturalistic assumptions as its two predecessors – Nietzsche was concerned at the time to divide his past works into periods. But what it disguises is that *Wanderer* constitutes a significant shift in his conception of the nature and purpose of philosophy from that subscribed to by *Human*.

To understand this shift, two facts need emphasising. The first is the truly appalling state of Nietzsche's health while he was writing *Wanderer*. To his Frankfurt doctor, the infamous Eiser (pp. 239–40 above), he writes,

> My existence is a terrible burden. I would have discarded it long ago if it wasn't for the most instructive tests and experiments in the spiritual-moral area...precisely during this period of illness and almost total deprivation – this joy, thirsting for knowledge, raises me to heights where I triumph over martyrdom and hopelessness. On the whole I'm happier than ever before in my life: and yet! Constant pain for several hours a day, with a feeling closely related to sea sickness during which I find it difficult to speak. By way of a change, raging seizures (the last one forced me to vomit three days and nights – I thirsted after death). Can't read! Only seldom can I write! No contact with human beings! Not able to listen to music! Solitude and solitary walks, mountain air, milk and egg diet. All inner means of amelioration useless...My consolations are my thoughts and perspectives.[32]

And in *Ecce Homo* he records that during the writing of *Wanderer* his health reached its very lowest point in his entire life:

> In 1879 I relinquished my Basel professorship, lived through the summer like a shadow in St. Moritz and the following winter, the most sunless of my life, *as* a shadow in Naumburg. This was my nadir: 'The Wanderer and His Shadow' came into existence during the course of it. I undoubtedly knew all about shadows in those days.[33]

* * *

The second fact crucial to understanding *Wanderer* is that during the period of its writing, Nietzsche experienced an ever-increasing affection for, and sense of affinity with, the Athenian philosopher Epicurus (341–270 BC). Mentioned only briefly in *Human, All-Too-Human*, and with no more than respect in *Assorted Opinions and Maxims*, Epicurus has become, by *Wanderer*, 'one of the greatest men' who ever lived.[34] The notebooks and letters of the period are full of warm references to Epicurus's 'refined heroism'[35] and his 'garden happiness'.[36] (Epicurus owned a garden in Athens where he met and taught his followers. For this reason his school became known as 'The Garden'.) In the letters and notebooks of the period, Nietzsche sets himself the task of 'renewing the garden of Epicurus',[37] of living 'philosophically' in the manner of the Epicureans.[38]

Though Nietzsche feels an especial affinity with Epicurus, it is not with Epicurus *as opposed to* other philosophers of the ancient world but rather Epicurus *as representative of* ancient philosophy in general. What engages Nietzsche are ideas common to all ancient philosophers rather than the differences of detail between them. What we find, therefore, is a merging or homogenising of ancient philosophy. Already in *Human* he suggests that the difference between Cynics (extreme Stoics, rather than 'cynics' in the modern sense) and Epicureans is merely one of 'temperament',[39] while *Assorted Opinions* treats Epicurus as, along with the Stoic Epictetus, the repository of a single lost 'wisdom'.[40] In *Wanderer* itself, the Sophist Hippias is said to share this single wisdom,[41] as does Socrates, who, banished to the dog-house in *The Birth of Tragedy*, undergoes an amazing rehabilitation in *Wanderer*:

> If all goes well, the time will come when one will take up the memorabilia of Socrates rather than the Bible as a guide to morals and reason...the pathways of the most various

philosophical modes of life lead back to him: at bottom they are modes of life of the various temperaments, confirmed and established by reason and habit, and all of them directed towards joy in living and in one's own self.[42]

* * *

Three features of ancient philosophy in general and Epicurus's philosophy in particular are important to understanding *Wanderer*. First, as Pierre Hadot's wonderful *Philosophy as a Way of Life*[43] has recently reminded us, the ultimate point and justification of philosophy was, for the ancients, practical rather than theoretical. Specifically, the point of philosophy was to provide a body of 'wisdom' that demonstrated how, by living 'philosophically', one could achieve eudaemonia, happiness. All ancient philosophy was eudaemonic.

In the Hellenistic period which is the object of Nietzsche's special attention (the period between the death of Alexander in 323 BC and Rome's annexation of Greece in 146 BC), all the various schools of philosophy, the Cynics, Stoics, Epicureans, Sceptics and others, conceived of happiness in a particular way: they thought of it as, above all, *ataraxia*, unshakeable tranquillity, serenity, peace of mind. More specifically – perhaps on account of the disorderly condition of the times – philosophy aimed at discovering the wisdom of how to achieve serenity in the face of an at best uncertain, and usually hostile, fate: how to overcome adversity, how to retain peace of mind *whatever happens*.

The second important feature of ancient philosophy is that the theoretical is subservient to the practical, to the goal of achieving happiness. The very word 'philosophy' tells us this: philosophy was (and, I would suggest, still ought to be) *philo-sophia*, love of wisdom, not *philo-theoria*, love of theory. This does not at all mean that theory was irrelevant to philosophy and its goal. Epicurus believed, for example, that our world is but one of a series of worlds created in an infinite void and that meditation on this fact reduced the ability of human affairs to upset our peace of mind. It does, however, mean that theoretical questions with no possible relevance to human happiness are not a part of philosophy, properly so called.

The third important feature common to all ancient philosophers is a kind of asceticism. In order to guarantee happiness, no matter how hostile one's fate, all the Hellenistic philosophers propose versions of the same strategy. Since pain is the non-satisfaction of desire, one is advised to give up, or at least achieve 'detachment' from, all desires which are (a) unnecessary and (b) uncertain in their fulfilment: for example, the desire for wealth, power or fame.

Thus, Epicurus, in particular, though believing, like the Nietzsche of the positivist period, that human beings both do and should pursue pleasure as the highest goal, advocates two sorts of 'modesty' as the paths to a life of guaranteed pleasure (*Lathe biosas*! – Live modestly! – was his motto). One should be modest, first, in the gratification of one's sensuous appetites: 'joy of the spirit and soul in place of frequent indulgence in . . . sensual pleasures' is Nietzsche's description of Epicurus's recommendation.[44] And one should be modest, second, in the sense of withdrawing from social ambition, living privately in a 'garden' rather than publicly in the market place: 'A little garden, figs, little cheeses, three or four good friends, these were the sensuous pleasures of Epicurus', comments Nietzsche.[45] Although Epicurus advocates a kind of asceticism as the path to a peaceful and pleasant life, it is essential to distinguish his asceticism – 'eudaemonic asceticism', one might call it – as a means to a pleasant life from asceticism as an expression of Schopenhauerian world-denial.

Of course, to live in this 'philosophical' manner is not easy since it requires both self-discipline, the disciplining of the passions by reason, and self-knowledge, knowledge of what passions and appetites one really has. As Nietzsche puts it in the notebooks, a happy life requires that we set 'grounds in the place of habits, intentions in the place of drives', goals which, in turn, require 'knowledge in the place of belief'.[46]

* * *

It is now possible to see the connection between the two facts that provide the essential background to *Wanderer*: Nietzsche's health and the Epicurean turn. Hellenistic philosophy, we have seen, was eudaemonic, was about achieving serenity in the face of adversity. But adversity was just what Nietzsche faced: his appalling bodily 'torture',[47] reached, we have seen, its worst point in 1879. His own bodily condition was, in other words, *precisely* the kind of hostile fate Greek philosophy was designed to overcome. It made him a paradigm case for treatment by Epicurean therapy. Given the deep knowledge of ancient philosophy lodged in his mind since his days as a philologist, it was almost inevitable that he would turn to someone like Epicurus.

In his youth Nietzsche found consolation for suffering in religion. In his Wagnerian period he found it in quasi-religious art; he was, he recalls, a very 'art-needy' man.[48] But neither the comforts of religion nor those of art were any longer available to him in 1879. Moreover, his suffering had become acute in a way that the resources of nineteenth-century medicine had shown themselves powerless to ameliorate. Given, then, that religion, art and medicine had all failed, spiritual, philosophical 'self-doctoring' remained his only option.[49]

The notebooks for 1879 are completely explicit that this is what occurred in the period during which *Wanderer* came into being. Since the 'consolations of Christianity' are becoming an 'antiquity', he writes, 'the means of comfort provided by ancient philosophy come once again to the fore with a renewed radiance'.[50] And again, speaking in a directly personal way – some of the entries in the notebooks are as much diary entries as sketches of philosophical thoughts – 'I need the boxes of salves and medicine bottles of all the ancient philosophers',[51] which leads to the self-directed injunction, 'Become ancient!'[52]

Of course, Nietzsche's concern is not just for himself. His appropriation of the style and much of the content of ancient philosophy for the purpose of self-doctoring is intended to be exemplary, to communicate to others how they, too, may engage in self-administered therapy, whatever their own particular form of adversity. Otherwise there would have been no point in allowing *Wanderer* to emerge from the privacy of the notebooks. In the September 11 letter to Köselitz accompanying the manuscript to be made print-ready, he writes:

I am at end of my 35th year, mid-life and so 'encircled by death'.* Because of my health I must think of sudden death … and so I feel like an old man, but also because I have done my life work … Basically I have put my observation of life already to the test: many will do that in the future. My spirit had not been cowed by prolonged and painful suffering, indeed I seem more cheerful and benevolent than ever before. Where have I got this new condition from? Not from people, who have mostly, with a few exceptions, irked me. Read this new manuscript through, dear friend, and ask yourself whether you find any trace of

---

* A fifteenth-century hymn contains the line *dedia vita in morte sumus*, 'in the middle of life we are in death', or, in Luther's translation, 'encircled by death'.

suffering or oppression. I think you won't find any, and this is a sign of the hidden powers in this outlook, not weakness and exhaustion.[53]

Having successfully 'tested' the 'hidden powers' of Epicurean philosophy on himself, having achieved happiness in spite of a terrible fate he describes in the letter to Eiser (p. 278 above),* he now wants to make them available to his readers : 'I see the suffering ones taking to the mountain air of the Engadine' (i.e., to the health spa of St. Moritz), he writes. And continues, 'I too send my patients into my mountain air',[54] in other words into the 'heroic-idyllic'[55] mood of Epicurus's philosophy.[56]

The Wanderer and His Shadow

Turning to *The Wanderer and His Shadow* itself, and viewing it against the above background, it becomes impossible to miss how thoroughly it is impregnated by Epicurean philosophy.

There is, first of all, an explicit affirmation and appropriation of the Epicurean conception of the goal of philosophy as eudaemonia, personal happiness. This personal orientation makes *Wanderer* a very different work both from its positivist predecessors and from Nietzsche's mature works, which, though concerned with human well-being in a general sense, pay little or no attention to the techniques of individual happiness. Nietzsche writes,

If we are sensible, the only thing that need concern us is that we should have joy in our hearts. Alas someone added, if we are sensible the best thing we can do is to be wise.[57]

Given, in other words, that happiness does not grow on trees, it has to be worked for and cultivated under the guidance of *philosophia*, of the philosopher's wisdom. Moreover, though they are not, as we shall see, identical, Nietzsche's concept of happiness at least includes Epicurean *ataraxia* as a crucial ingredient. Thus, as we have seen, 'joy in the heart', 'quieting of the heart', the 'idyllic mood', and 'Epicurus's garden happiness', as well as 'soothing of the soul',[58] are all epithets that necessarily apply to a happy person.

* * *

That the point of philosophy is to provide happiness-promoting wisdom explains the presence of much of *Wanderer*'s content which, if one approaches the work with a purely theoretical paradigm of philosophy in mind, should not be there. A great deal of the work, that is to say, has nothing to do with the big questions of metaphysics, epistemology, or even ethics, but is, rather, quite explicitly, *Lebensweisheit*, 'life-wisdom', or, as we might now say, 'life-coaching'. Nietzsche's observations as a life coach are of two basic sorts: advice on how to promote happiness in dealing with oneself, and advice on how to do so in dealing with others.

---

* Notice that in the letter to Eiser he describes his 'thoughts and perspectives' as 'consolations', positive pleasures. A theme in Hellenistic philosophy is that since a hostile fate cannot deprive one of the life of the mind, intellectual desires, since they are *not* uncertain of satisfaction (some of them, at least), are exempt from the requirements of eudaemonic asceticism.

The overall instruction with respect to dealing with oneself is to become a 'good neighbour' to 'closest' things, to experience *'peace all around me and goodwill to all things closest to me'*.[59] The contrast, here, is with the 'furthest' things of Christian metaphysics: hell, heaven, death, and judgment.[60] Since the 'nearest things' pertain to diet and health, it is likely that Nietzsche is influenced, here, by nineteenth-century German materialism (which he knew through his 1866 reading of Friedrich Lange's *History of Materialism* (pp. 89–90 above)). The spirit of German materialism is summed up in Feuerbach's famous remark that 'man is what he eats': more fully, 'If you want to improve people then give them better food instead of declamations against sin. Man is what he eats.'

People just don't realize, Nietzsche laments, that longer eggs taste better, that thunderstorms are beneficial for the bowels, or that speaking or listening intently at mealtimes is harmful to the digestion. People fail to attend to these humble, everyday things that, cumulatively, are of crucial importance since 'almost all our physical and psychological frailties' stem from this failure of attention:

> Not knowing what is beneficial to us and what is harmful...in the division of the day, in for how long and with whom we enjoy social intercourse, in profession and leisure, commanding and obeying, feeling for art and nature, eating, sleeping and reflecting; being *unknowledgeable in the smallest and most everyday things* and failing to keep an eye on them – this is what transforms the earth for so many into a 'vale of tears'.[61]

In the notebooks, under the heading 'The Doctrine of Nearest Things', he includes 'purpose of the day (divided into periods), food, company, nature, solitude, sleep, employment, education...use of mood and atmospheric conditions, health, retreat from politics'.[62] 'Use of mood' is perhaps explained by the remark in Nietzsche's next book, *Dawn*, that 'peace of soul' depends on the mood of our domestic environment:[63] after a hectic day dealing with the complexities of the modern world one needs, perhaps, to return to a simple, spacious, cool-coloured home environment, as Alain de Botton suggests in *The Architecture of Happiness*.

As to dealing with others, navigating the minefields of society, Nietzsche offers himself and us *inter alia* the following. Since the postman is an agent of rude intrusions into one's solitude, one should open one's letters only once a week and take a bath afterwards.[64] (An updated version would be the office wisdom that advises one to avoid opening one's e-mails first thing and, moreover, to do a great deal of deleting, so as not to allow other people to dominate one's day.) One should try to be a true *listener*, that is, focus on listening to what is said rather than on constructing one's reply.[65] One should avoid those who are embittered by coming home empty-handed after a hard day's work.[66] One should (this comes from Hesiod) return borrowed gain in extra measure so that, simultaneously, the lender is gratified by the profitability of his act and one expunges the humiliation of having had to be a borrower in the first place.[67] One should bear in mind that a man who has just been greatly honoured and has just eaten is at his most generous.[68] And so on.

* * *

For *The Wanderer*, then, the aim of philosophy is eudaemonia. The second way in which it both affirms and appropriates Epicurean philosophy is in the exclusion from philosophy of angels-on-a-pinhead questions, questions that have no practical relevance to our lives:

Epicurus, the soul-soother of late antiquity, had that wonderful insight, which is still today so rarely to be discovered, that to quieten the heart it is absolutely not necessary to have solved the ultimate and outermost theoretical questions. Thus to those tormented by 'fear of the gods' it is sufficient to say, 'If the gods exist they do not concern themselves with us', instead of indulging in fruitless...disputation over the ultimate question of whether the gods do in fact exist.[69]

Epicurus argued that the gods, if they existed, could take no interest in human affairs since that would disturb the blissful condition that belongs to the very concept of what it is to be a god. (Gods never go to horror movies.) So we do not need to suffer from fear of divine wrath: if gods exist they are not interested in us and if they do not exist they are not interested in us either. The moral Nietzsche derives is that we should develop 'indifference' to theoretical questions whose answers can make no difference to our lives:

I mean the questions: what is the purpose of man? How can he be reconciled with God?...Just as little are we concerned with the questions of the philosophical dogmatists, whether they be idealists or materialists or realists. Their object, one and all, is to compel us to a decision where neither faith nor knowledge is needed...[for] a full and excellent human life.[70]

Nietzsche concludes the passage by admitting there is a 'realm of darkness' beyond the 'closest' world, the world of nature, but says that it is something we should not bother our heads about. He admits once again, in other words, the *possibility* that the 'closest' world might be, as Kant claimed, a world of mere 'appearance' beyond which lies a reality 'in itself' of a quite different character. But since Kantianism would make absolutely no difference to our lives even if it were true, we do not need to read the *Critique of Pure Reason*.

Like Epicurus, however, Nietzsche recognises that theoretical knowledge is by no means irrelevant to philosophy, that it can be an important route to peace of mind. Thus, paralleling Epicurus's advice to achieve imperturbability by meditating on the vanishing insignificance of human affairs in the vastness of space and time, Nietzsche advises us to engage in 'mocking laughter' at humanity's treating itself as 'the goal and purpose of existence'. He advises us to become like those astronomers 'to whom there is sometimes given a horizon that really is free of the earth, [and who] give us to understand that the drop of *life* in the universe is without significance for the total character of the tremendous ocean of becoming and passing away'. Such a long-distance view of things enables us to understand how our traditional self-aggrandizement makes us like 'the ant in the forest [who] imagines that it is the goal and objective of the forest'.[71] What Nietzsche is pointing to here is the therapeutic benefit of the post-metaphysical, positivist 'horizon': by abandoning the idea of the world as a mere stage set for the playing out of the human drama under God's watchful and wrathful eye, we see self-aggrandizing man as 'the comedian of the world',[72] as, in the language Sartre borrows from *The Birth of Tragedy*, 'absurd'.[73] And this helps us to cut our troubles down to size, helps us achieve *ataraxia*.

Attainment of the 'astronomer's' horizon on human affairs is, of course, something which comes and goes. Hence, to preserve tranquillity, it will need constant repetition as a kind of meditative practice or spiritual exercise; spiritual 'gymnastics', as Nietzsche calls it.[74] Another such exercise is meditation upon death. The fact of its inevitability ought, says

Nietzsche, to 'introduce into every life a precious, sweet-smelling drop in levity [*leichtsinn* – literally 'lightness of mind']'.[75] This again seems to me a therapeutic use of Sartrean 'absurdity': knowing that death will inevitably puncture all our projects, that the mere 'wave' in the vast ocean of becoming that we are (p. 275 above) will soon be no more, should overcome *obsession* – our disposition to become obsessed with, for instance, office politics. Spiritual health, Nietzsche is suggesting, requires that we carry the absurd, and so a kind of Stoic detachment, always in the back of our minds.

Of course, the threat to serenity of spirit comes from only one source: desire and emotion, 'the passions'. So, for Nietzsche, as for Epicurus, serenity requires self-discipline, the 'overcoming of the passions'[76] by reason, the disciplining of one's soul into rigorous adherence to a rational life plan. Epicurus, we have seen, advocates the quasi-ascetic elimination of all 'unnecessary' desires that are uncertain of fulfilment, and so does Nietzsche:

> To satisfy one's necessary requirements [one's *needs*] as completely as possible oneself, even if only imperfectly, is the road to *freedom of the spirit and person*. To let others satisfy many of one's requirements...is a training in *unfreedom*. The sophist Hippias, who...himself produced everything he wore, within and without, represents, in this, the road to the highest freedom.[77]

Self-mastery is, of course, easier said than done. Hence, in addition to spiritual exercises such as adopting the 'astronomer's' perspective and meditating on mortality, Nietzsche recommends the regular practice of self-denial:

> *The most needful gymnastic.* – A lack of self-mastery in small things brings about a crumbling of the capacity for it in great ones. Every day is ill employed, and a danger for the next day, in which one has not denied oneself some small thing at least once: this gymnastic is indispensable if one wants to preserve oneself in the joy of being one's own master.[78]

Of course, self-mastery cannot be achieved without self-knowledge, and so accurate 'psychological observation' is as highly valued in *Wanderer* as it was in its positivist predecessors. Now, however, Nietzsche's account of the value of such observations takes a decisive step away from the malice of 'réealism', from Rée's 'belittling' 'contempt and scorn' (pp. 256, 236 above) for human nature, as well as from the 'macho' idea that the unconditional pursuit of 'scientific' truth is an end in itself. Those whose 'dissection' of morality can be approved of – and they should never be more than a small minority – do so not as an end in itself, nor out of sadistic glee in 'hitting the black', but 'only for the sake of better knowledge, better judgment, better living'.[79] Unlike the 'trivial' and cynical moralists who want to show, behind all apparent greatness of soul, 'a paltriness similar to their own' (one can see that, even if Lou Salomé had not come between them, a break between Nietzsche and Rée was inevitable), moralists such as himself do not '*deny the existence*' of 'great and pure' states of the soul, of 'truly good men and women', but seek rather to '*explain*' those states by exhibiting their origins and complexity.[80] In other words, *Nietzsche's* 'psychological observations' on human excellences are designed not to debunk but rather to provide *depth-psychological analyses*. These are important because if we are to cultivate and master our passions and so achieve fine and happy states of the soul, it is important that we overcome all false sentimentality, that we achieve a clear-eyed understanding of what those states really consist in. As all the ancient philosophers insisted, only if one 'knows oneself' can one hope to become either good or happy.

Building Walden Two

Nietzsche would not, of course, be Nietzsche if his philosophy were an exact repetition of Epicurus. The crucial respect in which he departs from the Epicurean injunction to 'live modestly' is his ongoing concern for the regeneration of culture, his mission to build – not by direct political action but by the quiet exercise of small-scale 'spiritual leadership' – a new society. Possessing a life-unifying 'task', a life-defining meaning, is, as we know, an essential ingredient of happiness as Nietzsche conceives it, and cultural regeneration – through the writing of his books – is his own life-task. This grandeur of ambition that is, in a broad sense, political seems to me something like the opposite of Epicurean inconspicuousness, of Epicurus's recommended 'inner emigration' from politics.* Nietzsche writes,

> the man who has overcome his passions has entered into possession of the most fertile ground, like the coloniser who has mastered the forests and swamps. To *sow* the seeds of good spiritual works in the soil of the subdued passions is then the immediate urgent task. The overcoming is only a *means* not a goal: if it is not so viewed, all kinds of weeds and devilish nonsense will quickly spring up in this rich soil now unoccupied, and soon there will be more rank confusion than there ever was before.[81]

This, I think, is a criticism of Epicurus: *he* is the one who views a rational mastery of the passions along the guidelines supplied by his philosophy as an end rather than a means. He is the one who fails to see that happiness requires a 'goal' other than itself. Happiness has to be more than Epicurean *ataraxia*; it demands a life-defining task. Indeed, there cannot be *ataraxia* in the absence of a life-defining task. Nietzsche's own task is building a new culture; 'building Walden Two', as I call it.

By way of constructing a blueprint for Walden Two, *Wanderer* both elaborates on themes already introduced in *Human* and introduces some new and startling ideas of its own. I begin with the former.

* * *

Economics. The new world, we know, will be one in which the dangers of the 'machine culture' are avoided. In the present age we have lost the pride in production characteristic of the craft economy and we have lost the *'bestowing of distinction on individuals'* that a purchase used to constitute. Workers are reduced to 'an anonymous and impersonal slavery'. So not 'paying too high a price' for the alleviation of labour, restoring the worker's job-satisfaction, will be a desideratum.[82] There is an echo, here, of Nietzsche's near-contemporary William Morris. Though an implacable opponent of socialism, remarks such as these show Nietzsche to be by no means unsympathetic to all strands of nineteenth-century socialism. They also

---

* Epicurus taught in Mytilene, Lesbos, but because his philosophy challenged prevailing orthodoxy, he was threatened with a charge of impiety and had to flee in danger of his life. This convinced him that it was better to have nothing to do with politics, even indirectly.

show, as far, at least, as *Wanderer* is concerned, the erroneousness of thinking that only the well-being of the exceptional individual has any value for him.

Nietzsche arrives at this same conclusion by appealing to capitalist self-interest. In setting wage levels, the exploitation of the worker will be avoided since that makes him less efficient and will produce a class alienated from society as a whole and thereby social unrest.[83] (The 1848 workers' uprising was, recall, a living memory for Nietzsche.)

On the other hand, Plato's and the socialists' intention of abolishing private property is based on the lack of proper knowledge of human nature. Such an abolition is a mistake since people are diligent in pursuit only of what they can own, and diligent in the care only of what they do own. Nonetheless, since a large gap between rich and poor causes envy and social unrest, the concentration of enormous wealth in private hands will be avoided. Businesses, in particular banks, that generate such wealth will be state-owned.[84] This passage makes two things clear: that, at least in *Wanderer*, Nietzsche's 'anti-socialism' is in fact anti-*communism*, and that the social-democratic ideal of partial nationalisation of the means of production and exchange is something he actually *endorsed*.

One last stipulation: since, in the free market, products are judged not by experts but only by consumers, who can go only on appearances, a strong consumer protection agency will be needed to maintain the quality of products.[85]

Art and Character. In general terms, the art and life of Nietzsche's new world will be 'classical' rather than 'romantic' in both mood and design.* All great art and every man of 'moral consequence', Nietzsche asserts, possesses the opposite of the romantic (Wagnerian) desire to 'show more feeling than one actually has'. 'Greatness likes to arrest...feelings on their course and not allow them to run quite to their conclusion'. The 'modesty' of greatness requires feelings to 'present themselves as more sober than they are'.[86] 'Arcadia', to repeat, is a Poussin landscape populated with Hellenic heroes.[87]

War and Peace. Since, as we know, there is no free will, 'wrath and punishment' are 'logical sins' which, one day, will be returned to the animal world from which they came. But we have the capacity to transcend these 'sins', so that one day they will wither away.[88] (This is why I call this section 'Building Walden Two' – B. F. Skinner's *Walden Two*, too, dreams of the demise of anger. Notice that Nietzsche's view that legitimate punishment – exile, imprisonment – is a matter of 'reminding' the transgressor of the advantages of community he has forfeited by harming it[89] resembles Skinner's faith in 'operant conditioning'.)

Speaking of hostility between nations, Nietzsche says that the so-called 'armed peace', in which one has not an army but a 'defence force', is no real peace at all, because by demonising the neighbour it creates the seeds of future warfare. True peace, the time when we can truly say that there is 'on earth peace, goodwill to all men',[90] will only be achieved when the strongest nation voluntarily disarms, understanding that it is better to perish than to live in mutual hate and fear.[91] (Nietzsche would have supported the Campaign for Nuclear Disarmament.)

Of course, human aggression, as we know, can never be wholly eradicated. So here we must learn from 'Greek prudence', from the Greeks' institution of gymnastic and artistic

---

* A letter to Rée written in September 1879 contains an amusing comment on Nietzsche's own romantic period: '*On my first five Books*. Once I thought, A and O/My wisdom stands within;/Now I think no more so:/ Only the eternal Ah! and Oh!/My youth stands within' (KGB II.5 879). The 'five books' are, of course, *The Birth of Tragedy* and the four *Untimely Meditations*.

contests by means of which the 'drive for victory and eminence' could be discharged without imperilling the political order.[92] Aggression must be sublimated. Good Eris in place of bad Eris. The World Cup in place of World War.

Women

The aspects of Nietzsche's Walden Two discussed so far are, to some degree, familiar from *Human, All-Too-Human*. What is new, however, and calls for a reconsideration of the popular picture of Nietzsche as, from start to finish, a virulent anti-feminist, indeed misogynist, are his remarks about women.

Some quotations: 'Many a woman has the spirit of sacrifice and can no longer enjoy life when her husband refuses to sacrifice her'.[93] 'What women now think of the male mind can be divined from the fact that when they adorn themselves ['put on a face'], the last thing they have in mind is to emphasise the intellectual qualities of their face'. They prefer to present an appearance of 'lustful sensuality and mindlessness... Their conviction that men are terrified of intellectual women is so firm that they are even ready to deny they have any sharpness of mind and deliberately impose on themselves a reputation for *shortsightedness*'[94] (of being a 'dumb blonde' in need of a guiding male hand). What women privately say among themselves, however, is 'stupid as a man'. And that indeed is where stupidity belongs: 'stupidity is, in woman, the *unwomanly*'.[95]

Properly read, these kinds of remarks seem to me not only to 'hit the bullseye' but also to be extremely sympathetic to the plight of women in nineteenth-century, paternalist society. More precisely, they strike me as remarkably *empathetic* – a quality many noticed as one of the salient features of Nietzsche's personality. Their butt is not women but the male culture which forces them into devalued roles. And, consistent with his battle to have women admitted to Basel University (p. 191 above), he clearly sees women as *at the very least* as intellectually gifted as men – so that their being debarred from using their intelligence is a tragic waste with respect to the project of building a better, more intelligently designed, world. It is not, then, surprising that, as we shall see, most of the company he chose for himself during the last decade of his sanity was female.

After reading through the manuscript of *Wanderer* in preparation for making the print-ready copy, Köselitz, as was his habit at the time, suggested some alterations:

> You write, 'The domestic animal which understood how to create itself a right within humanity is the woman'. The comparison of women with domestic animals is unworthy and unphilosophical; women are as little animals as men are women. Women have, particularly in intellectual matters, advantages which men could do well to emulate.[96]

Nietzsche replies:

> Many thanks for picking me up on that. I do not wish to present the appearance of diminishing women and have cut out the whole passage. What is true is that, originally, only men were held to be human beings... the recognition of women as human beings was a great moral advance. My – or our – view of women should not be brought into contact with the word 'domestic animal'. – I was judging according to [the travel writer Sir Henry Veel] Huntley's description of the situation of women in primitive tribes.[97]

When we compare this with Schopenhauer's view, more typical of the age, that

> women are qualified to be the nurses and governesses of our earliest childhood by the very
> fact that they are themselves childish, trifling, and short-sighted ['shortsightedness' again!],
> in a word, are all their lives grown up children; a kind of intermediate stage between the
> child and the man, who is the human being in the real sense,[98]

we can see that the exchange actually does considerable credit to both men. Of course, the view that Nietzsche was anti-feminist, indeed 'anti-woman', is by no means without grounds in his later philosophy. Soon we shall have to attend to the question of what it was that altered his views on the 'women's question'.

Is Nietzsche a Democrat?

Will democracy be part of Nietzsche's Walden Two? Various remarks in *Wanderer* might seem to suggest that it will.

Nietzsche most often uses 'democracy' to refer to a *cultural* phenomenon: the levelling of everyone down to the lowest cultural denominator, the creation of a 'mass' culture. 'Democratization' of this sort he always opposes. But with respect to democracy as a *political* system *Wanderer* has a different attitude. Thus, commenting on the growth of political democracy in the Europe of his day, he observes, first, that it is inevitable, since even the opponents of democracy, 'the spirits of [reactionary] revolution', have to employ democratic methods and thereby strengthen democratic institutions. Second, he seems to say that this is a *desirable* development since the political 'democratization of Europe' is one of those 'tremendous *prophylactic measures* which are the conceptions of modern times through which we separate ourselves from the Middle Ages' and which provide the 'foundations' on which 'the whole future can safely be built'. The reason democracy provides a 'prophylactic' foundation for the future is that it 'makes it impossible for the fruitful fields of culture again to be destroyed overnight by wild and senseless torrents'. In establishing democratic institutions 'we erect stone dams and protective walls against barbarians, against pestilences, against *physical and spiritual enslavement*'.[99] Again, 'Democratic institutions are quarantine arrangements to combat that ancient pestilence, lust for tyranny; as such they are very useful and very boring'.[100] This is a defence of democracy Churchillian in its orthodoxy: for all its failings, democracy is a bastion against tyranny.

Before we decide, however, that Walden Two will be a democratic state, *Wanderer*'s remarks need to be set against a long and complex discussion entitled 'religion and government' in section 472 of *Human, All-Too-Human*. In brief, the argument, here, is this. The traditional, 'tutelary' (i.e., 'paternalistic', non-democratic) state was essentially dependent on religion for two things: validation of the legitimacy of the ruler (the 'divine right of kings') and validation of the lot of the ruled. Divine authorisation made the traditional state an object of reverence and so a powerful force for social order. The arrival of democracy, however, is draining it of such reverence because it is now 'the people' who are becoming the 'sole sovereign power'. Democracy thus constitutes 'the *decay of the state*'. Though this threatens social anarchy it need not be viewed with absolute horror, since history shows humanity's fecundity in creating new forms of social organisation. It might be, for example (another of Nietzsche's prescient moments), that the traditional business of the state will be transferred to 'private contractors'. Nonetheless, this general faith in a viable humanity following the collapse of the democratic state does not mean we should actively seek to *work* for its death. On the contrary, we must hope that it survives 'for some time yet'. And, of course, *Wanderer* tells us why: the collapse of the democratic state may well lead to tyranny (to Hitler and Mussolini).

It is not that easy to determine just what Nietzsche's view of democracy is during the positivist period. Some things are, however, clear. The democratic state is *not* the best form of the state since it constitutes the 'decay of the state'. It is only the best form *for now* since, given the current state of human nature, its disappearance would likely lead to tyranny. As we shall see, a question that exercises Nietzsche's late philosophy is what (at least some) human beings would have to be like for the replacement of democracy by a different kind of state not to be its replacement by tyranny. What would conditions have to be like for the death of democracy to be a blessing rather than a curse?

* * *

The most insightful reaction to *Wanderer* came from Rohde, who, recall, had been appalled by *Human, All-Too-Human*. The book, he wrote Nietzsche, 'causes pain to anyone who knows what suffering lies beneath its calm spirit, but really we should all be pleased that your "shadow conversation" raises you so high and far above all personal things', bestowing on the reader, as it does, so many exemplary 'victories over sickness'.[101] To Overbeck Rohde wrote that 'the Réeness has become less dogmatic... Nietzsche looks about himself more freely and wins back his own being which [in *Human*] he suppressed through a forced free-spiritedness... to a considerable degree Nietzsche has overcome the cold wind of Réeism that succeeded the heat of Wagnerism'.[102] These remarks seem to me basically correct.

Naumburg, Riva, Venice, Marienbad, Stresa

With the approach of the autumn of 1879, Nietzsche's three months in St. Moritz came to an end. Influenced, perhaps, by the various doctors who had advised him to abandon his perverse habit of challenging the cold, he decided that the cold of the Engadine winter would be as bad for his health as the heat of the Basel summer. He decided, in other words, that what was particularly bad for his health was *extremes* of climate. And so began a pattern that would remain with him for the final nine years of his sanity: high mountain valleys in summer, warmer places at sea level in winter. Though by the following year he would search out these warmer places on the French and Italian Rivieras, for the moment the (marginally) warmer place was Naumburg, where he would stay until the middle of February 1880. On September 17 he caught the train to Chur, where he met up with Elizabeth – they discussed George Eliot's *Middlemarch*,* which she was in the

---

* It had appeared five years earlier in 1874. One assumes it was already in German translation since Elizabeth certainly could not read English.

middle of reading – and from there they travelled on to Naumburg, where they arrived on September 20.

Nietzsche's project in Naumburg was what he called a 'rational…winter-cure programme'. The idea behind the 'cure' was the advice that would be given by his next book, *Dawn*, that the best cure for physical and spiritual depression is

> a great deal of sleep literal or metaphorical. Then one will recover one's morning. The apogee of the wisdom of life (*Lebensweisheit*) consists in knowing how to fall asleep in either sense at the right time.[103]

Writing to Overbeck on arrival in his 'winter station', he says that the 'chief thought' behind the programme is metaphorical sleep: 'as much rest as possible from my constant inner work, recuperation from myself, such as I have not had for years'.[104] One recalls Immermann's advice that he would feel better if he 'became more stupid'(p. 171 above). Or Shakespeare's about knitting up the ravelled sleeve of care.

Under the influence of his own, Epicurean philosophy, Nietzsche had begun to plan the recovery of his health and spirits the previous July. At that time the plan had been to rent from the city a room in a tower in the city wall right by his mother's house at the end of the Weingarten street. There he would supplement his income by tending the nearby orchard and vegetable garden during the spring and summer months. The plan, in other words, was to dwell quite literally in 'Epicurus's garden'. On July 21 he asked his mother to inform the city authorities that he would formally commit himself to renting the room for six years at (the very modest) seventeen-and-a-half talers per year. The vegetable gardening, he continued,

> is just what I want and is in no way unworthy of an aspirant 'wise one'. You know that I yearn ever more strongly for a simple and natural life-style, there is no other cure for my health. Real work which takes time and makes one tired without straining the head is what I need. Did not father once say that I would become a gardener?[105]

Nietzsche's plan, in short, was to take his own Epicurean advice to 'live unobtrusively', to live, for the time being at least, in a state of intellectual 'sleep'. In the end the plan came to nothing because the room was rented to someone else. And in the event, Nietzsche, who could no more give up on his 'task' than he could fly, was really somewhat relieved to get out of the rental contract (which, *inter alia*, forbade him to hang up washing in the tower room or to open a tavern there).[106]

Nietzsche's health did not improve in Naumburg. In fact, with the onset of winter cold, it reached its ultimately lowest point. In January 1880 he wrote the already-quoted letter to Dr. Eiser (p. 278 above) itemising the alternation between pain and nausea and seizures so violent that he sometimes lost consciousness. At the same time, striking a 'heroic', Epicurean pose, he informed Malwida of his imminent demise:

> This will no doubt be my last [letter]! For the terrible and unrelenting martyrdoms of my life make me thirst for the end; according to certain symptoms, it seems that the saving brain stroke is close enough to grant me hope. As far as torture and deprivation are concerned,

my life during the past few years can measure up to that of any ascetic...Nevertheless I
have attained much during these same years towards the purifying and polishing of my
soul – and I no longer need either religion or art to that end...I believe I have fulfilled my
life's work...No pain has been able to seduce me into bearing false witness against life, *life
as I know it*, nor should I ever be able to do so.[107]

Death, however, turned out to be less imminent than he thought. And so he began to
reflect, once more, on the relation between climate and health. Naumburg, indeed northern
Europe in general, he decided, was very bad for him. Accordingly, on February 13, he set
off for Riva, on the northern shore of Lake Garda, in the Trentino-Alto Adige region of
northern Italy. Nestling at the foot of the snow-streaked Dolomites, Riva was an oasis of
trees and flowers. The spacious grounds of his hotel, the Seevilla (today the Hôtel du Lac
et du Parc), extended to the shore of the lake. Nietzsche had now entered what was to be,
for the rest of his sanity, his nomadic homeland. Though he was regularly on the move and
often liked to pose as a homeless 'wanderer', from now on he was really, as he indeed saw
himself, in the proper sense, a 'nomad':[108] one, that is to say, who, though mobile, is mobile
in a defined pattern and within a defined space. In Nietzsche's case, apart from occasional
excursions elsewhere, mostly business or duty trips to Leipzig or Naumburg, his space was
defined, in the north, by the southern valleys of the Swiss Alps, and, in the south, by the
sea; either the Adriatic (Venice) or the Mediterranean (Genoa and Nice).

In Riva, Nietzsche began work on the notes that would become *Dawn*. But after a
month of cold, wet weather and no improvement in his health, he decided on the adopted
home town of his friend Köselitz and moved to Venice, where he would remain until the
beginning of July. Here, in the eternal quest for better health, he began a 'very necessary
experiment' to see whether the supposedly medically 'depressing' climate might not actually
benefit his headaches.[109] (With its marshy lagoon, mosquitoes, and honeycomb of dubious
canals, Venice was regarded, throughout the nineteenth century, as a place where one easily
succumbed to a fatal infection.) For several weeks he stayed with Köselitz near the Campo
San Canciano, in the working-class neighbourhood of Cannaregio, at number 5256 on the
narrow Calle Nuova. From there he moved to his own apartment not many blocks away
with a view onto San Michele, Venice's island cemetery.

Nietzsche loved Venice. He loved his spacious and elegant apartment, the peaceful doves
on St. Mark's Square, the open-air cafés where he discovered Italian coffee to be the best
in the world, the warm early summer sun, the dark alleys that shaded his eyes, the sea air
and sea bathing. He began to sleep better than for a long time and his health and appearance began to improve.[110] Work on *Dawn* continued under the provisional title *L'Ombra
di Venizia*.[111]

Relations with Köselitz were not, however, without tension. On the one hand, Köselitz
was able to write to a friend that Nietzsche was 'a saint in the most solemn sense...he is the
only one of his type on the earth, there has never been his sort on the earth nor will there ever
be again'.[112] But on the other, he wished he could get on with his own work as a composer,
which, on account of his role as Nietzsche's friend, amanuensis, and general spirits-raiser,
had come to a complete halt. But then he would lambaste himself as a 'complete bastard'
to begrudge a little time to 'this poor man who has only me to lean on'. Yet he could not
help telling his friend that not only did Nietzsche wake him up in the small hours to write

down some idea that had just come to him, but he also demanded at other times that he play Chopin or go bathing, with the result that 'often, at night, I realised I'd done nothing for myself so that I got angry and wished Nietzsche would go to the devil'.[113] Later on he wrote in exasperation to the same friend, 'I've spent several weeks writing up a book [*Dawn*] of more than two hundred pages from an almost illegible manuscript produced by an almost blind man – ask me if my head hurts!'[114]

Nietzsche's letters show he was not insensible to the strain he was placing on his friend. If only to save the friendship, it thus became imperative to leave Venice – though by July it was in any case becoming too hot and mosquito-ridden for him. Having received a recommendation for the Bohemian spa town of Marienbad (now Mariánské Lázně in the Czech Republic), he decided to spend July and August there, staying in the Hotel Ermitage. It was not, however, a good move. He liked neither the people nor the steak, the weather was wet, and he was overcome with nostalgia for the old Tribschen days. The break with Wagner, he wrote Köselitz, was 'the hardest sacrifice my path of living and thinking has demanded of me'. In the same letter (conveniently forgetting the Brahms episode), he began the falsification of his personal relation with Wagner that would persist through all his later accounts of the relationship: 'a cross word has never been spoken between us', he claimed.[115]

Surrounded by a language he did not understand, Nietzsche felt completely isolated in Marienbad. The only bright spot was the forest and the fact that people took him for a Pole.[116] (Another fantasy in his later writings is that he was Polish.) A moment of excitement occurred when the sounds of digging came from the hotel's garden in the middle of the night. The next morning it turned out that the police had dug up a machine for forging banknotes and had carted the hotel's owner off to jail.[117] Among the locals Nietzsche was referred to as 'the sad professor from Switzerland', while fellow residents reported him as being 'extremely silent' and speaking mostly only to children.[118]

After spending September in Naumburg, hoping, no doubt, that a good dose of mother love would enable him to recover from the misery of Marienbad, he travelled south once more, this time to Stresa, on the southwestern shore of Lake Maggiore, which, however, he found 'not southerly enough', shivering already from 'the frosty breath of winter'.[119] Here he resumed work on *Dawn*, thinking now to recycle the title, *Ploughshare*, originally planned for *Human, All-Too-Human*. He was forced to remain in Stresa much longer than he wished – from October 14 to November 8 – impatiently awaiting the arrival of a trunk his sister had sent from Naumburg. A note written during this time gives an indication of the mood brought on by the windless, clammy mists of autumnal Maggiore:

> One gets older, and it is hard for me to be quite satisfied with a place however famous a name it may bear. The anaemic beauty of the Lago Maggiore in late autumn, a beauty which spiritualises all the contours and makes the countryside almost a vision, does not enchant me, but speaks to me in a tone of infectious sadness – I know such tones elsewhere than in nature.[120]

Finally the trunk arrived and the next day he was off to Genoa, where he had decided to spend the winter.

Genoa, Recoaro, and Sils Maria

After a few false starts, Nietzsche settled in the Salita della Battistine 8, about twenty minutes' uphill walk from Genoa's Brignole railway station. He describes the walk to Elizabeth with his usual mathematical precision:

> Yes there's a lot of walking! And climbing! For in order to reach my little garret I have to climb 164 steps, and the house itself is very high up in a steep street of palaces.[121] This street, being so steep and ending in a great flight of steps, is very quiet and there is grass growing between the stones.[122]

The house was well chosen, with pleasant fellow-lodgers and a sympathetic landlady, Signora Settima Stagnetti, who added to his culinary repertoire (he had, remember, learnt to make risotto in Sorrento) a Genoese dish of artichokes and eggs.[123] The house was adjacent to a wooded park, the Villeta Dinegro, with excellent walking paths that wound up to a stunning view over the entire city and harbour. The only drawback was the absence of heating in his attic room. In his quiet backwater, he came to feel 'so much at home that everyone with whom my basic needs bring me into contact has a friendly face and word for me'.[124] His landlady confirmed to Elizabeth that he was indeed on friendly terms with fellow lodgers, reporting that he shared in their joys and sorrows to such a degree that he was known as 'il piccolo santo'.[125]

Nietzsche was determined to live in solitude and anonymity in Genoa – to live with Epicurean 'modesty'. He was, he wrote his publisher, 'living philosophically'.[126] 'Don't tell anyone where I am', he repeatedly enjoined his few correspondents:

> All my efforts [he wrote Overbeck] are directed towards developing an idealistic garret-solitude in which – as much, much suffering has taught me – the necessary and simplest demands of my nature find their satisfaction ... For a good period of time I must live without company, in the middle of a town whose language I don't understand ... I live as though the centuries were nothing, without thinking of the date or the newspapers.[127]

Nietzsche was, in short, withdrawing into the deep solitude ('solipsism therapy', one might call it) that will be reflected in Zarathustra's ten-year solitude in a mountain cave. Rée had visited in Naumburg but, Nietzsche decided, the visit had been too stimulating. His effort now was to recover physical and mental harmony through the elimination of external stimuli:

> I am again making the attempt [he wrote home] to discover a life that is harmonious for me, and believe it will also be the path to health: all the life-paths I have followed to date have simply forfeited my health. I want to be my own doctor and that means, for me, that I have to be true to the depths of myself and no longer listen to anything alien. I can't put into words how much good this solitude does me. Don't think it lessens my love for you! Help me rather to keep my anchorite-existence a secret! Only in this way can I advance myself in every sense (and in the end perhaps also be useful to others). Here, this great, bustling port city where over 10,000 ships dock in a year – it gives me peace and being-for-myself.

An attic with an excellent bed: simple, healthy food, sea air, vital for my head, excellently paved paths, and, for November, a lovely warmth (lots of rain, unfortunately).[128]

Though Nietzsche's health was not as good as it had been in Venice, he developed an intense love of Genoa. As the home city from which Columbus sailed over the horizon to discover the new world, it came to symbolise his own search for a new dawn for Western culture – he had by now settled on *Dawn* as the title of the current project. In *The Gay Science*, also written largely in Genoa, the city has its own section where it is celebrated as the home of people who, 'in their thirst for what is new, placed a new world beside the old one.[129] He loved the baroque palaces on the Strade Nuova* five minutes walk from his lodgings, loved the combination of competitive - 'agonistic' – individuality with an overarching unity of style that made it 'competition' rather than chaos.[130] He loved being able to walk six to eight hours a day, the brevity of the winter (it lasted only a month, he claimed), and being able to 'sit or lie almost every day on remote rocks by the sea like a lizard in the sun, quiet and engaged in adventures of the spirit'.[131] And he developed a mystical love for Genoa's sea as an occasion for absorption into the pantheistic totality of things:

> Here is the sea, here we can forget the city...Now all is still! The sea lies there pale and glittering, it cannot speak. The sky plays its everlasting silent evening game with red and yellow and green, it cannot speak. The little cliffs and ribbons of rock that run down into the sea...none of them can speak. This tremendous muteness which suddenly overcomes us is lovely and dreadful, the heart swells at it...I begin to hate speech, to hate even thinking;...O sea, O evening!...You teach man to cease to be man! Shall he surrender to you? Shall he become as you are now, pale, glittering, mute, tremendous, reposing above himself? Exalted above himself?[132]

By March of 1881 *Dawn* was basically finished and the manuscript sent to Schmeitzner. Its presiding spirits, he writes Köselitz, are 'my three Genoese guardian angels, Columbus, Mazzini, and Paganini'.[133] As a place to meet to deal with the proofs, he and Köselitz decided upon Recoaro, about halfway between Genoa and Venice. Nietzsche arrived there on May 3 for a two-month stay.

Set in the Dolomites east of Lake Garda, Recoaro was yet another spa resort. Nietzsche was able to take the famous Recoaro waters (now available in bottles). The two friends stayed in the Albergo Tre Garofani, an elegant yet unpretentious hotel not far from the Fonti Centrali. They must have had access to a piano because here, for the first time, Nietzsche gained a proper knowledge of Köselitz's music, specifically his comic opera, *Joke, Cunning, Revenge*. 'He is a composer of the first rank without peer among all living composers' (i.e., superior to Wagner), he decided. With its 'cheerfulness, grace, inwardness and great range of feeling from harmless fun to innocent sublimity',[134] Köselitz's music was, he asserted, 'precisely the music to which my philosophy belongs'.[135]

As in most other places, Nietzsche's health did badly in Recoaro. The thunderstorms caused by the collision of warm, Adriatic air with the cool air of the Alps upset him, as

---

* Peter Paul Rubens was so struck by the beauty of the Strada Nuova that in 1622 he published a two-volume collection of architectural drawings of its palaces called *I Palazzi di Genova*. Now called the Via Garibaldi, the Strada Nuova is a World Heritage site.

did the lack of forest shade for his eyes. By July he was suffering his awful seizures every day. And so he decided to return to the Engadine. A nightmare journey of missed train connexions, from which he needed a week to recover, brought him to St. Moritz. Here, the impossibly high prices and a chance recommendation from a local inhabitant combined to send him onwards and upwards to the tiny farming village of Sils Maria. Here he found a relatively cheap room above a grocery shop in a simple, two-storey house conveniently abutting a pine forest, owned by the local mayor, Herr Durisch. Thus, on Monday, July 4, 1881, Nietzsche discovered the place that was to become, more than anywhere else, the heart of his spiritual homeland.

16

Dawn

Published in July 1881, *Dawn* (or *Daybreak*) was a Genoa book. Though he had begun the preparatory sketches a year and a half earlier in Riva, and had continued them in Venice and Stresa, the book itself came into being in Genoa: 'Almost every sentence was thought, was *tracked down*, among the confusion of rocks near Genoa'.[1] It is the concluding work of Nietzsche's positivist period.

A Book for Slow Readers

As with *Human, All-Too-Human*, *Dawn* is once again, clearly, a book that is addressed to 'free spirits', potential and actual. It is addressed to a 'company of thinkers', to, that is, 'we adventurers and birds of passage [*Wandervögel*]';[2] we who resist current customs and conventions and so are denounced by the mainstream as 'criminals, free-thinkers, immoral persons' and 'put under the ban of outlawry [*Vogelfreiheit*]'.[3] As in *Human*, Nietzsche senses the gathering of a movement of life-reform: 'at the present time ... those who do not regard themselves as bound by existing laws and customs are making the first attempts to organise themselves and therewith to create for themselves a *right*'.[4] This movement he wishes to encourage and guide, even though, with the collapse of the old morality, 'it may make the coming century a dangerous one in which it will be necessary to carry guns'.[5] At present, he observes, there are in Europe 'perhaps ten to twenty million people who no longer "believe in God"', so they should 'give a sign to one another' in order to become an organized 'power in Europe'.[6] Since this discussion takes place under the heading *in hoc signo vinces* ('in this sign you will conquer' – Constantine was referring to the cross), Nietzsche probably means 'sign' quite literally: we free spirits should identify ourselves to each other with, as it were, a counter-cross, some kind of lapel badge or logo. (Prometheus breaking free of his chains, perhaps, which was used on the cover of the first edition of *The Birth of Tragedy*.)

Since *Dawn* is for free spirits – always the exception rather than rule, remember – one can expect it to be a book intended for, once again, 'the few'. This shows up in the remarks on marriage. Nietzsche is clearly in favour of marriage *in general*, since 'breeding', i.e., eugenics, is a major part of his hope for the future: he wants, for example, an interbreeding of Jewish toughness and intelligence with the idealism and leadership qualities of the best of the European aristocracy.[7] But on the other hand *Dawn* is deeply sceptical about the suitability of marriage for his primary audience.[8] The implication seems to be that while some free spirits will marry, given that the 'breeding' of excellent human beings of the future must require procreation by excellent human beings of the present, Nietzsche's few and primary disciples will, like himself, remain unmarried. Or so he thinks.

What kind of a work is *Dawn*? How is it intended to be used? The book, says Nietzsche, is not 'for reading straight through or reading aloud, but for dipping into, especially when out walking or on a journey; you must be able to stick your head into it and out of it again and again and discover nothing familiar around you'.[9] It is intended, in other words, not as a *theoretical treatise* but as a spiritual *resource* – like, for example, the Bible. This idea of a text for meditation and rumination rather than instant consumption is referred to in the 1886 Preface to the work's second edition. The book, Nietzsche writes, is *only* for 'slow reading'; it must be read '*lento*'. To this end, and to combat the 'perspiring haste' of the present age which 'wants to get everything done at once', he deliberately writes, he says, in a way designed to 'reduce to despair' the hurried reader.[10] The reference is to the condensation of thought into shorter and longer aphorisms so that understanding becomes a matter of slowly puzzling out. The intended result is that the book should become as vibrantly alive for the reader as it was for its author. The same goes, I think, for its apparent lack of structure. Even more than *Human*, it gives the appearance of being written in a 'stream of consciousness': the five 'books' have no titles and there is no obvious reason why one stops and another starts. But I think this is motivated in the same way as is the aphoristic style: there *is* a structure, but one has to *work* to find it, work the wrong kind of reader, the 'hasty' one, will not put in.*

So *Dawn* is a text for meditation. Not, however, in the Eastern sense of putting the intellect out of action, but rather the opposite: the basis for the work is the use, even the passionate use, of reason. Nietzsche comments on the 'intoxication' with the newly discovered art of reasoning that speaks through 'every line' of Plato's dialogues, and deplores the glorification of anti-reason in 'how philosophy is done today'.[11] (The contemporary attack on 'logocentrism' would not engage his sympathy.)

Happiness

Nietzsche writes that while German morality, for example, Kant's categorical imperative ('Act only on that maxim which you can will to be a universal law'), is a morality of 'unconditional obedience', the 'morality of antiquity' was utterly different:

> All those Greek thinkers, however varied … seem, as moralists, like a gymnastics teacher who says to his pupil; 'Come follow me! Submit to my discipline! Then perhaps you will succeed in carrying off the prize before all Hellenes'.[12]

* That being said, there may also be an element of making a virtue out of necessity. Large-scale structure is something Nietzsche's fine-grained sensibility was never good at, a sensibility attuned, as he put it, to 'quarter-tones' (KGB III.5 960).

What was the prize? Nietzsche tells us that when philosophy became matter of public competition in the third century BC there was a premium on appearing happy in order to discombobulate the opposition. The result (by a kind of reverse causation) was that eventually one *became* happy.[13] He mentions the Cynics, whose main competitors were the Stoics, the Epicureans, the Aristotelians, and the Platonists. The prize, then, for which they competed was happiness. As we know, all the Hellenistic schools agreed that the point of philosophy was to achieve happiness.

Following the Hellenistic model, as he did in *The Wanderer and His Shadow*, Nietzsche conceives of *Dawn* as teaching a spiritual 'gymnastics', a soul-therapy the aim of which is happiness. The purpose of the book, he says, is simply to 'translate into reason a strong and constant drive, a drive for gentle sunlight, bright and buoyant air, southerly vegetation, the breath of the sea'.[14] Written in Genoa, the book, *Ecce Homo* suggests, is infused with the genius loci, the southern happiness that is the spirit of the place. The result is that it contains 'no malice' (none of Rée's sadistic joy in 'hitting the black').* Rather, like its author, 'it lies in the sun, round, happy, like a sea-beast sunning itself among the rocks'.[15] So the book *expresses* happiness. And since happiness is infectious it *promotes* happiness.

Of course, the happiness that is to be restored to us is what has long been denied under the gloomy skies of Christianity. That is why the book is called *Dawn* – I prefer *Dawn* to *Daybreak* as a translation of its title since it calls to mind 'dawn of a new age'. The sun is beginning to shine (*Sunrise* would be another possible translation of *Morgenröte*) after a long absence. Actually, since the book's motto tells us that 'there are so many dawns that have not yet broken', it is not a single new age Nietzsche is looking for but an indefinite series of new ages, each rising above the other,[16] an ascending series of 'new dawns'.

* * *

Dawn, then, is not a theoretical treatise but a spiritual therapy aimed, like the philosophies of antiquity, at happiness. The spirit of Epicurus presides over *Dawn* as it did over its predecessor. This explains why roughly a third of its aphorisms have no theoretical content at all but are, rather, exercises in 'life-wisdom',[17] very concrete pieces of advice on the art of living, on how to live a happy life, such as 'get plenty of sleep' and 'don't trust flatterers'.

It also explains Nietzsche's suggestion that the 'right' philosophy for one individual may be different from the 'right' one for another. Just as one medical regimen will not suit all patients, so philosophies, while containing, perhaps, elements that are beneficial to all, will need to vary from person to person. As the ancient world believed, the question of which philosophy best suits one will ultimately be a matter of individual 'temperament'.[18]

---

* This claim seems to me true: the malice (though not the taste for depth psychology) of *Human* really has disappeared. In the notebooks of the period Nietzsche finally realises what is fundamentally wrong with Rée's and La Rochefoucauld's taste for the dark side. 'Up to now there have been glorifiers and vilifiers of man but both proceeded from the moral standpoint. La Rochefoucauld and the Christians both found mankind ugly: this is a moral judgment, a different kind of morality was unknown! We however regard man as belonging to nature which is neither evil nor good' (KSA 9 6 [382]). The venom behind Rée's 'psychological observations' – and the despair that marked his character – comes, Nietzsche now sees, from the fact that, though he had rejected Christian metaphysics, he had not been able to free himself from Christian morality. His psychological observations are experienced and presented as exposing the 'dark' in human nature only via an implicit subscription to a Christian conception of the 'light'.

Fundamentally, claims Nietzsche, a philosophy is nothing but 'an instinct for a personal diet', different philosophies being expressions of different 'personal drives'. For this butterfly fluttering 'high on the rocky sea coast . . . a philosophy could no doubt be found: though it would not be my philosophy'.[19]

The Theoretical Framework

As I emphasised in the last chapter, the Epicurean conception of the goal of philosophy as happiness-promoting 'wisdom' rather than knowledge-promoting 'theory' by no means excludes theory from philosophy. All it excludes is irrelevant theory, theory for theory's sake. In *Dawn* there is a clear theoretical foundation.

First, the work emphatically rejects Kantian/Schopenhauerian idealism. What Plato and Schopenhauer wanted to discover behind the so-called 'veil of appearances' 'does not exist'. It is, Nietzsche writes, simply 'nothing'.[20] The 'thing in itself' is thus abolished. There is only one world, not two. Moreover, this world is emphatically the world of nature; in particular, Darwin's nature. (Though never mentioned by name, Darwin seems to have returned to favour in *Dawn*: for the moment there is no attempt to repeat *Human, All-Too-Human*'s feeble attempt to refute him.) Thus Nietzsche observes, approvingly, that the ape now stands grinning before the portal to the supposedly divine origins of man:[21] Darwin demolishes the metaphysical by showing the human-all-too-human (or rather animal-all-too-animal) origins of man. And he observes that anyone studying evolution now knows that 'vision was *not* the intention behind the creation of the eye, rather . . . vision appeared only after chance (random mutation) had put the apparatus together'. 'A single instance of this kind', Nietzsche continues, 'and "purposes" fall away like scales from the eyes!'[22]

Naturalism then reigns in *Dawn*: there is only the one world of nature, and the human being is nothing more than an organism that has evolved within it. And rationalism reigns, too: 'reason', and more specifically natural science, is the authoritative way to find out about this one world.[23]

As in *Human*, Nietzsche takes it as obvious that naturalism entails causal determinism and that determinism in turn entails the absence of 'free will': there are *no* actions performed of a free will, he asserts bluntly.[24] This in turn entails the absence of moral responsibility.[25] (From this absence he concludes, as before, that we should no more punish people for breaking the law than we punish them for being sick. Criminals indeed *are* mentally sick and should therefore be regarded as cases for *treatment* rather than punishment.)[26]

The final element in *Dawn*'s theoretical framework is psychological egoism: 'If only those actions are moral which are performed for the sake of another and only for his sake . . . then there are no moral actions'.[27] And, though it is less prominent than in *Human*, it seems that Nietzsche still adheres to the hedonistic version of egoism. This is suggested in various places,[28] but the strongest evidence is that though the 'will to power' almost makes its first significant appearance in Nietzsche's writings, what he actually talks about is the will not to power but rather to the *feeling* of power [*Machtgefühl*] – in other words a form of pleasure.[29]

In a word, then, the theoretical framework of *Dawn* consists in the same three axiomatic doctrines that we first met in *Human*: naturalism, determinism, and psychological egoism/hedonism. This is what makes it sensible to regard *Dawn* as belonging, still, to Nietzsche's positivist period.

Critique of Christian Metaphysics

As in *Dawn*'s positivist predecessors, Nietzsche offers no direct argument for abolishing the 'thing in itself', for naturalism. He does, however, indirectly support it through a critique of Christian supernaturalism, an essential prelude, he believes, to the 'dawn' of a new happiness. As before, some of the criticisms are 'genealogical' in character, employing the 'historical method' (p. 249). This method, he says, replaces the attempt to tackle religious belief head-on by proving the non-existence of God: 'in the past one sought to prove that there is no God – today one indicates how the belief that there is a God could *arise* and how this belief acquired its weight and importance; a counter-proof that there is no God thereby becomes superfluous'.[30] In other words, by showing the causes of belief in God to be something quite other than sound reasons one shows it to be – not false – but rather irrational, unworthy of belief.

Nietzsche's inquiry concerns the earliest origins of Christian belief. The question arises, therefore, as to how that inquiry is relevant to current believers. However suspect the grounds of our ancestors' beliefs, could not current believers base their belief on much better grounds? I think Nietzsche's discussion has to be understood in conjunction with *Human*'s remark that nearly everyone who adopts a religion does so unreflectively in the way in which, in wine-drinking countries, one grows up drinking wine.[31] In a family such as Nietzsche's, for example, you are simply *born into* a 'geography' of earth, heaven, and hell as you are born into the landscape of Saxony. Religious, like political, belief is usually inherited rather than adopted on the basis of reasons. This being so, it becomes relevant to look at what kind of epistemological authority Christianity's first believers had. For implicitly, as with a message passed back along a column of soldiers, the modern believer's grounds for belief can be no better than those of the original believers. In fact, however, when we look at these grounds we see that they have no epistemological authority at all.

The Bible, for instance, that supposedly divinely inspired source of infallible truth, was actually cobbled together by Paul, out of hatred for the Jewish law. Frustrated by his inability to fulfil the law on account of the all-too-human in his nature, this fanatical and tortured soul invented, as it were, a new game with a new set of rules, in order to destroy the old law. Even if it were still possible to sin, he made it no longer possible to sin against the Jewish law.[32]

Similarly, the reason Christianity spread so rapidly through the Roman Empire, elbowing aside all rival religions, had nothing to do with the power of truth or evidence. It spread, rather, as one might put Nietzsche's point, on account of effective 'marketing techniques'. Its 'proselytisers'[33] (i.e., 'sales people'), by engaging in dramatic sales techniques such as voluntary martyrdom,[34] fooled their audiences into accepting the tripartite geography of heaven, earth, and hell, and so were able to proffer both a stick and a carrot: they were able to terrify with threats of eternal damnation for unbelievers and seduce with promises of eternal bliss for the faithful.[35] In the notebooks Nietzsche adds that Christianity spread in an 'epidemic of panic' because it had been prophesied that the world would end very soon.[36] In general, then, the power of Christianity has never had anything to do with truth. From the point of view of reason and truth, it has, rather, a '*pudenda origo* (shameful origin)'[37] in Paul's revenge and in the deployment of sophisticated marketing techniques. In a word, Christianity is a 'con-job'.

In *Human*, Nietzsche proudly presented the 'historical method' as his sole method of criticising metaphysical belief. But now he admits that 'there are no scientific methods which alone lead to knowledge'.[38] In line with this methodological pluralism, we find him deploying other methods of criticism – two additional methods, I shall suggest. This is actually necessary since the 'historical' approach will deal with neither (a) the 'born again' Christian who does not rely on tradition but has had a 'conversion experience' nor (b) the *reflective* Christian – the Christian who has reasoned his way to belief via the thought, for example, that since the world exhibits 'intelligent design' it must have a designer, or the thought that *something* must have caused the 'big bang'. It is not, that is, in every instance true that the historical method renders the need for 'a counter-proof that there is no God . . . superfluous'.

The first supplementary critical method Nietzsche deploys is what might be called 'internal anti-theology', the hunt for contradictions within Christian dogma. Nietzsche poses, for example, the rhetorical question: if, as the doctrine of original sin holds, we are thoroughly contemptible, how could anyone, and in particular God, love us as he is supposed to? [39] Again, how, Nietzsche asks, could a wholly loving and wholly powerful God fail to make his intentions clear, how could he allow thousands of years of dispute as to what those intentions are? Does he not look more like a *cruel* than a loving god?[40] More important than these pinpricks, however (to which any skilful Jesuit would produce a ready response without raising a sweat), are Nietzsche's remarks, directed not like the 'historical method' to the origins but rather to the unhealthy *consequences* of Christian belief: fear and guilt.

So, with regard to fear, Nietzsche observes that Christianity blots out the sun: the true believer's life is rendered permanently 'gloomy' by 'fears of hell'. 'How much superfluous cruelty proceeds from those religions which invented sin'.[41] And, again, on the theme of cruelty and fear, he claims that Christianity turns the deathbed into a 'torture chamber'.[42] There is a palpable element of autobiography, here: recall what I called the 'gothic' undertone (pp. 7–8 above) to his memories of his father's church in Röcken.

Nietzsche's discussions of death during the positivist period can appear trite. One needs, however, to recognise that, for him, the fact that 'science has reconquered' 'the idea of definitive [*endgültig*] death',[43] the fact that modern thought has disposed of the immortality of the soul, is a genuine liberation from the fear of hell and damnation, a fear still genuinely experienced by many nineteenth-century believers. Kant called God, freedom, and immortality the 'postulates of practical reason', the necessary presuppositions of morality. Nietzsche denies each of them and each denial is a liberation.[44]

Along with mortal fear, the other effect of Christian belief is guilt, irredeemable guilt, the 'bad conscience'[45] about our inescapable condition as natural, animal beings. Aphrodite and Eros, divinities in the ancient world, are turned into 'diabolical hobgoblins' by Christianity – a demonizing of regularly recurring feelings that is yet another act of appalling Christian cruelty.[46] In addition, while the Greeks had the concept of genuine misfortune, Christianity, with its just God, turns every misfortune into a punishment.[47]

Critique of Christian Morality

Nietzsche views Christianity as a package deal: the metaphysics and the morals are inseparable. The former, God, freedom, and immortality, constitute the backdrop of punishment and reward without which the commandments of Christian morality make no sense. Following Schopenhauer, he thinks that Kant's idea of a '*categorical* imperative' – a command divorced from any associated punishment or reward – makes no sense: commandments make sense only as the prescription of means to desired ends,[48] the ends, for example, of attaining eternal bliss and avoiding eternal torment. Nonetheless, old habits die hard. Although Christian metaphysics is dying of its own accord, its morality, to which we have over so many generations become habituated, lives on and, by demanding of us impossible standards of virtue, destroys our self-esteem. It needs, therefore, an independent critique.[49]

Schopenhauer claimed that his own ethics capture the essence of Christian ethics, and Nietzsche agrees. Thus, since Schopenhauer reduces virtue to the single quality of altruism, which, combined with pessimism, turns into *Mitleid* (the word means both 'pity' and 'compassion'), Nietzsche sees pity as the heart of Christian ethics. Concerning pity he makes, basically, two points: first that it is really disguised egoism, and second that it in fact harms rather than helps its recipient.

As we have already seen, Nietzsche's psychological egoism commits him to the view that if compassionate action is conceived as action performed 'for the sake of another and only for his sake'[50] it never occurs. So-called compassion is in fact *always* motivated by one's own interests rather than the interests of another. The interest Nietzsche identifies most prominently is in 'the feeling of power'. In giving alms or visiting the poorhouse I experience the pleasant feeling of superiority.[51] There are, however, other interests apparently compassionate action can serve. If, for example, 'without thinking about it' I leap in to save a drowning man, unconsciously I am thinking of my own honour.[52]

Why does Nietzsche take the claim that Schopenhauerian altruism does not exist to be important? For, I think, two reasons. First, since '"ought" implies "can"'[53] – since we cannot be under an obligation to do, or be, something unless we *can* do, or be, it – psychological egoism, if true, liberates us from the demands of Christian morality. Second, because the kinds of acts which a morality of compassion encourages us to perform, acts of *apparent* compassion, harm the recipients of those actions.

Acts of pity harm their recipient in two ways. First, just as they produce the pleasant feeling of power in the pitier, so do they produce an unpleasant feeling of powerlessness and inferiority in the pitied.[54] The notebooks refine this point in an insightful way, observing that 'we can only help the neighbour in that we locate him in a class (patient, prisoner, beggar, artist, child) and thus humiliate him: the individual can't be helped'.[55]

Second, pity as an emotion blocks the performance of genuinely benevolent acts. Nietzsche considers, first, the Schopenhauerian saint who empathises with the suffering of the whole world (p. 85 above). Such empathy, he says, would destroy us: were we really to empathise with all of suffering Africa, were we to take all that suffering on board 'as demanded by the philosophy of pity', we would experience a psychological collapse that would render us incapable of genuinely benevolent action[56] – 'unhinge all the wings of the soul', as he put it in *The Birth of Tragedy*.[*,57] Even on a less universal level, says Nietzsche, *Mitleid* 'will paralyse...the helpful hand'. The Jews, 'whose charity is more effective than that of

---

* This point is actually taken from Schopenhauer, who holds, as we saw, that it is universal compassion which produces the 'transition from virtue to asceticism', from love to world-denial. The difference is that while Schopenhauer thinks this a good thing, Nietzsche thinks the opposite.

other nations', are particularly not given to weepy emotionalism.[58] The surgeon's scalpel will shake if he starts weeping over the condition of the patient: 'only when one knows about the other's suffering without oneself suffering can one act for his sake, like the doctor'.[59]

This second line of criticism makes it apparent that Nietzsche does not in fact deny that the emotion of pity/compassion occurs. This is very surprising since it appears to be incompatible with the psychological egoism in which he professes to believe. He tries to deal with this problem by saying that when we have the feeling of sympathy or empathy (the latter word, he observes, better describes what Schopenhauer is talking about),[60]

> it is misleading to call the *Leid* [suffering] we may experience *Mit-leid* [literally with-suffering] for it is under all circumstances a suffering which he who is suffering in our presence is free of: it is our own, as the suffering the other feels is his own. But it is *only this suffering of our own* which we get rid of when we perform deeds of pity.[61]

So suppose I give money to the beggar, this time not (or not solely – pity, Nietzsche observes, is a richly 'polyphonous' phenomenon)[62] to acquire a feeling of superiority but because it pains me to see you suffering. In this case, Nietzsche claims, I act to relieve *my* pain.

This, surely, is confused. If I had no desire for your well-being, if I was completely indifferent to the well-being of anyone but myself, the sight of your suffering would not cause me pain and so there would be nothing for me to seek to relieve. What emerges, therefore, though Nietzsche refuses to admit it, is that, once he gets down to the details of human emotional life, the psychological egoism to which he is theoretically committed in fact collapses. If there are genuine feelings of compassion on which we sometimes act, psychological egoism cannot be true.

So what valid points emerge from *Dawn*'s critique of 'morality of pity'? First, that acts of *apparent* compassion are in reality often egoistic in their primary motivation: in particular, they are often aimed at feeling superior to their 'victims'. Second, genuine benevolence will only be hindered by gushy feelings of sympathy. Effective love is, as one might put it, *tough* love. The problem, though, with the intended universality of Nietzsche's critique of Christian morality is that a thoughtful Christian would have little difficulty in agreeing with both these points. And what this suggests is that the target Nietzsche actually hits – with his novelist's fine-grained and subtle insight – is not, in fact, Christian morality as such but rather the kind of middle-class, drawing-room woman who, Pharisee-like, congratulates herself on her 'good works' and 'fine feelings', on her 'beautiful soul'.[63] The notebook remark, 'Not to be able to look at blood – is that moral?'[64] seems to be so targeted. If this is true, then what Nietzsche really targets, sometimes consciously, sometimes not, is *moral narcissism*, a phenomenon – as Dickens, too, was acutely aware – all too prevalent in bourgeois, Victorian society. What he attacks is the 'thirst for appearing morally *excited* at all costs'[65] (an appearance contemporary postmodernism often cultivates to disguise its lack of substance). The attack is effective and legitimate. But it is one that would surely be endorsed by any thoughtful Christian.

The Counter-Ideal to Christianity

Nietzsche wants us to reject, we have seen, not only Christian metaphysics but also that part of Christianity which still survives, its morality. We are to reject the Christian worldview in its totality. And, as we know, we are to replace it with a worldview whose presuppositions* are naturalism, determinism (with the consequent denial of free will and moral responsibility) and psychological egoism. But how are we to live within such an outlook? What new way of living are we free spirits to adopt in place of the old, Christian way?

First of all, we must become ethical egoists. If, that is, psychological egoism is true, then since, as observed, we can only be obligated to do what we *can* do, we must adopt a moral code that is a frank endorsement of acting out of self-interest.

'Ought', however, does not merely entail 'can'; it also entails 'can *not*'. Nietzsche recognises this: the chief commands of any moral code reveal where, from the point of view of the survival and thriving of a community, its chief *failings* have been.[66] (*Zarathustra* observes that a people's moral code reveals what is 'needful *and difficult*' for them.)[67] Only the Jews, the best haters in the world, could have invented the commandment to love one's enemy.[68] So there has to be something Nietzsche thinks we ought to do which, even given the truth of psychological egoism, we can fail to do. What we can fail to do is to recognise where our true interests lie. A great deal of *Dawn* is devoted, therefore (as was the conversation in Pisa with Isabella von Prahlen (p. 230 above)), to establishing the nature of our true self-interest, the character of *enlightened* egoism.

Self-Creation

The first requirement of acting out of enlightened self-interest is that there be a self. But a self – a unitary self as opposed to a chaos of conflicting desires – is not a birthright. It is not something to be *discovered* but rather, in a certain sense, needs to be *created*. In the notebooks of the period, Nietzsche writes that

> it's a myth to suppose that we will find our true self by leaving behind this or that or forgetting it. That way we find ourselves back in the infinite. Rather, we have to make ourselves, have to give form to all elements – that is the task. Always a sculptor! A productive human being! Not through knowledge but through practice, and so become a [role] model ourselves! [Self-] Knowledge is at best a means.[69]

There is, however, a problem with this injunction to self-creation, namely, a new kind of way in which Nietzsche at least appears to argue for the absence of free will. He appears, that is (and has often been taken), to argue along the following lines. We have no real idea what the true causes of our actions are since they happen below the level of consciousness. Hence we are as little responsible for our actions as we are for our dreams.[70] Mostly, we

---

* *Dawn*'s subtitle, 'Thoughts on the *Vorurteile* of Morality', is generally translated as 'Thoughts on the Prejudices of Morality'. However, since *Vor-urteile* literally means 'pre-judgment', 'Presuppositions' or 'Preconceptions' offer themselves as alternative translations. This certainly is the best translation of the notebooks' remark that 'Someone for whom the usual presuppositions [of morality] don't begin to sound paradoxical has not reflected enough' (KSA 9 3 [72]). If we think of the subtitle in this way then the structure of *Dawn* becomes more perspicuous. The work is an attack on the 'presuppositions' of Christian morality – God, freedom, and immortality – with the intention of replacing them with his own 'presuppositions' – which he would not want to call 'prejudices'.

lack even the language to describe those causes – words such as 'hate', 'love' and 'desire' only describe *extreme* states, not the mild and intermediate states that usually govern our actions.[71] Hence someone who thinks that his willing causes his actions is as much in error as someone who says 'I will the sun to rise' and then, when it does, thinks his willing has caused it.[72]

At first glance these and other passages seem to reduce us to mere passengers riding on the shoulders of our unconsciousnesses, mere observers of our lives. But this cannot really be what Nietzsche means. One reason is that it would be an affirmation of 'Islamic fatalism', already identified as an error (p. 268 above). Another reason is the theme of 'self-creation' itself, the fact that, as we are about to see, Nietzsche actually allows us a considerable degree of control over who we are to be and hence what we do.

So the above remarks are, I think, to be read as preceded by an implicit 'mostly' or 'typically' and so end up making a Freudian (or Schopenhauerian or La Rochefoucauldian) point: *mostly* we have little or no understanding of the viper's nest of 'drives' and emotions that are inside us, *mostly* what we tell ourselves about our motives has as little to do with the real causes of our actions as it has to do with the real causes of the rising of the sun. The point of the remarks is really, then, I think, to *define a task*: if we are to take control of our lives – if we are to be 'selves' rather than 'failed selves' (or 'ex-selves') – a precondition is, as Epicurus emphasised, to 'know oneself', to understand our own natures – through precisely the kinds of unflinching, unsentimental, 'psychological observations' presented by the La Rochefoucauld–Schopenhauer–Rée tradition. *Dawn* complains, for example, that since, typically, we do not attend to what our 'drives' really are, the question of which ones are to be strengthened by 'nutrition', and which allowed to wither through lack of it, is left to chance.[73]

Suppose we do achieve a good degree of self-knowledge, come to a good understanding of the 'drives' that operate within us. How should we then proceed in our task of 'self-creation'? How, indeed, *can* we proceed? 'What', asks Nietzsche, given the truth of determinism, 'are we at liberty to do?'

One can, he writes in a crucial passage,

> dispose of one's drives like a gardener and, though few know it, cultivate the shoots of anger, pity, curiosity, vanity as productively and profitably as a beautiful fruit tree on a trellis; one can do it with the good or bad taste of a gardener and, as it were, in the French or English or Dutch or Chinese fashion; one can also let nature rule and only attend to a little tidying-up here or there; one can, finally, without paying any attention to them at all, let the plants grow up and fight their fight out among themselves...all this we are at liberty to do: but how many know we are at liberty to do it? Do not the majority *believe* in *themselves* as in complete *fully-developed facts*? Have not the great philosophers put their seal on this prejudice with the doctrine of the unchangeability of character?[74]

Though this might seem a critical reference to Schopenhauer, who makes a big parade of his doctrine of the 'unchangeability of character', it is, in fact, a repetition of his view of 'acquired character'. Nietzsche talks, for example, of self-'sculpting' or self-'gardening' (self-landscaping, one might say) as a matter of allowing undesirable drives to wither by removing oneself from places and company which stimulate them.[75] This, word for word, is what Schopenhauer says with respect to acquiring 'what in the world is called "character"'.[76]

But, one might object, does not Nietzsche's commitment to determinism and the denial of 'free will' commit him precisely to *denying* this 'liberty' of self-creation or, less misleadingly, self-cultivation? Not so. All that determinism entails is that *whether or not I am going to be the gardening type of person and what kind of gardening person I might be is already determined*: '*that* one *desires* to combat the vehemence of a drive, does not stand within our power; nor . . . the choice of method; nor . . . the success or failure of this method'.[77] Nonetheless, since Nietzsche clearly *advocates* 'self-mastery'[78] through self-'cultivation' and *disapproves* of 'letting the plants grow up and fight their fight out among themselves' (the Platonic theme that you can't do anything until you make yourself 'one man' runs through all his thinking), he presupposes that his readers will be predetermined as 'gardening' types, so that reading his book will act as a stimulus that activates their horticultural disposition.[79] And this is a reasonable presupposition, since if they were not they would not be reading the book. They would not, at least, be the 'perfect readers' for whom that reading would be a significant event.[80]

Continuing the 'gardening' theme, Nietzsche emphasises the potentially misleading character of the phrase 'self-creation'. The ideal condition of the soul, he says, is 'fruitfulness'; spiritual 'pregnancy', being 'pregnant' with some 'idea' or 'deed' (the character of which I shall shortly discuss). But as with literal pregnancy, 'self-making' is a matter of 'bringing forth' (as a sculptor 'brings forth' the figure slumbering in the marble), a fact which 'ought to blow to the winds all presumptuous talk of "willing" and "creating"'.[81] So it is a mistake to think of Nietzschean self-creation as a matter of creating, like God, *ex nihilo*. Self-creation is, to repeat, self-cultivation.

Nietzsche (from childhood, we have seen, a devotee of the 'Protestant work ethic') emphasises that self-cultivation is a matter of hard *work*. One of his more telling complaints against (some) Christians is that they are spiritually *lazy*, want to avoid 'the burden of the demands of morality' by finding a 'shorter route to perfection': one born-again leap to 'salvation' is the route taken by the 'exhausted and despairing'.[82] Though he knew him at best by hearsay, this may be intended as a critique of Kierkegaard's 'leap of faith'.

It is not just Christians, however, who fail to put in the hard yards. Even self-professed egoists practise a mere 'pseudo-egoism' since 'whatever they say about their "egoism", the great majority nonetheless do nothing for their ego their whole life long' since they actually have no ego. They act, rather, for the sake of a socially constructed 'fiction' which they mistake for themselves.[83] Glossy magazines, for example, tell me that what I really want is fast cars, fast women, golf, and fishing. And so I devote all my energies to retiring at forty so I can enjoy doing what *I* want to do. Sadly, however, I quickly find out that fast cars, fast women, golf, and fishing are boring, the reason being that none of these 'manufactured desires' are to be found among the desires I really have.

Nietzsche identifies six modes of 'working on oneself', of pruning those aspects of one's nature one wishes to deny expression: one can deny a drive gratification so it eventually withers (giving up smoking, for example), restrict its expression to certain limited times and places (carnivals, ancient and modern),[84] overindulge it so as to generate disgust (risky, Nietzsche points out, because the horse-rider often breaks his neck), associate the drive with some painful thought, as when the Christian associates the idea of the devil with sex (aversion therapy), build up a rival drive by constant gratification, and finally, like the ascetic, one can weaken the whole bodily system so that all drives, including the one to be dealt with, are deprived of vehemence.[85]

These are *techniques* of self-cultivation. Further technical advice (this becomes much more prominent in Nietzsche's next book, *The Gay Science*) is to learn from artists how to cultivate one's character, particularly with respect to one's 'weaknesses': those drives, that is to say, which do not fit into the master-plan of the self. If we cannot get rid of them – there are bound to be some indelible drives, Nietzsche suggests – we should learn to 'deploy [them] like an artist'. We should study Beethoven, for instance, and learn to imitate his use of the 'coarse, obstinate, impatient' elements in his nature to highlight, make us 'ravenously hungry' for, his virtues.[86] Another strategic use of weaknesses is to humanize our characters: we may, Nietzsche suggests, allow a little 'folly' to show in order to stop ourselves becoming *too* perfect, too unapproachable.[87]

But what should we *do* with techniques such as these? What principle should guide their deployment? The most general principle is that one should organise one's life around, ideally, a single defining drive. As *The Wanderer and His Shadow* observes (echoing Cézanne's instruction to the painter always to discover the 'cube, cone, and sphere' in nature), land-scapes do not please unless they possess 'beneath all their multiplicity, a simple geometrical shape'. And the same, Nietzsche now suggests, is true of human beings. A pleasing char-acter and life will have a 'mathematical substratum'.[88]

As in the case of Napoleon and 'the mankind of antiquity', the ideal shape of a life (the pyramid, we shall discover, is the ideal shape of the soul) is a straight line: 'a single drive worked through to the end with perfect consistency', with the result that one's life becomes 'the inventive elaboration and variation on a single motif'.[89] 'Multiplicity in *unity*'[90] is the watchword of all Nietzsche's thought about society and the soul: Malwida von Meysenbug records him telling her that 'of all lives, it was that of Mazzini which he envied most, this absolute concentration on a single idea [Italian unification] which burnt like a powerful flame within the individual'.[91] So one should become the 'one man' of Plato's *Republic* rather than a flickering (as Plato calls it, 'democratic') chaos in which sometimes one drive assumes dominance and sometimes another. But how? What kind of character should one's life-defining motif have?

Let us recall that the fundamental goal of Dawn is *happiness*: to roll away the dark clouds of Christianity so as to reveal a sunlit landscape. What Nietzsche wants to do is show his readers, in a word, how to be happy. Of course, his ultimate concern is for the 'culture' as a whole – our culture is to become a happy, or at least happier, culture through the efforts of his readers and their successors. For the moment, however, I should like to set that concern to one side. That being done, the question becomes: what kind of life-defining principle will lead to *personal* happiness?

The Paradox of Happiness

Nietzsche issues a warning concerning this question: '*insofar* as the individual is seeking happiness, one ought not to tender him any prescriptions as to the path to happiness: for individual happiness springs from one's own unknown laws, and prescriptions from without can only hinder it'.[92] The conditions of individual happiness, like the conditions of individual health, are so variable that no general prescription can be given. However, though Nietzsche gives no concrete 'recipe' for happiness, he does say quite a lot of a more abstract character about how to be happy.

The clue to the direction of his thinking is the remark that 'sacrificing' yourself for the future of humanity is actually no sacrifice at all but rather 'a positive enhancement of *happiness*'.[93] What he is referring to here is the so-called 'paradox of happiness', briefly touched upon earlier: experience shows that aiming directly at happiness is counterproductive, that precisely the 'pursuit of happiness' is what puts happiness out of reach. ('Desperate housewives' are permanently miserable.) The reason for this is that happiness is a by-product of passionate engagement in some activity *other than* the pursuit of happiness, an engagement which demands that not happiness but rather the goal of *this* activity be the focus of one's attention. Happiness, Nietzsche is pointing out (correctly, it seems to me), can only be pursued indirectly since it is, in philosophical jargon, an 'epiphenomenon' of passionate commitment to something else: of doing well – or at least hopefully – something one considers important. That this is Nietzsche's point comes out very clearly in an already-quoted passage from *Zarathustra*. Nietzsche's alter ego says, 'What does happiness matter to me? . . . I am striving after my work', to which his 'animals' reply 'but are you not basking in a sky-blue lake of happiness?' which forces Zarathustra, ruefully amused that the animals have divined his secret strategy, to admit that he is.[94] Happiness is a by-product of 'work'. But just what kind of 'work'? Before answering this question, I should like to digress for a moment to attend to an apparent conflict implicit in Nietzsche's conception of happiness as outlined in the previous chapter but not there addressed.

The Heroic-Idyllic

In discussing *The Wanderer and His Shadow*, I suggested that the Nietzsche of the late 1870s should be viewed in relation to the Hellenistic philosophers of life, above all Epicurus. The goal of their 'wisdom' was the achievement of a happiness in which the main ingredient was *ataraxia*, serenity. As I observed, much of this Hellenistic conception of happiness reappears in *Wanderer*: we are encouraged, for example, to meditate on the inevitability of death and our vanishing insignificance in the infinity of space and time in order to elevate ourselves above the seriousness of human affairs, to see such seriousness as 'comic', and so preserve peace of mind (p. 283 above). This Hellenistic conception of happiness is even more prominent in the notebooks of the period. They speak, for example, of the 'threefoldness of joy' as consisting in 'elevation' (above human seriousness), 'illumination' (the enjoyment of intellectual pleasures, presumably), and 'peace' (of mind). Best of all, though, is a fourth thing: the 'three in one', the trinity of elevation, illumination and peace gathered together in a unity.[95] A little later, returning to the idea of 'elevation', Nietzsche writes that he is tempted to name the 'feeling [of spiritual] . . . floating and flying' as 'the highest good'.[96] The problem, though, with all these *ataraxia*-centred delineations of happiness is that they look very passive, scarcely compatible with the idea of passionate commitment to a cause. They do not look compatible with Zarathustra's 'work', nor with Nietzsche's own passionate commitment to the regeneration of Western culture. Is there not, then, a contradiction concealed within Nietzsche's conception of happiness, a contradiction between the passive and the active?

Contrary to appearances, I think the answer is that there is not. Another note from the *Wanderer* period, referring to the summer landscape around St. Moritz, records that

> the evening before last I was so absorbed into a Claude Lorraine-like rapture that eventually
> I broke into heavy weeping. That I should still be allowed to experience this! I never knew

that the earth could display such a thing; I thought the good painters had invented it. The heroic-idyllic is now the discovery of my soul.[97]

The theme of this note reappears in the already-quoted *Wanderer* passage entitled '*Et in Arcadia ego*', 'Arcadia' being the pastoral paradise of classical mythology. Here Nietzsche says that his idea of paradise is a Poussin or Claude Lorraine landscape populated by Hellenic heroes. He adds that his ideal is a feeling which, like theirs, is 'at one and the same time heroic and idyllic'.[98] What he's referring to is the seemingly paradoxical combination of pastoral landscapes with heroic – one might also say 'epic' – dramas on themes typically taken from Graeco-Roman mythology. So, for example, while the dominant mood of a Claude painting is one of serenity, and the dominant scene is a pastoral paradise – the figures are usually dwarfed by nature – the subject matter is indicated by startling titles such as 'Mercury Stealing Apollo's Oxen', 'The Rape of Europa', 'The Trojan Women Setting Fire to the Fleet', and so on.

An anticipation of the heroic-idyllic is to be found in *Human, All-Too-Human*, where Nietzsche speaks of 'the artist's and philosopher's vision of happiness' as a kind of 'serene agitation', a kind of active 'floating'.[99] What this indicates, I think, is that Nietzsche's 'heroic-idyllic' is close to what Martin Heidegger called *Gelassenheit* ['releasement'], a serenity that is simultaneously active, the kind of serenity that goes with the mastery of any kind of art or craft. Nietzsche refers to it in *Beyond Good and Evil* as the 'necessity', the effortless flow, the absence of conscious choice, which every artist recognises as characterizing his highest creative moments.[100] Think, for example, of the concert violinist's serene relaxation that is yet at the same time an intensely concentrated, supremely skilful state. Nietzsche is, I think, quite right: serenity and activity – including 'heroic' activity – are not opposites, but capable of combination in a single state.

Benevolent Egoism

To return from this digression, the question that faces us is this: What kind of 'work', what kind of 'task' – 'heroic' or otherwise – should define the life that has happiness as a by-product? Before answering it, let us briefly review the strategic situation. Negatively, we have seen, Nietzsche wants to abolish the old, Christian morality of compassion, unselfishness, 'putting others first', of 'looking away from oneself' while being 'lynx-eyed' for the distress of others.[101] Provocatively, as he will for the rest of his career, he habitually refers to this as, simply, 'morality'. (To distinguish it from other uses, this use of the word has been usefully dubbed '"morality" in the pejorative sense'.)[102] In its place he advocates 'egoism' – acting exclusively out of self-interest. But does this not amount to the abolition of not merely morality in the pejorative sense but morality *as such*? Soon, Nietzsche will begin to call himself – provocatively – an 'immoralist'. But, one needs to ask rather urgently, does not his avocation of egoism make him not just polemically but *really* an immoralist, an immoral thinker?

What is morality? A moral code is, Nietzsche points out, 'nothing other…than obedience to custom'.[103] (Since *Sittlichkeit*, morality, comes from *Sitte*, custom, this, in German, is almost a tautology.) The point of custom is the well-being of the moral community – social 'utility', Nietzsche calls it.[104] But does this not actually *demand* something like morality – morality 'in the pejorative sense'? Is not Nietzsche's elevation of egoism to a life-guiding principle precisely an invitation to moral chaos and social collapse? Can we not, indeed, in the spirit of works such as Alan Bloom's *The Closing of the American Mind*, see the moral collapse of the present age – the age in which *our* public, communal space has been atomised into '*My* Space' and the solidarity of friendship dissolved into the egoistic manipulations of 'networking' – as at least partially attributable to the influence of Nietzsche's validation of egoism?

Nietzsche is extremely anxious to reject the charge that his form of ethical egoism leads to social collapse, to the disappearance of action possessing communal 'utility'. He wants, indeed, to show that, after a perhaps difficult period of transition, society as a whole will be *better off*, will be a happier society, if it follows his prescription than it was under the old, Christian code of selfless pity. For this reason he emphasises that

> it goes without saying that I do not deny – unless I am a fool – that many actions called immoral [under the Christian code] ought to be avoided and resisted, and many called moral ought to be done and encouraged – but . . . *for other reasons than hitherto*.[105]

Many, that is, of the socially beneficial actions performed and validated by Christian morality will continue to be performed under the new 'egoistic' morality – but from different motives. Why should this be so? Why should the Nietzschean egoist find himself promoting the welfare of the community as a whole?

The basic shape of Nietzsche's answer is, it seems to me, encapsulated in his view of sex: what a 'benevolent arrangement' it is, he comments, that 'the one person by doing what pleases him gives pleasure to another person'.[106] In a letter to Köselitz he remarks that 'One stops loving oneself properly when one stops practicing love of the other on account of which one is advised not to stop the latter (in my experience)'.[107] And, in the notebooks, evidently repeating a popular jingle, he says we should never forget that 'Making joyful makes you joyful yourself [*Freude machen selber Freude macht*]'.[108]

What Nietzsche wants to show is that the kind of life-focus that is needed for one's own happiness is *also* one that promotes the long-term well-being of the community as a whole. We might call this 'the coincidence requirement'. What is to be shown is that the *enlightened* pursuit of one's own happiness *coincides* with the promotion of the happiness of the community as a whole; that one is not involved (in today's ghastly jargon) in a 'zero-sum game' but in, rather, a 'win–win situation'.

Nietzsche makes it clear that at least *some* forms of egoism satisfy the coincidence requirement. He identifies his own guiding mission, the life-defining 'task' which Horst Hutter calls his 'ministry to the world',[109] as that of being an 'educator' of humanity to a better future,[110] a 'doctor of the spirit' (or 'soul')[111] ministering to the confused and troubled condition of the present age.[112] (He was proud and delighted when he heard, in 1877, of a Hungarian noblewoman in Vienna (Freud's city, of course) who was using his works for the purpose of counselling people cast into turmoil by religious doubt.)[113] In what is clearly an idealised description of his *own* psychological condition, he describes what he calls an 'ideal selfishness' that is based on defining one's life in terms of this kind of mission. In letters he calls it 'holy selfishness'.[114] 'Ideal selfishness', the highest form of happiness, is, he says, spiritual 'pregnancy'. It consists in a 'state of consecration . . . of pride and gentleness . . . a balm which spreads . . . onto restless souls'. It is a matter of being pregnant with an 'idea' and 'continually to watch over and nurture and keep our soul still, so that our fruit-fulness shall *come to a happy fulfilment…for the benefit of all*'.[115] (Notice the 'idyllic-heroic' combination, here, of one's 'mission' with a kind of Madonna-like serenity.)

What Nietzsche here calls 'pregnancy', pregnancy, in his own case, with his culture-regenerating writings, is what, in another section, he calls 'being overfull' so that one 'wants to be emptied'.[116] The same idea appears in a section which describes 'the first effect of happiness' as 'the *feeling of power*', a feeling which 'wants to *express itself*'.[117] (This is a feeling shared by many creative people. Iris Murdoch, for instance, writes in a letter to a friend, 'I feel, even at the lowest moment, such endless vitality within me', a vitality she describes as 'joy'.)[118] Nietzsche refers to this 'pregnancy' as *ideal* selfishness, first, I think, because it is to represent the kind of happiness his chosen readers – the free-spirited heralds of the new culture – are to aim at but, second, because it satisfies the coincidence requirement. He, and the 'disciples' he hopes to attract, will find their – and Murdoch's – 'joy' in thinking and acting, overflowing, giving birth, 'for the benefit of all'.

Nietzsche recognises, of course, that there is another kind of 'selfishness'.* Whereas 'ideal' or 'holy' selfishness is 'overfull and wants to be emptied' – is 'gift-giving' – this other kind 'is hollow and wants to be full'[119] – is 'hungry' in the language of *Zarathustra*. In letters it is associated with cats. To Lou Salomé he writes, 'What I hate most in men is that cat-egoism that can't love any more, which is committed to nothing: worse than any other evil'.[120] The real challenge, therefore, to his view that enlightened egoism coincides with promoting 'the benefit of all' is to show that the 'hollow' selfishness which *takes* rather than *gives*, which 'looks at everything with the eye of a thief'[121] is *unenlightened*. Why should the fabulously wealthy drug baron, the priest of perverted sexual tastes, or the nihilistically-minded terrorist, provided they are clever enough not to get caught, *not* be satisfying their own (admittedly non-standard) best interests?

Though Nietzsche does not make his answer to this question immediately apparent it is, I think, or at least should be, the following. Nietzsche says that 'educators' such as himself 'find their *dignity* in their own eyes' and in the eyes of those they respect in 'the *task* of their life'.[122] And as we have seen, he speaks with immense pride of the state of being 'pregnant' with an 'idea' that will benefit humanity as a whole. 'It is in this *state of consecration*', he says, 'that one should live'.[123] What this says, I think, is that human beings are (for reasons it would not be difficult to explain socio-biologically) *just so constituted* as to achieve self-respect only if they regard themselves, in some way or other, as 'making a contribution' to the well-being of society as a whole. (Abraham Maslow intends, I think, a similar point in attributing to us a fundamental 'need for self-esteem'.) One sign of this is the fact that drug barons, terrorists, and sometimes, perhaps, even perverted priests, if they are not out-and-out psychopaths, try to rationalise their actions in terms of benefit to others: the drug baron does it all 'for the family', the terrorist does it to wipe The Great Satan off the face of the earth, the priest (like Plato's Lysias) may claim that, under the guidance of Eros, his wan-dering hand is also an educating hand. Nietzsche's point, I think, is that if one really does recognise the guiding theme of one's life as destructive, if one really does define oneself as, for example, a *femme fatale*, a wrecker of marriages and destroyer of the happiness of others,

---

* 'Selfish' action is action in which (to be brief), in pursuing my own interests, I *harm* the interests of another. Strictly, therefore, there can be no such thing as 'benevolent selfishness'. What Nietzsche is really talking about is benevolent *self-interest*. But he uses 'selfish', I think, as a provocation that is of a piece with his rejection of 'morality'.

then in one's heart of hearts one cannot but despise oneself. Just like Nietzsche's Christian, the 'hollow' egoist lives his life under the gloomy skies of the 'bad conscience'.

If this is the correct reading of Nietzschean egoism then what emerges, once again, is the fundamentally communitarian character of his philosophy. Nietzsche says that one of the major pleasures of being a thinker, a 'doctor of the spirit' such as himself, is that one satisfies one's need to experience the 'feeling of power' through the exercise of a 'concealed' 'dominion' over the community.[124] This is because, however little they may realise it, 'practical people' take their understanding of 'the palatableness of things' from 'we thinkers'.[125] As already noted, practical people are too absorbed in action to be able to think about goals and values: one should never ask a banker the purpose of his activity. Evaluation of goals is the province of the *vita contemplativa*.[126] In an unobvious way, therefore, thinkers such as Nietzsche are the 'spiritual leaders' of the community, the hidden 'philosopher kings'. Not everyone can exercise that kind of power, of course. But everyone can, in a way that fits their expertise and station in life, contribute to the well-being of the community as a whole and in that way secure self-respect and their own kind of feeling of power: their own happiness, in other words. In the end, therefore, Nietzsche's portrait of his own 'ideal selfishness' is an ideal not just for his target audience of contemplative, spiritual leaders but for everyone.

Concrete Advice

I have emphasised that the goal of *Dawn* is to provide 'life-wisdom' – specifically, advice on how to live a happy life. But of course the advice we have received so far has been very abstract: create ('landscape') yourself as a unitary self that is governed by a life-defining fundamental project which benefits the community as a whole. Many sections, however – sections which find Nietzsche at his most aphoristic – are concerned to give quite concrete advice on how to be happy, advice that may be more or less relevant to individual cases. This counselling can be arranged under three headings: care of self, navigating the world of others, and influencing others.

Care of Self. Under this heading we are told, for example, to avoid social environments where we can neither remain silent nor speak of what really matters to us[127] (often the problem with one's in-laws), and that we need plenty of solitude to escape the malice of 'little people'[128] (office politics?). Other sections show how Nietzsche's concerns intersect with those of psychotherapy and yoga. He observes, for example, that chronic sicknesses of both body and soul usually arise not from a single traumatic event but from bad habits engaged in over a long period. Shallow breathing, for instance, can lead to lung infections for which the only cure is to regularly lie on the floor breathing deeply for a quarter of an hour with a clock which chimes the quarter. Along similar lines, if one feels at odds with one's environment one should reflect whether it is not one's own habits that are to blame. In both cases the cure is bound to be a slow one.[129] Again, sleep, both literal and metaphorical, is the best cure for depression: 'the apogee of the wisdom of life consists in knowing how to fall asleep in either sense at the right time'.[130] As we saw, this was the advice that lay behind the Naumburg tower project of 1879 (p. 290 above).

Navigating Society. A number of sections point to facets of human nature against which one needs to be on guard to avoid harm. For example: one pat and the dog is all over you – 'like any other flatterer'.[131] Too much sex develops a habit in young wives that will lead them into serious temptation later on when their husbands grow old or infirm.[132] '"Woman is our enemy"– from a man who speaks so to other men there speaks an immoderate drive which hates not only itself but its means of satisfaction'.[133] (This illustrates well the acrostic quality of some of Nietzsche's aphorisms. One had to think quite hard to get the point which is, surely, that the misogynist is really in the grips of the Christian demonisation of sexual desire: an interesting observation in view of Nietzsche's own reputation for misogyny.) A fanatical prosecutor 'believes in all innocence that the assailant of a crime and a criminal must of necessity be of good character or count as such – and so he ... *discloses* himself'[134] – as, presumably, someone with good reason to *doubt* that he has a good character. (One might think of the feeding-frenzy that occurs whenever the hidden sin of a public figure is uncovered.) Don't bother arguing with old philosophers since they are interested not in a genuine intellectual challenge but in erecting a 'temple'.[135]

How to Make Friends and Influence People. The maxims in the first two categories can be of interest to anyone. But those in this third category are, I think, specifically intended for Nietzsche's target audience, the free spirits who will become the 'educators' of tomorrow. To these Nietzsche offers, for instance, the following. A man of rank does well to have a courteous memory of others, to remember only the good things about them, for that keeps them in a state of pleasant dependence.[136] (The politician's gift of remembering everyone's name and the great time you had last time you saw them.) Again, to become 'the prophet and miracle worker of one's age' – to become a 'guru' – one must live apart so that the belief finally arises that 'mankind cannot get on without us *because we ourselves quite clearly* can get along without mankind'.[137]

The Status of the Theoretical Framework

I have emphasised that, following the Hellenistic model, the ultimate goal of *Dawn* is practical 'wisdom' rather than theoretical 'knowledge'. But as we have seen, adopting the 'right' theoretical outlook – adopting the basic assumptions of naturalism and positivism – Nietzsche takes to be an essential precondition of genuine happiness, of achieving practical wisdom. This raises the question of the epistemological status of *Dawn*'s theoretical framework.

Every claim to knowledge is, says Nietzsche, at best a *Versuch*, an 'experiment' or 'attempt'.[138] This suggests that his own theoretical framework – naturalism, causal determinism, psychological egoism – he regards as itself no more than an 'experiment', something he does not count as certain knowledge. This impression is confirmed by *Dawn*'s emphasis that all our attempts at knowledge are confined by an 'horizon' (constituted, obviously, à la Kant, by the filters of our minds) which represents a 'prison' from which 'there is absolutely no escape, no backway or bypath into the *real world*!' If our horizons were different the world would disclose itself in a different way to us. From this it follows that all our so-called knowledge is 'error'.[139]

Such a conclusion, of course, by no means follows if by 'error' Nietzsche means 'falsehood'. Let our world-picture be ever so subjectively constituted and different from the world-picture of other cognitive beings, still, it might be the case that, unlike, say, the ant's world-picture, ours just happens to correspond to the way the world really is. Nietzsche recognises this in the notebooks: 'The possibility that the world is similar to the world that appears to us is not ruled out by this admission of subjective factors'.[140] Actually, however, as we have already seen, Nietzsche virtually never uses 'error' to mean 'falsehood'. The word is rather used, like Wagner's *Wahn* (p. 117 above), to mean 'goes beyond what we have evidence for', 'lacks an epistemological guarantee of truth'.

Sometimes Nietzsche is tempted to see the inescapability of 'error' as nauseating: sometimes he finds the Genoa sea (a metaphor for the infinitude of reality) malicious in its mute refusal to speak to him and 'begin[s] to hate speech and even thinking', hearing 'behind every word the laughter of error, of imagination, the spirit of delusion [*Wahn*]'.[141] But this is just a passing mood. More typically, he finds the inescapability of 'error', our inability definitively to capture the 'sea' of reality in the 'spider's net' of human 'knowledge',[142] exciting:

> In the midst of the ocean of becoming we awake [human consciousness arises] on a little island no bigger than a boat, we adventurers and birds of passage [*Wandervögel*], and look around us for a few moments: as sharply and inquisitively as possible, for how soon may a wind not blow us away . . . and thus we live a precarious minute of knowing and divining, amid joyful beating of wings and chirping with one another, and in spirit we adventure out over the ocean, no less proud than the ocean itself.[143]

Really, it is better that we cannot escape from 'error' since otherwise there would be no possibility of 'adventure', of the 'joy' of travelling. A world in which we were 'error'-free, in which we were granted God's supposed 'intellectual intuition' (knowledge unmediated by any mental filters) of reality, would be unbearably claustrophobic. In *The Birth of Tragedy* Nietzsche quotes Gotthold Lessing's remark that the search for truth means more than the truth itself,[144] and this, I think, remains his predominant sentiment.

Notice that his insistence on the inescapability of 'error' can be grounded in two different ways. His point might be that we can never have complete justification in claiming that a particular proposition corresponds to reality, or it might be that the idea of an interpretation-independent reality makes no sense, so that the very idea of correspondence between thought and reality is a mistake. The choice, as we might put it, is between a 'Kantian' and a 'postmodernist' view: the former is an epistemological thesis which denies the possibility of fully *justifying* claims to know something to be true, the latter is a thesis in metaphysics (or perhaps 'philosophical logic') which denies the very possibility of truth.

It is pretty clear from the remarks quoted already that Nietzsche is not – not yet, at least – a postmodernist. There is a reality out there – a '*real world*', as *Dawn* says without a hint of irony – to which, for all we know, our world-picture *might* more or less accurately correspond.[145] Other remarks from the notebooks make it clear that Nietzsche's focus is on epistemology rather than metaphysics. For example: 'what is new about our current view of philosophy is the conviction . . . that we don't know the truth. All previous men "possessed the truth", even the sceptics'.[146] Remarks such as these seem to presuppose that, however inaccessible, there is such a thing as 'the truth'.

Nietzsche's insistence on the inescapability of error has created the hoary question of his supposed self-refutation: if he does not claim his philosophy to be *true*, why should we be interested in it? But this seems to me a non-problem once it is realised that 'error' does not mean 'falsehood'. Nietzsche's point, surely, is just the point W. V. Quine made a hundred years later concerning the 'theory-ladenness' of observation, the 'horizon'-bound character of all human knowledge. 'We can never', says Quine, 'do better than occupy the standpoint of some theory or other, the best we can muster at the time'.[147]

By 'best theory' Quine means 'theory of maximum power': the theory that explains and predicts the maximum number of experienced phenomena in the most efficient manner. But what does Nietzsche means by 'best theory'? Why does he think that his own theoretical framework is a better theory than any of its rivals? Why, in particular, does he think the positivist worldview a better theory than the Christian – or more generally, metaphysical – worldview it seeks to replace?

One answer he might give is in terms of the consequences of the two worldviews: whereas the Christian worldview makes us depressed and passive with respect to the condition of our world, the positivist worldview makes us optimistic and active. Nietzsche has, however, pointed out enough times that the happiness-making propensity of a belief has nothing to do with its truth, and has done so with sufficient scorn, to make one think that he *cares* about truth and believes his 'experiment' in knowledge, if not necessarily the final word, is at least more likely to be true than its Christian rival. How might he have wished to argue that?

Recall my suggestion, at the beginning of Chapter 14, that what impresses Nietzsche about the positivist outlook of his age – the outlook that, up until the mid-1870s, he had been resisting – was its technological power and explanatory efficiency: railways, the telegraph, the telephone, as well as Darwin's demonstration of the redundancy of the 'God hypothesis'. The positivist worldview offered a theory of the world of incredible power and efficiency in comparison with that which had preceded it. And that, surely, one can imagine Nietzsche saying, is some kind of evidence of truth. Creatures, that is to say, who are radically mistaken about the nature of the world tend to die out before reproducing. Conversely, those whose power over their environment enables them to survive and thrive are probably close to the truth.

17

The Gay Science

First Summer in Sils Maria

THE PUBLICATION of *Dawn* coincided, almost exactly, with Nietzsche's arrival, on July 4, 1881, in Sils Maria, where he would remain until October 1. This established the pattern for the rest of his life. Save for 1882, during which normal life was disrupted, as we shall see, by the traumatic events of the 'Salomé affair', every year until his final collapse at the end of 1888 he would spend roughly three summer months in Sils.

The (still) small village of Sils Maria is located on a neck of land between Lake Sils and Lake Silvaplana in the upper Engadine Valley at a height of 2,000 metres. Above the valley, seemingly in every direction, tower the Alps, the foot of Mount Corvatsch, the most breathtaking of all, a mere ten minutes' walk from the village. Nietzsche fell in love with Sils at first sight: with the grandeur of the scenery, the hard and simple life of the peasants, the thoughtful shade of the forests, the turquoise clarity of the lakes, the level walking paths around them, the tranquil silence broken only by cow- and church-bells, and the sense of the 'meta-physical', of being above and beyond the affairs of the world.

Shaded by a fir tree outside its small, solitary window and panelled in dark, light-absorbing pine, Nietzsche's room on the second floor of the Durisch house, lit only by a solitary spirit lamp, was dark and unheated (see Plates 21, 22). It was here that, every day at five, Nietzsche would rise, wash his entire body in cold water, and think for an hour, before breakfasting on two raw eggs, bread rolls, tea, and aniseed rusks at six-thirty. Three or more hours of – weather and health permitting – walking and thinking were followed by lunch consisting of steak and macaroni with an occasional glass of beer. Always the same, it was taken in the Alpenrose Hotel, a hundred metres from his lodgings, and always at eleven-thirty, to avoid the mid-day rush. Following another three or four hours walking, the evening meal was taken at six-thirty and consisted – again every day the same – of tea, two raw eggs, and (two staples of the local peasant diet) polenta and aniseed rusks. Nietzsche appears to have eaten absolutely no fruit or vegetables during this summer, which must have had an appalling effect on his always suspect digestion. In the evenings, as had been his practice in Genoa, he sat quietly in the dark from seven to nine, conserving, so he believed, his 'spiritual powers'. And so to bed.[1]

Nietzsche called Sils his 'rescue-place', the place where 'it is quiet in a way I have never before experienced and all the 50 conditions of my poor life are fulfilled...an unexpected and unearned gift'.[2] On the face of things this was a peculiar judgment since he had already decided that 'clear skies for months on end' were an absolute requirement of his health[3] – clear skies day after day would be the very last thing to expect in the notoriously moody high mountains. And indeed this first summer in Sils was a summer of constant cloud. July was hot, with regular thunderstorms. Nietzsche was convinced that atmospheric electricity brought on his seizures, so it is no surprise that each storm laid him low with a debilitating attack of headaches and nausea. August was extremely cold, even by Engadine standards, and in his unheated room he began to suffer from chilblains. September was equally bad, with the days alternating between rain, thunderstorms and snow. Writing home, Nietzsche commented that in Sils the snow does not start to melt until June and can still fall in July and August, so that many a winter day in Genoa is warmer than a summer day in Sils.[4] Far from any centre of civilisation, he reverted to his practice of sending shopping lists to his mother. Among other supplies, he asked her to send German sausage, the wick for a spirit lamp, a brush and comb, cake, and a needle and thread (evidently he could sew as well as cook). Above all, however, he requests warm gloves and socks,[5] and when the latter do not arrive writes again, piteously, 'I'm so cold: socks! Lots of socks!'[6]

Nietzsche continued his efforts at self-doctoring, convinced both that the root of his troubles lay in a hard-to-diagnose condition of the brain and that he knew more about his condition than any doctor.[7] He also believed that the key to ameliorating his condition lay in the effects of climate on health – every new place, he wrote Elizabeth, is a new health 'experiment'.[8] He read Pierre Foissac's *On Meteorology*, which, despite its title, was actually a study of the effects of such things as air pressure and atmospheric electricity on the human body, but found, to his regret, that the 'science' was still in its infancy.[9]

Despite (or because of) his strict daily regimen, his health remained as bad as ever. Often days would pass during which nausea would allow him to eat nothing at all.[10] The whole summer, he wrote Köselitz at the end of September, 'death looked over my shoulder': there had been only ten bearable days, the attacks being as bad as they had ever been in Basel (where, of course, they had forced him to give up his professorship).[11]

In spite of its lack of success, Nietzsche continued to believe in his self-doctoring: 'people will say that I have been a good doctor – and not just for myself', he added, referring to the just-appeared *Dawn*.[12] What he means is that in settling in Sils his doctoring of the *spirit* has been a great success. As Epicurean philosophy teaches, bodily suffering is the kind of hostile fate the spirit can rise above, even welcome into a productive life: 'There are many ways of becoming strong and of making strong wing-beats: austerity and pain belong here, are means that belong to the economy of wisdom', he writes Marie Baumgartner.[13] What matters is spiritual health and that, Nietzsche finds, thrives in Sils. Writing to his mother to comfort her on the death of 'the nicest of the Oehlers', his uncle Theobald, who had committed suicide by throwing himself into the Saale, he says, turning to himself, that 'never was there a man to whom the word "depressed" applied less...I have weightier matters to consider than [bodily] health'.[14]

Enter Eternal Return

These 'weightier matters' were of course philosophical thoughts. Given that these were bubbling away, nothing else in the final analysis mattered. And bubbling they were. 'Now, my good friend', he wrote Köselitz on August 14 (anticipating in a somewhat disturbing way some of the behaviour that marked his final breakdown),

> the August sun is above us, the year passes by, it is becoming quieter and more peaceful on the mountains and in the forests. Thoughts have climbed above my horizon of a kind I have never before seen – I cannot speak of them…the intensity of my feelings makes me shiver and laugh…walking yesterday I…wept not sentimental tears but tears of jubilation; and as I wept I sang and talked nonsense, filled with a new vision that I have had in advance of all other human beings.[15]

The thoughts of which he refuses to speak (calling to mind the way in which Jews do not pronounce the name of God) are those contained in the master thought of the 'eternal return of the same':* the thought that the entire history of one's life and the cosmos will repeat itself, *down to the very last detail*, throughout all eternity. The thought, in other words, that time is a circle. Eternal return is the central topic of *Thus Spoke Zarathustra* and, as I noted, was regarded by Nietzsche as the most important thought that ever came to him. It is one of the two key themes – the other is the 'will to power' – that constitute the heart of his mature philosophy. Here, then, at the beginning of August 1881, we are standing on the cusp between the end of Nietzsche's positivist period and the beginning of his maturity.

Nietzsche recalls the arrival of his thought of thoughts in *Ecce Homo*:

> the basic conception [of *Zarathustra*], the idea of the eternal return, the highest formula of affirmation that can possibly be attained, belongs to August of the year 1881. It was jotted down on a piece of paper with the inscription: '6000 feet beyond man and time'. I was that day walking through the woods beside the lake of Silvaplana. I stopped beside a mighty pyramidal block of stone [see Plate 23] which reared itself up not far from Surlei. It was there that this thought came to me.[16]

In later years, Nietzsche would fall silent when walking with a companion past the pyramidal stone (thirty minutes' walk from Sils), as if entering a holy precinct. The arrival of the thought had, for him, the character of a visitation.

Relying on memory, Nietzsche, as usual, misquotes himself. What he actually wrote in his notebook was a heading, '*The Return of the Same: Sketch*', followed by five numbered points, followed by the subscript 'Beginning of August in Sils-Maria, 6000 feet above sea level and much higher still above all human things!', followed by a long comment on the fourth of the five points.[17] The note is cryptic to the point of unintelligibility – it is no surprise that in the letter to Köselitz he refers to himself as speaking 'nonsense' at the time of writing it. Several relatively clear points do, however, emerge.

---

* Nietzsche's word for 'return', *Wiederkunft*, possesses a certain religious aura. Christians speak of the *Wiederkunft* of Christ, the 'second coming'. Later on, I shall suggest an important continuity between eternal return and the Christian piety of Nietzsche's youth.

The first is that at no point is the *truth* of eternal return asserted. The form of the discussion seems to be: *suppose* the eternal return were true, what would be the existential consequences of recognising that truth? And here he seems undecided. On the one hand, he thinks that an attitude of 'indifference' might arise: seeing that there was no ultimate point or meaning to life, no last judgment, no entry into paradise either heavenly or earthly, in general no 'end of history', one might come to regard life as nothing but an absurd 'game'. Whether Nietzsche regards this as a good or bad thing is unclear. On the one hand, he talks of 'aesthetically enjoying' the game, which recalls what, in discussing *The Wanderer and His Shadow*, I called 'the therapeutic use of the absurd' (pp. 283–4 above): meditating on the pointlessness of our existence as a spiritual 'gymnastic' in order to relieve stress, to attain Epicurean 'elevation' above life and thus peace of mind. But on the other hand, he says that the truth of eternal return would raise 'the question of whether we still want to live'. A quite different response to eternal return, however, is what he calls 'the new weight of gravity' with respect to which our 'errors' and 'habits' acquire 'infinite importance'. This seems to suggest the response to eternal return suggested in Milan Kundera's *The Incredible Lightness of Being*: were one to come to believe that whatever one did next would be repeated throughout all eternity the result would be to attach incredible importance – 'weight', 'gravity' – to each and every action one performed. If one responded this way to eternal return the effect would be to eliminate all cowardice, compromise, and evasion. One would begin to live with incredible *intensity*.

The peculiar thing, however, about these various possible responses to the eternal return recorded in the note written by the pyramid is that none of them give any idea of why eternal return should be the 'highest formula of [life] affirmation'. Becoming 'indifferent' to life looks more like life-*denial*, while deciding to live one's life with extreme intensity is compatible with both the affirmation and denial of life. (One might think it would be better never to have been born yet decide that, having been born, one might as well make the most intense job of living as possible.) The actual content of the note, in short, gives no clue as to why eternal return should be associated with life-affirmation.

One possibility is that only many months later did the connexion between eternal return and life-affirmation occur to Nietzsche. I am, however, more inclined to think that, though it does not appear in the note itself, the association had, in fact, occurred to him by August 1881. The cause, I suspect, was his discovery of Spinoza.

* * *

Sometime in June 1881, some 'instinct'[18] told Nietzsche that he needed to find out about the great seventeenth-century Portuguese-Jewish-Dutch philosopher Baruch Spinoza. As a consequence, and with his usual penchant for taking a short cut via the secondary literature, he wrote to Overbeck at the beginning of July asking him to post to Sils Volume I of Kuno Fischer's *History of Modern Philosophy*, the volume dealing with Spinoza. (This was the same six-volume work he had used in 1866 to gain a working knowledge of Kant.) By July 30 he had become an ecstatic Spinozist:

> I am completely astounded [he wrote Overbeck], completely enraptured! I have a forerunner. And what a forerunner! I knew Spinoza hardly at all…It is not only that his whole tendency is like mine – to produce through knowledge the most powerful affect – but also that in five central points of this massive and solitary thinker I discover myself in his teaching: he denies freedom of the will, purpose, a moral order to the world, the unegoistic,

evil … In sum, my aloneness which often, like being on high mountains, robs me of breath, is now at least a two-ness.[19]

Spinoza was a pantheist. God is not a separate world-creator but rather just *is* the world. 'God' and 'nature' are simply different aspects of one and the same totality. This is why a Spinozist must deny 'evil': if the world is divine there can be no evil in it. The point of Spinoza's philosophy, embodied in his great book called, simply, *Ethics*, is to enable one to achieve happiness through love of a divine world.

Since boyhood, Nietzsche had loved the nineteenth-century American mystic and Unitarian Ralph Waldo Emerson. He was re-reading Emerson during this first summer in Sils. The title page of the first edition of *The Gay Science*, on which he was now working, contains the following quotation from Emerson: 'To the poet and the sage, all things are friendly and sacred, all experiences profitable, all days holy, all men divine'. This is the pantheistic, world-affirming vision of a Spinozist – the 'instinct' that led him to Spinoza may, indeed, have been the sense of him as Emerson's forerunner.

On July 30, 1881, then, Nietzsche declared himself a Spinozist. Immediately thereafter – at 'the beginning of August' – the thought of eternal return came to him beside the pyramid. It seems reasonable to assume, therefore, that Spinoza–Emerson pantheism was very much in his mind as the thought of eternal return came to him. If we make this assumption it becomes, for the first time, clear just why eternal return – *desiring* the eternal return – should be the 'highest formula' for the expression of the highest possible love of life. For if *all* things are (somehow) 'profitable', 'holy', 'divine' then, of course, one wants none of them ever to go away. And that is what, if true, eternal return would secure. More accurately, what it would secure is the nearest approximation to permanent presence that is possible in a world where time and transitoriness are inescapable.

Second Winter in Genoa

On October 2, with winter closing in, Nietzsche returned to his old quarters in Genoa's Salino della Battestine, where he would remain until the end of March 1882. After recovering from the uncomfortable downhill trip, he sent a postcard to Overbeck telling him of his delight in being

> once more in my city … the most unmodern that I know and yet bustling with life – it's completely unromantic and yet the opposite of vulgar. And so I shall live on under the protection of my local guardian angels, Columbus, Paganini and Mazzini, who together are very good ambassadors for their city.[20]

Columbus, the discoverer of new horizons and dawns, is an obvious hero for Nietzsche, and Mazzini, we already know, Nietzsche admired for his monomania – the subordination of his entire life to the single idea of Italian unification. But why should that (some suspected demonically inspired) magician of the violin, Niccolò Paganini, be a Nietzschean hero?

Nietzsche was at this time becoming more and more enraptured by Köselitz's music. He admired Köselitz for turning against the Wagnerian style of composition. His ('Peter Gast's') comic opera, *Joke, Cunning, Revenge*, Nietzsche believed, was a work of such 'bright cheerfulness'[21] as to justify calling him 'the new Mozart'.[22] 'What Carlsbad [mineral water] is for the sick stomach', he writes, 'Köselitz is for a sick spirit'.²³ This, presumably, the replacement of heavy, Germanic, metaphysical, northern seriousness by southern brightness and elegance, is what he admired in Paganini's light, even frivolous, displays of violinistic virtuosity. He refers to this taste for lightness in the Preface to *The Gay Science*: what 'we convalescents' need, he writes, is not 'the theatrical scream of passion … the whole romantic [Wagnerian] uproar and tumult' but rather 'a mocking, light, fleeting, divinely untroubled, divinely artificial art that, like a bright flame, blazes into an unclouded sky'.²⁴

Though his health still left much to be desired, Nietzsche now decided that 'I can live only on the sea'. In Genoa there was a 'human possibility' of living with his condition, 'whereas in 'Engadine, Marienbad, Naumburg and Basel my life was that of a tortured animal'.²⁵ Once again he begins to take a keen interest in Italian cooking: German *Stollen* is, he claims, but a pale imitation of Genoa's *pane dolche* (a kind of Christmas cake made with heavy, sweet bread dough).²⁶ He appears to have shifted rooms in his boarding house, for now he has 'a very bright room with a high ceiling – which is good for my mood'. And also for reading: his eyes are getting so weak that he often stumbles and breaks things, which makes him relieved that Genoa's large, flat paving stones provide a safe surface on which to walk.²⁷ His eyes are so bad, in fact, that his handwriting has become illegible even to himself and so he takes serious steps to acquire a typewriter.²⁸ (The first commercially successful typewriter was invented in 1867; the first Remington appeared in 1873.)

As Beethoven's deafness forced him to give up listening to music and turn to his own, inner, resources, so Nietzsche's 'half-blindness' decided him to get rid of his books, which he sent to be stored with Ida Overbeck's mother in Zurich: 'what do half-blind animals need with books?' he asked.²⁹ With the abandonment of reading, the writing of *The Gay Science* – conceived at this stage as Books 6 to 10 of *Dawn*³⁰ – proceeded apace.

Carmen, St. Januarius, Rée, and Sarah Bernhardt

Nietzsche's hopes that the move to Genoa would produce better weather than the miserable summer in Sils Maria were disappointed. Even at sea level, the closing months of 1881 were unusually cold, wet, and miserable. But then, at the end of November, there was something to cheer about:

> Hurrah friend! [he wrote Köselitz] finally something good again, an opera from François [sic] Bizet (who is that?): *Carmén* [sic] … witty, strong, here and there profoundly moving. An authentic French talent for comic opera, not at all disoriented by Wagner, a true pupil of H[ector] Berlioz. I had not thought that something like this was possible! It seems that the French have a better approach to dramatic music. And they have a head start over the Germans in one essential point: with them passion is nowhere near as dragged out (as for example all the emotions are in Wagner).³¹

The following month he attended another performance and simultaneously heard that the composer he had only just discovered was, in fact, dead. (Bizet died in 1875 at the age of thirty-six, shortly after the first performance of *Carmen*.) He was devastated:

> It was a deep blow [he wrote Köselitz] to hear that Bizet is dead. I heard *Carmen* for a second time – and again I had the impression of a novella of the first rank, like something

by Mérimée.* So passionate and so graceful a soul! For me this work is worth a journey to Spain – a completely southern work…badly ill in the meantime, but recovered through *Carmen*.[32]

Nietzsche was lucky enough to hear in the title role the stunning Célestine Galli-Marié, the singer who had made the role her own in the opera's first performance. What he liked was *Carmen*'s hot, this-worldly, 'southern' sensuality, the perfect opposite of (looking at things through Nietzsche's eyes) Wagner's metaphysical lugubriousness – a lugubriousness that reaches its peak in *Parsifal*, about to receive its first performance.[33]

The beginning of 1882 brought a dramatic change in the weather. It became and remained

> like spring: already in the mornings one can sit outside even in the shade – without freezing. No wind, no clouds, no rain! An old man told me that there had never been such a winter in Genoa. The sea calm and sunk deeply into itself. The peach-trees are blossoming! – …I see the soldier in the lightest linen suits, I myself wear the same on my walks, as in summer in the Engadine.[34]

Though the local fruit growers feared that a sudden frost would devastate the crop, the early spring persisted, so that by the following month Nietzsche was regularly swimming in the sea.[35] The January weather (as well as some fan mail from Baltimore)[36] transported him into a state of bliss: 'I begin and end every day with the question "Was there ever such good weather?" It's as if made for my nature, fresh, pure mild'. So much so that he decided to dedicate the fourth, and originally final, book of *The Gay Science* to the month, entitling it 'St. Januarius', the saint after whom the month is named.

Januarius was an early Christian martyr. A vial supposed to contain his blood is kept in the Cathedral in Naples, which Nietzsche visited during his stay in Sorrento. On certain feast days it is said miraculously to become fluid again. Nietzsche begins book IV with a poem:

> *You who with your lances burning*
> *Melt the ice sheets of my soul*
> *Speed it towards the ocean yearning*
> *For its highest hope and goal:*
> *Ever healthier it rises*
> *Free in fate most amorous: –*
> *Thus your miracle it prizes*
> *Fairest Januarius.*
> *Genoa, January 1882.*

In a word, with the melting of the winter ice, Nietzsche feels his own blood beginning to flow again. A new formula for world-affirmation comes to him, the idea of *amor fati* – 'love of fate', of *everything* that has happened – and becomes his New Year's resolution.[37]

To add to the excitement, Rée arrived on February 4 for a five-week visit, accompanied by a Danish typewriter, which, however, had been damaged in transit. It was repaired by a local

---

* The libretto *was*, in fact, by Mérimée, taken from his novella of the same name.

craftsman and Nietzsche used it to write thirteen letters. But finding it both 'aggressive' and 'temperamental, like a small animal' he was relieved rather than annoyed when, towards the end of March, it gave up the ghost. Large and chunky, it was, in any case, hardly consistent with his itinerant life-style.

Rée reported to Elizabeth that he had never seen Nietzsche looking so well or in such high spirits since their first meeting in Basel in 1872.[38] The day after his arrival Nietzsche took him down to the beach where they lay in the warm sun 'like a couple of sea urchins'.[39] A great deal of laughter and high jinks – though Nietzsche blamed them for the onset of one of his attacks – led to him sending Köselitz a typewritten bunch of silly ditties such as

Glattes Eis ein Paradeis [in proper German *Paradies*]
Für Den der gut zu tanzen weiss

(roughly, 'Smooth ice a paradice [sic]/ For he who is in dancing wise').[40]

One of the 'sea urchins'' outings was to see the famous Sarah Bernhardt. They hit a bad night, however:

> We attended the first performance. After the first act she collapsed as if dead. After an embarrassing hour of waiting, she played on but in the middle of the third act broke a blood vessel on stage. It made an unbearable impression particularly since she was playing that kind of a sick person ([the consumptive heroine of] *la dame aux camellias* by Dumas the younger) – Nonetheless she had a tremendous success the following night and the night after, which convinced Genoa that she was 'the leading living artist' – She reminded me in appearance and manner of Frau [Cosima] Wagner.[41]

(The collapse obviously did Bernhardt no lasting damage, since she did not die until March 1923. Born just a week after Nietzsche, she outlived him by a quarter of a century.)

Another 'urchin'-like escapade was a three-day visit to Monte Carlo at the beginning of March. Puritanical as ever, and anyway appalled by the price of everything on the French Riviera, Nietzsche had nothing to do with the casino, but Rée, a compulsive gambler in the Dostoyevskian mould, did. Though Nietzsche claimed, writing to his mother, that Rée 'at least didn't lose'[42] he must in fact have lost heavily, since when he left to visit Malwida von Meysenbug in Rome he had to borrow the train fare from Nietzsche.

On a more serious level, Rée's visit clearly turned Nietzsche's mind to scientific matters, since in March he wrote Köselitz of his admiration for Copernicus and Roger Boscovich,* 'the two greatest opponents of how things look to the untutored eye'. Boscovich, he continues, has 'thought atomic theory through to its ultimate conclusion', which is that 'matter does not exist'. Consistently thought out, that is, physics leads to the conclusion that 'nothing exists but force'[43] – gravity, electromagnetism, and so on.

---

* Roger Boscovich (1711–89) was a Dalmatian monk, mathematician and astronomer. Nietzsche first borrowed his *Philosophiae Naturalis Theoria* (p. 178 above) from the Basel University library in 1873, but re-read it on a number of subsequent occasions, as part of his programme of making up for the absence of natural science from his Pforta education.

Messina

At the end of March 1882, Nietzsche suddenly left Genoa for Messina in Sicily, where he spent the first three weeks of April. The departure was abrupt and disrupted his established pattern of seeking the high mountains as soon as the weather started to become warmer. Nothing is known about Nietzsche's stay in Messina, apart from four brief post-cards, on one of which he quotes Homer's description of Sicily as 'the edge of the world' and 'the place where happiness dwells'.[44] The apparently surprising choice of Messina, together with the dearth of concrete information about his time there, is the centrepiece of the thesis of Joachim Kohler's *Zarathustra's Secret: The Interior Life of Friedrich Nietzsche*, that the 'secret' of Nietzsche's 'interior life' is that he was (Shock! Horror!...Book sales!!) gay.[45] There was, it appears, a colony of gay artists in Taormina, not far from Messina.

Unfortunately for Kohler's thesis, there is not a shred of evidence that Nietzsche ever visited Taormina. That he enjoyed waking up with the sight of palm trees through the window and found the Messina locals friendly is about all we know about his stay in Sicily. Still the question remains, if it was not to indulge his 'interior secret', why did he go there?

Curt Janz suggests that the secret 'magnet' was the presence of the Wagners in Sicily; that Nietzsche hoped, accidentally on purpose, to bump into them. (They had been there but had, in fact, left by the time he arrived.) There is, however, no evidence for this hypothesis either. And actually, it seems to me, there is no real mystery about Nietzsche's visit to Messina since his letters offer a perfectly plausible account of his motives.

What needs to be remembered is the utter centrality of health to Nietzsche's life, the fact that he regarded every place he stayed in as a health 'experiment', together with the fact that the previous summer in Sils the weather had been terrible.[46] To Overbeck he wrote from Messina, 'reason has triumphed: – after last summer in the mountains turned out so badly and the proximity of clouds was always connected with a worsening of my condition, all that remained to try was to see what a summer by the sea would achieve'.[47] It is not that he abandoned the mountains that is surprising, but rather, given his belief that only clear skies cleared his head, that he ever went there in the first place. A subsidiary motive – remembering that his pension was barely enough to live on – was the 'astonishing cheapness of the prices'[48] in the impoverished South.

Still, Genoa was on the sea, too, so why not stay there? Because, I suspect, he thought that by going still further south he would obtain even clearer skies. The previous summer he had written Overbeck from Sils that since 'clear skies for months on end' were an essential condition of his health he would probably be forced to emigrate from Europe[49] – to settle in, perhaps, Mexico.[50] Hearing in March 1882 – three weeks, that is, before leaving for Messina – that Elizabeth's friend and future husband, Bernard Förster, was planning to found a colony in South America, and combining this news with the ongoing dream of a 'monastery for free spirits', led him to fantasize about founding a colony in the Mexican high country.[51]

The Sicilian 'health experiment' did not, however, work. After three weeks Nietzsche was driven out by his 'greatest enemy', the Sirocco[52] – hardly something that would have deterred someone finally able to indulge his hidden 'secret'! Relevant too, however, is the fact that, while in Messina, he received a letter from Rée informing him that a young, brilliant, and beautiful Russian woman was in Rome, staying with Malwida and 'desperate' to meet him[53] – Lou Salomé. Nietzsche's response to this summons is, we shall see, yet another blow to the 'hidden secret' hypothesis.

Idylls from Messina

While in Messina Nietzsche completed a set of eight poems, *Idylls from Messina*,[54] which he published in Schmeitzner's new journal, the *Internationale Monatschrift*, in May 1882. He had been becoming increasingly alienated from Schmeitzner and suspected that his house journal was intended to be Wagnerian, nationalistic, and anti-Semitic. (He was right – in 1883 it received the subtitle 'Magazine for General Combat against the Jews'.) He had, nonetheless, been pleasantly surprised by the cosmopolitan tone of its first editorial. Contrary to Schmeitzner's intention, Bruno Bauer talked about the need to overcome national rivalries and establish a united Europe as 'our spiritual homeland'. Amazed to see 'how harmonious with my thought' the editorial was, Nietzsche decided he had misjudged the journal and so gave Schmeitzner his poems.[55] I shall make a few comments on the more interesting ones.

Prince Vogelfrei (Prince Free-as-a-Bird or Prince Outlaw – the word has both meanings) is a celebration of, first, flight, flying with and at the 'invitation' of a bird far out above the sea, forgetful of goal, harbour, fear, praise, and blame. It recalls the notebooks' inclination to regard 'floating and flying', Epicurean 'elevation', as 'the highest good'.[56] It also celebrates time off from the tough business of thinking: whereas 'step by step' thinking often stumbles, floating effortlessly on the wind is much more joyful. And finally, while the thinking requires solitude, to sing in solitude is 'stupid'.

Song of a Goatherd. The lovesick poet lies in bed 'sick in his stomach' while 'she dances over there in light and noise'. 'She promised to sneak off with me'. I wait 'like a dog' but there is no sign of her. 'She lied'. 'Does she run after everyone just like my goats?' 'Where is her silken skirt?' How 'curled up inside and poisonous the waiting of the lover'. 'Love consumes me like a seventh hell/I eat almost nothing/Goodbye onions [sic]'. One is tempted to see this as an instance of Nietzsche's startling gift of second sight (or, alternatively, his disposition to act out literary roles) for it recounts, quite precisely, the tragic tale of his love for Lou Salomé that is just about to begin.

The Little Witch. She speaks: As long as I've still a pretty little bodice /It's still worth being pious/One knows God loved a pretty woman/Particularly the pretty ones/He will surely forgive the dutiful little monk/That he like many a monk likes to be with me./He is often like the greying tomcat/Rife with jealousy and want/ . . . Everyone will forgive me'. The song of a flirt who is likely to advertise more than she will deliver, again a pre-echo of Lou as Nietzsche came to experience her.

The Nocturnal Mystery. Neither opium nor the good conscience will bring the poet sleep, so he goes down to the warm beach where he finds a man (himself, it would seem) and a boat and puts out to sea. 'One hour, or perhaps two/ Or was it a year?/ Suddenly all my thought and mind/ sank into an eternal sameness/ And an abyss without limits/ Opened up'. And yet 'nothing happened'. There was no blood. 'We were sleeping, sleeping all, so well, so well.' A dream, it seems, embodying Freud's 'oceanic feeling', dissolution of individuality, absorption into the All.

Bird Judgement. To refresh myself/I recently sat under dark trees/I heard ticking, a soft ticking/Delicately as if following bar and measure./I got angry grimaced a bit/But finally gave up/Until I myself, like a poet, spoke in tick-tock too.//I kept making verses/Syllable by syllable they hopped out/Until I had to laugh, laugh a quarter of an hour./You a poet? You a poet?/Are you so sick in the head? -/Yes good sir, you are a poet/-Thus spoke the woodpecker.' A self-undermining poem to finish the set on a light-hearted note.

In 1887 Nietzsche published a revised version of the *Idylls* as an appendix to the second edition of *The Gay Science*, entitling the collection 'The Songs of Prince *Vogelfrei*'. In *Ecce Homo* he recalls that these songs, 'composed for the most part in Sicily, call to mind quite explicitly the Provençal concept of *gaya scienza*, that union of *minstrel, knight and free spirit* that was characteristic of the culture of medieval Provence.[57] That the poems are written by a 'free-as-a-bird' minstrel makes clear the need to finish on a light-hearted note.

The Gay Science

*L*a gaya scienza was the subtitle – or perhaps a translation of the title – of Nietzsche's next book, *The Gay [or Joyful] Science*. Concerning the title itself Nietzsche says the following:

> For most people, the intellect is an awkward, gloomy, creaking machine that is hard to start; when they want to work with the machine … they call it 'taking matters *seriously*' … and where laughter and gaiety are to be found [they suppose that] thinking is good for nothing' – that is the prejudice of this serious beast against all 'gay science'. Well then, let us prove it a prejudice.[58]

Thinking can be fun; serious fun!

As we saw, Nietzsche began the fourth and (originally) final book of the work in January 1882. It was almost finished by the time he left Messina on about April 21, but work was then interrupted by the events that will be narrated in the next chapter. The book was completed in Naumburg between May 18 and June 15 with the help of Elizabeth: she dictated the manuscript to a bankrupt Naumburg businessman, who made a print-ready copy, with Nietzsche looking on and interrupting where necessary.[59] Since Brauer's editorial in the *Internationale Monatschrift* had temporarily relieved Nietzsche's disquiet concerning his publisher, it appeared with Schmeitzner at the end of August. Book V was added much later, in 1887, and save for glancing references will not be discussed in this chapter.

The Main Argument

*T*he Gay Science is about everything under the sun. There is, however, a central argument which, in spite of its aphoristic formulation, is remarkably, even rigorously, systematic. Before turning to this main argument, however, as with all Nietzsche's works, the first question that needs to be raised is: for whom is the book written?

In the Prologue to *Zarathustra*, as we shall see, the eponymous hero begins his mission to the world by setting up a soap box in the market-place and preaching the 'superman' as the 'meaning of the earth'. The audience, seeing nothing but a ranting buffoon, laugh at him. After much soul searching this leads Zarathustra to the conclusion that he needs to conduct his mission in a different way, specifically, that he needs to find a new way of communicating his message. The 'insight' comes to him that he should 'speak not to the people but to companions'.[60]

This, in part, is autobiography. Nietzsche's first five books, the 'Bayreuth' works, were written for the (of course literate) world at large, were contributions to the culture wars of the times. And some of them were indeed, wholly or in part, rants – the 'Summons to the Germans', for example, the reason the Wagner Society decided it was useless (pp. 173–4 above). By *Human, All-Too-Human*, we have seen, he had given up writing for 'the people' at large, writing now, explicitly, 'for free spirits' alone. These remain the target audience in *The Gay Science*. 'We', he says, drawing himself and his chosen readers into an intimate circle, do not wish to conform to current mores but wish to become individuals 'who are new, unique, who give themselves laws'.[61] Though he wants 'disciples', they must be 'free-spirited' enough to say 'No' even to him: disciples who cannot do so he wishes on his enemies.[62] Once more, then, we have a book 'for free spirits', a book for that same select audience of Nietzsche's 'friends'[63] as have been all his books since *Human, All-Too-Human*. I turn now to the main argument he addresses to them.

The Gay Science's central argument can be divided, it seems to me, into three stages. First, it develops a general account of what it is to be a thriving 'culture' or 'people', a general theory of cultural 'health'. This, the theory of cultural evolution which, as we saw, made its first, embryonic appearance in the third of the *Untimely Meditations*, receives a more detailed statement in *The Gay Science* than in any other work. Second, it uses the general theory to diagnose and display the unhealthy condition of the present age. Finally, it derives from the general theory an account of the direction in which our culture must move if it is to recover its health. This outline of a future world is then offered as the ideal whose realisation is to constitute the life-defining mission of the free spirits for whom the book is written.

Cultural Evolution

The background to the general theory of cultural health is Darwinism, Nietzsche's second-hand knowledge of which was first derived, as we saw, from his reading of Lange's *History of Materialism* (pp. 89–90 above). 'Life' in general, he writes, is to be defined as the 'continual shedding of something that wants to die', of, that is, 'the old and weak'.[64] It is, in other words, the 'survival of the fittest' in a competitive and, at least potentially, hostile environment. Nietzsche applies this theory to human society, which makes him a 'social Darwinist': he regards human societies as organisms subject to the same laws as organisms in general.

All organisms, including human individuals and human societies, aim to be victorious in the struggle to survive: the 'instinct to do whatever favours the preservation of the human race … constitutes the essence of our species'.[65] Nietzsche identifies two main conditions a healthy community must satisfy in order to be 'fit' for survival. The first is what he calls a 'universally binding … faith',[66] sometimes also 'morality' or 'custom'. It is such a faith that constitutes the community as a community, orders the relations between individuals in such a way as to enable the social organism to function as an efficient survival machine. For that reason, the loss of such a faith, a faith to which the great majority subscribe, constitutes 'the greatest danger that hovered and still hovers over humanity'.[67] Without the social glue of a communal faith a society loses its capacity for collective action and becomes ripe for destruction, either through internal disintegration or through colonisation by a more successful society.

The principal means by which the community – or 'herd'[68] – preserves conformity to communal faith consist in more or less crude forms of social ostracism. What makes this effective is the individual's basic need for community. 'Even the strongest person ... fears a cold look or a sneer on the face of those among whom he has been brought up. What is he really afraid of? Growing solitary'.[69] Nietzsche calls this 'the herd instinct' in the individual.[70] The 'herd instinct' has thus two aspects. On the part of the community it is the instinct to exert pressure on the individual to conform. And on the latter's part it is the instinct to give in to that pressure.

The basic effect of a 'faith' or 'morality' is to turn individuals into 'functions'[71] or 'instruments'[72] of the community. For those who are, by nature, 'herd-types', this does them no harm. But for other, rarer, individuals this is not the case: their development into the kinds of people they potentially are is fatally harmed if they succumb to the herd instinct. And paradoxically, the community, too, is harmed thereby.

Communal faith, communal morality, ensures the durability of a community – 'and durability is a first-ranked value on earth'.[73] But sometimes its power to do so begins to diminish. The reason is change, changes in the human and natural environment in which the community finds itself. (Traditional notions of property, the right, for example, to do anything one wishes with one's land, including cutting down its trees, might become, in the age of global warming, positively damaging to the well-being of the community.) Environmental change demands change in communal morality, demands the community's capacity to mutate with respect to its fundamental 'laws of agreement'. In a Darwinian world the law is: mutate or die.

The agents of such mutation are the non-'herd' types, those who resist the pressure to conform to current norms, free themselves from the chains of current morality: the 'free spirits'. 'The celebrated European capacity for constant *transformation*' depends on such 'malcontents'. China, on the other hand, Nietzsche claims, is a country in which large-scale discontent became extinct centuries ago, and with it the capacity for change.[74] (Hence, presumably, its history of colonisation and exploitation by European powers, and later Japan.)

Free spirits may be of either 'second' or 'first rank'.[75] The former simply say 'No' to current conventions but live lives that are otherwise without significance. The latter, Nietzsche's true readers, are 'the seed bearers of the future, the spiritual colonizers and shapers of new states and communities',[76] the Columbus-types who discover new 'lands' and horizons. The essential difference between the two is between creation and destruction. Whereas the former simply transgress current norms, the latter, by 'creating new names and valuations',[77] create 'new life-possibilities to weigh against the old ones'.[78] Though many of these will fall by the wayside through lack of influence, social utility, or both, the community's best hope of successfully adapting to a new environment in which its old faiths and customs no longer work is that one of these new forms of life will both become influential and be just what it needs to survive and once more thrive. (The eccentric who knits his own sweaters, refuses to drive a car, never flies, and has his own electricity-generating windmill suddenly finds himself, perhaps, transformed from 'weirdo' into role model: in

Nietzsche's language, he is recognised as an 'Argonaut of the ideal' and herald of 'the great health'.)[79]

As already observed, Nietzsche's central insight is that both the 'herd instinct' and free-spiritedness are essential to a thriving community. The former binds individuals together as an adaptive unity capable of collective, in particular self-preserving, action. The latter – which in a healthy community must be possessed only by a minority[80] – prepares for the day when communal faith will need to mutate in order to remain adaptive. Nietzsche's insight, then, an insight which some might regard as tragic, is that a healthy society exists *always* in a state of dynamic tension. More or less open and more or less acute tension between the forces of reform and reaction does not represent a temporary, social malfunction but is, rather, an essential condition of communal health. There is no paradise at the 'end of history' in which all conflict will be washed away. We must reconcile ourselves to the 'eternal recurrence of war and peace'.[81]

The Way We Are Now

The second stage in Nietzsche's central argument is to apply this general theory to our current condition. The most central fact about Western modernity is the 'death of God' – first officially announced in *The Gay Science*.[82] From one point of view this abandonment of Christian belief is to be welcomed with open arms. For Christianity produced an unhappy humanity. Unlike the Greeks, who 'gilded and deified' all things human,[83] Christianity produced (as many pictorial representations of our expulsion from the Garden of Eden make clear) a humanity fundamentally ashamed of itself.[84] And this made us not only unhappy but also dangerous. By teaching us self-hatred, it disposed us to hateful action towards others.[85]

This is the familiar aspect of Nietzsche's reaction to the secularisation of European society. Less often noticed, however, is his keen sense of the *downside* of God's 'death'. Whatever its deficiencies, Christianity did provide a 'universally binding faith' that preserved European culture for two thousand years. But now it has gone, leaving us in a 'faith'-less condition. In the modern West, where free spirits (of the second rank) have become the rule rather than the exception, the lack of a socially binding faith means that 'it is with little confidence that one may speak of the future of humanity'.[86] In Book V, foreseeing the death of God as leading to the collapse of 'our entire European morality', Nietzsche seems to have a premonition of the twentieth century's world wars and even of nuclear war.[87]

Modernity, then, is in a state of decay, 'corruption': the old faith has gone, leaving us with a chaos of second-rank free spirits each pursuing a private egotism. Yet there is no reason to become entirely downcast, for among the free spirits there are likely to be the 'seed-bearers of the future': corruption, after all, is 'just a rude word for the autumn of a people'.[88] What kind of future should we hope for from these seed-bearers?

In the famous passage in which 'the madman' (who is, of course, far from mad) announces not only that God is dead but also that we moderns have 'murdered' him with our human and natural sciences, he goes on to say that we must 'atone' for the deed.[89] The general theory of cultural health explains this immediately: what we must atone for is the destruction of our community-preserving faith. And the only way we can do that is by providing a new faith, one that will both be adapted to the conditions of modernity and will produce a happier breed of humanity than its Christian predecessor. This is the task Nietzsche assigns to his chosen readers. Since a new faith can only come from creative free spirits, Nietzsche's madman is informing the chosen ones of their fundamental task in life.

But what are we supposed to understand by 'faith'? How close to the traditional religious meaning of the word is what he has in mind? And what content does he have in mind for the new faith that is to replace the dead faith of Christianity? To answer these questions we need to turn, once more, to Nietzsche's gaze into his hoped-for future.

Nietzsche's Future

Nietzsche's 'madman' says that the only way we can 'atone' for the destruction of Christianity is by the construction of new 'festivals' and 'sacred games'.[90] This points to two features of the hoped-for future. First, that Nietzsche's use of 'faith' is not at all far removed from 'religion', where the heart of any religion is taken to be the festive gathering of a community in a sacred place in affirmative re-collection of its conception of the right way to live. Second, that the new faith will be inspired by Greece – for the 'sacred games' are, of course, the Olympics, the festive occasion dedicated to Zeus.

In short, therefore, we have returned yet again to the 'rebirth of Greek tragedy' theme and to the Wagnerian *ideal*. Though the thought that Wagner's own art might redeem the West is by now, of course, completely rejected – the last thing we need is the art of 'intoxication', of 'hashish-smoking and betel-chewing'[91] – the Wagnerian quest to redeem the West from its current decadence through a reanimation of the Greek festival remains Nietzsche's guiding star, as it will until the end of his thinking.[92]

What we know, then, is, first, that the future society for which Nietzsche's select band of readers is to work will (like, in *this* respect, the Christian society of the past) find its unifying heart in a new 'faith', a faith that will be a union of religion and morality and be centred upon the sacred festival. And second, the reference to the Greeks as a guiding ideal tells us that, though the new religion may have structural and institutional similarities to the medieval Church, in terms of content it will be utterly different: in place of Christian vilification, it will be a celebration of the human that will help create a humanity that is once again free from guilt and self-hatred. Both these points are summed up in a cryptic but important notebook entry of the period:

> Insofar as we don't need morality any more – we don't need religion either. The 'I love [the Christian] God' – the only old form of the religious – is transformed into the love of an ideal – has become creative – pure God-Men. Morality is necessary: for what should we act, and act we must? Whatever we have done we must evaluate . . . Morality is a condition of life, 'You should'.[93]

(Notice that this note deploys first the 'pejorative' (p. 309 above) and then the non-pejorative sense of 'morality'.)

* * *

Further elaboration of the hoped-for religious festival occurs in *The Gay Science's* discussion of art. Alluding to the fact that virtually all art prior to the modern period was more or less immediately religious art, Nietzsche writes:

What do all our art of artworks matter if we lose that higher art, the art of festivals! Formerly, all artworks were displayed on the great festival road of humanity as commemorations of high and happy moments. Now one uses artworks to lure poor, exhausted and sick human beings to ... a little intoxication and madness.[94]

The art of the future must, then, be associated with the new 'faith'. Since the artists of whom Nietzsche approves 'constantly glorify – they do nothing else', they help create the faith of the future.[95] Roughly speaking, as the 'Apollonian' artists of Greece glorified their gods and heroes and the Christian artists their saints and martyrs, so the art of the future will create 'pictures one can live by',[96] role models who will collectively embody the new faith. As we saw Nietzsche putting it in *Human, All-Too-Human* (p. 265 above), the art of the future will 'imaginatively develop a beautiful image of man', which it will elevate to 'the status of a model, and in so doing, through the excitation of envy and emulation, help create the future'.

The Gay Science places great emphasis on the power of art: its 'soft' power, its power to create feeling, thought, and action not by coercion but by attraction. Sometimes this power is a matter of suspicion: 'the poets tell many lies' but get away with it on account of the power of poetic rhetoric to disable reason.[97] Overwhelmingly, though, Nietzsche's view is that the power of art is an essential ingredient in the establishment of the new 'festival'. Above all the Orphic power of music:

'I am thirsting for a master composer' said an innovator to his disciple 'who can learn my thoughts from me and hereafter speak them in his language: in that way I will better penetrate into people's ears and hearts. With tones one can seduce people into every error and every truth: who could refute a tone?' 'So you would like to be considered irrefutable?' said his disciple. The innovator replied: 'I wish for the sprout to become a tree. For a teaching to become a tree, it has to be believed for a good while; for it to be believed, it has to be considered irrefutable ...[98]

The reason the new faith and festival are essentially dependent on the power of art in general and music in particular is not hard to find. Since God is dead, since fear of hell and hope of heaven no longer exist, the morality that creates and preserves a community can no longer derive its power and authority from a supernatural judge and morality-enforcer. So the morality of the new faith must find a new source of authority. No longer able to base itself on the 'hard' power of threat and reward, it must turn to 'soft' power – power without coercion – the power of art.

Nietzsche's notion of a 'new faith' sustained and empowered by (in Wagner's still entirely appropriate language) the 'artwork of the future', a faith and art which replaces Christian denigration of the human with 'Greek' deification, sounds very abstract. But actually it very much anticipates the spirit of the early twentieth century. To gain a notion of a faith and art inspired by something like Nietzschean ideas one only has to think of the glorification of soldiers, workers, and farmers in the Soviet art of the early twentieth century – the 'faith' in question incorporating the eventual arrival of the communist utopia, a faith which also inspired Fernand Leger's monumental swimmers and cyclists. Or, to change 'faiths', one might think of Leni Riefenstahl's Aryan-humanity-glorifying films of the Nuremberg 'festival' and the 'sacred games' of 1936.[99] (Though the Nazi appropriation of Nietzsche was an abysmal perversion of his thought, one needs, nonetheless, to acknowledge the genuine similarities and continuities between him and them, for otherwise it becomes inexplicable how and why the appropriation occurred.)

* * *

As well as a communal faith, let us recall, a healthy society (unlike Nazism) also harbours, nurtures even, the countervailing force of (creative) free-spiritedness, so that, as the old faith becomes non-adaptive, it possesses at least the hope of modifying its way of life in order to meet altered conditions. This generates the second aspect of Nietzsche's vision of a healthier future.

Section 329 of *The Gay Science* sums up the critique of modernity we have seen running through all Nietzsche's previous works. 'The Americans', Nietzsche reflects, above all

> strive for gold; and their breathless haste in working…is already spreading to the old Europe…Already one is ashamed of keeping still; long reflection almost gives people a bad conscience. One thinks with a watch in hand, as one eats lunch with an eye on the financial pages…all forms are being destroyed by the haste of the workers…one no longer has time and energy for ceremony…more and more it is work that gets all good conscience on its side; the desire for joy already calls itself 'the need to recuperate'…'one owes it to one's health' – that is what one says when caught on an excursion in the countryside. Soon we may well reach the point where one cannot give in to the desire for a *vita contemplativa* [contemplative life] (that is, taking a walk with ideas and friends)…[100]

The last line is the punch line. For the most serious danger posed by 'American haste' is the destruction of contemplation.

The reason this is the greatest danger is that it is the contemplative types of human being (in other words, the creative free spirits) who create the possibility of a new future:

> Higher human beings distinguish themselves from the lower by…thoughtfully seeing and hearing immeasurably more…The higher human being…calls his nature contemplative and thereby overlooks the fact that he is also the actual poet and ongoing author of life. To be sure, he differs greatly from the actor of this drama, the so-called man of action; but he is even less like a mere spectator and festival visitor in front of the stage. As the poet, he certainly possesses *vis comtemplativa* [contemplative power]…but the same time and above all *vis creativa* [creative power] which the man of action lacks, whatever appearances and universal belief may say. It is we, the thinking-receptive ones, who really and continually make something that is not yet there: the whole perpetually growing world of valuations, colours, weights, perspectives, scales, affirmations and negations. This poem that we have invented is constantly internalised, drilled, translated into flesh and reality, indeed into the commonplace, by the so-called practical human beings (our actors)…but we have created the world…[101]

This vision of the contemplative, creative free spirit as the 'playwright' who creates the script we others then live out sounds the very German theme of *geistige Führung* [spiritual leadership], of being the spiritual 'shepherd of the herd'.[102] Contrary to appearances, the real leaders are those among us who are thinkers rather than actors but are yet (far from being head-in-the-clouds professors) 'receptive' to the realities of their world. The real leaders, in other words, are those who are, in the broadest possible sense of the word, philosophers. True leadership, Nietzsche plausibly holds, is spiritual-intellectual leadership: in *Zarathustra*'s beautiful words, 'thoughts that come on doves' feet direct the world'.[103] Changes to common valuations and opinions happen 'through individuals – powerful, influential…who announce…their *hoc est ridiculum, hoc est absurdum* [this is ridiculous, this is absurd]'.[104] Hence – a theme that goes back to the 1872 lectures, *On the Future of Our Educational Institutions* (see pp. 142–7 above) – if we kill the spiritual-intellectual life by, for example, turning universities into mere training schools for the life of work, then we kill the possibility of there being 'educators' who will lead us towards a more successful response to the changing world we find ourselves inhabiting.* To avoid this fate, our new culture must be organised so as to combat 'haste' and the over-valuation of work, production, and profit. It must be organized so as to foster the contemplative life for those who are suited to it. Architecture and gardening, for example, must nurture contemplation:

> One day, and probably soon, we will need some recognition of what is missing primarily in our big cities: quiet and wide, expansive places for reflection – places with long, high-ceilinged arcades for bad or all-too-sunny weather [as in Genoa or Turin], where no shouts or noise from carriages can penetrate…a whole complex of buildings and sites that would give expression to the sublimity of contemplation and of stepping aside…We want to have *us* translated into stone and plants; we want to take walks *in us* when we stroll through these hallways and gardens.[105]

* * *

Nietzsche's future society values spiritual leadership. But leadership, or what he will call 'rank-ordering', is a principle that permeates all aspects of social life – for example, relations between men and women. To this end he goes to considerable lengths to make the point that the correlative of leadership, subordination, is not the same as oppression. Nietzsche's underlying thesis, here, is the obvious truth that people are different, that there is no such thing as 'health [or happiness] as such', that one person's meat may be another's poison.[106] Some people derive joy from leadership, but in many others there is a 'drive to submit' which results in their experiencing a positive 'joy' in becoming a 'function' of someone else.[107] Many women, for example, exhibit

> a surplus of strength and pleasure in wanting to become a function; they press towards and have the most delicate sense for all places where precisely they can be a function. Here belong those women who turn themselves into some function of a man that is especially weakly developed in him, and to that extent become his purse, or his politics, or his sociability.[108]

(Almost certainly, he is thinking, here, of Cosima Wagner. On hearing of Richard's death he wrote her that she could be proud of 'having made every sacrifice' for him.)[109] Of course, the essential condition of a non-oppressive relation of leading and following is that the

---

* Implicit in Nietzsche's philosophy of education is, I think, a plea for the funding of what we would now call 'blue-sky' research – in the broadest sense of the phrase. Obviously, if all research is tied to current goals, there is no possibility of opening up new goals, either technical or cultural. Talented researchers need to be allowed to follow their noses wherever they may lead.

leaders should legitimise themselves in the eyes of the led. Thus, whereas the factory owner is mostly seen by his workers as nothing but 'a cunning bloodsucking dog of a man', the military leader is often treated with respect. The crucial point is that the leader should have some kind of nobility, should appear to be of a 'higher race' than the led. 'The masses are basically prepared to submit to any kind of slavery provided that the superiors constantly legitimize themselves as higher, as born to command, through refined demeanour'.[110]

Nietzsche's examples, here, may be dubious. The reason talented women of Nietzsche's time usually made themselves a man's 'function' almost always lay not in an innate disposition to follow rather than lead but simply in the fact that, denied formal education and so the possibility of an independent income, the culture of the time left them no other choice. Yet the point Nietzsche is making, that subordination is not the same as oppression, is surely correct. The captain of the football team (mostly) does not oppress those he leads, and neither does the leader of a string quartet. (That Michel Foucault thinks that subordination always implies oppression suggests that he never played football or belonged to a string quartet.) That Nietzsche's future society will contain leaders and followers of all sorts – in provocative language 'masters' and 'slaves' – is not in itself an objection to it. And he may in fact be right that a society with a 'rank-ordering' is typically happier than one without. As Alexis de Tocqueville pointed out in his observations on America – a point later recycled by Alain de Botton – when one's station in society is one's station for life one is at least free of 'status anxiety'.

Life as an Artwork

Many of the more celebrated passages of *The Gay Science* discuss individual rather than social life – which has given rise to the widely accepted interpretation of Nietzsche as an 'elitist' and 'individualistic' philosopher concerned with the well-being of a few, select individuals but unconcerned with the well-being of society as a whole.

There is no denying that the work contains a strong 'individualistic' element: much of the time Nietzsche is concerned to tell his chosen readers not what kind of future society to work for but how to live fulfilled, happy lives here and now. At the same time, however, it needs to be remembered that his chosen readers are the creative free spirits, the potential 'seed-bearers and colonisers of the future'. This is why he stresses the uniqueness of his readers; why he says, to repeat, that 'we' want to become 'new, unique, incomparable',[111] i.e., embodiments of new, and potentially community-saving, life-forms. (Had he been writing a self-help book for that great majority whose happiness is best served by becoming 'instruments' of communal morality he would have omitted all talk of uniqueness.) So there must be a connexion between the advice to his readers on how to become happy and the communal concerns that are ultimately most important to him.

The connexion, I think, lies in the idea of exemplification or modelling – an idea which underlies Nietzsche's persistent desire to set up a 'colony for free spirits' (as well as, in many cases, underlying the general attempt by nineteenth-century Germans to set up literal colonies in far-away places). Nietzsche's chosen readers are, that is, 'preparatory human beings' whom he calls 'signs' of a higher form of human existence. He says – and here we see, once more, his affinity with the 'life-reform' movement (pp. 244–6 above) – that they must become 'human beings with their own festivals, their own working days, their own periods of mourning…more fruitful, happier human beings'.[112] They must also possess 'a self-sufficiency that overflows and communicates to men and things'.[113] What this amounts to, I think, is the idea that just as art glamorises and so empowers new life-forms by 'exciting envy and emulation' (p. 265 above), so will the lives of the creative free spirits. They will become our 'educators', inspirational role models of the new culture. But of course they can only do that if they radiate a manifest health and happiness. (One might think, here, of how the Dalai Lama's own radiant personality is by far the best advertisement for his teaching.) In short, then, the discussion of individual happiness is, I think, integrated after all into Nietzsche's overriding social concerns. The happiness exemplified by his chosen 'preparatory human beings' is an important means of bringing the new culture into existence. How, then, are Nietzsche's chosen readers to become happy?

* * *

As we saw in the previous chapter, the self is not something we simply discover. Rather it has to be created: not created from scratch, but created by 'sculpting', 'pruning', 'gardening', or 'landscaping' the set of drives which *are* things we simply discover ourselves to have (pp. 304–7 above). In order, therefore, to become a happy person we have first to 'sculpt' the person we are to be. *Dawn*, as we saw, offered some advice on self-sculpting. *The Gay Science* elaborates on its account. The heart of what it adds is the idea of making one's life into an artwork.

To sculpt ourselves into genuine persons, Nietzsche writes, we must 'learn from artists' but be wiser than they are. For whereas 'their delicate powers usually stop where art ends and life begins' – stereotypically, great artists live messy lives – 'we want to become poets of our lives'.[114]

What one needs to learn from artists, and 'especially those of the theatre', is to see oneself 'simplified and transfigured' in order to recognise 'the hero that is concealed in everyday characters'. As a skilful novelist or playwright selects and displays events so as to build up a coherent and believable portrait of the character who is the work's 'hero' (Elizabeth Bennett, Henry V), so we need to tell ourselves the story of our life in such a way as to reveal the 'hero' that we decide to be. To do this, we need to learn from artists how to observe ourselves 'from a distance as something past and whole', for otherwise we are 'nothing but foreground'.[115]

Mostly, that is, we are so 'close up' to our lives that we miss the wood on account of the trees. Particularly in bustling modernity, our lives rush from one incident to the next – the report that was supposed to be on the manager's desk last week, the breakfast quarrel with one's spouse, one's child's bad behaviour at school, the overdraft at the bank, the shopping needed for dinner, the train for which one is already late – with the result that they are nothing more than a succession of incidents with no overarching theme. To become a coherent self we need less action and more reflection: for a time, at least we need the *vita contemplativa* (pp. 260, 312 above).

A concrete example makes Nietzsche's thought easier to grasp. Let us imagine Gauguin, a successful Paris stockbroker but also a painter. His life is a miserable and confused jumble of incidents devoid of overall coherence. To determine who is to be the 'hero' of his life, he needs to distance himself from all its incidents, 'learn the art of "putting [himself] on the stage"',[116] and decide on his life story. He has (to simplify for the sake of illustration) two options. According to the first story he is a painter of genius who, through a cowardly attachment to bourgeois comforts and constraints, has so far failed to live the life he really wants, has failed to live up to the Nietzschean injunction to 'become who you are'.[117] A second story (the one that in real life, of course, he rejected) is that he is a brilliant manipulator of financial markets who has been making himself miserable with romantic desires for the bohemian life of a painter for which he has a minor but unremarkable talent. Notice that each story tells Gauguin *how to go on*. The result of committing himself to one story or the other leads to coherent and decisive action. The consequence of failing to make any choice is to remain a victim of circumstance; to remain a mere locus of incidents rather than an authentic, tangible person.

Of course, being a literary 'hero' is not everything. Lady Macbeth, Richard III, and Lear are all 'heroes' in the sense of being central characters, but since the aim is to become a *happy* person, something more than becoming a coherent self is required. One needs to *like* the life one has decided to narrate, the person one has decided to be.

'Like', of course, is much too weak a word for Nietzsche. For him, to fully match up to the ideal of happiness one must *love* one's life, love it *ecstatically*, love, indeed, *everything* about it. Nietzsche's New Year's resolution for 1882, which, as noted, begins Book IV of *The Gay Science*, reads:

> I want to learn more and more how to see what is necessary in things as beautiful. *Amor fati* [love of fate]: let that be my love from now on! I do not want to wage war against ugliness...Let looking away be my only negation!...some day I want only to be a Yes-sayer![118]

Since all the facts in one's life are 'necessary' in the sense that, being past, they are unalterable, ideal happiness consists in loving absolutely everything that one had done and had happened to one. And what this means – since even a single 'negation' is a failure of *amor fati* – is, in a word, that one needs to be able to love the 'eternal return'. Suppose, Nietzsche asks, a 'demon' were to whisper in your ear that

> this life as you now live it and have lived it you will have to live once again and innumerable times again; and there will be nothing new in it, but every pain and every joy and every thought and sigh and everything unspeakably small or great in your life must return to you – even this spider and this moonlight between the trees, and even this moment and I myself,

would you 'throw yourself down and gnash your teeth and curse the demon' or, on the contrary, could you say, "You are a god and never have I heard anything more divine"?'[119] Only if you are capable of the latter response, according to Nietzsche's stringent criterion, do you match up to the ideal of happiness.

How on earth could anyone love *everything* in their life? Surely, though most of us would be willing to live the broad outline of our lives once again, we can all think of episodes – the death of a child, the broken marriage, the time one lectured for a whole hour, only realising at the end that one's zip was undone – we would rather excise from our second life? Surely we can all remember things in our lives we would rather, in our second life, censor out, 'negate'?

One thing we need to learn from those pianists who are (like himself) 'masters of improvisation', says Nietzsche, is the ability to incorporate what in most hands would be a bad mistake into the beauty of the whole.[120] We must, that is, have the flexibility to modulate our life-narrative in the face of new exigencies. At any point in our lives we must, that is, deploy our 'skill in interpreting and arranging events' – our 'literary' skill in constructing the 'hero' of our lives – to enable us to discover, as it were, a 'personal providence' running through them. We need to be able to show how

> everything that befalls us continually turns out for the best. Every day and every hour life seems to want nothing else than to prove this proposition again and again; be it what it may – bad or good weather, the loss of a friend, a sickness, slander, the absence of a letter, the spraining of an ankle, a glance into a shop, a counter-argument, the opening of a book, a dream, a fraud – it shows itself immediately or very soon to be something that must not be missing',[121]

as, in other words, an essential part of a life-narrative we can wish to recur for ever and ever. Of course, narrating one's life so that there is *nothing* one would prefer to be without is easier said than done. But the one Nietzsche line known to almost everyone – 'what does not kill me makes me stronger'[122] – indicates one important technique: we need to have turned, or be confident we will turn, a traumatic event into a 'learning' or, in some other way, 'growth' experience.

This then – desiring the eternal return, i.e., *amor fati* – is Nietzsche's ideal of happiness. Guiding our attempt to 'sculpt' our lives into a unitary self is the requirement that everything that happens to us – everything we *remember* happening to us – turns out 'for the best'. Of course, few if any of us match up to the ideal – Nietzsche himself did not, not at least in January 1882, since *amor fati* was merely his New Year's *resolution*. That, however, is no criticism of the ideal: it is the nature of ideals that people almost always fall short of them. Nietzsche's thought, presumably, is that the fewer the episodes in our lives which remain as undigested traumas, the closer we come to the ideal, the happier we become.

Reality, Truth, and Knowledge

A number of passages in *The Gay Science* concern the traditional, 'big' theoretical questions of what there is and what we can know. One passage, for instance, though critical of many aspects of his philosophy, refers to Schopenhauer's 'immortal [i.e., timelessly true] doctrine of the intellectuality of intuition … and the instrumental nature of the intellect'.[123] All our experience is filtered through the intellect, filtered in a way that is geared – is 'instrumental' – to practical ends. Schopenhauer thought there was just one end, namely survival, but Nietzsche is more sophisticated: he recognises that we have many 'drives' and that each of them presents a 'one-sided' view of reality,[124] a one-sided 'perspective'[125] on the world: the building that shows up to the condemned man as the house of death may show up to the criminologist as a school for crime and to the architectural historian as a fine example of late-nineteenth-century Gothic.

Nietzsche rejects the idea that behind the various ways in which the world appears lies, as an 'unknown X', a 'thing in itself'.[126] Kantian idealism is definitively rejected. Our various world-appearances are not 'dreams': they are not false presentations of reality in the way that dreams are false presentations. But neither, on the other hand, can we privilege any one perspective as uniquely true, particularly not that of the 'sober' scientific 'realist' who claims that 'before [natural science] alone reality stands unveiled'.[127] There is no perspective on the world that uniquely captures the truth about it.

This leaves us with two possible ways of understanding Nietzsche's position. The first possibility is that he subscribes to what in the last chapter I called 'postmodernism': we have numerous world interpretations serving different practical purposes, but the idea that any of them could correspond to reality makes no sense. Our world interpretations cannot be false to reality, but neither can they be true to it. The second possibility, which I shall call 'plural realism',[128] is that Nietzsche, like Spinoza, thinks of reality as multi-aspected, so that different perspectives reveal – *truly* reveal – different aspects of it. Each of them reveals *a* truth though none reveals *the* truth. The building before me may be the house of death *and* a school for crime *and* a fine example of neo-Gothic architecture. Of course, there are some things the building almost certainly is not: an alien settlement or a film set, for instance. How would we rule these descriptions to be false? Nietzsche speaks of 'the sublime consistency and interrelatedness of all knowledge',[129] which suggests the following idea. The perspectives of the condemned man, the criminologist, and the architectural historian all *cohere* with each other: collectively they help build up a coherent and rounded picture of the object. But the idea that it is a film set or an alien settlement almost certainly *fails* to cohere with this relatively rounded picture. And so we should decide that it is very probably false.

The Gay Science's discussion of truth and knowledge takes place on a level of high metaphor which makes it hard to decide whether it subscribes to postmodernism or plural realism. My own inclination is to read Nietzsche as a plural realist, though it is possible that he was, at this stage, not entirely clear in his own mind as to what his position was. The issue will recur when we come to discuss the *Genealogy of Morals*, written near the end of his career. Since our chief interest is in his final position I shall defer further discussion until then.

One final point. The foregoing discussion of truth and knowledge has the appearance of being disconnected from what I called 'the main argument', the discussion of the free spirit's role in promoting cultural health. But this, I think, is not at all the case. For remember that the role of the free spirit is to promote cultural change by providing 'new names and valuations' for things.[130] This is what, for instance, environmental science does: what was previously a 'forest' as well as a 'supply of timber' acquires the new name 'carbon sink', an acquisition that powerfully alters our 'valuation' of and behaviour towards it. Cultural change, in other words, happens through shifts in perspective. This makes it tremendously important to Nietzsche to insist that our access to the world *is* perspectival, indeed that there are indefinitely many possible perspectives on it.[131] Were things to be otherwise, cultural change would be impossible.

18

The Salomé Affair

Lou Salomé

O N OR about April 26, 1882, in St. Peter's Basilica, Rome, Nietzsche kept an appointment with a young Russian who, beautiful and brilliant, was to be the cause of the most traumatic events of his life and a significant change in his intellectual outlook. The meeting had been arranged by Paul Rée, who sat in a nearby pew, pretending to read some notes but actually, for reasons that will become apparent, keeping a sharp eye on proceedings. Though the Messina poems suggest the intimation that its course might not be entirely smooth, they also suggest that Nietzsche was already in love with love, was ready to be rescued from his life of solitude. And so he greeted her with an echo of *Romeo and Juliet* almost certainly prepared beforehand: 'what stars', he asked, 'have brought us here together?' (In the just completed *Gay Science* he says farewell to Wagner with the thought that different 'stellar orbits' have drawn them apart:[1] here he suggests the reverse.)

The recipient of this portentous introductory line was Lou Salomé (see Plate 24), at twenty-one eleven years younger than Rée and sixteen years younger than Nietzsche. Lou was the daughter of a Baltic German who, in the pro-German atmosphere of late-nineteenth-century St. Petersburg (both Tsars Nicholas I and Alexander II had German wives and mothers), had risen to the rank of general in the Tsar's army. She loved her handsome father as much as she detested her anxiously bossy mother, Louise, who, though of mainly Russian blood, was also, like Rée, of part Huguenot descent.

Born into a masculine household (the youngest of six siblings, she had five elder brothers), Lou developed characteristics – intelligence, resoluteness, courage, and clarity of purpose – that were regarded as 'mannish' by the standards of the day. Her mother, whom she frequently exasperated, called her 'stubborn and determined to get her own way in everything'. Rée referred to her as the 'high-commanding Fräulein Lou', and Nietzsche described her as 'sharp-eyed as an eagle and courageous as a lion', though at the same time 'very maidenly'.[2] Köselitz called her 'heroic' of character, with a face taken from ancient Rome.[3]

Born into the revolutionary times of the liberation of the serfs, Lou was determined to liberate herself from the 'children–church–kitchen' role that was then the almost invariable destiny of women. Above all, she was determined to overcome the denial to women of all but an elementary education. Subject to early religious doubts, she refused confirmation into the German Reformed church, much to the disappointment of her dying father. To compensate, she started attending sermons delivered by the ultra-liberal Hendrik Gillot, pastor of the Dutch Reformed church in St. Petersburg. Mesmerised by his modernised theism, she found in it an antidote to the incipient atheism of the Russian intelligentsia. At the age of eighteen she persuaded him to accept her as a pupil. As well as French and German literature, he taught her Eastern religion and philosophy.

Gillot was twenty-five years her senior, with two daughters of almost her own age. This did not prevent him from falling in love with her, offering to leave his wife, and proposing marriage. Lou refused. This established the pattern for much of the rest of her life. Almost every man she had any serious contact with wanted to marry her (or at least get her into his bed), whereas what she wanted from them was intellectual stimulation without strings. Lou's passionate desire to enjoy the same independence as men led her to refuse every marriage offer. She knew that marriage entailed sex, which, in an age without reliable contraception, entailed children, which entailed imprisonment in the traditional female role. In her memoirs she recalls telling Rée that her 'love-life was closed for the duration of [her] life', a decision to which she was impelled by her 'completely unbridled thirst for freedom'. Even though, after passing out of Nietzsche's life, she eventually did marry the linguist Carl Friedrich Andreas (who in the course of their stormy engagement stabbed himself in the chest, just missing an artery) she did so only on the condition that the marriage remain celibate.

In 1880, showing symptoms of possible consumption, she was allowed, accompanied by her mother, to escape the harsh Russian winter. They settled in Zurich, where she gained permission to audit lectures on Hegel, Hinduism, Confucianism and the pre-Socratic Greek philosophers, at the university. Eager to meet Malwida von Meysenbug, whose *Memoirs of a Female Idealist* had made her a heroine to women of Lou's cast of mind, she arrived in Rome in February 1882, still chaperoned by her mother. She began to attend Malwida's salon at the Via Polveriera 6, held in her drawing-room, which looked out onto the Colosseum. When Rée arrived back from visiting Nietzsche in Genoa, having gambled away all his money in Monte Carlo (p. 323 above), he seemed rather dashing and 'free-spirited' in comparison with, in Lou's eyes, the rather stuffy, middle-aged ladies of Malwida's circle.

Nietzsche in Rome

Initially, Rée's interest in Lou seems to have been purely intellectual. Insofar as he thought of her in any different way, he seems to have had Nietzsche rather than himself in mind. A letter (now lost) written during his first week in Rome caused Nietzsche to reply from Genoa on March 21:

> If there is any point, greet the Russian girl for me. I have been lusting [*lüstern*] after this kind of soul. Indeed I'm soon going on the hunt for it – in view of what I have planned for

the next ten years I need it. But marriage is a completely different matter – I could at most agree to a two-year marriage, and this only in relation to what I have to do in the next ten years.[4]

This suggests that Rée recommended Lou as both an intelligent amanuensis and as a possible future marriage prospect. Nietzsche's airy raising of the possibility of taking her on as a temporary, part-time lover would soon have catastrophic consequences.

A month later, on April 20, Rée proposes a three-way rather than a two-way relationship. The 'Russian', he says, is

an energetic, incredibly smart creature with the most peculiar, even child-like, characteristics...I give talks about my book [probably *The Genesis of Conscience*] which helps me a great deal, since the audience includes the young Russian who misses nothing. She even, in an extremely annoying fashion, appears to know what will be coming up next, and what the purpose of it all is.[5]

What she wants, he reports, is that the three of them should live together for a year (chastely of course), possibly in Genoa, with an older woman, perhaps Malwida, on site for the sake of propriety:[6] effectively, a 'monastery for free spirits', a recreation of Sorrento about which Lou had, of course, heard a great deal. Later on, Vienna, and, still later, Paris, replace Genoa as the proposed site. Malwida, however, keen that 'free-spiritedness' should at the same time not give rise to cheap gossip, was appalled when she heard of the idea. 'It is dangerous to tempt fate', she told them presciently; 'that way one exposes oneself to mishaps with the result that what could remain pure, clear and beautiful both at the time and in retrospect, turns discordant and turbid' – which is exactly what happened.

The change of plan from a twosome to a threesome was of course a response to Lou's wishes – and fitted very much with Rée's and Nietzsche's long-standing hopes of a 'Return to Sorrento', of re-establishing an intellectual commune. What, however, Rée did not tell Nietzsche was that he no longer wished to offer him Lou, as it were, on a plate, since in the meantime he had fallen in love with her himself. On their evening walks à deux through the streets of Rome prior to Nietzsche's arrival (scandalous by the standards of the day) his dormant emotional life had been aroused. Through her mother, he proposed marriage. Lou, of course, gently rejected the proposal, telling him that sex was off and that they should live together 'as brother and sister'. The fact, however, that Rée concealed his change of attitude meant that there was a note of deception from the start. And it meant, too, that he and Lou were always one step ahead of Nietzsche; that he was, in fact, their dupe. They needed him for his intellectual firepower but neither of them, for their own, very different reasons, wanted him to fall in love with Lou.

Nietzsche arrived in Rome from Messina on or about April 24. After the usual post-travel collapse he was ready for his first, as he hoped, historic encounter with Lou in St. Peter's. Lou later recorded her first impressions of a man of 'solitude' possessing a 'deep inner life'. He struck her as 'very polite' and given to 'social formalities and careful dress', while displaying 'an almost feminine mildness and benevolent equanimity'. 'From what a man allows to be visible', she concluded, turning Nietzsche's own words on himself, 'one can wonder what it is he conceals'.[7]

With the same extraordinary gaucheness displayed six years earlier towards Mathilde Trampedach, Nietzsche decided immediately on a (proper rather than just 'two-year') marriage proposal. Knowing nothing of Rée's feelings, he entrusted his best friend with the mission of proposing on his behalf. A couple of days later, with one imagines acute embarrassment, Rée relayed the proposal to Lou. She of course rejected her second offer in a month. Letting Nietzsche down gently, she pointed out that marriage would mean the loss of the small pension left her by her now-deceased father for her *unmarried* years, and hence of her financial independence. Nietzsche appears to have accepted these grounds. Since he could only just support himself, he was hardly in a position not to.

The Mystery of Sacro Monte and the 'Whip' Photograph

At the beginning of May the badly balanced trio, together with Lou's mother, Louise, set off for Lucerne, breaking the journey for most of the first week in Orta San Giulio. Orta is a small peninsula town jutting out into Lake Orta, overlooked by the perpetually snow-covered Monte Rosa, just west of Lake Maggiore in the Piedmont region of northern Italy. They had idyllic weather, made boat trips around the lake and out to the monastery island of San Guilio and were enchanted by the singing of the nightingales. Nietzsche must have delighted in the shaded alleyways of the ancient town.

One day, managing somehow to escape the supervision of both Louise and Rée, Nietzsche and Lou walked up Sacro Monte, a hill behind Orta dedicated to St. Francis of Assisi. Sacro Monte (now a World Heritage site) is so called for the devotional spiral of twenty little chapels that encircles it. Each is a kind of peep show telling a scene from the life of St. Francis by means of a lively, three-dimensional tableau composed of life-sized painted terracotta figures. Here, inspired perhaps by the saint's call to authenticity, something of an intense nature occurred. Possibly Nietzsche revealed the secret of the eternal return, to which he had just given definitive form in *The Gay Science* (p. 336 above). Possibly there was an embrace and possibly a kiss. When asked many years later if Nietzsche kissed her (by which time he was a world star) Lou replied, nonchalantly, that she 'couldn't remember any more'. Whatever it was that happened on the hilltop had two consequences. First, Nietzsche received his own kind of stigmata: his love of being in love was transformed into real love. Later on he whispered to Lou, 'Monte Sacro[8] – the most delightful dream of my life; I owe it to you'.[9] And second, it made their reunion with the other members of their party considerably later than the appointed time, with the result that, when they eventually returned, they found Louise angry and Rée sulking.

Leaving Orta, the party agreed to meet again in Lucerne a week later. Nietzsche made a detour to Basel to catch up with the Overbecks. There he spoke of his desire to emerge from solitude and amazed Franz with his apparently vibrant good health. While in Lucerne, where Nietzsche remained from May 13 to 16, he and Lou made a, for him, nostalgic visit to Tribschen. Lou recalls that for a long time he sat silently on the shore of the quiet lake lost in melancholic memory. Slowly, head bowed and scratching in the soft, gravelly sand with a stick, he began to speak of his days there with Wagner. And when he looked up she saw that he was crying.

Another occasion on which Nietzsche managed to have Lou to himself was in the 'Lion Garden', Lucerne's city park. According to Lou, feeling that Rée had done a less than convincing job, he repeated the marriage proposal in person, only to be again rejected on the same grounds as before.

While in Lucerne, the trio visited the photographic studio of Jules Bonnet, where the infamous 'whip' photograph was taken (Plate 25). It shows Lou standing in a small cart drawn by Rée and Nietzsche as 'horses' and brandishing a 'whip' made out of a sprig of lilac. The tableau vivant was arranged by Nietzsche, whose high spirits overrode Rée's lifelong antipathy to having his photograph taken. Writing to Rée three months later,[10] Lou comments that whereas Nietzsche's face is totally inscrutable, in photograph as in life, his is a complete give-away. His entire character, she observes, is easily readable from his face – his keen powers of observation and intelligence from the eyes and forehead, his weary disdain of life from the soft droop of the mouth. Though she is actually writing with reference to a different photograph, these observations seem perfectly to fit the contrasting presences of the two 'horses' in the Lucerne photograph. And they explain, all too acutely, I think, why Rée hated being photographed. (Nietzsche's friend Resa von Schirnhofter observed, equally acutely, that the two horses seem to be pulling in different directions.)

Given the famous remark in *Zarathustra* – 'Do you go to women? Don't forget the whip' (p. 373 below) – there have been many speculative attempts to give a sadistic edge to Nietzsche's alleged misogyny. Given, however, that in the Lucerne photograph it is *Lou* who has the 'whip hand', such a line of interpretation seems unpromising. The most sensible interpretation comes from Curt Janz,[11] who suggests that (particularly since the photograph was taken but a half-hour's walk from Tribschen) the allusion is probably to Fricka in Wagner's *Ring* cycle, who is literally equipped with a whip and a horse-drawn chariot as well as almost always holding the whip hand over her husband, the supposedly supreme, but actually severely henpecked god, Wotan. Nietzsche's point, in arranging the tableau vivant, I would suggest, is to give ironic expression to both his own and Rée's enslavement to Lou. If this is true it suggests that he has, by now, caught onto the fact that Rée's feelings towards Lou mirror his own – but also that he wrongly assumes them to be on an equal footing with her.

Underhand Dealings

On May 16 the visitors left Lucerne for various destinations: Rée to return to his family home in Stibbe in northern Germany and Lou to return to her studies in Zurich. She took with her a copy of *Schopenhauer as Educator*, which Nietzsche had recommended as an expression of his fundamental stance.[12] Giving them only a couple of hours notice by telegram, Nietzsche descended on the Overbecks in Basel full of high spirits. Seemingly oblivious to the disruption of their lives, he kept them up until well after midnight with animated chatter. Once again they were astonished by the healthy colour of his skin and general appearance of good health. Two days later he arrived at his mother's house in Naumburg, which would remain his base until June 24.

Casting aside all obligations of decency, let alone of best friendship, Rée now began a subtle, underhand, long-distance battle to win Lou's heart entirely for himself. His letters to her shift to the intimate *du*, whereas Nietzsche never advanced beyond the formal *Sie*. 'It gives me great delight to call you *du*', he writes her at the end of May. And he tells his 'dear, dear Lu', a nickname he invents for her, that he 'yearns' for her since she is the only person he loves in the world. His mother's plan of more or less adopting her is a good idea, he writes, because if she does, 'when you are with my family and myself Nietzsche will grasp all the more quickly that you wish to reject the idea of being for a long time with him, *particularly with him alone*'. He tells her that he has not communicated the 'adoption' plan to Nietzsche because 'if he hears of it he is likely to see it as a manoeuvre to keep you from him' (which of course it was) and is liable to become 'agitated and angry'. A momentary attack of conscience 'that, in my relations with Nietzsche, I have not been completely open and honest, particularly since a certain young woman appeared from out of the blue' is dismissed with an appeal to the overpowering demands of love: 'But quite honestly I never stood to him as I do to you.' Repeatedly he tells Lou not to mention his 'money story' – his gambling losses in Monte Carlo. As I suggested earlier, these gave him a certain Dostoyevskian glamour in Lou's eyes. But the point of the concealment (in fact Nietzsche *knew* about the gambling losses since he had to lend Rée the train fare to Rome (p. 323 above)) is surely to draw Lou into a conspiracy of naughty schoolchildren against Nietzsche, cast into the role of stiff and stuffy schoolmaster.[13]

Meanwhile, from Naumburg, Nietzsche, too, begins to write love letters to Lou. More honourable and much more inhibited than Rée's, they are at the same time more self-deceiving. 'When I am quite alone', he writes on May 24, 'I often, very often, speak your name out loud – with very great pleasure'. But the same letter comments generously that 'Rée is in all ways a better friend than I am or can be: take good note of this difference!'[14] He adds that (since she is bound to find the idea scandalous) he has not breathed a word of the proposed *ménage à trois* to his mother.[15] To Ida Overbeck he writes that 'Rée and I have *the same feelings* towards our brave and honourable friend . . . he and I trust each other completely in this matter',[16] which seems to be an attempt to convince both Ida and himself that (a) the friendship with Rée is undamaged and (b) while neither of them is unaware of Lou's nubile capacity to, as he wrote Köselitz, cause 'the wild beast' in a man to 'poke its head out of the cage' [sic],[17] they will both quite certainly keep the wild beast firmly in check in the interests of the higher life of the mind.

At the end of May, Nietzsche's endeavour to preserve the official story that both he and Rée are interested solely in a celibate 'monastery for free spirits' begins to fracture. Learning that Lou plans to travel to Berlin en route to Rée's family in Stibbe, he says that he, too, will go to Berlin to meet her in the forested suburb of Grunewald (shade for his eyes, of course) since 'to be frank, I desire very much, to be completely alone with you as soon as possible'.* 'Solitaries such as myself', he continues, 'must become accustomed slowly to others, even those that are most dear to them'.[18] Another suggestion put forward in the same letter for being-alone-together-in-the-woods was the Thuringian village of Tautenburg, not far from Naumburg, with Elizabeth on hand as chaperone. And he suggests Vienna as a site for the three of them in the autumn.[19] (He favoured the intellectually advanced Vienna since, after putting the finishing touches to *The Gay Science*, his 'last book', he planned to spend the next decade studying scientific subjects to remedy the gap in his Pforta

---

* On June 16 he did in fact make a one-day dash from Naumburg to Berlin, the big city he always hated, in an unsuccessful attempt to meet up with Lou. He was appalled that the woods of Grunewald were full of litter and day-trippers.

education.) A week later he writes, referring to *Dawn*, which Lou was reading and by which she was profoundly impressed,

> I too have dawns around me, none of them printed. It now seems to me possible, something I have never believed in, to find a friend of my deepest happiness and suffering – as the golden possibility on the horizon of all my future life. I am moved whenever I think of the brave and deeply intuitive soul of my dear Lou.[20]

Here, clearly, the idea of a 'two-year marriage' is dead and buried. Nietzsche longs for a lifelong partnership – marriage – with Lou. Finally, it seems to him, he has found his Cosima.

Nietzsche in Tautenburg

On June 25 Nietzsche decamped to Tautenburg, where he would remain until August 27. The village is nine kilometres east of Jena and twenty kilometres southwest of Naumburg, an hour's walk from the better-known village and castle of Dornburg on the river Saale. Tautenburg is a picturesque village of (now as then) about 300 inhabitants. It nestles in a horseshoe of wooded hills beneath the protective gaze of the tower which is all that is left of the former Tautenburg castle from which the village derived its name. Since the rail line along the Saale Valley had been extended to Dornburg in 1875, Tautenburg was just beginning to become known as a holiday destination where the city folk of Jena could breathe the pure forest air and recuperate from the stresses of urban life.

That Tautenburg became known as a place to holiday was largely due to the efforts of the energetic and forward-looking pastor Hermann Stölten, who was keen to minister to the bodily as well as the spiritual needs of his countrymen. To that end, he started to take paying guests in the vicarage.

Elizabeth, who had visited Tautenburg previously, had been trying to get Nietzsche to adopt it as a summer retreat for a couple of years. According to her biography, she favoured it, and recommended it to her brother, on account of the shade the surrounding forest offered his eyes. Beneath this attraction, however, lay a covert purpose. She and her mother had the idea that Stölten would be able to reason with Nietzsche on his own level and thereby bring him back to the straight and narrow of Christian belief.[21] The idea was not quite totally stupid – in Leipzig Stölten had studied not only theology but also logic and philosophy – but he, of course, saw immediately that he had nothing like the intellectual firepower needed to combat Nietzsche's informed and by now highly developed critique of Christianity. He retained nonetheless a very good opinion of Nietzsche as a person, remarking merely that he found it impossible to grasp how 'so spiritual and richly endowed' a man could 'spout such poison in his writings'. It is clear that in Stölten's generous mind the man took precedence over the writings, since in September of 1882 he had Nietzsche elected an honorary member of the Tautenburg Beautification Society[22] – the only honorific title he ever received.

The Beautification Society figures in Nietzsche's correspondence. It has resolved, he proudly told Elizabeth at the beginning of July, to construct five benches in and around the woods solely for his use on his walks. They are to be called collectively 'The Gay Science' (he was correcting the final proofs in Tautenburg). By July 11 he reports that the benches are in place, though by now their number is reduced to two. 'I have promised to have two plaques put on them … On one will be written "The Dead Man. F. N." ['The Dead Man' was the quaint name of the part of the forest in which Nietzsche liked to walk] on the other "The Gay Science. F. N."' And he asks his mother to have the plaques made and to see that they are 'fine and beautiful, and something that does me an honour'.[23]

There is something odd about this whole story.[24] Why should the farmers who constituted the main membership of the Society treat someone who was at the time almost completely unknown outside a very small circle of intellectuals as if he were a famous philosopher? It seems most likely that what actually happened was that *Nietzsche* originally proposed the benches and badgered the society until a couple were erected, and then embellished the truth to impress his mother and sister.

Elizabeth versus Lou

It was agreed that, after a visit to Bayreuth, Lou would join Nietzsche in Tautenburg, chaperoned by Elizabeth. Unlike Rée, Lou, and Wagner (who had lived, remember, in open sin with Cosima in pious Switzerland), Nietzsche cared deeply about not becoming a 'topic of European gossip'.[25] The bait he used to entice Lou to Tautenburg was the offer of becoming her 'teacher', which would make her his spiritual 'heir', together with the promise of esoteric disclosures that appeared in none of his books. He now had no option but to tell Elizabeth of the proposed visit, explaining to her that Lou was to come to Tautenburg for a cram course in preparation for the planned 'monastery'. In mid-July he let Köselitz into the secret of the proposed threesome, trying to preserve the official story by adding that Köselitz 'will please do the two of us the honour of keeping the concept of a love affair far distant from our relationship'.[26]

On July 24 Elizabeth met up with Lou in Leipzig to accompany her to Bayreuth for the first performance of Wagner's *Parsifal* (conducted on the twenty-sixth by Hermann Levi). Keeping well clear of the event itself, Nietzsche nonetheless made an excursion from Tautenburg to Naumburg in order to 'prepare my sister a little for *Parsifal*'. In May he had studied the piano reduction. He told her, by way of alerting her to the religiosity of the work, that 'just *this* kind of music I wrote as a boy when I wrote my Oratorio' (p. 28 above). To Köselitz he commented that he had played through his old work and had seen that 'the identity of mood and expression is extraordinary'. One passage, in his Oratorio, 'the death of the king', he claimed, is 'completely Parsifalesque'. He was shocked to realise 'once again how intimately related Wagner and I are'.[27] On August 1 he reported hearing that 'the old magician has once again had a tremendous success' and that Elizabeth and Lou have both had a private invitation to visit Cosima.[28]

In Bayreuth, Elizabeth and Lou at first pretended to like each other and soon adopted the familiar *du*. Within a week, however, friendship had collapsed into open warfare. On account of her brother's defection, Elizabeth was not entirely persona grata in Bayreuth. She was, moreover, thirty-six, husbandless, poorly educated, somewhat dowdy and hobbled by a small-town mentality. Lou, on the other hand, was young, beautiful and clever, entirely at ease with the international glitterati assembled for the occasion. Effortlessly, she charmed the male members of the Wagner entourage, gaining immediate access to Wagner's inner circle. With the painter Paul Joukowsky – he had been working on the scenery for the production and had recently finished a portrait of Cosima – she flirted and discussed spiritualism; with Heinrich von Stein, tutor to Wagner's children, she discussed philosophy, displaying, according to Nietzsche's later friend Resa von Schirnhofer, 'astounding dialectical virtuosity'. (Rée had prepared her to combat von Stein's Schopenhauerian metaphysics by saying she should deploy the positivist dictum that 'all causes have to be verified in experience'.)

Elizabeth, desperately wishing to escape the restrictions of Naumburg and a bigoted mother, was consumed by horrified jealousy at the free and easy manner of a rival who had waltzed into Bayreuth's inner circle, with which she did not feel at ease and to which she was not admitted. She was horrified, too, by the gossip Lou created by circulating the 'amusing' 'whip' photograph, with its suggestion that she had both men in her power. (Resa von Schirnhofer, too, thought circulating the photograph 'in poor taste' (see p. 388 below).) In a fury Elizabeth sent her brother a telegram saying she could manage the scandalous girl no longer and was leaving Bayreuth.

Part of the documentation of what happened next is missing (destroyed, probably, by Elizabeth), but it is clear that Elizabeth provided her brother with a damning account of Lou's behaviour in Bayreuth that would have mixed a little fact with plenty of fiction. What seems to have cut him to the quick was the claim that, currying favour with the Wagnerians, Lou had been consistently scornful of their enemy, Nietzsche. 'My sister has a hundred stories' of Lou's 'putting me down' in Bayreuth, he wrote later.[29] The result was Nietzsche's cancellation of the Vienna commune project[30] and some maudlin mutterings about a bird having flown past which, grasping at straws as the lonely do, he took to be an eagle symbolizing a 'higher world', but which 'the whole world' now wants to prove to be a delusion. This leads on to more general reflections on whether it is better to be 'deluded' or 'undeluded'.[31]

Rapidly, however, love overcame suspicion. Recovering from Elizabeth's poison, he replies on August 4 to a (missing) letter from Lou that the bird he took to be an eagle *is* an eagle. 'Do come' to Tautenburg as originally planned, he writes; 'I suffer too much from having made you suffer. We will bear it better together'.[32]

She Said She Said He Said

Somehow matters were patched up and the Tautenburg project put back on track. On about August 6 Lou and Elizabeth arrived together to spend the night in Jena with family friends of the Nietzsches, the Gelzers, en route to Tautenburg. Here, however, a violent argument occurred.

The background to the argument is this. Rée had certainly told Lou of Nietzsche's proposal of a two-year 'marriage' – 'concubinage' in the language of the times. Nietzsche himself may have repeated the proposal in the Lion Garden in Lucerne, offering it as a prelude to real marriage. It was, after all, not unknown in artistic circles of the time – the Wagners had given birth to Siegfried in such a state. Rée may also have told Lou that Nietzsche had had dealings with prostitutes during the Sorrento period. A further background point – one on which both Nietzsche and Lou were agreed – is that Nietzsche was an 'egoist'. Indeed, since Lou was profoundly impressed by *Dawn*, which she had just finished reading, she would have agreed that she, too, was one (as was manifestly the case) since a fundamental thesis of that work is, of course, that *everyone* is an egoist (p. 299 above). The crucial question is, however: as just what kind of egoist did Lou see Nietzsche? Writing to him from Hamburg the month before accompanying Elizabeth to Bayreuth, she says that

> I've understood why people like Malwida like your work better than Rée's even though from her standpoint you say the more unpalatable things. Whereas Rée's egoist ... says to himself 'our only goal is a comfortable, happy course of life' you say – somewhere – 'if one must do without a happy life there still remains the heroic one'.[33] These deeply different representations of the egoistic, which in a certain sense give expression to the writer's own innermost drive, mark the difference. And these different outlooks would, if embodied in two different people, stamp the one with the features of Rééian egoism and the other with those of a hero'.[34]

This shows that Lou had understood *Dawn*'s distinction between the overflowing kind of – as she puts it here – 'heroic' egoism that needs to *give*, and the 'hungry' egoism that merely *takes*, as well as the idealised self-portrait implicit in the work (pp. 309–12 above). Later on, when disappointed love turned to hate, Nietzsche will attribute to Lou a 'cat-egoism which cannot love any more'.[35] But Lou would certainly have viewed her own egoism, her need to achieve equality in a man's world to do the important work she felt herself capable of, as being, as she here assesses Nietzsche's, of the giving, 'heroic' kind.

The quarrel at the Gelzers seems to have been started by Elizabeth praising Nietzsche as a 'saint' and 'ascetic'. She must have overdone this theme (a reflection of her own quasi-incestuous possessiveness), since eventually Lou's patience snapped, causing her to spill the beans about the 'two-year marriage' proposal. Elizabeth's account of Lou's rage is contained in a letter written after the event to her friend Frau Gelzer:

> 'Who first dragged our plan of a communal household into the dirtiest mud, who first thought in terms of marriage?' [Lou demanded.] 'That was your brother!' And to emphasize it once more, she said: 'Yes, it was your noble, pure-minded brother who first had the dirty idea of a concubinage!' And on it went late in the evening.

Later on, in Tautenburg, Elizabeth's letter claims – the argument seems to have simmered on for some weeks – Lou said, 'Don't think for a moment that I am interested in your brother or in love with him; I could sleep in the very same room as him, without getting any wild ideas'.[36] This claim has a strong ring of truth since, by now, Lou must have been thoroughly fed up with (from her point of view) old men trying to get her into bed.

The other allegation Elizabeth claimed Lou to have made at the Gelzers' is that Nietzsche was an egoist: according to her letter to Frau Gelzer an egoist 'in the grand [i.e., 'heroic'] style', according to what she told her mother, a 'common egoist'.[37] Elizabeth, of course, a woman of very little philosophical brain, would have been quite incapable of noticing the important distinction both Nietzsche and Lou drew between the different species of egoism (a distinction which, in its own way, actually reasserts Christian morality's distinction between egoism and altruism). But it is entirely possible that, aware by now of his more-than-intellectual designs on her, Lou precisely judged him in terms of his own standards and accused him of falling from his own 'heroic' ideal into a low, and very 'hungry', egoism.

The argument in Jena was brought to an abrupt halt by Elizabeth becoming so upset that she succumbed to an attack of vomiting.

Lou in Tautenburg

Amazingly, given this background and its undoubtedly coloured reporting back to Nietzsche – 'she [Lou] abused my whole character and will in Jena', he later wrote[38] – the Tautenburg project went ahead. Lou arrived with Elizabeth on August 7 to stay with pastor Stölten, a couple of minutes' walk from Nietzsche's lodgings. In spite of the difficulty of the situation she stayed until August 26, 1882, the very day on which *The Gay Science* appeared. That it assumed its final form under her gaze Nietzsche took as a good omen.

Nietzsche and Lou went for long walks in the forest shade (pausing, no doubt, to sit on the famous benches), engaged in intense, philosophical discussions that lasted many hours, and wrote aphorisms together. All of these activities excluded Elizabeth. Most of the time they escaped her company completely, reducing her to a chaperone in name only. Lou records in her diary spending an entire day with Nietzsche:

> We spent a beautiful day alone in the quiet, dark spruce forest with squirrels and the sunshine filtering through. Elizabeth had gone to visit the Dornburg [castle] with some acquaintances. At the village inn, when I arrive wearing my cap and Nietzsche without Elizabeth, and where one sits under the linden trees with their big branches, they consider us to belong together as much as do you and I.

The 'you' referred to, here, is Rée. Extraordinarily, she kept a detailed Tautenburg diary explicitly to contain his jealousy. Unable to prevent this disruption to his plan for keeping her all to himself, Rée had warned her on August 4 that ever since she agreed to go to Tautenburg Nietzsche had regarded her as his betrothed.[39] Unbeknownst to Nietzsche, therefore, Rée was able to 'see' everything that went on in Tautenburg, to assure himself that there was no hanky-panky.

The diary,[40] with – given its intended reader – its brutally frank objectivity, provides us with snapshots of life in Tautenburg. Nietzsche, Lou records, continually dropped by at her lodgings and sometimes kissed her hand. When confined to bed (she had a bad cough and was, remember, suspected of consumption), he would write her little notes or speak to her through the bedroom door. Nietzsche, she writes, is 'a man of violent mood swings' and there were sometimes 'stormy emotions' particularly early on in her stay. (Nietzsche himself records that 'every five days or so we have a little drama'.)[41] But also, she records, they had lots of fun. To Elizabeth's outrage – she no doubt thought that spiritualism, along with the 'other world' in general, should be taken more seriously – they pretended to hear a 'ghostly knocking' as soon as Nietzsche entered her lodgings. And (another joke with, like the 'whip' photograph, not-quite-pleasant undertones) Nietzsche decorated a photograph of Rée with ivy leaves. Lou asserts (correctly in my judgment) a deep intellectual affinity between Nietzsche and herself – 'we often take the words out of each other's mouth' – so that their discussions sometimes lasted all day and into the evenings, when Nietzsche would cover the lamp with a red cloth to shield his eyes. His growing respect for her intellect led him to abandon entirely his plan to be her 'teacher'; as Zarathustra tells his 'disciples', he told her to create independently and never behave like a pupil. Sometimes their communication transcends the kind of words that would be intelligible to a third party as they look together 'into the abyss' – of, one may guess, a God-deserted world.

In spite of this deep communion, Lou informs a no doubt relieved Rée that there is a 'shadow' between them. In the 'deep recesses of our natures', she writes, 'we are worlds apart'. Nietzsche's nature contains 'many a dark dungeon and hidden cellar that does not surface in the course of a brief acquaintance, yet could contain his very essence'. These 'concealed cellars', it occurs to Lou, mean that 'some day, we could even confront each other as enemies'. One might suspect that what is going on here is the over-psychoanalysing by the future Freudian psychoanalyst of a very simple fact: Nietzsche wanted to sleep with Lou but Lou did not want to sleep with Nietzsche.

To Pain

The remarkable thing about the contact between Lou and Nietzsche is that they genuinely were, for long periods of time, able to ascend to the realm of pure thought, to put all personal passions aside and relate to each other as pure minds. Lou notes in her diary Nietzsche's capacity for this kind of elevation: whereas, she tells Rée, you work with a 'clock in the hand', Nietzsche is, like her, obsessed with his work. 'Every emotion that is not related to it appears to him as a kind of unfaithfulness'. 'You', she continues, 'do not have your heart stuck in your brain and indissolubly connected with it to the same degree as Nietzsche – the egoist in the grand style'.*

What, on these occasions on which they transcended the personal, did Nietzsche and Lou talk about? Ida Overbeck comments that the radical transformation of Nietzsche's style from the witty aphorisms of *The Gay Science* to the 'religious' and 'prophetic' mode of expression in *Zarathustra*, his next work, was due to his contact with Lou. 'He later told my husband', she recalls, 'that religion was really the only topic they discussed'.[42]

Like Nietzsche, Lou lost her faith in the Christian God during her adolescence. Even more precocious than he, she rejected not merely Christian supernaturalism but, as her diary makes clear, 'metaphysics' in general. By the age of twenty-one, she had already arrived at the positivistic outlook that was the bond between Rée and Nietzsche. Throughout her life she continued to describe her 'loss of God' as a 'misfortune', though one that came to be compensated for by a 'dimly-awakening never relenting and always present' pantheistic sense of 'eternal union with all that is'.[43] In Nietzsche she found the same sense of loss and the same 'search for God': the search for a new god to fill the place left by the death of the old god. As I have already indicated, Nietzsche, too, under the influence of Spinoza and Emerson, was moving towards pantheism.

---

* Of course, for everyone of this period, the paradigm of the 'egoist in the grand style' was Wagner. Lou, it seems to me, is here making the insightful point that in terms of the scale of his ambition and his readiness to sacrifice to it both himself and those nearest and dearest to him, Nietzsche is no less 'grand' an egoist than Wagner. In effect, I think, she sees that part of her problem with Nietzsche parallels his with Wagner – given the 'tyrannical' nature of genius, he is the great tree under whose shade nothing else can grow. Not only the constant sexual tension but also her need for intellectual autonomy showed her the need for a break with Nietzsche. In both regards she saw that Rée, a smaller and milder man in every way, was a more satisfactory companion.

The fundamental problem for any such move is the 'problem of evil'. If the totality of nature is divine, the object of ecstatic affirmation and reverence, how is it possible that it contains so much pain? This is just a reformulation of the problem confronted by traditional Christian theology: if God is wholly good and wholly powerful, why does he allow so much evil in the world? In Christian theology the project of providing a convincing answer to this question is called 'theodicy'. And that, in essence, is Lou and Nietzsche's project.

At the beginning of July 1882, Nietzsche sent Köselitz a poem called 'To Pain', apparently written by himself. It begins:

> Who can escape you when you have seized him/When you fasten him with your serious gaze?/I will not curse when you grip me/I never believe that you merely destroy!/I know that every earthly existence must go to you/Nothing on earth is untouched by you./Life without you – would be beautiful/And yet – experiencing you has value./Certainly you are no ghost of the night/You come to warn the spirit of your power/Struggle is what makes the greatest great/The struggle for the goal, on impassable paths . . . [44]

Two weeks later he discloses that the poem (which may have been occasioned by the death of her father) is not by him but by Lou. And he adds that it 'belongs to the things that have a total power over me. I have never been able to read it without tears; it sounds like a voice that since my childhood I have waited and waited for'.[45]

In the piety of his childhood, as we saw, Nietzsche prayed for submission to God's will:

> May the dear Lord give me strength and power to carry out my intentions and protect me on my life's way. Like a child I trust in his grace: He will preserve us all, that no misfortune may befall us. But His holy will be done! All He gives I will joyfully accept: happiness and unhappiness, poverty and wealth, and boldly look even death in the face . . . (p. 18 above)

When, at the beginning of 1882, he hit upon *amor fati* (i.e., desiring the eternal return) as the formulation of his fundamental goal (p. 322 above) he described it as an expression of 'submission to God'.[46] In short, once he had cast off the shackles of doctrinaire positivism, his most fundamental problem became the question of how to recover the religious attitude to life – without backsliding into supernatural myths. Lou's poem goes to the heart of this problem: how is one to adopt the religious attitude to life, to affirm, love, reverence it in spite of all its pain and in the absence of any kind of metaphysical compensation? And it offers one kind of path to a solution: pain is the possibility of growth. Without suffering and struggle there can be no 'victory', no 'greatness'. What, as Nietzsche puts it in 1888, does not kill makes one stronger. There was, then, a deep intellectual affinity between Nietzsche and Lou. At the age of twenty-one she was already occupied with his fundamental problem: as she put it in the title of her 1885 novel, the problem was the 'Struggle for God',* more specifically the struggle to find 'God' *in spite* of evil, in spite of the pain of life.

Nietzsche describes this fundamental sense of *the* problem and *the* goal, this fundamental, governing mood of yearning for God that shapes both his own and Lou's thinking and feeling, as 'musical'. As she left Tautenburg, Lou gave him another poem, the 'Prayer to Life', the first verse of which he promptly set to music for voice and piano[47] (track 17 on

---

* A thinly disguised roman à clef depicting her life with Rée and Nietzsche.

the Web site for this book). A couple of weeks later he wrote Köselitz that he wanted a public performance of the piece 'in order to seduce men to my philosophy'.[48] The poem reads

> *It is certain – a friend loves a friend the way*
> *That I love you, enigmatic life –*
> *Whether you gave me joy or pain,*
> *I love you with your happiness and harm,*
> *And if you must destroy me,*
> *I wrest myself painfully from your arms,*
> *As a friend tears himself away from a friend's breast.*
> *I embrace you with all my strength!*
> *Let all your flames ignite my spirit,*
> *And me in the ardour of the struggle*
> *To find the solution to your riddle.*
> *To live and think millennia!*
> *Throw your content completely into me:*
> *If you have no more happiness to give me –*
> *Well then – give me your pain.*[49]

Even with all the muddy water that had passed under the bridge, for the rest of his life, Nietzsche never lost his conviction that the sense of life as sacred, as something to be prayed to in spite of all its pain, expressed in Lou's poem, captured the essence of his own spirit. In *Ecce Homo* he refers to his and her musical work – in a new setting of 1886 for chorus and orchestra that he retitled *Hymn to Life* – as expressing the 'greatness' of soul that underlies *Zarathustra*.[50]

Family Rupture

On August 27, Nietzsche travelled home to Naumburg. But it must have been with a heavy heart. For, after weeks of trying to smooth things over, he had finally to admit that Elizabeth had 'turned into Lou's mortal enemy'.[51] And given that she was, in her own way, as strong-willed as Lou, and endowed with considerable skill in petty intrigue, he must have known that a radical collapse in relations with his family was inevitable. Though Elizabeth stayed on in Tautenburg 'so that mamma shan't see my teary eyes' and to allow Nietzsche to 'tell mamma everything himself',[52] she in fact wrote her mother, as Nietzsche reported to Overbeck, that

> in Tautenburg she has seen my philosophy translated into life and is shocked: I love evil while she loves the good. If she was a good Catholic she'd go into a nunnery and do penance for all that wickedness which will result from it.[53]

She also gave her mother an – of course embroidered – account of Lou's alleged denigration of Nietzsche among his enemies in Bayreuth and of her displaying the 'whip' photo to all and sundry. The result was that, as he concludes his letter to Overbeck, 'I now have Naumburg "virtue" against me'[54] – provincial, small-town, petite-bourgeois, conventional, legalistic, narrow-minded morality. Matters came to a head when Franziska said she would never have Lou in the house and called Nietzsche 'a disgrace to his father's grave'. The result was that Nietzsche packed his bag on September 8 and left the following morning for Leipzig where, finding lodgings at Auenstrasse 26, he remained until November 15.

The End of the Affair

In spite of all that had happened, Nietzsche still retained hopes of forming a harmonious trinity, a 'three-in-one',[55] with Lou and Rée. Surely, he wrote Rée, two acute 'psychologists' such as themselves would be 'clever enough' to manage any difficulties. And he added, combining an appeal for sympathy with an assurance of the platonic nature of his intentions towards Lou, that 'having lost a natural sister I must be given a more than natural one'.[56]

On October 1 Lou and Rée gave in to his entreaties and paid a five-week visit to Leipzig. On the evening of their arrival Nietzsche arranged for them to attend a séance (given the joking about 'ghostly knockings' in Tautenburg, it was probably intended as light entertainment), which they found to be obvious trickery. The many unspoken undercurrents, however, cast a strained and melancholy mood over the visit. Lou probably thought mainly of avoiding Nietzsche's lust and forceful personality and the friendship between Nietzsche and Rée was effectively over. When the latter's *Genesis of Conscience* appeared three years later it was not dedicated to Nietzsche – though Nietzsche later claimed he had refused the dedication.

Nonetheless, lip service was still paid on all sides to the notion of the 'three-in-one', the idea being, at Lou and Rée's departure on November 5, that they would soon meet up again in some agreed city, though no longer, seemingly, to set up house together. On November 7 Nietzsche wrote to his old flame, Louise Ott, asking her if she would recommend Paris for the winter. But it took him less than a week to admit to himself that Lou and Rée had never been serious about the idea and that he had, in fact, been dumped. Abruptly, therefore, he cancelled all thoughts of Paris, returning once more to his practice of wintering in the South.

On November 23 he arrived, via Basel, in Genoa. Finding, however, his old lodgings rented he moved twenty kilometres eastwards along the coast to Portofino, a charming fishing village nestling at the foot of the mountains around a horseshoe harbour. Nietzsche loved the village, observing that the 'proud and calm balance' with which its mountains fall into the sea completes the 'melody' of the gulf of Genoa – the model of a perfect ending that only master composers can emulate.[57] Lodgings proved equally difficult to find in Portofino, however, so he edged another twenty kilometres eastwards along the coast to Rapallo, where he arrived on about November 23.

Aftermath

Following Nietzsche's appearance in Basel (on November 16), the unfailingly sympathetic Overbeck wrote to Rohde describing their friend's condition:

This summer and autumn he has experienced the worst time of his life, the result of which is that he is now condemned to a new kind of loneliness that even he can't bear. Following the events of this summer loneliness is the worst poison for him ... I was powerless to help him ... His health has astonishingly recovered and is the least of his worries ... What has absolutely shattered him (next to the story of the separation from the Russian – which in the circumstances is a blessing) is the complete break with his family ... his future is a very dark place.[58]

Overbeck did not exaggerate. Having lost the love of his life, his closest intellectual companion, and a mother and sister to whom, for all their faults, he was viscerally attached, Nietzsche now indulged in an orgy of recriminations. In a series of letter sketches, sometimes to Lou and sometimes to Rée (some but not all of which were sent), he calls Rée a wastrel: an exceptional nature collapsing through laziness and lack of genuine intellectual commitment,[59] a 'noble nature in decay'.[60] His main abuse, however, is reserved for Lou. He describes her (alleged) slandering and ridiculing of his character in Bayreuth, Jena, and Tautenburg as the 'ugliest' way in which anyone has ever acted towards him in his entire life[61] – which confirms the success of Elizabeth's attempts to poison his mind against her. He calls her a 'cat',[62] one who practices not his own 'holy selfishness' but rather a 'cat-egoism which cannot love'.[63] In place of love she has a 'cunning self-control when it comes to the sensuality of men (she is, in polite language, a manipulative coquette) which she deploys to satisfy her 'powerful will'.[64] He complains that he gave her *Schopenhauer as Educator* to show her his fundamental cast of mind (p. 343 above), which he thought she would share, but discovers her to be utterly 'superficial', lacking in 'respect, gratitude, piety, politeness and wonder'.[65] 'You don't really think that the "free spirit" is my ideal" he adds.[66] The force of this last remark is to contrast the intense, morally serious idealism demanded by *Schopenhauer as Educator* with the idea that 'anything goes'. The accusation is, in a word, nihilism: Lou tramples roughshod over current social conventions (and people's hearts) without having anything to put in their place: she is a free spirit of the worthless 'second rank', light years away from the creative 'first rank' (p. 329 above).

Sometimes Nietzsche reveals how deeply his conception of the properly dominant role of the male has been wounded: he writes that he has always disliked hearing her voice 'except when you beg'[67] and that she is a woman who 'belongs on the lowest level of humanity [i.e., is a slut]' despite her good brain.[68]

Interspersed with the hatred, however, are other moods: moments of abject self-pity, moments in which he purports to be above it all and moments in which he attempts a reconciliation. 'You'll be glad to be rid of me for a while', he writes Rée at the end of November, 'and I wish the two of you all the best'. But, he continues, 'we will all see each other from time to time won't we? Don't forget that this year I have been suddenly deprived of [Elizabeth's] love and am thus in great need of love'.[69] Again: 'Lou, dear heart, do create a clear sky above us', in other words make everything as it was before. Just before Christmas he tells Lou and Rée he can neither sleep nor work, that he has taken a huge dose of opium, and that they must just regard him as a crazy person 'driven half-mad by solitude'. He adds, pathetically, that they are 'not to worry too much if he kills himself'.[70] On Christmas Day, 1882, at the same time as telling his mother that 'she must take a quite different tone with him' if she wants him to open any more letters from Naumburg,[71] he writes Overbeck that he cannot sleep despite the strongest sleeping drugs and 'marching' six to eight hours a day. 'This bite of life', he continues, 'is the hardest I have ever had to chew'. And then he connects the Salomé affair in all its ramifications with his philosophy. I am, he says, 'going through all phases of self-overcoming'. But he wonders whether he will be able to complete the process, whether he will be able to 'swallow' the Salomé 'bite of life'. And then he indicates what the 'swallowing' will consist in:

> If I don't invent the alchemist's art of making gold from shit – from this too – I am lost. Here I have the best possible opportunity to prove that, to me, 'all experiences are useful, all days holy and all men divine'!!!⁷² All men divine. – My mistrust is at the moment very great. From everything I hear I am scorned on all sides.⁷³

'Swallowing', in other words, will consist, as Lou's poems indicate, in finding a 'theodicy' that will embrace even the storm of which she is the eye.

In spite of his efforts at self-overcoming, Nietzsche remained, as we shall see, locked into the pain of the Salomé affair until at least the end of 1883. Reconciled for a time with Elizabeth in midyear (communications with his family had, in fact, never been completely severed) he connived with her to get Lou sent back to Russia as an 'immoral person'.

* * *

Did Lou really deserve all this? Most Nietzsche scholars, women as much as men, surprisingly, think she did. Curt Janz, for instance, regards Lou as almost a psychopath, someone who 'was aware that she caused other people pain but nothing more. She never achieved a sense of responsibility or guilt'. 'For deep love and dutiful commitment…she had no capacity.'⁷⁴ But, one might ask, who *is* so committed at the age of twenty-one – particularly when the objects of possible 'dutiful commitment' that kept thrusting themselves upon one are getting on for one's father's age. One of Nietzsche's complaints is that Lou has treated him as if he were a twenty-year-old student.⁷⁵ But how else, one might ask, *could* a twenty-year-old have treated him? Her 'dumping' of Nietzsche, and later of Rée, surely represents 'experimental' behaviour entirely typical of someone her age. Both Janz and Nietzsche demand of Lou an emotional maturity beyond her years.

Leaving aside the fact that her suitors, Gillot, Nietzsche and Rée, were from her point of view old men, Lou's refusal to sleep with any of them was entirely understandable. As already remarked, sex meant the likelihood of children and thus of imprisonment in the traditional female role. Moreover, she seems to have been entirely explicit about the fact that sex was off the menu 'for the duration of my life'. Was she wrong, though, to remain in their company, knowing of their repressed lusts? Lou had the misfortune to live in a world in which education past the age of fourteen was almost entirely a man's prerogative. One might well feel, therefore, that she was entitled to use almost any means at her disposal in order to gain the admission to the world of ideas her brilliant mind craved.

Was she really a 'cat egoist', a 'taker' who never 'gave'? In 1897, at the age of thirty-six, she met the poet Rainer Maria Rilke, who was fifteen years her junior. (It was she who persuaded him to change his name from René to Rainer.) With him she had her first, or at least first truly satisfying, sexual experience. Though Rilke abandoned her three years later to marry Clara Westhoff, she remained his friend and correspondent for the rest of his life, mothering the perpetual hypochondriac through to the end. Lou was not just a brilliant mind. She eventually disclosed herself as, in many ways, a 'wonderful and wonderfully caring woman'.⁷⁶

* * *

The last word on the Salomé affair should be given to Schopenhauer. Writing in 1844, he observes that, next to the will to live, sexual lust

> shows itself…as the strongest and most active of all motives, and incessantly lays claim to half the powers and thoughts of the younger portion of mankind. It is the ultimate goal of almost all human effort; it has an unfavourable influence on the most important affairs, interrupts every hour the most serious occupations, and sometimes perplexes for a while even the greatest minds. It knows how to slip its love-notes and ringlets even into… philosophical manuscripts,[77]

one of which, we shall shortly see, was *Zarathustra*. This, I think, is about all that needs to be said. Even (or perhaps especially) philosophers are liable to behave foolishly and badly when 'the wild beast in man pokes its head out of the cage' (p. 344 above). In his passion for Lou, Nietzsche behaved both foolishly and badly. Like the rest of us, he was human – all-too-human, as Ida Overbeck told him to his great displeasure.[78]

19

Zarathustra

Retreat to Rapallo

As often happens, the pain of the Salomé affair spread out to engulf the place where it happened. Nietzsche could bear to be in Germany no longer[1] and so, in Overbeck's word, 'fled' to Italy.[2] Settling finally, as we saw, in Rapallo at the end of November 1882, he would remain there until the end of February of the following year. He found an albergo directly on the palm-lined waterfront with cheap off-season rates.

Predictably, his recently vibrant health now declined to a point as low as it had ever reached. Suffering prolonged attacks of vomiting, headaches, eye pain and insomnia – he could only sleep with high doses of chloral hydrate[3] – he became, once again, extremely depressed. Above all, his mother's words about his being a 'disgrace to his father's grave' went round and round in his head, making 'the barrel of a pistol' a tempting thought.[4] Only his mission, his overriding commitment to his 'main task', prevented him from taking the beckoning exit from an 'extraordinarily painful life'.[5]

Local conditions did not help. Food in the albergo was bad, and, for the normally mild Gulf of Genoa, it was extremely cold, the wind lashing the palms on the promenade and the windows of the hotel with grey sea-spray. Nietzsche blamed not only Germany but also his unaccustomed return to sociability for the Salomé affair. For the sake of his mental and physical health, he decided, he had to return to his 'hermit's regimen' of strict isolation.[6] But the cold turned isolation into alienation. 'A cold room affects the mood', he observed, producing a feeling of 'world-alienation', of being an exile and 'wanderer'.[7] This is the *Winterreise* mood captured in the following year by his memorable poem 'Farewell':

The crows caw/And make their whirring flight to the town:/Soon it will snow/Fortunate is he who still has a homeland!/Now you stand stiffly,/Looking backwards! O how long already!/What are you, fool,/Fled into the world before winter?/The world – a gate/To a thousand wastelands, mute and cold!/Whoever has lost/What you have lost finds no resting-place./Now you stand there, pale/Condemned to winter-wandering/That, like smoke,/Always seeks colder skies./Fly bird, croak/Your song to the tune of a wasteland bird!/Hide, you fool,/Your bleeding heart in ice and scorn./The crows screech/and make their whirring flight to the town:/Soon it will snow/Woe to him who has no homeland![8]

In spite of this pall of misery, an unexpected break in the weather – ten clear, fresh days in January 1883 – produced, as it had in January of the previous year, a mood of gratitude: 'we sufferers', Nietzsche reflects, 'are very modest [in our expectations] and given to immoderate gratitude'.[9] It was in this mood that, in the ten clear days, he produced 'Part I' (originally conceived as the entirety of a work which ended up with four 'Parts') of his most famous book, *Thus Spoke Zarathustra*.[10]

Anti-anti-Semitism

Though finished in January, *Zarathustra* Part I was not actually published until the end of August – very slow by nineteenth-century standards. This was partly due to the fact that Teubners, the Leipzig firm Schmeitzner had commissioned to print the work, had a rush job of printing half a million hymn books, and had, moreover, it seems, serious reservations about *Zarathustra*'s anti-Christian content.[11] Nietzsche experienced this as something of a defeat, since he had, by now, in a mood of jocular seriousness, accepted 'Antichrist' as the most accurate description of its author and most succinct summary of its main point.[12] Partly, however, the delay was also due to Schmeitzner himself, to his frequent absences from the office on account of his anti-Semitic activities as head of the 'Anti-Jewish Alliance'. Nietzsche was furious. First the 'Christian obstacle' stood in the way and now the 'anti-Semitic obstacle'. 'Who', he demanded of Overbeck, 'will free me from a publisher who thinks anti-Semitic agitation more important than publicising my thoughts?'[13]

This marks the beginning of Nietzsche's strident anti-anti-Semitism. To understand what he opposed, however, it is important to recognise that, in the nineteenth century, the meaning of the word 'anti-Semitic' – as noted, it was first coined in 1879 – was rather different from its current meaning.

At the beginning of the nineteenth century, on account of being regarded, by both religion and ethnicity, as a non-European 'people', Jews suffered many civil disabilities: debarred from voting and often required to live in designated ghettoes, they were also excluded from many trades and professions. Napoleon and later the liberal impetus behind German unification gave rise to a movement towards Jewish emancipation, towards the removal of all special restrictions and to treating Jews as full citizens of the German Reich. It was as a counter-movement to this liberal impulse that, in the 1870s, the anti-Semitic movement came into being, with Schmeitzner, Elizabeth's future husband Bernhard Förster, and the Christian socialist preacher Adolf Stöcker playing leading roles.

It is important to note that it was this *political* movement (a movement belonging, generally, to the political Left rather than, as now, to the Right) with its quite specific agenda towards which Nietzsche became ever more violently opposed. His main objection to it, as he bluntly told Schmeitzner, was that it was a politics of envy which threatened 'anarchic' disruption of the social order: 'Seen from a distance', he wrote, '" anti-Semitism" looks like nothing other than the fight against the rich and the established middle classes for the sake of becoming rich'.[14]

Since what Nietzsche opposed was a *political* movement, his opposition was in principle compatible with the harbouring of *cultural* prejudices against Jews. (The classic exponent of this compatibility was the gay English mandarin and member of the Bloomsbury group Harold Nicholson, who said, in 1945, 'I loathe anti-Semitism but I do dislike Jews', and habitually described them as 'oily'.) And though, by nineteenth-century standards, Nietzsche was reasonably free from such prejudices, he was not entirely so – particularly in the immediate wake of, as he saw it, his betrayal by his erstwhile Jewish friend Paul Rée. So, for example, in his notebooks for 1883, one finds the claim that 'One can't mistake the deep absence of nobility in Christ, his Jewishness, the good business deal',[15] the bargain offer being 'going without earthly happiness in favour of a heavenly one a thousand times greater'.[16] This being said, however, it should be noted that, as we have seen (p. 237 above) and will see further, in most respects Nietzsche in his maturity was positively philo-Semitic.

Nietzsche as Wagner's 'Heir'

On February 13, 1883, Wagner suffered a heart attack in his hotel, the Palazzo Vendramin, on the Grand Canal in Venice. He had retreated there in order to recuperate after conducting *Parsifal* at the second Bayreuth Festival in August of the previous year. He died in Cosima's arms. The following day Nietzsche read a brief announcement of his death in a Genoa newspaper. He immediately suffered one of his attacks that put him in bed for several days. From his sickbed he wrote Malwida that it had been 'extraordinarily hard for six long years to be the opponent of someone whom one has honoured and loved as I loved Wagner', adding, however, that a 'deadly insult' had come between them[17] – a reference, as we have seen, to Wagner's claim that the root of his problems was 'masturbation … with indications of pederasty' (p. 239 above).

Nietzsche wrote an interesting letter of condolence to Cosima to which, of course, he received no reply: 'You have lived for a goal and made every sacrifice for it', he wrote. 'Over and above the man you discovered his ideal, and this is something which does not die, which belongs to you, belongs to you for ever'.[18] The distinction, here, between Wagner's higher self, the ideal he strives to realise – his 'inner truth and greatness', to borrow a phrase from Heidegger – and the actual, warts-and-all human being, is the same as that made in *Wagner in Bayreuth* (p. 218 above). In the 1883 notebooks he uses this distinction to justify his opposition to Wagner the man: 'Whoever has seen someone's ideal becomes his implacable judge and at the same time his bad conscience'.[19] In a letter to Köselitz the same dichotomy appears as a distinction between the young and the old Wagner: 'In the end', Nietzsche writes, 'it was the aged Wagner against whom I had to protect myself',[20] the one whose 'creep back to Christianity and the church I experienced as a personal insult';[21] an insult and a betrayal since the mission that had bound them together had been the rebirth of *Greek*, not Christian, culture. Concerning the 'authentic' Wagner, Nietzsche continues,

> I will still to a great extent become his heir. Last summer I realised that he had taken away from me all the people [Rohde, von Stein, von Seydlitz, etc.] in Germany on whom it makes any sense to have an influence, and he began to drag them into the confused and desolate enmity of his old age.[22]

What these reactions to Wagner's death make clear – a point which, because it is almost universally denied, I have been emphasising for some time – is that though Nietzsche rejects Wagner the all-too-human *man and artist*, the Wagnerian *ideal* is something which, in 1883, he *still* adheres to. They also make clear that, with Wagner's passing, he himself, as standard-bearer for that ideal, sees it as his task to lead the 'higher men' of his acquaintance back from Wagner the man to Wagner the ideal.

Throughout the notes of the 1880s, Nietzsche never wavers from his demand that we 'become better Wagnerians than Wagner',[23] nor his support for Wagner's conceiving of art as an 'important and magnificent phenomenon';[24] conceiving of it as not the light entertainment of Franco-Italian opera but a festival of deep significance. In the future, Nietzsche writes, there will be 'festivals in which the many individual [artistic] inventions will be united in the collective artwork of the festival'[25] for which 'temples' will need to be specially constructed.[26] Even in late 1886 Nietzsche still affirms his adherence to the Wagnerian ideal. Referring to the fact that 'all the world' still accounted him a member of the Bayreuth circle, he writes to Overbeck,

> It is wonderful how all these followers of Wagner remain true to me. You know, I think, that today I still believe in the ideal in which Wagner believed as firmly as ever – why should it be important that I stumbled over the many human-all-too-human obstacles that R[ichard] W[agner] placed in the path of his ideal?[27]

These and other remarks, it seems to me, place beyond doubt the fact that the Wagnerian ideal remained with Nietzsche to the very end of his thinking. From which we can conclude that something like the original Wagnerian programme – the redemption of Western culture through the rebirth of 'the Greek', aided in a central way by art and religion – remains, to the end, the central commitment of Nietzsche's thinking about art, religion, and society.

Second Summer in Sils Maria

At the end of January, Nietzsche received a letter from Malwida inviting him for a prolonged stay in Rome. As bait, she offered him a young woman, Cécile Horner, as amanuensis. But since she had also invited Elizabeth, her real purpose was to godmother a reconciliation between brother and sister. Nietzsche prevaricated, objecting to the humid climate in Rome and insisting that his health required proximity to the sea. But his real reason was that he did not feel able to face Elizabeth, who had, he wrote Köselitz, declared 'open war' on him until such a time as he should have abandoned his 'cold-hearted egoism' and become, once again, 'a good and true person'.[28]

For the time being, therefore, Nietzsche avoided Rome. Instead, on February 23, unable to stand conditions in Rapallo any longer, he moved back into his old lodgings in Genoa. He remained there until May 3, on which day he did, finally, depart for a six-week visit to Rome. What occasioned the visit was a letter from Elizabeth toward the end of April suggesting they had taken everything much too 'tragically' and that they should kiss and make up. Since the alienation from mother and sister caused him terrible anguish,[29] he wrote conciliatory letters to both Elizabeth and his mother and rushed off to Rome where, according to Elizabeth, the status quo ante was almost immediately reestablished.

Save for a week vainly searching for a summer residence for Fritz in southern Italy, brother and sister stayed in Rome until June 14, on which day they travelled together to Milan and then parted, she to return to Naumburg, he to Sils Maria, where he arrived on June 18, 1883, for a seven-week visit.

Though the weather in Sils was exceptionally cold, with snow down to the village, he was delighted to be back in the Durischs' house, where all, including little Adrienne Durisch, greeted him almost as a returning native. He enjoyed the convenience of being able to buy many of the things he needed in the grocery shop on the ground floor – English biscuits, corned beef, tea and soap – though he still needed, and now that normal relations had been restored, received, regular food parcels from home containing items such as ham, sausage and honey (which sometimes leaked in transit).[30]

Sils felt to Nietzsche like home. 'Here, and nowhere else', he wrote von Gersdorff, 'is my proper homeland and place of meditation'.[31] He yearned to build a two-room, wooden 'dog-kennel' of a house on the Chasté peninsula that projected into Lake Sils.[32] Ten minutes' walk from his lodgings, Chasté was, he believed, 'without equal either in Switzerland or in the whole of Europe'.[33] And he hoped that Sils would be the place where, as he wrote at the beginning of July, he would one day die and be buried.[34]

In this idyllic mood he completed, probably in the first ten days of July, the final draft of Part II of *Zarathustra*, describing it as 'justifying' and giving 'new meaning' to the whole year: the enforced idleness of Rome, his attacks of pain and sleeplessness, and, above all, his decision to return to his source of inspiration, the Engadine.[35]

Continuation of the Salomé Affair

The idyllic mood was not, however, to last. Moved by an intimation that Lou and Rée might be going to the Engadine to seek a reconciliation and implacable in her hatred, Elizabeth wrote a long letter to Rée's mother abusing Lou as a man-hunter disguised as an intellectual, and her son as a false friend and Mephistophelean figure who had fed Lou the slanders she had perpetrated on Nietzsche.[36] And an advanced copy of the letter she sent to her brother.

Though the letter consists of nothing but uncorroborated abuse, it had a deep effect on Nietzsche – solely on account, it would seem, of Elizabeth's rising to a level of literary excellence never before achieved. (Evidently he forgot his own observation that 'the poets lie too much'.) The letter, he wrote Ida Overbeck, '(incidentally a masterpiece of woman's literature!) ... gave me light [on the situation] and what light! Dr. Rée steps into the fore-ground'.[37]

Given his new 'insight', Nietzsche now wrote to Rée, calling him a false friend and complete cad, asserting specifically that it was he, Rée, who was the origin of the assertion that 'under the mask of idealism' Nietzsche had, 'with respect to Fräulein Salomé pursued the filthiest of intentions'. (But (see p. 341 above) Nietzsche *had* suggested a 'two-year marriage'!) The letter concludes, 'I would have a strong desire to give you a lesson in practical morality with a couple of bullets', but regrets (using an anti-Semitic slur) that such an engagement could only be for 'clean hands not oily fingers'.[38] Not content with that, he wrote an equally abusive letter to Georg Rée telling him what a creep his brother was and describing Lou as 'a dried up, dirty monkey with bad breath and false breasts',[39] a letter he imagined might lead to a duel (but who would fight a duel with someone three-quarters blind?). In fact it led to nothing more than a threat of legal action if the abusive letters did not cease. At the same time he wrote a pompous letter to Lou's mother telling her that 'my sister and I have struck your daughter from our social calendar'.[40] Initially, though drafted, these letters were not sent. But then, thrown into a panic by the mistaken belief that the Rée family were coming to Sils (there was a confusion about names of future arrivals in a hotel register), he fired them off.[41]

Even as he wrote these abusive letters, Nietzsche had glimmers of insight that he was being manipulated by Elizabeth into feeling and acting against his own best interests – cunningly, she claimed to have long shielded him from most of the real horror of Rée's and Lou's behaviour.[42] 'My sister wants her revenge on that Russian', he wrote Ida Overbeck – this was the attempt to have Lou sent back to Russia as an 'immoral person' – 'that's all right, but up to now the victim of everything she has instigated in this matter has been myself'.[43] Mainly, however, he remained a hundred percent on Elizabeth's side. Up until the end of July 1883, he still asserted Elizabeth's 'perfect right' to seek her revenge on Lou,[44] and that he and his sister were 'better friends than ever'.[45] Of course the subtext to all this was that Elizabeth was forcing him to choose between her and Lou: the price of her ending the 'war' was his agreement to fully endorse her 'take' on the whole affair, the necessary proof that he had returned to being a 'good and true person'.

By mid-August, however, Nietzsche's doubts about Elizabeth's machinations, and about the way he himself has behaved under their influence, begin to get the upper hand. No doubt he has been lied to and misused and has had his honour besmirched, he writes his ever-sympathetic, but gently objective, confidante Ida Overbeck, so that when his friends demand 'satisfaction' on his behalf he cannot complain:

> I call it 'my sister's perfect right'. The downside is that all these hostile measures are directed at persons I once loved and perhaps still love. I, at least, am prepared to drop the whole business of insult and disgraceful behaviour towards me at any moment.[46]

Lou, he adds, whatever might be said about her moral character, is a spirit 'of the first rank', and even Rée must have something good about him to have earned Malwida's good opinion during the Sorrento year.[47] The next letter to Ida goes on to say that the only person who Elizabeth really damages is himself, and that he misses Lou terribly since he has never talked philosophy so productively with anyone else, and that, anyway, the whole affair is so complicated (as the reader of this book is by now likely to agree) that it's impossible really to assign blame to anyone.[48] By the end of August he makes the crucial point to Köselitz. He has, he now realises, been led, by Elizabeth, into a 'nervous fever'. His mind had been confused. 'I have been wound up for a whole year into feelings which I had disavowed and thought I had overcome at least in their cruder forms: feelings of revenge and *"ressentiment"*'.[49] Since, on a personal level, his deepest philosophy is the drive towards *amor fati* and willing the eternal return – the affirmation of everything, *including* the Salomé affair – what he belatedly sees is that Elizabeth has been manipulating him in the direction diametrically opposite to that taken by his philosophy: by, that is to say, the ideal which is his 'true self' and which it is his task to become.

On August 22 Nietzsche made the short coach trip down the Engadine Valley to Schuls (or in Romansch, Tarasp) to spend three days with the ever-loyal and forbearing Overbeck.

On the return journey, as he wrote him on August 26, he experienced 'a true hatred for my sister':

> With her silence at the wrong times and speaking at the wrong times she has killed the success of my best self-overcomings: so that, in the end, I became the victim of a ruthless lust for revenge, while precisely my innermost mode of thinking has rejected all revenge and punishment.'[50]

Three days later he wrote Elizabeth asking her not to mention the Salomé affair again.[51] And at the beginning of 1884, describing Lou as the 'most gifted and reflective' of all his acquaintances, he begged Elizabeth to make peace with her.[52] (In vain – Elizabeth pursued her vendetta against Lou long after his death.) At the same time, he wrote Overbeck that for the sixth time in two years he has received a letter from his sister that

> interrupted my highest and most blessed feelings (feelings which have seldom appeared on earth) with the base smell of the all-too-human. I have been furious each time over the dirty, abusive way my sister has spoken about Fr. Salome ... I have never found a more gifted reflective mind.[53]

For a man whose social life was, by now, conducted almost exclusively by letter, *The Gay Science*'s advice to take a bath after reading one's mail was good advice indeed.

The Shadow of Bernhard Förster

The approach of winter forced Nietzsche to bring his stay in Sils to an end. In spite, therefore, of his less than cordial feelings towards his sister he travelled, on September 5, to Naumburg, where he would remain for five tense weeks. The tension was partly caused by mother and sister demanding, in unison, that he should return to university work, and their complaints that he no longer mixed with respectable people. Mainly, however, the tension was caused by the looming shadow of Dr. Bernhard Förster, and here, for once, mother and son found themselves on the same side.

Bernard Förster, a Berlin high-school teacher, had been, since 1880, a leader of the anti-Semitic movement and, following the war against France, an ardently jingoistic Prussian patriot. His heroes were Ernst Hasse and Adolf Stöcker. Hasse was a former Prussian army surgeon who helped found the Pan-German League, aimed at promoting the creation of German colonies in Africa, South America and Eastern Europe. Stöcker was a former Prussian army chaplain who based his rabid anti-Semitism on a version of Christian socialism which saw the Jews as inextricably linked to the exploitation of workers by modern capitalism. Förster was also an admirer of Wagner (and of Nietzsche's early works). In 1880 he wrote to Wagner asking him to sign a petition demanding that the German chancellor take stern measures to halt the takeover of the Berlin press and 'corruption' of established religious values by Jewish plutocrats. To his credit, Wagner refused.

Förster's mother was a Naumburg acquaintance of Franziska and it was through her that Elizabeth and Förster became acquainted, sometime in 1882. Deprived, now, of the ability to make her brother the emotional centre of her life, Elizabeth was soon to find a new (and opposite) centre in Förster. She and Förster, she informed (the surely horrified) Köselitz on one occasion, 'gorged ourselves...on compassion, heroic self-denial, Christianity, vegetarianism, Aryanism, southern colonies etc. All this is very sympathetic to me and with these notions I find myself completely at home'.

In the autumn of 1882 Förster was involved in a bloody, anti-Semitic brawl in the streets of Berlin and lost his teaching post as a result. Embarrassed, his colleagues in the German People's Party, which he had helped found, encouraged him to abandon the 'polluted' atmosphere of Berlin for a time, and further the noble cause of German racial purity by founding a 'model' Aryan community in South America. In February 1883, therefore, he set sail for South America, intending to find a site for a colony near the river Plate.

Förster was, of course, everything Nietzsche loathed. Franziska, however, realising from the frequent exchange of letters that Elizabeth had set her sights on him, regarded him with equal disapproval. Partly she feared the disappearance to South America of her only daughter, and partly, though not free herself from cultural anti-Semitism, she considered that a street-brawling, politically anti-Semitic agitator fell beneath the minimum standard of respectability.

The more, however, that Nietzsche and his mother attacked, the more the mule-willed Elizabeth dug in her heels, insisting that poor Förster was a martyr to truth and goodness. Underlying her stubbornness, of course, was the stark fact that, as she approached her fortieth year, Förster almost certainly represented her last chance at the marriage that would release her from the claustrophobic life of a small-town spinster.

With the family at war, it must have been with relief that Nietzsche left Naumburg on October 2 to travel, again via the Overbecks, to Genoa for his final stay in this much-loved city. He returned to his old lodgings with Signora Stagnetti in the Salita della Battestine, though this time inhabiting a new room on the fifth floor. Once more, however, his health declined. He had, moreover, exhausted all the walks near to his lodgings and began to find the city too noisy. Accordingly he decided to move to Nice, a three-hour train ride westwards along the Riviera coast, through Ventimiglia, Menton and Monte Carlo. He arrived on December 2 and would stay there for the next four-and-a-half months.

First Winter in Nice

Originally Italian, Nice – or 'Nizza' in both Italian and German – had been peacefully ceded to the French Empire of Napoleon III in 1860. A fast-expanding resort for well-to-do Northern European sun-seekers, with its palm-lined Promenade des Anglais and red and orange facades, it remained reassuringly Italian.

Initially Nietzsche refused to recognise that Nice was in France. '*Nizza* as a *French* city', he wrote, 'I find disagreeable and a kind of stain on this southern splendour'. It was, he believed, 'still an Italian city – in the old town, where I have rented a place, people speak, when it is necessary to speak, Italian; and then it is like a Genoese suburb'. What attracted him to Nice was research in guidebooks which revealed, he decided, that Nice had 220 days of clear skies per year – twice as many as Genoa. With his health in mind, this was a decisive consideration. And so, with much regret, 'I said farewell to the beloved city of Columbus – it was never anything other than this to me'.[54]

To start with, Nietzsche found lodgings with a German landlady on the second floor of the six-storey Rue Ségurane 38, ten minutes' walk from the seafront. For company at mealtimes he had a Prussian general and his daughter, the wife of an 'Indian prince' (implausibly named 'Lady Mehmet Ali') likewise accompanied by a daughter, and a 'magnificently clad Persian'.[55]

Disappointingly, however, the move did not improve Nietzsche's health: 'as bad as at the worst times...vomiting, insomnia, depressing thoughts about the old things, general head pain, sharp pain in the eyes'.[56] His room, moreover, was once more without heating and dreadfully cold. So he decided to move again, to a place where he could return to his regimen of solitude, particularly at mealtimes. Just before Christmas, therefore, he moved to the Villa Mazzolini in the Chemin de St. Phillipe (today Rue de Châteauneuf 39). Here, his landlady, again German, cooked special meals for him and even installed a stove in his room which produced, 'if not warmth, at least a thick smoke'. His Spanish fellow lodger, with whom he spoke Italian, treated him 'come un fratello'.[57]

Two Disciples

On Christmas Eve Nietzsche reported to Overbeck that he had been receiving letters from an admirer, a Paul Lanzky, 'the first person who had addressed me in letters as "honoured Master" (which affected me with various feelings and memories)'[58] – memories, of course, of his own manner of addressing Wagner. Lanzky was the wealthy Jewish part-owner of a hotel in Vallombrosa, in Tuscany. After reading *Human, All-Too-Human*, he had decided that Nietzsche was the most important living German writer and proposed the use of a house on the grounds of his hotel as a 'nest' for Nietzsche's philosophy (presumably something along the lines of a 'monastery for free spirits'). Nietzsche thought he would probably accept the offer for part of 1884.[59]

Another admirer who made contact was Dr. Joseph Paneth, also Jewish, though non-religious and anti-Zionist. They had a long talk on December 26 about Spinoza, Schopenhauer, Wagner, and anti-Semitism. Paneth taught physiology at Vienna University and would later (with Lou Salomé) belong to Freud's inner circle. Freud greatly respected him and it was at his instigation that, later on, Freud began reading Nietzsche for himself.

Paneth described to his fiancée Nietzsche's manner and appearance in this, his thirty-ninth year:

> He was extraordinarily friendly and there is no trace of false pathos or the air of a prophet about him, which I had feared after the last work [*Zarathustra* Part I]. Much more, he comes over as quite harmless and natural...He told me, but without the least affectation or self-consciousness, that he always felt himself the bearer of a mission and now, as far as his eyes allowed, wanted to carry it out...he had an uncommonly clear and high brow, plain brown hair, veiled, deeply set eyes corresponding to his half-blindness, bushy eyebrows, a rather full face and a mighty moustache, otherwise he was clean-shaven.[60]

* * *

The meeting with Paneth occurred just as Nietzsche was putting the finishing touches to the third and, as he thought at the time, final part of *Zarathustra*. On January 25, 1884, he informed Overbeck of the work's completion, adding that 'the whole work has come into being in the course of precisely one year: strictly, in the course of 3 × 2 weeks: I have *never* sailed such a journey over such a sea'.[61] The '3 × 2 weeks' exhibits a persistent tendency on Nietzsche's part to exaggerate the inspirational nature of *Zarathustra*, to represent it as a gift of the gods. In reality, a glance at the notebooks reveals literally hundreds of pages of preparatory work for sections of *Zarathustra* and plans for its overall structure. As we saw Nietzsche himself observing in *Human, All-Too-Human*, artists promote themselves by disguising perspiration as inspiration.[62]

A New Bible

Nietzsche described *Zarathustra* as a great 'bloodletting' in which the stirrings of the blood by the torments of the Salomé affair found their 'retrospective justification'.[63] But he found it hard to decide what kind of book he had written. Sometimes the notebooks refer to its parts as 'acts', which suggest a kind of theatre piece, while at other times he calls it a 'symphony'. Sometimes he insists it is 'nothing literary' but rather a 'great synthesis' of his philosophy to date.[64] But at other times he calls it 'poetry', poetry which goes beyond everything he has written as a 'philosopher' and expressing for the first time his 'most essential thoughts'.[65]

What he is clear about, and correct to insist upon, is that, above all, the book is conceived as a *religious* work. In the first place, the eponymous hero whose 'speeches' make up the great bulk of the work is a religious figure – Zarathustra is Zoroaster, the founder of Zoroastrianism. Second, the style of his speech is overwhelmingly that of the Bible – he seems to have thought of its author as Luther leavened with elements of Goethe.[66] The work has the 'air of [being written by] a prophet' that Paneth objected to (p. 365 above), as do many others, even Nietzsche-fans, who find *Zarathustra* their least favourite work. Third, Nietzsche actually calls it a religious work, referring to it variously as 'a fifth Gospel'[67] and a 'new "holy book"' which 'challenges all existing religions',[68] especially, of course, Christianity. *Zarathustra* is, in a word, intended to be the central, sacred text of the new religion that is to replace the now-'dead' Christianity. (Had his 'colony for free spirits' project come to fruition, one can imagine a copy of *Zarathustra*, like the Gideon Bible, in every bedroom.) Retrospectively, in *Ecce Homo*, he says that the book was written by 'God himself':[69] as a book superior to the Bible and the *Vedas* – the authors of these works are not even worthy of 'unlatching the shoes' of *Zarathustra*'s author[70] – Nietzsche believed he had written one of the two or three most important books in human history.

This of course convinced him that he had far surpassed Wagner's failed attempt to create a new religion. With poetic licence, he claims that Part I of *Zarathustra* was finished 'in the very hour' in which Wagner died',[71] and that with it he has begun his own *Ring* cycle.[72] That the notebooks refer to *Zarathustra* as both a musical work and a theatre piece suggests that one can think of it as the libretto for a sacred music-drama.

Zarathustra is intended, then, to be the Bible of a new religion – a religion, Nietzsche would of course add, 'of life' rather than of 'after-life'. As the New Testament narrates Jesus's exemplary life and spiritual journey, so Nietzsche's text narrates Zarathustra's. Among other things, that is, it is a *Bildungsroman*, a story of its hero's spiritual development, his progress towards that ultimate 'greatness'[73] of soul that consists in embracing the eternal return, a story that is supposed to inspire us to follow in his footsteps. In Nietzsche's earlier language, Zarathustra is the great 'educator'.

His choice of his hero's name is, however, something of a surprise. Zarathustra/Zoroaster did, after all, found a religion based on a stark and absolute contrast between light and dark, good and evil, spirit and body – the *epitome* of all that Nietzsche is dedicated to abolishing. In *Ecce Homo* he explains that, as the oldest of all religious thinkers, he has had the time to correct himself. Jesus, he adds elsewhere, was great enough to have done the same, but he died too soon.[74]

* * *

Two further preliminary questions before we proceed to the text itself. First, what is the relationship between its central character and its author? Persistently, in his letters, Nietzsche refers to 'my son Zarathustra'.[75] So Nietzsche is Zarathustra's 'father'. In part, of course, this is just a metaphor for authorship: an author is 'parent' to the characters he creates. But there is, I think, more to the metaphor than this. The son, Nietzsche writes (one can imagine him thinking, here, of Leopold and Wolfgang Mozart), is 'often only the unveiled soul of the father'.[76] Often, 'the father understands himself better once he has a son'.[77] In a sense, therefore, Zarathustra *is* Nietzsche. Not of course the warts-and-all Nietzsche but rather the ideal Nietzsche; Nietzsche's 'true' self, the self that, in the words of *Schopenhauer as Educator*, 'draws [his] soul aloft' (p. 195 above). Zarathustra is Nietzsche's 'avatar', the person he would like to become in his Second Life.

There is a quite specific aspect to this 'identity' between author and hero. As Nietzsche retrospectively observes in *Ecce Homo*, the greatest challenge which confronts Zarathustra on his path of spiritual development is to overcome his '*great disgust*' at the petty ugliness of current humanity.[78] But as we have seen, *Nietzsche's* greatest task, during the period in which *Zarathustra* was written, was to overcome – by 'turning into gold' – his disgust and feelings of '*ressentiment*' over the Lou affair. In one important aspect, therefore, the writing of *Zarathustra* was Nietzsche's expiation, in effigy, as it were, of his *own* disgust.

A final, preliminary question: for whom is *Zarathustra* written? The subtitle addresses this question in a paradoxical way. *Zarathustra* is 'A Book for Everyone and No One'. 'Everyone' is easy to decipher: rather than being written in the dense, technical style of philosophy, the book is written, Nietzsche observes, in a style which (like the Bible) is 'accessible to everyone'.[79] And it has a biographical storyline: biographies (including this biography, one hopes) sweeten the hard-to-swallow pill of philosophy.

But why 'Nobody'? Because, I think, like all the works since *Human, All-Too-Human*, it is written for 'free spirits' (of the 'first rank'), the kinds of people who at various points in the work are described as Zarathustra's 'companions', 'friends', and 'brothers'. The point behind 'Nobody' is Nietzsche's fear that – particularly because the few promising spirits have been 'seduced' away from him by Wagner, and because Lou has left the scene – he has *no* proper readers among his contemporaries. At best in 'my children's land',[80] Nietzsche fears, will he find proper readers.

Thus Spoke Zarathustra: The Prologue

In the main, *Zarathustra* is little more than a collection of its hero's 'speeches'. Its Prologue, however, contains a great deal of narrative, more than any other part of the book. Here we learn that when he was thirty years old Zarathustra left his home by the lake and went to live in a cave in the mountains for ten solitary years. (There is an obvious parallel between Zarathustra's mountain retreat and Nietzsche's Sils Maria. Often, indeed, he refers to his room in the Durisch house as his 'cave'.) His only companions are his snake and his eagle, but since the former is said to be his own 'wisdom' and the latter his 'pride',[81] the animals are no more than personifications of aspects of his own personality; inner rather than outer voices.

After ten years a change comes over Zarathustra. In a conversation with the sun – Strauss's famous tone poem, *Thus Spoke Zarathustra* (otherwise, the music from the movie *2001*), begins with the sun's rising – he explains that as the sun *needs* to shine on him so he *needs* to shine on humanity with the accumulated wisdom of his ten years of solitary meditation. (I shall return to this conversation later on.) And so he descends to the lowlands, back to human society. Passing on the way down an old hermit who has not heard the news that 'God is dead', he descends to the city called 'Motley Cow'.

The Motley Cow ('motley' is the word Plato's *Republic* uses to describe and condemn the democratic state)[82] is just Western modernity.[83] As we have seen (p. 176 above), a society possesses, for Nietzsche, a 'culture' to the extent that it possesses a unified (though not homogeneous) form of life. Already, therefore, in the first *Untimely Meditation*, Nietzsche is condemning modernity as a 'fairground motley': in place of a genuine culture, what we moderns have is a 'chaotic jumble', a 'grotesque juxtaposition and confusion of different styles' (p. 177 above).

So 'Motley' signifies the semi-'barbarism' we have repeatedly seen ascribed to modernity by Nietzsche's cultural criticism. 'Cow', obviously, signifies that the town is inhabited by 'the herd'. That modernity is herd-like might seem inconsistent with motleyness, but I think that what Nietzsche has in mind is the capacity of politicians and the press to whip up mass hysteria – for example, the anti-French hysteria that preceded the Franco-Prussian war. Plainly we only have to think for a moment about our own recent history to see that Nietzsche is right in seeing motleyness and mass hysteria as capable of coexisting: 'multicultural' though we are, we regularly engage in, and are manipulated into, mass hysterics – the death of Princess Di, the threat of paedophilia, the 'war on terror'.

In the town's marketplace a rope is strung between two towers (as, according to Elizabeth, it was in the Naumburg marketplace during Nietzsche's childhood).[84] A crowd has assembled, waiting for a tightrope walker (tightrope 'dancer' in German) to begin his act. With the abruptness of a deranged, born-again Christian (as well, perhaps, as the relief of speaking after ten years of silence), Zarathustra spews out the sum of his decade of wisdom-gathering. Man, he shouts, is a 'rope stretched between beast and superman'. The superman is the 'meaning of the earth'. Beloved are those who take the dangerous path of dedicating themselves to making the world a 'house for the superman'. Man needs an 'ideal'. But since the supernatural is a delusion, we must reject all other-worldly ideals. Our 'greatest hour' is when we see that we fall as far short of the superman as the ape does of us.

Understandably, the crowd can make nothing of this. They take Zarathustra to be a sort of clownish ringmaster whose job it is to introduce the tightrope walker (the 'man' who will soon be 'super', above, their heads) and demand that the act start without further ado. Frustrated, Zarathustra has another go at getting his message across. He tries to convey a sense of impending catastrophe by warning of the immanent arrival of 'the last man': a man, the size of a flea, who hops over a tiny earth saying 'we have invented happiness', and merely 'blinks' short-sightedly at anyone who suggests that there might be more to life than the pleasure of cheap narcotics. There remains in us, Zarathustra yells, still enough 'chaos', enough free-spiritedness, to 'give birth to a star'. But only just. Soon it will be gone and that will be the end of 'man'.

It is unclear in just what sense the 'last man' is 'last'. Possibly and most radically, what Nietzsche envisages, given his theory of cultural health (pp. 327–9 above), is that the failure to produce creative free spirits will lead to the literal end of humanity – in the face, for example, of global warming. A slightly less radical possibility is that he envisages the 'death of man' in the sense of the disappearance of all those characteristics that distinguish human beings from the non-human animals. Less radical still is the possibility that what he is talking about is the death of *European* man, the possibility that European culture will be absorbed by some stronger culture. I shall return (more decisively) to this issue in discussing *Beyond Good and Evil*.

The 'last man' speech meets with no more success than the 'superman' speech : the crowd calls out – one of Nietzsche's frequent, satirical allusions to the New Testament[85] – 'Give us the last man. You can keep the superman'.

Meanwhile, the tightrope walker has begun his act. Suddenly a jester-like figure appears on the rope behind him, taunts him, and finally jumps over him. This causes the walker to lose his balance, drop his pole, and fall to his death. Zarathustra comforts the dying man with the observation that he has had the dignity of 'making danger his calling'. Free-spiritedness, as Nietzsche observes elsewhere,[86] often ends in 'martyrdom' – which suggests that the jester may represent conventional opinion, surer of foot than the free spirit because it follows a path (a 'neural pathway') it has trodden a thousand times before.

The beginning of Zarathustra's ministry to the world thus begins in total disaster. But it is, nonetheless, a learning experience for him. 'A light has dawned for me,' he reflects. 'Let Zarathustra talk not to the people but to companions', companions who, of course, he first needs to 'lure away from the herd'. This, to repeat, mirrors Nietzsche's own progression from addressing the world at large to writing books 'for free spirits' alone.

Zarathustra Part I: The Speeches of Zarathustra

Zarathustra's Prologue is followed by 'The Speeches of Zarathustra', each with its own title, a heading that embraces all the four 'Parts' that constitute the final version of the work. Interspersed between some of the speeches are snatches of narrative which locate Zarathustra in physical and spiritual space. Sometimes there are 'songs' at the end of which 'Thus sang Zarathustra' replaces the usual 'Thus spoke Zarathustra'. In what follows I summarise (in italics) and then comment upon (in normal font) what seem to me – an inevitably subjective choice – the most important speeches, beginning with those in Part I of the work.

On the Three Metamorphoses.[87] *First, the spirit becomes a desert-dwelling camel who 'bears much'; for example, 'feeding on the acorns and grass of knowledge and for the sake of truth, suffering hunger in the soul' as well as 'parting from our cause when it celebrates its victory'. Next the camel changes into a lion who slays the dragon called 'thou shalt', wishing to become 'master in his own desert'. Finally the lion becomes a child. This final transformation is necessary if one is to become a world-redeeming spirit, since though the lion pronounces the 'sacred No' it does not create anything to replace what it denies. For that, for the creation of 'new values', the child is needed. The child is 'innocence and forgetting, a new beginning, a play, a self-propelling wheel, a first movement, a holy Yes-saying'.*

The 'cause' from which Nietzsche parted in the moment of victory was, of course, Bayreuth, so that the 'camel' is the positivist Nietzsche – Nietzsche, however, as exemplifying the predicament of all positivists, of those who have abandoned the old, meaning-giving faith for the sake of truth but, since they have yet to find a new faith, inhabit the camel's spiritual 'desert'.

The camel has to change into the lion because, although he has renounced the old God, he is still a 'reverent spirit'. Though he has renounced Christian *metaphysics*, he still clings to Christian *ethics*. It is, indeed, the Christian virtue of truthfulness that forces him to admit to himself that the old God is 'dead'. The lion, seeing that Christian ethics makes no sense without the Christian God to back it up, drops, as it were, the other shoe.

Rather clearly the 'lion', as merely destructive of existing values, corresponds to *The Gay Science*'s free spirit 'of the second rank'. Since the 'child', on the other hand, is creative, creates a new form of life, it is a free spirit 'of the first rank'. Two things, however, are worrying about the 'child'.

The first is that the idea of a 'self-propelled first movement' looks very like an affirmation of precisely the doctrine of 'free will' Nietzsche has up to now been at pains to dismiss as a damaging myth. Since universal causal determinism is reaffirmed in *Zarathustra*,[88] we need to understand the child's 'self-propelling' nature, not in the sense of its being free of causal determination but in the sense of having *become a genuine self* rather than a 'herd animal' propelled by the 'herd instinct'. And the child's 'first movement' should be understood not as its being an uncaused cause but rather as constituting, *relative to existing social norms*, a new form of life.

The second and more troublesome worry, however, about the 'child' is that its 'innocence and forgetting' seems to amount to what is sometimes called 'decisionism': the idea that fundamental values are things which we just *decide upon* for ourselves, things we can and must *create* – out of nothing. The problem with decisionism, as Jean-Paul Sartre has shown, is that *if* one's fundamental values are based on nothing but one's own free choice, then they are 'absurd', devoid of genuine authority. If, for example, my communism is grounded in nothing but my own ungrounded decision, then, if it comes to fighting against your fascism, there is *nothing* I can do to show that my fundamental choice is in any way preferable to yours. And that means that I can have no genuine belief in what I am fighting for.

As we have already seen, a great deal of Nietzsche's social thinking is far from being decisionistic since it revolves around the idea of recovering 'the Greek'. Far from 'forgetting', this involves a reappropriation, a creative *remembering*. But perhaps what Nietzsche attributes to the child is only a *relative* forgetting – a forgetting of the past two millennia – which clears the way for a deep, deep remembering: one needs to go a long way back, he observes elsewhere, if one 'wants to make a great leap' forwards.[89]

On the Behind-the-Worldly.[90] *'At one time Zarathustra too cast his delusion beyond the human, like all believers into a world behind [the veil of appearances]. The work of a suffering and tortured god the world seemed to me then. A dream it seemed to me, and the fable of a god, coloured smoke before the eyes of one divinely discontented.' But this other world is a 'heavenly nothing'.*

This accurate summary of the *Birth of Tragedy* makes clear how closely Zarathustra's spiritual development is modelled on Nietzsche's own. One major function of *Zarathustra* is, under the guise of fiction, to present Nietzsche's path of spiritual development as exemplary, to present his idealised self as an 'educator'.

To be noted in this passage is the rejection of metaphysical idealism, showing, should there be any doubt, that Nietzsche still endorses the naturalistic presuppositions of the positivist period. 'Materialist' presuppositions indeed: 'soul', pronounces Zarathustra, 'is merely a word for something about the body'.[91]

Of Joys and Passions.[92] *'May your virtue be too exalted for the familiarity of names'*. As an at least relatively 'new beginning', 'the child's' new mode of life will not be covered by existing language, not, at least, by its words of praise.

'My brother you are fortunate if you have only one virtue. It is a distinction to have many but a hard lot indeed'. If you only have one central drive you are fortunate. If you have several you have the potential for inner richness, but a great deal of self-discipline is required to order the soul into a hierarchical unity. If you cannot achieve this 'rank-ordering' of the drives you will become a 'battle and battlefield of virtues'. (This explains the misery of the *'Pale Criminal'* discussed by Nietzsche in the speech immediately following *Joys and Passions*. Since his soul is a 'ball of wild snakes' he has no inner peace and so inflicts his misery on the world around him.)[93]

'At one time you had wild dogs in your cellar; but in the end they transformed themselves into birds and lovely singers'. This is the sublimation theme, again, the transformation of bad Eris into good, violence into *agon*, war into 'competition'. Unlike Christianity, which is ashamed of, and wants to *extirpate*, the warrior instinct, Nietzsche celebrates it as something which, when properly 'spiritualised', is the essential agent of personal and communal growth: 'War (but without gunpowder!) between different thoughts and their armies'[94] needs to be cherished and cultivated.

On the Thousand Goals and One.[95] This major speech makes a sequence of points about 'good and evil', the 'greatest power on earth'.

'No people could live without evaluating'. A 'people' or 'culture' is simply *defined* as such through the possession of a communal ethos. There can be no genuine community without a shared understanding of the right way to live.

'If a people wants to preserve itself it may not evaluate as does its neighbour'. If Europe wants to preserve itself as distinctively European it must avoid, for example, American values, becoming 'Americanised'. If it does not, it will simply become, culturally speaking, a part of America.

Neighbouring peoples regard each other as incomprehensible and wicked. All cultures are morally chauvinistic: to believe that it alone possesses moral truth promotes, after all, the survival of one's group.

Whatever is both necessary and difficult is what is valued. Morality is a 'tablet of a people's overcomings'. Obviously, if a character trait or mode of behaviour is *useless* to a community it will not be valued by communal ethos. And neither will it be valued if everyone does it anyway: there would be no point in a moral commandment to breathe. Morality is essentially a *discipline*, a matter of 'overcoming'. The next paragraph tells us the goal of that overcoming.

Morality is 'the voice of [a people's] will to power'. This is the first published appearance of 'will to power', a conception central to Nietzsche's later philosophy. The previous paragraph suggests that, in the first instance, the power in question is power over *oneself*, *self*-discipline. Almost immediately, however, the notion is extended to power over others: 'whatever allows a people to rule and conquer and shine to the horror and envy of its neighbour counts as the lofty, the measure, the meaning of all things'. Notice that this is simply *historical, sociological comment* on the 'many lands and peoples Zarathustra has seen'. Nietzsche is not *endorsing* the 'horrors' nations inflict on each other – indeed, as we have just seen, he wants the 'horrifying' manifestations of aggression to be sublimated into 'war ... *without* gunpowder'.

'Once you have recognised a people's need and land and sky and neighbour you can surely guess the law of its overcomings'. A community's morality expresses its 'will to power'; its drive to grow and expand, to achieve hegemony over its neighbours, either through the 'hard' power of military intimidation and conquest or by the 'soft' power of cultural 'shining' (iphones and rock music). But to expand *one needs first of all to survive*. And that means that a successful community's 'table of values' will be appropriate to the environment, both human and natural, in which it finds itself. People in cold climates, for example, needing to store food for winter, will attach a high value to habits of frugality and accumulation (which is probably why capitalism started in northern Europe rather than the South Pacific).

'Creators were first peoples and only later individuals ... pleasure in the herd is older than pleasure in the I, and as long as the good conscience is called herd only the bad conscience says I ... the cunning I is not the origin of the herd'. Partly this is advice to the free spirit not to be surprised if he finds himself feeling bad about his rejection of convention but not to take much notice of this affective remnant of his evolutionary past. But it is also an attack on Thomas Hobbes's account of the origin of society and the state as consisting in a group of full-fledged rational individuals making the game-theoretic calculation that since the 'state of nature' is 'nasty, brutish and short' it is in all their interests to set up a state to which everyone sacrifices a degree of autonomy. As history this cannot be correct, Nietzsche argues (surely correctly), since communal life came into being millennia before people came to conceive of themselves as individuals possessing interests distinct from the interests of the tribe.

'A thousand goals have there been so far, for there have been a thousand peoples. Only the shackles for the thousand necks are still lacking, there is lacking the one goal. Humanity still has no goal'. In the notebooks Nietzsche writes, 'in the *superman* ... individuals have become one'.[96] This is his cosmopolitanism, the demand for a European community, a new, supra-national, European culture that will overcome the warring nationalisms of the past and eventually spread throughout the entire globe (pp. 266–7 above). Only some form of world government offers the possibility of world peace. Cosmopolitanism is the basis of Nietzsche's admiration for Napoleon, the reason he calls him, like himself, a 'good European'.

A puzzle, however, is this: why does not the sublimation of aggression offer an alternative to world government? If aggression can be sublimated into 'competition' on the individual level, why cannot it happen on the collective level? Why cannot competitive 'shining' between nations offer an alternative to war? The answer is, perhaps, this: genuine *argon*, whether one thinks of the Olympic games or of competitions to write the best tragedy, requires *rules* of competition, rules that require enforcement. As games require umpires and disciplinary bodies, so inter-national 'shining' requires some form of global authority. (Something like the World Trade Organization might be part of it.)

On Old and Young Little Women.[97] One of Nietzsche's weaknesses as a philosopher is, on certain topics, his inability to tell the difference between the profound and the pathological. Though the formal point of this passage is to advise the potential free spirit on how to comport himself with women, its main value is as a manifestation of how deeply the Lou affair had damaged Nietzsche's attitude to women.

Zarathustra addresses a 'little old woman'. Everything about women, he tells her, has pregnancy as a solution. A man should be brought up for war and the woman for the recreation of the warrior. The woman's task is to bring out the child in the man. The happiness of a man is 'I will', of a woman 'he wills'. Her world becomes 'perfect' when she obeys out of total love. The old woman replies with 'a little truth': 'You are going to women? Then don't forget the whip'.

This, of course, is the infamous 'whip' remark. (It seems to me quite irrelevant that it is put in the mouth of the old woman – this is merely a rhetorical device designed to intensify the force of Zarathustra–Nietzsche's views on women: 'You see, even old, that is, wise, women agree with me', he implies.) As noted, there are two ways of interpreting the remark: one might take it that Nietzsche is encouraging sadistic behaviour towards women or alternatively – particularly if one connects the remark with the 'whip' photograph taken in Basel (see Plate 25 and p. 343 above) – take it as a warning that, given half a chance, women will seek to gain the whip hand in any relationship, thereby upsetting the natural order of things. It seems to me, however, that it makes little difference which of these interpretations one adopts. In either case, the message of the passage is a radical denial of the movement for female emancipation that was gathering force around him, a reactionary reaffirmation of the traditional repression of women. Repression is to continue either *with his* 'whip' or *because of her* whip.

There is a very marked contrast between Nietzsche's empathetic stance towards the plight of women in nineteenth-century Europe in the pre-Lou period (pp. 287–8 above) and this raising of male chauvinism to the point, even by nineteenth-century standards, of caricature, this insulting slapping down of everything Lou (and Malwida) aspired to. It is not hard to see what has happened. The previous year Nietzsche had staged the 'whip' photograph which, in a joking-rueful way, reflected reality by showing the, by nineteenth-century standards, 'mannish' and self-willed Lou holding the whip hand. Now, in the aftermath of the affair, Nietzsche eases his pain by taking a kind of fictional revenge. The passage, in other words, is cut from the same cloth as the pathologically disturbed letters he wrote Rée and Lou at precisely the same time as he was writing Part I of *Zarathustra* – remember the awful remark that he can bear Lou's voice 'only when she begs'.[98] It is, as he himself says of those letters, incompatible with the rejection of *'ressentiment'* by his innermost mode of thinking.

To be set against *Zarathustra*'s awful remarks about women in Part I, however, is the fact that in its two 'dance-songs,' one in Part II and the other in Part III, 'Life' (whom Zarathustra claims to love unreservedly) is portrayed as a woman, 'wild and not virtuous',[99] who dances in an ecstatic circle with 'flaming, flying hair'[100] (in part, surely, a portrait of the heroine of Nietzsche's favourite opera, *Carmen*). One can analyse this divided attitude to women in terms of Nietzsche's own categories of the 'Dionysian' and the 'Apollonian'. Women attract Nietzsche because the erotic represents transcendence of suffering individuality (à la *Tristan und Isolde*), the 'intoxicated' absorption into a 'higher community'[101] as described in *The Birth of Tragedy*. Burnt by the Lou affair, however, he reacts with the exaggerated Apollonianism represented by *The Birth* as the Doric response to the harmful side of Dionysianism: Apollo's 'majestic rejection of all licence'.[102] So dangerous are women that they must be pressed back into the cage of nineteenth-century chauvinism.

By Part III of *Zarathustra*, written towards the end of 1883 as he was beginning to recover a certain, at least temporary, equilibrium after the Lou affair, Nietzsche's text has calmed down somewhat, and even performs a kind of penance for the whip remark. In *The Other*

Dance-Song[103] Zarathustra tries to make Life dance to his tempo by cracking his whip – as seemingly advised to do in Part I. Life asks him to stop. Surely he knows that 'noise murders thoughts', in particular the 'tender' thoughts she is beginning to have about him. (There is an amusing allusion, here, to Schopenhauer's essay 'On Din and Noise', which complains bitterly about how coachmen cracking their whips disturb the thoughts of genius.) Even in Part III, however, Nietzsche remains opposed to female emancipation: 'women are becoming mannish,' he claims, because there is so little 'manfulness' in men – only a properly mannish man will *redeem the woman* in women'.[104] This still sounds pretty awful to modern ears. But it is embedded in an important and seriously philosophical thesis, the thesis we have already confronted that people are by nature different, so that the proper and most satisfying kind of life varies radically from one kind of individual to another, and possibly from one gender to the other (see further p. 425 below).

On Child and Marriage.[105] *Continuing to discuss how the free spirit should comport himself in relation to women, Zarathustra asserts that one has the right to marry only if one is a 'victor, self-compeller, commander of the senses, master of one's virtues'.* As we have seen, Nietzsche favours eugenics, the creation of a 'spiritual-physical aristocracy' through the 'promotion and prevention of marriages'.[106] But he is also a Lamarckian, that is, believes in the inheritability of traits first acquired during an individual's lifetime.[107] So he believes in the *biological* significance of *Bildung*, self-development. If the father has, through self-discipline and good education, developed into a fine person, his virtues are liable to be transmitted genetically to his son. 'Breeding' by those lacking *Bildung*, however, has the effect of transmitting precisely what should not be transmitted. (Since there is cultural as well as biological transmission between generations, this thesis does not seem to me essentially dependent on Lamarckianism.)

On the Free Death.[108] *Die at the 'right time', Zarathustra exhorts. Do not let yourself hang on the branch like a wizened apple. Your death should be a 'consummation' and a spur and promise for the living. Death should become a festival that 'consecrate[s] the oaths of the living'. In your dying your spirit shall still 'glow like a sunset'.*

Not just eugenics, then, but also self-elected euthanasia.* The justification offered is a social one and takes us back to the exemplary, 'monumental' figures of the second *Untimely Meditation*. Just as a good work of art must finish at the right point, so must a good life, a life that can become an inspiring role model for future generations. The problem with the analogy between life and literature, however, is that in real life, since one never knows what the future will bring, it is usually hard or impossible to know what the 'right time' is. Viewing *Parsifal*'s quasi-Christianity as a decline into senility, Nietzsche claims that Wagner conspicuously failed to die at the 'right time'.[109] Many, however, would argue that *Parsifal* is in fact Wagner's crowning achievement – that if he had taken Nietzsche's advice he would have, like Jesus, 'died too early'. Leaving Wagner aside, the sad fact is that the person who really did, conspicuously and dramatically, fail to die at the right time, who hung on in a completely 'wizened' condition for eleven years after losing his faculties, was Nietzsche himself.

On the Gift-Giving Virtue.[110] *There are two kinds of selfishness: the 'sick selfishness' of 'cats and wolves' which always wants to take and the 'holy selfishness' which wants to give, which is a 'gift-giving love'.*

---

* Given the similarity of surnames, one wonders whether the Australian euthanasia campaigner Dr. Philip Nitschke was inspired by this passage.

A consistent refrain throughout the notebooks for 1883 is that 'egoism is not a principle but a fact'.[111] During the writing of at least the first three parts of *Zarathustra*, therefore, Nietzsche *thinks* he is a believer in psychological egoism, the view, to repeat, that no one ever acts save out of perceived self-interest. This, it will be remembered, was a central point of difference between him and Rée, who agreed with Schopenhauer that altruism, though rare, genuinely occurs.

In place of the Rée/Schopenhauer distinction between egoism and altruism Nietzsche wants to introduce a distinction between good and bad egoism: the 'cat' selfishness of which he accused Lou less than a month before writing this passage,[112] on the one hand, and 'holy' selfishness, on the other. The latter is supposed to be exemplified by Zarathustra in his interaction with the sun in the Prologue. As the sun would be miserable if it did not have human beings to shine upon, says Zarathustra, he himself resembles a bee that has gathered too much honey: he needs to 'overflow' with his wisdom, and that is why he will 'go down' to the world of men.[113]

The question, though, is whether Zarathustra's 'going down' is motivated by the desire for the orgasmic relief of 'discharging' his uncomfortable fullness of metaphorical 'honey' or simply by the desire to bestow his wisdom on men. Since the latter desire contains no reference to Zarathustra's pleasure or relief from pain – it is an entirely other-regarding desire – Nietzsche must, surely, suppose Zarathustra to be motivated by the former desire.

Two years later, however, at the beginning of *Zarathustra*'s Part IV, Nietzsche pens the following passage, to which reference has already been made:

> 'O Zarathustra', they [his 'animals'] said, 'are you perhaps looking out for your happiness?' – 'What does happiness matter?', he [Zarathustra] answered. 'I have long ceased to strive after happiness: I am striving after my work'. 'O Zarathustra', said the animals again...are you not lying in a sky-blue lake of happiness? 'O you pranksters', replied Zarathustra, 'How well you choose that image!'[114]

This, quite explicitly it seems to me, rejects an egoistic account of Zarathustra's motivation. All that matters to him is his mission, his 'work'. True, he knows that a by-product of that will be his happiness – the 'paradox of happiness' – but that is not his aim.

Zarathustra's having 'long ceased' to strive after happiness is code for *Nietzsche's* having given up on psychological egoism well before finishing Part IV in 1885. He has finally, and rather reluctantly, seen that what motivates his hero really has to be admitted to be altruism and cannot be reduced to any kind of 'selfishness'. Since, as we have seen throughout this book, absolute commitment to his mission characterises Nietzsche every bit as much as Zarathustra, we must conclude that Nietzsche has, by 1885, understood that for a long time he had misdescribed his own nature and motivation. We must also conclude that, in her naivety, Elizabeth actually hit upon the truth in insisting that at heart her brother was no kind of egoist.

Zarathustra Part II

Following the speech on the gift-giving virtue, like a 'sower who has cast forth his seed', Zarathustra withdraws once more from the world of men – from friends as well as foes – into his mountain solitude. Demanding that his followers become autonomous 'brothers' rather than slavish 'disciples', he tells them that he will only return to them when (like St. Peter) they have 'denied' him, are 'ashamed' of having known him.

Years pass until one night a dream tells him that his enemies have distorted his teaching and his friends are indeed ashamed of him.[115] And so he returns, turning up on the 'Isles of the Blessed' where the whole of Part II is set. Nietzsche explained to Köselitz that the 'Isles' are in fact Ischia, in the northern Bay of Naples, which he knew from his Sorrento days.[116] The identifying clue is that in 'The Dance Song'[117] the country girls dance with 'Cupido', which is the Ischian dialect for 'Cupid'.[118]

In *Ecce Homo*, to digress for a moment, Nietzsche makes the point that the Dionysian, absent from his thought since the beginning of the positivist period, returns (though not by name) to centre stage in *Zarathustra*. The work is 'my concept "Dionysian" become supreme deed'.[119] The Dionysian is closely connected with dance (and so of course music) since ecstatic dance was the main characteristic of the Dionysian revellers in the ancient world. *The Birth of Tragedy* makes the connexion explicit. The crowds dancing through the streets in the medieval carnivals were 'Dionysian enthusiasts' expressing their sense of belonging to a 'higher community' in which the individuality and division of everyday life is abolished.[120]

As Nietzsche intimates, dancing is essentially *communal*. In dance we gain or reaffirm our sense of community with others. It is, it seems, part of the fundamentally religious character of Nietzsche's thought that he wants us to recover the capacity for festive, community-affirming dance.

Upon the Isles of the Blessed.[121] *'Once one said "God" when one looked on distant seas. But I have taught you to say: superman ... Everything must be humanly thinkable, humanly visible, humanly feelable'.* This calls to mind Nietzsche's repeated contrast between the Christian God and the Greek gods. Whereas the former is an anti-human ideal, an impossible standard designed to make us feel our human attributes to be *all-too*-human, the Greeks saw their gods as 'the most successful exemplars of their own stock', saw themselves and their gods as 'two castes living side by side', one 'mightier and nobler', but both 'of one species'.[122] Nietzsche is saying something similar here: whoever the superman is, he is a *human*, not an anti-human figure.

In the notebooks, commenting on the reduction of contemporary man to a cog in the 'machinery' of economic interests (an aspect of the 'Last Man' theme), Nietzsche writes that it remains possible to conceive of a 'higher type' of human being. And then he adds: 'As is well known, my concept, my *metaphor* for this type is the word "superman"'.[123] Why is 'metaphor' stressed here? Because, I think, Nietzsche wants to reject the idea of the superman as designating some *particular species* of humanity: we are *not* to think of 'super-man' as belonging to some such series as 'Neanderthal man', 'Cro-Magnon man', 'Aryan man'...In particular, we are not to think of the superman as an 'end of history' (or – Heidegger's misreading of Nietzsche – as a blond, blue-eyed SS tank commander.)

Towards the end of the speech, Zarathustra says that 'permanence is merely an allegory', that, in their praise of permanence, 'the poets lie too much'. This affirmation of the inexorability of change must apply to the superman, too. Though the superman is an ideal, 'the meaning of the earth' (p. 368 above), he can never be an eternal, *fixed* ideal of human being. Rather, like the horizon, the ideal will always lie ahead of whatever state of flourishing human society has arrived at. (Nietzsche's hope, we saw, was for not *a* 'dawn' but rather an *unending series* of 'new dawns' (p. 298 above).) Fugitive though it is, however, we do know some things about the superman ideal: that it will always be a human rather than anti-human ideal, and that it will always be a *communal* ideal: 'in the *superman*', as we saw, 'individuals have become one' (p. 372 above).

On those who pity.[124] *Pity [Mitleid], the central human virtue according to Christian [and Schopenhauerian] ethics, is in fact not a virtue at all but rather a cause of suffering. It injures the pride of the recipient and generates resentment. But it also injures those who pity. God died of his pity for man.*

In German, as already observed, *Mitleid* has to do duty for both 'pity' and 'compassion'. One's natural inclination is to say that Nietzsche's point about *Mitleid* harming its recipient is well taken but one-sided. Certainly, *pity* turns its object into an inferior being to whom one feels superior ('I pity you, you miserable little lump of vomit!') and so makes the pitied feel bad. But, one might continue, surely *Mitleid* in the sense of *compassion* is quite different: here one does not turn the other into an object separate from and lower than oneself but rather (as 'com-passion' tells us) *suffers-with* him. As Schopenhauer puts it, in compassion one sympathetically 'identifies with' the sufferer.[125] One takes his suffering on board as one's own.

In discussing *Dawn*'s critique of *Mitleid*, we saw that while admitting the existence of empathetic, Schopenhauerian compassion, Nietzsche argues that, like pity though in a different way, compassion harms other people: empathetic identification with the woes of the entire cosmos convinces one of the futility of attempts to relieve suffering and so causes active benevolence to wither and die (pp. 302–3 above). Here Nietzsche looks at this same phenomenon from a different angle: cosmic, Schopenhauerian compassion harms the *subject* by generating psychological collapse, deep depression. This is the idea, I think, that Nietzsche encapsulates in the poetic conceit that God died from compassion for the awfulness of human existence. And so Nietzsche discovers a further reason to reject compassion along with pity: compassion does not just harm the potential recipients of benevolent action, it also harms the compassionate, to varying degrees, kills their ability to 'affirm life'. This is a major reason that Nietzsche says that 'creators' must be 'hard'.[126] If we are to remake the world we must, for the sake of both others and ourselves, harden our hearts to compassion.

Compassion, I have already observed, was an unusually prominent element in Nietzsche's own personality. That is why he was, for instance, 'the little saint' to the Genoese. His conviction that compassion damaged the compassionate was strongly based on self-analysis. To Overbeck he wrote in September 1884:

> the total depression I was suffering from ... has lifted: I now think that I have taken the difference with my family a hundred times too seriously ... My trouble is the eternally repeated mistake of representing the suffering of others as greater than it is. From childhood the sentence, 'In *Mitleid* lies my greatest danger', has repeatedly confirmed itself. (Perhaps it is the bad consequence of the extraordinary nature of my father – everyone who knew him reckoned him to belong more to the 'angels' than to 'men'.) It's sufficient that through these bad experiences with *Mitleid* I have been stimulated to a theoretically very interesting alteration in the valuation of it.[127]

The Night Song.[128] *'This is my loneliness that I am girded round with light ... I do not know the happiness of the receiver ... this is my poverty that my hand never rests from gift-giving'.*

The most salient aspect of the 'new speech'[129] which is said to distinguish Part II from Part I is the introduction of the 'songs' Zarathustra 'sings' as distinct from the speeches which he 'speaks'. These, it seems to me (remembering that Nietzsche sometimes thinks of *Zarathustra* as a musical work) can be taken as 'arias' which, rather than advancing the narrative or the matter of discussion, express Zarathustra's feelings as he proceeds along his path of spiritual development. (A project for some composer of the future might be to turn *Zarathustra* into an opera.)

In *Ecce Homo* he calls the 'Night Song' a 'Dionysian Dithyramb' and describes it as 'the loneliest song ever written'. It expresses Zarathustra's 'immortal lament that through his superabundance of light and power, through his nature as a *sun*, he is condemned not to love'.[130]

That a 'sun' or 'superman' cannot *be* loved is easy to grasp: it can, one might say, only be revered. The kind of love that includes friendship (as we have seen, Nietzsche's letters frequently speak of 'loving' his friends) demands equality. But why should the 'gift-giver' be incapable of *loving*? For, I think, the very same reason. The kind of love the song is talking about can only be between equals and, sadly, Zarathustra–Nietzsche (like God) has no equals. This is what condemns the one who is 'higher' than all his contemporaries to loneliness. It is cold at the top. In March 1885 Nietzsche wrote to his sister the following:

> ...some of the best minds in Germany believe that I am mad or even say that I will die in a madhouse. I am too proud to believe that any human being could love me: that would presuppose he knew who I was. Equally little do I believe that I will ever love someone: that would presuppose that I had found – wonder of wonders – a human being of my rank – don't forget that ... I find the founder of Christendom superficial in comparison with myself.[131]

On Self-Overcoming.[132] *The will to truth is really the will to the 'thinkability' of all beings. We want to make things thinkable since we doubt, with healthy suspicion, that they really are. The will to the thinkability of beings is really the 'will to power' – which means things have to be 'smooth', a 'mirror' of our own spirit – even when it comes to good and evil. Wherever I found life I found the will to power. Even the weak seek power over the weakest and even the weak seek to steal power from the stronger by covert means. 'Life ... is that which must always overcome itself'.*

In the notebooks for 1883 we find Nietzsche entering a phase of global scepticism as to whether anything in reality corresponds to the network of concepts – matter, thing, cause, effect – in terms of which we make the world intelligible to ourselves. (Later on, we will see, he grows out of it.) But, Nietzsche–Zarathustra asserts, this actually does not matter since the point of intelligibility is technological; the achievement of 'power' over our environment and ourselves. Even morality serves this end – a development of the earlier idea that moralities always serve the 'existence conditions' of a community. Nietzsche now asserts that it is not mere existence but rather communal 'power' that moralities serve: some kind of increase and expansion, some kind of – a frequent synonym for 'power' – 'growth'.[133]

And now we come to the general claim: life is the will to power. This is implicit in the claim that 'life is that which must always overcome itself' since that claim, clearly, is derived from the premises that (a) life is the will to power and (b) the will to power is always the will to more power. Notice that this general claim falls short of the full-blown thesis of *Beyond Good and Evil* that 'life' (indeed 'the world') is 'will to power – *and nothing besides*'.[134] Unlike the full-blown thesis, *Zarathustra* does not exclude the possibility of motives other than power.

What is the status of the general claim? Zarathustra says he has found the will to power 'wherever I have found the living'. This is a quite cautious formulation: not a dogmatic assertion but, I would suggest, a working assumption based on a certain amount of observation; an inductive *hypothesis*. Schopenhauer asserts that his 'will to live' best 'deciphers', makes unified sense of, the 'riddle' of experience.[135] Nietzsche proposes the 'experiment' of seeing whether 'will to power' might not do better. (The fate of this experiment will be discussed in detail in Chapter 26.)

On Salvation.[136] The fact that *Erlösung*, 'salvation' or 'redemption', is a religious word brings to the fore, yet again, the fact that *Zarathustra* is intended as a religious text. Both in traditional Christianity and in Schopenhauer's mystical synthesis of Christianity and Buddhism, salvation consists in ascent from the mundane world of pain to a supernatural realm of bliss. Nietzsche, we have seen, from his pious youth onwards, yearns for salvation, for a world made not simply tolerable but, like the ultimate world of Christianity, *perfect*. In *The Antichrist* he says that the 'most spiritual' human beings are those who can affirm that 'the world is perfect',[137] and in Part IV of *Zarathustra*, in a state of 'strange drunkenness' caused by fumes from a grapevine, Zarathustra does, for a moment, experience the world as 'perfect'.[138] Zarathustra rejects, of course, the supernatural. His task, therefore, is to show how salvation, perfection, bliss, can be discovered within the confines of naturalism, how the 'kingdom of heaven' can be discovered in the heart.*

A hunchback tells Zarathustra he must cure the cripples if he is to convince the people of his teaching. 'Not so', Zarathustra replies. 'If one takes away the hunch from the hunchback one takes away his spirit'. This reveals Nietzsche's basic strategy: theodicy – showing that problematic phenomena are really blessings in disguise, showing that, as the notebooks put it, 'Furies – that is just a bad word for the graces'.[139] The rest of the speech shows us how to perform the theodicy.

'I walk among men as … over a battlefield or butcher-field'. (Here, surely, Nietzsche is experiencing one of his post-traumatic flashbacks to the stinking body-parts on the battlefield of Wörth (pp. 137–8 above).) Everywhere I see only 'fragments, limbs and terrible accidents – but no human being'. We must 'compose into one', 'poeticize' into a unity, all that is 'fragment, riddle and terrible accident'. We must learn to 'will backwards' so as to re-create all 'It was' as 'Thus I will it'.

The Gay Science has already told us what it is to 'will backwards': it is to narrate one's life so that 'everything that happens turns out for the best', turns out to be something that 'must not be missing' from the *Bildungsroman* of one's life: the story of one's spiritual development towards the goal of becoming the person who, according to one's ideal, one is (pp. 336–7 above). In narrating one's life in this way one is, of course, giving it unity, 'composing into one' all that was previously meaningless 'accident'. Apparent accidents become parts of 'personal providence'. To authentic 'selves' accidents never happen. For the rest, everything is an accident.

What Zarathustra outlines here is the *concept* of salvation: what one would have to do to 'redeem' one's life and – since that life is lived, inextricably, *in the world* – the history of

---

* In section 34 of *The Antichrist*, as we shall see, Nietzsche says that for the *historical* Jesus 'the kingdom of heaven' is not 'above' us but is rather a 'state of the heart'. Though he calls Jesus a *décadent*, in *this* respect, it seems to me, he is in profound agreement with him.

the world as a whole. This, however, does not at all mean that he (or Nietzsche) is capable of carrying out the task of redemption. And in fact the final two speeches of Part II make it clear that, as yet, he cannot. For what they reveal is his 'disgust' at even the 'highest and best' of those with whom he is compelled to share his world, his inability to 'redeem' them. This inability expresses itself as his inability to will, or even utter, the thought of the eternal return. What this shows is that eternal return is just a dramatic expression of redemption. Redemption, salvation, finding the world perfect, *amor fati*, embracing the eternal return, are one and all simply different expressions of the same thing.

Zarathustra Part III

Since Zarathustra's spiritual development – the *Bildungsroman* of his life – is not yet complete, he must return to the solitude of his mountain-top for further reflection. Part III (published in April 1884) discovers him en route from the Blessed Isles to the mountain. (Notice how Zarathustra's to-ing and fro-ing between sea and mountain reflects the life-cycle of his 'father'.)

On the Vision and the Riddle.[140] *With great difficulty Zarathustra finally manages to articulate his 'most abysmal' thought, though only by reporting it as the content of a 'vision'. The gate called (present) 'Moment' has two paths leading from it, one to the past, the other to the future. But actually they are one and the same path. Time is a 'circle'. And because every event is 'knotted to' a cause, what happens now must have happened an infinite number of times before – for example, this spider in this moonlight. After Zarathustra has finished explaining his vision, the howl of a dog is heard. And then the scene changes. A young shepherd is convulsed by a black snake hanging out of his mouth [as Nietzsche often was by vomit]. After a ferocious struggle he succeeds in biting off its head and jumps up laughing 'as no human being has ever laughed before'.*

To understand the content of the 'vision', think of a model train with an inexhaustible battery in eternal motion on a circular track: since the carriage now passing under the bridge called 'Moment' is 'knotted to' the engine in front of it, that same carriage has passed under the bridge an infinite number of times already and will do so an infinite number of times in the future. The speech indicates that the idea of eternal return is capable of being taken in two ways: it can be the cause of a canine 'howl' and a 'snake' of black bile, or it can be a thought that generates the joyful laughter of the superman, generates the words of *The Gay Science*, 'never have I heard anything more divine' (p. 336 above). Why should eternal return – supposing one discovered it to be true – have the capacity to generate both of these reactions?

Why, first of all, might someone – Zarathustra, for example, for at least most of the work – find the eternal return 'abysmal'? *Not*, let us be clear, because of the incredible tedium of living the very same life over and over again. Since I now have no memory of a previous existence, were my *exact* life to recur I would similarly have no memory of a previous existence.

Christianity, as well as most other world religions, thinks of 'salvation', whether of the individual or the world, as a blissful state which brings history, in at least the ordinary sense, to an end. Time is, as it were, an arrow which reaches the target and then stops. But if time is a circle then there is no such 'end of time'. This is the potentially 'abysmal' aspect of eternal return: in cancelling the arrow, the circle cancels the salvation that has always been believed in. There is no 'final solution' to the 'riddle' of life.

But suppose that we can find salvation *in* life. Suppose we can 'redeem', turn to 'gold' (p. 355 above), everything painful and problematic that has happened? Then our world is *already* 'perfect', 'salvation' has been achieved, and we have no need for any other kind of salvation. The kingdom of heaven is *here and now*, so that we have no need of a kingdom somewhere else and in the future. Having fallen in love with the circle, we lose all desire for the arrow. In some unexplained way, the young shepherd has performed the great theodicy and so made the transition from nausea to joy.

Before Sunrise.[141] *'O Heaven above, so pure, so deep . . . into your height I cast myself – that is my depth . . . my innocence . . . The God is veiled by his beauty . . . together we . . . learnt to climb above ourselves . . . and to smile down cloudlessly from luminous eyes and far-off distances, while beneath us constraint, and purpose, and guilt, stream like rain. At drifting clouds I am aggrieved . . . they take from you and me . . . the enormous and unbounded Yea- and Amen-saying . . . A blesser I have become and a Yea-sayer . . . But this is my blessing: to stand over each and every thing as its own heaven, as its rounded roof, its azure bell and eternal security, and blessed is he who blesses thus. For all things are baptised in the fount of eternity and are beyond good and evil . . . The world is deep, deeper than ever the day has thought'.*

Two aspects of this passage of, as *Ecce Homo* says, 'divine tenderness'[142] are of crucial importance. The first is that in it, Zarathustra, for a moment, has become a 'Yea-sayer', has achieved an 'emerald happiness'. For a moment, he shares in Emerson's experience of finding 'all things profitable, all days holy, and all men divine'. For a moment he can love the eternal return. The second important feature is the style and feeling of the passage – ecstatic, Dionysian. *Ecce Homo* makes this explicit: 'Before Sunrise' is the 'dithyramb' of 'a Dionysus'.[143] Dionysus, suppressed throughout Nietzsche's positivist period, refers us back to *The Birth of Tragedy* and to the 'metaphysical comfort' for the suffering of life brought by Dionysian consciousness.[144] Of course, since Nietzsche has now rejected the 'metaphysical world', has rejected idealism in favour of naturalism, the Dionysian can no longer be conceived in the way it was in the early period. But there must, nonetheless, be a link.

In *The Birth*, the Dionysian state consisted in two kinds of transcendence: of nature and of individuality, the latter being accounted the source of all suffering.[145] Since the possibility of the former is now rejected, the Dionysian, as conceived in Nietzsche's mature period, must consist in the latter. This indeed is what Nietzsche says. In a note from 1888 he says that 'the word Dionysus means an urge to unity reaching out beyond personality, the everyday, a passionate painful overflowing'.[146]

How can there be a Dionysian transcendence of individuality which is yet no longer thought of as a behind-the-worldly transcendence to something metaphysical? Later on in Part III, Zarathustra describes himself as a 'soul which, fleeing from itself, retrieves itself in the widest sphere',[147] a soul, that is, which rediscovers itself – not 'behind' but rather – *in* the totality of all existence. And this, I suggest, is what happens in the section under consideration: for a moment, Zarathustra *becomes* the all-embracing 'azure bell' of the sky – you are '*my* depth' he tells it – becomes the totality of all things.

'Before Sunrise' returns, then, to the idea that enlightenment consists in transcendence of individuality. *Zarathustra* offers us, as it were, transcendence in a new key. Lou Salomé described this as Nietzsche's 'unequivocal plunge into the eternal riddle of mysticism'.[148] But though on the right lines, the implication that Dionysian transcendence takes us beyond, or even against, reason is, I think, mistaken. For Nietzsche's soberly rational philosophising, too, tells us that, from an ultimate point of view, individuality is an illusion. If, as we have seen on numerous occasions, the everyday 'self' thinks that *it* acts and is 'responsible' for those actions, then it is deluded. What is really responsible for 'my' actions, in a world completely 'knotted together' by cause and effect, is the total causal history of the world, and from this it follows that the enlightened use of the 'I' is to apply it to that total history. As *Twilight of the Idols* will put it, rational insight, just as much as poetic ecstasy, consists in seeing that 'one belongs to the whole, one *is* the whole'.[149]

We have, then, a connexion between supreme 'affirmation', willing the eternal return, on the one hand, and the Dionysian state of (non-metaphysical) transcendence of individuality, on the other.[150] This is a connexion Nietzsche draws in many places. Only, says *The Gay Science*'s Book V, the 'Dionysian god or man' can achieve an unqualified affirmation of life – its 'terrible and questionable' aspect would defeat any lesser being.[151] The 'unbounded Yea-and-Amen-saying' *is*, says *Ecce Homo*, 'the concept of Dionysus'.[152] The hard question, however, is *why* Nietzsche makes this connexion. Why can the eternal return never be willed from an everyday, individual perspective? Why is it only possible for those who 'widen their souls' so as to become the totality of, in Nietzsche's preferred language, 'becoming'?

In Book IV of *The Gay Science* we were told to use our 'theoretical and practical skill in interpreting and arranging events' to discover a 'personal providence' in our lives, a narrative which discloses everything that happens as being 'for the best'.[153] Here there is no hint that the 'redemption' of the past necessary to affirming the eternal return required anything more than the ordinary, individual perspective on the world. But, then, in the very next section, Nietzsche descends into 'melancholy' at the 'thought of death': the thought of how all this 'thirsty life' will 'soon be so silent', how 'everyone's shadow stands behind him as his dark fellow traveller'.[154] (Notice how the 'shadow' in *The Wanderer and His Shadow* turns out to be death.) This suggests that, so far as (the original)[155] *The Gay Science* can see, death, and my knowledge of its inevitability, constitutes an insuperable objection to willing the eternal return.

And, of course, it does. If I am the passionate life-affirmer Nietzsche wants me to be then the *last* thing I want to do is to die. (No one wants to abandon a terrific party that is still in full swing.) For the healthy life-affirmer, one's own death can *never* turn out 'for the best'. For an unhappy life-denier, of course, death may well be for the best, but for him there are a myriad of other obstacles to affirming the circle. Death, then, is the fly in the ointment: because of the omnipresent 'shadow' of death the circle *cannot* be affirmed from the ordinary perspective but demands the extra-ordinary: transcendence to identification with the totality. From *that* point of view the situation is transformed: the death of that individual I once thought I was appears, now, as a triviality. And a necessity, too, since I see that the death of the old is a prerequisite of the birth of the new.

In *Zarathustra*, we have seen, Nietzsche wanted to write the founding book of a new religion. But any religion worth the name has to have something profound and comforting to say about death. For death is, for human beings, the *summum malum*, the worst evil, our most primal fear. For Nietzsche, in particular, it must have that status since it is the ultimate negation of what he is increasingly coming to identify as the human essence; the will to power. No existence, no power!

In *The Birth of Tragedy* Nietzsche did indeed address this primal need: seeing through the 'illusion' of individuality to the realisation of one's identity with the 'Primal Unity' was the 'metaphysical comfort' for, above all, mortality. But then, as he entered his positivist period, he became silent on the topic of death; or, when forced to speak, trite and/or evasive. *Human, All-Too-Human*, it is true, experienced a moment of nostalgia for his youthful idea that great art could assure us of eternal life: Beethoven's Ninth makes the receptive person feel that 'he is hovering above the earth in a dome of stars with the dream of *immortality* in his heart' (p. 251 above). (Notice that the 'dome of stars' links Beethoven's 'dream' to the 'azure bell' of 'Before Sunrise'.) But this is quickly debunked as the kind of sentimental backsliding that tests the free spirit's 'intellectual probity'.

The Gay Science's discussion of the melancholy 'thought of death' is as evasive as the positivist works: the best it can think of to say is that we should try to ignore the elephant in the sitting-room, try 'not... thinking the thought of death'.[156] Even Part I of *Zarathustra* remains superficial about death. As we saw, it recommends that we 'die at the right time' by opting for the 'free death' – as if choosing to end one's life were of no more moment or difficulty than choosing to cancel one's subscription to *Time* magazine. But finally, in 'Before Sunrise', he knows how to say something deep and instructive about death *without* lapsing into supernaturalism, something that is, in fact, implicit in the fundamentals of his philosophy. In effect, and perhaps with their help, he follows both Malwida (p. 231 above) and Lou (p. 350 above) into pantheism: death is of no moment to the enlightened since one's true identity is the ecstatic, pantheistic 'All'. By becoming the 'azure bell' that is the 'fount of [the enlightened soul's] eternity', Zarathustra achieves the immortality Nietzsche was forced to ridicule by the limited perspective of his positivist period. For the enlightened, fear of death is replaced by the 'eternal security' of a soul that has expanded into the 'widest sphere'.

Zarathustra Part IV

On January 18, 1884, Nietzsche wrote Schmeitzner that *Zarathustra* was finally complete.[157] The following November, however, he announced that he was working on a fourth part (and projecting even a fifth and sixth part, on the grounds that Zarathustra would allow him no peace until he had seen him through to his death).[158] In February of the following year he announces the completion of Part IV as a 'sublime finale' to the whole work, but one that was meant only for private distribution among friends, not for publication. In April 1885 forty-five copies were printed and privately distributed – to the usual suspects plus, among others, one Helene Druskowitz, of whom more anon. Initially, Nietzsche's purported reluctance to publish seems to have been a matter of making a virtue out of necessity. For, given that he could not contemplate publishing anything more with the appalling Schmeitzner, he did not actually *have* a publisher.[159] By 1886, however, his letters make clear that he genuinely did not want to publish Part IV: on account of its extremely blasphemous nature, he feared 'the police' and the possible loss of his pension.[160] As well as gratuitously offending people like his mother, Part IV, he feared, might result in the banning of the whole of *Zarathustra*.

Scholars often try to explain the non-appearance of Part IV in the supposedly 'complete' *Zarathustra* of 1886 (the appearance of Parts I to III together for the first time) by reference to an alleged falling off in the quality of the writing in comparison with the first three parts. While it is certainly true that the style is *different* to that of the first parts – biblical solemnity has been replaced by burlesque – I myself find no evidence of decline. More importantly, there is no evidence that Nietzsche was doubtful about the quality of Part IV.

There is a pleasing symmetry to the work. Wandering around in the vicinity of his cave the by now white-haired Zarathustra meets eight 'higher men' – presumably candidates for the status of being the 'free spirits' for whom Nietzsche's books have been written – and invites all of them to a feast in his cave. Though they turn out to fall short of his high expectations, they are, nonetheless, all genuinely 'higher' than the flea-sized rabble of modernity's 'last men'. The eight are: the 'soothsayer', a Schopenhauerian figure who says that life is meaningless; 'two kings' (these are treated as a single person), reactionary figures who rant and rave against the 'rabble' and the lack of hierarchy and respect in the modern world (the manner and matter of the rant sounds suspiciously like Nietzsche himself); the 'conscientious of spirit', a scholarly type interested only in truth, no matter how narrow; the 'magician', an 'actor' in the sense of 'fake', clearly a parody of Wagner; the 'last pope',* who knows that God is dead and suggests that it is Christian piety (towards truth) which forbids both Zarathustra and himself to believe in him any longer; the 'voluntary beggar', discovered preaching to the cows, a kind of Jesus figure; 'the shadow', who describes himself as a 'wanderer'; and finally 'the ugliest man', the sight of whose ugliness caused God to die. Fairly clearly, these are all aspects of Nietzsche's own personality and history. To the extent Zarathustra finds the higher men 'not high enough', they represent aspects of his life and personality Nietzsche now regards himself as having 'overcome': he was a Schopenhauerian, he ranted and raved against modernity, he was a scholar of meaningless philological minutiae, he was a Wagnerian, he was forced to give up God by Christian truthfulness, he lived a life of voluntary poverty (and also, as we shall see, preached to cows), he has many 'ugly' parts to his soul, manifested especially in the Salomé affair, and he was, in his positivist period, a wanderer and a shadow of his former self.

The Ass Festival

The higher men all assemble as instructed in Zarathustra's cave. Returning to the cave himself, he hears a 'cry of distress' that seems to be coming from their combined chorus. Zarathustra tells them to lighten up, that what they need is some dancing and cheerful buffoonery to make them laugh.[161] Finding the air in the cave oppressive, he goes for a walk. Returning, he hears the sound of giggling and notices the smell of incense (or perhaps marijuana) and 'burning pine cones' coming from his cave. Inside he discovers the higher men worshipping an ass. The high point of the Ass Festival is a descent into a mood of mock solemnity in which is sung a 'litany' in praise of the ass, who is treated as the incarnation of God. It begins, 'Amen: and praise and honour and wisdom and thanks and strength be unto our God', to which the ass predictably responds, 'Yea-Ah'.[162]

* * *

Historically the Ass Festival, otherwise known as the Feast of Fools, was a carnivalesque letting off of steam which happened in medieval Europe, particularly in France, usually in midwinter. Condemned, though usually somewhat half-heartedly, by the Church hierarchy, it involved such things as playing dice and eating black (i.e., blood) sausage on the altar (a

---

* Described as 'a tall man in black with a haggard, pale face', he looks suspiciously like Franz Liszt, particularly as he appears in the well-known 1839 portrait by Henri Lehmann. Since Liszt became a Catholic abbé, this looks like a piece of incidental naughtiness on Nietzsche's part.

parody of the Eucharist), wearing masks, dressing up as women or animals, and, after the ceremony, raging round town in a generally riotous manner. Not infrequently the day ended in minor bloodshed.

In the ceremony itself the ass was the centre of attention. Led into the cathedral, often covered by a golden cloth with its four corners held by the cathedral's four most eminent canons, it would be the object of hymns of praise.

The 'burning pine cones' mentioned in Nietzsche's Ass Festival come from a description of a particular version of the medieval festival by the eighteenth-century aphorist Georg Lichtenberg, an author Nietzsche knew well and was reading shortly before writing Part IV of *Zarathustra*.[163] The thirteenth-century version of the festival Lichtenberg describes is a representation of the Virgin Mary's flight into Egypt. A young woman representing Mary would be led into the cathedral, followed by a procession of clergy and congregation, and then the Mass would be read with great solemnity. After every section, however, the refrain was not 'Amen' but, rather, 'Yea-Ah'. And if the donkey itself joined in so much the better. At the end of the Mass, instead of the familiar blessing, the priest 'Yea-Ah'ed three times and the congregation did the same. The ceremony ended with a hymn of praise to the ass, half in Latin and half in French. It contained the lines '*Adventabat asinus/pulcher et fortissimus* (Here comes the ass, beautiful and strong)'.[164] Nietzsche quotes these lines as 'a lovely motto from an old mystery' in a letter to von Gersdorff written within a few days of the completion of Part IV of *Zarathustra*,[165] and the following year in *Beyond Good and Evil*.[166]

* * *

Discovering them celebrating the Ass Festival transforms Zarathustra's attitude to the higher men. Though they are still not really what he has been waiting for (they are not, in Nietzsche's other language, free spirits 'of the first rank'), their 'brave nonsense' and new 'joyfulness' pleases him enough for him to call them his 'new friends'. Two elements of the historical festival explain, I think, Zarathustra's altered attitude. First, it is wonderfully blasphemous, quite at odds with the 'age-of-gloomy-piety' stereotype of the Middle Ages. This, of course, would have greatly appealed to, as he now regarded himself, the 'Antichrist'. And second, it represents a continuation into the Middle Ages of the Dionysian festivals of the ancient world. This continuity is recognised in *The Birth of Tragedy*'s description of the dancing and singing crowds celebrating the festivals of St. John and St. Vitus as 'Dionysian enthusiasts', reincarnations of the 'Dionysian chorus' of Greek tragedy.[167] Given, as we now know, that stepping out of Apollonian 'sobriety' (the ordinary perspective on the world) and into Dionysian 'intoxication' (the extra-ordinary perspective) is necessary to willing the eternal return, one can see why the higher men, even if their Dionysianism is a momentary drunkenness rather than an enduring insight, at least point in a hopeful direction.

* * *

Zarathustra ends with an 'Intoxicated Song',*,[168] clearly another 'Dionysian dithyramb'. 'All joy wants eternity, wants return', sings Zarathustra. But since he also sings 'just now my world became perfect', we learn that, finally, he is able, at least for a moment, to will

---

* At its conclusion, the 'Intoxicated Song's' poetic prose develops into a proper poem. This appears on the memorial stone erected in 1900 on Sils Maria's Chasté peninsula (where Nietzsche had wished to be buried) by Nietzsche's organist friend Carl Fuchs and the concert pianist Walther Lampe (see Plate 26). As already noted, Gustav Mahler set the same words to music in his Third Symphony.

the eternal return. Then day breaks and 'The Sign'[169] appears: a laughing lion surrounded by doves. Having sobered up, the higher men run away.

The doves signify, presumably, that though the (rather C. S. Lewisish) lion is a fierce warrior, his war is 'without smoke or gunpowder'.[170] He is, presumably, at least a relative of the lion of the 'Three Metamorphoses' with which *Zarathustra* began (pp. 369–70 above) and, as such, a 'sign' of the 'child', the genuine creator. That he laughs rather than roars, however, suggests that he is a more effective lion than his relative since, as Nietzsche observes, 'Not by wrath does one kill but by laughter'.[171] This suggests what is wrong with the higher men – with the previous stages of Nietzsche's spiritual journey that he (or at least Zarathustra) has now overcome. In those previous stages he combated the decadence of modern culture with a foaming *fury* that shows him still to be a part of that culture. Only when one has overcome anger, only when one finds the old God *ludicrous* rather than evil, has one genuinely 'moved on'. Only then is one genuinely free to create new gods.

20

Nietzsche's Circle of Women

P ARTS II and III of *Zarathustra* were written, we saw, in Nice, where Nietzsche had decided to spend the entire winter of 1883–4. This migratory life-style – summers in Sils alternating with winters in Nice – was designed to produce the 'permanent, mild winter'[1] he now considered best for his health and would last almost to the end of his productive life. Not that, at first, he liked Nice at all: 'a poor imitation of Paris, a pretentious half-big-city incredibly deficient in forest, shade and quietness'[2] was his initial impression. The search for silence drove him to his third move within as many months, taking him from the Villa Mazollini to the Pension de Genève in the Petite Rue St. Etienne, which recommended itself particularly on account of the Savorin family's excellent Swiss cuisine.

Joseph Paneth

M ost of this first winter in Nice was punctuated by regular visits from Joseph Paneth. Paneth's record of these encounters recalls Nietzsche referring to the anti-Semitic movement as a 'swinishness' that had invaded even his own family, and as insisting on his Polish ancestry: his surname, Nietzsche gleefully claimed, came from '*Niecki*', meaning 'destroyer' or 'nihilist'. (Overbeck, too, records Nietzsche as harping at rather tedious length on the same theme, but suggests that it was more a conceit than a serious belief.) Paneth recalls Nietzsche saying that his letters should never be published, and that he would require his friends, after his death, only to release for publication those he himself had selected and prepared for that purpose. A man, he said, should not be required to appear in public 'in his shirt-sleeves'. The conversation then turned to the connexion between genius and madness. The similarity, suggested Nietzsche, is that in both cases one is obsessed by a single idea. And he quoted Goethe's bon mot, 'Man strives only so long as he is crazy'. In the fifth of their encounters, in early March, Nietzsche disclosed as his fundamental aim 'the improvement of the human race and culture', an improvement he called 'the superman'. Only weak ages, he added, strive for pleasure; strong ones strive for goals. In their final meeting, at the end of March, Nietzsche attacked the Germans as a 'servile' race always ready to sacrifice their individuality to the supposed good of society as a whole. Cataloguing the further crimes of the Germans, he complained that Luther had seriously delayed the collapse of Christianity and that it was the Germans who were responsible for thwarting Napoleon's heroic attempts to create a united Europe.[3]

Resa von Schirnhofer

Initially planning to leave Nice for Venice at the beginning of April 1884, Nietzsche remained in his winter quarters until the twentieth on account of a letter from Resa von Schirnhofer (see Plate 27), whose 'motherly friend', Malwida von Meysenbug, had suggested she visit him. Nietzsche enthusiastically welcomed the proposal with the result that she visited him from April 3 to April 12.

Born in 1855 (she died in 1948 at the age of 93), Resa arrived in Zurich in 1882 to study for her Ph.D., which she eventually completed in 1889. (At the time, Zurich was the only German-speaking university to admit women.) Earlier in 1882, she had met Malwida in Bayreuth at the first performance of *Parsifal*, where she also met Lou, whom she did not like very much. Lou's 'dialectical virtuosity', she thought, often lapsed into 'sophism', and, as noted, her display of the 'whip' photograph to all and sundry she considered poor taste (p. 347 above).

Nietzsche proved a charming host throughout her visit, Resa's initial awe quickly disappearing before his modest friendliness and the familiarity of his 'professorial' manner. He took her to a bullfight (in which the bull was not allowed to be killed) and on his favourite walks. One of these, a climb up Mont Boron, was particularly memorable:

> It was a heavenly day [Resa records] with the Mistral whipping everything up as, after a short tram ride, we began to climb up the mountain. Nietzsche was in a dithyrambic mood praising the wind as a redeemer from earthly gravity: for him there was some kind of healthy release in the gusts of wind. At a certain height, French sentries blocked our path... to the fortified summit. On this level spot we found a simple *osteria* [cheap café] with wooden tables and benches under a pergola. We sat down amidst the heavenly mountain nature. It alternated picturesquely between the surrounding hills and, below us, the graceful coastline with its charming bays. The bays were surrounded by a crescent of green, from which clusters of houses gleamed forth like bright flowers. Here I had my first taste of 'Vermouth di Torino' which Nietzsche poured for me... in a sparkling mood and full of humorous inspirations. The 'guarded mountain' was the occasion for a series of verses which tumbled out from him one after the other. I was amazed and began then to put in my pennyworth. It was no improvisation of any high art but amusing doggerel that showed me an unanticipated Nietzsche.[4]

Nietzsche told Resa she should not be offended by *Zarathustra*'s famous whip passage, which, her recollections add, at this stage in their acquaintance she was not inclined to do, taking it as a 'poetic generalisation' applying not to all women but only to particular cases. (Elizabeth, interpreting the 'whip' remark in the same, probably mistaken, way, makes the same claim – that the remark applies only to certain women who stand in need of a 'manly hand' to keep them in their 'proper bounds' – and it is not hard to guess whom she has in mind as a suitable case for treatment.) On another occasion he took her for a walk along the Promenade des Anglais and pointed out Corsica, just visible as a smudge on the horizon. This led to a disquisition on Napoleon, whom Nietzsche regarded as intermediate between contemporary humanity and 'the superman'. And he pointed out that Napoleon had the same pulse beat as himself – sixty beats per minute.

Nietzsche was able to relax with Resa as with few other people; 'a droll one who makes me laugh a lot', he described her to Overbeck.[5] It is true that he also complained that she was not very good looking, indeed downright 'ugly',[6] but, likely, it was precisely the lack of sexual tension that lightened his heart, enabled him to relax, and, as with his sister, make up silly verses.

The 'Other' Nietzsche

On one occasion during the Nice visit, however, Resa experienced a quite different persona:

> As Nietzsche rose to leave suddenly his manner changed. With a rigid expression in his face and looking reluctantly all around as though some terrible danger threatened were anyone to overhear his words, and putting his hand to the mouth in order to dampen the sound, he announced to me the 'secret' which Zarathustra had whispered in Life's ear ... There was something bizarre, even uncanny, in the way in which he told me of the 'eternal return' and the enormous weight of this idea. Far more than the content of the idea, it was Nietzsche's manner of communicating it that was alien to me. Another Nietzsche had suddenly stood there and terrified me ... Then, without explaining the idea further, he returned to his normal way of speaking and usual self. I had the impression he had intentionally played fortissimo on the instrument of my sensibility to mark the magnitude of his discovery.[7]

There are other records of this sudden switch of personality. Resa experienced it again the following August in Sils Maria (p. 392 below), and Overbeck, too, records the sudden switch to a solemn 'whispering' in which Nietzsche disclosed the 'secret doctrine' of eternal return.[8] In the letters of this period, moreover, there begin to appear occasional flashes of, if not megalomania, at least grandiosity. In February 1884, for example, he claims that, following Luther and Goethe, *Zarathustra* takes the final step which brings the German language to perfection,[9] and in March that his work will 'divide the history of humanity into two halves'.[10] In March of the following year he makes the already noted claim that, compared to himself, Christ is a 'superficial' figure (p. 378 above), remarks that it is a pity God does not exist since then he would have at least one friend on the same level as himself, and that it is a complete enigma how he could be biologically related to the likes of Elizabeth.[11] It seems, then, that lurking within mild-mannered, bespectacled Friedrich Nietzsche was another being (whom one has, of course, to call 'Zarathustra'), a prophetic figure carrying with him a 'secret' message of world-historical significance. I shall postpone, for now, further discussion of the significance of this 'other' Nietzsche. In Chapter 28, however, I shall attend to the question of what light his relatively early appearance might cast on the nature and cause of the madness that engulfed him in 1889.

Meta von Salis

Nietzsche left Nice at the end of April 1884, and made a slow journey via Venice, Basel and Zurich to Sils Maria. In Zurich he met Resa's friend and fellow university student Meta von Salis (1855–1929). A handsome and intelligent member of the upper Swiss aristocracy (see Plate 28), Meta was, like Resa and their mutual friend and role model Malwida von Meysenbug, a passionate feminist dedicated to freeing women (upper-class women, at least) from their traditional housewifely bondage. In 1887 she completed her Ph.D. (a study of the medieval empress Agnes of Poitou), becoming the first Swiss woman to obtain a doctorate. She had, she said, little interest in the title for its own sake, but had been determined to complete the thesis 'in the interest of the women's question'.

Nietzsche admired Meta's aristocratic manners, particularly the fact that she spoke high German rather than Swiss dialect. She, in turn, was bowled over by him – the encounter, she said, cast a 'golden shimmer' over the rest of her life,[12] a life during which she never abandoned the cause of promoting his philosophy. (It was Meta who, in 1897, purchased the Villa Silberblick in Weimar, which provided a home for Nietzsche and Elizabeth during the final three years of his life and the site for the Nietzsche Archive.) Meta would remain a friend of Nietzsche's for the remainder of his sanity.[*] But by now, as we know, he had lost all sympathy for the guiding ideal of her life, women's emancipation. When she tried to move from Zurich to Basel to study with Burckhardt in the spring of 1885 and was rejected by that still women-excluding university, Nietzsche's unsympathetic response was to 'laugh over the subtlety of the agent provocateur: she wanted to achieve precisely what she did, a rejection, so as to increase the stock of the "agitation"'.[13] This is the man, remember, who, in his previous incarnation as Basel's dean of humanities, had fought vigorously for the *admission* of women (p. 191 above).

Third Summer in Sils Maria

Nietzsche finally arrived in Sils Maria for his third summer retreat on July 18 and would remain until September 25. Durisch greeted him off the post coach from Chur with both hands outstretched, to which Nietzsche responded with 'finally I am home again'.[14]

Durisch regarded Nietzsche as 'one of us'. For all his education, Nietzsche had, as Meta von Salis observes, 'the gift of simplicity' (the same is said of Martin Heidegger), which enabled him to enter quite naturally into the lives of uneducated country people. He empathised, Meta continues, with his landlord's worry that his ox would fall victim to the outbreak of foot-and-mouth disease and engaged in animated conversation about the coming harvest. This was the chief event in the economy of the Engadine because winter feed for the cattle was absolutely dependent on it.[15]

· Nietzsche returned to his low-ceilinged 'cave', his dark, resin-scented, pine-panelled room at the back of the second floor of the Durisch house. With the Spartan self-discipline ingrained since Pforta, he would rise well before dawn, wash himself in cold water from the

---

[*] Since Meta and her already close friend and fellow feminist Hedwig Kym were still sharing a house in 1910, there was probably a helpful absence of sexual tension between her and Nietzsche: she was appalled when it was suggested that they got on so well they should marry (Gilman (1987) p. 198).

pitcher, and after drinking some warm milk, work uninterruptedly until eleven. A two-hour walk around one of the lakes would be followed by a solitary lunch at the Alpenrose. Long after Nietzsche had been overtaken by madness, Herr Krämer, the owner of the hotel, who, like Durisch, regarded Nietzsche as 'one of us', judged that his guest had had 'no faults' save for eating too much meat.[16]

After lunch, dressed in a long, well-cut brown jacket, he would be off on an even longer walk, either alongside one of the lakes or up the Fex Valley as far as its majestic glacier. Sometimes he would be accompanied by a visitor but was more often alone, armed always with a notebook, a pencil, and a grey-green parasol to shade his eyes. Returning home between four and five, he would immediately begin work again, sustaining himself on biscuits, peasant bread, honey, sausage, ham, and fruit, with tea to drink which he brewed in the little upstairs kitchen. At 11 o'clock he would retire to bed with a notebook and pencil by his side to capture night thoughts should they arrive.

Though Nietzsche avoided most of Sils's summer residents (many of whom were convalescing from some malady, either mental or physical), he made exceptions for two women in particular. The first was an elderly Russian spinster, the Countess Mansuroff, not quite recovered from a nervous breakdown. As a not-quite-right-in-the-head former lady-in-waiting to the Russian Tsarina, aunt of the current Russian ambassador in Paris, composer, pianist, and former student of Chopin, Mansuroff appealed simultaneously to Nietzsche's taste for the offbeat, the well-bred, and the musical, so that he became extremely attached to her.

Helen Zimmern

The second woman whose company he enjoyed was Helen Zimmern (1846–1934), Jewish, born in Hamburg but transplanted to London at the age of four. Feeling sorry for a man she found 'lonely, so terribly lonely',[17] she often accompanied him on his afternoon walks.

Bilingual, intelligent, and educated, Zimmern (whom Nietzsche had met briefly in Bayreuth in 1876) was chiefly responsible for introducing Schopenhauer to the English, both by translating his works and by writing his first English-language philosophical biography. Yet another of Nietzsche's feminist friends, Zimmern told Nietzsche she wanted to introduce Malwida's *Memoirs of a Female Idealist* to the British.[18]

Nietzsche's attitude to Zimmern, who belonged to his circle of women friends for several summers in Sils, was ambiguous. On the one hand, knowing now the pain a woman holding the 'whip-hand' could inflict, he felt his masculine security threatened by this 'protagonist for women's rights'.[19] 'Curious', he writes Köselitz, 'one had defended oneself well enough against women's emancipation: yet a paradigm of the little literary woman has arrived here to join me'.[20] On the other hand, he responded very positively to her Jewishness. 'It is', he continues his letter to Köselitz, 'crazy how much this race has the "intellectual life" of Europe in its hand'. This might suggest a conspiracy-theory paranoia worthy of Bernhard Förster. In fact, however, writing a little later to his by no means philo-Semitic mother, he says, with reference to Helen's Jewishness, 'God help European understanding if one were to abandon Jewish understanding'. The letter continues by noting that the author of a favourable review of *Zarathustra* Part III 'was once again a Jew (a German would not so easily allow his sleep to be disturbed), pardon the little joke, dear mother'.[21]

Zimmern has left a touching record of Nietzsche's sympathetic identification with Countess Mansuroff. The countess, she writes,

> suffered from obsessive ideas. It was already September and had become cold, and the patient's friends ordered a coach to the hotel [Alpenrose] every day to take her to a warmer climate in Italy. Every day, however, the coach had to leave without the patient who refused to leave her room. One day Nietzsche ... said to her worried friends 'Leave her to me!' And one day at noon, when the coach had once more appeared, he suddenly appeared at the front entrance to the hotel with the sick lady who followed him like an obedient dog, even though she had otherwise always gone into a fury if anyone spoke of a departure. None of us, however, had any idea of what Nietzsche had done. The famous whip had certainly not been used...[22]

The levity of this reference to 'the whip' by a committed feminist raises an issue to which I shall return shortly.

* * *

In the middle of August, accompanied by her fellow student and feminist Clara Wildenow, Resa von Schirnhofer made the eleven-hour journey from Zurich to visit Nietzsche for a second time. Having made reservations at the Alpenrose, he collected the two women from the post-coach in Silvaplana village. One day he took Resa for his favourite walk along the eastern shore of Lake Silvaplana (see Plate 29). As they came to the pyramidal 'Zarathustra Stone', Resa recalls, a 'plethora' of 'dithyrambic ... thoughts and pictures' tumbled out with Nietzsche in a state of 'high emotional and intellectual tension'– the 'other' Nietzsche, again. But as soon as they had passed the 'zone of Zarathustra magic' his words lost their 'secretive vibrations' and he relaxed once more into his natural manner.

One day, puzzled by Nietzsche's non-appearance at the Alpenrose, Resa walked round the corner to the Durisch house to find out where he was. Since, in Nice, he had appeared to be in vibrant good health, she was terribly shocked when he eventually appeared, leaning against the frame of the half-open door to his room, with a pale and haggard face. He began straight away to speak of his sufferings. He said that he could not sleep and that as soon as he closed his eyes he saw fantastic arrays of flowers. Then, with 'dark terrified eyes' fixed on her, he asked if this could be the beginning of madness, recalling that his father has died of a brain disease. Not until later did it occur to her that the hallucinations could be the result of the chloral hydrate and other drugs, possibly including hashish, that he had obtained in Rapallo, mostly by the simple expedient of signing a prescription with 'Dr. Nietzsche', his credentials never once having been questioned. He also mentioned that he had been drinking English (Irish?) stout and pale ale.[23]

Heinrich von Stein

Another pilgrim who made his way up the magic mountain to the self-styled 'hermit of Sils Maria' was Baron Heinrich von Stein, who, though confessing he had understood no more than twelve of its sentences, had been greatly impressed by *Zarathustra*. 'Tall as a giant and slim, the face fresh and rounded, the hair blond and the eyes bright blue and wide open', as a contemporary described him,[24] this Franconian nobleman was, in appearance, the perfect Siegfried. (Von Stein was not merely handsome, he was also tragic. Having completed his Habilitation (second doctorate) under Wilhelm Dilthey in 1887, he was awarded a professorial chair at the University of Berlin only to die of a heart attack, aged thirty, the day after hearing the news.)

Von Stein's fundamental quest was to rediscover the religious, but to do so in a way that would accommodate rather than deny the materialist outlook of modern science. Having followed a study of theology with a study of Darwinian science, he completed a doctorate on aesthetics that was strongly influenced by the materialistic and optimistic philosophy of the positivist Eugen Dühring. His first book, which appeared in 1878, was entitled *The Ideal of Materialism: A Lyrical Philosophy*. Though deeply impressed by Nietzsche, von Stein belonged to the Wagnerian inner circle and had been, for a year, tutor to Wagner's son Siegfried. For him, the rediscovery of the religious lay in art, specifically in Wagner's art.

Nietzsche had great hopes of von Stein and regarded his visit to Sils as '*the* event of the summer'.[25] He called him a 'splendid example of humanity and manhood who is, through and through, comprehensible and sympathetic to me on account of the heroism of his fundamental mood'. Since the 'lyrical materialism' of von Stein's book-title is a rather good description of Nietzsche's mature position, one can understand his affinity with the young man. 'Finally, finally, a new man', he continues his letter to Overbeck, 'someone who belongs to me and has instinctive reverence for me! Admittedly still a little *trop Wagnetisé* [sic], but on account of the rational training he's had in Dühring's proximity, well prepared for me'.[26] Nietzsche felt, in other words, that the young man, following in his own footsteps, would soon grow out of his Wagnerianism and transfer allegiance wholeheartedly to himself. In von Stein's presence, Nietzsche continues, he has the clearest grasp of the '*practical* task that belongs to my life', a task he can discharge 'if only I possess enough young people [such as von Stein] of a quite definite quality'.[27] Nietzsche yearned for disciples, in other words, where by 'disciple', he told von Stein, 'I understand one who makes an unconditional vow to me'[28] – rather than to Wagner.

Nietzsche's 'practical task' was, of course, the establishment of a 'colony for free spirits', albeit conceived, here, more along the Wagnerian lines of guru and disciple than in the egalitarian and democratic manner of the Sorrento period. What he wants is to set up a Europe-wide order of men which, semi-humorously, he now calls 'the knighthood and brotherhood of the *gay* science' as well as, in Nice, 'a small, but extremely good community that will represent this belief in the gaya scienza'.[29] And he is overjoyed that, during his visit to Sils, von Stein, 'a man after my own heart', 'has of his own volition promised … to join me in Nice'.[30]

Soon, alas, von Stein turned into a great disappointment. At the end of November, Nietzsche sent him a poem, 'Hermit's Yearning', dedicated to him 'in Memory of Sils-Maria'. It begins and ends with the verse

> *O life's noonday! Solemn time!*
> *O summer garden!*
> *Unquiet happiness in standing and watching and waiting!*
> *I tarry, awaiting the friend, ready day and night:*
> *Where is the new friend? Come! It's time, it's time!*[31]

Von Stein's amazing answer to this summons (which reappears as the 'Aftersong' to *Beyond Good and Evil*) was to invite Nietzsche to join a commune of disciples dedicated to the interpretation of *Wagner's* works – which Cosima had commissioned him to index. 'Would not this', he asked, 'count as the ideal monastery?'[32] – demonstrating thereby that he spoke only the literal truth when he said he had grasped no more than twelve sentences of *Zarathustra*. Dedicated to his dead hero, von Stein remained a Wagnerian to the end. In a note written at the beginning of January 1885 Nietzsche recorded his disappointment: 'What a dim letter the good von Stein has written me…He doesn't know how to behave any more'.[33]

Reconciliation with Elizabeth in Zurich

The arrival of the 'blue-fingered-cold'[34] of September 1884 told Nietzsche that it was time for the annual flight to warmer climes. So it was that, almost the last of the migratory 'birds', he left Sils on September 24. Dragging his 'club foot' of 104 kilos of books behind him, he arrived in Zurich two days later, where he would spend a month at the Pension Neptune. The main point of the visit was to attempt yet another reconciliation with Elizabeth.

For much of 1884 he had been immersed, once again, in deep hatred. January and February letters accuse her, and his mother, of ruining his life. He writes that he has known since childhood the 'moral distance' between himself and them. And he finds it 'disgusting' to be related to people such as the 'dirty and abusive' Elizabeth, people who constantly interrupted his 'highest and most blessed feelings' with the 'base smell of the all-too-human'.[35] In April he writes Köselitz that he is making a 'complete break' with his sister and with all who take her part. Her plan to emigrate to Paraguay with the lamentable Förster he regards as good riddance to bad rubbish.[36] By mid-May, however, he thought he had managed to rise above the whole business[37] – one of his heroes was the French republican statesman the Marquis de Mirabeau, who 'was unable to forgive an insult simply because he forgot'[38] – and finally, in September, he felt ready to attempt reconciliation.

Since the strong visceral affection between the two remained intact, a reconciliation of sorts occurred almost immediately. Nietzsche wrote Franziska that she would be relieved to hear her children were getting on again, while Elizabeth reported Fritz returning to his habit of making up verses of silly doggerel about mundane matters such as buying a 'tea machine', and as being in a generally relaxed and jolly mood. And soon Nietzsche would indeed be writing letters addressed, as of old, to 'My Dear Lama'.[39] To Overbeck, on the other hand, he confided the relative superficiality of the reconciliation: 'one must bury a great deal in order to live well', he wrote, adding that 'one can't expect the old intimacy'.[40]

Nietzsche had two other objectives in Zurich. The first was to meet the Swiss writer Gottfried Keller, whose novel *Green Henry*, often regarded as the greatest Swiss novel, he admired intensely. They did indeed meet, though Keller (a liberal and a Marxist sympathiser) later told a friend '*Ich glaube dä Kerl ischt verrucht*' – Swiss dialect for 'I think the fellow's crazy'. Nietzsche's other task was to persuade the conductor of the Zurich symphony orchestra, Friedrich Hegar, whom he had first met at Tribschen in the Wagner days, to perform some of Köselitz's music – Hegar did indeed give a rehearsal performance of the overture to *The Lion of Venice*. Nietzsche never gave up on his loyal, but in the end always unsuccessful, attempts to establish 'Peter Gast's' career. It belongs to the 'office of a friend', he wrote Overbeck, to see that one's friend does not have to beg.[41]

Helene Druskowitz

An important encounter, during Nietzsche's stay in Zurich, was with Helene Drusko-witz, yet another member of Malwida von Meysenbug's circle of feminist admirers. Born in Vienna in 1856, Druskowitz completed her doctorate in the University of Zurich's philosophical faculty in 1878 at the age of twenty-two, only the second woman to receive a doctorate from (Section I of) that faculty. In 1884 she published *Three English Writers*, a study of Joanna Baillie (a playwright), Elisabeth Barret Browning and George Eliot. Druskowitz and Nietzsche went on long philosophical walks together, leading Nietzsche to describe his 'new friend' to Elizabeth as a 'noble and honest' person who, 'of all the women I know, has had by far the most serious engagement with my books, and not without profit'.[42] It is therefore no surprise that Helene was one of the privileged few to receive, the following year, a copy of the privately printed Part IV of *Zarathustra*.

Alas, the mutual admiration did not last long. Describing her enthusiasm for Nietzsche's philosophy as a 'passion of the moment', Druskowitz returned the book with a critical letter which Nietzsche described to her as at least 'honest, if not exactly kind or insightful and not particularly "modest"'.[43] In 1886 she published a book, *The Quest for a Substitute for Religion*, that was highly critical of *Zarathustra*. In February 1887, the book came to Nietzsche's attention: 'it appears', he wrote Malwida, affecting injured innocence,

> that a Fräulein Druskowitz has written a precious piece of literary gossip against my son Zarathustra: it seems that through some kind of a crime I have turned the feminine pen against my breast – that's O.K.! For as my friend Malvida [sic] says "I'm even worse than Schopenhauer".[44]

By September it was all over with Druskowitz: using his familiar, patronising (but also defensive) diminutive for women with the temerity to stray into his domain of letters, he writes that the 'little literary-goose' is 'anything but my "pupil"'.[45]

As she got older, Druskowitz's feminism became ever more radical, so that among her literary remains was found a pamphlet, *The Male as Logical and Moral Impossibility and Curse of the World*, containing sentences such as 'the male is an intermediate stage between the human being and the animal' (a direct reversal of Schopenhauer's infamous sentence (p. 288 above)). Shortly after Nietzsche's collapse Druskowitz suffered her own mental breakdown and was herself forced into a mental institution where, continuing to write, she remained until her death in 1918.[46]

Second Winter in Nice

From Zurich, ever on the hunt for a new 'health experiment', Nietzsche travelled to Menton on the French Riviera near the Italian border (he always referred to it under its Italian name of 'Mentone'), arriving on November 9. He had received a recommendation for the German-run Pension des Étrangers. But though he found the landscape superb and the town pleasantly quiet in comparison with Nice, he blamed his poor health, again at an especially low ebb, on its lack of wind. He had, moreover, already designated Nice as the site of the 'colony' he expected soon to be up and running. And so he returned to the familiar environment of the Pension de Genève, the invigorating mistral, and the clear skies of Nice. Arriving on November 28, he would remain until April 8, 1885.

Timing his arrival badly, however, Nietzsche was met by a uniquely hard winter, with below-zero temperatures and a heavy snowfall. January saw the worst storm in fifty years, a storm which inflicted severe damage on the famous avenue of palms lining the Promenade des Anglais.[47] Nonetheless, intermittently clear skies inspired the creative mood out of which Nietzsche completed the 'divine blasphemy' of *Zarathustra*'s final part. Meanwhile, a mysterious Dutchman supplied Nietzsche with a strange white powder – probably cocaine – for his health problems and the respectful but lugubrious Paul Lanzky arrived to stay in the same pension for – to Nietzsche's dismay – three months. Increasingly, this dismal and not very bright person got on his nerves. 'He sighs a lot' and 'deprives me of solitude without providing me with company',[48] Nietzsche complained to his mother.

After he had finally departed, Lanzky's lugubriousness led Nietzsche to send him some advice on being cheerful: 'the cheerfulness [*Heiterkeit* – *heiter* means both 'clear' and 'cheerful'] of the "sky" depends on there being very many good things to do: and that life is too short to do them all'.[49] This reveals, perhaps, something important about Nietzsche's psychology: that, like many high achievers, his obsessive fixation on his 'task' and 'goal' had something to do with fear of boredom, fear of having more time on his hands than meaningful activity to fill it with.

Fourth Summer in Sils Maria

Nietzsche spent most of April and May of 1885 in Venice which, in spite of the humidity, which he thought very bad for his health,[50] he nonetheless loved – not merely on account of Köselitz's useful presence, and the shade provided by its endless maze of narrow alleyways, but also, one imagines, because in that carriage-less city, there was no chance of the half-blind professor being run over in the street. This time, however, he loathed the apartment Köselitz had found him, so it was with relief that on June 6 he left for Sils.

A high point of this fourth summer in Sils was a visit by Countess Mansuroff's piano teacher, Adolf Ruthardt, who journeyed from Geneva to give her composition lessons. During his stay he gave a recital in the Alpenrose on the excellent piano Mansuroff had shipped in from Chur especially for the occasion. He played Liszt's transcription of Bach's A minor organ fugue, a Chopin nocturne, and Schumann's *Kreisleriana*. Though Nietzsche and Ruthardt strongly disagreed on Schumann's merits – Nietzsche now thought him formless, romantic slush – they went for walks together and got on well. Ruthardt has left a vivid description of Nietzsche in this forty-first year of his life:

Above middle height, slender, well-formed, with a stance that was erect but not stiff, his gestures harmonious, calm and economical: the almost black hair, the thick Vercingetorix moustache,* his light-coloured but distinguished-looking suit of the best cut and fit, made

* Or, as we might say, 'Asterix moustache' – Vercingetorix was a Gallic leader and thorn in the side of the Romans.

him so little like a German scholar that he rather called to mind a Southern French noble-man or an Italian or Spanish higher officer in civilian clothes. His noble features expressed deep seriousness, but by no means the sombre, angular, demonic expression that has been attributed to him in pictures and busts.[51]

As well as working on *Beyond Good and Evil*, Nietzsche was, during this summer in Sils, concerned to gather his earlier works into a unity by reissuing them with new introductions. Two of these introductions would be for *Human, All-Too-Human*, which was now to absorb *Assorted Opinions and Maxims* and *The Wanderer and His Shadow* as a second volume. For the first month, he had an older woman, Louise Röder-Wiederhold, yet another of the Zurich feminists, acting as amanuensis. Considering, he wrote Resa von Schirnhofer, that she was 'baptised in the blood of 1848' (the emancipatory uprising that led to hopes of, *inter alia*, women's emancipation), she bore his 'horrifying, anti-democratic' views, and particularly his views on 'woman as such', 'with the patience of an angel'.[52] She must, however, have found it more difficult than Nietzsche suggests, since she cried a lot and jiggled her legs in a way he considered unladylike and which eventually got on his nerves. In the end he was glad to see her go.[53]

It is during this 1885 stay in Sils that Emily Fynn and her daughter, also Emily, make their first appearance in Nietzsche's correspondence. But since, at the beginning of his stay, he is already eagerly anticipating the arrival of 'my two English ladies', and since they were the inseparable companions of Countess Mansuroff, whom he had met the previous sum-mer, it is probable that the friendship dates from the summer of 1884. (In fact, as is obvious from the surname, Emily Fynn was an elderly *Irish* woman who had settled in Geneva and had somehow acquired excellent German.)[54] Resa von Schirnhofer reports that Emily was the centre of Nietzsche's summer 'circle' of women. Like almost everyone else visiting Sils, Emily was convalescing from some (unspecified) ailment. And like Nietzsche, she had lost a sister, though, as he put it to her, to death rather than to anti-Semitism.[55] Nietzsche had a strong affection for Emily, calling her a 'noble and tender soul',[56] and seems to have regarded her as something of a surrogate mother. A committed Catholic, she told Resa von Schirnhofer that, with tears in his eyes, Nietzsche had begged her not to read his books, since they contained much that would hurt her feelings.[*, 57] A letter Emily wrote Nietzsche's mother in 1890 discloses the relaxed and charming relation between the trio. Nietzsche, she recalls,

was very graciously interested in my daughter's paintings, and always said that she ought to paint something ugly in addition, in order to heighten, even more, the beauty of her [alpine] flowers. And then, one morning, he brought her, as a model, a live, hopping toad, which he himself had caught; and he greatly enjoyed his successful prank! In return we sent him after a few days what looked like a jar of jam, but as he was carefully opening it, grasshoppers sprang out at him![58]

---

* Nietzsche defends the supposed 'obscurity' of his 'dangerous' books on the grounds that he wanted them to be unintelligible to 'old maids of both sexes' in order not to 'corrupt' them (GS 381). It cannot be emphasised too strongly that, for all his anti-'herd' rhetoric – which, like Zarathustra's 'Last Man' speech, has the specific purpose of arousing the free spirit's slumbering sense of differ-ence and distinction – Nietzsche held that 'old maids *should always form the majority*', and that he valued and, on a personal level, sometimes *loved* them.

Nietzsche and His Feminist Friends

I should like, for a moment, to interrupt the narrative to reflect on the paradoxical nature of Nietzsche's relationships with women. As we have seen, after the pain he suffered at the hands of that 'self-willed', 'whip'-cracking, 'masculine', 'pseudo girl',[59] Lou Salomé, his previously sympathetic stance towards women's emancipation – at least so far as it concerned women's access to higher education – reversed itself. From the end of 1882 (when the famous 'whip' remark first appears in the notebooks)[60] he became unrelentingly opposed to the feminist movement, a fact he made no attempt to disguise: I am the movement's 'big bad wolf', he kept repeating.

Nietzsche's views on women are not merely offensive to modern opinion. They were offensive, too, to progressive opinion in the nineteenth century, including of course the opinion of many educated women.[61] Already in 1869 John Stuart Mill had written his seminal *On the Subjection of Women*, arguing for female equality. Yet the extraordinary thing about the friendships and acquaintances Nietzsche formed from 1883 onwards is that, with the exception of Countess Mansuroff and Emily Fynn, all of them were not merely women – in Sils and Nice Nietzsche generally avoided the male professors who came his way – but *feminist* women: Malwida von Meysenbug, Meta von Salis, Resa von Schirnhofer, Helen Zimmern, Louise Röder-Wiederhold, Helene Druskowitz and others. This paradoxical fact raises two questions. First, why was it that, notwithstanding their feminism, feminist women were attracted to Nietzsche? And second, why was Nietzsche, notwithstanding his anti-feminism, attracted to feminist women?

In the early years of the twentieth century there appeared the unlikely phenomenon of a Nietzsche-inspired feminist movement – a movement which remains, to this day, alive and well. What attracted women to Nietzsche's philosophy was the coincidence between his message of liberation and their own. To reconcile their feminism with the apparently anti-feminist elements in Nietzsche's philosophy, Nietzschean feminists deployed one of two basic strategies:[62] they either held it superficial to read Nietzsche as an anti-feminist – his attack, Valentine de Saint Pont insisted in 1912, was not on women but on 'the feminine', something which could appear as easily in men as in women[63] – or they admitted and rejected his anti-feminism but held that his basic, emancipatory message was nonetheless true and important.

For women who actually knew Nietzsche, the first of these strategies – the 'creative misreading' strategy, we might call it – was not available, since he admitted, went out of his way to *emphasise*, his anti-feminism, reducing Louise Röder-Wiederhold, as we saw, to tears. To Elizabeth he wrote gleefully in May 1885 that 'on all of those who rhapsodize about the "emancipation of women" it has slowly, slowly dawned that I am the "big bad wolf" for them'. In Zurich, he continues (basing his report on Köselitz's information), 'there is great fury against me among the female students'. Though this circle included his good friends Resa von Schirnhofer and Meta von Salis, he concludes the letter with an expression of gratitude that the feminists were beginning to get the point: 'Finally! And how many such "finally's" do I still have to wait for!'[64]

Since the creative misreading strategy was not available to them, Nietzsche's feminist friends were thus forced, at least implicitly, to treat his anti-feminism as a personal quirk and error rather than an essential part of his philosophy. This is surely the force of Helen Zimmern's joking dismissal of 'the famous whip' (p. 392 above).

That Resa von Schirnhofer took the same line is suggested by the way she reports and elaborates on a 'favourite thought' Nietzsche communicated to her in July 1884, the thought that

> human beings know only the smallest part of their possibilities, which corresponds to aphorism 336 of *Dawn* with its final sentence 'Who knows to what we *could* be driven by circumstances!', aphorism 9 of *The Gay Science*, 'We all have hidden gardens and plantations...', and aphorism 274 of *Beyond Good and Evil*...'Fortunate coincidences are necessary...for the higher human being "to erupt"...Mostly this does *not* happen, and in every corner of the earth people sit waiting...'[65]

One can see here, I think, Resa reading Nietzsche's philosophy in a manner designed to emphasise his message of personal liberation and self-realisation while quietly ignoring the fact that it is addressed to 'men only'.

Meta von Salis deploys the strategy of separating the anti-feminism from the essential philosophy more explicitly. Noting Nietzsche's 'increasing sharpness of tone' on the 'women question' in the post–*Gay Science* (i.e., post-Lou) years, she says that it never made her cross or indignant since 'a man of Nietzsche's breadth of vision and sureness of instinct has the right to get things wrong in one instance'. Pointing out the mistake 'more on his behalf than on ours', she identifies its source as the 'shameful fact that what he says is still accurate with regard to the majority of women'. In other words, Nietzsche made a reasonable, but in fact false, inductive generalisation from the run of contemporary womanhood to 'the eternal feminine' and so failed to see that, while 'the woman of the future who realises a higher ideal of power and beauty in harmonious coexistence has not yet arrived', she *will* arrive. 'God be praised', she concludes, 'for the fate which allowed me to see and reverence, beyond the ephemeral significance of the women question, elite human beings – men and women'.[66] In short, the aristocratic Meta, every bit as anti-democratic as Nietzsche, makes just one adjustment to his philosophy: the future belongs to 'superwomen' as well as 'supermen'.

Concerning the second question, the question of why the chauvinist Nietzsche was attracted to feminist women, one needs to attend, I think, to *Zarathustra*'s conception of woman as man's 'playmate', his 'recreation' when he comes home from the serious, masculine business of 'war' (p. 373 above); someone, as they say, who 'brings out his inner child'. 'Play', we have seen, is an important element in Nietzsche's relations with women: the toad joke with the Fynns, the silly verse sessions with Elizabeth and Resa. What needs to be remembered, however, is that, right up until the end – when he wrote her love letters – Nietzsche's ideal woman was Cosima Wagner and his ideal marriage, therefore, that of the Wagners. Here, the possibilities of play take on a much wider scope: play can include not merely jars of crickets but also the play of ideas, both verbal and musical. With Cosima, it will be remembered, four-handed piano playing and long philosophical conversations were major elements in their relationship (pp. 109, 112 above).

Putting these facts together, one thing becomes obvious: for a man such as Wagner or himself, a woman capable of being his ideal 'playmate' would *have* to possess a high level of intelligence and education, would *have* be someone, such as Cosima – or Lou – who *did* read his books, rather than like Emily Fynn, whom he begged not to. The higher type of warrior's 'recreation' cannot consist *solely* of toad jokes and silly verses since, on a daily basis, that would become boring. One can surmise, therefore, that, beneath his confusion, Nietzsche never really lost his initial disposition in favour of access to higher education for suitably gifted women. What terrified him was women's access to power, a monstrous regime of women such as Lou: 'women are always less civilized than men', he remarks. 'At the base of their souls they are wild'.[67] This I think is what lies behind the often-repeated sentiment that 'One wants the emancipation of women and achieves thereby the emasculation of men'.[68] To be sure, he himself observes, apropos 'the labour question', that 'If one wants slaves it is foolish to educate them to be masters',[69] since one sows thereby the seeds of social discontent and even revolution. But it is a by no means unusual human failing for insights in one domain to fail to be carried over into another, particularly when strong emotions are involved.

The Försters

From early in 1885 it became clear that nothing could prevent Elizabeth from marrying the execrable Förster. The wedding of these two rabid Wagnerians occurred in Naumburg on May 22 of that year – the deceased composer's birthday – after which they honeymooned in Tautenburg. Elizabeth had wanted Fritz as best man, but in spite of the Zurich reconciliation nothing would have persuaded him to give such a seal of approval to her marriage to a jingoistic, anti-Semitic street brawler. Walking a fine line between publicly endorsing the marriage and destroying the reconciliation, he opened a superficially friendly correspondence with Förster and sent his print of Dürer's *Knight, Death and Devil* as a (rather weird) wedding present. Resisting sustained pressure to invest money in the projected racially pure Paraguayan colony of *Nueva Germania* by investing in a plot of land (money he would certainly have lost), he remarked that such a project would be unsuitable for a 'dyed-in-the-wool European and anti-anti-Semite'[70] such as himself. And though he had read Förster's book evangelising on behalf of colonisation – *German Colonies in the Upper La Plata Region. Results of Extensive Tests, Practical Work and Journeys with a Map of Paraguay Drawn and Revised by Myself* – he expressed to both the Försters and his mother dire misgivings over the suitability of a middle-class German woman to the company of illiterate farmers and a life of breaking in the jungle. He predicted, absolutely correctly, that Paraguay's lack of proper infrastructure and bureaucracy, as well as the stranglehold Argentina had over its access to the sea, would render timber export, the intended economic base of the colony, impossible. He further suggested that an educated man like Förster would be better employed setting up an 'independent educational institution' that would be an alternative to Germany's 'state-slave-drilling schools'.[71]

Nothing, however, would deter the colonists from their ill-considered and ill-fated enterprise. Reluctantly, therefore, as autumn announced the time for the annual migration from Sils, the need to farewell his sister took Nietzsche off to Germany for a month and a half, where he divided his time between Naumburg and Leipzig (an hour's train journey apart). On October 28 he had what would prove to be the final meeting with Elizabeth before his mental collapse. She sailed from Hamburg on February 15, 1886.

The 'Schmeitzner Misère'

Apart from saying goodbye to his sister, Nietzsche had a second, pressing reason for returning to Germany – the urgent need to do something about his dire publishing situation. The first pangs of dissatisfaction with his publisher occurred, as we saw, in early 1883, when he realised that Schmeitzner's anti-Semitic activities were delaying publication of his works, which, he feared, would themselves be branded as anti-Semitic. The real 'Schmeitzner misère',[72] however, began in April 1884, when it became clear that the publisher was on the verge of bankruptcy. For several reasons, this threw Nietzsche into a state of great agitation. First, with Schmeitzner going out of business, he would become a writer without a publisher. Second, he had lent Schmeitzner 7,000 marks to help set up his business, the loss of which, in his straitened circumstances, would be a disaster. Third, he wanted Schmeitzner to release the rights to the works he had published (*Human, All-Too-Human, Assorted Opinions and Maxims, The Wanderer and His Shadow*, and Parts I–III of *Zarathustra*) in order to relaunch them as a unified body of work with new introductions, something for which Schmeitzner would, of course, demand payment from the new publisher. And fourth, he wanted Schmeitzner to release the unsold copies of the first editions of those works so that they could be rebound with the new introductions so as to constitute their second editions.

To recover his money, Nietzsche started legal proceedings, conducted first by a lawyer uncle and finally by a clever Leipzig lawyer named Kaufmann who, after many dates for payment had come and gone, finally managed to extract over 5,000 marks from Schmeitzner (or rather from his father, who had decided to guarantee his son's debts) in November 1885. On receiving the money, after paying off some book bills, Nietzsche insisted that he, and not his mother, should pay for a properly inscribed gravestone to be laid on his father's grave[73] – in order, surely, to erase her remark that he was a 'disgrace to his father's grave' (p. 353 above).

As far as the question of copyrights and unsold books was concerned, Schmeitzner attempted several, in Nietzsche's view, dirty tricks. One was a plan to sell his whole business, including Nietzsche's works, to a convicted Leipzig pornographer and (far worse) 'social democrat',[74] Albert Erlecke. Another was to demand, as Nietzsche saw it, an exorbitant sum for the same deal from the more respectable Leipzig publisher Hermann Credner.

As good fortune would have it, Nietzsche ran into his first publisher, Ernst Fritzsch (pp. 124, 190 above), in a Leipzig street in the middle of June 1886.[75] Fritzsch was back in business and eager to re-establish a professional relationship with Nietzsche. It soon became clear, in fact, as Nietzsche wrote Overbeck, that

> he lays great value on having in his publishing house not merely the complete Wagner [prose works] but also the complete Nietzsche (a neighbourliness I feel really good about since Wagner was the only, or at least the first, person to have any idea of what I was on about).[76]

Fritzsch opened negotiations with Schmeitzner, which dragged on for some time – Schmeitzner's demands being somewhat justified by the fact that he possessed nearly 10,000 unsold Nietzsche books including, in the case of *Zarathustra*, out of a print run of 1,000 copies in each case, 915 copies of Part I, 907 of Part II, and 937 of Part III. It was thus not until August 5 that Fritzsch was able to telegraph triumphantly, 'finally in possession', and Nietzsche was at last able to celebrate the severance of all relations with Schmeitzner.

Third Winter in Nice

Leaving Leipzig on November 1, 1885, Nietzsche had a notion of deviating from his usual migratory pattern. His first stop was Munich, where he spent a couple of days with Reinhart von Seydlitz, who was doing a thriving business selling Japanese interior design (the craze for 'Japonism' was infecting Van Gogh in Paris in the same year). Von Seydlitz, still president of the Munich Wagner Society, was the only one of Nietzsche's post-university friends with whom he used the familiar *du*. With his 'merry, pretty and young' Hungarian wife, Irene – she would have been his own perfect 'life companion', Nietzsche wrote Elizabeth enviously – he felt so relaxed as almost to be able to call her *du* as well.[77] With Irene he travelled to Florence, where he was delighted to find the chief astronomer with a copy of *Human, All-Too-Human* by his side. A quick trip to Lanzky's hotel in nearby Vallombrosa persuaded him, for unclear reasons, to abandon his plan of spending the winter there (possibly it was the thought of months of undiluted Lanzky that proved too much), and so, on November 11, 'the Hamlet-like mole of Nice'[78] found himself, via Genoa, once more in his familiar winter quarters. Once again the Nice air had triumphed over flirtations with alternatives.

Flirtation with the unfamiliar had the effect of opening Nietzsche's eyes to the delights of the familiar. His initial Francophobic dislike of the place changed into something like love. To the Försters, making their final preparations for emigration, he wrote at the beginning of January that it was as if he was seeing Nice 'for the first time', his eyes suddenly opened to its 'fine air and tender colours'.[79] He particularly loves, another letter tells them, the St. Jean peninsula with its 'young soldiers playing boules, fresh roses and geraniums in the hedges, and everything green and warm' (in December!). 'I drank [he adds] three large glasses of sweet *vin ordinaire* in your honour and was almost *a bitzeli betrunken* [Swiss-German for 'a bit drunk']'. Unable to resist a dig at his brother-in-law's racial views, he ends the letter by saying that the banning of garlic is 'the only form of anti-Semitism which smells good to your cosmopolitan rhinoceros – sorry!'[80] (Evidently some nineteenth-century stereotype associated Jews with garlic.)

Initially Nietzsche returned to the tried and true Pension de Genève, with its excellent Swiss cuisine, but dissatisfaction with his room led him to move, three days later, to cheaper accommodation in a large establishment on the Rue St. François de Paule 26, 'second floor, on the left', as he wrote at the top of letters. Though the room was cold and he often preferred to eat at the Genève, he enjoyed the stunning view from his window over houses, forest, and sea in the distance and, at his feet, the 'Square des Phocéens'. Nietzsche loved the 'incredible cosmopolitanism of this combination of words', English, French, and Greek ('Phocéens' refers to the Greek tribe who founded Nice). 'Something victorious, and pan-European sounds out of the name' he wrote Köselitz, 'something very comforting which says to me "Here you are in your right place"'.[81] Continuing the same theme a few days later in a letter designed to induce Köselitz to abandon Venice for Nice, Nietzsche asks him to consider the beautiful concept 'Nice' (the name is Greek and refers to a victory).* – It's a 'cosmopolis', if only Europe would one day become one! One is nearer to the fine French spirit but yet not too near...my street with the great Italian theatre is a superb example of the Italian style...the orchestra in Monte Carlo is directed by a German...there are many trattoria where one can eat as well as in the [Venice hotel] Panada (actually better and cheaper)...and a good selection of Russians and Poles.[82]

A melting pot indeed.

Nietzsche's Cosmopolitanism

As we saw (p. 117 above), German nationalism was intrinsic to the outlook of the later Wagner. Though given strong impetus by direct experience of the horrors of warfare on the Franco-Prussian battlefields, Nietzsche's turn to cosmopolitanism really began with the rejection of the all-too-human side of Wagnerianism in *Human, All-Too-Human*. There, it will be remembered (pp. 266–7 above), he extols the idea of European union as a way of overcoming warfare, and sees European unification as a prelude to the globalisation of European culture, Europe's colonisation of the entire world. In *The Gay Science* he admires the pan-Europeanism of the medieval Church (what he admires is the 'Roman' rather than the 'Catholic' in it) and praises Napoleon for striving to bring about 'one Europe'.[83] In the about-to-appear *Beyond Good and Evil* he praises the developing appearance of a 'European' type of person detached from all 'national feeling',[84] and says that it is time to abandon petty, nationalistic politics for 'grand' (i.e., global) politics. We must move to the latter, he says presciently, since the 'future of humanity' is at stake.[85]

For Nietzsche, 'European' always means 'classical'. He never escaped the idealisation of the Greeks that permeated his training as a philologist. In *Assorted Opinions and Maxims* the classical ideals of 'harmony', 'proportion', 'strength', 'mildness', 'repose' and 'an involuntary, inborn moderation' are to form the 'all-embracing golden ground' on which the future is to be constructed.[86] The 'golden' moments in modern history are the Renaissance and Napoleon, in other words, the attempted 'rebirths' of the classical ideal. That he repeatedly calls Christianity 'oriental'[87] indicates his view that it was an alien invasion and must be excluded from any truly 'European' revival.

The revival of Western culture is, then, a matter of rediscovering classical values, and, of course, reinterpreting them so that they make sense in the modern world (only derision would greet a return to togas and sandals). As I suggested in the last chapter, it is important to keep Nietzsche's classicism in mind as a corrective to the impression he sometimes gives that he is a 'decisionist', that he adheres to the – as I suggested, self-undermining – thesis that ultimate values are a matter of ungrounded, and hence arbitrary, *choice*. Really, it seems to me, this is not at all what he believes. When he asks us to 'give style to' our characters and culture, what he means is *classical* style. It follows, then, that though Nietzsche speaks of the type of person he hopes the future will bring as (like himself) a 'nomad',[88] he does not mean by this a rootless wanderer. He means, rather, someone who, like himself, is

---

* The name 'Nice', 'Nicaea' in Greek, is based on 'Nike', the goddess of victory. Nice was founded by the Greeks in about 350 BC.

rooted within a homeland which, because it is 'supra-national',[89] allows easy mobility across national boundaries. This homeland is 'the European', that is to say, 'the classical'.

Were one to ask just what is so special about classical values, I think Nietzsche would answer that classical values are the only ones that secure either an individual or a community against 'anarchy' and 'barbarism', always, for him, terms of final condemnation.[90] Only classical, that is, Apollonian, values rescued the Greeks from the Dionysian 'barbarism' of their neighbours;[91] only classical values will rescue us from the anarchic 'barbarism' of modernity's unbridled liberalism. Classical values are the only ones that promote integration, wholeness, and so persistence, the only ones that promote, in a word, 'life'. Classical values are, in sum, a matter not of taste but of survival. The opponent of classicism, 'romanticism', is thus 'anti-life', 'decadent'; ultimately, as he will argue in his final creative year, the 'will to death'.

One can see from Nietzsche's cosmopolitanism – closely connected, of course, to his anti-anti-Semitism, since 'rootless cosmopolitanism' was, well into the twentieth century, a familiar anti-Semitic slur – the precise character of his loathing of his brother-in-law. It was not Förster's colonialism he objected to: on the contrary, Nietzsche was all for Europe colonising the entire world. What he objected to was the nationalistic and racist character of Förster's colonialism. What Nietzsche wanted was *European* not *German* colonialism, a *Nueva Europa* rather than a *Nueva Germania*. And what he wanted was colonisation not by the decadent European culture of the present age but by a *revived and unified* European culture – which is why he told Förster that, rather than going to Paraguay, he should found an alternative high school, education being always, for Nietzsche, together with art and religion, the key to the revival of a culture.

Publishing *Beyond Good and Evil*

In mid-January 1886, Nietzsche approached Hermann Credner (the same Leipzig publisher who had engaged in fruitless negotiations with Schmeitzner) with a view to publishing *Beyond Good and Evil*, now well on its way to completion. Initially he thought of it as a second volume of *Dawn*, but by March, as it neared completion, he saw that it needed to be presented as an independent work.[92]

Meanwhile, however, Credner had read some of *Dawn* and, finding it shocking, severed all communication with Nietzsche. Another approach in April, to the Carl Dunker Verlag in Berlin, was no more successful, even though, in desperation, Nietzsche offered to forego all royalties[93] – desperation since the whole point of his books was, as he wrote in the midst of the Schmeitzner affair, to fashion 'fishing rods'[94] with which to catch people for his cause. Accordingly, now in possession of the balance of the money recovered from Schmeitzner, he decided to publish the work at his own expense, with the printing to be done by the Leipzig firm of Naumann.

* * *

Leaving Nice at the end of April 1886 for a short visit to Venice, Nietzsche spent most of May keeping his lonely mother company in Naumburg. From there he moved to Leipzig to take personal charge of the printing of *Beyond Good and Evil*. In Leipzig he had a few sad, final meetings with Rohde, who had foolishly moved from Tübingen, where he had been very happy, to take up a chair in Leipzig, their joint alma mater, only to quarrel almost immediately with his new colleagues. Nietzsche found him distracted and homesick for Tübingen, with no understanding of his current philosophy. Rohde, in turn, confided to Overbeck that he could no longer recognise his one-time best friend, finding it 'as if he came from a land where no one else lives'.[95] Leaving Leipzig on June 27, Nietzsche arrived in Sils Maria three days later for his fifth summer retreat.

Beyond Good and Evil appeared on August 4, 1886. Blaming his terrible sales of previous works on Schmeitzner's increasing reluctance to distribute review copies to literary opinion-moulders, Nietzsche asked Naumann to distribute the exceptionally large number of sixty-six complimentary copies not merely to the usual suspects (plus a few new ones such as Helen Zimmern) but also to the editors of twenty-five journals and newspapers in Leipzig, Dresden, Berlin, Munich, Hamburg, Cologne, Vienna, Zurich and London, where copies were sent to the editors of the *Atheneum*, the *Academy* and the *Westminster Review*.[96]

'Dynamite', 'Junker Philosophy', 'Pathological'

Thanks to this confetti of complimentaries, *Beyond Good and Evil* received quite a number of early reviews. Since book reviewers, then as now, tended to be of a left-liberal persuasion, collectively, the reviews represented Nietzsche's first major collision with the liberal opinion of his day. Nearly all were hostile, though some raised issues that, to this day, remain central to an evaluation of the work.

The earliest was by Joseph Widmann (a friend of Brahms) in the Swiss journal *Der Bund* for September 1886.[97] Borrowing Nietzsche's own image,[98] he calls the book 'dynamite' and says that it should be marked with a 'black flag'. The reference is to the flag that marked the stacks of dynamite used to blast the Gotthard railway tunnel (one of the first uses of the explosive in construction work), completed five years previously at the cost of 214 lives. Widmann comments, shrewdly, that the book is a brave attempt to find a way out of the traditional duality between morality and reality, but complains that it too often sacrifices philosophical rigour for the sake of a good turn of phrase. Its reactionary views on women and democracy are, Widmann asserts, dead wrong.

Gustav Glagau in Berlin's *Deutsche Literaturzeitung* for October 1886 complains that the book represents a quite different sort of 'free-spiritedness' to that of the 'democratic enlightenment' of the last hundred years (the phrase is taken from Nietzsche's own preface) and that one is offered nothing one can accept or reject but merely snippets from someone's worldview. Glagau also complains that rather than offering rational arguments, it tries to 'numb' one into submission with repeated hammer-blows of rhetoric to the head.

P. Michaelis, in Berlin's *Nationalzeitung* for December 4, 1886,[99] says that the work is 'worth careful consideration if only to combat it'. At times, Michaelis suggests, the work reads like a satire on the 'arrogant demands of the reactionary aristocracy', though, in reality, it is no satire but rather 'a symptom of a definite direction in modern life'. Nietzsche is 'the philosophical defender of the aristocratic current of our time', providing us with 'the philosophy of the Junker aristocracy' (Bismarck's class). Nietzsche's principle, Michaelis continues, is 'unlimited devotion towards those above, unlimited scorn towards those below'. 'Religion is an anachronism, a superseded standpoint, but a useful device for controlling the herd'. And 'morality is only for the rabble'. The watchword of the masters is 'might is right'. What reconciles one to the book, though, is the 'impudence' with which its author expresses his thoughts. (Nietzsche called this a 'good though hostile' review, 'the most creditable recapitulation of my path of thinking'. 'That it repulses the reviewer', he adds, 'doesn't bother me at all'.)[100]

Heinrich Welti's review in Zurich's *Neue Zürcher Zeitung* for December 13, 1886, though it does call the work 'a rare and unique book', is mostly flim-flam designed to disguise the fact that the reviewer is completely out of his depth – one suspects he wrote the review as a chore rather than choice. Nietzsche later complained of the incompetence of most of his reviewers.

Johannes Sclaf in the *Allgemeine Deutsche Universitätszeitung* for January 1887 claims, rather amazingly, that 'what gives backbone to the aphorisms is the not particularly original idea of the will to power and "revaluation of all values"', and goes on to complain that the author exaggerates the value of individuality, exhibiting the sick self-consciousness of those who isolate themselves from society, even though they cannot exist without it. The author, he concludes, wants to create either fools or dangerous parasites.

An anonymous review in Breslau's *Nord und Süd* for May 1887 insightfully calls the work an interesting attempt to build an 'ethic' on 'the will to power as a fundamental moral principle'. G. von Gizycki, in Volume 13 of the *Deutsche Rundschau* for the same year, describes the work as 'bordering on the pathological', while Thomas Frey, in *Antisemitic Letters* for December 1887, referring to Nietzsche's remarks on the 'Jewish question', thanks God that only half a dozen people will ever read the book.

A final reaction to the book occurs in a letter to Overbeck in which Rohde describes his old friend's book as the after-dinner product of someone who has drunk too much wine, 'almost childish' in its philosophical and political views, the totality a mere point of view resting on nothing but a mood. The work's point of view is treated as the only possible one, even though in his next work Nietzsche will surely inhabit its opposite. 'I can't take these eternal metamorphoses seriously any more',[101] Rohde writes, revealing the real source of his estrangement: Nietzsche's abandonment of the standpoint he, Rohde, had defended so bravely and passionately against Wilamovitz (pp. 150–1, 156 above), he takes as a personal betrayal.

What we now need to determine is whether any of these reviews and reactions does anything like justice to the book.

21

Beyond Good and Evil

The Heart of Darkness

WHAT IS the fundamental aim of *Beyond Good and Evil*? As we shall see, the work develops a distinction (greatly expanded in the *Genealogy of Morals*) between the 'slave' morality (a morality of 'good' versus '*evil*'), introduced by Christianity, and the ancient world's '*master*' morality (a morality of 'good' versus '*bad*') that preceded it. And so what the title tells us is that we must advance 'beyond' the 'good and evil' morality that we have grown up in. Presumably we are also told that we must recover some version of the 'good and bad' morality. We need, the title tells us, a moral revolution.

The subtitle, *Prelude to a Philosophy of the Future*, tells us the same thing in a different way. To understand it one has to notice its double reference to Wagner, the composer who called *Das Rheingold* a 'Prelude' to the remainder of the *Ring* cycle, and his music-dramas, collectively, the 'artwork of the future'.* As well as making clear Nietzsche's continuing power-struggle with his former 'Master', the function of the subtitle is to identify *Beyond Good and Evil* as a 'preview', a brief 'prelude' to a future work which will actually *be* the 'philosophy of the future'. A letter written just after the appearance of *Beyond Good and Evil* makes this clear: he is now planning, Nietzsche writes Elizabeth, to spend the next four years producing a 'four-volume masterwork with the fearsome title of *The Will to Power. Attempt at a Revaluation of All Values*'.[1] 'Revaluation of all values' is Nietzsche's term for 'moral revolution'. So, again, what we need is a moral revolution. Why should this be so?

Nietzsche repeatedly describes his book in the darkest of terms: the work is, he writes on its completion, 'something completely terrible and repellent',[2] 'a terrifying book . . . very black and squid-like'. In it, he continues, he has 'grasped something "by the horns": quite certainly it's not a bull'.[3]

---

* Wagner set out his revolutionary artistic programme in an 1849 pamphlet entitled 'The Artwork of the Future'. The work is dedicated to Ludwig Feuerbach and clearly derives its title from Feuerbach's *Principles of a Philosophy of the Future* (1843). Indirectly, therefore, *Beyond Good and Evil*'s subtitle comes from Feuerbach.

The 'squid-like' thing *Beyond Good and Evil* 'grasps' is, it seems to me, modern, that is to say, Darwinian science. As we shall see, Nietzsche's concept of the 'will to power', which comes in *Beyond Good and Evil* to a prominence it possesses in no other published work, is conceived as a modification of Darwinism. What was devastatingly problematic for the late nineteenth century in general, and for Nietzsche in particular, was not merely the 'death of God' but rather the fact that what takes the place of divine providence is 'survival of the fittest'. More exactly, in Nietzsche's 'improved' version of Darwin, a world that is '"will to power" and nothing besides'.[4] What makes the new science so 'repellent' is that it introduces the 'duality between morality and reality' mentioned in Widmann's review (p. 405 above). As Nietzsche puts it in a letter, it requires us to face the fact that 'that which has hitherto been the most hated, feared and despised', namely, 'the lust for power and sensuality', is, in fact, the reality of life and the world.[5] Christian morality, that is to say, tells us that we ought to be 'selfless', ought to love our neighbour as ourselves. But 'Darwinian' science tells us not that we occasionally fall short of that ideal but that, as a matter of scientific necessity, we *always* do, that the true motives on which we always act are in fact always the *opposite* of the motives on which we ought to act, that we act always out of the selfish lust for power. This is why Nietzsche writes that it is not a bull he grabs 'by the horns' and pulls into the light of day but rather, from the perspective of traditional morality, the devil.

Schopenhauer anticipated something very like the Darwinian worldview. And this led him to conclude that the world is something which 'ought not to be'.[6] This shows what is so deadly about the radical dualism between the 'ought' and the 'is': it leads to disgust and despair, to 'world-denial', Silenus's 'nihilism', as described in *The Birth of Tragedy* (p. 125 above).

Given that 'world-affirmation' is always the mature Nietzsche's prime aim – ecstatic world-affirmation, indeed – the primary aim of *Beyond Good and Evil* is to overcome moral dualism, the gap between the 'ought' and the 'is'. And since the 'is' would appear to be unalterable, it follows that the 'ought' has to be changed. A fundamental 'revaluation of values' needs to take place. Gordon Gekko, the 'hero' of the movie *Wall Street*, announces his great insight that 'greed – for want of a better word – is good'. Though this is not Nietzsche's 'revaluation', it does suggest the radical, to traditional eyes shocking, nature of what he proposes.

Nietzsche does not merely comment on the blackness of the book after its completion. He goes out of his way, in the book itself, to *emphasise* the blackness of its worldview – from the point of view of traditional morality from which, of course, as a child of his age, Nietzsche himself is by no means entirely free. (This, I think, is why one sometimes senses him to be, like a rabbit in the headlights, frozen rigid with horror at the blackness of the world he describes.) The reason for this emphasis is that *Beyond Good and Evil*'s primary target of attack is a position he describes as 'idealism'.

Idealists, 'the darling "idealists"', are those who 'wax lyrical about the good, the true, and the beautiful'.[7] The term (which, for the sake of simplicity, it is best to regard as having nothing to do with metaphysical idealism) undoubtedly takes its meaning from Malwida von Meysenbug's *Memoirs of a Female Idealist*. Though Nietzsche had once admired Malwida's book intensely, during his final years of sanity he became increasingly antagonistic to her.

Though regarding 'idealism' as the dominant condition of nineteenth-century culture in general, Nietzsche thinks of it as a particular affliction of educated women. Later he will accuse the 'little blue-stocking', George Eliot, of the same thing.[8] Its ground is the failure to follow the rejection of Christian metaphysics with the rejection of Christian morality. Having given up Christianity's metaphysics, idealists cling, all the more intensely, to its morality. They are thus threatened by the dualism between the 'ought' and the 'is' that, in someone possessing both Schopenhauer's commitment to Christian morality and his ruthless honesty about the way the world actually is, leads to world-denial.[9] The idealists, however, to avoid such despair, close the gap between the 'ought' and the 'is'. They do so, however, *not* via Nietzsche's strategy of 'revaluing' the 'ought' but rather by the strange alternative of 'revaluing' the 'is'. Malwida, Nietzsche writes Meta von Salis, populates the world with 'beautiful souls so as not to see reality', a project which forces her to 'lie with every sentence'.[10] To avoid the gap that leads to moral despair, in other words, idealists *fake* their account of reality. They deceive, above all, themselves into thinking that the world is full of 'nice' people who really do act out of unselfish 'neighbour love' most of the time. Really, they tell themselves, we can all be 'nice' people. Deep down we all have 'beautiful souls', and if we act in unbeautiful ways we, our better selves, our consciences, feel bad about it.

What, actually, is wrong with 'idealism'? Nietzsche's answer to this question is less than perspicuous. Idealists are 'dishonest', tell themselves 'lies', to be sure, but it is far from clear what objection Nietzsche has to self-deception. In the same letter to Meta von Salis he says that Malwida's 'seeing the best in everyone' is not in fact 'innocence' but rather an 'extreme arrogance'. What he is referring to, I think, is the arrogance of insisting that the world *must be* the way one thinks it *ought* to be ('the "ought"–"is" fallacy', one might call it), a lack of respect for the reality of things; an arrogation to oneself of the godly power of world-creation. But again, it is not clear why 'arrogance' should be an objection – particularly coming from the admirer of, as we shall see, 'master morality'. Nietzsche admits that Malwida's 'rose-tinted superficiality' has enabled her to 'keep afloat in a difficult life'.[11] And he himself, in a new preface to *The Gay Science*, is on the point of praising (from the point of view of a 'convalescent') Greek 'superficiality' – 'superficiality out of profundity'. This is a reference to *The Birth of Tragedy*'s account of Homer's 'Apollonian' art as casting a shining veil over its 'terrors and horrors' of life and so making 'life-affirmation' possible (pp. 126–7 above).

What, then, to repeat, can really be wrong with 'idealism'? Why must we remove our 'rose-tinted' glasses and look with unflinching Schopenhauerian courage into the heart of darkness? I think that Nietzsche would wish to make two points. First, that the idealists' evasion of the truth about the world is not merely the strategy of the psychologically weak but is also a strategy that declines the opportunity to overcome weakness. 'Feel the fear and do it anyway' is a familiar slogan from pop psychology. The advice is to build one's 'confidence' and so become a more 'powerful' (and probably 'loving') person, not by evading but rather by making a virtue of fronting up to the fearful as it comes one's way. As with a great deal of pop psychology – a fact which makes Nietzsche's 'life-wisdom' seem less original than it is – this derives ultimately from Nietzsche. For what it says is just what the famous 'what doesn't kill me makes me stronger'[12] aphorism says. The point, then, is that 'idealism' is a turning of one's back on the possibility of personal growth. The idealists' self-deception, *Beyond Good and Evil* points out, is motivated by the belief that populating the world with 'beautiful souls' will make them happy.[13] But what they turn their backs on is the possibility of a more *robust*, and so better, kind of happiness.

And in fact – this, it seems to me, has to be the main point – idealism does not really make its practitioners happy at all. Recall that Nietzsche's idealists are *educated* people. So they *know about* modern science, know perfectly well with one chamber of the mind that according to our best (effort at) knowledge, reality is a world of cutthroat competition denuded of 'neighbour love'. So, underlying the idealists' lyricism, moral despair is really present all along. Malwida just about 'keeps afloat', but 'keeping afloat' is hardly happiness.

This is why Nietzsche became increasingly frustrated with her. He knew she was not happy and knew, too, that in spite of her long exposure to his mode of thinking she had refused to get the point. And this is why, in *Beyond Good and Evil*, as we shall see, he emphasises, in brutal rhetoric, the *gruesomeness*, from the idealists' point of view, of a world governed by will to power. He *shouts* his slogan that 'the world is will to power, and nothing besides' in order to break through the idealists' self-imposed deafness. The aim is to *force* them to abandon their strategy of 'revaluing', fudging, the facts, to force them to see the absolute necessity of his own strategy of 'revaluing *values*'.

Notice that if this general understanding of *Beyond Good and Evil* is correct, two things follow. First, there is no room in Nietzsche's thought for postmodernist scepticism about truth: what generates its central problem is the fact that Darwinian science is *true* – more exactly, it is our best understanding of the truth about the world and as such *demands* rational acceptance. Second, there is no room for trying to airbrush the will to power. Sometimes, in order to make Nietzsche less shocking, scholars suggest that 'will to power' just means 'power over oneself'. But this misses the fundamental point that Nietzsche *wants* to be shocking. When he says that the 'overpowering' and 'exploiting' of the weaker by the stronger belongs to the essence of life,[14] he means exactly what he says.

* * *

The phrase 'beyond good and evil', I have suggested, directs us towards the moral revaluation necessary to properly 'affirm life' in a (among other things, socially) Darwinian world. It directs us towards a morality which contrasts the good with the 'bad' rather than the 'evil'. Sometimes, however, as in for instance *Zarathustra*'s 'Before Sunrise' (p. 381 above), Nietzsche uses the same phrase not to call for the replacement of a 'good–evil' moral perspective with a 'good–bad' perspective but rather to express an ecstatic state in which one is 'beyond' good and evil *because everything is good*, at least when seen in the context of 'becoming' as a whole. In a letter of 1888 expressing the perfection of living in Turin, he writes, 'Evenings on the Po bridge: heavenly! Beyond good and evil!!'[15] This suggests a connexion between being 'beyond good and evil' and willing the eternal return.

Nietzsche makes this connexion explicit in a letter of 1888 to Georg Brandes (as we shall see, the Dane who first made him famous):

'Revaluation of values' – Do you understand this trope? – Fundamentally the gold-maker is the kind of man to whom we owe most. I mean he who, out of the meanest, the most scorned, makes something worthwhile and even golden. My task is very odd this time: I have asked myself what has been until now most hated, feared, despised by humanity: – and out of that I've made my 'gold'.[16]

When we recall Nietzsche's connexion between the 'alchemy' of 'turning shit into gold' and the Emersonian state of finding all things 'divine' when viewed in the totality of existence (p. 355 above), it becomes apparent that the goal of becoming 'beyond good and evil' is not just that of 'affirming life'. It is, rather, the affirming of life *without reservations of any kind* that enables one to embrace the eternal return.

* * *

One further preliminary question. As I have insisted, of every one of Nietzsche's texts one must ask: for whom is it written? Who is the intended audience?

As with all its post-1876 predecessors, *Beyond Good and Evil* is written for 'the few'. 'Books written for the general public always stink', it asserts. 'The stench of petty people sticks to them'.[17] Books written for the airport bookstore always level themselves down to the lowest common denominator. As we know, the 'few' Nietzsche hopes to attract – to the 'Nietzschean' cause in general and, in selected cases, to the 'monastery for free spirits' – are the exceptional few, the creative free spirits who are to become the 'colonisers of the future', the seed-bearers of a regenerated culture. *Beyond Good and Evil* has, however, an even more specific goal: in the forefront of his mind is the goal of attracting Heinrich von Stein to his side. For, as noted, the poem that appears as its 'Aftersong' under the title 'From High Mountains' is, in fact, a revised and expanded version of the poem Nietzsche sent von Stein in November 1884 (pp. 393–4 above), imploring him to come to the 'high mountains' of Sils Maria and of Nietzschean thought.

Theoretical Philosophy: The 'Prejudices' of Metaphysicians

So much for generalities; now for *Beyond Good and Evil*'s specific content. What makes it perhaps the hardest of all Nietzsche's works is the difficulty of finding a thread through the labyrinth of aphorisms. The thread I shall employ consists in regarding the work as consisting, really, of two books of unequal size, one concerned with 'theoretical' philosophy, the other with 'practical' philosophy, 'ethics' in the very broadest sense of the word. The first is largely, but by no means exclusively, to be found in Part I, the second in the remaining eight parts.

As observed, the book aims to change the lives of its proper readers and via them to transform human culture as a whole. And so, like Marx, Nietzsche wants to redefine the notion of philosophy. Philosophy will no longer be mere 'critique' – Kant, the 'great Chinaman'* of Königsberg', was a 'great critic' and worthy 'philosophical labourer', but not a true philosopher.[18] Philosophy, Nietzsche adds, cannot any longer be reduced to 'epistemology', for how could mere epistemology 'dominate', how could it change the world?[19]

On the other hand, the new philosophers are ill advised to ignore the traditional areas of philosophy or the great names in its hall of fame. Kant and Hegel, who have carried out the 'noble task' of codifying and abbreviating traditional ideas in morality and metaphysics, represent 'steps' the true philosopher, in at least many cases, needs to tread, 'preconditions' of his undertaking his true task of 'creating values'.[20] It is not entirely clear why Nietzsche believes this. Perhaps the thought is that in order to create a new way of apprehending the world the true philosopher will be greatly aided by a comprehensive grasp of what it is that is to be replaced. Whatever the reason, Part I of the work, entitled 'On the Prejudices of Philosophers', sums up the fruits of Nietzsche's study of traditional philosophy, his time

---

* Presumably a reference to the immutability of Kant's 'forms' of experience, his failure to perceive the historical variability of the structures of human consciousness.

in, as it were, philosophical boot camp. Its aim is to settle some scores with a number of theoretical positions all of which he himself has inhabited at one time or another.

* * *

Metaphysical Dualism. The work begins by targeting the postulation by 'metaphysicians' of a dichotomy between a 'true' and a merely 'apparent' world. He has particularly in mind, here, Plato, Christianity ('Platonism for the people')[21] and Kant.[22] Since Nietzsche always uses 'metaphysics' – meta-physics – to mean supernaturalism, the target is the supposed duality between a natural and a supernatural world.*

What is unusual in Nietzsche's critique of two-worldism is its genealogical character. The 'fundamental belief of metaphysicians', he claims, is in 'opposition of values', together with the assumption that things of higher value must have a totally different origin from things of lower value.[23] What the difference-of-origin thesis attributes to metaphysicians is, I think, the insistence that, as a totality, reality be a moral order. What is attributed to them is a version of what I earlier called the 'ought–is' fallacy: since only the higher value of an opposing pair is what *ought* to exist, really, only it *does* exist.

Some examples of what I think Nietzsche has in mind: Plato, like all conservatives, hated change. He hated 'becoming' and admired 'Egyptian' immobility, 'being'. And so he postulated a 'true' world of unchanging 'Forms'. Change was relegated to mere appearance. Christians hate pain and mortality. So, again employing the hidden premise that deep down reality must be as it ought to be, they postulate a true world in which there is neither pain nor death. Kant hates sensuality as the source of selfish behaviour. And so he postulates an 'intelligible' self consisting of a pure, 'moral' will free of all sensual distractions. And so on.

Nietzsche's critique of metaphysical dualism makes two claims. First, that the traditional value-oppositions get things the wrong way round. This is his by now familiar point that egoism, for instance, has more value 'for life' than its opposite, the traditional 'good and honourable'. Nietzsche's second claim is that there are no absolute value oppositions: a higher value always has an 'incriminating link' to, is in fact 'essentially the same' as, its opposite. This, again, is the familiar theme of sublimation. Without, for instance, bad Eris there can be no good Eris, without the aggressive will to power that can lead to war there cannot be the 'competition' that creates culture (pp. 139–41 above). The Christian exclusion of aggression from its 'true world' is, therefore, doubly mistaken. It is a mistake to suppose that how reality is follows from any notion of how it ought to be, but it is also a mistake to suppose that drives such as the will to power and selfishness ought not to exist. Notice that the theme of sublimation bears importantly on the task of turning the seemingly 'squid-like' into 'gold', of 'loving fate', embracing the eternal return: to see aggression as a precondition of culture is to accept its presence in a totality one can love without reservation.

As with all Nietzsche's genealogical critiques, there is a question of what exactly the critique of dualism is supposed to establish. I suggest that what he is implicitly arguing here is something like the following. Naturalism is the most obvious and most plausible general account of the nature of reality. Prima facie, supernaturalism is highly implausible. Why then would anyone want to become a metaphysical dualist? The fundamental answer is: *value* dualism. But this, as demonstrated above, is a bad reason. So we should accept

---

* There is a tiresome ambiguity in philosophers' use of the term 'metaphysics'. Sometimes it means 'account of the fundamental nature of reality', sometimes '*supernatural* account of the fundamental nature of reality'. Nietzsche's own account of the world as 'will to power' is 'metaphysics' in the first but not, of course, the second sense.

naturalism. Kant, and even Plato, have, of course, arguments for metaphysical dualism that have nothing to do with values. Nietzsche's background assumption must be (a) that for metaphysicians these are rationalisations rather than reasons and (b) that none are powerful enough to make dualism more plausible than naturalism. The task of demonstrating (b) is left as an exercise for the reader.

Schopenhauerian Idealism. Schopenhauer's idealism is, of course, a version of metaphysical dualism. Nietzsche nonetheless provides a critique that is independent of the accusation of value dualism. 'The material world is merely our representation and is created by our sense organs' – a position Schopenhauer often lapses into – is, Nietzsche points out, self-refuting, since the first clause entails that the sense organs are mere fictions and so cannot cause or create anything.[24] This criticism is entirely correct. To render the position coherent one must either reformulate the claim into something like *'the commonsense picture of the world* is the product of our cognitive organs' or else deny that any physical organ is the origin of consciousness. As we will see, Nietzsche's own position corresponds to the first of these options.

Commonsense Realism. Two 'noble' spirits, Nietzsche writes, both Poles (like, he fantasises, himself), are Copernicus and Boscovich. Both deny the testimony of the senses, and disdain the over-valuing of sense perception that is characteristic of the modern age. Copernicus denied that the earth stood still, while Boscovich denied 'matter'. He did this by showing that this last refuge of the 'atomic' thing is 'merely an abbreviation'; an abbreviation of, as we saw (p. 178 above), centres of force which Boscovich called 'puncta'.

The passage continues by saying that Boscovich's war on atoms needs to be pushed further, so that we deny the 'atomic soul' that is the basis of Christianity. We need to deny 'soul atomism' to understand that the atomic soul, like the 'thing' in general, is merely the product of subject–predicate grammar. To the simple and indivisible soul we should prefer the idea of the soul as a 'multiplicity of subjects'. The idea of the soul as a 'social structure of drives and emotions' should be granted 'rights of citizenship in science'.[25]

The point I want to draw attention to, here, is Nietzsche's low esteem for common sense which he views as based on a naive faith in sense perception and grammar as faithful reflections of the nature and structure of reality. The commonsense image of the world is 'plebeian'[26] ('I hope *I don't* have *common* sense', Lord Bertrand Russell once remarked), greatly inferior to the scientific image.

Scientific Realism. That natural science is preferable to common sense does not mean, however, that it is the final arbiter of truth: 'physics is only an interpretation and arrangement of the world (according to ourselves! if I may say so) and *not* an explanation of the world'.[27] This, almost word for word, is a repetition of Schopenhauer's view that the scientific image of the world is essentially facile, two-dimensional; 'like a section of a piece of marble showing many different veins side by side but not letting us know the course of the veins from the interior . . . to the surface'.[28] The so-called 'laws' of science, Schopenhauer argues, are grounded in 'natural forces'. But as to the nature of these forces, as to what gravity, impenetrability, electricity, and so on really are, science has nothing to say. To it they are 'occult', 'unknown X's'.[29] Natural science, Schopenhauer concludes, is incomplete:

> *Physics* in the widest sense of the word [is] concerned with the explanation of the phenomena of the world; but it lies in the nature of these explanations that they cannot be sufficient. *Physics* is unable to stand on its own feet but needs a *metaphysics* on which to support itself, whatever fine airs it may adopt towards the latter.[30]

In repeating Schopenhauer's view of natural science Nietzsche appears to be preparing the way for his own, philosopher's account of the nature of reality. 'Science' in the broad German sense, he seems to be saying, needs to go beyond natural science. To his attempt to correct and complete natural science I now turn.

The Metaphysics of Power

As indicated, Nietzsche's positive metaphysics is above all naturalistic. Nothing exists outside nature, outside space and time. The starting point for his metaphysics is, it seems to me, Darwin's theory of evolution. Though he calls Darwin a 'mediocre Englishman',[31] one suspects this is intended to disguise how much his worldview, like those of all his thinking contemporaries, was moulded by Darwin's 'dangerous idea'.

One element of his positive view of reality has already been touched upon: Boscovich's demolition of the material atom in favour of a world made up of forces. This dematerialising of nature in favour of force seems to Nietzsche to be on the right track. The question remains, however, as it did for Schopenhauer, as to what the force in question actually *is*. In the notebooks of the period he writes,

> The victorious concept of 'force' with which our physicists have created God and the world needs a supplement: it must be given an inner world which I designate as 'will to power', i.e. as the insatiable drive to manifest power; or as the employment and exercise of power, as creative drive etc.[32]

As we have just seen, this 'needs a supplement' is just Schopenhauer's claim that since forces are, to natural science, 'unknown X's', 'physics' must be supplemented by 'metaphysics' in order to rescue science from fundamental meaninglessness.

Schopenhauer's master concept for 'supplementing' physics, giving meaning to 'force', is, as we know, will – 'will to live'. But Nietzsche criticises Schopenhauer's metaphysics, not as wrong but rather as failing to get to the bottom of things. His own master concept, 'will to power', is, he claims, more fundamental than Schopenhauer's 'will to live'. In attacking Schopenhauer, however, he takes himself to be simultaneously attacking Darwin. In *Twilight of the Idols* he explicitly attributes the will to live, the 'struggle for existence',[33] to Darwin – with good reason, since the full title of the first edition of the famous book is: *On the Origin of Species by Means of Natural Selection, or the Preservation of Favoured Races in the Struggle for Life*.

'Physiologists', says Nietzsche,

> should think twice before positing the drive for self-preservation as the cardinal drive of organic being. Above all, a living thing wants to *discharge* its strength – life itself is the will to power [or 'growth'[34]] – self-preservation is only one of the indirect and most frequent *consequences* of this.[35]

Nietzsche's claim, in other words, is that the fundamental drive of every organism, including every human being, is 'power'. Evidently, however, since existence is a precondition of power, there is a subsidiary drive to existence. Schopenhauer and Darwin are subsumed under a more fundamental view of the world.

Since life in general is will to power, when it comes to human life in particular, 'psychology', a branch of physiology, should be grasped as 'the morphology and the *doctrine (Lehre) of the development of the will to power* which is what I have done'.[36] Some human behaviour, of course – power politics, for example – is quite evidently motivated by power. But the universality of Nietzsche's thesis commits him to discovering the will to power at work in cases where motivation *seems* to be something quite different. So, for example, as we will see, the rise of Christian morality was really a 'covert'[37] and cunning power-grab on the part of the slaves of the ancient world, an attempt to disempower their masters. And pity, as we have already seen, is an exercise of power over the pitied. In general 'psychology', the study of human motivation becomes, for Nietzsche, the 'hermeneutic of suspicion'. Since conventional self-esteem usually represses the real power-springs of action, Nietzschean psychology is governed by the 'suspicion'[38] that what is decisive in action usually occurs below the level of conscious intention.

Nietzsche writes that 'moral prejudices' have created 'unconscious resistances' on the part of investigators which have prevented 'all psychology so far' from 'venturing into the depths'.[39] This is an exaggeration which disguises his own debt to the 'hermeneutics of suspicion' of La Rochefoucauld, Schopenhauer, and Paul Rée, on which he drew so extensively in *Human, All-Too-Human*. But what he is really talking about is the everyday psychology deployed by the 'darling idealists'. Wedded as they are to their Christian moral 'prejudices', they cannot face up to what really makes things happen and are thus forced, like Malwida, to 'lie with every sentence' so as 'not to see the reality of things'. This is why, as I have said, Nietzsche expresses his will-to-power metaphysics with deliberate harshness, the aim being to shock the idealists out of their sentimental dream – for, ultimately, their own good. The closing pages of the work contain a particularly brutal expression of his metaphysics of power:

> Life itself is *essentially* a process of appropriating, injuring, overpowering the alien and the weaker, oppressing, being harsh, imposing your own form, incorporating, and, at least, at the very least, exploiting.[40]

Nietzsche gives this conclusion special reference to Marxist utopianism which, as he sees it, is a version of the 'deep-down-we-all-have-beautiful-souls' psychology underlying Christianised, Western consciousness. 'Every body', he writes,

> that is living and not dying ... will have to be the embodiment of will to power, it will want to grow, spread, grab, win dominance ... But there is no issue on which base European consciousness is less willing to be instructed than this: these days people everywhere are lost in rapturous enthusiasms, even in scientific [i.e., Marxist] disguise about a future state of society where 'the exploitative character' will fall away [the 'withering away of the state']: – to my ears that sounds as if someone is promising to invent a life that dispenses with all organic functions. 'Exploitation' does not belong to a corrupted or imperfect primitive society: it belongs to the *essence* of being alive as a fundamental organic function.[41]

It is thus sentimental drivel to think that a 'beast of prey' such as Cesare Borgia suffers from some 'disease'. To be sure, something has to be done about such 'tropical monsters' (I shall return in Chapter 26 to the question of just what), but to suppose, as does Kant, that they are suffering from the inner 'hell' of a beautiful 'higher' self being oppressed and overcome by an ugly, sensual, 'lower' self is absurd.[42]

Epistemology

Evidently, Nietzsche's startling claim that life – indeed 'the world' – is just '"will to power" and nothing besides'[43] calls for close critical scrutiny. I shall postpone this task until I come to discuss his proposed masterwork, *The Will to Power*, in Chapter 26. What I shall, however, address here is the question of the intended epistemological status of Nietzsche's metaphysics of power.

Intellectual 'honesty' is, he says, the cardinal virtue of 'we free spirits' – of philosophers such as himself.[44] We have already seen him arguing the need to be ruthlessly honest about the world that is the object of investigation. But equally, he insists, we need to be ruthlessly honest about ourselves as investigators, about the limitations of our capacity to gain knowledge of that world.

Honesty that has become in this way self-reflexive forces us to face up to the fact that we have to give up the 'dogmatism' that was the hallmark of traditional philosophy. Traditional philosophy, that is, claimed to offer the absolutely certain, fundamental truth about the world. (Its 'proofs' of God's existence, for instance, did not claim to show that his existence was a reasonable hypothesis but that it was an *absolute certainty*.) That was what 'metaphysics' was. The reason we have to give up such dogmatism, Nietzsche says in the Preface, is the fact that 'perspectivism' is a 'fundamental condition of all life'.

Perspectivism is Nietzsche's Kantian inheritance that we have met in earlier chapters: whatever we perceive or think is moulded by the structure of our minds, a structure which constitutes a 'horizon' we can never cross, a 'corner' we can never 'look round'.[45] The epistemological consequence of this (so far, Nietzsche is just treading in Kant's footprints) is that, since we can never remove the 'sunglasses' of the mind, we can never check up that the world really is the way we think it is. We can never, that is, be certain that our theories of the world correspond to reality. In particular, then, *Nietzsche* can never be certain that his metaphysics of will to power is true. What, then, is its intended epistemological status?

Nietzsche rejects 'scepticism': there are 'puritanical fanatics of conscience who would rather lie dying on an assured nothing than an uncertain something', but this is 'nihilism', a 'sickness' of the soul.[46] Since perspectivism is a 'condition of life' so is 'uncertainty': to reject uncertainty is to reject life. To love life is to love 'error',[47] by which, as I have emphasised several times, Nietzsche does not mean 'falsehood' but simply 'belief that is less than certainly true'.

This tells us the status of the metaphysics of will to power: it is not certain knowledge but rather a 'theory' or 'teaching' (*Lehre*)[48] which should be granted 'rights of citizenship in science'.[49] Another 'theory', however, is astrology. Why should Nietzsche's theory be granted citizenship rights and not astrology? How in general do we choose one theory over another? Nietzsche's answer is that one should choose that theory which best 'promotes and preserves life'.[50] This, as I intimated in discussing the similarities between *Dawn* and the work of W. V. Quine (pp. 314–15 above), is very like the outlook of American pragmatism (which actually has its roots in Schopenhauer's and Nietzsche's philosophy). The best theory is that which 'works', which, in other words, gives us power over ourselves and our environment. Nietzsche's claim for the will to power – his, as he sees it, corrected and completed version of Darwinian science – is that it comprehends reality in a way that is more comprehensive and powerful than any rival theory. He would, I think, also add, as I suggested in discussing *Dawn*, that the fact that a theory 'works' well is evidence – less than completely conclusive evidence, to be sure, but still evidence – that it is true.

Cultural Criticism

I turn now to the practical philosophy in *Beyond Good and Evil*. In all his writings, Nietzsche's practical philosophy – his discussion of social, political, religious, artistic and moral themes – received its overall shape from his conception of the philosopher as the 'doctor of culture',[51] from the medical paradigm of description, diagnosis, and prescription. The description and diagnosis of what is wrong with the way we are now constitutes his 'cultural criticism', which *Beyond Good and Evil*, once again, makes a defining condition of the philosopher: the philosopher is, he says, the 'bad conscience' of his age.[52] In earlier language, he is an 'untimely man'.

As we have seen, the town that is the object of Zarathustra's scorn and love is called the 'Motley Cow'. These two words seem to me to pick out the two main strands of Nietzsche's cultural criticism: one thing wrong with modernity is its motleyness, the other is its 'cow'- or 'herd'-like, character.

The Motleyness of Modernity. Modern humanity, says Nietzsche, has a 'hybrid, mixed, soul'. It treats history as a storage closet of 'costumes' which it is constantly trying on but finding none that quite fits. It constantly tries out new styles in 'customs and the arts': one day it is the romantic, the next the baroque. Again and again 'a new piece of antiquity or foreign country' is taken up and then cast aside. (As noted in the previous chapter, Reinhardt von Seydlitz was cashing in on the European craze for Japonism as Nietzsche wrote these words.) Modern European culture has been invaded by fragments of every past and alien culture, turning it into a motley 'chaos'.[53] Several factors are responsible for this: the democratic mixing of classes, the mixing of nationalities, the unparalleled quantity of scholarly information about the past and the foreign. Above all, it is due to our 'historical sense', our tolerant empathy for all that is past and alien.

What Nietzsche is talking about is essentially globalisation, multiculturalism, and the 'postmodern' mixing of styles, all of them the effects of the new technology of railways and electronic communication. As Wagner was the first to observe, what we call 'postmodernism' is not really 'post' at all but is, rather, an integral part of modernity itself. That Nietzsche really does have postmodernism in his sights becomes particularly clear when he says that the only way of inhabiting (rather than opposing) the motleyness of modernity is to become a 'parodist' given to 'carnivalesque laughter'[54] – whimsy and 'play' figure, of course, as big (and serious) words in celebrations of postmodernism.

What is supposed to be wrong with motleyness? Nietzsche calls our 'plebeian curiosity' about everything under the sun an ignoble lack of 'good taste'. Whereas we have a taste for everything ('ethnic' cuisine, for example), a 'noble and self-sufficient' culture is marked by the 'very precise yes and no of their palate, their ready disgust, their hesitant reserve about everything strange and exotic'.[55] Nietzsche calls modernity a 'half-barbarism':[56] 'half' because we have civilisation – plumbing and the police – 'barbarism' because we lack culture. 'Culture', recall, is defined as 'unity of artistic style in all the expressions of the life of a people';[57] a *unified* conception of the beautiful, including the beautiful (i.e., good) life. Not only do we lack cultural unity, our taste for infinite variety makes us positively 'hostile' to it, hostile to that 'ripened aspect of every art and culture' which comes into being when 'a great force stands voluntarily still … in a sudden harnessing and fossilizing … on still shaking ground'. This hostility, he says, places us in great danger.[58]

The danger is 'the total degeneration of man'[59] – *Entartung* literally means falling out of the species 'man' – in some sense, the 'death of man'. The danger, in other words, is that we are *Zarathustra's* 'last men' (pp. 368–9 above). Nietzsche repeatedly talks of 'species' of humanity (an indication of the biological, Darwinian, character of his thought). But his talk of the degeneration of 'man' cannot apply to all 'species' of humanity since the scope of his cultural criticism is entirely confined to Western, 'European', modernity. What, therefore, this 'good European' fears is, I believe, the 'death' of the 'European' species of humanity.

A 'species' of humanity such as a Greek city-state or the Venetian Republic of the later Middle Ages, Nietzsche says, in order to 'be a species', must 'succeed and make itself persevere in constant struggle with its neighbours or with its own oppressed who are, or threaten to become, rebellious'. To do this it requires 'hardness, uniformity and simplicity of form'. He adds that experience teaches it which qualities enable it to survive and 'keep prevailing'. These it calls its 'virtues', and constitute its morality. To ensure that people acquire the virtues, it deploys measures of extreme 'harshness'.[60]

Morality, we have seen, is a survival kit. More exactly, since survival is merely a prerequisite of power, a morality is, in *Zarathustra's* words, 'the voice of a people's will to power'.[61] But why does such a morality require 'hardness, uniformity and simplicity'? Any football coach would, I think, find this an easy question to answer. 'Uniformity' refers to the idea of a 'game plan' in which every member of the 'team' contributes to the common goal. 'Simplicity', the exclusion of all unnecessary complexity, is a desideratum since the more complex the plan the more chance there is of something going wrong. And, of course, to ensure that everyone sticks to his appointed task, the plan must be enforced with 'hard' discipline. This, then, is why the motleyness of European modernity threatens its 'death': lacking a shared 'game plan', it lacks the capacity for effective collective action, in particular, for action directed at its own preservation and expansion. Nietzsche takes it as self-evident that the death of European humanity would be a bad thing. Those with a more jaundiced, more *guilty*, view of the European tradition might think otherwise.

The 'Cow' in Modernity. Nietzsche attributes the 'herd' nature of modernity to Christianity and its various 'shadows'. Christian morality was, he says, the first great European 'revaluation of values'.[62] By means of the 'slave revolt' it reversed all the values of antiquity. Moralities, he says, fall into two basic types depending on whether they are generated by 'masters' or by 'slaves'. (In higher cultures the two types often coexist in a confused mixture.) 'Master' or 'noble' morality, that for example of the Vikings, was 'self-glorifying'. It elevated to the status of virtues the 'hard' warrior qualities – strength, the will to power, resoluteness, self-discipline, courage, loyalty – which had enabled them to succeed. (Hearing of the success of Georg Brandes's 1888 lectures on his philosophy in Copenhagen, which represented the beginning of his fame, Nietzsche wrote that *of course* the Scandinavians understood what he was on about since they had read the Icelandic Sagas, the 'richest source material' for 'my theory of master morality'.)[63] The masters' value distinction was between 'good and bad', between 'noble' types such as themselves and the 'bad' types (badly formed, bad, as it were, efforts at manhood), the contemptible slave-types whom they had conquered.

Master morality was, then, *self*-focused. Slave morality, by contrast, was *other*-focused. It was based on hatred and fear of the slaves' oppressors. So it was that the hate-filled word 'evil' replaced 'bad', the expression, merely, of contempt. In the ethical 'revolt' of the slaves the good–evil dichotomy came to replace the good–bad dichotomy of the masters. The hard qualities of the masters were given new names – 'self-confidence' becomes 'arrogance', 'resoluteness' becomes 'ruthlessness', and so on – and were designated as 'evil'. Simultaneously, the formerly despised 'soft' qualities were also given new names – 'powerlessness' became 'humility', 'cowardice' became 'friendliness', and so on – and were elevated to the status of virtues.[64]

The culture of ancient Greece and Rome was, of course, very different from the rape-and-pillage life-style of the Vikings. But it still had the same set of master virtues, with the difference that it valued their sublimated expression more highly than their natural expression. What was prized most highly, as we have observed on several occasions, was not bad Eris – aggression – but good Eris – competition. As, however, slave morality gradually became the dominant morality of the Roman Empire, Christian morality took over and the 'revaluation' was complete.

The triumph of Christianity and its morality was, in two crucial respects, a disaster. First, it made Europe sick for two millennia by teaching humanity self-hatred; hatred of the physical in general and of human physicality in particular.[65] It taught hatred of the natural drives, above all hatred of sex. Eros, a god to antiquity, was given poison, which did not kill him, but rather turned him into a vice.*,[66]

The second disastrous consequence of the triumph of Christianity is that it 'keeps the type "man" on a low...level'.[67] It does this in two ways: by preserving life's 'failures' and by disabling its potential 'successes'. It preserves failures on account of the supposed virtue of compassion. Compassion means that a Christianised culture preserves 'too much of what should have perished'.[68] Though there is no reason to think of the extermination camps here, there is no getting away from the harshness of this view. What Nietzsche is talking about, I believe, is the eugenics – 'breeding'[69] – we have already seen him to be committed to. Through 'indulgent, preserving care' of those 'who suffer life like a disease',[70] through Christian welfare, those who would otherwise perish survive and breed so that their 'failure'-making characteristics are passed on into the gene pool. Hence the average strength and power of individuals remains at a low level.[71]

Christian morality disables life's potential successes because it 'throw[s] suspicion on delight in beauty, skew[s] everything self-glorifying, manly, conquering, autocratic, every instinct that belongs to the highest and best-formed type of "human", twist[ing] them into uncertainty, crisis of conscience, self-destruction at the limit'.[72] Slave morality destroys the will to rise above the average, to be a 'tall poppy', and so brings it about that there are *no* tall poppies. It does this by destroying the 'pathos of distance',[73] the gifted, exceptional person's sense of being higher than, *worth* more than, others. Christianity's preaching of the 'equality before God' of all souls produces guilt about the pathos of distance which results in its eventual destruction. Christian 'equality' reduces everyone to a 'herd animal'.[74]

* * *

God is dead. Christian metaphysics is unbelievable for modern, educated Europeans. But God's moral 'shadow',[75] in the disguised form of what Nietzsche variously calls 'the

---

* A telling example of hatred of the body and of sex occurs in Anne Enright's Booker-prize-winning *The Gathering*, a book which arises out of a background of Irish Catholicism. Veronica, Enright's heroine, tells us how she hates waking up next to her husband, Tom: 'I wake to a livid tumescence on his prone body; a purple thing on the verge of decay...a cock so purple and dense it was a burden to him'. Later on she includes her own body in her disgust for all flesh: 'I would love to leave my body. Maybe this is what they are about, these questions of which or whose hole, the right fluids in the wrong places, these infantile confusions and small sadisms: they are ways of fighting our way out of all this meat. (I would like to just swim out, you know? – shoot like a word out of my own mouth and disappear with a flick of the tail.)'

democratic movement', 'the democratic enlightenment' and 'modern ideas',[76] lives on. His claim is that the excellence-destroying moral consciousness of Christianity lives on in 'modern ideas'.

What Nietzsche calls 'modern ideas' stem from that great revival of slave morality, the French Revolution, which leads him to offer 'French ideas' as a synonym.[77] Under 'modern ideas' he includes political democracy and universal suffrage,[78] 'utilitarianism' (for John Stuart Mill and the nineteenth century in general primarily a movement of social emancipation rather than an abstract doctrine in philosophical ethics), 'socialism' (a term covering both social democracy and communism),[79] and finally, and particularly vociferously, feminism.[80] All these movements are applications of the doctrine of 'equal rights', which makes them 'heirs'[81] to Christianity's doctrine of the equality of all souls before God. And all are moved by the idea that 'sympathy for all that suffers' is a virtue, which makes them heirs to Christianity's doctrine of 'neighbour love'.[82]

Since the 'democratic enlightenment' is the continuation of Christian moral consciousness in a disguised form, it has the same effect of undermining the drives that develop into the tall poppy. The 'high independent spirit', a 'high and hard and self-reliant nobility', is viewed as 'offensive' and 'dangerous'; the 'lamb' or even better 'sheep', the 'herd animal', continues to be the ideal. Like Christianity, the democratic enlightenment seeks to 'level' everyone down to the same low mean. In the potential higher type it produces a 'pathological enervation', kills the will to rise above the average.[83] It produces, in other words, a society of 'cows'.

What is so wrong with a society composed entirely of 'cows', of 'herd animals'? The answer, of course, rests on Nietzsche's theory of cultural health. This appears only in dribs and drabs in *Beyond Good and Evil*, but Nietzsche presupposes, of course, that we have read all his works to date.

To recapitulate. A social 'organism' requires, as we know, a disciplined communal morality, a 'game plan' which enables it to survive and grow in the 'Darwinian' jungle. But it also requires the capacity to change, to respond well to changing circumstances. It requires the 'random mutation' (pp. 261–2 above), the creative 'free spirit' who will reject current practices, social norms, and offer us signposts towards a 'new morality'. As Nietzsche now puts it, we need a small number of those who will show us 'how much of present-day morality is *out of date*' and will say (in the spirit of Columbus) 'We need to go out there, out there, out where *you* feel least at home today'.[84]

* * *

Is it really true that the Christian/'democratic' commitment to 'equality' necessarily leads to a society of 'cows', a society in which there will be fewer and fewer creators of new ways of thinking and living? The equality on which modern, liberal thinkers agree is equality of *desert*: all human beings are equally deserving of moral respect and concern. When dividing up social goods it is immoral to say that people with IQs of less than 90 get nothing. Nietzsche claims that this notion of equality hinders the nurturing of genius because it denies 'all special claims, special rights, special privileges'.[85] But that, surely, is mistaken. *Equality of concern does not entail equality of treatment.* He himself shows this by emphasising[86] that one man's meat is another man's poison – radically different states constitute the happiness of different people. One person's happiness may be very cheap (training to become a car mechanic), another's expensive (education to become a brain surgeon). So Nietzsche is wrong to suppose that elitist treatment of the highly talented cannot be justified in an 'equal' (in the specified sense) society.

This leaves the psychological objection: the morality of equality disables the sense of superior 'worth'[87] that is inseparable from genius. It gives the tall poppy a complex about his height, makes him, as it were, stoop. One has only to observe a class of high-school students to appreciate the force of this remark: '*Streber*' ('striver' or perhaps 'swot' in English) is a familiar term of abuse in the German classroom. The student of superior talent and ambition is well advised to keep his light under a bushel, and without sufficient determination may well find it extinguished. But this, surely, is the 'herd instinct' that exists in all communities and sub-communities *whatever* their moral code, not something caused by Christian morality in particular. A popular summary of Christian morality (taken over by Marx) is, 'To each according to his needs'. But the summary adds, 'From each according to his abilities'. This recognises that some people have greater and more precious abilities than others, that some people are of greater 'worth' to the community than others. Properly thought out, therefore, there is no reason that the morality of equality of deserts should deny the genius his 'pathos of distance', his knowledge that he is of greater 'worth' – to the community – than most others.

* * *

A potentially serious difficulty in Nietzsche's cultural criticism is presented by an apparent inconsistency between the two strands of the 'motley cow' critique. On the one hand, he claims modernity to be a motley 'chaos'. But on the other, he seems to attribute to it an unhealthy *order*: that of (disguised) Christian morality.

Nietzsche does not explicitly address this problem, but I think his implicit answer is this. Democracy, socialism, and feminism are, for Nietzsche, essentially *negative*, destructive values. This is due to the negative, reactive nature of the 'slave revolt' in which modern liberalism has its roots: as we have seen, whereas the masters created values by glorifying themselves, the slaves simply negated those values. In a clear sense, slave morality *creates* nothing. So democracy, socialism, feminism, and so on are, really (like anti-Semitism (see p. 358 above)), nothing but the 'politics of envy'. 'Modern ideas', in short, seek to overthrow the 'rank-ordering' of the old morality, but can do nothing to overcome the resulting 'chaos' since they have nothing *positive*, no positive ideal, to put in its place. This point, I think, is implicit in Nietzsche's habitual treatment of 'socialism' as synonymous with 'anarchism'.

That the values of modernity are all 'should nots' rather than 'shoulds' is the reason the notes of the period characterise the condition of modernity as one of 'nihilism', a term which means, Nietzsche says, '*that the highest values devalue themselves*'. '*The aim is lacking, the "Why?" finds no answer*'.[88] *Beyond Good and Evil* makes this point by pointing out that, in the post-death-of-God world, the 'Where to?' and 'What for?' – a positive conception of the good life – are missing.[89]

A final critical question: does Nietzsche misdiagnose the root cause of modernity's 'cow'-like character? Western modernity is, everyone recognises, a 'mass culture'. This seems to give some validity to Nietzsche's claim that there are powerful, perhaps uniquely powerful, forces at work in modernity which 'level'[90] people down to a very low 'average'. The question, though, is whether Nietzsche correctly identifies those forces. According to him, the root cause of modernity's herd-like character is the legacy of Christian morality. But an alternative candidate is modern technology, the tendency of modern industrial, communications and administrative technology to turn human beings into 'human resources', parts of a great machine which differ from each other as little as do machine parts. Technology, not Christianity, it could well be argued, is the real cause of the 'cow'-like character of modernity. Particularly in the earlier works, as we have seen, Nietzsche is well aware of this effect of technology. It is arguable, however, that his ever-increasing determination to saddle Christianity with the blame for absolutely everything leads him to take his eye off this important ball.

How to Overcome Diseased Modernity: Philosophers of the Future

Nietzsche's 'motley' critique of modernity leads, as we have seen, to the conclusion that we need a new 'game plan': a new shared understanding of the right way to live that will give us the 'harness, uniformity and simplicity of form' necessary to be successful competitors in a socially Darwinist world. For this we require the appearance of 'spiritual colonisers and shapers of new states and communities'.[91] Although the resurgence of the slave revolt in the form of 'modern ideas' threatens the appearance of such types, we have not yet reached the condition of being the 'last men'. It is still possible for us to 'give birth to a star'. What we need, then, are new leaders who will 'teach humanity its future' – 'the image of such a leader (*Führer*) hovers before our eyes'.[92] (As I have said before, one should avoid making it impossible to see what the Nazis saw in Nietzsche.)

Here, Nietzsche's practical task and his theoretical writing come together. We need new leaders – the likes of Heinrich von Stein – and *Beyond Good and Evil* is designed to attract them. The book, as *Ecce Homo* puts it (repeating Hölderlin's phrase and gesture), is 'the slow search for those related to me'.[93] Several passages are devoted to presenting the 'image' of the new leader, a kind of profile of a suitable candidate for membership of the 'colony for free spirits'. (Since Nietzsche is searching for 'those related to me', the profile is at the same time an idealised self-portrait.) What then will they be like, these new leaders? Earlier they were called 'free spirits'. Now, however – partly, I think, to avoid confusion with the 'free thinker', that paradigm proponent of 'modern ideas' – he calls them 'philosophers of the future'.[94] What are they like?

The first thing to notice about this phrase is the ambiguous genitive (present also in the *Prelude to a Philosophy of the Future* subtitle). The phrase can mean either 'philosophers who – literally – *inhabit the future*' or 'philosophers who philosophise *towards or about the future*'. Nietzsche speaks of 'the philosopher' as being out of step with his time because he is 'necessarily of tomorrow and the day after tomorrow',[95] so one could say the second kind of philosopher inhabits the future, too – but only metaphorically. The philosopher of the first kind I shall call the 'philosopher-triumphant'. (Nietzsche's madness, we shall see, took the form of thinking he *was* the philosopher-triumphant – in the megalomania which overtook him, he believed he had the power to depose the crowned heads of Europe.) The second kind, 'the philosopher-visionary', one might call him, is just the creative free spirit, the 'random mutation' – such as Nietzsche himself – who represents and communicates a new way of thinking and living.

This ambiguity carries over into the notion of the philosopher as 'commander and legislator'.[96] Sometimes there is an unmistakable resurrection of Plato's philosopher-king. Nietzsche speaks, for example, of philosophers as a 'new ruling caste'[97] and of their 'making use of religion for breeding and educational purposes'.[98] These remarks have to be about the 'philosopher-triumphant'. On the other hand, when the philosopher's 'command' amounts to 'teaching humanity its future',[99] what with luck it will do one day rather than what it is to do *now*, that, clearly, has to concern the philosopher-visionary. Philosophers in this sense, rather than being themselves philosopher-kings, are, as Nietzsche puts it, the 'heralds' and precursors of the 'approaching' philosopher-kings.[100] I shall return to the philosopher-kings shortly, but for the moment I shall use 'philosopher of the future' to refer exclusively to 'we [creative] free spirits',[101] the philosophers-visionary. What are they like?

As observed earlier, *Beyond Good and Evil* sets out, in a Marxian spirit, to redefine 'philosopher'. The 'philosopher as *we* understand him'[102] will not, like Kant and Hegel, be a mere codifier of current values. Such activity is the mere 'under-labour'[103] of 'genuine philosophy'.[104] Rather than codifying and endorsing current values, this new type of philosopher will deconstruct – 'dynamite'[105] – such values as a prelude to his 'master task',[106] which is to *create [new] values*: 'true philosophers...reach for the future with a creative hand', legislating for their community a new 'Where to?' and 'What for?'[107]

Whereas, then, old-style philosophers have merely sought to understand the world, the new style seeks to change it, seeks to '*dominate*' the future:[108] philosophy in the new style is an expression of the philosopher's will to power. This means that the philosopher must get his hands dirty, 'play the rough game'. Though 'untimely', he must be intellectually engaged with his times rather than retreating to Spinoza's 'icy heights',[109] the disengaged heights of a mere onlooker. Neither will he indulge in mere scepticism,[110] mere criticism,[111] or mere scholarship.[112] And though he needs to *have* a philosophy, it need not be one he puts, or can put, into books. Von Stein, for example, Nietzsche decided, had 'no head' for the philosophy of books.[113] But, at the time, that did not bother him at all. His 'heroic fundamental mood' was the embodiment of a new way of living.[114] Nietzsche mentions Frederick II of Sicily, Caesar, Leonardo, and, above all, Napoleon, as heroes very much 'after his taste' – as, I think, *philosophers* according to the new conception. Hegel called Napoleon 'history on horseback'. Nietzsche, it seems to me, thinks of him as philosophy on horseback.

Nietzsche's 'Republic'

What does the philosopher-visionary work *towards*? Nietzsche says he knows a new 'greatness'.[115] But what will that be like?

He does not say in any detail. Partly this is because a successful ethos is a function of the circumstances in which a community finds itself: since Nietzsche has no crystal ball, he is not in a position to say what kind of morality will enable a community to survive and thrive in the future. But partly, too, it is because he does not want to stifle the creativity of his 'disciples' – as Zarathustra points out, a teacher is ill served by pupils who remain eternally pupils. The notebooks offer a charming evocation of this mystery at the heart of Nietzsche's philosophy:

> 'You seem to have in mind to lead me into something bad, one could well think you wanted the destruction of humanity?' – I once said to the god Dionysus. 'Perhaps', answered the god, 'but something can come out of it for you'. 'What then?' I asked inquisitively. 'Who then', you should ask. Thus spoke Dionysus and was silent in his own way, namely seductively. You should have seen him! – It was spring, and all the wood was full of sap.[116]

As we shall see, Nietzsche 'became' Dionysus as he entered his insanity.

In fact, though, the mystery is not as deep as this suggests, for Nietzsche actually says quite a lot about his new society. What he offers is a highly abstract, formal description of what any successful society must look like, a quasi-Kantian, quasi-*a-priori* template on which any healthy society must be constructed. As *Ecce Homo* modestly puts it, *Beyond Good and Evil* offers a set of 'signposts' to a society 'antithetical' to diseased modernity.[117] Let us examine these signposts one by one.

Hierarchy

Nietzsche writes,

> Every enhancement of the type 'man' has been the work of an aristocratic society – and so it will always be: a society which believes in a long ladder of rank-order and differences in worth between man and man and needs slavery in some sense or other. Without the *pathos of distance* as it grows out of an ingrained difference between stations, out of the ruling caste's constant looking out and looking down on subjects and instruments,* and from its equally continuous exercise in obeying and commanding...that *other*, more mysterious pathos could not have grown at all, the pathos which leads to 'expansions of distance within the soul', to 'self-overcoming'.[118]

To this idea that social distance is a prerequisite for psychological distance one is immediately inclined to object that Nietzsche himself hardly came from an aristocratic background. But that, I think, would be a misunderstanding. What Nietzsche says is that the psychologically superior type must be able to *see* social superiority, not that he should necessarily *inhabit* a socially superior position. And in any case, Nietzsche did, in fact, stem from a kind of aristocracy – the spiritual aristocracy of the Lutheran priesthood.

'Aristocracy' in its Greek origin simply means 'rule by the best'. And, as we have seen, for Nietzsche as for Plato, 'the best' at ruling are the philosophers (triumphant). 'Commanding and legislating' are their business. Together with Plato, then, Nietzsche believes in the 'philosopher-king'.

One is inclined to find something absurd in the idea of philosophers (hardly competent, usually, to run even their own university departments) ruling the world – 'childish' as Rohde put it (p. 406 above). Two points, however, should be borne in mind. The first is that just as the philosophers-visionary are, as just observed, not necessarily book-writing or even book-reading philosophers, neither, surely, are the philosophers-triumphant. If a Napoleon can be the first kind of 'philosopher' he can, surely, be the second. The second point, as will become clear when we discuss *The Antichrist*,[119] is that, like Plato, Nietzsche does not think of the philosopher-king as conducting the executive business of government. He is a 'big picture' rather than a nuts and bolts man. Rather than initiating executive decisions, he provides the community with spiritual leadership – the role that Wagner advised the King of Bavaria to adopt (p. 117 above). One might think of the relation between the President of Iran and

---

* Book I of Aristotle's *Politics* calls those who are by nature slaves 'instruments'.

the Ayatollah, who is the nation's 'supreme leader',* or between the government of pre-Chinese Tibet and the Dalai Lama, as providing approximate models of Nietzsche's ideal. These models are quite appropriate, for, as we will see, Nietzsche's alternative to democracy is, in fact, his own version of something approximating the 'theocratic state'. Though this is not calculated to endear his political theory to Western readers, it makes one thing clear: since theocratic states actually exist, whatever else one might think about it, one should not dismiss Nietzsche's ideal of the 'philosopher-king' as hopelessly impractical.

Nietzsche believes, then, in spiritual leadership by the philosopher-king. But, in fact, his proximity to the ideal state as described in Plato's *Republic* is even greater than this. For, like Plato, he believes that the 'rank-ordering' of any healthy society will consist of just three basic classes: the spiritual leaders; an educated and self-disciplined middle class who aspire to a 'higher spirituality' and from whom, one day, future leaders might arise (Plato's 'auxiliaries'); and finally, 'the common people, the great majority' (Plato's 'craftsmen').[120]

Plato defines 'justice' in the state as everyone fulfilling their proper role in the community, that role being defined by the class to which they are suited by nature. Similarly, Nietzsche believes in what I shall call a 'stratification of the virtues' thesis. Virtue is 'station'- or 'role'-specific.[121] Personality traits that are virtues in lower types would be vices if they appeared in the philosopher. 'Self-denial and modest retreat', praiseworthy in those born to follow, would be vices in one born to command.[122] And conversely, the will to command would be a vice in one born to follow. So Christian universalism, the view Nietzsche attributes to Christian ethics that 'what's right for one is right for all', is in fact *'immoral'*.[123]

In 'The Greek State' of 1871 (discussed on pp. 160-1 above) Nietzsche writes that *'Plato's perfect state* is...certainly something even greater than is believed by his warmest-blooded admirers, to say nothing of the superior smirk with which our 'historically' educated reject such a fruit of antiquity'.[124] Since the tripartite rank-ordering of society proposed in *Beyond Good and Evil* is identical with that explicitly borrowed from Plato in 1871, one can say that Nietzsche's ideas on the *structure* of society (as well as on the need for an 'iron hand'[125] to enforce that structure) have altered not at all since 1871.

The Slavery Issue

Nietzsche says, to repeat, that 'every enhancement of the type "man" has been the work of an aristocratic society and needs slavery in some sense'.[126] This returns us to the 'immoralism' issue raised in discussing *Dawn*. Is Nietzsche *really*, and not just polemically, an 'immoralist'? The issue, I think, is whether or not he thinks that *only* higher types have a claim to well-being, whether or not he thinks that the mediocre masses are to be *nothing but* a support system for the higher types. If Nietzsche treats 'lower' types as *mere* means, if he treats them as things rather than people, then he really is an immoral (and ontologically blind) thinker.

The key passage is section 258, in which Nietzsche says that, unlike the pre-Revolutionary French aristocracy, which 'thr[ew] away its privileges with a sublime disgust and sacrifice[d] itself to an excess of its moral [i.e., Christian] feeling', thereby entering a

* It is said that Ayatollah Khomeini read the *Republic* while in Qum in the 1920s and was inspired by Plato's vision of the philosopher-king in the creation of his Islamic republic.

state of 'corruption', a healthy aristocracy 'does *not* feel that it is a function (whether of the kingdom or the community), but instead feels itself to be the *meaning* and highest justification (of the kingdom or community)'. Only thus can it accept in good conscience

> the sacrifice of countless people who have to be pushed down and shrunk into incomplete human beings, into slaves, into tools, all *for the sake of the aristocracy*. Its fundamental belief must be that society *cannot* exist for the sake of society, but only as the substructure and framework for raising the exceptional type up to its...higher state of *being*. In the same way, the sun-seeking, Javanese climbing plant called *sipo matador* will wrap its arms around the oak tree, so often and for such a long time that finally, high above the oak, although still supported by it, the plant will be able to unfold its highest crown of foliage and show its happiness in the full, clear light.

It is this passage more than any other that has led to the charge of 'immoral elitism', the charge that nothing matters to Nietzsche other than a couple of Goethes per millennium: in a slogan, 'only the superman counts'. This is the way in which he has usually been interpreted, beginning with P. Machaelis's 'Junker-philosophy' accusation in 1886 (p. 405 above). Bertrand Russell, for example, claims that, for Nietzsche, 'the happiness of common people is no part of the good *per se*', that 'what happens to the...[non-elite] is of no [moral] account',[127] while the influential John Rawls thinks that Nietzsche believes in an elite of Socrates and Goethe types, of philosophers and artists, and has no independent concern for the well-being of 'the mediocre'. This, he suggests, is an immoral attitude which elevates a taste for aesthetic 'perfection'[128] above the claims of 'justice'. For Nietzsche, he claims, Greek philosophy justified Greek slavery.[129]

Nietzsche values neither art nor philosophy for its own sake: 'art for art's sake' is a form of 'nihilism', a 'paralysis of the will' to create *important, socially beneficial*, art[130] (see further pp. 508–9 below). And, as we have seen, he attributes a triple social responsibility to philosophers: they must be the 'bad conscience', the diagnosticians of the sicknesses of their age, the 'doctors of culture'; they must be the creative free spirits who herald a new way of life; and, in the best of all worlds, they must be the spiritual 'commanders and legislators' of the community. All in all, 'the philosopher as *we* understand him...[is] the man with the most comprehensive responsibility, whose conscience bears the weight of the overall development of mankind'.[131] In attributing, then, to Nietzsche the view that society exists for the sake of the artist and philosopher, Rawls gets him exactly back to front.

The inconsistency of the standard reading of the vine-climbing-the-oak passage with so much else of what Nietzsche says provides a motive for trying to read the passage in something other than a standard way. And this is not difficult to do. The crucial point to notice is that Nietzsche does not say '*my* fundamental belief' is that the 'aristocrats' are the 'meaning and justification' of everything else. He is reporting, rather, the way *the aristocrats* feel, reporting the fundamental 'faith' healthy aristocracies have had, something that may well be quite alien to his own point of view.

What Nietzsche is doing in section 258, I think, is simply surveying the past, in the anthropological fashion he often adopts,* and noting that, in thriving aristocracies of the

---

* 'Many lands has Zarathustra seen and many peoples: thus he discovered the good and evil of many peoples...' (Z 1 15).

past, the aristocrats have had a sublime arrogance which, when it collapses, leads to the decay, the 'corruption', of that society. The passage no more commits Nietzsche to endorsing aristocracy as the best order of society than his description of 'master-morality' societies as healthier than 'slave-morality' societies commits him to endorsing the rape and pillage of the Vikings.

And in fact, it seems to me, Nietzsche does *not* endorse aristocracy in the standard sense of the word. It is important to notice that the concluding Part 9 of the book in which section 258 occurs is not called 'What is Aristocratic (*adelig*)?' but rather 'What is Noble (*vornehm*)?' The relevant difference appears in Nietzsche's final letter to Brandes: 'If we win', he writes, 'we have overcome the absurd boundaries between race, nation, and classes (*Stände*): there exists from now on only order of rank (*Rang*) between human beings'.[132] The difference between rank and class is the difference between ability and birth. What Nietz-sche seeks, as we shall see in detail in discussing *The Antichrist*, is a hierarchy not of blood but of natural ability and aptitude.

Still, the question remains: what about the 'slaves'? Slavery 'in some sense', Nietzsche asserts, clearly in his own voice, is the condition of any higher culture.[133] Since he himself believes in slavery, is he not reducing a large section of the population to mere scaffolding, so that he really does have to be adjudged an immoral thinker?

The answer is not immediately clear. Though section 258's talk of the slaves being 'shrunk into incomplete human beings' out of the need to support the aristocracy is, I have suggest-ed, best read as an account of the aristocrats' rather than Nietzsche's view of things, section 61 speaks of the masses as existing only for 'general utility', and here it is unclear whether it is Nietzsche the anthropologist or Nietzsche the normative philosopher who speaks.

Nietzsche recognises that the traditional position assigned to women is one of slavery: it is 'slavish and serf-like'.[134] And so, since his views on women are emphatically his own, one should be able to infer his views on slavery in general from his views on women.

Women Again

*B*eyond Good and Evil's views on women* are an attack not so much on women as on the movement for women's emancipation that was gathering serious strength as he was writing the work. Often it is the emancipationists who are his quite explicit target: proponents of the movement for 'female self-determination', he says, fail to realise that

---

* In section 231 Nietzsche says that his views on 'woman as such' are idiosyncratic. They are only '*my* truths', a 'spiritual fate', a 'great stupidity that . . . *will not learn*'. He concedes, in other words, that his views may be infected by a degree of prejudice. The source of prejudice this extremely self-aware man has in mind is surely obvious: the trauma of the Salomé affair, which dramatically changed his stance to women (Chapters 18 and 19 above). By 1885, we have seen, the majority of Nietzsche's friends and admirers were not just women but *feminist* women. This tells us, I think, to whom the admission of possible prejudice is made: Malwida von Meysenbug, Helen Zimmern, Meta von Salis, Resa von Schirnhofer, Helene Druscowitz and others. Obviously Nietzsche does not wish to undermine his views on women completely; otherwise there would be no point in presenting them. But recognising, I think, his feminist friends' need to render their own position consistent, he invites them, as Zarathustra invites his followers, to scrutinise his views very carefully with an eye to separating the philosophical from the possibly pathological. That, it seems to me, is our task, too.

setting up Madame de Staël or George Sand as examples of how fine an emancipated woman can be is counter-productive since men find these women comical, *counter-examples* to emancipationist aspirations.[135] Four major themes run through Nietzsche's discussion.

(1) *'Woman as such', the 'eternal feminine', lacks the capacity for 'manly' pursuits.* Women have no concern for truth – their great talent is in the (slavish) practice of lying. They have no capacity for 'enlightenment' (rational objectivity) and so should be silent on religion and politics – and on the question of 'woman as such'. Women do not even know how to cook, though they have been at it for millennia: our terrible diet is clear proof of 'lack of reason in the kitchen'.[136] (As we know, when it comes to the serious business of the barbecue, the man always takes over!) Even women themselves admit that there has never been a female mind as profound as a man's. (How come there have never been any great women composers or philosophers???) Even women admit that the female heart can never be as just as a man's (and so women are unfit to rule either the state or the family).[137] It follows from all this that the proper role for women is the traditional one of bearing and bringing up children.[138] A woman scholar has something wrong with her sexuality.[139]

Is this *just* a mass of prejudices – or, at best, 'period errors' – or is there a serious point mixed in with this, as it now seems, unintentionally comic rave? I think there is, namely, as I remarked earlier, Nietzsche's 'station' or 'role' ethics, his anti-universalist, Platonic insistence that virtues are specific to the type of person one innately is. While it is not established that any intellectual or emotional capacities are gender-specific, the idea is not a silly one. It *might* really be true that men are better at some things and women at others – though empirical evidence is rapidly undermining Nietzsche's idea that art, science and government are specifically 'manly' aptitudes. Another point that needs to be recognised is that while physical capacities are clearly gender-specific, they can be modified by technology: though women of the past could not be soldiers, they can now become tank commanders and fighter pilots.

(2) *Women are terrifying and potentially barbaric.* Nietzsche refers to 'woman' as 'the beautiful and dangerous cat'. (Since it was Lou he called a 'cat', the possessor of a 'cat-egoism',[140] this comes close to naming names.) Inside the woman's glove are her tiger claws. In love and revenge women are terrifying. ('Hell hath no fury like . . . ')[141]

(3) *Women must be subject to tight masculine control.* This follows immediately from their capacity for barbaric terrorism. The oriental treatment of women as 'property' is thus 'enormously rational'. Woman must not lose her 'fear of man'.[142] (Thus spoke Ayatollah Nietzsche!)

(4) *The emancipationist movement, equal rights, is part of the democratic destruction of hierarchy, the levelling of Europe.* Feminism, in other words, is part of the general levelling of Western modernity down to a mediocre 'herd' which is destroying its capacity to produce the exceptional individual necessary to survival and growth.[143] As earlier noted, Meta von Salis, an aristocrat by birth, was as strongly antidemocratic as Nietzsche: her only disagreement with him lay in her belief that there could be 'superwomen' as well as 'supermen'. Nietzsche does not seem to have noticed that 'equal rights' for women does not necessarily imply 'equal rights' for all.

* * *

So far, the discussion of women seems to view them as mere tools, mere 'property', as Nietzsche indeed says. In fact, however, even the post-Lou Nietzsche evinces a concern for women which one does not have for tools. The democratic movement, he says, for instance, actually *decreases* women's real power, which depended on mystique and quiet cunning.[144] Since he now defines 'happiness' as 'the feeling of the increase of power – that a resistance has been overcome',[145] one of his objections to the emancipation movement is that it is actually making women less happy than they were before. This recapitulates *The Gay Science's* claim that women exercise 'a surplus of strength and pleasure' in being the 'function' of a man, his purse or social secretary (p. 333 above) – in being the 'power behind the throne'. (Though women cannot speak on the marae, Maori culture is often described as being closer to a matriarchy than a patriarchy.) Nietzsche is thus concerned that, in their own way, women, like men, should exercise the will to power. He is concerned, in short, that women should be happy. This is why he says that women are 'predestined to servitude *and fulfilled by it*'.[146] Underneath all the bluster, then, Nietzsche's views on women make him not an immoralist but rather a very traditional *paternalist*. And the same, we can assume, is true of his views on 'slavery' in general.

This becomes crystal clear in Nietzsche's final work, *The Antichrist*. Here he makes clear his view that those who are natural 'instruments' are happiest *being* instruments. 'For the mediocre, mediocrity is happiness'. What makes them unhappy is socialist rabble-rousers who make them want to rise above their happy level of life.[147] Not just virtue, then, but also happiness, is relative to the type of person you are. This makes it clear that, *for Nietzsche*, there is no question of 'pushing down' or 'shrinking' people into slavery, since *his* only 'slaves' – 'the mediocre' – are destined *by nature* for that role.

In sum, Nietzsche's views on hierarchy, slavery, and women do not make him an immoral thinker. What they show him to be, rather, is a 'compassionate' – or as the British used to say, 'one-nation' – conservative. Notice, however, that one is very liable to miss this conclusion if one dismisses his views on women as an embarrassing side issue, unrelated to his philosophy proper.

Morality, Religion, and Art in the New World

The first characteristic, then, of Nietzsche's utopia is social hierarchy with 'slaves in some sense' – those destined by nature to take rather than give orders – at the bottom of the social 'pyramid'.[148] The second characteristic is that, unlike 'motley' modernity, it will possess a shared morality: it will have the 'hardness, unity and simplicity of form' which 'an [any] aristocratic community enforces upon itself'.[149] It will, in short, possess that shared 'game plan' which, according to the theory of cultural health, is essential to evolutionary success.

Not that such unity will demand uniformity all the way down. A noble society will not be North Korea but will, rather, exemplify that human 'greatness' which consists in 'the very scope and variety of humanity, in unity in multiplicity'.[150] Again, the analogy of a football team comes to mind. Evidently, a good team is not one in which every player does the same thing but is one, rather, in which a multiplicity of different functions are coordinated by a unifying game plan so as to achieve a common goal. Notice that Nietzsche's theses of the stratification – 'station'-relative nature – of both virtue and happiness find a ready explanation in terms of this analogy.

Nietzsche's ideal society, then, will have a shared but non-totalitarian ethos. But to be effective, an ethos needs to have authority. Here Nietzsche sees a central place for a communal religion in the 'noble' society: not a religion based, like Christianity, on fear, but rather a 'noble' religion based, like that of the Greeks, on 'gratitude' for communal success in the evolutionary struggle, a religion in which a 'noble' people projects idealised images of itself as moral 'touchstones' – paradigms of human excellence.[151]

To be effective, such models need to possess authority, to become objects of reverence, objects that produce an 'involuntary hush'. One of the few beneficial legacies of Christianity is that it has accustomed us to the idea that certain things demand such reverence, that it has 'bred into people the understanding that they cannot touch everything, that there are holy experiences which require them to take off their shoes and keep their dirty hands away'.[152] In *Assorted Opinions and Maxims* it was the task of, above all, artists to use their subtle techniques of 'transfiguration'[153] to produce shining images of 'beautiful souls' which, through their charismatic power, excite emulation.[154] That *Beyond Good and Evil* speaks of (the right sort of) art as belonging to 'the genuinely noble elements'[155] of a culture indicates that this remains his view.

It should by now be clear why I spoke of Nietzsche's alternative to democracy as a kind of (non-metaphysical) theocracy. What he still seeks, it seems to me, as he sought in his first book, is the 'rebirth of Greek tragedy', the rebirth of a 'collective artwork' which, as its sacred heart, collects the community together in a clarifying affirmation of its fundamental ethos.

* * *

Nietzsche says that the philosophical leader of the ideal state, charged as he is (and as Wagner charged King Ludwig (p. 117 above)) with 'the most comprehensive responsibility' for the 'overall development of mankind' will make use of one religion or another 'for his breeding and education work'. Since he mentions the Hindu caste system in this connexion, what he has in mind, here, seems to be the buttressing of the eugenics, in which we know he believes, with religious sanctions. Religions, he adds, have many social benefits: for example, they 'bind the ruler together with the ruled' and 'give the common people an invaluable sense of contentment with their situation and type'.[156] In other words, they provide a clarifying and authoritative exposition of, as I put it, communal ethos.

Given, however, Nietzsche's enthusiasm for Plato's *Republic*, this picture of the philosopher as 'using' religion to social ends might seem to conjure up the idea of religion as a 'noble lie' and of the ruler as a cynical outsider who is himself not for a moment taken in by the 'pious fraud':[157] a picture of the philosopher-king as, like Dostoyevsky's Grand Inquisitor, all too aware that religion is the opium needed to control the masses while regarding it himself as nothing but infantile superstition. This is what Michaelis's review suggests in representing Nietzsche as holding 'religion' to be 'an anachronism, a superseded standpoint, but a useful device for controlling the herd' (pp. 405–6 above).

Actually, though, this cannot be Nietzsche's account of the philosophical leader, since, if it were, he would become indistinguishable from the 'free thinker': the man of 'modern ideas' who looks down on religion 'with an air of superior, almost gracious amusement . . . mixed with slight contempt for what he assumes to be "uncleanliness" of spirit that exists when anyone supports a church'.[158] What, then, does the 'philosopher-king' believe?

Returning to the passage which claims that 'every enhancement of the type "man" has been the work of an aristocratic society', note that, as with Plato's philosopher-king, whose rule is governed by his knowledge of the 'Forms' (the divine 'blueprint' of how the world ought to be), Nietzsche's philosophical leader does not rule by arbitrary fiat. Rather, he is engaged 'in a continuous exercise '*in obeying* and commanding'.[159] What, given that, along with all metaphysical worlds, Nietzsche has rejected Plato's supernatural realm of the Forms, does his ideal leader obey?

He will obey communal ethos, that 'morality' which is a function of the unique character, history, and current circumstances of his community. Since the religion of the community is – is nothing more than – an empowering articulation of that ethos, he will know that the gods are not supernatural beings but rather human projections. (Homer and the Greek poets in general, Nietzsche remarks, cannot have 'believed' in their gods; otherwise they would not have allowed themselves such freedom of 'invention' in representing them.)[160] Yet along with Feuerbach,* Wagner and Nietzsche himself, he will know that they are none the worse for that, that being fictions (or fictionalised versions of real people) impairs in no way their functioning as 'touchstones' of human excellence.

Nietzsche grasps here, I think, an important point about religious discourse: 'Jesus would never do that' can have just as much ethical force for someone who believes Jesus never existed as for someone who believes he did. As *The Jane Austen Book Club* illustrates, 'This is what (Jane Austen's) Emma would do in this situation' can have ethical force. What this shows is that though religion might be a 'noble lie' told to the masses, this does not at all confine the enlightened ruler to cynical detachment. Rather, in reverencing the gods, he knows he is reverencing the best in his community. The situation is like that between mother and child: both can agree that 'Santa wouldn't like that' even though one knows Santa to be a fiction while the other believes him to be real.

Nietzsche says that 'there is a high and horrible price to pay when religions do *not* serve as means for breeding and education in the hands of the philosopher but instead serve themselves and become *sovereign*, when they want to be the ultimate goal instead of a means alongside other means'.[161] This might be read as enjoining the leader to use religion to manipulate the masses while preserving himself in cynical detachment. But in fact, I think, all it means is that a good religion must serve human well-being rather than, as with Christianity, subordinating human life to religious prescriptions damaging to human health. 'The gods' should serve man, not man the gods.

---

* Ludwig Feuerbach's *Essence of Christianity* (1841), which had a profound effect on Wagner (and on George Eliot, who translated it into English), is the origin of the idea that gods are fictional projections of human desires (for immortality, for example) and virtues.

22

Clearing the Decks

Fifth Summer in Sils Maria

THE APPEARANCE of *Beyond Good and Evil* found Nietzsche once again in Sils Maria. Arriving on June 30, 1886, he would stay, as usual, until the end of September. Though the place was becoming too crowded with middle-class tourists for his liking – by August he records the unwelcome presence of ten professors, four, including himself, in the Durisch house alone – he could find no better way of supporting the 'permanent, mild winter' he believed his health required (the 'bland weather cure', we might call it). For company he had his usual circle of women, the two Emily Fynns, Countess Mansuroff, and, on a more intellectual level, Helen Zimmern. Meta von Salis visited for two days, together with her mother and her friend (and lover) Hedwig Kym. Having taken her place at the communal dining table, Meta recalls,

> I looked around, and my short-sighted eyes gradually assured themselves that it was Nietzsche at the top end of the table. He seemed to me more youthful than at our first meeting and was engaged in lively conversation with the lady on his right, who was introduced to me the next day as Miss Helen Zimmern ... That evening, I was able to observe how finely and attentively – quite unlike his ill-founded reputation – he related to women, especially older women. Shortly before everyone left the table I sent my card across to him. When he came over to us I introduced my mother and friend. He was quite charming ... to my mother. There was no trace of forcedness ... He attempted to persuade her to remain in Sils for the following day ... He wanted to show her the fine spots of the region [and] described its particular charms, the [Chasté] peninsula, the two lakes ... For me Nietzsche is inseparable from ... the silent mountain world of the upper Engadine ... the most solitary, proud, tender man of our century stepped into his ancestral realm, like a king's son born in exile.[1]

There were, however, less regal moments: pausing during a long walk around Lake Silvaplana, Meta records, he delivering an impassioned and lengthy speech to the cows grazing around them (recall the 'voluntary beggar' from *Zarathustra* Part IV).[2]

Explosions Below

It was in Sils that Nietzsche first heard, like the sound of distant explosions in the low-lands, the initial reactions to *Beyond Good and Evil*. Initially he was pleased by Wid-mann's 'dynamite' review (p. 405 above), quoting a whole paragraph from it in a letter to Malwida.[3] At last he was getting some respectful attention. And he welcomed the idea that his books were considered 'dangerous' – he himself had called them that.[4] Soon, however, he began to think that 'danger' had been stressed too much, so that soon he would have 'all sorts of police' onto him.[5] Similarly, although his initial reaction to Welti's review (p. 406 above) was pleasure at the 'great respect' shown him by 'the Swiss',[6] he was soon forced to recognise its essential vacuousness as well as the ultimate superficiality of all his reviewers, claiming in January of the following year that in fifteen years of book-writing he had not received a single even competent review.[7]

On the other hand, he was delighted with Burckhardt's reaction to the book. To Nietz-sche's suggestion that they were both working on the same problem – the 'conditions for the growth of culture'[8] (what I have been calling the 'theory of cultural health'), Burck-hardt responded by saying that, as a humble historian, he lacked a 'philosophical head' and so could not be said to share Nietzsche's research programme. Much of the book, indeed, he was incapable of understanding. But he agreed on the 'herd nature' of mo-dernity; on democracy as the heir of Christianity; and 'very particularly on the future strong ones on earth'. 'Here', Burckhardt wrote, 'you describe the probable generation and life con-ditions of a mode of being in a way that must arouse the strongest agreement'.[9] No wonder Nietzsche was delighted by this, in fact, high level of comprehension and agreement expressed by the revered Burckhardt's 'heavenly' letter.[10]

Another reader who received a complementary copy of the book and responded with a letter that 'takes me as seriously as I could wish'[11] was the French historian and literary theorist Hippolyte Taine. Nietzsche respected Taine almost as much as he did Burckhardt; they, he wrote, were his only true readers.[12] And he wrote a furious letter to Rohde, who had called Taine's work 'contentless', telling him that the remark showed how stupid he was, adding that, unlike Taine's, his (Rohde's) own life was meaningless.[13] He was full of admiration for Taine's biography of Napoleon: 'it was you', he wrote Taine, 'who gave us the tremendous problem of monster and superhuman (*Unmensch und Übermensch*)',[14] a judgment on Napoleon that reappears in the *Genealogy of Morals*. On the other hand, he did not agree with Taine's '*milieu*' theory, the theory that works of art are absolute functions of their physical and cultural '*milieu*'. Genius, Nietzsche writes in his notes, is not explained by its environment. Different individuals may respond differently to one and the same envi-ronment.[15] In *Twilight of the Idols* he explains what is really wrong with the theory: it is incompatible with the appearance of individual genius.[16] If, in other words, creativity is entirely a function of milieu there is neither the necessity for, nor the possibility of, as I have called him, the 'random mutation'.

Hymn to Life

During August 1886, unwilling to abandon his aspirations as a composer entirely, Nietzsche completed his *Hymn to Life*. This was his earlier *Prayer to Life* (track 17 on the Web site for this book), his 1882 setting of Lou Salomé's poem (p. 352 above), but with two differences. First, the original work for tenor and piano (itself a recycling of the melody from his 1873 *Hymn to Friendship*) was transformed into a work for choir and orchestra, the orchestration, beyond Nietzsche's technical competence, being done by Köselitz. And second, he now set the second as well as the first verse of Lou's poem.

Seeking the approval of his Zurich conductor friend Friedrich Hegar (p. 394 above), he describes the closing bars of the work as containing 'a tragic accent that comes from my innermost "entrails"'. He wanted it to be sung, he continued, 'in memory of me', that is, 'in something over a hundred years when it has been grasped what I was talking about'.[17] Though Hegar was unenthusiastic about (or so he said) the orchestration, the work was eventually published by Fritzsch in October 1887.

In *Ecce Homo* Nietzsche gives extraordinary prominence to the *Hymn*, connecting it closely with the idea of eternal return and with the inspiration that gave rise to *Zarathustra*, a work which itself 'might perhaps be reckoned as music'. The setting of 'Fräulein Lou von Salomé's' poem, he says (treating the *Prayer* and the *Hymn* as the same work), arose out of a time

> when I was possessed to the highest degree by the *affirmative* pathos, *par excellence*, which I call the tragic pathos ... He who knows how to extract any meaning at all from the closing words of the poem will divine why I preferred and admired it: they possess greatness. Pain does *not* count as an objection to life: 'Have you no more happiness to give me, well then! *Still do you have your pain* ...' Perhaps my music is also great at this point. (Last note of the clarinet in A is C sharp not C. Printing error.)[18]

This comment helps explain the change in the title from Lou's 'prayer' to his own 'Hymn'. Both 'prayer' and 'hymn' are religious words, but while a 'prayer' is a conversation with a personal deity, 'hymn' is appropriate to the expression of wonder and praise before an impersonal one. It is significant that the notebooks of this period are full of favourable remarks about 'pantheism', the pantheistic attempt at 'thinking out a way in which evil, error and suffering are not arguments against divinity'. Habitation of pantheistic consciousness generates, he writes, a life-affirming 'gratitude for existence' which finds natural expression in the 'dithyramb'; in, in other words, a *Hymn* – not to the 'moral God' of Christianity but rather to Dionysus.[19]

Schopenhauer held (rightly, it seems to me) that the essence of music is that it gives the *feeling* of feeling, of emotion. 'Sad' or 'happy' music, even purely instrumental music, is called 'sad' or 'happy' because that is how it makes us feel. If the words are set to that music they give the conceptual mind a particular 'example' of something that makes one sad (the poet's beloved has deserted him) or happy (she has returned). The intimate connexion Nietzsche always sees between his philosophy and his music – the original *Prayer to Life* was, remember, intended to 'seduce' people to his philosophy[20] – is, I think, to be explained in Schopenhauer's way. While the words of the works from *Zarathustra* onwards announce Nietzsche's message of life-affirmation, only his music (including the 'music' of his poetry and poetic prose) can communicate the fundamental, 'dithyrambic' emotion that underlies and unifies those works, communicate it by making us *feel* that emotion.[21] Philosophy,

philosophy that aims to change people's lives, *cannot*, then, do without music. It follows that music was not something Nietzsche wrote *in addition* to philosophy. Philosophy and music are ultimately the same enterprise.*

A Month in the Country

As September drew to a close, Nietzsche's plan of keeping his ambient temperature between 9 and 12 degrees (Celsius) throughout the year[22] dictated that it was time once again for the annual migration. He had already stayed too long and was this year, he told his mother, 'the last bird to fly out of Sils'.[23] To avoid the still considerable heat in Nice, he opted for a month-long intermezzo in the hills above his beloved Gulf of Genoa, in Ruta Lugure.

Nietzsche loved Ruta. Sending Köselitz a letter headed 'Circa 400 meters above sea level, on the road that leads over the peninsula of Portofino', he feels impelled to offer

a word from this wonderful corner of the world...Think of an island in the Greek Archipelago, with forests and mountains strewn about at random which, one day, by accident, swam to the mainland and never came back. There is without doubt something Greek about it, but also something piratical, sudden, hidden, dangerous.[†,24]

Though he found the Venetian style cooking in Ruta's Albergo Italia, with its absence of 'proper meat', 'dreadful', he was able to live for a mere '5 francs a day, including wine'. And he loved the view from his room. 'To the left', he wrote Emily Fynn, 'the Gulf of Genoa as far as [Genoa's landmark] lighthouse; beneath my window and as far as the mountains, everything green, dark, refreshing to the eye'.[25] And he loved, too, the invigorating air, the walks 'between two seas' (the Gulf of Genoa and the Gulf of Tigullio), and the cool evenings: 'three times already', he writes, 'we have lit great, outdoor fires:...there is nothing more beautiful than seeing the flames blazing into...a cloudless sky'.[26] (As an image for art, these fires find their way into a new preface to *The Gay Science* (p. 409 above) composed during the month in Ruta: what 'we convalescents' need is 'a mocking, light, fleeting, divinely untroubled, divinely artificial art that, like a bright flame, blazes into a cloudless sky'.)

Though he at first found in Ruta the 'Robinson- [Crusoe] isolation'[27] he needed to work, once again it was interrupted by the tedious but adhesive Lanzky. Too polite to give Lanzky his marching orders, Nietzsche was thankful he would not be following him to his winter quarters in Nice.[28]

* As one might put it, they constitute a *Gesamtkunstwerk*, a 'collective artwork'. The idea that only a *musical* artwork can attain sufficient emotional power to change people's lives was the core of Wagner's aesthetic theory.
† For all Nietzsche's love of Greek antiquity, he never even contemplated setting foot in Greece. One suspects he wanted it to remain a place of the imagination, feared that reality would spoil the dream.

Fourth Winter in Nice

Nietzsche arrived in Nice, on October 20, for his fourth winter stay (seventh in the Nice–Genoa corner of the Mediterranean), and would remain there until the beginning of April 1887. Though the palms on the Promenade des Anglais led him to describe Nice as 'African',[29] this year it was bitterly cold, particularly in his north-facing, stove-less room in the Villa Speranza, the neighbouring building into which the Pension de Genève had expanded in order to acquire forty extra rooms.

'Blue fingers' made writing difficult.[30] Reluctantly, therefore, at the beginning of January, he moved to new lodgings in the Rue des Ponchettes 29 (now Number 17), which provided both sunlight and a stove. Perversely spartan as ever, however, he bragged that he had used the stove not once,[31] while continuing to add the blue of his fingers to his palette of local colours: 'The near mountains have been white for a long time (what a coquette nature seems in this colour-saturated landscape). To this "colourfulness" belongs also my blue fingers [and] black thoughts'.[32]

Shortly after his arrival in Nice, his peace of mind was disturbed by money demands from the Försters in Paraguay. The demands were presented once again in the form of an investment in a plot of land to which, it was suggested, he should one day emigrate. Nietzsche was impressed by the size of the land *Nueva Germania* had acquired: twelve square miles, he observed, was larger than some German principalities. And he wished them well in their dream of a major railway being constructed through their land, thus enabling them to export their timber. But, as he wrote Köselitz, he refused to have any personal involvement in this 'anti-Semitic enterprise',[33] and feared, moreover, that the Baselers, on hearing he was buying real estate, would decide that he obviously needed his pension no longer.[34] He declined the purchase while, in a somewhat cowardly way, laying the responsibility on Overbeck's shoulders. Overbeck (his man on the spot in Basel), he said, had advised him of serious problems with his pension that the purchase could cause.[35]

Preparations for Greatness

Following the completion of *Beyond Good and Evil*, Nietzsche's literary project for the remainder of 1886 was the reissue, in a revised form, of all of what he considered his major philosophical works to date. Thus, by the beginning of September, working with lightning speed, he had completed new prefaces to *Human, All-Too-Human* and to *The Birth of Tragedy*. A further preface was written to *Assorted Opinions and Maxims* and *The Wanderer and His Shadow*, which were now combined to form the second volume of *Human, All-Too-Human*. All four works, in these second editions, were published by Fritzsch on October 31. By the end of 1886, moreover, Parts I–III of *Zarathustra* had been bound together and published as a single work for the first time.

Not content with this, by the middle of November, Nietzsche had ready for the printers a new preface for a second edition of *Dawn* and, by the end of December, a preface for a new edition of *The Gay Science*. This second edition included a new motto on the title page, the new preface written in Ruta, and, at the end of the work, a whole new fifth book, followed by 'The Songs of Prince Vogelfrei', an expanded version of the 'Idylls of Messina' (pp. 325–6 above). Due to tiresome printing delays, these two works did not appear until June 1887.

Nietzsche had several complementary motives for this re-presentation of all his work to date. The first was that Fritzsch had acquired from Schmeitzner not only the rights to all his works but also the large number of unsold copies (pp. 401–2 above). Nietzsche hoped that rebinding the old copies with new prefaces would give them 'new wings' and so generate 'new interest, from a book-dealing point of view'.[36]

A second, less commercial, motive lay in Nietzsche's certainty that he was, as he puffed himself to Fritzsch, 'by far the most independent thinker of the present age, one who thinks far more than any other in the grand style'. He was, moreover, someone whose development as a thinker in the face of the ills and uncertainties of the present age was exemplary for his contemporaries. This made it a matter of urgency to present his works as a developmental whole, thereby showing, by example, how to 'inaugurate for Germany a new literature (the prelude to a moral self-education and culture which the Germans have lacked up to now)'.[37]

A final motive was provided by the sense that he had reached a turning point in his career. On completing the project of self–re-presentation he felt that 'a phase of my life has come to an end' so that 'now I have the whole, enormous task before me. Before me and, still more, on top of me'.[38] As we know, this enormous task, this work 'in the grand style' that would systematically sum up his entire philosophy (and thereby allow him entry into the ranks of the truly great German philosophers), was to bear the grandiose title *The Will to Power: Attempt at a Revaluation of all Values*. This project appears for the first time in the notebooks from late 1885[39] and, in the letters, for the first time in August 1886, he thinks that a 'pilgrimage' to Corte in Corsica, the place of Napoleon's conception, is an appropriately world-historical preparation for the task ahead.[40] Hence a bringing-to-closure of the totality of his works to date, a clearing of the decks, was a necessary prelude to focusing his efforts on this crowning project. A mark of his sense of closure was the momentary experience of nausea at all these works: 'between ourselves', he wrote Köselitz, 'I can't stand them'.[41]

The Prefaces of 1886

In the same letter, Nietzsche tells Köselitz that he regards it as 'a piece of luck' that he had neither *The Birth of Tragedy* nor *Human, All-Too-Human* to hand as he was writing (in Sils Maria) their new prefaces.[42] The reason he regards this as fortunate is that, apart from selling books, the point of the new set of prefaces is something other than providing accurate guides to the contents of the books. Rather, as already noted, their point is to present 'a kind of narrative of spiritual development',[43] a *Bildungsroman*, a story of his 'self-education' that will be exemplary for the Germans (and Western modernity as a whole). In the prefaces Nietzsche seeks to present himself as a spiritual *hero*. But, as *The Gay Science* observes (p. 335 above), to discover the hero that is 'concealed in everyday characters' one needs artistic 'distance' from one's subject matter to avoid losing the forest on account of the trees. Aesthetic distance means, however, that 'there is a good deal one no longer sees, and much our eye has to add if we are to see anything at all'.[44] In a word, one needs to *fake* things a bit. It follows, then, that we should not expect scholarly accuracy from the 1886 prefaces. In order for him to present himself as a 'monumental', exemplary figure, the thinker he portrays has to be to a certain degree, like all role models, an artistic fiction. (Art, Picasso once observed, is the lie that tells the truth.)

That the new prefaces are not to be regarded as anything like scholarly reports is particularly evident with respect to the 'Attempt at a Self-Criticism' that precedes the second edition of *The Birth of Tragedy*. The problem is not that Nietzsche ungenerously lambastes the style of his first book – 'badly written, clumsy, embarrassing, with a rage for imagery and confused in its imagery, emotional, here and there sugary to the point of effeminacy'. It is rather that he tries to modulate a work which, in reality, as we saw, is every bit as committed to metaphysical idealism and to pessimism about human life as is Schopenhauer into a work whose true message is naturalism and life-affirmation. That message, he claims (without, remember, the work before him), 'fundamentally ran counter to both the spirit and taste of Kant and Schopenhauer' but was spoilt by the attempt to express it 'in Schopenhauerian and Kantian formulations'. Trying, for the sake of his narrative, to paint a picture of the 'true' Nietzsche as already present, in embryo, in *The Birth*, he gives a thoroughly unreliable account of its content. (It is notable that the new Book V of *The Gay Science*, written at the same time but not under the same constraints, is much more accurate: 'It may be recalled, at least among my friends, that initially I approached the modern world [and in particular] . . . the philosophical pessimism of the nineteenth century as if it were a symptom of a higher force of thought'.)[45]

Similarly, in the new preface to *Human, All-Too-Human* (now Volume I of the expanded work), he seeks to suggest he was never *really* either a Schopenhauerian or a Wagnerian. Lacking the courage he later acquired to face up to the isolation of the radical thinker, he suggests,

> I *knowingly-wilfully* closed my eyes before Schopenhauer's blind will to [Christian] morality at a time when I was already sufficiently clear-sighted about morality. Likewise *I deceived myself* over Richard Wagner's incurable romanticism, as though it were a beginning and not an end [my emphases].

Writing to Fritzsch (who, as we know, was also Wagner's publisher) concerning the preface to Volume II of the expanded *Human, All-Too-Human*, Nietzsche says that its point is 'to make an end of the eternal misunderstanding in relation to my break with R. Wagner . . . to say the main thing clearly'.[46] And what he says is that at the time of writing *Human, All-Too-Human* it was, for him,

> high time indeed to *say farewell*: and I immediately received a confirmation of the fact. Richard Wagner, seemingly the all-conquering, actually a decaying, despairing romantic, suddenly sank down helpless and shattered before the Christian cross [Nietzsche's account of *Parsifal*] . . . Was there no German with eyes in his head . . . for this dreadful spectacle?

Actually, though, Nietzsche's attitude to Wagner was much more nuanced than this. Less than a month after writing this he wrote the already-quoted letter to Overbeck (pp. 359–60 above) affirming his continuing belief 'in the ideal in which Wagner believed' and saying that it was only the 'human-all-too-human' in Wagner over which he 'stumbled'. In an important sense he *never* said farewell to Wagner. But the idea of a dramatic and total break makes a better story.

The Gay Science, Book V: Being Scientific about Science

The most substantial part of the self-re-presentation project was the new Book V added to *The Gay Science* almost five years after the appearance of the first four books. Since the serene luminosity of 'We Fearless Ones' reveals Nietzsche at the height of his powers, it deserves an extended discussion.

* * *

In German, I have pointed out, everything is 'science' (*Wissenschaft*). The humanities, including, importantly, philosophy, are the 'spiritual-intellectual sciences' (*Geisteswissenschaften*). 'Science' in the English sense corresponds to the *Naturwissenschaften*, the 'natural sciences'. When Nietzsche speaks simply of 'science' he is speaking collectively of both the natural and human sciences, though usually it is the latter that are foremost in his mind. Though science is supposed to be defined and distinguished from other forms of human belief by being free of irrational 'prejudice', 'conviction', and 'faith' – 'in science, convictions have no rights of citizenship'[47] – several major sections of Book V are concerned to expose ways in which science is frequently free of none of these things. A major concern, therefore, is to render 'science', and in particular philosophy, truly scientific.

One target of criticism is natural science, or, more exactly, 'materialist' natural science, posing as metaphysics. The target is the physicist who makes two claims which together amount to arrogant stupidity. First, that his 'interpretation' of, or 'perspective' on, the world, which discloses it as measurable chunks of matter pushed around by mathematically quantifiable mechanical forces, grasps reality *as it really is*. Second, that his is 'the *only* rightful interpretation of the world'.[48] I shall call the combination of these two claims – science is true and nothing else is – the 'absolutising' of the scientific perspective.

Nietzsche mentions the 'pedantic Englishman', Herbert Spencer, as someone who claimed to have produced an 'ultimate perspective', but one may suspect that he also has his erstwhile friend Paul Rée, a dogmatic scientific naturalist, in mind. Were he alive now he would surely target dogmatic materialists such as Daniel Dennett and Richard Dawkins as prime exemplars of unscientific science-worship.

Nietzsche points out that the two elements of the absolutiser's position are both 'prejudices'. Since, as already noted, we 'cannot look around our corner',[49] cannot step outside our minds, we can have no *certainty* that *any* world-interpretation produced by our 'four-cornered little human reason'[50] corresponds completely, or even partially, to reality. And since we cannot be certain that our interpretation grasps the world as it really is, we have no grounds for being dismissive of other interpretations: 'good taste' demands 'reverence for everything that lies beyond [one's own] interpretation'.[51]

Instead of scientistic arrogance, the watchword for the truly scientific spirit is 'modesty'. The very word 'philosophy', '*lover* of wisdom', Nietzsche points out, was coined by modest Greeks who, apart from 'conceited' exceptions such as Pythagoras and Plato, never claimed to *be* wise or to *know* anything of real importance.[52] A truly scientific person is modest about his own world-interpretation – a modesty that requires 'sovereignty and strength'.

Every kind of 'fanaticism', whether it takes the form of socialism, Russian nihilism, the 'realism' of Flaubert and Zola or the 'scientific-positivist' outlook of the present age, is actually a sign of a weak and timid will that lacks the courage to live in a world of uncertainty. Lacking, as Nietzsche puts it, the courage to 'maintain [himself] on the lightest of ropes and possibilities', to dance 'beside abysses', the weak-willed fanatic needs to be 'commanded' by some prepackaged 'faith', needs to become a 'believer' in a 'single point of view'.[53]

Being a good scientist or philosopher is, then, as one might put it, a matter of being of good character. People who are of such a character live, Nietzsche writes, in the awareness of a world which has 'become infinite': become infinite because, particularly when we take into account the possibility of world-perspectives belonging to non-human creatures, we see that there is no limit to the number of possible world-interpretations, each quite possibly, in its own way, as good as every other one. Living in such a world, 'we' (Nietzsche and the 'friends' for whom Book V is written)[54] are far away from 'the ridiculous immodesty of decreeing from our angle that perspectives are *permitted* only from that angle'.[55]

What we confront, here, once again, is Nietzsche's doctrine of 'perspectivism': the human mind moulds all its input, and since we can never step outside it, we can never have absolute certainty that any of our world interpretations are true. To this, as I called it, 'Kantian' inheritance (p. 416 above), Nietzsche now makes two modifications. First, there are *many* different human perspectives on the world (as well, possibly, as non-human perspectives). And, second, each perspective is the product of some particular need, desire, emotion or interest.[56]

What kind of metaphysical account of reality is implied by perspectivism? As I have suggested, there are two possible interpretations of Nietzsche's position. The first is the 'postmodernist' reading: since there are many different interpretations of reality none of which can claim to be *truer* than the others, it follows that *no* interpretation can claim to represent the world as it really is. And since no representation can make that claim, it makes no sense to say that reality *has* any particular character – from which it follows that the very idea of an interpretation being true of reality is incoherent. The second interpretation, the 'plural realist' reading, as I called it (p. 338 above), suggests, in an ecumenical spirit, that the fact that we have many, in their own way, equally good interpretations of the world suggests that *all*, or at least many, of them are true of a multi-faceted reality – true of a reality that has many aspects, one aspect being revealed by one interpretation, another by a different one.

It is not easy to decide between these interpretations. There is no doubt that, in the notebooks at least, Nietzsche sometimes says things which suggest postmodernism.[57] As earlier indicated, though I incline to the plural realist reading, I want to defer a firm decision between these rivals until we come to the final discussion of perspectivism in the *Genealogy of Morals*. Here, however, I would like to reemphasize one point from the previous chapter. The whole purpose of the violent language in which the will-to-power metaphysics is expressed in *Beyond Good and Evil* is to force the sentimental 'idealists' to face up to *reality* – to, at least, an account of reality which demands of rational beings that they accord it strong, though always provisional, acceptance as being *true*. If, then, we read Nietzsche as undermining the very idea of truth, we emasculate *Beyond Good and Evil*. It might, of course, be that Nietzsche's philosophy as a whole is inconsistent, that he says one thing when talking about truth and reality and a different thing when talking about the will to power. But inconsistency should be attributed to him only as a very last resort.

* * *

Perspective-absolutisers, those who do not realise that their perspectives *are* perspectives, represent one kind of 'prejudice' in science. Another is exposed in a section with the intriguing title 'To What Extent We, Too, Are Still Pious'.[58]

'Convictions', to repeat, have no 'rights of citizenship' in science. Permitted only is the 'hypothesis', a 'tentative experimental standpoint', which, however, always remains 'under police supervision, under the police of mistrust'.[59] Yet, Nietzsche asks, is it not the case that in order for conviction-rejecting science even to *begin* there must be the prior conviction that '*Nothing is more* necessary than truth'? The practice of science, in other words, rests on 'the unconditional will to truth', the will to truth 'at any price'. What, Nietzsche now asks, is the ground of this will? It must, he decides, rest either on the will not to deceive or (at first sight the most obvious answer) the will not to be deceived. In fact, however, it cannot rest on the latter, on prudential calculation, since it is perfectly obvious that on many occasions it is more beneficial to be deceived than to know the truth. (Suppose my partner is guilty of just one infidelity that is now well over and long in the past, but that I am the type of person whom knowledge of the infidelity would drive to murderous anger and suicidal despair. In this situation it is more beneficial for all concerned that I should be deceived about my partner's fidelity.) Hence, contrary to expectations, the unconditioned will to truth must actually be based on the will not to deceive anyone – including oneself – and here, says Nietzsche, 'we stand on moral grounds': the will to truth at any price is a *moral* commitment. But whence does truthfulness acquire this unconditional value? For reasons already given, it cannot acquire it from any benefit that accrues to us in the natural world. So, Nietzsche concludes, it must derive from benefits which supposedly accrue to us in *another* world: 'those who are truthful in that audacious and ultimate sense which faith in science presupposes *thereby affirm another world than that of life [and] nature*'. Nietzsche concludes the section by saying that what he has demonstrated is that 'even we knowers of today, we godless anti-metaphysicians, take our fire from the…Christian faith which was also Plato's faith that God is truth, that truth is divine…But what if God himself turned out to be our longest lie?'

Nietzsche obviously does not mean that those with 'faith in science' consciously affirm the existence of the Christian heaven, for that is what modern men of science actively deny. What he means, rather, is that their commitment to the overriding value of truthfulness is, first, a hangover from our Christian past and, second, completely irrational given that, as we now know, Christian metaphysics is a 'lie'.

One's immediate response to this peculiar argument, I think, is to say that it is completely naive to suppose that the practice of science rests on the unconditional will to truth. People practise science for all sorts of reasons, the most obvious being to make a living. But Nietzsche is perfectly aware of this. In the early part of *The Gay Science* he observes that 'even *without* this new passion – I mean the passion for knowledge – science would be promoted: up to now it has grown and matured without it', and he goes on to observe that, in the past, the 'scientific drive' has often been motivated by status-seeking, curiosity, or fear of boredom.[60] On a more institutional level, the notebooks of this period remark (in *apparent* contradiction to the *Gay Science* passage) that '*fear of the unpredictable* [is] *the hidden instinct* of science'.[61] And in the *Genealogy of Morals*, the book he was constructing as this final book of *The Gay Science* appeared, he explicitly distinguishes 'believers' in truth from the majority of scientists as 'the rarer cases…the last idealists we have today among philosophers and scholars'.[62]

Contrary to appearances, therefore, those who are 'still pious' – still *too* pious – are not scientists (natural scientists, philosophers, and scholars) in general but rather that tiny minority for whom the practice of science *is* motivated by the unconditional will to truth. The overly pious are the 'idealists' of truth, those for whom the search for truth *is* an absolute ideal, who believe that in all circumstances they ought to ascertain the truth 'whatever the cost'. The question is: who might they be?

We are told quite explicitly: it is 'we' who are 'pious', 'we God-less anti-metaphysicians'. Paradigmatically, in other words, it is *himself and Rée* in the period of their collaboration on the 'positivist' programme of demolishing, as they repeatedly put it, 'metaphysics'. For it was in that period, it will be remembered, that Nietzsche recognised, with Byron, that 'the tree of knowledge is not that of life' (p. 256 above), that, as often as not, knowledge brings sorrow rather than joy – the knowledge, for example, that there is no God. Nonetheless, he insisted at that time, 'any degree of . . . melancholy is better than . . . incurably dirtying one's intellectual conscience and prostituting it' through a 'romantic return . . . to Christianity'.[63] It is true that in the privacy of the notebooks of the positivist period he worried that Rée's sardonic 'psychological observations' would make people contemptuous of themselves and suspicious of others,[64] but none of these private doubts were allowed to disturb the truth-at-any-cost ethos of the official programme.

What, in short, section 344 of *The Gay Science* really constitutes is another part of his long goodbye to Rée together with an explanation of why, intellectually, the two had to part; why Nietzsche outgrew – why *one should* outgrow – his 'réealism' of the late 1870s. (In a similar way, Book V's critique of 'scholars' – they have cramped digestions from sitting too much, and cramped minds from forcing them into a narrow speciality whose importance they vastly overestimate – is a farewell to Rohde and an explanation of why he, too, has to be outgrown. Nietzsche makes this almost completely explicit by saying that he is describing the 'friends of [his] youth' who have become 'cramped beyond recognition'.)[65]

In what way does Nietzsche think he has outgrown the will to truth-at-any-price and what are the consequences of that development? Nietzsche never abandons the idea of intellectual honesty as a supreme virtue. In the notebooks of this period one finds 'The ultimate virtue . . . *our* virtue is called: honesty. For the rest we are only the heirs . . . of virtues that were not collected and treasured by us'.[66] In Book V he honours Schopenhauer's 'integrity [his] unconditional honest atheism', his unflinching honesty about the pain of life which, combined with his adherence to Christian morality, demolished the possibility of interpreting the world as the product of a benevolent creator. And he claims that it is the *Christian* virtue of truthfulness that triumphs, in Schopenhauer, over Christian metaphysics: it was 'Christian conscience, translated and sublimated into a scientific conscience, into intellectual cleanliness at any price' that 'triumphed over the Christian God'.[67]

But, to repeat the question, 'what if God turns out to be [a] lie'? What if the unconditional will to truth 'presupposes' God, heaven, and the immortal soul, but we become convinced that there is no God? Then – this is the conclusion Nietzsche is leading us towards – we must proceed beyond Schopenhauer by turning an 'honest' eye not only on Christian metaphysics but also on Christian morality, *including the supposed virtue of truthfulness*. And the result of that – the result of being completely *honest* about the will to truth – is to see that no justification exists for pursuing truth 'at any price', that truth, knowledge of truth, is *not* the highest value. The unconditional will to truth auto-destructs. This does not mean, of course, that we give up doing science. But it means that we do it, when we do it, for prudential rather than moral reasons. Truth 'at any price' gives way to truth 'when the price is right'. If, for example, we really became convinced that the La Rochefoucauld–Rée programme of 'psychological observations' had the effect of undermining life, then we should have to abandon it. For ultimate value attaches not to the 'tree of knowledge' but rather to 'the tree of life'. There is more to be said on this topic, which, however, I shall reserve for the next chapter.

The Wanderer Speaks

As with all Nietzsche's writings, the driving force behind Book V is an 'untimely' stance towards Western modernity, the alienated stance of, as he again calls himself, a 'homeless...wanderer'.[68] It is a stance thoroughly critical of the current state of Western culture, though at the same time full of hope for – indeed, as we shall see, 'faith' in – its future. The main fact about how we are now is, of course, the death of God:

> The greatest recent event – that 'God is dead'; that belief in the Christian God has become unbelievable – is already casting its first shadow over Europe...Some kind of sun seems to have set, some old, deep trust turned to doubt.

But, Nietzsche continues, very few have grasped 'how much must collapse because it was built on this faith...for example, our entire European morality'. Few have grasped the 'monstrous logic of horror' that must follow, 'the long dense succession of demolition, destruction, downfall, upheaval that now stands ahead'.[69]

Nietzsche thinks – prophetically – of a century of warfare as one of the traumatic consequences of the collapse of the old faith and the old morality. Another is the malaise of pessimism and nihilism. Schopenhauer's pessimism – his denial of the 'value of existence' – is, says Nietzsche, a 'pan-European' phenomenon: Schopenhauer speaks not just for himself but for post-Christian Western consciousness in general. And his refutation of the Christian meaning of life immediately raises the 'terrifying' question: '*does existence have any meaning at all?*'[70] Since, in other words, a meaningless life is a worthless life, the loss of the old faith means that, deep down, modern Western humanity thinks that life is not worth living.

A further consequence of the collapse of the old morality is the 'Americanisation' of the West – Nietzsche expands, here, on what I have called his 'motley' critique of modernity. In the past, he reflects, a man's profession was, or more accurately 'became', his character; through accident of birth and allied forms of social 'coercion' what was originally 'artifice' became 'nature'. A man's professional role in society was accepted as his 'destiny'. This faith was embodied in the medieval guilds and class distinctions, and so enabled one to build the 'broad-based social pyramid' of feudalism. Whatever one might say against the coercive character of the Middle Ages, one can 'at least credit it' with social 'durability' – and 'durability', Nietzsche adds, is a 'first-rank value on earth'. Now, however, with the collapse of the old faith, we live in an age of 'democratic' anarchy. We are dominated by the 'American faith...according to which the individual is convinced he can do just about anything *and is up to playing any role,* and everyone experiments with himself'. This means that profession or role no longer constitutes 'character' or 'destiny', that roles are simply *acted out* on a temporary basis. Western modernity is thus an age of *actors* (who, as we know, 'play many parts'). It is an age of fluidity and unpredictability which has the consequence that the capacity for social 'architecture', 'the strength to build', is now 'paralysed':

> what is dying out is that fundamental faith on the basis of which someone could calculate, promise and project, and sacrifice the future to his plan – namely, the basic faith that man has value and meaning only insofar as he is *a stone in a great edifice*; to this end he must be *firm*, above all a 'stone'…above all not an actor!…what from now on *can* never be built is a society in the old sense of the term…*We are all no longer material for a society*.[71]

The West is, then, in a parlous condition. In its 'motley' state it lacks the 'hardness, uniformity and simplicity of form' of a shared, as I called it, 'game plan' (p. 418 above) possession of which is necessary to survive and thrive in a competitive world. But the situation is not hopeless. For one thing, for all the difficulties it creates, the collapse of Christianity, since it made our culture sick, is fundamentally a cause for celebration. For another, we possess a secret 'faith', a vision of what should and must redeem us from the present and the past. To what end, Nietzsche asks rhetorically, have we 'overcome' our Christian past? For the sake of 'unbelief'? 'No', he replies, 'you know better than that, my friends! The hidden Yes in you is stronger than all Nos and Maybes that afflict you and your age like a disease'. Far from being a whimpering 'end of history', modernity is, Nietzsche believes, a 'time of transition'.[72] To what?

Nietzsche's Undiscovered Land

The bulk of *The Gay Science* was written, it will be remembered, in Columbus's city of Genoa. Book V, completed within sight of Genoa, in Ruta, is, like its predecessors, permeated by the sight and smell of the sea. What, more than anything else, binds it to the earlier books is the persistence of the Columbus image: we 'friends' of Nietzsche, we 'free spirits', he tells us, rejoice in the sight of the 'open sea'.[73] We who 'must sail the seas' are willing 'emigrants'.[74] As for all seafarers, however, our journey must have a destination: a hope and vision of the future which transforms us from mere sailors into 'argonauts of the ideal'. Though we have often suffered 'shipwreck,' we are voyaging on towards 'an as yet undiscovered land the boundaries of which no one has yet surveyed…a world so over-rich in what is beautiful, strange, questionable, terrible [by today's standards], and divine'.[75]

What is this 'land'? Even though its exact 'boundaries' are unknown, surely we must know *something* of its character, for otherwise why would it be our destination? At the very least, surely, something of its character must be inferable from Nietzsche's critique of the present.

The main feature of the promised land is that, in contrast to the 'sickness' of Christian culture, it will exhibit 'the great health'.[76] But what is that? Nietzsche's discussion suggests that the ideal 'we argonauts' pursue consists in fact of two ideals, one pertaining to the health of the community, the other to the health of individuals.

Communal Health

One has to leave a city, observes Nietzsche, in order to see the height of its towers. (He is surely thinking of Naumburg, where the imposing height of the cathedral towers, visible for miles over the flat landscape, really can only be appreciated from a distance.) Similarly, one has to 'leave' our present morality and 'wander' among other moralities in order to grasp ours for what it is. One needs to be careful, however, to view it from a position outside every morality, for otherwise our observations about morality will simply be 'prejudices about prejudices'.[77] The product of this wandering, he writes, is to see how utterly 'childish' it is to suppose that Christian morality is universally binding, the only 'true' morality. It is *equally* 'childish', however, to infer from the fact of many moralities the conclusion that *no* morality is binding. Every society needs a morality, for without it there can be no society.[78]

Morality, Nietzsche continues, is a kind of medicine, 'the most famous of all medicines'.[79] If it is good medicine, in other words, what it will produce is communal *health*. This view of morality has two consequences. First, what kind of morality a society needs at a given point in its history will vary according to the conditions it finds itself in, the 'diseases' that threaten it. And second, as emphasised earlier, since Nietzsche cannot know what 'diseases' will threaten in the future, his account of the morality of his future 'land' has to be highly abstract: all he can provide are the structural features which, he believes, any healthy morality must exhibit.

One of these structural features – Nietzsche elaborates, here, on the point made in *Beyond Good and Evil* – is that morality will be closely allied to religion. Religions, he writes, do not invent 'ways of life'. The function of a religion, rather, is to validate a form of life that already exists but has, as yet, no sense of its special worth. The founder of a religion selects a particular culture and provides a narrative which explains why it is the highest way of life ('God's chosen people', and so on). A religion, in other words, collects together a group of people 'who have not yet recognised each other as allies', making it 'a long festival of recognition'.[80] (A *Bayreuth* Festival, purged of the all-too-human, is, I suggest, the subtext here.)

'Way of life' is just another – more revealing – word for what Nietzsche means by 'morality'. So what a religion does is to validate a morality, provide it with *authority*. It establishes a '*disciplina voluntatis* (discipline of the will)'[81] by, as we know, raising selected figures to exemplary status, to the status of gods or heroes, and (with the help, I suggested, of the 'collective artwork') endowing them with charismatic authority. This is not so difficult to do since man, by nature, is 'a venerating animal':[82] given half a chance, he will revere and be moved to live in imitation of an effectively presented life-model.

Religions, Nietzsche says, do, in general, two other things. First, they establish a kind of governance by the better type of person:

> A church is above all a structure for ruling that secures the highest rank to the *more spiritual* human beings and that *believes* in the power of spirituality to the extent of forbidding itself the use of all cruder instruments of force; and on that score alone the church is under all circumstances a *nobler* institution than the state.[83]

Second, the way of life which it presents as possessing the highest worth it elevates into 'a good for which one fights and under certain circumstances even gives one's life'.[84] Religion illuminates a communal way of life in such a way that one's contribution to the preservation and flourishing of that community becomes one's highest value, *the meaning of one's life*, a meaning for which, sometimes, one is prepared to die. In the ideal, meaning-giving, nation you do not ask what your nation can do for you, but what you can do for your nation.

It is, I think, obvious that these remarks about morality and religion are not mere history but rather 'signposts' to the future society which is Nietzsche's guiding 'ideal'. Since he knows perfectly well, for instance, that, historically, the Church has by no means always abjured 'cruder instruments of force', it is clear that he is describing an ideal 'church'. What, then, we can take from this discussion is further evidence that Nietzsche is far from being the 'atheist' he is often represented as being. For all his rejection of *Christian* religion, his future society will be a religious society: it will be led, at least spiritually, by something resembling a priesthood, will have some kind of pantheon of 'monumental' figures so that it validates a form of life which gives meaning to individual lives and overcomes, thereby, the meaninglessness of modernity. And regular 'festive' occasions will gather the community in celebratory reaffirmation of its fundamental morality: the 'collective artwork' will collect the community into a cohesive unity, thereby endowing it with that 'first-rate value on earth', 'durability'.

Mental Health

Nietzsche writes that as well as his ideal of *communal* 'health', 'another ideal runs before us ... the ideal of a human, superhuman well-being and benevolence',[85] an ideal of *individual* health. Nietzsche elaborates on this conception of 'the superman', a conception we should aspire to emulate, in a brilliant section entitled *What is Romanticism?*[86]

'Pessimism', Nietzsche assures us (attaching a new and unusual meaning to the term), is true: life and suffering are inseparable. There are, however, two kinds of 'pessimism': 'romantic' and 'Dionysian'. Romantic pessimism takes suffering to be an insuperable objection to life. In art or philosophy, therefore, what the romantic seeks is 'quiet, stillness, calm seas, redemption from themselves ... or else intoxication, paroxysm, numbness, madness'. Romanticism, in short, is escapism. It 'denies' life. Naturally, it is the usual suspects, Wagner, Schopenhauer, and the Christians, who are identified as romantics.*

Nietzsche treats romanticism as a symptom of a physiological condition: of an 'impoverishment of life', a condition of low energy. The 'antithesis' is a 'superabundance of life'

---

* Surprisingly, however, Nietzsche adds Epicurus to the list: 'the "Christian"', he writes, 'is really simply a kind of Epicurean and, like him, essentially a romantic' (GS 370). This rejection of the hero of *Dawn* is startling, since in Book I of the very same book, he still remains a great love: 'Yes, I am proud to experience Epicurus's character in a way unlike perhaps anyone else, and to enjoy, in everything I hear and read of him, his happiness' (GS 45). What has happened, of course, between 1882 and 1886, is the will to power: if the human essence is the will to power, happiness, Nietzsche thinks, has to be conceived as increasing one's power over the world rather than withdrawing from it into 'Epicurus's garden'. What he seems, at least temporarily, to have forgotten, however, is his notion of the 'heroic-idyllic' (pp. 308–9 above), a conception that seemed to make it possible to *combine* Epicurean serenity with a life of challenge and action.

(which as we know is 'will to power'), an 'overflowing of energy pregnant with future'. This is the underlying condition of the 'Dionysian pessimist' who not only finds suffering no objection to life but positively welcomes it. The ideal of this condition is 'the Dionysian god or man' who (unlike the 'idealist' attacked in *Beyond Good and Evil*)

> can allow himself not only the sight of what is terrible and questionable but also the terrible deed and every luxury of destruction, decomposition, negation; in his case, what is evil, absurd, and ugly seems, as it were, permissible owing to an excess of procreating, fertilizing forces capable of turning any desert into lush farmland.[87]

He elaborates on this idea in the notebooks:

> the decision on what excites pleasure and unpleasure depends on the degree of power: the same thing which, in the case of a small quantum of power, appears as a danger and as having to be repulsed immediately, with a greater consciousness of a plenitude of power, can result in voluptuous stimulation, a feeling of pleasure...Pleasure and unpleasure are never 'original facts'...[They are variable] *reactions of the will (affects).*[88]

In other words, that which seems 'evil, absurd, and ugly' to someone who possesses only a small 'quantum' of power will appear exciting and delightful, an occasion for exercising and expanding one's 'will to power', to someone with a large quantum. Nietzsche's ideal of individual mental health is, then, someone so richly endowed with the will to power that *everything* that to most people appears 'terrible and questionable' is welcomed as an occasion for 'overcoming', an overcoming one is sublimely confident one can achieve.

As he recognises, Nietzsche's ideal is set extraordinarily high: only a 'Dionysian god or [super]man' can fully achieve it. (I shall return, in Chapter 24, to the question of the significance that 'Dionysian' has here.) Nonetheless, though it may seem to verge on megalomania, it is based, I think, on quite familiar experiences. When we are 'down' everything seems impossible, too hard, the whole world against us. We wish – 'romantically' – we were somewhere else. But when we are 'up' nothing seems too difficult; the world is at our feet. We feel full of energy and confidence, confidence in our power to overcome the 'terrible and questionable'. And so we (we who are full of 'the power of positive thinking', another sub-Nietzschean concept) *welcome* the stressful in the way in which a mountain climber welcomes the challenge of the mountain. And we feel this way not just about what lies within our own direct control but also about the world in general: that in one way or other, it will all work out for the best in the long run. Nietzsche's ideal of spiritual health imagines this state of 'Dionysian' ecstasy as not just a momentary condition but a permanent state:

> Most people simply do not believe in elevated moods, unless these last for moments only or at most a quarter of an hour...But to be a human being with one elevated feeling – to be a single great mood incarnate – that has hitherto been a mere dream...as yet history does not offer us any certain examples. Nevertheless history might one day give birth to such people [to the feeling of]...a continual ascent as if on stairs and at the same time a sense of resting on clouds.[89]

The mark of having reached that ideal of health is, of course, the ability to will the eternal return, to 'redeem' the 'terrible and questionable' by seeing how it fits as an essential component into a divine totality. Perfect mental health, we know, is being able to cry '*Da capo!*' *Encore!* to the 'whole play and performance'[90] down to the very last detail.

'A Lovely Thought: Via Sils to Greece!'[91]

Nietzsche calls the joyful 'pessimism' that he opposes to romanticism 'classical'. Understood properly, he says (not, that is, as meaning '*serenely* rational'), the 'vision' of a restored classicism belongs to his 'innermost' self,[92] the self that, ever since Pforta, has been in love with classical antiquity. In a properly qualified sense, therefore, the watchword for the attainment of individual health (and of communal health, too, since the structure of Nietzsche's ideal community is, we have seen, taken, almost word for word, from Plato) is 'back to the Greeks'.

This is the key to understanding the meaning of Nietzsche's claim that he and his notional 'friends' are, though 'homeless' in the present, 'at home' somewhere else. We are at home, he says, because we are

> – and let this be our word of honour – *good Europeans*, the heirs of Europe (*Europa*), the rich heirs of millennia of European spirit, the rich, oversupplied, but also overly obligated heirs of thousands of years of European spirit. As such we have outgrown Christianity and are averse to it.[93]

It is very important to see that by 'the European' Nietzsche means 'the classical'. Unlike thinkers such as Hölderlin and Heidegger, he looks for no synthesis between the classical and the Christian. Rather, he *excludes* 'oriental'[94] Christianity from the authentically 'European' – as does the name 'Europe'.* The picture he offers, then, is this. We are 'heirs' to millennia of 'European' values. But the mixture is muddy and confused, we are 'oversupplied' with conflicting obligations – our morality is a 'battle-ground' (see p. 460 below) of competing and conflicting moralities, slave and master, classical and Christian. The task is to recover consistency by 'outgrowing', overcoming, the Christian. Of course, we cannot and do not want to literally re-create 'the Greek': 'we do not want to return to any past period'.[95] But that just means that, like the French of the seventeenth century, we need to reinterpret, to 'translate' the classical so that it makes sense in a modern context:

> The French of Corneille's age as well as those of the Revolution took possession of Roman antiquity in a way for which we would no longer have courage enough...And Roman antiquity itself: how forcibly and at the same time how naively it took hold of everything good and lofty of Greek antiquity. How they translated things into the Roman present!... They did not know the delights of the historical sense ['cultural safety']...translation was a form of conquest. Not only did one omit what was historical; one also added allusions to

---

* The word Nietzsche uses, *Europa*, is, of course, the standard German word for 'Europe'. Steeped as he is, however, in Greek mythology, the knowledge that 'Europa' originally applied solely to Greece would never have been far from his mind. (The name derived from that of a Phoenician princess, raped by Zeus in the form of a bull, who later became queen of Crete.)

the present and, above, all, struck out the name of the poet and replaced it with one's own –
not with any sense of theft but with the very best conscience of the *Imperium Romanum*.[96]

This, surely, gives us the key to Nietzsche's vision of the future. What inspires and provides
the outline of the 'great health' is the classical, ultimately the Greek. What provides the
medium into which that structure is to be 'translated' is the modern.

23

The Genealogy of Morals

Parsifal, Dostoyevsky, and a 'Well-Intentioned' Earthquake

THE YEAR 1887 began with a deep freeze: 'Europe', Nietzsche wrote Elizabeth, sweltering in Paraguay, 'has transformed itself into a snow-mountain and polar bear'. Though there was none in Nice itself, the hills surrounding his winter quarters were powdered with snow.[1] In spite of his new, south-facing room in the Rue des Ponchettes (p. 436 above) the 'blue-finger' problem persisted, as did a lowering of health and spirits, the cumulative effect, he thought, of two months of frost and rain.[2] Towards the end of January, however, his spirits received a lift from an unexpected quarter: a visit to Monte Carlo to hear the prelude to *Parsifal*. 'Leaving aside the question of the use of such music and regarding it purely aesthetically', he wrote Köselitz,

> has Wagner ever done anything better? The highest psychological awareness and definiteness with regard to what should be said, expressed, *communicated*, the shortest and most direct form thereof, every nuance of feeling reduced to the epigrammatic: a clarity of music as a descriptive art...and a sublime and extraordinary feeling, experience, eventfulness, of the soul at the very heart of the music which honours Wagner to the highest degree.[3]

And in the notebooks he calls it 'the greatest masterpiece of the sublime that I know'. 'Nothing else grasps Christianity so deeply or brings one to have such intense sympathy with it', he writes, adding that 'no painter had painted such a dark, melancholy vision' as do its final bars, 'not Dante, not Leonardo'.[4] A couple of months later he writes Köselitz that what is wrong with modern music is that it has become 'theatrical', subordinated to the conventions of drama. There should be, he adds 'a return of music from its theatrical un-nature to the nature of music'.[5] Two connected points emerge from these reflections on Wagner: first, a repetition of the Schopenhauerian view that music is a far deeper spiritual phenomenon than words or drama, and, second, Nietzsche's continuing valuing of ecstatic self-transcendence – his word for 'sublime' is *erhoben*, which means, literally, 'raised up above'.

* * *

The second event that helped lift the oppression of winter was the discovery, at the beginning of February, of Dostoyevsky. Chancing, in a Nice bookshop, upon a French translation
of *Notes from the Underground* by an author he had never heard of, he quickly progressed to
Humiliated and Oppressed, 'one of the most human books ever written',[6] and to *House of the
Dead*. With joy he recognised in the 'great psychologist' a view of the human condition to
which he felt 'instinctively related'.[7]

That Nietzsche should have felt Dostoyevsky and himself to be 'on the same wavelength'
comes as no surprise to a reader of *Zarathustra*. The similarity between Nietzsche's 'Pale
Criminal' and Dostoyevsky's Raskolnikov, the former as puzzled about the motives for
the murder he has committed as the latter, has led many people to believe that Nietzsche
must have known *Crime and Punishment* by 1883. In fact, though, there is no reason to
doubt his assertion that he had never heard of him before 1887.[8] In connexion with the
Nietzsche–Dostoyevsky affinity it is worth noticing that both men (Dostoyevsky after his
mock execution and exile to Siberia) were strong opponents of 'socialism', 'anarchism',
and 'nihilism', and that both believed in the retention and restoration of the firm, aristocratic, religiously sanctioned social hierarchy of the past. The difference, however, was
that Dostoyevsky believed in a *Christian* aristocratic society. This is why Nietzsche writes
Brandes that while he esteems Dostoyevsky as 'the most valuable psychological material
that I know', he is, nonetheless, 'in a strange way thankful to him that he is quite contrary
to my basic instinct'.[9] Had the affinity between the two been complete there would have
been nothing left for Nietzsche to say.

* * *

The third, strangely cheering event was a major earthquake which claimed two thousand
lives on the French Riviera as a whole. In Nice, it emptied the hotels and pensions of their
panic-stricken guests in the early hours of February 24. Having slept soundly through the
quake itself, Nietzsche, as a man of Prussian bearing and training, 'strolled'[10] through the
town, 'attending to people I knew who were sitting in the open, on benches or in coaches,
hoping to escape the danger'. 'I myself', he adds, pleased to have acquitted himself well in
the face of mortal danger for a second time, 'experienced not a moment of fear – even a
great deal of irony'.[11] (The irony, presumably, was that his own stick of 'dynamite', *Beyond
Good and Evil*, had conspicuously *failed* to cause an earthquake in the world of letters.)

Not only did Nietzsche feel no fear, he felt positive glee:

> We are living in the most interesting expectation of *perishing* thanks to a well-intentioned
> earthquake which made more than dogs howl, far and wide. What a pleasure it is when the old
> house above one rattles like a coffee-grinder! When the inkwell declares its independence!
> When the streets fill up with terrified, half-clothed figures with shattered nervous systems.

Nice, he continues his letter to von Seydlitz, looked as though it had been transformed into
a military bivouac: 'I found all my men and lady friends pitifully stretched out under green
trees – well towelled and blanketed, for the cold was piercing – and thinking with every
tiny tremor that the end of the world had arrived'.[12]

Nietzsche's glee is probably explained by an entry in the notebooks written a few months
later. Whereas in primitive times 'evil' consisted in 'chance, the uncertain, the sudden',
in the modern world, made safe and predictable by science and technology, the sudden
and unexpected presents itself as something *positive*: a 'titillation' that breaks through the

tedium of predictability.[13] (Stock-market crashes can create this kind of horrified glee – even in those who are losing money hand over fist.)

The earthquake emptied Nice. By the third week in March the sixty-eight guests round the *table d'hôte* at the Pension de Genève (where Nietzsche continued to lunch in spite of his shift to the rue des Ponchettes) were reduced to six, including himself. And the fourth, the top, floor of the pension, where he had written the third and fourth parts of *Zarathustra*, was so badly damaged that it had to be removed.

Youths and Anti-Semites

Though he enjoyed the earthquake, other interruptions of Nietzsche's work routine were less welcome. One was a visit from a half-German, half-American, recently graduated Dr. Adams who had studied classics with Rohde but now wanted Nietzsche, his 'Master', to teach him how to 'become a philosopher'.[14] Nietzsche neither liked Adams nor discerned in him any gift for philosophy. But with his innate politeness and his respect for the Rohde connexion he entertained him patiently. He was greatly relieved when Adams left, complaining to Overbeck that '"young people" are a burden, particularly when they come to me as fans of my writings, since it ought to be obvious that they are quite unsuitable for "young people"'.[15] His attitude to 'young people' was in no way improved by the fact that the impecunious Adams borrowed the money for his hotel bill and never repaid it.[16]

Equally unwelcome were letters from one Theodor Fritsch (not to be confused with the publisher Fritzsch), who thought he had discovered his own chauvinistic anti-Semitism reflected in *Zarathustra*. Nietzsche wrote him that he had no sympathy at all for the so-called 'German spirit' and, as for the Jews versus the Germans, he found the former far more worthy of attention than the latter. Eventually, forced out of his habitual shell of politeness, he returned all Fritsch's correspondence, together with the poisonous anti-Semitic literature he had been receiving, finishing his letter with the question, 'How do you think I feel when anti-Semites mouth the name Zarathustra?'[17] The question is answered in the privacy of the notebooks: 'A very peculiar Herr Fritsch has been corresponding with me. Since he was very persistent, there was nothing for it but to give him a couple of friendly kicks in the guts. These "Germans" of today make me ever more sick'.[18] In return, having failed to get Nietzsche to see the error of his philo-Semitic ways, Fritsch attacked him in the *Antisemitic Correspondence* as a man of 'Jewified book learning' devoid of any understanding of the 'German essence'.

The Fritsch episode caused Nietzsche to reflect wryly on his strange 'underground influence' on all the wrong people: 'In all the radical parties (socialists, nihilists, anti-Semites, orthodox Christians, Wagnerians) I enjoy a strange, almost mysterious respect'[19] (a situation, one might reflect, that persists to this day).

Intermezzo

Nietzsche hated spring and autumn, the 'intermezzo' seasons he called them, since they challenged his programme of living within 9–12 degrees at all times. At the beginning of April, it being too warm in Nice but too cold yet for Sils, he decided on Cannobio for the spring intermezzo between his two 'homes'. An ancient and beautiful town 200 metres above sea level on the western shore of Lake Maggiore, it had been recommended to him as a 'heavenly' spot where he would be well cared for in the Villa Badia, a pension run by a reliable Swiss couple. His first reaction was rhapsodic: 'this spot,' he wrote Köselitz, 'is more beautiful than anywhere on the Riviera – how did I come so late to this insight? The sea has, like all great things, something stupid and indecent about it. That is absent here'.[20] (Unlike the sea, therefore, lakes are intelligent and modest! In the *Genealogy of Morals* he calls them 'eyes'.) Soon, though, while his 'inner eye' continued to 'say Yes' to the beauty of the place and the 'incomparable purity' of the sky, his outer eyes 'said No' to the bright sunlight and lack of shade.[21] At the end of the month, therefore, he reluctantly decided he must wait out the rest of the intermezzo in his old haunt, the Pension Neptun in Zurich.

Mostly, as we have seen, Nietzsche had had good times in Zurich, times of, for him, unusual sociability. On this occasion, however, though Overbeck came over from Basel for a couple of days, he found it hard to catch up with people. Meta von Salis was under pressure to finish her doctoral thesis while at the same time needing to help her sister refurbish her house, recently gutted by fire. He did manage to meet up with Resa von Shirnhofer, but only after she returned from Paris at the end of his stay. Like him, she had discovered Dostoyevsky, which led to an intense discussion about *House of the Dead*. He also told her how much he admired her fellow Austrian, the lieder writer Hugo Wolf (destined to follow Nietzsche into insanity in 1897). Loyal as ever, he attempted to persuade several people, including his conductor friend Friedrich Hegar, of the merits of Köselitz's opera, *The Lion of Venice*, but, as Resa remarks, tended to put people off by 'letting the points against Wagner be too clearly felt'.[22]

Lacking the usual stimulus of society and feeling sick in the warm, humid atmosphere, Nietzsche became once again depressed – 'the worst of all penalties that exists on earth', he wrote Malwida.[23] Unable to arrange lodgings in his beloved Venice, he decided after a week to move on to Chur, roughly halfway between Zurich and Sils in both travel-time and elevation. Here he lodged cheaply in a schoolteacher's house, waiting for the moment when he could return to Sils 'without freezing to death'.

Depressed in Chur

Chur, however, proved a bad move. Though he escaped Zurich's humidity, what replaced it were days of cold, wintery rain, ruling out walks in the surrounding pine forests. His physical and mental health decreased further, intensified by the thought of how much nicer it would be to be with Köselitz in sunny Venice: 'no music, no Palazzo San Marco, no gondolas, only ugly mountain peasants',[24] he moaned. Later he did hear some music, Schumann's oratorio, *Paradise and the Peri*, which, however, as a self-pitying 'sea of lemonade', only made him feel worse.[25] He thought of again trying out Plato's assertion (according to Nietzsche) that massage can cure even a bad conscience, though he had not found it helpful to date.[26]

In Chur, he received the news of Lou Salomé's engagement to (the future distinguished orientalist) Friedrich Carl Andreas. (As mentioned earlier, Lou only agreed to marry him on the condition that the marriage would be sexless.) 'Fräulein Salomé has announced to me her engagement', he wrote Malwida on May 12, 'but I have not replied...One must avoid this kind of person, someone who is without respect. No one knows who this Dr. Andreas is'.[27] Six months later, however, he wrote his sister that he felt unable to visit the Overbecks in Basel since he could not forgive Ida the 'dirty and unworthy remarks she made concerning a woman of whom I myself have said that she is the only nature related to me that I have met in my entire life'.[28] Clearly he was still far from forgiving and forgetting the Salomé affair, and from sorting out what his true feelings about Lou were – something, I think, he never in fact achieved.

And neither was he able to overcome his choking animosity towards his sister and her husband. Whereas their attempts to extract money from him had, in the past, been couched in the idea that he should purchase land in the *Nueva Germania* colony, in Chur Nietzsche received an outright *demand* that he should guarantee for them a bank loan of 4,500 marks. This he flatly refused to do.[29] While the letter he actually sent Elizabeth (he could no longer bear to write to her and his brother-in-law jointly, and in fact never addressed another letter to the latter) excused the refusal on the grounds of his own precarious financial situation,[30] an unsent sketch of the letter reveals his true feelings: he will not support any anti-Semitic undertaking, he does not trust her any more, he hopes all the anti-Semites will leave Germany and join them, and he hopes that the Jews come to power in Europe.[31] The sketch of another letter at the end of the year reveals even more clearly his true feelings towards Elizabeth:

> How I have suffered from your mixing our good name in with this [anti-Semitic] movement through your marriage! In the last 6 years [i.e., going back to the time of the Salomé affair] you have lost all capacity for understanding and respect. God, how hard it has been for me! I have never demanded, which would have been easy, that you understood my stance to the times. Nonetheless, given even a little of the instinct of love, you would have refrained from shacking up with my antipode. I now think about sisters what Schopenhauer thought, more or less – they are superfluous, they create nothing but mischief.[32]

Fifth Summer in Sils Maria

Miserable in Chur, Nietzsche made his way to Sils as early as he possibly could, arriving on June 12, the first guest of the summer season. The remains of an avalanche behind the Durisch house reminded him how early he was. Though happy to be back on home soil, his health was, if anything, even worse than it had been in Zurich and Chur. A week after arriving he suffered a twelve-hour attack of headaches and vomiting coupled with insomnia and a fever which made him sweat in spite of the cold.[33] He decided that he was suffering 'a deep, physiological obstruction of unknown cause and location on account of which the average state of feeling...is permanently below zero'. 'Without exaggeration', he wrote Overbeck, 'I have now had a whole year without a single day of feeling fresh and light-hearted in body and spirit...[and suffering from] a permanent depression'.[34]

By the end of June, however, he was at least well enough to think of provisions, sending SOS messages to his mother and to the Overbecks for, *inter alia*, honey, sausages, '12 dozen Roeder steel pens, no. 15 broad', and tea:

> 'the only tea I trust...is Horniman's English tea...there are kilo tins which cost 12 francs ...This tea is not particularly fine, but it has remained absolutely the same (for forty years*) so that it is not, as with other teas one buys, a matter of experiment'.[35]

---

* Actually for 61 years. Horniman's was a famous Victorian brand and was probably the first tea to be sold in tins. In 1918 the company was bought by J. Lyons, but the name lived on in Britain into the 1960s and in the United States until the 1990s.

In late June Nietzsche received the news of the death of Heinrich von Stein, almost his last bridge to the Wagner circle. He died on June 20, at the age of thirty. Nietzsche was devastated for weeks:

> Inwardly, I am quite beside myself [he wrote Köselitz]. Heinrich von Stein is dead … quite suddenly, heart attack. I truly loved him. He seemed to me to be reserved for me at a later date. He belonged to the very few people whose existence gave me joy; and he had great faith in me. He said that in my presence thoughts came to him for which he otherwise would lack the courage: I 'freed' him. And how much we laughed together up here … He was by far the most beautiful species of human being among the Wagnerians.[36]

And to Overbeck he added: 'I had no doubt that he was saved for me at a later date: for men like him, rich and deep, who necessarily have a slow development, must be given plenty of time. And that was not allowed to him!'[37] Von Stein, as we have seen, had been the focus of Nietzsche's hopes of seducing the better sort of Wagnerian to his own cause. Given time, he now felt (forgetting, as one does in the face of death, how badly von Stein had disappointed him (pp. 393–4 above)), von Stein would have traversed his own path from Wagnerianism to 'free-spiritedness'.

July opened with the exciting discovery that the mysterious 'Muthgen' mentioned in Goethe's diaries as an affair of the young poet's heart was none other than his paternal grandmother Erdmuthe. Alas, enquiries showed that Erdmuthe was certainly too young to have been 'Muthgen', a conclusion Nietzsche was extremely reluctant to accept.[38] Since Goethe was his greatest hero, his paradigm of mental health, a personal connection – perhaps he even entertained the possibility of Goethe's blood flowing in his own veins – would have been a great joy.

In mid-July, the Emily Fynns and Countess Mansuroff arrived once more in the Engadine, but this time they stayed not in Sils but in the Grand Hotel in Maloja, about an hour and a half's walk away on the opposite, southeastern end of Lake Sils. Nietzsche's report of nine hundred vehicles in the forecourt of the hotel, making Maloja very 'Nicelike',[39] sounds exaggerated, but contemporary photographs of the hotel dining room, with seating for three or four hundred people at a time around huge, communal tables, shows that, by the 1880s, mass tourism had arrived in the Engadine.

High summer saw the whole of Europe gripped by an intense heat wave, leading Nietzsche to write Köselitz that, in Venice, he must be 'more omelette than man'.[40] Though Nietzsche was grateful to be six thousand feet above the worst of it, even in Sils the humidity was high, accompanied by frequent thunderstorms. These did nothing to improve his health or spirits, though there were some good days which allowed him to dash off his 'little polemic', the *Genealogy of Morals*, in three weeks.

At the beginning of August he decided on yet another new dietary experiment.* Though not invaded by tourists to the extent of Maloja, the dining room at Sils's Alpenrose still had over a hundred people dining at the *table d'hôtel*, among them many children. Nietzsche decided, on account of both the noise and the 'dangerous' nature of the food, that he was

---

* As we have seen, Nietzsche always insisted on the 'experimental' nature of his own thought and of rational thinking in general. His constant experiments with climate and diet in the effort to improve his health reflect that view of rationality, and perhaps helped generate it. A failure of rationality, however, was his failure to consider the likelihood that his digestion would have been happier had his diet been more settled.

'too tender an animal to take his fodder with the masses'. He decided to eat lunch half an hour before the rush and, abandoning the set menu, concocted a comprehensive regimen: every day for lunch, beefsteak with spinach, followed by a large omelette with apple jam; in the evenings, a few slices of ham with two egg yolks and two bread rolls. For the mornings, he decided to replace his five a.m. cup of tea with unsweetened cocoa (van Houten's Dutch cocoa was his preferred brand, though later on he decided to experiment with the Swiss Sprügli). Then, after an hour's further sleep, he rose, dressed, had a cup of tea and began work.[41] Unsurprisingly, this appalling, fruit-less and almost vegetable-less diet made no visible improvement to his health. And then he made it even worse by giving up the spinach at lunchtime and replacing the steak with ham, following the by now (unsurprisingly) deceased Dr. Wiel's (pp. 208–12 above) 'ham cure' for diseases of the stomach.[42]

Throughout August, Nietzsche enjoyed the regular company of (now Dr.) Meta von Salis, who arrived with her friend Hedwig Kym, with whom she now shared a house. Meta recalls that Nietzsche made the two-minute walk from his lodgings to hers almost every morning and sometimes in the afternoons, too. His non-appearance meant that he was ill that day. If it was not too hot they went for a walk, otherwise remaining in 'intimate conversation' in her room. Mostly, Nietzsche was very cheerful and given to harmless jokes – as was his wont with those women (Elizabeth in earlier times) to whom he stood in a 'brotherly' relation. The women taught him to row and he enjoyed the slight shiver of danger when there was a wind. To Hedwig's expression of guilt after a trip during which she had done none of the rowing, he replied that he would remember her always as 'welcome ballast'.

Meta's visit came to an end in early September:

> I will never forget our parting … we were walking along the shore of Lake Silvaplana, at the foot of [Mount] Corvatsch. The air had that silvery, autumnal tone which Nietzsche liked to call 'otherworldly'. The lake was slightly agitated and the little ripples in which the rosy evening clouds were reflected ran murmuring onto the sandy shore and back again. 'As if they too wanted to shake your hand in farewell' said our companion in his melodious voice. Then, as we were walking home across a bleak stretch of field between the lake and the side of Sils facing it, he remarked with a small sigh: 'Now I am widowed and orphaned again'.[43]

A final meeting in early September was with his old school friend Paul Deussen. Nietzsche had received a complimentary copy of Deussen's new book, an extensive translation of and commentary on the *Sutras of the Vedanta*.[44] Far from patronising Deussen as he had usually done in the past, Nietzsche was impressed by his gaining, in Berlin, a chair of philosophy, the first Schopenhauerian to do so. And he was tremendously impressed by Deussen's – indeed major – book. 'Subtle and refined,' he wrote, it made Deussen the foremost orientalist in Europe. And it made one aware, he added, that 'the clever positions of the most modern European philosophy (Kantianism, atomism, nihilism, and so on) had all happened in Indian philosophy several millennia earlier'.[45] Deussen visited from September 2 to 4, together with his wife, Marie, Jewish and half his age, en route to Greece. Deussen recalls that

> it was with a beating heart that I met my friend for the first time after fourteen years of separation and, greatly moved, embraced him. But how changed he had become during

this period. No longer the proud bearing, the elastic step, the fluent talk of the past. Only slowly, and leaning somewhat to one side, he seemed to drag himself along. And his speech was often laboured and hesitant...The next morning he led me into his apartment or, as he called it, his 'cave'. It was a simple room in a peasant house, three minutes from the main road...To the one side stood his books, mostly well-known to me from earlier times. Next to them was a rustic table with coffee cups, egg-shells, manuscripts, toilet articles, all in colourful confusion, then a boot-jack with a boot on it, and finally the unmade bed. Everything pointed to slack service and an indulgent gentleman...As we parted there were tears in his eyes, which I had never seen before. I would never again see him in his right mind.[46]

* * *

With autumn in the air it was once again time to leave Sils. A few days before leaving, Nietzsche wrote to Widmann (author of the 'dynamite' review of *Beyond Good and Evil*) asking him to show his *Hymn to Life* to his friend Johannes Brahms.[47] Perhaps he thought that his break with the Wagnerians would make Brahms, Wagner's musical antipode, his natural ally. Alas, Brahms merely sent a formal note of receipt of the work. To Widmann he wrote that he had Nietzsche's *Beyond Good and Evil* to hand (presumably on Widmann's recommendation) but also an Italian novella so that he could choose 'whether to walk under grey or blue skies'.[48] Evidently Brahms had at least dipped into that 'squid-like' work.

* * *

Nietzsche left Sils on September 21, having once more sought out an 'intermezzo' between his two 'homes'. This time he had luck with Venice, finding lodgings at Calle Dei Preti 1263, close to both his beloved St. Mark's Square and his friend Köselitz. Importantly, here as in Nice, there was a mosquito net above the bed. It would be his last visit to Venice, and the last time Köselitz would see him before his collapse. Alas, the sun proved too bright, so that, although he enjoyed the cool breeze and clear sky, the intended two-month stay was reduced to one. After a tortuous journey involving a two-hour delay in a train tunnel between Genoa and Milan, he arrived in Nice on October 23, with a burst suitcase and a bursting head.

Fifth and Final Winter in Nice

In spite of the stress of the journey he was delighted to be back. Noticeably warmer than Venice, there was, he wrote Köselitz, something 'intoxicating' about Nice's cheerful, worldly elegance, big-city feel, and exotic, 'African' vegetation.[49] This time there was no question of staying anywhere other than the tried and true Pension de Genève, no question of departing from the tried and true in any respect: 'I have arrived at a point', he wrote Franziska, 'where I can do nothing...other than stick to the few proved things (Nice among them) and allow my work – which is the meaning of my life – to be disturbed as little as possible by external things'.[50] Avoiding distractions of all sorts is a matter, he wrote Carl Fuchs, of finding one's 'centre':

When I was a philologist, I was 'eccentric [ex-centric]', outside my centre (which...is not to say that I was a bad philologist). Today it seems to me an eccentricity that I was a Wagnerian...Gradually one disciplines oneself back towards one's innermost unity; that passion for which, for a long time, one has no name, rescues one from all digressions and dispersions, that task of which, one is, without any freedom of choice, the missionary.[51]

Predictably, the return to a cheap room in the Pension de Genève meant once again a cold, tree-shaded north-facing room which, in a cold January, he found 'no joke'.[52] Facing the usual 'blue-finger' problem, he thought of renting a stove. But since it would have cost 50 francs (without fuel) for the season he had Franziska send one from Naumburg. Overjoyed when it arrived and bathing in the luxury of a room heated for the first time, he confessed to Köselitz that he had performed a 'pagan dance' around the 'fire god'.[53]

* * *

At the beginning of December, Nietzsche received a letter from the Danish scholar and critic Georg Brandes. Brandes (born Morris Cohen) had made a name for himself as the author of a many-volumed study of the nineteenth century's principal literary trends. He wrote Nietzsche that he knew *Human, All-Too-Human, Beyond Good and Evil*, and the *Genealogy of Morals* and now wanted to read all of his works. Brandes wrote that he was amazed to find that Nietzsche was a professor and congratulated him on sounding so little like one. He endorsed the attack on Christianity and on democratic mediocrity as well as Nietzsche's 'aristocratic radicalism'. No sycophant, however, he said he was uncertain about the attack on compassion and did not agree with the attack on women. And there was, he added, a great deal he didn't understand.[54]

Nietzsche replied by calling Brandes a 'good European'. As for difficulties in compre-hension, he attributed them to the fact that 'as an old musician I have a good ear for quarter tones', making the texture of his works denser, and to his 'distrust of dialectics, even of the giving of reasons'.[55] Delighted to have caught the eye of this widely influential figure, Nietzsche had Fritzsch send him all the works he did not already possess. To Köselitz he wrote that Brandes was 'the intellectually richest Dane there is at the moment i.e. is a Jew' and that the description 'aristocratic radicalism' was 'well said and experienced'.[56] Aside from discussions of philosophy, Brandes, who had spent time with them in Berlin, report-ed that Rée and Lou Salomé were living together 'like brother and sister'.[57]

* * *

Christmas 1887 was, in Nice, Nietzsche wrote, something 'fantastic and absurd':

Deep snow: something new for me even for many of the Niçois. Palms weighed down with snow, the yellow oranges peering out of the snow, above, an unbelievable sky, radiant with joy. Under these circumstances I envy myself my little stove (which I light every morning at precisely six o'clock).[58]

Shortly before Christmas, Nietzsche had attended his fourth performance of *Carmen* in the Nice Opera's newly opened Italian theatre. Once again it was a 'true event – I learnt and understood more in these four hours than in the previous four weeks',[59] he wrote, sounding his often-repeated theme that music, or at least musical mood, emotion, gives birth to thought. Reflecting on the same experience a month later, he wrote Köselitz,

Music now gives me sensations as never before. It frees me from myself, it sobers me up from myself, as though I survey the scene from a great distance, overwhelmed. It strengthens me … and every time, after an evening of music, I am full of resolute insights and thoughts the following morning. It is very strange. It is as though I had bathed in some natural element. Life [and evidently thought] without music is simply a mistake, exhausting, an exile.[60]

Notice, once again, Nietzsche's continuing attachment to the experience of self-transcendence through music.

Literary Projects

As we saw in the previous chapter, with his set of new prefaces to old books and with the expanded new edition of *The Gay Science*, Nietzsche felt, in June 1887, that he had 'performed the last rites over, bade a fond farewell to, the totality of my writings to date'.[61] He had, he wrote, brought a 'segment of my life' to an end so that what lay before him, now, was 'the vast task' of producing *The Will to Power*[62] – that 'philosophy of the future' to which all his work to date, as the subtitle of *Beyond Good and Evil* had announced, was merely a 'prelude'. As noted, this project makes its first appearance in his letters in August 1886. Since that was the month in which *Beyond Good and Evil* appeared, it seems clear that the original plan was that full-time work on the magnum opus should immediately succeed the appearance of its 'prelude'.

Things did not, however, go to plan. For in spite of the sixty-six complimentary copies and the appearance of a few reviews, *Beyond Good and Evil*'s effect on the book-reading public at large was, as usual, non-existent. In June 1887, Nietzsche complained to Overbeck that of the complimentary copies, only a fifth had produced any response at all, and that to date only 114 copies had been sold. The proceeds, he added, did not even begin to cover the 100 talers he had paid for the private printing of *Zarathustra* Part IV, the 300 for *Beyond Good and Evil* itself, and the 150 for correcting and expanding older works.[63] Accordingly, Nietzsche decided to interrupt his plans for the *Will to Power* by writing a short work, the *Genealogy of Morals*, which would be 'an expansion and elaboration' of *Beyond Good and Evil* and must therefore be printed so as to look exactly like its predecessor.*

As its subtitle announces, the *Genealogy* was intended to be 'A Polemic' whose 'relevance' to the current situation would stir up interest in, and sales of, its predecessors.[64] (Nietzsche had, I think, difficulty in judging the effect his works had on readers, since one could hardly describe any of them as *un*polemical. The important thing about the *Genealogy*, he wrote, was that it was a 'declaration of war on morality'[65] – but that war, surely, had been well and truly declared way back in *Human, All-Too-Human*. His description of *Beyond Good and Evil*

---

* KGB III.5 946. Since the 'expansion and elaboration…' phrase appeared on the back of the title page of the first edition of the *Genealogy*, and since this was the only edition to appear under Nietzsche's supervision, it is unfortunate that it no longer appears in the Colli-Montinari collected works or in standard English translations. In February 1888, Nietzsche wrote to Naumann, his printer, that instead of *Genealogy of Morals*, he should, perhaps, have retained the catchier title *Beyond Good and Evil*, coupled to the subtitle: *Appendix. Three Essays* (KGB III.5 994). It is a matter of regret that, in the past decade, Anglo-Saxon moral philosophers have become obsessed with the *Genealogy* but rarely discuss *Beyond Good and Evil*.

as exhibiting a 'studied neutrality' in contrast to the '*allegro feroce*' of the *Genealogy*[66] seems particularly wide of the mark.)

The substance of the *Genealogy* was written in the three weeks from July 10 to 30.[67] He was, however, still adding bits and pieces at the end of August.[68] Since it is the most organic of all Nietzsche's works, tightly organised, by his standards, in accordance with a guiding conception of the whole as no other, it is an extraordinary tour de force. It appeared on November 16, 1887, again with Naumann, and again at Nietzsche's own expense, since he now regarded Fritzsch as, though well-meaning, incompetent.

Having written the *Genealogy*, Nietzsche now decided that *it*, and not the expanded *Gay Science*, was the work that concluded an 'epoch', completed his 'narrative of development', 'drew a line under my existence to date'.[69] 'I stand', he wrote at the end of December, 'at high noon: one door closes and another opens up', the door to 'the chief thing of my existence', *The Will to Power*.[70]

On the Genealogy of Morals

The central aim of the *Genealogy* is to liberate Nietzsche's – as usual 'few' – proper readers from the power of Christian morality and point them towards a better morality. As we shall see, it is definitive of the 'higher' type to whom the *Genealogy* is addressed that he is not completely taken in by received, Christian morality but is, rather, the 'battleground' of a fight between it and the older, classical morality that it supplanted. Nietzsche's aim is to bring into the open the subterranean battle between 'Rome' and 'Judea' and to make sure that 'Rome' comes out the victor.

As with most of Nietzsche's prefaces, the preface to the *Genealogy* is not a particularly reliable guide as to its content. 'My problem', he writes, is 'under what conditions did man invent the value judgments good and evil? *and what value do they themselves have?*'[71] So, we are led to believe, the aim is to establish the (of course negative) value of Christian morality and the method consists in a 'genealogy', an account of its 'origins'.[72] One thing that is misleading about this is that by making the work seem entirely critical it obscures its fundamentally constructive intention of securing a victory for 'Rome'. Another is that the genealogical investigation of Christian morality is, in fact, confined, almost entirely, to the first two of its three essays. Principally in the third essay, that is, the work contains substantial and significant discussions of issues that have little or nothing to do with either the origin or the value of Christian morality.

Still, there is no doubt that the genealogy of Christian morality is the central feature of the work. And this, the idea that 'value' can be determined by an investigation of 'origins', is liable to set off alarm bells. Is it not, one is inclined to ask, an affirmation of the well-known 'genetic fallacy'? Take nuclear power. It originated in the intention to cause death and destruction on an inhuman scale. But now it is increasingly valued as a source of clean, 'green' energy. The vicious character of its origin does not, therefore, establish its current value. Given, then, that the genetic fallacy is a failure in logic, plus the fact that Nietzsche seems to be aware that it is,[73] plus the fact that the *Genealogy* is subtitled 'A Polemic', many scholars have concluded that Nietzsche is not interested in logic or rationality. His aim, they believe, is to liberate his chosen reader from the clutches of Christian morality by hook or by crook. And, in fact, they suggest, his preferred method is not the hook of rational critique but rather the crook of emotional rhetoric. The *Genealogy*, it is suggested, is a work addressed not at all to the head but only to the heart.

This view of the work seems to me entirely wrong. As, however, it is impossible properly to discuss the rationality or otherwise of Nietzsche's genealogical procedure until we see it in action, I shall postpone discussing the issue until we get to the very end of the text.

First Essay: 'Good and Evil', 'Good and Bad'

The *Genealogy*'s first essay is an expansion of *Beyond Good and Evil*'s account of the historical origins of Christian morality in the 'revolt' of the ancient world's slaves against the morality of their masters.

The first moralities, Nietzsche suggests, originated with warrior-nobles: the Vikings or the Homeric Greeks, for example. Experiencing the 'pathos of distance' between themselves and the 'plebeian' or 'common',[74] they designated themselves as 'the good' and their salient characteristics as virtues: health, physical strength, courage, military skill, truthfulness, loyalty, and ruthlessness towards enemies. Those who were unlike themselves, either foreign tribes they knew they were stronger than or else their own slaves, they designated as 'bad'. As in 'bad egg', 'bad' was an expression not of hatred but rather contempt, contempt often tinged with genuine sympathy for the misfortune of 'not being like us'. To the Greek nobility the bad were 'the unlucky'.[75]

Calling on his training as a philologist, Nietzsche's evidence for the priority of master moralities consists in the claim that 'good' in many, perhaps all, European languages seems to lead back ultimately to words for describing the warrior nobility. *Bonus* in Latin probably derives from *duonus*, warrior, and German *gut*, he suggests, surely derives from *gott* and so originally meant 'of godlike race'.[76] The concept of social superiority, Nietzsche suggests, always generates the concept of psychological superiority which can then, over time, become detached from actual social standing.[77] Conversely, the concept of low social standing generates the concept of low psychological standing: *schlecht* (bad) is simply a typographical variant on *schlicht* (plain, simple).[78]

(In a note at the end of the first essay Nietzsche invites linguistics to consider the question '*What signposts does linguistics, especially the study of etymology, give to the history of the evolution of moral concepts?*' suggesting that the history of morality sketched in the first essay is offered not as knowledge but rather as an hypothesis proposed as the basis of a research programme. Brandes accepted the invitation and consulted Danish etymologists about Nietzsche's claims. His experts confirm, he wrote Nietzsche, the *bonus–duonus* derivation but say that in Gothic German *gut* and *gott* have, in fact, no connexion.[79] One can think of other examples to support Nietzsche's case: in both English and German, of course, 'noble' as an attribute of character derives from 'noble' as a designation of social status, 'vulgar' in the sense of 'uncouth' derives from 'vulgar' in the sense of lower-class, and 'villain' in the sense of scoundrel must surely derive from 'villein', meaning a type of feudal serf.)

So much for 'noble morality'. 'Slave morality' originated, says Nietzsche, with the enslaved Jews. It was they who, out of 'unfathomable hatred', first conquered the nobles by bringing about the replacement of noble morality's equation, 'good = noble = powerful = beautiful = happy = blessed', with slave morality's 'good = suffering = poor = powerless = lowly'.[80] This is what *Beyond Good and Evil* called 'the first revaluation of values'.[81] (Notice that 'revaluation' means simply 'reversal', which provides a clear 'signpost' as to the character of Nietzsche's second 'revaluation'.) The reason the Jews responded to oppression in this way is that they were a 'priestly people', a nation led by priests.

Two characteristics of the Jewish priests – which are also characteristics of priests in general – are crucial to the 'slave revolt'. First, lusting after power but being in a physically powerless, oppressed situation, the priests were 'cauldrons of unassuaged hatred', their souls 'poisoned' by – a central term throughout the *Genealogy* – *ressentiment*.*[82] Second, the priests were *clever*: only that explains their position of influence within Jewish society. It was the priests' intelligence that enabled them to work out 'a very deliberate act of revenge', the cunning plan of enervating the oppressive nobles, and so relieving the oppression of the Jews, by persuading them to adopt a new morality according to which qualities they used to regard as virtues became vices, and qualities they regarded as vices became virtues.[83]

Entirely unanswered in the *Genealogy* is the question of when the Jewish slave revolt occurred and against whom it was directed. In a letter to Overbeck Nietzsche admits that the *Genealogy* omits a great many details for the sake of the overall sweep of the story.[84] But in *The Antichrist*, written the following year, he makes clear that the revolt in fact occurred not, as one might think, in the Roman Empire but during the Babylonian Exile (597 BC).[85] The picture is thus the following. The Jews first invented 'slave morality', a morality that validated the life they had no option but to lead, during the Babylonian Captivity. Hundreds of years later the Christians took over this well-developed tool of disempowerment, added some refinements to it that we will come to shortly, and directed it against the Roman nobility. The existence of this earlier history is why the *Genealogy* says that Christianity was the 'heir' to the slave revolt[86] (and why, strictly, Christian morality is only one species of 'slave morality')[87]. And it is also why Nietzsche says that when Constantine made Christianity the official religion of the Roman Empire in 312 AD, not 'Christianity' but rather '*Israel* triumphed': 'with its revenge and revaluation of all former values', Israel was victorious and continues to be so to the present day.[88] The focus of Nietzsche's interest, certainly, is the transition from the morality of classical antiquity to that of the Christian Middle Ages. But that transition he views as the completion of a process that began in Babylon.

* * *

How exactly did this 'first revaluation of values' work? What was the *mechanism* of value reversal? Nietzsche points to two things: I shall call them 'moral spin' and 'the invention of metaphysical clip-ons'.

Viewed through the 'poisonous eyes of *ressentiment*' the noble qualities were 'retouched and reinterpreted':[89] in other words, 'spun'. Self-assurance becomes selfishness, strength becomes barbarism, habit of command arrogance, truthfulness cruelty, and so on. Conversely, in imitation of the masters' self-glorification, the slaves turn the characteristics they *had to* exhibit into virtues. Quite literally, they made virtues out of necessities: huddling together for warmth with fellow slaves became 'love of neighbour', timidity became humility, slavishness became obedience, 'having to wait at the door' became patience. In general

---

* Though he would have met the word in Emile Dühring's *The Value of Life*, which he read in 1875, Nietzsche takes the concept from Hippolyte Taine's three-volume *The French Revolution*, which is why he consistently uses the French word rather than the German *Groll*. Taine, to whom he sent a complimentary copy of the *Genealogy*, would have been pleased to see his fundamental explanatory concept at work in Nietzsche's book.

'impotence becomes goodness'.⁹⁰ (Notice that 'spin' amounts to a shift in perspective: one and the same character trait that was once viewed from the master's perspective is now viewed from the slave's. This provides a link to the important discussion of 'perspectivism' in the *Genealogy*'s third essay.)

According to Christian morality, 'not only are [the slaves] better, but they have a "better time", or at least will have a better time one day'.⁹¹ As, that is, Christianity developed (according to *The Antichrist*, St. Paul was the chief architect of this development), its morality acquired two metaphysical 'clip-ons' which increased its grip.

The first was the attribution, to every human being, of a 'free will'. The aim was twofold: first, to make the nobles free, and thus responsible, and thus guilty, and thus deserving of punishment for their oppressive acts, and, second, to enable the slaves to represent their own weaknesses as *accomplishments*, freely chosen virtues, deserving moral credit and reward.⁹²

The second clip-on was the supernatural: God, heaven, and the immortal soul. Since the 'wicked' prosper all too evidently and all too often in this life, for 'justice' (i.e., revenge) to arrive, there has to be another, eternal life in which the tables will be turned. 'Eternal hate', Nietzsche claims, created the afterlife, in support of which he quotes Aquinas's claim that 'the blessed in the heavenly kingdom will see the torment of the damned *so that they may even more thoroughly enjoy their blessedness*',⁹³ a momentary slip of the mask that reveals the reality behind 'Christian love'.

* * *

Nietzsche thinks that there are two fundamental contrasts between slave and noble morality. The first lies in their different creative origins. Whereas with the nobles *self-esteem* is what creates, the slave revolt begins when '*ressentiment* becomes creative'. Whereas the noble says 'Yes' to himself, the slave says 'No' to the other. So while noble morality is *self*-focused slave morality is *other*-focused, reactive. This is why, while the focal word in noble morality is 'good' – 'bad' being just a pale and conceptually necessary contrast – the focal word in slave morality is the hate-filled 'evil' – 'good' being just its pale and necessary contrast. Noble morality starts with the *virtues* and adds vices as an 'after-thought'; slave morality does the opposite.⁹⁴

The second fundamental contrast is between the 'diseased' condition of the slaves and the psychological 'health' of the nobles. Whereas the 'squinting' souls of the slaves, especially their priests, are disfigured, 'poisoned', and eaten away by cancerous 'worms' of *ressentiment*,⁹⁵ the nobles are psychologically 'magnificent' – 'blond beasts of prey avidly prowling round for spoils and victory', for the exercise, that is, of their will to power. It is true that, in contrast to the untrammelled rapaciousness of their behaviour towards outsiders, within the tribe the warrior-nobles suffer their own kind of oppression: they are 'strongly held in check by custom, respect, habit, gratitude and even more through spying on one another and through peer group jealousy'. This, however, did no lasting damage to their health since their regular infliction of barbaric savagery on outsiders 'compensat[ed] for the tension of being closed in and fenced in by the peace of the community'.⁹⁶ Because they were able to 'let off steam', to relieve the frustration of their will to power quickly and often, it did not fester, did not poison their souls.⁹⁷ (Notice how this perhaps over-simple, hydraulic model of the soul has seeped into much of contemporary psychotherapy: the psychodramatist invites one to 'kill' the cushion in order to 'vent' one's hatred of an abusive but now-dead parent.)

The First Essay's Contribution to a Vision of the Future

*E*cce Homo describes the *Genealogy* as comprising 'three decisive preliminary studies...for a revaluation of all values',[98] for the replacement of Christian morality with a new kind of morality. As, therefore, with its mother-work, *Beyond Good and Evil*, we should expect that, collectively, the three essays will provide some 'signposts' to a morality 'antithetical' to that of today.[99]

Contrary to the 'free thinker' who says, 'Look Nietzsche, you make noble morality sound very attractive but let's face facts – the Jews have won, there is no turning the clock back',[100] Nietzsche thinks that, though slave morality is indeed dominant within our culture, there are still plenty of places where the 'battle' between slave and noble morality is undecided. Indeed, precisely what defined a potentially higher kind of person is that his soul is a genuine moral 'battlefield'. As we know, the battle to be fought is 'Rome against Judea' (the battle, I suggested, between Pforta's worship of Greece, on the one hand, and its Christianity on the other (pp. 25–6 above)). The 'well-being and the future of the human race', Nietzsche suggests, depends on a moral revolution which will bring about the 'unconditional rule of aristocratic values, Roman values'.[101] (We will need to return to the unexplained jump from the Vikings to the Romans, to the assumption that, somehow, they share the same kind of morality.)

And then Nietzsche provides us with a potted history of Europe viewed through the prism of 'Rome (and so, of course, Greece) versus Judea'. Rome was defeated by the pious Middle Ages, but then there was a 'brilliant, uncanny reawakening of the classical ideal, of the noble method of valuing everything' in the Italian Renaissance. Soon, however, the Renaissance was silenced by the Reformation's reinvigoration of Christianity. That was followed by the triumph of an even more slavish kind of morality in 1789, the French Revolution. A final, brief flare-up of the classical arrived with Napoleon, an embodiment of noble morality in whom 'the problem of the *noble ideal itself* was made flesh', since (as Taine revealed (p. 433 above)) Napoleon is a 'synthesis of *Unmensch* (the inhuman) and *Übermensch* (the superhuman)'.

* * *

As Nietzsche says, this description of Napoleon reveals in a nutshell what is problematic about his desire for a return to 'Rome', for a resurrection of noble morality: the problem is how to do away with the *Unmensch* without destroying the possibility of the *Übermensch*. Nietzsche emphasises time and again the incredible barbarism, the savage 'delight in destruction' of the Vikings and of the Germanic tribes which invaded the dying Roman Empire. Though the 'blond beast' is 'magnificent' in its health, strength, and joie de vivre, it is also 'shockingly violent', so that we are 'entirely justified' in wanting to protect ourselves from it. The rest of Europe is entirely right to view with 'deep and icy mistrust' the rise of German power, such mistrust being the 'aftermath of that inextinguishable horror with which, for centuries, Europe viewed the raging of the blond, Germanic beast'.[102] (In a year's time Nietzsche will be demanding that European nations erect a 'ring of steel' around the aggressive and powerful German Reich.)

So, Nietzsche freely admits, one can empathise with the *motive* of the slave moralists and even admire the skill with which, from a position of powerlessness, they nonetheless tamed the beast. But precisely here is the point: the victory of slave morality has had the effect of turning the blond beast into a 'tame...household pet', a sick mediocrity, in other words, contemporary Western humanity: the 'man of today' is 'stunted ... wasted away ... poisoned' with a soul that no longer seeks to 'expand'.[103] Christian morality is destroying the possibility of the creative free spirit.

What we see, then, is that we – Europe – went about civilising the blond beast in the wrong way. This, I think, is the principal conclusion of the first essay. What, then, is the right way? The answer we know already: it is the 'Greek solution'. What we need in place of Christian emasculation is Greek sublimation: we need not the abolition of Eris but rather the transformation of her 'bad' into her 'good' manifestations, the transformation of war into 'competition'. We need to *preserve* war and the warrior instinct, but, to repeat, it should be 'war without gunpowder and smoke'.[104] In this way we avoid the *Unmensch* while not destroying the possibility of the *Übermensch*, a being that will be 'beyond' the morality of good and evil though emphatically *not* beyond the morality of good and bad.[105] If we do this then we can retain our '*faith in mankind*',[106] our faith that man – European man (see pp. 417–18 above) – has a future. But otherwise we will discover that we are the 'last men', that we have reached the 'end of (Western) history'.

Second Essay: The Morality of Custom and the Sovereign Individual

The *Genealogy*'s second essay has an odd beginning: though the title announces an essay on '"Guilt", "Bad Conscience" and Related Matters', it begins with a discussion of promise-making and the 'sovereign individual', neither of which is mentioned in the title. In section 4 Nietzsche speaks of *returning* to the issue of the genealogy of morality, so the first three sections must constitute a discussion of the promised 'Related Matters' as a prelude to the main discussion.

The essay begins by observing that, surprisingly, *the* problem of humanity, that of 'breeding an animal capable of making promises', has been largely solved. What makes this surprising is that 'active forgetfulness' is not an isolated malfunction of the human mind but is essential to 'happiness and cheerfulness': we become 'dyspeptic' without it.[107] If, that is, we retain a vivid memory of a past injury (the Salomé affair, for example), if we dwell on it, we become consumed by the undischarged thirst for revenge; by *ressentiment*. Nietzsche's paradigm of healthy forgetting is given in the first essay: the already mentioned Marquis de Mirabeau, a statesman at the time of the French Revolution, who, reputedly, could never forgive an insult simply because he forgot it.[108]

The reason promising is *the* problem of humanity is that it alone – the making and keeping of promises, explicit or implicit – makes man 'undeviating, uniform, predictable'. From pre-historic times, Nietzsche continues, what made man predictable was 'the morality of custom', which is – here he refers us back to *Dawn* – 'the first proposition of civilization', present even among the most primitive tribes.[109] As we have seen, in order to survive in a competitive, Darwinian environment, a community must have a morality which provides the 'hardness, uniformity and simplicity' of, as I put it, a shared 'game plan' (p. 418 above). Nietzsche now adds 'predictability' to the list of requirements: unless there is social trust, unless individuals can be relied upon to perform the task allotted to them, the game plan will be ineffective.

Since forgetting is so powerful a force and predictability so important, horrendous means were needed to 'burn' into the individual's psyche the memory of his promise to the community as a whole: in order to enjoy the advantages of society he implicitly promised to follow the rules of its customary morality. Since pain is 'the most powerful of all mnemonics', castration, hanging, drawing and quartering, and the sacrifice of one's first born were among the typical means used to 'remind' lawbreakers of their promise.[110]

Nietzsche's term 'morality of custom' refers, of course, to any communal morality. The second essay's focus, however, is on the morality of 'pre-historic',[111] pre-Greek, tribes. What we are trying to discover, he says, are the first 'origins of responsibility', responsibility for keeping the rules one has implicitly promised to follow. This generation of responsibility, and so of predictability, is what first made man a 'peer among peers', a member of the tribe rather than an isolated individual.[112]

Recall the passage in the first essay which observed that while the Vikings and Gothic tribes acted as 'uncaged beasts of prey' towards outsiders, within the tribe they were 'held in check through custom, respect and even more through spying on each other and peer group jealousy' (p. 463 above). With this in mind one can see how the present talk about responsibility and predictability weaves the second essay back into the first: the discussion of the 'morality of custom' is an expansion of the brief earlier reference to the *internal* workings of the barbarian tribes. Another continuity between the two essays is the second essay's discussion of the 'bad conscience', which, as we will shortly see, is an account of what happened to the 'beast of prey' when rape and pillage were taken off the menu. Before we get to the bad conscience, however, there is an important digression concerning the 'sovereign individual'.[113]

The end, and 'ripest fruit', of the 'immense process' covering many millennia of subordinating individuals to the 'social straightjacket' of the morality of custom, is, says Nietzsche, the 'sovereign individual'. *Zarathustra* says something similar: 'creators [of moralities] were first peoples, only later individuals; verily the individual is itself just the most recent creation'.[114]

The idea is this. Over many millennia the enforcement of 'custom' ingrained the habit of 'responsibility', of fulfilling the implicit promise to obey the rules of custom. Man became a being with an ingrained habit of being true to his commitments. One day – Nietzsche makes no attempt to explain how this happens, there is just, in the language I have been using, a 'random mutation' – an individual arises in whom the habit of responsibility, the 'long, unbreakable will', fixes itself onto a new target: its *own* 'standard of value'. The individual, while every bit as 'responsible' as the custom-driven person, becomes 'free', not, of course, in the sense of having an uncaused 'free will' (an illusion, Nietzsche consistently believes), but in the sense of 'autonomy', of being a *self-* rather than custom-driven individual. He becomes, in the language of *The Gay Science*, a 'free spirit', free to follow his *own* 'dominant instinct'. As free, he is 'supra-customary' 'since "autonomous" and "customary" are mutually exclusive'.[115] Nietzsche describes this process in the notebooks:

> *Development of Humanity.* (A) Conquering nature and *thereby* a certain power over oneself. Morality was necessary in order for humanity to prevail in the battle with nature and with the 'wild beast' [in itself]. (B)...Power over nature achieved, one can use this power in order to shape oneself freely: will to power as self-elevation and strengthening.[116]

Nietzsche speaks of the long history of customary morality as a 'means to' the sovereign individual. This sounds like Hegel's telling of history as a story building up to a happy ending, which seems very odd coming from Nietzsche, since he repeatedly denies the existence of purpose in the world: as *The Gay Science* put it, 'the world is to all eternity chaos', and every projection of pattern, order, or purpose a mere 'anthropomorphism'.[117] What, however, I think he means is that if, from the point of view of willing the eternal return (always at the back of Nietzsche's mind), we look at the horrendous means used to enforce the habit of responsibility and wonder how they can possibly be 'redeemed' in the totality of human existence, then from this, retrospective, point of view, a point of view which does not project any prior purpose or intention into the world, we can see the morality of custom as the 'means to' (i.e., justified by) the sovereign individual. Nietzsche makes an oblique reference to this retrospective arranging of events into means and ends in a letter: 'The intentional character of ... fate ... is no fable if we understand it as such'.[118]

Who, exactly, is the sovereign individual? Given that the *Genealogy* is an 'elaboration' of *Beyond Good and Evil*, he is, surely, a reappearance of the 'philosopher of the future'. Recall that both 'conscience' and 'responsibility' were there attributed to him: 'the philosopher as *we* understand him ... [is] the man with the most comprehensive responsibility, whose conscience bears the weight of the future development of mankind'.[119] Given that 'philosopher of the future' referred both to the 'philosopher-visionary' and the 'philosopher-triumphant' (p. 422 above), 'sovereign individual', I suggest, has a similar double reference. When he talks of the sovereign individual's 'self-mastery' as qualifying him for 'mastery over ... all creatures of less durable and reliable will'[120] he is talking simultaneously about the spiritual leadership exercised by the philosopher-visionary in leading his fellows towards the ideal community and about the leadership of the philosopher-triumphant within the ideal community.

Why has Nietzsche prefaced the discussion of the main business of the essay, the 'bad conscience', with this discussion of the sovereign individual? Let us recall that, in one way or another, virtually all of Nietzsche's works are concerned to present a profile – as it were, a 'job description' – which determines whether or not one is a potentially suitable recruit for his cause. Usually, the profile consists in an idealised self-portrait. Here, I believe, it consists in the portrait of the sovereign individual (which is actually a not-so-idealised self-portrait.)* This being so, it is important for him to emphasise that though the bulk of the essay attempts to show the 'bad conscience' to be a type of sickness, *he is by no means opposed to conscience as such but, on the contrary, demands it*. He has, that is, no interest in attracting 'anarchists', those 'free thinkers' ('free spirits of the second rank') who reject current morality but have no other morality, no 'conscience', no consistent personality or life-style, to put in its place. Rather, a potential recruit will only be one who can measure up to the sovereign individual's 'self-mastery'; his disciplining of the soul into a coherent and unified hierarchy. The sovereign individual will subordinate all his drives to a 'dominant instinct' which he 'will [rightly] call his *conscience*'.[121] 'Being answerable to oneself, and proudly too',[122] being answerable to the ideal that is one's higher self and task, is the condition of being a sovereign individual. Only those who can develop this kind of 'conscience' have the potential to become 'philosophers of the future'.

---

* Nietzsche's biography is very much that of a 'sovereign individual'. Pforta-Prussian self-discipline remains with him his entire life but, after 1876, finds itself harnessed to a new, and very anti-Prussian, 'standard of value'.

Origins of the Bad Conscience

Having completed the discussion of the sovereign individual, Nietzsche finally gets to the point, the genealogy of Christian 'guilt'. The inspiration for the genealogy is once again etymology: the fact that 'guilt (*Schuld*)' descends from the 'very material' concept of 'debt (*Schuld*)'.*,123 This derivation is suggested by the fact that, in modern German, *Schuld* (still) means both 'debt' and 'guilt'. The *Schuld–Schuld* connection thus suggests the idea of 'debt' as the origin of 'guilt': of the 'bad conscience'. Nietzsche now tells what he regards as a compelling story of how the one grew into the other.

In the earliest communities (we seem to start off, once again, inside the warrior tribes), promises of repayment were made, on the basis of which services were rendered. But since the debtor often had nothing by way of a commodity to offer as security for the promise, he offered instead his wife, freedom, life or even his afterlife. In general, the debtor offered a 'pound of flesh' that was understood to be equivalent to the service and could be claimed in the event of failure to keep the promise of repayment. Every society has, Nietzsche observes, its creditor–debtor (and so of course promising) relationships. In all but the most primitive, these are formalised into an all-embracing system of 'justice' which arises on the basis of the premise that 'everything has its price, *everything* can be compensated'.

Nietzsche observes *en passant* that the horrendous punishments of undischarged debtors force us to face up to the (once again 'dark and squid-like') fact that cruelty, 'disinterested malice', is a basic ingredient in human nature. To see someone suffer is nice, to make them suffer even nicer. In the ancient world no pain meant no festival. The most delectable gift the Greeks could offer their gods was the Trojan wars – as it were, a horrific sex and violence movie screened for their entertainment. (The Greeks, Nietzsche engagingly suggests, lived their entire lives in the omnipresent sense of the gods as their audience – as it were, the *Truman Show* with the actors fully aware that their world was a film set.)124

As well as obtaining between individuals, and between the individual and the community, on account of the promise to obey customary morality, the debtor–creditor relation obtained between the community as a whole and the founding ancestor. The tribe feels it exists only because of the efforts and sacrifices of its founders, who continue to exist as powerful guardian spirits. The more flourishing the tribe, the more powerful the ancestor and the greater the debt that must be paid through festivals and very major sacrifices (e.g., of the first born). (Abraham seems to have regarded it as par for the course that Jehovah would demand that he sacrifice his son, Isaac.) Eventually, the ancestor is pushed into a realm of 'divine mystery and transcendence', transfigured into a god. In the main, therefore, gods originate in fear, fear of what they will do if the debt is not repaid.125

This is the point at which Christianity comes into the picture. Having inherited the pagan idea of debt to the creditor-god, Christianity invented the idea of a 'maximal' – monotheistic and so all-powerful – god, and hence a maximal debt.126 Its 'stroke of genius', however, was the crucifixion: God's sacrificing himself for man's debt – the creditor sacrificing himself for the debtor – supposedly out of 'love'. The implication is that, worthless as we are, the

---

* This is not just a peculiarity of German. The etymology of the English 'guilt' is uncertain. But the choice seems to be between an ancestry in the Old English *gieldan*, 'debt', and in *gylt*, 'delinquency'.

possibility of our repaying the debt ourselves is forever 'foreclosed'. Only God himself can discharge the debt.[127]

This is the point at which what Nietzsche calls the 'moralization' of debt occurs, the point at which pagan *Schuld*, 'debt', is transformed into Christian *Schuld*, 'guilt'.[128] The essential difference, I think, is the difference between *necessary* and *contingent* debt. Christian guilt consists in our '*original* sin', our *in principle* incapacity ever to return to God what we owe him. *Schuld* has exited the realm of exchange and entered that of metaphysics.

* * *

Meanwhile – here Nietzsche's complex narrative structure takes a step back in time – another development was taking place. Imprisoned in peace – Nietzsche may well have in mind, here, something approximating to the transition from hunter–gatherer to farming communities – man finds himself clumsy in discharging the requirements of his new life and alienated within it. He feels like a 'sea animal forced to live on land' (a 'fish out of water').*,[129] The old warrior instincts are there but can no longer find their natural gratification. So they are forced to seek an 'underground' satisfaction. Because it is allowed no external satisfaction, aggression becomes *self*-directed.[130] Warrior-man is transformed into self-hating man. Aggression – 'in my language the will to power'[131] – turns inwards.[132] Like the tiger in the zoo gnawing at its own foot, man (women seem to play no part in this story) becomes deeply sick.

* * *

Before us, now, are two genealogical stories. One tells of the transformation of ancestor-debt into *undischargeable* debt, into guilt before the Christian God. The other tells of the development of self-hatred on the part of the warrior nobles forced into conditions of peace. (What they *should* have done, of course, is to continue with *other*-directed aggression but, like the Greeks, in sublimated form. They should have invented the Olympic Games or the tragic festival. But then – that was the genius of the Greeks.)

In section 22 the two stories meet (Nietzsche's coup de théâtre resembles that of a detective-story writer suddenly revealing the convergence of plot and subplot). The self-hating human being, with all the natural outlets for his aggressive instincts blocked, seizes on religious precepts in order to 'sharpen his self-torment', to give focus and shape to his previously inarticulate self-hatred. The God 'of love' becomes, on the one hand, Jesus, the antithesis of his animal instincts (and as the embodiment of the new ideal, serves to intensify his self-loathing), and on the other, the 'hangman God' who serves to terrify him with fear of eternal torment. The world becomes weirdly exciting, but also a 'madhouse' that we have inhabited far too long.

* * *

The first of the *Genealogy*'s essays contains two lacunae. The first is the lack of any account of how Christian morality first gained traction: of what it was that enabled the slaves of the Roman Empire to *succeed* in winning over the hearts and minds of the nobles to their new morality. As we shall see, this lacuna is removed in Nietzsche's final works. But since that

---

* In *Straw Dogs*, John Grey argues that the transition from the footloose and fancy-free life of hunter–gathering to the sedentary life of farming resulted in a radical diminution of human health, longevity, and happiness. He agrees with Jared Diamond that the introduction of farming was, as the title of the latter's article in *Discover* magazine (May 1987) puts it, *The Worst Mistake in the History of the Human Race.*

removal required a major modification of the claim that 'life is will to power and nothing besides', which did not happen until those final works, I need to postpone discussing the matter until after I discuss that modification in Chapter 26. The second lacuna concerns the question of how Christian morality spread beyond the Roman Empire, how it conquered the hearts and minds of the barbarian tribes. We are now in a position to understand Nietzsche's answer to this second question.

In the first essay, we saw that the internal constraints of custom did no lasting harm to warrior individuals since they were able to 'let off steam' externally. The second essay continues the story of these tribes by moving on to the time when rape and pillage is no longer possible, a time when life becomes *nothing but* constraint. And so aggression turns inwards. It was this that constituted the fertile ground that enabled Christianity to expand beyond its original home in the Roman Empire, to conquer the world. As *The Antichrist* puts it, what enabled Christianity to conquer the barbarian tribes was the fact that (having turned to farming) they had 'become self-lacerating and inwardly feral'.[133] The ex-warrior tribes needed a stick to beat themselves with, and Christianity provided a bigger and better stick than anyone else.

The Second Essay's Contribution to a Vision of the Future

At the end of the second essay Nietzsche asks, 'Is an ideal set up or destroyed here?' He answers, 'If a shrine is to be set up *a shrine has to be destroyed*'.[134] This indicates two things: first, that he has a certain positive alternative – a 'counter-ideal'[135] – to Christianity in mind, and, second, given that 'shrine' is a religious term, that Nietzsche's counter-ideal will not simply replace Christianity with atheism but will offer something like an alternative religious outlook. In order to glimpse something of this alternative 'ideal', let us return to the origins of religion in the sense of a 'debt' to the powerful, transcendentalised ancestor. These origins, he points out, have nothing to do with 'piety': religion originates in 'fear'.[136] Nietzsche, of course, does not want us to live in fear of the gods, so even though the *ultimate* sickness of the 'moralized' bad conscience only arrives with Christianity, the relationship to the gods that preceded it was far from healthy.

Or rather, mostly it was. For it turns out that certain 'noble tribes' provide exceptions to the thesis that religion originates in fear.[137] That there are ways of making use of the 'invention' of gods other than self-crucifixion and self-abuse can, Nietzsche says, 'fortunately be deduced from a glance at the *Greek gods*, these reflections of noble and proud men in whom the *animal* man felt deified'.[138] As we have seen, the Greek gods, in Nietzsche's view, were glorified self-portraits, expressions of profound self-esteem. From this we can infer, yet again, that gods who promote not human self-loathing but rather human self-esteem will inhabit the 'shrine' that belongs to Nietzsche's ideal future. This is why he speaks of his own ideal as the 'reverse' of Christianity:[139] his second 'revaluation of values' is, in outline, simply a cancellation of the first.

Notice, here, the *constructive* role played by the genealogical method. By enabling us to identify the points at which religion becomes, to one degree or another, antithetical to human 'health', the points at which health dissolves into sickness, it 'signposts' the route to a healthier conception of the gods and our relation to them. To repeat *Beyond Good and*

Evil's observation, if one wants to prepare for a 'great leap' forwards it is a very good idea to go a long way 'backwards'.[140]

Third Essay: What Do Ascetic Ideals Mean?

*E*cce Homo says that 'the third essay gives the answer to the question of the tremendous power of the ascetic ideal'.[141] In fact, however, the essay talks as much about 'ascetic ideals' as about 'the ascetic ideal'. It is, I think, clarifying to take 'ascetic ideals' to mean 'ascetic practices'. Given this substitution, what the essay's first, introductory section tells us is that ascetic practices, that is, practices exhibiting the traditional, monastic virtues of poverty, chastity, and humility,[142] have 'meant' many different things. If we are talking about artists they have meant 'too many things' for a snappy summary; with philosophers and scholars they are signs of 'a nose for favourable conditions of higher intellectuality' (Nietzsche's standard argument against marriage); with priests they are 'their best instrument of power and ultimate sanction of their power'. Nietzsche also mentions women – their chastity is just 'one more seductive charm' (he has *still* not got over Lou Salomé's alleged coquetry (p. 354 above)) – and he mentions saints, whose asceticism is supposed to give them a foretaste of the beyond. Women and saints, however, figure no further in the discussion. Nietzsche's central concern is with priests, though he says quite a lot, first of all, about artists and philosophers and, after the discussion of priests, about scholars and scientists.

Wagner and the Ascetic Ideal

*S*ections 2–5 of the essay are supposed to discuss subscriptions to the ascetic ideal on the part of artists. But actually only one artist (the only one who matters) is discussed: Wagner, of course. What is the significance of the fact that, in old age, he 'pays homage to chastity?' Nietzsche points out, correctly, the contradiction between the affirmation of animal and sensual life by the early, world-affirming, anarchist-socialist Wagner (not to mention a more than average number of love affairs in his personal life) and the world-denial of his later works, above all his last opera, *Parsifal*, with its theme of redemption through denial of sex. Nietzsche attributes this turn to Wagner's discovery of Schopenhauer in mid-career (pp. 119–24 above).

For Wagner, what was really important in Schopenhauer's philosophy was, Nietzsche claims, the 'sovereignty' of music over drama. (According to Schopenhauer, as we saw (p. 84 above), while all the other arts deal in the world of mere 'representation', music penetrates to the heart of the 'thing in itself', transports us to the Absolute.) Nietzsche now says that Wagner's egoism, which would do anything for 'the greater glory of music' – of, that is, the musician – made him latch on to this conception of the composer as an oracle and priest, as 'God's ventriloquist', the possessor of 'a telephone ['hot line'] to the beyond'. Since he was thus setting himself up as a priest, it is hardly surprising that he adopted the trappings of a priest, in particular chastity.[143] The suggestion here is that the later Wagner's asceticism is the *fake* asceticism; the asceticism of – Nietzsche's regular term for abusing Wagner – an *actor*. Wagner is like the guru with his simple loincloth and begging bowl, but with his white Rolls Royce hidden around the corner.

Sex and the Philosopher

The main function of the Wagner discussion (apart from getting a bit more spleen out of Nietzsche's system) is to introduce Wagner's and his own former hero, Schopenhauer, and with him the question: what is the significance of the preaching of the ascetic ideal *by philosophers*? Though the question is ostensibly a general one, Nietzsche really uses it to introduce a discussion of Schopenhauer and, under a thin veneer of impersonality, himself.

Though now his opponent, Nietzsche still has tremendous respect for Schopenhauer. Whereas Wagner is a fake, or at least derivative from the philosopher he took as his 'front man', with Schopenhauer we come to a 'more serious question: what does it mean when a genuine *philosopher* pays homage to the ascetic ideal, a genuine, independent mind like Schopenhauer, a man and a knight of brazen countenance who has the courage to be himself, knows how to stand alone?'[144]

The focus of the *Genealogy*'s critique is Schopenhauer's philosophy of art, specifically his definition of the aesthetic state as 'disinterested'. Though he took this term over from Kant's aesthetic theory, he interpreted it, claims Nietzsche, in a closely personal way. When he writes that aesthetic experience is a mode of perception in which we 'celebrate the Sabbath from the penal servitude of willing' (p. 84 above), what he really means is release from *sexual* willing.[145] In the notebooks Nietzsche writes: '"The World as Will and Representation" – translated in a closely personal way back into Schopenhauerianese: the World as Sex-drive and Tranquillity'.

Stendhal, Nietzsche observes, was a sensualist. He defined beauty as 'a promise of happiness', in other words, an erotic *rousing* of the will. Schopenhauer, too, was a sensualist, but, unlike the 'happily adjusted' Stendhal, a *guilty* one. Here we see the first 'hint' of what it means when a philosopher pays homage to ascetic practices: he wants to escape a kind of *torture*.[146] Nietzsche, here, is implicitly repeating the point that, though he has freed himself from Christian metaphysics, Schopenhauer remains saturated by Christian morality. What makes sexual desire a torment for him is the Christian designation of physicality, animality, sexuality, as sinful.

In section 7 this psychoanalysis of Schopenhauer is followed by another coup de théâtre – philosophers *as a type* are partial to ascetic practices. If they are not, they are only 'so-called' philosophers. It turns out, however, that the kind of asceticism Nietzsche is talking about, here, is quite different from Schopenhauerian life-denial: the reason that philosophers abhor marriage – a married philosopher (the hen-pecked Socrates) is a comic figure – is that a true philosopher refuses to allow his 'independence' to be compromised. What leads the genuine but non-guilty philosopher to practice asceticism is not Christian life-denial but rather a desire to enjoy the 'conditions of the highest and boldest spirituality'.[147] The crucial point here is that ascetic practices can have radically different motives and therefore, in the language of the third essay's title, different, even opposite, 'meanings'.

Section 8 continues a discussion of the asceticism of the 'genuine philosopher' that is already close to being confessional in a manner that is – to Nietzsche's 'friends' at least – overtly autobiographical. In his own way 'the philosopher' (aka Nietzsche) practices the monastic virtues of poverty, chastity, and humility – though not as *virtues* but simply as *means* to being a philosopher: it is a matter of his '*predominant* instinct imposing itself on the others'. The philosopher practices 'poverty', goes, that is, into the 'desert'. Though probably inclined to sensual luxury, he takes to the mountains: not, however, dead ones but ones with 'eyes, by which I mean lakes' (the lakes of Sils Maria). Here he takes a Spartan room in a hotel. (It is not made explicit why such 'poverty' is conducive to philosophising. Probably it is a matter of denying drives that are liable to confuse and countermand one's central drive so that they eventually 'wither', as recommended in *Dawn* (p. 305 above).) He practices 'humility' in that he lives in hotels where no one knows who he is, so he can talk to anyone with impunity – as Nietzsche did, when in the mood, in Genoa, Nice and Sils. He avoids 'shiny loud things' (unlike Wagner) such as fame and royal patronage. He avoids animosities, even friendships (as we know, save for Overbeck, Nietzsche had lost all his intimate friendships by this time). In sum, the philosopher's humility consists in *keeping a low profile*. (Actually, though, this is not real humility at all since 'he inhabits his age like a shadow: the more the sun sinks the greater he becomes'. Nietzsche's will to power aims far above contemporary celebrity.)

The philosopher's avoidance of marriage is partly, as we have seen, a matter of preserving his 'independence', by which Nietzsche means, perhaps, freedom from distraction. And it is also a matter of 'humility', of keeping a low profile. (The incurable sociability of women inevitably drags one into society.) But it is also avoided on grounds of maintaining 'chastity': this has nothing to do with hatred of the senses but is rather cultivated because, as every 'athlete or jockey' knows, sex dissipates vital energy needed for creation. (Rugby coaches to this day forbid their players to have sex on the eve or even in the week of a big match.) Writing books is another way of having children.

The main point of this discussion of asceticism and the philosopher seems to be Nietzsche's somewhat anxious attempt to distinguish himself from the Schopenhauerian ascetic. Though his life-style may look very like that of a life-denier (though he may have kept his foot in a bucket of cold water through winter nights at Pforta), the reality behind the appearance is, he wants to convince us, very different.

Perspectivism and Objectivity

Section 6 observes that in making objectivity, 'disinterestedness', the hallmark of art Kant wanted to attribute to it what he took to be the 'glories of knowledge, namely, impersonality and universality'. But then Nietzsche drops the subject of knowledge in favour of the just-surveyed discussion of Schopenhauer's sex life. In section 12, however, the complex structure of the essay returns us to a discussion of objectivity and knowledge.

Schopenhauer made the same connexion between knowledge and objectivity as Kant, describing 'genius' as 'pure objectivity'.[148] Indeed the whole Western scientific tradition makes the connexion: science, everyone insists, must be 'objective', 'impersonal', 'disinterested', 'value-free'. Subjectivity, interest, the tradition assumes, distorts perception and therefore undermines knowledge. It is this entire tradition Nietzsche sets out to attack.[149]

His basic point is that interest-free knowledge is impossible: the 'pure willless painless timeless subject of knowledge' (a direct quotation from Schopenhauer), 'pure reason', and 'contemplation without interest' are 'conceptual fairy-tales', 'non-concepts', 'absurdities'. 'Here', he says, 'we are asked to think of an eye turned in no direction at all, an eye where the active and interpretive powers are to be suppressed, absent, but through which seeing still becomes a seeing-something'. And then he asserts: 'There is *only* a perspectival seeing, *only* a perspectival knowing'.[150]

'Perspectivism', to take up the discussion of the previous chapter (pp. 440–3 above), seems to entail *two* things: first, the post-Kantian commonplace that there is no epistemic encounter with the world, a 'seeing *something*', that is not mediated by a particular conceptual scheme or 'horizon', and, second, that there are no interest-free epistemic encounters with the world. Perspectivism is thus a double denial: it denies both concept-free and interest-free perception of the world.

But these denials are surely connected. Concepts are tools, tools for making sense of the world. In German their tool-like nature is particularly obvious: the word for 'concept', *Begriff*, comes from *greifen*, 'to grasp'. Concepts are tools for 'grasping' the world. But how one grasps, which 'tool' one will use, will depend on one's 'interest'. If one is a farmer one will 'grasp' the land by means of concepts to do with stock-feed, if a conservationist by means of concepts to do with eco-systems, if a real estate developer by means of concepts to do with apartment-space per square meter. In general, then, concepts are always interest-related. Nietzsche makes this point explicitly in *The Gay Science*, acknowledging it as something he has learnt from Schopenhauer: part of Schopenhauer's greatness, he says, is his 'immortal doctrine of the intellectuality of perception [and]...the instrumental nature of the intellect.'[151] What he criticises in Schopenhauer is his failure to make this account of things *comprehensive*, his attempt to make aesthetic perception an *escape* from the 'instrumentality', interest-impregnatedness, of perception.

If Nietzsche's doctrine of perspectivism stopped at this point (and if one ignored the fact that he calls scepticism a nihilistic 'disease' (p. 416 above)) it might be reasonable to take him to be a 'postmodernist' sceptic about truth and knowledge: there are many world-interpretations, all serving some interest or other, none of which can claim to be 'truer' than the others. Hence no interpretation can claim to represent reality as it is and so it makes no sense to suppose there *is* any particular way reality is.* 'There is nothing but the text', no firm land, only a sea of interpretations. In fact, though, Nietzsche's discussion does *not* stop at this point. Having criticised the traditional idea of objectivity, he feels it incumbent on him to develop his own account. Rather than thinking of objectivity as disinterestedness, he suggests, we should think of it as '*having in our power* our "fors" and "againsts" so that, with respect, precisely, to the *difference* in perspectives and affective interpretations, one knows how to make them useful from the point of view of knowledge'. Since there is *only* perspectival 'knowing', he continues,

> the *more* affects we allow to speak about a thing, the *more* eyes, various eyes we know how to bring to bear on the same thing, the more complete will be our 'concept' (*Begriff*) of the thing, our 'objectivity'. But to eliminate the will completely and turn off all the emotions without exception, assuming we could, would that not be to *castrate* the intellect?[152]

---

* Actually, there is some seriously shonky reasoning here. For it does not, in fact, follow from the fact that there are many, equally good, interpretations of the world that none can be truth-revealing. It only follows if one adds the premise that no interpretation can be true unless it is *uniquely* true. What this suggests is that the postmodernist is, in fact, to deploy a term I coined in the previous chapter, a frustrated 'absolutiser': someone with the 'bad taste' to want his own interpretation to be 'the only rightful interpretation of the world' (GS 373). Having had his metaphysician's yearning to be sole owner of the truth frustrated by perspectivism, he goes into a kind of sulk and claims that 'Well, then, no one can say anything true about the world'. Since postmodernism is the result of seriously bad reasoning one should avoid saddling Nietzsche with it, if at all possible.

The basic idea, then, is to admit the perspectival, interest-impregnated nature of knowing and then assemble as many perspectives as possible. The big question is: how can a bunch of 'affective interpretations', perspectives, possibly end up producing something one could call 'objectivity'? How can adding a whole lot of, as one might again call them, 'spins', add up to something that is unspun?

The first thing to notice is that being driven by interest or emotion by no means makes an interpretation of the world false, or even suspect. This was always a weak point in Schopenhauer's argument that only disinterested perception can yield knowledge: he regularly speaks of the 'falsification' of reality by ordinary, interested consciousness but, in fact, his impressive examples only point to *simplification*. To the traveller in a hurry, he points out, the beautiful bridge over the Rhine is reduced to little more than a dash intersecting with a stroke, to the engaged chess player the beautifully carved Chinese pieces are reduced to mere Xs that play their defining role, to most of us most of the time people are reduced to their job-description or social standing. In sum, Schopenhauer points out, in perception governed by practical interest, the world shows up 'as a landscape does on a general's map of a battlefield'.[153] Schopenhauer's 'general' with his simplified worldview reappears in Nietzsche's notebooks:

> Just as there are many things a general doesn't want to know, so our conscious mind must be above all a drive to exclude. Logic, our sense of time, our sense of space are prodigious capacities to abbreviate. A concept is an invention to which nothing corresponds wholly but many things slightly. Yet with this invention of the rigid world of concepts ... man seizes a huge number of facts by means of signs.[154]

These reflections on the general and his simplifying map surely provide the clue to understanding Nietzsche's conception of objectivity as a matter of building up a 'complete' concept of a thing. Maps, that is to say, represent only an aspect of the world they map; one represents the roads, another the contours of hills and valleys, another the types and distribution of vegetation, another the geological make-up of the terrain, another the ethnic diversity of the population, another its religious diversity, and so on. To move towards a 'complete' knowledge of the terrain one needs to possess all these maps and more.[155] In principle there is no limit to the number of world-representations, 'maps' of different types one might assemble, so that although one can acquire *more* 'complete' knowledge of the world one can never acquire *absolutely complete* knowledge. Science, the acquisition of knowledge, can never come to an end, since with the recognition of perspectivism, our world, as *The Gay Science* puts it, 'becomes infinite'.[156] That this is the correct understanding of Nietzschean objectivity is suggested by the following notebook entry:

> A thing in itself is just as wrong-headed as a meaning in itself. There is no fact in itself. Instead, for there to be a fact a sense ['horizon', 'perspective'] has first to be projected into it. A thing not 'defined' until all possible perspectives of all possible beings have been considered.[157]

The foregoing discussion supports the idea, canvassed in Chapter 17 (p. 338 above), that Nietzsche really is a 'plural realist'. Reality is multi-aspected.* Some perspectives (not all,

---

* In *The Gay Science* he calls it *vieldeutig*: 'ambiguous' is the best English can do, but the word actually means not 'of two' but rather 'of *many* meanings' (GS 373). A further point: the first great Western philosopher to view reality as multi-aspected was Spinoza. It is possible, therefore, that 'plural realism' was part of the affinity Nietzsche felt for the Amsterdam lens-grinder (pp. 319–20 above).

of course) genuinely reveal aspects of reality. The more genuine perspectives one has command of, the more 'knowledgeable' one is, the closer one comes to the – unattainable but inspiring – goal of 'completing science'.

One aspect of Nietzsche's discussion I have not yet attended to: the idea that assembling one's (interested) perspectives on a thing will be a matter of assembling one's 'fors' and 'againsts'. Though it is not impossible to imagine, one does not normally think of a contrast between hostile and favourable perspectives on, say, a tomato. For this reason, when Nietzsche speaks of assembling pros and cons he has primarily in mind, I think, his own special topics, such as religion and morality. One of his great strengths as a philosopher, which coexists, paradoxically, with his taste for radically biased polemics, is his fair-mindedness. Consistently, his itemising of the downside of, for example, Christianity is balanced, sooner or later, by an admission of its upside. (He has, of course, to be able to do this if he is to embrace the eternal return.) Christianity gave us a meaning of life, made us more spiritual, more interesting, gave us a sense of reverence for holy things, the Catholic Church was a great, supra-national institution, and so on. The more aspects of Christianity one assembles the more 'complete' is one's knowledge of it and the better placed one is to decide whether it has been, *on balance*, a good or a bad thing. It is this *roundedness* and *fair-mindedness* that makes Nietzsche's overall discussion of his central topics 'objective' rather than *merely* 'polemical', intellectually serious rather than mere propaganda. In sum, then, what Nietzsche's completed doctrine of perspectivism does is to replace the traditional idea of objectivity as a God-like gaze which penetrates to the heart of being and grasps it all at once, neat and entire – the view from nowhere and from no interest – with a new and impressive notion of objectivity as the slow and careful survey of a thing that *builds up* our knowledge of it.

A final question: why would 'turning off' the emotions '*castrate* the intellect'? Why would it represent the *absence* of cognition? The point becomes clear if we return to the analogy between concepts and tools. If one does not want to construct anything, one does not reach for a hammer. Analogously, if we did not wish to survive – more exactly, if we lacked the drive to increase our power – knowing would never start. As the notebooks put it, 'it is the will to power which *interprets*', the point of interpretation being '*to become master of something*'.[158]

The Ascetic Ideal as Practised and Propagated by Priests

The discussion of perspectivism is a digression from the main topic of the third essay, the ascetic ideal. With section 11 we return to, and approach the heart of, that topic. Only when we turn to the 'ascetic priest', Nietzsche writes, 'can we seriously get to grips with our problem; what does the ascetic ideal mean?' Save in the case of Schopenhauer, in other words, we have been dealing with ascetic 'ideals', ascetic *practices*, that are in varying ways useful, *and so life-affirming*. But now we come to asceticism as genuinely *life-denying*. 'The' ascetic ideal, the doctrine preached by the priest, is a 'valuation of our life':

He relates this (together with all that belongs to it, 'nature', 'the world', the whole sphere of what becomes and passes away) to a quite different sphere of existence which is opposed to it and excludes it *unless* it should turn against itself and *deny itself*; in this case, the case of the ascetic life, life counts as a bridge to that other existence. The ascetic treats life as a wrong path.[159]

Life and the world are, in other words, as Schopenhauer puts it, things that 'ought not to be'.

The third essay's focal question is, then: what does the ascetic priest's denial of life 'mean'? 'Mean' is a vague word. It seems to me that what Nietzsche is really asking is: how is it possible that a living being should disvalue life? He thinks that this is something 'astonishing', 'paradoxical',[160] 'self-contradictory' when viewed from a 'physiological standpoint'.[161] And given that 'physiological' means, essentially, 'Darwinian', it is easy to see that it is: if a type of human being really and unequivocally did subscribe to the view that 'exiting life is better than living', it would surely have been either self- or other-genocided by now. It follows that 'life against life' must in fact be a misleading description, 'merely provisional'. In reality there must be something *life-preserving* about the ascetic ideal.[162] Its real 'meaning' will be, then, this life-preserving function.

What is really going on, Nietzsche says, is that *'the ascetic ideal springs from the protective and healing instinct of a degenerate life'*.[163] He continues by saying that the priest's *success* in gaining widespread acceptance of the ascetic ideal 'reveals a major fact, the *sickliness* of the type of man who has lived up to now, at least of the tamed man'. The ascetic priest is the 'incarnation of his wish…to be elsewhere', his 'nausea' and 'fatigue'. The ascetic priest makes himself the leader of 'the whole herd of failures, the disgruntled and underprivileged' and – in ways we will come to – actually persuades them to 'retain their hold on life'. He achieves this because the ascetic ideal's big 'No' brings with it a host of 'tender Yeses'.[164]

This talk of the 'tamed man' – in section 20 Nietzsche talks of the 'caged animal' – returns us to the second essay's identification of the groundwork for Christian 'guilt' and the 'bad conscience' as consisting in the internalisation of aggression by the former warrior-nobles no longer able to 'let off steam' in rape and pillage.

Now, however, there is a surprise: whereas the 'animal bad conscience'[165] looked to be universal to all humans when (as I suggested) hunter-gathering gave way to farming, we now learn that only a certain group – the 'failures, the disgruntled and the underprivileged' – suffered it. But it is not hard, I think, to grasp Nietzsche's point: even in conditions of peace the nobles remain healthy because they can carry on venting their aggression. The only difference from their footloose and fancy-free days as wandering warriors is that now they vent their violence on their own slave class rather than foreign tribes, throw them to the lions and so on. (As I write, the eighty-five-year-old Robert Mugabe continues to torture and murder his fellow Zimbabweans. One notices, however, his amazing skin tone.) So it seems that the need for aggression against oneself only afflicts 'the underprivileged, the unfortunate'.[166] This returns us to the 'slave revolt' of the first essay.

So how, contrary to appearances, does the ascetic priest with his Christian propaganda, the ascetic ideal, preserve the life of the 'slave' classes? In four ways. First, the priest defends the 'sick' against the healthy nobles. He protects them from suffering violence at the hands of the nobles by means of a 'war of cunning' which converts the nobles to slave morality and so makes them 'sick', too, by depriving them of their release of aggression. This (a) lessens the violence the slaves have to suffer and (b) increases the following, and so power, of the priests.[167]

Second, the priest protects the slaves against envy of the healthy (and so against the futility of a 'ghetto uprising').[168] He tells the slaves 'it's easier for a camel to go through the eye of a needle than for a rich man to enter the kingdom of God',[169] so that the slaves even come, perhaps, to pity their oppressors, the nobles.

Third, the ascetic priest defends the herd against 'anarchy and the ever-present threat of inner dissolution'. The threat exists because, as Zarathustra puts it, 'the weak who have to serve the strong seek to be masters of the weaker still'.[170] (One can think, here, of the prevalence of child abuse in the underclasses of the contemporary West.) The priest prevents inner dissolution by deploying the concepts of guilt, sin, and damnation to defuse the explosive material of *ressentiment*. He defuses it by turning its direction inwards, thus making it relatively 'harmless'. Finding someone guilty for one's suffering is the great 'anesthetiser', but the priest says 'you yourself are to blame'. In other words, interpreting my misery as *my own* fault – on account of my original sinfulness – leads me to flagellate, literally or metaphorically, myself rather than another.[171]

The fourth and, it seems to me, by far the most important life-preserving effect of the ascetic ideal, Nietzsche reserves, for dramatic effect, to the very end of the essay, section 28. Whatever its downside, the ascetic ideal gave us a 'meaning' of life. This meant that 'the will was saved', saved from 'non-meaning'. And the fact is that 'man would rather will nothingness than not will'. 'Any meaning', that is to say, 'is better than no meaning at all'.

In *The Gay Science*, as we saw, Nietzsche says that we need to construe ourselves as the 'hero' of a life-unifying narrative. And then he adds that at least the following can be said for Christianity: by surrounding him with 'eternal perspectives' it taught man to view himself as a dramatic, meaningful whole, a 'grand criminal' in quest of redemption.[172] In other words, it made his life meaningful. Why do we need meaning? Because without it we cannot *will*; willing has to have a direction, a goal, it has to be a willing-*towards*. (It has to have a *sens*, which, in French, means both 'meaning' and 'direction'.) Nietzsche's point, then, is that Christianity made our lives *exciting*. It gave us a *project* to work on so that, in fact, we did *not* wish to exit the world before our time. In other language, it enabled us to exercise our will to power, to growth, even if the power in question was only power over oneself. It provided an outlet for the will to power without which we suffer 'depression', a 'physiological feeling of obstruction'.[173]

The Ascetic Ideal in Modernity

Nietzsche is at pains to emphasise that the discussion of the ascetic ideal is not merely an excursion into ancient history. Even though we have given up 'theological astronomy', the ideal's 'denial' of life is still with us as the dominant force in our culture. Far from 'Copernican' (i.e., modern) science meaning an end to 'man's self-depreciation', it has actually increased it by turning humanity into a mere animal 'rolling faster and faster away from the centre ... into nothingness'. The result is that 'since Kant, every sort of transcendentalism has had a winning hand'.[174]

The basic point, here, is that because we have retained Christian morality we have inevitably retained the thought of man as a flawed, sinful being. The gap between the Christian 'ought' and the natural 'is' is as large as ever. But this, Nietzsche suggests, leaves post-metaphysical humanity even worse off than before. We have retained the disease, the perceived need for 'redemption' from the flesh, but have lost the remedy. The result is that any kind of an Eastern guru, or a salvation-mongering artist like Wagner, has a ready market, since the will to abandon this world for a better one – life-denial, in other words, 'nihilism' in Nietzsche's most fundamental use of the term – is the basic character of modernity.[175]

This claim seems to me to be strongly located in the fin de siècle mood of the period in which Nietzsche was writing. In the last two decades of the nineteenth century Schopenhauer was becoming the dominant European philosopher while *décadence*, the cult of decay, deviance, and death, was all the rage in art: in France with Baudelaire, and in England with Oscar Wilde and Aubrey Beardsley. In music, Wagner was writing *Tristan* and *Parsifal* while Mahler – *the* composer of *Weltschmerz* – was writing his 'Resurrection Symphony'. Nietzsche actually uses '*Weltschmerz*', which he parses as 'lethargy' and 'depression', to describe the prevailing mood of the Europe of his time.[176]

The question is: how relevant is this to us? Are we still 'nihilistic' or is Nietzsche's claim about the dominance of the ascetic ideal *merely* a report on the fin de siècle mood of his times? Do we still have, in our culture and psyches, at least an element of the 'I'd rather be out of here' feeling? Is global warming generating in us a kind of fatalistic nihilism? Or is environmentalism becoming the new, meaning-giving religion that is reoccupying the gap left by the 'death of God', a new religion with the power to rescue us from the 'will to nothingness'? Notice that on Nietzsche's line of thinking one might well conclude that *we* need environmentalism just as much as the planet does. Heidegger calls environmentalists 'guardians' of the earth. Can 'guardian of the earth' replace 'grand criminal' as a meaning-giving description of the human essence that will enable us to find a new, and healthier, means of expressing our will to power?

What Is Wrong with the Ascetic Ideal?

In his customary, fair-minded – 'objective' – way, Nietzsche has pointed out several advantages of the ascetic ideal – which, so far as it concerns mainstream European history, just means Christianity. It preserves social order, prevents ghetto uprisings, prevents the underclasses from taking their misery out on each other, reduces the violence of masters against slaves, and on top of all that gives us a meaning of life, a goal that allows the will to power to express itself. The question, therefore, becomes acute: what, actually, is wrong with the ascetic ideal?

Nietzsche's fundamental objection is simple and has been with him since *Human, All-Too-Human*: the priest, the 'doctor' to the sick who is sick himself, combats 'only the suffering itself, the discomfort of the sufferer … *not* its cause, *not* the actual state of being ill – this must constitute our most fundamental objection to priestly medication'.[177] The main means is to produce an 'excess of feeling',[178] 'strong emotions', 'paroxysms of unknown happiness', which, when released, 'combat lethargy'. Afterwards, however, like a 'narcotic', they only leave the sick sicker than they were before.[179]

In its most general form, we know, the suffering in question is the 'caging' of the wild beast's will to power,[180] Freud's 'discontents' that are the price of 'civilisation'. What is the religious 'narcotic' used to combat this 'physiological feeling of obstruction' and consequent 'depression' and '(world-) weariness'?[181] Since, as we have seen, Nietzsche persistently refers to Wagner's music as a 'narcotic', what he has in mind, I think, is the vision of paradise offered by Christian or quasi-Christian art. Why does the narcotic make the sick sicker? Nietzsche's claim, it seems to me, is that though the 'big picture', which reduces our earthly existence to a brief chapter in a long story with a happy ending, lifts 'depression' for a brief moment, its overall effect is to make the 'little picture' even worse. Once one has been 'in paradise', the resulting nostalgia makes it even harder to be enthusiastic about mundane life than it was before. The 'up' of all drugs, Nietzsche believes (he had, as we have seen, considerable experience of drugs), is always outweighed by the 'down' of the withdrawal symptoms.

Science and the Ascetic Ideal

What, Nietzsche asks, is it about human nature that has enabled the ascetic ideal to dominate Western culture for two millennia? The answer, he suggests, is simple: 'up to now' there has been no alternative, no 'counter-ideal' to the ascetic ideal.[182] Given, then, that 'man would rather will nothingness than not will', the fact that there have been no rival candidates means that the ascetic ideal has been, as it were, elected unopposed.[183]

The 'up to now' makes clear the point I have been emphasising throughout this book, that Nietzsche is no mere critic, that he conceives himself as offering a positive 'counter-ideal' to Christianity. In *Ecce Homo*'s comments on the *Genealogy*[184] he says there had been no counter-ideal '*until the advent of Zarathustra*'. This work, as we know, is supposed to 'divide history into two halves'[185] by, quite evidently, providing, or at least clearly 'signposting', a 'counter-ideal'.

Surveying the current scene, the third essay now asks: where are the 'counter-idealists'? Are there any 'opponents' of the ascetic ideal?[186] Where is the 'counterpart' to the ascetic ideal that mirrors it by offering its own 'one goal' to override all others?[187] (Notice the equation between 'opponent' and 'counter-idealist', an equation which implies that the 'opponent' cannot be a *mere* critic: to repeat *The Gay Science*'s assertion once again, 'only as creators *can* we destroy'.)[188]

Nietzsche begins with a negative point: 'science' is *not* a genuine opponent of the ascetic ideal. The modern age sets up science as the opponent of the ascetic ideal with its own 'one goal' (namely truth), but in fact science is only the ascetic ideal's 'most recent and noble manifestation'.[189] Under 'scientist' Nietzsche includes 'philosophers' and 'scholars' and characterises them as 'unbelievers' and 'atheists'.[190] So he is talking about human as well as natural scientists, and particularly about those of an anti-metaphysical cast of mind. Conspicuously, therefore, he is talking about himself.

Why are 'scientists' manifestations rather than opponents of the ascetic ideal? Because they have an 'unconditioned will to truth' and so, without knowing it, they 'affirm another world'. To understand this, Nietzsche refers us to section 344 of *The Gay Science*,[191] which we discussed in the previous chapter (pp. 441–3 above). There, to recapitulate, he argued that since false beliefs are sometimes more beneficial to life than true ones, a commitment to truth at whatever cost commits one to valuing something higher than life. In affirming 'truth at any price' we are affirming a principle that is hostile to life. In doing so – here there appears for the first time a phrase that plays a crucial role in Nietzsche's final works – there exists a 'hidden will to death'.[192] Far, then, from opposing it, 'science' is a closet *affirmer* of the ascetic ideal.

As I pointed out in the previous chapter, Nietzsche knows perfectly well that the real-life motives of scientists only rarely include the 'will to truth at any price'. What, therefore, he is really attacking, I suggested, is *himself and Rée*, who *really did* subscribe to truth, 'intellectual cleanliness', at any price in their programme of 'psychological observation' – more accurately, of psychological undermining. What, however, about the author of the *Genealogy of Morals*? Does *he* fail to be a genuine opponent of the ascetic ideal because, covertly, he – still – subscribes to it?

'All great things', Nietzsche writes, succumbing to a Hegelian moment, 'bring about their own demise through an act of self-cancellation (*Selbstaufhebung*)'.[193] So it is that, through the agency of modern 'scientists', Christianity has overcome itself. Christian morality has overcome Christian metaphysics. 'Christian morality itself, the concept of truthfulness' – here Nietzsche quotes directly from section 357 of *The Gay Science* – 'translated and sublimated into scientific conscience, into intellectual cleanliness at any price', is what has '*conquered* the Christian god'.[194]

Are we then to conclude that (a) Nietzsche *approves* of this final manifestation of the ascetic ideal and (b) sees himself as part of it? Not so. For at this point he identifies a further task for 'Christian' truthfulness: having demolished the Christian God, it must now turn its attention to Christian morality – *including the very 'will to truth' itself*. What we must now recognise is that the will to truth is itself a 'problem'.[195] Thus, Nietzsche would say, by questioning the validity of the unconditional will to truth, he has raised himself *out of* the ascetic ideal. Having used the ladder of 'Christian' truthfulness to climb out of Christian metaphysics, he is now kicking it away beneath him. Notice, here, the plausibility of my earlier suggestion that Nietzsche is best seen not as an opponent but rather as a radical *continuation* of the Protestant – Protest-ant – tradition in which he was brought up. What overcomes first Christian metaphysics and then Christian morality is Christian morality – Christian truthfulness* – itself.

What does 'questioning' the will to truth, turning it into an *issue*, mean for Nietzsche? It means elevating life, *healthy life*, into a higher value than truth. If self-deception, illusion, is what best promotes *your* psychic health, that is what you should go for. This, however, by no means represents the demise of the 'will to truth', for here is Nietzsche's very last word, in *Ecce Homo*, on the question of the relative value of truth and illusion:

> How much truth can a spirit *bear*, how much truth can a spirit *dare*? That became for me more and more the real measure of value. Error (- belief in the ideal[†] -) is *cowardice* ... Every step forward in knowledge is the result of courage, of severity towards oneself, of cleanliness with respect to oneself.[196]

---

* The idea that the Christian virtue of truthfulness entails telling the truth 'at all costs' strikes me as an evident and strange weakness in Nietzsche's argument. For one would think it obvious that Christian compassion would accommodate, even encourage, the occasional 'white' lie. I can only assume that an unconditional prohibition on lie-telling was part of the Protestant tradition in which Nietzsche grew up. (Kant, his fellow Protestant and fellow Prussian, famously wrote an essay denying that there could *ever* be a right to tell a 'white' lie.) I have suggested already that the 'scientific conscience' Nietzsche is talking about is, centrally, that belonging to the author of *Human, All-Too-Human*. Only, I think, if the argument is taken in this autobiographical way is it at all plausible.

† In other words, the sentimentalised falsification of reality by 'darling idealists' such as Malwida von Meysenbug (pp. 408–9 above).

If, in other words, one is a supremely healthy, supremely 'noble', type one *will* have the 'will to truth at any price' since one will be confident that one can 'pay' any price. As *The Gay Science* puts it, 'He who is richest in fullness of life, the Dionysian god or man, can afford the sight of what is most terrible and questionable' because he is conscious of 'an overflow of procreating fertilizing forces capable of transforming every desert into bountiful farmland'.[197] Unlike the weaker spirit who needs the crutch of illusion and the 'convalescent' who needs 'superficiality – out of profundity' (p. 409 above), the supremely healthy can (in a manner that will be discussed in the next chapter) will the eternal return in full and unflinching knowledge of all that is 'black and squid-like' in the world. At the end of the story, therefore, the unconditional will to truth becomes the criterion of psychic health.

Masters of the Universe

Some time ago we set out to discover what the third essay has to say by way of characterising Nietzsche's 'counter-ideal' to Christianity, his vision of a better future. Its really positive contribution occurs in section 9.

All 'good' things were once 'bad' things, Nietzsche writes, expounding once again his theory of cultural development. Marriage used to be considered an infringement of communal rights, law was once viewed as an infringement of the right to a vendetta. It is thus imperative that we protect and promote the few spiritually exceptional people, 'man's stroke[s] of luck' ('random mutations' as I have called them), as the agents of the capacity for cultural change that is essential to a healthy community. The forces of conservatism will, of course, turn most of them into 'martyrs' but with luck, among the survivors, there will be those who promote the change that we need.

One of the 'good' things which used to be 'bad', Nietzsche continues, is our will to mastery of the earth. Though we are – rightly, he seems to say – proud of this, for pre-modern man, 'even using the yardstick of the ancient Greeks', our 'whole modern existence'

> is nothing but *hubris* and godlessness in so far as it is strength and awareness of strength
> . . . *hubris* today characterises our whole attitude towards nature, our rape of nature with
> the help of machines and the completely unscrupulous inventiveness of technicians and
> engineers. *Hubris* characterises our attitude to God, or rather some alleged spider of pur-
> pose and ethics . . . and it characterises our attitude to *ourselves* – for we experiment on our-
> selves in a way we would never allow on animals, we merrily vivisect our souls out of curi-
> osity . . . Afterwards we heal ourselves . . . We violate ourselves . . . we are nutcrackers of the
> soul, questioning and questionable, treating life as though it were nothing but the cracking
> of nuts.

The first observation to make about this passage is that it does not *endorse* hubris – overweening, unjustified pride, which, in Greek tragedy, leads to retribution and downfall. Rather, it says that modernity's stance to nature and to human nature *would have been considered* hubris even by the Greeks, who were by no means deficient in pride. The second thing to be noticed is that since Nietzsche himself – Nietzsche the undermining 'psychological observer' and genealogical deconstructor of 'ethics' – is the 'nutcracker of the soul' *par excellence*, the passage has to be self-reflexive. This means that though the use of the word 'questionable' might suggest that he intends to condemn the modern stance to nature, this cannot in fact be the case since that would be to condemn all his own work.

What the passage does, it seems to me, is to *endorse* modernity's unlimited will to power over both nature and human nature. It is one of those things which used to be considered 'bad' – 'playing God' – but is really good. And here, it seems, Nietzsche offers us a new 'one goal' to override all other goals, an ultimate goal to replace the 'one goal' of Christianity: making ourselves masters of the universe.

A glance into the notebooks of the period makes this clear. So we read, for example, that 'what is necessary' in place of the old morality is a 'reversal of values' which will produce 'a morality that has the intention of breeding a ruling caste – the future *masters of the earth*'.[198] In *The Gay Science* Napoleon is admired for wanting to make Europe 'mistress of the earth',[199] an admiration which incorporates the desire for the domination of the globe by European culture that goes back to *Human, All-Too-Human* (pp. 266–7 above). In the notebooks of 1886–7 we see Nietzsche dreaming of a time when science will have such a 'superabundance of [e.g., nuclear] force' at its disposal that man will be able to bring about the '*slavery of nature*'.[200] And since mastery of nature includes mastery of human nature, he dreams of a 'master race', the future 'masters of the earth', who will be the 'artists' who 'sculpt' 'herd' types into 'flexible tools' and humanity in general into a more perfect, that is more powerful, species.[201] Recall *Human, All-Too-Human*'s enthusiasm for eugenics.

Nietzsche's language of 'rape', 'violation', and 'mastery' closely resembles that used by Martin Heidegger to describe the world of modern technology. The difference, however, is that whereas Heidegger condemns modernity's unlimited will to power, here at least, Nietzsche endorses it.

Living in the times we do, we may well find ourselves agreeing with Heidegger's condemnation. We may well find Nietzsche's approval of the unlimited will to power repellent, find it to be *indeed* hubris, the fateful recompense for which – the meltdown of our climate – we are now experiencing. That, however, is something we have to live with. For all his criticisms of many of the effects of modern technology, at least some of the time, Nietzsche inhabited the modernist spirit of the age that invented railways, electric power, the telephone, and the bureaucratic state, the age in which the world seemed technology's inexhaustible oyster. Perhaps the best that can be said for him is that if he were alive now he would certainly classify the unlimited will to power as one of those things that used to be considered 'good' but is now 'bad'.

The Question of Method

Let me bring this discussion of the *Genealogy* to a close by returning to the issue raised at the beginning, the question of whether the genealogical method employed in the first two essays is, from a rational point of view, fallacious, whether the anti-Christian persuasive power of the work is, whether by design or accident, rhetorical rather than rational.

In the first essay, as we saw, Nietzsche takes it as a *datum* that the 'man of today' is sick; 'stunted ... wasted away ... poisoned'.[202] And he observes that, in the past, humanity enjoyed blooming good health. He then – recall that he frequently describes himself as the 'doctor of culture' – sets out to diagnose the origin of the 'patient's' sickness. And so he, as it were, asks the patient: did you ingest anything new and unusual at about the time you began to feel sick? And the patient reports that it did indeed ingest something new and unusual, namely slave morality. Lead poisoning provides an analogy of Nietzsche's procedure. If lead is what you ingested shortly before you first became sick then, quite probably, that is the reason you are still sick.

Nietzsche backs this up by looking at the origins of slave morality in *ressentiment*. He exhibits it as a kind of device deliberately designed for the purpose of 'poisoning' and so disempowering the oppressive nobles. The intention with which a device is designed is, generally, a reliable indicator of its effects.[203] If we know that the canister of gas was designed as a weapon of war we can conclude that, almost certainly, the gas it contains is poisonous. And so, understanding better the potential effects of slave morality, we can add to the fact that Western culture became sick after 'ingesting' slave morality the fact that what it 'ingested' was in fact poisonous. Clearly there is not the slightest hint of irrationality in this procedure. It is, on the contrary, a paradigm of powerful, rational, 'medical' reasoning.

The argument of the second essay is a slightly more complicated application of the same diagnostic procedure. The datum is a specific aspect of modern humanity's sickness, our 'bad conscience', lack of self-esteem. The question once again is, what has caused it? And the answer is that it originated in the internalised aggression of the human animal 'caged' behind the bars of civilisation, an aggression that was then shaped, endorsed, and massively intensified by Christianity. From this, Nietzsche concludes that Christianity is the major contributory cause of our current sickness. His therapy is a morality that returns humanity to an esteem for its basic instinct of aggression, but one which has the same civilisation-preserving *effect* as Christian morality by endorsing cultural rather than natural, sublimated rather than crudely physical, forms of its expression. Once again we are presented with a paradigm of 'medical' reasoning, a paradigm that contains not the slightest hint of the irrational or the merely polemical.

24

1888

Winter in Nice

THE YEAR 1888 began, as its predecessor had finished, cold. Sitting in his room in the Pension de Genève, redecorated with his own choice of dark, reddish-brown wallpaper, Nietzsche found the stove imported from Naumburg 'de rigueur' with respect to the otherwise intractable 'blue-finger' problem. Seated at his large writing table he had begun serious work on what was intended to be the main event of his life, the production of his 'systematic masterwork',[1] *The Will to Power*, to which all his previous works were the mere prelude. This was to be a four-volume work of 'extreme' and 'rigorous serious-ness'[2] that would provide a grounding and synoptic exposition of his entire philosophy. By February 13 he had completed the first detailed plan (with the title now altered to *Attempt at a Revaluation of All Values*). But though he continued to work steadily, he suffered from diarrhoea and insomnia, with his spirits – not improved by failing to win the half-million-franc prize in the Nice lottery – under the weather.

Since many of his fellow guests were, like him, hoping the Nice climate would ameliorate their various conditions, dinner-table conversation in the pension centred on climate and health. A lady from Berlin, for example, suffering from 'a kind of melancholic desperation' at home and scarcely able to leave the house, had, she claimed, been completely cured by the dry air of Nice. A short sharp 'change of air', Nietzsche agreed, had much to recommend it.[3]

As well as the right climate, a rigorous and unchanging daily routine was, he felt, essential: to bed at nine, up at six-thirty, tea with two rusks, an hour's walk in the morning, lunch at noon, three hours walking in the afternoon, always the same route, dinner at six, no wine, beer, spirits, or coffee, always the same, day after day.[4]

To relieve the monotony, at the beginning of January he took himself off to another concert in Monte Carlo. This, however, proved a disaster: César Franck and other 'mod-ern French music or, to speak more clearly, bad Wagner...nervous, brutal, insufferable, demanding, and boastful – and so tarted up'.[5] It was, he concluded, pure '*décadence*', just like Baudelaire – 'libertine, mystical, "satanic", but above all Wagnerian'.[6] (On the Baudelaire–Wagner affinity see pp. 493–5 below.) A couple of months later, on the other hand, he was charmed by three pieces by Offenbach, 'buffoonery but in the form of classical taste, completely logical...wonderfully Parisian',[7] a comment manifesting the ever-increasing taste for light music that marked his final year of sanity. (*The Gay Science*, we know, speaks of 'we convalescents' as needing 'superficiality out of profundity', as needing an 'untroubled, divinely artificial art'.[8] It is possible to suspect that it was a dim intimation of the approaching abyss that led to Nietzsche's increasing need for 'superficial' music.)

As 1888 progressed, Nietzsche became ever more concerned by the European political situation, by the 'armed peace' between, on the one side, Russia and France, and on the other, the 'Triple Alliance' of Germany, the Austro-Hungarian Empire, and Italy. 'Triple Alliance – with the *Reich* an intelligent people can only enter a *mésalliance*' he wrote at the end of the year.[9] 'Bristling like a hedgehog with weapons' under the aggressive policies of Bismarck and the ninety-year-old Emperor William I, Germany, he believed, was the principal danger to European peace. His experiences on the battlefield of the Franco-Prussian war seared into his memory, Nietzsche feared that Europe was on the brink of a catastrophe of unprecedented scale. His final hope for the house of Hohenzollern was the crown prince, Friedrich, who finally became Emperor of the *Reich* on March 9, 1888. By this time, however, he had developed throat cancer, from which he would die ninety-nine days later in Postdam.

Nietzsche admired Friedrich. He was distraught by the news that, in San Remo, he was dying and, fed information by his neighbour at dinner, a Baroness Pläncker, who claimed to be a close friend of the Empress, suspected that dark forces, either English or German, were conniving to obstruct a potentially life-saving tracheotomy.[10] 'You will be surprised', he wrote Köselitz, 'that I am seriously affected by the news from San Remo'.[11] Nietzsche's concern is indeed surprising, since Friedrich, unlike his antiquated and ultra-conservative father, was a liberal. Married to Princess Victoria, Queen Victoria's daughter 'Vicky', and strongly influenced by his fellow German, the estimable Prince Albert, he was an admirer of British cabinet government and parliamentary democracy. (Had he not died and been succeeded by his arrogantly macho son, William II, the First World War might never have happened.)

As well as being a superb horseman and general, Friedrich was a man of wide culture with a command of five languages. What Nietzsche admired in him was not his political but rather his cultural liberalism – 'the last glimmer of free-thinking in Germany'[12] – as well as his freedom from anti-Semitism. 'The death of the Emperor [Friedrich]', he wrote Köselitz in mid-June, 'has greatly moved me: in the end, he was the last hope for Germany. Now begins the regime of Stöcker: – I draw the conclusion and know already that now my 'Will to Power' is going to be confiscated first of all in Germany'.[13] (As noted already, Stöcker – appropriately christened Adolf – was a leading anti-Semite.)

First Visit to Turin

Spring and autumn, the 'intermezzi' between his summer and winter homes, were, as we know, the worst times of the year for Nietzsche. As it once again became time to leave Nice, he lay awake a whole night agonising about his 'spring problem'. The Italian lakes were too humid and depressing, Zurich was impossible at all times of year, and, in spring, everywhere else in Switzerland was still too enveloped in low cloud, mist, and winter.[14] And then came a suggestion from Köselitz: Turin.

The journey there was more than usually disastrous. Short-sighted and dithery, Nietzsche changed into the wrong train and ended up in Genoa where, too sick to continue, he wandered around for two days, lost in old memories. His clear-headed luggage, on the other hand, 'kept to the original intention' and arrived, as planned, in Turin.[15] When, however, he finally arrived, on April 5, it was love at first sight:

> What a noble and serious town! Not at all a big city [its population was about 300,000], not at all modern, as I'd feared. Rather, a princely residence of the 17th century which has only one commanding taste everywhere, that of court and nobility. An aristocratic quietness is preserved in everything: there are no shabby suburbs; a unity of taste down to the matter of colour (everything is either yellow or red-brown).[16]

As if designed expressly for his needs, Turin possessed nearly twenty kilometres of covered arcades through which he could walk in all weathers. And the sight of the Alps, the mountain air and water, the bookshops, well-stocked in three languages, the excellent food – cheap on account of the many young people attending the university and the military academy – the serene river Po bounding the city on the east with parkland and a shaded boulevard on the other side, all occasioned ecstasies of praise. 'Evenings on the Po bridge', he wrote, 'heavenly! Beyond good and evil!!'[17] He loved the café life (as he had as a student in Leipzig), became a connoisseur of gelato, which he found to be 'of the highest culture', and loved the palm court orchestra which sometimes accompanied it (without raising the price above the usual thirty cents).[18] 'The café ... a demi-tasse of paradise' he wrote in his notebooks.[19]

Nietzsche loved Turin's rich musical life. He listened to Rossini, Tchaikovsky and Goldmark ('a hundred times better than Wagner'),[20] and congratulated the city for extending *Carmen*'s run at the Teatro Carignano to two months at the expense of three other operas. And he loved the fact that operetta was available almost all the time due to the existence of two competing operetta companies. In Turin his taste for light music became ever more indiscriminate, to the point where he loved almost anything, as long as it was the opposite of Wagnerian portentousness. The only exception was Johann Strauss: since Germanic sentimentality is as bad as Germanic earnestness, '*Wienerei = Schweinerei*', he decided.[21]

Strangely, Nietzsche found, his health rapidly improved even though the weather, miserable on arrival and continuing often overcast, rainy, and foggy, was the opposite of what he had prescribed for himself. (He never seems to have properly conceded, however, the refutation of all his theories about the dependence of health on climate.) He took up residence in the apartment of a newspaper-kiosk owner, Davide Fino, on the 'superb' Piazza Carlo Alberto. His balconied window on the fourth floor (the Fino family lived below on the third) of 6 Via Carlo Alberto presented the suitably aristocratic sight of the statue of Carlo Alberto, King of Piedmont from 1831 to 1849, in full military uniform with his sabre raised to the sky.

Sic Incipit Gloria Mundi

From Turin, Nietzsche's correspondence with Brandes continued to flourish. They agreed that modern civilisation is a problem rather than a solution. Nietzsche told Brandes that Part IV of *Zarathustra* could well bear the title 'The temptation of Zarathustra' and that it is the best answer to his doubts about Nietzsche's critique of pity. He told him that 'the gold-maker' such as himself, who makes 'golden' what mankind most fears and despised, is its greatest benefactor.[22]

The most exciting news Brandes delivered was that he had held a cycle of five lectures between April 10 and May 8 devoted to Nietzsche's entire philosophy up to and including the *Genealogy*, and that it had been a tremendous success, each lecture being attended by over three hundred people. Nietzsche was given to claiming that while composers without fame are like girls no one will dance with, philosophers find fame merely 'burdensome'.[23] Nonetheless, bursting with joy, he reported news of the lecture series – with imaginative embellishments – to nearly every correspondent. In his notebooks he adopts the pompous tone of a public proclamation:

> It will be of value to the friends of the philosopher Friedrich Nietzsche to hear that last winter the intelligent Dane, Dr. Georg Brandes, delivered an extended lecture cycle at the University of Copenhagen devoted to the aforementioned philosopher... The audience of over 300 people showed such lively interest for this new and bold mode of thinking in German philosophy that they gave the speaker and his theme a standing ovation.[24]

Köselitz pointed out that Brandes's lectures constituted Nietzsche's breakthrough to fame. To have caught the eye of a man of Europe-wide reputation, a man who wrote in French, German, Swedish, Russian and Polish, as well as in his native Danish, ensured that he would become famous. Nietzsche agreed. '*Sic incipit Gloria mundi*', he wrote with affected indifference on a postcard to Deussen – 'Thus begins worldly glory', a pun on the familiar antidote to hubris, 'Thus passes (*Sic transit*) worldly glory'.[25]

To aid the PR process, Nietzsche decided Brandes needed an up-to-date curriculum vitae, which he provided, mixing truth and fiction in equal proportions. He was born on the battlefield of Lützen (near, not on), descended from Polish nobility (completely false). His grandmother belonged to the Schiller–Goethe circle in Weimar (a modified version of the 'grandma was Goethe's lover' story, but still false). And so on.[26]

Usually as a result of Brandes's efforts, Nietzsche began to receive letters from New York and St. Petersburg which (though in the end the suggestions of translating him into English and Russian came to nothing) led him to believe he was becoming famous in America and Russia – everywhere, indeed, save in Germany. This had the effect of increasing his fury against the country of his language and birth. Though they have 'celebrated me this winter in Denmark [as]... the most independent spirit in Europe and the only German writer', he wrote Malwida, and though 'something similar is about to happen in New York', 'in the dear Fatherland, if they notice me at all, they treat me as someone who "belongs in a mad house"' (a reviewer, recall, had declared *Beyond Good and Evil* to be 'bordering on the pathological' (p. 406 above)). 'The cretinism of Bayreuth', he continued, riding roughshod over Malwida's known loyalty to Wagner, 'stands in my way. The old seducer, Wagner, even after his death, takes away from me those remaining men on whom I could have an effect'.[27]

Brandes persuaded the great Swedish playwright August Strindberg, one of the fathers of modern realistic theatre, to read Nietzsche, with the result that he became an ardent fan, parroting Nietzsche's own judgment (p. 519 below) that *Zarathustra* was 'undoubtedly the most profound book man possesses'.[28] Since Brandes had described Strindberg as 'a true genius', even if 'slightly mad',[29] this more than anything, perhaps, persuaded Nietzsche that he had finally arrived. A lively correspondence grew up between the two 'slightly mad' writers. Nietzsche read Strindberg's play, *Père*, a domestic tragedy concerning a power struggle between husband and wife. 'I was deeply moved', he wrote Strindberg, and was 'amazed to find a work expressing in such a grand way my own conception of love – the means are war and the ground is deadly hatred between the sexes'.[*,30] To Overbeck he bragged, 'The Swedish genius, Strindberg, holds me to be the greatest psychologist of the "eternal feminine"'[31] – with in fact some justice, since Strindberg wrote Brandes, 'Nietzsche is my man... naturally a woman-hater like all gifted men'. (Strindberg bore the scars of three marriages and three bitter divorces.)

On one occasion Nietzsche addresses Brandes as 'honoured Herr Cosmopoliticus'[32] – thereby turning a familiar anti-Semitic slur into the virtue of being a 'good European'. (As 'cosmopolitan' in outlook, Jews, the anti-Semites claimed, had no loyalty to the state, a slur that undoubtedly contributed to the 'Dreyfus affair' about to break out in France.) One major ground of Nietzsche's anti-anti-Semitism was his grateful knowledge that whatever fame he might achieve was due, almost entirely, to the efforts of Jews: among others, Lipiner, Zimmern, Lanzky, Paneth, and, above all, Brandes. 'Without Jews there is no immortality',[33] he wrote Köselitz.

Elizabeth was aware of the same thing. Writing to Overbeck at Christmas 1888, Nietzsche reported that the Paraguay venture was collapsing: the settlers, seduced there by false promises, were demanding their money back, but it had all vanished and violence had broken out. Yet, Nietzsche continued, this had not deterred Elizabeth from writing 'with the utmost contempt, that I might well want to become "famous". That's very nice! And what a rabble I've chosen as a means – Jews, like Georg Brandes, who have licked in every pot'[34] (a version, presumably, of the 'cosmopolitan' slur). Clearly, in his last weeks of relative sanity, relations between Nietzsche and his sister were at the lowest possible ebb. As a response to her slur on Brandes, he sketched a letter bidding her a final farewell.[35]

Last Summer in Sils Maria

As June arrived, it was again time for Nietzsche to escape the summer heat. He knew that the evidence no longer supported his self-prescription of permanent 'mild winter' – 'Strange', he wrote Köselitz, 'though it was 31 degrees day after day going down only to 22 at night I, the most sensitive person to heat, didn't suffer at all[36] – but stuck doggedly to his routine. As usual, therefore, he decided on summer in the mountains, on his seventh summer in 'my old summer residence, Sils Maria: the upper Engadine – my landscape, so distant from life, so metaphysical [meta-physical]'.[37]

The move, however, proved a bad one. Though there was now a direct train from Turin to Chiavenna, just short of the Swiss border, the long train journey, followed by the post coach

---

* This view of love finds its way into the second section of *The Wagner Case*. Unlike Wagner, who represents love as self-sacrificing – 'Senta-sentimentality' – *Carmen* presents love as it really is: '*fatality*, cynical, innocent, cruel. . . . Love whose method is war, whose basis is *deadly hatred between the sexes*'. One may guess that this represents Nietzsche's current feelings towards Lou Salomé and surmise that, as only death terminates Don Jose's love–hate for Carmen, only his own spiritual death terminated his love–hate for Lou.

to Sils, where he arrived on June 5, prostrated him with a week-long attack of headaches and vomiting. And for the next couple of months, indeed, his health continued in very bad shape indeed; 'absurd',[38] as he put it.

The weather that greeted him was also 'absurd'. Its exceptional warmth and humidity caused many avalanches – one stopped just short of the Durisch house – which removed whole forests from their hillsides. (Nietzsche notes with interest a local law to the effect that trees uprooted by an avalanche are deemed to belong to the owner of the land they end up on, so that many landowners received unexpected gifts of firewood.) By mid-June, however, it was snowing. Nietzsche reported that 'I sat in my cave wondering whether the weatherman had taken leave of his senses'.[39] He changed into his winter clothes and put two duvets on his bed at night.

Something that took his breath away in mid-July was the receipt of two thousand marks, via Paul Deussen, as a contribution to the costs of his programme of self-publication.[40] (Meta von Salis later donated a further thousand marks.) Nietzsche suspected Deussen himself of having gifted the money, but in fact it came from a young, recently graduated *Dozent* (junior lecturer) in Berlin, Richard M. Meyer – yet another Jewish contribution to the promotion of his career.

Visitors

L eaving the family castle in Chur, Meta von Salis visited for the first three weeks of August. Together they did the five-hour walk from Sils to the post office in Silvaplana village, and on another occasion walked from Maloja to see, for the first and only time in Nietzsche's life, the dark Lake Cavloccio. And in rough water they rowed round his beloved Chasté peninsula in Lake Sils. Given his solitary life, Meta recalls, every interruption of his work-filled days was a special event.[41] She noticed, she later recalled, no signs of mental derangement at all.[42]

Nietzsche's other walking companion was Julius Kaftan, who visited for the same three weeks of August. Formerly a close colleague of Overbeck's, now professor of theology in Berlin, Kaftan had known Nietzsche in Basel. On their walks they engaged in serious philosophical conversations centring, from their opposing viewpoints, on the topic of religion – conversations which may have stimulated the writing of the *Antichrist* and possibly, too, *Twilight of the Idols*, both of which were begun very soon after his departure. Kaftan recalls that, one day,

> we walked up the Fex valley towards the glacier … By a little [symbolic] bridge … he came to a halt on the narrow street and spoke in a quiet voice of the great transformation he had experienced. It was as when a pious person discovers the nothingness of the world and given his soul to God. What he had in mind was the [1876] transition from No to Yes. That is the basis of all his teaching.[43]

In his memoir, Kaftan, noting that he was almost certainly the last person to have an extended philosophical conversation with Nietzsche, makes a point of stating, like Meta, that he saw not the slightest hint of the mental collapse that was but four months away.[44]

Two other visitors caught Nietzsche's attention. One was the Hamburg pianist Karl von Holten, who played a private concert of excerpts from Köselitz's compositions –

'Köselitziana', Nietzsche calls them, after Schumann's 'Kreisleriana'.[45] They also discussed the influential theory of musical phrasing propounded by Hugo Riemann, which, with its insistence that even the smallest musical element should be stressed and phrased, Nietzsche felt, dissolved the musical whole into its atomic elements, a typical manifestation of Wagnerian *décadence*.

He also continued a long intermittent discussion of this same issue with Carl Fuchs, which had started way back in October 1884,[46] the latter writing ten or more pages at a time. He had become somewhat cool towards Fuchs on account of the latter's trying to remain in good standing with the Wagnerians. Moreover, Nietzsche suspected (possibly unfairly) that as organist of the synagogue in Danzig (Gdansk), Fuchs had spoken of the Jewish service 'in the dirtiest possible way'.[47] Eventually, overwhelmed by page after page of Fuchs on musical phrasing, he treated him to a dose of Monty Python:

> Letters about 'phrasing' to the philosopher of the revaluation of all values!...In Nice they tried to interest me in the question of Martians – they had the largest stellar telescope in Europe. What is actually closer to me, Martians or phrasing? I'd like to continue to interest myself in Dr. Fuchs but with the exclusion of his Martians...P.S. They try to interest me here in the largest trout ever caught, 30 pounds in weight: who knows, in this case, supposing there to be a good mayonnaise sauce...[48]

Another visitor who interested Nietzsche from afar was Fritz Baedeker, the Leipzig publisher of the famous Baedeker travel guides and son of the firm's founder. 'Herr Baedeker and wife distinguished, "starred", my hotel (Alpenrose) the whole summer', he wrote von Seydlitz, excitedly.[49]

* * *

Two records of Nietzsche's final stay in Sils allow us to step out of the perspective of his letters and catch a glimpse of how local people saw him. A Frau Fümm recalled, in 1938, that

> there were three women from Geneva, a Frau Choindron with her two daughters staying with us in the Fex valley. On account of the Geneva ladies with whom Nietzsche was friendly, he came to us the whole summer twice a week to drink fresh milk. The friendly convalescent never spoke a great deal...With us he spoke *Schwyzerdütsch* [Swiss dialect, impenetrable to most Germans]. In the end he sought ever more to be alone. We had great respect for the strange man with the bushy eyebrows. Later, he suffered headaches all the time. When he did, he walked without a hat and with large damp leaves on his forehead and head. He would stand for a long time motionless as if rooted to the spot staring into the sky. And when he walked, swinging his arms and legs in a strange way, everyone laughed at the poor man. Later they wanted to erect a memorial to him on Chasté [see Plate 26 and p. 385 above]...That's the way it goes: one only becomes famous after one is dead.[50]

A second perspective is through the cruel eyes of children. A Herr Zuan, son of the local schoolteacher, told the visiting philosopher Theodor Adorno, many years later, that

> a band of children, to which he [Zuan] belonged, had fun by practicing throwing stones into Nietzsche's closed umbrella, so that as soon as he opened it they all fell on his head.

Then he would run after the children, threatening them with a raised umbrella, but he never caught them.[51]

In another recollection recorded in 1938, Zuan recalls that Nietzsche

> walked for hours every day mostly in the direction of Chasté. There on the huge stone, known now as the Nietzsche-stone [Plate 26], he would sit staring thoughtfully in front of him. And we children would then make fun of him, teasing him, pulling at his red umbrella, and would try to put stones in his pocket without him noticing. For the man with the huge moustache didn't notice what was going on around him. We called him just 'the idiot'.[52]

* * *

As autumn approached, Nietzsche's departure from Sils was delayed by massive floods. Much of the village was under water; the Chasté peninsula (*Halbinsel*, 'half-island', in German) became a complete island. With his never-flagging taste for statistics, Nietzsche reported to Deussen that 220 millimetres of water had fallen in four days, whereas the whole of September normally received only 80.[53] Finally, on September 20, the waters relented a little, and so he departed once more for Turin.

Writings in Sils Maria: The Wagner Case

Towards the end of the Turin spring, Nietzsche decided to take time out from work on the 'masterwork' to write *The Wagner Case*. Why he did this is unclear. On the one hand, he describes it as a 'recreation'[54], on the other as (yet another) 'declaration of war' on Richard Wagner.[55] Since, as we have seen, Nietzsche was still full of resentment against 'the old seducer' for, even posthumously, continuing to deprive him of potential followers, one would hardly think the declaration of war a mere 'recreation'. The truth, I think, is that relative to the – as Nietzsche was finding – increasingly difficult task of making the *Will to Power* the masterpiece he wanted it to be, descent to the level of polemics was a relaxation, a release of intellectual tension.

War with Wagner, and all he now stood for – German chauvinism, anti-Semitism, *décadence* in art – was, then, one motive for the work. But another, pretty clearly, was the desire to be noticed. In the 1880s, Wagner remained a 'hot' cultural topic. The German Emperor (Friedrich) had declared the Wagner movement a matter of national importance.[56] Moreover, the last of Nietzsche's works to have been widely read was his *Wagner at Bayreuth* – a work in which he appeared as a protagonist *for* Wagner. Why not, then, re-enter the fray, but this time on the other side? Anything to do with Wagner, one way or the other, could be guaranteed to sell.

And Nietzsche's calculations were not wrong. Naumann's booksellers' catalogue produced over a thousand advance orders before the pamphlet had even been printed. Malwida, too, knew that it would be a cause célèbre, writing to Olga Herzen that, for better or worse, it would put Nietzsche back on the map. In tandem with Brandes's efforts, *The Wagner Case* made a considerable contribution to the fame – or notoriety – that would soon be Nietzsche's.

Nietzsche completed much of a first draft in Turin – the work is subtitled 'Letter from Turin, May 1888' – but finished it in Sils, from whence he sent it to Naumann on July 17th.

The printer, however, promptly returned it as completely unreadable. Thereupon Nietzsche rewrote the whole manuscript with a new, thick-nibbed pen (a Sönnecken Rundschrift Number 5), which forced him to give up the microscopic chicken-scribble his previous nibs had permitted. The final parts of the new manuscript were returned to the Leipzig printer on August 2 and appeared on September 22. As with all his works from *Beyond Good and Evil* onwards, it was published at his own expense. To date, he wrote Malwida in July, self-publishing had cost him 4,000 francs[57] – a thousand francs more than the annual income from his Basel pension.

Décadence

A s the description 'Letter' suggests, *The Wagner Case* is a relatively slight work. To someone familiar with his earlier works from *Human, All-Too-Human* onwards, most of the Wagner-critique is familiar, even tiresomely so: Wagner is the purveyor of cheap feelings of transcendence-to-bliss that offer his world-and-work-weary audience a vague substitute for the now-no-longer-believable 'redemption' of Christianity. (In 1888, of course, hardly anyone *was* familiar with those earlier works, so readers *then* would have found nothing tiresome in the critique.) Not only Wagner's art is criticised, but also his character. Above all, Nietzsche tells us, yet again, that Wagner is an *actor*, which means that his effects are not merely cheap but also fake. (Something similar might be said of that other *Ring* saga: 'Tolkienesque' comes to mind as a summation of Nietzsche's 'actor'-critique of Wagner.) In addition to the 'actor' criticism, Nietzsche attempts to hoist Wagner with his own anti-Semitic petard: Wagner was probably the son of his supposed stepfather, Ludwig Geyer, who was probably Jewish. (Wagner may have confided worries about his paternity to Nietzsche in the days of their intimacy.) So he was not really German, merely *acted* being German, gave a very good imitation of Germanness[58] – precisely the objection to Jewish musicians in general, and Mendelssohn in particular, raised in Wagner's infamous 'On Jewishness in Music'.

Mixed in, however, with these essentially familiar claims are two matters that are both new and interesting. The first concerns the notion of '*décadence*', the second the genesis and nature of the *Ring* cycle.

* * *

Wagner is an interesting case-study, Nietzsche holds, because the '*décadence*' of his art sums up – and its overwhelming success proves – the '*décadence*' of modernity in general. Only the decadent appreciate the decadent. But just what is '*décadence*'?

As the French accent indicates, Nietzsche takes over the term – which from now on becomes his favourite summation of all that is wrong with modernity – from the French literary movement of the later nineteenth century personified by Baudelaire's *Fleurs du mal*, a movement characterised by a taste for the 'gothic', a fin de siècle obsession with decay, deviance, and death. As the virtually contemporary 'impressionists' defiantly described themselves with a term originally used to abuse them, so the *décadents* wore that term as a badge of honour.[59]

Nietzsche defines *décadence* as a 'neurosis' in which the 'exhausted are *attracted* by what is harmful' to life.[60] In *Twilight of the Idols* he says something similar: 'to choose instinctively what is harmful to *yourself*…is practically the formula for *décadence*'.[61] This is an accurate description of the (mainly) French literary movement: obsessed with the death-infected, exhibiting a kind of 'death-wish', Keats's being 'half in love with easeful death', the aesthetic decadents were precisely 'attracted to the harmful'. Even more *décadent* than Baudelaire, however, is Wagner, who, after reading Schopenhauer, Nietzsche points out, is overcome by the yearning for 'nothingness' which he presents, at the end of the *Ring* (and even more explicitly in *Tristan*), as his final account of 'salvation'. Wagner, in short, is the embodiment of the defining feature of *décadence*, the 'will to death'.[62] Notice that, thus defined, *décadence* implies the seismic shift in Nietzsche's metaphysics that will be discussed in Chapter 26: the abandonment of the claim that 'life' and 'the world' are 'will to power and nothing besides'. Now, there *is* something 'besides' – the 'will to death'.

The death wish, the 'hidden will to death', makes its first appearance in section 344 of Book V of *The Gay Science* and is then incorporated into section 24 of the *Genealogy*'s third essay, where it is treated as identical with 'the ascetic ideal'. In the *Genealogy*, however, Nietzsche still adheres to his will-to-power metaphysics and so, in a certain sense, he cannot take the ascetic ideal seriously: since everyone wills power, and so of course life, the *appearance* that the ascetic ideal 'denies life', wills death, has to be deceptive. So, as we saw, the ascetic priest's big 'No' is actually outweighed by a host of 'tender Yeses' (p. 477 above) and Wagner's *purported* subscription to the ideal is mere pretence (p. 471 above). Now, however, having (without anywhere announcing the fact) abandoned the universality of his will-to-power metaphysics, he finally treats the ascetic ideal, the will to death, with the seriousness it merits. Wagner really *does* will death; the yearning for 'nothingness' is *genuine*, and so genuinely *décadent*.

So much for *The Wagner Case*'s most prominent explication of *décadence*. What makes the notion tricky, however, is that he now proceeds to offer a second explication of the concept which at first sight seems to have nothing to do with the first. This is derived from the long discussion with Carl Fuchs of Riemann's theory of musical phrasing (p. 491 above) – Riemann is mentioned by name in section 11 – and proceeds as follows. The infallible 'sign' of *décadence* in literature is that

> life no longer dwells in the whole. The word becomes sovereign and leaps out of the page, the page gains life at the expense of the whole – the whole is no longer a whole. But this is the simile of every style of *décadence*: there is always the anarchy of atoms, disintegration of the will, 'freedom of the individual', to use moral terms – expanded into political theory, '*equal* rights for all'. Life, *equal* vitality, the vibration and exuberance of life pushed back into the smallest forms, the rest *poor* in life. Everywhere paralysis, torpidity *or* hostility and chaos: both more and more obvious the higher one ascends ... the whole no longer lives at all; it is composite, calculated, artificial, and artefact.[63]

Applying this explication of '*décadence*' to Wagner, Nietzsche says that he is infected by the 'decline in the power to organize' characteristic of all aspects of modern life.[64] The result is that his works are structureless – the principle of 'infinite melody' is merely an attempt to make a virtue out of necessity. In reality Wagner is nothing more than a gifted '*miniaturist*'.[65]

The extension of this second characterisation of *décadence* into the realm of politics and modern life in general is, of course, just a new formulation of the 'motley' critique. The 'democratisation' of Western modernity has reduced it to an 'anarchy of atoms'. And since it lacks the disciplined unity of a shared morality (a 'game plan' as I called it) that is necessary to survive in a competitive world, it suffers from 'declining life',[66] and is moving inexorably towards collapse and death. (As something that is 'artificial' and imposed rather than an organic expression of communal 'morality', the modern state, Nietzsche believes, cannot command the loyalty of its subjects and so cannot arrest its decline towards death.)

The introduction of death, here, helps one to see that there is, in fact, a connexion between the two explications of *décadence*. Discussion of the precise character of the connexion, however, I shall reserve for Chapter 26 (pp. 547–8 below).

The Story of The Ring

The second passage in which *The Wagner Case* offers something more than the routine case against Wagner is section 4, which offers 'the story of the *Ring*', an analysis of the genesis and nature of his *Ring* cycle.

Like all Wagner's operas, Nietzsche observes, the four operas of the cycle add up to a 'story of redemption'. Halfway through its composition, however, Wagner radically altered his conception of the nature of redemption. For the first half of his creative life, he believed in revolution 'as much as any Frenchman'. In Siegfried he thought he had found the essence of the revolutionary. All the world's problems come from 'old contracts'. Only by declaring war on them – on morality, on tradition – can the old society be abolished. This is what Siegfried does: he overthrows all reverence for tradition and authority, overthrows all *fear*. (The revolution is completed when he breaks Wotan's spear, the guarantor of the old contracts.) Siegfried's revolutionary nature, his 'war on morality',* is already prefigured in his incestuous birth. His love affair with Brünnhilde signifies the birth of a new golden age with free love as its central feature. This is the age that will succeed the 'twilight' and death of the old gods and the old contracts.

Thus the original story line. But then, midway through the composition of the *Ring*, Wagner's 'ship' struck the 'reef' of Schopenhauer's philosophy. Under Schopenhauer's spell, Wagner realised with shame that what he had done was to 'translate *optimism* into music'. Then, however, the inspiration came to him that perhaps the shipwreck was in fact *the goal*.

> And so he translates the *Ring* into Schopenhauer's terms. Everything goes wrong, everything perishes, the new world is as bad as the old: the *nothing*, the Indian Circe, beckons. Originally Brunhilde was supposed to take her farewell with a song in honour of free love, comforting the world with the vision of a socialist utopia in which 'all turns out well' – but now she gets something else to do. She has to study Schopenhauer first: she has to transpose the fourth book of *The World as Will and Representation* [Schopenhauer's advocacy of world-denial and ascent into 'the nothing'] into verse.[67]

Redemption in the *Ring* is thus transformed from socialist utopianism into death and nothingness – which is what makes it a work of *décadence par excellence*. (Notice that Wagner's turn to life-denial, his 'shame' at his previous 'optimism', is here treated as *genuine*. The persistence of the 'actor', 'fake', critique[68] introduces inconsistency into *The Wagner Case*.)

---

* Here, perhaps, we have the origin of the 'lion' of *Zarathustra*'s 'Three Metamorphoses' (pp. 369–70 above). As Siegfried slays the dragon, Fafner, so the lion slays the dragon, 'Thou Shalt'. And also the origin of the 'Metamorphoses'' 'child': knowing neither his parentage nor fear, Siegfried has the innocence of a child.

This penetrating and completely correct account of the impact of Schopenhauer on the composition of the *Ring** is, if my account of *The Birth of Tragedy* in Chapter 7 is correct, something Nietzsche had been aware of since 1872. As I argued there, early Nietzsche tried as hard as possible to square the circle by showing how Wagner could be *both* a socialist *and* a Schopenhauerian. Now he sees Wagner as *abandoning* the former for the latter, and so lapsing into '*décadence*'.

Notice, to make a small digression, how easy, in a sense, it was for Wagner to achieve the transformation of the *Ring* Nietzsche attributes to him. Since the destruction of Valhalla (the death of the gods) at the end of the cycle could represent *either* the ending of everything *or* the beginning of the new and better age, either the onset of night or arrival of dawn, it remains open to a director to present the cycle as either a socialist or a Schopenhauerian work. All it needs is a slight inflection at the end to lean it one way or the other. Harry Kupfer's 1996–9 Deutsche Staatsoper production, for example, portraying the destruction of Valhalla as the nuclear holocaust, needed only to introduce a small and appealing child (who appears to have wandered in from *Les Misérables*) emerging from the rubble at the very end to offer the suggestion that, ultimately, 'all turns out well'. Since, however, the child has absolutely no justification in the libretto, one might well feel that the production panders to an audience assumed to be incapable of stomaching Wagner's final nihilistic message.

* * *

A notable deficiency in *The Wagner Case* is the absence of any discussion, any mention even, of *Die Meistersinger*,[69] Wagner's most obviously life-affirming, un-transcendentalist celebration of a community and art flexible enough to accept novelty while preserving tradition. (The message, here, is virtually identical with, possibly even the inspiration for, Nietzsche's own theory of cultural development.) Even if the *Ring* ends up being *décadent*, it would be most implausible to apply that epithet to *Die Meistersinger*. This, one suspects, is precisely why Nietzsche pretends it does not exist: its admission would destroy the simplicity of the polemical flow.

A further weakness in the work is the absurdity of calling Wagner a musical 'miniaturist', incapable of large-scale organisation. It is true that his music is not unified by the logic of Mozart and Haydn. But, like *Die Meistersinger*'s Walther von Stolzing, Wagner was in the business not of following the old but of inventing a new musical logic. Nietzsche's denying him the right to do so merely reveals, once again, his own innate musical conservatism. The person who really was a miniaturist was *Nietzsche himself*. As a composer of anything longer than five minutes he rambles,[†] his music exhibiting neither the old logic nor a new one, and

---

* In 1852 Wagner created the so-called 'Feuerbach ending' to the *Ring*'s libretto, in which Brunhilde sings of the death of the gods and their replacement by a human society ruled by love. In 1856, two years after discovering Schopenhauer, he sketched a 'Schopenhauer ending' in which she now sings of will- and world-denial and redemption through absorption into nirvana. In the event, neither ending was set to music. Both, however, were included as footnotes to the final version of the score, together with the remark that though the Schopenhauer ending was the right one, its setting was unnecessary since the meaning was better expressed by the music alone.

† His Zurich conductor friend Friedrich Hegar, through friendlier towards Nietzsche's *Manfred Meditation* than von Bülow (see pp. 154–5 above), commented nonetheless that 'the whole is missing the architectural conditions to give form to the musical ideas, so that it gives me the impression of being an atmospheric improvisation rather than a properly thought-out artwork' (J I pp. 580–1).

as a philosopher, his works easily degenerate into a 'chaos of atoms', of aphorisms. Even the, by his standards, organically organised *Genealogy* sometimes loses the plot on account of an excess of digressions. In Chapter 26 we will see how his one attempt to produce a large-scale, genuinely systematic masterpiece ended in disaster.

Writings in Sils Maria: Twilight of the Idols

On September 7 Nietzsche wrote Malwida that on two recent nights he had woken up at two o'clock with ideas buzzing around in his head and had immediately committed them to paper. Then, on a third night, he continued, 'I heard my landlord, Herr Durisch, carefully opening the front door as he slipped out to hunt chamois. Who knows! Perhaps I too was out hunting chamois...'[70] The 'chamois-hunt', another 'relaxation'[71] from work on the masterwork,[72] was *Twilight of the Idols*. It was begun, Nietzsche reports, on August 18 and finished twenty days later on September 7.[73] Though it incorporates notebook material that was originally intended for the masterwork, there are no notebook sketches of this specific work, so Nietzsche's implication that it was a work of inspiration rather than per-spiration is partially correct.

Originally it was to have had the rather downbeat title *Idleness of a Psychologist*. But it took little effort on Köselitz's part to persuade Nietzsche that this was inadequate to the major significance of its content. Since, he quickly agreed, he had deployed his 'heavy artillery' against the 'highest mountains', there was nothing 'idle' in the book and the false modesty of the original title was inappropriate.[74] So the work became *Twilight of the Idols*. Though this brilliant pun on Wagner's *Twilight of the Gods* was intended to allow the work to follow *The Wagner Case* in cashing in on the Wagner market – he called it a 'twin' of that work, which should be published in a format that made this clear[75] – it is actually a somewhat misleading title since, for once, Wagner hardly appears.

The work, Nietzsche wrote Köselitz, contained many contemporary references and spoke some hard truths to the Germans that provide the justification for his low opinion of their *Reichsdeutsch* (jingoistic) mentality.[76] Though this is true it is again somewhat misleading, since, as the Preface notes, the work is, in the main, concerned to demonstrate the hollow-ness of 'not just idols of our age but *eternal* idols'. Unlike *The Wagner Case*, polemics against contemporary targets form a relatively minor part of the book.

The style, Nietzsche wrote Köselitz, is light and charming – 'French' rather than Ger-man – so that the work can be guaranteed to 'whet the appetite' for the masterwork.[77] As the Preface puts it, though the subtitle is, 'How One Philosophises with a Hammer', the hammer that 'sounds out' the idols is used as if it were a tuning fork (a railwayman checking carriages to see if they have wheels of clay, perhaps).

Since it would be inappropriate to produce an at least seemingly light work after the appearance of the masterwork, the latter a treatise of 'rigorous seriousness...a hundred miles beyond all tolerance and pleasantness',[78] Nietzsche decided that *Twilight* should be published as soon as possible. In the event, as we shall see, other elements of his publishing plans intervened, delaying its appearance until January 24, 1889.

* * *

Although it was finished but a few weeks before his collapse into madness, *Twilight* is a brilliant work. Unlike its successors, there are no pre-echoes of the approaching madness, which confirms the testimony of both Meta von Salis and Julius Kaftan that Nietzsche exhibited no traces of mental derangement during his final summer in Sils (p. 490 above). The style is effortless and graceful, the concision and compression masterly. The majority of his most famous epigrams come from *Twilight*. One suspects that the euphoria of release from the unrewarding slog on the masterwork produced a moment of effortless creative intensity.

Though light in style, Nietzsche was under no illusions that it was light in content. He calls it 'a complete introduction to my philosophy',[79] a 'summary of my essential heterodoxies',[80] which indeed it is. In *Ecce Homo* Nietzsche comments that, in *Twilight*, 'you do not get hold of things that are open to question any more, you get hold of decisions'.[81] What are these decisions? I shall try to bring them to light by thinking of the work as a series of answers to questions that might have been put to Nietzsche by an intelligent reader of his earlier works – Brandes, for example. Thought of in this way, it seems to me, at least nine important questions receive decisive answers.

What Is the Nature of Reality?

The fourth of the work's eleven parts, which runs to half a page, is titled 'How the True World Became a Fable'. There are six stages. First the 'true' (the term is of course ironic), supernatural world of 'being', the opposite of this natural world of pain and 'becoming', was immediately accessible to the sage's – Plato's – mental gaze. Then it became something one had to wait for; Christianity postponed the true world, transmuted it into the future home of the virtuous. With Kant it receded further, since it could no longer be *known* to exist. Yet as a consoling *hope* and as something we *had to believe* in for morality to make sense, it lingered on in a twilight state. But then came the 'cockcrow of positivism', the thought that something unknown could hardly be consoling. 'Gray morning', Nietzsche's stage direction, as it were, reads at this point, 'first yawn of reason, cockcrow of positivism'. This leads to the coup de grâce. Positivism, when it finally arrives, *abolishes* the true world (denies it, one might say, 'rights of citizenship in science'). Nietzsche applauds from the sidelines: 'Bright day; breakfast; return of good sense; Plato blushes in shame; pandemonium of all free spirits'. And now the conclusion arises that since there is no 'true' world, it makes no sense to call 'this' one a merely 'apparent' world. There is only one world and 'this' is it.[82] As *Ecce Homo* puts the conclusion: the 'true world' is a *'made up* world', so that what used to be called 'the world of appearances' is, in truth, 'reality'.[83]

This is not only the most brilliant *A Very Short History of Western Philosophy* ever written but also, save for the first stage, autobiography. It recounts Nietzsche's own passage from the Christianity of his boyhood, via a Kantian–Schopenhauerian 'true' world, to positivism, and from there to the naturalism of his mature philosophy. For Nietzsche, too, 'this' world is the only world.

But what is 'this' world? Nietzsche continues to promote scientific over commonsense realism. It is not just the 'true world' that is a fable; 'things' are as well, a projection of our inner life. We mistakenly think there is a thing called the 'I' which causes our actions* and

---

* The *Genealogy* argues that this is an illusion of grammar. Because grammar demands a subject for every predicate, we think that every action demands a substantial thing which causes it to happen.

then extend this schema to the outer world so that it becomes populated with a whole lot of 'I'-like things causing 'actions' to happen. But this is mere projection. Things in general, including material atoms, not to mention Kant's *'thing in itself'*, are projections. Boscovich's conception of a world of forces remains our best account of the nature of fundamental physical reality.[84]

But what is the character of these forces? At the time of writing *Beyond Good and Evil* the concept of force needed 'supplementing' by the notion of will to power (p. 414 above). Yet in *Twilight* Nietzsche is strangely reticent. There is no mention of supplementation, indeed the very phrase 'will to power' only occurs four times in the entire work, and never in conjunction with natural forces. The suggestion arises, once again, that the grand metaphysics of reality as 'will to power and nothing else' has been abandoned, leaving us to understand forces purely in terms of their effects.

What Is Freedom?

A fundamental presupposition of all science, Nietzsche assumes, is causal determinism. This means that 'free will', understood as one's being the uncaused cause of one's own actions, must be rejected. It was, in any case, a theological invention designed to make us feel responsible, and so guilty, and so deserving of punishment, and so dependent on the intercession of the priest for our salvation. So to understand ourselves as nothing more than a 'piece of fate', the summation of the causal history of the world to date, restores (as was argued way back in *Human, All-Too-Human*) our lost 'innocence'.[85]

Of course, some parts of the past are more directly relevant to the person one is than others. From the general rejection of 'things' it follows that 'individuals' are not 'atoms', not 'links in the chain'. An individual is, rather, 'the entire single line of humanity up through himself'.[86] 'Single line' looks to be another term for a family. And Nietzsche's idea, here, looks to be something like what we would now call genetic determination: the idea that an individual 'is' the sum of the genes inherited from both parents, which they have inherited from their parents, and so on. Notice that this idea explains Nietzsche's continued belief in the importance of eugenics.[87] Freedom, then, cannot be the freedom of the theologians, the nonsense of the *causa sui*, the self-caused cause.[88] But Nietzsche by no means rejects the notion of freedom as such. 'My idea of freedom', he writes, is that it is a matter of 'being responsible for oneself', maintaining one's 'distance', 'becoming indifferent to hardship', 'being prepared to sacrifice people to your cause, yourself included'. To be free means that 'the instincts which take pleasure in war and victory have gained control over the other instincts', the instinct to 'happiness', for instance, happiness, at least, as conceived by 'grocers, Christians, cows, females, Englishmen, and other democrats'. Freedom is not a birthright. Rather one *'becomes* free' by being a 'warrior' on the internal battlefield of the soul. The degree of freedom one possesses is measured by the degree of 'resistance one has overcome, the amount of effort it costs to stay *on top*'.[89]

Philosophers distinguish between 'positive' and 'negative' freedom. The latter consists in freedom from *external* barriers to doing what one wants – more generally, in being who one

But this, he suggests, is like thinking that the lightning in 'The lightning flashed' is something over and above the flashing (GM I 13).

wants to be – the former in the absence of *internal* barriers to being who one wants to be. If one is a slave in the nineteenth-century American South one lacks, to a very large degree, negative freedom. If one is enslaved by desire, by, for example, an uncontrollable lust for sex or drugs, one lacks, to a very large degree, positive freedom. The idea of positive freedom goes back to Plato's *Republic*. For Plato, freedom to be the person you are demands long and arduous disciplining of the passions. One is not born free but rather makes oneself free – or does not.

The valuing of negative freedom, says Nietzsche, the 'modern concept of freedom' as 'anything goes', is merely a proof of the *décadence* of modern society and is 'what I do *not* mean by freedom'.[90] Rather, the freedom Nietzsche endorses is very clearly positive freedom, closely related to Plato's conception. One must become a 'warrior', engage, first and foremost, in the battle with one's own desires, the battle to arrange them into a coherent hierarchy in which it is one's leading desire that achieves satisfaction at the expense, where necessary, of subordinate desires.

Notice that one cannot become free unless one *has* a leading desire, one that is more important than anything else, that defines one's life, determines one's identity. One cannot, as it were, shape the soul into a pyramid unless one knows what should constitute its apex. This is why Nietzsche speaks of 'one's cause', one's life-shaping meaning, for which one must make 'sacrifices'.

Notice that positive freedom is completely compatible with universal causal determinism, with one's being 'a piece of fate'. All that follows from the truth of determinism is that if one succeeds in 'becoming free' there are causally sufficient grounds, antecedent to one's birth, for that to happen.

What Is Happiness?

A s the above remarks suggest, Nietzsche's notion of freedom is closely connected to his notion of happiness. 'Formula for my happiness', he writes, 'a yes, a no, a straight line, a *goal*':[91] in other words a life-defining cause. (As noted, he told Malwida that the life he envied most was that of the Italian patriot Giuseppe Mazzini, on account of his 'absolute concentration on a single idea' – that of Italian Unification – which 'burned within him like a powerful flame'.)[92] This same point emerges in one of *Twilight*'s most memorable aphorisms:

> If you have your *why?* in life you can put up with almost any *how?* Man does *not* strive for happiness; only the Englishman does.[93]

The 'Englishman', here, is John Stuart Mill,[94] protagonist of the 'Utilitarian' principle that we should all seek to produce 'the greatest happiness of the greatest number'. The aphorism is a reappearance of the 'paradox of happiness' (pp. 307–8 above). The only kind of happiness that can be directly sought is 'English happiness',[95] a 'stupid ease and contentment doctrine', stupid because the pursuit of English happiness leads ultimately to boredom and frustration. True happiness is always a *by-product* of one's 'work', of active commitment to the 'straight line' of one's life, one's life-defining 'goal'.

More, however, than focused commitment is required for happiness. As Nietzsche emphasises – overemphasises – a socialist may be committed to the cause of the worker's revolution, yet be consumed by *ressentiment* against the capitalist oppressors and so be far from happy. Happiness requires the overcoming of *ressentiment*, of repressed hatred and lust for revenge: one must 'redeem' evils done to one in the past (for example, the Salomé affair) by showing that, as Nietzsche's most famous (but not best) epigram puts it, 'What does not kill me makes me stronger'.[96] And it requires, too, the overcoming of guilt. St. Paul, for example (my example, not Nietzsche's), was committed to the cause of spreading the gospel, but the commitment was motivated by deep guilt – *ressentiment* against himself – at his former persecution of them. Again, therefore, such a person must be far from happy. If you want to be happy, *Twilight* instructs, 'Don't be cowardly about your actions! Don't abandon them afterwards! The pang ['bite' in German] of conscience is obscene'.[97] As one must 'redeem' evils done *to* one, so one must redeem actions done *by* one. In short, the 'straight line' that defines both one's goal and one's identity must 'narrate' one's life in such a way that everything that is done to or by one finds its justification, its 'redemption', within one's life as a whole.

Nietzsche sums all this up with a panegyric to Goethe – the human personality he admires more than any other. A spirit like Goethe, he says,

> who has *become free*, stands in the middle of the world with a joyful and trusting fatalism, in the *faith* that only what is individual is reprehensible, that everything is redeemed and affirmed in the whole – *he does not negate any more* . . . a faith like this is the highest of all possible faiths: I have christened it with the name *Dionysus*.[98]

This 'highest faith' is of course the faith that constitutes *amor fati* (love of fate), the faith that allows one to will the eternal return. Perfect happiness is the ability to will the eternal return.

Notice two things. First, that 'Goethe's faith' has expanded to embrace not merely things done directly to and by him but *everything* that happens. One cannot be *perfectly* happy unless one's faith in 'redemption' becomes *universal*, embraces the entire universe. If something in the world seems to me irredeemable (Auschwitz, for example) then, whether or not it belongs directly to my individual life, my happiness is less than complete. Notice, second, Nietzsche's emphasis on '*faith*'. At any point in time there will always be glaringly 'unredeemed' phenomena (Auschwitz, again) so that, since we possess no crystal ball, we can never *know for certain* that they will be 'redeemed' in the whole. To claim such knowledge would be to claim that optimism is *true*. And that, Nietzsche points out, like all judgments of the value of life, can never be known: 'judgments, value judgments concerning life, for and against, can ultimately never be true: they have value only as symptoms . . . [since] *the value of life can never be estimated*'.[99] What is important, then, about Goethe's 'faith', about willing the eternal return, is not that it represents superior cognition but rather that it is a 'symptom', the defining test, of the ideally happy state of mind.

Why Is Willing the Eternal Return 'Dionysian'?

Why does Nietzsche 'christen' Goethe's faith, the precondition of willing the eternal return, 'Dionysus'? A great deal of *Twilight* conveys the sense of closing the circle, of returning to the beginning of Nietzsche's path of thinking, of re-embracing the central insights of *The Birth of Tragedy*, albeit cast in a new, naturalistic form. The informed and insightful Lou Salomé understood this: 'Nietzsche's philosophy', she wrote, 'forms a circle … towards the end, the man again approaches the youth through several of his most intimate and concealed experiences'.[100] One aspect of this circling back to the beginning (cancelling the *rapprochement* of the positivist period) is a return to *The Birth*'s assessment of Socrates as representing the decay of Greek culture.[101] Most strongly, however, the sense of return is generated by the reappearance of the Dionysian. 'I was', Nietzsche observes, looking back to *The Birth*, 'the first to take seriously the wonderful phenomenon that bears the name "Dionysus"'. Without understanding this '*fundamental fact* of the Hellenic instinct – its "will to life" – which expresses itself only in the Dionysian mysteries, in the psychology of the Dionysian state', one cannot understand the Greeks. In the Dionysian festivals, Nietzsche continues, the Greeks communicated their 'fearlessness in the face of the fearful'.* In the festivals, that is, they

> guaranteed for themselves … *eternal* life, the eternal return of life: the future promised by the past, the past consecrated in the future: the triumphal yes to life over and above all death and change: the *true* life as the overall continuation of life through procreation, through the mystery of sexuality. This is why the *sexual* symbol was the symbol to be venerated above all others, the truly profound element in the whole of ancient piety. All the details about the acts of procreation, pregnancy and birth inspired the highest and most solemn feelings. In the doctrine of the mysteries, *pain* is pronounced holy: the 'woes of a woman in labour' sanctify pain in general, – all becoming and growth, everything that guarantees the future involves pain … there has to be the 'agony of the woman in labour' so there can be an eternal joy of creation. The word 'Dionysus' means all of this.[102]

And then, at the conclusion of the whole book, Nietzsche turns from the Dionysian mysteries in general to Greek tragedy in particular:

> The psychology of the orgiastic, as an overflowing feeling of life and strength where even pain acts as a stimulus, gave me the key to the concept of *tragic* feeling … Saying yes to life even in its strangest and harshest problems, the will to life rejoicing in its own inexhaustibility through the *sacrifice* of its highest types – *that* is what I call Dionysian, *that* is the bridge I found to the psychology of the tragic poet.

As *The Birth of Tragedy* showed, *Twilight* continues, what drew one to tragedy was not Aristotle's 'catharsis', the purgation of pity and fear. It was rather,

> beyond all fear and pity, *to be oneself the eternal joy of becoming* – that joy which includes even joy in destruction. And with this I return to the place that once served as my point of departure – the *Birth of Tragedy* was my first revaluation of all values: and now I am back on that soil where my wants, my *abilities* grow – I the last disciple of the philosopher Dionysus, – I the teacher of eternal return.[103]

And so the circle closes.

---

* Kant's *Critique of Judgment* uses this phrase to define the 'feeling of the sublime', the feeling of transcending one's everyday self.

Two things are to be noticed about these passages. First, *cognitive insight* occurs in the Dionysian state. In the state, one guarantees to oneself 'eternal life' by rising above 'all death and change'. One transcends life as an individual by identifying with, *identifying oneself as*, 'the overall continuation of life'. This 'being *oneself* the eternal joy in becoming' is the state in which one identifies with, understands, what one's '*true* life' is. As I emphasised earlier, a great deal of Nietzsche's philosophy has been a preparation for this validation of Dionysian feeling, for validation of the idea that one's 'true' life is universal, that individual life is 'untrue': the persistent theme of the individual as the summation of the causal history of the universe to date, the individual as nothing substantial but rather a temporary conglomeration of forces that will soon reconfigure itself, a momentary 'wave in the necessary wave-play of becoming'.[104] This *anatta*, no-self ontology, as well as the broader rejection of 'things' in general, is a meeting point between Nietzschean and Buddhist ontology. But it is grounded in solid Western philosophising, in the thinking of 'the philosopher, Dionysus', the thinking of all those who follow Heraclitus (in whose company Nietzsche feels 'warmer and in better spirits than anywhere else')[105] in rejecting being and beings as 'an empty fiction'.[106]

The second point consists in noticing how much this ontological insight indeed recapitulates *The Birth of Tragedy*. 'Saying yes to life even in the face of its hardest problems' requires transcendence of the ego, transcendence to, indeed, a 'primal unity'. Only now, Schopenhauerian metaphysics having been left behind long ago, the 'primal unity' in question is nothing *behind* the phenomena but is, rather, *the totality of natural phenomena*, the 'eternal . . . continuation of life', itself.

Saying 'the triumphal yes to life' even in the face of its most terrible aspects is, of course, willing the eternal return. So, to return to our original question, in calling 'Goethe's faith', willing the eternal return, 'Dionysian', Nietzsche's point is that it can only be achieved through transcendence of the ego, identification with the totality of existence. Why should this be so? Ultimately, as I have suggested, because of the intractable problem of death. If I love life the last thing I want to do is to leave it and so the last thing I can embrace is my own death – the ultimate defeat of my will to power. As long, therefore, as I remain attached to my ego, willing the eternal return remains beyond my grasp. Only by transcending the ego, only by 'becoming oneself the eternal joy of becoming', can I 'guarantee for [myself] *eternal* life'. The happiness, of 'we Hyperboreans',* Nietzsche writes at the beginning of *The Antichrist*, consists in dwelling in a realm that is 'beyond death'.[107]

How Can an 'Immoralist' Deal with Harmful Actions?

Nietzsche, we know, objects to the 'domestication' of human beings by Christian morality. But this raises the urgent question: how does *he* propose to deal with the disposition of human beings to inflict harm on others and on themselves?

Nietzsche concedes there is a problem: 'all passions go through a phase when they are just a disaster, when they drag their victim down with the weight of their stupidity'.[108] Aggression lands one in a fight in the pub, jail, and the end of one's education. Greed leads to fraud and a similar destination. There are, he continues, two ways of dealing with the stupidity of

---

* Hyperborea is a paradise in Greek mythology located 'beyond' (*hyper*) Thrace, where 'the north wind' (*Boreas*) comes from. 'Beyond the black stump', as Australians would say.

drives and emotions: the Christian prescription of 'extermination' and his own prescription of 'spiritualization', sublimation.

Christian indoctrination directs one to become, like Christ, *free* of 'negative' drives such as aggression and (especially) sexual lust. To the extent one has such drives (even if one's adultery is only 'in the heart'), one is supposed to feel bad. The ultimate aim is their 'castration', becoming unable ever to experience them again. 'Castration' is the preferred technique of the weak-willed in general. Trappists have so little faith in their ability not to be corrupted by worldly things that they have to leave the worldly world entirely.[109] The disastrous, incredibly wasteful, mistake underlying Christian 'castration', however, is its failure ever to ask how the passions might be 'spiritualized, beautified, deified':[110]

> The spiritualization of sensuality is called *love*. It is a great triumph over Christianity. Another triumph is our spiritualization of *hostility*. It consists in a deep appreciation of the value of having enemies: in brief, one comes to act in the opposite way to the way one used to act.[111]

One values one's enemies, Nietzsche continues, because one only discovers one's identity when faced with opposition. This is as true of individuals as of political parties.

Spiritualisation, sublimation, is a matter of providing a drive with a new, spiritual expression in place of its old, crudely physical one, so that it becomes no longer harmful. Notice, however, an element in Nietzsche's conception of sublimation not previously made fully explicit: sublimation does not merely *vent* the dangerous drive (so that it becomes something merely neutral, as when aggression is vented on the football field) but rather transforms it into something that is the 'opposite' of what it used to be, something *positively beneficial*. Thus – this presumably is what Nietzsche's cryptic remark means – the setting of the sex drive in the context of love transforms the 'other' from a sex object to be used into a person to be respected and cared for. And the spiritualisation of hostility becomes a kind of competitive friendship.

This second example takes us back to Nietzsche's reflections on bad and good Eris, and shows why spiritualisation is a better solution to the problem of violence than 'castration'. As we have seen on several occasions, the Greeks spiritualised aggression into 'competition', and it was this 'agonistic' energy that fuelled not merely the Olympic Games but the tragic festival and Greek cultural life in general. To deal with violence via castration is to deprive humanity of the energy it needs to fuel creation. The same idea appears in the notes from the period of *Twilight* with respect to sex:

> The artist is, of necessity perhaps, a sensual man...Yet usually, under the pressure of his task, of his will to mastery, he is actually moderate, even chaste. His dominant instinct demands this of him...The force that one expends in artistic conception is the same as that expended in the sexual act: there is only one kind of force. An artist betrays himself if he squanders himself here.[112]

As the *Genealogy* observed, it is a commonplace known to every 'athlete or jockey' that sex dissipates vital energy that is needed for creation (p. 473 above). If then sex is 'squandered' in a crudely physical manner, then there is no art. But equally, if sex is 'exterminated', there can be no art.

Isn't Selfishness Harmful?

Spiritualisation is the response, then, to the charge that Nietzsche offers nothing to deal with the harmful effects of human drives and passions. But we are not yet finished with the question of the harmful, for we have still to deal with the issue of selfishness. Is not, the worried questioner might persist, the rejection of 'unegoism' and advocacy of 'selfishness' a positive *advocacy* of the harmful? Does not the positive *admiration* of Cesare Borgia[113] give the game away?

At the centre of 'all religions and moralities', says Nietzsche, is the idea that virtue is the path to happiness: 'do this, don't do that – and then you'll be happy! Otherwise ...'. We, however, he continues, say exactly the opposite:

> a well-formed person, a 'happy one', *has to* perform certain acts and will instinctively avoid others. In a word: his virtue is the *effect* of his happiness.

Nietzsche emphasises the importance of this insight by calling it the first example of his 'revaluation of all values',[114] meaning, presumably, that the first injunction of his new morality is: Become a 'happy', 'well-formed', (in his favourite terminology) 'healthy' person! Socrates asserted that no man knowingly does evil. Nietzsche proposes a modified version of this: no fully *healthy* (well-formed, happy) person knowingly does evil. Why, however, should we believe this to be true?

Nietzsche writes, 'Selfishness (or 'self-seeking' – *Selbstsucht*) is worth only as much as the physiological value of the selfish person: it can be worth a lot or it can be worthless and despicable'.[115] This repeats the distinction going back to *Zarathustra* and the positivist period between the 'hungry', 'cat' selfishness that wants to *take*, and the 'holy' selfishness of, for instance, Zarathustra that wants to *give*, to 'overflow', and so expresses itself as 'gift-giving' love (pp. 374–5 above). As observed earlier, it is the fact that the gift-giver is doing what he *wants* to do that moves Nietzsche to use the word 'selfish'. This, to repeat, is an unfortunate use of the word since, given that every action is motivated by some desire or other, it reduces 'everyone always acts egoistically' to a vacuous tautology.* We just have to put up with the fact, however, that 'selfish' is the word Nietzsche uses, bearing in mind that all it actually means is 'something one wants to do'.

The 'selfishness' of fully healthy people has, says Nietzsche, 'extraordinary value' since 'the whole of life *advances* through them'.[116] Healthy, happy people benefit us all. Who are they? The answer to this question we know already: they are people like Goethe and Mirabeau who, the *Genealogy* observes, being free of the 'worm' of *ressentiment*, exhibit *true* love of their neighbours.[117] The people who benefit us all are those who are never motivated by guilt, fear, hatred, or *ressentiment*, people who, 'trusting' that even the most repellent things and persons contribute to some greater good, display an extraordinary and universal benevolence towards the world that 'negates' nothing. The more like Goethe we become, the greater the value of our (unselfish) selfishness. Of course, the best laid plans of mice and men sometimes go astray. Fools, too, may possess gift-giving love. So far as

---

* Revealingly, Nietzsche's account of being '*un*selfish' is applying Kant's categorical imperative 'without any inner need, any deep personal choice, any pleasure', being 'an automaton of duty' (A 11). In other words, only computers can be 'unselfish': *human* action is, *by definition*, 'selfish'.

motivation is concerned, however, the 'joyful and trusting fatalism' that can will the eternal recurrence is the ideal to which we should aspire.

What, though, about Cesare Borgia (not his sister, Lucrezia, the flamboyant poisoner, but rather the general admired by Machiavelli for the utter ruthlessness of his methods)? What indeed about the *Genealogy*'s Vikings and Goths? Were they not, like Cesare, healthy and happy, and yet a barbaric blight upon the earth? In a passage designed to be deliberately 'audacious', *Twilight* calls Cesare 'a "higher man" ... a type of superman'.[118] In *Beyond Good and Evil*, on the other hand, he calls him a 'healthy ... monster'.[119] This conjunction of epithets, 'superman' and 'monster', puts him in the same category as Napoleon: he is a 'synthesis of monster (*Unmensch*) and superman (*Übermensch*)'.[120]

So what, then, does Nietzsche have to say about such 'healthy monsters'? Do they not represent a counter-example to his claim that no healthy person knowingly does evil, that a well-formed person, a 'happy' one, never knowingly performs harmful actions? I think not. For Borgia, Napoleon and the Vikings, though healthy and happy, are not, in Nietzsche's sense, 'well-formed'. And for that reason (just as von Bülow thought that Nietzsche's *Manfred Meditation* was not 'well-formed' enough to count as music (pp. 154–5 above)) they are not, in the full sense, *persons*. So long, that is, as one retains elements of the *Unmensch* one is not fully a *Mensch*, let alone an *Übermensch*. To be fully a human person one must have sublimated one's sub-human drives into ones that are human and humane.

This, however, leaves a question unanswered: why should one be *bothered about* becoming, in Nietzsche's sense, a 'fully human person'? One can imagine a Borgia-type responding by suggesting, first, that Nietzsche's account of 'person' is stipulative rather than descriptive and, second, that he himself has no interest in becoming a 'person' in the stipulated sense, but prefers to carry on with rape and pillage. If he was feeling clever he might even take a leaf out of Nietzsche's own book and suggest that the proffered concept of a 'person' is a *slave* conception and that he himself has his own 'master' conception, which he much prefers. Nietzsche's likely treatment of this response I shall discuss at the end of Chapter 26.

What's Wrong with the Germans?

The modern stereotype of Germany places technology in the centre of the picture. As Audi tell us, Germany is the place of *Vorsprung durch Technik*, a high-tech powerhouse. During the eighteenth and the first half of the nineteenth century, however, the stereotype was quite the opposite. The Germans were, even to the Germans themselves, *Das Volk der Dichter und Denker*, 'the people of poets and thinkers', to be found not in laboratories or factories or on battlefields but wandering about in their dark and mysterious forests, in lederhosen, carrying pens rather than swords. Essentially it is the transition to the modern stereotype, which happened with remarkable speed at about the time of the Franco-Prussian war, that Nietzsche lamented in the first of the *Untimely Meditations*,[121] and it is the foundation of *Twilight*'s critique: under Bismarck, he complains, the Germans have abandoned the life of the spirit for power politics. (Note that, had he been a contemporary figure, Nietzsche would have levelled this same complaint against Cesare Borgia.) Once a – indeed 'the' – nation of thinkers, there are no longer *any* German thinkers (apart from Nietzsche and he, of course, is 'Polish'). '*Deutschland, Deutschland über Alles*' (the first line of the German national anthem) was, Nietzsche claims, the end of German philosophy.

The German intellect has been destroyed by the chauvinistic *Reichsdeutsch* mentality and by being filled up with 'beer' and 'pyjamas'.¹²² (What Nietzsche had against pyjamas will never be known.)

It is no mere coincidence that, with the arrival of German power, German spirit, German culture, has disappeared. For, as we know, there is an 'either–or' choice to be made. If – either as an individual or a nation – one expends all one's energy on 'economics, world commerce...power, and power politics', one will have none left for culture. Since 'no one can give more than they have...culture and state – let us be honest with ourselves – ...are adversaries.'¹²³ Good Eris or bad Eris – one cannot have both.

* * *

As always, a major focus of Nietzsche's critique of the current German scene is higher education. Repeating the critique of *On the Future of our Educational Institutions* (pp. 142–7) – the views expressed there remain remarkably constant throughout his career – he observes that whereas the true goal of the university is to create fine human beings, those of both outstanding intellect and character, the university of the *Reich* has become a factory for turning men into machines, machines designed for the civil service. (He adds a nicely satirical summary of Kant's 'Prussian' metaphysics of duty: 'the civil servant as thing in itself raised up in judgment over the civil servant as phenomenon'.)¹²⁴ In line with its function as a factory, the universities have been filled with 'scholarly morons'. And this is a disaster, for what we need is *educators who are themselves educated* – Jacob Burckhardt is the one exception to the rule. Of course the 'democratisation' of the universities makes this impossible – genuine 'higher education and *horde* are contradictions'. To 'educate', to promote the growth of 'higher types of humans' (those 'random mutations', remember, on whom the future of community and culture depends), the university must remain the privilege of the few rather than the right of the masses.¹²⁵

* * *

A final strand in Nietzsche's critique of modern Germany, and by implication Western modernity in general, a critique of what he takes to be a developing trend, is his rejection of 'liberal institutions' – by 'liberal' he seems to mean institutions governed by the idea of 'equal rights for all', which makes this critique part of the ongoing critique of 'equal rights'. 'Liberal institutions' would thus seem to include women's emancipation, universal education, parliamentary democracy, social welfare, trades unions, and the like.

'Modern institutions', Nietzsche writes, 'are no good':

> For there to be institutions, there needs to be a type of will, instinct, imperative, that is anti-liberal to the point of malice: the will to tradition, to authority, to a responsibility that spans the centuries, to *solidarity* in the chain that links the generations, forwards and backwards *ad infinitum*. Where this will is present one finds something like the *Imperium Romanum*: or like Russia, the *only* power that can wait, that can still make promises, whose body can endure.

Adumbrated here is the conservative side of Nietzsche's theory of communal health: along with the occasional 'random mutation', a thriving community requires a powerful 'will to tradition', a tough, authoritarian conservatism that makes departure from tradition difficult. This is where 'liberal institutions' fail. Take marriage. It used to be 'indissoluble for life' with sole 'juridical authority' invested in the husband, a clarity in the chain of command which gave it a 'centre of balance'. Now, however, it is based on love, a notoriously fickle foundation on which to base anything at all. And with 'equal rights' for women its former clarity of purpose has gone. Instead of walking, modern marriage 'limps along on both legs'. It is, consequently, disappearing; social degeneration (the decay of 'family values', a similar spirit would say today) is the effect.[126]

Notice the rationale, here, for authoritarian conservatism – as his reviewers thought, a kind of 'Junker philosophy' (p. 405 above), for all Nietzsche's loathing of Bismarck. Without it, the capacity for resolute collective action disappears, so that the community degenerates and eventually disappears. In the language of Plato's *Republic*, a society – or soul – that fails to make itself 'one man' can do nothing, nothing in particular to protect itself from external and internal collapse. This is why, in the modern world, only Tsarist Russia is capable of 'making promises': only its promises will be believed, for only it has the capacity to keep them.

What Would You Like to See Replace Modern Culture?

Evidently, *Twilight*'s better society will be one of *illiberal* institutions. It will be a society that, while supporting elitist educational institutions that nurture the exceptional types who carry the seeds of its future development, will at the same time make it *difficult* for them to carry out their task. It will be, moreover, a society of firmly maintained hierarchy. Take the question of the workers. What the modern machine economy demands is, effectively, industrial *slaves*. But at the same time, wishy-washy liberalism insists on providing them with education, the right to vote and the right to unionise. The result is that they develop the desire to become themselves the masters. And the consequence of that is social strife and misery. 'If you want slaves', Nietzsche concludes, 'it is stupid to train them to be masters'.[127]

What any society needs, he continues, is a stratum of 'modest and self-sufficient types, Chinese types'[128] – coolies. As we have seen, the basic shape of society needs to be the 'pyramid' of Plato's *Republic* with a stratum of workers forming its 'broad base' (p. 160 above and p. 515 below). Within that basic shape, however, there will be many fine-grained distinctions. Since 'reality shows us an enchanting wealth of types' it is stupid to say, as 'moralists' do, that 'man *ought* to be thus and thus!' to 'paint a picture on the wall and say *ecce homo*'.[129] Whatever morality the new society possesses, it will have differential rights and duties for different kinds of people. Though hierarchical, it will be the opposite of homogeneous.

What Is the Place of Art in Your New Society?

'Art for art's sake' is, Nietzsche says, a legitimate protest against the subordination of art to Christian morality. (He is referring to the 'aesthetic' movement, an aspect of the *décadent* movement which was in high fashion as he was writing.) From the fact, however, that art should not be Christian propaganda it by no means follows that it has no ulterior purpose at all. What art does, good art, is to 'select' and 'dignify'. It 'strengthens' certain 'valuations' and weakens others. Specifically, it strengthens life-enhancing valuations and weakens life-denying ones. The subject matter of Raphael's wonderful art was, of course,

Christian. But let us not be 'childish': 'Raphael said yes, Raphael *did* yes, ergo Raphael was no Christian'.[130]

'Every healthy morality', Nietzsche asserts, every 'natural' morality, serves 'some rule of life'.[131] It is, we know, 'the voice of a people's will to power' (p. 371 above), its will to live and thrive. And so, too, we have just seen, is its art. There is thus a coincidence between healthy art and healthy morality: the 'valuations' that are validated by a community's art are the valuations of its morality. This takes us back to the task assigned to art in *Human, All-Too-Human* of 'imaginatively developing' shining images of the 'great and beautiful soul', back to the 'monumental' figures of the second *Untimely Meditation* and, ultimately, back to Wagner and *The Birth of Tragedy*'s assertion that 'art and people, myth and morality' are 'necessarily and closely intertwined' (p. 130 above) in a healthy community. On the connexion between art and society nothing has changed.

Last Stay in Turin

As noted (p. 492 above), serious flooding delayed Nietzsche's departure from Sils for Turin until September 20. As usual, the journey was a disaster involving, near Como, a night-time crossing of a narrow footbridge over flooded terrain – 'just the thing for a blind cow like me!' he lamented. (Evidently, not all of the Italian leg of the journey could be completed by train.) The arrival, however, instantly made up for the journey. 'Strange!' Nietzsche reported, 'as before, in a moment everything in order. Wonderful clarity, autumn colours, an exquisite feeling of well-being spreading over all things'. The welcome in the Fino household and in his local trattoria was all that could be desired. As before, he loved being just two minutes' walk from the magnificent castle on the Piazza Castello, loved the open-air theatre where one could eat gelato while watching a performance, loved going to operetta after operetta (the only fly in the ointment being Strauss's *Gipsy Baron*).[132] For the first time in his life he had his own tailor.

Though the weather was bad on arrival, this had no effect on either his health or productivity.[133] And it soon picked up, developing into a glorious autumn: from the beginning of October until well into November there was 'golden beauty, day after day, *da capo*'.[134] When not working, Nietzsche played four-handed piano with Fino's twelve-year-old daughter, Irene, for whom he had developed the same affection as for Adrienne Durisch. (Sixteen-year-old Giulia, on the other hand, regarded him as weird and would sit staring at him for long periods.) He frequently visited the excellent bookshops, browsing through new books, though never buying anything. And of course, he was a regular visitor to his favourite cafés, café Livorno in the afternoons, café Florio (famous, still, for its gelato) in the evenings.

The Antichrist

Throughout 1888 Nietzsche regards himself as 'at war', engaged in a spiritual 'war to the knife' against 'the present', but more specifically against the German present; against German chauvinism and anti-Semitism and the decay of its culture.[135] On September 30 he finished fashioning one of his major artillery pieces, *The Antichrist* (or *Antichristian* – the

German has both meanings), which at that time he regarded as Book I of the projected four-book masterwork (now, for reasons that will be explored in Chapter 26, retitled *Revaluation of All Values*). By mid-November, however, he had come to regard it as constituting the *totality* of the masterwork. This makes it an important document, in a sense, Nietzsche's last will and testament.

The Antichrist is an uneven work in both tone and content. Some passages, the account of the historical Jesus, for instance, are as fine as anything he wrote. But others amount to little more than a rage against Christianity that goes on much too long and says nothing that has not been said before. The subtitle, 'A Curse on Christianity', added at the last moment as Nietzsche was dipping into insanity, captures the quality of this rage. Gone is the former judicious weighing up of Christianity's 'pros' and 'cons' (see p. 476 above); in its place is simply the crude judgment that Christianity is 'the greatest corruption conceivable'.[136] The work ends with the promulgation by 'The Antichrist' of a seven-part 'Law against Christianity', subtitled 'Given on the Day of Salvation, on the first day of the year one (– 30th September, 1888, according to the false calculation of time)'.* The 'laws' contradict each other, since whereas the first calls for all priests to be 'locked up', the fifth calls for them to be ostracised at mealtimes. It is hard to believe Nietzsche had proper possession of his faculties when he wrote this addendum to the work.

Judaism and the Origin of Slave Morality

The essential thing about Christianity, writes Nietzsche, is its Jewish origin. It was the Jews who invented 'slave morality', the 'morality of *ressentiment*'.[137] Originally invented during the Babylonian Exile,[138] it was subsequently adopted by the Christians in the early Roman Empire. *The Antichrist* now proceeds to offer an account of the origin of slave morality in *ressentiment* which, since he refers us back to that, he clearly believes to be no more than an expansion of the account presented in the *Genealogy*'s first essay (pp. 462–3 above):

> Looked at psychologically the Jews are the people with the toughest life force; when transplanted into impossible conditions they took sides with all the instincts of *décadence*...out of the most profoundly shrewd sense of self-preservation – *not* because they were dominated by these instincts, but because they sensed that these instincts had a power that could be used to prevail against 'the world'. The Jews are the opposite of *décadents* – they had to *act* like decadents, to the point of illusion...a *non plus ultra* of theatrical genius...for the type of person who wields power inside Judaism...a priestly type, *décadence* is only a means.[139]

Originally, then, we now learn, slave morality was just *theatre*, a 'noble lie' that the Jewish priests used to disempower their Babylonian oppressors. By encouraging and validating the *décadent* instincts of the nobles (pp. 547–8 below), they persuaded them to transfer their allegiance from 'master' to 'slave' morality and so cease their oppression.

* Recall that *Zarathustra* is supposed to 'split history into two halves' (pp. 389, 480 above): 'Before *Zarathustra*' and 'After *Zarathustra*' is supposed to replace the old BC/AD system.

What makes this story initially startling in relation to the *Genealogy*'s account of the 'slave revolt' is that, there, the Jewish priests – 'cauldrons of unassuaged hatred', their souls 'poisoned' by *ressentiment* against their oppressors – appeared as paradigms of *sickness* (p. 463 above). Here, however, what look to be those same priests seem to appear as paradigms of *health* – 'the opposite of *décadent*'. Has Nietzsche then changed his mind about the slave revolt? Contrary to appearance, I think not – that what he is doing here, actually, is expanding rather than contradicting the *Genealogy*.

Crucial is the fact that *The Antichrist* is talking about not the Christian revolt against the Romans but Judaism's revolt against the Babylonians. Nietzsche portrays these *early* Jewish priests as, though naturally *resentful* of their oppression by the Babylonian masters, *not* infected by the poison of *ressentiment*. The reason they are not, evidently, is that they *do something* – something *effective* – about their oppression, and so 'assuage', *vent*, their resentment. Of course, they do not do so in the manner in which the Vikings vent their resentment against the internal constraints imposed by the tribe (p. 463 above). Under their 'impossible conditions', that option is not available to them. Rather than the sword, their weapon is, and has to be, the pen – black propaganda. What this means, in effect, is that – like Nietzsche himself – they are engaged in a spiritual *agon*. They view their oppressors as enemies, to be sure, even hate them, but they do not poison their souls with the *unvented* hatred that is *ressentiment*.

When we turn to the *later* Jewish priests, however, the Christian ones, the story is very different. What makes it different is the fact that the Christian priests have *internalised* slave morality: what for their predecessors was mere 'theatre' is for them the ultimate truth. And that demands, of course, that one 'turn the other cheek'; it forbids them the practice of health-restoring revenge.

The crucial contrast, then, is between the priests of Judaism and the priests of Christianity. That *The Antichrist* calls 'Jewish priests' healthy while the *Genealogy* calls 'Jewish priests' sick is not a contradiction since the former focuses on priests of Judaism while the latter focuses on the priests of Christianity. *The Antichrist* is, I think, making this point when it says that, while the priests of Judaism are 'the opposite of *décadents*', 'the Christianity of Paul' is a 'movement of *décadence*'.[140] And perhaps the *Genealogy* makes the same point by specifying the target of its attack as not, in fact, 'priests' in general, but rather 'ascetic priests' (p. 477 above).

The Historical Jesus

The real, historical Jesus, Nietzsche claims, had nothing to do with ideas of sin and punishment. Afflicted by a neurotic oversensitivity to suffering, he preached a doctrine of universal love, of never resisting, always 'turning the other cheek'. Presumably the suffering, here, is the suffering of division, of enmity. If one loves, forgives, everyone then whatever they do they can never be one's enemy. Nietzsche calls this a kind of hedonism, closely related to Epicureanism. Both Jesus and Epicurus are *decadent*,[141] on the grounds, evidently, that they lack the will that craves 'victories' and therefore 'enemies'. They lack, in a word, the will to power (see further pp. 547–8 below).[142]

The real Jesus was no metaphysician, had no supernatural beliefs whatsoever. For him, 'the kingdom of heaven' is a 'state of the heart'. It lies neither 'above the earth' nor 'after death' but is achieved here and now in the practice of universal love. Jesus taught by parable and by example. His death was not an expiation of human sins but rather the ultimate demonstration of his doctrine of non-resistance.[143] He was, in short, a kind of Buddhist, Buddhism being also a non-metaphysical life-practice engendered by hypersensitivity to pain.[144] Jesus represented a 'Buddhistic peace movement'.[145] This true, original Christianity represents a 'life that is still possible today, for *certain* people it is even a necessity'.[146] Possible and in the 1960s, surely, actual. On Nietzsche's impressive account, Jesus turns out to be the first hippie.

Paul's Perversion

In the immediate aftermath of Jesus's death, Nietzsche continues, the traumatised disciples asked: who killed him? The answer was: the Jewish upper classes. Gripped by *ressentiment*, they quickly began to misunderstand Jesus as a radical opponent of the Jews. Jesus's death could not, therefore, be the end of the matter: there would be a 'second coming', judgment and punishment. This is the torch that soon passed to that 'priestly tyrant' Paul, who, welding Jewish notions of judgment to Plato's metaphysics, invented Christianity as we know it: original sin, a supernatural heaven and hell, an all-powerful judge, and Christ's death as the hope of redemption. Above all, Paul propagated that ridiculous flattery of human vanity, the idea of personal immortality. This proved the trump card in the spread of Christianity.[147]

The Charges against Christianity

The trope in terms of which *The Antichrist* is constructed is that of a law court. The 'prosecution' brings series of charges upon which (there is no 'defence') the 'prisoner in the dock' is condemned as 'the greatest corruption conceivable'. Though there is nothing new in the charges, they do provide a useful compendium of Nietzsche's main objections to Christianity. There are eight of them.

First, and most easily overlooked, Nietzsche complains of Christianity's (Malwida's, for example (see p. 409 above)) 'idealist' 'arrogance', an arrogance that 'does not allow any scrap of reality to be honoured, or even expressed'.[148] As *Ecce Homo* puts it, 'to the extent one *fabricates* an ideal world one deprives reality of its meaning, value and truthfulness'.[149]

Second, Christianity both produces and intensifies the sickness of self-hatred.[150] It demonises all the natural instincts, in particular sex,[151] interpreting them as 'sins' that put us in danger of eternal damnation save for the intercession of Christ – i.e., the priests. In so doing, as we saw (p. 470 above), it caters to, and so intensifies, the self-loathing of the 'inwardly feral' human being caught in the cage of civilisation, provides him with a stick with which to satisfy the desire to inflict pain that has, perforce, turned inwards.[152]

Third, Christianity destroys all life-enhancing instincts, all 'public spirit'. Faced with the task of saving one's immortal soul, all attempts to promote the common good shrink into irrelevance. Indeed, concern to improve 'worldly' things might well come to be seen as a positive distraction from the real task of saving one's soul.[153] (No doubt the doctrine of 'salvation by works' was introduced to counteract this kind of theology.)

Fourth, via the 'poisonous doctrine "*equal* rights for everyone"' (notice that Nietzsche does not object to 'rights'), the idea that we are all equally valuable in the eyes of God, 'Christianity has waged a deadly war on every feeling of respect and distance between people, which is to say the *presupposition* of every elevation, of every growth of culture'. By destroying all 'aristocratism of mind' the 'evangel of the lowly *makes* things lower',[154] a process which, as we know, is carried on by the 'modern ideas'.

Fifth, Christianity is an incredibly cunning form of hypocrisy. 'If *ye* forgive not men their trespasses, neither will your father forgive your trespasses' (Matthew 6:15). And 'Whosoever shall offend one of these little ones that believe in me, it is better for him that a millstone were hanged about his neck and he were cast into the sea' (Mark 9:42). In pronouncements such as these 'Chandala hatred' disguises itself as love. Jesus's original message of love is perverted into a slave's threatening the powerful with hell fire and damnation.[155]

Sixth, modern Christian theologians lie through their teeth. They *know* 'there is no "God" anymore', that the 'God-hypothesis' is incompatible with all the other furniture of the modern, educated mind. Everyone knows that there is no 'last judgment', no 'sin', and no 'redeemer', yet everything goes on as before. It is notable that the 'Law against Christianity' that concludes *The Antichrist* reserves the harshest punishments for *liberal* Christians, on the grounds that 'the criminality of being Christian increases with one's proximity to science'.

Seventh, Christianity does not merely lie, it lies to a bad end. All the great world religions, Nietzsche suggests, indulge in the 'holy lie': Islam, Christianity, Confucius, the Lawbook of Manu, not to mention that would-be founder of a new religion, Plato. It makes a tremendous difference, though, why the 'lie' is told.

Take the Lawbook of Manu. (Nietzsche's source, here, is undoubtedly Deussen's book on Hinduism, which he had read the previous year (p. 456 above).) At a certain point, the spiritual leaders of ancient Indian society decided that the age of moral experimentation should be brought to a close: that their society had now arrived at *the* code that best served the health of their community. And so they recorded that code as the 'Laws of Manu', the central feature of which is the division of society into five levels: Brahmins (priests), Kshatriya (ruler-warriors), Vaishya (merchants), Schudra (craftsmen and farmers), and the Chandala, untouchables. In reality, the Lawbook was an empirical summary of the social order which long experience had suggested to work best. But to prevent further experimentation (the conservative dynamic in Nietzsche's account of cultural health), this empirical character had to be disguised. The Lawbook was, the priests pronounced, the product of divine revelation and had once, in a past golden age, been faithfully followed by the ancestors. 'Revelation' and 'tradition' were two 'walls' the priests erected to prevent further experimentation.[156]

Thus Manu's 'holy lie'. Shortly we will see that Nietzsche does not, in fact, support any kind of holy lie. Yet, at least on the surface, he observes, there seems to be a huge difference between Manu's lie and that of Christianity: whereas Christianity's lie is designed for the 'poison, slander [and] negation of life', Manu at least seems to aim at promoting human well-being, seems to 'say Yes to life'.[157] Reflection on Manu shows that some 'holy lies' are worse than others, and that Christianity's 'lie' is the worst of all.

The Antichrist's eighth, final, and in the end by far the most serious charge against Christianity (the root-cause of Nietzsche's hatred) is that it 'cheated us out of the fruits of ancient culture'.[158] Manu, Nietzsche writes, was an attempt to '"eternalise" the supreme condition for a *thriving* life, a great organisation of society'. But, ultimately, it does not provide a model we should follow, given that it creates and persecutes an underclass of 'untouchable' Chandalas. This not only represents a tremendous social 'harm', something we, quite properly, find 'outrageous', but also prepares the seeds of its own destruction at the hands of the 'Chandala revenge', a slave revolt.[159]

The same is true of a much finer example of the effort to 'eternalise' the conditions of thriving life, the Roman Empire: 'In this society, the revenue of reason from long ages of experiment and uncertainty *should* have been invested for the greatest long-term advantage, and the greatest, richest, most perfect crop possible should have been harvested'.[160] The Roman Empire, Greece's heir, brought the moral wisdom of the ancient world, antiquity's wonderful understanding of the 'art of life', into a political structure 'more enduring than bronze',[161] a design that *ought* to have lasted for, and '*proved*' its worth over, millennia. (It should, in other words, have become a 'Thousand Year Reich'.) No one since has even dreamt 'from the eternal point of view' in such a 'grand style', no one has dreamt of such a magnificent piece of social 'architecture'. But we were destined never to enjoy the 'fruits' of this wonderful European 'beginning' on account of its one design flaw, the creation of a 'Chandala' underclass. Though the structure was strong enough to survive both bad emperors and barbarian attacks, it was not able to resist the 'worm' of internal corruption, Christianity's 'Chandala revenge', the spread of slave morality which 'gradually alienated the "souls" [of the Roman nobility] from that tremendous structure'.[162] Rome died, Nietzsche agrees with Gibbon, on account of Christianity, the 'vampire' within it which gradually sucked out its life-blood.[163] And so the West's magnificent 'beginning' turned into a tragic end.

The Great Noon

In the light of this case for the prosecution (there is, as I said, no defence), 'The Antichrist' delivers his judgment that Christianity is the worst disaster ever to have befallen the human race. In promulgating his concluding 'Laws against Christianity' he condemns it to having all its priests either expelled or imprisoned, along with all preachers of chastity. All its churches are to be razed to the ground with farms for poisonous snakes erected on their sites ('holocaust' memorials, as it were). But then what? What kind of post-Christian world should we hope for and work towards?

Nietzsche's fury at the loss of the great 'beginning' (Hölderlin and Heidegger used the same word to lament the same loss, though neither blames it on Christianity) suggests – the point I have been emphasising throughout this book – that our new beginning should derive its inspiration from classical antiquity. What, Nietzsche asks in the notebooks, do we need in order to construct a new and stronger kind of human being out of the 'chaos' of modernity? What we need is a revival of 'classical taste ... the will to simplification, strengthening, to the visibility of happiness'.[164] In *Ecce Homo* the 'back to the Greeks' theme is even more explicit: the 'world-historical' task, announced already in *Wagner at Bayreuth*, is 'the imminent return of the Greek spirit, the need for *counter-Alexanders** to *retie* the Gordian knot of Greek culture after it had been undone'.[165] How are we to achieve this work of recovery that will restore the health of our culture? How are we to achieve 'The Great Noon'? (In the

* Nietzsche views the Alexandrian period as the decay of high Greek culture.

very last of Nietzsche's sketch-plans for a book to be called *The Will to Power*, the fourth and final book, evidently intended to contain his vision for the future, is entitled *The Great Noon*.)[166]

Manu, Nietzsche believes, represents a far from perfect social order. Yet the general idea of a 'caste system' is absolutely right; 'caste order, order of rank, is just a formula for the supreme law of life itself', a '*natural order*, lawfulness *par excellence*'.[167] What 'nature' dictates, however, is not the four (or five, counting the Chandala) social strata of Manu but rather three:

> In every healthy society, three mutually conditioning physiological types separate out and gravitate in different directions, each one having its own hygiene, its own area of work, its own feeling of perfection and field of mastery. Nature, *not* Manu, separates from each other: predominantly spiritual people, people characterised by muscular and temperamental strength, and a third group of people who are not distinguished in either way, the average.[168]

The smallest of the three castes are the rulers. 'They do not rule because they want to, but rather because they *exist*, they are not free to be second'. Buoyed up by a natural charisma that in a healthy society generates natural respect, neither their nature nor their fellows allow them not to rule. What, here, is meant by 'rule'? In *Ecce Homo* Nietzsche repeats *Zarathustra*'s beautiful and profound statement that 'thoughts that come on doves' feet guide the world'.[169] So the kind of leadership the rulers – *Beyond Good and Evil*'s 'philosophers of the future' (pp. 422–3 above) – exercise is *spiritual* rather than directly political in character. Rather like, as I suggested, the 'supreme leader' of an Islamic republic, Nietzsche's 'philosopher-king' is a *spiritual* king, which is why, in the future, 'the concept of politics will ... merge into spiritual warfare'.[170]

The second caste, the spiritually or physically muscular types, are the 'attendants, the right hand and best pupils' of the spiritual leaders and provide the custodians of the law as well as the military. They are 'the executives of the most spiritual', and take over everything '*crude*' in the work of government. The third caste is responsible for 'craft, trade, farming, science, and most of art'. Because this caste is by far the most numerous, 'a high culture is a pyramid' with a 'broad base'.[171] This is an exact repetition of 'The Greek State' of 1872 (see p. 160 above), indicating that Nietzsche's political views at the end of his career are identical with those at the beginning.

To anyone familiar with Plato's *Republic*, this scheme of things looks to approach plagiarism. The castes are not merely the same in number as Plato's castes but identical in function. The idea that one belongs *by nature rather than inherited social privilege* to one of the castes is what Plato embodies in the 'noble lie' of souls being born as either gold, silver, or bronze. (Notice that from Nietzsche's point of view this is not really a 'lie' at all but rather a metaphorical expression of a natural *truth*.) Even the details are taken from Plato: that the leaders lead out of necessity rather than mere desire, and that there is a natural affinity between the first and second castes.

To us there is something extraordinary in taking a two-and-a-half-thousand-year-old document as a blueprint for the future of the West, as indeed there would have been for many of Nietzsche's contemporaries: this is why, as we have seen, he felt compelled to defend himself against 'the superior smirk with which our "historically"-educated reject such a fruit of antiquity' (p. 425 above). What we need to understand is that to those moulded by the reverence for Greece that permeated, almost defined, the German *Gymnasium* well into the twentieth century, the idea was quite normal that political theory (like geometry and logic) had been completed by the Greeks. Martin Heidegger believed the same thing.

* * *

What Nietzsche offers, however, is not, in fact, pure plagiarism. For Plato, the reason philosophers must rule is that they alone have knowledge of the 'Forms': the eternal and perfect paradigms of justice and virtue, knowledge of which is the prerequisite of being a wise ruler. But Nietzsche, as we know, dismisses this 'true world' as a 'fable'. And so he offers something else as a condition of leadership:

> The highest cast – which I call *the few* – being the perfect caste also has the privilege of the few: this includes being [exemplary] models of happiness, beauty, goodness on earth. Only the most spiritual human beings are allowed … to be [morally] beautiful: only among them is goodness not a weakness … On the other hand nothing can be tolerated less in this type than ugly manners or a pessimistic look … Indignation is the privilege of the Chandala, pessimism too. '*The world is perfect*' – this is how the instinct of the most perfect speaks, the yes-saying instinct.[172]

Finding the world 'perfect' is, of course, just Goethe's 'highest of all possible faiths' (p. 501 above), the faith that all is redeemed in the totality of existence that enables one to embrace the eternal return. This brings out another, perhaps the most important, aspect of the test of willing the eternal return.

If one rejects democracy, as both Nietzsche and Plato do, if one believes – to call a spade a spade – in dictatorship, the question arises of how to ensure it is a *benevolent* dictatorship. Plato's answer, we have seen, is not available to Nietzsche since the Forms are a myth. More broadly, it seems to me, Nietzsche does not believe that the *most* essential thing to good politics is *any* kind of cognitive expertise. Though the spiritual rulers must indeed be 'the most circumspect (which is to say far-sighted and hind-sighted)',[173] their most essential feature is a quality of the heart. What we need are leaders who are *genuinely* 'good', those in whom 'goodness is not a weakness', those who are 'the kindest' and who 'treat the average more delicately than they treat themselves or their equals'.[174] The ideal leader, therefore, is someone like Zarathustra or Goethe (or King Ludwig, as Wagner wished him to be (p. 117 above)), who looks upon the world with universal love – who, that is to say, can will the eternal return.[175] Transported into politics, being able to will the eternal return is the crucial criterion of fitness to rule.[176] Notice that this is essentially a restatement of Nietzsche's view that 'virtue is a *consequence* of happiness' (p. 505 above). If this is true, then the supreme virtue of the ideal leader demands supreme happiness.

It might seem that one can look on the world with universal love and yet remain an entirely private person, but this is not so. Love is action, needs, as in the case of Zarathustra, to 'overflow'. Love for the community (for humanity) as a whole demands action for the sake of the community as a whole. Hence the ideal leader will be like 'those valuable, those masculine-noble natures that saw Rome's business as their own business, their own seriousness, their own *pride*'.[177] For the ideal leader, indeed for any truly healthy person, the prosperity of the community (of humanity) as a whole is the defining meaning of their lives. For the healthy person, personal meaning is communal meaning.

* * *

What, however, about the 'average'? Since 'Nietzsche's Republic' denies them 'equal rights',[178] do they not, in fact, for all the claimed benevolence of the leaders, form a class of oppressed slaves? As we have seen, Nietzsche argues that the fatal design flaw in both the society of Manu and in the Roman Empire was the creation of a 'Chandala' class: by allowing the development of an alienated underclass both societies sowed the seeds of their own downfall. He needs, therefore, to be able to demonstrate that his own future society is free of this design flaw.

Each of the three natural castes has, he say, a kind of happiness specific to itself. One man's meat is another man's poison, as he emphasises in *Beyond Good and Evil* (p. 420 above). An 'average' type, for instance, would be 'crushed' by the burden of leadership and ascetic life-style that is the happiness of the spiritual type: 'life becomes increasingly difficult the *higher* up one goes – it gets colder, there are more responsibilities'.[179] For the average, those with average desires and abilities, 'being average is happiness'. For one born an 'intelligent machine', a 'wheel' in the system, living the life of a wheel (or cog) *is* happiness. This is a principal objection to socialism – it makes those it purports to benefit *unhappy*, 'undermine[s] workers' instincts and pleasures, their feelings of modesty about their little existences'. 'Injustice', concludes Nietzsche, endorsing, exactly, Plato's definition of justice as everyone's adhering to the station in society to which they are, by nature, suited, 'is never a matter of unequal rights but is a matter of claiming "*equal*" rights'.[180]

Religion in Nietzsche's 'Republic'

The Christian God, we have seen, is 'the greatest corruption'. But does Nietzsche also reject gods in general; will his new world be a religion-free zone? Since the *Antichrist* is, essentially, his last creative work of philosophy, it will be as well to get his final word on the subject of gods.

'A people', writes Nietzsche,

> which still believes in itself [i.e., possesses a unifying morality in which to believe] still also has its own god. In him it venerates the conditions through which it has prospered, [i.e.] its virtues – it projects its joy in itself, its feeling of power, onto a being whom one can thank for them. He who is rich wants to bestow; a proud people needs a god in order to *sacrifice*...Within the bounds of such presuppositions religion is a form of gratitude. One is grateful for oneself: for that one needs a god. – Such a god must be able to be both useful and harmful, both friend and foe.[181]

Nietzsche is talking, here, about what the *Genealogy* called a 'noble' religion, the religion of a healthy people: the religion, paradigmatically, of the Greeks (p. 470 above), who 'repay with interest their founders, their ancestors (heroes and gods) with all the attributes which, in the meantime, had become manifest in themselves, the *noble* attributes'.[182] The reason the god has to be capable of both harm and help is that 'one would not understand' a god 'who knew nothing of anger, revengefulness, envy, mockery, cunning, acts of violence'. One needs a natural god as opposed to the '*anti-natural*' god of Christianity.[183] This is just the point, first expressed in *The Birth of Tragedy*, that a *non*-human role model is an *anti*-human role model since the effect of such a figure is depressing rather than inspiring; the point that a genuinely inspiring model with whom we can identify must be human, with a dash, even, of the all-too-human.

Nietzsche makes the point that before the Babylonian captivity de-natured him, the god of the Jews, too, was a healthy god:

> Originally, particularly in the time of the kings, Israel had a *correct*, which is to say, natural relation to all things. Its Yahweh allowed people to express a consciousness of power, Israel's joy in itself and hope for itself: Yahweh allowed people to expect victory and salvation, he allowed people to trust that nature would provide what they needed – above all rain … Festival cults expressed these two sides of a people's self-affirmation: they are grateful for the magnificent destiny that elevated them to their present position, they are grateful for the yearly cycle and all the luck they have had in agriculture and breeding cattle.[184]

Healthy societies of the past have had, then, gods who allowed them, in one way or another, to celebrate themselves. 'There has never been a [successful] people without a religion' he writes in the notebooks;[185] 'culture' *means* 'the gods'.[186] And a healthy society of the future will be the same: 'Almost two thousand years and no new god!' he laments. That we have had only the same old 'monoto-theism' says very little for Europe's 'skill in religion'.[187]

Notice the gesture, here, towards Greek polytheism: since Judaism, like Christianity (and Islam), is monotheistic,[188] Yahweh will not, in the end, count as an ideal god. Since the principal function of healthy gods is to be exemplary embodiments of the virtues of the community, and since Nietzsche insists that virtue, like happiness, is relative to one's station in the social totality,* there must be, in the end, no 'one size fits all' kind of god but rather, as in Greece, a plurality – and presumably a hierarchy – of gods.

That it is the gods of Greece who are Nietzsche's primary love and inspiration is confessed in a directly personal way in the final notebooks:

> We few or many, we who dare once again to live in a *de-moralized world*, we pagans of faith: we are perhaps the first who grasp what a pagan faith is: having to imagine *higher beings* than man, but these as beyond good and evil; having to assess all being-higher as also being [in Christian terms] immoral. We believe in Olympus – and *not* in the 'crucified'.[189]

The return of the 'Greek' gods in and through the rebirth of Greek tragedy was, of course, the aspiration of Nietzsche's first book. With respect to the gods, it is clear, nothing essential has changed.

Ecce Homo

A weapon in his 'war against the present' which Nietzsche regarded as even more potent than *The Antichrist* was, in the order of composition, his last work, *Ecce Homo*. Begun on his birthday, October 15th, he regarded it as, in principle, finished by November 4, though he continued to make alterations up until January 6, 1889.

---

* 'A man as he ought to be: that sounds to us as tasteless as "a tree as it ought to be"', he writes in the notebooks (KSA 13 11 [132]).

In the Preface, Nietzsche writes that 'Since I plan shortly to have to confront humanity with the heaviest demand that has ever been made on it, it seems indispensable to say *who I am*'. The reference, here, is to the immanent appearance of the masterwork (reduced, we shall see, in size) and its urgent demand that we 'revalue all values'. Since he anticipated the masterwork being even more 'black and squid-like' than *Beyond Good and Evil*, he felt it imperative first to abolish the notion that its author was, as the reviewer had suggested (p. 406 above), a sadistic misanthrope, a 'pathological' case. The idea that he is a 'bogey man' or 'moral monster', he says in the Preface,[190] someone who (as he now summarises Widmann's review of *Beyond Good and Evil*) 'strives to abolish all decent feelings', is completely mistaken.[191] By presenting a human, even intimate, portrait of himself as someone with a normal human background, who has had to struggle every step of the way with ill health, and who has *himself* been infected with the *décadence* he criticises, he wants to show, I think, that the fundamental impulse of his work is (as he wrote Elizabeth, in one last attempt to penetrate that thick skull) 'not hardness but the opposite, a true humanity which strives to prevent needless disaster'.[192]

Ecce Homo – 'behold the man', the words with which Pilate presented Jesus to the crowd baying for his crucifixion – is, then, a self-presentation. The subtitle – *How One Becomes What One Is* – indicates that this will be done by means of a kind of autobiography. But since self-realisation is, for Nietzsche, our primary task, it also indicates the *exemplary* nature of the narrative. In telling 'the story of my life'[193] Nietzsche intends to set himself forth, once again, as a life model, as, in his own language, an 'educator'.*

Given that Nietzsche's collapse came right on the heels of *Ecce Homo*, the question inevitably arises as to whether, or to what extent, the work is infected by the approaching madness. What sharpens the question is the fact that the work contains what look to be manifest delusions: that he was descended from Polish aristocracy, that even in childhood he never took the Christian God seriously, that the influence of Schopenhauer on *The Birth of Tragedy* was minimal, that he never had any enemies, that his greatness is obvious to everyone he meets, and many more.

What, however, complicates the situation is the fact that, given that he is presenting his life as exemplary for the reader, fictionalising, 'idealising', 'staging' one's life so that 'there is a good deal one no longer sees and much our eye has to add if we are to see [anything] ... at all',[194] is a legitimate, indeed essential, part of the project, as it was in the 1886 prefaces. Thus, given that he is presenting himself as having become a model of 'Dionysian' health and puissance, a certain amount of 'Muhammad Ali' hyperbole – the chapter headings 'Why I Am So Wise', 'Why I Am So Clever', 'Why I Am a Destiny', the claim that *Zarathustra* is better than Goethe, Shakespeare and the Vedas combined[195] – might be regarded as a legitimate part of the project. And the same might be claimed, too, for the apparent lies or delusions mentioned above.

This being said, however, a great deal of the fictionalising actually has no particular literary justification. The claim to descent through his father from Polish nobility,[196] to be sure, allows him to find *nothing* redeeming about the Germans, allows almost every page to drip – in the end, it has to be said, tediously – with bile against these 'vulgar' 'cattle' who

---

* *Ecce Homo* remarks that since it is really a portrait not of Schopenhauer but of himself, *Schopenhauer as Educator* could be more accurately titled *Nietzsche as Educator* (EH III UM 3). In 1914, a work entitled *Nietzsche as Educator* did in fact appear, written by the 'life-reformer' Walther Hammer.

have perpetrated all the cultural crimes of the last four hundred years. But given that he is supposed to be a picture of psychic health, he ought to be free of *ressentiment* and should not, therefore, have had any bile to spit in the first place. *Ressentiment* is, it should be noted, exactly the right word here. For, far too obviously, the bitterness that he is read, as he thinks, 'by nothing but *choice* intelligences... in Vienna, St. Petersburg, Stockholm, Copenhagen, Paris and New York, everywhere *except* in Europe's flatland, Germany',[197] betrays the fact that the readers who *really* matter to him are none other than his fellow Germans – who, however, either ignore him or dismiss him as a madman.

What, moreover, has to be recognised is that a great deal of the hyperbole has a megalomaniac character which, as we shall see in the next chapter, is directly continuous with themes in the letters he wrote as he was unmistakably losing his mind. The claim, for instance, that 'wherever I go, here in Turin, for example, every face grows more cheerful and benevolent at the sight of me... the old market women take great pains to select together for me their sweetest grapes'[198] appears, as we shall see, several times in the 'crazy letters', as does the claim to be God: the idea he is related to his mother and sister is, *Ecce Homo* claims, in a passage Elizabeth managed for many years to suppress, a 'blasphemy against my divinity'.[199]

Ecce Homo is, then, a flawed work. Other signs of Nietzsche's failing powers are repetition, wandering organisation, self-quotation at disproportionate and self-indulgent length, and, when he comes to review his earlier works, a lack of a sense of their relative importance: whereas the *Genealogy* receives less than a page, *The Wagner Case* receives six. For all this, however, Nietzsche being still, for the most part, Nietzsche, it remains a book full of interest and sublime moments.

Basically, the work does two things. First, it tells the reader how Nietzsche became 'what he is', how *one* becomes what one is. And second, it tells us *what it is* that he has become.

How One Becomes What One Is

In *Schopenhauer as Educator* Nietzsche tells one to 'become oneself' by living up to one's 'true self'. This is not something 'concealed deep within you' but is, rather, 'immeasurably high above you, or at least above that which you usually take yourself to be'. It is that 'ideal' and 'task' which 'draws the soul aloft' (p. 195 above). In *Wagner in Bayreuth* (which, he now says, was not really about Wagner but about himself)[200] he applied this formula to Wagner, explaining how he overcame his 'lower' inclinations and became his 'ideal' self. This understanding of 'becoming what one is' through passionate moral idealism is preserved unchanged in *Ecce Homo*: to become who we are we must become, he says, 'argonauts of the ideal'.[201]

How does one become one's true, ideal self? Through 'self (*Selbst*)-seeking (*sucht*)' – the standard translation of *Selbstsucht* as 'selfishness' fails to convey the tautological character of this claim. Self-seeking is how one discovers one's 'self'. And if one is Nietzsche, or one of the higher types who are his proper readers, one's higher self is the world-historical 'destiny' that one is. In *Schopenhauer as Educator* one discovered one's true self by allowing one's admiration for 'educators' to disclose what one has 'truly loved'.

Without rejecting the importance of role models, *Ecce Homo* expands on the techniques of self-discovery in an interesting way:

> That one becomes what one is presupposes that one does not have the remotest idea *what* one is. From this point of view even life's *mistakes* have their own meaning and value, the occasional side roads and wrong turns, the delays, the ... seriousness wasted on tasks that lie beyond *the* task.[202]

To, as it were, discover who one is by discovering who one is *not*, one must keep the 'surface of consciousness ... free of all the great imperatives' and 'big words', otherwise one will 'understand oneself too early'; one's self-definition will run down worn, all-too-worn, paths. To become a 'higher' type, something new and unique, one must preserve a kind of passivity while, 'in the mean time, the organizing, governing idea' that is the 'meaning' of one's life 'keeps growing deep inside'. Soon it 'starts commanding and slowly leads *back* from out of the side roads and wrong turns'.[203] In a word, 'self-seeking' is, through a process of trial and probably lots of error, a matter of *finding* rather than *creating* oneself, rather as the sculptor 'finds' rather than creates the figure 'slumbering' in the marble. Especially if one lives the life of the mind, a book like *Zarathustra* is a matter not of creation but of reception, of

> revelation in the sense of something suddenly becoming *visible* and audible ... you listen, you do not look for anything, you take, you do not ask who is there; a thought lights up in a flash, with necessity ... I never had any choice ... All of this is involuntary ... things approached on their own and offered themselves up.[204]

The idea of allowing one's 'self' and 'destiny' to emerge through one's mistakes provides the narrative structure of the work, a narrative that centres, inevitably, on Wagner. The 'most affectionate and profound' relation of his life, Nietzsche says, was with Richard Wagner. 'None of my other personal relationships amounts to much, but I would not give up my Tribschen days for anything'.[*,205] But then came the Bayreuth Festival:

> Where was I? I did not recognise anything. I hardly recognised Wagner. I sifted through memories in vain. Tribschen – a distant Isle of the Blessed: not a shadow of similarity. The incomparable days when we laid the cornerstone [of the opera house – notice that Nietzsche *still* endorses the *original* enterprise], a small society of people who belonged there ... *What had happened*?

What had happened was that Wagner had been 'translated into German',[206] had allowed himself to be captured by the Wagnerians and in the process become *Reichsdeutsch*,[207] an anti-Semitic German chauvinist. (With *Parsifal* things went from bad to worse; on top

---

* After a lifetime of administering Nietzsche's finances, offering him, on a moment's notice, a bed and a shoulder to cry on, considerable intellectual companionship, and unfailing loyalty, this must have cut poor Overbeck to the quick. Köselitz was probably too much in awe to be much affected.

of everything else Wagner slid back into Christian 'piety'.)[208] And so, as we know, Nietzsche fled the festival halfway through for Klingenbrunn, saw that it was time to consider whether his life had taken a seriously wrong turn. He began writing *Human, All-Too-Human*, the work 'in which I liberated myself from that in my nature which did not belong to me'.[209] Notice the phrase 'in my nature'. Wagnerian *décadence*, the impulse to world-denial, is, Nietzsche emphasises, 'in' rather than 'outside' his nature. Becoming 'what one is' is more a matter of ordering the inner world than of resisting alien influences.

Under the guiding spirit of Voltaire, Nietzsche continues, he made, in *Human, All-Too-Human*, the turn from Wagnerian romanticism to Enlightenment thinking. (He might have mentioned, here, the influence of Paul Rée, but, unforgiving to the end, goes out of his way to deny that *Human* represented any kind of 'higher réealism'.)[210] Shortly after, through the fortunate intervention of sickness and fading eyesight, he had to give up the bookwormish life of philology – another wrong turning – and began writing his own philosophy.

And that, essentially, is that: the end of *Ecce Homo*'s, in fact, rather meagre narrative. Since the rest of Nietzsche's life was writing books, all that remains is to review the books. With the turn away from Wagner, the turn away from *décadent*, life-denying romanticism and towards health and life-affirmation, Nietzsche had essentially become 'what he was'. But exactly what was that? Who did he become?

What Nietzsche Became

'I am', Nietzsche declares, 'a *bearer of glad tidings* as no one ever was before'.[211] (Given this allusion to the angel's announcement of the impending birth of Christ as well as the '*Ecce Homo*' title, the diagnosis 'Messiah complex' hovers in the air.) What are these 'tidings'? What is Nietzsche's message to the world? Most of it, of course, is by now familiar. Yet, as always, Nietzsche's pronouncement of his basic message receives a novel nuance.

'So far', he writes, referring to Christian morality, 'humanity' has 'worship[ped] values that are the reverse of those that might begin to guarantee it prosperity, a future, a high *right* to a future'.[212] Since he has exempted European antiquity from this critique, and has no knowledge of what values are worshipped in contemporary, say, Africa, what he must mean by 'humanity' is the *European, post-antiquity* 'species' of humanity. As I have emphasised before, Nietzsche's philosophy is deeply 'Euro-centric'.

What, then, is wrong with the current state of Western culture is that its 'future' is in doubt. 'The good', as defined by current standards, live at the expense of both 'the truth' and 'the future'. 'In this sense', he explains, 'Zarathustra sometimes calls the good men "the last men", and sometimes "the beginning of the end"'.[213] They are the beginning of the end because, to repeat, without the capacity to adapt to its changing environment – which requires, of course, a clear-eyed acknowledgment of 'the truth' about that environment[214] – a species of humanity, a 'people', must go under.

To adapt and grow, we know, a people must 'give birth to a star',[215] to a 'free spirit': in my language, a 'random mutation'. *Ecce Homo* identifies 'superman' as just another name for this bearer of the future: the superman 'is a superman specifically when compared to the *good*' – he stands 'super', above, their morality. Nietzsche adds, recalling the *Genealogy*'s point that most free spirits will be 'martyred' by the forces of social conservatism, that 'the good and just would call [Zarathustra's] ... superman a *devil*.'[216]

What will a 'superman' propose in the way of cultural reform? In a nutshell, 'the imminent return of the Greek spirit'. Community will be once more created, gathered together, and preserved by the *authentic* collective art work, 'the supreme art in the affirmation of life, tragedy, will be reborn'. And this takes us back, yet again, to Wagner, to a Wagner purified of cheap showmanship, anti-Semitism, German chauvinism, romanticism, Christianity and life-denial: the 'idea of Bayreuth [will have] transformed itself into . . . that *great noon* . . . who knows? the vision of a festival that I will live to see someday'.[217]

If, however, we are to abandon the Christian worldview what are we to do about that most problematic of all life's features, its finitude, to which, it has to be admitted, Christianity provided *a* solution? The answer, again, is 'Dionysus': entering into the 'psychology of the tragic poet' in which 'over and above all fear and pity *one is oneself* the eternal joy of becoming', 'the will to life rejoicing in its own inexhaustibility through the *sacrifice* of its highest types'. To become fully healthy, to enter the Dionysian state, is to be able to rejoice, *inter alia*, over the eventual 'sacrifice' of one's own, everyday self. Through transcending the illusion of individuality, through realising one's identity with the totality of existence, one not merely overcomes death but achieves a positive 'affirmation of [in particular, *one's own*] passing away'.[218]

Deploying the Artillery

By mid-November Turin's halcyon autumn – a 'permanent Claude Lorraine', Nietzsche called it[219] – was over and winter had arrived. The Alps were already covered with a 'light wig'.[220] Nietzsche acquired his first gas stove, amazed that all one had to do to get it going was light a match.[221] Completely free for the first time in twenty years from the appalling attacks of headaches and vomiting, he abandoned giving health bulletins in his letters. 'Health', he wrote Meta von Salis, is a 'standpoint that had been overcome'.[222] In the mirror he looked 'ten years younger'.[223]

Mental well-being followed the physical. Gratitude for release from pain cast a benign glow over everything. Everyone, it seemed, treated him as 'a person of distinction', for example, opening the door for him whenever he entered a building. To live up to his new dignity he bought a superb pair of English leather gloves and attended the funeral of Count Robilant, the 'best sort' of Piedmont aristocrat, he confided to Meta.[224] (Count Robilant, the natural son of King Carlo Alberto, had been ambassador to London, where he died on October 17.) For the first time in his adult life he felt completely at home. His days as a nomad were over. In Turin he felt (as Socrates did about Athens) that he had discovered 'a place one never wants to leave, not even to walk in the countryside, a place where it is a joy just to walk along the streets! – Previously I would have held that to be impossible'.[225]

An event occurred, however, which, for a moment, interrupted the halcyon mood. On October 25 Nietzsche's Leipzig publisher, Fritzsch (see pp. 401–2 above), allowed to appear in his *Weekly Musical Review* a review of *The Wagner Case* by a rabid Wagnerian, one Richard Pohl. (In Fritzsch's defence it needs to be remembered (a) that he was also Wagner's publisher and (b) that controversy sells books.) Entitled 'The Nietzsche Case: A Psychological Problem', the review claimed Nietzsche to believe himself to be the greatest composer alive, whereas he was, in fact, completely unmusical. Pohl asserted further – claiming to have this directly from Wagner's mouth – that Nietzsche had shown Wagner the opera he had composed, which Wagner had been obliged to tell him was rubbish, thereby generating Nietzsche's anti-Wagner animus. Though some Wagnerians believe this story to this very day, Nietzsche had, of course, never even attempted to write an opera.

Nietzsche was paralytic with fury when he discovered the review. 'You have', he wrote Fritzsch, 'the distinction of having the first man of the century in your publishing house. That you can allow an utter fool like Pohl to write about me is one of those things that could only happen in Germany'. Particularly galling was the appearance of the review at the very time when 'letters of homage are arriving from all quarters calling it [*The Wagner Case*] a masterpiece of psychological sagacity without equal'.[226] (Predictably, this is high exaggeration – most of the letters were either from friends or were acknowledgments of receipt of complimentary copies. None went in for hyperbole.) The result of this insult was that Nietzsche decided to take all his works out of Fritzsch's ownership and spent the final days before his collapse trying to raise the huge sum of 10,000 talers Fritzsch demanded for the sale of copyright.

In mid-December another article on *The Wagner Case* appeared, written by Ferdinand Avenarius, yet another of Nietzsche's Jewish supporters. Though generally appreciative, Avenarius lamented the fact that a deep thinker such as Nietzsche could express his 'recent change of mind' about Wagner in the style of a mere journalist. Indignantly, Nietzsche pointed out that his published criticisms of Wagner went back a full decade, to *Human, All-Too-Human*.[227] Since this trivialising misunderstanding was likely to be widespread and might undermine the reception of *Ecce Homo*, Nietzsche decided that its publication must be delayed so that *Nietzsche contra Wagner* (subtitled *From the Files of a Psychologist*), a collection of seventeen excerpts from earlier books dating back to 1878, could appear first. The point was to demonstrate the long and deeply considered nature of his Wagner-critique.[228] It would also, of course, enable Nietzsche, yet again, to cash in on the Wagner market.[229]

A quite different motivation for delaying the publication of *Ecce Homo* is suggested by a strange remark in a letter to Köselitz written on December 16: 'I don't see why I should accelerate too much the tragic catastrophe of my life which begins with "Ecce".[230] This suggests that Nietzsche knew that his mind was slipping away from him* and knew that *Ecce Homo* was the appropriate closure to his life's work. The implication is that by delaying its publication he could extend his life a little longer. Life would, as it were, imitate art. And perhaps he was right: it is well known that the terminally ill often cling to life until a significant event, Christmas or a birthday, has passed.

The manuscript of *Nietzsche contra Wagner* was sent to Naumann on December 15. Five days later, however – the generalship of his 'war against the present' becoming increasingly erratic – Nietzsche decided, for barely comprehensible reasons, that after all *Ecce Homo* should appear first.[231] In the event, though both works appeared when he was beyond caring about them, the original order was maintained. *Nietzsche contra Wagner* appeared in February 1889, while *Ecce Homo* did not appear until 1908.

---

* Ernst Horneffer, a collaborator on the first attempt to produce an edition of Nietzsche's collected works, comments on the 'nervous excitement' that 'trembles' through all the last manuscripts, on how, in 1888, 'his handwriting changes completely. He suddenly uses the most incredible abbreviations, leaving out letters and syllables, and finally writing almost only in consonants' (Gilman (1987) p. 256). This, together with his incredible rush of productivity and the refusal to listen to anything but very light music, further suggests that Nietzsche in some sense knew, some time in advance, that his life was rushing towards its effective close.

In his final weeks of at least intermittent sanity, Nietzsche had effectively given up serious philosophical thinking, feeling either that he had completed everything he had to say or that he was no longer capable of saying it. He still wrote furiously, but since the task was now to deploy his 'artillery' rather than to manufacture it, what he wrote were letters. Between December 1, 1888, and January 6, 1889, he wrote more letters than in the whole of either 1884 or 1885. The objective of most of these letters was to win to his cause of 'revaluing all values' opinion-moulders throughout Europe and to arrange for translations of his works into first two, then three, then seven, then finally *all* foreign languages[232] by the leading writers of Europe such as August Strindberg. (Strindberg told him there was little point in translating into 'Greenlandese' (i.e., Swedish, Norwegian and Danish) since no one read it.)

Hand in hand with the project of winning opinion-makers to his cause went a revival of the idea of a 'monastery for free spirits' in a newly institutionalised form: a network of 'Nietzsche societies' (mirroring the network of Wagner societies) was to be set up. In *Ecce Homo* he looks forward to the day when there will be 'institutions in which people live and teach in the way I understand living and teaching', as well as chairs of philosophy devoted to the interpretation of *Zarathustra*.[233] 'A last word', he wrote in his December notebooks:

> From now on I will need unlimited numbers of helping hands – immortal hands. The *Revaluation* shall appear in two languages. It will be a good idea to found societies everywhere so as to deliver into my hands at the right time a million disciples. It is particularly important to recruit first of all officers and Jewish bankers. Both together represent the will to power. If I ask who my natural allies are I see that above all they are officers. With military instincts in the body one cannot be a Christian ... In the same way, Jewish bankers are my natural allies, as the only international power which, by origin and instinct, binds nations together after accursed interest-politics has made the arrogance and egoism of nations into a duty.[234]

When relaxing from the stresses of being 'on campaign', Nietzsche spent his last days of sanity enjoying Turin's café life:

> In the evenings [he wrote Köselitz on December 16] I sit in a splendid high-ceilinged room: an excellent, small orchestra (piano, 4 strings, two woodwind) which produces a muted sound, just as one would wish. There are three salons next to each other. They bring me my *Journal des débats* [a contributor was Jean Bourdeau, his, as he thought, influential French disciple] – I eat a portion of excellent ice-cream: it costs 40 cents including the tip (a practice I observe since it is the custom here) – In the Galeria Subalpina (which I look across to when I leave my front door) are the loveliest rooms of this sort that I know, they play the *Barber of Seville* every evening.[235]

Nietzsche's Mental Condition

Several strands are entwined in Nietzsche's mental state during the final weeks of 1888. One was the already noted state of almost continuous euphoria produced (or least contributed to) by the release from, as he often called it, the 'animal torture' of his body. This not only cast a halcyon glow over all things but also made the production of three major works, one minor work, and several other publications within the year virtually effortless: 'I am' he wrote Overbeck in October, sounding an unmistakable note of closure, 'the most grateful man in the world – in autumnal mood in the best sense of the word. It is my great harvest time. Everything comes easily...even though, probably, no one has ever had such great things in hand'.[236]

At the same time the tendency to megalomania, flashes of which, recall, go back to the *Zarathustra* period, becomes more and more pronounced. The theme that his work will explode the history of the world into two halves[237] since he is 'more dynamite than man'[238] becomes more and more strident, as does the claim that he is the 'first man' of 'the century' – later of 'the millennium', finally of 'all millennia'.[239] Commensurate with the sense of his own world-historical importance is the belief that it is entirely visible to others:

> It's strange [he writes Overbeck] that here in Turin I exercise the most complete fascination on people although I am the most modest and undemanding person. If I enter a large shop every face changes; the women in the street look at me – my old market ladies search out the sweetest grapes for me and reduce the price.[240]

In general, 'they treat me like a prince – as perhaps I am'.[241]

Accompanying a sense of exceptional importance is a belief in his telekinetic power: 'I read the *Journal des débats* – it was brought to me instinctively on my first visit to my first café. – There are no accidents any more: when I think of someone a letter appears promptly through the door'.[242] (In *The Gay Science* (p. 337 above) he talks about the importance of interpreting one's life so that everything that happens is non-accidental, significant. Now, however, retrospective *interpretive* power is replaced by *causal* power.)

Of course, the more megalomania took over, the weaker became his grasp of reality. The tentative contacts Brandes had made on his behalf with, save for Strindberg, quite average people – people, moreover, who were generally interested in, but hardly converts to, his philosophy – were transformed into 'a discipleship' composed solely of 'the most elevated natures: of exclusively high-placed and influential people in St. Petersburg, in Paris, in Stockholm, in Vienna, in New York'. In his mind he had become 'incredibly famous', a superstar: 'there is no name that is treated with such reverence as mine'.[243] Jean Bourdeau, actually no more than an occasional contributor, got promoted to the editor-in-chief of the *Journal de débats* and the *Revue des deux mondes* and as such was 'the most influential man in France'.[244] And in reality, far from admiring Nietzsche, Bourdeau regarded his writings as 'cruel and perverse'.

Of course, in a very few years Nietzsche *would* be a superstar, in part, indeed, precisely on account of his self-assessment: sooner or later, Disraeli remarked, the world takes a man at his own estimate of himself. None of this, however, alters the fact that Nietzsche's estimation of his celebrity in 1888 was almost entirely delusional.

Connected with the megalomania were eruptions into the benign landscape of lahars of molten fury, fury directed against those who failed to recognise his genius. First and foremost against the Germans, 'herd people', 'idiots', 'swine', world-historical 'criminals' (Luther killed off the Renaissance, the misnamed 'wars of liberation' killed off Napoleon, and Kant killed off scientific thought)[245] who fail to recognise that Nietzsche and Nietzsche alone 'justified' their miserable existence[246] by having written the 'profoundest book in the German language'.[247]

Outbursts of fury were also directed against individuals. Against Fritzsch, as we have seen, for allowing Pohl to criticise 'the foremost man of the millennium'. Against von Bülow who, living the life of a travelling conductor, had been slow to respond to an – as it were regal – request to take an interest in Köselitz's *Lion of Venice*. 'You have not answered my letter', Nietzsche wrote. 'I shall not trouble you again, I promise you that. I think, you understand that the foremost spirit of the age has expressed a wish to you'.[248] Unforgivably, Malwida von Meysenbug became a target of abuse. Always attempting to square the circle by remaining loyal to both Wagner and Nietzsche, Malwida had responded to *The Wagner Case* by gently suggesting that he devalued his own former love for Wagner by applying the word 'tomfool (*Hanswurst*)' both to him and to Liszt.[249] Nietzsche replied imperiously that Wagner 'is not a matter in which I permit contradiction'. And, going out of his way to be offensive, he refers to Wagner once again as 'this *Hanswurst*' (literally 'Hans-sausage') – effectively, and for such a polite person astonishingly, calling his friend and surrogate mother of more than fifteen years a silly old cow.[250] As we have seen (p. 490 above), Nietzsche (wrongly) believed the 2,000-mark donation towards the costs of self-publication he had received via Deussen came from Deussen himself. This emboldened him to approach his old friend for the 10,000 talers needed to buy back the rights to his books from Fritzsch. Deussen, of course, replied that (as a married man on a professorial salary) he had unfortunately no means of raising such an enormous sum, whereupon Nietzsche dismissed him in a letter to Köselitz as 'too stupid for us – too common'.[251]

25

Catastrophe

Becoming God

THE FIRST time the Finos noticed that all was not well with their tenant – they were, of course, unaware of the increasingly strange letters he had been writing for some time – was at the beginning of December 1888. Nietzsche asked them to remove all the hangings from the walls of his room since he was expecting a visit from the King and Queen of Italy, and the room needed to look like a temple to receive them.[1] They also began to find torn-up banknotes in his wastepaper basket. Darkness did not, however, descend all at once; there were still moments of lucidity. Even though, at the beginning of December, he had begun to write letters that were unmistakably deranged – one to Bismarck, for instance, was signed, 'The Antichrist/ Frederick Nietzsche/ Fromentin'[2] (the last a French romantic painter who died in 1876) – he was still capable of writing an entirely normal letter to Emily Fynn on December 6 and a reasonably normal one to Köselitz on December 16.[3] Progressively, though, his loss of contact with reality became ever more marked.

With respect to his body, for instance, he himself notes a sporadic loss of control, a kind of emotional incontinence. Such idiotic, 'private-tomfool-notions' came to him as he walked the streets, he writes on November 25, that for a full half hour he would be unable to stop grinning. One of these inspirations was the truly crazy, quasi-obscene idea of having Malwida (the most virginal of women) appear in *Ecce Homo* as Kundry, the evil (though ultimately redeemed) whore from Wagner's *Parsifal*: 'I couldn't keep a straight face for four days', he tells Köselitz.[4] On another occasion, following a wonderful concert, he reports, again, dissociation from his body: 'my face was making continual grimaces in order to try to control my extreme pleasure including, for ten minutes, the grimace of tears'.[5]

The megalomania noted in the previous chapter took him increasingly into a realm of political fantasy. To Brandes he writes, at the beginning of December,

> I am preparing an event which will very probably split history into two halves, to the point where we will have a new way of reckoning time: 1888 will be the year one [see p. 510 above]...We will have war like no other, but between neither nations nor classes. All that

is exploded – I am the most terrible dynamite there is. I will instruct the printing of *The Antichrist: Revaluation of All Values* to proceed in three months time. It's a secret – it will serve as a work of agitation. I will need translations into all European languages...in the first edition I reckon a million copies in each language.

The war, Nietzsche continues, will be a 'war of extermination' against Christianity. World-wide laws banning it will be promulgated, the 'brown fool' of an Emperor will be deposed and the 'Triple Alliance' (the political-military order of continental Europe) will be abolished. Nietzsche concludes with the already quoted sentence:

If we win, we will have world-government in our hands – world peace will be established...we [will] have overcome the absurd boundaries between race, nation, and class; only an order of rank between man and man will remain, indeed an exceedingly long ladder of rank-ordering.[6]

This exercise in 'world-historical' politics, 'grand politics par excellence',[7] is followed by further letters abolishing the Emperor, indeed the whole house of Hohenzollern,[8] and, again, the Triple Alliance. On December 31 he writes Strindberg that he has ordered a public holiday to celebrate the execution of the young Emperor, signing the letter 'Nietzsche Caesar'.[9] Strindberg, who himself only narrowly escaped confinement in a psychiatric institution, replied that 'It sometimes helps to be mad'.

By January 3 victory has been achieved and world peace established: 'Do you not see how the heavens rejoice?' he writes Meta von Salis. 'I have entered into possession of my realm, I am throwing the Pope in jail and having Wilhelm [the Emperor], Bismarck and Stöcker [the anti-Semite] shot'.[10] The following day (his own kind of 'final solution') he is 'just now having all anti-Semites shot'.[11]

All this, of course, is madness. Yet there is method in it, a vein of fragmented sanity that runs back to his best writings. There remains, first of all, a vein of political sanity, generated by his experience of the Franco-Prussian battlefields. His remarks in the closing pages of the notebooks on the 'madness' of the dynastic squabbles which 'place the flower of youth and energy and power in the cannon's mouth',[12] and on the madness of spending twelve billion marks a year on preserving the 'armed peace' of the Triple Alliance, a peace which is no peace at all but merely a recipe for future war,[13] are models of sanity. And the underlying presentiment of the Great War that would break out a mere fourteen years after his death is prophetic. Entirely sane, too, is the idea that war can only finally be overcome through the abolition of national and dynastic egoisms, an abolition that requires European unification and, in the end, world government. These ideas, Nietzsche's cosmopolitanism and his understanding that only the abandonment of armed nationalism can produce genuine peace, are paragons of sanity that reach all the way back to *Human, All-Too-Human*.[14]

Sane, too, is what we may call the 'books make a difference' thesis, the thesis that the 'spiritual leadership' of great thinkers can and does make a difference to culture, politics, and life, that the ideas that change the world 'come on doves' feet'. Nietzsche called his war against Christianity and the house of Hohenzollern a 'war of the spirit'. What, however, was insane was the idea that spiritual warfare could achieve results overnight rather than over centuries, that all he needed to do to bring about the collapse of governments and of the Church was to send complimentary copies of *Ecce Homo* and *The Antichrist* to the crowned heads of Europe and to the Pope.[15] And totally insane, of course, was the conviction that the new order was already happening.

Increasingly, then, Nietzsche lost contact with his body and with political reality. And in the end he lost contact with his own identity. On December 31 he wrote Köselitz that he could no longer remember his street address, but added, 'Let's assume it's the Palazzo del Quirinale'[16] (the residence, in Rome, of the King of Italy). Many letters were signed 'The Crucified',[17] and even more 'Dionysus'.[18] (One link between Jesus and Dionysus is that both overcame death. Both were killed – Dionysus was torn to pieces by the Titans – and were then resurrected to eternal life.) In his last letter to Burckhardt, written on January 6, he explains what has happened to his identity:

> Dear Herr Professor, ultimately, I would rather be a Basel professor than God. But I have not ventured to push a private egoism so far as, on its account, to cease creating the world. But I have rented a small student-room directly opposite the Palazzo Carignano (– in which I was born as Victor Emmanuele). Don't take the case of Prado too seriously [Prado had been condemned to death in Paris on November 14 for the murder of a prostitute]. I am Prado, I am also the father of Prado . . . basically I am every name in history . . . everything in 'God's realm' comes from God. This autumn, as modestly dressed as possible, I was twice at my funeral: first as count Robilant (No, that is my son insofar as I am Carlo Alberto) . . . [19]

Two things are noteworthy about this extraordinary letter. First, it reports a kind of 'out of body' experience (which perhaps explains Nietzsche's loss of control over his body), a transcendence of the everyday ego. Second, the transcendence Nietzsche undergoes is a transcendence to a new kind of universal identity: he becomes a kind of 'primal unity'. This shows a certain continuity between his philosophy and his madness: that the circling back of his final philosophy to the 'most intimate and concealed experiences' underlying its beginning, noted by Lou Salomé (p. 502 above), continues in the 'crazy letters'. The ecstatic side of Nietzsche's madness consisted in a habitation of the Dionysian state. That habitation is now, however, a confused one. On the one hand, the 'primal unity' he becomes is an *immanent, natural* unity: he 'is' Caesar, Robilant, Carlo Alberto, Prado, Prado's father, whoever comes to mind – the totality of all natural beings. This is the *non-metaphysical* understanding of the Dionysian state presented by his final philosophy. But on the other hand, he becomes the *nature-transcendent, meta-physical* primal unity of *The Birth of Tragedy*. He becomes the supernatural child–artist–god who – the very phrase used in the letter – 'creates the world'; creates, and so can alter at will, the 'battlefield-painting' that is the world we, as individuals, all inhabit (p. 126 above). The ecstatic side of Nietzsche's madness can thus be described as an entry into the Dionysian state that is the foundation of his philosophy. But it has become, now, a confused, oscillating, version of that state.

As 1888 turned into 1889, then, Nietzsche, in a confused way, 'becomes' the god Dionysus. And with this new identity comes an intensification of the mood of holy joy that he has inhabited since his arrival in Turin at the end of September. 'Sing me a new song: the world is transfigured and all the heavens rejoice',[20] he commands Köselitz, reverting to the New Testament language of his upbringing. And he commands Cosima to announce 'the glad tidings' from Bayreuth.[21] (As in *The Birth of Tragedy*, one feels, the 'new song' ought to sound very like Beethoven's 'Ode to Joy' (p. 128 above)).

In line with this transfiguration of the world into perfection and with his new identity as both the Dionysian and 'the Crucified' God, Nietzsche now engages in a general 'forgiveness of sins', combined, sometimes, with a little wit and mischief. To Malwida he writes that 'much is forgiven, for you have loved me much'.²² To von Bülow (Cosima's first husband, remember) he sends a complex, acrostic joke: 'as the third Veuve Cliquot-Ariadne [the third bottle of champagne, i.e., husband of Ariadne, i.e., Cosima] I don't want to spoil your game: rather I condemn you to [perform for ever] the *Lion of Venice*' (Köselitz's opera which von Bülow had failed to take an interest in).²³ To Deussen (who, recall, had been too 'stupid' to supply the money to buy the books back from Fritzsch) he writes that he, too, has been assigned a place in the new 'world-plan' – as a satyr.²⁴ Placing the blame for their squabble over Taine on his own 'blindness', Nietzsche assigns Rohde a place among the gods, 'right next to the nicest goddess'.²⁵ Even Wagner is forgiven, or at least excused, on grounds of 'being of unsound mind'.²⁶

All this is, of course, Nietzsche's fulfilling his own injunction to *amor fati*, to embracing the eternal return. *Amor fati* reappears in the final pages of the notebooks:

A last point of view, the highest perhaps. I myself justify the Germans, I alone…I would not be possible without the opposite kind of race…without Bismarck, without 1848, without the [anti-Napoleon] 'war of liberation', without Kant, without Luther himself…The great cultural crimes of the Germans justify themselves in a higher economy of culture. I want nothing to be different, not backwards either… *Amor fati*…Even Christianity was necessary; the highest form, the most dangerous, the most seductive No to life challenges forth its highest affirmation – myself.²⁷

The Horse Story

As Christmas turned to New Year, life at the Finos' became impossible. Nietzsche's piano-playing had progressed from endless Wagner, always from memory, to the frenzied bashing out of tone clusters, often with his elbows, accompanied by wild singing and shouting at all hours of day and night. For three nights in a row no one in the house was able to sleep. On one occasion Fino peered through the keyhole of Nietzsche's room to find him shouting, jumping, and dancing round the room, stark naked, in what seems to have been a one-man re-creation of a Dionysian orgy. Overbeck's restrained report of this event casts a veil over 'other things' too vulgar to be mentioned. What he may have concealed was the satyr's erect penis.

On or about January 3, 1889, matters came to a head. Seeing a coachman thrashing his horse with a whip in one of Turin's piazzas, Nietzsche threw his arms around the horse's neck, tears streaming from his eyes, and then collapsed onto the ground.

The uncanny thing about this story is that, if it is true, Nietzsche partially scripted the scene half a year earlier. (Recall, here, his own youthful suggestion that Hölderlin's madness was partially 'scripted' by his identification with Empedocles (p. 42 above) and his own close identification with Hölderlin.) In the middle of a letter to von Seydlitz, he abruptly breaks off chatting about mundane things to recount a vision of 'moral tearfulness' that came to him out of the blue: 'winter landscape. An old coachman with an expression of the most brutal cynicism, harder than the surrounding winter, urinates on his horse. The horse, the poor, ravaged creature, looks around, thankful, very thankful.'[28] An even more exact script for the scene – recall *The Gay Science*'s talk of 'staging oneself'[29] – is to be found in *Crime and Punishment*, where Raskolnikov has a dream in which, overcome by compassion, he throws his arms around a horse that has been beaten to death. (*Twilight of the Idols*' discussion of the criminal as a strong type made sick by unfavourable circumstances attributes this insight to the '*profound*' Dostoyevsky, which strongly suggests that, by 1888, he had included *Crime and Punishment* in his reading of the Russian.)[30]

The reliability of the horse story has been questioned on the grounds that the original source is an anonymous newspaper article written eleven years after the supposed event. Yet it does have a ring of truth for, as we have seen, Nietzsche had an unusually powerful disposition to compassion (a leading motive for his critique of its debilitating effects on the compassionate, I suggested) and had always been easily moved to tears.

Returned to the house on the Via Carlo Alberta by two policemen, Nietzsche was persuaded to go to bed to await the arrival of the psychiatrist Dr. Carlo Turina. The moment he appeared, however, Nietzsche shouted '*Pas malade!*' '*Pas malade!*' and refused to see him. Only by later presenting Turina as a friend of the family did Fino finally persuade Nietzsche to receive him. Bromide, widely used as a tranquiliser in the nineteenth century, was ordered from the Rossetti pharmacy (still) in the Piazza Carignano.

Meanwhile, in Basel, Burckhardt, much perturbed by the 'I'd rather be a Basel professor than God' letter, visited Overbeck on January 6. The latter, who had been worried about Nietzsche's mental condition for several weeks, consulted his colleague Ludwig Wille, professor of psychiatry at the university and director of the local psychiatric clinic. The latter advised him to bring Nietzsche back to Basel immediately, lest he find himself incarcerated in some dubious Italian institution.

On the afternoon of January 7, Overbeck arrived at Nietzsche's lodgings, to the great relief of Davide Fino, who, soft-hearted but desperate, had been on the point of calling the police. Overbeck found his old friend, a shadow of his former self, sitting in the corner of a sofa, chewing, and reading what turned out to be the final proofs of *Nietzsche contra Wagner*. Nietzsche embraced him passionately and then collapsed back on the sofa, where he lay shivering and groaning. Overbeck's knees gave way too. The sick man was given a further dose of bromide and finally became quieter. He began to speak cheerfully of the great reception he had planned that evening (presumably for the Italian King and Queen). He lived, Overbeck wrote Köselitz the following week,

> entirely in his deranged world from which, in my presence, he never again emerged. Quite clear about who I and other people were, he was in complete darkness about himself...In ever more intense attacks of singing and crashing about on the piano, he came forth with fragments of the world of thought he had recently inhabited. Sometimes, in a whisper, he produced sentences of wonderful luminosity. But also uttered terrible things about himself as the successor of the now-dead God, the whole performance continuously punctuated on the piano, following which there would be more convulsions and a new outbreak of unspeakable suffering.[31]

On January 9, Overbeck decided Nietzsche must be removed from Italy without delay. Since the police were already apprised of his condition, the alternative was a Turin jail.

Mild-mannered Overbeck was, however, unable to exercise any control over the patient so that, alone, he could never have managed the journey. Fortunately, however, a deus ex machina appeared, a Dr. Bettmann, recommended by the German consul as having a way with the mentally disturbed, and offered to accompany the patient to Basel. (Bettmann was, in fact, a Jewish dentist, the last in the long line of Jews who had promoted and protected Nietzsche throughout his adult life.) Since Nietzsche followed all Bettmann's instructions with the childlike obedience with which Countess Mansuroff had, in happier days, followed his own (p. 392 above), the journey was now possible. Bettmann persuaded Nietzsche that a great reception was being prepared for him at the end of the journey and so brought him to the railway station.

During the journey Nietzsche was kept sedated with chloral hydrate, though when the drug began to wear off he wanted to embrace everyone and kept singing a gondolier song which Overbeck later realised was his own poem from *Ecce Homo*.[32] Arriving in Basel on January 10, Nietzsche was brought without fuss into Wille's sanatorium.

26

The Rise and Fall of
The Will to Power

IN CHAPTER 24 we saw that, during his final years, the project of writing a book to be called *The Will to Power* became Nietzsche's principal philosophical project. This chapter is devoted to investigating the reasons it was never completed.

The idea of the will to power first occurs in Nietzsche's published works in 1878, in *Human, All-Too-Human*'s discussion of selected psychological phenomena: deep down, we learn, gratitude is the equalising revenge of the powerful, the desire to excite pity is a quest for control on the part of the weak, ostentatious asceticism is the quest for spiritual power on the part of the saint, and the bad conscience is the quest for power forced to turn inwards.[1] The *phrase* 'will to power' first appears in January 1883 in Part I of *Zarathustra*. Here, in the context of group psychology, the idea begins to take on a more systematic look. A 'people's' morality, we are told, is 'the voice of its will to power', of its will to 'rule and conquer and shine, to the horror and envy of its neighbour'.[2] By the summer of 1883, in Part II of *Zarathustra*, the idea has expanded to embrace the whole of life:

> Wherever I found the living, there I found will to power: even in the will to serve I found the will to be master…And life itself confided this secret to me: 'Behold', it said, "*I am that which must always overcome itself*".[3]

Two years later, in April 1885, Nietzsche conceives the idea of extending will to power so that it would be the underlying ground not just of the biological but of the inorganic realm, too: in his notebook shorthand he writes 'that the will to power is what governs the inorganic world, or rather that there is no inorganic world'.[4] By August of that year, he had come up with the first of about twenty plans for a book with *The Will to Power* as its main title.[5] And by the summer of 1886 he had conceived the work as a massive, four-volume enterprise[6], a 'masterwork'[7] that would provide a 'synoptic'[8] account of his entire philosophy. This 'task' became both his central literary project and, as we have seen, the meaning of his life until shortly before his collapse into madness.

But though he produced well over a thousand pages of preparatory notes for the masterwork, he never published it. The posthumous work that appeared in 1901 under the title *The Will to Power: Attempt at a Revaluation of All Values*, and again in 1906 and 1911 – expanded eventually to contain 1,067 snippets from his notebooks – was a philologically disgraceful[9] concoction on the part of the appalling Elizabeth, aided by, in particular, Köselitz, who had by now gone over to the enemy.

Given the seriousness with which Nietzsche took the project and the apparent plausibility of attributing its non-appearance to the onset of madness, it is by no means unreasonable that many philosophers and Nietzsche scholars have taken the unpublished notebooks, the *Nachlass*, to be the repository of Nietzsche's 'real' philosophy.* Martin Heidegger took this view, writing at the beginning of his four-volume Nietzsche study that

> Nietzsche's philosophy proper, the fundamental position on the basis of which he speaks in...all the writings he himself published, did not assume a final form and was not itself published in any book...What Nietzsche himself published during his creative life was always foreground...His philosophy proper was left behind as posthumous, unpublished work.[10]

Alfred Bäumler, the Nazi Nietzsche scholar, also took this view and on the basis of the *Nachlass* turned Nietzsche into a proto-Nazi. From a different perspective, Heidegger also turned Nietzsche into a proto-Nazi. At the end of his four-volume study, finally waking up to the horror of the Nazi reality gathering around him in the early years of the war (though remaining a member of the Nazi party), he decides that his lifelong admiration of Nietzsche has been misplaced: 'at the end of [Nietzsche's] metaphysics', he writes, 'stands the statement *Homo est brutum bestiale*', the 'blond beast'.[11] The embodiment of the Nietzschean 'superman', he claims, is the SS tank commander. (This reading of the *Nachlass* produced something close to a nervous breakdown: *Nietzsche hat mich kaputt gemacht*, Heidegger lamented.)

It is not merely dubiously motivated German philosophers, however, who have taken the 'real' Nietzsche to be located in the notebooks. Anglophone philosophers with backgrounds in the 'analytic' tradition have, more often than not, done the same. In Richard Schacht's monumental study, for instance, out of a total of 1,718 Nietzsche-quotations, 861 – over half – are taken from the 'book' Nietzsche never published. And in the chapter devoted to Nietzsche's alleged metaphysics, out of 199 quotations, 152 are taken from Elizabeth's potpourri.[12]

Schacht and Heidegger share a common perception of Nietzsche. For both of them he is a philosopher in the traditional mould, according to which the heart of the discipline is metaphysics. Although they have different stances to metaphysics – Heidegger thinks it something to be 'overcome', Schacht is more neutral – both see Nietzsche as, first and foremost, a 'metaphysician'. Specifically, they believe he offers a 'cosmological' doctrine according to which everything is, at bottom, 'will to power'. Since, in the 3,130 pages Nietzsche chose to publish,[13] only one passage, totalling barely a page, section 36 of *Beyond Good and Evil*, actually argues for the cosmological doctrine, and even that in a somewhat qualified way,[14] the determination to read Nietzsche as offering a metaphysical cosmology has to be based on the *Nachlass*.

---

* This idea was encouraged by Elizabeth, who, trying to bolster the legitimacy of her own *Will to Power* project, put it about that Franz Overbeck had destroyed a complete manuscript of the 'work'.

The Heidegger–Schacht approach to Nietzsche is by no means silly. For, as I now want to show, Nietzsche's own original impetus to the *Will to Power* project was precisely to fit himself into the traditional mould of philosophical greatness. But as I shall go on to show, it was an impulse that he eventually rejected, and, with it, the entire *Will to Power* project. It was not the onset of madness but rather Nietzsche's conscious, sane, and, as I shall show, well-grounded decision that deprived us – or ought to have deprived us – of *The Will to Power*.

The Casaubon Impulse

The Reverend Edward Casaubon spends the duration of George Eliot's *Middlemarch* slaving over his *Key to All Mythologies* – a book he never finishes. This impulse to discover the one 'key' to unlock an entire universe is what lay behind Nietzsche's first conception of the 'masterwork'. The 1885 notebook entry in which the conception makes its first, grandiose appearance reads:

The Will to Power
Attempt at a new Explanation[15] of all Events[16]
by
Friedrich Nietzsche.[17]

The same title and subtitle are preserved in a second sketch for the work a month or so later.[18]

Nietzsche's only lifelong friend, his unfailing support in each and every emergency, Franz Overbeck, produced a surprisingly qualified posthumous assessment of Nietzsche's character. He was not, Overbeck writes, 'a great man in the genuine sense'. Rather, 'what really governed and possessed him was the *aspiration* to greatness, ambition in the competition of life'.[19] That Nietzsche had to an extraordinary degree a yearning for greatness is beyond doubt. Ambition verging on the megalomania that became a central feature of his madness was, as we have seen, already present in 1884: *Zarathustra*, he said – yearning disguising itself as prophesy – would 'split history into two halves' (p. 389 above).

To become 'great' in nineteenth-century Germany was to write a 'big' book. None of Nietzsche's publications prior to the projected 'masterwork' fitted the bill – brevity alone disqualified them. So the task which came to absorb all his energies after the completion of the *Genealogy of Morals* in August 1887 was to produce something which would equal, indeed surpass, the *Critique of Pure Reason,* the *Phenomenology of Spirit*, and – particularly – *The World as Will and Representation*.

As an ex-classicist who never had a proper education in the history of philosophy, Nietzsche only really *knew* the Greeks – his admiration being reserved for the pre-Socratics – and his 'one and only educator', Arthur Schopenhauer. With this background, it was inevitable that greatness as he, like Casaubon, conceived it, would be a matter of producing a 'theory of everything', a theory of the form 'it's all X'. The pre-Socratics had developed these kinds of theories – for them everything is either water, matter, atoms, being, or becoming – as did Schopenhauer, for whom everything is 'will', 'will to live'.

Nietzsche specifically endorses this taste for the sweeping statement, observing in the notebooks that Democritus and Empedocles 'criticised and improved on' Anaxagoras's work on the basis of the conviction that the heart of 'scientific method' is the 'law of parsimony', the law that 'the hypothesis which deploys the smallest number of presuppositions and means to explain the world takes precedence over all rivals'.[20] Schopenhauer, too, appeals to the law of parsimony in justifying his expansion of 'will' beyond its natural home in the realm of human motivation to become the metaphysical ground of all events. The justification for this expansion, he writes, lies in the 'divine Plato's' 'law of homogeneity', which requires us to seek out the highest genus under which all natural species can be subsumed.[21] Inevitably, then, Nietzsche's quest for greatness required him to produce, as his proposed subtitle put it, 'an explanation of all events' that would reduce them to a single principle, and with the exciting concept of will to power to hand, he thought he had a good chance of providing such a reduction.

The Explanation of All Events

As noted, Nietzsche's 'theory of everything' begins to appear in the notebooks in the summer of 1885. He continues his underground work on it until about the middle of 1888, but only once, in the middle of 1886, in section 36 of *Beyond Good and Evil*, is it allowed to poke its head, and then, as remarked, only tentatively, into the light of publication.

The construction of the theory begins with an attack on substantival thinking, which, as we know, had long been a theme in both the notebooks and the published works. Substances, 'things', are, Nietzsche holds, 'errors': illusions, myths, fictions. Though useful, indeed essential, for purposes of survival, there is nothing corresponding to them in reality. Even the substances of natural science are myths: to Boscovich's replacement of the 'material atom' by extensionless *puncta* of force, he says in *Beyond Good and Evil*, we owe the insight that matter does not exist (p. 413 above).

Beneath the folk mythology of common sense, then, reality consists of 'forces'. But what are forces? To attach any meaning to the key term of Boscovichian physics, Nietzsche reflects, we must render 'force' intelligible in terms of our own sense experience: 'a force we cannot imagine is an empty word and should be denied rights of citizenship in science'.[22] From this it follows, to repeat the quotation, that

> the victorious concept of 'force' with which our physicists have created God and the world needs a supplement: it must be given an inner world which I designate as 'will to power', i.e. the insatiable drive to manifest power or as the employment and exercise of power, as creative drive etc.'.[23]

Up to this last point Nietzsche's train of thought follows exactly in Schopenhauer's footsteps. For he, too, had argued that matter is a fiction, that fundamental reality is force (he attributed the discovery to Joseph Priestley, but Priestley was in fact influenced by Boscovich), and that, left to their own devices, the forces of natural science are mere 'unknown Xs'.[24] So, Schopenhauer concludes, in order to rescue science from meaninglessness, forces must be thought of in terms of 'will', since that is the only plausible experiential candidate. Schopenhauer's will, however, is the 'will to live', the will to mere self-preservation, and at this point Nietzsche makes his claim to originality, his claim to outdo his onetime 'Master': the world is not will *to live* but rather will *to power*: 'self-preservation', he writes in *Beyond Good and Evil*, 'is only one of the indirect and most frequent consequences of this'. One should, he adds, appealing again to the 'law of parsimony', 'watch out for *superfluous* teleological principles'.[25]

Of course, if the will to live were the basis of an *adequate* theory of everything it would *not* be 'superfluous'. Schopenhauer's theory would then have a single principle and be just as parsimonious as his rival's. Nietzsche's view must be, therefore, that Schopenhauer's theory cannot 'save the phenomena', cannot in fact explain the character of the world as we observe it. The reason for this, he thinks, is that the world of our experience is not the 'celebrated struggle for existence' postulated with one voice by Schopenhauer and that 'mediocre Englishman'[26] Charles Darwin, but rather a struggle for *power*, because what we observe is that life 'often enough risks and sacrifices self-preservation' for the sake of an *'expansion of power'*.[27]

In the underground world of the notebooks, Nietzsche's power-theory begins with the transformation of Boscovich's puncta into 'quanta', 'quant[a] of will to power'.[28] These strive to 'dominate', to 'master', every other quantum, to incorporate it, take it over. The results of these power struggles, these subatomic efforts at colonisation, are organised systems of quanta – the 'things' of everyday experience – which try to dominate other systems of power-quanta. This explains the observed character of life as one enormous power struggle. It explains why, if we look at the world with an unsentimental eye, we cannot avoid seeing that, to repeat the words of *Beyond Good and Evil*, 'life itself is *essentially* a process of appropriation, injuring, overpowering the alien and the weaker, oppressing, being harsh, imposing your own form, incorporating, and at least, at the very least, exploiting'.[29]

Two further features of this grand theory merit mention. Since the will to power is, as we have seen, 'insatiable'[30] (the will to power is always the will to more power) and since the more complex systems of quanta become the more unstable they are, it follows that every organised power structure in the end collapses. They grow bigger and bigger until – like the Roman Empire or General Motors – they explode and everything returns, more or less, to the beginning. This leads Nietzsche to speculate as to whether the return to the beginning might not be an *exact* return, whether, in other words, the 'eternal return of the same', no more than a thought experiment designed as a test of spiritual health in the published works, might not also be a metaphysical truth. And according to at least one note it is; since the total quantity of force in the world is finite, it follows, Nietzsche postulates, that every possible state is realised over infinite time, so that the return of the *exact* present state of the world is guaranteed.[31]

Nietzsche sums up this vision of the totality of things in a note of 1885 which, ignoring the fact that Nietzsche's thought continued to change and develop for a further three years, Elizabeth chooses as the ecstatic finale of *her Will to Power*:

> This world: a monster of energy without beginning, without end, a firm iron magnitude of force that does not grow bigger or smaller...a play of forces, and waves of forces...increasing here and at the same time decreasing there...eternally changing, eternally flooding back, with tremendous years of recurrence, with an ebb and flow of forms out of the simplest forms striving towards the most complex...and then returning home to the simple...out of the play of contradictions...the eternally self-creating, the eternally self-destroying, 'beyond good and evil'... *This world is the will to power – and nothing besides! And you yourself are will to power – and nothing besides!*[32]

Revaluation of All Values

Thus the 'new explanation of all events'. By the summer of 1886, however, Nietzsche had come to prefer a new subtitle for the projected masterwork: *Revaluation of All Values*.[33] This was not because he had abandoned the idea of universal explanation, for it was during this summer that he actually *published* the claim that 'the world...is will to power and nothing besides' in section 36 of *Beyond Good and Evil*. Rather, it is because he has something to *add* to it, something that bears on 'values'.

What might Nietzsche's 'new explanation of all events' have to do with values? Modernity, we know, is in a condition of 'nihilism'. The upside of the demise of Christianity is the demise of a system of belief that has made humanity sick with self-loathing for two millennia. But the downside is that we have lost our account of the meaning of life. 'The highest values devalue themselves. The aim is lacking; "why?" finds no answer.'[34] But now, as a result of the foregoing metaphysics, we at least know what life *is*: 'will to power and nothing besides'. From this it follows, Nietzsche believes, that the meaning of life has to be the acquisition of (ever more) power.[35] Moreover, since values are just the 'voice of [either an individual's or] a people's will to power' – less poetically, 'the conditions of preservation and growth with respect to complex structures of relative permanence of life within becoming'[36] – it follows that morals are just, as it were, an instruction manual for the 'preservation and growth' of either of an individual or a community. The new understanding of what the world is, the new ontology, thus provides a new meaning of life and demands of us a new morality; a 'revaluation of all values'. It demands a return to the world of Machiavelli (that Henry Kissinger of the Florentine Renaissance), a return to 'virtue in the Renaissance style, virtù [in other words, efficiency], moraline-free virtue'.[37]

According to tradition, the three fundamental questions of philosophy are: What is there? What can we know? and What should we do? With the introduction of the 'revaluation' theme, it becomes clear that Nietzsche has answered all three. For the first time the grandeur of his vision and ambition stands before us in its stark simplicity. The answer to each of the first two questions is, 'The world is the will to power and nothing besides', and the answer to the third question is, 'Will power!'

But, one might object, is not this inference from 'life is the will to power' to 'power is what we ought to pursue', this attempt to derive ethics from ontology, a blatant instance of the well-known 'naturalistic fallacy', the fallacy of trying to derive an 'ought' from an 'is'? That power is desired does not, surely, make it *a fortiori* desirable.

Nietzsche goes out of his way to emphasise that, in relation to current moral sensibilities, sensibilities which, to some degree, he himself shares, his metaphysical vision is one of horror: 'a hundred miles beyond...everything pleasant', he describes the massive thing taking shape in the notebooks,[38] and the book in which the tip of that submerged mass becomes visible, *Beyond Good and Evil*, is, we know, 'very black and squid-like'. In the sketch of a possible preface to the masterwork, he writes:

> The conception of the world which one discovers in the background of this work is extraordinarily gloomy and unpleasant: among the types of pessimism known up to now, none appears to have reached this degree of malignancy. The contrast between a true and apparent world is missing here [there is no exit to a saving 'beyond'], there is only one world, and it is a false, cruel, contradictory world...without meaning.[39]

This emphasis on the blackness of Nietzsche's vision, as we know, is intended to bring to the fore the radical nature of the disjunction between, on the one hand, the traditional Christian morality of selfless love and, on the other, the reality of the world, as disclosed by modern, post-Darwinian scientific thinking. And the point of highlighting the disjunction is to compel that rare being, Nietzsche's proper reader, to a choice between two fundamental stances towards the world. The first option is to remain loyal to traditional morality. But in this case, since 'selflessness' is *impossible* in a world in which 'life itself is *essentially* a process of appropriating, injuring, overpowering the alien and the weaker, oppressing…exploiting',[40] one is forced to 'deny life'; to conclude, with Schopenhauer, that the world is something which 'ought not to be' and our existence in it is a kind of 'error…or mistake'.[41] The second stance to the world is to insist on 'affirming life', in which case one is *compelled* to advance 'beyond [traditional] good and evil' and is committed to Nietzsche's fundamental 'revaluation of values'. One has no option but to adopt the new morality, according to which only power has value[42] and 'good' simply *means* 'increases power' and 'bad' means 'decreases power'.[43] To make the first of these choices, however, is to succumb to the sickness of 'nihilism', a sickness that is the road to despair and suicide. It follows that making the second choice, revaluing all values, is a condition of mental health, something a healthy human being *must* do. That health requires world-affirmation is thus the premise that mediates the inference from the ontology of power to the ethics of power.

This is the lesson Ernst Jünger took from Nietzsche. As a special operations officer during the First World War (wounded fourteen times, he was one of Germany's most decorated war heroes), he experienced himself as a cog in a giant process which was the cosmic will to power expressing itself in its latest, mechanised form. Initially he found this process to be one of utmost horror. Yet unexpectedly, as he records in *Storm of Steel*, his memoir of the trenches, he found that by submitting to the process, he experienced a feeling of unparalleled elevation and intensity which seemed to him an encounter with his true being. And this became his guiding ethic for life in modernity. Since not just overt war but the 'totally mobilized' world of modernity in general is nothing but the mechanised ('electronic', he might now say) will to power in action, it follows that to live in harmony with such a world one must affirm – even ecstatically affirm – the will to power in its current, technological expression. In a nutshell, the lesson Jünger took from Nietzsche was: if you cannot mould the world to fit your morality you must mould your morality to fit the world. (If you can't beat them, join them!)

This, then, was the philosophy gathering itself in the notebooks – fascist (or perhaps 'neo-con') philosophy, one might agree with Heidegger, bearing in mind that Jünger was one of Hitler's heroes. This was the masterwork almost ready to spring out and astonish the world, almost ready to do what *Zarathustra* had failed to do, namely, 'split history into two halves'. But apart from its momentary surfacing in *Beyond Good and Evil*, it never saw the light of day. Nietzsche decided to abandon *The Will to Power*.

History of a Failed Literary Project

Work on *The Will to Power* project reached a peak in February 1888, with, as noted, a planned total of 374 aphorisms divided up into four books.[44] But Nietzsche was deeply dissatisfied with what he had produced. Writing to Köselitz on February 13, he says that 'the first version of my "Attempt at a Revaluation" is ready: it was, all in all, a torture, I haven't had the audacity for it. In ten years time I'll make it better'.[45] (Note the use of the subtitle rather than the main title, itself an indication that something is amiss with the original scheme.) Thirteen days later he tells Köselitz that he has abandoned all thought of publishing the work.[46]

Deeply reluctant, however, to abandon his brilliant key to the unravelling of all mysteries, Nietzsche compelled himself to soldier on with the project as originally conceived until the end of August 1888. But it went from bad to worse. On August 22, he wrote Meta von Salis from Sils Maria that the work of the entire summer was

'down the plug hole [*ins Wasser gefallen*]'. I'm devastated by this [he continued] since compared with last year, the first of my spring[47] visits [to Sils] to turn out really well, I brought even more energy with me this time. Also, everything had been prepared for *one grand and very specific task*.[48]

On August 26, Nietzsche sketched one final plan for a book with *Will to Power* as its main title.[49] But just four days later, he wrote his mother that 'a well and long prepared work which should have been completed this summer, has literally "gone down the plug hole"'.[50]

In the same letter Nietzsche told his mother that he was 'once again fully in action' – there is an unmistakable feeling of liberation now that he has finally cut his losses with respect to *The Will to Power*. The focus of his renewed productivity was a new publishing strategy which emerges in the notebooks at the beginning of September. The plan was to publish salvageable bits of the *Will to Power* material in a series of 'excerpts from my philosophy'.[51] One of these collections of repackaged material was to be called *Idleness of a Psychologist* (soon, we know, to be retitled *Twilight of the Idols*), another *Revaluation of All Values*, with *The Antichrist* as the title of the first of its four books.

Though this *Revaluation* was to be somewhat shorter than the original *Will to Power*, Nietzsche still thought of it as the masterwork which, as he wrote Paul Deussen on September 14, by demanding 'a value decision of the first order', would (yet again!) 'split the history of humanity into two halves'. All his other publishing intentions, he wrote, represented mere 'relaxations and diversions' from this main task.[52] The continued centrality of this work to Nietzsche's conception of his life-defining 'task', the continued grandeur of ambition, and the continued presence of 'Revaluation' in the proposed title make it legitimate, I think, to regard the *Revaluation* as a continuation of the 'masterwork' project.

On September 30, 1888, Nietzsche completed both *Twilight of the Idols* and *The Antichrist*, continuing to describe the latter as 'the first book of the *Revaluation of All Values*'.[53] On November 20, however, he wrote Georg Brandes – referring to *The Antichrist* – that 'the *Revaluation of All Values* lies complete before me' and claimed that 'in a couple of years [it] will bring the whole earth into convulsions'.[54] And six days later he wrote Deussen that 'my *Revaluation of All Values*, with the main title *The Antichrist*, is ready', adding that a million copies in seven languages will need to be produced.[55] The planned four-volume work had thus contracted into the one book of *The Antichrist*.

On or about December 29 – close to the time of his tearful embrace of the beaten horse in the Turin piazza and complete mental breakdown – Nietzsche made one final adjustment to the masterwork project: he crossed out *The Antichrist*'s subtitle, *Revaluation of All Values*, and replaced it with *A Curse on Christianity*.

One might well, therefore, come to the conclusion that the last of the many permutations of the masterwork-project resulted in cutting *The Antichrist* loose as a free-standing work and therefore in the complete abandonment of the project. I am, however, inclined to resist this conclusion – in spite of the relative brevity of *The Antichrist*. I am inclined, that is, to discount the 'Curse on Christianity' subtitle on several grounds. First, because Nietzsche was almost certainly insane when he created it – outbursts of fury would increasingly become one of the characteristics of his insanity. Second, because 'Curse on Christianity' is an inaccurate guide to the work's content, which comprises, as we have seen, a great deal more than a critique of Christianity. And third, because this additional material contains significant amounts of the material which had been planned for the *Revaluation*. The very last plan, that is, for a four-booked *Revaluation* has *The Antichrist* as Book I, a critique of 'morality' as Book II, a critique of philosophy hitherto as Book III, while Book IV is entitled 'Dionysus. Philosophy of the Eternal Return'.[56] As we have seen, however, in abbreviated form the 'philosophy of eternal return' is incorporated into *The Antichrist*: being able to will the eternal return as the condition of becoming a leader of Nietzsche's ideal community turns out to provide the apex of his political philosophy (p. 516 above). And the material of Books III and IV had, in any case, been presented already in many previous works. I am inclined to conclude, therefore – as we have seen, Nietzsche knew on December 16, if not before, that the 'tragic catastrophe' was fast approaching (p. 524 above) – that he packed everything he now felt essential to the masterwork project but had not yet published into *The Antichrist*.

* * *

Nietzsche, then, abandoned the *Will to Power* project, transmuting it into the *Revaluation* project, which in the end abbreviated itself into *The Antichrist*. This leaves us with two questions. First, what was it that caused Nietzsche so much trouble and caused him, finally, at the end of August 1888, to abandon the attempt to publish a book called *The Will to Power*? And second, what, if anything, remains in the philosophical works produced after that abandonment – *The Wagner Case*, *Twilight of the Idols*, *Ecce Homo*, and *The Antichrist* – of the original project? What role, if any, is played by the will to power in the works completed during the final four months of 1888?

Intellectual Cleanliness

Why, then, first of all, did Nietzsche abandon *The Will to Power*? If we return to the point at which his dissatisfaction with the project first emerged, February 1888, two things stand out as important. First, the fact that nearly all of the time from that point onwards (though with moments of nostalgia for his original title) he thinks of the project as the *Revaluation* rather than *The Will to Power*. And second, the following notebook comment on, and apparently for, the projected work:

> I mistrust all systematisers and go out of my way to avoid them. The will to system, for a thinker at least, is something compromising, a form of immorality...Perhaps one will guess by looking underneath and behind this book which systematiser it is doing its best to avoid – me myself.[57]

As we saw, the original impetus behind the masterwork project was utterly systematic. The reduction of 'all events' to a single principle was, following the pre-Socratics and Schopenhauer, a defining condition of the 'greatness' for which Nietzsche yearned. The rejection of his own systematising ambitions in early 1888 is thus an indication that the project was in deep trouble.

This aphorism also lets us understand something of the character of that trouble. Pressing on with the systematic reduction of everything to will to power would, it tells us, 'compromise' Nietzsche's integrity as a philosopher, would be a form of intellectual 'immorality'. What we see, then, is that, at the beginning of 1888, Nietzsche was in a state of spiritual turmoil caused by a clash between, on the one hand, his will to greatness, greatness in the traditional mould, and, on the other, his intellectual integrity, which was in danger of being compromised.

In Nietzsche's published works, as we have seen, intellectual integrity – 'honesty', the 'intellectual conscience',[58] 'intellectual cleanliness',[59] the 'will to knowledge'[60] – is presented time after time as the highest personal virtue of both himself and thinkers he admires.[61] And in the end – a fact greatly to his credit – after a long and agonising struggle, it is his will to intellectual integrity, his will to truth, that wins out over his will to greatness and causes him to abandon the original project. What, however, was it that convinced him that intellectual integrity required him to reject his original, all-embracing system?

* * *

The grand, 'synoptic' attempt to 'explain all events' as will to power involves three elements, three, in Schopenhauer's language, 'extensions'[62] of the will. I shall refer to them as follows:

(1) *The psychological doctrine*: the 'extension' of will to power from being the depth psychology of selected events such as gratitude, pity, and asceticism to being the depth psychology of *all* human motivation. This thesis is clearly stated in *Beyond Good and Evil* as the programme of 'grasp[ing] psychology as the morphology and *doctrine of the development of the will to power*'.[63]

(2) *The biological doctrine*: the claim that not just human actions but rather all organic phenomena are to be reduced to will to power; *Beyond Good and Evil*'s claim that '*life*' – all life – is 'will to power, and nothing besides'. [64]

(3) *The cosmological doctrine*: the claim that absolutely everything – '*the world*' – is 'will to power, and nothing besides'.[65]

With respect to each of these increasingly daring 'extensions', one can ask whether there was something, and if so what, that offended Nietzsche's intellectual integrity and caused him to reject it. I shall work backwards, from the third doctrine to the first.

The Cosmological Doctrine

In section 36 of *Beyond Good and Evil*, Nietzsche recapitulates his route to the cosmological doctrine in the form of an argument. The essence of a not very clear presentation is the following:

(1) It is possible to 'explain our entire life of drives as the organisation and outgrowth of one basic form of will (namely the will to power which is *my* claim)'. It is possible, that is, to portray the entirety of human motivation in terms of the 'causality of the will to power' ('The psychological doctrine').

(2) It 'follows from the definition' of scientific 'method' that 'multiple varieties of causation should not be postulated until the attempt to make do with a single one has been taken as far as it will go (– *ad absurdum* if you will)'[66] ('The law of parsimony' (p. 537 above)).

So (3) we should make the attempt to regard all 'forces' underlying the manifest world, including those underlying the 'so-called mechanistic world', as essentially the same as those underlying our own psychological life and hence regard the 'inner nature' of the whole world as 'will to power, and nothing besides' ('The cosmological doctrine').

In short, a procedure that mimics exactly Schopenhauer's 'extension' of will all the way to inorganic nature (p. 537 above), the psychological doctrine, plus the principle of parsimony, gives birth to the cosmological doctrine.

Nietzsche's own formulation of this argument is, in fact, even more tentative than I have represented it. What he actually says is: '*supposing*'[67] that the premises are true *then* the cosmological doctrine follows. That at this stage he still feels reasonably confident about the psychological doctrine is indicated by the parenthetical remark 'this is *my* claim' in premise (1). But that he is already worried by the 'law of parsimony' is indicated by the appearance of the defensive '*ad absurdum*, if you will' in premise (2). What might have worried him about the principle?

One of the many bad things about Elizabeth's *Will to Power* is that, by arranging her brother's aphorisms thematically rather than chronologically, she disguises the fact that the notebooks are *notebooks*, a confused and often contradictory jumble of *experiments* in the laboratory of thought, not ex cathedra pronouncements of final doctrine. Like most philosophers, Nietzsche jots down an idea but then sets it aside for a period of time while haring off in a different, often opposing, direction.

Now in fact, already in 1885, Nietzsche had doubts about the law of parsimony, observing in a note the 'self-deception' involved in the belief that a 'complex of ideas is truer' when it can be organised into a 'great "system"'. The 'fundamental prejudice' on which the notion is based, he continues, the idea that 'order, clarity of arrangement, the systematic, must reflect the true being of things while the opposite – disorder, the chaotic, the incalculable – brings to appearance only a false or inadequately understood world', is a 'pedantic' and quite unprovable 'moral prejudice' which 'views things according to the prescription of a model civil servant'.[68]

This is a critique of the 'will to system', and so of the 'law of parsimony', as such. According to the point he himself makes (but then forgets or represses), Nietzsche the systematiser evinces the mentality of a Prussian civil servant – one of his satires on Kant's moral philosophy, recall, consists in summarising it as 'the civil servant as thing in itself raised up in judgement over the civil servant as phenomenon'.[69]

A related matter that may have contributed to *Beyond Good and Evil*'s unease about the cosmological doctrine is *The Gay Science*'s conviction that every kind of 'aesthetic anthropomorphism' leads to a false (or, at least, unjustified) conception of reality: that the 'total character of the world' is 'to all eternity chaos', 'in the sense not of lack of necessity but of a lack of order, arrangement, form, beauty [or] wisdom.[70] For nothing, surely, is more 'anthropomorphic' than *Beyond Good and Evil*'s use of the law of parsimony to exhibit 'the mechanistic world as belonging on the same plane of reality as our affects themselves – as a ... *pre-form* of life'.[71] And is there not, moreover, the projection of an eerie kind of 'beauty' onto the world in picturing it as forming and reforming itself in a giant circle? As with Schopenhauer, Nietzsche's version of the cosmological doctrine is anthropomorphic as well as systematic, which makes it doubly suspect.

The Biological Doctrine

I turn now to the biological doctrine, the claim that not just human but *all* organic life is 'will to power and nothing besides'. The basic problem with this, as Nietzsche must surely have come to realise, is that it is obviously false. (This entails, of course, that the cosmological doctrine is obviously false, too.)

As we saw earlier, in the grip of his will to systematic greatness, Nietzsche claimed that his own concept of 'will to power' was superior to both Schopenhauer and Darwin's 'struggle for existence' in doing justice to the observed fact that life is a universal power-struggle. In line with this notion of what the facts are, we find him claiming in the notebooks that what 'trees in the primeval forest fight each other for ... [is not mere existence but rather] for power'.[72]

This is, of course, absurd. Though trees do, I suppose, in the language of *Beyond Good and Evil*, 'injure', 'oppress', and 'overpower' 'weaker' trees, as well as 'appropriating' their light and soil, the point of such activity is simply *to survive*, not to 'grow, spread, win dominance',[73] to become lord of the forest. Nietzsche claims, contra Schopenhauer, that the will to live is merely a *means to* the will to power (p. 414 above). But in non-human, organic nature, I suggest, one finds precisely the opposite: the drive to 'power', insofar as it exists at all, is a means to satisfying the drive to survive. In short, to the extent one is willing to speak at all of a 'will' in non-human, biological nature, Schopenhauer's 'will to live' looks a much better bet than Nietzsche's 'will to power'.

If we look more closely at the train of thought that leads Nietzsche to the idea that trees fight each other for power, we see that the suggestion that the idea is grounded in empirical evidence is really a sham. He writes:

> 'Man strives for happiness', what is true about that! To understand what life is, what kind of striving and tension life is, the formula must apply just as well to tree and plant ... What do the trees in the primeval forest fight each other for? For 'happiness'? – For power ...[74]

What, in other words, is really motivating the biological doctrine is once more the psychological thesis plus the law of parsimony: human life is driven by power; 'method' demands the homogenising of reality, that it be human nature writ large;[75] ergo, plant and animal life *must* be driven by power.

Nietzsche continues to be 'anti-Darwin' in the works completed at the end of 1888. But in these works, his objection is entirely to *social* Darwinism. *Twilight of the Idols*, for example, claims that Darwin (whom, as I noted, he almost certainly never read) 'forgot the spirit', forgot that the mediocre herd cunningly gangs up to undermine the higher type so that 'species do *not* grow more perfect'.[76] This, of course, is a silly objection – Darwin's theory is not a theory of *cultural* evolution, and in any case he claims not that species become more 'perfect' but only that they become more *adaptive*. But the introduction of 'spirit' makes it evident that the focus is entirely on 'species' of *humanity*. In the works published after the abandonment of the *Will to Power* project the biological doctrine, for very good reasons, disappears without trace.

The Psychological Doctrine

Intellectual integrity, then, forced Nietzsche to abandon both the cosmological and the biological doctrines. Neither is even mentioned, let alone endorsed, in the published works of 1888. What, then, of the psychological doctrine, the claim that all human motivation can be reduced to will to power? That, too, is abandoned in the works of 1888. We need now to discover why.

Two important things happen in these late works. First, 'the anti-systematiser' aphorism reappears but *without*, now, the earlier identification of *Nietzsche himself* as the systematiser *par excellence*: 'I distrust all systematisers and avoid them. The will to system is a lack of integrity' is all he writes in *Twilight of the Idols*.[77] This modification of the aphorism is a fair indication, I think, that his own will to an all-embracing system has now been overcome, his integrity recovered.

The second thing that happens is that he becomes open to the rich variety of human motivations and no longer tries to force them all onto the procrustean bed of the will to power. In discussing 'the psychology of the artist', for instance, *Twilight of the Idols* recognises *three* fundamental impulses: Apollonian 'intoxication', which excites the eye and inspires great visual art, Dionysian 'intoxication', which inspires music and dance, and 'the highest feeling of power', which inspires great architecture – but, it seems, none of the other arts.[78] Throughout 1888, moreover, sexual intoxication (as distinct from marriage which, we have seen, *is* viewed as a power struggle) is viewed as a cause of perception and action alongside, and not reducible to, will to power: a note from the spring of that year, for instance, itemises the 'yes-saying affects' as 'pride, joy, health, sexual love, enmity and war, reverence . . . the strong will' *as well as* 'the will to power' as affects which transfigure things, make them 'golden, eternal and divine'.[79]

Another motive for action recognised by the late works as being distinct from the will to power – here, it seems to me, they face up to an obstacle to Nietzsche's reductive drive that had been lurking in his thought for over a decade – is *Mitleid* ('pity' or 'compassion'). Earlier works, to be sure, made a valiant effort to exhibit pity as an attempt to humiliate the other, thereby gaining the 'feeling of power' – and hence, one might argue, power itself.[80] But the attempt to make all compassion an exercise of, or quest for, power was always an uphill battle which, I think, Nietzsche never fully believed in. The reason for this lies in the theme, present from the earliest discussions, that pity harms the pitier as well as the pitied. Influenced by Schopenhauer's notion that compassion produces a 'transition from virtue to asceticism',[81] Nietzsche holds, we saw (pp. 302–3 above), that pity, sympathetic identification with the suffering of others, causes depression. If I take to heart the entire pain of Africa, then I become overwhelmed by the quantity of pain in the world and am thereby rendered incapable of *any* acts of benevolence. Nietzsche alludes to this theme in *Ecce Homo*, where he points out that pity for humanity's 'cry of distress' is Zarathustra's final 'temptation' (see pp. 487–8 above): he must resist it because it threatens to 'seduce' him from the 'elevation of his task' of leading humanity to a new and better world, both by diverting him into 'short-sighted' acts of benevolence and by destroying his faith in the possibility of improving the human condition.[82] True love is tough love.[83]

Clearly this theme presupposes the reality of pity as *genuine* empathy with the pain of others, as an emotion that has nothing to do with the attempt to feel superior to or gain power over them. As we have seen, the fact that Nietzsche himself was exceptionally prone to being overwhelmed by feelings of compassion is what makes the story of his embrace of the tormented horse in the Turin piazza inherently plausible.

What Remains of the Will to Power?

The late works abandon, then, the reductive psychological doctrine and allow human motivation to blossom into the richness it actually has. Yet beneath this richness Nietzsche detects an underlying pattern. This pattern, however, abandons the monism of 'will to power and nothing besides' in favour of a *dualism* between two kinds of human life, a dualism which, I think, is intended to gather human motives into two camps. On the one hand, there is healthy or 'ascending' life, the governing 'principle' of which *is* the will to power.[84] Healthy life, says *The Antichrist*, is 'an instinct for growth, for the accumulation of force, of *power*'.[85] But as a counter-balance to the will to power, there now appears what Freud would later call the 'death instinct'. 'Where there is no will to power', the *Antichrist* tells us – note the *explicit* rejection of the psychological doctrine – 'there is decline', '*décadence*'.[86]

'*Décadence*' makes its first appearance as a significant philosophical term in Nietzsche's published works in 1888. As already observed (p. 494 above), what makes the notion a difficult one is that Nietzsche defines it in two ways. According to the first definition, *décadence* is the yearning for 'nothingness', the 'will to death', that is implicit in Baudelaire's taste for decay and deviance, and explicit in Wagner's later operas. According to the second, *décadence* is defined in terms of atomisation: whether we are talking of art or society, the *décadence* of modernity consists in the decay of the power to maintain complex unities, in 'the exuberance of life' being 'pushed back into its smallest forms' and so reducing former wholes to rubble, to 'chaos'.[87]

These characterisations do not, however, seem to me incompatible. Nietzsche says that those who become *décadent* are 'the weak and exhausted'.[88] They develop a hatred of life and the will to exit it because they are no longer able to face up to its challenges. And the reason for that, for their fin de siècle *Weltschmerz* and life-weariness, lies in atomisation: in the 'anarchy' of their 'instincts',[89] their failure to organise themselves into disciplined wholes, capable of the coherent, single-minded action necessary to 'victory' – and confidence in victory – over life's challenges. *Décadents* are those who, as they might have said at Pforta, can no longer 'pull themselves together'. They have forgotten how to be 'warriors'.

Together with Wagner and Baudelaire, we have seen, (the real) Jesus and the Buddha are also classified as *décadents* on account of their inability to confront opposition, enmity.[90] And the success of Christianity (finally the question of how the 'slave' moral-ists were able to capture the hearts and minds of the nobles (see p. 510 above) receives an answer) was in part due to *décadence*. The reason, that is, that the Jewish priests were able to persuade their former oppressors to adopt the Christian metaphysico-moral package was by appealing to their world-weary 'instincts of *décadence*'.[91] The 'morbid'[92] condition of the souls of their target audience, their will to nothingness, was the fertile soil in which Chris-tianity – that sanctification of the will to nothingness – took root.

* * *

In the late works, we have now seen, Nietzsche abandons each of the three elements that had constituted the grand vision of the world as 'will to power and nothing besides'. This should not, however, be understood as returning the will to power to the modesty of its role in the works of the 1870s – no more than a useful tool for uncovering the depth psy-chology of selected kinds of human behaviour. For the will to power remains, to the end, the governing 'principle' of *healthy* life. What really happens to it in the final works is that it is transformed from a principle of universal *explanation* into a principle of *demarcation*, demarcation between the healthy life and *décadent* life.

Healthy life, that is, remains the 'insatiable' quest for power – or 'growth'[93] – remains 'that which must always overcome itself'.[94] Moreover, Nietzsche assumes, health is the highest desideratum. Even the *décadent*, I think he assumes, would prefer to be healthy, and only become *décadent* when the capacity for health deserts them. From this it follows that the constant quest for power remains the meaning of (healthy) life, the 'why?' that makes healthy life able to withstand any 'how?'[95] and hence the standard of value.[96] With a certain inflection, all this can still be said by the formula 'life is the will to power'. But now 'life' has exchanged description for evaluation. It functions as it does when one tells someone to stop being a neurotic pedant and 'Get a life!'

The Problem of the 'Healthy Monster'

As we have seen, Nietzsche holds that morality, 'virtue', comprises 'the most basic laws of the preservation and growth' of either a community or an individual. But, opposing Kant's one-size-fits-all conception of morality in *The Antichrist*, he argues that since the nature of growth varies from individual to individual and community to community, it follows that each individual or community 'should invent its *own* virtues, its *own* categorical imperatives',[97] its own prescription for the growth of its own kind of power. Yet not just any kind of exercise of power goes. Bismarck's power politics, we have seen, is absolutely rejected. On two grounds. First, because it is a squandering of the energy, discipline, and intelligence needed to create what *Twilight of the Idols* calls 'cultural power'.[98] And second, because it is incompatible with one of Nietzsche's most fundamental aims, world peace. The 'good European' theme which runs through all his writings from 1878 onwards, and even into the 'crazy letters' (p. 529 above), is, we have seen, the desire to overcome the petty nationalisms that lead to militarism and war.

What, then, Nietzsche approves, as we know, is the *sublimated* or, as he calls it, 'spiritu-alised'[99] expression of the will to power: 'war', by all means – healthy people are always, like Nietzsche himself, 'warriors' – but 'war without gunpowder'.[100] The 'strongest instinct' of the Greeks, for example, was the will to power. Yet the high point of their marvellous culture arrived when they sublimated it into the 'agonistic instinct' that gave rise to culture, to the tragic festival, philosophy, art and science.[101]

Nietzsche's heart, then, is in the right place. Violence, brutality and barbarism ought to be expelled from human life. The question, though, is whether his head is, too, whether he can in fact justify such an expulsion in terms of his fundamental principle of value. If the good for me is whatever fosters my kind of power, why should I not decide – particularly if I have big muscles and am not particularly good at dialectics or writing tragedies – that brutal rather than sublimated power is the thing for me? After all, Cesare Borgia, we have been told, though a 'monster', was one in whom no trace of 'disease' is to be found.[102] And, on other occasions, he says the same of the marauding Vikings.

Nietzsche's answer to this question is, I think, simple. 'All passions', he says, 'go through a phase...when they drag their victim down with the weight of their stupidity'.[103] And the truth about the brutal exercise of power is that it is, almost certainly, stupid. Repeatedly, that is, he emphasises how the 'mediocre' gang up on the exceptional individual, 'martyr'[104] him for the sake of conventional norms. How much more, therefore, will they do so if his exceptionality takes a violently sociopathological form. The barbaric individual may be healthy. But he is likely to come to a bad end. Cesare Borgia died, in exile, at the age of thirty-one.

Nietzsche's view is not only that this almost certainly *will* happen. It is also that it *should* happen. Since, as I have argued throughout this book, his overriding concern is the flourishing of the community as a whole, the community is *right* to suppress those who threaten it with destruction, those who threaten *its* will to power. Generally he laments the 'herd's' destruction of the exceptionality of the exceptional individual. But not always. About its right to protect itself from criminal harm he has no doubts.

27

The End

In the Basel Clinic

O N JANUARY II, 1889, Franz Overbeck informed Nietzsche's only other remaining human contact, Heinrich Köselitz, that the previous day he had delivered Nietzsche,

> or more exactly the rubble of what only a friend would recognise as him, to the psychiatric clinic [in Basel]. He suffers from delusions of infinite grandeur, but also from much else – it's hopeless. I have never seen such a horrific picture of destruction.[1]

He delivered his friend to the care of Dr. Ludwig Wille, whom Nietzsche recognised immediately. 'I believe we have met', he greeted Wille with the urbane dignity of a Basel professor, 'but I am sorry to say that I have forgotten your name. Would you –' *'Wille*, I am Wille', replied the doctor. 'Ah yes, Wille', Nietzsche agreed. 'You are a psychiatrist. Some years ago we had a conversation about religious insanity'.[2] Clearly, though the recollection was perfectly correct, Nietzsche had no idea of where he was or why.

Wille diagnosed 'progressive paralysis', in other words, neurosyphilis, a diagnosis that was possibly encouraged by the fact that this was his research speciality. (To those good at hammering, it is said, everything is inclined to look like a nail.)

According to the patient records, Nietzsche's voluble conversation during his week in the asylum was a 'colourful confusion of former experiences' jumbled together 'without logical connexion'. Knowledge of his philosophy does, however, reveal a kind of pattern to his behaviour, a continuation of the parody of the Dionysian state that marked his final weeks in Turin.

There was, first of all, a continuation of the euphoric megalomania of his last days in Turin. 'The patient feels extraordinarily well and elevated', the patient book records. And it also records that, apologising to the staff for the terrible weather they had been having, he told them he had prepared 'the most splendid day for tomorrow'. When his mother arrived he spoke at length and entirely coherently about family matters before suddenly exclaiming 'Behold the tyrant of Turin!' and then lapsing into incoherent mumbling. Second, the 'psychology of the orgiastic'[3] continued to manifest itself. He loved, wanted to embrace, everyone he saw and was given to singing, dancing, and leaping about in goat-like bounds in an apparent re-creation of the Dionysian orgy. And he experienced a heightened sensuality (akin, perhaps, to the effect of marijuana). He ate massively, constantly asked for more food, reported erotic dreams, and regularly demanded 'females' (one more nail in the coffin of the Nietzsche-was-gay theory).

On January 17 he was taken to the Basel railway station to be transferred to the clinic in Jena, close to Naumburg, where his mother would be able to visit him on a regular basis. He was accompanied by Franziska, a young Dr. Mähly (whom Nietzsche had taught in secondary school), and a warder. Overbeck went to the station to say a final goodbye. The departure, he wrote Köselitz,

> was the most terrible and unforgettable moment. I saw Nietzsche at about nine o'clock in the luridly lit entrance hall of the central station closely led by his two companions. He had a quick but stumbling walk and an unnaturally stiff bearing, his face was like a mask...I am plagued by the thought that it would have been the office of a friend to take his life rather than delivering the poor man to the asylum. I now have no other wish than that it will soon be taken...With Nietzsche it's all over (*Mit Nietzsche ist es aus*).[4]

Overbeck found his friend in his compartment on the train, upon which he 'pressed me stormily to his heart and said that I was 'the man whom he had loved most of all"[5] – an affection Overbeck had earned many times over.

In the Jena Asylum

The psychiatric clinic of the University of Jena was directed by Professor Otto Binswanger. Nietzsche was admitted on January 18, 1890, and would remain there until March 24. Since he had had an attack of fury directed against his mother on the train, he was immediately placed under sedation. In the patient book he was entered as 'religion: Protestant, condition: progressive paralysis, cause: syphilis'. (The account of his 'religion' hardly inspires confidence in the account of his condition.) Wille's diagnosis, in other words, was accepted without question or examination by Binswanger – who also had progressive paralysis as a speciality.

Physically Nietzsche was still in good shape. The increased weight brought on by his gargantuan appetite made him look good, and for at least the next two years he was capable of walking three to four hours without difficulty. From now on, however, though interspersed with fragments of sanity, his mental condition went into steep decline. Produced on stage in a lecture to medical students (patient dignity was evidently a low priority), he was engaged in conversation by Binswanger, a conversation in which, as a student recorded, he spoke about the wonders of Turin and the relative advantages of large and small cities with a 'cogency of content and spell-binding style' the student had never before experienced, but then lost the plot and collapsed into mumbling incoherence.[6] His musicianship, on the other hand, remained unimpaired: Köselitz visited and reported him improvising flawlessly on the piano. There were clusters of chords, 'full of the spirit of *Tristan*', with wonderful orchestral effects: 'dramatic pianissimos, choruses of trombones, and trumpet fanfares of Beethoven-like grimness'.⁷

From time to time there were still moments of 'Dionysian' euphoria. He was inclined to introduce himself as the Duke of Cumberland or the German Emperor, and as the husband of Cosima Wagner. When a certain 'Baron X' (a patient's report preserves, here, the anonymity of a fellow patient) started to play his zither, Nietzsche would leap to his feet and dance until a warder quietened him down. 'He must have been a dashing dancer in his youth', the anonymous patient remarks.⁸

There were, however, less attractive aspects of his loss of (as his philosophy would say, 'Apollonian') control. He regressed into a kind of infantilism, smearing excrement over walls, wrapping faeces in paper and putting them in the drawer of a table, and urinating in a boot and drinking the result.

In spite of the moments of euphoria, which became ever less frequent, Nietzsche's overall state in the Jena clinic seems to have been one of great unhappiness. Outbursts of fury were frequent: on one occasion he kicked a fellow patient and on another put his fist through a window. And – the probable cause of most of the fury – he suffered frequent attacks of paranoid delusion. He thought that he was being tortured during the night and that an archduchess was trying to poison him. He smashed another window pane because he saw the barrel of a rifle behind it. He asked for a pistol for self-defence.

Towards the end of 1889, Julius Langbein, art historian, Nietzsche fan, and author of *Rembrandt as Educator*, half-persuaded Franziska that her son was being ill-treated in the clinic and that what he needed was talk therapy rather than drugs. Langbein, a forerunner of Nietzsche's Nazi appropriators, was an anti-Semitic mystagogue who claimed the Germans to be the inheritors of the greatness that was Greece. Aiming to make Nietzsche the figurehead of his movement, he demanded legal custody of him for two years, as well as control of his pension. Nietzsche still had enough sense to take an instant dislike to the man, overturning a table and shaking his fist at him on their first encounter. Nonetheless, he was forced to take several walks with this reptilian figure until Overbeck eventually managed to convince Franziska that he was very bad news.

At the end of March 1890, Franziska decided to move him into a private residence in Jena where, though remaining under medical surveillance, he seemed happier and quieter. He still played the piano beautifully – *inter alia*, Beethoven's Opus 31 sonatas – and went on long walks with his mother. On one of these walks, however, disaster struck. Escaping maternal supervision, he wandered off looking for the public baths. Finding them closed, and having, since his schooldays, been a keen and able swimmer, he decided to swim in a city lake and stripped naked. Franziska eventually found him chatting amiably with a policeman, and two of them brought him home without difficulty. The clinic, however, was furious, fearing that its reputation for security would be compromised. Anticipating reincarceration, mother and son beat a hasty retreat to Naumburg.

In Naumburg

On May 12, 1890, Nietzsche found himself back in the house in the Weingarten street from which, thirty-two years earlier, he had set out for Pforta. Until her death seven years later, Franziska's devotion to and care for her son, aided by the faithful servant Alwine, was extraordinary. One can perhaps surmise that she experienced a kind of happiness that Fritz's antithetical mind no longer existed to frustrate the expression of her love, that she had finally recovered her son. Though he was in reasonable shape to start with, Nietzsche's physical condition began to deteriorate rapidly. By the end of 1891 his loss of manual control destroyed his piano playing and by the end of the following year he was mainly bed- and wheelchair-ridden. The following year Franziska had a door put into the wall of his upstairs room so he could be wheeled out to take the air on the veranda. Massage became necessary to prevent bedsores. He now failed to recognise old friends such as Paul Deussen and even became uncertain as to his mother's identity. He sank more and more into apathy; little interested him apart from dolls and other children's toys. He still spoke occasionally, but mainly to produce stock sentences in the style of a brainwashed schoolboy. Franziska made a record of some of them: 'I translated much'. 'I lived in a good place called Naumburg'. 'I swam in the Saale'. 'I was very fine because I lived in a fine house'. 'I love Bismarck'. 'I don't like Friedrich Nietzsche'. It would be a mercy to think that he experienced at least a kind of vegetative contentment, but this seems not to have been the case. He suffered from his lifelong curse of insomnia, and visitors downstairs were often disturbed by groans and howls coming from the upstairs bedroom. Towards the end of 1893 Franziska recorded him uttering 'More light!' (Goethe's dying words) and 'In short, dead!' suggesting that that is what he wanted to be.

Becoming a Star

With fate's fickle irony, Nietzsche's spiritual decline was accompanied by the exponential growth of his fame. Already in February 1889, the *Allgemeine Schweizer* newspaper had got wind of his collapse and, borrowing from Shakespeare (Ophelia on Hamlet), observed 'what a noble mind is here o'erthrown'. The same month an eighteen-page essay, 'Friedrich Nietzsche: The Outline of His System and His Personality', appeared in the magazine *Unsere Zeit*, an essay which, the following year, its author, Ola Hansson, expanded into a book, *Friedrich Nietzsche: His Personality and His System.* (Evidently Hansson missed the aphorism 'the will to system is a lack of integrity'.) In May of 1889 a translation of twelve of Nietzsche's aphorisms appeared in the *New York Century Magazine*. Books on Nietzsche now began to follow thick and fast: Lou Salomé's work of intuitive insight in 1894 (p. 502 above) – Overbeck thought it the best available – and, among the following year's crop, Volume I of Elizabeth's two-volume attempt to make a killing on the Nietzsche market.[9] (This fundamentally toxic work was designed to narrate Nietzsche's life in a way that would (a) destroy Lou Salomé (when Lou's book appeared Elizabeth put it about that she was a Finnish Jew), (b) exclude her mother as a significant factor in her brother's life, and (c) reveal herself as its true co-star.) Pilgrims from all over Germany and beyond began to come to Naumburg to stand before the house on Weingarten, hoping to catch a glimpse of the deranged philosopher at his upstairs window. In the age of mad-women-in-the-attic Victorian novels, Nietzsche's madness can only have increased the fascination with his philosophy.

Elizabeth Cashes In

Almost from the beginning, the Försters' Paraguayan venture found itself in deep trouble. Based on Aryan ideology rather than skill and planning, it soon found itself short of water and, with no roads or railways, unable to transport the timber that was to have been its economic foundation to any market. There was strife over the price the Försters charged their settlers for basic household supplies, and the size of their own grand house caused great resentment. The land they sold the settlers as freehold had in fact merely been rented from the government, so that when disgruntled settlers wished to leave they found that their deposits had disappeared into rental payments. On June 3, 1889, Bernhard Förster poisoned himself with a combination of morphine and strychnine, dying alone in the bedroom of a Paraguayan hotel. This was the beginning of Elizabeth's long career as a counterfeiter. (As well as faking *The Will to Power*, expurgating *Ecce Homo* and *The Antichrist*, and forging letters from Nietzsche to herself, she also represented her father's death as due to falling down stairs and her brother's madness to a combination of overwork and sleeping-tablet abuse.) She bribed a local doctor to produce a fake death certificate for her husband citing a heart attack as the cause of death – to no avail, since news of the suicide had already reached the local newspapers.

Elizabeth returned to Europe at the end of 1890, where she remained until the middle of 1892 attempting, amazingly, to gain further recruits and money for the project. In the main settler newspaper, the *Südamerikanische Kolonial-Nachrichten*, one of her settlers, Fritz Neumann, accused her of perpetrating a 'crime' by continuing to lure settlers to *Nueva Germania*. After investigation, the newspaper itself agreed, describing the whole venture in an editorial as 'a plundering of inexperienced and credulous people, performed without conscience and in a most ruthless way'. In the following year a former ally of Elizabeth's, Paul Ulrich, wrote to the paper calling her a liar, thief and disaster for the colony, and urging the settlers to turn her out.[10]

In September 1893, seeing that the game was finally up, Elizabeth liquidated what assets she had and returned to Europe for good, determined to cash in on something far more glamorous and potentially lucrative, the Nietzsche business. Legally changing her name to Förster-Nietzsche (a contradictory combination of anti-Semitism and anti-anti-Semitism), she devoted her enormous reserves of energy, ruthless lack of scruple, and unlimited will to power to taking complete control of the Nietzsche business, to obtaining sole control over both his works and what remained of his life.

As much given to the 'warrior' mentality as her brother (though in a vulgar, un-'spiritualised' form), Elizabeth pursued a two-pronged strategy for taking control of his literary works, both published and unpublished. First, she had the idea of the Nietzsche Archive, which was to be a repository for documents and Nietzsche-memorabilia, a setting for special 'Nietzsche events' and, in general, a shrine for Nietzsche-worship. On November 18, 1893, she furnished and opened the Archive in two rooms on the ground floor of her mother's house. By the following year there were regular assemblies to hear readings from the sacred texts, including the still unpublished *Antichrist*, readings which were, however, sometimes disturbed by shouts and groans from above.

Since 1891, with Franziska's approval, Overbeck's advice, and Naumann's encouragement (the financial health of his firm having become heavily dependent on the Nietzsche texts),

Köselitz had been working hard to produce an edition of Nietzsche's complete works, each with an introduction by himself. Judging by the description he gave Overbeck of the general line of interpretation, these introductions were judicious, interesting, accurate, and, to a suitable degree, detached. 'Honoured teacher', he wrote Overbeck,

> in the introduction to *Zarathustra*...I've emphasized a particular aspect of Nietzsche's teaching – that man must first achieve *self-mastery*: master morality within the world of drives in the individual person. The rest – mastery of others – then happens by itself. The 'superman' I've made into a quality, an abstraction, though I know Nietzsche meant it otherwise. I want to leave it a decade until the reader has become accustomed to this conception before speaking of the great masters of discipline (*Zucht*) that Nietzsche thought necessary...I confess I have never found anything similar to what Nietzsche says on the question of rank: the nearest is Plato...Nietzsche wants to *organise a people* in a democratic age.[11]

This is precisely the communitarian, Plato-dependent reading of Nietzsche's philosophy I have been urging through this book and, coming from someone who knew his intentions better than anyone else, an important confirmation.

By the end of 1893, five volumes of these collected works had been printed. Unable to tolerate work not carried out under her oversight, however, Elizabeth instructed Köselitz that his services were no longer required. 'Who made *you* editor, then?' she demanded, and ordered all copies of his edition pulped. The following year she appointed in his place a young, piano-playing poet with a doctorate in philosophy and a fervent admiration of Nietzsche, the very good looking Fritz Kögel. He was instructed to begin work on a second attempt at a collected works.

Meanwhile there was the problem that, legally, it was Franziska, together with a figurehead cousin, who owned all the rights to the Nietzsche texts. Eventually, after a long campaign to wear down her resistance (during which Elizabeth stole the bundle of Nietzsche's letters to his mother), Franziska agreed to make over the rights to the Archive, that is, Elizabeth, for a down-payment of 30,000 marks and an annual royalty of 1,600 marks. Elizabeth's argument, which clinched the deal, was that a group of admirers had banded together to offer the 30,000 marks specifically in order to buy the rights for the Archive. In fact, the money was a bank loan arranged by Elizabeth which she had persuaded the 'admirers' to guarantee.

Initially, work on the new collected works proceeded smoothly, Elizabeth very much enjoying her collaboration with the attractive young Kögel. Soon, however, relations became strained. He began to see that she planned to suppress, and even forge, parts of the texts and began to make a private record of what they actually said. And from Elizabeth's point of view Kögel committed the ultimate sin of falling in love, not with her but with the daughter of a Weimar professor.

In the middle of 1896 Elizabeth decided to study philosophy with Rudolf Steiner, who was helping the Archive organise Nietzsche's library, in order to equip herself better for her philological task. Steiner (later the founder of anthroposophy) effectively gave her a failing grade, commenting that 'she lacks all understanding of fine, and even of crude, logical distinctions', and that 'even the remotest respect for facts and objectivity escapes her'.[12] He must, however, have concealed this opinion effectively, because Elizabeth offered him the collected-works editorship in place of Kögel. Wisely, Steiner refused. Kögel was sacked the following year and his edition abandoned. Finally, in 1898, a third effort at a collected works, known as the *Grossoktav* edition on account of the size of paper used, began under six editors, including Köselitz, whom, realising his unrivalled qualifications, Elizabeth had lured back to the Archive. Why Köselitz succumbed to the overtures of a woman he loathed is unclear. Possibly he hoped to prevent at least the worst perversions of the texts. If he did he was unsuccessful, since the edition, which appeared, volume by volume, between 1899 and 1913, was, as already noted, a philological disgrace.

* * *

Elizabeth's second strategic objective was to gain control of her brother's body, still a cultural object of considerable potency. Soon after her final return from Paraguay she began a campaign of persecution against her mother with this aim in mind. She tried to persuade medical authorities that the (in fact exemplary) care provided by Franziska and the devoted family doctor, Oscar Gutjahr, was inadequate, demanding that Nietzsche be delivered to her care in her now separate Naumburg residence. And then, in 1895, she tried to get the Basel pension stopped on grounds of alleged superfluity, knowing that without the pension Franziska would have no option but to hand over the booty. Overbeck put a stop to this particular machination, earning for himself and for anyone who had anything to do with Basel Elizabeth's undying hatred.

Worn out by her daughter's campaigns of persecution, Franziska became ill and two months later, on April 20, 1897 (Hitler's eighth birthday), died at the age of 71. Elizabeth had finally achieved her second strategic goal.

The Shrine in Weimar

As the home of Germany's greatest literary figure, Goethe, and now the home of the Goethe–Schiller Archive, Weimar, fifty kilometres from Naumburg, represented the heart of German *Kultur*. With her shrewd marketer's eye, Elizabeth had for some time seen that by relocating herself, the Archive, and the remnants of her brother to Weimar she could promote the idea that Nietzsche, too, belonged to that heart. The opportunity came through the generosity of Meta von Salis, who, in May 1897, purchased the Villa Silberblick (Silver-view), a four-storied house, half an hour's walk from the city centre, surrounded, at that time, by cornfields and possessing the panoramic view over the city implied by its name. Meta placed the house entirely at Elizabeth's disposal, both as a residence for her brother and herself and as a home for the Archive.

Running true to form, Elizabeth, immediately and without consultation, ordered extensive alterations and renovations to the house in order to make it suitable not merely for the Archive but also for the grand style in which she intended to live – all of them to be paid for by the owner of the house. Meta was furious and, after further recriminations, broke off all relations with Elizabeth the following year. In 1899 she sold the house to Elizabeth's cousin, Adalbert Oehler, who finally made it over to Elizabeth in 1902. Thereupon Elizabeth employed the Belgian Henry van der Velde to reconstruct the whole building, inside and out, in the art nouveau style that it has today (see Plate 30).

In August 1897, brother and sister moved into the Villa. Elizabeth now began to live in the style she felt she deserved. Visitors were met at the railway station by liveried servants, while she herself would use her carriage and a retinue of servants for even the shortest trip into town. (In the 1930s she welcomed many of the Nazi bigwigs, including Hitler himself, to the house (see Plate 32) – their stench somehow remains to this day. There is no trace of Nietzsche.)

Elizabeth set up the Archive as a shrine to her brother, with portraits, books, and manuscripts laid out as quasi-sacred relics. Especially favoured guests were escorted upstairs into the presence of the great thinker, now very thin, almost skeletal, his eyes receded deep into the sockets. He was paralysed down his right side, which he would rub ineffectually. One visitor remarked that when Elizabeth persuaded him to extend his hand, with its prominent green-violet veins and cool, waxy feel, it was more like shaking hands with a corpse than with a living person. Another visitor during the last year of Nietzsche's life was Richard Strauss, who had already gifted a score of his tone-poem *Also Sprach Zarathustra* to the Archive in 1896.

What the visitors saw was a man without qualities, a blank slate onto which they could project whatever fantasy they liked. Almost always, though, it was the prophet and seer, the Zarathustra–Nietzsche, they wanted to see: someone who was not mad but rather, as Ernst Bertram (one of those who would soon attempt to mythologise Nietzsche into a Nazi hero) wrote, had undergone an 'ascent into the mystic', a 'proud transition' to a higher state. Ernst Horneffer, one of the editors of the *Grossoktav* edition, saw 'a prophet of divine simplicity . . . I stood still, awestruck with reverence. The first thing I saw was the mighty forehead. There was something Goethean, Jupiter-like in its form', the form of a forehead belonging to a man who 'no longer denied his own greatness'.[13] Rudolf Steiner, too, succumbed to the quasi-religious mood:

> Whoever saw Nietzsche at the time [he wrote] as he reclined in his white, pleated robe [see Plate 31] – with the glance of a Brahman in his wide- and deep-set eyes beneath bushy eyebrows, with the nobility of his enigmatic, questioning face and the leonine, majestic carriage of the thinker's head – had the feeling that this man could not die, but that his eye would rest for all eternity upon mankind and the whole world of appearance in this unfathomable exultation.[14]

Elizabeth, of course, encouraged such mythologising – to be the sister and guardian of a demigod could hardly fail to be good for both self-esteem and business. In 1898 she commissioned a bust by a Friedrich Krause making visible Nietzsche's 'eternal eye' resting upon mankind's future, and a bronze relief by Curt Stoeving showing the philosopher's eager face bathed in light streaming from the future and with Zarathustra's eagle (the symbol of his 'pride' and also, conveniently, of Germany's) in the background. Fritz Schumacher designed a Nietzsche memorial showing, in his own words, 'a still, round temple on lonely, high ground with, on top, the genius of humanity with arms raised to the heavens and below dark gigantic forms bound in their chains',[15] a design which, unsurprisingly, won him an invitation to Weimar. Other objects were mass-produced for the tourist market: picture postcards showing the Archive together with Nietzsche's youthful head and, again, the eagle, and a plaster model of Nietzsche sitting in an armchair, designed for the mantelpiece.

Nietzsche's Death

Nietzsche suffered a stroke in the summer of 1898 and a more serious one in May of the following year. On August 25th, 1900, eight months into the century[16] that would fulfil the direst of his fears for Germany and the world, he died. Köselitz (who now insisted on being called by the pseudonym Nietzsche had given him, 'Peter Gast') closed his eyes, although the right one kept opening so that, even in the coffin, the white of the eye and the bottom of the iris was visible under the eyelashes. A ceremony was held in the Archive with an important, and self-important, art-historian, Kurt Breisig, being wheeled in from Berlin by the Archive's leader to deliver the eulogy. Fritz Schumacher takes up the tale:

> An obvious feeling commanded that the mood of the hour be captured in a few solemn, deeply felt words . . . Instead, the speaker pulled out a thick manuscript and began to read. Since he had trouble holding his manuscript, a lecture-stand was improvised for him out of Frau Förster's sewing box. And now he mercilessly read to us a cultural-historical analysis of the Nietzsche phenomenon. Seldom have I experienced a grimmer moment. Scholarship pursued this man to the grave. If he had revived he would have thrown the speaker out of the window and chased us out of the temple.[17]

Contrary to his wishes – he had written Elizabeth in 1886 that he wished to be buried on the Chasté peninsula in Sils Maria[18] – Nietzsche was buried between his parents by the church in Röcken next to which he had been born. The church bells were rung and the funeral oration, delivered by Köselitz, now fully absorbed into the mythologising business, ended with the words 'Peace be with thine ashes! Holy be thy name to all future generations!'

When Elizabeth died in 1935, Hitler, who had been providing financial support to the Archive, attended the funeral, together with several high-ranking Nazi officials. In death she inflicted the last of the many indignities she had visited on her brother. On her orders, he was dug up and placed to one side so that *she* could be placed between the parents. When it came to power politics Elizabeth won every time.

28

Nietzsche's Madness

WHAT WAS wrong with Nietzsche? Why did he go mad? The question has been much discussed, partly by members of the medical profession who have taken to diagnosing the great dead as a recreation, and partly by Nietzsche scholars. The latter usually have a vested interest in the outcome. Broadly, if they are admirers of Nietzsche, they favour a purely physiological diagnosis – usually the traditional one of syphilis – while if they are opponents they favour a psychological one. If, that is, Nietzsche's madness was the product of psychological factors arising from within his personality, it becomes possible to make the argument that his philosophy is tainted by those same factors; that it is, as the reviewer of *Beyond Good and Evil* claimed (p. 406 above), 'pathological'. Opponents generally wish to open up this possibility, admirers to close it down.

Nietzsche suffered, we have seen, time after time, awful bouts of depression that sometimes brought him close to suicide (p. 357 above). In June 1887 he describes himself as having been depressed for an entire year,[1] a condition (Winston Churchill's 'black dog') which he describes as a worse form of suffering than all his physical ailments, 'the worst penalty there is for life on earth'.[2] Yet at other times he experienced moments of great elation, elation coloured by touches of grandeur, and increasingly by megalomania. As early as 1884, the 'other' Nietzsche presents himself: the 'superman' lurking within mild-mannered, bespectacled Friedrich Nietzsche, to whom has been vouchsafed the secret thought of the eternal return, a thought that will 'split history into two halves' and reveal Jesus a 'superficial' figure in comparison with its possessor (p. 389 above). And perhaps the 'other' Nietzsche manifested himself already in 1869, in the threat to terminate the friendship with Deussen on account of the latter's inadequate realisation of the honour of having a university professor for a friend (p. 79 above). (The special elevation of professors in Germanic culture is indicated by the phrase 'God-professor'.) What this oscillation – Lou Salomé observed that Nietzsche was subject to 'violent mood swings' (p. 349 above) – calls to mind is the label 'manic-depressive'; in more anodyne language, 'bipolar disorder'. To the extent that it is plausible to think of Nietzsche as having been, for many years, at least incipiently manic-depressive, 'almost permanent habitation of the manic phase of manic depression' seems an appropriate description of his final weeks in Turin.

Here, courtesy of Oliver Sacks,[3] are some descriptions of the mania of certified manic-depressives (generally they come from the patients themselves, though occasionally from their therapists): 'He started to see himself as a messiah'; 'I believed I could stop cars and paralyze their forces by merely standing in the middle of the highway with my arms outspread' (this comes from the poet Robert Lowell); 'intoxication'; 'the apotheosis of health'; 'a super-positive state'; 'you're feeling [so]...well, you must be ill'; 'the release of a deep, previously suppressed self'; 'not only did everything make perfect sense, but it all began to fit into a marvellous kind of cosmic relatedness'; 'My sense of enchantment with the laws of the natural world caused me to fizz over [at]...how beautiful it all was'.

Three themes run through these descriptions: pantheistic ecstasy, the sense of the world as a perfect totality; believing oneself to be a messiah; and the possession of the causal power to alter the world at will (stopping cars). These themes exactly characterise Nietzsche's condition in his final weeks in Turin. He was constantly euphoric, believed the world to be 'beyond good and evil' because it was completely good. He believed himself a messiah – the bringer of 'glad tidings' (p. 530 above). And, having 'become God', he believed himself to possess telekinetic powers capable, for example, of deposing the crowned heads of Europe. All in all, therefore, 'bipolar mania' seems a plausible description of the initial phase of his madness.

The mania, as we have seen, did not last. Within a few weeks he began to display symptoms of serious psychosis; hallucinations, paranoid delusions, grossly disorganised behaviour, incoherent thought and speech (though interspersed with coherent fragments of memory), catatonic withdrawal degenerating, eventually, into a vegetative state. It is commonly assumed that psychotic symptoms such as these represent the point at which a diagnosis of bipolar disorder must give way to one of schizophrenia. This would lead to the idea of a dual psychiatric diagnosis: that Nietzsche's condition is to be described as one of manic depression degenerating, after 1889, into schizophrenia. Such, indeed, is Dr. Richard Schain's diagnosis.[4] In fact, however, modern psychiatric thinking recognises psychotic, schizophrenia-like episodes as, in many cases, indicative not of schizophrenia but of bipolar disorder. And counting against Schain's diagnosis is the fact that whereas Nietzsche's psychotic symptoms appeared only in his forties, those of schizophrenics typically appear in the late teens or early twenties. Probably the most plausible description of Nietzsche's condition is, therefore, 'bipolar disorder with, in its later stages, psychotic features'. The question arises, however, as to whether this ought to be regarded as a diagnosis or merely as a description; whether there might not have been a physical pathology underlying the psychological symptoms. Let us consider the options.

* * *

The original and still, I think, most widely supported story is that Nietzsche suffered from syphilis. This, as we saw, was Wille's diagnosis in the Basel clinic, a diagnosis repeated by Binswanger in Jena. Both psychiatrists decided that Nietzsche was suffering from 'general paresis [partial paralysis] of the insane'; in other words, dementia caused by neurosyphilis, the form of tertiary syphilis in which the spirochetes (bacteria) attack the brain. Because syphilis was extremely widespread (the HIV of the day), this was the nineteenth century's default diagnosis for middle-aged men suffering from dementia. But it was by no means the only possible cause.

Recent critiques have revealed at least six weaknesses in the syphilis diagnosis. First, the fact that Nietzsche suffered from chorioretinitis – inflammation of the retina – was taken to have been caused by syphilis, which it indeed can be. But it can also be caused by a wide variety of other conditions, including simple myopia, from which, we know, Nietzsche had suffered since childhood. Second, at the time of his admission to the Jena clinic, Nietzsche exhibited no physical tremors, an almost universal symptom of 'paretic' syphilis. Third, though severe migraines can be a symptom of tertiary syphilis, they typically begin only a few weeks, or at most months, before a general collapse. Nietzsche's, however, began while he was still a schoolboy. Fourth, for someone with paretic syphilis, Nietzsche lived an extraordinarily long time, eleven years, after the Turin collapse. In one late-nineteenth-century study, out of 244 patients with the disease, 229 had died within five years of diagnosis, 242 within nine. Fifth, whereas paretic syphilis affects both hemispheres equally, a number of Nietzsche's physical symptoms (which we will come to in a moment) suggest a process confined to the right hemisphere. Finally, there is Dr. Eiser's report that although Nietzsche admitted to gonorrhoea infections from his student years, he explicitly denied ever having contracted syphilis (p. 240 above). Given his frankness about the one, it is unlikely he would have dissembled about the other. He might, of course, have had syphilis without knowing it, but given his constant and minute observation of his own condition, this seems unlikely.

Given all these difficulties it is worth attending to an alternative diagnosis proposed by Dr. Leonard Sax.[5] Since his teenage years, Sax suggests, Nietzsche had probably suffered from a meningioma, a non-malignant brain tumour positioned on the right optic nerve.

Psychiatric symptoms, which may range from mania to dementia, Sax explains, are common in patients with such tumours. Their development, he claims, is slow but inexorable, and sometimes may stop completely for a number of years. Headaches are also common, typically severe and intermittent, and are often confused with migraines. A tumour of the right optic nerve beneath the right frontal lobe of the brain would account for the right-sided predilection of Nietzsche's headaches, recorded independently by two doctors in 1889, for the larger size of the right pupil that his mother noted at the age of five and for the fact that the right eye bulged more than the left (the reason, clearly, that his right eyelid refused to stay properly shut as he lay in his coffin (p. 558 above)). At a certain point, Sax concludes, the growth of the tumour would have led to a de facto frontal lobotomy, which would account for the lapse into a quasi-vegetative apathy of Nietzsche's final years.

We have, then, three possibilities before us: the syphilis story, Sax's brain tumour, and the possibility that Nietzsche's condition was a *purely* psychiatric one, manic depression with late-developing psychotic features. In light of the recent critique, syphilis seems the least likely of the options. Sax's brain tumour is an elegant attempt to account for all of Nietzsche's health problems, mental and physical, in one fell swoop: the lifelong headaches, the mania, and the eventual apathy, all caused by the brain tumour. Unfortunately, however, it seems that Sax's elegant diagnosis – he is a medical generalist rather than a specialist ophthalmologist – is inconsistent with basic ophthalmological facts. For, first, meningiomas in childhood, as postulated by Sax, are actually extremely rare. Second, when they grow, they grow, contra Sax, quickly and aggressively (unlike meningiomas in adulthood, which may indeed grow slowly and insidiously). Third, they do not produce a change in pupil size unless they also affect the eye muscles. But in that case one would expect Nietzsche's right eyeball to have been, since childhood, turned permanently down and out and the eyelid to droop. But this was never the case. Finally, had the protrusion of Nietzsche's right eye been caused by a tumour one would have expected it to increase with the increasing size of the tumour. But the many photographs taken throughout his life provide no evidence that this was the case.[6]

It seems, then, that Sax's brain tumour diagnosis is no more likely to be true than the syphilis story. Because the theoretical possibility of exhuming Nietzsche's body and performing an autopsy using the latest medical technology will never be realised, we will never know for certain whether his mental condition was caused by an underlying physical pathology. Nonetheless, the most plausible conclusion appears to be that Nietzsche's madness was, in fact, a purely psychological condition.

This means that we cannot avoid facing up to the issue of the continuity between his philosophy and his madness: the continuity, observed earlier, between the Dionysian side of his philosophy and the 'Dionysian' character of the 'crazy letters' and of his final days in Turin. Does the continuity disclose his philosophy as, in major respects, 'pathological'? Does madness infect the foundations of Nietzsche's philosophy?

* * *

Nietzsche's philosophy places an unusually high value on ecstasy: a state of mind in which one transcends one's everyday identity while at the same time finding the world 'perfect' and so being able to will its 'eternal return'. This valuing of the ecstatic goes right back to the beginning, to the very first section of *The Birth of Tragedy* with its celebration of the state in which 'all the rigid hostile barriers' between man and man dissolve so that, 'singing and dancing', one feels oneself to 'belong to a higher community' (p. 128 above). What is important about this description of the Dionysian state is that it is one we can all recognise and empathise with. For it is, as I pointed out, the 'rock-concert' or 'football-crowd' feeling. Since we all encounter the Dionysian state in ourselves, we are in no position to detect anything 'mad' in the Dionysianism that appears in Nietzsche's philosophy.

What, however, we cannot recognise in our own experience is the belief that we can, at will, control any aspect of the world we choose. But that is a salient characteristic of bipolar mania and of Nietzsche's final days in Turin. There is therefore, it seems to me, a clear line of demarcation between the Dionysianism of the philosophy and the mad Dionysianism of his final days. Though Nietzsche's philosophy was likely produced by a manic-depressive (as, probably, were the works of Plato, Newton, Mozart, Hölderlin, Coleridge, Schumann, Byron, Van Gogh, Georg Cantor, Winston Churchill, Sylvia Plath, John Lennon, Leonard Cohen and many other great human beings), there is nothing 'pathological' about it – apart from the views on women.

Chronology

1844	*October 15:* N is born, first child of Karl Ludwig and Franziska Nietzsche (née Oehler), in Röcken, near Lützen, near Leipzig.
1846	*July 10:* Elizabeth born.
1849	*July 30:* Father dies of a brain disease, aged 35.
1850	*January 4:* Death of N's brother, Ludwig Joseph, aged 2. *Early April:* Moves to Naumburg. Enrolls in town primary school.
1851	*Spring:* Transfers to Weber's private school, where friendship with Krug and Pinder begins. All three transfer to Cathedral Grammar School in 1854.
1858	*October:* Family moves to 18 Weingarten, where Franziska will remain until her death in 1897. N begins to attend Pforta School.
1859	Meets Paul Deussen.
1860	*July 25:* N, Krug and Pinder found *Germania* society. Schopenhauer dies in September. Beginning of friendship with Paul Deussen.
1861	*January–February:* Suffers very bad headaches. *March:* Confirmed. Discovers Wagner's *Tristan* in this or the following year. *October 19:* Calls Hölderlin 'my favourite poet'.
1863	*September:* First signs of N's moustache.
1864	*September:* Becomes friends with Carl von Gersdorff. Graduation and departure from Pforta. Rhineland holiday with Deussen. *October:* Begins studies in Bonn; joins *Franconia* fraternity.
1865	*February:* Decides to switch from theology to philology. Visit to the Cologne brothel. *October 19:* Enrols at university in Leipzig, where Rohde will become N's closest friend. *November:* Discovers Schopenhauer's *The World as Will and Representation*.
1866	*Summer:* Discovers Lange's *History of Materialism*.
1867	*August:* Hiking trip in Bohemian forest with Rohde. *Summer:* Becomes increasingly enthusiastic about Wagner, mainly on account of *Die Meistersinger*. *September:* Begins military service in Naumburg.
1868	*March:* Chest wound in riding accident, which terminates military service in June. *October:* Returns to studies in Leipzig. *November 8:* First meeting with Wagner.
1869	*February 12:* Appointed professor of classical philology at Basel. *April 19:* Takes up residence in Basel. *May 17:* First of twenty-three visits to Wagners in Tribschen. *July 1:* Moves into Schützgraben 45 (the 'Poison Hut' and later 'Baumann's Cave').

1870   *April:* Franz Overbeck moves into Schützgraben 45.
        July 19: French parliament declares war on Prussia.
        August 13: Arrives in Erlangen for training as medical orderly.
        August 23 : Sets off for front, passing through recent battlefields. Horrified by body
        parts on Wörth battlefield.
        August 25: Wagner marries Cosima.
        September 2: N at the front, which has now moved to Ars-sur-Moselle, near Metz.
        Three days in closed railway wagon accompanying wounded back to Karlsruhe.
        Catches dysentery and diphtheria and is hospitalised for a week on return to
        Erlangen.
        September 14–October 21: Recuperation in Naumburg.
        November: Teaching again in Basel; reads Wagner's *Beethoven* essay; audits
        Burckhardt's lectures on historiography.
        Christmas Day: Present at first performance of *Siegfried Idyll* on Tribschen staircase
        as birthday present for Cosima.

1871   *January 18:* Second German Reich declared and William I crowned Kaiser.
        February 28: End of Franco-Prussian war.

1872   *January 2: The Birth of Tragedy* appears with Fritzsch.
        January 16: Begins lecture series *On the Future of Our Educational Institutions*,
        which runs until March 23. Declines offer of chair in Greifswald during this month.
        April 22: Wagner leaves Tribschen to take up residence in Bayreuth.
        May 22: Together with Rohde and von Gersdorff, attends laying of foundation
        stone of Festspielhaus in Bayreuth. Meets Malwida von Meysenbug, a close friend
        of the Wagners.
        Late May–September: Rohde's review of *The Birth of Tragedy* and Wilamowitz's
        critique. Long conversations with Burckhardt arising out of the latter's lectures on
        Greek cultural history.

1873   *Spring:* Begins intensive reading of books on natural science, including African
        Spir's *Thought and Reality*.
        May: First meeting with Paul Rée, invited to Basel for the summer by N's friend
        Heinrich Romundt.
        August 8: First *Untimely Meditation, David Strauss, the Confessor and the Writer*,
        appears.
        November: N's *Summons to the Germans* (to support the Bayreuth project) rejected by
        the Wagnerians.

1874   *January 15:* Appointed dean of Basel's faculty of humanities.
        February 22: Second *Untimely Meditation, On the Uses and Disadvantages of History
        for Life*, appears with Fritzsch.
        July 9: Headhunted by publisher Ernst Schmeitzner.
        August: Appears with Brahms's *Song of Triumph* in Wahnfried, the Wagners' house
        in Bayreuth. Wagner furious.
        October 15: Third *Untimely Meditation, Schopenhauer as Educator,* appears with
        Schmeitzner.
        December: Completes, but does not publish, *Philosophy in the Tragic Age of the
        Greeks.*

1875   *January–mid-July:* Works on *We Philologists* but never completes it.
        July 15–August 12: 'Cure' in Steinabad.
        Autumn: Moves to Spalenthorweg 48 with Elizabeth as housekeeper. Reads Rée's
        Psychological Observations.
        November: First meeting with Heinrich Köselitz ('Peter Gast'), who comes to Basel
        to attend N's lectures.

1876   *January:* Relieved of Pädegogium teaching due to poor health. Headaches make
        university teaching difficult.
        February: Beginning of friendship with Rée.
        April 11: Marriage proposal to Mathilde Trampedach rejected.
        July 10: Fourth *Untimely Meditation, Richard Wagner at Bayreuth*, published by
        Schmeitzner. French translation by Marie Baumgartner appears in February
        1877.
        July 23: Final visit to Bayreuth to attend first Bayreuth Festival. Suddenly leaves on
        August 4 for Klingenbrunn, where he begins work on *Human, All-Too-Human.*
        August 8: Overbeck marries Ida Rothpletz.
        August 12–26: Back in Bayreuth for first performance of *Ring* cycle. Meets
        Reinhardt von Seydlitz; flirts with Louise Ott.
        October 27: Arrives in Sorrento, where he will remain at the Villa Rubinacci, rented
        by Malwida von Meysenbug, until May 8, 1877.

1877   *June 11–September 1:* Works on *Human, All-Too-Human* in Rosenlaui.
        Meets Croom Robertson, editor of *Mind.*
        October 5: Examination by Dr. Otto Eiser and ophthalmologist Gustav Krüger in
        Frankfurt.

1878   *January:* Receives libretto of *Parsifal.*
        May 7: Human, All-Too-Human appears with Schmeitzner.

1879   *March 20: Assorted Opinions and Maxims* appears with Schmeitzner as an 'Appendix'
        to *Human, All-Too-Human.*
        May 2: Resigns from Basel University on grounds of ill health.
        June 21–September 16: In St. Moritz. Health reaches lowest point.
        Works on *The Wanderer and His Shadow*, which appears with Schmeitzner on
        December 18.

1880   *February–March:* Works on *Dawn* in Riva del Garda.
        March–July: With Köselitz in Venice.
        July–August: Depressed in Marienbad.
        November: First winter in Genoa, where he remains until the following May.

1881   *July 4–October 1:* First summer in Sils Maria.
        July 8: Dawn appears with Schmeitzner.
        Early August: Thought of eternal return occurs to N.
        October 2: Second winter in Genoa, where he will stay until the end of March 1882.
        November 27: Hears *Carmen* for the first time at Genoa's Politeana theatre.

1882   *January–March:* Working on *The Gay Science*. Rée visits, bringing a typewriter.
        March 29–April 21: In Messina, Sicily.
        End of April: In Rome. Meets Lou Salomé. Proposes marriage to her, via Rée.
        Rejected.

First half of May: With Lou on Sacro Monte. A possible kiss. Proposes marriage to her again in Lion Garden in Lucerne. Again rejected. 'Whip' photograph taken.

First week in June: *Idylls from Messina* appears in Schmeitzner's monthly magazine.

June 16-17: One day in Berlin in vain attempt to meet up with Lou.

June 25–August 27: In Tautenburg. Lou and Elizabeth both there, August 7–26. Lou presents N with her 'Prayer to Life', which he immediately sets to music, using melody of his 1874 'Hymn to Friendship'.

July 26: First performance of *Parsifal*.

August 26: *The Gay Science* (Books I–IV) appears with Schmeitzner.

September 7: Leaves Naumburg for Leipzig, having quarrelled with his mother, who is outraged by the N–Rée–Lou affair as reported by Elizabeth.

October: Final meeting with Lou and Rée.

November 23: Via Genoa and Santa Marguerita Ligure to Rapallo, where he settles until the end of the following February.

1883   *February 13:* Wagner dies in Venice.

February 24: N returns to old apartment building in Genoa.

June 18–September 5: Second summer in Sils Maria.

End of August: *Zarathustra Part I* appears with Schmeitzner.

September: Elizabeth announced her engagement to Bernhard Förster.

December 2: First winter in Nice, where he will stay until April 20, 1884.

1884   *January:* *Zarathustra Part II* appears with Schmeitzner.

April: *Zarathustra Part III* appears with Schmeitzner. Resa von Schirnhofer visits N in Nice.

June: Meets Meta von Salis in Zürich.

July 18–September 25: Third summer in Sils Maria. Meets the two Emily Fynns.

October: Meets Helene Druscowitz in Zürich.

November 28: Second winter in Nice; stays until April 8, 1885.

1885   *First week in May:* *Zarathustra Part IV* privately printed by Naumann at N's expense.

June 7–mid-September: Fourth summer in Sils Maria. First plans for *Will to Power*.

September–October: In Naumburg, last meeting with Elizabeth while sane.

November 11: Third winter in Nice; stays until beginning of May 1886.

1886   *February:* The Försters set off for South America.

June 30: Fifth summer in Sils Maria; stays until September 25. Meets Helen Zimmern.

August 4: *Beyond Good and Evil* appears, printed and published by Naumann at N's expense.

August 5: Fritzsch takes over unsold copies and rights to N's works from Schmeitzner.

September 25–October 20: In Ruta Lugure. Writes new preface to *The Gay Science*.

October 20: Fourth winter in Nice; will stay until April 2, 1887.

October 31: New edition of *The Birth of Tragedy* (prefaced by *Attempt at a Self-Criticism*) appears with Fritzsch. New, two-volume edition of *Human, All-Too-Human* (incorporating *Assorted Opinions and Maxims* and *The Wanderer and His Shadow*) appears with Fritzsch.

End of December: *Zarathustra Parts I–III* appear as a single volume with Fritzsch.

1887   *February 24:* Nice earthquake.
       June 12: Fifth summer in Sils Maria; will remain until September 19.
       June 24: New edition of *Dawn* appears with Fritzsch. New edition of *The Gay Science* (including the new Book V) appears with Fritzsch.
       October 20: Hymn to Life (for choir and orchestra) appears with Fritzsch.
       October 23: Fifth winter in Nice, where N will stay until April 8, 1888.
       November 16: Genealogy of Morals appears with Naumann at N's expense.

1888   *April 5:* First stay in Turin, where N will remain until June 5.
       April 10–May 5: Brandes's lectures on N in Copenhagen.
       June 6: Seventh and last summer in Sils Maria; will remain until September 20. von Salis and Kaftan observe no signs of madness.
       September 21: In Turin; will remain until January 9.
       September 22: The Wagner Case appears with Naumann.
       December: Collapse into madness.

1889   *January 10–17:* In the mental institution in Basel.
       January 18: In the mental institution in Jena, where he will remain until March 24, 1890.
       January 24: Twilight of the Idols appears with Naumann.
       February: Nietzsche contra Wagner appears with Naumann.
       June 3: Bernhard Förster commits suicide.

1890   *March 24–May 12:* In a private residence in Jena.
       May 12: With his mother in Weingarten 18 in Naumburg, where N will remain until July 19, 1897.

1891   Köselitz begins complete edition of N's works.

1892   *March: Zarathustra Part IV* appears with Naumann.

1893   *October:* Elizabeth orders Köselitz to abandon his edition of N's works. New edition begun under editorship of Fritz Kögel. Elizabeth begins Archive in mother's house.

1894   *November: The Antichrist* appears with Naumann.

1895   *April:* First volume of Elizabeth's biography of N published by Naumann.
       December: Elizabeth in sole control of N's works.

1896   *August 1:* Archive moves to Weimar. Rooms rented with financial support from Meta von Salis. Archive will move to Villa Silberblick later in year.

1897   *April 20:* Franziska dies. Second volume of Elizabeth's biography of N appears with Naumann during this spring.
       June: Kögel dismissed as editor of collected works.
       July 20: In Villa Silberblick, Weimar, where N will remain until death.

1898   *Grossoktav* edition of collected works begun under six editors, including Köselitz.

1900   *August 25:* Nietzsche dies.

1901   *October 28:* Paul Rée dies, aged 52.

1903   *April 23:* Malwida von Meysenbug dies, aged 87.

1905   *June 26:* Overbeck dies, aged 68.

1930   *April 1:* Cosima dies.

1935   *November 8:* Elizabeth dies, aged 92.

1937   *February 5:* Lou Salomé dies, aged 75.

Notes

1. DA CAPO

1. EH 1 3. (see KSA 14 p. 472).
2. TI 1 44.
3. KGW 1.1 4 [77].
4. EH 1 7.
5. YN p. 32.
6. Ibid.
7. KGW 1.1 4 [77].
8. YN p. 15.
9. YN p. 16.
10. EH 1 3. This is actually an early version of the passage in question. In December 1888 Nietzsche rewrote it to include serious abuse of his sister, a revision that remained suppressed until the 1960s.
11. KGB 1.1 296.
12. KGW 1.2 10 [10].
13. KGW 1.1 4 [77].
14. Ibid.
15. YN p. 15.
16. It is notable that the very first fragment preserved in Nietzsche's literary estate is a sketch for a play, written at the age of ten, in which a king, as the hero, faced a riot (KGW 1.1 1 [1]). In a fragment preserved from his eighteenth year, Nietzsche writes that monarchical states always do best in everyday affairs and particularly in war. The Greeks understood this by making Zeus reign over all the other gods; the might of the Persian Empire came about not because the Persians were particularly clever, but because of their intense devotion to the king (KGW 1.2 10 [33]). In 1883, commenting on the decadence of Western modernity, he writes that 'the age of kings is past since the people are no longer worthy of them: they do not *want* to see the symbol of their ideals in kings, but a means for their profit' (WP 725). In his late thought, as we shall see, Plato's 'philosopher-king' looms large.
17. KGW 1.1 4 [77].
18. KGB 111.3 652.
19. KGW 1.1 4 [9].
20. KGW 1.1 4 [77]. Nietzsche says that Joseph died 'at the end of 1850', but his memory is at fault here. Joseph actually died in February of that year (see J I p. 47).
21. KGW 1.1 4 [77].
22. GM 11 22.
23. TI vi 3.
24. EH 1 1.
25. AOM 17.
26. KGW 1.1 4 [77].
27. YN pp. 21–2.
28. KGB 11.3 364.
29. YN p. 22.

30. KGW 1.1 4.
31. YN p. 24.
32. KGW 1.1 4 [77].
33. Ibid.
34. Ibid.
35. YN p. 46.
36. KGW 1.1 4 [77].
37. Mendelssohn's incidental music to Shakespeare's eponymous play.
38. KGW 1.1 4 [77]. Elves 'dancing in airy rings' is a quotation from Schiller's 'The Dance'.
39. Z 1 14.
40. KGW 1.1 4 [77].
41. Z 1 14.
42. Ibid.
43. KGW 1.1 4 [77].
44. YN p. 30.
45. KGW 1.1 4 [77].
46. YN p. 42.
47. KGW 1.1 4 [77].
48. YN p. 25.
49. KGW 1.1 4 [77].
50. Ibid.
51. Ibid.
52. WS 350.
53. YN pp. 33–4.
54. YN p. 25.

2. PFORTA

1. YN pp. 74–5.
2. Ibid.
3. YN p. 107.
4. J I p. 66.
5. YN p. 75.
6. Janz's analogy. See J I p. 66.
7. KGW 1.2 6 [77].
8. Hayman (1980) p. 28.
9. KGW 1.2 6 [77].
10. KGB 1.1 21, 22.
11. KGW 1.2 6 [77].
12. KGB 1.1 55.
13. KGW 1.2 6 [77].
14. KGB 1.1 257.
15. KGB 1.1 69.
16. KGW1.2 6 [77].
17. UM II 7.
18. YN pp. 107–8. Unless otherwise noted, emphasis is in the original text.
19. D 195.
20. The name was probably suggested by that of the university fraternity in Jena to which Fritz's uncle by marriage, Emil Schenk, belonged. It has obviously nationalistic connotations.
21. YN pp. 91–3.
22. Ibid.
23. Or possibly at the end of 1860. See KGB 1.1 To Nietzsche 33.
24. YN p. 98.

25. Listed by Nietzsche at KGW 1.2 13 [28].
26. KGB 1.2 Reply 41.
27. Deussen (1901) p. 4.
28. KGB 1.1 230.
29. KGB 1.1 288.
30. Deussen (1901) p. 4.
31. KGB 1.1 343.
32. KGB 1.1 324.
33. KGB 1.1 To Nietzsche 56.
34. KGB 1.1 350.
35. EH II 1.
36. KGB 1.1 353.
37. KGB 1.1 352.
38. Schlechta III p. 151.
39. YN 110.
40. Kohler (2002).
41. J I pp. 125–6.
42. KGB 1.1 217. That he disclosed this in a letter *to his mother* and asked for a photograph of her to add to the collection indicates that no guilty secret was involved.
43. C p. 594.
44. J I pp. 124–5.
45. KGW 1.2 10 [3].
46. KGW 1.2 13 [6].
47. GS 58.
48. HH 153.
49. KGB 1.1 301.
50. J I p. 103.
51. Feuerbach (1855).
52. TI IX 5.
53. KGW 1.1 4 [77].
54. Ibid.
55. KGB 1.1 203.
56. HKG II p. 172.
57. Not to be confused with his tutor, Robert Buddensieg.
58. KGB 1.1 435.
59. HH I 150.
60. HKG II p. 114.
61. HKG II pp. 371–4. Note from April–May 1864.
62. HKG pp. 368–9. Note from April–May 1864.
63. Ibid.
64. Heidegger (1977 onwards) Vol. 39, pp. 290–4.
65. Z. An allusion not noticed by Parkes is the motto at the beginning of Part III of the work: 'He who climbs the highest mountains laughs at all tragedies real and imaginary (*Trauer-Spiele und Trauer-Ernste*)'. '*Trauer-Spiel*' reappears in *Beyond Good and Evil*: 'There are heights of the soul from whose vantage point even tragedy stops having tragic effects' (BGE 30). Given that Empedocles, standing on the summit of Mt. Etna, before throwing himself to his mortal death in the crater believed himself to have become immortal, this probably echoes the title of Hölderlin's *Der Tod des Empedocles: Fragmente eines Trauerspiels*.
66. C p. 308.
67. Wilhelm is interested in Hölderlin already in November 1858 (KGB 1.1 To Nietzsche 24), but not until August 1861 does Fritz show any interest (KGB 1.1 252). In October 1861 he writes from Pforta asking his mother to send him the biography of Hölderlin (Wilhelm Neumann's *Moderne Klassiker. Deutsche Literature-Geschichte der neuern Zeit in Biographien, Kritiken und Proben: Friedrich Hölderlin*) that is sitting in his bookcase at home and which

he needs for the essay he is writing (KGB 1.1 281), an essay completed on the nineteenth of that month.

68. Through the biography mentioned in the previous footnote.

69. I owe these parallels to Thomas Brobjer's useful *Beiträge zur Quellenforschung: Abhandlungen* (Brobjer 2001).

70. It turns out that about half of this essay is, as we would now describe it, 'plagiarized' from the biography of Hölderlin mentioned in endnote 67 above. It appears that parts of this work were, in turn, 'plagiarized' from works by C. T. Schwab and Alexander Jung. Nietzsche's youthful notebooks are full of passages copied verbatim from other authors. In his maturity he often 'plagiarized' – the Bible, Schopenhauer, Hölderlin, and, frequently and inaccurately, himself. But to speak of plagiarism here is anachronistic. The idea of 'intellectual property' had no purchase at all anywhere in Europe until the Bern Convention of 1886, so that unacknowledged borrowing was commonplace at the time. In Germany it was commonplace until the middle of the twentieth century. The elevation of plagiarism from a venal to a mortal sin is a very recent phenomenon, a product of the absorption of, in particular, the university into postmodern, Western capitalism. I am told that the concept still does not exist in Japanese culture nor, one would guess, in China. The only question that concerns us here is whether the 'plagiarism' might indicate that the essay was written as a tedious chore, so that little or no weight is to be placed on the description of Hölderlin as 'my favourite poet'. But the clear answer is that it does not. For, quite apart from the likelihood of personal identification already alluded to, Nietzsche's letters of the time suggest that he was fully engaged with the composition of the essay. Writing to his friend Rohde on September 3, 1869, moreover, he refers again to Hölderlin as, among the poets, 'my favourite from my time at secondary school'. Nietzsche re-read Hölderlin in the 1870s, referring to him as 'the glorious Hölderlin', and recommended him, and particularly *Hyperion*, to his student Louis Kelterborn (see the Brobjer article mentioned in endnote 69).

71. KGW 1.2 12 [1].

72. BT 10.

73. These excerpts from *Hyperion* are all taken from Hölderlin (1965).

74. KGW 1.2 13 [6].

75. HKG II pp. 359–63.

76. HKG II pp. 336–42.

77. See Chapter 1 endnote 16. Notable in this remark is the habit Nietzsche never abandoned of basing political conclusions on evidence drawn entirely from the ancient world. It hardly ever occurs to him that different and perhaps sounder conclusions might be drawn from modern history. This of course reflects the fact that, within the walls of Pforta, classical antiquity was the 'real' world, the world without the walls something of a dream.

78. KGW 1.2 12 [9].

79. KGW 1.2 [12A.1]. Nietzsche is here paraphrasing an historian called Guizot. But he would not have 'plagiarized' into his notebooks – which he did out of interest rather than in relation to any school assignment – had he not found the sentiments impressive. And as we have seen, they correspond to those expressed in the lecture on Napoleon, which itself is based on notes from Menzel's *History of the Last Forty Years* (see KGW 1.2 12A [9]).

80. KGW 1.2 [12A 6]. These notes are again copied – from Theodor Mundt's *History of Society* – but again the fact that the copying was voluntary indicates Fritz's strong sympathy with Mundt's sentiments.

81. It is sometimes suggested that Nietzsche's school-leaving essay on Theognis of Megra, a poet-aristocrat of sixth-century Greece who fought against an attempted popular revolution, anticipated the rejection of democracy in Nietzsche's mature writings. As Curt Janz points out, however, what Nietzsche says is simply that although 'Theognis designated the nobility as "the good" and the party of the people as "the bad (*schlecht*)"', his stance simply represented 'a typical aristocrat who sees his special privileges threatened by an oncoming popular revolution'. He expresses no admiration for Theognis; on the contrary, he calls him a 'Junker' with a sad and somewhat confused longing for the past (J I pp. 123–4).

82. KGW 1.2 12 [9].
83. KGW 1.2 12A.
84. KGW 1.2 9 [2].
85. KGW 1.2 6 [65–6].
86. HKG II pp. 343–4.
87. KGW 1.2 13 [7].

3. BONN

1. KGB 1.2 471.
2. KGB 1.2 446.
3. KGB 1.2 445.
4. Hayman (1980) p. 59.
5. KGB 1.2 446.
6. KGB 1.2 448.
7. Ibid.
8. KGB 1.2 470.
9. KGB 1.3 To Nietzsche 95.
10. KGB 1.2 467.
11. S III p. 128.
12. Hayman (1980) p. 58.
13. KGB 1.2 449.
14. KGB 1.2 470.
15. KGB 1.2 449.
16. KGB 1.2 453.
17. KGB 1.3 To Nietzsche 96.
18. Hayman (1980) p. 62.
19. JN p. 113.
20. J I p. 138.
21. Z IV 16.
22. KGB 1.2 469.
23. J I pp. 137–8.
24. Mann (1947) p. 359ff.
25. KGB 1.2 480.
26. KGW 1.4 29 [1].
27. KGW 1.4 35 [1].
28. KGW 1.4 29 [1].
29. KGW 1.4 36 [1].
30. KGB 1.3 To Nietzsche 86.
31. KGB 1.3 To Nietzsche 87.
32. JN p. 135.
33. J I p. 147.
34. KGB 1.3 To Nietzsche 97.
35. KGB 1.2 469. The letter is dated June 11, 1865.
36. KGB 1.2 469.
37. KGB 1.2 470.
38. KGB 1.2 454.
39. KGB 1.2 454, 460.
40. KGB 1.2 454.
41. KGB 1.2 455.
42. In *The Gay Science* he will look to *art* for the ability to view oneself 'from a distance' in order to see the overall shape of one's life rather than a mere mass of 'foreground' details (GS 78).
43. KGB 1.2 458.
44. KGB 1.2 479. This poem is quoted again in HH 109.

45. Z IV I.
46. GS 344.
47. KGB 1.2 478.
48. J I pp. 167–8.

4. LEIPZIG

1. KGB 1.2 481.
2. KGW 1.2 60 [1].
3. Ibid.
4. Ibid.
5. YN p. 166.
6. KGB 1.2 523.
7. KGB 1.2 554.
8. KGW 1.4 60 [1].
9. KGB 1.2 583.
10. KGB 1.2 497.
11. KSA 10 12 [1] 16.
12. KGB 1.2 538.
13. GS 277.
14. KGW 1.4 57 [30].
15. KGB 1.2 595.
16. KGW 1.4 57 [30].
17. KGB 1.2 559.
18. KGB 1.2 595.
19. KGW 1.4 57 [27].
20. AOM 218.
21. KGB 1.2 569.
22. KGW 1.4 60 [1].
23. KGW 1.4 60 [1].
24. KGB 1.2 540.
25. KGB 1.2 512.
26. KGB 1.2 509.
27. KGB 1.2 511.
28. KGB 1.2 510.
29. KGB 1.2 517.
30. KGB 1.2 258.
31. KGB 1.2 512.
32. KGB 1.2 509.
33. KGB 1.2 512.
34. See KGB 1.2 470 and 509.
35. KGB 1.2 512.
36. KGB 1.2 513.
37. KGB 1.2 To Nietzsche 151.
38. KGB 1.2 536.
39. For an outstanding discussion of the militarisation of Prussian society see Rohkrämer (2007).
40. KGB 1.2 511. Emphasis added.
41. KGB 1.2 512.
42. Tanera (1896) p. 10.
43. Meinecke (1963) p. 25.
44. KGB 1.2 509.
45. YN p. 130.

46. KGB 1.2 559.
47. Ibid.
48. YN p. 237.
49. KGB 1.2 565.
50. KGB 1.2 593.
51. KGB 1.2 596.
52. KGB 1.2 591.
53. KGB 1.2 523.
54. KGB 1.2 591.
55. KGB 1.2 596.
56. KGB 1.2 625.
57. KGB 1.2 599.
58. KGB 1.2 604.
59. J I pp. 254–5.
60. KGB 1.2 610.
61. This is reported in Deussen's memoirs and quoted at KGB 1.4 p. 561.
62. KGB 1.2. 608.
63. KGB 1.3 To Nietzsche 211.
64. KGB 1.2 632. This is, I think, the first occurrence of the idea of the 'herd' man, a notion destined to play a central role in Nietzsche's mature philosophy. *Fachmensch* means, literally, 'specialist', but Nietzsche uses it pejoratively to mean someone whose life is absorbed into the robotic fulfilment of a narrow professional function; 'nerd' might be a contemporary approximation.

5. SCHOPENHAUER

1. HKG III pp. 297–8.
2. For a detailed account of Schopenhauer's philosophy see Young (2005).
3. WR I p. 17.
4. WN p. 216.
5. WR II p. 578.
6. WR II p. 540.
7. WR I pp. 312–13, PP II p. 295.
8. WR I p. 179.
9. WR I p. 196.
10. WR I p. 256.
11. WR I p. 264.
12. WR I p. 380.
13. Ibid.
14. WR II p. 159.
15. WR I p. 411.
16. Ibid.
17. WR II pp. 612–13.
18. GM III 5.
19. GM III 25.
20. GS 125.
21. HKG III pp. 297–8.
22. WR I p. 383 WR II 627–8.
23. HKG III pp. 297–8.
24. KGB 1.2 493.
25. KGB 1.2 554.
26. KGB 1.2 595.
27. KGB 11.2 585.

28. KGB 11.2 493.
29. KGB 11.2 625.
30. KGB 1.3 letter to Nietzsche 193: see, also, letter to Nietzsche 190.
31. KGB 1.2 585.
32. KGB 1.2 500.
33. WR II Chapter 17.
34. WR I p. 411.
35. WR II p. 463.
36. WR II p. 493.
37. The title of Chapter 46 of WR II is 'On Death and Its Relation to the Indestructibility of Our Inner Nature'.
38. WR II p. 491.
39. Fischer (1860).
40. Kant (1964) B xxxiv.
41. Lange (1925) pp. 215, 223.
42. Lange (1925) p. 227.
43. Lange (1925) pp. 224–5.
44. KGB 1.2 562. This recommendation was actually made in February 1868. But Nietzsche evidently forgot that he had recommended Lange to von Gersdorff much earlier – in August 1866 (KGB 1.2 517) – just after his first discovery of the book. The remaining quotations concerning Nietzsche's recommendation of Lange to von Gersdorff all come from the earlier letter.
45. KGB 1.2 517.
46. Lange (1925) p. 219.
47. KGB 1.2 517.
48. KGW 1.4 57 [51–5].
49. KGB 1.2 517.
50. WR I p. 354.
51. WR II p. 583.
52. WR II pp. 349–50.
53. WR I section 63 passim.
54. WR II pp. 197–8.
55. Young (2005) p. 97.
56. Nietzsche's thoughts, here, and Lange's, too, are somewhat muddled, so that the following is the product of a certain amount of tidying up. It needs to be remembered that at this stage of his life Nietzsche was, though a professional philologist, only an *amateur* philosopher.
57. Kant (1964) B xxx.
58. WR II p. 641.
59. PP II pp. 9–11.
60. WR II p. 612.
61. WR II pp. 614.
62. See p. 85 above.
63. WR p. 411.
64. WR II p. 368, WR I pp. 370–71.
65. KGB 11.2 517. Compare 'Who could *refute* a tone' (GS 106).
66. KGB 1.2 595.
67. KGB 11.2 517.
68. HH 131. Nietzsche almost always quotes from memory and usually, therefore, slightly inaccurately. Here, however, he has Schopenhauer's remark word perfect, save for the addition of 'the glance of'.
69. HH 153.
70. HH 15.
71. EH III HH 1. Some English translations omit the crucial 'in my nature'.

6. BASEL

1. YN p. 207.
2. KGB II.1 1.
3. KGB II.1 3.
4. YN p. 208.
5. KGB II.1 16.
6. KGB II.1 7.
7. KGB II.1 67.
8. KSA 13 24 [1] 4. The claim made in the second sentence appears in *Ecce Homo* itself (EH I 4).
9. YN pp. 227–8.
10. J I p. 522.
11. YN p. 205.
12. KGB III.5 1245.
13. KGB II.5 528.
14. KSA 8 10 [14].
15. KGB II.1 58.
16. KGB II.1.
17. KGB II.3 301.
18. KGB II.3 300.
19. KGB II.5 894.
20. KGB II.1 16.
21. KGB II.1 58.
22. Ibid.
23. YN p. 223.
24. EH III HH 2.
25. KGB II.2 To Nietzsche 16.
26. J I pp. 293–5.
27. KGB II.1 58.
28. J I p. 393.
29. KGB II.1 4.
30. KGB II.1 19.
31. KGB II.1 81.
32. GS 119.
33. J I pp. 426–8.
34. KGB II.1 7.
35. YN pp. 223–4.
36. KGB II.1 81.
37. J I p. 356.
38. KGB II.1 212.
39. KGB II.1 214.
40. EH II 5.
41. KGB II.3 393.

7. RICHARD WAGNER AND THE BIRTH OF "THE BIRTH OF TRAGEDY"

1. KGB II.1 19.
2. KGB II.1 4.
3. KGB II.1 108.
4. KSA 1 p. 754.

5. A startling omission in Thomas Brobjer's otherwise useful book (Brobjer (2008)) is that though it is devoted to discussing contemporary philosophical influences on Nietzsche, Wagner receives no discussion at all. (Another omission is Hippolyte Taine.)

6. KSA 7 19 [303] et passim.

7. *Philologischer Anzeiger* Vol. 5, No. 3, 1873, pp. 134–9.

8. WMD p. 59.

9. WMD p. 68.

10. WMD p. 59.

11. WMD p. 65.

12. WMD pp. 85–7.

13. WMD p. 62.

14. WPW p. 120.

15. WMD pp. 37–41.

16. WPW V pp. 113–15.

17. WMD p. 65.

18. WMD p. 63.

19. Ibid.

20. KSA 7 1[1].

21. WMD p. 63.

22. WMD p. 81.

23. Ibid.

24. WMD p. 63.

25. WMD p. 89.

26. WMD p. 84.

27. WMD pp. 85–7.

28. WMD pp. 399–401.

29. WMD p. 85.

30. WMD p. 65.

31. WMD pp. 90–1.

32. WMD pp. 399–421.

33. BGE 212.

34. EH II 5, EH VI 2.

35. WMD p. 422.

36. WMD p. 235.

37. WC 7.

38. WMD pp. 228–9.

39. WMD p. 215.

40. WMD p. 228.

41. WMD p. 229, Wagner's emphases.

42. WMD p. 52.

43. Heidegger (1979) Vol. I, p. 88.

44. BT Preface.

45. KGB 11.2 To Nietzsche 32.

46. KGB 11.1 19.

47. Ibid.

48. Magee (1983) p. 355.

49. WMD p. 402.

50. WMD p. 413.

51. WPW pp. 71–2.

52. WMD pp. 420–1.

53. WMD p. 413.

54. Ibid.

55. WPW pp. 80–1.

56. In *Wagner at Bayreuth* (1876), Nietzsche deals with the conflict between the reservations he is now beginning to have about Wagner and the still overriding desire to praise the composer and promote the cause of Bayreuth, by narrating Wagner's career as a kind of *Bildungsroman*, a 'novel of education', in which his 'higher self' gradually triumphs over his 'lower self'. It seems to me likely that the structure of this essay consciously alludes to the structure of the 'Beethoven' essay.

57. WPW p. 77.

58. WPW pp. 78–81.

59. Wagner actually says 'symphony in F', which could mean either the Sixth or the Eighth. The former, however, seems far more likely.

60. WPW pp. 91–4. Later on, Nietzsche will seize on this as a *criticism* of 'other-worldly', romantic music. As with drugs, he will suggest, the withdrawal symptoms more than outweigh the brief moment of ecstasy.

61. PP II pp. 432–6.

62. KSA 7 8 [21], BT 21.

63. Wagner coined the term 'absolute' to refer to purely instrumental music. One can to some degree trace the process of Nietzsche's thinking his way into Wagner's later theoretical stance via his use of 'absolute' in the notebooks of the period. In the autumn of 1869, for instance, in line with Wagner's earlier theory, with which Nietzsche was familiar prior to the Tribschen period, 'absolute', as applied to music, functions as a term of clear disapproval (KSA 7 1 [54]). But by the end of the year – a year in which Nietzsche celebrated Christmas at Tribschen – it has lost its critical connotation (KSA 7 3 [2]), and by the end of 1870 it has become a term of high approbation (KSA 7 5 [110]).

64. KSA 7 3[70].

65. WPW p. 104.

66. WR I p. 261.

67. WR I p. 263, WR II p. 449.

68. WPW p. 121.

69. Heidegger (1979) pp. 86–8.

70. Might not a society composed of world- and will-'negating' ascetics waiting patiently for death to absorb them into a better world count as a 'redeemed civilisation'? Hardly. For in the absence of will, of action, such a society would soon get wiped out by willfully aggressive neighbours. The idea of a will-denying civilisation is, in short, an oxymoron. To live is to act, and as Nietzsche says, 'action is world-affirmation' (KSA 7 5 [32]).

71. WPW p. 121; my emphasis.

72. WMD p. 404.

73. WMD pp. 353–69.

74. KGB 11.1 133.

75. Wagner himself speaks of such a split. In a letter to his friend August Röckel, written in August 1856, he observes that the theme of 'renunciation, the negation of the will' appears already in pre-Schopenhauerian works such as *Tannhaüser* and *Lohengrin*. He explains this as a split between artist and early theoretician: 'with my conscious reason, I was working in direct opposition to the intuitive ideas represented in these works. While as an artist I *felt* [the need for world-denial] ... as a philosopher I sought to discover a totally opposite interpretation of the world', one, namely, supportive of socialism (Magee (1983) p. 341).

76. KGB 11.1 4.

77. BT 5.

78. BT 9, 10.

79. BT 7.

80. Ibid.

81. 'On the Pathos of Truth', the first of the *Five Prefaces for Five Unwritten Books* Nietzsche dedicated to Cosima (KSA 1 p. 756).

82. This is how the 'wisdom of Silenus' is formulated in 'The Birth of Tragic Thought', a lecture of 1871 (KSA 1 p. 588). It strikes me as more interesting than the slightly different formulation given in *The Birth* itself (BT 3).
83. AOM 218.
84. BT 1, 2, 9.
85. BT 1,4, 16.
86. BT 3. Notice the first appearance of the idea that being 'beyond good and evil' is a good state to be in.
87. 'The Dionysian Worldview', BT pp. 119–38, p. 124.
88. BT 3.
89. BT 3, 7, 16.
90. BT 3; my emphasis.
91. BT 12.
92. BT 15.
93. BT 16.
94. BT 5.
95. BT 11.
96. BT 10.
97. BT 21, 24.
98. BT 2, 5.
99. BT 1.
100. BT 23.
101. 'The Greek Music Drama', a lecture of January 1870 (KSA 1 p. 521).
102. BT 1.
103. Strictly, of course, it is *Schiller's*, not Beethoven's, 'Ode to Joy' that is set to music in the last movement of the Ninth Symphony. Or rather, it is *mainly* Schiller's Ode. As he reports in the 'Beethoven' essay, Wagner discovered, on inspecting the original score, that for Schiller's *Was die Mode streng getheilt* (what fashion has *strictly* separated) Beethoven had substituted *Was die Mode frech getheilt* (what fashion has *impudently* separated). He suggests that 'strict' was not strong enough to express Beethoven's rage at the division between man and man. Because he knew the 'Beethoven' essay intimately, Nietzsche is engaging, surely, in a quiet piece of scholarship in referring to 'Beethoven's Ode to Joy'.
104. BT 1.
105. BT 8.
106. Ibid.
107. BT 5.
108. BT 17.
109. BT 24.
110. BT 24. In the notebooks Nietzsche identifies the child-sculptor as Zeus (KSA 1 p. 758).
111. BT 6.
112. BT 21.
113. BT 21. In the *Genealogy of Morals* the 'will to nothingness' provides the definition of 'nihilism' (GM III 14).
114. Compare with this the description of the ecstatic state in *Thus Spoke Zarathustra*'s 'Before Sunrise': identifying himself with the 'azure bell' of the sky, Zarathustra learns 'to smile uncloudedly down from bright eyes and from miles away when under us compulsion and purpose and guilt stream like rain'.
115. KSA 1 p. 595; compare BT 7.
116. BT 21.
117. Ibid.
118. BT 7.
119. BT 9.
120. BT 23.
121. Ibid.

122. KSA 1 p. 518.
123. KSA 7 3[1].
124. BT 21. Did Wagner the artist ever achieve this combination of 'metaphysical comfort' with the 'noble illusion' that enables us to carry on with life? Perhaps just once. Arguably, one of the things Nietzsche achieves in *The Birth* is an articulation of the mysteriously ambivalent character of *Die Meistersinger*. If one attends to Hans Sachs (who is, of course, Wagner himself), and in particular to his great *Wahn! Wahn! Überall Wahn* (Illusion! Illusion! Everything illusion) monologue, the work appears to be, like its immediate predecessor, *Tristan*, an expression of Schopenhauerian life-denial. Yet it has a 'happy ending': Walter's new music both reinvigorates the moribund tradition of the mastersingers and wins him Eva's hand in marriage. True music and true love have won the day. And so, in spite of the centrality of the Schopenhauerian Sachs, one leaves the theatre with a sense of life wonderfully affirmed.
125. One might wish to object that the 'noble deception' that shields us from nihilism can only work on someone who has never read *The Birth*. If 'action requires the veil of illusion' and this is irrevocably shattered by the revelation of the truth of Schopenhauerian idealism, then action, world-affirmation, becomes impossible. But this, I think, assumes that beliefs are more stable than they really are. As we have seen, Nietzsche was, in his youth, a passionate Prussian who enthusiastically supported Bismarck's 1866 war against Austria. Yet at the same time he was able to tell his friend von Gersdorff (himself in mortal danger in the field) of moments when 'I free myself for minutes from temporal consciousness, from my subjective natural sympathy for the Prussians, and then I have before me the theatre-piece of a great state action of the stuff that history is now made of. Admittedly it's not moral, but for the observer rather beautiful and uplifting' (KGB 1.2 517). In other words, Nietzsche oscillates between the engaged perspective of the everyday human individual and the disengaged, 'aesthetic' perspective which, in *The Birth*, he will identify as belonging to the 'primal unity'. And so did Wagner, who, while writing of the world as a 'game of play' and of 'nothingness' as the only redemption, was simultaneously engaged in the Bayreuth project. This, as Nietzsche later points out, is probably the greatest exercise of the 'will to power' in the history of art. Switching perspectives is, I think, much more common than is usually recognised. I may, for example, most of the time, recognise that the 'office politics' of my workplace are vicious, trivial and pathetic. But in the office I am still likely to find myself as fully and nastily engaged as everyone else. The psychological truth of the matter is that one inhabits different belief-systems at different times. That in some moments I believe the world of the *principium individuationis* to be ideal does not exclude my believing at a different time that it is real. Human beings are made of many souls.
126. KGB 11.4 To Nietzsche 513.
127. BT 11.
128. BT 15.
129. BT 18.
130. Ibid.
131. BT 17.
132. UM IV 4.
133. BT 23.
134. Compare Z 1 15.
135. GS 78.
136. BT 23.
137. BT 23; my emphasis.
138. BT 23.
139. Ibid.
140. Ibid.
141. Ibid.
142. BT 19.
143. Ibid.

8. WAR AND AFTERMATH

1. KGB 11.1 86.
2. KGB 11.1 87.
3. KGB 11.1 88.
4. BT pp. 117–38.
5. KGB 11.1 89; Nietzsche's emphasis.
6. YN pp. 233–4.
7. KSA 7 4 [1].
8. YN p. 234.
9. KGB 1.2 95.
10. To Vischer he writes that it was 'two days and two nights' (KGB 11.1 99) but to von Gersdorff it is back to three and three (KGB 11. 1 103).
11. KGB 11.1 103.
12. KGB 11.1 100.
13. KGB 11.1 103.
14. Ibid.
15. KGB 11.1 104.
16. KGB 11.1 103.
17. KGB 11.1 102.
18. YN p. 235.
19. KGB 11.3 313.
20. KSA 7 32 [62].
21. KSA 1 pp. 783–92; GM pp. 187–94.
22. GM p. 189.
23. BT 2.
24. GM p. 189.
25. KSA 7 16 [26], 16 [18].
26. BT p. 123.
27. D 94.
28. GM p. 187.
29. KGB 11.1 107.
30. KGB 11.1 111.
31. EI p. 98.
32. EI p. 35.
33. EI p. 64.
34. Ibid.
35. EI p. 65.
36. EI pp. 36–7.
37. EI p. 77.
38. EI p. 74.
39. EH p. 77.
40. EI p. 67.
41. EI p. 75.
42. EI p. 79.
43. EI pp. 76–8.
44. EI p. 19.
45. Ibid.
46. EI pp. 18, 83.
47. EI pp. 82–3.
48. Ibid.
49. EI p. 97.
50. WR II Chapter 31.
51. EI p. 96.

52. EI p. 60.
53. EI p. 54.
54. EI p. 55.
55. EI p. 60.
56. EI p. 99.
57. EI p. 63.
58. KSA 7 1 [29].
59. Kant (1972) section 46.
60. WR II pp. 376, 391.
61. EI pp. 66–7.
62. Ibid.
63. EI p. 67.
64. Ibid.
65. Ibid.
66. KSA 7 14 [14].
67. KSA 7 8 [92].
68. EI p. 119.
69. EH p. 77.

9. ANAL PHILOLOGY

1. KGB II.1 113.
2. KGB II.1 156.
3. KGB II.1 195.
4. KGB II.1 207.
5. KGB II.1 168. He adds, using a Hölderlinian trope, 'Since these best moments obviously alienate us from the spirit of the present age, but since we must find a homeland somewhere, I think we have, in these moments, a dim sense of that which is coming (*des Kommenden*)'.
6. KGB II.1 197. Compare the last section of *Zarathustra*: 'My suffering... – what does that matter? Am I striving for *happiness*? I am striving for my *work!*'
7. KGB II.1 194.
8. KGB II.1 192.
9. KGB II.1 218.
10. KGB II.1 170.
11. Janz I pp. 462–3.
12. KGB II.3 223.
13. J I p. 469.
14. KGB II.1 194.
15. KGB II.2 285.
16. KGB II.4 335.
17. J I pp. 511–12.
18. WPW pp. 292–8.
19. KSA 7 19 [269].
20. KGB II.3 227.
21. KGB II.3 242.
22. KGB II.4 To Nietzsche 347.
23. KGB II.3 268, 269.
24. KGB II.3 267.
25. The source of this suggestion is Wolfgang Bottenberg, who is responsible for the most extensive recording of Nietzsche's music and for the versions available at the Web site for this book. Some support for the suggestion is to be found in Cosima's diary entry for January 10, 1869: 'Never', she records, 'would he [von Bülow] have lost me if fate had not brought

me together with the man [Wagner] for whom I had to recognise it as my task to live or die'.

26. KGB 11.3 236. The performance was conducted by von Bülow. Since Nietzsche sent him the 'Manfred Meditation' a month later, this may have been partially inspired by his experience of the performance.
27. KGB 11.3 244.
28. KGB 11.3 257.
29. I owe this suggestion to David Krell and Donald Bates's wonderful coffee-table book, *The Good European* (Krell and Bates (1997) p. 82).
30. YN p. 274.
31. KSA 7 23 [15].
32. KSA 8 3 [62]; my emphasis. See, also, AOM 218.
33. JI p. 465.
34. KGB 11.4 To Nietzsche 326.
35. YN p. 280.
36. KGB 11.4 To Nietzsche 333.
37. KGB 11.3 298.
38. KSA 1 pp. 753–92.
39. JI p. 496.
40. KSA 1 pp. 873–90; BT pp. 141–53.
41. KSA 7 19 [158].
42. GM pp. 176–86.
43. See KSA 7 10 [1].
44. GM p. 181. This is perhaps a version of *The Birth*'s rather silly conceit according to which the world only exists as entertainment for its 'sole author and spectator' (BT 6), the primal unity.
45. GM pp. 185–6.
46. Z I 15.
47. GM pp. 178–9.
48. GM p. 180.

10. UNTIMELY MEDITATIONS

1. KGB 11.5 656.
2. KGB 11.3 300.
3. KGB 11.3 302.
4. KGB 11.3 301.
5. Hayman (1980) p. 160.
6. KGB III.1 148.
7. KGB 11.3 299.
8. JI pp. 595–6.
9. KGB 11.3 299.
10. PTA pp. 73–160.
11. KSA 7 16 [18].
12. KGB 11.3 304.
13. KGB 11.4 To Nietzsche 431.
14. KGB 11.3 309.
15. KSA 7 19 [303]
16. KSA 7 19 [269]. It has been suggested by C. Landerer and M.-C. Schuster (Landerer and Schuster (2002) pp. 114–33) that the long note from the spring of 1871 (KSA 7 12 [1]), in which Nietzsche defends Schopenhauer's view that music does not have any *need* for words, and argues that Schiller's words are inessential to the last movement of Beethoven's Ninth Symphony, shows that, privately, he was critical of Wagner and sympathetic to his

arch-opponent, Eduard Hanslick, even before *The Birth* was published. But this is not so. All that Nietzsche is doing, as we have seen him doing on other occasions, is agreeing with late Wagner – the Wagner he knew, the author of the 'Beethoven' essay – in criticising Wagner's *early* theory of opera. Wagner *himself*, that is to say, would have agreed with every word of the note. It is significant that in the letter confessing to von Gersdorff his need for a 'sanitary' distance, immediately adjacent to this confession, he praises Wagner's 'State and Religion' as essential reading, reading that is 'edifying in the noblest sense' (KGB 11.3 298). And far from being a sympathetic figure, Hanslick finds himself (along with *inter alios* the butt of the first *Untimely Meditation*, David Strauss) on a 'to be attacked' list dating from the period late 1872 to early 1873 (KSA 7 19 [259]). In short, when Nietzsche speaks of needing personal distance to 'remain true in a higher sense' he speaks the exact truth. And this is not such an odd truth either: writers are quite typically only able to write at a distance from where their emotions are most passionately engaged, only when emotion can be recollected 'in tranquillity'.

17. KGB 11.3 304.
18. KGB 11.4 To Nietzsche 431.
19. KGB 11.3 307.
20. KSA 7 23.15. In a March letter to von Gersdorff he refers to a projected 'companion piece for *The Birth*' that will perhaps be called 'the philosopher as physician of culture' (KGB 11.3 298).
21. EH v 2.
22. EH v 1.
23. A 28.
24. UM I 2.
25. UM I 4.
26. UM I 7.
27. KSA 7 29 [53].
28. UM I 6.
29. KGB 11.3 303.
30. UM I 6.
31. UM I, KSA 7 26 [16].
32. UM I 7.
33. UM I 6, KSA 7 27 [1].
34. UM I.
35. UM I 7.
36. KGB 11.3 316.
37. C p. 305.
38. C p. 302.
39. C p. 306.
40. C p. 302.
41. C p. 307.
42. KGB 11.3 345.
43. KGB 11.3 313. The suggestion that his left eye gave him the most trouble is strange, since almost always the right eye was the weakest. Perhaps he was carried away by the literary neatness of the contrast.
44. C p. 307.
45. C p. 299.
46. C p. 300.
47. KGB 11.3 318.
48. KSA 7 27 [32].
49. KSA 1 pp. 891–7.
50. Z 1 15.
51. KSA 7 32 [80].
52. KGB 11.4 To Nietzsche 474.

53. C pp. 304–5.
54. KGB 11.3 330.
55. UM II 1.
56. UM II 2.
57. UM III 4.
58. UM II 7. In the notebooks Nietzsche, using Wagner's word, speaks of the '*Wahn* of the monumental' as 'promoting greatness' (KSA 7 29 [38]), so 'illusion' should, I think, as in *The Birth*, be decoupled from the notion of falsehood. He also writes that the potential power of art is so great that, even now, 'a great artist could still re-create Christianity, above all its festival' (KSA 7 27 [15]).
59. UM II 10.
60. UM II 3.
61. UM II 2.
62. UM II 3.
63. UN II 3, 6.
64. UM II 3.
65. UM II 2.
66. UM II 4, UM I 1. The most crucial word here is 'unity'. Time and again the notes insist that an authentic culture creates unity, 'unity out of multiplicity' (KSA 7 26 [16]; see, too, BGE 212). Above all culture creates, as one might put it, *e pluribus unum*. The notes draw a sharp distinction between 'fashion' and 'convention' (KSA 7 29 [122]). The former is all that modernity possesses, the latter is the 'glue' necessary to there being a genuine culture. The paradigm of the convention-created human being is the Prussian soldier who is created, from the ground up, by convention (KSA 7 29 [119]). But conventional forms of behaviour can become, with practice, a 'second nature', so that 'to be simple and natural' is the 'highest goal' of culture (KSA 7 29 [118]).
67. UM II 4, UM I 1. So presumably even Nietzsche's 'slaves' belong to the culture he believes can only be built on the backs of their labour.
68. UM II 4.
69. KSA 7 27 [66].
70. UM I 1.
71. UM I 1, UM II 4.
72. UM II 7.
73. KSA 7 29 [40], [139], [149].
74. UM II 10.
75. 'Attempt at a Self-Criticism' (BT pp. 5–6).
76. KSA 7 29 [143].
77. KSA 7 29 [147].
78. KSA 7 29 [108].
79. KSA 7 29 [205]; that is, 'multiplicity in unity'.
80. KSA 7 31 [7].
81. KSA 7 19 [125]. This is what Nietzsche learnt from Lange (see p. 90 above).
82. KSA 7 27 [77].
83. KSA 7 19 [125].
84. KSA 7 28 [1].
85. KSA 7 19 [24].
86. KSA 7 19 [34].
87. KSA 7 19 [132]; see, too, 19 [87].
88. KSA 7 27 [37].
89. KSA 7 30 [8].
90. KSA 7 19 [1].
91. KSA 7 24 [8].
92. KSA 7 7 [160].
93. KSA 7 7 [157].

94. See KSA 7 19 [314], for instance.
95. KSA 27 [24].
96. KSA 7 29 [141].
97. KSA 7 23 [14].
98. Ibid.
99. KSA 7 19 [73].
100. KSA 7 31 [8].
101. KSA 7 28 [6].

11. AIMEZ-VOUS BRAHMS?

1. KGB 11.3 335.
2. KGB 11.3 338.
3. KGB 11.3 346.
4. KGB 11.3 356.
5. KGB 11.3 364.
6. KGB 11.3 368.
7. KGB 11.4 To Nietzsche 544.
8. KGB 11.4 To Nietzsche 529a.
9. KGB 11.4 To Nietzsche 544.
10. KGB 11.3 367.
11. KGB 11.3 361.
12. KGB 11.3 398.
13. KSA 8 18 [8].
14. KGB 11.3 368.
15. KGB 11.3 356.
16. KGB 11.3 404.
17. KGB 11.3 343.
18. KGB 11.3 361.
19. KGB 11.3 365.
20. KGB 11.3 364.
21. '…*in's Begrenzste und Heimische*' (KSA 7 32 [15]).
22. KGB 11.3 373.
23. The notes from the beginning of 1874 contain the first sketch plan for the fourth *Meditation* (KSA 7 32 [17]).
24. KSA 7 32 [15].
25. KSA 7 32 [25].
26. KGB 11.3 346.
27. KSA 7 32 [8].
28. KSA 7 32 [16].
29. KSA 7 32 [34].
30. KSA 7 32 [58].
31. KSA 7 32 [35].
32. KSA 7 32 [32].
33. KSA 7 [10].
34. KSA 7 32 [42].
35. KSA 7 32 [58].
36. KSA 7 32 [43].
37. KSA 7 32 [30].
38. KSA 7 32 [44].
39. BT 21.
40. KSA 7 32 [22].
41. KSA 7 32 [14].

42. KSA 7 32 [58].
43. KSA 7 32 [28].
44. KSA 7 32 [61].
45. KSA 32 [29].
46. KSA 7 32 [31].
47. KSA 7 32 [10].
48. KSA 7 33 [7].
49. KSA 7 32 [12].
50. KSA 7 32 [21].
51. KGB 11.3 360.
52. KGB 11.5 440.
53. KGB 11.3 341.
54. KGB 11.3 353.
55. YN p. 310.
56. YN pp. 314–15.
57. KGB 11.4 To Nietzsche 553.
58. KGB 11.4 To Nietzsche 542.
59. KGB 11.3 370.
60. KGB 11.5 424.
61. UM I 1.
62. J I p. 650.
63. J I pp. 624–5.
64. KGB 11.3 380.
65. KGB 11.3 383.
66. KGB 11.3 381.
67. Ibid.
68. KGB 11.3 252.
69. KGB 11.3 382.
70. KGB 11.3 371.
71. C p. 321.
72. Ibid.
73. C pp. 321–2.
74. YN p. 332.
75. Ibid.
76. C p. 322.
77. C pp. 523–4.
78. KGB 11.3 390.
79. KGB 11.3 395.
80. KGB 111.1 352.
81. UM III 1.
82. Ibid.
83. Ibid.
84. Ibid.
85. UM III 3.
86. UM III 2, 4, 6.
87. *Human, All-Too-Human*, Preface to Volume II, section 1.
88. UM III 2.
89. UM III 4.
90. UM III 3.
91. UM III 5.
92. Ibid.
93. Ibid.
94. Ibid.
95. BT 5.

96. UM III 6.
97. UM III 5.
98. UM III 6.
99. KSA 7 19 [132], 19 [87].
100. At this stage in his thought, Nietzsche's concept of the 'higher' is an uneasy mixture of the 'more adaptive' and the 'more admirable', i.e., more 'spiritual'.
101. UM III 7.
102. UM III 6.
103. EH v 2.
104. C p. 330.
105. KGB II.4 To Nietzsche 619.
106. KGB II.4 To Nietzsche 599.
107. KGB II.4 To Nietzsche 598.
108. KGB II.4 To Nietzsche 603.
109. YN p. 320.
110. KGB II.4 To Nietzsche 610.
111. YN p. 324.
112. EH v 3; my emphasis.
113. UM III 3.
114. YN pp. 320–1.
115. KGB II.3 404.
116. KGB II.5 414.
117. Ibid.
118. KGB II.5 422.

12. AUF WIEDERSEHEN BAYREUTH

1. KGB II.5 412.
2. YN p. 340.
3. KGB II.5 414.
4. KGB II.5 422.
5. KGB II.5 414.
6. C pp. 332–3.
7. C p. 363.
8. KGB II.5 525.
9. KGB II.5 433.
10. KGB II.5 487.
11. KGB II.5 430.
12. KGB II.5 431.
13. KGB II.5 477.
14. KSA 8 3 [1]–[16].
15. KSA 8 3 [12].
16. KSA 8 3 [49].
17. KSA 8 3 [14].
18. KSA 8 3 [18].
19. KSA 8 17 [72].
20. KSA 8 5 [20].
21. KSA 8 5 [146].
22. KSA 8 3 [68]; my emphasis.
23. KSA 8 5 [65].
24. KSA 8 5 [47].
25. KSA 8 5 [143].
26. KSA 8 5 [58].

27. KSA 8 5 [58].
28. KGB 11.5 528.
29. KGB 11.5 443.
30. C pp. 334–6.
31. KGB 11.5 443.
32. KGB 11.5 430.
33. KGB 11.5 439.
34. KGB 111.5 449.
35. KGB 11.6/1 680.
36. KGB 11.6/1 691.
37. AOM 74.
38. KGB 11.5 466.
39. KGB 11.5 481.
40. KGB 11.5 469.
41. KGB 11.5 476.
42. KGB 11.5 470.
43. Ibid.
44. KGB 11.6/1 To Nietzsche 680.
45. KGB 11.6/1 To Nietzsche 455.
46. KGB 11.5 498.
47. KGB 11.5 475.
48. KGB 11.5 474.
49. KGB 11.5 471.
50. C p. 346.
51. KGB 11.5 495.
52. KGB 11.5 521.
53. KGB 11.5 520.
54. KGB 11.5 449.
55. KGB 11.5 474.
56. KGB 11.5 481.
57. On his last day in Steinabad Nietzsche wrote to Carl Fuchs 'may God grant that we become free spirits, you can keep the rest', which seems to be his first use of this key expression (KGB 11.5 479).
58. KGB 11.5 471.
59. KGB 11.5 479.
60. KGB 11.5 475.
61. KGB 11.5 481.
62. KGB 11.5 450.
63. KGB 11.5 493.
64. KGB 11.5 495.
65. KGB 11.5 493.
66. KGB 11.5 494.
67. KGB 11.5 498.
68. Cate (2002) p. 232.
69. Small (2005) p. 44.
70. KGB 11.5 492.
71. KGB 11 6.1 745.
72. KGB 11.5 505.
73. KGB 11.5 494.
74. HH 36.
75. WR II p. 210.
76. KGB 11.6/2 To Nietzsche 1084, EH III HH 6.
77. GS 335.
78. J I p. 695.

79. C pp. 351–3.
80. C p. 357.
81. KGB 11.5 516.
82. J I p. 630.
83. KGB 11.5 517.
84. KGB 11.5 529.
85. KGB 11.5 533.
86. KGB 11.5 490.
87. EH III BT 4.
88. EH III UM 3; my emphasis.
89. WB 1.
90. WB 4.
91. WB 8.
92. Ibid.
93. WB 1.
94. WB 4.
95. An impressive note from this period reads: 'Education is first a teaching of necessity, then of the changeable and alterable. One shows the pupil the universal sway of laws in nature; then the laws of civil society. With regard to the latter the question arises: *must* this be so? Gradually the student needs history in order to hear how it was in the past. But here he learns, too, that things can be otherwise. How much power does man have over things? This is the question of all education. And now to show how things could be quite different one shows him, for example, the Greeks. The Romans one needs in order to show how things became as they are' (KSA 8 5 [64]).
96. WB 11.
97. WB 5, 7, 10.
98. WB 2.
99. KSA 8 9 [1]. The phrase is taken over from Karl Eugen Dühring, whose *The Value of Life* Nietzsche had been reading intensively during the summer of 1875.
100. WB 9, 2.
101. WB 4.
102. WB 7.
103. KGB 11.5 490.
104. WB 7.
105. Ibid.
106. KGB 11.5 734.
107. WB 7.
108. It is unknown which ones were sent since after he became *persona non grata* in *Wahnfried* in the following year, Cosima destroyed most of his letters.
109. KGB 11.5 535, 536, 537, 538.
110. *Ecce Homo's* claim that 'Wagner failed to recognise himself in the essay' (EH III BT 4) is thus something of a fiction.
111. KGB 11.6/1 To Nietzsche 797.
112. KGB 11.6/1 To Nietzsche 796.
113. KGB 11.6/1 To Nietzsche 799.
114. KGB 11.6/1 To Nietzsche 800.
115. C p. 370.
116. YN p. 390.
117. KGB 11.5 544.
118. KGB 11.5 545.
119. KGB 11.5 544.
120. Ibid.
121. KGB 11.5 734.
122. Ibid.

123. YN p. 386.
124. YN p. 392.
125. EH III BT 4.
126. J I p. 724.
127. YN p. 385.
128. YN p. 389.
129. Ibid.
130. BT 23, UM II 2.
131. KGB 11.5 734.
132. YN pp. 376–7.
133. HH 153.
134. HH Volume II Preface 3.
135. EH III HH 2.
136. KGB 11.5 545.
137. YN p. 391.
138. He would marry on August 8, 1877, a year to the day after Overbeck's marriage.
139. KGB 11.6/1 To Nietzsche 711.
140. EH III HH 2.
141. KGB 11.5 549.
142. KGB 11.6/1 To Nietzsche 810.
143. KGB 11 6/1 To Nietzsche 814.
144. KSA 8 3 [76].
145. KGB 11.5 552.

13. SORRENTO

1. KGB 11.5 526.
2. KGB 11.5 555.
3. KGB 11 6/1 To Nietzsche 821.
4. KGB 11.5 556. Jacob Bernays had succeeded Ritschl as professor of classical philology at Bonn. In December 1872 Nietzsche had written Rohde, 'the latest is that Jacob Bernays has claimed that [the views presented in *The Birth of Tragedy*] ... are his views, only strongly exaggerated. I find it a divine cheek on the part of this educated and clever Jew, but at the same time a cheerful sign that the "cunning in the land" have scented what's up' (KGB 11.3 277).
5. J I p. 742.
6. C p. 382.
7. KGB 11.5 518.
8. J I p. 692.
9. Available on the Web in an English translation presented as an M.A. thesis at Brigham Young University by Monte Gardiner.
10. KGB 11.5 518.
11. *Memoirs of a Female Idealist*, Part I, Chapter 10.
12. William James cites this passage in his *Varieties of Religious Experience* (see Small (2005) p. 26).
13. KSA 8 32.19. Lambrettas, unfortunately, have changed all that.
14. C p. 385.
15. GS 77.
16. KGB 11.5 580.
17. HH 1.
18. Small (2005) p. 26.
19. C p. 394.

20. C p. 392.
21. KSA 21 [13].
22. KSA 8 19 [108].
23. KSA 8 21 [43]. In a couple of years time, when he had begun to use 'morality' as a pejorative term, Nietzsche could have made exactly this same remark with the implication 'so much the worse for socialism'. But as yet he has not hit on the pejorative use of 'morality'. Without exception, in the notebooks for 1877, the term is used in the traditional manner as an expression of high approval.
24. KSA 8 23 [14].
25. KSA 8 17 [44].
26. C p. 386.
27. GS 279.
28. KGB 11.5 581.
29. KGB 11.6 To Nietzsche 858.
30. KGB 11.5 567.
31. C p. 418.
32. KGB 11.5 606.
33. KGB 11.5 630.
34. HH 402, 424.
35. KGB 11.5 674.
36. KGB 11.5 642.
37. KGB 11.5 599.
38. KBG 11.5 628.
39. KGB 11.5 644.
40. KGB 11.5 654.
41. Ibid.
42. GS 381.
43. KGB 11.5 627.
44. KGB 11.5 661.
45. KGB 11.5 660.
46. Z II 10.
47. Janz (1976) I p. 782.
48. KGB 11.5 656.
49. KGB 11.5 652.
50. KGB 11.5 643.
51. C p. 414.
52. KGB 11.5 620.
53. KGB 11.5 654.
54. KGB 11.5 662.
55. Janz I p. 787.
56. C p. 422.
57. KGB 11.5 669.
58. C p. 417.
59. Magee (1983) p. 121.
60. C pp. 417–48.
61. KGB III.1 384.
62. KGB III.1 405. Note that 'Unnatural debauchery, with indications of pederasty' has Wagner's letter to Eiser word-perfect.

14. HUMAN, ALL-TOO-HUMAN

1. KGB 11.5 678.
2. EH III HH 5.

3. KGB 11.5 673.
4. KGB 11.5 679, 710.
5. KGB 11.5 676.
6. Mathilde was recipient of the letter referred to in endnote 106 to Chapter 12 and re-quoted in the next paragraph.
7. KGB 11.5 734.
8. TI iv. See below, p. 498.
9. WR II p. 164.
10. TI iv.
11. EH iii hh 6.
12. TI iv.
13. HH 630, 631.
14. EH iii hh 1. 'All-too' contains here, I think, at least two meanings: the sources of metaphysical belief are all-too-human for metaphysics to achieve, as it were, lift-off, and they are all-too-human in that they are all cases of the human intellect having a bad day.
15. *The Antichrist*, Preface.
16. GS 381. See, too, AOM 158.
17. Small (2005) p. 41.
18. KGB 11.5 76.
19. KGB 11.5 554.
20. HH 225.
21. Ibid.
22. WS 288.
23. Spir (1869) p. 55ff. Translated, the document's title reads, *Proposal to the Friends of a Rational Way of Living*.
24. EH ii 1, TI viii 2. Though in his youth, as we have seen, by no means unacquainted with alcohol, in later life he hardly ever drank it, save when he thought it might benefit his health.
25. UM II 10.
26. HH 282.
27. WS 218–19.
28. HH 290. See, too, AOM 49.
29. WS 295.
30. KGB 11.5 522.
31. KGB 11.5 656. Occasionally he says the opposite.
32. AOM 187.
33. That the dedication to Voltaire was removed from the 1886 edition says something about Nietzsche's intellectual development.
34. KSA 8 5 [30].
35. Small (2005) p. 31.
36. GS 58.
37. HH Preface 3, 4. In *Zarathustra* Nietzsche makes the same point by requiring the desert-inhabiting 'lion' to be transformed into the creative 'child' for the full development of the spirit to occur (z 1 1).
38. KGB 11.5 521.
39. KGB 11.5 554.
40. Ibid.
41. J I p. 750.
42. KGB 11.5 113.
43. KGB 11.5 589.
44. KSA 8 17 [50].
45. Ibid.
46. HH 109.
47. AOM 180.
48. HH 1.

49. HH 30.
50. HH 6.
51. HH 119.
52. HH 55, 142.
53. HH 126.
54. HH 115, 141. Here, in embryo, we have the second essay of the *Genealogy of Morals*.
55. HH 111.
56. HH 13.
57. HH 9.
58. BT 17.
59. HH 153.
60. HH 26, 37.
61. WR II Chap. 17.
62. HH 153.
63. HH 15.
64. Salomé (1988) p. 67.
65. HH 164.
66. HH 145, 155.
67. HH 162.
68. HH 132–3.
69. The 'Third Antinomy' of the *Critique of Pure Reason*.
70. See FW pp. 94–7, WR I pp. 113, 155–6, WR II pp. 319–21.
71. HH 37.
72. HH 106.
73. HH 18, 39.
74. HH 102.
75. HH 119.
76. HH 37.
77. HH 37, 46.
78. HH 107.
79. HH 103.
80. HH 54.
81. HH 133.
82. HH 20.
83. HH 22.
84. HH 34.
85. HH 1 325.
86. HH 327.
87. HH 37.
88. KSA 8 23 [41], a preliminary version of HH 36.
89. HH 36, 37.
90. HH 109. That Nietzsche is consistently in favour of literal prostitution ought to have led to reservations about this remark.
91. HH 147.
92. HH 141, 114, 119, 133.
93. HH 124.
94. HH 107.
95. HH 108.
96. HH 242.
97. HH 108.
98. HH 128.
99. HH 95.
100. HH 95.
101. Z IV 1.

102. KGB II 630.
103. KSA 8 23 [16].
104. HH 23–4.
105. HH 585.
106. HH 520.
107. Compare HH 237.
108. HH 235.
109. HH 442. In modern warfare, of course, leadership and danger are not so closely connected.
110. HH 439, 284, 283.
111. Compare AOM 131.
112. HH 226.
113. HH 231.
114. HH 224.
115. HH 225, 463.
116. HH 224.
117. Ibid.
118. KSA 8 17 [44].
119. KSA 7 19 [132], 19 [87].
120. HH 224.
121. HH 462.
122. HH 457. Compare the remarks in 'The Greek State', GM p. 180.
123. KSA 8 25 [1]; my emphasis.
124. HH 462.
125. HH 66.
126. HH 105, 70.
127. Z I 21.
128. HH 80.
129. HH 24.
130. KSA 10 5 [1] 38. I have no idea what occasioned this remarkable entry.
131. HH 251.
132. HH 278.
133. HH 276.
134. KSA 9 8 [2].
135. HH 111.
136. HH 114.
137. HH 111.
138. AOM 222.
139. BT 23.
140. HH 262. As we know, one crucial difference is that Greek religion is polytheistic, thus avoiding the 'one size fits all' character of the morality embodied in Christian 'monototheism' and allowing humanity to flourish in all its rich variety.
141. HH 224.
142. Durkheim (1995) p. 47.
143. HH 222. The quotation is from Goethe's poem 'The Bridegroom'.
144. AOM 99.
145. AOM 114.
146. KSA 8 30 [90].
147. KSA 8 30 [82].
148. WS 87.
149. HH 25.
150. WS 350.
151. WS 284.
152. HH 444.
153. HH 477.

154. WS 61.
155. KGB 11.5 674.
156. AOM 88.
157. HH 27.

15. THE WANDERER AND HIS SHADOW

1. KGB 11.6/2 To Nietzsche 1057.
2. KGB 11.5 744.
3. KGB 11.5 723.
4. KGB 11.6/2 To Nietzsche 1065.
5. LN p. 39.
6. KGB 11.6/2 To Nietzsche 1084.
7. KGB 11.6/2 To Nietzsche 1082.
8. KGB 11 6/2 To Nietzsche 1083.
9. KGB 11.5 743.
10. Salomé (1988) p. 74. Translation adjusted.
11. KGB 11.5 738.
12. KGB 11.5 744.
13. AOM 33, 50.
14. AOM 50.
15. AOM 33.
16. AOM 91.
17. AOM 321.
18. AOM 109.
19. AOM 89.
20. AOM 13.
21. AOM 5.
22. KGB 11.5 772.
23. KGB 11.5 832.
24. KGB 11.5 739, 839.
25. KGB 11.5 825.
26. LN pp. 57–9.
27. KGB 11.5 837.
28. KGB 11.5 859.
29. KGB 11.5 863.
30. KGB 11.5 864.
31. KSA 8 43.
32. KGB 111.1 1.
33. EH 1 1.
34. WS 295.
35. KSA 8 28 [15].
36. KSA 8 30 [31].
37. KGB 11.5 826.
38. KSA 9 7 [97].
39. HH 275.
40. AOM 224.
41. WS 318.
42. WS 86.
43. Hadot (1995).
44. KSA 8 41 [48].
45. WS 192.
46. KSA 8 41 [48].

47. KGB 11.5 842.
48. KSA 8 30 [52].
49. KGB 111.1 68, 125.
50. KSA 8 41 [32].
51. KSA 8 28 [41].
52. KSA 8 28 [40].
53. KGB 11.5 880.
54. KSA 8 27 [21].
55. This will be discussed further on pp. 308–9 below.
56. WS 295.
57. WS 300.
58. WS 7.
59. WS 350.
60. That these are on his mind is indicated by the title of section 300, 'One thing is needful', an oblique reference to John Bunyan's 'One Thing Is Needful; Or Serious Meditations Upon the Four Lasting Things: Death, Judgment, Heaven, and Hell'. Nietzsche of course rejects Bunyan's fourfold. The only thing 'needful' is 'joy in the heart', to be achieved through 'wisdom'.
61. WS 6.
62. KSA 8 40 [16].
63. D 283.
64. WS 261.
65. WS 241.
66. WS 250.
67. Ibid.
68. WS 253.
69. WS 7.
70. WS 16.
71. WS 14.
72. Ibid.
73. BT 7.
74. WS 305.
75. WS 322.
76. WS 88.
77. WS 318.
78. WS 305; compare WS 65.
79. WS 19.
80. WS 20.
81. WS 53.
82. WS 288.
83. WS 286.
84. WS 285.
85. WS 280.
86. WS 136.
87. WS 295.
88. WS 183.
89. WS 22.
90. WS 350.
91. WS 284.
92. WS 226.
93. WS 272.
94. WS 270.
95. WS 272.
96. KGB 11.6/2 To Nietzsche 1252.

97. KGB 11.5 900.
98. PP II pp. 614–15.
99. WS 275.
100. WS 289.
101. KGB 11.6/2 To Nietzsche 1265.
102. C pp. 453–4.
103. D 376.
104. KGB 11.5 884.
105. KGB 11.5 867.
106. KGB 11.5 896.
107. KGB 111.1 2.
108. BGE 242.
109. KGB 111.1 17.
110. KGB 111.1 16–32.
111. KSA 9 47–102.
112. C p. 457.
113. C p. 475.
114. C p. 483.
115. KGB 111.1 49.
116. Ibid.
117. KGB 111.1 42.
118. C p. 476.
119. KGB 111.1 40.
120. LN p. 79.
121. 'Palaces' is a flight of fancy. The street actually contains a terrace of four- and five-storey middle-class houses on one side, with the Villeta Dinegro park on the other.
122. KGB 111.1 69.
123. KGB 111.1 101.
124. Ibid.
125. LN p. 82.
126. KGB 111.1 85.
127. KGB 111.1 66.
128. KGB 111.1 68.
129. GS 291.
130. GS 290, 291. See pp. 139–41 above.
131. KGB 111.1 76.
132. D 423.
133. KGB 111.1 86.
134. KGB 111.1 110.
135. KGB 111.1 109. This should probably be taken as cancelling the earlier claim that his own 'Manfred Meditation' is the musical background to *Dawn* (KGB 111.1 83).

16. DAWN

1. EH III D 1.
2. D 314.
3. D 164.
4. Ibid.
5. Ibid.
6. D 96.
7. D 205, 201.
8. D 150, 359.
9. D 454.

10. D Preface 5.
11. D 544.
12. D 207.
13. D 367.
14. D 553.
15. EH III D 1.
16. D 575.
17. D 376.
18. HH 275.
19. D 553.
20. D 474.
21. D 117, 31.
22. D 122. This Darwinian deconstruction is surely a principal thought behind *The Gay Science*'s assertion that 'the total character of the world' is 'chaos', that any projection of order or wisdom onto it is a mere 'anthropomorphism' (GS 109).
23. D 33, 41, 72 453.
24. D 148, 128.
25. D 116.
26. D 202. Presumably Nietzsche would also allow protection of society and deterrence of others as rational considerations. What he denies rationality to is *retribution*.
27. D 148.
28. D 18, 109, 110, 339.
29. D 18, 23, 189, 204, 348, 356.
30. D 95.
31. HH 226.
32. D 68.
33. D 72.
34. D 18, 94.
35. D 72.
36. KSA 9 3 [117].
37. D 102.
38. D 431.
39. D 79.
40. D 91.
41. D 53.
42. D 77.
43. D 72.
44. In the notebooks Nietzsche writes, 'Kant: man is a moral being: therefore he is (1) free (2) immortal (3) there's a rewarding and punishing justice: God. – But the moral being is a fiction, therefore . . .' (KSA 9 7 [20]).
45. D 148.
46. D 76.
47. D 78.
48. D 108.
49. D 57, 99.
50. D 148.
51. D 224, 136, 334.
52. D 133. As Karl Popper remarks apropos Freud, claims like this are irrefutable.
53. But see endnote 6 of Chapter 21.
54. D 135, 224.
55. KSA 9 3 [14].
56. D 137.
57. BT 21.
58. D 134.

59. KSA 9 2 [40].
60. D 63.
61. D 133.
62. Ibid.
63. KGB III.5 1144.
64. KSA 9 2 [41].
65. D 190.
66. D 165.
67. Z I 15.
68. D 377.
69. KSA 9 7 [313].
70. D 128.
71. D 115.
72. D 124.
73. D 119.
74. D 560.
75. KSA 9 7 [30]; compare AOM 36.
76. WR I pp. 304–5. The 'character' that is unchangeable is one's repertoire of *basic* dispositions. 'Acquired' character has to do with the set of dispositions one allows to express themselves.
77. D 109.
78. Ibid.
79. This working out of the tension between *Dawn*'s 'fatalism' and the theme of 'self-creation' was originally achieved by Brian Leiter. See Leiter (2001).
80. D Preface 5.
81. D 552.
82. D 59.
83. D 105; see, too, KSA 8 2 [15].
84. AOM 220.
85. D 109.
86. D 218; see, too, 337, 468, and WS 120.
87. D 469.
88. WS 115.
89. D 245.
90. BGE 212.
91. C p. 399.
92. D 108.
93. D 146.
94. Z IV 1.
95. KSA 8 40 [16].
96. KSA 9 7 [37].
97. KSA 8 43 [3].
98. WS 295.
99. HH 611.
100. BGE 213.
101. D 174.
102. Leiter (2002).
103. D 9.
104. D 9, 165, 377.
105. D 103.
106. D 76.
107. KGB III.1 40.
108. KSA 8 29 [29].
109. Hutter (2006).

110. D 194.
111. D 52.
112. D 449.
113. KGB 11.5 671.
114. KGB III.1 348.
115. D 552, Nietzsche's emphases.
116. D 145. This is the idea that appears in the Prologue to *Zarathustra* and in its discussion of the 'gift-giving virtue' (Z 1 22) which suggests that the latter should be understood on the model of pregnancy.
117. D 355.
118. Quoted in Conradi (2001) and requoted by Stuart Hampshire (2001) in a review of Conradi's book in *The New York Review of Books*.
119. D 145.
120. KGB III.1 348.
121. Z 1 22.
122. D 194.
123. D 552.
124. D 449.
125. D 505.
126. HH 283.
127. D 364.
128. D 323.
129. D 462.
130. D 376.
131. D 258.
132. D 321.
133. D 346.
134. D 413.
135. D 542.
136. D 278.
137. D 325.
138. D 432.
139. D 117.
140. KSA 910 [D 82].
141. D 423.
142. D 117.
143. D 314.
144. BT 15.
145. Further support for the view that Nietzsche is a 'Kantian' rather than 'postmodernist' from the notebooks: 'Man in the end does not discover the world, but rather his tactile and sense organs and their laws – but isn't their existence a sufficient proof of reality? I think the mirror proves the things' (KSA 9 10 [D 83]). 'Our sensible world is not really present, it contradicts itself: it is a sensory illusion. But what then are the senses? The cause of the illusion must be real' (KSA 9 10 [E 93]).
146. KSA 9 3 [19]; see, too, WS 16.
147. Quine (1960) p. 22.

17. THE GAY SCIENCE

1. KGB III.1 142.
2. KGB III.1 122.
3. KGB III.1 135.
4. KGB III.1 142.

5. KGB III.1 137.
6. KGB III.1 142.
7. KGB III.1 125.
8. KGB III.1 121.
9. KGB III.1 167.
10. KGB III.1 145.
11. KGB III.1 153.
12. KGB III.1 125.
13. KGB III.1 128.
14. KGB III.1 125.
15. KGB III.1 136.
16. EH III z 1.
17. KSA 9 11 [141].
18. KGB III.1 135.
19. Ibid.
20. KGB III.1 158.
21. KGB III.1 144.
22. KGB III.1 326.
23. KGB III.1 198.
24. GS Preface 4.
25. KGB III.1 157.
26. KGB III.1 181.
27. Ibid.
28. KGB III.1 173.
29. KGB III.1 184.
30. KGB III.1 188.
31. KGB III.1 172.
32. KGB III.1 174.
33. On July 26, 1882.
34. KGB III.1 194.
35. KGB III.1 202.
36. KGB III.1 187.
37. GS 276.
38. KGB III.7/1 Appendix 31.
39. KGB III.1 195.
40. KGB III.1 201. This reappears in the collection of poems at the beginning of *The Gay Science*.
41. KGB III.1 197.
42. KGB III.1 206.
43. KGB III.1 213.
44. KGB III.1 220.
45. Kohler (2002).
46. KGB III.1 121.
47. KGB III.1 221.
48. KGB III.1 222.
49. KGB III.1 135.
50. KGB III.1 162.
51. KGB III.1 204–5.
52. KGB III.1 224.
53. KGB III.2 118.
54. KSA 3 pp. 334–42.
55. KGB III.1 195, 224.
56. KSA 9 7 [37].
57. EH III GS.
58. GS 327.

59. KGB III.1 230.
60. Z Prologue 9.
61. GS 335; see, too, 55.
62. GS 32; see, too, 255.
63. GS 381.
64. GS 26.
65. GS 1.
66. GS 76.
67. Ibid.
68. GS 116–17.
69. GS 50.
70. Ibid.
71. GS 116.
72. GS 5.
73. GS 356.
74. GS 24.
75. GS 23.
76. Ibid.
77. GS 58.
78. KSA 8 17 [44].
79. GS 382.
80. GS 55.
81. GS 285.
82. GS 108.
83. GS 139.
84. GS 274–5.
85. GS 294.
86. GS 76.
87. GS 343.
88. GS 23.
89. GS 125.
90. Ibid.
91. GS 86.
92. KGB III.1 381, 459, 769.
93. KSA 10 4 [90].
94. GS 89. In the notebooks: 'Against the art of artworks I want to teach a higher art: the invention of festivals' (KSA 9 11 [170]).
95. GS 85.
96. KSA 10 4 [265]. Nietzsche actually says 'many pictures', expressing his requirement that the polytheism of Greek religion should replace the monotheism of Christianity. This requirement is made explicit at GS 143.
97. GS 84.
98. GS 106.
99. *Triumph of the Will* and *Olympia*.
100. GS 329.
101. GS 301.
102. KSA 9 11.191.
103. Z II 22. Such thoughts may sometimes, of course, be very *bad* thoughts. The fundamental cause of the global financial meltdown of 2008 lay, surely, not in the greed of bankers but in the dominion of neoclassical economics, with the absurd assumption that economic agents are perfectly rational.
104. GS 39. This, at least at the time of writing, is the great hope of the Obama U.S. Presidency. For the first time in living memory we seem to be offered the combination of (benign) spiritual leadership with global power.
105. GS 280.

106. GS 120.
107. GS 118.
108. GS 119.
109. KGB III.1 380. See further p. 359 below.
110. GS 40.
111. GS 335.
112. GS 283.
113. GS 55.
114. GS 299
115. GS 78.
116. Ibid.
117. GS 335.
118. GS 276.
119. GS 341.
120. GS 303.
121. GS 377.
122. TI 1 8.
123. GS 99.
124. GS 333.
125. GS 374.
126. GS 54.
127. GS 57.
128. The term is Hubert Dreyfus's; see Dreyfus (1991).
129. GS 54.
130. GS 58.
131. GS 374.

18. THE SALOMÉ AFFAIR

1. GS 279.
2. KGB III.1 263.
3. C p. 536.
4. KGB III.1 215.
5. KGB III.2 118.
6. Ibid.
7. C p. 510.
8. The hill is actually, and always has been, called Sacro Monte, Sacro Monte d'Orta.
9. KGB III 7/1 p. 905.
10. Lou's Tautenburg diary Monday, the 21st of August 1882 (KGB III.7/1 pp. 904–11).
11. J II p. 130.
12. KGB III.1 352.
13. KGB III. 7/1 *Briefe, Erinnerungen und andere Materialien* pp. 48–59.
14. KGB III.1 231.
15. KGB III.1 233.
16. Ibid.
17. KGB III.1 250.
18. KGB III.1 234.
19. Ibid.
20. KGB III.1 237.
21. See Schaumann (1998) pp. 59–87. Professor Gerhard Schaumann suggested to me, when I visited Tautenburg in the summer of 2007, that Elizabeth was also half in love with the (married) pastor, which perhaps exaggerated her estimation of his ability to deal with Nietzsche on his own level.

22. The society still thrives. An interesting point of continuity is that Professor Schaumann, mentioned in the previous endnote, is an active member.
23. KGB III.1 262.
24. Tautenburg memories as to the location and number of benches contradict each other. Very recently the Beautification Society has erected two benches in memory of Nietzsche's visit, but without any pretence that they are placed where the original benches were.
25. KGB III.1 239.
26. KGB III.1 263.
27. KGB III.1 272.
28. KGB III.1 276.
29. KGB III.1 339.
30. KGB III.1 278.
31. Ibid.
32. KGB III.1 279.
33. See KGW III.1 p. 369.
34. KGW III.2 125.
35. KGB III.1 348, 347.
36. KGB III.7/1 pp. 912–18.
37. KGB II.2 152.
38. KGB III.1 339.
39. C p. 525.
40. KGB III.7/1 pp. 904–11.
41. KGB III.1 282.
42. C pp. 540–41.
43. Salomé (1968) p. 24.
44. KGB III.1 252.
45. KGB III.1 263.
46. KGB III.1 190, 236, 243.
47. KGB III.1 293.
48. KGB III.1 295.
49. Ibid. It is perhaps significant that he did not set the second verse, whose final lines seem inconsistent with his search for a God-less theodicy.
50. EH III z 1.
51. KGB III.1 301.
52. C p. 528.
53. KGB III.1 301. Nietzsche here appears to be quoting from a letter that has not survived.
54. *Naumburger 'Tugend'* (Ibid.).
55. KGB III.1 304.
56. KGB III.1 303.
57. GS 281.
58. C p. 538.
59. KGB III.1 348.
60. KGB III.1 353.
61. KGB III.1 339.
62. KGB III.1 347.
63. KGB III.1 348.
64. KGB III.1 351.
65. KGB III.1 352.
66. KGB III.1 335.
67. KGB III.1 352.
68. KGB III.1 362.
69. KGB III.1 334.
70. KGB III.1 360.
71. KGB III.1 363.

72. The Emerson quotation mentioned on p. 320 above.
73. KGB III.1 364, 365.
74. J II p. 167. The remark about Lou's incapacity for love is actually qualified by 'at least at this stage of her life and for many years to come'.
75. KGB III.1 364.
76. Banville (2006) pp. 61–4.
77. WR II p. 533.
78. KGB III.1 444.

19. ZARATHUSTRA

1. KGB III. 370.
2. C p. 538.
3. KGB III.1 372.
4. KGB III.1 370.
5. KGB III.1 403.
6. KGB III.1 384.
7. KGB III.1 431.
8. KSA 11 28 [64].
9. KGB III.1 369.
10. KGB III.1 373.
11. KGB III.1 399.
12. KGB III.1 400.
13. KGB III.1 431.
14. KGB III.1 399.
15. KSA 10 7 [227].
16. KSA 10 7 [213]. In *The Antichrist* this assessment of Jesus will be radically revised.
17. KGB III.1 382, 384.
18. KGB III.1 380.
19. KSA 10 [27].
20. KGB III.1 381.
21. KGB III.1 382.
22. KGB III.1 381.
23. KSA 8 30 [82].
24. KSA 8 30 [90].
25. KSA 9 3 [81].
26. KSA 9 3 [107].
27. KGB III.3 769.
28. KGB III.1 405.
29. Ibid.
30. KGB III.1 425, 426.
31. KGB III.1 427.
32. Ibid.
33. KGB III.3 741.
34. KGB III.1 428. See, also, KGB III.3 741.
35. KGB III.1 432.
36. KGB III. 7/1 pp. 952–7.
37. KGB III.1 443.
38. KGB III.1 434.
39. KGB III.1 435.
40. KGB III.1 436.
41. KGB III.1 444.
42. KGB III.1 443.

43. KGB III.1 438.
44. KGB III.1 442.
45. KGB III.1 443.
46. KGB III.1 448.
47. Ibid.
48. KGB III.1 449.
49. KGB III.1 457.
50. KGB III.1 458.
51. KGB III.1 459.
52. KGB III.1 481.
53. KGB III.1 483.
54. KGB III.1 474.
55. KGB III.1 475.
56. KGB III.1 478.
57. Ibid.
58. KGB III.1 477.
59. Ibid.
60. Janz II p. 257.
61. KGB III.1 480.
62. HH 145, 155.
63. KGB III.1 403.
64. KGB III.1 473.
65. KGB III.1 398.
66. KGB III.1 490.
67. KGB III.1 375.
68. KGB III.1 404.
69. EH III z 2.
70. EH III z 6.
71. KGB III.1 452. Since Wagner died on February 13, 1883, Part I of *Zarathustra* was actually completed at least two weeks earlier.
72. KGB III.1 370.
73. EH II 10.
74. Z I 21.
75. See, for example, KGB III.1 407, 421.
76. KSA 12 [43].
77. GS 9.
78. EH III z 8.
79. KGB III.1 375.
80. Z II 14.
81. Z Prologue 10.
82. *Republic* 558c.
83. Z II 14.
84. YN pp. 52–4. Elizabeth claims that a regular trick of the tight-rope walker, 'old Weizmann', was to have an accomplice, approaching from the opposite direction, jump over him – without disturbing his balance.
85. In Matthew 27:15–26 Pilate asks the crowd which prisoner he should release, Jesus or Barabbas. They choose Barabbas.
86. GM III 9.
87. Z I 1.
88. Z III 2.
89. BGE 280.
90. Z I 3.
91. Z I 4.
92. Z I 5.

93. Z I 6.
94. KSA 10 16 [50].
95. Z I 15.
96. KSA 10 4 [188].
97. Z I 18.
98. KGB III.1 352.
99. Z II 10.
100. Z III 15.
101. BT 1.
102. BT 2.
103. Z III 15.
104. Z III 5.
105. Z I 20.
106. HH 243.
107. GS 143, BGE 213.
108. Z I 21.
109. KGB III.1 382.
110. Z I 22.
111. See, for instance, KSA 10 7 [256].
112. KGB III.1 347.
113. Z Prologue 1.
114. Z IV 1. See, too, Z IV 20.
115. Z II 1.
116. Another 'Isle of the Blessed (*der Glückseligen*)' was, as we have seen, Tribschen (p. 106 above). The phrase first occurs in Hesiod's *Works and Days*.
117. Z II 10.
118. KGB III.1 452.
119. EH III z 6.
120. BT 1.
121. Z II 2.
122. HH 111.
123. KSA 12 10 [17].
124. Z II 3.
125. BM pp. 243–4, WR I pp. 375–6.
126. Z III 12.
127. KGB III.1 533.
128. Z II 9.
129. Z II 1.
130. EH III z 4, 7.
131. KGB III.1 583.
132. Z II 12.
133. BGE 259.
134. BGE 36; my emphasis.
135. WR II p. 182.
136. Z II 20.
137. A 57.
138. Z IV 10.10.
139. KSA 9 16 [22].
140. Z III 2.
141. Z III 4.
142. EH III z 7.
143. Ibid.
144. BT 17.
145. BT 10.

146. KSA 13 14 [14] (WP 1050).
147. Z III 12 19. A phrase which reappears in Rilke.
148. Salomé (1988) p. 35.
149. TI VI 8.
150. If (Apollonian) reason supports the idea of transcendence, why should there be anything especially Dionysian about it? I think Nietzsche's thought is that because the everyday perspective on the world that is centred on the everyday self is so engrained – it is, after all, its most essential piece of survival equipment – it takes something extraordinary (poetry, drugs, spring, strong emotion, some kind of 'intoxication') to achieve, as it were, lift-off: to propel one into the 'widest sphere', into the supra-individual perspective on the world.
151. GS 370.
152. EH III z 6.
153. GS 277. We are also warned not to remove the 'scare quotes' around 'personal providence', not backslide into belief in the old God.
154. GS 278.
155. Books I–IV.
156. GS 278.
157. KGB III.1 479.
158. KGB III.1 556.
159. KGB III.3 572 calls the publishing business in general a 'whorehouse', yet letters 573 and 580 make clear that, initially, he would have published if he could.
160. KGB III.3 761, 773.
161. Z IV 11.
162. Z IV 17, 18.
163. Lichtenberg (1867) p. 326ff.
164. KGB III 7/2 p. 76.
165. KGB III.1 601.
166. BGE 8.
167. BT 1.
168. Z IV 19. In a later edition the title was changed to 'The Sleep-walker's Song'.
169. Z IV 20.
170. EH III HH 1.
171. Z I 7.

20. NIETZSCHE'S CIRCLE OF WOMEN

1. KGB III.1 606.
2. KGB III.1 486.
3. C pp. 575–80.
4. C p. 581.
5. KGB III.1 526.
6. KGB III.1 528.
7. C pp. 580–2.
8. C p. 586.
9. KGB III.1 490.
10. KGB III.1 494. This idea actually originated with Köselitz, who, becoming ever more slavish, wrote Nietzsche in February 1884 that *Zarathustra* 'gives one the feeling that time should be newly dated from it' and that 'one day you will be accorded a higher reverence than that accorded to the founders of Asian religions' (KGB III.2 To Nietzsche 223). But as we shall see, Nietzsche took to it as a duck to water.
11. KGB III.3 583.
12. Gilman (1987) p. 159.

13. KGB 111.3 589.
14. C p. 588.
15. C p. 592.
16. C p. 594.
17. C p. 588.
18. KGB 111.1 528. Alas, the project never came to fruition.
19. KGB 111.3 750.
20. KGB 111.3 724.
21. KGB 111.3 750.
22. C pp. 588–9.
23. Gilman (1987) pp. 161–6.
24. J II p. 326.
25. KGB 111.1 514, 533.
26. KGB 111.1 533.
27. Ibid.
28. J II p. 289. This is a continuation of KGB 111.1 514 discovered by Janz's examination of the manuscript to be missing in KGB.
29. KGB 111.1 529.
30. KGB 111.1 528.
31. KGB 111.1 562. The word '*new*' appears only in the repetition of the verse at the end of the poem.
32. KGB 111.2 To Nietzsche 262.
33. J II p. 369.
34. KGB 111.1 531.
35. KGB 111.1 482, 483.
36. KGB 111.1 507.
37. KGB 111.1 512.
38. GM I 10.
39. KGB 111.1 547.
40. KGB 111.1 551.
41. Ibid.
42. KGB 111.1 549.
43. KGB 111.3 623.
44. KGB 111.5 809.
45. KGB 111.5 914.
46. These details about Druscovitz's life and works are derived from Robert C. Holub's excellent 'Nietzsche and the Woman's Question (BGE 231–8)', which appears to have no existence save on the Web.
47. KGB 111.3 571.
48. KGB 111.3 760.
49. KGB 111.3 582.
50. KGB 111.1 491.
51. Gilman (1987) pp. 182–4.
52. KGB 111.3 607.
53. KGB 111.3 613.
54. Gilman (1987) p. 213.
55. KGB 111.3 671.
56. KGB 111.3 661.
57. Gilman (1987) p. 195.
58. Gilman (1987) p. 213.
59. KGB 111.3 636.
60. KSA 10 3 [1] 367.
61. This point has been well emphasised by Robert Holub (op. cit.).
62. Ascheim (1992) p. 86.

63. Ascheim (1992) pp. 62–3.
64. KGB 111.3 600.
65. J II p. 300. A translation appears in Gilman (1987) p. 160. In Gilman's index this passage is given the quaint but appropriate title 'On *man's* potential' (my emphasis).
66. Salis-Marschlins (2000) pp. 31–6.
67. KSA 11 25 [92].
68. KGB 10 3 [1] 442.
69. TI ix 40.
70. KGB 111.3 669.
71. Ibid.
72. KGB 111.3 741.
73. KGB 111.3 652.
74. KGB 111.3 711.
75. Ibid.
76. KGB 111.3 720.
77. KGB 111.3 656.
78. KGB 111.3 644.
79. KGB 111.3 656.
80. KGB 111.3 654.
81. KGB 111.3 648.
82. KGB 111.3 650.
83. GS 362.
84. BGE 242.
85. BGE 208.
86. AOM 99.
87. WB 4, BGE 46.
88. BGE 242.
89. Ibid.
90. See KGB 111.1 399 and BGE 188, for example.
91. BT 2.
92. KGB 111.3 682.
93. KGB 111.3 687.
94. KGB 111.1 553.
95. C p. 635.
96. KGB 111.3 726.
97. Janz III pp. 257ff.
98. BGE 208.
99. KGW 111 7/3,2 Appendix 6.
100. KGB 111.5 918.
101. C p. 641.

21. BEYOND GOOD AND EVIL

1. KGB 111.3 741.
2. KGB 111.3 617.
3. KGB 111.3 690.
4. BGE 36.
5. KGB 111.5 1036. See also KSA 13 16[43].
6. The principle that '"ought" implies "can"' is generally regarded as a truism. But in that bald form it is, in fact, not really true at all. There is nothing incoherent in Schopenhauer's position that we both ought to be altruists and that (at least as natural beings) we cannot be. It is precisely the conjunction of 'ought' and 'cannot' which, if true, renders the project of life one which no one in their right mind would choose to participate in – any more than

one would choose to participate in a game in which he who makes the first move always loses and in which one always has to make the first move. The true principle is that *relative to the assumption that life is worth living*, 'ought' implies 'can'.

7. BGE 39.
8. TI ix 5.
9. Schopenhauer, Nietzsche remarks, was 'a stubborn man of morality who had to negate the world in order to be right about morality' (KSA 12 2 [106]).
10. KGB 111.5 1144.
11. KGB 111.3 678.
12. TI i 8.
13. BGE 39.
14. BGE 259, Z ii 12.
15. KGB 111.5 1013.
16. KGB 111.5 1036.
17. BGE 30.
18. BGE 210, 211.
19. BGE 204.
20. BGE 211.
21. BGE Preface.
22. BGE 2.
23. Ibid.
24. BGE 15.
25. BGE 12.
26. BGE 14.
27. Ibid.
28. WR I p. 98.
29. WR II p. 318.
30. WR II p. 172.
31. BGE 253.
32. KSA 11 36 [31].
33. TI ix 14.
34. BGE 259.
35. BGE 13.
36. BGE 23.
37. Z ii 12.
38. BGE 32.
39. BGE 23.
40. BGE 259.
41. Ibid.
42. BGE 197.
43. BGE 36.
44. BGE 227.
45. GS 374.
46. BGE 10, 208.
47. BGE 24, 4.
48. BGE 259, 23.
49. BGE 12.
50. BGE 4.
51. A 7, KSA 7 23 [15], D 52.
52. BGE 212.
53. BGE 223, 224.
54. BGE 223.
55. BGE 224.
56. Ibid.

57. UM II 4.
58. BGE 224.
59. BGE 203.
60. BGE 262.
61. See p. 371 above.
62. BGE 46.
63. KGB III.5 1041.
64. BGE 260.
65. BGE 62.
66. BGE 168.
67. BGE 62.
68. Ibid.
69. BGE 4, 24, 61.
70. BGE 62.
71. Notice that Nietzsche seems concerned, here, to raise the *average* level of the 'herd'. It is initially unclear whether this is because he thinks there is more chance of 'breeding' exceptional individuals from a high base or whether he thinks that a healthy society needs both exceptional types and a high and happy herd. But since a strong and happy herd surely makes an important contribution to a community's success in the evolutionary struggle, the latter interpretation must, I think, be the correct one.
72. BGE 62.
73. BGE 257.
74. BGE 62.
75. GS 108.
76. BGE 202, 203.
77. BGE 253.
78. BGE 202, KSA 11 25 [174], 25 [211].
79. BGE 202.
80. BGE 232, 233, 238, 239.
81. BGE 202.
82. BGE 44.
83. BGE 201, 202, 44.
84. BGE 212.
85. BGE 202.
86. BGE 194, 198.
87. BGE 257.
88. KSA 12 9 [35] = WP 2.
89. BGE 211.
90. BGE 44.
91. GS 23.
92. BGE 203.
93. EH III BGE 1. Compare Hölderlin's poem 'Homecoming/To the Relatives'.
94. BGE 44.
95. BGE 212.
96. Ibid.
97. BGE 208.
98. BGE 61.
99. BGE 211, 203.
100. BGE 44.
101. Ibid.
102. BGE 61.
103. BGE 211.
104. BGE 204.
105. BGE 208, 274. The metaphor elaborated on in Widmann's review (p. 405 above).

106. Ibid.
107. BGE 211.
108. BGE 204.
109. BGE 25, 26.
110. BGE 208.
111. BGE 210.
112. BGE 205–7.
113. KSA III.3 598.
114. KSA III.1 531, 533.
115. BGE 212.
116. KSA 12 4 [4].
117. EH III BGE 2.
118. BGE 257.
119. A 57.
120. BGE 61. The exactness of the correspondence to Plato's ideal state becomes even clearer in section 57 of *The Antichrist*.
121. BGE 30.
122. BGE 221.
123. Ibid. This idea that Christian ethics cannot accept stratification of the virtues, it might be argued, is the same error that Nietzsche makes when he supposes that moral 'equality' precludes all special 'privileges' (p. 420 above).
124. GM p. 185.
125. Ibid.
126. BGE 257.
127. Russell (1957) p. 796.
128. Hence 'consequential perfectionism' is another label for the position Nietzsche is accused of holding.
129. Rawls (1972) section 50. Save for the brief honeymoon around the time of *Dawn*, far from thinking of Socrates as a 'superman', Nietzsche actually thinks of him as a '*décadent*' (TI II, KSA 13 11 [375]). This suggests that Rawls's acquaintance with Nietzsche was relatively slight, that what he was after was a straw man rather than a genuine understanding of Nietzsche's philosophy.
130. BGE 208.
131. BGE 61.
132. KGB III.5 1170.
133. BGE 257, 239.
134. BGE 239.
135. BGE 233.
136. BGE 234.
137. BGE 232.
138. BGE 239.
139. BGE 144.
140. KGB III.1 347, 348.
141. BGE 239.
142. BGE 238.
143. BGE 239.
144. Ibid.
145. KSA 13 11[414].
146. BGE 238; my emphasis.
147. A 57.
148. Ibid.
149. BGE 262.
150. BGE 212.
151. BGE 49.

152. BGE 263.
153. TI IX 9–11.
154. AOM 99.
155. BGE 224.
156. BGE 61.
157. BGE 105.
158. BGE 58. See, too, 263.
159. BGE 257; my emphasis.
160. HH 125, GS 302.
161. BGE 62.

22. CLEARING THE DECKS

1. J II p. 480.
2. C p. 640.
3. KGB III.3 751, 756.
4. GS 76.
5. KGB III.3 761.
6. KGB III.5 803, 811.
7. KGB III.5 794. In June 1887, however, he reverted to calling Widmann's review 'very intelligent' (KGB III.5 865) and sent him, in gratitude, a complementary copy of *The Gay Science* (KGB III.5 869).
8. KGB III.3 754.
9. KGB III.4 403.
10. KGB III.3 760.
11. KGB III.3 769.
12. KGB III.3768, KGB III.5 849.
13. KGB III.5 849.
14. KGB III.5 872. See KSA 12 5 [90], which says that Taine showed that the 'intensity, coherence and inner logic' of Napoleon's 'dream' made him the brother of Dante and Michelangelo.
15. KSA 12 2. 175. *Zarathustra's* claim in 'The thousand and one Goals' that 'once you have recognised a people's need and land and sky and neighbour you can surely guess the law of its overcomings', its morality, looks to have been inspired by *milieu* theory.
16. TI IX 44. Compare KSA 12 7 [33] and 7 [25].
17. KGB III.3 735, KGB III.5 951.
18. EH III z 1.
19. KSA 12 2 [106], 2 [114], 2 [117].
20. KGB III.1 295; see p. 352 above.
21. KGB III.5 931, 940.
22. KGB III.3 773.
23. KGB 760.
24. KGB III.3 759.
25. KGB 757.
26. KGB III.3 757, 759.
27. KGB III.3 759.
28. KGB III.3 760.
29. KGB III.3 770.
30. KGB III.5 785.
31. KGB III.5 798.
32. KGB III.5 790.
33. KGB III.5 851.
34. KGB III.3 774.

35. KGB III.3 773.
36. KGB III.3 742. That the *Untimely Meditations* did not come within the scope of this project might suggest that Nietzsche did not consider them major works, but a more likely reason, I think, was that Fritzsch had inherited few, if any, unsold copies of these works.
37. KGB III.3 740, 730.
38. KGB III.5 834.
39. KSA 12 1 [126], 2 [73], 3 [4].
40. KGB III.3 734.
41. KGB III.3 770.
42. The unreliability of these prefaces from a scholarly point of view contrasts with much more accurate descriptions of earlier works such as *The Birth of Tragedy* in the notes of 1888 (see KSA 13 [14] passim).
43. KGB III.5 908.
44. GS 299.
45. GS 370. Z I 3 is also more accurate.
46. KGB III.2 747.
47. GS 344.
48. GS 373; my emphasis.
49. GS 374.
50. GS 373.
51. Ibid.
52. GS 351.
53. GS 347.
54. GS 381.
55. GS 374.
56. GS 354. Compare KSA 12 6 [11].
57. See, for example, KSA 12 9 [40].
58. GS 344.
59. Ibid.
60. GS 123.
61. KSA 12 5 [10].
62. GM III 24.
63. HH 109.
64. KSA 8 [23]; see pp. 255–6 above.
65. GS 366, 373, 381.
66. KSA 12 1 [144], [145].
67. GS 357.
68. GS 377, 380.
69. GS 343.
70. GS 357.
71. GS 356. Notice that Nietzsche rules out only the possibility of a society in which birth is 'destiny', not the possibility of building *any* kind of new society.
72. GS 377.
73. GS 343.
74. GS 377.
75. GS 382.
76. Ibid.
77. GS 380.
78. GS 345.
79. Ibid.
80. GS 353.
81. Ibid.
82. GS 346.
83. GS 358.

84. GS 353.
85. GS 382.
86. GS 370.
87. Ibid.
88. KSA 13 11 [710].
89. GS 288.
90. BGE 56.
91. KGB 111.5 899. In August 1887, Paul Deussen visited Nietzsche in Sils Maria en route to Greece.
92. GS 370. The same elevation of the classical occurs in his talk about music. He can think of no higher praise for the wonderful music of the new Mozart, Heinrich Köselitz, than to call it 'classical' (KGB 111.5 951).
93. GS 377.
94. See p. 403 above.
95. GS 377.
96. GS 83; see, too, D 191 and WC 9.

23. THE GENEALOGY OF MORALS

1. KGB 111.5 794.
2. KGB 111.5 792.
3. KGB 111.5 793.
4. KSA 12 5 [41].
5. KGB 111.5 824.
6. KGB 111.5 814.
7. KGB 111.5 804.
8. KGB 111.5 804. To point out that Widmann's review of *Beyond Good and Evil* (p. 405 above) begins with a quotation from Dostoyevsky's *The Younger Generation* would be to quibble.
9. KGB 111.5 1151.
10. KGB 111.5 807.
11. KGB 111.5 805.
12. KGB 111.5 807.
13. KSA 12 10 [21].
14. KGB 111.5 820.
15. KGB 111.5 847. Since, for example, Heinrich von Stein was twenty-seven when Nietzsche met and was entranced by him, this must express a momentary irritation rather than a considered judgment.
16. KGB 111.5 855.
17. KGB 111.5 819, 823.
18. KSA 12 5 [45].
19. KGB 111.5 820.
20. KGB 111.5 829.
21. KGB 111.5 827, 839.
22. Gilman (1987) p. 193.
23. KGB 111.5 884.
24. KGB 111.5 851.
25. KGB 111.5 863.
26. KGB 111.5 851. One wonders whether the brothels we know Nietzsche sometimes visited were also 'massage parlours'.
27. KGB 111.5 845.
28. KGB 111.5 968.
29. KGB 111.5 850.
30. KGB 111.5 855.

31. KGB iii.5 854.
32. KGB iii.5 968.
33. KGB iii.5 863.
34. KGB iii.5 870.
35. Ibid.
36. KGB iii.5 868.
37. KGB iii.5 870.
38. KGB iii.5 873, 878.
39. KGB iii.5 895.
40. KGB iii.5 883.
41. KGB iii.5 885.
42. KGB iii.5 887.
43. C p. 670.
44. It appeared in English translation as *The Sutras of the Vedanta with the Commentary of Cankara* in 1906.
45. KGB iii.5 899, 903.
46. C pp. 671–2.
47. KGB iii.5 907.
48. C p. 699.
49. KGB iii.5 937.
50. KGB iii.5 938.
51. KGB iii.5 963.
52. KGB iii.5 940.
53. KGB iii.5 958.
54. KGB iii.6 500.
55. KGB iii.5 960.
56. KGB iii.5 964.
57. KGB iii.6 505.
58. KGB iii.5 966.
59. KGB iii.5 964.
60. KGB iii.5 976.
61. KGB iii.5 858.
62. KGB iii.5 834.
63. KGB iii.5 858.
64. KGB iii.5 894.
65. KGB iii.5 949.
66. KGB iii.5 985.
67. KGB iii.5 1014.
68. KGB iii.5 879.
69. KGB iii.5 951, 908, 964.
70. KGB iii.5 965.
71. GM Preface 3.
72. GM Preface 5.
73. GS 345, GM ii 12.
74. GM i 2.
75. GM i 10.
76. GM i 5.
77. GM i 6. Presumably, then, when section 257 of *Beyond Good and Evil* claims that the 'pathos of distance' can only originate in an 'aristocratic society', it allows for the possibility that the society in question may be an aristocracy based on psychological attributes rather than on social class.
78. GM i 4.
79. KGB iii 6 542.
80. GM i 7.
81. BGE 46.

82. As we shall see, a quite different account of the priest's nature and motivation is given in *The Antichrist* (section 24). This may have been a response to Overbeck's criticism that *ressentiment* is too simple an explanation of the slave revolt (KGB 111.6 To Nietzsche 510).

83. GM I 6, 7, 10, 11.

84. KGB 111.5 971.

85. A 25.

86. GM I 7.

87. James Stewart has suggested that Buddhist morality might be regarded as another species, given that it grew out of a reaction against the oppressive practices of the Brahmins.

88. GM I 8; my emphasis.

89. GM I 11.

90. GM I 14.

91. Ibid.

92. GM I 13.

93. GM I 15. Aquinas is, in fact, précising the book of Revelation.

94. GM I 10.

95. Ibid.

96. GM I 11.

97. GM I 10.

98. EH III GM.

99. EH III BGE 2.

100. GM I 9.

101. GM I 16.

102. GM I 11.

103. GM I 11, 12.

104. EH III HH 1.

105. GM I 17.

106. GM I 12.

107. GM II 1.

108. GM I 10.

109. GM II 2.

110. GM II 3.

111. See GM III 9.

112. GM II 2.

113. Ibid.

114. Z I 15.

115. GM II 2.

116. KGB 12 5 [63].

117. GS 109.

118. KGB 1.2 538; see p. 67 above.

119. BGE 61; see p. 426 above.

120. GM II 2.

121. Ibid.

122. GM II 3.

123. GM II 4.

124. GM II 5, 6, 7, 8.

125. GM II 19.

126. GM II 20.

127. GM II 21.

128. Ibid.

129. GM II 16.

130. Ibid.

131. GM II 18.

132. Nietzsche adds two points here. First, the Christian ideal of self-sacrifice grows out of pleasure in cruelty to self. Only the will to self-violation provides the condition for valuing the 'unegoistic'. Second, the upside of this awful sickness is that man develops an inner life: acquiring what will later be called a 'soul', man becomes 'interesting' and full of 'future'. His sickness is like pregnancy (GM II 16, 19).
133. A 22.
134. GM II 24.
135. GM I 16.
136. GM II 19.
137. Ibid.
138. GM II 23.
139. GM II 24.
140. BGE 280.
141. EH III GM.
142. GM III 8.
143. GM II 2–5.
144. GM II 5.
145. GM II 6.
146. Ibid. Nietzsche tries to claim that Schopenhauer's aesthetic theory contradicts itself since he has the 'most personal interest possible' in entering the aesthetic state. But this is a bad mistake: that one has an interest in entering the aesthetic state by no means entails that the state itself is 'interested'.
147. GM II 7.
148. WR I pp. 185–6.
149. Christopher Janaway (2007) points this out in Chapter 12 of his *Beyond Selflessness*. Though I do not agree with Janaway on all matters, I have found this chapter an extremely helpful guide to the *Genealogy*'s third essay.
150. GM II 12.
151. GS 99.
152. GM II 12; compare KSA 12 1 [50].
153. WR II pp. 381, 372, PP II p. 69.
154. KSA 11 34 [131].
155. I believe that this 'map' analogy has recently been revived by Frijof Bergmann.
156. GS 374.
157. KSA 12 2 [149].
158. KSA 12 2 [148].
159. GM III 11.
160. Ibid.
161. GM III 13.
162. GM II 11.
163. GM III 13.
164. Ibid.
165. GM III 20.
166. GM III 13.
167. GM III 15.
168. Ibid.
169. Matthew 19:24.
170. Z II 12.
171. GM III 15–16.
172. GS 78.
173. GM III 17.
174. GM III 25.
175. GM III 14.
176. GM III 17.

177. GM III 17.
178. GM III 19.
179. GM III 20.
180. Ibid.
181. GM III 17.
182. GM III 24.
183. GM III 28.
184. EH III GM.
185. KGB III.1 494, III.5 1132. See p. 389 above.
186. GM III 24.
187. GM III 23.
188. GS 58. My emphasis. Nietzsche chooses *können* rather than *dürfen* – a descent from his normally elevated use of language – because, it seems to me, like the English 'can', it embraces both 'may' and 'can'. *Mere* criticism, he is saying, is *ineffective*, idle whinging. Without a counter-ideal to offer in place of the criticised ideal, criticism will be unable to prevent backsliding, since, as we know, the will to power prefers to have an unhealthy goal to no goal at all.
189. GM III 23.
190. GM III 23–4.
191. GM III 24.
192. GS 344.
193. GM III 27. 'Self-sublation' and 'self-sublimation' are other possible translations. The general principle is obviously either false or trivial, but that is not really important, since Nietzsche is only concerned with one instance of it. It is, I think, little more than a rhetorical flourish.
194. Ibid.
195. Ibid.
196. EH Foreword 3.
197. GS 370.
198. KSA 11 37 [8].
199. GS 362.
200. KSA 12 5 [61].
201. KSA 12 2 [57]. See, too, KSA 12 2 [76] and KSA 11 37 [8].
202. GM I 12.
203. I am indebted to John Richardson for making clear to me the relevance of this observation.

24. 1888

1. J II p. 577.
2. KGB III.5 1105, 1110.
3. KGB III.5 983.
4. KGB III.5 1005.
5. KGB III.5 973.
6. KGB III.5 1000.
7. KGB III.5 1007.
8. GS Preface 4.
9. NCW Preface.
10. KGB III.5 1003, 1005.
11. KGB III.5 998.
12. KGB III.5 1049.
13. Ibid.
14. KGB III.5 1007.
15. KGB III.5 1013.

16. Ibid.
17. Ibid.
18. KGB III.5 1022, 1025.
19. KSA 13 11 [296].
20. KGB III.5 1068. *The Wagner Case*'s Second Postscript, however, calls him Wagner's 'clever ape'.
21. KGB III.5 1122, 1148.
22. KGB III.5 1036.
23. KGB III.5 796.
24. KSA 13 16 [63].
25. KGB III.5 1026.
26. KGB III.5 1014.
27. KGB III.5 1078.
28. KGB III.5 1181.
29. KGB III.5 1130.
30. KGB III.5 1160.
31. KGB III.5 1163.
32. KGB III.5 1107.
33. KGB III.5 1207.
34. KGB III.5 1210.
35. KGB III.5 1145.
36. KGB III.5 1045.
37. KGB III.5 1018.
38. KGB III.5 1066.
39. KGB III.5 1048.
40. KGB III.5 1068.
41. Gilman (1987) p. 209.
42. Gilman (1987) p. 206.
43. J II p. 621.
44. J II p. 620.
45. KGB III.5 1115.
46. KGB III.1 551.
47. KGB III.5 1066.
48. KGB III.5 1101.
49. KGB III.5 1110.
50. C p. 700.
51. C p. 699.
52. C p. 700.
53. KGB III.5 1111.
54. KGB III.5 1108.
55. KGB III.5 1111.
56. KGB III.5 1134.
57. KGB III.5 1079.
58. WC Postscript, footnote.
59. Nietzsche seems to have taken over the term and part of the concept from the French writer and literary critic and self-styled *décadent* Paul Bourget (see Neumann (2001)), whom he first read in the winter of 1883–4 (KSA 10 24 [6]). The term does not, however, appear in his published works until 1888.
60. WC 5.
61. TI IX 35.
62. WC 4, KSA 12 2 [127].
63. WC 7.
64. WC Second Postscript.
65. WC 7.

66. WC Epilogue.
67. WC 4.
68. WC 8, 12.
69. The postscript contains one glancing and virtually meaningless reference to it, which may have been inserted in the attempt to cover over the weakening of the case against Wagner its omission represents.
70. KGB iii.5 1102.
71. KGB iii.5 1111.
72. No longer, however, for reasons to be discussed Chapter 26, to be called *The Will to Power*.
73. KGB iii.5 1115. In November Nietzsche claims it was written in ten days (KGB iii.5 1157), but by then he was beginning to lose touch with reality.
74. KGB iii.6 581, KGB iii.5 1122.
75. KGB iii.5 1105.
76. Ibid.
77. Ibid.
78. KGB iii.5 1105.
79. KGB iii.5 1104.
80. KGB iii.5 1105.
81. EH iii TI 2.
82. TI iv.
83. EH Preface 2.
84. TI vi 3.
85. TI vi 7–8.
86. TI ix 33.
87. TI ix 36.
88. BGE 21.
89. TI ix 38.
90. TI ix 42.
91. TI i 44.
92. C p. 399.
93. TI ix 12.
94. Surprisingly, in view of his Anglophobia, Nietzsche had read, or at least dipped into, no less than six works by Mill (Brobjer (2008) p. 251).
95. BGE 228.
96. TI i 8.
97. TI i 10.
98. TI ix 49.
99. TI ii 2.
100. Salomé (1988) p. 32.
101. TI ii.
102. TI x 4.
103. TI x 5.
104. AOM 33.
105. EH iii 'The Birth of Tragedy' 3.
106. TI iii 2.
107. A 1.
108. TI v 1.
109. TI v 2.
110. TI v 1.
111. TI v 3.
112. KSA 13 23 [2]. He goes on to suggest that Wagner betrayed himself in just this way, a passage expurgated by Elizabeth in the reappearance of the note as WP 815.
113. TI ix 37.
114. TI vi 2.

115. TI IX 33.
116. Ibid.
117. GM I 10.
118. TI IX 37.
119. BGE 197.
120. GM I 16.
121. UM I 1.
122. TI VIII 2.
123. TI VIII 4.
124. TI IX 29.
125. TI VIII 6.
126. TI IX 38–9.
127. TI IX 40.
128. Ibid.
129. TI V 6.
130. TI IX 9, 10, 24.
131. TI V 4.
132. KGB III.5 1122.
133. Ibid.
134. KGB III.5 1142.
135. KGB III.5 1112.
136. A 62.
137. A 24.
138. A 26; see p. 462 above.
139. A 24.
140. Ibid.
141. A 30.
142. A 2.
143. A 29, 30, 33, 35.
144. A 20, 22, 42.
145. A 42.
146. A 39.
147. A 41, 42. According to biblical scholars, Paul actually took over the doctrine of personal immortality not from Plato but from the Pharisee sect to which he originally belonged.
148. A 8, 9.
149. EH Preface 2.
150. A 21.
151. A 43.
152. A 22.
153. A 43, 58.
154. A 43.
155. A 44–7.
156. A 57.
157. A 56.
158. A 60.
159. TI VII 3–4.
160. A 58.
161. A 57.
162. A 58.
163. Ibid.
164. KSA 13 11 [31].
165. EH III BT 4.
166. KSA 13 18 [17]. See, too, EH III BT 4. Essentially, section 57 of *The Antichrist* offers, in abbreviated form, what would have been the content of that book.

167. A 57.
168. Ibid.
169. EH Preface 4.
170. EH 4 1.
171. A 57.
172. Ibid.
173. Ibid.
174. Ibid.
175. Given Nietzsche's view that the eternal return can only be embraced from a Dionysian perspective, this, I think, is the point of a cryptic note that reads, 'Dionysus – the type of the lawgiver' (KSA 13 23 [8]).
176. In the sketch of contents for the fourth book of *The Will to Power* (KSA 13 18 [17]) mentioned earlier, two of the three main topics (the third is too cryptic to be intelligible) are '"Order of Rank: the Principle of Life"' and 'The Eternal Return'.
177. A 58.
178. A 57.
179. Ibid.
180. Ibid.
181. A 16.
182. GM II 19.
183. A 16.
184. A 25.
185. KSA 13 11 [346].
186. KSA 13 11 [375].
187. A 19.
188. The Old Testament, at least, recognises only one 'true' god.
189. KSA 13 16 [16].
190. EH Preface 2.
191. EH III 1.
192. KGB III.5 1145.
193. EH Preface 4.
194. GS 299.
195. EH III z 6.
196. EH I 3.
197. EH III 2.
198. Ibid.
199. EH I 3.
200. EH III UM 3.
201. EH III z 2.
202. EH II 9.
203. Ibid.
204. EH III z 3.
205. EH II 5.
206. EH III HH 2.
207. EH II 5.
208. EH III HH 5.
209. EH III HH 1.
210. EH III HH 6.
211. EH IV 1.
212. EH Preface 2.
213. EH IV 4.
214. There is no room, therefore, for global-warming deniers.
215. Z Preface 5.
216. EH Why I Am a Destiny 5.

217. EH III BT 4.
218. EH III BT 3.
219. KGB III.5 1144.
220. KGB III.5 1143.
221. KGB III.5 1157.
222. KGB III.5 1144.
223. KGB III.5 1137.
224. Ibid.
225. KGB III.5 1192.
226. KGB III.5 1147.
227. KGB III.5 1184.
228. KGB III.5 1189.
229. KGB III.5 1192.
230. Ibid.
231. KGB III.5 1202.
232. KGB III.5 1156, 1203, 1213.
233. EH III 1.
234. KSA 13 25.11.
235. KGB III.5 1192.
236. KGB III.5 1132.
237. Ibid.
238. KGB III.5 1159.
239. KGB III.5 1147, 1158.
240. KGB III.5 1210.
241. KGB III.5 1186.
242. KGB III.5 1210.
243. KGB III.5 1204.
244. KGB III.5 1193.
245. KGB III.5 1132.
246. KSA 13 25 [7] 5.
247. KGB III.5 1050.
248. KGB III.5 1129.
249. KGB III.6 591.
250. KGB III.5 1131.
251. KGB III.5 1207.

25. CATASTROPHE

1. C p. 716.
2. KGB III.5 1173.
3. KGB III.5 1175, 1192.
4. KGB III.5 1157.
5. KGB III.5 1168.
6. KGB III.5 1170.
7. Ibid.
8. KGB III.5 1227.
9. KGB III.5 1229.
10. KGB III.5 1239.
11. KGB III.5 1249.
12. KSA 13 25.15.
13. KSA 13 25.19.
14. WS 284, 350; see pp. 266–7 above.
15. KGB III.5 1172, 1173, 1254, 1255.

16. KGB III.5 1128.
17. KGB III.5 1238, 1243.
18. KGB III.5 1235, 1244, 1249, 1250, 1251, 1252.
19. KGB III.5 1256.
20. KGB 1247; cf. 1239.
21. KGB III.5 1242.
22. KGB III.5 1248.
23. KGB III.5 1244.
24. KGB III.5 1246.
25. KGB III.5 1250.
26. KGB III.5 1252.
27. KSA 13 25 [7].
28. KGB III.5 1034.
29. GS 78.
30. TI IX 45.
31. J III p. 39.
32. EH II 7.

26. THE RISE AND FALL OF "THE WILL TO POWER"

1. HH 44, 50, 55, 137.
2. Z I 15.
3. Z II 12.
4. KSA 11 34 [247].
5. KSA 11 39 [1].
6. KSA 12 2 [100].
7. KGB III.3 741.
8. KGB III.5 973.
9. The plan Elizabeth uses, taken from a sketch of March 17, 1884, was a plan for a four-volume work containing 374 aphorisms. Of these, 104 were not used at all. Of the remaining 270 fragments, 137 are reproduced incompletely or with intentional alterations – deletion of headings or whole sentences, dismemberment of texts that belong together, and so on (see Montinari (2003) pp. 92–3). And, of course, 693 fragments of Elizabeth's 1906 edition were not intended to go with the 1884 plan at all. Many of these had in fact been consigned to Nietzsche's wastepaper basket in Sils, from which, for unknown reasons, Durisch retrieved them.
10. Heidegger (1979) Vol. I, pp. 8–9.
11. Heidegger (1979) Vol. IV, p. 148.
12. The chapter in question is Chapter IV of *Nietzsche* (Schacht (1983)). These statistics appear in Magnus (1986).
13. In the KSA edition.
14. Section 12 of the second essay in the *Genealogy of Morals* might be construed as *asserting* it.
15. Or 'interpretation' – *Auslegung*.
16. Why 'events' rather than 'things'? Because, we know, Nietzsche believes things in general to be an illusion of grammar (p. 498 above). Reality, he holds, is made up of events. The only question requiring discussion is the character of those events.
17. KSA 11 39 [1].
18. KSA 11 40 [2].
19. Bernoulli (1908), Vol. I, p. 269; my emphasis.
20. KSA 7 23 [30].
21. FR p. 1.
22. KSA 12 2 [88].
23. KSA 11 36 [31].

24. WR II p. 318.
25. BGE 13.
26. BGE 253.
27. GS 349.
28. KSA 12 14 [79].
29. BGE 259.
30. KSA 11 36 [31].
31. WP 1066. George Simmel proved this argument fallacious in 1907.
32. KSA 11 38 [12] = WP 1067.
33. KSA 12 2 [100].
34. KSA 12 9 [35] = WP 2.
35. KSA 12 10 [137].
36. KSA 13 11 [73].
37. KSA 13 11 [43].
38. KGB 111.5 1105.
39. KSA 13 11 [415].
40. BGE 259.
41. WR II p. 605.
42. WP 55.
43. KSA 13 11 [414].
44. KSA 13 12 [1].
45. KGB 111.5 991.
46. KGB 111.5 1000.
47. Nietzsche seems to think that he arrived unusually early in 1887, but this is a mistake. The earliest Nietzsche ever appeared in Sils was June 7, in 1885. In 1887 he arrived on June 12.
48. KGB 111.5 1094.
49. KSA 13 18 [17].
50. KGB 111.5 1098.
51. KSA 19 [2]–19 [8].
52. KGB 111.5 1111.
53. TI Preface.
54. KGB 111.5 1151.
55. KGB 111.5 1159.
56. KSA 13 22 [14].
57. KSA 13 11 [410].
58. GS 335.
59. BGE 210, GM III 24.
60. GM Preface 2.
61. See, too, EH Preface 3.
62. WR I p. 111.
63. BGE 23.
64. BGE 259 (my emphasis), BGE 36.
65. BGE 36; my emphasis.
66. See, too, BGE 13.
67. BGE 36; my emphasis.
68. KSA 11 40 [9].
69. TI ix 9.
70. GS 109.
71. BGE 36.
72. KSA 13 11 [111].
73. BGE 259.
74. KSA 13 11 [111].
75. Notice that a logical limit to the otherwise 'insatiable' will to power would be to 'become God'. Did, one wonders, Nietzsche's own insipient megalomania help support his

metaphysics of power? Is his faith in the psychological doctrine sustained, in part, by introspection?

76. TI ix 14.
77. TI i 26.
78. TI ix 9–11.
79. KSA 13 14 [11].
80. HH 54, D 135, 224.
81. WR I p. 380.
82. EH i 4.
83. This is surely a major part of the point behind the repeated assertion that 'Creators are hard', hard as 'diamond[s]' (Z iii 12, TI xi).
84. WC Epilogue.
85. A 6.
86. A 6, 17.
87. WC Second Postscript, WC 7.
88. WC 6.
89. TI ii 9.
90. A 30, 42.
91. A 24.
92. TI ix 35.
93. BGE 259.
94. Z ii 12.
95. TI i 12.
96. A 2.
97. A 11.
98. TI viii 4.
99. TI v 1.
100. KSA 10 16 [50].
101. TI x 3.
102. BGE 197.
103. TI v 1.
104. GM iii 9.

27. THE END

1. C p. 735.
2. C p. 736.
3. TI x 5.
4. C p. 739.
5. C p. 738.
6. C p. 743.
7. C pp. 755–6.
8. C p. 741.
9. YN and LN.
10. Hollingdale (1999) p. 249.
11. J III pp. 157–8.
12. C p. 793.
13. Gilman (1987) p. 254.
14. Hollingdale (1999) p. 253.
15. C p. 810.
16. Or, pedantically reckoned, four months before that century.
17. Gilman (1987) p. 248.

18. KGB 111.3 741. See also p. 361 above. It is appropriate, therefore, that at least the Nietzsche Memorial (Plate 26) is sited on Chasté.

28. NIETZSCHE'S MADNESS

1. KGB 111.5 870.
2. KGB 111.5 884.
3. Sacks (2008).
4. Schain (2001).
5. Sax (2003). The medical details of the above critique of the syphilis diagnosis are derived in part from Sax and in part from Schain (2001).
6. I am indebted for these facts to Helen Danesh-Meyer, W & L Stevenson Professor of Ophthalmology at the University of Auckland's Medical School and a world authority on, in particular, meningiomas. This entire chapter has been greatly improved as a result of her critique of an earlier draft.

Bibliography of Secondary Literature

Aschheim, S. (1992) *The Nietzsche Legacy in Germany 1890–1900* (Berkeley: University of California Press).

Banville, J. (2006) Review of *Rainer Maria Rilke and Lou Salomé: The Correspondence*, trans. E. Snow and M. Winkler (New York: Norton, 2006), in the *New York Review of Books* Vol. 53, No. 20, December, pp. 61–5.

Bernoulli, C. (1908) *Franz Overbeck und Friedrich Nietzsche. Eine Freundschaft*, 2 vols. (Jena: Eugen Diederichs).

Bertram E. (1918) *Nietzsche, Versuch einer Mythologie* (Berlin: Bondi).

Brobjer, T. (2001) 'Beiträge zur Quellenforschung: Abhandlungen. A Discussion and Source of Hölderlin's Influence on Nietzsche: Nietzsche's Use of William Neumann's Hölderlin', in *Nietzsche-Studien* Vol. 30, pp. 394–6.

———— (2008) *Nietzsche's Philosophical Context* (Urbana: University of Illinois Press).

Conradi, P. (2001) *Iris Murdoch: A Life* (New York: Norton).

Cate, C. (2002) *Friedrich Nietzsche* (London: Hutchinson).

Deussen, P. (1901) *Erinnerungen an Friedrich Nietzsche* (Leipzig: Brockhaus).

Dreyfus, H. (1991) *Being-in-the-World: A Commentary on Heidegger's Being and Time, Division I* (Cambridge, MA: MIT Press).

Durkheim, E. (1995) *Elementary Forms of the Religious Life*, trans. K. Fields (New York: Free Press).

Feuerbach, L. (1855) *The Essence of Christianity*, trans. Marian Evans (New York: Calvin Blanchard).

Fischer, K. (1860) *Geschichte der neueren Philosophen*, Vols. 3 and 4: *Entwicklungsgeschichte und System der kritischen Philosophie* (Mannheim: Bassermann'sche Verlag).

Gilman, S. (1987) *Conversations with Nietzsche*, trans. D. Parent (New York: Oxford).

Hadot, P. (1995) *Philosophy as a Way of Life : Spiritual Exercises from Socrates to Foucault*, trans. M. Chase (Oxford: Blackwell).

Hampshire, S. (2001) Review of *Iris Murdoch: A Life*, by P. Conradi (New York: Norton), in the *New York Review of Books* Vol. 48, No. 18, November, pp. 24–6.

Hayman, R. (1980) *Nietzsche: A Critical Life* (London: Weidenfeld and Nicolson).

Heidegger, M. (1977 onwards) *Heidegger: Gesamtausgabe*, ed. F.-W. von Hermann (Frankfurt am Main: Klostermann).

———— (1979) *Nietzsche*, 4 vols., trans. D. Krell (San Francisco: Harper & Row).

Hölderlin, F. (1965) *Hyperion, or the Hermit in Greece*, trans. W. R. Trask (New York: Friedrich Ungar).

Hollingdale, R. (1999) *Nietzsche: The Man and His Philosophy* (Cambridge: Cambridge University Press).

Hutter, H. (2006) *Shaping the Future: Nietzsche's New Regime of the Soul and Its Ascetic Practices* (Garfield, WA: Lexington Books).

Janaway, C. (2007) *Beyond Selflessness* (Oxford: Oxford University Press).

Janz, C. P. (1976) *Friedrich Nietzsche: Der musikalische Nachlass* (Basel: Bärenreiter).

Kant, I. (1964) *Critique of Pure Reason*, trans. N. Kemp Smith (London: Macmillan).

Kant, I. (1972) *Critique of Judgment*, trans. J. H. Bernard (New York: Hafner).

Kohler, J. (2002) *Zarathustra's Secret. The Interior Life of Friedrich Nietzsche*, trans. R. Taylor (New Haven, CT: Yale University Press).

Krell, D. and Bates, D. (1997) *The Good European* (Chicago: University of Chicago Press).

Landerer, C. and Schuster, M.-C. (2002) 'Nietzsches Vorstudien zur Geburt der Tragödie in ihrer Beziehung zur Musikästhetik Eduard Hanslicks', in *Nietzsche-Studien* Vol. 31, pp. 114–33.

Lange, F. (1925) *The History of Materialism and Criticism of Its Importance*, trans. E. Chester Thomas, intro. Bertrand Russell (New York: Arno Press).

Leiter, B. (2001) 'The Paradox of Fatalism and Self-Creation in Nietzsche', in J. Richardson and B. Leiter, *Nietzsche* (Oxford: Oxford University Press), pp. 281–321.

———— (2002) *Nietzsche on Morality* (London: Routledge).

Lichtenberg, G. (1867) *Vermischte Schriften*, Vol. 5 (Göttingen: Heinrich Dieterich).

Magee, B. (1983) *The Philosophy of Schopenhauer* (Oxford: Clarendon Press).

Magnus, B. (1986) 'Nietzsche's Philosophy in 1888: The Will to Power and the "*Übermensch*"', in *Journal of the History of Philosophy* Vol. 24, pp. 79–99.

Mann, T. (1947) 'Nietzsche's Philosophie im Licht unserer Erfahrung', in *Die neue Rundschau*, Vol. 58, pp. 58–82.

Meinecke, F. (1963) *Das Zeitalter der deutsche Erhebung* (1906), 7th ed. (Göttingen: Vandenhoeck and Ruprecht).

Mithen, S. (2005) *The Singing Neanderthals: The Origins of Music, Language, Mind and Body* (London: Weidenfeld and Nicolson).

Montinari, M. (2003) *Reading Nietzsche*, trans. G. Whitlock (Urbana: University of Illinois Press).

Neumann, V. (2001) 'Die französishe Krankheit: Nietzsches Rezeption des Begriffs "décadence" von Paul Bourget', in *Man ist viel mehr Künstler als man weiss*, ed. G. Seubold (Bonn: DenkMal).

Neumann, W. (1853) *Moderne Klassiker. Deutsche Literature-Geschichte der neuern Zeit in Biographien, Kritiken und Proben: Friedrich Hölderlin* (Kassel: Balde).

Quine, W. (1960) *Word and Object* (Cambridge, MA: MIT Press).

Rawls, J. (1972) *A Theory of Justice* (Cambridge, MA: Harvard University Press).

Rohkrämer, T. (2007) *A Single Communal Faith?* (New York: Berghahn).

Russell, B. (1957) *A History of Western Philosophy* (London: Allen and Unwin).

Sacks, O. (2008) 'A Summer of Madness', in the *New York Review of Books* Vol. 60, No. 14, September, pp. 57–61.

Salis-Marschlins, M. (2000) *Philosoph und Edelmensch: Ein Betrag zur Charakteristik Friedrich Nietzsches* (Schutterwald: Wissenschaftlicher Verlag).

Salomé, L. (Andreas-) (1968) *Lebensrückblick*, ed. E. Pfeiffer (Frankfurt: M. Suhrkamp).

———— (1988) *Nietzsche*, ed. and trans. S. Mandel (Redding Ridge, CT: Black Swan Books).

Sax, L. (2003) 'What was the cause of Nietzsche's dementia?' in the *Journal of Medical Biography*, Vol. 11, pp. 47–54.

Schacht, R. (1983) *Nietzsche* (London: Routledge and Kegan Paul).

Schain, R. (2001) *The Legend of Nietzsche's Syphilis* (Westport, CT: Greenwood Press).

Schaumann, G. (1998) *Tautenburg bei Jena: Kulturgeschichte einer thürinischen Sommerfrische* (Jena: Quartus-verlag).

Small, R. (2005) *Nietzsche and Rée: A Star Friendship* (New York: Oxford University Press).

Spir, A. (1869) *Vorschlag an die Freunde einer venüftighen Lebensführung* (Leipzig: J.G. Findel).

Tanera, K. (1896) *An der Loire und Sarthe* (Nördlingen: Beck).

Young, J. (2005) *Schopenhauer* (London: Routledge).

Index

Schopenhauer on, 82–3, 91–2, 95, 120–1
Wanderer on abandonment of, 267–8
French Revolution of 1789, 8–9
Freud, Sigmund, 365, 479
Friedrich Wilhelm IV (King of Prussia), 13
Friendships generally, 16–17, 472–3
Fritsch, Theodor, 452
Fritzsch, Ernst, 172–3, 190, 401–2, 434, 523–4
Foucault, M., 22
Fuchs, Carl, 189, 189n, 491, 590n
Fynn, Emily (daughter), 397, 432, 455
Fynn, Emily (mother), 397, 432, 435, 455, 528

Gast, Peter. *See* Köselitz, Heinrich
Gauguin, Paul, 335–6
Gay Science, The
  on Apollonian outlook on life, 127
  on art (music), 330–2
  audience, 327
  Book V: *Being Scientific about Science*, 439–43, 494
  contemplation, destruction of, 332–3, 333n, 604n
  on creation, destruction, 35, 247
  cultural evolution theme, 327–9
  death of God theme, 329–30, 383
  eternal return theme in, 318, 318n, 319
  on faith, 86–7
  on gender relations, 109
  on life as artwork, 334–7, 478, 485–6
  overview, 326, 327
  on pan-Europeanism, 403, 483
  perspectives in, 474, 475n, 476n
  preface, 1886, 437–9, 617n
  on rank-ordering in healthy society, 333–4, 604n
  on reality, truth, knowledge, 337–8
  "rebirth of Greek tragedy" theme, 330, 408–9, 604n
  reissue of, 436–7
  on self-cultivation, 306–7, 382
  self-development, reflection on, 60–1, 379, 573n
  on truth, 441
  on world as chaos, 299
Genealogy of Morals
  audience, 459–60
  bad conscience, origins of, 468–70
  as conclusion of epoch, 460
  First Essay: Good and Evil, Good and Bad, 461–5, 469–70, 483–4, 619n
  mastery of earth concept in, 482–3, 622n

methodology question, 483–4
modern obsession with, 459n
on Napoleon, 433
on objectivity, 473, 498n, 499n
overview, 460–1
perspectivism in, 440, 473, 474n, 476
Second Essay: Morality of Custom and the Sovereign Individual, The, 465–7, 470–1, 484
Third Essay: What Do Ascetic Ideals Mean?, 471, 494 (*See also* asceticism)
on truth, 441
writing, 455, 460
Genius, Nietzsche on, 145–6, 161, 161n, 179, 197–8, 433
Genoa, 293–4, 320–1
Germania Society, 27–8, 248n
German materialism, 281–2, 598n
German Reich, 25, 70, 486
Germany, hatred of, 488, 506–8
Gersdorff, Carl von, 31, 31n, 32, 53, 73, 87–8, 94n, 171–2, 227–8
Gillot, Hendrik, 339–40
Glagau, Gustav, 405
Globalisation, 266, 266n, 267
God's existence, Hegel on, 81–2
Goethe
  life at Leipzig, 63
  Nietzsche's admiration of, 15, 455, 501
Good and Evil, Good and Bad, 461–5, 469–70, 483–4, 619n
Great Noon, The, 514–17
Greece, 435, 435n
Greek art
  Nietzsche on, 124–5, 127–9, 265–6
  sublimation of violence in, 140
Greek culture
  religion in, 265–6, 596n
  as role model for Western civilisation, 203–5, 448, 448n, 449, 464–5
  sublimation of violence in, 139–41, 469
'The Greek State,' 160–1
Greek tragedy
  Apollonian/Dionysian duality in, 135–6
  death of, 132
  Wagner on, 114–15
Grey, John, 469n
Guerrieri-Gonsaga, Emma, 190, 199
Guilt, origins of, 468–70

Hammer, Walther, 519n
Handel, Georg Friedrich ('Händel'), 4, 16, 37, 60, 193, 255
Hanslick, E., 121, 124, 186, 584n, 585n

.